CW00743223

COLOUR PATCH

*The men of the
2/4th Australian
Machine Gun Battalion*

COLOUR PATCH

The men of the
2/4th Australian
Machine Gun Battalion
1940 – 1945

by

Murray Ewen

HESPERIAN
PRESS

First published 2003

by

Hesperian Press, P.O. Box 317, Victoria Park, Western Australia

National Library of Australia Cataloguing in Publication data.

ISBN 0 85905 312 1

© Ewen, Murray – Colour Patch

Bibliography
Includes index
ISBN 0 85905 312 1

Australia at war 1939 – 1945
Battle of Singapore, Battle of Java
7th Division 2nd A.I.F.
8th Division 2nd A.I.F.
Prisoner of War
Singapore, Java, Burma-Thailand Railway, Sumatra, Borneo, Japan, Korea, Manchuria

Main text typeset in Times New Roman and printed on 100gsm paper

Typesetting, Dossier Scans and indexing by Mike Tucker
Pre-Press, Colour Plates and Drum Scans by ColourboxDigital
Cartography by Marcel Maron
Artwork by Carol Fleming
Pre-Editing by Judith Anketell
Editing by Dr John Coe
Proof reading by Joan Westlake

The author gratefully acknowledges the support of the West Australian Newspapers Pty Ltd, Australian War Memorial, National Library of Australia, National Archives of Australia, Department of Veterans' Affairs, the ex-members of the 2/4th Machine Gun Battalion and members of the general public. Where applicable the copyright on some original photographs will, when desired, remain with their original owners and or family.

Disclaimer: Whilst great care has been taken to ensure that all maps are as accurate as possible, they are purely for reference purposes only and therefore not to exact scale.

The identification of the men as seen within group photographs has been accomplished by using existing records and private sources. Similarly the selection of photographs for the men's dossiers has been undertaken with the greatest possible care. However, some unavoidable errors may have occurred due to the factor of time.

Printed by Lamb Print, Perth, Western Australia

At least Once in Everyone's Life a True Friend is Lost

This Book is Dedicated to the Memory of

TREVOR JOHN EPIS

18.4.1947 − 13.12.1998

Foreword by Kim Beazley MP

1942 was Australia's year of living dangerously. Whatever confidence they may have had in the ultimate outcome of the Pacific war, no Australian political or military leader could be absolutely certain that the high watermark of Japanese military success would not include a successful invasion of all or part of the Australian continent. None of our decision makers could be confident that the defence of the Australian mainland would rate sufficiently highly in the calculations of the main allied statesmen that resources would be diverted from other theatres in sufficient amounts to guarantee our short term survival.

Curtin's stark wake up call to the nation on 27 December 1941 that Australia would look to the United States "free of any pangs as to our traditional links" with the United Kingdom was badly received in both London and Washington. It effectively announced, however, in advance of the fall of Malaya, Singapore and the Netherlands East Indies, that the Australian government had no confidence in Imperial defence and the broader European Asian empires which had been the focus of Australian defence planning since federation. Indeed Australian statesmen had been overtly hostile to much of the Pacific policy of the United States to that point of time, consistently siding with the United Kingdom when views clashed.

With a clear eye, the government saw the writing on the wall. Murray Ewen points out in this book that Churchill had said in December 1940 that, "if Australia is seriously threatened by invasion we should not hesitate to compromise or sacrifice the Mediterranean for the sake of our kith and kin". By January 1942 Churchill believed no such thing. Britain was fighting for its life, and with the US not yet mobilised the critical thing was to keep the Soviet Union in the war. British eyes were focused on the western Indian Ocean more than the East. For much of 1942 that was where the critical routes for allied supplies to the Soviet Union lay, and these could be threatened only by Japanese dominance of India or German success in the Middle East. With a clear and present danger to Australia obvious, this was sufficient for Churchill to argue vigorously with the Australian government to keep the sixth and seventh divisions, almost half Australia's fighting capacity, in the Middle East. As he gave way on that he tried to keep strategy intact by attempting to divert them to Burma on the way home.

Douglas MacArthur's appearance in Australia in 1942 was valued as much for its indication that the 'beat Hitler first strategy', combined with the United States navy's predilection to see the central Pacific – as opposed to the South West Pacific – as the road to Tokyo, would still see enough crumbs fall from the table for Australian survival. MacArthur was an Australian political hostage in 1942. He brought little else. Indeed I used to enjoy pointing out to my American counterparts when I was Defence Minister that it was not until 1944 that MacArthur had more US troops under his command than Australian.

Something of the mental agony of these calculations for Australian statesmen can be seen in these pages in Murray Ewen's account of the Advisory War Council's debate on sending the 2/4th Machine Gun Battalion to Singapore.

A thread of pessimism, as to their fate, runs through our leaders comments. There was a feeling that they might help to hold things up a bit. There is a concern for appearances. The previous war time Prime Minister, W.M. Hughes, said "If we don't send additional troops to Malaya, there will be a public outcry." J.A. Beasley however said what must have been in the hearts of many members of parliament, despite some comments to the contrary, "The disposition of Japanese forces is not confined to Malaya as they are also in the Philippines, Bonin Islands and elsewhere. How can we say that they won't attempt a landing at Darwin? Only Army Minister Forde seemed to believe that "properly equipped, Singapore can be defended". The best that any expected was summed up by Navy Minister Makin, "The longer the delay to the fall of Singapore, the more time it will give us to prepare for the defence of Australia".

So these statesmen, educated by the World War One experience of the value of machine guns defending trenches and barbed wire, consigned the 2/4 machine gun battalion to the hopeless task of adding some fire power to the doomed 8th Division in Singapore and those elements of the 7th Division deployed largely unarmed to Java. The members of the battalion fought with ferocity, but in vain and were effectively out of the war by mid-February 1942, the survivors in Japanese hands. The first victims in our dangerous year.

Murray Ewen details their fate. What follows interlaces the grand strategy of the war's progress with the fate of the members of 2/4th. He takes us through the agony of a small group of Australians who experienced all the horrors the war and imprisonment in Japanese hands could produce. This is a story of heroism, mateship, loyalty, honour, misery, humiliation, cruelty, deprivation, sorrow, savagery, brutality and survival.

It is an extraordinary story. Having suffered defeat in Singapore and Java, members of the 2/4th were despatched by their captors to every field of atrocity the Japanese, ignoring the Geneva Convention, could place them. Members were incarcerated in the infamous camp at Changi. They were slave labour on construction projects in Java, Borneo and Thailand. There were representatives at the notorious Hellfire Pass. There were others on the Sandakan death march. Some in Korea, Manchuria, Indo-China and in Japan. One prisoner from the 2/4th was down a coal mine in Nagasaki when the second atom bomb was detonated, climbing 800 feet out of the mine when the lifts no longer worked. Ironically if you were a prisoner in Nagasaki it was probably the best place to be.

They were humiliated, bashed and starved by their captors. They were bombed and torpedoed by their friends. Men from the battalion were on the *Rakuyo Maru* on the way to Japan when it was torpedoed by an American submarine in September 1944. Eleven battalion members were among the survivors picked up by the submarines. It was their information which for the first time gave the allies a comprehensive picture of the story of the enslavement and brutalisation of captured allied soldiers. As if the horrors all suffered weren't enough, the survivors in all the camps in the last months of the war lived under the shadow of a widely known Japanese order that they were not to survive an allied landing or push in the areas where they were held.

They also experienced the excesses of Australian officialdom. Sent when few had confidence they would return, they were denied leave in Fremantle on the way, having been promised it. When some took it anyway, rather than simply being put back on the road, they went through a period of incarceration to be despatched to Java in another fraught cause to join fellow machine gunners of the 2/3rd who arrived from the Middle East without their weapons. At the end of the war many were denied decorations for which they were justifiably recommended.

But this is not a book about horror, injustice and arm chair generalship. Murray Ewen has written the ultimate human story. He has followed every single member of the battalion he possibly can. He documents for us and particularly their relatives how each one fought, lived and died. He tries to get at their state of health, their mind and the location in which they found themselves. He documents a story of brotherhood. There are no mock heroics here. There are just simple tales lifted from diaries, official documents, interviews and regimental lore. There is no attempt to paint a false picture about their enemies. Often they are individualised as well. The horror was real, but not uniform. It was mitigated by extraordinary mateship. There are plenty of stories of sacrifice to help sick mates. What is clear is that this caring attitude ensured that some at least did come home.

Murray Ewen asks the question that many who found themselves imprisoned so early in the war also asked – was their sacrifice worthwhile? His compelling view is that it was. Certainly, despite, the strident opposition of the Japanese General who was their conqueror, Yamashita, the Japanese experience of the way the Australians in South East Asia and their brothers in New Guinea fought, meant that the Japanese leadership concluded an invasion of Australia would be too costly: *"If the invasion is attempted, the Australians, in view of their national character would resist to the end ... The invasion would require the main body of the combined fleet and an infantry force of 12 divisions. The shipping required for the army alone would amount to 1,500,000 tons. The progress of the invasion might require the army to make additional commitments of large strengths."*

As important as that contribution was, it was what they demonstrated about the Australian character that counts. The sense of personal responsibility for one's mate was not a view developed in a month, it had to be inculcated from birth. This is a story about a machine gun battalion. It is also a spiritual odyssey into the hearts of an extraordinary generation of Australians which can speak to generations of an era in which many feel some of those values may have eroded.

Kim Beazley MP

Contents

List of Maps

List of Colour Plates

List of Black and White Plates

1. Ferguson family
2. Gibbs family
3. Browning family
4. Bevis family
5. Bunce family
6. Laurence and Enid Harvey
7. George Hancock, Dorothy Letts and Bryan Manwaring
8. Tom Pascoe
9. Harry and Junor Elkins, Edward Popham and son, Bert and Nell Rubery
10. Vern Hoppe, Claude Anderson and John Mellor
11. William and John King and Sydney Osborne
12. No. 1 Platoon Signals
13. No. 2 Platoon Ack-Ack
14. No. 2 Platoon Ack-Ack and Drivers
15. Men of No. 3 Platoon during the march from Northam to Perth
16. No. 3 Platoon Drivers
17. Pioneers and A.A.O.C.
18. A.A.O.C.
19. 'A' Company
20. 'A' Company, No. 4 Platoon
21. 'A' Company, No. 5 Platoon
22. 'A' Company, No. 6 Platoon
23. 'B' Company
24. 'B' Company Headquarters
25. 'B' Company, No. 7 Platoon
26. 'B' Company, No. 8 Platoon
27. 'B' Company, No. 8 Platoon entraining
28. 'B' Company, No. 9 Platoon
29. 'C' Company
30. 'C' Company Headquarters
31. 'C' Company, No. 10 Platoon
32. 'C' Company, No. 11 Platoon
33. 'C' Company, No. 11 Platoon men starting out on weekend leave
34. 'C' Company, No. 12 Platoon
35. 'D' Company
36. 'D' Company, No. 13 Platoon
37. 'D' Company, No. 14 Platoon
38. 'D' Company, No. 15 Platoon
39. Reinforcement pool Northam
40. Anzac Day 1946

The Australian Soldier

Around Anzac Day, April 25th of each year, Australia prepares itself for its National Day of Remembrance for the servicemen and women who have fought and died for their country. Most Australian children are introduced to their 'Anzac Heritage' in primary school where they are told of the brave deeds of Pte. John Simpson and his donkey at Gallipoli during April and May of 1915. John Simpson Kirkpatrick was in fact born in England in 1892 and had jumped ship in Fremantle. He later enlisted in the A.I.F. and served as a stretcher bearer with the 3rd Field Ambulance. As Australia's ancestral roots were predominantly from English, Scottish, Welsh or Irish stock, it is natural that men from the British Isles would make up a large proportion of Australia's population and, therefore, Australia's Military Forces. The 2/4th Machine Gun Battalion was no exception to the rule, and in fact slightly less than 25% of the men in this battalion were not born in Australia. Furthermore, it is also likely that a very high number of the remainder were only first or second generation Australians.

One last point on this subject is the fact that although raised in Western Australia, not all the men who served with this unit were born in that state. In fact, every state of Australia was represented with the South Australians making up the highest number of these Australian imports. Perhaps the simplest explanation in this case was that men crossed the state border to seek their fortunes in the goldfields around Kalgoorlie or take up farming land. The following list shows the countries of birth of those men born overseas:

England	160
Scotland	46
Wales	17
Ireland	7
Canada	1
Ceylon	1
Germany	1
Greece	1
India	1
Macedonia	1
New Zealand	1
South Africa	2
	Total 239

Preface

After assisting Les Cody with his well documented unit history of the 2/4th Machine Gun Battalion, *Ghosts in Khaki*, I felt something was driving me on to continue the battalion's story. However, the dilemma was how to continue to research and document information on a battalion when their history has already been published? After a great deal of thought the solution to the problem was simple enough, as solutions so often are. The answer came from the families of the ex-members of the battalion. So many family members apparently knew very little about their relative who had served with the battalion. This was true not only for the actions on Singapore and Java but in particular during the three and a half years as prisoners of the Japanese. Information about this period of time is never easy to locate, so the first priority was to chat to as many of the men as possible to try and glean as much information as possible, thereby establishing a base from which to work. The difficulty here, as you would expect, is that memories aren't that clear after sixty years. In fairness how could you expect a man who on a good day in 1943 was possibly suffering from malnutrition, malaria and dysentery to remember his comings and goings. Turning next to the families of the ex-members, in most cases it was discovered that the men had not wished to reminisce about their experiences, but instead had preferred to forget them. Occasionally there was a humorous story, letter, postcard or photograph, but apart from these items there was little in the families' possession that could help me with regard to their relative's experiences.

Some of the men had managed to keep diaries but only at the risk of swift and savage reprisal by the Japanese or Korean guards if caught with these in their possession. Additionally, writing materials were scarce and paper does not stand up well to the test of time in the damp climate of the tropics. It was generally found that official reports and interrogation forms that did make it back to Australia, and were later stored at our archival institutions, had either been culled over the years or else it was extremely difficult to pin-point items of particular interest, such as of Prisoner of War nominal rolls. The best that could be hoped for was that enough information could be found on each man to fill in the jigsaw puzzle. Often it was the case that people would contact the author and say, 'Dad didn't talk about the war all that much and because his health wasn't the best we didn't like to ask'. Often a son or daughter would remark 'I wish I had talked to dad more about the war when he was still alive'. As a general rule we can track the men en-masse. As units attempted to stay together and mates tried to stay with mates it is often a simple task just to cross-reference each man's story with that of the group or otherwise his closest friends. It therefore makes sense to relate the individual's story through the experiences of the group.

As Les Cody once commented: 'Dont think of the Battalion as individuals but instead as a group of men all going in the same direction'. These were wise words in hindsight as this is the manner in which the individual's story must be related. Where a man's story varies from the group's this is reflected in his personal dossier or covered in more detail in the narrative. The narrative was written to support the dossiers and is intended to import a higher level of detail and understanding into the 2/4th story.

Although this book is predominately about the trials and tribulations of the 2/4th Machine Gun Battalion, two other points are to be noted. Firstly, that this was just one battalion from the 8th Division, 2nd Australian Imperial Force. The information provided about these men in the 2/4th Machine Gun Battalion could so easily be used as a general guide for other men that were members of Australian units who fought in the Second World War. Places of birth, ages, occupations, backgrounds and even previous military service in all the arms of the services in both the United Kingdom and Australia has been documented. The other point is that in attempting to explain the reasons behind the sending of Australian troops to Singapore and Java and the period as Prisoners of War, the spectrum is widened to include not only the whole of the 8th Division but also a portion of the 1st Australian Corps attatched to the 7th Division, the sailors from the HMAS *Perth* and of course, some R.A.A.F. personnel.

The book is structured in three main sections – the Honour Roll, the Nominal Roll and the Narrative. Every effort has been made to pay attention to detail so that what is being offered is not only a book that can be passed down from generation to generation, but an archival document which tells the story of an Australian battalion in the Far Eastern Theatre of War. And whilst it is true that these were our fighting men in uniform, it is not to be forgotten that they were also husbands, fathers, sons, and brothers. For this reason some family photographs have been included, to remind the reader that each photograph of a soldier in uniform represents a real person. Hopefully the reader will then see these men in a different light, not just as soldiers or Prisoners of War, but each and every one a personality with a heart and soul, a laugh and a smile that was surely missed by someone at home somewhere in Australia. It is hoped that this story about the men in the 2/4th Machine Gun Battalion will be looked upon as an important reference source concerning Australia's military and social heritage during World War II.

Murray Ewen

Acknowledgements

My heartfelt thanks go out to the following people who have assisted me in some way with the production of this book. Most importantly to my wife Nancy, who without choice since 1990 has been forced to re-live the years 1940–1945 with me, but more recently over the past six years since I initiated *Colour Patch*.

To Daniel and Kathryn, my son and daughter who on numerous occasions were the victims when I pushed them aside and immersed myself in this project.

To Les and Glynneath Cody who welcomed me into their home on that first Sunday morning back in 1990. Les Cody was my mentor and I will always be grateful for his direction on all matters concerning the battalion. Without Les's guidance I do not believe that I would have gone to depths that I have to quench my thirst for knowledge regarding this battalion and the Prisoner of War experience. To all the ex-members of the 2/4th Machine Gun Battalion and their wives who have embraced Nancy and I into their select group, some of whom have become our close friends.

To the relatives and friends of the men who have trustingly lent me photographs and material so this project might succeed.

To my saviour Jenny Kohlen at *The West Australian* Newspaper without whose help there would simply not be a *Colour Patch*.

To the Department of Veterans' Affairs who assisted me by way of a research grant.

To Jim Scott and Graham Whitworth at D.V.A. and to Graham Edwards, the Federal Minister for Cowan, himself a veteran and campaigner who stood behind me when I needed his help.

To Tony Fewings, Jen Forde and all the staff at the National Archives in Western Australia. Likewise to Tom Volmer, Mark Brennan and Joanna Leahy and all the staff at the National Archives in Melbourne. The staff at the Australian War Memorial including Elizabeth Dracoulis, Louise Burmester, Ian Smith and Geoff Brewster, to name a few who over ten years of research have helped me out of some tight spots.

To Mike Tucker who managed to make sense out of the mess I called a manuscript and prepared this book for pre-press.

To Neville Browning who came to my rescue on many occasions in the early days with his computer skills and personal interest in the project by way of his uncle Johny Browning, who perished at Sandakan in Borneo.

To Ian Gill, who offered me his friendship, his encouragement and his moral support through many of the difficult stages of this book. I can honestly say that I know no other person who is so in tune with our Australian military heritage from a grass roots level.

To Bill Haskell, an ex-member of the 2/3rd Machine Gun Battalion whose opinions and comments I regard highly and who helped me immensely with the 'Battle of Java' and difficult Hellfire Pass–Hintok sector of the rail link.

I also gratefully acknowledge the support of the ex-members of the 2/4th Machine Gun Battalion and members of the general public who helped me to turn my dream into reality so that these men from the 2/4th will 'Never Be Forgotten'. Finally, yet to no lesser an extent, I wish to thank the following people and organisations, and offer my sincere thanks, and my apologies to anyone that I may have omitted who is also deserving of my gratitude.

ABC Radio Western Australia
Max Anderson
Judith Anketell
Ron and Vera Badock
Hugh and Rosemarie Baird
John 'Banjo' Binstead
Barbed Wire and Bamboo
Barbara Brand
Peter Bridge
Margo Bunning
John Cecil
Bill Clayton
Dr John Coe
Cottesloe Surf Life Saving Club
Alan Cough
Alex Dandie
Jim Elliot
Peter Epps
Carrol Fleming
Captain Wayne Gardiner
Jim Gilmour
Tom Gough
Gary Gribben - *My Irish connection*
Les Hockey
Trevor and Ruth James
Laurie Jamieson
Phillip Kindleysides
Kraft Foods Ltd
Jack Kyros
John Lane
Marcel Maron

'Cowboy' and Marion Matthews
Graham Mayberry
Les McCann
Chris Mills and GWN Television
Our Lady of the Rosary Church-Adelaide
Barbara Page, *Sunday Mail* Adelaide
Tony Richards, Imperial War Museum
Ian Saggers
Soldier Career Management Agency
Geoff and Tammy Scougal
Doris Simkin
Peter Sirr
Hilton Stanton
Mike Tucker
The Community Newspaper
The City of Kalgoorlie-Boulder
The Fremantle Army Museum
The National Archives Canberra
The National Library of Australia
The ex-Prisoners of War Association of Australia
The Regional Press Network of W.A.
The Returned Services League of Australia
The Returned Services League of Western Australia
Snap Print Applecross
The State Library of Western Australia
Pat Toovey
Don Wall
Ted and Stas Wallin
Mick Wedge
Western Veteran Magazine
Joan Westlake

A Brief History of the 2/4th Australian Machine Gun Battalion 1940–1945

The first year of the 2/4th Battalion's war diary commences on 19th November 1940 and refers to the advance party of the unit assembling at the Lord Street Drill Hall (Perth) for movement by motor transport to Northam Camp. Lt-Col M. J. Anketell was to be the Commanding Officer. The battalion proceeded on leave for Christmas 1940, and in the New Year Vickers machine gun training commenced. The Colonel was a stickler for physical fitness, and so one of the main features of training was a sixty-mile route march from Northam to Perth from 4th to 7th March 1941, ending with a march through the city to the welcoming cheers and waves of family, city workers and shoppers.

Machine gun training continued at Lancelin Island and Waterman's Bay in May and June and on 12th July, the battalion began its transfer interstate and moved into Woodside Camp in the Adelaide Hills. In October 1941 the battalion moved by rail and motor transport to Winnellie Camp, Darwin. In December the battalion engaged in training in the Darwin area, but, with the entry of Japan into the war in December 1941, individual companies occupied battle stations on beach areas within the Darwin environs. On New Years Eve 1941-42, under embarkation orders, the battalion sailed from Port Darwin on the SS *Marella* and HMAS *Westralia.* Sailing to Port Moresby, personnel and stores were transhipped to HMT *Aquitania* which sailed on 4th January. The *Aquitania* berthed in Sydney on 8th January, where a further 2502 reinforcements for Singapore were taken on board before the ship departed on 10th January.

The battalion arrived at Fremantle on 15th January 1942 and HMT *Aquitania* dropped anchor off Gage Roads. An incident occurred at Fremantle when many of the men left the ship and proceeded on shore leave without authority. Once under weigh again, a head count revealed that nearly ninety machine gunners had failed to reboard the ship before she sailed. Departing Fremantle on the 16th under the escort of the cruiser HMAS *Canberra,* HMT *Aquitania* was joined on the 19th by two Dutch cruisers, two destroyers and one British destroyer. Arriving at the Sunda Straits off Java in the Netherlands East Indies on the 20th the battalion was transhipped to two smaller Dutch vessels for the forward sea journey to Singapore. Disaster was averted when a tropical storm developed and shielded the convoy of seven small ships from the eyes of the Japanese aircrew who had been out searching for targets. On 24th January the convoy tied up safely at Singapore docks and the battalion disembarked and moved by rail to Woodlands Station, thence by route march to the Singapore Naval Base Camp.

Singapore was already in the thick of the action, being subject to daily raids from Japanese bombers. The battalion moved immediately into the construction of weapons pits and slit trenches as the fighting in Malaya drew closer to Johore Bahru. The machine gun companies were allotted their various defensive and reconnaissance rolls, coming initially under the command of British regiments until later allotted to Australian battalions. With the demolition of a section of the Causeway at 0800 hours on 31st January 1942, the serious business of the defence of Singapore began.

At the end of the first week of February, Japanese aerial bombing and shelling had greatly increased. By 2200 hours on the night of 8th February, Vickers gunners of 'D' Company No. 13 Platoon and 'B' Company's 8 and 9 Platoons had seen action. Nothing further eventuated in 'B' Company's Causeway Sector until the night of 9th February – but on the west coast it was a different story. Even though heavy casualties were suffered on the receiving end of the Vickers machine guns, the Japanese 5th and 18th Divisions managed to cross the strait in pontoons and barges and gain a foothold on the island.

Hand to hand fighting followed all along the west coast as the Japanese attempted to move around the flanks of any opposition to gain further territory. As the Vickers positions along the west coast were over-run, the defenders were forced to fight their way out from the coast; the men often coming up against Japanese patrols which had managed to overtake them due to confusion of battle and the close nature of the terrain. Groups of men became separated and stories of machine gun tripods, bayonets and even captured Japanese swords being used against the enemy are now part of battalion folklore following these isolated actions.

On 9th February the companies moved to new positions and with further enemy landings at different points it was not long before the battalion was again engaging the Japanese, whilst coming under heavy bombing and shelling attacks. Further battalion withdrawals took place during the day. The days to follow were marked by heavy fighting and constant movement, ever closer to Singapore City. On 12th February at 1700 hours, orders were received for the battalion to join the 22nd Brigade perimeter in the vicinity of the crossroads of Ulu Pandan and Holland Roads. This move was completed by 1800 hours. Within the brigade perimeter, the 2/4th Machine Gun Battalion now consisted of Battalion Headquarters, Headquarter Companies, 'A', 'C' and 'D' Companies (less casualties), approximately 400 of all ranks.

During a move to reorganise on a smaller battalion perimeter, Lt-Col M. J. Anketell was mortally wounded. At this stage of the battle the battalion was almost completely surrounded. Of the 400 about 50 men were either killed or wounded. The battalion broke off contact with the enemy and further withdrawals took place. The morning of 14th February revealed that during the night, the left flank had been exposed and the new C.O., Maj. C. E. Green, after contacting Brigade Headquarters, decided to reform the battalion perimeter. The area was harassed all day by enemy aircraft machine gun fire. Major Green was called to a Brigade conference on 15th February and advised of the possibility of a ceasefire and the action to be taken.

During the day the perimeter was reorganised and 'C' Company was drawn into reserve with a counter attack role. Enemy troops were observed and engaged, causing many casualties to battalion personnel. Likewise, as the Battle of Singapore drew to a close, many battalion personnel were killed or wounded as the enemy stepped up their artillery and mortar fire on the Australian positions. The desperation by the Japanese to force a surrender is reflected in the number and nature of casualties incurred by the men of the battalion on the last day of fighting. At 2015 hours on 15th February 1942 a telephone message was received confirming the morning conference at Brigade Headquarters and, at 2030 hours, the ceasefire order was issued.

From 8th to 15th February 1942 the 2/4th Machine Gun Battalion fought to save Singapore. From 15th February 1942 to 15th August 1945 they would fight a very different battle.

Military Abbreviations

As cited in Colour Patch

AA	Anti-Aircraft		Lt-Col	Lieutenant-Colonel
A.A.M.C.	Australian Army Medical Corps		Lt-Gen	Lieutenant-General
A.A.O.C.	Australian Army Ordnance Corps		Maj.	Major
A.A.P.C.	Australian Army Postal Corps		Maj-Gen	Major-General
A.A.S.C.	Australian Army Service Corps		MBE	Member of the Order of the British Empire
A.G.H.	Australian General Hospital		MC	Military Cross
A.I.F.	Australian Imperial Force		MID	Mentioned in Despatches
A/Cpl.	Acting Corporal		MM	Military Medal
A/Sgt.	Acting Sergeant		M.O.	Medical Officer
A/Tk	Anti-Tank		M.G.	Machine Gun
AWL	Absent Without Leave		M.M.G.	Medium Machine Gun
BCOF	British Commonwealth Occupation Forces		MT	Motor Transport
Bde.	Brigade		NCO	Non Commissioned Officer
BEM	British Empire Medal		OR's	Other Ranks
Bn.	Battalion		Pln.	Platoon
Brig.	Brigadier		Pnr.	Pioneer
Capt.	Captain		POW	Prisoner of War
C.C.S.	Casualty Clearing Station		Pte.	Private
CDF	Call for Defensive Fire		QM	Quartermaster
C.G.S.	Chief of the General Staff		R.A.A.F.	Royal Australian Air Force
C.I.G.S.	Chief of Imperial General Staff		R.A.F.	Royal Air Force
Coy	Company		R.A.M.E.	Royal Army Medical Corps
C.Q.M.S.	Company Quartermaster Sergeant		RAP	Regimental Aid Post
C.O.	Commanding Officer		R.M.O.	Regimental Medical Officer
Col.	Colonel		R.N.	Royal Navy
Cpl.	Corporal		R.A.N.	Royal Australian Navy
C.S.M.	Company Sergeant Major		R.P.	Regimental Police
DCM	Distinguished Conduct Medal		R.Q.M.S.	Regimental Quartermaster Sergeant
Div.	Division		R.S.M.	Regimental Sergeant Major
DoW	Died of Wounds		2 i/c	Second in Command
Dvr.	Driver		SAA	Small Arms Ammunition
Fld.	Field		Sgt.	Sergeant
Gen.	General		Sig.	Signaller
G.O.C.	General Officer Commanding		SRBn.	Special Reserve Battalion
Govt.	Government		S/Sgt.	Staff Sergeant
HMAS	His/Her Majesty's Australian Ship		T/ or Temp	Temporary
HMHS	His/Her Majesty's Hospital Ship		T.G.	Trade Group
HMS/M	His/Her Majesty's Submarine		ToS	Taken on Strength
HMT	His/Her Majesty's Transport		U.S.	United States of America
H.Q.	Headquarters		U.S.A.A.C.	United States Army Air Corps
I.J.A.	Imperial Japanese Army		U.S.N.	United States Navy
I.J.N.	Imperial Japanese Navy		USS	United States Ship
I.O.	Intelligence Officer		WIA	Wounded in Action
KIA	Killed in Action		W.O.I	Warrant Officer Class 1 (R.S.M.)
L.A.D.	Light Aid Detachment		W.O.II	Warrant Class Class 2 (S/Sgt or C.S.M.)
LAS	Lost at Sea		W.A.G.R.	West Australian Government Railways
L/Cpl.	Lance Corporal		105 (A)MH	Adelaide Military Hospital
L of C	Line of Communication		110 (P)MH	Perth Military Hospital
L/Sgt.	Lance Sergeant		113 (C)MH	Concord Military Hospital
Lt.	Lieutenant		115 (H)MH	Heidelberg Military Hospital

Japanese Words

cho	town	kita	north	sempaku	shipping
dore	street	ko	lake	shi	city
gata	bay, inlet, lake	machi	town	shima	island
gawa	river	minami	south	shimo	lower
gun	country	mine	mountain	take	mountain
hama	beach, field	mura	village	umi	sea, lake
higashi	east	nada	sea	ura	lake, coast
jima	island	naka	middle	wan	bay
kami	upper	nishi	west	yama	mountain
kawa	river	saki	cape		

Malay Words

atap	roof	bukit	hill	perahu	fishing boat
bahru	new	kiri	left	pulau	island
danau	lake	kuala	river mouth/confluence	pasir	sand
gudang	warehouse	lalang	long grass	sungei	river
kampong	village	muara	estuary	tanjong	point or headland
kanan	right	makan	food	telok	bay
kechil	small	padi	wet rice field	ulu	headwaters

The 24 hour Clock

0100 hours = 1.00 am	1000 hours = 10.00 am	1900 hours = 7.00 pm
0200 hours = 2.00 am	1100 hours = 11.00 am	2000 hours = 8.00 pm
0300 hours = 3.00 am	1200 hours = 12.00 am	2100 hours = 9.00 pm
0400 hours = 4.00 am	1300 hours = 1.00 pm	2200 hours = 10.00 pm
0500 hours = 5.00 am	1400 hours = 2.00 pm	2300 hours = 11.00 pm
0600 hours = 6.00 am	1500 hours = 3.00 pm	2330 hours = 11.30 pm
0700 hours = 7.00 am	1600 hours = 4.00 pm	2359 hours = 11.59 pm
0800 hours = 8.00 am	1700 hours = 5.00 pm	0001 hours = 00.01 am
0900 hours = 9.00 am	1800 hours = 6.00 pm	

Imperial Weights and Measures

1 mile = 1,760 yds or 1.61 km.	1 inch = 25.40 mm.	1 pint = 568 ml.
1 yard = 36 ins or 0.91 m.	1 acre = 0.405 he.	1 quart = 1.136 l.
1 foot = 12 ins or 30.5 cm.	1 pound = 454 gm.	1 gallon = 4.55 l.

Currency

1d (penny) = 0.83 cents	1s (shilling) = 10 cents	1 pound = 2 dollars

JOHN ROUGHTON ABERLE

Rank	Corporal
Regimental Number	WX239
Company	'C' Company
Enlisted	11.12.1940
Date of Birth	3.12.1920
Place of Birth	Perth, Western Australia
Father	Frederick John Aberle
Mother	Margaret Rose Aberle
Religion	Church of England
Pre-War Occupation	Warehouseman

HISTORY

Epitaph
Singapore Memorial
Column 135
Age 21

Cause of Death	Killed in Action
Place of Death	Ulu Pandan
Date of Death	12.2.1942
Buried	Where killed at map reference 758128 by Major A. Cough Party on 21.12.1942.

ARTHUR ALFRED ADAMS

Rank	Private
Regimental Number	WX9828
Classification	Butcher
Company	'C' Company
Enlisted	6.12.1940
Date of Birth	14.12.1917
Place of Birth	Perth, Western Australia
Father	Victor George Adams
Mother	Alice Rebeca Adams
Religion	Church of England
Pre-War Occupation	Butcher

HISTORY

Kranji War Cemetery
Special Memorial 'C'
Plot 4
Row B
Grave 16
Age 24

Cause of Death	Killed in Action
Place of Death	Ulu Pandan
Date of Death	11.2.1942

CYRIL WILLIAM MAX ANDERSON
a.k.a. Cyril William Max Jubelski

Rank	Private
Regimental Number	WX9123
Company	'C' Company
Enlisted	30.10.1940
Date of Birth	10.3.1914
Place of Birth	Caulfield, Victoria
Father	Samuel Jubelski
Mother	Jessie Winifred Jubelski
Religion	Church of England
Pre-War Occupation	Traveller

HISTORY

Singapore	Selarang Camp Changi
Force	'B' Force Borneo
POW Number	389
Cause of Death	Malaria
Place of Death	Sandakan
Date of Death	16.6.1945

Epitaph
Labuan Memorial
Panel 18
Age 31

WILLIAM JOSEPH ANDREWS

Rank	Private
Regimental Number	WX17793
Company	'E' Company, Special Reserve Battalion
Enlisted	26.11.1941
Date of Birth	8.10.1917
Place of Birth	Mosman Park, Western Australia
Father	Frederick Samuel Andrews
Mother	Rosa Ellen Andrews
Religion	Methodist
Pre-War Occupation	Taxi Driver

HISTORY

Cause of Death	Killed in Action
Place of Death	South-West Bukit Timah
Date of Death	11.2.1942

Epitaph
Singapore Memorial
Column 135
Age 24

MICHAEL JOSEPH ANKETELL
Commanding Officer

Rank	Lieutenant-Colonel
Regimental Number	WX3376
Awards	Mentioned in Despatches
Company	Battalion Headquarters
Enlisted	5.11.1940
Date of Birth	10.10.1890
Place of Birth	Briagolong, Victoria
Father	Richard John Anketell
Mother	Annie Anketell
Religion	Church of England
Pre-War Occupation	Trustees Officer

Epitaph
Singapore Memorial
Column 135
Age 51

HISTORY

Cause of Death	Died of Wounds
Place of Death	Alexandra Hospital
Date of Death	0745 hours on 13.2.1942
Buried	In Slit Trench No. 17 near the main entrance of Alexandra Hospital with 32 other men on Monday 16.2.1942.
Additions	Wounded in action at Ulu Pandan 12.2.1942, receiving a gunshot wound to the groin. The Colonel was evacuated unconscious by ambulance to Alexandra Hospital. Major Bull R.A.M.C. stated that he was on duty in the officer's ward at Alexandra Hospital and that Lieutenant-Colonel Anketell was admitted there on Thursday, Feb 12 at 1700 hours. He was suffering from a compound fracture of the right upper femur and was in a profoundly shocked condition. He was sent to the resuscitation ward and was given 2 pints of plasma. When his condition was improved he was sent to the operating theatre whilst his wound was dressed and the limb splinted. He was sent to the ward in moderate condition but never rallied and died on the morning of Friday, Feb 13 1942. Report by the Surgeon in Charge-Major Webster, R.A.M.C.

DUDLEY ATHELSTAN ANNEAR

Rank	Private
Regimental Number	WX13457
Company	'D' Company
Enlisted	11.12.1940
Date of Birth	11.5.1910
Place of Birth	Kalgoorlie, Western Australia
Father	John Henry Annear
Mother	Ada Eva Frances Anne Annear
Religion	Church of England
Pre-War Occupation	Warehouseman

Epitaph
Singapore Memorial
Column 135
Age 31

HISTORY

Cause of Death	Died of Wounds
Place of Death	Johore Straits, Singapore
Date of Death	14.2.1942

FREDERICK JOHN ANNESLEY

Rank	Acting Corporal (Promoted on 14.2.1942)
Regimental Number	WX7905
Company	Headquarters Company
Enlisted	13.8.1940
Date of Birth	23.3.1916
Place of Birth	Collie, Western Australia
Father	Leslie Wenbam Annesley
Mother	Janet Annesley
Religion	Church of England
Pre-War Occupation	Printer

Epitaph
Labuan Memorial
Panel 18
Age 28

HISTORY

Java	'Blackforce'
'A' Force Burma	Java Party No. 4, Black Force
POW Number	3930
Japan	*Rakuyo Maru* Party, Kumi No. 37
Cause of Death	Lost at Sea
Place of Death	South China Sea
Date of Death	16.9.1944

ALBERT BRIAN WALTER ANNETTS

Rank	Lance Corporal
Regimental Number	WX13515
Company	'E' Company, Special Reserve Battalion
Enlisted	24.5.1941
Date of Birth	1.9.1918
Place of Birth	Subiaco, Western Australia
Father	Walter William Annetts
Mother	May Annetts
Religion	Church of England
Pre-War Occupation	Farmer

Kranji War Cemetery
Special Memorial 'C'
Plot 4
Row C
Grave 18
Age 23

HISTORY

Cause of Death	Killed in Action
Place of Death	South-West Bukit Timah
Date of Death	11.2.1942
Buried	In common grave at map reference 755150 on 21.12.1942.

FRANCIS ARMSTRONG

Rank	Lance Corporal
Regimental Number	WX7717
Company	'D' Company
Enlisted	10.8.1940
Date of Birth	21.8.1912
Place of Birth	Boulder, Western Australia
Father	Thomas Francis Armstrong
Mother	Catherine Armstrong
Religion	Church of England
Pre-War Occupation	Millhand

Labuan War Cemetery
Plot Q
Row AA
Grave 14
Age 31

HISTORY

Singapore	Selarang Camp Changi
Force	'B' Force Borneo
POW Number	1467
Cause of Death	Duodenal Ulcer
Place of Death	Sandakan
Date of Death	30.7.1942
Additions	Wounded in action North Lim Chu Kang Road on the west coast of Singapore on 9.2.1942. Admitted to the 2/10th Australian General Hospital with a gunshot wound to the right arm. Discharged to unit on 22.2.1942.

ARTHUR RICHARD ATTENBOROUGH

Rank	Private
Regimental Number	WX7444
Classification	Driver
Company	'D' Company
Enlisted	6.8.1940
Date of Birth	16.3.1917
Place of Birth	Warragul, Victoria
Father	Reppon Attenborough
Mother	Jean Maude Attenborough
Religion	Church of England
Pre-War Occupation	Tractor Driver

Epitaph
Labuan Memorial
Panel 18
Age 28

HISTORY

Singapore	Selarang Camp Changi
	Thomson Road (Caldecot Hill Estate Camp)
	River Valley Road Camp
Force	'B' Force Borneo
POW Number	392
Cause of Death	Acute Enteritis
Place of Death	Ranau area
Date of Death	12.4.1945

ROYAL JAMES BAGGS

Rank	Private
Regimental Number	WX9864
Classification	Cook
Company	'A' Company
Enlisted	6.12.1940
Date of Birth	21.9.1909
Place of Birth	Weymouth, Dorset, England
Father	John Randell Baggs
Mother	Eliza Jane Baggs
Religion	Church of England
Pre-War Occupation	Warehouseman

Epitaph
Labuan Memorial
Panel 18
Age 34

HISTORY

Singapore	Selarang Camp Changi
'A' Force Burma	Green Force, No. 3 Battalion
Camps Thailand	Tamarkan, Non Pladuk, Nacompaton
Japan	*Rakuyo Maru* Party, Kumi No. 37
Cause of Death	Lost at Sea
Place of Death	South China Sea
Date of Death	14.9.1944

NEVILLE ERNEST BAILEY

Rank	Private
Regimental Number	WX10920
Classification	Fitter and Technical Storeman
Attached 2/4th	88 Light Aid Detachment
Enlisted	12.2.1941
Date of Birth	21.6.1920
Place of Birth	Perth, Western Australia
Father	Paul Bert Bailey
Mother	Eliza Bailey
Religion	Methodist
Pre-War Occupation	Warehouseman

Epitaph
Labuan Memorial
Panel 29
Age 24

HISTORY

Singapore	Selarang Camp Changi
Force	'B' Force Borneo
POW Number	485
Cause of Death	Malaria
Place of Death	Sandakan
Date of Death	10.6.1945
Additions	Taken on Strength from 2/4th Field Workshops on 20.2.1941. Transferred to 88 L.A.D. on 27.12.1941.

ARTHUR JOSEPH BAKER

Rank	Private
Regimental Number	WX8720
Classification	Driver
Company	Headquarters Company
Enlisted	23.10.1940
Date of Birth	13.1.1914
Place of Birth	Coolgardie, Western Australia
Father	Arthur Joseph Baker
Mother	Helen Baker
Religion	Roman Catholic
Pre-War Occupation	Truck Driver

Epitaph
Labuan Memorial
Panel 18
Age 30

HISTORY

Singapore	Selarang Camp Changi
'A' Force Burma	Green Force, No. 3 Battalion
POW Number	3076
Camps Burma	Reptu 30km Camp
Japan	*Rakuyo Maru* Party, Kumi No. 37
Cause of Death	Lost at Sea
Place of Death	South China Sea
Date of Death	12.9.1944

WILLIAM ROBERT SAMUEL BAKER

Rank	Private
Regimental Number	WX8682
Classification	Driver
Company	'B' Company
Enlisted	23.10.1940
Date of Birth	27.4.1919
Place of Birth	Esperance, Western Australia
Mother	Lulu Esther Baker
Stepfather	William Edward Johnson
Religion	Methodist
Pre-War Occupation	Miner

Epitaph
Labuan Memorial
Panel 18
Age 25

HISTORY

Java	'Blackforce', attached to 2/3rd Machine Gun Battalion
'A' Force Burma	Java Party No. 4, Black Force
POW Number	4665
Japan	*Rakuyo Maru* Party, Kumi No. 38
Cause of Death	Lost at Sea
Place of Death	South China Sea
Date of Death	12.9.1944

ROBERT SHIPLEY BARR

Rank	Private
Regimental Number	WX7611
Company	'D' Company
Enlisted	10.8.1940
Date of Birth	13.5.1918
Place of Birth	Perth, Western Australia
Father	James Barr
Mother	Hannah Barr
Religion	Presbyterian
Pre-War Occupation	Labourer

Kranji War Cemetery
Special Memorial 'C'
Plot 4
Row D
Grave 20
Age 23

HISTORY

Cause of Death	Possibly Executed
Place of Death	Not known
Date of Death	Thought to be approximately 15.2.1942
Additions	Unconfirmed report stated that soldier was admitted to hospital and then discharged to unit on 15.2.1942. It is believed soldier was travelling in an ambulance when captured by the Japanese. No other details are known.

JOSEPH JOHN SAMUEL BARRASS

Rank	Private
Regimental Number	WX7796
Classification	Driver
Company	'D' Company
Enlisted	10.8.1940
Date of Birth	27.9.1912
Place of Birth	Maylands, Western Australia
Father	Joseph Barrass
Mother	Ada May Barrass
Religion	Roman Catholic
Pre-War Occupation	Hoist Driver

Epitaph
Singapore Memorial
Column 135
Age 29

HISTORY

Cause of Death	Died of Wounds
Place of Death	Tanjong Murai, Singapore
Date of Death	11.2.1942
Additions	Party scattered when it came under heavy fire. Last seen on Wednesday 11.2.1942 by WX8958 William Gibbs.

FREDERICK MARKWELL BARRYMORE

Rank	Private
Regimental Number	WX9589
Classification	Driver
Company	'D' Company
Enlisted	4.12.1940
Date of Birth	2.9.1908
Place of Birth	Peppermint Grove, Western Australia
Father	Frederick William Barrymore
Mother	Cora Henrietta Barrymore
Religion	Church of England
Pre-War Occupation	Traveller

Kanchanaburi War Cemetery
Plot 1
Row F
Grave 47
Age 35

HISTORY

Singapore	Selarang Camp and Barracks Changi
POW Number	1/6937
'D' Force Thailand	V Battalion
POW Number	2221
Camps Thailand	Kuii
Cause of Death	Malaria
Place of Death	Non Pladuk, Hospital Camp No. 2
Date of Death	21.12.1943
Buried	Non Pladuk, Grave No. 1
Additions	Wounded in action on 9.2.1942. Soldier made his way to the General Base Depot and was then admitted to the 2/13th Australian General Hospital on 10.2.1942 with shrapnel wounds to the left arm and chest. Discharged to unit on 21.2.1942.

MICHAEL ARTHUR BARTLETT

Rank	Private
Regimental Number	WX9361
Classification	Driver
Company	'C' Company Headquarters
Enlisted	2.11.1940
Date of Birth	16.4.1917
Place of Birth	Albany, Western Australia
Father	Michael Bartlett
Mother	Mary Baker Bartlett
Religion	Church of England
Pre-War Occupation	Farmhand

Kanchanaburi War Cemetery
Plot 1
Row K
Grave 47
Age 28

HISTORY

Singapore	Selarang Camp Changi
	Johore Bahru, Adam Park
	Selarang Barracks Changi
POW Number	3/6887
'D' Force Thailand	S Battalion
POW Number	8754
Cause of Death	Beri-Beri and Dysentery
Place of Death	Tarsau
Date of Death	7.12.1943
Grave Number	454 No. 2 Cemetery, Tarsau.

WILLIAM HERBERT BEARD

Rank	Private
Regimental Number	WX7883
Company	'C' Company
Enlisted	13.8.1940
Date of Birth	25.6.1911
Place of Birth	Subiaco, Western Australia
Father	Henry William Beard
Mother	Florence Eva Beard
Religion	Roman Catholic
Pre-War Occupation	Linesman

Epitaph
Labuan Memorial
Panel 18
Age 34

HISTORY

Singapore	Selarang Camp Changi
Force	'B' Force Borneo
POW Number	470
Cause of Death	Malaria
Place of Death	Sandakan
Date of Death	10.7.1945

WILLIAM JOHN BEER

Rank	Private
Regimental Number	WX7636
Company	'D' Company
Enlisted	10.8.1940
Date of Birth	7.2.1917
Place of Birth	Bunbury, Western Australia
Father	George Henry Joseph Beer
Mother	Margarette Mary Beer
Religion	Roman Catholic
Pre-War Occupation	Not Known

Epitaph
Labuan Memorial
Panel 18
Age 28

HISTORY

Singapore	Selarang Camp and Barracks Changi
POW Number	4/5912
Force	'E' Force Borneo
POW Number	1581
Cause of Death	Malaria
Date of Death	14.6.1945

ALBERT JAMES BELL

Rank	Private
Regimental Number	WX9063
Company	'D' Company
Enlisted	25.10.1940
Date of Birth	19.8.1918
Place of Birth	Boulder, Western Australia
Father	James Robert Bell
Mother	Mabel Bell
Religion	Methodist
Pre-War Occupation	Labourer

Epitaph
Singapore Memorial
Column 135
Age 22

HISTORY

Cause of Death	Killed by mortar fire during escape bid
Place of Death	Johore Straits
Date of Death	Thought to be 14.2.1942
Additions	Reported missing from 9.2.1942.

ROBERT JOSEPH BELL

Rank	Private
Regimental Number	WX16389
Company	'A' Company
Enlisted	8.9.1941
Date of Birth	6.5.1920
Place of Birth	Perth, Western Australia
Father	Robert John Bell
Mother	Kate Bell
Religion	Presbyterian
Pre-War Occupation	Farmhand

Epitaph
Labuan Memorial
Panel 18
Age 24

HISTORY

Singapore	Selarang Camp Changi
'A' Force Burma	Green Force, No. 3 Battalion
POW Number	1501
Japan	*Rakuyo Maru* Party
Cause of Death	Lost at Sea
Place of Death	South China Sea
Date of Death	14.9.1944

BERTRAM ALFRED BENDALL

Rank	Private
Regimental Number	WX17864
Company	'A' Company
Enlisted	3.12.1941
Date of Birth	13.11.1914
Place of Birth	Donnybrook, Western Australia
Father	William Alfred Bendall
Mother	Alice Matilda Bendall
Religion	Methodist
Pre-War Occupation	Farmhand

Epitaph
Labuan Memorial
Panel 18
Age 30

HISTORY

Singapore	Selarang Camp Changi
Force	'B' Force Borneo
POW Number	482
Cause of Death	Cardiac Beri-Beri
Date of Death	12.2.1945
Additions	Soldier was wounded in action at Buona Vista on 15.2.1942 and was admitted to the 2/13th Australian Hospital with a shrapnel wound to the back. Discharged to unit on 20.2.1942.

HENRY PATRICK BENNETT

Rank	Private
Regimental Number	WX9340
Classification	Driver
Company	Battalion Headquarters
Enlisted	30.10.1940
Date of Birth	10.7.1914
Place of Birth	Albany, Western Australia
Father	Albert Ernest Bennett
Mother	Margaret Cicely Bennett
Religion	Roman Catholic
Pre-War Occupation	Tractor Driver

Epitaph
Labuan Memorial
Panel 18
Age 30

HISTORY

Singapore	Selarang Camp and Barracks, Changi
POW Number	4/5916
Force	'E' Force Borneo
POW Number	1585
Cause of Death	Heart Paralysis
Date of Death	15.2.1945

GUY PERCIVAL BIGGS

Rank	Private
Regimental Number	WX8798
Classification	Driver
Company	'B' Company Headquarters
Enlisted	23.10.1940
Date of Birth	17.8.1905
Place of Birth	Monmouth, Wales
Father	Percy James Biggs
Mother	Miriam Biggs
Religion	Church of England
Pre-War Occupation	Truck Driver

Thanbyuzayat War Cemetery
Plot A5
Row E
Grave 11
Age 39

HISTORY

Singapore	Selarang Camp Changi
'A' Force Burma	Green Force, No. 3 Battalion
POW Number	6272
Cause of Death	Cardiac Beri-Beri, Dysentery and Tropical Ulcers
Place of Death	Khonkan 55km Camp
Date of Death	21.8.1943
Buried	Grave No. 61, Khonkan.

CHARLES ROLAND BIRD

Rank	Private
Regimental Number	WX9017
Company	'A' Company
Enlisted	25.10.1940
Date of Birth	22.9.1911
Place of Birth	North Fremantle, Western Australia
Father	Roland Bird
Mother	Beatrice Agnes Bird
Religion	Church of England
Pre-War Occupation	Bread Carter

Epitaph
Labuan Memorial
Panel 18
Age 28

HISTORY

Singapore	Selarang Camp Changi
Force	'B' Force Borneo
POW Number	487
Cause of Death	Acute Enteritis
Date of Death	26.7.1945

HECTOR JOHN BISHOP

Rank	Private
Regimental Number	WX8650
Classification	Driver
Company	Headquarters Company
Enlisted	23.10.1940
Date of Birth	16.12.1912
Place of Birth	Bayswater, Western Australia
Father	John Bishop
Mother	Lizzie Anne Bishop
Religion	Church of England
Pre-War Occupation	Truck Driver

Kranji War Cemetery
Joint Grave
Plot 23
Row A
Grave 15-16
Age 29

HISTORY

Cause of Death	Died of Wounds
Place of Death	Ulu Pandan
Date of Death	12.2.1942
Additions	A witness stated that this soldier received a gunshot wound to the chest and that 'he was given a drink of water, but was not in a good state at this time.' It is alleged by survivors of this action that Japanese troops moved into the area and were seen bayoneting the wounded. Soldier was reported as missing in action in the vicinity of Reformatory Road following the withdrawal to the new line. This was caused by friendly artillery fire forcing the line back approximately one mile.

JOHN HAROLD BLACKBORROW

Rank	Private
Regimental Number	WX12469
Company	'D' Company
Enlisted	6.5.1941
Date of Birth	29.3.1920
Place of Birth	London, England
Father	Charles Blackborrow
Mother	Gladys Maud Blackborrow
Religion	Church of England
Pre-War Occupation	Metal Polisher

Epitaph
Singapore Memorial
Column 135
Age 21

HISTORY

Cause of Death	Killed in Action
Place of Death	West coast, Singapore
Date of Death	9.2.1942
Additions	Badly shell shocked by Japanese artillery barrage. Not seen again after 9.2.1942 when his party withdrew. Reported to have been with Lieutenant Meiklejohn's group when they were ambushed by the Japanese.

HAROLD VERNON BOOTH

Rank	Lance Corporal
Regimental Number	WX8766
Classification	Driver
Company	'B' Company
Enlisted	23.10.40
Date of Birth	14.11.1907
Place of Birth	Western Australia
Father	George Booth
Mother	Freda Evelyn Booth
Religion	Church of England
Pre-War Occupation	Farmhand and Miner

Djakarta War Cemetery
Plot 1
Row D
Grave 19
Age 37

HISTORY

Java	'Blackforce'
Camps Java	Leles, Garoet, Bandoeng, Bicycle Camp, Batavia
POW Number	5273
Force	Java Party, No. 22
Cause of Death	Beri-Beri
Place of Death	Pakan Baroe, Sumatra
POW Number	3696
Date of Death	15.4.1945
Buried	Camp cemetery, 4 km from Pakan Baroe.

JOSEPH BORROW

Rank	Private
Regimental Number	WX8712
Company	'A' Company
Enlisted	23.10.1940
Date of Birth	4.12.1916
Place of Birth	Newcastle-upon-Tyne, England
Father	John Joseph Borrow
Mother	Sarah Borrow
Religion	Church of England
Pre-War Occupation	Yardman

Kranji War Cemetery
Special Memorial 'C'
Plot 22
Row E
Grave 20
Age 25

HISTORY

Cause of Death	Died of Wounds
Place of Death	St Andrew's Anglican Cathedral, Singapore
Date of Death	15.2.1942
Buried	St Andrews Anglican Cathedral grounds
Additions	Wounded in action at Buona Vista on the afternoon of 15.2.1942. Soldier was admitted to the 2/9th Field Ambulance suffering from a gunshot wound fracture to the lower right leg. He was transferred to hospital but died as a result of his wounds. Soldier was buried on 16.2.1942 in the south-east corner of St Andrew's Cathedral grounds.

'Joe Borrow shared the fate of so many of his generation. Born during a war, grew up in a depression and killed in another war. He did not know what it was like to have a secure job, home and family of his own. And like so many other victims of war, his remains lie in foreign soil, far from his homeland.'

Doreen Borrow

ARTHUR AMOS MURRAY BRAZIER

Rank	Lance Corporal
Regimental Number	WX14226
Company	'A' Company
Enlisted	16.6.1941
Date of Birth	14.2.1908
Place of Birth	Kirup, Western Australia
Father	Lt-Col Noel Brazier, 10th Light Horse Regiment
Mother	Edith Maud Brazier
Religion	Church of England
Pre-War Occupation	Farmer and Grazier

Thanbyuzayat War Cemetery
Plot A11
Row B
Grave 13
Age 38

HISTORY

Singapore	Selarang Camp Changi
'A' Force Burma	Green Force, No. 3 Battalion
POW Number	1500
Cause of Death	Bacillary Dysentery
Place of Death	Thanbyuzayat Base Hospital
Date of Death	18.3.1943
Buried	Grave A30 Thanbyuzayat Cemetery, A.I.F. Section
Additions	Evacuated by truck from Thetkaw 14km Camp to the Base Hospital at Thanbyuzayat on 3.3.1943. Soldier died at 0122 hours on 18.3.1943. Funeral service was conducted by Chaplain F. H. Bashford from the 2/4th Casualty Clearing Station.

MAURICE JOHN BRENNAN

Rank	Corporal
Regimental Number	WX9031
Classification	Chiropodist
Company	Battalion Headquarters
Enlisted	25.10.1940
Date of Birth	5.7.1913
Place of Birth	Perth, Western Australia
Father	George Brennan
Mother	Mary Brennan
Religion	Roman Catholic
Pre-War Occupation	Labourer

Kanchanaburi War Cemetery
Plot 1
Row O
Grave 70
Age 30

HISTORY

Singapore	Selarang Camp and Barracks Changi
POW Number	4/4451
'D' Force Thailand	V Battalion
POW Number	2211
Cause of Death	Beri-Beri
Place of Death	Kuii Camp
Date of Death	27.9.1943
Buried	Grave No.182, Kuii.

JOHN ARTHUR BRIGGS

Rank	Lance Sergeant
Regimental Number	WX5050
Classification	Driver
Company	Headquarters Company
Enlisted	23.7.1940
Date of Birth	22.8.1914
Place of Birth	North Perth, Western Australia
Father	Frederick George Briggs
Mother	Edith Briggs
Religion	Church of England
Pre-War Occupation	Motor Mechanic

Thanbyuzayat War Cemetery
Plot A8
Row B
Grave 20
Age 29

HISTORY

Singapore	Selarang Barracks Changi
'A' Force Burma	Green Force, No. 3 Battalion
POW Number	2723
Cause of Death	Post Leg Amputation
Place of Death	Khonkan 55km Hospital Camp
Date of Death	11.9.1943
Buried	Grave No. 136, Khonkan
Additions	Evacuated to Khonkan 55km Camp from Aungganaung 105km Camp with a tropical ulcer to the ankle.

JOHN ALLEN BROOKER

Rank	Private
Regimental Number	WX9288
Classification	Driver
Company	'A' Company
Enlisted	30.10.1940
Date of Birth	16.4.1917
Place of Birth	Medstead, England
Father	John Alfred Brooker
Mother	Innocence Eleanor Brooker
Religion	Church of England
Pre-War Occupation	Labourer

Kranji War Cemetery
Collective Grave
Plot 30
Row A
Grave 5-8
Age 24

HISTORY

Cause of Death	Killed in Action
Place of Death	Buona Vista
Date of Death	15.2.1942
Buried	Where killed in common grave at map reference 784112. Soldier was killed during an enemy artillery barrage.

ALLAN ROY BROWN

Rank	Private
Regimental Number	WX7947
Classification	Driver
Company	Headquarters Company
Enlisted	13.8.1940
Date of Birth	24.7.1908
Place of Birth	Perth, Western Australia
Father	Henry Robert Brown
Mother	Annie Jane Brown
Religion	Church of England
Pre-War Occupation	Mechanic

Kranji War Cemetery
Collective Grave
Plot 28
Row C
Grave 10-14
Age 33

HISTORY

Cause of Death	Killed in Action
Place of Death	Reformatory Road, Ulu Pandan
Date of Death	12.2.1942
Buried	Where killed at map reference 761126 by Major A. Cough Party on 21.12.1942.
Additions	This soldier was ordered to stay near his truck during the action at Ulu Pandan on account of his small stature of 5 foot and one half inch. His body was discovered by several men from the 2/4th Machine Gun Battalion who went under the wire at Adam Park Camp on the night of 28/29 May 1942.

JAMES BROWN

Rank	Private
Regimental Number	WX17754
Classification	(acted as Clerk, advanced Headquarters Orderly Room)
Company	Battalion Headquarters
Enlisted	8.10.1941
Date of Birth	22.4.1921
Place of Birth	Brown Hill, Victoria
Father	James Reed Brown
Mother	Mabel Wilson Brown
Religion	Church of England
Pre-War Occupation	Trainee Teacher

Epitaph
Singapore Memorial
Column 135
Age 20

HISTORY

Cause of Death	Executed by a Japanese firing squad
Place of Death	Not Known
Date of Death	19.2.1942
Additions	Taken by Imperial Japanese Army on 16.2.1942 from Raffles College Square along with Lieutenant Raphael and Captain Thompson. The Japanese stated that they required drivers. Neither of these two officers or this soldier were ever seen again.

REGINALD JAMES BROWN

Rank	Private
Regimental Number	WX10805
Company	'D' Company
Enlisted	15.1.1941
Date of Birth	22.10.1920
Place of Birth	McGill, South Australia
Father	Albert James Brown
Mother	Dorothy Brown
Religion	Roman Catholic
Pre-War Occupation	Bootmaker

Kranji War Cemetery
Collective Grave
Plot 6
Row C
Grave 12-14
Age 22

HISTORY

Cause of Death	Killed in Action
Place of Death	Lim Chu Kang Road
Date of Death	9.2.1942
Additions	When withdrawing from the coast, this party came under Japanese small arms fire. This soldier along with several others were never sighted again. There is reason to believe that this soldier enlisted underage and that he was closer to 18 years of age.

SYDNEY THOMAS BROWN

Rank	Private
Regimental Number	WX8789
Classification	Batman/Runner
Company	'D' Company
Enlisted	23.10.1940
Date of Birth	23.7.1911
Place of Birth	Burracoppin, Western Australia
Father	Sydney Thomas Brown
Mother	Emma Brown
Religion	Church of England
Pre-War Occupation	Miner

Epitaph
Singapore Memorial
Column 136
Age 30

HISTORY

Cause of Death	Died of Wounds
Place of Death	2/9th Field Ambulance
Date of Death	8.2.1942
Additions	Wounded in action at the 14 mile peg on Lim Chu Kang Road on 8.2.1942. Soldier was taken to the 2/9th Field Ambulance in the same truck that evacuated Lieutenant Wankey. It is believed that soldier died of shock in hospital as a result of his wounds.

MAURICE LESTER BROWNE

Rank	Private
Regimental Number	WX7148
Company	'D' Company
Enlisted	1.8.1940
Date of Birth	2.4.1903
Place of Birth	Ballarat, Victoria
Father	John Browne
Mother	Isabella Browne
Religion	Roman Catholic
Pre-War Occupation	Truck Driver

Kranji War Cemetery
Collective Grave
Plot 6
Row C
Grave 12-14
Age 38

HISTORY

Cause of Death	Killed in Action
Place of Death	14 mile peg Lim Chu Kang Road
Date of Death	9.2.1942

JOHN HENRY BROWNING

Rank	Private
Regimental Number	WX9283
Company	'D' Company
Enlisted	30.10.1940
Date of Birth	13.1.1920
Place of Birth	Northam, Western Australia
Father	James Leonard Browning
Mother	Ellenor Florence Browning
Religion	Church of England
Pre-War Occupation	Butcher

Epitaph
Labuan Memorial
Panel 18
Age 25

HISTORY

Singapore	Selarang Camp Changi
Force	'B' Force Borneo
POW Number	489
Cause of Death	Malaria
Date of Death	16.7.1945
Additions	Wounded in action Lim Chu Kang Road at 0930 hours on 9.2.1942. Admitted to 2/9th Field Ambulance on 9.2.1942 with a gunshot wound to the calf muscle of the right leg. Transferred to the 2/13th Australian General Hospital on 16.2.1942. Transferred to the 2/9th Field Ambulance on 7.3.1942. Discharged to unit on 21.3.1942.

JOHN SCOTT BUCKLEY

Rank	Private
Regimental Number	WX15989
Company	Headquarters Company
Enlisted	25.8.1941
Date of Birth	14.12.1906
Place of Birth	Perth, Western Australia
Father	John William Buckley
Mother	Edith Buckley
Religion	Church of England
Pre-War Occupation	Labourer

Kanchanaburi War Cemetery
Collective Grave
Plot 3
Row D
Grave 37-40
Age 36

HISTORY

Singapore	Selarang Camp Changi
	River Valley Road Camp
	Selarang Barracks Changi
'D' Force Thailand	V Battalion
POW Number	2226
Cause of Death	Malaria, General Debility and Tropical Ulcers
Place of Death	Kuii Camp
Date of Death	19.9.1943
Buried	Grave No. 170, Kuii.

FREDERICK BUGG

Rank	Private
Regimental Number	WX7629
Company	'C' Company
Enlisted	10.8.1940
Date of Birth	6.5.1914
Place of Birth	Maylands, Western Australia
Father	George Bugg
Mother	Jessie Maude Bugg
Religion	Church of England
Pre-War Occupation	Farmhand and Tractor Driver

West Terrace Cemetery
South Australia
Plot 1S
Row 31
Grave 20E
Age 27

HISTORY

Cause of Death	Not Determined
Place of Death	Woodside Army Camp, South Australia
Date of Death	29.9.1941 at 0100 hours
Additions	Frederick had a bony lump on his head which caused him discomfort when he wore his steel helmet. Whether this caused his death, is not known. A Court of Enquiry failed to determine the cause of death, but did determine that there was no evidence to suggest foul play.

LEONARD NEVILLE WILLIAM BULLOCK

Rank	Private
Regimental Number	WX13442
Classification	Clerk (relinquished 30.1.1942)
Company	Battalion Headquarters
Enlisted	11.12.1940
Date of Birth	27.11.1921
Place of Birth	Kalgoorlie, Western Australia
Father	Thomas Charles Bullock
Mother	Jessie Isabelle Bullock
Religion	Church of England
Pre-War Occupation	Clerk at Chamber of Mines, Kalgoorlie

Kanchanaburi War Cemetery
Collective Grave
Plot 1
Row F
Grave 51
Age 22

HISTORY

Singapore	Selarang Camp Changi
	Johore Bahru, Adam Park
	Selarang Barracks Changi
POW Number	3/7129
'D' Force Thailand	V Battalion
POW Number	2227
Cause of Death	Beri-Beri
Place of Death	Non Pladuk (evacuated from Kuii)
Date of Death	31.12.1943
Buried	Grave No. 21, Non Pladuk
Additions	It is believed that this soldier enlisted underage.

RONALD BURCHELL

Rank	Corporal (Promoted on 7.2.1942)
Regimental Number	WX14022
Company	'E' Company, Special Reserve Battalion
Enlisted	11.6.1941
Date of Birth	26.5.1920
Place of Birth	Devon, England
Father	Thomas William Burchell
Mother	Violet Lilian Burchell
Religion	Church of England
Pre-War Occupation	Farmhand

Epitaph
Singapore Memorial
Column 135
Age 21

HISTORY

Cause of Death	Killed in Action
Place of Death	South-West Bukit Timah
Date of Death	11.2.1942
Additions	Kingsley Fairbridge Farm Schoolboy.

CLIFFORD EDWARD BURNS

Rank	Private
Regimental Number	WX7702
Company	'A' Company
Enlisted	10.8.1940
Date of Birth	5.12.1916
Place of Birth	Dandenong, Victoria
Father	William Joseph Burns
Mother	Amy Maude Burns
Religion	Church of England
Pre-War Occupation	Miner

Epitaph
Labuan Memorial
Panel 18
Age 28

HISTORY

Singapore	Selarang Camp Changi
Force	'B' Force Borneo
POW Number	490
Cause of Death	Cardiac Beri-Beri
Date of Death	4.2.1945
Additions	Wounded in action at Buona Vista and admitted to the 2/13th Australian General Hospital on 15.2.1942 with a shrapnel wound to the back. Discharged to unit on 20.2.1942.

EDWARD GEORGE BURTON

Rank	Private
Regimental Number	WX7007
Company	'A' Company
Enlisted	30.7.1940
Date of Birth	13.8.1922
Place of Birth	Edmonton, London
Father	George Edward Burton
Mother	Dorothy Ethel Burton
Religion	Church of England
Pre-War Occupation	Labourer

Epitaph
Labuan Memorial
Panel 18
Age 22

HISTORY

Singapore	Selarang Camp and Barracks Changi
POW Number	3/6262
Force	'E' Force Borneo
POW Number	1506
Cause of Death	Malaria
Date of Death	21.2.1945

MANSON WILLIAM FRANK BUTCHER

Rank	Private
Regimental Number	WX17755
Company	'E' Company, Special Reserve Battalion
Enlisted	24.11.1941
Date of Birth	18.9.1922
Place of Birth	Palmyra, Western Australia
Father	Frank Gunn Butcher
Mother	Francis Elizabeth Butcher
Religion	Church of England
Pre-War Occupation	Trainee School Teacher

Epitaph
Singapore Memorial
Column 136
Age 19

HISTORY

Cause of Death	Missing believed killed in action
Place of Death	South-West Bukit Timah
Date of Death	11.2.1942

THOMAS JOSEPH BUTLER

Rank	Private
Regimental Number	WX7469
Classification	Driver
Company	Headquarters Company
Enlisted	6.8.1940
Date of Birth	15.4.1907
Place of Birth	Perth, Western Australia
Father	Thomas Edward Butler
Mother	Bridget Butler
Religion	Roman Catholic
Pre-War Occupation	Insurance Agent

Kranji War Cemetery
Plot 3
Row E
Grave 8
Age 34

HISTORY

Cause of Death	Contracted pneumonia and died in hospital
Place of Death	2/13th Australian General Hospital
Date of Death	14.2.1942
Buried	Martia Road Military Cemetery, Katong on 15.2.1942 Roman Catholic Section, Section 1, Grave No. 14
Additions	Soldier received a gunshot wound to the upper chest during a bayonet charge at Hill 200, Ulu Pandan. A second witness stated that soldier was wounded in the throat.

HENRY DAVID CAIN

Rank	Private
Regimental Number	WX17860
Company	'A' Company
Enlisted	3.12.1941
Date of Birth	13.12.1920
Place of Birth	Donnybrook, Western Australia
Father	Richard Cain
Mother	Vera Hildegarde Cain
Religion	Church of England
Pre-War Occupation	Farmhand

Kranji War Cemetery
Collective Grave
Plot 28
Row C
Grave 10-14
Age 21

HISTORY

Cause of Death	Killed in Action
Place of Death	Hill 200, Ulu Pandan
Date of Death	12.2.1942
Buried	Believed buried where killed.

WILLIAM CAMERON

Rank	Private
Regimental Number	WX20026
Company	'E' Company, Special Reserve Battalion
Enlisted	8.9.1941
Date of Birth	8.7.1908
Place of Birth	Inverness, Scotland
Father	Angus Cameron
Mother	Christina Cameron
Religion	Presbyterian
Pre-War Occupation	Labourer

Epitaph
Singapore Memorial
Column 136
Age 33

HISTORY

Cause of Death	Killed in Action
Place of Death	South-West Bukit Timah
Date of Death	11.2.1942

REGINALD FRANCIS CANNON

Rank	Private
Regimental Number	WX7479
Classification	Signaller
Company	Headquarters Company
Enlisted	6.8.1940
Date of Birth	2.9.1912
Place of Birth	Carnarvon, Western Australia
Father	Desmond Ernest Cannon
Mother	May Cannon
Religion	Roman Catholic
Pre-War Occupation	Salesman

Kranji War Cemetery
Plot 1
Row A
Grave 14
Age 29

HISTORY

Cause of Death	Killed in Action
Place of Death	Hill 200, Ulu Pandan
Date of Death	12.2.1942
Buried	Where killed at map reference 763132 by Major A. Cough Party on 21.12.1942.

ROBERT JAMES CARLILE

Rank	Private
Regimental Number	WX8192
Company	'C' Company
Enlisted	16.8.1940
Date of Birth	25.12.1913
Place of Birth	Meekatharra, Western Australia
Father	Edwin Joseph Carlile
Mother	Ellen Kathleen Carlile
Religion	Roman Catholic
Pre-War Occupation	Barman

Kranji War Cemetery
Plot 1
Row B
Grave 11
Age 28

HISTORY

Cause of Death	Killed in Action
Place of Death	Vicinity of Reformatory Road, Ulu Pandan
Date of Death	11.2.1942

JOHN MURRAY CARR

Rank	Private
Regimental Number	WX15690
Company	'B' Company
Enlisted	11.8.1941
Date of Birth	13.1.1915
Place of Birth	Katanning, Western Australia
Father	John Augustine Carr
Mother	Evelyn Mary Carr
Religion	Church of England
Pre-War Occupation	Maltster's Labourer

Kanchanaburi War Cemetery
Plot 1
Row J
Grave 48
Age 28

HISTORY

Singapore	Selarang Camp Changi
	Johore Bahru, Adam Park
	Selarang Barracks Changi
POW Number	4/5977
'D' Force Thailand	S Battalion
POW Number	8766
Cause of Death	Cerebral Malaria and Beri-Beri (evacuated to Tarsau)
Place of Death	Tarsau Base Hospital
Date of Death	23.7.1943
Buried	Grave No. 51, No. 2 Cemetery, Tarsau.

RAYMOND FRANCIS CARRUTHERS

Rank	Private
Regimental Number	WX7325
Company	'B' Company
Enlisted	6.8.1940
Date of Birth	1.1.1920
Place of Birth	Subiaco, Western Australia
Father	James Victor Carruthers
Mother	Lucy Carruthers
Religion	Roman Catholic
Pre-War Occupation	Labourer

Kranji War Cemetery
Special Memorial 'C'
Plot 6
Row E
Grave 11
Age 22

HISTORY

Cause of Death	Killed in Action
Place of Death	On a slope about 300 yards from Mandai Road
Date of Death	11.2.1942

ALFRED HENRY CARTER

Rank	Private
Regimental Number	WX9326
Company	'D' Company
Enlisted	30.10.1940
Date of Birth	28.8.1920
Place of Birth	Northam, Western Australia
Father	Lewis Basil Carter
Mother	Mary Jane Carter
Religion	Church of England
Pre-War Occupation	Labourer

Epitaph
Labuan Memorial
Panel 18
Age 24

HISTORY

Singapore	Selarang Camp Changi
'A' Force Burma	Green Force, No. 3 Battalion
POW Number	1536
Japan	*Rakuyo Maru* Party, Kumi No. 35
Cause of Death	Lost at Sea
Place of Death	South China Sea
Date of Death	12.9.1944

REGINALD CHARLES CARTER

Rank	Private
Regimental Number	WX8445
Company	Headquarters Company
Enlisted	18.10.1940
Date of Birth	1.7.1913
Place of Birth	Guildford, Western Australia
Father	Charles Henry Carter
Mother	Sophia Elizabeth Carter
Religion	Presbyterian
Pre-War Occupation	French Polisher

Kanchanaburi War Cemetery
Plot 10
Row D
Grave 10
Age 31

HISTORY

Singapore	Selarang Camp Changi
	Thompson Road (Caldecott Hill Estate Camp)
	Adam Park, River Valley Road Camp
	Selarang Barracks Changi
POW Number	3/7236
'D' Force Thailand	S Battalion
POW Number	8763
Camps Thailand	Konkoita
Cause of Death	Blackwater Fever
Place of Death	Chungkai
Date of Death	18.2.1945
Buried	Grave No. B129
	Reburied at Kanchanaburi Allied War Cemetery, Row N, Plot 1, Grave No. 23.

WILLIAM CECIL CASE

Rank	Private
Regimental Number	WX11584
Company	'C' Company
Enlisted	9.4.1941
Date of Birth	6.2.1915
Place of Birth	London, England
Father	William Frank Case
Mother	Susan Case
Religion	Church of England
Pre-War Occupation	Farmhand

Epitaph
Singapore Memorial
Column 136
Age 27

HISTORY

Cause of Death	Killed in Action
Place of Death	Hill 200, Ulu Pandan
Date of Death	12.2.1942
Buried	Where killed at map reference 758128 by Major A. Cough Party on 21.12.1942.

FREDERICK CHARLES CHAMBERS

Rank	Private
Regimental Number	WX16795
Company	'E' Company, Special Reserve Battalion
Enlisted	1.10.1941
Date of Birth	30.11.1906
Place of Birth	Menzies, Western Australia
Father	Charles Henry Chambers
Mother	Myrtle Anne Chambers
Religion	Roman Catholic
Pre-War Occupation	Truck Driver

HISTORY

Cause of Death	Missing believed killed in action
Place of Death	South-West Bukit Timah
Date of Death	11.2.1942

Epitaph
Singapore Memorial
Column 136
Age 35

DESMOND BRUCE CHAPMAN

Rank	Staff Sergeant
Regimental Number	WX7504
Company	'C' Company Headquarters
Enlisted	6.8.1940
Date of Birth	18.3.1916
Place of Birth	Queensland
Father	William George Chapman
Mother	Ethel Lloyd Chapman
Religion	Church of England
Pre-War Occupation	Cashier

HISTORY

Singapore	Selarang Camp Changi
'A' Force Burma	Green Force, No. 3 Battalion
POW Number	2650
Cause of Death	Tropical Ulcer, Malaria and Dysentery
Place of Death	Khonkan 55km Hospital Camp
Date of Death	11.9.1943
Buried	Grave No. 130, Khonkan
Additions	Evacuated to the 55km Camp from Aungganaung 105km Camp on 1.7.1943 due to an irregularly large 8 inch by 8 inch tropical ulcer that exposed the bones and tendons on the right foot. Soldier's right leg was amputated below the knee. The surgical re-amputation of stump was conducted due to gangrene.

Thanbyuzayat War Cemetery
Plot A3
Row C
Grave 19
Age 27

HERBERT ALFRED THOMAS CHILVERS

Rank	Private
Regimental Number	WX8123
Classification	Driver
Company	'D' Company
Enlisted	16.8.1940
Date of Birth	21.4.1911
Place of Birth	Sutton, England
Father	Alfred Chilvers
Mother	Eleanor Maria Chilvers
Religion	Church of England
Pre-War Occupation	Labourer

Epitaph
Labuan Memorial
Panel 18
Age 33

HISTORY

Singapore	Selarang Camp and Barracks Changi
POW Number	4/5990
Force	'E' Force Borneo
POW Number	1634
Cause of Death	Malaria
Date of Death	31.3.1945

ROBERT WILLIAM CHIPPERFIELD

Rank	Private
Regimental Number	WX8397
Company	'A' Company
Enlisted	7.10.1940
Date of Birth	5.5.1916
Place of Birth	London, England
Father	R. W. Chipperfield
Mother	Not Known
Religion	Church of England
Pre-War Occupation	Labourer

Labuan War Cemetery
Plot R
Row AA
Grave 15
Age 28

HISTORY

Singapore	Selarang Camp Changi
	Serangoon Road Camp
Force	'B' Force Borneo
POW Number	591
Cause of Death	Cardiac Beri-Beri
Date of Death	11.2.1945
Additions	Shell shocked at Ulu Pandan. Admitted to the 2/13th Australian General Hospital on 13.2.1942. Discharged to unit on 15.2.1942. Kingsley Fairbridge Farm Schoolboy.

JOHN CLARE

Rank	Private
Regimental Number	WX7163
Company	'C' Company
Enlisted	2.8.1940
Date of Birth	15.3.1909
Place of Birth	Manchester, England
Father	John Clare
Mother	Florence Clare
Religion	Roman Catholic
Pre-War Occupation	Labourer

Epitaph
Singapore Memorial
Column 136
Age 32

HISTORY

Cause of Death	Killed in Action
Place of Death	Ulu Pandan
Date of Death	11.2.1942
Buried	Where killed at map reference 758128 by Major A. Cough Party on 21.12.1942.

JOHN MOSTYN CLARE

Rank	Corporal
Regimental Number	WX6976
Classification	Clerk (relinquished 26.6.1941, but acted as a clerk)
Company	'A' Company
Enlisted	30.7.1940
Date of Birth	14.7.1907
Place of Birth	Kapunda, South Australia
Father	William Rutherford Clare
Mother	Emma Catherine Clare
Religion	Church of England
Pre-War Occupation	Linotype Operator

Kanchanaburi War Cemetery
Plot 1
Row G
Grave 77
Age 36

HISTORY

Singapore	Selarang Camp and Barracks, Changi
POW Number	3/7278
'D' Force Thailand	V Battalion
POW Number	2230
Cause of Death	Chronic Diarhorrea
Place of Death	Hindane Camp
Date of Death	8.8.1943
Buried	Linson Camp Cemetery, Grave No. 16.

FRANCIS DENIS JOHN CLARK
a.k.a. Francis Denis John Stevens

Rank	Private
Regimental Number	WX7714
Classification	Driver/Mechanic
Company	'D' Company Headquarters
Enlisted	10.8.1940
Date of Birth	18.8.1913
Place of Birth	Worsely, Western Australia
Father	(1) Not Known
Mother	(1) Catherine Edith Stevens
Father	(2) John Stephenson Clark
Mother	(2) Margaret Caroline Clark
Religion	Roman Catholic
Pre-War Occupation	Storekeeper

Kanchanaburi War Cemetery
Plot 3
Row G
Grave 35-39
Age 30

HISTORY

Singapore	Selarang Camp Changi
	Johore Bahru, Adam Park
	Selarang Barracks Changi
POW Number	4/5995
'D' Force Thailand	V Battalion
POW Number	2231
Cause of Death	Malaria and Cardiac Beri-Beri
Place of Death	Kuii Camp
Date of Death	10.10.1943
Buried	Grave No. 196, Kuii
Additions	Margaret Clark was Catherine's sister so this made her Frank's aunt. Although never officially adopted he changed his name from Stevens to Clark before he married and enlisted in the A.I.F. as such.

JAMES SYDNEY CLARKE

Rank	Private
Regimental Number	WX7625
Company	'C' Company
Enlisted	10.8.1940
Date of Birth	9.6.1918
Place of Birth	Bunbury, Western Australia
Father	James Charles Clarke
Mother	Nellie Margaret Clarke
Religion	Roman Catholic
Pre-War Occupation	Abattoir Worker

Thanbyuzayat War Cemetery
Plot A3
Row C
Grave 20
Age 25

HISTORY

Singapore	Selarang Camp Changi
'A' Force Burma	Green Force, No. 3 Battalion
POW Number	1475
Cause of Death	Pellagra and Cardiac Failure
Place of Death	Khonkan 55km Camp
Date of Death	13.8.1943
Buried	Grave No. 44, Khonkan
Additions	Soldier was evacuated sick from Aungganaung 105km Camp on 7.7.1943.

SAMUEL CLARKE

Rank	Private
Regimental Number	WX6632
Company	'C' Company
Enlisted	5.6.1940
Date of Birth	24.6.1919
Place of Birth	Essex, England
Father	George Clarke
Mother	Ada Elizabeth Clarke
Religion	Church of England
Pre-War Occupation	Labourer

Thanbyuzayat War Cemetery
Plot A11
Row B
Grave 1
Age 23

HISTORY

Singapore	Selarang Camp Changi
'A' Force Burma	Green Force, No. 3 Battalion
POW Number	1511
Cause of Death	Dysentery
Place of Death	Thanbyuzayat
Date of Death	1910 hours on 23.1.1943
Buried	POW Cemetery, A.I.F. Section, Grave No. 22, Thanbyuzayat. The funeral service was conducted by Chaplain F. H. Bashford, 2/4th Casualty Clearing Station.
Additions	Soldier's possessions at time of his death were as follows; one whistle on a lanyard, one half rupee note and two ten cent notes.

GORDON DAGLEY CLIFTON

Rank	Private
Regimental Number	WX16436
Company	'A' Company
Enlisted	10.9.1941
Date of Birth	1.4.1915
Place of Birth	Bunbury, Western Australia
Father	Richard Henry Clifton
Mother	Rachael Isabella Clifton
Religion	Methodist
Pre-War Occupation	Skipman

Kranji War Cemetery
Plot 30
Row A
Grave 5-8
Age 26

HISTORY

Cause of Death	Killed in Action
Place of Death	Buona Vista
Date of Death	15.2.1942
Buried	Where killed at map reference 784112 in a common grave on 16.2.1942.
Additions	Soldier was killed by shrapnel during an enemy artillery barrage.

AUSTIN NEWMAN CLIMIE

Rank	Corporal (Promoted on 12.2.1942)
Regimental Number	WX4927
Company	'C' Company
Enlisted	23.7.1940
Date of Birth	23.10.1907
Place of Birth	Perth, Western Australia
Father	Murray Climie
Mother	Eliza Martha Climie
Stepfather	William Thomas Jacks
Religion	Anglican
Pre-War Occupation	Truck Driver

**Yokohama British
Commonwealth Cemetery**
Australian Section
Plot A
Row A
Grave 15
Age 37

HISTORY

Singapore	Selarang Camp Changi
'A' Force Burma	Green Force, No. 3 Battalion
POW Number	2896
Japan	*Rakuyo Maru* Party, Kumi No. 36 (rescued)
Camps Japan	Kawasaki Camp No. 14D
POW Number	6103
Cause of Death	Killed during an Allied air raid
Place of Death	Kawasaki Camp No. 14D
Date of Death	13.7.1945

EDWIN HENRY COLE

Rank	Private
Regimental Number	SX11457
Attached 2/4th	88 Light Aid Detachment
Enlisted	24.2.1941
Date of Birth	29.7.1909
Place of Birth	England
Father	William Cole
Mother	Not Known
Religion	Church of England
Pre-War Occupation	Carpenter

Epitaph
Labuan Memorial
Panel 18
Age 35

HISTORY

Singapore	Selarang Camp and Barracks Changi
Force	'E' Force Borneo
POW Number	1646
Cause of Death	Not Known
Date of Death	18.5.1945
Additions	Taken on Strength from 2/4th Field Workshops, Australian Army Ordnance Corps on 14.1.1943.

ALEXANDER JOHN COLQUHOUN

Rank	Private
Regimental Number	WX9109
Company	'C' Company
Enlisted	30.10.1940
Date of Birth	10.6.1906
Place of Birth	Midland Junction, Western Australia
Father	Robert Colquhoun
Mother	Mary Ann Colquhoun
Religion	Church of England
Pre-War Occupation	Labourer

Epitaph
Labuan Memorial
Panel 18
Age 38

HISTORY

Singapore	Selarang Camp Changi
'A' Force Burma	Green Force, No. 3 Battalion
POW Number	1481
Japan	*Rakuyo Maru* Party
Cause of Death	Lost at Sea
Place of Death	South China Sea
Date of Death	15.9.1944

HUGH MYLES COOPER

Rank	Private
Regimental Number	WX15707
Company	Battalion Headquarters
Enlisted	12.8.1941
Date of Birth	8.4.1905
Place of Birth	Tenterdon, Western Australia
Father	William Cooper
Mother	Sarah Cooper
Religion	Church of England
Pre-War Occupation	Labourer

Kanchanaburi War Cemetery
Collective Grave
Plot 10
Row D
Grave 1-3
Age 38

HISTORY

Singapore	Selarang Camp Changi
	Serangoon Road Camp
	Selarang Barracks Changi
POW Number	4/6017
'D' Force Thailand	V Battalion
POW Number	2232
Cause of Death	Dysentery
Place of Death	Kuii
Date of Death	3.10.1943
Buried	Kuii Cemetery Grave No. 191. Exhumed from Kuii Cemetery and re-interred at Kanchanaburi War Cemetery, Plot 1, Row P, Grave No. 55-77. Exhumed and re-interred in Plot 10, Row D, Grave No. 1-3.
Additions	Wounded in action on 11.2.1942. Admitted to Field Ambulance with a shrapnel wound to right thigh. Transferred to the 2/13th Australian General Hospital on 16.2.1942. Discharged to unit on 16.2.1942

ARNOLD VIVIAN COUSINS

Rank	Private
Regimental Number	WX9092
Company	'C' Company
Enlisted	25.10.1940
Date of Birth	26.11.1913
Place of Birth	Mt Helena, Western Australia
Father	William Robert Moore
Mother	Clara Matilda Moore
Religion	Church of England
Pre-War Occupation	Baker

Epitaph
Labuan Memorial
Panel 18
Age 30

HISTORY

Singapore	Selarang Camp Changi
'A' Force Burma	Green Force, No. 3 Battalion
POW Number	1480
Japan	*Rakuyo Maru* Party
Cause of Death	Lost at Sea
Place of Death	South China Sea
Date of Death	14.9.1944
Additions	Previous service, 10th Light Horse Militia.

DAVID CHARLES CRIPPS

Rank	Private
Regimental Number	WX15783
Company	'A' Company
Enlisted	13.8.1941
Date of Birth	15.12.1921
Place of Birth	Geraldton, Western Australia
Father	David Williams Cripps
Mother	Mary Grace Cripps
Religion	Methodist
Pre-War Occupation	Labourer

Epitaph
Labuan Memorial
Panel 18
Age 22

HISTORY

Singapore	Selarang Camp Changi
'A' Force Burma	Green Force, No. 3 Battalion
POW Number	1502
Japan	*Rakuyo Maru* Party, Kumi No. 35
Cause of Death	Lost at Sea
Place of Death	South China Sea
Date of Death	12.9.1944

ALBERT CRYER

Rank	Private
Regimental Number	WX9004
Classification	Despatch Rider
Company	'D' Company
Enlisted	25.10.1940
Date of Birth	17.9.1910
Place of Birth	England
Father	Charles Henry Cryer
Mother	Martha Cryer
Religion	Church of England
Pre-War Occupation	Shop Assistant

Kanchanaburi War Cemetery
Plot 1
Row H
Grave 73
Age 32

HISTORY

Singapore	Selarang Camp Changi
	Johore Bahru, Adam Park,
	Selarang Barracks Changi
POW Number	4/6037
'D' Force Thailand	S Battalion
POW Number	8760
Cause of Death	Typhus
Place of Death	Kanu 1 River Camp
Date of Death	28.7.1943
Buried	Kanu 1 River Camp Cemetery, Grave No. 75.

ALFRED THOMAS CUNNINGHAM

Rank	Private
Regimental Number	WX17706
Company	'C' Company
Enlisted	19.11.1941
Date of Birth	5.10.1916
Place of Birth	Fremantle, Western Australia
Father	Charles Herbert Cunningham
Mother	Elizabeth Cunningham
Religion	Church of England
Pre-War Occupation	Farmhand

Kranji War Cemetery
Special Memorial 'C'
Plot 28
Row D
Grave 7
Age 22

HISTORY

Cause of Death	Died of Wounds
Date of Death	10.2.1942
Additions	Soldier was wounded in action at Jurong Road and was evacuated to an Indian Regimental Aid Post but was not seen again. Soldier's date of birth and age at death do not correspond.

FRANCIS LYLE CURNOW

Rank	Lieutenant
Regimental Number	WX3446
Company	Headquarters Company (replaced by Lt. K. Lee)
Enlisted	2.11.1940
Date of Birth	7.8.1917
Place of Birth	Kalgoorlie, Western Australia
Father	Carlyle Curnow
Mother	Naomi Curnow
Religion	Methodist
Pre-War Occupation	Clerk

Kranji War Cemetery
Plot 1
Row A
Grave 10
Age 24

HISTORY

Cause of Death	Killed in Action
Place of Death	Hill 200, Ulu Pandan
Date of Death	12.2.1942
Buried	Where killed at map reference 763162 by Major A. Cough Party on 21.12.1942.

ALBERT EDWARD DAHLBERG

Rank	Corporal
Regimental Number	WX9561
Classification	Fitter
Attached 2/4th	88 Light Aid Detachment
Enlisted	4.12.1940
Date of Birth	23.7.1911
Place of Birth	Hamelin Bay, Western Australia
Father	Charles Dahlberg
Mother	Bertha Dahlberg
Religion	Church of England
Pre-War Occupation	Truck Driver

Epitaph
Singapore Memorial
Column 139
Age 30

HISTORY

Cause of Death	Killed in Action
Place of Death	Reformatory Road, Ulu Pandan
Date of Death	10.2.1942

GORDON ALEXANDER DALRYMPLE

Rank	Private
Regimental Number	WX14068
Company	'E' Company, Special Reserve Battalion
Enlisted	11.6.1941
Date of Birth	19.5.1920
Place of Birth	Dundee, Scotland
Father	James Alexander Dalrymple
Mother	Mary Conway Dalrymple
Religion	Methodist
Pre-War Occupation	Coppersmith and Welder

Epitaph
Singapore Memorial
Column 136
Age 20

HISTORY

Cause of Death	Killed in Action
Place of Death	Bald Hill, Bukit Timah
Date of Death	11.2.1942

SYDNEY JAMES DARBY

Rank	Private
Regimental Number	WX15873
Company	'E' Company, Special Reserve Battalion
Enlisted	19.8.1941
Date of Birth	16.7.1922
Place of Birth	Epping Green, Essex, England
Father	William Robert Darby
Mother	Edith Hannah Darby
Religion	Church of England
Pre-War Occupation	Shop Assistant

Epitaph
Singapore Memorial
Column 136
Age 19

HISTORY

Cause of Death	Killed in Action
Place of Death	Sungei Kranji-Sungei Jurong Defence Line
Date of Death	10.2.1942
Additions	Soldier is thought to have been killed by a Japanese sniper whilst on patrol.

ROY WILLIAM DAVEY

Rank	Private
Regimental Number	WX8681
Company	A' Company
Enlisted	23.10.1940
Date of Birth	25.4.1915
Place of Birth	East Perth, Western Australia
Father	Herbert Davey
Mother	Ethel Olive Davey
Religion	Church of England
Pre-War Occupation	Miner

Kanchanaburi War Cemetery
Plot 1
Row L
Grave 3
Age 28

HISTORY

Singapore	Selarang Camp and Barracks Changi
'D' Force Thailand	S Battalion
POW Number	8768
Cause of Death	Dysentery and Avitaminosis
Place of Death	Tarsau
Date of Death	1.7.1943
Buried	Tarsau No. 1 Cemetery, Grave No. 156.

THOMAS DAVIDSON

Rank	Acting Lance Corporal (Promoted 22.1.1943)
Regimental Number	WX7909
Classification	Signaller
Company	Headquarters Company
Enlisted	13.8.1940
Date of Birth	15.1.1910
Place of Birth	Perth, Western Australia
Father	William Davidson
Mother	Jeanie Davidson
Religion	Congregational
Pre-War Occupation	Miner

Kanchanaburi War Cemetery
Collective Grave
Plot 10
Row A
Grave 1-4
Age 33

HISTORY

Singapore	Selarang Camp Changi
	Johore Bahru, Adam Park
	Selarang Barracks Changi
POW Number	4/6053
'D' Force Thailand	V Battalion
POW Number	2230
Cause of Death	Acute Enteritis
Place of Death	Kuii
Date of Death	18.9.1943
Buried	Kuii Cemetery, Grave No. 169.

DAVID JOHN DAVIES

Rank	Private
Regimental Number	WX8855
Company	Headquarters Company
Enlisted	23.10.1940
Date of Birth	10.11.1906
Place of Birth	Pontyberem, Carmarthenshire, Wales
Father	Benjiman Davies
Mother	Mary Davies
Religion	Methodist
Pre-War Occupation	Labourer

Kanchanaburi War Cemetery
Plot 1
Row D
Grave 61
Age 37

HISTORY

Java	'Blackforce'
'A' Force Burma	Java Party No. 4, Williams Force
POW Number	4656
Camps Thailand	131km-133km (26.12.1943)
	departed 133km Camp arrived Kanchanaburi 13.1.1944
Cause of Death	Cerebral Malaria
Place of Death	Tamarkan
Date of Death	0815 hours on 10.7.1944
Buried	Tamarkan Cemetery, Row AX, Grave No. 37
Additions	Funeral service conducted by Chaplain F. X. Corry 2/4th Machine Gun Battalion. Chaplain was assisted by Lt-Col C. Green and Lt. C. Blakeway. Soldier was selected and marched out on Japan Party on 27.6.1944 but returned sick on 5.7.1944.

GUSTAVE DAVIES

Rank	Private
Regimental Number	WX20086
Company	'E' Company, Special Reserve Battalion
Enlisted	1.10.1941
Date of Birth	22.10.1921
Place of Birth	Crumlin, Wales
Father	Charles Davies
Mother	Agnes Mabel Davies
Religion	Church of England
Pre-War Occupation	Farmhand

Epitaph
Singapore Memorial
Column 136
Age 20

HISTORY

Cause of Death	Died of Wounds
Place of Death	Buona Vista
Date of Death	15.2.1942
Additions	Soldier had been listed as missing following the ambush at South-West Bukit Timah on 11.2.1942. Kingsley Fairbridge Farm Schoolboy.

HAROLD ALLAN DAVIS

Rank	Private
Regimental Number	WX16420
Company	'A' Company
Enlisted	10.9.1941
Date of Birth	14.4.1917
Place of Birth	Kulyalling, Western Australia
Father	Edward Benjamin Davis
Mother	Annie Rebecca Davis
Religion	Baptist
Pre-War Occupation	Farmhand

Epitaph
Singapore Memorial
Column 136
Age 24

HISTORY

Cause of Death	Died of Wounds
Place of Death	St Andrews Cathedral, Singapore
Date of Death	15.2.1942
Buried	South-east corner of St Andrew's Cathedral grounds on 16.2.1942.
Additions	Wounded in action at Buona Vista on 15.2.1942. Admitted to the 2/9th Australian Field Ambulance with a gunshot wound to right shoulder.

THOMAS MEDLAND DAVISON

Rank	Private
Regimental Number	WX7804
Classification	Driver
Company	Headquarters Company
Enlisted	10.8.1940
Date of Birth	26.4.1908
Place of Birth	Streatham, London, England
Father	Augustus Harry Davison
Mother	Bessie Mabel Davison
Religion	Church of England
Pre-War Occupation	Storeman

Thanbyuzayat War Cemetery
Plot A8
Row D
Grave 16
Age 34

HISTORY

Singapore	Selarang Camp Changi
'A' Force Burma	Green Force, No. 3 Battalion
POW Number	3091
Camps Burma	Reptu 30km Hospital Camp
	To Khonkan 55km Hospital Camp from Aungganaung 105km Camp on 4.7.1943 to amputate left leg above the knee due to a 3 inch by 2 inch tropical ulcer. Three amputations were conducted by Colonel Coates, A.A.M.C.
Cause of Death	Chronic Diarrhoea and Malnutrition
Place of Death	Khonkan 55km Camp
Date of Death	25.10.1943
Buried	Grave No. 204, Khonkan 55km Camp.

DONALD ALEXANDER DAY

Rank	Private
Regimental Number	WX7240
Company	'B' Company
Enlisted	1.8.1940
Date of Birth	21.10.1913
Place of Birth	Jarrahdale, Western Australia
Father	William Frederick Day
Mother	Vertue Day
Religion	Church of England
Pre-War Occupation	Shop Assistant

Epitaph
Singapore Memorial
Column 136
Age 28

HISTORY

Cause of Death	Died of Wounds
Place of Death	West Mandai Road
Date of Death	11.2.1942
Additions	Wounded whilst withdrawing No. 3 gun back 100 yards to new position on Mandai Road.

MARTIN WILLIAM DAY

Rank	Private
Regimental Number	WX17391
Company	'E' Company, Special Reserve Battalion
Enlisted	27.10.1941
Date of Birth	18.8.1920
Place of Birth	Jarrahdale, Western Australia
Father	Horace William Day
Mother	Amelia Day
Religion	Church of England
Pre-War Occupation	Wood Cutter

Epitaph
Singapore Memorial
Column 136
Age 21

HISTORY

Cause of Death	Killed in Action
Place of Death	South-West Bukit Timah
Date of Death	11.2.1942

HARRY THOMAS DELAPORTE

Rank	Private
Regimental Number	WX8011
Company	'A' Company
Enlisted	10.8.1940
Date of Birth	14.8.1914
Place of Birth	Capel, Western Australia
Father	Henry Thomas Delaporte
Mother	Emily Ada Delaporte
Religion	Church of England
Pre-War Occupation	Labourer

Epitaph
Labuan Memorial
Panel 18
Age 30

HISTORY

Singapore	Selarang Camp Changi
'A' Force Burma	Green Force, No. 3 Battalion
POW Number	3088
Japan	*Rakuyo Maru* Party, Kumi No. 37
Cause of Death	Lost at Sea
Place of Death	South China Sea
Date of Death	12.9.1944

HENRY FRANCIS DeMOULIN

Rank	Lieutenant
Regimental Number	WX9389
Company	Headquarters, 'E' Company, Special Reserve Battalion
Enlisted	16.11.1940
Date of Birth	16.4.1920
Place of Birth	Perth, Western Australia
Father	Harry Thomas DeMoulin
Mother	Elizabeth Ann DeMoulin
Religion	Church of England
Pre-War Occupation	Clerk

Epitaph
Singapore Memorial
Column 135
Age 21

HISTORY

Cause of Death	Killed in Action
Place of Death	South-West Bukit Timah
Date of Death	11.2.1942

GORDON DORIZZI

Rank	Private
Regimental Number	WX9274
Classification	Driver
Company	'A' Company
Enlisted	30.10.1940
Date of Birth	30.5.1916
Place of Birth	Perth, Western Australia
Father	Thomas John Dorizzi
Mother	Mary Ann Dorizzi
Religion	Roman Catholic
Pre-War Occupation	Truck Driver

Epitaph
Labuan Memorial
Panel 18
Age 28

HISTORY

Singapore	Selarang Camp Changi
Force	'B' Force Borneo
POW Number	622
Cause of Death	Malaria
Place of Death	Sandakan
Date of Death	11.2.1945

HERBERT DORIZZI

Rank	Private
Regimental Number	WX7997
Classification	Driver
Company	'D' Company Headquarters
Enlisted	13.8.1940
Date of Birth	29.4.1918
Place of Birth	Toodyay, Western Australia
Father	Thomas John Dorizzi
Mother	Mary Ann Dorizzi
Religion	Roman Catholic
Pre-War Occupation	Truck Driver

Epitaph
Labuan Memorial
Panel 18
Age 26

HISTORY

Singapore	Selarang Camp Changi
	Johore Bahru, Adam Park
Force	'B' Force Borneo
POW Number	623
Cause of Death	Heart Failure
Place of Death	Sandakan
Date of Death	11.2.1945
Additions	Soldier received a shrapnel wound to the head on 9.2.1942 but remained on duty.

THOMAS HENRY DORIZZI

Rank	Private
Regimental Number	WX12884
Classification	Driver
Company	'A' Company
Enlisted	14.5.1941
Date of Birth	24.2.1914
Place of Birth	Perth, Western Australia
Father	Thomas John Dorizzi
Mother	Mary Ann Dorizzi
Religion	Roman Catholic
Pre-War Occupation	Truck Driver

Epitaph
Labuan Memorial
Panel 18
Age 31

HISTORY

Singapore	Selarang Camp Changi
POW Number	4/6079
Force	'E' Force Borneo
POW Number	1678
Cause of Death	Beri-Beri
Place of Death	Ranau No. 1 Camp
Date of Death	11.3.1945
Buried	No. 1 Camp Cemetery, Ranau
Additions	Wounded in action at Bouna Vista on 15.2.1942. Admitted to the 2/13th Australian General Hospital with a shrapnel wound to the right leg on 15.2.1942. Discharged to unit on 23.2.1942.

ALEXANDER McDOUGAL DONALD DRUMMOND

Rank	Private
Regimental Number	WX8830
Company	'B' Company Headquarters
Enlisted	23.10.1940
Date of Birth	21.6.1911
Place of Birth	Kinross, Scotland
Father	George Watt Drummond
Mother	Agnes Henderson Drummond
Religion	Presbyterian
Pre-War Occupation	Miner

Epitaph
Labuan Memorial
Panel 18
Age 33

HISTORY

Java	'Blackforce'
'A' Force Burma	Java Party No.4, Williams Force
POW Number	4641
Japan	*Rakuyo Maru* Party, Kumi No. 38
Cause of Death	Lost at Sea
Place of Death	South China Sea
Date of Death	15.9.1944

CHARLES HENRY DUNN

Rank	Corporal
Regimental Number	WX8092
Attached 2/4th	Australian Army Postal Corps
Enlisted	16.8.1940
Date of Birth	11.9.1899
Place of Birth	Staplehurst, Kent, England
Father	Not Known
Mother	Not Known
Religion	Church of England
Pre-War Occupation	Dairyhand

Epitaph
Labuan Memorial
Panel 31
Age 44

HISTORY

Singapore	Selarang Camp Changi
Force	'B' Force Borneo
POW Number	190
Cause of Death	Malaria
Place of Death	Sandakan
Date of Death	21.3.1945

WILLIAM ANDREW DWYER

Rank	Private
Regimental Number	WX10390
Company	'D' Company
Enlisted	18.12.1940
Date of Birth	21.12.1921
Place of Birth	Kalgoorlie, Western Australia
Father	John Joseph Dwyer
Mother	Marie Annie Dwyer
Religion	Roman Catholic
Pre-War Occupation	Labourer

Kanchanaburi War Cemetery
Plot 1
Row H
Grave 22
Age 24

HISTORY

Singapore	Selarang Camp and Barracks Changi
POW Number	3/7649
'D' Force Thailand	V Battalion
POW Number	2237
Cause of Death	Malaria and Dysentery
Place of Death	Brankassi
Date of Death	22.8.1943
Buried	Grave No. 47, Brankassi
Additions	Admitted to the 2/10th Australian General Hospital on 12.2.1942 badly shell shocked and suffering from nervous exhaustion. Discharged to unit on 20.2.1942.

WILLIAM DWYER

Rank	Private
Regimental Number	WX20076
Company	Headquarters Company
Enlisted	24.9.1941
Date of Birth	7.2.1907
Place of Birth	Kunanalling, Western Australia
Father	John Westby Dwyer
Mother	Georgina Alexandra Dwyer
Religion	Roman Catholic
Pre-War Occupation	Miner

Labuan War Cemetery
Plot H
Row D
Grave 15
Age 38

HISTORY

Singapore	Selarang Camp and Barracks Changi
POW Number	4/6090
'D' Force Thailand	V Battalion
Camps Thailand	Brankassi, Hindaine, Chungkai, Tamuang, Non Pladuk
Japan	*Aramis* Party
Place of Death	Fukuoka sub-Camp No. 1
Date of Death	5.5.1945
Cause of Death	Acute Colitis
Additions	Soldier's ashes are believed to have been carried from Japan to Labuan by an unknown serviceman.

WILLIAM HOWARD EARNSHAW

Rank	Private
Regimental Number	WX6262
Company	'B' Company
Enlisted	13.7.1940
Date of Birth	20.8.1919
Place of Birth	Kalgoorlie, Western Australia
Father	William Howard Earnshaw
Mother	Faith Daisy Earnshaw
Religion	Church of England
Pre-War Occupation	Rigger's Mate

Epitaph
Labuan Memorial
Panel 18
Age 25

HISTORY

Singapore	Selarang Camp Changi
	Johore Bahru, Adam Park
	Selarang Barracks Changi
POW Number	4/6092
Force	'E' Force Borneo
POW Number	1684
Cause of Death	Malaria
Place of Death	Sandakan
Date of Death	15.3.1945

HAROLD EASTWOOD

Rank	Private
Regimental Number	WX10114
Classification	Signaller
Company	Headquarters Company
Enlisted	13.12.1940
Date of Birth	3.5.1908
Place of Birth	Manchester, England
Father	William John Eastwood
Mother	Violet Eastwood
Religion	Church of England
Pre-War Occupation	Oil Grader

Kranji War Cemetery
Plot 1
Row 4
Grave 15
Age 33

HISTORY

Cause of Death	Killed in Action
Place of Death	Reformatory Road, Ulu Pandan
Date of Death	10.2.1942
Buried	Where killed at map reference 763132 by Major A. Cough Party on 21.12.1942.

GEORGE HENRY EDWARDS

Rank	Private
Regimental Number	WX7266
Company	'B' Company
Enlisted	1.8.1940
Date of Birth	3.11.1910
Place of Birth	Newcastle-upon-Tyne, England
Father	Not Known
Mother	Not Known
Religion	Church of England
Pre-War Occupation	Miner

Epitaph
Labuan Memorial
Panel 18
Age 34

HISTORY

Singapore	Selarang Camp Changi
	Johore Bahru, Adam Park,
	Selarang Barracks, Changi
POW Number	4/6096
Force	'E' Force Borneo
POW Number	1686
Cause of Death	Malaria
Place of Death	Sandakan
Date of Death	20.3.1945

THOMAS HENRY EDWARDS

Rank	Private
Regimental Number	WX7620
Company	'D' Company
Enlisted	10.8.1940
Date of Birth	3.9.1900
Place of Birth	Shropshire, England
Father	Henry Edwards
Mother	Francis Edwards
Religion	Church of England
Pre-War Occupation	Labourer

Epitaph
Singapore Memorial
Column 136
Age 42

HISTORY

Cause of Death	Died of Wounds
Place of Death	Hill 200, Ulu Pandan
Date of Death	0500 hours on 12.2.1942
Buried	On the padang above lowest level of flat ground NNW of Oldham Hall Singapore, Grave No. 9.
Additions	Wounded in trench by a shell burst from enemy artillery fire at Hill 200, Ulu Pandan. Stretcher bearers carried him to the Regimental Aid Post where 100 yards away, Captain Anderson from the 2/4th Machine Gun Battalion pronounced soldier dead.

HARRY LAURENCE ELKINS

Rank	Private
Regimental Number	WX7562
Classification	Pioneer
Company	Headquarters Company
Enlisted	6.8.1940
Date of Birth	31.3.1906
Place of Birth	Margate, England
Father	Harry Elkins
Mother	Emily Elkins
Religion	Church of England
Pre-War Occupation	Railways Yardman

Kanchanaburi War Cemetery
Plot 1
Row H
Grave 13
Age 37

HISTORY

Singapore	Selarang Camp and Barracks Changi
POW Number	4/6097
'D' Force Thailand	V Battalion
POW Number	2239
Cause of Death	Dysentery and Acute Enteritis
Place of Death	Brankassi
Date of Death	12.8.1943
Buried	Brankassi Cemetery, Grave No. 37.

RONALD EDWARD ELLIS

Rank	Private
Regimental Number	WX13079
Company	'D' Company
Enlisted	17.5.1941
Date of Birth	2.11.1920
Place of Birth	Wagin, Western Australia
Father	George Christopher Ellis
Mother	Olive Ellen Ellis
Religion	Church of England
Pre-War Occupation	Fitter's Assistant

Kranji War Cemetery
Plot 3
Row C
Grave 19
Age 21

HISTORY

Cause of Death	Died of Wounds
Place of Death	2/13th A.G.H. at St Patricks School
Date of Death	11.2.1942
Buried	Martia Road Military Cemetery, Katong. Protestant Section, Grave No. 6.
Additions	Wounded in action on 10.2.1942. Soldier received a gunshot wound to the right arm and shrapnel wound to the chest. Admitted to the 2/13th Australian General Hospital in a badly shocked state, where an amputation of the arm, 2 inches below the shoulder joint was conducted.

ROBERT PHILIP ELVISH

Rank	Private
Regimental Number	WX8381
Company	'A' Company
Enlisted	13.9.1940
Date of Birth	18.9.1901
Place of Birth	Clacton on Sea, Thorpe-le-Soken, Essex, England
Father	Robert Elvish
Mother	Emily Elvish
Religion	Church of England
Pre-War Occupation	Stationhand

Kanchanaburi War Cemetery
Plot 1
Row M
Grave 54
Age 42

HISTORY

Singapore	Selarang Camp and Barracks Changi
POW Numbers	1/7621 and 7995
'D' Force Thailand	V Battalion
POW Number	2240
Cause of Death	Pellagra and Tropical Ulcers
Place of Death	Chungkai
Date of Death	9.10.1943
Buried	Grave No. 643, Chungkai.

WALTER CYRIL EVANS

Rank	Private
Regimental Number	WX9230
Company	'A' Company
Enlisted	30.10.1940
Date of Birth	3.5.1902
Place of Birth	England
Father	William George Evans
Mother	Annie Evans
Religion	Methodist
Pre-War Occupation	Stevedore

Labuan War Cemetery
Plot R
Row AA
Grave 16
Age 43

HISTORY

Singapore	Selarang Camp Changi
Force	'B' Force Borneo
POW Number	1465
Cause of Death	Malaria
Place of Death	Sandakan-Ranau track
Date of Death	14.6.1945

ALBERT BARNETT FACEY

Rank	Private
Regimental Number	WX4915
Classification	Driver
Company	'A' Company
Enlisted	23.7.1940
Date of Birth	3.2.1919
Place of Birth	Bunbury, Western Australia
Father	Albert Barnett Facey
Mother	Evelyn Mary Facey
Religion	Church of England
Pre-War Occupation	Market Gardener and Truck Driver

Kranji War Cemetery
Collective Grave
Plot 30
Row A
Grave 9-13
Age 23

HISTORY

Cause of Death	Killed in Action
Place of Death	Cemetery Hill, Buona Vista
Date of Death	15.2.1942
Buried	Chinese Cemetery Hill, map reference 784112
Additions	Soldier was wounded in the back by shrapnel and died a few minutes later. Buried where killed with eight others in two separate graves, one grave with four bodies and the other with five bodies. The bodies were buried by denomination, one containing Roman Catholics and the other Protestants. Albert was the son of Albert Barnett Facey, author of *A Fortunate Life*.

HUGH ROBERT NELSON FAWCUS

Rank	Corporal
Regimental Number	WX4945
Classification	Cook
Company	'A' Company Headquarters
Enlisted	23.7.1940
Date of Birth	16.6.1901
Place of Birth	Melbourne, Victoria
Father	Robert Flynn Fawcus
Mother	Sarah Fawcus
Religion	Roman Catholic
Pre-War Occupation	Horse Breaker

Kranji War Cemetery
Plot 3
Row C
Grave 11
Age 40

HISTORY

Cause of Death	Died of Wounds
Place of Death	2/13th Australian General Hospital
Date of Death	20.2.1942
Buried	Martia Road Military Cemetery, Katong. Section No. 20, Grave No. 20, Roman Catholic Section. Map reference 927113.
Additions	Wounded by shell fire on the afternoon of 15.2.1942 at Cemetery Hill, Buona Vista. Admitted to the 2/13th Australian General Hospital on 16.2.1942 with shrapnel wounds to both legs and a gunshot wound to the left elbow. Soldier's right leg was amputated on 16.2.1942, but due to toxaemia an emergency operation was conducted on 17.2.1942. Funeral service was conducted by Chaplain Lionel T. Marsden from the 2/13th Australian General Hospital on 20.2.1942. The soldier's body was re-interred at Kranji War Cemetery on 1.5.1946.

REGINALD PAUL FERGUSON

Rank	Private
Regimental Number	WX7999
Company	'D' Company Headquarters
Enlisted	13.8.1940
Date of Birth	8.3.1913
Place of Birth	Toodyay, Western Australia
Father	Robert Lewis Ferguson
Mother	Ada May Ferguson
Religion	Church of England
Pre-War Occupation	Labourer

Epitaph
Labuan Memorial
Panel 18
Age 32

HISTORY

Singapore	Selarang Camp Changi
Force	'B' Force Borneo
POW Number	692
Cause of Death	Acute Intestinalitis
Place of Death	Ranau
Date of Death	23.3.1945
Buried	Ranau
Additions	Shell shocked at Ulu Pandan and evacuated on 12.2.1942.

ALEXANDER WILLIAM FINDLAY

Rank	Private
Regimental Number	WX8874
Classification	Clerk
Company	Headquarters Company
Enlisted	25.10.1940
Date of Birth	28.6.1898
Place of Birth	Inverness, Scotland
Father	George Findlay
Mother	Elizabeth Findlay
Religion	Presbyterian
Pre-War Occupation	Orchardist

Kanchanaburi War Cemetery
Plot 1
Row F
Grave 39
Age 44

HISTORY

Singapore	Selarang Camp Changi
	Johore Bahru, Adam Park
	Selarang Barracks Changi
POW Number	4/6116
'D' Force Thailand	V Battalion
POW Number	2241
Cause of Death	Malaria
Place of Death	Non Pladuk
Date of Death	19.1.1944
Buried	Non Pladuk Cemetery, Grave No. 43
Additions	Fought with the 51st Highland Division in WW1 and was a Prisoner of War in Germany.

RICHARD NEWELL FITZPATRICK

Rank	Sergeant
Regimental Number	WX9039
Classification	Driver
Company	Headquarters Company
Enlisted	25.10.1940
Date of Birth	21.3.1911
Place of Birth	Wiluna, Western Australia
Father	Francis Joseph Fitzpatrick
Mother	Rebecca Fitzpatrick
Religion	Church of England
Pre-War Occupation	Truck Driver

Kranji War Cemetery
Collective Grave
Plot 28
Row C
Grave 10-14
Age 30

HISTORY

Cause of Death	Killed in Action (bayonet charge)
Place of Death	Hill 200, Ulu Pandan
Date of Death	12.2.1942
Buried	Where killed at map reference 761126 by Major A. Cough Party on 21.12.1942.

CHARLES HENRY FLETCHER

Rank	Private
Regimental Number	WX17745
Company	Battalion Headquarters
Enlisted	24.11.1941
Date of Birth	28.12.1901
Place of Birth	Cork, Ireland
Father	Samuel Fletcher
Mother	Laura Fletcher
Religion	Church of England, converted to R.C. at Non Pladuk
Pre-War Occupation	Pastry Cook and Orderly at Fremantle Hospital

Kanchanaburi War Cemetery
Plot 1
Row F
Grave 44
Age 43

HISTORY

Singapore	Selarang Camp Changi
	Johore Bahru, Adam Park
	Selarang Barracks Changi
POW Number	4/6125
'D' Force Thailand	V Battalion
POW Number	2242
Cause of Death	Colitis
Place of Death	Non Pladuk
Date of Death	21.2.1944
Buried	Non Pladuk Cemetery, Grave No. 87
Additions	Soldier acted as a cook although not trade grouped as such.

ARTHUR ERNEST FLOYED

Rank	Private
Regimental Number	WX12663
Company	'C' Company
Enlisted	9.5.1941
Date of Birth	29.6.1918
Place of Birth	Narrogin, Western Australia
Father	John Bertram Floyed
Mother	Ada Clara Floyed
Religion	Baptist
Pre-War Occupation	Labourer

Epitaph
Labuan Memorial
Panel 18
Age 26

HISTORY

Singapore	Selarang Camp Changi
	Johore Bahru, Adam Park
	Selarang Barracks Changi
POW Number	4/6128
Force	'E' Force Borneo
POW Number	1709
Cause of Death	Malaria
Place of Death	Sandakan
Date of Death	12.3.1945

THOMAS RANTOUL FOTHERINGHAM

Rank	Private
Regimental Number	WX10803
Classification	Rangetaker
Company	'B' Company
Enlisted	15.1.1941
Date of Birth	25.3.1921
Place of Birth	Newcastle, England
Father	John Rantoul Fotheringham
Mother	Annie Fotheringham
Religion	Church of England
Pre-War Occupation	Wire Drawer

Epitaph
Labuan Memorial
Panel 18
Age 24

HISTORY

Singapore	Selarang Camp Changi
	Johore Bahru, Adam Park
Force	'B' Force Borneo
POW Number	715
Cause of Death	Beri-Beri
Place of Death	Sandakan-Ranau track
Date of Death	7.6.1945

STUART EDWARD FOXALL

Rank	Corporal
Regimental Number	WX7569
Company	'C' Company
Enlisted	6.8.1940
Date of Birth	7.5.1920
Place of Birth	Cottesloe, Western Australia
Father	John Stuart Foxall
Mother	Mary Josephine Foxall
Religion	Christian Scientist
Pre-War Occupation	Clerk

Thanbyuzayat War Cemetery
Plot A10
Row E
Grave 7
Age 22

HISTORY

Java	'Blackforce'
Camps Java	Bandoeng, Bicycle Camp Batavia
'A' Force Burma	Java Party No. 4, Williams Force
POW Number	3866
Cause of Death	Cholera
Place of Death	Beke Taung 40km Hospital Camp
Date of Death	7.7.1943
Buried	Grave No. 12, by Lieutenant-Colonel Eadie from the 2/2nd Casualty Clearing Station.
Additions	Wounded in action on 22.2.1942 during an enemy air raid at Semplak Airfield with the 2/2nd Pioneer Battalion. Evacuated to a Dutch Military Hospital in the Batavia area.

NORMAN WILSON FRASER

Rank	Private
Regimental Number	WX10366
Classification	Driver
Company	'C' Company
Enlisted	18.12.1940
Date of Birth	10.6.1913
Place of Birth	Claremont, Western Australia
Father	George Duncan Fraser
Mother	Frances Marion Fraser
Religion	Methodist
Pre-War Occupation	Insurance Agent

Thanbyuzayat War Cemetery
Plot A7
Row D
Grave 3
Age 29

HISTORY

Singapore	Selarang Barracks Changi
'A' Force Burma	Green Force, No. 3 Battalion
Cause of Death	Cholera
Place of Death	Aungganaung 105km Camp Cemetery
Date of Death	2345 hours on 4.6.1943
Buried	Funeral service conducted by Chaplain H. Cunningham on 5.6.1943 Grave No. 11 Aungganaung 105km Camp Cemetery.
Additions	Wounded in action at Ulu Pandan on 11.2.1942. Admitted to the 2/13th Australian General Hospital with a shrapnel wound to abdominal wall. Discharged to unit on 21.2.1942. Soldier's illness at the Aungganaung 105km Camp began at 0830 hours on 4.6.1943 after drinking contaminated water. Soldier had a smuggled camera which he used during his captivity. The undeveloped films were buried at the head of his grave, but when they were recovered by the War Graves Party at the end of the war they had deteriorated beyond use.

THOMAS JOSEPH FURY

Rank	Private
Regimental Number	WX9270
Company	'A' Company
Enlisted	30.10.1940
Date of Birth	13.8.1907
Place of Birth	Kalgoorlie, Western Australia
Father	Thomas Joseph Fury
Mother	Sarah Fury
Religion	Roman Catholic
Pre-War Occupation	Miner

Thanbyuzayat War Cemetery
Plot A11
Row D
Grave 14
Age 35

HISTORY

Java	'Blackforce'
Camps Java	Bandoeng, Bicycle Camp Batavia
'A' Force Burma	Java Party No. 4, Williams Force
POW Number	4659
Cause of Death	Killed during an Allied air raid
Place of Death	Thanbyuzayat
Date of Death	15.6.1943
Buried	Thanbyuzayat Cemetery, Australian Section, Grave No. 59. Funeral service was conducted by Chaplain F. X. Corry from the 2/4th Machine Gun Battalion.

DONALD JAMES GARDNER

Rank	Corporal (Promoted 7.2.1942)
Regimental Number	WX15041
Company	'E' Company, Special Reserve Battalion
Enlisted	14.7.1941
Date of Birth	22.7.1920
Place of Birth	Cannington, Western Australia
Father	John Donald McKay Gardner
Mother	Margaret Gardner
Religion	Church of Christ
Pre-War Occupation	Joiner

Epitaph
Singapore Memorial
Column 135
Age 22

HISTORY

Cause of Death	Killed in Action
Place of Death	South-West Bukit Timah
Date of Death	11.2.1942

MICHAEL HERBERT GEARY

Rank	Private
Regimental Number	WX8000
Company	'D' Company Headquarters
Enlisted	13.8.1940
Date of Birth	12.8.1911
Place of Birth	Toodyay, Western Australia
Father	Edward James Geary
Mother	Ellen Geary
Religion	Roman Catholic
Pre-War Occupation	Rabbit Trapper

Kanchanaburi War Cemetery
Plot 1
Row H
Grave 2
Age 31

HISTORY

Singapore	Selarang Camp Changi
	Johore Bahru, Adam Park
	Selarang Barracks Changi
POW Number	4/6153
'D' Force Thailand	V Battalion
Camps Thailand	Kinsaiyok, Brankassi, Hindaine
POW Number	2244
Cause of Death	Acute Enteritis
Place of Death	Linson
Date of Death	9.8.1943
Buried	Linson Camp Cemetery, Grave No. 19.

LACEY GORDON GIBBS

Rank	Private
Regimental Number	WX16407
Company	'D' Company
Enlisted	25.8.1941
Date of Birth	25.8.1917
Place of Birth	Cannington, Western Australia
Father	Jabez Gibbs
Mother	Florence Adeline Gibbs
Religion	Church of England
Pre-War Occupation	Market Gardener

Epitaph
Labuan Memorial
Panel 18
Age 27

HISTORY

Singapore	Selarang Camp Changi
'A' Force Burma	Green Force, No. 3 Battalion
POW Number	3123
Camps Burma	Khonkan 55km Camp
Japan	*Rakuyo Maru* Party, Kumi No. 37
Cause of Death	Lost at Sea
Place of Death	South China Sea
Date of Death	14.9.1944

STUART HENRY GIBBS

Rank	Private
Regimental Number	WX9255
Company	'A' Company
Enlisted	30.10.1940
Date of Birth	29.11.1903
Place of Birth	Cardiff, Wales
Father	Henry Gibbs
Mother	Catherine Jemma Gibbs
Religion	Methodist
Pre-War Occupation	Dairy Manager

Epitaph
Labuan Memorial
Panel 18
Age 41

HISTORY

Singapore	Selarang Camp and Barracks Changi
POW Number	3/7872
Force	'E' Force Borneo
POW Number	1717
Cause of Death	Acute Enteritis
Place of Death	Sandakan
Date of Death	24.2.1945

WILLIAM HERBERT GIBBS

Rank	Private
Regimental Number	WX8958
Company	'D' Company
Enlisted	25.10.1940
Date of Birth	16.4.1916
Place of Birth	Cannington, Western Australia
Father	Jabez Gibbs
Mother	Florence Adeline Gibbs
Religion	Church of England
Pre-War Occupation	Market Gardener

Epitaph
Labuan Memorial
Panel 18
Age 28

HISTORY

Singapore	Selarang Camp Changi
'A' Force Burma	Green Force, No. 3 Battalion
POW Number	3110
Japan	*Rakuyo Maru* Party, Kumi No. 37
Cause of Death	Lost at Sea
Place of Death	South China Sea
Date of Death	12.9.1944

LIONEL STEPHEN GIBSON

Rank	Private
Regimental Number	WX17974
Company	'E' Company, Special Reserve Battalion
Enlisted	10.12.1941
Date of Birth	27.10.1922
Place of Birth	Bunbury, Western Australia
Father	Clarence Gibson
Mother	May Gibson
Religion	Church of England
Pre-War Occupation	Farmhand

Epitaph
Singapore Memorial
Column 136
Age 19

HISTORY

Cause of Death	Killed in Action
Place of Death	South-West Bukit Timah
Date of Death	11.2.1942

NORMAN ALLEN GIBSON

Rank	Private
Regimental Number	WX10994
Classification	Driver
Company	'C' Company
Enlisted	12.3.1941
Date of Birth	10.8.1919
Place of Birth	Mt Lawley, Western Australia
Father	Norman Frank Gibson
Mother	Ebba Gibson
Religion	Church of England
Pre-War Occupation	Jackeroo

Labuan War Cemetery
Plot 20
Row E
Grave 6
Age 25

HISTORY

Singapore	Selarang Camp Changi
Force	'B' Force Borneo
POW Number	720
Cause of Death	Acute Enteritis
Place of Death	Sandakan-Ranau track
Date of Death	24.6.1945
Additions	Wounded in action at Reformatory Road, Ulu Pandan. Admitted to Field Ambulance with a shrapnel wound to the back. Transferred to the 2/10th Australian General Hospital and discharged to unit on 29.3.1942.

PHILIP ARTHUR GIESE

Rank	Corporal (Promoted on 24.1.1942)
Regimental Number	WX7998
Classification	Rangetaker
Company	'D' Company
Enlisted	13.8.1940
Date of Birth	27.4.1918
Place of Birth	Wyalkatchem, Western Australia
Father	Ernst Emil Giese
Mother	Ellen Giese
Religion	Methodist
Pre-War Occupation	Clerk

Kanchanaburi War Cemetery
Plot 1
Row L
Grave 59
Age 25

HISTORY

Singapore	Selarang Camp Changi
	Thomson Road (Caldecot Hill Estate Camp)
	Selarang Barracks Changi
POW Number	3/6333
'D' Force Thailand	V Battalion
POW Number	2212
Cause of Death	Dysentery
Place of Death	Brankassi
Date of Death	28.9.1943
Buried	Brankassi, Grave No. 72
Additions	Wounded in action at Ulu Pandan and admitted to the 2/10th Australian General Hospital with a shrapnel wound to the right leg. Discharged to unit on 23.2.1942.

THOMAS EDWIN GITTOS

Rank	Private
Regimental Number	WX8870
Company	'A' Company
Enlisted	23.10.1940
Date of Birth	15.3.1920
Place of Birth	Guildford, Western Australia
Father	Thomas Gittos
Mother	Doris Gittos
Religion	Church of England
Pre-War Occupation	Labourer

Kanchanaburi War Cemetery
Plot 1
Row E
Grave 55
Age 23

HISTORY

Singapore	Selarang Camp and Barracks Changi
POW Number	3/7897
'D' Force Thailand	S Battalion
POW Number	8782
Cause of Death	Post Leg Amputation and Dysentery
Place of Death	Tamarkan
Date of Death	26.9.1943
Buried	Grave E24, Tamarkan.

RICHARD EDWARD GODFREY

Rank	Private
Regimental Number	WX7606
Classification	Batman/Runner
Company	'C' Company
Enlisted	10.8.1940
Date of Birth	5.11.1919
Place of Birth	Perth, Western Australia
Father	Frederick Godfrey
Mother	Alice Godfrey
Religion	Church of England
Pre-War Occupation	Farmhand

Epitaph
Singapore Memorial
Column 136
Age 22

HISTORY

Cause of Death	Killed in Action
Place of Death	South-West Bukit Timah
Date of Death	11.2.1942
Additions	Killed by a Japanese patrol whilst fetching water for Lieutenant V. Warhurst following his wounding at South-West Bukit Timah. Soldier had been transferred to 'E' Coy Headquarters, Special Reserve Battalion from 'C' Company No. 10 Platoon as Lieutenant Warhurst's Batman.

JAMES McLAUGHLAN GOLDIE

Rank	Private
Regimental Number	WX7627
Company	'C' Company
Enlisted	10.8.1940
Date of Birth	1.11.1918
Place of Birth	Clydesbank, Scotland
Father	Thomas Goldie
Mother	Sarah Hamil Goldie
Religion	Congregational
Pre-War Occupation	Labourer

Epitaph
Labuan Memorial
Panel 18
Age 26

HISTORY

Singapore	Selarang Camp Changi (Forest Party)
Force	'B' Force Borneo
POW Number	739
Cause of Death	Acute Enteritis
Place of Death	Sandakan-Ranau track
Date of Death	4.6.1945

REUBEN GOODWIN

Rank	Private
Regimental Number	WX9131
Company	'B' Company
Enlisted	30.10.1940
Date of Birth	14.8.1916
Place of Birth	Essex, England
Father	Not Known
Mother	Not Known
Religion	Church of England
Pre-War Occupation	Farmhand

Thanbyuzayat War Cemetery
Plot A16
Row D
Grave 8
Age 27

HISTORY

Singapore	Selarang Camp Changi
	Havelock Road Camp
	Selarang Barracks Changi
POW Numbers	1/7826 and 3/7917
Force	'F' Force Thailand
Cause of Death	Beri-Beri and Dysentery
Place of Death	Tanbaya Hospital Camp, Burma
Date of Death	0900 hours on 6.11.1943
Buried	Grave No. 579, Tanbaya
Additions	Funeral service was conducted by Chaplain Duckworth (British Army) on 15.11.1943. Rueben was a Kingsley Fairbridge Farm Schoolboy and therefore an orphan which accounts for the fact that his parents names are not listed.

GLEN ALVAN GORMAN

Rank	Lance Corporal
Regimental Number	WX12575
Company	'A' Company
Enlisted	9.5.1941
Date of Birth	7.5.1905
Place of Birth	Zeehan, Tasmania
Father	Thomas Gorman
Mother	Lilly Gorman
Religion	Church of England
Pre-War Occupation	Truck Driver

Kranji War Cemetery
Collective Grave
Plot 30
Row A
Grave 9-13
Age 36

HISTORY

Cause of Death	Killed in Action
Place of Death	Buona Vista at map reference 784112
Date of Death	16.2.1942
Buried	Where killed in a common grave
Additions	Soldier was killed during an enemy artillery barrage.

GEORGE JOHN GOSSAGE

Rank	Private
Regimental Number	WX9062
Classification	Signaller
Company	Headquarters Company
Enlisted	25.10.1940
Date of Birth	12.4.1915
Place of Birth	Kalgoorlie, Western Australia
Father	George Victor Gossage
Mother	Annie Elizabeth Gossage
Religion	Roman Catholic
Pre-War Occupation	Crane Driver with the W.A.G.R.

Kranji War Cemetery
Plot 1
Row A
Grave 13
Age 26

HISTORY

Cause of Death	Killed in Action
Place of Death	Ulu Pandan
Date of Death	12.2.1942
Buried	Where killed at map reference 763132 by Major A. Cough Party on 21.12.1942. Soldier is believed to have received a gunshot wound to the stomach during the bayonet charge at Hill 200, Ulu Pandan.

ROBERT STUART GOULDEN

Rank	Private
Regimental Number	NX10420
Classification	Cook
Attached 2/4th	ToS from 2/9th Field Ambulance 2.4.1942
Enlisted	13.5.1941
Date of Birth	18.10.1917
Place of Birth	Lakemba, New South Wales
Father	Frederick William Goulden
Mother	Mary Goulden
Religion	Presbyterian
Pre-War Occupation	Fencer

Thanbyuzayat War Cemetery
Plot A12
Row B
Grave 11
Age 24

HISTORY

Singapore	Selarang Camp Changi
'A' Force Burma	Green Force, No. 3 Battalion
POW Number	Pre issue of POW Numbers at Victoria Point
Cause of Death	Japanese firing squad
Place of Death	Victoria Point Aerodrome Camp Burma
Date of Death	1200 hours on 12.7.1942
Buried	Christian Cemetery Victoria Point, Grave No. 30
Additions	Soldier embarked at Sydney on 10.1.1942 as 8/10 reinforcements for the Australian Army Medical Corps and was taken on strength with the 2/9th Field Ambulance. He was transferred to the 2/4th Machine Gun Battalion so that Claude Webber could transfer across to the 2/9th Field Ambulance to join his brother George. Soldier was reported missing from the Victoria Point Aerodrome Camp from 1000 hours on 8.7.1942.

JAMES HENRY GRACE

Rank	Private
Regimental Number	WX6258
Classification	Cook
Company	Headquarters Company (transferred to SRBn.)
Enlisted	13.7.1940
Date of Birth	17.5.1917
Place of Birth	Kalgoorlie, Western Australia
Father	John Grace
Mother	Catherine Grace
Religion	Roman Catholic
Pre-War Occupation	Diamond Driller

Epitaph
Singapore Memorial
Panel 136
Age 24

HISTORY

Cause of Death	Killed in Action
Place of Death	South-West Bukit Timah
Date of Death	11.2.1942

LINDSAY CAMPBELL GRAY

Rank	Private
Regimental Number	WX15872
Company	Headquarters Company
Enlisted	19.8.1941
Date of Birth	27.5.1919
Place of Birth	Manjimup, Western Australia
Father	Charles Hill Gray
Mother	Edith Anne Gray
Religion	Church of England
Pre-War Occupation	Truck Driver

Kranji War Cemetery
Plot 1
Row A
Grave 16
Age 22

HISTORY

Cause of Death	Killed in Action
Place of Death	Reformatory Road, Ulu Pandan
Date of Death	12.2.1942
Buried	Where killed at map reference 763132 by Major A. Cough Party on 21.12.1942.

HENRY FREDERICK GREEN

Rank	Lieutenant
Regimental Number	WX10788
Company	'E' Company, Special Reserve Battalion
Enlisted	15.1.1941
Date of Birth	31.8.1919
Place of Birth	Perth, Western Australia
Father	John Green
Mother	Mildred Alice Green
Religion	Roman Catholic
Pre-War Occupation	Printer's Assistant at Sands & McDougall

Epitaph
Singapore Memorial
Panel 135
Age 22

HISTORY

Cause of Death	Killed in Action
Place of Death	South-West Bukit Timah
Date of Death	11.2.1942
Additions	This officer was killed in the ambush at South-West Bukit Timah when at close range he received a burst from a Japanese light automatic weapon. Lieutenant J. Till rushed at this light automatic section and killed the gun crew with his Thompson machine gun. Lieutenant Till was also wounded in the shoulder in his action.

THOMAS WILLIAM GREEN

Rank	Private
Regimental Number	WX8540
Classification	Driver
Company	Headquarters Company
Enlisted	18.10.1940
Date of Birth	3.1.1918
Place of Birth	Not Known
Father	Thomas William Green
Mother	Elsie May Green
Religion	Church of England
Pre-War Occupation	Truck Driver

Epitaph
Labuan Memorial
Panel 18
Age 24

HISTORY

Java	'Blackforce'
Camps Java	Bicycle Camp Batavia
'A' Force Burma	Java Party No. 4, Black Force
POW Number	1716
Cause of Death	Not Known
Place of Death	Sandakan
Date of Death	22.1.1945
Additions	Transported to Kuching and joined 'E' Force at Sandakan.

JOHN EDGAR JAMES GREGORY

Rank	Private
Regimental Number	WX8674
Company	'B' Company
Enlisted	23.10.1940
Date of Birth	2.11.1903
Place of Birth	Kalgoorlie, Western Australia
Father	George Henry Gregory
Mother	Janet Margaret Ronald Gregory
Religion	Presbyterian
Pre-War Occupation	Miner

Thanbyuzayat War Cemetery
Plot A6
Row D
Grave 12
Age 39

HISTORY

Singapore	Selarang Camp and Barracks Changi
POW Number	3/7954
Force	'F' Force Thailand
Camps Thailand	Nikhe, Old and New Headquarters Camps
Cause of Death	Cholera
Place of Death	Shimo Sonkurai
Date of Death	1.6.1943
Buried	Grave No. 33, at the 126km peg Thailand.

ALEXANDER MEORA HACK

Rank	Private
Regimental Number	WX8003
Classification	Batman/Runner (transferred to SRBn. Headquarters)
Company	'A' Company
Enlisted	3.10.1940
Date of Birth	7.7.1906
Place of Birth	Bridgetown, Western Australia
Father	William Wilton Meora Steven Hack
Mother	Charlotte Scott Hack
Religion	Church of England
Pre-War Occupation	Shearer

Epitaph
Labuan Memorial
Panel 18
Age 38

HISTORY

Singapore	Selarang Camp Changi
Force	'B' Force Borneo
POW Number	779
Cause of Death	Beri-Beri and Heart Failure
Place of Death	Sandakan-Ranau track
Date of Death	4.2.1945

ALBERT HACKSHAW

Rank	Private
Regimental Number	WX7801
Company	'B' Company
Enlisted	10.8.1940
Date of Birth	5.4.1900
Place of Birth	Epsom, Surrey, England
Father	Henry Frank Hackshaw
Mother	Rose Edith Hackshaw
Religion	Church of England
Pre-War Occupation	Foreman with the Main Roads Department

Thanbyuzayat War Cemetery
Plot A16
Row C
Grave 19
Age 43

HISTORY

Singapore	Selarang Camp Changi
	Johore Bahru, Adam Park
	Selarang Barracks Changi
POW Number	1/11818
Force	'F' Force Thailand
Cause of Death	Tropical Ulcers
Place of Death	Tanbaya Hospital Camp Burma
Date of Death	2.11.1943
Buried	Grave No. 548, Tanbaya
Additions	Funeral service conducted by Chaplain Duckworth (British Army) on 15.11.1943. Actual burial was conducted at 0130 hours on 2.11.1943.

FRANCIS HALBERT

Rank	Private
Regimental Number	WX8250
Company	'C' Company
Enlisted	16.8.1940
Date of Birth	16.6.1907
Place of Birth	Menzies, Western Australia
Father	Joseph Halbert
Mother	Jane Halbert
Religion	Roman Catholic
Pre-War Occupation	Prospector

Thanbyuzayat War Cemetery
Plot A6
Row B
Grave 7
Age 35

HISTORY

Singapore	Selarang Camp and Barracks Changi
POW Numbers	1/7898 and 3/7950
Force	'F' Force Thailand
Cause of Death	Cholera
Place of Death	Shimo Sonkurai
Date of Death	4.6.1943
Buried	Grave No. 24, at the 126km peg, Thailand

ROBERT WILLIAM HALDANE

Rank	Private
Regimental Number	WX8433
Company	'B' Company
Platoon	9 Platoon
Enlisted	18.10.1940
Date of Birth	28.3.1923
Place of Birth	Broome, Western Australia
Father	William Haldane
Mother	Charlotte Esther Haldane
Religion	Presbyterian
Pre-War Occupation	Labourer

Presbyterian Cemetery
Botany Sydney
Section B
Grave 473
Age 18

HISTORY

Cause of Death	Drowning
Place of Death	Sydney Harbour
Date of Death	9.1.1942
Additions	A court of inquiry was held at Sydney on board HMT "PA" (*Aquitania*) on 9.1.1942

A court of inquiry was held at Sydney on board HMT "PA" (*Aquitania*) on 9.1.1942 inquiring into the absence of WX8433 Pte. Haldane, following the receipt of a report that a member of the ship's complement had fallen overboard. The court found that WX8433 Pte. Haldane. W. was a member of 'B' Company 2/4th Machine Gun Battalion A.I.F. and was absent from Company muster parade at 06.30 Hours on 9.1.1942 and was still so absent. A search had been made of the unit area but Pte. Haldane was not sighted on the ship. In view of the evidence of Pte. Grundy and Pte. Gossage had been taken. (Pte. Haldane had spoken to members of the Battalion and was it was thought that Pte. Haldane did not appear to be in an intoxicated state). The court considered that the evidence submitted indicated a connection between the absence of Pte. Haldane and the reported disappearance overboard of a member of the ship's complement. The Funeral service was conducted by Reverend G. W. McAlpine.

DOUGLAS CHARLES JOHN HALL

Rank	Private
Regimental Number	WX10370
Classification	Driver
Company	'B' Company
Enlisted	18.12.1940
Date of Birth	23.2.1919
Place of Birth	Kalgoorlie, Western Australia
Father	Algernon William John Hall
Mother	Kathleen Rose Hall
Religion	Church of England
Pre-War Occupation	Truck Driver

Kranji War Cemetery
Plot 2
Row C
Grave 5
Age 25

HISTORY

Singapore	Selarang Camp and Barracks Changi
	Sarangoon Road Camp
'H' Force Thailand	'H' Force Group No. 3
Singapore	Sime Road Camp
Cause of Death	Septic Thrombosis
Place of Death	Australian General Hospital at Roberts Barracks Changi
Date of Death	0830 hours on 21.5.1944
Buried	A.I.F. Cemetery Changi, Grave No. 134
Additions	Soldier was evacuated to the A. G. H. Roberts Barracks with septic thrombosis pyaemia of the right iliac vein. He was buried on 21.5.1944 at 1430 hours. The funeral service was conducted by Chaplain M. K. Jones from 8th Division Headquarters. Captain Tom Bunning wrote that he was buried with the greatest possible approach to full Military Honours and on the sounding of the 'Last Post' all within earshot stood to attention in respect of him. Soldier had also been wounded at West Mandai.

WILLIAM HARRISON HALL

Rank	Private
Regimental Number	WX8747
Classification	Section Orderly
Company	'B' Company
Enlisted	23.10.1940
Date of Birth	23.5.1901
Place of Birth	Abergavenny, Wales
Father	John Harrison Hall
Mother	Mary Hall
Religion	Church of England
Pre-War Occupation	Railways Ganger

Kanchanaburi War Cemetery
Collective Grave
Plot 10
Row F
Grave 2-10 L4
Age 42

HISTORY

Singapore	Selarang Camp and Barracks Changi
POW Number	1/1963
'H' Force Thailand	'H' Force Group No. 3
Cause of Death	Beri-Beri, Cerebral Malaria and Cholera
Place of Death	Kanu II, Malayan Hamlet
Date of Death	17.7.1943
Buried	Grave No. 38 (soldier's body was not cremated).

JACK HALLIGAN

Rank	Private
Regimental Number	WX8819
Classification	Motorcycle Orderly
Company	'B' Company
Enlisted	23.10.1940
Date of Birth	26.10.1919
Place of Birth	Menzies, Western Australia
Father	James Edge Halligan
Mother	Nellie Francis Halligan
Religion	Roman Catholic
Pre-War Occupation	Bogger

Epitaph
Labuan Memorial
Panel 18
Age 25

HISTORY

Singapore	Selarang Camp Changi
Force	'B' Force Borneo
POW Number	781
Cause of Death	Malaria
Place of Death	Sandakan-Ranau track
Date of Death	4.2.1945

STANDISH O'GRADY HALY

Rank	Private
Regimental Number	WX14830
Classification	Driver
Company	'C' Company
Enlisted	3.7.1941
Date of Birth	25.1.1916
Place of Birth	Toowong, Queensland
Father	Arthur Haly
Mother	Doris Christabel Haly
Religion	Church of England
Pre-War Occupation	Station Overseer and Truck Driver

Labuan War Cemetery
Collective Grave
Plot 16
Row E
Grave 4-9
Age 29

HISTORY

Singapore	Selarang Camp Changi
Force	'B' Force Borneo
POW Number	800
Cause of Death	Not Known
Place of Death	Sandakan Estate, 12 miles from Sandakan
Date of Death	15.6.1945

BENJAMIN EDWIN HANSEN

Rank	Sergeant
Regimental Number	WX10678
Classification	Signaller
Company	Headquarters Company
Enlisted	15.1.1941
Date of Birth	24.5.1912
Place of Birth	Coolgardie, Western Australia
Father	Albert Leach Hansen
Mother	Ursella Foster Hansen
Religion	Church of England
Pre-War Occupation	Timekeeper

Kranji War Cemetery
Plot 1
Row A
Grave 2
Age 29

HISTORY

Cause of Death	Killed in Action
Place of Death	Reformatory Road, Ulu Pandan
Date of Death	12.2.1942
Buried	Where killed at map reference 763132 by Major A. Cough Party on 21.12.1942.
Additions	This NCO was killed by a gunshot wound to the stomach at Hill 200, Ulu Pandan.

ARTHUR MACK HARGREAVES

Rank	Private
Regimental Number	WX16793
Company	'E' Company, Special Reserve Battalion
Enlisted	1.10.1941
Date of Birth	14.10.1914
Place of Birth	Perth, Western Australia
Father	Richard Lupton Hargreaves
Mother	Laura Agnes Hargreaves
Religion	Church of England
Pre-War Occupation	Farm Manager

Epitaph
Singapore Memorial
Column 136
Age 27

HISTORY

Cause of Death	Killed in Action
Place of Death	South-West Bukit Timah
Date of Death	11.2.1942
Additions	*'Mack was kindness itself to my brother and I in the years before he went away',*

Maisie Cullum.

CHARLES HARRIS

Rank	Private
Regimental Number	WX7851
Company	'A' Company
Enlisted	13.8.1940
Date of Birth	20.5.1914
Place of Birth	Picton Junction, Western Australia
Father	Edward Harris
Mother	Ellen Curley Harris
Religion	Church of England
Pre-War Occupation	Farmhand

Epitaph
Labuan Memorial
Panel 18
Age 31

HISTORY

Singapore	Selarang Camp Changi
Force	'B' Force Borneo
POW Number	797
Cause of Death	Not Known
Place of Death	Sandakan
Date of Death	27.5.1945

HENRY RALPH HARRISON

Rank	Private
Regimental Number	WX8733
Company	Headquarters Company
Enlisted	23.10.1940
Date of Birth	18.2.1916
Place of Birth	Perth, Western Australia
Father	Arthur Ellis
Mother	Louisa Ellis
Religion	Church of England
Pre-War Occupation	Miner

Kanchanaburi War Cemetery
Plot 1
Row P
Grave 34
Age 27

HISTORY

Singapore	Selarang Camp Changi
	Johore Bahru, Adam Park
	Selarang Barracks Changi
POW Number	1/7963
'D' Force Thailand	V Battalion
POW Number	2251
Cause of Death	Malaria
Place of Death	Kuii
Date of Death	15.9.1943
Buried	Grave No. 163, Kuii
Additions	It is believed that Henry and his brother Thomas were adopted and that they kept their parents, who were both blind. Arthur's blindness was caused as a result of service during WW1.

LAURENCE JOHN HARVEY

Rank	Corporal (Promoted on 7.2.1942)
Regimental Number	WX10822
Company	'C' Company
Enlisted	15.1.1941
Date of Birth	24.12.1919
Place of Birth	Kent, England
Father	William Harvey
Mother	Margaret Emma Harvey
Religion	Roman Catholic
Pre-War Occupation	Labourer

Epitaph
Labuan Memorial
Panel 18
Age 24

HISTORY

Singapore	Selarang Camp Changi
'A' Force Burma	Green Force, No. 3 Battalion
POW Number	2928
Camps Burma	Khonkan 55km Camp (medical orderly)
Japan	*Rakuyo Maru* Party, Kumi No. 37
Cause of Death	Lost at Sea
Place of Death	South China Sea
Date of Death	12.9.1944

ALBERT GEORGE HAYES

Rank	Private
Regimental Number	WX8408
Company	Headquarters Company
Enlisted	18.10.1940
Date of Birth	6.9.1911
Place of Birth	Kalgoorlie, Western Australia
Father	Ernest George Hayes
Mother	Sarah Hayes
Religion	Roman Catholic
Pre-War Occupation	Labourer

Epitaph
Labuan Memorial
Panel 18
Age 33

HISTORY

Java	'Blackforce'
'A' Force Burma	Java Party No. 4, Williams Force
POW Number	4654
Camps Thailand	131km, 133km, Kanchanaburi (13.1.1944)
Japan	*Rakuyo Maru* Party, Kumi No. 38
Cause of Death	Lost at Sea
Place of Death	South China Sea
Date of Death	12.9.1944

KEITH THOMAS HAYES

Rank	Private
Regimental Number	WX11202
Classification	Driver
Company	'C' Company
Enlisted	18.3.1941
Date of Birth	10.11.1919
Place of Birth	East Perth, Western Australia
Father	Thomas Joseph Hayes
Mother	Eileen Hayes
Religion	Roman Catholic
Pre-War Occupation	Truck Driver

Kranji War Cemetery
Collective Grave
Plot 2B
Row C
Grave 10-14
Age 22

HISTORY

Cause of Death	Killed in Action
Place of Death	Hill 200, Ulu Pandan
Date of Death	12.2.1942
Buried	Where killed at map reference 761126 by Major A. Cough Party on 21.12.1942.
Additions	Soldier's body was riddled with machine gun bullets.

HERBERT WILLIAM HEAL

Rank	Private
Regimental Number	WX9320
Company	'A' Company
Enlisted	30.10.1940
Date of Birth	29.5.1910
Place of Birth	Perth, Western Australia
Father	Herbert William Heal
Mother	Elizabeth Heal
Religion	Presbyterian
Pre-War Occupation	Hotel Yardman

Thanbyuzayat War Cemetery
Plot A16
Row E
Grave 2
Age 33

HISTORY

Singapore	Selarang Camp and Barracks Changi
POW Number	4/6208
Force	'F' Force Thailand
Cause of Death	Beri-Beri and Dysentery
Place of Death	Tanbaya Hospital Camp Burma
Date of Death	1645 hours on 22.12.1943
Buried	Grave No. 737, Tanbaya
Additions	Funeral service conducted by Chaplain Duckworth (British Army).

FREDERICK JOSEPH HEINZ-SMITH

Rank	Private
Regimental Number	WX18022
Company	'E' Company, Special Reserve Battalion
Enlisted	11.12.1941
Date of Birth	12.11.1902
Place of Birth	Paddington, New South Wales
Father	Frederick Joseph Heinz-Smith
Mother	Ada Maude Heinz-Smith
Religion	Roman Catholic
Pre-War Occupation	Labourer

Thanbyuzayat War Cemetery
Plot A10
Row G
Grave 18
Age 40

HISTORY

Singapore	Selarang Camp Changi
	Johore Bahru, Adam Park
	Selarang Barracks Changi
POW Number	1/12940
Force	'F' Force Thailand
Cause of Death	Malaria, Dysentery and Tropical Ulcers
Place of Death	Kami Sonkurai
Date of Death	23.10.1943
Buried	Grave No. 18, Kami Sonkurai.

LEONARD HELLIWELL

Rank	Lance Corporal
Regimental Number	WX9755
Classification	Clerk
Company	'C' Company Headquarters
Enlisted	6.12.1940
Date of Birth	20.7.1898
Place of Birth	North Perth, Western Australia
Father	Isaac Helliwell
Mother	Rosina Helliwell
Religion	Salvation Army
Pre-War Occupation	Fire Insurance Officer

Epitaph
Singapore Memorial
Column 135
Age 43

HISTORY

Cause of Death	Killed in Action
Place of Death	Hill 200, Ulu Pandan
Date of Death	12.2.1942
Buried	Where killed at map reference 775128 by Major A. Cough Party on 21.12.1942.

LESLIE CLIVE HELLMRICH

Rank	Private
Regimental Number	WX8638
Classification	Driver
Company	'A' Company
Enlisted	18.10.1940
Date of Birth	31.3.1910
Place of Birth	Bunbury, Western Australia
Father	John Mathieson Hellmrich
Mother	Hester Hellmrich
Religion	Church of England
Pre-War Occupation	Truck Driver

Kanchanaburi War Cemetery
Plot 1
Row B
Grave 62
Age 33

HISTORY

Singapore	Selarang Camp and Barracks Changi
POW Numbers	1/8005 and 1/291
Force	'F' Force Thailand
Cause of Death	Malaria, Beri-Beri and Dysentery
Place of Death	Kanchanaburi
Date of Death	1030 hours on 22.12.1943
Buried	Grave No. 62, Kanchanaburi
Additions	Funeral Service conducted by Major Cordingley. Taken on Strength 2/6th Field Park Company on 5.1.1943 to join his brother Noel.

JOHN FREDERICK HELSIN

Rank	Corporal
Regimental Number	WX10095
Company	'B' Company
Enlisted	13.12.1940
Date of Birth	3.4.1919
Place of Birth	London, England
Father	John Helsin
Mother	Edith Emily Helsin
Religion	Church of England
Pre-War Occupation	Warehouseman

Epitaph
Labuan Memorial
Panel 18
Age 25

HISTORY

Singapore	Selarang Camp Changi
'A' Force Burma	Green Force, No. 3 Battalion
POW Number	1371
Camps Burma	Khonkan 55km Camp, ex-Aungganaung 105km Camp
Japan	*Rakuyo Maru* Party, Kumi No. 35
Cause of Death	Lost at Sea
Place of Death	South China Sea
Date of Death	12.9.1944

COLIN LESLIE HEPPELL

Rank	Corporal (Promoted on 24.1.1942)
Regimental Number	WX9348
Company	'C' Company
Enlisted	30.10.1940
Date of Birth	3.7.1906
Place of Birth	Niangel, Victoria
Father	Robert Heppell
Mother	Agnes Heppell
Religion	Church of England
Pre-War Occupation	Storekeeper

Kanchanaburi War Cemetery
Collective Grave
Plot 10
Row C
Grave 3-5
Age 38

HISTORY

Singapore	Selarang Camp and Barracks Changi
POW Number	4/4505
'D' Force Thailand	V Battalion
POW Number	2213
Cause of Death	Colitis
Place of Death	Kuii
Date of Death	6.10.1943
Buried	Grave No. 93, Kuii.

ERNEST THORNTON HILL

Rank	Private
Regimental Number	WX7029
Company	'D' Company
Enlisted	30.7.1940
Date of Birth	16.2.1918
Place of Birth	Greenhills, Western Australia
Father	Charles Cogar Hill
Mother	Flora May Hill
Religion	Methodist
Pre-War Occupation	Farmhand

Epitaph
Labuan Memorial
Panel 18
Age 27

HISTORY

Singapore	Selarang Camp Changi
	Thomson Road (Caldecot Hill Estate Camp)
Force	'B' Force Borneo
POW Number	830
Cause of Death	Malaria
Date of Death	28.5.1945

JOHN HILL

Rank	Lance Corporal
Regimental Number	WX8756
Classification	Driver/Mechanic
Company	'B' Company
Enlisted	23.10.1940
Date of Birth	1.1.1912
Place of Birth	Fremantle, Western Australia
Father	Arthur Hill
Mother	Margaret Hill
Religion	Church of England
Pre-War Occupation	Truck Driver

Kranji War Cemetery
Plot 2
Row C
Grave 20
Age 31

HISTORY

Cause of Death	Bacillary Dysentery
Place of Death	A. G. H. Roberts Barracks Changi
Date of Death	11.3.1943
Buried	A.I.F. Cemetery Changi, Grave No. 80
Additions	Wounded in action at Pasir Panjang and admitted to Field Ambulance with gunshot wounds to the left arm and head on 14.2.1942. Admitted to the 2/13th Australian General Hospital on 16.2.1942. Soldier died at approximately 1330 hours on 11.3.1943 at the Australian General Hospital at Roberts Barracks Changi from mycotoxicosis, diphtheria and acute but resolving bacillary dysentery. Soldier's body was cremated by order of the Imperial Japanese Army and his ashes buried on 11.3.1943. The funeral service was conducted by Chaplain G. Polain of the 2/26th Battalion.

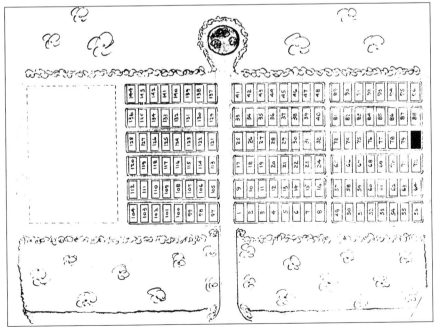

Sketch of Grave Plan at A.I.F. Cemetery
John Hill's grave position number 80, is darkened.

JACK HARRIS HILL

Rank	Captain
Regimental Number	WX3434
Company	Battalion Headquarters
Enlisted	5.11.1940
Date of Birth	11.11.1919
Place of Birth	Victoria
Father	Stanley Albert Hill
Mother	Agnes May Hill
Religion	Church of England
Pre-War Occupation	Staff Corps, Royal Military College Duntroon

**Toowoomba War Cemetery
Queensland**
Plot B
Row B
Grave 16
Age 26

HISTORY

Singapore	Selarang Camp Changi
	Johore Bahru, Adam Park
	Selarang Barracks Changi
'D' Force Thailand	V Battalion
Camps Thailand	Hindaine (evacuated sick), Non Pladuk
Return Details 1945	Thailand-Singapore by aircraft
	Singapore-Fremantle, HMT *Highland Brigade*
Cause of Death	Basal Fracture to the skull
Place of Death	Cabarlah, Queensland
Date of Death	24.1.1946
Additions	

This Officer was appointed Adjutant of the 2/4th Machine Gun Battalion with the rank of Temporary Captain on 1.11.1940. After his return to Western Australia on 15.10.1945 Jack (or John as he was known) married Elizabeth Ashton on 14.11.1945. Sadly Elizabeth would soon find herself widowed. At 1600 hours on 24.1.1946 John was travelling in an army truck along Allora Road, Toowoomba, Queensland. Due to the tropical rains the road was flooded and John leant out over the back of the truck to place his map case over the truck's exhaust. The vehicle suddenly lunged and John was thrown from the vehicle and under one of its wheels, where upon his skull was crushed. The tradegy was compounded by the fact that this officer had endured so much heartache and hardship as a Prisoner of War.

HERBERT ROY HINDLE

Rank	Lance Corporal
Regimental Number	WX8869
Classification	Driver/Mechanic
Company	'B' Company
Enlisted	25.10.1940
Date of Birth	17.4.1904
Place of Birth	Pindar, Western Australia
Father	William Lawrence Hindle
Mother	Bridget Emily Hindle
Religion	Roman Catholic
Pre-War Occupation	Store Foreman

Labuan War Cemetery
Plot H
Row D
Grave 2
Age 40

HISTORY

Singapore	Selarang Camp Changi
	River Valley Road Camp
	Selarang Barracks Changi
POW Number	4/4509
'D' Force Thailand	S Battalion
POW Number	8739
Camps Thailand	Kanu II, Tamuang
Japan	*Rashin Maru* Party
POW Number	1548
Camps Japan	Yamane
Additions	Soldier was killed by a fall of rock at the Sumitomo Besshi copper mine at Yamane on Shikoku Island Japan on 30.9.1944. His body was cremated and his ashes were carried as far as Labuan Island.

CLIFFORD HOBSON

Rank	Private
Regimental Number	WX16446
Company	Headquarters Company
Enlisted	10.9.1941
Date of Birth	8.11.1905
Place of Birth	Leeds, Yorkshire, England
Father	Charles Hophni Hobson
Mother	Charlotte Ann Hobson
Religion	Church of England
Pre-War Occupation	Miner

Epitaph
Labuan Memorial
Panel 18
Age 38

HISTORY

Singapore	Selarang Camp Changi
'A' Force Burma	Green Force, No. 3 Battalion
POW Number	1517
Japan	*Rakuyo Maru* Party, Kumi No. 35
Cause of Death	Lost at Sea
Place of Death	South China Sea
Date of Death	12.9.1944

LEONARD SYDNEY HODGSON

Rank	Private
Regimental Number	WX9231
Classification	Rangetaker
Company	'A' Company
Enlisted	30.10.1940
Date of Birth	20.8.1919
Place of Birth	London, England
Father	John Henry Hodgson
Mother	Minna Bertha Hodgson
Religion	Church of England
Pre-War Occupation	Dairy Farmer

Thanbyuzayat War Cemetery
Plot A8
Row D
Grave 13
Age 24

HISTORY

Singapore	Selarang Camp Changi
'A' Force Burma	Green Force, No. 3 Battalion
POW Number	2902
Cause of Death	Post Leg Amputation and Toxaemia
Place of Death	Khonkan 55km Camp
Date of Death	24.9.1943
Buried	Grave No. 13 Khonkan
Additions	Soldier was wounded in action at Buona Vista on 15.2.1942 and was admitted to the 2/13th Australian General Hospital with a gunshot wound to the back. Discharged to unit on 20.2.1942. Evacuated to Khonkan 55km Hospital Camp on 4.7.1943. Left leg was amputated below the knee as a result of tropical ulcers. The leg was re-amputated above the knee.

NORMAN PHILLIP HOLDMAN

Rank	Private
Regimental Number	WX7465
Classification	Driver
Company	Headquarters Company
Enlisted	6.8.1940
Date of Birth	10.10.1910
Place of Birth	Cottesloe, Western Australia
Father	Henry Hugh Holdman
Mother	Elizabeth Holdman
Religion	Church of England
Pre-War Occupation	Transport Worker

Kanchanaburi War Cemetery
Plot 1
Row L
Grave 37
Age 34

HISTORY

Java	'Blackforce', attached to 'A' Coy 2/3rd M.G. Bn.
Camps Java	Bicycle Camp Batavia
'A' Force Burma	Java Party No. 4, Williams Force
POW Number	4657
Camps Burma	Beke Taung 40km Camp, Reptu 30km Camp
Camps Thailand	Kanchanaburi, Bangkok
Cause of Death	Killed during an Allied air raid
Place of Death	Go-downs Bangkok, wharf area
Date of Death	27.3.1945

HAROLD WILLIAM HOLLAND

Rank	Private
Regimental Number	WX17636
Company	'B' Company
Enlisted	12.11.1941
Date of Birth	22.9.1914
Place of Birth	East Perth, Western Australia
Father	William George Holland
Mother	Minnie Norris Holland
Religion	Church of England
Pre-War Occupation	Labourer

Epitaph
Labuan Memorial
Panel 18
Age 30

HISTORY

Singapore	Selarang Camp Changi
Force	Johore Bahru, Adam Park
	Thomson Road (Caldecot Hill Estate Camp)
	Selarang Barracks Changi
POW Number	4/6228
Force	'E' Force Borneo
POW Number	1742
Cause of Death	Malaria
Place of Death	Sandakan-Ranau track
Date of Death	15.6.1945

DAVID HOLM

Rank	Sergeant
Regimental Number	WX8986
Company	'B' Company
Enlisted	25.10.1940
Date of Birth	18.4.1917
Place of Birth	Water End, Herts, England
Father	Hugh Crawford Holm
Mother	Lilian May Frances Holm
Religion	Church of England
Pre-War Occupation	Farmhand

Kranji War Cemetery
Plot 3
Row B
Grave 5
Age 24

HISTORY

Cause of Death	Died of Wounds
Place of Death	2/10th Australian General Hospital
Date of Death	2.3.1942
Buried	70 yards south of the 13 mile peg on the main Singapore-Changi Road in the British Cemetery.
Additions	Wounded in action at Pasir Panjang on 14.2.1942. Gunshot wounds to the skull, right hand and legs. Died of cerebral abscess at 1900 hours on 2.3.1942 at Changi. The funeral service was conducted by Chaplain F. X. Corry from the 2/4th Machine Gun Battalion. NCO's body was exhumed and placed into Grave No. 90, A.I.F. Cemetery Changi on 22.6.1943.

CHARLES HOLME

Rank	Private
Regimental Number	WX16416
Company	Not Known
Enlisted	10.9.1941
Date of Birth	22.3.1922
Place of Birth	Harvey, Western Australia
Father	Karle Holme
Mother	Alma Holme
Religion	Church of England
Pre-War Occupation	Farmhand

HISTORY

Singapore	Selarang Camp Changi
	Thomson Road (Caldecot Hill Estate Camp)
	Selarang Barracks Changi
POW Number	3/8155
Force	'E' Force Borneo
POW Number	1744
Cause of Death	Malaria
Place of Death	Sandakan-Ranau track
Date of Death	7.6.1945

ERIC JOSEPH HOLST

Rank	Private
Regimental Number	WX8678
Company	'A' Company
Enlisted	23.10.1940
Date of Birth	9.11.1913
Place of Birth	Perth, Western Australia
Father	Andrew Mathias Holst
Mother	Rose Theresa Holst
Religion	Roman Catholic
Pre-War Occupation	Prospector

HISTORY

Singapore	Selarang Camp Changi
	Johore Bahru, Adam Park
	Selarang Barracks Changi
POW Number	4/6231
Force	'E' Force Borneo
POW Number	1745
Cause of Death	Malaria
Place of Death	Sandakan
Date of Death	20.3.1945

WILLIAM JOHN HOLT

Rank	Private
Regimental Number	WX7550
Company	Headquarters Company
Enlisted	6.8.1940
Date of Birth	9.7.1903
Place of Birth	Cottesloe, Western Australia
Father	Frederick William Holt
Mother	Margaret Ellen Holt
Religion	Church of England
Pre-War Occupation	Pastry Cook

Thanbyuzayat War Cemetery
Plot A8
Row A
Grave 15
Age 40

HISTORY

Singapore	Selarang Camp Changi
'A' Force Burma	Ramsay Force, No. 1 Battalion
POW Number	6286
Cause of Death	Cerebral Malaria
Place of Death	Aungganaung 105km Camp
Date of Death	1618 hours on 20.8.1943
Additions	Wounded in action at Ulu Pandan and admitted to 2/13th Australian General Hospital with a shrapnel wound to the right ear. Discharged to unit on 26.2.1942. Admitted to camp hospital at Aungganaung on 19.8.1943 with cerebral malaria. Soldier died at 1618 hours on 20.8.1943. Body was buried in grave No. 23 in the camp cemetery located 192 degrees from 104.65km point on the rail link at a distance of 170 yards from this point. The funeral service was conducted by Padre J. K. W. Mathieson of the Royal Australian Navy.

EDWIN JAMES HOPE

Rank	Private
Regimental Number	WX7022
Company	'D' Company
Enlisted	30.7.1940
Date of Birth	7.6.1920
Place of Birth	Buntine, Western Australia
Father	Ivan Meredith Hope
Mother	Edith Hope
Religion	Church of England
Pre-War Occupation	Clerk

Thanbyuzayat War Cemetery
Plot A3
Row C
Grave 6
Age 23

HISTORY

Singapore	Selarang Camp Changi
'A' Force Burma	Green Force, No. 3 Battalion
POW Number	3080
Cause of Death	Beri-Beri
Place of Death	Khonkan 55km Camp
Date of Death	8.8.1943
Buried	Grave No. 43, Khonkan
Additions	Wounded in action at Hill 200, Ulu Pandan. Admitted to Alexandra Hospital on 12.2.1942 with a gunshot wound to the left elbow. Discharged to unit on 24.2.1942.

VERNON THOMAS WILLIAM HOPPE

Rank	Private
Regimental Number	WX10635
Classification	Signaller
Company	Headquarters Company
Enlisted	14.1.1941
Date of Birth	26.5.1910
Place of Birth	Day Dawn (near Cue), Western Australia
Father	Willy Hoppe
Mother	Ellen Morris Hoppe
Religion	Church of England
Pre-War Occupation	Wool Scourer

Kanchanaburi War Cemetery
Collective Grave
Plot 10
Row B
Grave 2-5
Age 33

HISTORY

Singapore	Selarang Camp and Barracks Changi
POW Number	1/8080
'D' Force Thailand	V Battalion
POW Number	2253
Cause of Death	Cerebral Malaria
Place of Death	Kuii
Date of Death	19.11.1943
Buried	Grave No. 208, Kuii

EDWARD MASON HOPSON

Rank	Private
Regimental Number	WX9241
Company	'B' Company
Enlisted	30.10.1940
Date of Birth	7.2.1909
Place of Birth	Albany, Western Australia
Father	Alfred Joseph Hopson
Mother	Mary Jane Hopson
Religion	Presbyterian
Pre-War Occupation	Farmhand

Dutch Cemetery
Atjeh
North Sumatra
Age 35

HISTORY

Force	Atjeh Party Sumatra
POW Number	338
Cause of Death	Appendicitis
Place of Death	Tenal Gajoe
Date of Death	26.4.1944
Buried	Soldier's body was buried at a point 200 yards to the south of the 28 kilometre peg on the Blang Kenjeren-Tekencong Road at location 3.59N-97.20E.
Additions	Listed as missing from Pasir Panjang on Sunday evening 15.2.1942. Soldier had appendicitis but due to the fact that he also had dysentery doctors were unable to operate.

BERNARD JAMES HOWARD

Rank	Private
Regimental Number	NX73270
Classification	Trade Group I
Attached 2/4th	88 Light Aid Detachment
Enlisted	September 1941
Date of Birth	19.10.1914
Place of Birth	Quirindi, New South Wales
Father	Frederick William Howard
Mother	Annie Mary Howard
Religion	Roman Catholic
Pre-War Occupation	Truck Driver

Epitaph
Labuan Memorial
Panel 29
Age 29

HISTORY

Singapore	Selarang Camp Changi
'A' Force Burma	Green Force, No. 3 Battalion
POW Number	3086
Camps Burma	Reptu 30km Camp
Camps Thailand	Tamarkan
Japan	*Rakuyo Maru* Party, Kumi No. 37
Cause of Death	Lost at Sea
Place of Death	South China Sea
Date of Death	12.9.1945

EDGAR JOSEPH HOWARD

Rank	Sergeant (Promoted on 7.2.1942)
Regimental Number	WX7628
Company	'A' Company
Enlisted	10.8.1940
Date of Birth	25.6.1912
Place of Birth	Armadale, Western Australia
Father	George Joseph Howard
Mother	Beatrice Victoria Howard
Religion	Church of England
Pre-War Occupation	Ticket Inspector, W.A.G.R.

Kanchanaburi War Cemetery
Collective Grave
Plot 10
Row F
Grave 2-10 L4
Age 31

HISTORY

Singapore	Selarang Camp Changi
	Mount Pleasant Camp
	River Valley Road Camp
	Selarang Barracks Changi
POW Number	3/6204
'H' Force Thailand	'H' Force Group No. 3
Cause of Death	Cholera
Place of Death	Kanu II, Malayan Hamlet
Date of Death	1.7.1943
Buried	Grave No. 22 Malayan Hamlet (NCO's body was not cremated)
Additions	Suffered shell shock at Ulu Pandan.

KENNETH JACK HOWELL

Rank	Private
Regimental Number	WX5181
Company	'C' Company
Enlisted	26.7.1940
Date of Birth	1.10.1913
Place of Birth	Bridgetown, Western Australia
Father	David Howell
Mother	Clara Howell
Religion	Church of England
Pre-War Occupation	Miner

Epitaph
Singapore Memorial
Column 136
Age 28

HISTORY

Cause of Death	Killed in action by a mortar bomb
Place of Death	West Ulu Pandan
Date of Death	11.2.1942
Buried	Where killed at map reference 758128 by Major A. Cough Party on 21.12.1942.

RONALD EDWARD HUGHES

Rank	Private
Regimental Number	WX10795
Company	'A' Company
Enlisted	15.1.1941
Date of Birth	10.7.1920
Place of Birth	Manjimup, Western Australia
Father	John Arthur Hughes
Mother	Jeanette Hughes
Religion	Methodist
Pre-War Occupation	Carpenter's Labourer

Epitaph
Labuan Memorial
Panel 18
Age 24

HISTORY

Java	'Blackforce', attached to the 2/2nd Pioneer Bn.
'A' Force Burma	Java Party No. 4, Williams Force
POW Number	4646
Camps Burma	Reptu 30km Camp (25.3.1943)
Japan	*Rakuyo Maru* Party, Kumi No. 38
Cause of Death	Lost at Sea
Place of Death	South China Sea
Date of Death	12.9.1944

EDGAR HAROLD HUNT

Rank	Corporal (Promoted on 11.2.1942)
Regimental Number	WX9327
Classification	Cook
Company	'D' Company
Enlisted	30.10.1940
Date of Birth	14.1.1914
Place of Birth	Beverley, Western Australia
Father	Percival Harold Hunt
Mother	Alice Matilda Hunt
Religion	Church of England
Pre-War Occupation	Farmhand

Kanchanaburi War Cemetery
Plot 1
Row H
Grave 4
Age 29

HISTORY

Singapore	Selarang Camp Changi
	Johore Bahru, Adam Park
	Selarang Barracks Changi
POW Number	4/6247
'D' Force Thailand	V Battalion
POW Number	2255
Cause of Death	Bacillary Dysentery
Place of Death	Hindaine
Date of Death	10.8.1943
Buried	Linson Camp Cemetery, Grave No. 22.

JOHN WILLIAM HUNT

Rank	Private
Regimental Number	WX16375
Classification	Stretcher Bearer
Company	Battalion Headquarters
Enlisted	8.9.1941
Date of Birth	31.8.1918
Place of Birth	York, Western Australia
Father	William Thomas Hunt
Mother	Amy Evelyn Hunt
Religion	Church of England
Pre-War Occupation	Horse Breaker

Kranji War Cemetery
Collective Grave
Plot 30
Row A
Grave 9-13
Age 23

HISTORY

Cause of Death	Killed during an enemy artillery barrage
Place of Death	Buona Vista
Date of Death	15.2.1942
Buried	In a common grave at map reference 784112.

PATRICK GEORGE HURST

Rank	Private
Regimental Number	WX17351
Company	'E' Company, Special Reserve Battalion
Enlisted	22.10.1941
Date of Birth	11.1.1922
Place of Birth	London, England
Father	Not Known
Mother	Not Known
Religion	Church of England
Pre-War Occupation	Farmhand

Epitaph
Singapore Memorial
Column 136
Age 20

HISTORY

Cause of Death	Killed in Action
Place of Death	South-West Bukit Timah
Date of Death	11.2.1942
Additions	Kingsley Fairbridge Farm Schoolboy.

ROBERT BAMFORD HUTCHISON

Rank	Private
Regimental Number	WX7646
Classification	Cook
Company	'D' Company
Enlisted	10.8.1940
Date of Birth	23.4.1912
Place of Birth	Subiaco, Western Australia
Father	Thomas Hutchison
Mother	Violet Denmead Hutchison
Religion	Church of Christ
Pre-War Occupation	Fetter

Epitaph
Labuan Memorial
Panel 18
Age 32

HISTORY

Singapore	Selarang Camp Changi
'A' Force Burma	Green Force, No. 3 Battalion
POW Number	1508
Camps Thailand	Tamarkan
Japan	*Rakuyo Maru* Party, Kumi No. 35
Cause of Death	Lost at Sea
Place of Death	South China Sea
Date of Death	12.9.1944
Additions	Wounded in action 12.2.1942, receiving a shrapnel wound to the back.

WILLIAM LEONARD INNES

Rank	Sergeant
Regimental Number	WX9552
Company	Headquarters Company (replaced L/Sgt. C. Phillips)
Enlisted	4.12.1940
Date of Birth	29.7.1919
Place of Birth	Subiaco, Western Australia
Father	Robert Leonard Innes
Mother	Edith Innes
Religion	Church of England
Pre-War Occupation	Labourer

Kranji War Cemetery
Plot 1
Row A
Grave 1
Age 22

HISTORY

Cause of Death	Killed in action, by a gunshot to the chest
Place of Death	Hill 200, Ulu Pandan
Date of Death	12.2.1942
Buried	Where killed at map reference 763132 by Major A. Cough Party 21.12.1942.

LAWRENCE JAENSCH

Rank	Private
Regimental Number	WX15402
Company	Headquarters Company
Enlisted	25.7.1941
Date of Birth	30.6.1907
Place of Birth	Adelaide, South Australia
Father	John Friederich Wilhelm Jaensch
Mother	Ellen Jaensch
Religion	Roman Catholic
Pre-War Occupation	Farmhand

Kanchanaburi War Cemetery
Collective Grave
Plot 10
Row C
Grave 3-5
Age 36

HISTORY

Singapore	Selarang Camp and Barracks Changi
POW Number	4/6259
'D' Force Thailand	V Battalion
POW Number	2259
Cause of Death	Acute Enteritis and Malaria
Place of Death	Kuii
Date of Death	6.10.1943
Buried	Grave No. 193, Kuii.

JAMES MORGAN JENKINS

Rank	Private
Regimental Number	WX5118
Company	'C' Company
Enlisted	23.7.1940
Date of Birth	15.5.1901
Place of Birth	Cardiganshire, Wales
Father	Not Known
Mother	Ann Jane Morgan Jenkins
Stepfather	Arthur Davies
Religion	Church of England
Pre-War Occupation	Driver

Thanbyuzayat War Cemetery
Plot A11
Row C
Grave 2
Age 41

HISTORY

Java	'Blackforce'
POW Number	1904
'A' Force Burma	Java Party No. 4, Williams Force
POW Number	4538
Cause of Death	Dysentery and Heart Failure
Place of Death	Thanbyuzayat
Date of Death	11.11.1942
Buried	Grave No. 2 (A.I.F. Section) Thanbyuzayat
Additions	Soldier apparently collapsed on the parade ground at Thanbyuzayat on 10.11.1942 and died the following day. The funeral service was conducted by Padre F. H. Bashford from the 2/4th Casualty Clearing Station.

BENJAMIN CHARLES JONES

Rank	Acting Corporal (Promoted on 24.1.1942)
Regimental Number	WX9112
Company	'C' Company
Enlisted	30.10.1940
Date of Birth	24.8.1913
Place of Birth	Pingelly, Western Australia
Father	Benjamin Jones
Mother	Maude Eliza Jones
Religion	Church of England
Pre-War Occupation	Clerk

Kanchanaburi War Cemetery
Plot 1
Row N
Grave 13
Age 30

HISTORY

Singapore	Selarang Camp and Barracks Changi
POW Number	4/4523
'D' Force Thailand	S Battalion
POW Number	8732
Camps Thailand	Kanu II
Cause of Death	Avitaminosis
Place of Death	Chungkai
Date of Death	5.11.1943
Buried	Grave No. 849, Chungkai.

EDGAR CHEETHAM JONES

Rank	Private
Regimental Number	WX7453
Company	Headquarters Company
Enlisted	6.8.1940
Date of Birth	10.9.1901
Place of Birth	Manchester, England
Father	John Hugh Jones
Mother	Mary Alice Jones
Religion	Church of England
Pre-War Occupation	Railway Shunter

Djakarta War Cemetery
Plot 5
Row E
Grave 10
Age 40

HISTORY

Java	'Blackforce'
Camps Java	Bicycle Camp Batavia
Cause of Death	Bacillary Dysentery
Place of Death	Bicycle Camp Hospital Batavia
Date of Death	6.7.1942
Buried	Dutch Cemetery about 6 miles from camp. Funeral service conducted by Padre Frank Kellow from the 2/2nd Pioneer Battalion. Buried in Grave No. 102 but reburied later in the British Section, Grave No. 65.

IVOR WILLIAM JONES

Rank	Private
Regimental Number	WX7234
Company	'D' Company
Enlisted	1.8.1940
Date of Birth	28.9.1900
Place of Birth	Abergavenny, Monmouthshire, Wales
Father	William Jones
Mother	Ada Jones
Religion	Church of England
Pre-War Occupation	Fireman

Thanbyuzayat War Cemetery
Plot A13
Row B
Grave 18
Age 43

HISTORY

Singapore	Selarang Camp and Barracks Changi (Forest Party)
POW Number	3/8326
Force	'F' Force Thailand
Cause of Death	Beri-Beri
Place of Death	Kami Sonkurai
Date of Death	14.11.1943
Buried	Grave No. 340, Kami Sonkurai.

NORMAN JONES

Rank	Private
Regimental Number	WX9433
Company	'C' Company
Enlisted	4.12.1940
Date of Birth	30.12.1905
Place of Birth	Mostyn, North Wales
Father	John Jones
Mother	Ann Jones
Religion	Methodist
Pre-War Occupation	Stevedore and Tractor Driver

Kanchanaburi War Cemetery
Plot 1
Row P
Grave 8
Age 37

HISTORY

Singapore	Selarang Camp Changi
	A. G. H. Roberts Barracks Changi (Beri-Beri)
	Selarang Barracks Changi
'D' Force Thailand	S Battalion
POW Number	8792
Cause of Death	Avitaminosis and Beri-Beri
Place of Death	Chungkai
Date of Death	1600 hours on 11.11.1943
Buried	Grave No. 886, Chungkai
Additions	Six years previous service with the Royal Tank Corps.

COLIN JOYNES

Rank	Private
Regimental Number	WX9297
Company	'C' Company
Enlisted	30.10.1940
Date of Birth	15.1.1914
Place of Birth	Wagin, Western Australia
Father	Arthur Thomas Joynes
Mother	Annie Joynes
Religion	Roman Catholic
Pre-War Occupation	Farmer

Epitaph
Labuan Memorial
Panel 18
Age 31

HISTORY

Singapore	Selarang Camp Changi
Force	'B' Force Borneo
POW Number	860
Cause of Death	Not stated by Japanese
Place of Death	Sandakan
Date of Death	7.6.1945

VIVIAN ALBERT KEAY

Rank	Warrant Officer II (Promoted on 7.2.1942)
Regimental Number	WX8431
Classification	Clerk
Company	'E' Company Headquarters, Special Reserve Battalion
Enlisted	18.10.1940
Date of Birth	13.6.1905
Place of Birth	Glenshee, Scotland
Father	John Keay
Mother	Christine Keay
Religion	Presbyterian
Pre-War Occupation	Clerk

Epitaph
Labuan Memorial
Panel 18
Age 39

HISTORY

Singapore	Selarang Camp Changi
	A. G. H. Roberts Barracks, Changi (dengue fever)
Force	'B' Force Borneo
POW Number	258
Cause of Death	Malaria
Place of Death	Sandakan
Date of Death	10.5.1945

CHARLES GEORGE McQUEEN KELLY

Rank	Private
Regimental Number	WX7612
Classification	Driver
Company	'D' Company
Enlisted	10.8.1940
Date of Birth	27.7.1904
Place of Birth	Wigtown, Scotland
Father	Charles Kelly
Mother	Agnes Kelly
Religion	Presbyterian
Pre-War Occupation	Wheat Bin Attendant

Kanchanaburi War Cemetery
Plot 1
Row E
Grave 42
Age 39

HISTORY

JAVA	'Blackforce'
'A' Force Burma	Java Party No. 4, Williams Force
POW Number	4490
Camps Burma	Beke Taung 40km Hospital (2.7.1943) Reptu 30km Hospital (22.7.1943)
Cause of Death	Cerebral Malaria
Place of Death	Tamarkan
Date of Death	1915 hours on 13.1.1944
Buried	Grave F24, Tamarkan
Additions	Funeral service conducted by Chaplain H. Cunningham, General base Depot.

ROBERT JAMES KELT

Rank	Private
Regimental Number	WX9151
Classification	Bricklayer
Company	Headquarters Company
Enlisted	30.10.1940
Date of Birth	29.11.1907
Place of Birth	Scotland
Father	Dr James Alexander Mailor Kelt
Mother	Helen Mary Kelt
Religion	Presbyterian
Pre-War Occupation	House Painter

Kanchanaburi War Cemetery
Plot 1
Row F
Grave 49
Age 36

HISTORY

Singapore	Selarang Camp and Barracks Changi
POW Number	4/6288
'D' Force Thailand	V Battalion
POW Number	2261
Cause of Death	Beri-Beri
Place of Death	Non Pladuk
Date of Death	19.1.1944
Buried	Grave No. 49, Non Pladuk.

THE KELTS

Ray Kelt recalls the last time he saw his father, Robert James Kelt.

'When the war broke out we were living in Palmyra. Dad was trying to earn a quid as a house painter but was battling a bit as things were very tough in those days and eventually he joined the A.I.F. Mum and I left Palmyra and moved into the Town Hall apartments. We only had one room where we slept, cooked our meals and dined. I can remember looking out the window across St John's Church and watching the trams go past and listening to the Salvation Army play outside Nicholson's music store. The last time I saw my dad was outside the entrance of our apartment building in High Street. He said to me: "Dad's got a job to do, now you're in charge so look after your mother until I return". He then marched down High Street turned and waved, then disappeared down towards the Round House at the end of the street. I was 12 years old, my mum died at 95 years of age. We were always close and good mates through all 'the years'.'

Robert James Kelt was one of the few survivors from Major Alf Cough's 'D' Force V Battalion but passed away at Non Pladuk camp on 19th January 1944. This war had claimed one more man from the A.I.F. and created yet another widow and fatherless child.

GEORGE KIDD

Rank	Private	
Regimental Number	WX7250	
Company	'B' Company	
Enlisted	1.8.1940	
Date of Birth	1.6.1904	
Place of Birth	Newcastle, England	
Father	James Alexander Hunter Kidd	
Mother	Christina Ross Kidd	
Religion	Presbyterian	
Pre-War Occupation	Painter	

Kanchanaburi War Cemetery
Plot 1
Row A
Grave 47
Age 37

HISTORY

Singapore	Selarang Camp and Barracks Changi
POW Number	3/8402
'H' Force Thailand	'H' Force Group No. 3
POW Number	639
Cause of Death	Cardiac Beri-Beri
Place of Death	Kanchanaburi
Date of Death	0900 hours on 24.10.1943
Buried	Grave No. 214, Kanchanaburi.

ALFRED VICTOR KING
a.k.a. Albert John King

Rank	Private
Regimental Number	WX16236
Enlisted	27.8.1941
Discharged	23.1.1946
Date of Birth	22.2.1922
Place of Birth	Birmingham, England
Father	Not Known
Mother	Not Known
Religion	Church of England
Pre-War Occupation	Miner and Stationhand

Sukchon Cemetery Korea
Portion 2
Plot and Row 11
Grave 126
Age 26

HISTORY

Singapore	Selarang Camp and Barracks Changi
	Forest Party
'D' Force Thailand	S Battalion
POW Number	8800
Camps Thailand	Chungkai
Japan	*Rashin Maru* Party
POW Number	1648
Camps Japan	Yamane, Niihama
Return Details 1945	Wakayama-Okinawa, USS *Sanctuary*
	Okinawa-Manila, USS *Bingham*
	Manila-Sydney, HMS *Speaker*
	Sydney-Fremantle, HMT *Strathmore*
Additions	Soldier had been a Kingsley Fairbridge Farm school boy and had absconded and changed his name to avoid detection. Soldier re-enlisted and was killed in action after only 42 days in Korea on 8.11.1950.

EDRIC HERBERT KING

Rank	Private
Regimental Number	WX8007
Classification	Driver
Company	'A' Company
Enlisted	13.8.1940
Date of Birth	1.3.1911
Place of Birth	Northam, Western Australia
Father	Albert Thomas King
Mother	Eleanor Rose King
Religion	Church of England
Pre-War Occupation	Labourer

Kanchanaburi War Cemetery
Plot 1
Row D
Grave 74
Age 32

HISTORY

Singapore	Selarang Camp and Barracks Changi
POW Number	4/6295
'D' Force Thailand	S Battalion
POW Number	8799
Cause of Death	Pulmonary Tuberculosis
Place of Death	Tamarkan
Date of Death	12.11.1943
Buried	Grave AX 9, Tamarkan.

JOHN KINGDON

Rank	Private
Regimental Number	WX15700
Company	'E' Company, Special Reserve Battalion
Enlisted	11.8.1941
Date of Birth	7.4.1916
Place of Birth	Mandurah, Western Australia
Father	Roger Audley Kingdon
Mother	Alice Maud Kingdon
Religion	Church of England
Pre-War Occupation	School Teacher

Kanchanaburi War Cemetery
Plot 1
Row F
Grave 23
Age 27

HISTORY

Singapore	Selarang Camp and Barracks Changi
POW Number	3/8420
'D' Force Thailand	V Battalion
Cause of Death	Pulmonary Tuberculosis
Place of Death	Kanchanaburi
Date of Death	13.10.1943

RONALD JAMES KINGSWELL

Rank	Sergeant
Regimental Number	WX4949
Company	'C' Company
Enlisted	23.7.1940
Date of Birth	2.11.1916
Place of Birth	Isle of Wight, England
Father	Not Known
Mother	Rose Ellen Kingswell
Religion	Church of England
Pre-War Occupation	Farmhand

Djakarta War Cemetery
Plot 3
Row H
Grave 11
Age 25

HISTORY

Java	'Blackforce'
Cause of Death	Acute Bacillary Dysentery and Appendicitis
Place of Death	No. 1 Allied General Hospital, Bandoeng
Date of Death	25.3.1942
Buried	Grave No. 58, Bandoeng
Additions	Soldier was a Kingsley Fairbridge Farm Schoolboy. Funeral service conducted by Padre F. J. Camroux on 26.3.1942. It appears that the surgeons were unable to operate on this NCO due to his having contracted dysentery.

GERRY BROWN KLUTH
a.k.a. Gerry Brown Cluth

Rank	Private
Regimental Number	WX16391
Company	'D' Company
Enlisted	8.9.1941
Date of Birth	28.3.1920
Place of Birth	Subiaco, Western Australia
Father	Henry Adolph Kluth
Mother	Matilda Brown (mother died 14 days after child birth)
Religion	Church of England
Pre-War Occupation	Labourer and Professional Cyclist

Kanchanaburi War Cemetery
Plot 1
Row H
Grave 49
Age 23

HISTORY

Singapore	Selarang Camp and Barracks Changi
POW Number	4/6003
'D' Force Thailand	S Battalion
POW Number	8761
Cause of Death	Cholera
Place of Death	Kanu II
Date of Death	5.7.1943
Buried	Grave No. 12, Kanu II.

LAURANCE ANZAC CHRISTIAN KUHLMANN

Rank	Private
Regimental Number	WX8077
Company	'C' Company
Enlisted	16.8.1940
Date of Birth	19.4.1916
Place of Birth	Ravensthorpe, Western Australia
Father	Herman Robert Kuhlmann
Mother	Bertha Matilda Kuhlmann
Religion	Church of England
Pre-War Occupation	Miner

Kanchanaburi War Cemetery
Plot 1
Row F
Grave 59
Age 27

HISTORY

Singapore	Selarang Camp and Barracks Changi
	A. G. H. Roberts Barracks Changi
POW Number	1/8312
'D' Force Thailand	V Battalion
POW Number	2263
Cause of Death	Acute Colitis
Place of Death	Non Pladuk
Date of Death	3.3.1944
Buried	Grave 9B, Non Pladuk
Additions	Wounded in action Jurong Road. Admitted to 2/9th Field Ambulance with shrapnel wounds to the left chest and back on 9.2.1942. Discharged to unit on 21.6.1942.

GEORGE LAKE

Rank	Private
Regimental Number	WX17582
Company	'E' Company, Special Reserve Battalion
Enlisted	6.11.1941
Date of Birth	13.4.1921
Place of Birth	Collie, Western Australia
Father	George Lake
Mother	Ann Lake
Religion	Methodist
Pre-War Occupation	Wheeler

Epitaph
Labuan Memorial
Panel 18
Age 23

HISTORY

Singapore	Selarang Camp and Barracks Changi
Force	'E' Force Borneo
POW Number	1782
Cause of Death	Not Stated
Place of Death	Sandakan
Date of Death	8.4.1945
Additions	Wounded in action Bukit Timah. Admitted to Field Ambulance on 11.2.1942 with a shrapnel wound to the right thigh. Transferred to the 2/10th Australian General Hospital on 6.3.1942.

PERCIVAL HENRY CHARLES LAKEMAN

Rank	Private
Regimental Number	WX8767
Company	'D' Company
Enlisted	23.10.1940
Date of Birth	19.10.1898
Place of Birth	Bunbury, Western Australia
Father	Henry Rosewarne Lakeman
Mother	Alice Lakeman
Religion	Church of England
Pre-War Occupation	Bogger

Kanchanaburi War Cemetery
Plot 1
Row H
Grave 50
Age 44

HISTORY

Singapore	Selarang Camp and Barracks Changi
POW Number	4/6037
'D' Force Thailand	S Battalion
POW Number	8802
Cause of Death	Malaria
Place of Death	Kanu I River Camp
Date of Death	20.6.1943
Buried	Grave No. 10, Kanu I River Camp
Additions	Soldier was shell shocked at Buona Vista on 14.2.1942.

KENNETH LALLY

Rank	Private
Regimental Number	WX9318
Company	'D' Company
Enlisted	30.10.1940
Date of Birth	20.2.1915
Place of Birth	Northam, Western Australia
Father	Thomas Henry Lally
Mother	Jessie Lally
Religion	Church of England
Pre-War Occupation	Storeman and Manager

Yokohama War Cemetery
Plot E
Row A
Grave 9
Age 30

HISTORY

Singapore	Selarang Camp Changi
	Johore Bahru, Adam Park
	Selarang Barracks Changi
POW Number	4/6307
'D' Force Thailand	V Battalion
Camps Thailand	Tamarkan Hospital (7.5.1943 Beri-Beri and Malaria), Non Pladuk
Japan	*Aramis* Party
Camps Japan	Fukuoka sub-Camp No. 17, Omuta
Cause of Death	Suffocation
Place of Death	Below ground in a coal mine
Date of Death	23.3.1945
Additions	Soldier was wounded in action on the west coast of Singapore at 2100 hours on 8.2.1942. He was admitted to the 2/13th Australian General Hospital with shrapnel wounds to the right leg. Discharged to unit on 21.2.1942. In Japan soldier was crushed between two coal trucks, dislocating his cervical vertebrae.

DENNIS RICHARD LANE

Rank	Private
Regimental Number	WX16439
Company	'A' Company
Enlisted	10.9.1941
Date of Birth	23.10.1920
Place of Birth	Shipton, England
Father	George Lane
Mother	Elizabeth Lane
Religion	Church of England
Pre-War Occupation	Plasterer, Fixer and Greaser

Epitaph
Labuan Memorial
Panel 18
Age 24

HISTORY

Singapore	Selarang Camp and Barracks Changi
POW Number	4/6312
Force	'E' Force Borneo
POW Number	1783
Cause of Death	Beri-Beri
Place of Death	Sandakan
Date of Death	16.1.1945

RONALD GUY LANGDON

Rank	Private
Regimental Number	WX9293
Classification	Driver
Company	'D' Company
Enlisted	30.10.1940
Date of Birth	5.2.1911
Place of Birth	Boulder, Western Australia
Father	Alfred John Langdon
Mother	Agnes Langdon
Religion	Methodist
Pre-War Occupation	Farmer

Kranji War Cemetery
Plot 15
Row C
Grave 10
Age 32

HISTORY

Singapore	Selarang Camp Changi
	Johore Bahru, Adam Park
	Selarang Barrracks Changi
POW Number	1/8329
'H' Force Thailand	'H' Force Group No. 3
Camps Thailand	Kanu II, Malayan Hamlet (evacuated to Kanchanaburi with cholera and beri-beri)
Singapore	Sime Road Camp
Cause of Death	Cardiac Beri-Beri
Place of Death	Sime Road Camp
Date of Death	24.1.1944
Buried	Diagonally opposite golf house, Grave No. 10.

EDWARD JOHNATHAN LEADBITTER

Rank	Private
Regimental Number	WX8425
Company	'D' Company
Enlisted	18.10.1940
Date of Birth	5.12.1918
Place of Birth	London, England
Father	George Leadbitter
Mother	Maud Leadbitter
Religion	Church of England
Pre-War Occupation	Gardener

Kanchanaburi War Cemetery
Collective Grave
Plot 3
Row G
Grave 35-39
Age 24

HISTORY

Singapore	Selarang Camp and Barracks Changi
POW Number	3/8489
'D' Force Thailand	V Battalion
POW Number	2266
Cause of Death	Cholera
Place of Death	Kuii
Date of Death	10.10.1943
Buried	Kuii, Grave No. 196
Additions	This soldier had been sent out to Australia as an orphan to the Kingsley Fairbridge Farm School. His father had died in the Battle of Jutland and his mother had passed away when he was 11 years old. Soldier was listed as missing from 8.2.1942. He had been captured by the Japanese on the west coast of Singapore but had escaped and rejoined unit after the surrender. In Thailand soldier had been suffering from malaria and was delirious. He was kicked and beaten for 30 minutes by the Japanese Engineer Corporal known as 'Black Cat'. Soldier died of cholera 14 days later.

Edward Leadbitter and his wife Winifred, on their wedding day

HAROLD BERNARD LEAR

Rank	Private
Regimental Number	WX7043
Classification	Driver
Company	'A' Company
Enlisted	30.7.1940
Date of Birth	21.7.1919
Place of Birth	Midland Junction, Western Australia
Father	Alfred Frederick Lear
Mother	Maud Isabel Lear
Religion	None Stated
Pre-War Occupation	Labourer

Epitaph
Labuan Memorial
Panel 18
Age 25

HISTORY

Singapore	Selarang Camp Changi
	A. G. H. Roberts Barracks Changi
	Selarang Barracks Changi
POW Number	3/8493
Force	'E' Force Borneo
POW Number	1785
Cause of Death	Malaria
Place of Death	Sandakan
Date of Death	17.3.1945
Additions	Wounded in action at Buona Vista on 15.2.1942. Admitted to the 2/13th Australian General Hospital with a shrapnel wound to the right leg. Discharged to unit 25.3.1942.

JOHN LEE
a.k.a. George Lee

Rank	Private
Regimental Number	WX9214
Classification	Driver
Company	'A' Company
Enlisted	16.4.1941
Date of Birth	21.5.1907
Place of Birth	Woodford Bridge, Bromley, Essex, England
Father	William Henry Lee
Mother	Elizabeth Lee
Religion	Church of England
Pre-War Occupation	Labourer

Thanbyuzayat War Cemetery
Plot A3
Row D
Grave 2
Age 36

HISTORY

Singapore	Selarang Camp Changi
'A' Force Burma	Green Force, No. 3 Battalion
POW Number	2920
Cause of Death	Cardiac Beri-Beri
Place of Death	Khonkan 55km Camp
Date of Death	26.8.1943
Buried	Grave No. 87, Khonkan
Additions	Wounded in action at Hill 200, Ulu Pandan on 12.2.1942. Admitted to the 2/13th Australian General Hospital with a shrapnel wound to the right foot. Discharged to unit on 21.2.1942. Soldier was evacuated from Aungganaung 105km Camp to Khonkan 55km Hospital Camp on 28.5.1943.

FORREST LEE-STEERE

Rank	Lance Corporal
Regimental Number	WX7640
Classification	Driver
Company	'D' Company Headquarters
Enlisted	10.8.1940
Date of Birth	17.7.1907
Place of Birth	Bridgetown, Western Australia
Father	Wilfred Lee-Steere
Mother	Laura Francis Lee-Steere
Religion	Church of England
Pre-War Occupation	Farmer

Kanchanaburi War Cemetery
Collective Grave
Plot 10
Row D
Grave 1-3
Age 36

HISTORY

Singapore	Selarang Camp and Barracks Changi
POW Number	4/6324
'D' Force Thailand	V Battalion
POW Number	2219
Cause of Death	Cholera
Place of Death	Kuii
Date of Death	3.10.1943
Buried	Grave No. 189, Kuii.

GEORGE RICHARD LEIPOLD

Rank	Private
Regimental Number	WX16355
Company	'E' Company, Special Reserve Battalion
Enlisted	3.9.1941
Date of Birth	29.8.1922
Place of Birth	Jessop's Well, Western Australia
Father	George William Leipold
Mother	Ida Evelyn Leipold
Religion	Methodist
Pre-War Occupation	Labourer

Epitaph
Singapore Memorial
Column 136
Age 19

HISTORY

Cause of Death	Killed in Action
Place of Death	South-West Bukit Timah
Date of Death	11.2.1942

JOHN SCOTT LIVINGSTONE

Rank	Private
Regimental Number	WX17759
Company	'E' Company, Special Reserve Battalion
Enlisted	24.11.1941
Date of Birth	18.7.1922
Place of Birth	Queenstown, Ireland
Father	Robert Livingstone
Mother	Ellen May Livingstone
Religion	Church of England
Pre-War Occupation	Plasterer

Kanchanaburi War Cemetery
Plot 1
Row J
Grave 68
Age 21

HISTORY

Singapore	Selarang Camp Changi
	Thomson Road (Caldecot Hill Estate Camp)
	River Valley Road Camp
	Selarang Barracks Changi
	Garden Control Party
'D' Force Thailand	S Battalion
POW Number	8801
Cause of Death	Malaria and Tropical Ulcers
Place of Death	Tarsau
Date of Death	4.9.1943
Buried	Cemetery No. 2, Grave No. 180, Tarsau.

FREDERICK JOHN LUDGE

Rank	Private
Regimental Number	W17778
Company	'E' Company, Special Reserve Battalion
Enlisted	26.11.1941
Date of Birth	1.2.1907
Place of Birth	Claremont, Western Australia
Father	Frederick William Ludge
Mother	Caroline Rose Ludge
Religion	Church of England
Pre-War Occupation	Labourer

Epitaph
Singapore Memorial
Column 136
Age 35

HISTORY

Cause of Death	Killed in Action
Place of Death	South-West Bukit Timah
Date of Death	11.2.1942

JOSEPH JOHN LYNCH

Rank	Private
Regimental Number	WX8639
Classification	Section Orderly
Company	'B' Company
Enlisted	18.10.1940
Date of Birth	22.12.1908
Place of Birth	Subiaco, Western Australia
Father	Bernard Lynch
Mother	Marion Lynch
Religion	Roman Catholic
Pre-War Occupation	Builder's Labourer

Kanchanaburi War Cemetery
Plot 1
Row H
Grave 71
Age 34

HISTORY

Singapore	Selarang Camp and Barracks Changi
POW Number	4/6534
'D' Force Thailand	S Battalion
POW Number	8805
Cause of Death	Cholera and Typhus
Place of Death	Kanu I River Camp
Date of Death	1.8.1943
Buried	Grave No. 78, Kanu I River Camp.

ROY DAVID MACONACHIE

Rank	Private
Regimental Number	WX9801
Classification	Signaller
Company	Headquarters Company
Enlisted	6.12.1940
Date of Birth	31.5.1920
Place of Birth	Dundee, Scotland
Father	David Hugh Maconachie
Mother	Flora McLeod Maconachie
Religion	Presbyterian
Pre-War Occupation	Clerk

Epitaph
Labuan Memorial
Panel 18
Age 25

HISTORY

Singapore	Selarang Camp Changi
Force	'B' Force Borneo
POW Number	1067
Cause of Death	Malaria
Place of Death	Sandakan-Ranau track
Date of Death	5.6.1945

JOHN MacDONALD

Rank	Private
Regimental Number	WX224
Classification	Mechanic
Company	'D' Company
Enlisted	11.12.1940
Date of Birth	11.5.1912
Place of Birth	England
Father	John MacDonald
Mother	Hannah MacDonald
Religion	Roman Catholic
Pre-War Occupation	Truck Driver

Epitaph
Singapore Memorial
Column 136
Age 29

HISTORY

Cause of Death	Missing believed killed in action
Place of Death	Near Ama Keng Village
Date of Death	9.2.1942

LINDSAY MURRAY MacDONALD

Rank	Private
Regimental Number	WX9279
Company	'D' Company
Enlisted	30.10.1940
Date of Birth	25.10.1914
Place of Birth	York, Western Australia
Father	Douglas Grant MacDonald
Mother	Laura Jessie MacDonald
Religion	Presbyterian
Pre-War Occupation	Farmhand

Epitaph
Singapore Memorial
Column 136
Age 27

HISTORY

Cause of Death	Believed killed in action
Place of Death	Lim Chu Kang Road
Date of Death	9.2.1942

HECTOR CECIL STANLEY MacMASTER

Rank	Corporal (Promoted on 11.2.1942)
Regimental Number	WX8689
Company	'B' Company
Enlisted	23.10.1940
Date of Birth	22.11.1908
Place of Birth	Leslie, Scotland
Father	John MacMaster
Mother	Catherine MacMaster
Religion	Presbyterian
Pre-War Occupation	Carpenter

Kanchanaburi War Cemetery
Plot 1
Row J
Grave 53
Age 37

HISTORY

Singapore	Selarang Camp and Barracks Changi
'D' Force Thailand	S Battalion
POW Number	8741
Camps Thailand	Kanu II
Cause of Death	Beri-Beri
Place of Death	Tarsau
Date of Death	25.7.1943
Buried	Cemetery No. 2, Grave No. 146, Tarsau on 26.7.1943.

DONALD THOMAS MANNING

Rank	Private
Regimental Number	WX7660
Company	'C' Company
Enlisted	10.8.1940
Date of Birth	26.6.1915
Place of Birth	Dwellingup, Western Australia
Father	Thomas Manning
Mother	Margaret Adeline Manning
Religion	Church of England
Pre-War Occupation	Miner

Kanchanaburi War Cemetery
Collective Grave
Plot 3
Row F
Grave 48-53
Age 28

HISTORY

Singapore	Selarang Camp Changi
	Thomson Road (Caldecot Hill Estate Camp)
	Selarang Barracks Changi
POW Number	3/8612
'D' Force Thailand	V Battalion
POW Number	2271
Cause of Death	Avitaminosis
Place of Death	Kuii
Date of Death	22.10.1943
Buried	Grave No. 205, Kuii.

HERBERT JOHN MANNING

Rank	Lieutenant
Regimental Number	WX8484
Company	'A' Company (took over command of No. 4 Platoon)
Enlisted	18.10.1940
Date of Birth	28.12.1914
Place of Birth	Subiaco, Western Australia
Father	Herbert Melville Manning
Mother	Jane Amelia Manning
Religion	Methodist
Pre-War Occupation	Warehouseman and Salesman

Kranji War Cemetery
Plot 3
Row C
Grave 13
Age 27

HISTORY

Cause of Death	Died of Wounds
Date of Death	12.2.1942
Buried	Martia Road Military Cemetery, Katong
	Protestant Section, Section 1 Grave No. 7
Additions	Wounded in action at Hill 200, Ulu Pandan. This Officer was hit in the neck by a fragment of shrapnel that exited through the chest. The time was 2100 hours on 12.2.1942 at map reference 764127. He was put onto a truck and driven 300 yards to the rear and placed on a bench in a (village) kampong. He was later moved by truck to the corner of Holland and Farrer Roads and attended to by a Medical Officer. He lived for approximately one and a half hours after receiving his wound. Officer was buried on 13.2.1942.

ALFRED NORMAN MANTLE

Rank	Sergeant (Promoted on 11.2.1942)
Regimental Number	WX11455
Classification	Clerk
Company	Battalion Headquarters
Enlisted	8.4.1941
Date of Birth	27.4.1909
Place of Birth	Wrexham, North Wales
Father	Alfred Mantle
Mother	Nina Isabel Mantle
Religion	Church of England
Pre-War Occupation	Clerk

Kanchanaburi War Cemetery
Plot 1
Row D
Grave 68
Age 36

HISTORY

Singapore	Selarang Camp Changi
'A' Force Burma	Green Force, No. 3 Battalion
POW Number	1348
Cause of Death	Dysentery and Malaria
Place of Death	Tamarkan
Date of Death	22.6.1944
Buried	Grave AX 34, Tamarkan
Additions	Detached to 2nd Echelon A.I.F. Malaya, for duty on 24.1.1942.

ROBERT WALTER MARSH

Rank	Private
Regimental Number	WX17639
Company	'E' Company, Special Reserve Battalion
Enlisted	12.11.1941
Date of Birth	20.1.1923
Place of Birth	Pinjarra, Western Australia
Father	Walter James Marsh
Mother	Beatrice Kathleen Marsh
Religion	Methodist
Pre-War Occupation	Labourer

Kranji War Cemetery
Plot 1
Row C
Grave 9
Age 18

HISTORY

Cause of Death	Died of Wounds
Place of Death	A. G. H. Roberts Barracks Changi
Date of Death	5.4.1942
Buried	A.I.F. Cemetery Changi, Grave No. 19
Additions	Soldier was wounded in action at South-West Bukit Timah on 11.2.1942. He stayed out with Laurence Kearney until captured by the Japanese on 7.3.1942. Admitted to the Australian General Hospital at Roberts Barracks Changi in a delirious state with gunshot wounds to the left hip and stomach. Soldier died from his wounds on 5.4.1942. Funeral Service was conducted by Padre F. Bashford from the 2/4th Australian Casualty Clearing Station on 6.4.1942.

DONALD ANGUS MATHESON

Rank	Private
Regimental Number	WX9296
Classification	Driver
Company	'C' Company
Enlisted	30.10.1940
Date of Birth	27.2.1908
Place of Birth	Rogart, Scotland
Father	William Matheson
Mother	Esther Matheson
Religion	Presbyterian
Pre-War Occupation	Farmhand

Thanbyuzayat War Cemetery
Plot A3
Row B
Grave 3
Age 36

HISTORY

Singapore	Selarang Camp Changi
'A' Force Burma	Green Force, No. 3 Battalion
POW Number	3078
Cause of Death	Cardiac Beri-Beri
Place of Death	Aungganaung 105km Camp
Date of Death	10.3.1944
Buried	Grave No. 120, Aungganaung
Additions	For this soldier to have died at Aungganaung in March 1944 it is probable that he was attached to Williams Force.

ANGELO ENRICO MAZZA

Rank	Lieutenant
Regimental Number	WX7216
Company	'E' Company, Special Reserve Battalion
Enlisted	1.8.1940
Date of Birth	19.8.1919
Place of Birth	Gwalia, Western Australia
Father	Bernard Mazza
Mother	Elena Boudoni Mazza
Religion	Non denominational
Pre-War Occupation	Butcher

Epitaph
Singapore Memorial
Column 135
Age 22

HISTORY

Cause of Death	Killed in Action
Place of Death	South-West Bukit Timah
Date of Death	11.2.1942
Additions	Believed killed in the vicinity of the atap huts at map reference 752148.

ROBERT RAMSAY McASKIL

Rank	Private
Regimental Number	WX8261
Company	'C' Company
Enlisted	17.8.1940
Date of Birth	2.1.1901
Place of Birth	North Coburg, Victoria
Father	Donald McAskil
Mother	Jessie McAskil
Religion	Presbyterian
Pre-War Occupation	Prospector

Djakarta War Cemetery
Plot 2
Row B
Grave 17
Age 44

HISTORY

Java	'Blackforce'
Camps Java	Bandoeng No. 4 Camp, Bicycle Camp Batavia, Makasura
Force	Java Party No. 20
POW Number	4394
Cause of Death	Cardiac Beri-Beri
Place of Death	Kampoeng 106km near Kota Baroe, Sumatra
Date of Death	0300 hours on 28.3.1945
Additions	Soldier missed draft to Japan due to illness. He later joined Java Party No. 22 and worked on the Pakan Baroe-Moearo Railway until his death in 1945.

ROBERT McCANN

Rank	Private
Regimental Number	WX8435
Attached 2/4th	88 Light Aid Detachment
Enlisted	18.10.1940
Date of Birth	24.12.1904
Place of Birth	Moora, Western Australia
Father	Arthur McCann
Mother	Margaret McCann
Religion	Church of Christ
Pre-War Occupation	Stationhand

Thanbyuzayat War Cemetery
Plot A5
Row G
Grave 8
Age 35

HISTORY

Singapore	Selarang Camp and Barracks Changi
POW Number	4/6360
Force	'F' Force Thailand
Cause of Death	Beri-Beri
Place of Death	Kami Sonkurai
Date of Death	23.11.1943
Buried	Grave No. 464, Kami Sonkurai.

JACK McCARTHY

Rank	Private
Regimental Number	WX9324
Company	'D' Company
Enlisted	30.10.1940
Date of Birth	18.9.1918
Place of Birth	Dangin, Western Australia
Father	Michael McCarthy
Mother	Catherine McCarthy
Religion	Church of England
Pre-War Occupation	Farmhand

Kanchanaburi War Cemetery
Plot 1
Row G
Grave 70
Age 24

HISTORY

Singapore	Selarang Camp Changi
	Johore Bahru, Adam Park
	Selarang Barracks Changi
POW Number	4/6361
'D' Force Thailand	V Battalion
POW Number	2277
Cause of Death	Malaria
Place of Death	Linson Camp
Date of Death	21.7.1943
Buried	Linson Camp Cemetery, Grave No. 1.

RONALD DUNCAN McCRACKEN

Rank	Private
Regimental Number	WX5584
Classification	Signaller
Company	Headquarters Company
Enlisted	11.12.1940
Date of Birth	11.12.1918
Place of Birth	Narrogin, Western Australia
Father	James Owen McCracken
Mother	Dorothy Kathleen McCracken
Religion	Roman Catholic
Pre-War Occupation	Radio Dealer

Epitaph
Labuan Memorial
Panel 18
Age 24

HISTORY

Singapore	Selarang Camp Changi
'A' Force Burma	Green Force, No. 3 Battalion
POW Number	3090
Japan	*Rakuyo Maru* Party, Kumi No. 37
Cause of Death	Lost at Sea
Place of Death	South China Sea
Date of Death	15.9.1944
Additions	Soldier was involved in the bayonet charge at Hill 200, Ulu Pandan where he was wounded in action. Admitted to the 2/10th Australian General Hospital with a gunshot wound to the right foot. Discharged to unit on 28.2.1942.

WALLACE PATRICK McCUDDEN

Rank	Private
Regimental Number	WX8820
Company	'C' Company
Enlisted	23.10.1940
Date of Birth	18.5.1907
Place of Birth	Esperance, Western Australia
Father	John Patrick McCudden
Mother	Emma Ann McCudden
Religion	Roman Catholic
Pre-War Occupation	Labourer

Kanchanaburi War Cemetery
Plot 1
Row M
Grave 12
Age 36

HISTORY

Singapore	Selarang Camp and Barracks Changi
POW Number	3/8859
'D' Force Thailand	S Battalion
POW Number	8819
Cause of Death	Cardiac Beri-Beri and Typhus
Place of Death	Chungkai
Date of Death	21.8.1943
Buried	Grave No. 274, Chungkai.

KEITH KITCHENER McDONALD

Rank	Private
Regimental Number	WX8621
Company	'A' Company
Enlisted	18.10.1940
Date of Birth	17.5.1918
Place of Birth	Geraldton, Western Australia
Father	William Donald McDonald
Mother	Beatrice Maude McDonald
Religion	Church of England
Pre-War Occupation	Factory Hand at Bristle Tiles

Kanchanaburi War Cemetery
Joint Grave
Plot 1
Row O
Grave 48-49
Age 25

HISTORY

Singapore	Selarang Camp and Barracks Changi
POW Number	1/12015
'D' Force Thailand	S Battalion
POW Number	8812
Cause of Death	Cholera
Place of Death	Tarsau
Date of Death	25.11.1943
Buried	Cemetery No. 3, Grave No. 123, Tarsau.

HENRY ELVIN McDONOUGH

Rank	Private
Regimental Number	WX9052
Company	'C' Company
Enlisted	25.10.1940
Date of Birth	5.6.1915
Place of Birth	Melbourne, Victoria
Father	Joseph Albert McDonough
Mother	Maud Mary McDonough
Religion	Spiritualist
Pre-War Occupation	Bootmaker

Kanchanaburi War Cemetery
Collective Grave
Plot 1
Row P
Grave 37-52
Age 28

HISTORY

Singapore	Selarang Camp and Barracks Changi
POW Number	3/8865
'H' Force Thailand	'H' Force Group No. 3
Cause of Death	Cholera
Place of Death	Kanu II, Malayan Hamlet
Date of Death	27.6.1943
Buried	In an unmarked cemetery approximately 300 yards North of Kanu IIIa (Tampie North), on the Kanu-Hintok Road, Grave No. 18.

OSWALD SYDNEY McEWIN

Rank	Captain
Regimental Number	WX3442
Company	Company Headquarters
Enlisted	19.11.1940
Date of Birth	15.7.1910
Place of Birth	Greenwich, Sydney, New South Wales
Father	James Guthrie McEwin
Mother	Eva Rosina McEwin
Religion	Presbyterian
Pre-War Occupation	Sales Manager

Kranji War Cemetery
Plot 1
Row A
Grave 9
Age 31

HISTORY

Cause of Death	Killed in Action
Place of Death	Hill 200, Ulu Pandan
Date of Death	12.2.1942
Buried	Where killed at map reference 763132 by Major A. Cough Party on 21.12.1942. This Officer died as a result of a gunshot wound to the skull whilst leading a bayonet charge up Hill 200, Ulu Pandan.

DONALD SPENCER McGLINN

Rank	Private
Regimental Number	WX11580
Company	'C' Company
Enlisted	9.4.1941
Date of Birth	22.3.1915
Place of Birth	Dangin, Western Australia
Father	James Edmund McGlinn
Mother	Victoria Elizabeth McGlinn
Religion	Methodist
Pre-War Occupation	Railways Platelayer

Kanchanaburi War Cemetery
Plot 1
Row J
Grave 44
Age 28

HISTORY

Singapore	Selarang Camp and Barracks Changi
POW Number	3/8883
'D' Force Thailand	S Battalion
POW Number	8817
Camps Thailand	Kanu II
Cause of Death	Dysentery and Avitaminosis
Place of Death	Tarsau
Date of Death	15.7.1943
Buried	Cemetery No. 2, Grave No. 45 Tarsau, on 16.7.1943.

ARCHIBALD JAMES LIVIE McINTOSH

Rank	Private
Regimental Number	WX9849
Classification	Signaller
Company	Headquarters Company
Enlisted	6.12.1940
Date of Birth	16.6.1920
Place of Birth	Scotland
Father	John Ramsay McIntosh
Mother	Mary McLeod McIntosh
Religion	Presbyterian
Pre-War Occupation	Ledger Keeper

Thanbyuzayat War Cemetery
Plot A16
Row D
Grave 16
Age 23

HISTORY

Singapore	Selarang Camp Changi
	Thomson Road (Caldecot Hill Estate Camp)
	River Valley Road Camp
	Selarang Barracks Changi
POW Number	3/8580
Force	'F' Force Thailand
Camps Thailand	Shimo Sonkurai
Cause of Death	Beri-Beri and Dysentery
Place of Death	Tanbaya Camp, Burma
Date of Death	1000 hours on 10.11.1943
Buried	Grave No. 598, Tanbaya
Additions	Funeral service was conducted by Chaplain Duckworth (British Army) on 15.11.1943. Soldier was actually buried on 10.11.1943.

WILLIAM McKAY

Rank	Private
Regimental Number	WX7138
Company	'C' Company
Enlisted	1.8.1940
Date of Birth	2.7.1908
Place of Birth	Colspie, Scotland
Father	Hugh McKay
Mother	Sarah McKay
Religion	Presbyterian
Pre-War Occupation	Prospector

Kanchanaburi War Cemetery
Plot 1
Row L
Grave 56
Age 35

HISTORY

Singapore	Selarang Camp and Barracks Changi
POW Number	1/8536
'D' Force Thailand	V Battalion
POW Number	2276
Cause of Death	Acute Enteritis
Place of Death	Brankassi
Date of Death	23.9.1943
Buried	Grave No. 68, Brankassi.

THOMAS MEMBURY McMAHON

Rank	Private
Regimental Number	WX8760
Company	'A' Company
Enlisted	23.10.1940
Date of Birth	8.3.1920
Place of Birth	Loxton, South Australia
Father	Thomas Michael McMahon
Mother	Ethel Joan McMahon
Religion	Church of England
Pre-War Occupation	Hoist Driver

Epitaph
Labuan Memorial
Panel 18
Age 24

HISTORY

Singapore	Selarang Camp Changi
'A' Force Burma	Green Force, No. 3 Battalion
POW Number	1495
Japan	*Rakuyo Maru* Party, Kumi No. 35
Cause of Death	Lost at Sea
Place of Death	South China Sea
Date of Death	14.9.1945
Additions	Wounded in action at Ulu Pandan on 12.2.1942. Admitted to the 13th Australian General Hospital with a schrapnel wound to the left foot. Discharged to unit on 24.2.1942.

STANLEY SCOTT McNEIL

Rank	Warrant Officer II (Promoted on 7.2.1942)
Regimental Number	WX15720
Company	'E' Company Headquarters, Special Reserve Battalion
Enlisted	13.8.1941
Date of Birth	7.2.1900
Place of Birth	Bootle, Liverpool, England
Father	Arthur McNeil
Mother	Louisa McNeil
Religion	Church of England
Pre-War Occupation	Farmer

Epitaph
Singapore Memorial
Column 135
Age 42

HISTORY

Cause of Death	Killed in Action
Place of Death	South-West Bukit Timah
Date of Death	11.2.1942

KENNETH LAWRANCE MEADS

Rank	Corporal
Regimental Number	WX10388
Classification	Cook
Company	Headquarters Company
Enlisted	18.12.1940
Date of Birth	17.1.1905
Place of Birth	St Lennards on Sea, Hastings, England
Father	Adolphus Kingsworth Meads
Mother	Ethel Meads
Religion	Church of England
Pre-War Occupation	Cook

Thanbyuzayat War Cemetery
Plot A8
Row D
Grave 2
Age 38

HISTORY

Singapore	Selarang Camp Changi
'A' Force Burma	Green Force, No. 3 Battalion
POW Number	1372
Cause of Death	Toxemia
Place of Death	Khonkan 55km Camp
Date of Death	14.9.1943
Buried	Grave No.139, Khonkan
Additions	Soldier was evacuated to Khonkan 55km from Aungganaung 105km Camp around 10.9.1943 due to tropical ulcers to his right foot. The right leg was amputated above the knee, but soldier died post leg amputation as a result of toxemia.

JOHN THOMPSON MEIKLEJOHN

Rank	Lieutenant
Regimental Number	WX9393
Company	'D' Company
Enlisted	16.11.1940
Date of Birth	17.5.1919
Place of Birth	Katanning, Western Australia
Father	John Meiklejohn
Mother	Lilian Grace Meiklejohn
Religion	Church of England
Pre-War Occupation	Warehouseman

Epitaph
Singapore Memorial
Column 135
Age 22

HISTORY

Cause of Death	Missing believed killed in action
Place of Death	West coast of Singapore
Date of Death	8.2.1942
Additions	Wounded in the chest whilst in action on the west coast of Singapore. This Officer was last seen firing his revolver at a Japanese Corporal whilst fighting his way out from the coast. Officer was in the company of several men from his No. 15 Platoon, including Sergeant Solly.

RUPERT JOHN MILLHOUSE

Rank	Private
Regimental Number	WX16675
Company	'E' Company, Special Reserve Battalion
Enlisted	22.9.1941
Date of Birth	14.8.1919
Place of Birth	Port Lincoln, South Australia
Father	Hugh Percy Millhouse
Mother	Joan Margaret Millhouse
Religion	Roman Catholic
Pre-War Occupation	Farrier

Kranji War Cemetery
Plot 32
Row C
Grave 13
Age 23

HISTORY

Cause of Death	Executed by a Japanese firing squad
Place of Death	Singapore
Date of Death	19.2.1942
Additions	Wounded in action South-West Bukit Timah receiving four gunshot wounds to the right leg. Missing in action from 11.2.1942. Executed by a Japanese firing squad for no apparent reason at map reference 753097.

ALEC RANDOLPH MINCHIN

Rank	Corporal (Promoted on 18.1.1942)
Regimental Number	WX7662
Company	'C' Company
Enlisted	10.8.1940
Date of Birth	4.4.1914
Place of Birth	Dangin, Western Australia
Father	Frederick Minchin
Mother	Lilly May Minchin
Religion	Methodist
Pre-War Occupation	Farmer

Epitaph
Labuan Memorial
Panel 18
Age 30

HISTORY

Singapore	Selarang Camp Changi
'A' Force Burma	Green Force, No. 3 Battalion
POW Number	1367
Camps Burma	Reptu 30km Camp
Japan	*Rakuyo Maru* Party, Kumi No. 35
Cause of Death	Lost at Sea
Place of Death	South China Sea
Date of Death	15.9.1944

KENNETH MOHER

Rank	Private
Regimental Number	WX17737
Company	'E' Company, Special Reserve Battalion
Enlisted	21.11.1941
Date of Birth	25.9.1914
Place of Birth	Gwalia, Western Australia
Father	William Moher
Mother	Mary Moher
Religion	Roman Catholic
Pre-War Occupation	Clerk and Baker

Thanbyuzayat War Cemetery
Plot A5
Row E
Grave 8
Age 28

HISTORY

Singapore	Selarang Camp Changi
'A' Force Burma	Green Force, No. 3 Battalion
Cause of Death	Amoebic Dysentery
Place of Death	Khonkan 55km Camp
Date of Death	24.7.1943
Buried	Grave No. 27, Khonkan.

ANDREW DONALD MOIR

Rank	Private
Regimental Number	WX9337
Classification	Driver
Company	'D' Company
Enlisted	30.10.1940
Date of Birth	13.11.1919
Place of Birth	Albany, Western Australia
Father	John Andrew Moir
Mother	Gladys Emma Moir
Religion	Church of England
Pre-War Occupation	Farmhand

Kranji War Cemetery
Plot 30
Row B
Grave 20
Age 22

HISTORY

Cause of Death	Killed in Action
Place of Death	West coast of Singapore
Date of Death	8.2.1942
Additions	Soldier is believed to have been killed on the night of 8.2.1942 by mortar fire. He was last seen with his vehicle. Soldier's body was located and identified on 11.12.1946.

EDWARD GEORGE MOIR

Rank	Private
Regimental Number	WX15905
Company	'D' Company
Enlisted	20.8.1941
Date of Birth	14.5.1911
Place of Birth	Donnybrook, Western Australia
Father	McLaren John Moir
Mother	Edith Alice Moir
Religion	Roman Catholic
Pre-War Occupation	Labourer

Kanchanaburi War Cemetery
Collective Grave
Plot 3
Row D
Grave 71-73
Age 32

HISTORY

Singapore	Selarang Camp and Barracks Changi
'D' Force Thailand	V Battalion
POW Number	2273
Cause of Death	Malaria and Dysentery
Place of Death	Kuii
Date of Death	1.10.1943
Buried	Grave No. 187, Kuii
Additions	Soldier was admitted to the 2/9th Field Ambulance on 2.2.1942. Transferred to the 2/10th Australian General Hospital with a fever. Discharged to unit having recovered from malaria on 8.3.1942.

KEVIN GEORGE MOIR

Rank	Private
Regimental Number	WX8012
Classification	Rangetaker
Company	'C' Company
Enlisted	13.8.1940
Date of Birth	8.4.1919
Place of Birth	Collie, Western Australia
Father	Charles John Moir
Mother	Agnes Theresa Moir
Religion	Roman Catholic
Pre-War Occupation	Teamster

Kanchanaburi War Cemetery
Collective Grave
Plot 1
Row Q
Grave 2-78
Age 24

HISTORY

Singapore	Selarang Camp and Barracks Changi
'D' Force Thailand	S Battalion
POW Number	8822
Cause of Death	Cholera
Place of Death	Hintok River Camp
Date of Death	7.8.1943
Buried	Grave No. 83, Hintok River Camp
Additions	Wounded in action at Hill 200, Ulu Pandan on 12.2.1942, receiving a gunshot wound to the arm.

GEORGE GABRIEL MONGAN

Rank	Lance Corporal
Regimental Number	WX8973
Classification	Technical Storeman
Company	'A' Company Headquarters
Enlisted	25.10.1940
Date of Birth	6.10.1904
Place of Birth	Perth, Western Australia
Father	John Thomas Mongan
Mother	Sara Mongan
Religion	Roman Catholic
Pre-War Occupation	Storeman

Kranji War Cemetery
Collective Grave
Plot 30
Row A
Grave 9-11
Age 37

HISTORY

Cause of Death	Died of Wounds
Place of Death	Buona Vista
Date of Death	15.2.1942
Buried	Where killed in a common grave at map reference 784112 on 16.2.1942.
Additions	Soldier was wounded by mortar fire at Cemetery Hill, Buona Vista near Holland Village at 1700 hours on 15.2.1942.

FRANK CLIFFORD MOORE

Rank	Private
Regimental Number	WX8076
Company	'A' Company
Enlisted	16.8.1940
Date of Birth	20.6.1911
Place of Birth	Northam, Western Australia
Father	Frank Randell Moore
Mother	Margueretta Valeria Agnes Moore
Religion	Presbyterian
Pre-War Occupation	Teamster

Epitaph
Labuan Memorial
Panel 18
Age 33

HISTORY

Singapore	Selarang Camp Changi
'A' Force Burma	Green Force, No. 3 Battalion
POW Number	2898
Japan	*Rakuyo Maru* Party, Kumi No. 36
Cause of Death	Lost at Sea
Place of Death	South China Sea
Date of Death	12.9.1942

RONALD KEITH MORAN

Rank	Private
Regimental Number	WX15386
Company	'A' Company
Enlisted	24.7.1941
Date of Birth	25.6.1922
Father	William Moran
Mother	Charlotte Olive Moran
Stepfather	Charles Noel Cleale
Religion	Church of England
Pre-War Occupation	Tractor Driver

Epitaph
Labuan Memorial
Panel 18
Age 21

HISTORY

Singapore	Selarang Camp and Barracks Changi
POW Number	3/8755
Force	'E' Force Borneo
POW Number	1827
Cause of Death	Malaria
Place of Death	Sandakan
Date of Death	28.6.1945
Additions	This soldier may have been as young as 16 years of age on enlistment.

JOHN ERNEST MULDOON

Rank	Corporal
Regimental Number	WX15684
Company	'E' Company, Special Reserve Battalion
Enlisted	11.8.1941
Date of Birth	3.8.1923
Place of Birth	Brisbane, Queensland
Father	William Ernest Muldoon
Mother	Mabel Muldoon
Religion	Church of England
Pre-War Occupation	Clerk

Epitaph
Singapore Memorial
Column 135
Age 19

HISTORY

Cause of Death	Killed in Action
Place of Death	Bald Hill, Bukit Timah
Date of Death	11.2.1942

ERNEST MONTAGUE MUNDAY

Rank	Private
Regimental Number	WX17390
Company	'E' Company, Special Reserve Battalion
Enlisted	27.10.1941
Date of Birth	24.3.1916
Place of Birth	Guildford, Western Australia
Father	Harry James Munday
Mother	Fanny Munday
Religion	Church of England
Pre-War Occupation	Labourer

Epitaph
Singapore Memorial
Column 136
Age 25

HISTORY

Cause of Death	Killed in Action
Place of Death	Sungei Kranji-Sungei Jurong Defence Line
Date of Death	10.2.1942

JAMES JOSEPH MURPHY

Rank	Private
Regimental Number	WX16674
Company	'E' Company, Special Reserve Battalion
Enlisted	22.9.1941
Date of Birth	17.1.1917
Place of Birth	Pinnaroo, South Australia
Father	James Vincent Murphy
Mother	Gwendoline Ellen Murphy
Religion	Methodist
Pre-War Occupation	Farmhand

Epitaph
Singapore Memorial
Column 136
Age 25

HISTORY

Cause of Death	Killed in Action
Place of Death	South-West Bukit Timah
Date of Death	11.2.1942

JOHN PATRICK MURPHY

Rank	Private
Regimental Number	WX7426
Company	Headquarters Company
Enlisted	6.8.1940
Date of Birth	13.3.1916
Place of Birth	Boulder, Western Australia
Father	Thomas Bernard Murphy
Mother	Arimathea Goine Callaway Murphy
Religion	Roman Catholic
Pre-War Occupation	Truck Driver

Kanchanaburi War Cemetery
Plot 1
Row O
Grave 73
Age 27

HISTORY

Singapore	Selarang Camp and Barracks Changi
POW Number	4/6434
'D' Force Thailand	V Battalion
POW Number	2274
Cause of Death	Cholera
Place of Death	Kuii
Date of Death	30.11.1943
Buried	Grave No. 219, Kuii.

ALFRED CHARLES MUSSMAN

Rank	Private
Regimental Number	WX9887
Classification	Rangetaker
Company	'C' Company
Enlisted	9.12.1940
Date of Birth	25.4.1911
Place of Birth	Adelaide, South Australia
Father	Lawrence Mussman
Mother	Maud Mussman
Religion	Agnostic
Pre-War Occupation	Fitter's Assistant

Epitaph
Singapore Memorial
Column 136
Age 30

HISTORY

Cause of Death	Killed in Action
Place of Death	Reformatory Road, Ulu Pandan
Date of Death	11.2.1942
Buried	Where killed at map reference 758128 by Major A. Cough Party on 21.12.1942.
Additions	This soldier had received a wound to the head.

CHARLES MUTTON

Rank	Private
Regimental Number	WX7181
Classification	Scout
Company	'B' Company
Enlisted	1.8.1940
Date of Birth	14.7.1913
Place of Birth	Perth, Western Australia
Father	Arthur Stephen Mutton
Mother	Bridget Agnes Mutton
Religion	Methodist
Pre-War Occupation	Truck Driver

Epitaph
Labuan Memorial
Panel 18
Age 31

HISTORY

Singapore	Selarang Camp Changi
'A' Force Burma	Green Force, No. 3 Battalion
POW Number	3109
Japan	*Rakuyo Maru* Party, Kumi No. 37
Cause of Death	Lost at Sea
Place of Death	South China Sea
Date of Death	12.9.1944
Additions	This soldier it is believed, worked down into Thailand with Williams Force.

CLAUDE OCEA NASH

Rank	Private
Regimental Number	WX17363
Company	'D' Company
Enlisted	22.10.1941
Date of Birth	10.5.1919
Place of Birth	Subiaco, Western Australia
Father	Richard Harry Nash M.P.
Mother	Ruby Nash
Religion	Church of England
Pre-War Occupation	Shop Assistant

Epitaph
Labuan Memorial
Panel 18
Age 26

HISTORY

Singapore	Selarang Camp Changi
	Thomson Road (Caldecot Hill Estate Camp)
	River Valley Road Camp
	Selarang Barracks Changi
POW Number	3/8964
Force	'E' Force Borneo
POW Number	1831
Cause of Death	Acute Intestinalitis
Place of Death	Ranau
Date of Death	23.3.1945
Additions	Wounded in action on 9.2.1942 and admitted to the 2/13th Australian Hospital with small fragments of shrapnel in the arm. Discharged to unit on 16.2.1942.

FRANCISCO NAZZARI

Rank	Corporal (Promoted on 11.2.1942)
Regimental Number	WX8707
Company	'A' Company
Enlisted	23.10.1940
Date of Birth	31.1.1916
Place of Birth	Kalgoorlie, Western Australia
Father	Onrato Nazzari
Mother	Vincenza Nazzari
Religion	Roman Catholic
Pre-War Occupation	Miner

HISTORY

Singapore	Selarang Camp and Barracks Changi
POW Number	12090
Force	'E' Force Borneo
POW Number	1832
Cause of Death	Acute Intestinalitis
Place of Death	Sandakan
Date of Death	24.4.1945

STANLEY EDWARD NEALE

Rank	Private
Regimental Number	WX9260
Classification	Trade Group I
Attached 2/4th	88 Light Aid Detachment
Enlisted	30.10.1940
Date of Birth	18.7.1914
Place of Birth	Northampton, Western Australia
Father	Edward Neale
Mother	Ruby Elizabeth Neale
Religion	Roman Catholic
Pre-War Occupation	Miner

HISTORY

Singapore	Selarang Camp Changi
Force	'B' Force Borneo
POW Number	835
Cause of Death	Not stated on Japanese Death Certificate
Place of Death	Sandakan (presumed)
Date of Death	28.2.1945
Additions	2/4th Field Workshops, 11th Recovery Section. Taken on Strength at Darwin, no date.

JOHN WILLIAM HAYNES NEEDHAM

Rank	Lance Corporal
Regimental Number	WX8137
Classification	Driver/Mechanic
Company	'C' Company
Enlisted	16.8.1940
Date of Birth	26.8.1913
Place of Birth	Broome, Western Australia
Father	Richard William Needham
Mother	Isabella Needham
Religion	Church of England
Pre-War Occupation	Motor Mechanic

Thanbyuzayat War Cemetery
Plot A9
Row D
Grave 10
Age 30

HISTORY

Singapore	Selarang Camp Changi
'A' Force Burma	Green Force, No. 3 Battalion
POW Number	1451
Camps Burma	Khonkan 55km Camp (tropical ulcers on right foot)
Cause of Death	Pneumonia
Place of Death	Khonkan 55km Camp
Date of Death	5.12.1943
Buried	Grave No. 259, Khonkan.

PETER JAMES NEGRI

Rank	Lance Corporal
Regimental Number	WX12985
Company	'C' Company
Enlisted	14.5.1941
Date of Birth	12.2.1920
Place of Birth	Greenbushes, Western Australia
Father	Peter Negri
Mother	Florrie Negri
Religion	Methodist
Pre-War Occupation	Millhand

Epitaph
Labuan Memorial
Panel 18
Age 25

HISTORY

Singapore	Selarang Camp and Barracks Changi
POW Number	1/12091
Force	'E' Force Borneo
POW Number	1836
Cause of Death	Cardiac Beri-Beri
Place of Death	Sandakan
Date of Death	21.1.1945

FRANK HENRY NEW

Rank	Private
Regimental Number	WX5196
Company	Headquarters Company
Enlisted	26.7.1940
Date of Birth	7.11.1902
Place of Birth	Gloucestershire, England
Father	John Henry New
Mother	Caroline New
Religion	Church of England
Pre-War Occupation	Cook

Thanbyuzayat War Cemetery
Plot A4
Row A
Grave 6
Age 40

HISTORY

Singapore	Selarang Camp Changi
'A' Force Burma	Green Force, No. 3 Battalion
POW Number	2907
Cause of Death	Post Leg Amutation
Place of Death	Khonkan 55km Hospital Camp
Date of Death	21.10.1943
Buried	Grave No. 201, Khonkan
Additions	Soldier was evacuated to Khonkan on 4.7.1943. Two tropical ulcers had developed on the lower right leg. The leg was amputated above the knee but soldier died post operation. He was also suffering from malaria and dysentery at the time of his death.

OSWALD KITCHENER NEWLING

Rank	Private
Regimental Number	WX17458
Company	Headquarters Company
Enlisted	27.10.1941
Date of Birth	10.6.1915
Place of Birth	Leederville, Western Australia
Father	William John Newling
Mother	Lillian Mary Newling
Religion	Church of England
Pre-War Occupation	Boat Repairer

Kanchanaburi War Cemetery
Collective Grave
Plot 3
Row F
Grave 48-53
Age 28

HISTORY

Singapore	Selarang Camp and Barracks Changi
POW Number	4/6448
'D' Force Thailand	V Battalion
POW Number	2279
Cause of Death	Malaria
Place of Death	Kuii
Date of Death	22.10.1943
Buried	Grave No. 205, Kuii
Additions	Admitted to Alexandra Hospital with appendicitis. Posted on the sick list on 27.1.1942.

REXFORD FRANK NEWLING

Rank	Private
Regimental Number	WX8432
Classification	Bricklayer
Company	Headquarters Company
Enlisted	8.10.1940
Date of Birth	28.4.1913
Place of Birth	Perth, Western Australia
Father	William John Newling
Mother	Lillian Mary Newling
Religion	Church of England
Pre-War Occupation	Bricklayer

Kanchanaburi War Cemetery
Collective Grave
Plot 3
Row D
Grave 71-73
Age 30

HISTORY

Singapore	Selarang Camp and Barracks Changi
POW Number	4/6449
'D' Force Thailand	V Battalion
POW Number	2278
Cause of Death	Malaria
Place of Death	Kuii
Date of Death	29.9.1943
Buried	Grave No. 187, Kuii.

ROLF WALKER NEWLING

Rank	Private
Regimental Number	WX8865
Classification	Section Orderly
Company	'B' Company
Enlisted	25.10.1940
Date of Birth	15.6.1911
Place of Birth	Perth, Western Australia
Father	William John Newling
Mother	Lillian Mary Newling
Religion	Church of England
Pre-War Occupation	Labourer

Epitaph
Labuan Memorial
Panel 18
Age 33

HISTORY

Singapore	Selarang Camp Changi
Force	'B' Force Borneo
POW Number	1071
Cause of Death	Malaria
Place of Death	Ranau
Date of Death	13.6.1945

CECIL WILLIAM NEWMAN

Rank	Private
Regimental Number	NX73279
Attached 2/4th	88 Light Aid Detachment
Enlisted	Not Known
Date of Birth	24.4.1920
Place of Birth	Scone, New South Wales
Father	William Newman
Mother	Mercy Beatrice Newman
Religion	Church of England
Pre-War Occupation	Cabinet Maker

Epitaph
Labuan Memorial
Panel 29
Age 24

HISTORY

Singapore	Selarang Camp Changi
Force	'E' Force Borneo
POW Number	1837
Cause of Death	Not Known
Place of Death	Sandakan
Date of Death	11.3.1945
Additions	Taken on Strength at Sydney on 9.1.1942.

WILLIAM JAMES NICHOLLS

Rank	Private
Regimental Number	WX7645
Classification	Signaller
Company	Headquarters Company
Enlisted	10.8.1940
Date of Birth	12.7.1910
Place of Birth	Donnybrook, Western Australia
Father	Albert Edward Nicholls
Mother	Elizabeth Ann Nicholls
Religion	Methodist
Pre-War Occupation	Butcher

Djakarta War Cemetery
Plot 4
Row L
Grave 9
Age 32

HISTORY

Java	'Blackforce'
POW Number	7838
Cause of Death	Bacillary Dysentery
Place of Death	Bicycle Camp Hospital, Batavia
Date of Death	13.10.1942
Buried	Petamboran Cemetery, British Section Grave No. 102
Additions	Soldier became sick on 30.9.1942.

WALTER GEORGE NICHOLSON

Rank	Private
Regimental Number	WX7940
Company	'B' Company
Enlisted	13.8.1940
Date of Birth	14.12.1907
Place of Birth	Norwich, England
Father	Walter George Nicholson
Mother	Margaret Rebecca Nicholson
Religion	Church of England
Pre-War Occupation	Farmhand

Epitaph
Labuan Memorial
Panel 19
Age 36

HISTORY

Singapore	Selarang Camp Changi
'A' Force Burma	Green Force, No. 3 Battalion
POW Number	1886
Japan	*Rakuyo Maru* Party, Kumi No. 35
Cause of Death	Lost at Sea
Place of Death	South China Sea
Date of Death	13.9.1944

FRANK RICHARD NOBLE

Rank	Private
Regimental Number	WX9413
Classification	Rangetaker
Company	'B' Company
Enlisted	28.11.1940
Date of Birth	7.4.1920
Place of Birth	Perth, Western Australia
Father	Richard William Noble
Mother	Kathleen May Noble
Religion	Church of England
Pre-War Occupation	Clerk

Epitaph
Labuan Memorial
Panel 19
Age 25

HISTORY

Singapore	Selarang Camp and Barracks Changi
POW Number	1/8831
Force	'E' Force Borneo
POW Number	1843
Cause of Death	Malaria
Place of Death	Sandakan
Date of Death	26.5.1945

EDWIN LESLIE NOLAN

Rank	Private
Regimental Number	WX7659
Classification	Driver
Company	'C' Company
Enlisted	10.8.1940
Date of Birth	21.2.1910
Place of Birth	Durham, England
Father	Not Known
Mother	Grace Isabel Nolan
Religion	Church of England
Pre-War Occupation	Farmhand

Epitaph
Labuan Memorial
Panel 19
Age 34

HISTORY

Singapore	Selarang Camp Changi
'A' Force Burma	Green Force, No. 3 Battalion
POW Number	2925
Camps Burma	Reptu 30km Hospital Camp ex-Aungganaung
Japan	*Rakuyo Maru* Party, Kumi No. 37
Cause of Death	Lost at Sea
Place of Death	South China Sea
Date of Death	12.9.1944

HARRIS HERBERT THOMAS NORTON

Rank	Private
Regimental Number	WX16293
Company	'E' Company, Special Reserve Battalion
Enlisted	1.9.1941
Date of Birth	15.4.1925
Place of Birth	Boulder, Western Australia
Father	Harris Charles Norton
Mother	Amy Norton
Religion	Church of England
Pre-War Occupation	Farmhand

Epitaph
Singapore Memorial
Column 136
Age 17

HISTORY

Cause of Death	Killed in Action
Place of Death	Bald Hill, Bukit Timah
Date of Death	11.2.1942
Additions	The exact date of birth for this soldier is not known, however it is believed that he enlisted underaged and may have been as young as 16 at the time of his death.

LAWRANCE ROY NYBO

Rank	Private
Regimental Number	WX14327
Company	Headquarters Company
Enlisted	18.6.1941
Date of Birth	6.2.1919
Place of Birth	Broken Hill, New South Wales
Father	Herman Nybo
Mother	Ivy Elizabeth Nybo
Religion	Church of England
Pre-War Occupation	Greengrocer

Kanchanaburi War Cemetery
Plot 1
Row L
Grave 46
Age 22

HISTORY

Singapore	Selarang Camp Changi
	Johore Bahru, Adam Park
	Selarang Barracks Changi
POW Number	4/6460
'D' Force Thailand	V Battalion
Cause of Death	Beri-Beri
Place of Death	Hindaine
Date of Death	4.9.1943
Buried	Grave No. 33, Hindaine.

DANIEL MARTIN O'LEARY

Rank	Lance Sergeant
Regimental Number	WX8174
Company	'A' Company
Enlisted	16.8.1940
Date of Birth	3.3.1910
Place of Birth	Kalgoorlie, Western Australia
Father	Jeremiah O'Leary
Mother	Honorah Ethel O'Leary
Religion	Roman Catholic
Pre-War Occupation	Railway Fireman

Thanbyuzayat War Cemetery
Plot A13
Row C
Grave 2
Age 33

HISTORY

Singapore	Selarang Camp and Barracks Changi
POW Number	3/6123
Force	'F' Force Thailand
Cause of Death	Malaria and Dysentery
Place of Death	Kami Sonkurai
Date of Death	14.11.1943
Buried	Grave No. 344, Kani Sonkurai
Additions	NCO's leg was amputated by Captain. J. L. Taylor, A.A.M.C.

LESLIE O'NEIL

Rank	Private
Regimental Number	WX5222
Classification	Driver
Company	'B' Company
Enlisted	26.7.1940
Date of Birth	15.12.1908
Place of Birth	Kalgoorlie, Western Australia
Father	David O'Neil
Mother	Annie Edith O'Neil
Religion	Church of England
Pre-War Occupation	Driver

Epitaph
Labuan Memorial
Panel 19
Age 36

HISTORY

Singapore	Selarang Camp Changi
	A. G. H. Roberts Barracks Changi
	Selarang Barracks Changi
POW Number	1/8885
Force	'E' Force Borneo
POW Number	1852
Cause of Death	Acute Gastroenteritis
Place of Death	Sandakan
Date of Death	0630 hours on 16.12.1944
Additions	Soldier contracted disease on 12.12.1944. Death Certificate was signed by Lieutenant Yamamato Katsuki.

HAROLD BERTRAM OCKERBY

Rank	Private
Regimental Number	WX7336
Classification	Driver
Company	Battalion Headquarters
Enlisted	6.8.1940
Date of Birth	24.4.1899
Place of Birth	Sulphur Creek, Tasmania
Father	Alfred Lockton Ockerby
Mother	Amy Ockerby
Religion	Church of England
Pre-War Occupation	Truck Driver

Kranji War Cemetery
Special Memorial 'C'
Plot 32
Row D
Grave 13
Age 42

HISTORY

Cause of Death	Executed by a Japanese firing squad
Place of Death	Singapore
Date of Death	19.2.1942
Additions	This soldier was Lt-Col. Anketell's driver and like the Colonel was a veteran of WWI having served with the 51st Battalion in France.

CHARLES PERCIVAL ODGERS

Rank	Lieutenant
Regimental Number	WX9406
Attached 2/4th	Reinforcement Officer (Taken on Strength at Darwin)
Company	Battalion Headquarters, Special Reserve Battalion
Enlisted	21.11.1940
Date of Birth	5.1.1919
Place of Birth	Narrogin, Western Australia
Father	Percival William Clunes Odgers
Mother	Florence Mary Odgers
Religion	Church of England
Pre-War Occupation	Taxation Department

Epitaph
Singapore Memorial
Column 135
Age 22

HISTORY

Cause of Death	Killed in Action
Place of Death	South-West Bukit Timah
Date of Death	11.2.1942
Additions	This officer was last seen with a Lewis gun across his shoulder.

STIRLING JOHN OLIVER

Rank	Acting Corporal (Promoted on 27.12.1941)
Regimental Number	WX12628
Company	'C' Company
Enlisted	9.5.1941
Date of Birth	1.2.1904
Place of Birth	Boulder, Western Australia
Father	George Oliver
Mother	Alma Oliver
Religion	Methodist
Pre-War Occupation	Shop Assistant

Epitaph
Singapore Memorial
Column 135
Age 41

HISTORY

Cause of Death	Wounded in action at Ulu Pandan on 11.2.1942
Place of Death	Singapore
Date of Death	13.2.1942

ERIC FRANCIS OSBORNE

Rank	Private
Regimental Number	WX16279
Company	'A' Company
Enlisted	1.9.1941
Date of Birth	31.8.1922
Place of Birth	Perth, Western Australia
Father	Henry Joseph Osborne
Mother	Edith Beatrice Osborne
Religion	Roman Catholic
Pre-War Occupation	Farmhand

Kranji War Cemetery
Collective Grave
Plot 30
Row A
Grave 9-13
Age 19

HISTORY

Cause of Death	Killed in Action
Place of Death	Buona Vista
Date of Death	15.2.1942
Buried	In a common grave at map reference 784112
Additions	Soldier received a shrapnel wound to the skull. He had spent most of his life in an orphanage.

JOHN ROBERT OSBORNE

Rank	Private
Regimental Number	WX9287
Company	'D' Company
Enlisted	30.10.1940
Date of Birth	15.1.1915
Place of Birth	Bruce Rock, Western Australia
Father	John Osborne
Mother	Alice Osborne
Religion	Methodist
Pre-War Occupation	Farmhand

Thanbyuzayat War Cemetery
Plot A5
Row G
Grave 14
Age 28

HISTORY

Singapore	Selarang Camp Changi
	Johore Bahru, Adam Park
	Selarang Barracks Changi
POW Number	4/6480
Force	'F' Force Thailand
Cause of Death	Pneumonia
Place of Death	Kami Sonkurai
Date of Death	27.9.1943
Buried	Grave No. 170, Kami Sonkurai
Additions	Shell shocked at Buona Vista on 15.2.1942 but remained on duty. Soldier marched into Shimo Sonkurai with malaria and dysentery but recovered well. Captain George Gwynne spoke to soldier on his way up to Tanbaya in Burma. At the time soldier was at Kami Sonkurai (24.8.1943) and Captain Gwynne recalled that he appeared to be well.

SYDNEY ALBERT OSBORNE

Rank	Private
Regimental Number	WX7634
Classification	Driver
Company	'D' Company
Enlisted	10.8.1940
Date of Birth	23.5.1919
Place of Birth	London, England
Father	Not Known
Mother	Not Known
Religion	Church of England
Pre-War Occupation	Truck Driver

Labuan War Cemetery
Plot 20
Row C
Grave 13
Age 31

HISTORY

Singapore	Selarang Camp Changi
Force	'B' Force Borneo
POW Number	1105
Cause of Death	Malaria
Place of Death	Sandakan
Date of Death	21.6.1945
Buried	Sandakan
Additions	Wounded in Action at Ulu Pandan. Admitted to the 2/13th Australian General Hospital on 16.2.1942 with shrapnel wounds to the back, shoulder and left buttock. Discharged to unit on 7.3.1942. Kingsley Fairbridge Farm Schoolboy.

HENRY CHRISTOPHER OSWALD
a.k.a. Hugh Christopher Oswald

Regimental Number	WX16931
Company	'E' Company, Special Reserve Battalion
Enlisted	22.7.1941
Date of Birth	5.2.1921
Place of Birth	Perth, Western Australia
Father	Andrew Oswald
Mother	Not Known
Religion	Roman Catholic
Pre-War Occupation	Timber Worker

Kanchanaburi War Cemetery
Plot 1
Row F
Grave 29
Age 21

HISTORY

Singapore	Selarang Camp and Barracks Changi
POW Number	1/8897
'D' Force Thailand	V Battalion
POW Number	2281
Cause of Death	Dysentery
Place of Death	No. 3 Base Hospital, Kanchanaburi
Date of Death	7.11.1943
Buried	Kanchanaburi Cemetery
Additions	Soldier was a stowaway on the HMT *Aquitania* at Fremantle on 16.1.1942. Soldier was transferred to the 2/4th Machine Gun Battalion on 16.1.1942, (Routine Order 5/1791 of 28.1.1942) from the 2/16th Battalion reinforcements. Soldier was shell shocked and was admitted to the 2/9th Field Ambulance on 15.2.1942. Admitted to the 2/13th Australian General Hospital on 16.2.1942. Discharged to unit on 21.2.1942.

NOEL JAMES OUTTRIM

Rank	Corporal (Promoted on 11.2.1942)	
Regimental Number	WX10802	
Classification	Rangetaker	
Company	'B' Company	
Enlisted	15.1.1941	
Date of Birth	5.7.1920	
Place of Birth	Ravensthorpe, Western Australia	
Father	Edwin Kingston Outtrim	
Mother	Annie Florence Genevra Outtrim	
Religion	Church of England	
Pre-War Occupation	Letter Carrier	

Kanchanaburi War Cemetery
Plot 1
Row E
Grave 57
Age 24

HISTORY

Singapore	Selarang Camp Changi
	Thomson Road (Caldecot Hill Estate Camp)
	River Valley Road Camp
	Selarang Barracks Changi
POW Number	1/12120
'D' Force Thailand	Captain Fred Harris Party
Cause of Death	Cerebral Malaria
Place of Death	Kinsaiyok
Date of Death	22.11.1944
Buried	Grave H38, Kinsaiyok
Additions	Soldier was with Captain Fred Harris Party at Non Pladuk on 4.3.1944 and it is likely that he went back up the line on a maintenance party.

ERNEST JESSE OVENS

Rank	Private
Regimental Number	WX9129
Classification	Signaller
Company	30.10.1940
Date of Birth	20.1.1918
Place of Birth	York, Western Australia
Father	Meshacha Thomas Ovens
Mother	Lily Ovens
Religion	Church of England
Pre-War Occupation	Farmhand

Kranji War Cemetery
Plot 1
Row A
Grave 11
Age 24

HISTORY

Cause of Death	Killed in Action
Place of Death	Ulu Pandan
Date of Death	12.2.1942
Buried	Where killed at map reference 763132 by Major A. Cough Party on 21.12.1942.

RONALD ARTHUR PAGE

Rank	Private
Regimental Number	WX4934
Company	'C' Company
Enlisted	23.7.1940
Date of Birth	28.12.1917
Place of Birth	Athelstone, South Australia
Father	Albert Lloyd Page
Mother	Bessie Page
Religion	Church of England
Pre-War Occupation	Labourer

Epitaph
Labuan Memorial
Panel 18
Age 26

HISTORY

Singapore	Selarang Camp Changi
Force	'B' Force Borneo
POW Number	1127
Cause of Death	Acute Enteritis
Place of Death	Ranau
Date of Death	17.2.1945
Additions	Soldier contracted disease on 3.2.1945 and died at 1230 hours on 17.2.1945 Death Certificate completed by Japanese Probationary Officer Ferai.

WILLIAM JAMES PATERSON

Rank	Corporal (Promoted on 11.2.1942)
Regimental Number	WX9073
Company	'D' Company
Enlisted	25.10.1940
Date of Birth	1.3.1916
Place of Birth	Melbourne, Victoria
Father	William James Paterson
Mother	Jessie Paterson
Religion	Church of England
Pre-War Occupation	Farmhand and Timber Worker

Thanbyuzayat War Cemetery
Plot A7
Row C
Grave 1
Age 27

HISTORY

Singapore	Selarang Camp Changi
	Woodlands Camp Kranji (Clothing Store)
	Selarang Barracks Changi (C.Q.M.S.)
POW Number	1/8931
Force	'F' Force Thailand
Cause of Death	Cerebral Malaria and Colitis
Place of Death	Shimo Sonkurai
Date of Death	25.7.1943
Buried	Row 1, Grave No. 4, Sonkurai
Additions	Wounded in action North Lim Chu Kang Road at 'D' Company No. 13 Platoon position at 1130 hours on 8.2.1942. Admitted to the 2/13th Australian General Hospital with shrapnel wounds to the left and right forearms and face. Soldier also suffered bone damage to the right elbow. Admitted to the 2/9th Field Ambulance and transferred to the 2/10th Australian General Hospital on 6.3.1942. Transferred to No. 2 Convalescent Depot ex-Australian General Hospital on 12.8.1942. Discharged to unit on 27.9.1942. It is reported that soldier collapsed into a coma and died suddenly but peacefully. Body was cremated at Shimo Sonkurai and casket returned to Sonkurai for burial.

HARRY WALTER PEARCE

Rank	Private
Regimental Number	WX8856
Company	'C' Company
Enlisted	23.10.1940
Date of Birth	25.1.1914
Place of Birth	Fremantle, Western Australia
Father	Harry Arnell Pearce
Mother	Ellen Ada Pearce
Religion	Methodist
Pre-War Occupation	Truck Driver

Epitaph
Labuan Memorial
Panel 19
Age 30

HISTORY

Java	'Blackforce'
'A' Force Burma	Java Party No. 4, Williams Force
POW Number	4663
Camps Thailand	131km-133km, Kanchanaburi Camps
Japan	*Rakuyo Maru* Party, Kumi No. 38
Cause of Death	Lost at Sea
Place of Death	South China Sea
Date of Death	12.9.1944

JOHN EYRES PEARSON

Rank	Sergeant
Regimental Number	WX8118
Company	'B' Company
Enlisted	16.8.1940
Date of Birth	13.9.1900
Place of Birth	Kalgoorlie, Western Australia
Father	John Pearson
Mother	Mary Isabella Pearson
Religion	Church of England
Pre-War Occupation	Clerk

Kanchanaburi War Cemetery
Plot 10
Row B
Grave 15
Age 43

HISTORY

Singapore	Selarang Camp Changi
	Johore Bahru, Adam Park
	Sime Road Camp
	Selarang Barracks Changi
POW Number	4/4555
'D' Force Thailand	S Battalion
POW Number	8720
Cause of Death	Beri-Beri and Enteritis
Place of Death	Chungkai
Date of Death	0830 hours on 13.2.1944
Buried	Grave No. 1195, Chungkai
Additions	This NCO was highly respected and held the temporary rank of Lieutenant as a Prisoner of War. He had acted as the Commanding Officer of No. 7 Platoon when Lieutenant P. V. Dean was evacuated to hospital. He had held the rank of Lieutenant in the militia in which he served from 1924-1929.

LEONARD OSWALD PEAT

Rank	Private
Regimental Number	WX7458
Classification	Batman/Runner
Company	Company Headquarters
Enlisted	6.8.1940
Date of Birth	8.7.1916
Place of Birth	Fremantle, Western Australia
Father	Bertie Peat
Mother	Lucy Florence Peat
Religion	Protestant
Pre-War Occupation	Stationhand

Kranji War Cemetery
Plot 1
Row A
Grave 4
Age 25

HISTORY

Cause of Death	Killed in Action
Place of Death	Ulu Pandan, Reformatory Road
Date of Death	12.2.1942
Buried	Where killed at map reference 763132 by Major A. Cough Party on 21.12.1942.

JOHN EDGAR PEERS

Rank	Private
Regimental Number	WX9197
Company	'C' Company
Enlisted	30.10.1940
Date of Birth	6.6.1903
Place of Birth	Western Australia
Father	Harley Edwin Daniel Peers
Mother	Annie Genevieve Peers
Religion	Church of England
Pre-War Occupation	Road Worker

Kranji War Cemetery
Plot 2
Row A
Grave 20
Age 38

HISTORY

Cause of Death	Died of Wounds
Place of Death	A. G. H. Roberts Barracks Changi
Date of Death	6..3.1942
Buried	Grave No. 2, A.I.F. Cemetery, Changi
Additions	Soldier was admitted to the 2/10th Australian General Hospital with a shrapnel wound to the left groin and a fractured left pelvis. He died of wounds at 0500 hours on 6.3.1942. The funeral service was conducted by Chaplain F. X. Corry from the 2/4th Machine Gun Battalion.

JOHN STANLEY PETERS

Rank	Private
Regimental Number	WX17414
Company	'E' Company, Special Reserve Battalion
Enlisted	27.10.1941
Date of Birth	6.9.1921
Place of Birth	Perth, Western Australia
Father	John Charles Peters
Mother	Blanche Ethel Peters
Religion	Methodist
Pre-War Occupation	Orchardist

HISTORY

Cause of Death	Killed in Action
Place of Death	South-West Bukit Timah
Date of Death	11.2.1942

Epitaph
Singapore Memorial
Column 136
Age 20

CECIL ALLEN PHILLIPS

Rank	Lance Sergeant
Regimental Number	WX10389
Company	Headquarters Company
Enlisted	18.12.1940
Date of Birth	5.9.1918
Place of Birth	Northam, Western Australia
Father	Cecil William Phillips
Mother	Rosalind Martha Phillips
Religion	Church of England
Pre-War Occupation	Labourer

HISTORY

Cause of Death	Killed in Action
Place of Death	Ulu Pandan, Reformatory Road
Date of Death	12.2.1942
Buried	Where killed at map reference 763132 by Major A. Cough Party on 21.12.1942.

Kranji War Cemetery
Plot 1
Row A
Grave 3
Age 23

WILLIAM HAWKSLEY PHILP

Rank	Private
Regimental Number	WX7902
Classification	Driver
Company	Headquarters Company
Enlisted	13.8.1940
Date of Birth	17.12.1907
Place of Birth	Mt Barker, Western Australia
Father	William John Philp
Mother	Maud Ethel Philp
Religion	Church of England
Pre-War Occupation	Bus Driver

Kanchanaburi War Cemetery
Collective Grave
Plot 10
Row A
Grave 1-4
Age 35

HISTORY

Singapore	Selarang Camp and Barracks Changi
POW Number	1/8982
⟨D⟩ Force Thailand	V Battalion
POW Number	2283
Cause of Death	Malaria
Place of Death	Kuii
Date of Death	18.9.1943
Buried	Grave No. 169, Kuii
Additions	Wounded in action and admitted to Australian General Hospital on 12.2.1942 with a bayonet wound to the right thigh. Discharged to unit 20.2.1942.

NORMAN WILLIS PLATTS

Rank	Sergeant (Promoted on 7.2.1942)
Regimental Number	WX16883
Company	⟨E⟩ Company, Special Reserve Battalion
Enlisted	6.10.1941
Date of Birth	14.3.1910
Place of Birth	Bunbury, Western Australia
Father	Herbert Sceath Platts
Mother	Ethel Jane Platts
Religion	Methodist
Pre-War Occupation	Water Engineer

Epitaph
Singapore Memorial
Column 135
Age 31

HISTORY

Cause of Death	Killed in Action
Place of Death	South-West Bukit Timah
Date of Death	11.2.1942
Additions	NCO pulled Lieutenant J. Till back after he was wounded at South-West Bukit Timah.

WILLIAM NEIL POOLE

Rank	Private
Regimental Number	WX13429
Company	'E' Company, Special Reserve Battalion
Enlisted	23.5.1941
Date of Birth	22.5.1921
Place of Birth	Carlisle, Western Australia
Father	John Arthur Poole
Mother	Fanny Poole
Religion	Church of England
Pre-War Occupation	Coach Painter

Epitaph
Singapore Memorial
Column 136
Age 20

HISTORY

Cause of Death	Killed in Action
Place of Death	South-West Bukit Timah
Date of Death	11.2.1942

ALLEN ETHELBERT POWELL

Rank	Private
Regimental Number	WX8840
Classification	Driver
Company	'B' Company
Enlisted	23.10.1940
Date of Birth	26.10.1909
Place of Birth	Northam, Western Australia
Father	Albert Charles Powell
Mother	Margaret Powell
Religion	Church of England
Pre-War Occupation	Prospector and Road Grader Operator

Kanchanaburi War Cemetery
Plot 1
Row L
Grave 66
Age 33

HISTORY

Singapore	Selarang Camp and Barracks Changi
POW Number	3/9223
'D' Force Thailand	V Battalion
POW Number	2284
Camps Thailand	Tarsau, Hindaine
Cause of Death	Dysentery
Place of Death	Brankassi
Date of Death	6.9.1943
Buried	Grave No. 58, Brankassi.

LESLIE ANDREW POYSER

Rank	Private
Regimental Number	WX7320
Company	'D' Company
Enlisted	6.8.1940
Date of Birth	28.6.1906
Place of Birth	Mansfield Woodhouse, Nottinghamshire, England
Father	Harry Poyser
Mother	Sarah Elizabeth Poyser
Religion	Methodist
Pre-War Occupation	Labourer

Kanchanaburi War Cemetery
Plot 10
Row E
Grave 14
Age 37

HISTORY

Singapore	Selarang Camp and Barracks Changi
POW Number	4/6522
'D' Force Thailand	S Battalion
POW Number	8831
Cause of Death	Amoebic Dysentery and Avitaminosis
Place of Death	Chungkai
Date of Death	21.10.1943
Buried	Grave No. 748, Chungkai.

ROBERT WILLIAM PRATT

Rank	Private
Regimental Number	WX8705
Company	'D' Company
Enlisted	23.10.1940
Date of Birth	10.8.1918
Place of Birth	Gloucester, England
Father	Robert William Pratt
Mother	Edith Pratt
Religion	Church of England
Pre-War Occupation	Bogger

Epitaph
Singapore Memorial
Column 136
Age 23

HISTORY

Cause of Death	Killed in artillery barrage
Place of Death	North Lim Chu Kang Road
Date of Death	8.2.1942
Additions	Killed by the same bomb that wounded Joe Pearce and Bill Paterson at the No. 13 Platoon position on the west coast of Singapore.

ERIC LINCOLN PREEDY

Rank	Private
Regimental Number	WX7416
Classification	Carpenter
Company	Headquarters Company
Enlisted	6.8.1940
Date of Birth	5.7.1913
Place of Birth	Subiaco, Western Australia
Father	Charles Edward Preedy
Mother	Anna Augusta Preedy
Religion	Church of England
Pre-War Occupation	Truck Driver

Kanchanaburi War Cemetery
Plot 1
Row H
Grave 11
Age 30

HISTORY

Singapore	Selarang Camp Changi
	Serangoon Road Camp
	Selarang Barracks Changi
POW Number	4/6523
'D' Force Thailand	V Battalion
POW Number	2285
Cause of Death	Acute Enteritis
Place of Death	Brankassi
Date of Death	7.8.1943
Buried	Grave No. 34, Brankassi.

LEONARD PURCHON

Rank	Private
Regimental Number	WX8826
Classification	Batman/Runner
Company	'E' Company, Special Reserve Battalion
Enlisted	23.10.1940
Date of Birth	27.7.1903
Place of Birth	Castleford, Yorkshire, England
Father	George Purchon
Mother	Catherine Purchon
Religion	Church of England
Pre-War Occupation	Labourer

Epitaph
Singapore Memorial
Column 136
Age 38

HISTORY

Cause of Death	Killed in Action
Place of Death	South-West Bukit Timah
Date of Death	11.2.1942

HAROLD RADBURN

Rank	Private
Regimental Number	WX15829
Company	'A' Company
Enlisted	15.8.1941
Date of Birth	30.10.1919
Place of Birth	Worcestershire, England
Father	Charles Radburn
Mother	Mary Josephine Radburn
Religion	Church of England
Pre-War Occupation	Tobacco Burner

Epitaph
Singapore Memorial
Column 136
Age 22

HISTORY

Cause of Death	Killed in Action
Place of Death	Hill 200, Ulu Pandan
Date of Death	12.2.1942

HENRY WALDOCK RALPH

Rank	Private
Regimental Number	WX20068
Company	'E' Company, Special Reserve Company
Enlisted	22.9.1941
Date of Birth	23.2.1919
Place of Birth	Toodyay, Western Australia
Father	Henry Waldock Ralph
Mother	Rose Ellen Ralph
Religion	Church of England
Pre-War Occupation	Farmhand

Epitaph
Singapore Memorial
Column 136
Age 22

HISTORY

Cause of Death	Killed in Action
Place of Death	South-West Bukit Timah
Date of Death	11.2.1942

GEORGE ROBERT RAMAGE

Rank	Sergeant
Regimental Number	WX9059
Classification	Signaller
Company	Headquarters Company
Enlisted	25.10.1940
Date of Birth	24.6.1905
Place of Birth	Cape Leeuwin, Western Australia
Father	George Ramage
Mother	Ellen Ramage
Religion	Church of England
Pre-War Occupation	Guard, W.A.G.R.

Thanbyuzayat War Cemetery
Plot A3
Row B
Grave 15
Age 38

HISTORY

Java	'Blackforce'
'A' Force Burma	Java Party No. 4, Williams Force
POW Number	3931
Camps Burma	Reptu 30km Camp
Cause of Death	Dysentery
Place of Death	Payathonzu 108km Camp
Date of Death	23.9.1943
Buried	Grave No. 17, Payathonzu
Additions	Funeral service conducted by Major A.F. Hobbs, 2/4th C.C.S.

ERNEST EDWARD RANDALL

Rank	Private
Regimental Number	WX16356
Company	'A' Company
Enlisted	3.9.1941
Date of Birth	2.5.1908
Place of Birth	Northampton, Western Australia
Father	Edward Harrison Randall
Mother	Manda Randall
Religion	Roman Catholic
Pre-War Occupation	Stationhand

Epitaph
Labuan Memorial
Panel 19
Age 36

HISTORY

Singapore	Selarang Camp Changi
'A' Force Burma	Green Force, No. 3 Battalion
POW Number	1505
Camps Burma	Thanbyuzayat (detached for hospital duty)
	Kendau 4.8km (medical orderly)
	Reptu 30km (medical orderly)
	Aungganaung 105km ex-Reptu 30km on 22.8.1943
Camps Thailand	Tamarkan
Japan	*Rakuyo Maru* Party, Kumi No. 35
Cause of Death	Lost at Sea
Place of Death	South China Sea
Date of Death	12.9.1944

GEOFREY WYATT ALFRED RAPHAEL

Rank	Lieutenant
Regimental Number	WX3447
Company	Battalion Headquarters
Enlisted	21.11.1940
Date of Birth	29.7.1916
Place of Birth	West Perth, Western Australia
Father	Alfred Raphael
Mother	Maria Raphael
Religion	Jewish
Pre-War Occupation	Trainee Executive

HISTORY

Cause of Death	Executed by the Imperial Japanese Army
Place of Death	Singapore
Date of Death	19.2.1942

Epitaph
Singapore Memorial
Column 135
Age 25

LESLIE ROBERT RAYNER

Rank	Private WX9357
Company	'A' Company
Enlisted	30.10.1940
Date of Birth	26.2.1918
Place of Birth	Perth, Western Australia
Father	Henry Richard Rayner
Mother	Emily Rayner
Religion	Church of England
Pre-War Occupation	Farmhand

Kranji War Cemetery
Plot 2
Row E
Grave 6
Age 24

HISTORY

Cause of Death	Died of Wounds
Place of Death	2/13th Australian General Hospital
Date of Death	27.2.1942
Buried	Military Cemetery Changi on the main road approximately 70 yards north of the 13 mile peg and approximately 40 yards on the south side of the road, map reference 014188. Funeral service conducted by Senior Chaplain M. Jones A.I.F. Details were noted and left in a bottle at the head of the grave by Captain A.W. Thomas. Soldier had been wounded in action on 15.2.1942 at Buona Vista. Admitted to the 2/13th Australian General Hospital with shrapnel wounds to both legs, one leg being amputated.

RICHARD CHARLES REED

Rank	Private
Regimental Number	WX8503
Classification	Batman/Runner
Company	'A' Company
Enlisted	18.10.1940
Date of Birth	11.5.1918
Place of Birth	Bassendean, Western Australia
Father	Stephen Francis Reed
Mother	Jane Isabella Reed
Religion	Roman Catholic
Pre-War Occupation	Gardener

Kranji War Cemetery
Special Memorial 'C'
Plot 23
Row D
Grave 11
Age 23

HISTORY

Cause of Death	Died of Wounds
Place of Death	St Andrews Cathedral, Singapore
Date of Death	16.2.1942
Buried	South-East corner of St Andrew's Cathedral
Additions	Soldier was wounded in action on 15.2.1942 at Chinese Cemetery Hill. He was admitted to the 2/9th Field Ambulance with shrapnel wounds. Both legs were amputated and soldier died at 0500 hours on 16.2.1942. Funeral service was conducted by Reverend G. Chambers from the 35th Light Anti Aircraft Regiment, Royal Artillery.

SYDNEY REID

Rank	Private
Regimental Number	WX9295
Classification	Batman/Runner
Company	'D' Company
Enlisted	30.10.1940
Date of Birth	18.12.1908
Place of Birth	Cumberland, England
Father	Joseph Reid
Mother	Christine Reid
Religion	Church of England
Pre-War Occupation	Farmhand

Kranji War Cemetery
Joint Grave
Plot 17
Row D
Grave 1-2
Age 33

HISTORY

Cause of Death	Wounded and missing in action
Place of Death	Tanjong Murai, west coast of Singapore
Date of Death	9.2.1942

ROBERT GEORGE STANTON RENNIE

Rank	Private
Regimental Number	WX7493
Classification	Carpenter
Company	Headquarters Company
Enlisted	6.8.1940
Date of Birth	11.11.1905
Place of Birth	India
Father	Robert Henry Rennie
Mother	Winifred Alice Rennie
Religion	Church of England
Pre-War Occupation	Labourer

Kanchanaburi War Cemetery
Plot 1
Row E
Grave 58
Age 37

HISTORY

Java	'Blackforce'
'D' Force Thailand	Java Party No. 6, P Battalion
POW Number	12210
Cause of Death	Post Leg Amputation
Place of Death	Tamarkan
Date of Death	4.10.1943
Buried	Grave E31, Tamarkan
Additions	Soldier had his right leg amputated at the thigh due to a tropical ulcer.

JOHN THOMAS RIDLEY

Rank	Private
Regimental Number	WX20074
Company	'E' Company, Special Reserve Battalion
Enlisted	24.9.1941
Date of Birth	15.9.1903
Place of Birth	Durham, England
Father	John Ridley
Mother	Martha Ridley
Religion	Church of England
Pre-War Occupation	Farmhand

Kanchanaburi War Cemetery
Plot 1
Row F
Grave 28
Age 40

HISTORY

Singapore	Selarang Camp and Barracks Changi
POW Number	4/6547
'D' Force Thailand	V Battalion
POW Number	2286
Cause of Death	Tropical Ulcers and Malaria
Place of Death	Kanachanaburi Base Hospital No. 3
Date of Death	8.11.1943

RONALD WESTON ROBERTS

Rank	Private
Regimental Number	WX16618
Company	'E' Company, Special Reserve Battalion
Enlisted	22.9.1941
Date of Birth	1.11.1921
Place of Birth	Wonnerup, Western Australia
Father	Edmund Henry Roberts
Mother	Alice Ivy Roberts
Religion	Congregational
Pre-War Occupation	Farmhand and Timber Worker

Epitaph
Singapore Memorial
Column 136
Age 20

HISTORY

Cause of Death	Killed in Action
Place of Death	South-West Bukit Timah
Date of Death	11.2.1942

WILLIAM CHARLES ROBERTS

Rank	Private
Regimental Number	WX9358
Company	'C' Company
Enlisted	30.10.1940
Date of Birth	20.10.1907
Place of Birth	Ravensthorpe, Western Australia
Father	Hugh Roberts
Mother	Mary Lee Roberts
Religion	Church of England
Pre-War Occupation	Farmer

Thanbyuzayat War Cemetery
Plot A5
Row C
Grave 5
Age 35

HISTORY

Singapore	Selarang Camp Changi
'A' Force Burma	Green Force, No. 3 Battalion
POW Number	1477
Cause of Death	Cardiac Failure following Bacillary Dysentery
Place of Death	Khonkan 55km Camp Burma
Date of Death	2315 hours on 16.8.1943
Buried	Grave No. 60, Khonkan
Additions	Soldier had been evacuated from Aungganaung 105km Camp on 1.6.1943.

JAMES WILLIAM ROBINSON

Rank	Private
Regimental Number	WX15941
Company	Battalion Headquarters
Enlisted	20.8.1941
Date of Birth	4.4.1915
Place of Birth	Grangetown, Sunderland, England
Father	William Luddington Robinson
Mother	Elizabeth Robinson
Religion	Congregational
Pre-War Occupation	Miner and Truck Driver

Kanchanaburi War Cemetery
Plot 1
Row M
Grave 36
Age 28

HISTORY

Singapore	Selarang Camp and Barracks Changi
POW Number	4/6552
'D' Force Thailand	S Battalion
POW Number	8841
Cause of Death	Acute Enteritis
Place of Death	Chungkai
Date of Death	28.8.1943
Buried	Grave No. 317, Chungkai.

WILLIAM JOSEPH ROBINSON

Rank	Acting Sergeant (Promoted on 14.2.1942)
Regimental Number	WX5200
Company	'B' Company
Enlisted	26.7.1940
Date of Birth	22.4.1918
Place of Birth	Victoria Park, Western Australia
Father	Charles Stewart Robinson
Mother	Henrietta Robinson
Religion	Church of England
Pre-War Occupation	Labourer

Kanchanaburi War Cemetery
Collective Grave
Plot 1
Row Q
Grave 2-78
Age 25

HISTORY

Java	'Blackforce', attached to 2/3rd M.G. Bn.
'D' Force Thailand	Java Party No. 6, O Battalion
POW Number	6910
Cause of Death	Dysentery
Place of Death	Hintok Road Camp
Date of Death	17.7.1943
Buried	Grave No. 30, Hintok Road Camp.

JOHN ROCHESTER

Rank	Private
Regimental Number	WX10808
Company	'E' Company, Special Reserve Battalion
Enlisted	15.1.1941
Date of Birth	1.8.1905
Place of Birth	England
Father	Edward Anderson Rochester
Mother	Jane Rochester
Religion	Church of England
Pre-War Occupation	Farmer

Epitaph
Singapore Memorial
Column 136
Age 36

HISTORY

Cause of Death	Killed in Action
Place of Death	South-West Bukit Timah
Date of Death	11.2.1942
Additions	This soldier was at Woodside Camp South Australia when he contracted meningitis and was returned to Western Australia on 25.11.1941. He was transferred to the 2/4th Machine Gun Battalion reinforcements on 9.1.1942. Soldier was originally a member of 'A' Company No. 6 Platoon.

ARTHUR WILLIAM RODDA

Rank	Private
Regimental Number	WX7509
Company	'D' Company
Enlisted	6.8.1940
Date of Birth	28.4.1900
Place of Birth	Midland, Western Australia
Father	Henry Rodda
Mother	Jane Rodda
Religion	Presbyterian
Pre-War Occupation	Railway Employee

Kanchanaburi War Cemetery
Plot 1
Row G
Grave 52
Age 44

HISTORY

Singapore	Selarang Camp Changi
	Selarang Barracks Changi (Forestry Party)
POW Number	4/6554
'D' Force Thailand	S Battalion
POW Number	8838
Camps Thailand	Tarsau, Tamuang, Chungkai
Cause of Death	Cerebral Malaria
Place of Death	Nacompaton
Date of Death	1800 hours on 20.2.1945
Buried	Row E, Grave No. 1, Nacompaton
Additions	Wounded in action on 13.2.1942. Soldier received a shrapnel wound to the leg but remained on duty. This soldier also had a history of repeated malaria attacks. On 8.4.1944 at Chungkai in Thailand Lieutenant 'Mick' Wedge signed an I.O.U. for 12 Pounds and 10 Shillings for a small jar of Vegemite to help Bill recover from beri-beri, a B group vitamin deficiency disease.

DONALD ROSS

Rank	Private
Regimental Number	WX9253
Classification	Driver
Company	'A' Company
Enlisted	30.10.1940
Date of Birth	8.3.1913
Place of Birth	Albany, Western Australia
Father	Alexander Ross
Mother	Lillian May Ross
Religion	Presbyterian
Pre-War Occupation	Quarry Worker and Driver

Epitaph
Labuan Memorial
Panel 19
Age 32

HISTORY

Singapore	Selarang Camp Changi
POW Number	4/6560
Force	'E' Force Borneo
POW Number	1885
Cause of Death	Malaria
Place of Death	Sandakan
Date of Death	23.5.1945

GEORGE ROBERT ROUSE

Rank	Private
Regimental Number	WX7656
Company	'D' Company
Enlisted	10.8.1940
Date of Birth	30.12.1914
Place of Birth	Pingelly, Western Australia
Father	George Henry Rouse
Mother	Harriet Lucy Rouse
Religion	Methodist
Pre-War Occupation	Labourer

Epitaph
Singapore Memorial
Column 136
Age 27

HISTORY

Cause of Death	Killed in Action
Place of Death	Tanjong Murai, west coast of Singapore
Date of Death	2300 hours on 8.2.1942
Additions	Soldier was captured by the Japanese and was shot whilst attempting to escape.

EDWARD JOHN ROWELL

Rank	Corporal
Regimental Number	WX10793
Company	'C' Company
Enlisted	15.1.1941
Date of Birth	9.8.1916
Place of Birth	Fremantle, Western Australia
Father	George Thomas Rowell
Mother	Gertrude Alma Rowell
Religion	Methodist
Pre-War Occupation	Hairdresser

Epitaph
Singapore Memorial
Column 135
Age 25

HISTORY

Cause of Death	Killed in Action
Place of Death	Hill 200, Ulu Pandan
Date of Death	12.2.1942
Buried	Where killed at map reference 758128 by Major A. Cough Party on 21.12.1942.

JOHN DOUGLAS ROYCE

Rank	Lieutenant
Regimental Number	WX9383
Company	Headquarters Company (replaced by Lt. K. Lee)
Enlisted	16.11.1940
Date of Birth	30.6.1919
Place of Birth	Katanning, Western Australia
Father	Sydney George Royce
Mother	Amy Royce
Religion	Church of England
Pre-War Occupation	Clerk, Wool Classer's Assistant

Kranji War Cemetery
Plot 1
Row A
Grave 12
Age 22

HISTORY

Cause of Death	Died of Wounds
Place of Death	Hill 200, Ulu Pandan
Date of Death	12.2.1942
Buried	

Where killed at map reference 763132 by Major A. Cough Party on 21.12.1942. This Officer was wounded in action at the crest of Hill 200 in during a bayonet charge. He crawled back to his men who wanted to evacuate him to the Regimental Aid Post, but he refused. His men cut his webbing off to make him more comfortable. His body was discovered by the 2/4th Party who went under the wire from Adam Park on 28/29 May 1942.

HERBERT MICHAEL RUBERY

Rank	Private
Regimental Number	WX7474
Company	'A' Company
Enlisted	6.8.1940
Date of Birth	7.3.1918
Place of Birth	Gosnells, Western Australia
Father	Michael John Rubery
Mother	Esther Mary Rubery
Religion	Roman Catholic
Pre-War Occupation	Labourer

Kranji War Cemetery
Plot 2
Row C
Grave 6
Age 24

HISTORY

Singapore	Selarang Camp and Barracks Changi
POW Number	1/12199
Cause of Death	Dysentery, Pneumonia and Toxemia
Place of Death	A. G. H. Roberts Barracks Changi
Date of Death	23.2.1943
Buried	Grave No. 79, A.I.F. Cemetery Changi
Additions	Funeral service was conducted by Chaplain C. G. Sexton from the 2/20th Battalion.

DOUGLAS NORMAN RUSSELL

Rank	Private
Regimental Number	WX10164
Company	'B' Company
Enlisted	18.12.1940
Date of Birth	18.1.1915
Place of Birth	Leederville, Western Australia
Father	Norman Charles Russell
Mother	Gladys Hamilton Russell
Religion	Church of England
Pre-War Occupation	Bank Officer

Thanbyuzayat War Cemetery
Plot A8
Row B
Grave 12
Age 28

HISTORY

Singapore	Selarang Canp Changi
'A' Force Burma	Green Force, No. 3 Battalion
POW Number	1472
Cause of Death	Cerebral Malaria
Place of Death	Aungganaung 105km Camp
Date of Death	21.1.1944
Buried	Grave No. 105, Aungganaung 105km Camp.

JOHN MAURICE RUTHERFORD

Rank	Sergeant (Promoted on 12.2.1942)
Regimental Number	WX10785
Classification	Signaller
Company	Headquarters Company
Enlisted	15.1.1941
Date of Birth	21.11.1920
Place of Birth	Maylands, Western Australia
Father	Harold Francis Walton Rutherford
Mother	Elsie Alice Mary Rutherford
Religion	Methodist
Pre-War Occupation	Salesman

Kanchanaburi War Cemetery
Plot 1
Row M
Grave 68
Age 22

HISTORY

Singapore	Selarang Camp and Barracks Changi
POW Number	1/9175
'D' Force Thailand	V Battalion
POW Number	2216
Cause of Death	Cardiac Beri-Beri
Place of Death	Chungkai
Date of Death	13.10.1943
Buried	Grave No. 676, Chungkai
Additions	NCO was promoted to Sergeant posthumously. This is due to the fact that Lieutenant Royce and Sergeant Hansen were both killed in action and Corporal Rutherford had taken over command of the Signals Platoon.

JOHN WILLIAM SANDERSON

Rank	Sergeant (Promoted on 15.2.1942)
Regimental Number	WX8777
Company	'B' Company
Enlisted	23.10.1940
Date of Birth	20.8.1907
Place of Birth	Morgan's, Western Australia
Father	John Matthew Sanderson
Mother	Anna Sanderson
Religion	Church of England
Pre-War Occupation	Commercial Traveller

Kanchanaburi War Cemetery
Plot 1
Row J
Grave 43
Age 35

HISTORY

Singapore	Selarang Camp and Barracks Changi
'D' Force Thailand	S Battalion
POW Number	8721
Camps Thailand	Kanu II, Kanu I (evacuated sick to Tarsau)
Cause of Death	Beri-Beri and Dysentery
Place of Death	Tarsau
Date of Death	18.7.1943
Buried	Grave No.17, Tarsau
Additions	This NCO was an original member of No. 7 Platoon. When Sergeant N. J. Harris was evacuated to hospital, Sergeant K. D. Tucker was promoted to Senior Sergeant and Corporal J. W. Sanderson was promoted to Sergeant and transferred to No. 9 Platoon. This NCO was a highly thought of 'B' Company member.

RICHARD HENRY SANDILANDS

Rank	Sergeant
Regimental Number	WX8809
Company	'B' Company
Enlisted	23.10.1940
Date of Birth	24.6.1913
Place of Birth	Perth, Western Australia
Father	Not Known
Mother	Not Known
Religion	Church of England
Pre-War Occupation	Miner

HISTORY

Cause of Death	Killed in Action
Place of Death	West Mandai Road
Date of Death	11.2.1942
Additions	This NCO was wounded during the withdrawal action on West Mandai Road. He was paralysed from the waist down

CLARENCE SAMUEL SAUNDERS

Rank	Lance Corporal
Regimental Number	WX7211
Classification	Technical Storemen
Company	'D' Company Headquarters
Enlisted	1.8.1940
Date of Birth	18.7.1900
Place of Birth	Perth, Western Australia
Father	Joseph Charles Saunders
Mother	Louisa Saunders
Religion	Church of England
Pre-War Occupation	Miner

Kanchanaburi War Cemetery
Plot 1
Row M
Grave 32
Age 43

HISTORY

Singapore	Selarang Camp Changi
	Johore Bahru, Adam Park
	Selarang Barracks Changi
POW Number	4/6579
'D' Force Thailand	S Battalion
POW Number	8743
Cause of Death	Post Leg Amputation, Haemorrhage
Place of Death	Chungkai
Date of Death	31.8.1943
Buried	Grave No. 334, Chungkai.

CLARENCE JOHN SAWYER

Rank	Private
Regimental Number	WX7939
Company	Battalion Headquarters
Enlisted	13.8.1940
Date of Birth	25.8.1907
Place of Birth	Mount Helena, Western Australia
Father	Joseph Archibald Sawyer
Mother	Mary Sawyer
Religion	Church of England
Pre-War Occupation	Farmhand

Djakarta War Cemetery
Plot 3
Row H
Grave 14
Age 34

HISTORY

Java	'Blackforce'
Cause of Death	Dysentery
Place of Death	No. 1 Allied General Hospital, Bandoeng
Date of Death	1720 hours on 1.4.1942
Buried	Grave No. 62, Dago Weg, Bandoeng
Additions	Funeral service was conducted by Chaplain F. J. Camroux on 2.4.1942.

HARRY WRIGHT SCADDAN

Rank	Private
Regimental Number	WX7617
Company	Headquarters Company
Enlisted	10.8.1940
Date of Birth	20.8.1914
Place of Birth	Ashington, England
Father	Harry Wright Scaddan
Mother	Winnie Scaddan
Religion	Roman Catholic
Pre-War Occupation	Butcher and Farmhand

Kanchanaburi War Cemetery
Plot 1
Row D
Grave 66
Age 29

HISTORY

Singapore	Selarang Camp Changi
'A' Force Burma	Green Force, No. 3 Battalion
POW Number	2906
Camps Burma	Khonkan 55km Camp (4.7.1943-19.10.1943)
Cause of Death	Cerebral Malaria
Place of Death	Tamarkan Hospital
Date of Death	2105 hours on 22.4.1944
Buried	Grave No. AX33, Tamarkan
Addition	Funeral service conducted by Padre (R.C.) Matheson. Soldier was a Kingsley Fairbridge Farm Schoolboy.

JAMES SCALES

Rank	Private
Regimental Number	WX8843
Company	'A' Company
Enlisted	23.10.1940
Date of Birth	18.2.1908
Place of Birth	County Clare, Ireland
Father	William Scales
Mother	Jane Scales
Religion	Roman Catholic
Pre-War Occupation	Labourer

Kanchanaburi War Cemetery
Plot 1
Row M
Grave 14
Age 35

HISTORY

Java	'Blackforce', attached to 2/3rd M.G. Bn.
'D' Force Thailand	Java Party No. 6, O Battalion
POW Number	6920
Cause of Death	Polyavitaminosis and Dysentery
Place of Death	Chungkai
Date of Death	11.9.1943
Buried	Grave No. 426, Chungkai
Additions	Soldier had been evacuated to Tarsau on 20.8.1943 suffering from malaria.

STANLEY GORDON SCOTT

Rank	Private
Regimental Number	WX17899
Company	'E' Company, Special Reserve Battalion
Enlisted	3.12.1941
Date of Birth	13.1.1921
Place of Birth	Westonia, Western Australia
Father	Edward Alexander Scott
Mother	Amy Scott
Religion	Church of England
Pre-War Occupation	Butcher

Epitaph
Singapore Memorial
Column 136
Age 21

HISTORY

Cause of Death	Killed in Action
Place of Death	South-West Bukit Timah
Date of Death	11.2.1942

JOSEPH SEVIER

Rank	Private
Regimental Number	WX8544
Classification	Driver
Company	Company Headquarters
Enlisted	18.10.1940
Date of Birth	5.8.1906
Place of Birth	Bristol, England
Father	Joseph Sevier
Mother	Florence Rose Sevier
Religion	Church of England
Pre-War Occupation	Truck and Tractor Driver

Epitaph
Labuan Memorial
Panel 19
Age 38

HISTORY

Selarang	Selarang Camp and Barracks Changi
POW Number	4/6597
Force	'E' Force Borneo
POW Number	1895
Cause of Death	Malaria
Place of Death	Sandakan-Ranau track
Date of Death	7.6.1945

ELLIS SHACKLETON

Rank	Private
Regimental Number	WX7330
Company	'D' Company
Enlisted	6.8.1940
Date of Birth	18.6.1914
Place of Birth	Perth, Western Australia
Father	Ellis Shackleton
Mother	Alice Maud Shackleton
Religion	Methodist
Pre-War Occupation	Wood Machinist

Epitaph
Singapore Memorial
Column 136
Age 27

HISTORY

Cause of Death	Missing in Action
Place of Death	West coast of Singapore
Date of Death	11.2.1942
Additions	Believed to have been killed or badly wounded.

JAMES HAROLD SHACKLETON

Rank	Private
Regimental Number	WX9252
Classification	Driver
Company	'A' Company
Enlisted	30.10.1940
Date of Birth	12.5.1904
Place of Birth	Kings Lynn, Norfolk, England
Father	Edward Shackleton
Mother	Alma Shackleton
Religion	Christian Scientist
Pre-War Occupation	Truck Driver

Kranji War Cemetery
Plot 3
Row B
Grave 7
Age 38

HISTORY

Singapore	Selarang Camp Changi
	Thomson Road (Caldecot Hill Estate Camp)
	River Valley Road Camp
Cause of Death	Acute Bacillary Dysentery
Place of Death	Regimental Aid Post, Bukit Timah
Date of Death	1330 hours on 6.9.1942
Buried	A.I.F. Cemetery Changi, Grave No. 62
Additions	Funeral service was conducted by Chaplain K. F. Saunders NX70157 who was attached to the 27th Australian Brigade. A Doctor Holmes planted a tree in this soldier's memory.

GEORGE TOM SHELTON

Rank	Private
Regimental Number	WX7623
Company	'D' Company
Enlisted	10.8.1940
Date of Birth	23.10.1918
Place of Birth	England
Father	George Tom Emmanuel Shelton
Mother	Avice Hilda Shelton
Religion	Roman Catholic
Pre-War Occupation	Labourer

Kanchanaburi War Cemetery
Plot 1
Row L
Grave 71
Age 24

HISTORY

Singapore	Selarang Camp Changi
	Johore Bahru, Adam Park
	Selarang Barracks Changi
POW Number	4/6606
'H' Force Thailand	'H' Force Group No. 3
Cause of Death	Post Pneumonia and Beri-Beri
Place of Death	Kanu II Malayan Hamlet
Date of Death	7.9.1943
Buried	Grave No. 80, Malayan Hamlet
Additions	Wounded in action at 1800 hours on 15.2.1942 and admitted to the 2/10th Australian General Hospital with a shrapnel wound to the left temple. Discharged to unit on 23.2.1942.

CHARLES BADEN SHELVOCK

Rank	Private
Regimental Number	WX5018
Classification	Cook
Company	'A' Company Headquarters
Enlisted	23.7.1940
Date of Birth	24.8.1906
Place of Birth	Shrewsbury, England
Father	Charles Shelvock
Mother	Sarah Elizabeth Shelvock
Religion	Roman Catholic
Pre-War Occupation	Mechanic

Epitaph
Labuan Memorial
Panel 19
Age 38

HISTORY

Singapore	Selarang Camp and Barracks Changi
POW Number	3/9519
Force	'E' Force Borneo
POW Number	1900
Cause of Death	Beri-Beri
Place of Death	Sandakan
Date of Death	17.6.1945

ARTHUR FRANCIS SHIRLEY

Rank	Private
Regimental Number	WX8535
Company	'D' Company
Enlisted	18.10.1940
Date of Birth	15.6.1908
Place of Birth	Albany, Western Australia
Father	Francis Shirley
Mother	Annie Shirley
Religion	Church of England
Pre-War Occupation	Clerk

Epitaph
Labuan Memorial
Panel 19
Age 36

HISTORY

Singapore	Selarang Camp Changi
Force	'B' Force Borneo
POW Number	1298
Cause of Death	Malaria
Place of Death	Sandakan
Date of Death	10.5.1942
Additions	Wounded in action at 1700 hours on 8.2.1942. Admitted to the 2/13th Australian General Hospital on 9.2.1942 with shrapnel wounds to the left forearm. Transferred to the 2/9th Field Ambulance on 22.2.1942 and discharged to unit on 8.3.1942.

FRANCIS KENNETH HERBERT SKINNER

Rank	Sergeant (Promoted on 11.2.1942)
Regimental Number	WX9282
Company	'D' Company
Enlisted	30.10.1940
Date of Birth	10.11.1903
Place of Birth	Melbourne, Victoria
Father	Francis Edward Skinner
Mother	Alice Marie Skinner
Religion	Church of England
Pre-War Occupation	Accountant

Epitaph
Labuan Memorial
Panel 18
Age 40

HISTORY

Singapore	Selarang Camp Changi
'A' Force Burma	Green Force, No. 3 Battalion
POW Number	2677
Japan	*Rakuyo Maru* Party, Kumi No. 36
Cause of Death	Lost at Sea
Place of Death	South China Sea
Date of Death	12.9.1944

ALBERT SLATER

Rank	Private
Regimental Number	WX17344
Company	'E' Company, Special Reserve Battalion
Enlisted	22.10.1941
Date of Birth	20.9.1921
Place of Birth	Perth, Western Australia
Father	Not Known
Mother	Not Known
Stepfather	William G. R. Linnerah
Religion	Methodist
Pre-War Occupation	Blacksmith's Assistant

Kanchanaburi War Cemetery
Joint Grave
Plot 10
Row C
Grave 13-14
Age 22

HISTORY

Singapore	Selarang Camp Changi
	Johore Bahru, Adam Park
	Selarang Barracks Changi
POW Number	4/6618
'D' Force Thailand	V Battalion
POW Number	2288
Cause of Death	Beri-Beri
Place of Death	Kuii
Date of Death	26.9.1943
Buried	Grave No. 181, Kuii.

ROBERT LEO SLOANE

Rank	Private
Regimental Number	WX7506
Classification	Driver
Company	Battalion Headquarters
Enlisted	6.8.1940
Date of Birth	17.9.1914
Place of Birth	Perth, Western Australia
Father	Walter John Sloane
Mother	Annie Lillian Sloane
Religion	Roman Catholic
Pre-War Occupation	Transport Driver and Mechanic

Epitaph
Singapore Memorial
Column 136
Age 27

HISTORY

Cause of Death	Killed in Action
Place of Death	Jurong Road
Date of Death	9.2.1942
Buried	Where killed at map reference 748162
Additions	Bombed by a Japanese aircraft.

CLIFFORD VAUGHAN SMITH

Rank	Sergeant (Promoted 24.1.1942)
Regimental Number	WX14644
Company	Battalion Headquarters
Enlisted	25.6.1941
Date of Birth	13.2.1905
Place of Birth	Perth, Western Australia
Father	Clifford John Smith
Mother	Annie Vaughan Smith
Religion	Church of England
Pre-War Occupation	Road Contractor and Truck Driver

Thanbyuzayat War Cemetery
Special Memorial 'C'
Plot A14
Row C
Grave 15
Age 38

HISTORY

Singapore	Selarang Camp Changi
	Johore Bahru, Adam Park
	Selarang Barracks Changi
POW Number	4/4587
Force	'F' Force, Thailand
Cause of Death	Cardiac Beri-Beri
Place of Death	Kami Sonkurai
Date of Death	22.10.1943
Buried	Grave No. 283, Kami Sonkurai.

GEORGE SMITH

Rank	Acting Corporal (Promoted on 24.1.1942)
Regimental Number	WX4891
Classification	Cook
Company	'B' Company Headquarters
Enlisted	16.7.1940
Date of Birth	19.9.1902
Place of Birth	Brechin, Angus, Scotland
Father	David Smith
Mother	Margaret Smith
Religion	Presbyterian
Pre-War Occupation	Bread Carter

Epitaph
Labuan Memorial
Panel 18
Age 42

HISTORY

Singapore	Selarang Camp Changi
	Johore Bahru, Adam Park
	Selarang Barracks Changi
POW Number	4/4580
Force	'E' Force Borneo
POW Number	1550
Cause of Death	Not Stated
Place of Death	Sandakan-Ranau track
Date of Death	7.6.1945

MONTAGUE JOSEPH SMITH

Rank	Private
Regimental Number	WX9143
Company	'C' Company
Enlisted	30.10.1940
Date of Birth	18.8.1916
Place of Birth	Queens Park, Western Australia
Father	Mathew Joseph Smith
Mother	Lily Monica Smith
Religion	Roman Catholic
Pre-War Occupation	Farmhand

Thanbyuzayat War Cemetery
Plot A15
Row A
Grave 4
Age 27

HISTORY

Singapore	Selarang Camp Changi
	Johore Bahru, Adam Park
	Selarang Barracks Changi
POW Number	4/6639
Force	'F' Force Thailand
Cause of Death	Dysentery and Tropical Ulcers
Place of Death	Tanbaya Hospital Camp, Burma
Date of Death	0900 hours on 13.11.1943
Buried	Grave No. 615, Tanbaya
Additions	Funeral service conducted by Capt. F. J. Cahill from the 2/9th Field Ambulance on 15.11.1943. Soldier was actually buried on 13.11.1943.

ROBERT LEIGHTON SMITH

Rank	Private
Regimental Number	WX8736
Company	'B' Company
Enlisted	23.10.1940
Date of Birth	19.8.1908
Place of Birth	Norseman, Western Australia
Father	Thomas William Smith
Mother	Sarah Jane Smith
Religion	Methodist
Pre-War Occupation	Truck Driver

Kranji War Cemetery
Collective Grave
Plot 6
Row E
Grave 13-16
Age 33

HISTORY

Cause of Death	Killed in Action
Place of Death	West Mandai Hill
Date of Death	11.2.1942

RAYMOND MATTHEW SMITH

Rank	Private
Regimental Number	WX7904
Company	Headquarters Company
Enlisted	13.8.1940
Date of Birth	2.2.1906
Place of Birth	Perth, Western Australia
Father	Matthew Dunlop Smith
Mother	Gertrude Josephine Smith
Religion	Roman Catholic
Pre-War Occupation	Mines Clerk

Kranji War Cemetery
Plot 2
Row D
Grave 15
Age 26

HISTORY

Singapore	Selarang Camp Changi
Cause of Death	Dysentery and Toxemia
Place of Death	A. G. H. Roberts Barracks Changi
Date of Death	19.4.1942
Buried	Grave No. 26, A.I.F. Cemetery, Changi
Additions	Soldier was admitted to the 2/10th Australian General Hospital with an infected cyst on 1.2.1942. He was operated on the same day and discharged to unit on 13.2.1942. He was admitted to the Australian General Hospital again on 9.4.1942, but died ten days later. Soldier was buried at 1000 hours on 20.4.1942, the funeral service being conducted by Chaplain F. X. Corry from the 2/4th Machine Gun Battalion.

THOMAS ERNEST SMITH

Rank	Private
Regimental Number	WX8731
Classification	Section Orderly
Company	'B' Company
Enlisted	23.10.1940
Date of Birth	9.4.1912
Place of Birth	Norseman, Western Australia
Father	Thomas William Smith
Mother	Sarah Jane Smith
Religion	Methodist
Pre-War Occupation	Miner

Epitaph
Labuan Memorial
Panel 19
Age 32

HISTORY

Singapore	Selarang Camp and Barracks Changi
Force	'E' Force Borneo
POW Number	1911
Cause of Death	Pulmonary Tuberculosis and Beri-Beri
Place of Death	Sandakan
Date of Death	18.12.1944

JOHN FREDERICK SOLLY

Rank	Sergeant
Regimental Number	WX7127
Company	'D' Company
Enlisted	1.8.1940
Date of Birth	25.1.1901
Place of Birth	Milparinka, New South Wales
Father	John Solly
Mother	Sarah Solly
Religion	Church of England
Pre-War Occupation	Miner

Epitaph
Singapore Memorial
Column 135
Age 41

HISTORY

Cause of Death	Killed in Action
Place of Death	Tanjong Murai
Date of Death	9.2.1942
Additions	Killed in action whilst fighting his way out from the west coast of Singapore during the early morning of 9.2.1942. This NCO was hit in the chest by enemy light machine gun fire.

RODERICK HESLOP CAMPBELL SPENCE

Rank	Lance Corporal
Regimental Number	WX8467
Attached 2/4th	88 Light Aid Detachment
Company	Headquarters Company
Enlisted	18.10.1940
Date of Birth	24.6.1904
Place of Birth	Boulder, Western Australia
Father	James Spence
Mother	Katherine Elizabeth Spence
Religion	Presbyterian
Pre-War Occupation	Clerk

Epitaph
Labuan Memorial
Panel 29
Age 40

HISTORY

Singapore	Selarang Camp Changi
Force	'B' Force Borneo
POW Number	1237
Cause of Death	Malaria
Place of Death	Sandakan-Ranau track
Date of Death	31.5.1945

ALEC SPOONER

Rank	Lance Corporal
Regimental Number	WX7337
Classification	Driver
Company	'C' Company Headquarters
Enlisted	6.8.1940
Date of Birth	13.12.1910
Place of Birth	Redhill, Surrey, England
Father	Arthur Spooner
Mother	Francis Elizabeth Spooner
Religion	Church of England
Pre-War Occupation	Truck Driver

Epitaph
Labuan Memorial
Panel 18
Age 33

HISTORY

Singapore	Selarang Camp Changi
'A' Force Burma	Green Force, No. 3 Battalion
POW Number	1447
Japan	*Rakuyo Maru* Party, Kumi No. 35
Cause of Death	Lost at Sea
Place of Death	South China Sea
Date of Death	14.9.1944

ARTHUR PERCIVAL SPOUSE

Rank	Lance Corporal
Regimental Number	WX8646
Company	'C' Company
Enlisted	18.10.1940
Date of Birth	8.9.1920
Place of Birth	Doodlakine, Western Australia
Father	Oswald Roy Spouse
Mother	Florence Amy Spouse
Religion	Church of England
Pre-War Occupation	Pastry Cook

Epitaph
Singapore Memorial
Column 136
Age 21

HISTORY

Cause of Death	Killed in Action
Place of Death	Possibly at Hill 200, Ulu Pandan
Date of Death	12.2.1942

SYDNEY FRANCIS SPOUSE

Rank	Private
Regimental Number	WX13553
Company	'A' Company
Enlisted	24.5.1941
Date of Birth	19.1.1921
Place of Birth	Subiaco, Western Australia
Father	Stanley Garfield Spouse
Mother	Elizabeth Valetine Spouse
Religion	Church of England
Pre-War Occupation	Miner

Kanchanaburi War Cemetery
Plot 1
Row K
Grave 7
Age 22

HISTORY

Singapore	Selarang Camp Changi
	Thomson Road (Caldecot Hill Estate Camp)
	River Valley Road Camp
	Selarang Barracks Changi
POW Number	3/9609
'D' Force Thailand	S Battalion
POW Number	8849
Camps Thailand	Kanu II
Cause of Death	Heart Failure
Place of Death	Tarsau
Date of Death	13.10.1943
Buried	Grave No. 261, Cemetery No. 2, Tarsau.

DUDLEY JOSEPH SQUIRE

Rank	Private
Regimental Number	WX9330
Company	'C' Company
Enlisted	30.10.1940
Date of Birth	6.5.1909
Place of Birth	Bideford, Devon, England
Father	Elias Edmund Squire
Mother	Ethel Jane Squire
Religion	Church of England
Pre-War Occupation	Farmer

Kranji War Cemetery
Collective Grave
Plot 28
Row C
Grave 10-14
Age 32

HISTORY

Cause of Death	Killed in Action
Place of Death	Hill 200, Ulu Pandan
Date of Death	12.2.1942
Buried	Where killed at Map reference 761126 by Major A. Cough Party on 21.12.1942.

OLIVER MOIR STANWELL

Rank	Corporal
Regimental Number	WX7789
Classification	Driver
Company	'D' Company Headquarters
Enlisted	10.8.1940
Date of Birth	24.7.1905
Place of Birth	Moora, Western Australia
Father	Richard Arthur Stanwell
Mother	Rachel Stanwell
Religion	Church of England
Pre-War Occupation	Shop Assistant and Truck Driver

Epitaph
Labuan Memorial
Panel 18
Age 39

HISTORY

Singapore	Selarang Camp and Barracks Changi
POW Number	4/459?
Force	'E' Force Borneo
POW Number	1556
Cause of Death	Malaria
Place of Death	Sandakan
Date of Death	12.3.1945

GEORGE CLIFFORD STONE

Rank	Private
Regimental Number	WX17594
Company	'E' Company, Special Reserve Battalion
Enlisted	10.11.1941
Date of Birth	18.3.1918
Place of Birth	Swanbourne, Western Australia
Father	George Bernard Stone
Mother	Caroline Stone
Religion	Church of Christ
Pre-War Occupation	Orchardist

Kanchanaburi War Cemetery
Plot 1
Row E
Grave 45
Age 25

HISTORY

Singapore	Selarang Camp Changi
'A' Force Burma	Green Force, No. 3 Battalion
POW Number	3092
Cause of Death	Malaria and Dysentery
Place of Death	Tamarkan Hospital
Date of Death	0630 hours on 1.3.1944
Buried	Grave No. 30, Tamarkan
Additions	Funeral service conducted on 1.3.1944 by Padre J. W. K. Mathieson.

JACK OLIVER STREET

Rank	Private
Regimental Number	WX9178
Classification	Driver
Company	'A' Company
Enlisted	30.10.1940
Date of Birth	5.4.1911
Place of Birth	Leederville, Western Australia
Father	William John Street
Mother	Isabelle Clare Street
Religion	Church of England
Pre-War Occupation	Farmhand

Kranji War Cemetery
Collective Grave
Plot 30
Row A
Grave 5-8
Age 30

HISTORY

Cause of Death	Killed in Action
Place of Death	Buona Vista
Date of Death	15.2.1942
Buried	Where killed at map reference 784112
Additions	Soldier was hit in the head by shrapnel during an enemy artillery barrage.

ALBERT WILLIAM STRIBLEY

Rank	Lance Corporal
Regimental Number	WX9080
Classification	Driver
Company	'D' Company Headquarters
Enlisted	25.10.1940
Date of Birth	7.11.1911
Place of Birth	Midland Junction, Western Australia
Father	Thomas William Stribley
Mother	Emily Stribley
Religion	Church of England
Pre-War Occupation	Truck Driver

Kranji War Cemetery
Special Memorial 'C'
Plot 6
Row A
Grave 13
Age 30

HISTORY

Cause of Death	Killed in Action
Place of Death	2/19th Battalion Headquarters
Date of Death	9.2.1942
Additions	The 2/19th Battalion Headquarters was located on the west coast of Singapore to the north of the Sungei Berih.

ALBERT JOHN STRUTHOFF

Rank	Private
Regimental Number	WX15869
Company	'C' Company
Enlisted	18.8.1941
Date of Birth	10.2.1914
Father	John Struthoff
Mother	Ellen Struthoff
Religion	Methodist
Pre-War Occupation	Farmhand

Kranji War Cemetery
Plot 26
Row C
Grave 1
Age 30

HISTORY

Singapore	Selarang Camp Changi
'A' Force Burma	Green Force, No. 3 Battalion
POW Number	1516
Japan Party	*Rakuyo Maru* Party, Saigon
POW Number	1657
Cause of Death	Pneumonia
Place of Death	Tan Son Nhut, French Indo-China
Date of Death	19.9.1944
Buried	Chi Hoa Cemetery, Saigon.

WILLIAM GEORGE RAYMOND STUART

Rank	Private
Regimental Number	WX14495
Company	'D' Company
Enlisted	23.6.1941
Date of Birth	16.4.1893
Place of Birth	Semaphore, South Australia
Father	Not Known
Mother	Not Known
Religion	Presbyterian
Pre-War Occupation	Carpenter's Trade Assistant

Kranji War Cemetery
Collective Grave
Plot 6
Row C
Grave 12-14
Age 49

HISTORY

Cause of Death	Killed in Action
Place of Death	14 mile peg, Lim Chu Kang Road
Date of Death	9.2.1942
Buried	Singapore Military Cemetery
	Collective Grave 12-14
Additions	Soldier was coming out from the west coast of Singapore when his group were split up under enemy small arms fire. He was not seen again after this time. This soldier was a veteran of WWI in which he was wounded in action with the 16th Battalion at Gallipoli. He was wounded again at Hill 63 Messines Ridge and was awarded a Military Medal for his actions at Proyart with the 48th Battallion in 1918. He was also a Staff Sergeant and a Vickers machine gun instructor with the 16th Battalion militia.

JOHN BOWE STUBBS

Rank	Private
Regimental Number	WX9332
Company	'B' Company
Enlisted	30.10.1940
Date of Birth	6.12.1918
Place of Birth	Narrogin, Western Australia
Father	William Stubbs
Mother	Margaret Stubbs
Religion	Church of England
Pre-War Occupation	Farmhand

Epitaph
Singapore Memorial
Column 136
Age 23

HISTORY

Cause of Death	Killed in Action
Place of Death	Tengah Aerodrome
Date of Death	9.2.1942

EDMUND HERBERT SULLIVAN

Rank	Private
Regimental Number	WX7563
Classification	Driver
Company	Headquarters Company
Enlisted	6.8.1940
Date of Birth	29.5.1910
Place of Birth	Cottesloe, Western Australia
Father	Edmund Archer Sullivan
Mother	Margaret Elsie Sullivan
Religion	Church of England
Pre-War Occupation	Tractor Driver

Kranji War Cemetery
Plot 1
Row A
Grave 6
Age 31

HISTORY

Cause of Death	Killed in Action
Place of Death	Hill 200, Ulu Pandan
Date of Death	12.2.1942
Buried	Where killed at map reference 763132 by Major A. Cough Party on 21.12.1942.

DONALD ELIAS SUTHERLAND

Rank	Private
Regimental Number	WX15967
Company	'A' Company
Enlisted	22.8.1941
Date of Birth	28.3.1921
Place of Birth	Fremantle, Western Australia
Father	William James Alexander Sutherland
Mother	Amelia Georgina Victoria Sutherland
Religion	Methodist
Pre-War Occupation	Farmhand

Kranji War Cemetery
Collective Grave
Plot 30
Row A
Grave 5-8
Age 20

HISTORY

Cause of Death	Killed in Action
Place of Death	Tanglin Halt, Buona Vista
Date of Death	15.2.1942
Buried	In a common grave, at map reference 784112 on 16.2.1942.

FREDERIC LAURENCE TAYLOR

Rank	Private
Regimental Number	WX8450
Company	'D' Company
Enlisted	18.10.1940
Date of Birth	1.4.1919
Place of Birth	Fremantle, Western Australia
Father	Samuel George Taylor
Mother	Olive Emily Taylor
Religion	Church of Christ
Pre-War Occupation	Civil Servant

Kranji War Cemetery
Joint Grave
Plot 17
Row D
Grave 1-2
Age 22

HISTORY

Cause of Death	Killed in Action
Place of Death	Tanjong Murai
Date of Death	9.2.1942
Additions	Soldier was badly shell shocked following a heavy artillery barrage. Not seen again after his party moved out from the west coast of Singapore.

GEORGE LANE TAYLOR

Rank	Private
Regimental Number	WX14775
Classification	Signaller
Company	Headquarters Company
Enlisted	2.7.1941
Date of Birth	18.10.1919
Place of Birth	Kalgoorlie, Western Australia
Father	Arthur Lane Taylor
Mother	Johanna Taylor
Religion	Roman Catholic
Pre-War Occupation	Clerk at Bunbury Court

Epitaph
Labuan Memorial
Panel 19
Age 25

HISTORY

Singapore	Selarang Camp Changi
Force	'B' Force Borneo
POW Number	1344
Cause of Death	Malaria
Place of Death	Sandakan-Ranau track
Date of Death	7.6.1945

GEORGE WILLIAM TAYLOR

Rank	Corporal (Promoted on 24.1.1942)
Regimental Number	WX8867
Classification	Driver/Mechanic
Company	'A' Company Headquarters
Enlisted	23.10.1940
Date of Birth	7.2.1902
Place of Birth	Derbyshire, England
Father	William Taylor
Mother	Fanny Taylor
Religion	Church of England
Pre-War Occupation	Truck Driver

Epitaph
Labuan Memorial
Panel 18
Age 43

HISTORY

Singapore	Selarang Camp and Barracks Changi
POW Number	4/4597
Force	'E' Force Borneo
POW Number	1560
Cause of Death	Malaria
Place of Death	Sandakan
Date of Death	2.3.1945

JAMES TEMPLETON TAYLOR

Rank	Sergeant
Regimental Number	WX4921
Classification	Armourer
Attached 2/4th	Australian Army Ordnance Corps
Enlisted	23.7.1940
Date of Birth	12.11.1905
Place of Birth	Dunkeld, Scotland
Father	James Templeton Taylor
Mother	Catherine Taylor
Religion	Church of Scotland
Pre-War Occupation	Truck Driver

Thanbyuzayat War Cemetery
Plot A13
Row A
Grave 19
Age 37

HISTORY

Singapore	Selarang Camp and Barracks Changi
POW Number	4/4598
Force	'F' Force Thailand
Cause of Death	Beri-Beri and Pneumonia
Place of Death	Kami Sonkurai
Date of Death	11.7.1943
Buried	No. 3 Cemetery, Grave No. 22, Kami Sonkurai.

CYRIL BERNARD THACKRAH

Rank	Corporal (Promoted on 14.2.1942)
Regimental Number	WX8699
Company	Headquarters Company
Enlisted	23.10.1940
Date of Birth	4.2.1903
Place of Birth	Reading, Berkshire, England
Father	Charles Thackrah
Mother	Maria Felcia Thackrah
Religion	Church of England
Pre-War Occupation	Labourer

Thanbyuzayat War Cemetery
Plot A16
Row F
Grave 2
Age 40

HISTORY

Singapore	Selarang Camp Changi
	Johore Bahru, Adam Park
	Selarang Barracks Changi
POW Number	4/6709
Force	'F' Force Thailand
POW Number	1490
Cause of Death	Dysentery and Malaria
Place of Death	Tanbaya
Date of Death	1000 hours on 19.9.1943
Buried	Grave No. 226, Tanbaya
Additions	Funeral service by Chaplain Duckworth (British Army) on 15.11.1943.

DAVID WILLIAM THOMAS

Rank	Private
Regimental Number	WX6623
Company	'D' Company
Enlisted	19.7.1940
Date of Birth	22.9.1919
Place of Birth	Perth, Western Australia
Father	Joseph John Thomas
Mother	Emily Coombes Thomas
Religion	Church of England
Pre-War Occupation	Butcher

Epitaph
Labuan Memorial
Panel 19
Age 23

HISTORY

Singapore	Selarang Camp Changi
'A' Force Burma	Green Force, No. 3 Battalion
POW Number	3093
Japan	*Rakuyo Maru* Party, Kumi No. 37
Cause of Death	Lost at Sea
Place of Death	South China Sea
Date of Death	12.9.1944

GEORGE ALAN JACK THOMPSON

Rank	Captain
Regimental Number	WX3448
Company	'C' Company Headquarters
Enlisted	5.12.1940
Date of Birth	8.1.1906
Place of Birth	Kalgoorlie, Western Australia
Father	George Thompson
Mother	Mary Jane Thompson
Religion	Church of England
Pre-War Occupation	Despatch Hand

HISTORY

Cause of Death	Executed by the Imperial Japanese Army
Place of Death	Singapore
Date of Death	19.2.1942

Epitaph
Singapore Memorial
Panel 135
Age 36

ERNEST JAMES THOMSETT

Rank	Private
Regimental Number	WX17615
Company	'E' Company, Special Reserve Battalion
Enlisted	11.11.1941
Date of Birth	17.12.1922
Place of Birth	Subiaco, Western Australia
Father	Albert Edward Charles Thomsett
Mother	Vera Alexandria Thomsett
Religion	Church of England
Pre-War Occupation	Grocer's Assistant

HISTORY

Cause of Death	Killed in Action
Place of Death	Sungei Kranji-Sungei Jurong Defence Line
Date of Death	10.2.1942

Kranji War Cemetery
Plot 6
Row C
Grave 11
Age 19

IVOR EDWIN THORLEY

Rank	Sergeant
Regimental Number	WX9562
Classification	Fitter
Attached 2/4th	88 Light Aid Detachment
Enlisted	4.12.1940
Date of Birth	7.7.1901
Place of Birth	Ballarat, Victoria
Father	Edwin Donald Thorley
Mother	Blodwyn Thorley
Religion	Church of England
Pre-War Occupation	Fitter

Epitaph
Labuan Memorial
Panel 28
Age 43

HISTORY

Singapore	Selarang Camp Changi
Force	'B' Force Borneo
POW Number	351
Cause of Death	Malaria
Place of Death	Sandakan
Date of Death	4.3.1945
Additions	Embarked on HMT *Zealander* at Fremantle on 30.5.1941 with 86 Light Aid Detachment attached to the 2/6th Field Park Company. Taken on Strength with 88 Light Aid Detachment and attached to the 2/4th Machine Gun Battalion on Singapore. The actual date this occurred is not known.

ARTHUR STANLEY THORNS

Rank	Private
Regimental Number	WX10289
Classification	Driver
Company	'B' Company
Enlisted	18.12.1940
Date of Birth	18.11.1917
Place of Birth	Trafalgar, Western Australia
Father	Albert Wilfred Thorns
Mother	Amy Matilda Thorns
Religion	Methodist
Pre-War Occupation	Pipe Fitter

Epitaph
Labuan Memorial
Panel 19
Age 27

HISTORY

Singapore	Selarang Camp Changi
	Johore Bahru, Adam Park
	Selarang Barracks Changi
POW Number	4/6721
Force	'E' Force Borneo
POW Number	1936
Cause of Death	Beaten to Death
Place of Death	Ranau
Date of Death	1.8.1945
Additions	This soldier was amongst the last group at Ranau to be massacred.

JAMES THORPE

Rank	Private
Regimental Number	WX8460
Company	'D' Company
Enlisted	18.10.1940
Date of Birth	11.11.1916
Place of Birth	Shotley Bridge, Durham, England
Father	John Thorpe
Mother	Margaret Thorpe
Religion	Roman Catholic
Pre-War Occupation	Milk Carrier

Kranji War Cemetery
Plot 30
Row A
Grave 16
Age 25

HISTORY

Cause of Death	Killed in Action
Place of Death	Buona Vista
Date of Death	15.2.1942
Buried	Chinese Cemetery in a common grave
Additions	Soldier was killed sometime between 1600 and 1700 hours. He was sheltering behind a house when it received a direct hit. The Chinese Cemetery was located at the head of Holland Village and Buona Vista Roads.

JAMES JOHN TILL

Rank	Lieutenant
Regimental Number	WX9382
Company	'E' Company, Special Reserve Battalion
Enlisted	27.11.1940
Date of Birth	19.7.1914
Place of Birth	Guildford, Western Australia
Father	George Phillip Till
Mother	Edith Mary Till
Religion	Church of England
Pre-War Occupation	Regular Soldier

Kranji War Cemetery
Plot 28
Row C
Grave 20
Age 27

HISTORY

Cause of Death	Died of Wounds
Place of Death	South-West Bukit Timah
Date of Death	13.2.1942
Buried	Where killed on 21.12.1942
Additions	This Officer rushed at a Japanese light automatic section, the same one that had killed Lieutenant Harry Green at close range. Lieutenant Till was wounded in the shoulder and was pulled back by Sergeant Norm Platts to a position where his wounds could be treated. It is believed that in the confusion of the ambush and during the withdrawal from the area that Lieutenant Till came across some more Japanese. His body was discovered at the crossing of a creek and Reformatory Road at Map Reference 763139 by the burial party led by Major Bert Saggers from Sime Road Camp on 21.12.1942.

RICHARD LLOYD TODD

Rank	Private
Regimental Number	WX7470
Company	Headquarters Company
Enlisted	6.8.1940
Date of Birth	22.4.1916
Place of Birth	Perth, Western Australia
Father	Joseph Todd
Mother	Leonora Todd
Religion	Church of England
Pre-War Occupation	Hairdresser

Kranji War Cemetery
Joint Grave
Plot 23
Row A
Grave 15-16
Age 25

HISTORY

Cause of Death	Killed in Action
Place of Death	Reformatory Road, Ulu Pandan
Date of Death	12.2.1942

FREDERICK WILLIAM TOMS

Rank	Private
Regimental Number	WX7664
Company	'C' Company
Enlisted	10.8.1940
Date of Birth	28.8.1904
Place of Birth	Aldershot, England
Father	Septimus Toms
Mother	Minnie Toms
Religion	Church of England
Pre-War Occupation	Truck and Tractor Driver

Epitaph
Labuan Memorial
Panel 19
Age 40

HISTORY

Singapore	Selarang Camp Changi
'A' Force Burma	Green Force, No. 3 Battalion
POW Number	1479
Japan	*Rakuyo Maru* Party, Kumi No. 35
Cause of Death	Lost at Sea
Place of Death	South China Sea
Date of Death	14.9.1944
Additions	Wounded in action at Buona Vista on 15.2.1942. Admitted to the 2/13th Australian General Hospital with splinter wounds to the back. Soldier was operated on the same day. Discharged to unit 18.3.1942.

FRANCIS ANDREW TOOVEY

Rank	Private
Regimental Number	WX15897
Company	'D' Company
Enlisted	20.8.1941
Date of Birth	12.4.1919
Place of Birth	Albany, Western Australia
Father	Henry Weir Toovey
Mother	Harriett Rosa Toovey
Religion	Roman Catholic
Pre-War Occupation	Shearer

Karrakatta War Cemetery
Plot M
Row C
Grave 7
Age 27

HISTORY

Singapore	A. G. H. Roberts Barracks Changi
	Changi Gaol Camp Hospital
POW Number	1/9519
Cause of Death	Died of Wounds
Place of Death	110 (P)MH
Date of Death	9.11.1945
Return Details 1945	Singapore-Darwin-Sydney, 1st Netherlands Military Hospital Ship, *Oranje*. Sydney-Melbourne-Perth by train. Admitted to 110(P)MH on 10.10.1945.
Additions	This soldier, known as Andy, was wounded in action at Hill 200, Ulu Pandan on 12.2.1942 where he was hit by shrapnel. He was evacuated to the 2/10th Australian General Hospital at Oldham Hall on 12.2.1942 where part of his right thumb was amputated. He was then transferred to a Field Ambulance on 15.2.1942 before being transferred again to the 2/13th Australian General Hospital on 17.2.1942. Apart from the damage he incurred to his thumb he had also received wounds to the left and right arms and his abdomen. On 6.3.1942 he was transferred to the Australian General Hospital at Robert Barracks Changi. The Japanese had given him an 'A' Medical Classification due to the severity of his wounds. Given little chance of survival by the doctors, Andy's battle for life was just beginning. Twelve months after his initial wounds, the hole in his shoulder had not healed and he had lost the partial use of his left arm. The Australian surgeons were in the process of reconstructing a thumb on his right hand by strapping his hand to his stomach, where they hoped to graft the flesh. Once this had succeeded they then intended to graft some bone from his shin in an attempt to reconstruct the thumb. Andy, it is said, remained cheerful during the whole affair and kept himself busy by making chess pieces. He survived his Singapore ordeal and returned to his loved ones in Perth but sadly passed away one month after his return to Western Australia. It was not until Andy's brother Pat, an ex-member of the 2/28th Battalion and himself an ex-Prisoner of War, met with the author and stated that Andy's name did not appear on the Cenotaph at the King's Park War Memorial overlooking the City of Perth. This obvious omission needed to be corrected because at the time of Andy's passing he was still a full serving member of the 2nd A.I.F. Over a period of fourteen months Andy's details were forwarded to and verified by the Commonwealth War Graves. Once these were accepted as being correct, the State Executive of the Returned Services League put their weight behind Pat's cause and, at an unveiling ceremony on 1st May 2000, the panel on which Andy's name had been added, was unveiled by Mr Ross O'Connor, the Vice President of the Returned Services League.

REGINALD GERALD TOOZE

Rank	Private
Regimental Number	WX16323
Classification	Batman/Runner
Company	'E' Company, Special Reserve Battalion
Enlisted	3.9.1941
Date of Birth	24.9.1920
Place of Birth	Somerset, England
Father	Not Known
Mother	May Tooze
Religion	Church of England
Pre-War Occupation	Farmhand

Epitaph
Singapore Memorial
Column 136
Age 21

HISTORY

Cause of Death	Killed in Action
Place of Death	South-West Bukit Timah
Date of Death	11.2.1942
Additions	Kingsley Fairbridge Farm Schoolboy.

FRANK McPHAIL TOWNSEND

Rank	Corporal (Promoted on 9.2.1942)
Regimental Number	WX10797
Company	'A' Company
Enlisted	15.1.1941
Date of Birth	15.5.1921
Place of Birth	Kalgoorlie, Western Australia
Father	Frank McPhail Townsend
Mother	Olivia Agnes Townsend
Religion	Presbyterian
Pre-War Occupation	Letter Carrier

Thanbyuzayat War Cemetery
Plot A8
Row D
Grave 18
Age 22

HISTORY

Singapore	Selarang Camp Changi
'A' Force Burma	Green Force, No. 3 Battalion
POW Number	1370
Cause of Death	Chronic Diarrhoea, Pellagra and Tropical Ulcers
Place of Death	Khonkan 55km Hospital Camp
Date of Death	16.8.1943
Buried	Grave No. 52, Khonkan.

JOHN TREASURE

Rank	Private
Regimental Number	WX9351
Classification	Driver
Company	Headquarters Company
Enlisted	30.10.1940
Date of Birth	5.4.1919
Place of Birth	Perth, Western Australia
Father	Leo Edward Treasure
Mother	Victoria Regina Treasure
Religion	Roman Catholic
Pre-War Occupation	Farmhand

Kanchanaburi War Cemetery
Collective Grave
Plot 1
Row O
Grave 58-59
Age 24

HISTORY

Singapore	Selarang Camp Changi
	Pulau Blakang Mati
	Adam Park
	Selarang Barracks Changi
POW Number	4/6728
'D' Force Thailand	V Battalion
POW Number	2293
Cause of Death	Cerebral Malaria
Place of Death	Kuii
Date of Death	13.9.1943
Buried	Grave No. 161, Kuii.

FREDERICK THOMAS TREGENZA

Rank	Private
Regimental Number	WX9280
Company	'D' Company
Enlisted	30.10.1940
Date of Birth	8.4.1910
Place of Birth	Dangin, Western Australia
Father	James Montague Tregenza
Mother	Mary Jane Tregenza
Religion	Church of England
Pre-War Occupation	Farmer

Epitaph
Singapore Memorial
Column 136
Age 31

HISTORY

Cause of Death	Missing in Action
Place of Death	2/20 Battalion Headquarters
Date of Death	9.2.1942
Additions	Whilst retiring from his gun position on the west coast of Singapore this soldier's convoy was ambushed and machine gunned by the enemy. The trucks were abandoned and the men scattered and attempted to make their way to the 2/20th Battalion Headquarters. Soldier was last seen with George Quinn who managed to escape to Sumatra. It is believed that this soldier was killed somewhere on or near Lim Chu Kang Road.

JOHN ERNEST TREGENZA

Rank	Sergeant (Promoted on 20.2.1942)
Regimental Number	WX9325
Company	'D' Company
Enlisted	30.10.1940
Date of Birth	14.10.1914
Place of Birth	Dangin, Western Australia
Father	James Montague Tregenza
Mother	Mary Jane Tregenza
Religion	Church of England
Pre-War Occupation	Farmer

Kanchanaburi War Cemetery
Plot 1
Row L
Grave 50
Age 28

HISTORY

Singapore	Selarang Camp Changi
	Johore Bahru, Adam Park
	Selarang Barracks Changi
POW Number	4/4604
'D' Force Thailand	V Battalion
POW Number	2218
Cause of Death	Cerebral Malaria
Place of Death	Brankassi
Date of Death	2.9.1943
Buried	Grave No. 54, Brankassi.

ALLAN GEORGE TRIGWELL

Rank	Private
Regimental Number	WX17882
Company	'C' Company
Enlisted	4.12.1941
Date of Birth	14.8.1920
Place of Birth	Donnybrook, Western Australia
Father	Thomas Frederick Trigwell
Mother	Mary Jane Hamshire Trigwell
Religion	Church of England
Pre-War Occupation	Farmhand

Epitaph
Labuan Memorial
Panel 19
Age 23

HISTORY

Singapore	Selarang Camp and Barracks Changi
Force	'E' Force Borneo
POW Number	1941
Cause of Death	Malaria
Place of Death	Sandakan
Date of Death	4.5.1945

VERNON CHAPMAN TRIGWELL

Rank	Private
Regimental Number	WX17863
Company	'C' Company
Enlisted	3.12.1941
Date of Birth	22.9.1919
Place of Birth	Donnybrook, Western Australia
Father	Alfred Trigwell
Mother	Mary Jane Trigwell
Religion	Church of England
Pre-War Occupation	Farmhand

Epitaph
Labuan Memorial
Panel 19
Age 24

HISTORY

Singapore	Selarang Camp Changi
'A' Force Burma	Green Force, No. 3 Battalion
POW Number	1485
Japan	*Rakuyo Maru* Party, Kumi No. 35
Cause of Death	Lost at Sea
Place of Death	South China Sea
Date of Death	14.9.1944

WILLIAM JOHN TUCKER

Rank	Private
Regimental Number	WX7484
Company	Headquarters Company
Enlisted	6.8.1940
Date of Birth	15.7.1906
Place of Birth	Northam, Western Australia
Father	Robert Henry Tucker
Mother	Jean Maxwell Tucker
Religion	Methodist
Pre-War Occupation	Labourer

Epitaph
Labuan Memorial
Panel 19
Age 38

HISTORY

Singapore	Selarang Camp Changi
'A' Force Burma	Green Force, No. 3 Battalion
POW Number	3074
Japan	*Rakuyo Maru* Party, Kumi No. 37
Cause of Death	Lost at Sea
Place of Death	South China Sea
Date of Death	12.9.1944

REGINALD GEORGE TUFFIN

Rank	Corporal
Regimental Number	WX8491
Company	'A' Company
Enlisted	18.10.1941
Date of Birth	10.1.1911
Place of Birth	Bath, England
Father	George Andrew Tuffin
Mother	Edith Henriette Tuffin
Religion	Church of England
Pre-War Occupation	Nurseryman

Kranji War Cemetery
Special Memorial 'C'
Plot 28
Row D
Grave 4
Age 31

HISTORY

Cause of Death	Killed in Action
Place of Death	Tengah (defending airfield)
Date of Death	9.2.1942
Additions	Soldier received a wound to the chest. It is uncertain whether soldier was shot by a Japanese sniper or a Sikh Bren gunner who was firing at an enemy aircraft.

HAROLD RAYMOND TURNER

Rank	Private
Regimental Number	WX17593
Company	'E' Company, Special Reserve Battalion
Enlisted	10.11.1941
Date of Birth	13.12.1919
Place of Birth	Perth, Western Australia
Father	Harold Herbert Turner
Mother	Elizabeth Ellen Turner
Religion	Baptist
Pre-War Occupation	Storeman

Epitaph
Labuan Memorial
Panel 19
Age 25

HISTORY

Singapore	Selarang Camp Changi
	Johore Bahru, Adam Park
	Selarang Barracks Changi
POW Number	4/6736
Force	'E' Force Borneo
POW Number	1944
Cause of Death	Malaria
Place of Death	Sandakan
Date of Death	8.5.1945

HARRY TYSOE

Rank	Private
Regimental Number	WX9226
Company	'A' Company
Enlisted	30.10.1940
Date of Birth	21.3.1908
Place of Birth	Burton on Trent, England
Father	Roger Tysoe
Mother	Martha Ann Tysoe
Religion	Methodist
Pre-War Occupation	Ganger

Yokohama War Cemetery
Plot B
Row A
Grave 14
Age 35

HISTORY

Singapore	Selarang Camp Changi
	Johore Bahru, Adam Park
	Selarang Barracks Changi
'J' Force Japan	*Wales Maru* Party
POW Number	702
Camps Japan	Kobe
Cause of Death	Chronic Beri-Beri and Influenza
Place of Death	Japanese Hospital, Osaka
Date of Death	1320 hours on 26.11.1943
Buried	Soldier's body was cremated and enshrined at Juganji Temple, Osaka
Additions	Soldier was admitted to hospital on 7.11.1943 with progressive cardiac failure and beri-beri.

FRANK VAUGHAN

Rank	Private
Regimental Number	WX5932
Classification	Cook
Company	'B' Company Headquarters
Enlisted	29.6.1940
Date of Birth	8.11.1910
Place of Birth	Surrey, England
Father	Frank Vaughan
Mother	Eliza Jane Vaughan
Religion	Church of England
Pre-War Occupation	Farmhand

Kanchanaburi War Cemetery
Plot 1
Row E
Grave 39
Age 33

HISTORY

Singapore	Selarang Camp Changi
'A' Force Burma	Green Force, No. 3 Battalion
POW Number	1473
Camps Burma	Khonkan 55km (evacuated from Meiloe 3.7.1943)
Cause of Death	Malaria and Dysentery
Place of Death	Tamarkan
Date of Death	1.4.1944
Buried	Grave G3, Tamarkan
Additions	Funeral service conducted by Padre J. K. W. Matheson. At Ye, soldier was admitted to the Dutch ward on 28.9.1942. Transferred to the Australian ward on 10.10.1942.

NORMAN JAMES VENEMORE

Rank	Private
Regimental Number	WX9292
Company	'D' Company
Enlisted	30.10.1940
Date of Birth	7.7.1916
Place of Birth	Cottesloe, Western Australia
Father	Joseph Munday Venemore
Mother	Rosa May Venemore
Religion	Church of England
Pre-War Occupation	Farmer

Epitaph
Labuan Memorial
Panel 19
Age 28

HISTORY

Singapore	Selarang Camp Changi
'A' Force Burma	Green Force, No. 3 Battalion
POW Number	3124
Japan	*Rakuyo Maru* Party, Kumi No. 37
Cause of Death	Lost at Sea
Place of Death	South China Sea
Date of Death	15.9.1945

HAROLD ALEXANDER WALKER

Rank	Private
Regimental Number	WX9224
Classification	Signaller
Company	Headquarters Company
Enlisted	30.10.1940
Date of Birth	25.6.1918
Place of Birth	Greenbushes, Western Australia
Father	John Walker
Mother	Ivy Alice Walker
Religion	Methodist
Pre-War Occupation	Baker

Kranji War Cemetery
Plot 1
Row A
Grave 7
Age 23

HISTORY

Cause of Death	Killed in Action
Place of Death	Reformatory Road, Ulu Pandan
Date of Death	12.2.1942
Buried	Where killed at map reference 763132 by Major A. Cough Party on 21.12.1942.

ROBERT JOSEPH WALKER

Rank	Private
Regimental Number	WX15614
Company	Headquarters Company
Enlisted	6.8.1941
Date of Birth	15.7.1905
Place of Birth	Bellevue, Western Australia
Father	Alfred Henry Walker
Mother	Flora Elizabeth Walker
Religion	Methodist
Pre-War Occupation	Labourer

Djakarta War Cemetery
Plot 4
Row J
Grave 8
Age 36

HISTORY

Java	'Blackforce'
Cause of Death	Dysentery
Place of Death	Bicycle Camp Batavia
Date of Death	5.5.1942
Buried	Petamboran Cemetery, British Section
	Grave No. 47
Additions	Funeral service conducted by Padre F. Kellow from the 2/2nd Pioneer Battalion.

LEO PATRICK WALSH

Rank	Private
Regimental Number	WX8776
Company	'B' Company
Enlisted	23.10.1940
Date of Birth	23.3.1907
Place of Birth	Kalgoorlie, Western Australia
Father	Joseph George Walsh
Mother	Mary Francis Walsh
Religion	Roman Catholic
Pre-War Occupation	Locksmith

Epitaph
Labuan Memorial
Panel 19
Age 36

HISTORY

Singapore	Selarang Camp Changi
'A' Force Burma	Green Force, No. 3 Battalion
POW Number	1512
Camps Thailand	Tamarkan
Japan	*Rakuyo Maru* Party, Kumi No. 35
Cause of Death	Lost at Sea
Place of Death	South China Sea
Date of Death	12.9.1944

VICTOR INGLEBY WARHURST

Rank	Lieutenant
Regimental Number	NX70433
Company	'E' Company Headquarters, Special Reserve Battalion
Enlisted	12.11.1940
Date of Birth	22.1.1918
Place of Birth	Adelaide, South Australia
Father	Victor Arnold Warhurst
Mother	Olive Drew Warhurst
Religion	Church of England
Pre-War Occupation	Regular Officer, Graduate of Duntroon

Epitaph
Singapore Memorial
Column 135
Age 24

HISTORY

Cause of Death	Died of Wounds
Place of Death	South-West Bukit Timah
Date of Death	11.2.1942
Additions	Wounded in action by mortar fire. Officer's thigh was shattered as a result of the blast. An eye witness stated that five Japanese soldiers appeared on the scene and ended this young man's life with his own rifle and bayonet.

NEIL WARNE

Rank	Private
Regimental Number	WX8626
Classification	Signaller
Company	Headquarters Company
Enlisted	18.10.1940
Date of Birth	2.3.1910
Place of Birth	Western Australia
Father	William Evans Warne
Mother	Adeline Warne
Religion	Methodist
Pre-War Occupation	Bank Clerk

Kranji War Cemetery
Plot 1
Row A
Grave 8
Age 31

HISTORY

Cause of Death	Killed in Action
Place of Death	Hill 200, Ulu Pandan
Date of Death	12.2.1942
Buried	Where killed, at map reference 763132 by Major A. Cough Party on 21.12.1942.

JOHN WARREN-SMITH

Rank	Private
Regimental Number	WX8765
Company	'B' Company
Enlisted	23.10.1940
Date of Birth	4.8.1897
Place of Birth	Perth, Western Australia
Father	Not Known
Mother	Not Known
Religion	Church of England
Pre-War Occupation	Prospector

Kanchanaburi War Cemetery
Plot 10
Row L
Grave 13
Age 47

HISTORY

Singapore	Selarang Camp Changi
	Johore Bahru, Adam Park
	Selarang Barracks Changi
POW Number	4/6722
'D' Force Thailand	S Battalion
POW Number	8860
Cause of Death	Not Known
Place of Death	Prachuab Kirikhan
Date of Death	1910 hours on 17.7.1945

THOMAS CLIFFORD WEARN

Rank	Lance Corporal
Regimental Number	WX12008
Company	'A' Company
Enlisted	29.4.1941
Date of Birth	27.4.1909
Place of Birth	Boulder, Western Australia
Father	Joseph Henry Wearn
Mother	Margaret Ann Wearn
Religion	Salvation Army
Pre-War Occupation	Moulder's Assistant

Thanbyuzayat War Cemetery
Plot A11
Row A
Grave 17
Age 33

HISTORY

Singapore	Selarang Camp Changi
'A' Force Burma	Green Force, No. 3 Battalion
POW Number	1510
Cause of Death	Dysentery
Place of Death	Thanbyuzayat
Date of Death	0115 hours on 20.11.1942
Buried	Grave No. 4, Thanbyuzayat
Additions	Soldier was evacuated fron Kendau 4.8km Camp to Thanbyuzayat Hospital on 8.11.1942 where he died in the Dutch isolation ward. Tom was a religious man and in his diary, which made it home to his family, he wrote the following verse:

'Not only by the things we do, not only by the deeds confessed,
But in the most unconscious way, is Christ expressed.
For from your eyes he beckons you, and from your heart his love is shed,
Till I lose sight of you, and see Christ instead.'

FREDERICK WILLIAM WEBB

Rank	Private
Regimental Number	WX9829
Company	'C' Company
Enlisted	6.12.1940
Date of Birth	18.11.1921
Place of Birth	Subiaco, Western Australia
Father	James Webb
Mother	Doris Webb
Religion	Roman Catholic
Pre-War Occupation	Hairdresser

HISTORY

Singapore	Selarang Camp Changi
'A' Force Burma	Green Force, No. 3 Battalion
POW Number	2917
Japan	*Rakuyo Maru* Party, Kumi No. 37
Cause of Death	Lost at Sea
Place of Death	South China Sea
Date of Death	12.9.1944

HERBERT STANLEY WERRETT

Rank	Private
Regimental Number	WX7166
Company	'C' Company
Enlisted	2.8.1940
Date of Birth	2.8.1899
Place of Birth	Perth, Western Australia
Father	Thomas Werrett
Mother	Annie Werrett
Religion	Church of England
Pre-War Occupation	Railways Porter, W.A.G.R.

HISTORY

Cause of Death	Died of Wounds
Place of Death	Alexandra Hospital Singapore
Date of Death	14.2.1942
Additions	Soldier was listed as missing in action from 11.2.1942 possibly from the Ulu Pandan area.

FRED WHITACKER

Rank	Private
Regimental Number	WX16274
Company	Headquarters Company
Enlisted	29.8.1941
Date of Birth	28.2.1907
Place of Birth	Sheffield, South Yorkshire, England
Father	James Whitaker
Mother	Sarah Whitaker
Religion	Church of England
Pre-War Occupation	Truck Driver

Kanchanaburi War Cemetery
Plot 1
Row G
Grave 76
Age 36

HISTORY

Singapore	Selarang Camp Changi
	Johore Bahru, Adam Park
	Selarang Barracks Changi
POW Number	1/9704
'D' Force Thailand	V Battalion
POW Number	2298
Cause of Death	Dysentery
Place of Death	Hindaine
Date of Death	6.8.1943
Buried	Linson Camp Cemetery, Grave No. 15.

ROBERT WHITFORD

Rank	Private
Regimental Number	WX7232
Company	'D' Company
Enlisted	1.8.1940
Date of Birth	6.4.1903
Place of Birth	Princess Royal, Western Australia
Father	Henry Whitford
Mother	Minnie Whitford
Religion	Church of Christ
Pre-War Occupation	Prospector

Kranji War Cemetery
Plot 30
Row A
Grave 17
Age 38

HISTORY

Cause of Death	Died of Wounds
Place of Death	Buona Vista
Date of Death	1800 hours on 15.2.1942
Buried	In a common grave, in a Chinese Cemetery, at the head of Holland Village and Buona Vista Road.
Additions	Soldier was killed during the last artillery barrage of the battle. He was hit in the chest by the same shell that killed Jim Thorpe. He was running towards a native hut which was hit by a shell and caught fire. The men managed to get soldier clear from the burning hut but he only lived for about 5 minutes after he was wounded.

JAMES WILKIE

Rank	Private
Regimental Number	WX8706
Company	Headquarters Company
Enlisted	23.10.1940
Date of Birth	27.7.1908
Place of Birth	Perthshire, Scotland
Father	Andrew Wilkie
Mother	Mary Anne Wilkie
Religion	Presbyterian
Pre-War Occupation	Plantation Owner

Epitaph
Labuan Memorial
Panel 19
Age 36

HISTORY

Singapore	Selarang Camp and Barracks Changi
POW Number	1/12380
Force	'E' Force Borneo
POW Number	1962
Cause of Death	Malaria
Place of Death	Sandakan
Date of Death	17.5.1945

LESLIE GEORGE WILLACOTT
a.k.a. Leslie George Willacott Williams

Rank	Private
Regimental Number	WX6071
Company	'A' Company
Enlisted	30.7.1940
Date of Birth	2.6.1907
Place of Birth	Cardiff, Wales
Father	George Williams
Mother	Olive Williams
Religion	Church of England
Pre-War Occupation	Fettler

Kanchanaburi War Cemetery
Plot 1
Row E
Grave 60
Age 36

HISTORY

Singapore	Selarang Camp Changi
'A' Force Burma	Green Force, No. 3 Battalion
POW Number	3137
Camps Burma	Ye (appendix operation 20.9.1942)
Cause of Death	Malaria and Dysentery
Place of Death	Tamarkan Hospital
Date of Death	7.2.1944
Buried	Grave No. G28, Tamarkan
Additions	Funeral service conducted by Padre J. W. K. Matheson on 7.2.1944. Soldier was wounded in action at Hill 200, Ulu Pandan on 12.2.1942. Admitted to the 2/13th Australian General Hospital with a gunshot wound to the right leg. Discharged to unit on 21.2.1942.

GEORGE EDWIN WILLIMOTT

Rank	Private
Regimental Number	WX11744
Classification	Fitter
Attached 2/4th	88 Light Aid Detachment
Enlisted	21.4.1941
Date of Birth	2.11.1910
Place of Birth	Oakleigh, Victoria
Father	Walter James Willimott
Mother	Annie Willimott
Religion	Church of England
Pre-War Occupation	Plumber

Thanbyuzayat War Cemetery
Plot A13
Row D
Grave 7
Age 32

HISTORY

Singapore	Selarang Camp Changi
'A' Force Burma	Green Force, No. 3 Battalion
POW Number	3071
Cause of Death	Dysentery
Place of Death	Thanbyuzayat
Date of Death	4.6.1943
Buried	Grave No. A46, Thanbyuzayat
Additions	It appears that this soldier reported sick to the Regimental Aid Post at Kendau 4.8km Camp on 17.11.1942 and may then have been evacuated to the hospital camp at Thanbyuzayat.

JAMES FREDERICK WILLIMOTT

Rank	Private
Regimental Number	WX11745
Classification	Fitter
Attached 2/4th	88 Light Aid Detachment
Enlisted	21.4.1941
Date of Birth	2.5.1904
Place of Birth	Worksop, England
Father	Walter James Willimott
Mother	Annie Willimott
Religion	Church of England
Pre-War Occupation	Not Known

Kanchanaburi War Cemetery
Plot 1
Row B
Grave 26
Age 39

HISTORY

Singapore	Selarang Camp Changi
	Johore Bahru, Adam Park
	Selarang Barracks Changi
Force	'F' Force Thailand
Cause of Death	Dysentery
Place of Death	Kanchanaburi
Date of Death	15.12.1943
Buried	Grave No. 368, No.2 Cemetery, Kanchanaburi.

JOHN WILSON

Rank	Private
Regimental Number	WX17973
Company	'E' Company, Special Reserve Battalion
Enlisted	10.12.1941
Date of Birth	23.3.1907
Place of Birth	Newcastle, England
Father	John Coutts Wilson
Mother	Ann Wilson
Religion	Church of England
Pre-War Occupation	Timber Worker

Kanchanaburi War Cemetery
Plot 1
Row L
Grave 7
Age 36

HISTORY

Singapore	Selarang Camp and Barracks Changi
POW Number	4/6828
'D' Force Thailand	V Battalion
POW Number	2295
Cause of Death	Dysentery
Place of Death	Brankassi
Date of Death	25.8.1943
Buried	Grave No. 48, Brankassi.

RONALD MATTHEW WILSON

Rank	Staff Sergeant (Promoted on 24.1.1942)
Regimental Number	WX8438
Company	'A' Company
Enlisted	18.10.1940
Date of Birth	30.12.1910
Place of Birth	Melbourne, Victoria
Father	Matthew Wilson
Mother	Marian Reva Wilson
Religion	Church of England
Pre-War Occupation	Estate Agent

Epitaph
Labuan Memorial
Panel 18
Age 35

HISTORY

Singapore	Selarang Camp Changi
Force	'B' Force Borneo
POW Number	374
Cause of Death	Menningitis and Malaria
Place of Death	Sandakan
Date of Death	25.12.1944
Additions	Contracted illness on 7.11.1944. Death certified by 1st Lt. Yamamoto Katsuji, Medical Officer. Shell shocked at Buona Vista on 15.2.1942. Admitted to the 2/13th Australian General Hospital suffering from exhaustion and anxiety neurosis as a result of being 10 days in the front line. discharged to unit on 26.2.1942.

WALTER GEORGE WORTH

Rank	Private
Regimental Number	WX10012
Classification	Signaller
Company Headquarters	Company
Enlisted	13.12.1940
Date of Birth	5.4.1912
Place of Birth	Guildford, Western Australia
Father	De Courcey Cleaver Worth
Mother	Olive Ernestine Worth
Religion	Church of England
Pre-War Occupation	Flour Mill Employee (Smutterman)

Thanbyuzayat War Cemetery
Plot A14
Row A
Grave 12
Age 31

HISTORY

Singapore	Selarang Camp Changi
	Johore Bahru, Adam Park
	Selarang Barracks Changi
POW Number	4/6845
Force	'F' Force Thailand
Cause of Death	Cholera
Place of Death	Kami Sonkurai
Date of Death	28.8.1943
Buried	Grave No. 92, Kami Sonkurai
Additions	Soldier was a member of both Colonel Kappe's and Pond's parties. This is the only member of the 2/4th that is known to have been on both parties although it is likely there were others.

HENRY EDWARD WRIGHT

Rank	Lance Corporal
Regimental Number	WX13161
Company	'B' Company
Enlisted	17.5.1941
Date of Birth	3.11.1920
Place of Birth	Wagin, Western Australia
Father	John Edward Wright
Mother	Elizabeth Margaret Wright
Religion	Church of England
Pre-War Occupation	Labourer

Kanchanaburi War Cemetery
Joint Grave
Plot 10
Row C
Grave 10-11
Age 22

HISTORY

Singapore	Selarang Camp Changi
	Thomson Road (Caldecot Hill Estate Camp)
	River Valley Road Camp
	Selarang Barracks Changi
POW Number	3/10080
'D' Force Thailand	V Battalion
POW Number	2296
Cause of Death	Avitaminosis
Place of Death	Kuii
Date of Death	5.10.1943
Buried	Grave No. 192, Kuii.

FREDERICK BERNARD YENSCH

Rank	Private
Regimental Number	WX7429
Company	Headquarters Company
Enlisted	6.8.1940
Date of Birth	18.12.1914
Place of Birth	Fremantle, Western Australia
Father	Frederick Yensch
Mother	Mary Jane Yensch
Religion	Roman Catholic
Pre-War Occupation	Shop Assistant

Kanchanaburi War Cemetery
Plot 1
Row D
Grave 72
Age 29

HISTORY

Singapore	Selarang Camp Changi
'A' Force Burma	Green Force, No. 3 Battalion
POW Number	3077
Cause of Death	Cerebral Malaria
Place of Death	Tamarkan
Date of Death	19.3.1944
Buried	Grave No. G2, Tamarkan
Additions	Soldier was travelling on a train between Nikhe and Tamarkan on 18.3.1944 when he drifted into a coma.

JOHN YOUNG

Rank	Private
Regimental Number	WX6958
Company	'A' Company
Enlisted	30.7.1940
Date of Birth	19.7.1899
Place of Birth	Glasgow, Scotland
Father	John Young
Mother	Mary Young
Religion	Presbyterian
Pre-War Occupation	Labourer

Kanchanburi War Cemetery
Plot 8
Row G
Grave 72
Age 46

HISTORY

Singapore	Selarang Camp and Barracks Changi
POW Number	4/6856
'D' Force Thailand	S Battalion
POW Number	8863
Camps Thailand	Chungkai
Cause of Death	Beri-Beri, Dysentery, Malaria and Odema
Place of Death	Nacompaton
Date of Death	15.8.1945

NORMAN LESLIE ABLETT

Rank	Private
Regimental Number	WX7622
Company	'C' Company
Enlisted	10.8.1940
Discharged	4.3.1946
Date of Birth	25.4.1918
Place of Birth	York, Western Australia
Father	Thomas Henry Ablett
Stepmother	Linda Doris Ablett
Religion	Church of England
Pre-War Occupation	Builder's Labourer

HISTORY

Singapore	Selarang Camp Changi
'A' Force Burma	Green Force, No. 3 Battalion
POW Number	1490
Japan	*Awa Maru* Party, Kumi No. 41
Camps Japan	Fukuoka sub-Camp No.17, Omuta
Return Details 1945	Nagasaki-Okinawa-Manila, USS *Cape Gloucester* Manila-Morotai-Darwin PBY Catalina aircraft A24-306 Darwin-Perth by aircraft 10.10.1945

EDWIN THOMAS ADAMS

Rank	Private
Regimental Number	WX8245
Company	'C' Company
Enlisted	16.8.1940
Discharged	12.3.1946
Date of Birth	6.4.1914
Place of Birth	Kellerberrin, Western Australia
Father	Horace John Adams
Mother	Edith Lucy Adams
Religion	Church of England
Pre-War Occupation	Carpenter

HISTORY

Java	'Blackforce'
Camps Java	Bandoeng, Bicycle Camp Batavia, Makasura
'D' Force Thailand	Java Party No. 6, P Battalion
Japan	*Rashin Maru* Party
POW Number	1559
Camps Japan	Yamane (carpenter's shop)
Return Details 1945	Niihama Wakayama-Okinawa, USS *Sanctuary* Okinawa-Manila, USS *Bingham* Manila-Sydney, HMS *Speaker* Sydney-Fremantle, HMT *Dominion Monarch*

GEORGE FREDERICK AIREY

Rank	Warrant Officer Class 1
Regimental Number	WX13977
Company	Battalion Headquarters
Enlisted	24.7.1939
Discharged	18.7.1950
Date of Birth	17.10.1898
Place of Birth	Kendal, Westmoreland, England
Father	James Airey
Mother	Dora Alice Airey
Religion	Church of England
Pre-War Occupation	Packer

HISTORY

Java	Taken on Strength with 2/3rd Machine Gun Battalion after escaping to Java
Camps Java	Bandoeng, Bicycle Camp Batavia, Makasura
'D' Force Thailand	Java Party No. 6, O Battalion
POW Number	6506
Camps Thailand	Hintok, Tarsau, Tamuang, Nacompaton
Return Details 1945	Bangkok-Rangoon by aircraft
	Rangoon-Singapore, HMT *Highland Brigade*
	Singapore-Fremantle, HMT *Moreton Bay*
Additions	WO.I Frederick George Airey had soldiering in his blood. He served with the British Army during the Great War and when the "Call to Arms" came for WWII, he was already serving with the Militia in Western Australia. Following the "Battle of Singapore", Fred, along with three other men from the 2/4th Machine Gun Battalion and eleven others, were marched off to a remote location to be shot. Fred was one of the lucky ones to survive and managed to escape to Java by way of Sumatra. Fred then later passed himself off as an Australian Officer during his time as a Prisoner of War, so as not to draw attention to his past.

JOHN ALDERTON

Rank	Private
Regimental Number	WX8599
Company	'A' Company
Enlisted	18.10.1940
Discharged	7.12.1945
Date of Birth	23.2.1911
Place of Birth	Kalgoorlie, Western Australia
Father	Not Known
Mother	Mary Elizabeth Alderton
Religion	Church of England
Pre-War Occupation	French Polisher

HISTORY

Singapore	Selarang Camp Changi
POW Number	3/6748
Camps	Mount Pleasant Camp
	Selarang Barracks Changi
	Changi Gaol Camp
	Pulau Blakang Mati
	Kranji Camp Woodlands
Return Details 1945	Singapore-Darwin-Sydney, HMT *Arawa*
	Sydney-Melbourne-Perth by troop train

THOMAS WILLIAM ALLEN

Rank	Private
Regimental Number	WX17915
Classification	Cook
Company	'E' Company Headquarters, Special Reserve Battalion
Enlisted	8.12.1941
Discharged	11.1.1946
Date of Birth	24.5.1905
Place of Birth	Durham, England
Father	Not Known
Mother	Margaret Ellen Prince
Religion	Church of England
Pre-War Occupation	Taxi Driver

HISTORY

Singapore	Selarang Camp and Barracks Changi
POW Number	4/5871
'D' Force Thailand	V Battalion
Camps Thailand	Kinsaiyok, Brankassi, Hindaine, Non Pladuk, Ubon
Return Details 1945	Bangkok-Singapore by aircraft
	Singapore-Fremantle, HMT *Highland Brigade*

BERT WINFIELD JAMES ALLPIKE

Rank	Private
Regimental Number	WX7064
Company	Battalion Headquarters
Enlisted	2.8.1940
Discharged	20.2.1946
Date of Birth	25.4.1920
Place of Birth	Hamilton Hill, Western Australia
Father	Bert Allpike
Mother	Elsie Allpike
Religion	Church of England
Pre-War Occupation	Abattoir Employee

HISTORY

Java	'Blackforce'
Camps	Bandoeng, Bicycle Camp Batavia
'D' Force Thailand	Java Party No. 6, O Battalion
POW Number	6921
Camps Thailand	Hintok, Kinsaiyok, Tarsau, Tamuang (March 1944-April 1945)
Return Details 1945	Thailand-Singapore by aircraft
	Singapore-Fremantle, HMT *Moreton Bay*

THEODORE ROSSLYN AMBROSE

Rank	Lieutenant
Regimental Number	WX10874
Company	'C' Company
Enlisted	24.1.1941
Appointment Terminated	27.11.1945
Date of Birth	14.1.1906
Place of Birth	West Perth, Western Australia
Father	Dr Theodore Ambrose
Mother	Clara Beatrice Ambrose
Religion	Church of England
Pre-War Occupation	Barrister and Solicitor

HISTORY

Singapore	Selarang Camp and Barracks Changi
POW Number	3/5818
'H' Force Thailand	H6 Officer's Party
POW Number	1/668
Camps Thailand	Hintok Valley Camp, Hintok River Camp
Singapore	Sime Road Camp
	Changi Gaol Camp
Return Details 1945	Singapore-Darwin-Sydney, HMT *Arawa*
	Sydney-Perth by aircraft
Additions	This Officer replaced Lieutenant J. G. Wilson on his wounding on 12.2.1942.

CLAUDE LEONARD ANDERSON

Rank	Captain (R.M.O.)
Regimental Number	WX3464
Attached 2/4th	A.A.M.C.
Awards	Mentioned in Despatches
Company	Battalion Headquarters
Enlisted	2.12.1940
Appointment Terminated	4.1.1946
Date of Birth	26.12.1909
Place of Birth	Curramulka, South Australia
Father	Ernest James Anderson
Mother	Edith Alice Anderson
Religion	Methodist
Pre-War Occupation	General Practitioner

HISTORY

Singapore	Selarang Camp Changi
'A' Force Burma	Green Force, No. 3 Battalion
POW Number	2618
Camps Burma	Khonkan 55km (1.9.1943-19.10.1943)
Camps Thailand	Tamarkan, Lopburi (See Danny Bevis Diary)
Return Details 1945	Bangkok-Singapore by aircraft
	Singapore-Fremantle, HMT *Moreton Bay*

Claude Anderson - 'The Man'

Claude Leonard Anderson was born on 26th December 1909 at Curramulka on the Yorke Peninsula, South Australia. He was schooled at Prince Alfred College before taking up six years medical training at Adelaide University. On graduation he attained a position at Royal Perth Hospital. After twenty-seven months at Royal Perth, Claude was appointed second-in-charge. When the Second World War erupted in 1939 Claude was a practicing G.P. with his own rooms in Nedlands. He decided to enlist with the 2nd A.I.F. where he was acting as Medical Officer at Northam Camp Recruit Training Depot. It was at Northam where Claude accepted the position of Regimental Medical Officer with the 2/4th Machine Gun Battalion. He moved to No. 2 Camp Northam where the battalion was being formed by Lieutenant-Colonel M. J. Anketell. If you asked Claude to describe himself he would probably say that he was just an ordinary bloke. But in reality Claude could be described as a quiet, softly spoken man, a true gentleman in every sense of the word, who just got on and did the job without complaint. His services during the action on Singapore Island and, of course, as a Prisoner of War Medico were recognised by his being Mentioned in Despatches. Beyond reward however, Claude never failed to command the respect and admiration from all who served with this battalion.

DANIEL FRANK ANDERSON

Rank	Lance Corporal
Regimental Number	WX8872
Classification	Clerk
Company	'A' Company Headquarters
Enlisted	25.10.1940
Discharged	26.4.1946
Date of Birth	17.2.1904
Place of Birth	Menzies, Western Australia
Father	Daniel Edward Anderson
Mother	Mary Anderson
Religion	Presbyterian
Pre-War Occupation	Clerk and Orchardist

HISTORY

Singapore	Selarang Camp Changi
'A' Force Burma	Green Force, No.3 Battalion
POW Number	1365
Camps Thailand	Tamarkan, Chungkai, Petchaburi, Kachu Mountain Camp
Return Details 1945	Thailand-Singapore by aircraft
	Singapore-Fremantle, HMT *Circassia*

JAMES LORIMER ANDERSON

Rank	Corporal
Regimental Number	WX15433
Company	'B' Company
Enlisted	28.7.1941
Discharged	4.2.1946
Date of Birth	16.11.1912
Place of Birth	Ottawa, Canada
Father	Alfred John Anderson
Mother	Ada Anderson
Religion	Church of St Andrews
Pre-War Occupation	Farmer

HISTORY

Singapore	Selarang Camp Changi
Camps	Johore Bahru, Adam Park
	Selarang Barracks Changi
POW Number	4/5872
Force	'F' Force Thailand
Singapore	X1 Party
	P Party
	Changi Gaol Camp
Return Details 1945	Singapore-Darwin-Sydney, 1st Netherlands Military Hospital Ship *Oranje*
	Sydney-Perth by troop train.

RONALD GEORGE ANDERSON

Rank	Private
Regimental Number	WX9289
Company	'D' Company
Enlisted	30.10.1940
Discharged	9.1.1946
Date of Birth	27.12.1918
Place of Birth	Narrogin, Western Australia
Father	George Edwin Anderson
Mother	Irene Anderson
Religion	Church of England
Pre-War Occupation	Not Known

HISTORY

Singapore	Selarang Camp Changi
'A' Force Burma	Green Force, No. 3 Battalion
POW Number	1535
Camps Thailand	Tamarkan, Chungkai, Linson Wood Camp, Pratchinburi, Nakom Nayok
Return Details 1945	Not Known

WILLIAM GEORGE HARVEY ANDERSON

Rank	Private
Regimental Number	WX14634
Company	'B' Company
Enlisted	25.6.1941
Discharged	22.3.1946
Date of Birth	5.6.1923
Place of Birth	Subiaco, Western Australia
Father	George Andrew Anderson
Mother	Doris Shirley Anderson
Religion	Church of England
Pre-War Occupation	Clerk

HISTORY

Singapore	Selarang Camp Changi
'A' Force Burma	Green Force, No.,3 Battalion
POW Number	2921
Japan	*Awa Maru* Party
POW Number	1525
Camps Japan	Fukuoka sub-Camp No. 17, Omuta
Return Details 1945	Nagasaki-Okinawa, USS *Cape Gloucester*
	Okinawa-Manila, USS *Bingham*
	Manila-Sydney, HMS *Speaker*

WILLIAM FRANCIS ANDERTON

Rank	Private
Regimental Number	WX8518
Company	'B' Company
Enlisted	18.10.1940
Discharged	6.12.1945
Date of Birth	5.8.1917
Place of Birth	Preston, England
Father	William Francis Anderton
Mother	Margaret Anderton
Religion	Roman Catholic
Pre-War Occupation	Butcher

HISTORY

Singapore	Selarang Camp and Barracks Changi
	X3 Party
	Changi Gaol Camp
POW Numbers	1/6549, 3/6786 and 12394
Return Details 1945	Singapore-Darwin-Sydney, HMT *Arawa*
	Sydney-Melbourne by troop train
	Melbourne-Fremantle, HMT *Strathmore*

RICHARD WINSTON ANNEAR

Rank	Private
Regimental Number	WX13468
Company	'D' Company
Enlisted	11.12.1940
Discharged	26.2.1946
Date of Birth	29.2.1908
Place of Birth	Kalgoorlie, Western Australia
Father	John Henry Annear
Mother	Ada Eva Frances Anne Annear
Religion	Church of England
Pre-War Occupation	Business Manager

HISTORY

Sumatra	Captured at Padang, Sumatra on 9.5.1942
Camps	Gloe Gloer Camp, (Medan)
	Harukiku Maru, SS Van Waerwjick Party (rescued)
POW Number	271
Singapore	River Valley Road Camp
Sumatra	Pakan Baroe-Moearo Railway
Return Details 1945	Sumatra-Singapore by aircraft
	Singapore (admitted to the 2/14th Australian General Hospital on 17.9.1945)
	Singapore-Perth, Duke of Gloucester's aircraft *'Endeavour'*
Additions	Soldier was reported missing from 10.2.1942

RONALD EDWARD ARBERY

Rank	Sergeant
Regimental Number	WX10787
Company	'D' Company
Enlisted	15.1.1941
Discharged	24.1.1946
Date of Birth	4.2.1919
Place of Birth	Perth, Western Australia
Father	John Thomas Arbery
Mother	Elizabeth Agnes Arbery
Religion	Church of England
Pre-War Occupation	Warehouseman

HISTORY

Singapore	Selarang Camp Changi
Camps	Johore Bahru, Adam Park
	Selarang Barracks Changi
POW Number	4/4433
'D' Force Thailand	S Battalion
Camps Thailand	Kanu II, (evacuated sick to Kanchanaburi 5.7.1943-30.11.1943)
	Chungkai (1.12.1943-20.4.1944)
	Tamuang (22.4.1944-22.6.1944)
POW Number	8716
Japan	*Rashin Maru* Party
Camps Japan	Yamane
	Niihama (blast furnace)
POW Number	1527
Return Details 1945	Wakayama-Okinawa, USS *Sanctuary*
	Okinawa-Manila, USS *Bingham*
	Manila-Sydney, HMS *Speaker*
	Sydney-Fremantle, HMT *Dominion Monarch*
Additions	Wounded in action at 0800 hours on 8.2.1942. Admitted to the 2/13th Australian General Hospital on 10.2.1942 with a gunshot wound to the scalp. Transferred to the 2/2nd Convalescent Depot on 12.2.1942 and discharged to unit on 20.2.1942.

CHARLES WILLIAM ARMSTRONG

Rank	Private
Regimental Number	WX7370
Company	'B' Company
Enlisted	6.8.1940
Discharged	9.1.1946
Date of Birth	10.4.1920
Place of Birth	Harvey, Western Australia
Father	Horace Lewis Armstrong
Mother	Jessie May Armstrong
Religion	Methodist
Pre-War Occupation	Miner

HISTORY

Singapore	Selarang Camp Changi
Camps	Johore Bahru, Adam Park
	Selarang Barracks Changi
POW Number	1/6862
'D' Force Thailand	S Battalion
POW Number	8747
Camps Thailand	Tarsau, Kanu 11, Tamuang
Japan	*Rashin Maru* Party
POW Number	1560
Camps	Yamane
	Niihama
Return Details 1945	Wakayama-Okinawa, USS *Sanctuary*
	Okinawa-Manila, USS *Bingham*
	Manila-Morotai-Darwin, PBY Catalina aircraft A24-306
	Darwin-Perth by aircraft 10.10.1945

LEONARD ARMSTRONG

Rank	Private
Regimental Number	WX8963
Company	'A' Company
Enlisted	25.10.1940
Discharged	13.12.1945
Date of Birth	25.2.1914
Place of Birth	Perth, Western Australia
Father	Horace Lewis Armstrong
Mother	Jessie May Armstrong
Religion	Methodist
Pre-War Occupation	Hairdresser

HISTORY

Singapore	Selarang Camp Changi
Camps	Johore Bahru, Adam Park
	River Valley Road Camp
	Selarang Barracks Changi
'D' Force Thailand	S Battalion
POW Number	8748
Camps Thailand	Tarsau, Kanu II, Tamuang
Japan	*Rashin Maru* Party
POW Number	1561
Camps	Yamane
	Niihama
Return Details 1945	Wakayama-Okinawa, USS *Sanctuary*
	Okinawa-Manila, USS *Bingham*
	Manila-Morotai-Darwin, PBY Catalina aircraft A24-306
	Darwin-Perth by aircraft 10.10.1945

MALCOLM ARMSTRONG

Rank	Corporal (Promoted on 11.2.1942)
Regimental Number	WX7046
Company	'A' Company
Enlisted	30.7.1940
Discharged	25.5.1946
Date of Birth	1.9.1915
Place of Birth	South Perth, Western Australia
Father	Not Known
Mother	Lillian Armstrong
Religion	Church of England
Pre-War Occupation	Miner

HISTORY

Singapore	Selarang Camp Changi
'A' Force Burma	Green Force, No. 3 Battalion
POW Number	1373
Camps Burma	Khonkan 55km (evacuated sick from 105km Camp on 1.7.1943)
Camps Thailand	Tamarkan, Tamuang, Bangkok, Ubon
Return Details 1945	Thailand-Singapore by aircraft
	Singapore-Fremantle, HMT *Moreton Bay*
Additions	Wounded in action at Buona Vista on 15.2.1942. Admitted to the 2/13th Australian General Hospital with a shrapnel wound to the right shoulder. Discharged to unit on 24.2.1942.

GERALD CHARLES ARTHUR

Rank	Corporal (Promoted on 1.2.1942)
Regimental Number	WX9011
Company	'B' Company
Enlisted	25.10.1940
Discharged	27.2.1946
Date of Birth	25.7.1913
Place of Birth	Yarloop, Western Australia
Father	Michael Thomas Arthur
Mother	Elizabeth Ann Arthur
Religion	Roman Catholic
Pre-War Occupation	Truck Driver

HISTORY

Singapore	Selarang Camp Changi
Camps	Johore Bahru, Adam Park
	Selarang Barracks Changi
'J' Force Japan	*Wales Maru* Party
POW Number	797
Camps Japan	Kobe House (Mitsubishi wharves, Toyo Steel), Maibara
	Osaka sub-Camp No. 10 (rice planting and irrigation work)
Return Details 1945	Maibara-Yokohama by train
	Yokohama-Okinawa-Manila by aircraft
	Manila-Sydney, HMS *Formidable*
	Sydney-Perth by troop train

LLOYD GEORGE ASHBOLT

Rank	Corporal	
Regimental Number	WX17251	
Company	'E' Company, Special Reserve Battalion	
Enlisted	15.10.1941	
Discharged	23.1.1946	
Date of Birth	6.5.1916	
Place of Birth	York, Western Australia	
Father	George Henry Ashbolt	
Mother	Edith Fanny Ashbolt	
Religion	Methodist	
Pre-War Occupation	Traveller	

HISTORY

Singapore	Selarang Camp Changi
Camps	Thomson Road (Caldecot Hill Estate Camp)
	Selarang Barracks Changi (Garden Control Party)
'D' Force Thailand	S Battalion
POW Number	8746
Camps Thailand	Kanu II, Hintok River Camp, Tamuang
Japan	*Rashin Maru* Party
POW Number	1562
Camps Java	Yamane
	Niihama
Return Details 1945	Wakayama-Okinawa, USS *Sanctuary*
	Okinawa-Manila, USS *Bingham*
	Manila-Sydney, HMS *Speaker*
	Sydney-Fremantle, HMT *Dominion Monarch*

HERBERT ATKINSON

Rank	Private
Regimental Number	WX9342
Classification	Driver
Company	'B' Company
Enlisted	30.10.1940
Discharged	11.12.1945
Date of Birth	19.5.1920
Place of Birth	Whitby, Yorkshire, England
Father	Herbert Atkinson
Mother	Ann Atkinson
Religion	Church of England
Pre-War Occupation	Farmhand

HISTORY

Singapore	Selarang Camp Changi
Camps	Thomson Road (Caldecot Hill Estate Camp)
	Selarang Barracks Changi
POW Number	3/6821
'D' Force Thailand	S Battalion
POW Number	8749
Camps Thailand	Kanu II (April 1943-July 1943)
	Tarsau (July 1943-January 1944)
	Tamuang (January 1944-June 1944)
Japan	*Rashin Maru* Party
POW Number	1563
Camps Japan	Yamine
	Niihama
Return Details 1945	Wakayama-Okinawa, USS *Sanctuary*
	Okinawa-Manila, USS *Bingham*
	Manila-Morotai-Darwin, PBY Catalina aircraft A24-306
	Darwin-Perth by aircraft 10.10.1945
Additions	Wounded in action Riley Road Singapore on 15.2.1942. Admitted to the 2/10th Australian General Hospital with a shrapnel wound to the right wrist. Discharged to unit on 23.2.1942.

RONALD COLLETT BADOCK

Rank	Private
Regimental Number	WX8729
Company	'B' Company
Enlisted	23.10.1940
Discharged	25.2.1946
Date of Birth	31.1.1919
Place of Birth	Kalgoorlie, Western Australia
Father	Charles Frederick Badock
Mother	Ivy Euphemia Badock
Religion	Church of England
Pre-War Occupation	Miner

HISTORY

Singapore	Selarang Camp Changi
Camps	Johore Bahru, Adam Park
	Sime Road Camp
	Selarang Barracks Changi
POW Number	4/5886
'D' Force Thailand	Captain Harris Party
Camps Thailand	Kanchanaburi, Tarsau, Kinsaiyok, Chungkai (evacuated sick by barge) Non Pladuk
French Indo-China	*Both* Party
Return Details 1945	Saigon-Bangkok-Singapore by aircraft
	Singapore-Sydney, HMT *Highland Chieftan*
	Sydney-Adelaide troop train
	Adelaide-Perth by aircraft.

JAMES BAGRIE

Rank	Private
Regimental Number	WX8829
Classification	Technical Storeman
Company	Headquarters Company
Enlisted	23.10.1940
Discharged	17.1.1946
Date of Birth	13.9.1897
Place of Birth	Glasgow, Scotland
Father	William Bagrie
Mother	Margaret Ross Bagrie
Religion	Presbyterian
Pre-War Occupation	Miner

HISTORY

Singapore	Selarang Camp Changi
'A' Force Burma	Green Force, No. 3 Battalion
POW Number	3096
Camps Thailand	Tamarkan, Banderra (bridge repair)
Return Details 1945	Thailand-Singapore by aircraft
	Singapore-Fremantle, HMT *Moreton Bay*

WILLIAM FINLAY BAILLIE

Rank	Private
Regimental Number	WX9294
Classification	Batman/Runner
Company	'D' Company
Enlisted	30.10.1940
Discharged	31.1.1946
Date of Birth	15.7.1920
Place of Birth	Bruce Rock, Western Australia
Father	William Finlay Baillie
Mother	Mary Baillie
Religion	Methodist
Pre-War Occupation	Hairdresser

HISTORY

Singapore	Selarang Camp Changi
Camps	Johore Bahru, Adam Park
	Selarang Barracks Changi
POW Number	4/5889
'D' Force Thailand	V Battalion
Camps Thailand	Kuii (evacuated sick), Non Pladuk, Ubon
Return Details 1945	Thailand-Singapore by aircraft
	Singapore-Fremantle, HMT *Highland Brigade*

ERIC REGINALD BAKER

Rank	Private
Regimental Number	WX8981
Classification	Driver and Stretcher Bearer
Company	Battalion Headquarters (transferred from 'B' Company)
Enlisted	25.10.1940
Discharged	18.1.1946
Date of Birth	9.3.1912
Place of Birth	Portsmouth, England
Father	Arthur Edward Baker
Mother	Blanche Roe Baker
Religion	Church of England
Pre-War Occupation	Builder's Labourer

HISTORY

Singapore	Selarang Camp Changi
'A' Force Burma	Green Force, No. 3 Battalion
POW Number	2813
Camps	Aungganaung 105km (Eric contracted cholera 29.5.1943, discharged 30.7.1943)
Camps Thailand	Tamarkan, Nacompaton
Return Details 1945	Thailand-Singapore by aircraft
	Singapore-Sydney, HMT *Highland Chieftan*
Additions	Soldier was detached from R.M.O. to the No. 8 and 9 Platoon area to keep casualty records. Soldier was wounded in action on 7.2.1942 and admitted to Field Ambulance on 9.2.1942 with a shrapnel wound to the back. Transferred to the 2/13th Australian General Hospital on 13.2.1942. Discharged to unit on 20.2.1942.

JOHN ANDREW BAKER

Rank	Corporal (Promoted 12.2.1942)
Regimental Number	WX8962
Company	'C' Company
Enlisted	25.10.1940
Discharged	22.2.1946
Date of Birth	21.3.1918
Place of Birth	Warminster, Wiltshire, England
Father	Henry Andrew Baker
Mother	Dorothy Winifred Baker
Religion	Church of England
Pre-War Occupation	Not Known

HISTORY

Singapore	Selarang Camp Changi
'A' Force Burma	Green Force, No. 3 Battalion
POW Number	1331
Camps Thailand	Tamarkan, Chungkai, Nikhe Wood Camp (commanded several parties of thirty or more POW's as wood cutters on the railway), Tamuang
Return Details 1945	Thailand-Singapore by aircraft
	Singapore-Fremantle, HMT *Circassia*

JOHN ROBERT BAKER

Rank	Private
Regimental Number	WX9367
Company	'A' Company
Enlisted	4.11.1940
Discharged	10.1.1946
Date of Birth	21.10.1907
Place of Birth	Perth, Western Australia
Father	William Baker
Mother	Rosa Baker
Religion	Church of England
Pre-War Occupation	Railway Linesman

HISTORY

Java	'Blackforce'
'A' Force	Java Party, No. 4, Black Force
Return Details 1945	Thailand-Singapore by aircraft
	Singapore-Fremantle, HMT *Moreton Bay*

LEO PATRICK BALL

Rank	Private
Regimental Number	WX7495
Classification	Butcher
Company	Headquarters Company
Enlisted	6.8.1940
Discharged	24.1.1946
Date of Birth	26.1.1905
Place of Birth	Bendigo, Victoria
Father	Patrick Ball
Mother	Not Known
Religion	Roman Catholic
Pre-War Occupation	Butcher

HISTORY

Singapore	Selarang Camp Changi
	Serangoon Road Camp
	Selarang Barracks Changi
POW Number	4/5592
'D' Force Thailand	V Battalion
POW Number	2223
Camps Thailand	Tamarkan Camp No. 2 Base Hospital, Nacompaton Base Hospital, Ubon
Return Details 1945	Thailand-Singapore by aircraft
	Singapore-Fremantle, HMT *Highland Brigade*

ALLAN WESLEY BAMFORD

Rank	Corporal (Promoted 14.2.1942)
Regimental Number	WX8485
Classification	Clerk
Company	Battalion Headquarters
Enlisted	18.10.1940
Discharged	8.1.1946
Date of Birth	6.7.1913
Place of Birth	Maylands, Western Australia
Father	Charles Wesley Bamford
Mother	Daisy Bamford
Religion	Church of England
Pre-War Occupation	Accountant

HISTORY

Singapore	Selarang Camp Changi
'A' Force Burma	Green Force, No. 3 Battalion
POW Number	2686
Camps Burma	Khonkan 55km (evacuated from 105km Camp Aungganaung 19.11.1943 with a tropical ulcer. Right leg amputated at middle thigh on 22.11.1943)
Camps Thailand	Tamarkan, Bangkok, Nacompaton
Return Details 1945	Thailand-Singapore by aircraft
	Singapore-Fremantle, HMT *Tamaroa*

NOEL EDWIN BANKS

Rank	Private
Regimental Number	WX10343
Company	'C' Company Headquarters
Enlisted	18.12.1940
Discharged	17.12.1945
Date of Birth	22.7.1916
Place of Birth	Mt Lawley, Western Australia
Father	James Albert Banks
Mother	Celia Lydia Banks
Religion	Methodist
Pre-War Occupation	Orchardist

HISTORY

Java	'Blackforce', attached to 2/2nd Pioneer Battalion
POW Numbers	4444, 12562 and 11825
Camps Java	Bandoeng, Tjimahi, Bandoeng, Glodok Prison, Bicycle Camp Batavia, Makasura
Singapore	Java Party No. 22
Sumatra	Pakan Baroe-Moearo Railway
Return Details 1945	Evacuated by aircraft to the 2/14 Australian General Hospital, Singapore. Evacuated to Perth, by the Duke of Gloucester's aircraft *'Endeavour'* on 24.9.1945.
Additions	Captured by the Japanese on 8.3.1942 whilst travelling in an ambulance in transit to Bandoeng. From 11.3.1942-18.4.1942 with the 2/2nd Casualty Clearing Station suffering from malaria. Attached to the 2/3rd Reserve Motor Transport Company for period of convalescence until 5.11.1942.

THOMAS BARBOUR

Rank	Private
Regimental Number	WX7587
Company	'C' Company
Enlisted	6.8.1940
Discharged	12.4.1946
Date of Birth	9.5.1912
Place of Birth	Ormiston, Scotland
Father	James Barbour
Mother	Doris Edna Barbour
Religion	Presbyterian
Pre-War Occupation	Miner

HISTORY

Java	'Blackforce', attached to the 2/3rd Machine Gun Battalion
'D' Force Thailand	Java Party No. 6, O Battalion
POW Number	6919
Camps Thailand	Tarsau, Non Pladuk, Nacompaton (evacuated to Tarsau 20.8.1943 suffering from malaria and a tropical ulcer. Left leg amputated on 9.10.1943 possibly at No. 2 Hospital Camp Non Pladuk)
Return Details 1945	Thailand-Singapore by aircraft Singapore-Sydney, HMT *Highland Chieftan* Sydney-Perth by troop train

FREDERICK BARKER

Rank	Private
Regimental Number	WX7164
Company	'C' Company
Enlisted	2.8.1940
Discharged	1.2.1946
Date of Birth	19.3.1905
Place of Birth	North Perth, Western Australia
Father	Harry Barker
Mother	Edith Maud Barker
Religion	Methodist
Pre-War Occupation	Dredgehand

HISTORY

Java	'Blackforce'
Camps Java	Bicycle Camp Batavia
'A' Force Burma	Java Party No. 4, Black Force
Camps Burma	Apalon 80km, Aungganaung 105km
Return Details 1945	Thailand-Singapore by aircraft
	Singapore-Australia by aircraft

ALFRED JOHN BARNES

Rank	Private
Regimental Number	WX6970
Classification	Driver
Company	'A' Company Headquarters
Enlisted	30.7.1940
Discharged	6.11.1946
Date of Birth	5.6.1917
Place of Birth	Northam, Western Australia
Father	Not Known
Mother	Doll Eanus Barnes
Religion	Church of England
Pre-War Occupation	Farmer

HISTORY

Java	'Blackforce', attached to 2/2nd Pioneer Battalion
'A' Force Burma	Java Party No. 4, Williams Force
POW Number	4386
Camps Burma	Aungganaung 105km
Camps Thailand	131km Camp, Tamarkan
Return Details 1945	Thailand-Singapore by aircraft
	Singapore-Fremantle, HMT *Tamaroa*

THOMAS JAMES BARNETT

Rank	Corporal (Promoted on 11.2.1942)	
Regimental Number	WX222	
Classification	Driver	
Company	'B' Company Headquarters	
Enlisted	11.12.1940	
Discharged	6.12.1945	
Date of Birth	28.1.1915	
Place of Birth	Rose Park, South Australia	
Father	John James Barnett	
Mother	Essie Barnett	
Religion	Christadelphian	
Pre-War Occupation	Dry Cleaner	

HISTORY

Singapore	Selarang Camp and Barracks Changi
POW Number	4/4439
'D' Force Thailand	Captain Harris Party
Camps Thailand	Non Pladuk
French Indo-China	*Both* Party
Return Details 1945	Saigon-Bangkok-Singapore by aircraft
	Singapore-Fremantle, HMT *Tamaroa*

VICTOR GEORGE BARNETT

Rank	Private	
Regimental Number	WX8429	
Company	'B' Company	
Enlisted	18.10.1940	
Discharged	29.11.1945	
Date of Birth	17.7.1912	
Place of Birth	Moora, Western Australia	
Father	Alfred Henry Barnett	
Mother	Marion Naomie Barnett	
Religion	Church of England	
Pre-War Occupation	Window Dresser	

HISTORY

Singapore	Selarang Camp Changi
'A' Force Burma	Green Force, No. 3 Battalion
POW Number	6297
Camps Thailand	Tamarkan, Non Pladuk
Japan	*Awa Maru* Party, Kumi No. 40
POW Number	1511
Camps Japan	Fukuoka sub-Camp No. 17 Omuta (coal mine and wharf labour)
Return Details 1945	Nagasaki-Okinawa-Manila, USS *Cape Gloucester*
	Okinawa-Manila, B24 Liberator aircraft
	Manila-Morotai-Darwin, PBY Catalina aircraft A24-306
	Darwin-Perth by aircraft 10.10.1945

JAMES JOSEPH BARRY

Rank	Private
Regimental Number	WX8185
Classification	Section Orderly
Company	'B' Company
Enlisted	16.8.1940
Discharged	13.2.1946
Date of Birth	31.9.1911
Place of Birth	Fremantle, Western Australia
Father	Dennis Edward Barry
Mother	Jessie Barry
Religion	Roman Catholic
Pre-War Occupation	Farmhand and Chaff Cutter

HISTORY

Singapore	Selarang Camp Changi
	Serangoon Road Camp
	Selarang Barracks Changi
'H' Force Thailand	'H' Force Group No. 3
Singapore	Selarang Barracks Changi
	X10 Party
	Changi Gaol Camp
Return Details 1945	Not Known

JAMES WILLIAM BASELL

Rank	Private
Regimental Number	WX9195
Classification	Driver
Company	'C' Company Headquarters
Enlisted	30.10.1940
Discharged	13.12.1945
Date of Birth	21.5.1916
Place of Birth	Kelmscott, Western Australia
Father	Alfred John Basell
Mother	Esther Basell
Religion	Church of England
Pre-War Occupation	Butcher

HISTORY

Singapore	Selarang Camp and Barracks Changi
POW Number	4/5901
'D' Force Thailand	S Battalion
Camps Thailand	Kanu II, Tamuang, Chungkai, Nakom Nayok
Return Details 1945	Thailand-Singapore by aircraft
	Singapore-Labuan-Morotai-Townsville-Brisbane, R.A.A.F. aircraft A65-89
	Brisbane-Perth by troop train. 10.10.1945

EDWARD NIMROD BATES

Rank	Private
Regimental Number	WX9018
Classification	Rangetaker and Technical Storeman
Company	'A' Company
Enlisted	25.10.1940
Discharged	6.12.1945
Date of Birth	16.8.1916
Place of Birth	Mount Lawley, Western Australia
Father	Edward Russel Bates
Mother	Ruth Bates
Religion	Baptist
Pre-War Occupation	Railways Fireman

HISTORY

Singapore	Selarang Camp Changi
'A' Force Burma	Green Force, No. 3 Battalion
POW Number	1493
Camps Burma	Thanbyuzayat, Reptu 30km (evacuated several times to hospital)
Camps Thailand	Tamarkan, Non Pladuk (selected for Japan but did not join party due to illness)
	Ubon, Bangkok (go-downs)
Return Details 1945	Thailand-Singapore by aircraft
	Singapore-Fremantle, HMT *Highland Brigade*

FRANCIS JOHN BAXTER

Rank	Private
Regimental Number	WX8140
Company	'C' Company
Enlisted	16.8.1940
Discharged	13.3.1946
Date of Birth	4.4.1910
Place of Birth	Boulder, Western Australia
Father	Not Known
Mother	Hannah Baxter
Religion	Roman Catholic
Pre-War Occupation	Labourer

HISTORY

Singapore	Selarang Camp and Barracks Changi
POW Number	4/5904
Force	'F' Force Thailand
Singapore	Sime Road Camp
	Changi Gaol Camp
Return Details 1945	Singapore-Darwin-Sydney, 1st Netherlands Military Hospital Ship *Oranje*
	Sydney-Perth by troop train

THOMAS JAMES BEARD

Rank	Private
Regimental Number	WX9277
Company	'D' Company
Enlisted	30.10.1940
Discharged	30.1.1946
Date of Birth	13.1.1917
Place of Birth	Northam, Western Australia
Father	Stephen James Beard
Mother	Johanna Beard
Religion	Church of England
Pre-War Occupation	Truck Driver

HISTORY

Singapore	Selarang Camp Changi
'A' Force Burma	Green Force, No. 3 Battalion
POW Number	2758
Camps Burma	Khonkan 55km (tropical ulcer)
Camps Thailand	Tamarkan, Bangkok, Nikhe area
Return Details 1945	Singapore-Melbourne by aircraft
	Melbourne-Perth by troop train 17.10.1945
Additions	Wounded in action Lim Chu Kang Road on 8.2.1942 during the pull out from the No.13 Platoon position on the west coast of Singapore. Soldier was admitted to the 2/13th Australian General Hospital on 10.2.1942 with shrapnel wounds to the left knee and left wrist. Discharged to unit on 21.2.1942.

ALAN ROBERT BEATTIE

Rank	Private
Regimental Number	WX10791
Classification	Driver
Company	'A' Company
Enlisted	15.1.1941
Discharged	12.3.1946
Date of Birth	9.11.1922
Place of Birth	Perth, Western Australia
Father	Robert Murdie Beattie
Mother	Sadie Beattie
Religion	Methodist
Pre-War Occupation	Driver and Storeman

HISTORY

Java	'Blackforce'
Camps Java	Bicycle Camp Batavia
'D' Force Thailand	Java Party No. 6, P Battalion
Camps Thailand	Tamarkan, Tamuang
Camps Japan	*Rashin Maru* Party
POW Number	1983
Camps Japan	Fukuoka sub-Canp No. 13, Saganoseki
	Fukuoka sub-Camp No.17, Omuta
Return Details 1945	Nagasaki-Okinawa-Manila, USS *Cape Gloucester*
	Manila-Sydney, HMS *Speaker*, Sydney-Perth by troop train

PETER RODERICK BEATON

Rank	Lance Corporal
Regimental Number	WX14855
Classification	Despatch Rider
Company	'C' Company
Enlisted	7.7.1941
Discharged	1.5.1946
Date of Birth	15.4.1918
Place of Birth	Claremont, Western Australia
Father	Charles Beaton
Mother	Elizabeth Beaton
Religion	Church of England
Pre-War Occupation	Farmhand

HISTORY

Singapore	Selarang Camp Changi
'A' Force Burma	Green Force, No. 3 Battalion
POW Number	1544
Camps Burma	Reptu 30km (medical orderly, to Aungganaung 8.9.1943)
Camps Thailand	Linson Wood Camp, Tamuang
Return Details 1945	Thailand-Singapore by aircraft
	Singapore-Fremantle, HMT *Moreton Bay*

RONALD CLIFFORD BECKHAM

Rank	Private
Regimental Number	WX13421
Attached 2/4th	2.3.1942 from the 4th Anti-Tank Regiment
Enlisted	12.5.1941
Discharged	15.7.1946
Date of Birth	28.9.1924
Place of Birth	Fremantle, Western Australia
Father	Reauban Thomas Beckham
Mother	Olive Clotilde Beckham
Religion	Church of England
Pre-War Occupation	Farmhand

HISTORY

Singapore	Selarang Barracks Changi
'H' Force Thailand	'H' Force Group No. 3
Singapore	Sime Road Camp
	Changi Gaol Camp
	X10 Party
Return Details 1945	Singapore-Darwin-Sydney, HMT *Arawa*
	Sydney-Melbourne by troop train
	Melbourne-Fremantle, HMT *Strathmore*
Additions	Ron, who at sixteen, had enlisted underaged was formerly a Home Service soldier (Regimental Number W4800) on strength with the 5th AA Battery. On 17.4.1941 he stowed away on a transport to Singapore. On arrival he was charged and admonished and allotted the A.I.F. Regimental Number WX13421. He was then Taken on Strength with Headquarters A.I.F. Australian Base Ordnance and later transferred to the 4th Anti-Tank Regiment.

PHILIP JAMES BEILBY

Rank	Private
Regimental Number	WX12765
Classification	Motor Transport Fitter
Attached 2/4th	A.A.O.C.
Enlisted	12.5.1941
Discharged	13.8.1945
Date of Birth	12.11.1911
Place of Birth	Collie, Western Australia
Father	Albert Kenny Beilby
Mother	Agnes Sarah Beilby
Religion	Church of England
Pre-War Occupation	Motor Mechanic

HISTORY

Singapore	Selarang Camp Changi
'A' Force Burma	Green Force, No. 3 Battalion
POW Number	1584
Japan	*Rakuyo Maru* Party, Kumi No. 35 (rescued by USS *Queenfish*)
Return Details 1944	Saipan-Guadalcanal-Brisbane-Perth by aircraft 1.11.1944

EDWARD BELL

Rank	Warrant Officer Class 2
Regimental Number	WX691
Classification	Clerk
Company	Headquarters Company
Enlisted	10.11.1939
Discharged	10.4.1946
Date of Birth	4.5.1910
Place of Birth	Durham, England
Father	William Andrew Bell
Mother	Edith Bell
Religion	Church of England
Pre-War Occupation	Farmhand

HISTORY

Singapore	Selarang Camp and Barracks Changi
'D' Force Thailand	V Battalion (appointed quartermaster in charge of the cookhouse and rations)
Camps Thailand	Brankassi, Hindaine, Hindato, Onte, Kuii, Non Pladuk, Bangkok, Ubon
Return Details 1945	Thailand-Singapore by aircraft
	Singapore-Fremantle, HMHS *Karoa*
Additions	Soldier was an original member of the 2/11th Battalion. Following an injury during training in N.S.W. he was transferred to Western Command for three months sick leave. Later he transferred from the 2/11th to the 2/4th Machine Gun Battalion on 5.12.1940 also making him an original member of this battalion.

DANIEL EDMUND BEVIS

Rank	Corporal
Regimental Number	WX9061
Company	'C' Company
Enlisted	25.10.1940
Discharged	15.2.1946
Date of Birth	21.1.1909
Place of Birth	North Perth, Western Australia
Father	Daniel Bevis
Mother	Mary Banks Bevis
Religion	Church of England
Pre-War Occupation	Railways Fireman

HISTORY

Singapore	Selarang Camp Changi
'A' Force Burma	Green Force, No. 3 Battalion
POW Number	1368
Camps Thailand	(See Danny Bevis Diary, Thailand 1944-1945)
Return Details 1945	Thailand-Singapore by aircraft
	Singapore-Fremantle, HMT *Tamaroa*

HAROLD GEORGE BLAKISTON

Rank	Private
Regimental Number	WX7937
Classification	Driver
Company	'B' Company
Enlisted	13.8.1940
Discharged	14.1.1946
Date of Birth	29.5.1912
Place of Birth	York, Western Australian
Father	George John Blakiston
Mother	Mary Ellenor Blakiston
Religion	Church of England
Pre-War Occupation	Farmhand

HISTORY

Singapore	Selarang Camp Changi
	Johore Bahru, Adam Park
	Selarang Barracks Changi (Garden Control Party)
'D' Force Thailand	S Battalion
POW Number	8750
Camps Thailand	Kanu II, Kanu I River Camp (evacuated to Tarsau with cholera),
	Tardan (bridge repairs), Nacompaton (3 months), Tamuang, Tamarkan, Tamuang,
	Nakom Chassi, Chumphon
Return Details 1945	Thailand-Singapore by aircraft
	Singapore-Fremantle, HMT *Highland Brigade*

LESLIE ANDREW BLAIR

Rank	Private
Regimental Number	WX7308
Company	'D' Company
Enlisted	6.8.1940
Discharged	25.2.1946
Date of Birth	21.10.1907
Place of Birth	Cottesloe, Western Australia
Father	Roderick John Blair
Mother	Elsie May Blair
Religion	Methodist
Pre-War Occupation	Farmhand

HISTORY

Singapore	Selarang Camp Changi
'A' Force Burma	Green Force, No. 3 Battalion
POW Number	1525
Camps Burma	Khonkan 55km (1.7.1943)
Camps Thailand	Tamarkan, Chumphon, Kachu Mountain Camp, Petchaburi
Return Details 1945	Thailand-Singapore by aircraft
	Singapore-Fremantle, HMT *Highland Brigade*
Additions	Wounded in action Lim Chu Kang Road at 0300 hours on 9.2.1942. Admitted to Field Ambulance with a gunshot wound to the left leg. Transferred to the 2/10th Australian General Hospital on 17.2.1942. Discharged to unit on 22.2.1942.

COLIN BLAKEWAY

Rank	Lieutenant
Regimental Number	WX10322
Escort Officer Only	Fremantle-Java
Enlisted	18.12.1940
Appointment Terminated	27.11.1945
Date of Birth	16.6.1908
Place of Birth	Swansea, South Wales
Father	Roger Herbert Blakeway
Mother	Fanny Olive Blakeway
Religion	Church of England
Pre-War Occupation	Mechanical Engineer

HISTORY

Force	'Blackforce', attached to 'C' Company 2/3rd Machine Gun Battalion
Camps Java	Leles, Bicycle Camp Batavia
'A' Force Burma	Java Party No. 4, Williams Force
POW Number	4732
Camps Thailand	131km Camp, Tamarkan, Nakom Nayok, Bangkok
Return Details 1945	Thailand-Singapore by aircraft
	Singapore-Fremantle, HMT *Tamaroa*

RICHARD BERNARD BLASCHEK

Rank	Private
Regimental Number	WX8709
Classification	Stretcher Bearer
Company	Battalion Headquarters
Enlisted	23.10.1940
Discharged	16.1.1946
Date of Birth	6.6.1914
Place of Birth	Murray Bridge, South Australia
Father	William Valentine Blaschek
Mother	Pearl Blaschek
Religion	Roman Catholic
Pre-War Occupation	Farmer

HISTORY

Singapore	Selarang Camp and Barracks Changi
	X8 Party
	Changi Gaol Camp
Return Details 1945	Singapore-Darwin-Sydney, HMT *Arawa*
	Sydney-Melbourne by troop train
	Melbourne-Perth, HMT *Strathmore*

SAMUEL JAMES BLEWETT

Rank	Private
Regimental Number	WX8631
Classification	Rangetaker
Company	'A' Company
Enlisted	18.10.1940
Discharged	17.10.1946
Date of Birth	4.1.1914
Place of Birth	Gwalia, Western Australia
Father	Not Known
Mother	Mary Blewett
Religion	Methodist
Pre-War Occupation	Railways Porter

HISTORY

Singapore	Selarang Camp Changi
	Johore Bahru, Adam Park
	River Valley Road Camp
	Changi Gaol Camp
POW Number	3/6981
Return Details 1945	Singapore-Darwin-Melbourne, 1st Netherlands Military Hospital Ship *Oranje*
	Melbourne-Perth by troop train
Additions	This soldier suffered from asthma and as a result was not sent 'up country' on a work party. It is also likely that like several other asthma sufferers from the 2/4th that he spent some time at the Kranji Hospital Camp at Woodlands.

GEORGE REGINALD BOUSFIELD

Rank	Private
Regimental Number	WX7600
Company	'D' Company
Enlisted	6.8.1940
Discharged	14.2.1946
Date of Birth	8.8.1914
Place of Birth	Liverpool, England
Father	George Bousfield
Mother	Henrietta Bousfield
Religion	Atheist
Pre-War Occupation	Stockman

HISTORY

Java	'Blackforce'
Camps Java	Bicycle Camp Batavia
'A' Force Burma	Java Party No. 4, Williams Force
Camps Burma	Marched out from Aungganaung 105km Camp to Tamarkan on 27.2.1944 which would indicate that this soldier had worked with Williams No. 1 Mobile Force, down into Thailand.
Camps Thailand	Tamarkan, Nakom Nayok
Return Details 1945	Thailand-Singapore by aircraft
	Singapore-Fremantle, HMT *Moreton Bay*

WALTER VERDUN BOW

Rank	Private
Regimental Number	WX7253
Classification	Driver
Company	'D' Company Headquarters
Enlisted	1.8.1940
Discharged	14.3.1946
Date of Birth	19.3.1916
Place of Birth	Perth, Western Australia
Father	Harry Bow
Mother	Rachel Lambert Bow
Religion	Church of England
Pre-War Occupation	Blacksmith's Striker

Singapore	Selarang Camp Changi
	Thomson Road (Caldecot Hill Estate Camp)
	River Valley Road Camp
	Selarang Barracks Changi
POW Number	3/7016
'D' Force Thailand	V Battalion
Camps Thailand	Brankassi, Hindaine, Hindato, Nacompaton, Bangkok (go-downs), Japanese Transport Camp just out of Bangkok to repair trucks. Accompanied by Swift and Manthorpe.
Return Details 1945	Thailand-Rangoon by aircraft
	Rangoon-Singapore, HMT *Highland Brigade*
	Singapore-Fremantle, HMT *Moreton Bay*
Additions	Wounded in action at Buona Vista on 15.2.1942. Admitted to the 2/13th Australian General Hospital on 16.2.1942 with shrapnel wounds to the left and right buttocks. Discharged to unit on 22.2.1942.

KEVIN CHARLES BOYLE

Rank	Lieutenant
Regimental Number	WX3483
Company	'C' Company
Enlisted	17.12.1940
Appointment Terminated	4.2.1946
Date of Birth	26.5.1911
Place of Birth	York, Western Australia
Father	Thomas William Boyle
Mother	Bertha Annie Boyle
Religion	Church of England
Pre-War Occupation	Grazier

HISTORY

Singapore	Selarang Camp Changi (Market Garden)
'A' Force Burma	Green Force, No. 3 Battalion
POW Number	1291
Camps Thailand	Joined Williams No.1 Mobile Force and worked down into Thailand to the Nikhe area. Tamarkan, Kanchanaburi (Officer's Group No. 7), Bangkok
Return Details 1945	Thailand-Rangoon by aircraft
	Rangoon-Singapore, HMT *Highland Brigade*
	Singapore-Brisbane-Perth by aircraft
Additions	Wounded in action Ulu Pandan on 12.2.1942 whilst on reconnaissance of Hill 200. Admitted to the 2/13th Australian General Hospital with bayonet wounds to the right leg and arm. Discharged to unit on 22.2.1942.

FRANZ BRACKLEMANN

Rank	Lance Corporal
Regimental Number	WX8796
Company	'D' Company
Enlisted	23.10.1940
Discharged	18.12.1945
Date of Birth	28.4.1905
Place of Birth	Kalgoorlie, Western Australia
Father	Peter Niclaus Franz Bracklemann
Mother	Lucy Anne Bracklemann
Religion	Presbyterian
Pre-War Occupation	Book Keeper and Traveller

HISTORY

Singapore	Selarang Camp Changi
	Johore Bahru, Adam Park
	Sime Road Camp
	Selarang Barracks Changi
	X3 Party
	Changi Gaol Camp
Return Details 1945	Singapore-Darwin-Sydney, HMT *Arawa*
	Sydney-Melbourne by troop train
	Melbourne-Fremantle, HMT *Strathmore*
Additions	Franz was admitted to the Australian General Hospital at Roberts Barracks Changi on 16.4.1943 with an abscess to the cornea. Previous to this he had been suffering from amblyopia (impaired vision) which might explain why Franz remained in Singapore. Soldier was wounded in action at Lim Chu Kang Road on the west coast of Singapore at 2100 hours on 8.2.1942. It is reported that Franz attacked a group of Japanese with bayonet and could have killed as many as eight of the enemy. He was evacuated to the 2/10th Australian General Hospital at Oldham Hall Singapore with a compound fracture to the scalp caused by a bullet wound. Transferred to the 2/13th Australian General Hospital at St Patrick's School on 17.2.1942. Discharged to unit on 22.2.1942.

No. 13 Platoon men relaxing. The man far left at rear is Franz.

NORMAN BRADSHAW

Rank	Lance Corporal
Regimental Number	WX9090
Company	'C' Company Headquarters
Enlisted	25.10.1940
Discharged	25.2.1946
Date of Birth	12.12.1916
Place of Birth	Perth, Western Australia
Father	John Bradshaw
Mother	Mary Ann Bradshaw
Religion	Church of England
Pre-War Occupation	Labourer

HISTORY

Singapore	Selarang Camp Changi
	Mount Pleasant Camp
	Selarang Barracks Changi
'D' Force Thailand	S Battalion
POW Number	8738
Camps Thailand	Kanu II, Chungkai, Tamunag
Return Details 1945	Thailand-Singapore by aircraft
	Singapore-Fremantle, HMT *Tamaroa*

GEORGE HOWARD BRANSON

Rank	Lieutenant
Regimental Number	WX10372
Company	'A' Company
Enlisted	18.12.1940
Appointment Terminated	22.11.1946
Date of Birth	23.2.1918
Place of Birth	Subiaco, Western Australia
Father	Howard Henry Branson
Mother	Ethel May Branson
Religion	Church of England
Pre-War Occupation	Sales Manager

HISTORY

Singapore	Selarang Camp Changi
	Johore Bahru, Adam Park
	Sime Road Camp
	Selarang Barracks Changi
POW Number	4/4079
'H' Force Thailand	H6 Officer's Party
	'H' Force No. 1 Sub-Section
Singapore	Sime Road Camp
	Serangoon Road Camp
	Changi Gaol Camp
Return Details 1945	Singapore-Darwin-Sydney, HMT *Arawa*
	Sydney-Melbourne by troop train
	Melbourne-Fremantle, HMT *Strathmore*
Additions	Replaced Lieutenant J. C. Morrison on his evacuation to hospital with dengue fever.

WALTER EDWARD BREED

Rank	Sergeant (Promoted 14.2.1942)
Regimental Number	WX9229
Company	'B' Company
Enlisted	30.10.1940
Discharged	15.1.1946
Date of Birth	25.6.1902
Place of Birth	London, England
Father	Alfred Breed
Mother	Agnes Breed
Religion	Church of England
Pre-War Occupation	Farmer

HISTORY

Singapore	Selarang Camp and Barracks Changi
POW Number	3/6014
'D' Force Thailand	S Battalion
POW Number	8726
Camps Thailand	Kanu II, Chungkai, Nacompaton
Return Details 1945	Singapore-Perth by aircraft on 9.10.1945
Additions	Missing in action from 10.2.1942. Known to have joined up with 'A' Company 2/4th Machine Gun Battalion and fought with this Company until the surrender on 15.2.1942.

GORDON GUYTON BREEZE

Rank	Lance Corporal
Regimental Number	WX11573
Company	'C' Company
Enlisted	9.4.1941
Discharged	27.2.1946
Date of Birth	23.6.1910
Place of Birth	Great Yarmouth, England
Father	Henry George Breeze
Mother	Edith Sarah Breeze
Religion	Salvation Army
Pre-War Occupation	Railway Repairer

HISTORY

Singapore	Selarang Camp Changi
	Johore Bahru, Adam Park
	Selarang Barracks Changi
POW Number	3/7055
'D' Force Thailand	S Battalion
POW Number	8757
Camps Thailand	Kanu II, Kanu I River Camp (evacuated sick), Chungkai, Nacompaton
Return Details 1945	Thailand-Singapore by aircraft
	Singapore-Fremantle, 2/1st H.M. Australian Hospital Ship *Manunda*

ROY ALBERT BRIGGS

Rank	Private
Regimental Number	WX7329
Classification	Rangetaker
Company	'B' Company
Enlisted	6.8.1940
Discharged	11.2.1946
Date of Birth	4.1.1915
Place of Birth	North Perth, Western Australia
Father	Frederick George Briggs
Mother	Edith Briggs
Religion	Church of England
Pre-War Occupation	Not Known

HISTORY

Singapore	Selarang Camp and Barracks Changi
'D' Force Thailand	S Battalion
POW Number	8751
Camps Thailand	Konkoita, (Sonkurai to Nikhe-Nikhe Defence Line from May 1945)
Return Details 1945	Thailand-Singapore by aircraft
	Melbourne-Perth by troop train

ALBERT BROOKSBANK

Rank	Private
Regimental Number	WX9316
Classification	Batman/Runner
Company	'B' Company Headquarters
Enlisted	30.10.1940
Discharged	11.1.1946
Date of Birth	16.11.1900
Place of Birth	Leeds, England
Father	Not Known
Mother	Martha Brooksbank
Religion	Salvation Army
Pre-War Occupation	Miner

HISTORY

Singapore	Selarang Camp and Barracks Changi (Garden Control Party)
	Changi Gaol Camp
POW Number	1/7100
Return Details 1945	Singapore-Darwin-Sydney, HMT *Arawa*
	Sydney-Melbourne by troop train
	Melbourne-Fremantle, HMT *Strathmore*

RONALD EDMUND BROWN

Rank	Private
Regimental Number	WX12335
Company	'B' Company
Enlisted	2.5.1941
Discharged	31.1.1946
Date of Birth	29.5.1917
Place of Birth	Arthur River, Western Australia
Father	Algenon Edmund Brown
Mother	Alice Rose Brown
Religion	Church of England
Pre-War Occupation	Timber Worker

HISTORY

Singapore	Selarang Camp Changi
	Serangoon Road Camp
	Selarang Barracks Changi
POW Number	4/5953
'D' Force Thailand	Captain Harris Party
French Indo-China	*Both* Party
Return Details 1945	Saigon-Bangkok-Singapore by aircraft
	Singapore-Sydney, HMT *Highland Chieftan*
	Sydney-Perth by troop train

ARTHUR CRIGHTON BRUCE

Rank	Private
Regimental Number	WX10841
Company	Battalion Headquarters
Enlisted	15.1.1941
Discharged	21.2.1946
Date of Birth	23.5.1915
Place of Birth	North Fremantle, Western Australia
Father	Robert Findley Bruce
Mother	Susan Bruce
Religion	Presbyterian
Pre-War Occupation	Labourer

HISTORY

Singapore	Selarang Camp and Barracks Changi
	X6 Party
	Changi Gaol Camp
POW Number	3/7112
Return Details 1945	Singapore-Darwin-Sydney, HMT *Arawa*
	Sydney-Melbourne by troop train
	Melbourne-Perth, HMT *Strathmore*

JOHN ROBERTSON BUCHAN

Rank	Private
Regimental Number	WX17545
Company	'E' Company, Special Reserve Battalion
Enlisted	4.11.1941
Discharged	3.5.1946
Date of Birth	24.10.1906
Place of Birth	Lerwick, Shetland Islands, Scotland
Father	James Walker Buchan
Mother	Flora Buchan
Religion	Church of England
Pre-War Occupation	Fettler

HISTORY

Singapore	Selarang Camp Changi
'A' Force Burma	Green Force, No. 3 Battalion
POW Number	1515
Camps	Williams No.1 Mobile Force, worked down into Thailand to the Nikhe area.
Camps Thailand	Tamarkan, Chungkai, Petchaburi, Nakon Nayok, Lopburi, Bangkok
Return Details 1945	Thailand to Rangoon by aircraft
	Rangoon-Singapore by aircraft
	Singapore-Brisbane by aircraft
	Brisbane-Perth by troop train 17.10.1945

EDWARD WILLIAM HENRY BUNCE

Rank	Private
Regimental Number	WX9278
Classification	Driver
Company	'D' Company
Enlisted	30.10.1940
Discharged	21.1.1946
Date of Birth	15.2.1913
Place of Birth	Aldershot, England
Father	Edward Bunce
Mother	Alice Bunce
Religion	Methodist
Pre-War Occupation	Farmer

HISTORY

Singapore	Selarang Camp and Barracks Changi
POW Number	4546
'D' Force Thailand	S Battalion
POW Number	8758
Camps Thailand	Kanu II, Tamuang
Japan	*Rashin Maru* Party
Camps Japan	Yamane
	Niihama
Return Details 1945	Wakayama-Okinawa, USS *Sanctuary*
	Okinawa-Manila, USS *Bingham*
	Manila-Darwin, B24 Liberator aircraft A72-121
	Darwin-Perth by aircraft 20.10.1945

HAROLD THOMAS BUNKER

Rank	Private
Regimental Number	WX9223
Classification	Rangetaker
Company	'A' Company
Enlisted	30.10.1940
Discharged	6.6.1945
Date of Birth	26.9.1920
Place of Birth	Mount Barker, Western Australia
Father	George Edward Bunker
Mother	Annie Ansit Bunker
Religion	Methodist
Pre-War Occupation	Orchardist

HISTORY

Singapore	Selarang Camp Changi
'A' Force Burma	Green Force, No. 3 Battalion
POW Number	1509
Japan	*Rakuyo Maru* Party, Kumi No. 35 (rescued by USS *Queenfish*)
Return Details 1944	Saipan-Guadalcanal-Brisbane-Perth by aircraft 1.11.1944
Additions	Wounded in action on 15.2.1942 at Buona Vista, but soldier remained on duty.

GAVIN McRAE BUNNING

Rank	Captain
Regimental Number	WX3452
Company	'B' Company Headquarters
Enlisted	21.11.1940
Appointment Terminated	20.12.1945
Date of Birth	20.7.1910
Place of Birth	Cottesloe, Western Australia
Father	Robert Bunning
Mother	Helen Marion Bunning
Religion	Presbyterian
Pre-War Occupation	Company Director

HISTORY

Singapore	Selarang Camp and Barracks Changi
	Changi Gaol Camp
POW Number	1/690
Return Details 1945	Singapore-Darwin-Sydney, HMT *Arawa*
	Sydney-Melbourne by troop train
	Melbourne-Perth, HMT *Strathmore*
Additions	Tom as he was more commonly known, acted as the Senior 2/4th Machine Gun Battalion Officer for two years and as the Changi Garden Control Officer from May 1942.

GREGORY LACHLAN BURDON

Rank	Private
Regimental Number	WX7542
Company	'C' Company
Enlisted	6.8.1940
Discharged	6.2.1946
Date of Birth	17.3.1920
Place of Birth	Perth, Western Australia
Father	John Jervis Burdon
Mother	Alice Burdon
Religion	Methodist
Pre-War Occupation	Carpenter

HISTORY

Singapore	Selarang Camp Changi
	Johore Bahru, Adam Park
	Sime Road Camp
	Selarang Barracks Changi
POW Number	4/5958
'D' Force Thailand	V Battalion
POW Number	2225
Camps Thailand	Hintok River Camp (3 weeks at Pack of Cards Bridge), Kinsaiyok, Rin Tin, Kuii, Chungkai (evacuated sick by barge), Non Pladuk No. 2 Hospital Camp, Tamajao Wood Camp, Nacompaton, Prachuab Kirikhan-Mergui Escape Road
Return Details 1945	Flown out to Kachu Mountain Camp by aircraft
	Kachu Mountain Camp-Singapore by aircraft
	Singapore-Fremantle, HMT *Highland Brigade*

ALFRED JOHN BURGESS

Rank	Private
Regimental Number	WX15756
Company	Battalion Headquarters
Enlisted	13.8.1941
Discharged	12.3.1946
Date of Birth	27.12.1919
Place of Birth	Maylands, Western Australia
Father	John Burgess
Mother	Margaret Burgess
Religion	Church of England
Pre-War Occupation	Labourer

HISTORY

Singapore	Reported missing from Ulu Pandan 12.2.1942
Sumatra Camps	Padang, Gloe Gloer Camp (Medan)
Singapore	*Harukiku Maru*, SS *Van Waerwjick* Party (rescued)
Camps	Changi Gaol Camp from 28.6.1944
Return Details 1945	Singapore-Darwin-Melbourne, 1st Netherlands Military Hospital Ship *Oranje*
	Melbourne-Perth by troop train
Additions	Originally Special Reserve Battalion then transferred to Battalion Headquarters from the 2/4th reinforcement pool. Escaped to Sumatra.

EDWARD JOHN BURGESS

Rank	Private
Regimental Number	WX16405
Company	'E' Company, Special Reserve Battalion
Enlisted	10.9.1941
Discharged	11.12.1945
Date of Birth	26.1.1906
Place of Birth	Boulder, Western Australia
Father	Sydney Albert Burgess
Mother	Emily Burgess
Religion	Methodist
Pre-War Occupation	Miner

HISTORY

Singapore	Selarang Camp Changi
'A' Force Burma	Green Force, No. 3 Battalion
POW Number	3114
Camps	Reptu 30km Hospital Camp from Aungganaung 105km Camp, (August 1943)
	Aungganaung 105km Camp from Reptu (September 1943)
	Joined Williams No. 1 Mobile Force and worked down into Thailand to the Nikhe area.
Camps Thailand	Tamarkan, Nikhe Wood Camp (1944)
Return Details 1945	Thailand-Singapore by aircraft
	Singapore-Fremantle, HMT *Tamaroa*

WILLIAM BURGESS

Rank	Warrant Officer Class 2
Regimental Number	WX8098
Company	'A' Company
Enlisted	16.8.1940
Discharged	12.6.1946
Date of Birth	12.12.1905
Place of Birth	Belfast, Ireland
Father	Thomas Henry Burgess
Mother	Not Known
Religion	Church of England
Pre-War Occupation	Gold Miner

HISTORY

Singapore	Selarang Camp Changi
	Johore Bahru, Adam Park
	Sime Road Camp
	Selarang Barracks Changi
POW Number	4/4455
'D' Force Thailand	S Battalion
POW Number	8714
Camps Thailand	Tamuang, Chungkai
Return Details 1945	Thailand-Singapore by aircraft
	Singapore-Fremantle, HMT *Tamaroa*
Additions	Unofficially held the rank of Captain. Adjutant of Major Cough's Adam Park group.

ARTHUR JOHN BURNS

Rank	Corporal (Promoted 16.9.1944)
Regimental Number	WX7333
Company	'B' Company
Enlisted	6.8.1940
Discharged	23.6.1945
Date of Birth	11.11.1919
Place of Birth	Subiaco, Western Australia
Father	Not Known
Mother	Not Known
Religion	Church of England
Pre-War Occupation	Dry Cleaner

HISTORY

Java	Embarked on HMT *Marella* for Java 30.1.1942, disembarked Java 13.2.1942. Evacuated sick to the 2/12th Australian General Hospital Ceylon on 4.3.1942. Disembarked Fremantle ex-Ceylon on 6.5.1942.
Australia	1. 25th Australian Divisional Cavalry
	2. Guerilla Warfare Group
	3. 43rd Water Transport Company

COPELAND JAMES BURNS

Rank	Private
Regimental Number	WX7316
Company	'B' Company
Enlisted	6.8.1940
Discharged	3.4.1946
Date of Birth	16.5.1917
Place of Birth	Moora, Western Australia
Father	William Burns
Mother	Ada Francis Burns
Religion	Church of England
Pre-War Occupation	Shop Assistant

HISTORY

Singapore	Selarang Camp Changi
	Johore Bahru, Adam Park
	Selarang Barracks Changi
'D' Force Thailand	S Battalion
POW Number	8752
Camps Thailand	Kanu II, Kanu I River Camp (evacuated sick to Tarsau by barge), Kinsaiyok, Konkoita, Tarsau, Chungkai, Nacompaton, Nihke-Nihke Wood Camp, Sonkurai, Kanchanaburi, Bangkok (Sports Stadium)
Return Details 1945	Thailand-Singapore by aircraft
	Singapore-Fremantle, HMT *Highland Brigade*

GEORGE NATHANIEL BURSLEM

Rank	Private
Regimental Number	WX7661
Company	'C' Company
Enlisted	10.8.1940
Discharged	17.5.1946
Date of Birth	13.5.1900
Place of Birth	Carlton, Victoria
Father	Not Known
Mother	W.T. Burslem
Religion	Roman Catholic
Pre-War Occupation	Miner

HISTORY

Singapore	Selarang Camp and Barracks Changi
'D' Force Thailand	S Battalion
POW Number	8756
Camps Thailand	Chungkai, Tamuang, Linson Wood Camp
POW Number (Linson)	16618
Return Details 1945	Thailand-Singapore by aircraft
	Singapore-Morotai-Sydney by aircraft
	Sydney-Perth by troop train 10.10.1945

THOMAS HENRY BUSCOMBE

Rank	Private
Regimental Number	WX7790
Classification	Scout
Company	'B' Company
Enlisted	10.8.1940
Discharged	14.2.1946
Date of Birth	2.5.1917
Place of Birth	Mt Hawthorn, Western Australia
Father	David Alexander Buscombe
Mother	Margaret Buscombe
Religion	Roman Catholic
Pre-War Occupation	Miner

HISTORY

Singapore	Selarang Camp Changi
	Johore Bahru, Adam Park
	Selarang Barracks Changi
'D' Force Thailand	S Battalion
POW Number	8753
Camps Thailand	Nakom Nayok, Bangkok
Return Details 1945	Thailand-Singapore by aircraft
	Singapore-Fremantle, H.M. Hospital Ship *Karoa*

LEO PATRICK BYRNE

Rank	Private
Regimental Number	WX6155
Company	'C' Company
Enlisted	13.7.1940
Discharged	29.6.1942 (medically unfit)
Date of Birth	12.1.1906
Place of Birth	York, Western Australia
Father	Frederick Byrne
Mother	Mary Byrne
Religion	Roman Catholic
Pre-War Occupation	Miner

HISTORY

Java	'Blackforce', attached to 2/3rd Machine Gun Battalion
	Admitted to hospital from 18.2.1942 to 25.2.1942.
	Embarked on H.M. Hospital Ship *Wuseh* on 25.2.1942.
	Admitted to the 2/12th Australian General Hospital at Columbo (Ceylon) on 4.3.1942.
	Returned by ship to Melbourne and by train to Perth.
Additions	The Hospital Ship *Wuseh* departed Singapore on 9.2.1942. This ship then departed Tanjong Priok, Batavia, crowded with patients.

JOHN NICHOLAS CAIMANOS

Rank	Private
Regimental Number	WX9261
Company	'B' Company
Enlisted	30.10.1940
Discharged	27.5.1946
Date of Birth	28.12.1898
Place of Birth	Albany, Western Australia
Father	Christophia Caimanos
Mother	Louisa Esther Caimanos
Religion	Church of England
Pre-War Occupation	Foreman with the Roads Board

HISTORY

Singapore	Selarang Camp and Barracks Changi
'D' Force Thailand	S Battalion
POW Number	8765
Camps Thailand	Kanu II, Kanu I River Camp, Tarsau (evacuated sick by barge), Kinsaiyok, Konkoita, Tarsau, Tamuang, Chungkai
Return Details 1945	Thailand-Singapore by aircraft
	Singapore-Fremantle, HMT *Moreton Bay*

WILLIAM ERNEST CAKE

Rank	Private
Regimental Number	WX12661
Company	'A' Company
Enlisted	9.5.1941
Discharged	6.3.1946
Date of Birth	15.1.1915
Place of Birth	Albany, Western Australia
Father	Ernest William Cake
Mother	Jane Cake
Religion	Church of England
Pre-War Occupation	Farmhand

HISTORY

Singapore	Selarang Camp Changi
'A' Force Burma	Green Force, No. 3 Battalion
POW Number	9353
Camps Burma	Tavoy, Ye, Tavoy (May-November 1942)
Japan	*Awa Maru* Party, Kumi No. 40
POW Number	1318
Camps Japan	Fukuoka sub-Camp No. 17, Omuta
Return Details 1945	Nagasaki-Okinawa-Manila, USS *Cape Gloucester*
	Manila-Morotai-Darwin, PBY Catalina aircraft A24-201
	Darwin-Perth, B24 Liberator aircraft 14.10.1945

MAURICE WILLIAM CALDWELL

Rank	Private
Regimental Number	WX10365
Company	Battalion Headquarters
Enlisted	18.12.1940
Discharged	10.1.1946
Date of Birth	7.1.1906
Place of Birth	Subiaco, Western Australia
Father	Maurice William Caldwell
Mother	Mary Ann Gordon Caldwell
Religion	Roman Catholic
Pre-War Occupation	Hairdresser

HISTORY

Java	'Blackforce', attached to 2/2nd Pioneer Battalion
Camps Java	Bandoeng, Soekamiskin Prison, Tjimahi Camp No. 4
Return Details 1945	Not Known
Additions	Listed as missing in action. Soldier had been sent to Bandoeng by Captain Albrecht to collect supplies but collapsed with dengue fever and was admitted to hospital by the Dutch and became separated from his unit. Soldier was captured by the Japanese on 15.4.1942.

COLIN CAMERON

Rank	Major (Promoted 14.2.1942)
Regimental Number	WX3451
Awards	Mentioned in Despatches
Company	'C' Company Headquarters
Enlisted	5.12.1940
Discharged	6.2.1946
Date of Birth	13.9.1900
Place of Birth	Digby, Victoria
Father	George Alexander Voege
Mother	Flora Ann Voege
Religion	Presbyterian
Pre-War Occupation	Farmer

HISTORY

Singapore	Selarang Camp Changi (Market Garden)
'A' Force Burma	Green Force, No. 3 Battalion
POW Number	2613
Camps Burma	Reptu 30km Camp from Aungganaung 105km Camp 28.10.1943
Camps Thailand	Tamarkan, Chungkai, Kanchanaburi
Return Details 1945	Thailand-Rangoon-Singapore-Perth by aircraft
Additions	Name change from Voege to Cameron in 1931. This Officer was promoted on the death of Lieutenant-Colonel M. J. Anketell.

GRAEME KEATS CAMERON

Rank	Corporal (Promoted on 15.2.1942)
Regimental Number	WX11226
Company	'B' Company
Enlisted	31.3.1941
Discharged	18.1.1946
Date of Birth	2.7.1917
Place of Birth	Perth, Western Australia
Father	Robert Alan Cameron
Mother	Lucy Gwendoline Cameron
Religion	Church of England
Pre-War Occupation	Broadcast Announcer and Law Student

HISTORY

Singapore	Selarang Camp Changi
	Johore Bahru, Adam Park
	Selarang Barracks Changi
POW Number	4/5971
'D' Force Thailand	V Battalion
Camps Thailand	Tamarkan Hospital Camp No. 2 (7.5.1943-15.10.1943)
	Kanchanaburi Base Camp No.1, Non Pladuk, Ubon
	(possibly worked on the Sonkurai-Nikhe Defence Line during 1945)
Return Details 1945	Thailand-Singapore by aircraft
	Singapore-Fremantle, HMT *Moreton Bay*
Additions	Soldier received a mortar blast to the left ear in the early stages of the fighting on Singapore. Missing in action from 10.2.1942 but joined 'A' Company 2/4th Machine Gun Battalion and fought with this Company until the surrender on 15.2.1942.

RANDOLF STUART CAMPBELL

Rank	Staff Sergeant
Regimental Number	WX9556
Company	'B' Company Headquarters
Enlisted	4.12.1940
Discharged	31.5.1946
Date of Birth	10.6.1906
Place of Birth	Kirkcubright, Scotland
Father	Randolf Stuart Campbell
Mother	Margaret Campbell
Religion	Presbyterian
Pre-War Occupation	Not Known

HISTORY

Singapore	Selarang Camp Changi
	Serangoon Road Camp
	Selarang Barracks Changi
	Changi Gaol Camp
Return Details 1945	Singapore-Darwin-Sydney, HMT *Arawa*
	Sydney-Melbourne by troop train
	Melbourne-Fremantle, HMT *Strathmore*

WILLIAM CARLYON

Rank	Private
Regimental Number	WX15785
Company	Headquarters Company
Enlisted	13.8.1941
Discharged	7.2.1946
Date of Birth	27.1.1905
Place of Birth	Northampton, Western Australia
Father	Not Known
Mother	Julia Carlyon
Religion	Salvation Army
Pre-War Occupation	Stationhand

HISTORY

Singapore	Selarang Camp Changi
'A' Force Burma	Green Force, No. 3 Battalion
Camps Thailand	Tamarkan, Chungkai, Linson Wood Camp, Nacompaton
POW Number (Linson)	12127
Return Details 1945	Thailand-Singapore by aircraft
	Singapore-Fremantle, H.M. Hospital Ship *Karoa*

FRANK VINCENT CARROLL

Rank	Private
Regimental Number	WX9551
Classification	Driver
Company	'C' Company
Enlisted	4.12.1940
Discharged	21.3.1946
Date of Birth	26.7.1908
Place of Birth	York, Western Australia
Father	Robert Carroll
Mother	Maud Carroll
Religion	Church of England
Pre-War Occupation	Labourer

HISTORY

Java	'Blackforce'
Camps Java	Bandoeng, Tjimahi, Bicycle Camp Batavia
Return Details 1945	Singapore-Fremantle, HMT *Tamaroa*

DOUGLAS NEWINGTON HUNTER CARTER

Rank	Sergeant (Promoted 28.2.1942)
Regimental Number	WX8240
Company	'B' Company
Enlisted	16.8.1940
Discharged	18.12.1945
Date of Birth	22.7.1916
Place of Birth	Claremont, Western Australia
Father	Rupert Newington Carter
Mother	Dorothy Margaret Carter
Religion	Presbyterian
Pre-War Occupation	Bank Teller

HISTORY

Java	'Blackforce', attached to 2/3rd Machine Gun Battalion then Composite Battalion.
Camps Java	Soekaboemi (2.4.1942-June 1942), Tjimahi, Bandoeng, Makasura
'D' Force Thailand	Java Party No. 6, O Battalion
POW Number	6909
Camps Thailand	Evacuated sick to Tarsau, suffering from malaria and enteritis 5.9.1943
Japan	*Rashin Maru* Party
POW Number	278
Camps Japan	Ohama Camp No.9B
Return Details 1945	Ohama-Wakayama by troop train
	Wakayama-Okinawa, USS *Sanctuary*
	Okinawa-Manila, USS *Haskel*
	No other details are known.

WILFRED THOMAS CASTLES

Rank	Corporal (Promoted on 11.2.1942)
Regimental Number	WX8792
Classification	Scout
Company	'B' Company
Enlisted	23.10.1940
Discharged	17.12.1945
Date of Birth	26.4.1917
Place of Birth	Subiaco, Western Australia
Father	Albert Thomas Castles
Mother	Not Known
Religion	Roman Catholic
Pre-War Occupation	Miner

HISTORY

Singapore	Selarang Camp Changi
'A' Force Burma	Green Force, No. 3 Battalion
POW Number	1531
Camps Burma	Evacuated to Khonkan 55km Hospital Camp on 5.7.1943
Camps Thailand	Tamarkan, Kanchanaburi, Hindato, Chungkai, Ratburi, Petchaburi, Bangkok, Nakom Nayok (see Danny Bevis Diary)
Return Details 1945	Bangkok-Singapore by aircraft Singapore-Morotai-Sydney-Perth by aircraft

ALFRED THOMAS JAMES CATO

Rank	Private
Regimental Number	WX9060
Classification	Despatch Rider
Company	'D' Company
Enlisted	25.10.1940
Discharged	28.2.1946
Date of Birth	12.6.1909
Place of Birth	Broken Hill, New South Wales
Father	James Edward Cato
Mother	Mabel Emily Cato
Religion	Methodist
Pre-War Occupation	Locomotive Fireman

HISTORY

Singapore	Selarang Camp Changi Johore Bahru, Adam Park Selarang Barracks Changi
POW Number	4/5981
'D' Force Thailand	S and U Battalions
POW Number	8759
Camps Thailand	Tarsau, Tarsau North, Tonchan South, Tonchan Central, Kanu I, Kanu II, Hintok River Camp, Kinsaiyok, Hintok Road Camp, Hintok River Camp, Tarsau, Tamuang, Wampo, Kinsaiyok, Kanu II, Kinsaiyok, Chungkai, Tamarkan, Tardan Bridge, Tarsau, Tamuang, Pratchai, Bangkok.
Return Details 1945	Thailand-Singapore by aircraft Singapore-Fremantle, HMT *Highland Brigade*

CYRIL NICHOLS CHAMBERLAIN

Rank	Private
Regimental Number	WX16425
Classification	Batman/Runner
Company	'E' Company, Special Reserve Battalion
Enlisted	10.9.1941
Discharged	30.5.1946
Date of Birth	22.8.1904
Place of Birth	Lancaster, England
Father	Ernest Chamberlain
Mother	Ivy Florence Chamberlain
Religion	Church of England
Pre-War Occupation	Pipe Fitter

HISTORY

Singapore	Selarang Camp and Barracks Changi
POW Number	4/5983
'D' Force Thailand	V Battalion
Camps Thailand	Tamarkan, Nacompaton
Return Details 1945	Thailand-Singapore by aircraft
	Singapore-Sydney, HMT *Highland Chieftan*
	Sydney-Melbourne-Perth by troop train

GEORGE KEITH CHATFIELD

Rank	Private
Regimental Number	WX11279
Company	'C' Company
Enlisted	5.4.1941
Discharged	14.2.1946
Date of Birth	22.8.1911
Place of Birth	Northam, Western Australia
Father	Levin Owen Chatfield
Mother	Catherine Chatfield
Religion	Church of England
Pre-War Occupation	Truck Driver

HISTORY

Singapore	Selarang Camp Changi
	Johore Bahru, Adam Park
	Selarang Barracks Changi
POW Number	4/5986
'D' Force Thailand	S Battalion
POW Number	8762
Japan	*Rashin Maru* Party
POW Number	1585
Camps Japan	Yamane
	Niihama
Return Details 1945	Wakayama-Okinawa, USS *Sanctuary*
	Okinawa-Manila, USS *Bingham*
	Manila-Sydney, HMS *Speaker*
	Sydney-Melbourne-Perth by troop train

JOHN MURRAY COLVILLE CHEYNE

Rank	Sergeant
Regimental Number	WX9388
Classification	Clerk
Attached 2/4th	Australian Army Postal Corps
Enlisted	19.11.1940
Discharged	12.12.1945
Date of Birth	24.10.1919
Place of Birth	Cottesloe, Western Australia
Father	Charles Campbell Cheyne
Mother	Ina Millicent Cheyne
Religion	Church of England
Pre-War Occupation	Clerk and Regular Soldier

HISTORY

Singapore	Selarang Camp Changi
'A' Force Burma	Green Force, No. 3 Battalion
POW Number	2671
Japan	*Rakuyo Maru* Party, Kumi No. 36 (removed from draft at Singapore)
Singapore	Changi Gaol Camp, (attached to Changi Administration 28.1.1945)
	Levelling Party Changi Aerodrome
Return Details 1945	Singapore-Darwin-Sydney, HMT *Arawa*
	Sydney-Melbourne by troop train
	Melbourne-Fremantle, HMT *Strathmore*

JAMES PATRICK CLANCY

Rank	Corporal (Promoted on 11.2.1942)
Regimental Number	WX7122
Company	'D' Company
Enlisted	1.8.1940
Discharged	11.2.1945
Date of Birth	27.11.1918
Place of Birth	Wagin, Western Australia
Father	Peter Clancy
Mother	Catherine Clancy
Religion	Roman Catholic
Pre-War Occupation	Miner

HISTORY

Singapore	Selarang Camp Changi
	Johore Bahru, Adam Park
	Selarang Camp Changi
Force	Japan 'B' Party Korea
POW Number	1199
Camps Korea	Keijo, Jinsen
Camps Manchuria	Hoten
Return Details 1945	Hoten-Port Arthur by train
	Port Arthur-Okinawa-Manila, USS *Refuge* and USS *Noble*
	Manila-Sydney, HMS *Formidable*
	Sydney-Perth by troop train
Additions	Admitted to the 2/10th Australian General Hospital suffering from shell shock and a leg wound on 11.2.1942. Discharged to unit 20.2.1942.

BASIL WILLIAM JAMES CLARKE

Rank	Lance Corporal (Promoted on 18.1.1942)
Regimental Number	WX9136
Company	'C' Company
Enlisted	30.10.1940
Discharged	22.2.1946
Date of Birth	25.12.1915
Place of Birth	Northam, Western Australia
Father	William Jesse Clarke
Mother	Daisy Linda Clarke
Religion	Methodist
Pre-War Occupation	Farmhand

HISTORY

Singapore	Selarang Camp Changi
'A' Force Burma	Green Force, No. 3 Battalion
POW Number	2743
Camps Burma	Evacuated from Aungganaung 105km to Khonkan 55km Camp on 3.7.1943 with a tropical ulcer. Soldier's right leg was amputated through middle of thigh 22.9.1943.
Camps Thailand	Tamarkan Hospital Camp No. 2, December 1943
	Bangkok, Nacompaton from April 1944 to September 1944
Return Details 1945	Thailand-Singapore by aircraft
	Singapore-Sydney, HMT *Highland Chieftan*
	Sydney-Melbourne-Perth by troop train

EDWIN JOHN CLARKE

Rank	Private
Regimental Number	WX9360
Company	'A' Company
Enlisted	31.10.1940
Discharged	23.1.1946
Date of Birth	13.8.1902
Place of Birth	Barking, Essex, England
Father	James Clajrke
Mother	Alice Clarke
Religion	Church of England
Pre-War Occupation	Dairy Farmer

HISTORY

Singapore	Selarang Camp Changi
	Johore Bahru, Adam Park
	Selarang Barracks Changi
POW Number	4/5996
'J' Force Japan	*Wales Maru* Party
POW Number	700
Camps Japan	Kobe House (Mitsubishi wharves, Toyo Steel)
	Maibara, Osaka sub-Camp No. 10 (irrigation works)
POW Number	197
Return Details 1945	Maibara-Yokohama by train
	Yokohama-Manila, USS *Goodhue*
	Manila-Sydney, HMS *Formidable*
	Sydney-Perth by troop train

JOHN WILLIAM CLAY

Rank	Private
Regimental Number	WX12488
Company	'C' Company
Enlisted	6.5.1941
Discharged	10.12.1945
Date of Birth	9.10.1916
Place of Birth	Fremantle, Western Australia
Father	Not Known
Mother	Not Known
Religion	Roman Catholic
Pre-War Occupation	Farmhand

HISTORY

Singapore	Selarang Camp and Barracks Changi
	Pulau Blakang Mati
	Changi Gaol Camp
	Kranji Camp Woodlands
POW Number	4/5998
Return Details 1945	Singapore-Darwin-Sydney, HMT *Arawa*
	Sydney-Melbourne by troop train
	Melbourne-Fremantle, HMT *Strathmore*

HAROLD THOMAS CLAYDEN

Rank	Private
Regimental Number	WX10354
Company	'C' Company
Enlisted	18.12.1940
Discharged	13.2.1946
Date of Birth	23.8.1917
Place of Birth	Perth, Western Australia
Father	Jesse Thomas Clayden
Mother	Elizabeth Clayden
Religion	Church of England
Pre-War Occupation	Timber Worker

HISTORY

Java	'Blackforce'
'A' Force Burma	Java Party No. 4, Williams Force
POW Number	4652
Camps Burma	Reptu 30km and Khonkan 55km Hospital Camps
Camps Thailand	Tamarkan
Japan	*Awa Maru* Party (remained in French Indo-China)
Return Details 1945	Saigon-Bangkok-Singapore by aircraft
	Singapore-Sydney, HMT *Highland Chieftan*
	Sydney-Melbourne-Perth by troop train

SYDNEY RICHARD CLAYDEN

Rank	Private
Regimental Number	WX10358
Company	'C' Company Headquarters
Enlisted	18.12.1940
Discharged	28.2.1946
Date of Birth	28.7.1915
Place of Birth	Perth, Western Australia
Father	Jesse Thomas Clayden
Mother	Elizabeth Clayden
Religion	Church of England
Pre-War Occupation	Millhand

HISTORY

Singapore	Selarang Camp Changi
'A' Force Burma	Green Force, No. 3 Battalion
POW Number	3094
Japan	*Rakuyo Maru* Party, Kumi No. 37 (rescued by a Japanese corvette)
Camps Japan	Kawasaki Camp No. 14D
	Shinagawa Main Hospital Camp
Return Details 1945	U.S.M.C. barge to a U.S. Navy Hospital Ship, Tokyo Bay-Manila
	Manila-Sydney, HMS *Speaker*
	Sydney-Fremantle, HMT *Dominion Monarch*

KENNETH CLIFTON

Rank	Private
Regimental Number	WX9243
Classification	Driver
Company	'A' Company
Enlisted	30.10.1940
Discharged	11.12.1945
Date of Birth	15.7.1903
Place of Birth	Norwood, South London, England
Father	Not Known
Mother	Not Known
Religion	Church of England
Pre-War Occupation	Farmhand

HISTORY

Singapore	Selarang Camp Changi
	River Valley Road Camp
	Selarang Barracks Changi
	Pulau Blakang Mati (from 5.11.1943)
	Changi Gaol Camp
	Kranji Camp Woodlands
POW Numbers	3/7303 and 1/7302
Return Details 1945	Singapore-Darwin-Sydney, HMT *Arawa*
	Sydney-Melbourne by troop train
	Melbourne-Fremantle, HMT *Strathmore*

WILLIAM ERNEST CLOTHIER

Rank	Private
Regimental Number	WX10739
Classification	Signaller
Company	Headquarters Company
Enlisted	15.1.1941
Discharged	6.2.1946
Date of Birth	8.6.1909
Place of Birth	Mt Barker, Western Australia
Father	Thomas Clothier
Mother	Mary Anne Clothier
Religion	Methodist
Pre-War Occupation	Farmhand

HISTORY

Singapore	Selarang Camp Changi
'A' Force Burma	Green Force, No. 3 Battalion
POW Number	3089
Camps Thailand	Tamarkan, Linson Wood Camp, Banderra (Chao Puraya River on bridge repair)
POW Number (Linson)	12132
Return Details 1945	Marched into Bangkok ex-Banderra
	Thailand-Singapore by aircraft
	Singapore-Fremantle, HMT *Moreton Bay*

ALFRED JOHN COCKING

Rank	Private
Regimental Number	WX16369
Company	'B' Company
Enlisted	28.9.1941
Discharged	25.5.1945
Date of Birth	28.3.1914
Place of Birth	Bunbury, Western Australia
Father	James Henry Cocking
Mother	Doris Maud Cocking
Religion	Methodist
Pre-War Occupation	Leading Hand at Westfarmers

HISTORY

Java	'Blackforce', attached to the 2/2nd Pioneer Battalion
Camps Java	Arinem, Leles, Bicycle Camp Batavia
'A' Force Burma	Java Party No. 4, Williams Force
POW Number	4591
Camps Burma	Beke Taung 40km, Khonkan 55km
Camps Thailand	131km, 133km, Kanchanaburi, Tamarkan
Japan	*Rakuyo Maru* Party, Kumi No. 38 (rescued by the USS *Pampanito*)
Return Details 1944	Saipan-Guadalcanal, Brisbane-Perth by aircraft 1.11.1944

LESLIE CODY

Rank	Staff Sergeant (Promoted 11.2.1942)
Regimental Number	WX9555
Company	'D' Company Headquarters
Enlisted	4.12.1940
Discharged	1.5.1946
Date of Birth	12.12.1918
Place of Birth	Boulder, Western Australia
Father	Richard Cody
Mother	Mabel Cody
Religion	Roman Catholic
Pre-War Occupation	Clerk

HISTORY

Singapore	Selarang Camp Changi
'A' Force Burma	Green Force, No. 3 Battalion
POW Number	1310
Camps Burma	Reptu 30km and Khonkan 55km Hospital Camps
Camps Thailand	Tamarkan Hospital Camp No. 2 (4.4.1944)
	Chungkai, Kachu Mountain Camp, Nakom Nayok, Lopburi (see Danny Bevis Diary)
Return Details 1945	Thailand-Singapore by aircraft
	Singapore-Fremantle, HMT *Circassia*
Additions	Wounded in action at Buona Vista on 15.2.1942. Admitted to Field Ambulance with a shrapnel wound to the thigh. Transferred to the 2/13th Australian General Hospital on 16.2.1942. Transferred to the 2/10th Australian General Hospital on 6.3.1942. Discharged to unit on 28.3.1942. Commonwealth War Graves Party under the command of Captain J. Leemon. This NCO was an original member of No. 13 Platoon until his appointment as 'D' Company C.Q.M.S.

JOHN CUTHBERT COLBEY

Rank	Private
Regimental Number	WX8808
Classification	Driver
Company	'B' Company Headquarters
Enlisted	23.10.1940
Discharged	14.12.1945
Date of Birth	10.7.1912
Place of Birth	Adelaide, South Australia
Father	Harold Colbey
Mother	Clara Colbey
Religion	Church of England
Pre-War Occupation	Gold Miner

HISTORY

Singapore	Selarang Camp Changi
	Thomson Road (Caldecote Hill Estate Camp)
	Selarang Barracks Changi (Forest Party)
	Pulau Blakang Mati
	Changi Gaol Camp
	Kranji Camp Woodlands
Force	Soldier selected for 'F' Force but was evacuated to the Australian General Hospital, Roberts Barracks on 18.4.1943 with amblyopia and missed the draft.
Return Details 1945	Not Known

JOHN VERDUN COLEVAS

Rank	Sergeant
Regimental Number	WX10609
Company	'D' Company
Enlisted	14.1.1941
Discharged	April 1961
Date of Birth	20.7.1916
Place of Birth	Richmond, Victoria
Father	Spiro Colevas
Mother	Faye Colevas
Religion	Greek Orthodox
Pre-War Occupation	Shop Assistant

HISTORY

Singapore	Selarang Camp Changi
	Johore Bahru, Adam Park
	Selarang Barracks Changi
'D' Force Thailand	S Battalion
POW Number	8718
Camps Thailand	Kanu II, Kanu I River Camp, Chungkai, Tamuang
Japan	*Rashin Maru* Party
Camps Japan	Yamane
	Niihama
Return Details 1945	Wakayama-Okinawa, USS *Sanctuary*
	Okinawa-Manila, USS *Bingham*
	Manila-Sydney, HMS *Speaker*
	Sydney-Melbourne-Perth by troop train
Additions	Wounded in action at Sungei Berih at 1000 hours on 9.2.1942. Admitted to Casualty Clearing Station then to Field Ambulance with a gunshot wound to left side of chest wall. Transferred to 2/13th Australian General Hospital on 15.2.1942. Discharged to unit 22.2.1942

CHARLES LESLIE COLLINS

Rank	Private
Regimental Number	WX10282
Classification	Motorcycle Orderly
Company	'B' Company
Enlisted	18.12.1940
Discharged	4.2.1946
Date of Birth	28.1.1922
Place of Birth	Perth, Western Australia
Father	Albert Collins
Mother	Jean Victoria Collins
Religion	Church of England
Pre-War Occupation	Apprentice Fitter

Singapore	A. G. H. Roberts Barracks Changi
	Selarang Barracks Changi
POW Number	1/7325
'H' Force Thailand	'H' Force Group No. 3
Camps Thailand	Kanu II Malayan Hamlet, Kanchanaburi Hospital 1.10.1943 (beri-beri)
Singapore	Sime Road Camp
	X10 Party
	Changi Gaol Camp
Return Details 1945	Singapore-Darwin-Sydney, 1st Netherlands Military Hospital Ship *Oranje*
	Sydney-Melbourne-Perth by troop train
Additions	Wounded in action at West Mandai on 14.2.1942. Admitted to the 2/10th Australian General Hospital which was located at the Cathay Building. Soldier was admitted with a fractured left elbow caused by shrapnel. Discharged to unit on 27.4.1942. He was given a 'B' Medical Classification and spent much of his time in the Changi area due to reconstructive surgery required to the elbow in question. Selected for 'H' Force, Group No. 3 and could have evaded the draft but soldier decided that he wanted to be included.

THOMAS JAMES CONWAY

Rank	Private
Regimental Number	WX4912
Classification	Rangetaker
Company	'C' Company
Enlisted	23.7.1940
Discharged	20.2.1946
Date of Birth	15.6.1920
Place of Birth	Wales, United Kingdom
Father	Alfred James Conway
Mother	Isabel Conway
Religion	Roman Catholic
Pre-War Occupation	Barman

HISTORY

Singapore	Selarang Camp and Barracks Changi
'D' Force Thailand	S Battalion
POW Number	8764
Japan	*Rashin Maru* Party
POW Number	1590
Camps Japan	Yamane
	Niihama (wharf)
Return Details 1945	Wakayama-Okinawa, USS *Sanctuary*
	Okinawa-Manila, USS *Bingham*
	Manila-Sydney, HMS *Speaker*
	Sydney-Fremantle, HMT *Dominion Monarch*

JOSEPH COOK

Rank	Private
Regimental Number	WX16306
Classification	Batman/Runner
Company	'E' Company, Special Reserve Battalion
Enlisted	1.9.1941
Discharged	17.6.1946
Date of Birth	9.5.1904
Place of Birth	Hartlepool, England
Father	Robert Moon Cook
Mother	Hannah Marshall Cook
Religion	Church of England
Pre-War Occupation	Prospector and Baker

HISTORY

Singapore	Selarang Camp and Barracks Changi
	X10 Party
	Kranji Hospital Woodlands
POW Number	1/7348
Return Details 1945	Singapore-Labuan by aircraft (evacuated to the 2/6th Australian General Hospital)
	Evacuated to the 2/2nd H.M. Australian Hospital Ship *Wanganella* for Morotai
	Morotai (evacuated to the 2/9th Australian General Hospital) 19.9.1945
	Morotai-Sydney, 2/2nd H.M Australian Hospital Ship *Wanganella*,
	Sydney-Melbourne by train, evacuated to 115 (H)MH
	Melbourne-Perth by train, evacuated to 110 (P)MH
Additions	Soldier had injured back and legs and was paralysed for three months prior to his release in 1945.

HENRY JAMES COOPER

Rank	Private
Regimental Number	WX8822
Classification	Equipment Repairer, A.A.O.C.
Company	Headquarters Company
Enlisted	23.10.1940
Discharged	11.1.1946
Date of Birth	10.8.1911
Place of Birth	Mandurah, Western Australia
Father	Clarence Cleland Cooper
Mother	Gertrude Cooper
Religion	Church of England
Pre-War Occupation	Miner and Timber Worker

HISTORY

Singapore	Selarang Camp Changi
'A' Force Burma	Green Force, No. 3 Battalion
POW Number	2938
Camps Burma	Evacuated to Khonkan 55km with a tropical ulcer to the heel on 4.7.1943. Information written on the back of a photograph indicates that this soldier was a member of Williams No. 1 Mobile Force and worked in the area of 114km and 126km points on the rail link in Thailand.
Japan	*Awa Maru* Party-Kumi No. 41 (joined party at River Valley Road Camp ex-Changi Gaol Camp Hospital)
POW Number	11033
Camps Japan	Fukuoka sub-Camp No. 17, *Omuta*
	Fukuoka sub-Camp No. 22
Return Details 1945	Nagasaki-Manila, USS *Lunga Point*
	Manila-Sydney, HMS *Speaker*
	Sydney-Melbourne-Adelaide-Perth by troop train

EDWARD AINSLEY CORNELL

Rank	Lance Corporal (Promoted on 7.2.1942)
Regimental Number	WX16260
Company	'E' Company, Special Reserve Battalion
Enlisted	27.8.1941
Discharged	1.2.1946
Date of Birth	17.9.1913
Place of Birth	Northampton, Western Australia
Father	Robert Charles Cornell
Mother	Mary Edith Cornell
Religion	Church of England
Pre-War Occupation	Farmer

HISTORY

Singapore	Selarang Camp Singapore
'A' Force Burma	Green Force, No. 3 Battalion
POW Number	3072
Camps Thailand	Tamarkan, Linson Wood Camp, Banderra (bridge repairs, Chao Puraya River)
POW Number (Linson)	12134
Return Details 1945	Singapore-Crawley Bay, Perth, PBY Catalina aircraft, 18.10.1945

RONALD HAMILTON CORNISH

Rank	Sergeant (Promoted on 7.2.1942)
Regimental Number	WX9035
Company	'A' Company
Enlisted	25.10.1940
Discharged	19.12.1945
Date of Birth	14.12.1915
Place of Birth	Perth, Western Australia
Father	Berham Hugo Cornish
Mother	Eva Grace Cornish
Religion	Church of England
Pre-War Occupation	Farmer

HISTORY

Singapore	Selarang Camp Changi
	Johore Bahru, Adam Park
	Selarang Barracks Changi
'D' Force Thailand	S Battalion
POW Number	8717
Camps Thailand	Konkoita
Return Details 1945	Thailand-Singapore by aircraft
	Singapore-Fremantle, HMT *Moreton Bay*

FRANCIS XAVIER CORRY

Rank	Chaplain
Regimental Number	NX76253
Attached 2/4th	Australian Army Chaplain's Department
Enlisted	9.8.1941
Appointment Terminated	16.1.1946
Date of Birth	20.3.1907
Place of Birth	Hawthorn, Victoria
Father	Not Known
Mother	Ellen Mary Corry
Religion	Dominican Order
Pre-War Occupation	Dominican Order of Preachers

HISTORY

Singapore	Selarang Camp Changi
'A' Force Burma	Green Force, No. 3 Battalion
POW Number	9441
Camps Burma	Reptu 30km Camp to Thanbyuzayat 28.10.1943. Remained at Thanbyuzayat until moved to Aungganaung 105km Camp. Joined Williams No. 1 Mobile Force to 133km Camp Thailand.
Camps Thailand	Kanchanaburi
Return Details	No details are known
Additions	Father Corry returned to **OUR LADY OF THE ROSARY CHURCH** at Prospect, South Australia. Father Corry's date of death is recorded as being 2.9.1965.

JOHN LIVINGSTON CORREY

Rank	Private
Regimental Number	WX20018
Company	Headquarters Company
Enlisted	3.9.1941
Discharged	29.11.9145
Date of Birth	25.2.1911
Place of Birth	Boulder, Western Australia
Father	John Richard Correy
Mother	Anne Correy
Religion	Church of England
Pre-War Occupation	Electrical Fitter

HISTORY

Singapore	Selarang Camp Changi
'A' Force Burma	Green Force, No. 3 Battalion
POW Number	2966
Camps Burma	Reptu 30km and Khonkan 55km Hospital Camps
Camps Thailand	Tamarkan, Kanchanaburi, Nacompaton (indications are that this soldier served as a medical orderly during his time as a POW)
Return Details 1945	Thailand-Singapore by aircraft
	Singapore-Perth from 16.9.1945 to 29.9.1945 by aircraft

EDWARD JAMES COSSON

Rank	Private
Regimental Number	WX10048
Classification	Signaller
Company	Headquarters Company
Enlisted	13.12.1940
Discharged	1.2.1946
Date of Birth	13.3.1910
Place of Birth	Melbourne, Victoria
Father	Edward James Cosson
Mother	Florence Mabel Beatrice Cosson
Religion	Church of England
Pre-War Occupation	Publican

HISTORY

Java	'Blackforce', attached to the 2/2nd Pioneer Battalion
'A' Force Burma	Java Party 5a, Robertson Force
Camps Thailand	Joined Williams No. 1 Mobile Force and moved as far the 133km Camp, Kanchanaburi (12.1.1944), Nacompaton, Prachuab Kirikhan-Mergui Escape Road, Kachu Mountain Camp.
Return Details 1945	Flown out to Kachu Mountain Camp by aircraft
	Kachu Mountain Camp-Singapore by aircraft, to the 2/14th Australian General Hospital for two weeks.
	Singapore-Fremantle, HMT *Moreton Bay*

ALFRED JOHN COUGH

Rank	Major
Regimental Number	WX3444
Company	'D' Company
Enlisted	21.10.1940
Appointment Terminated	18.1.1946
Date of Birth	18.1.1906
Place of Birth	Busselton, Western Australia
Father	Henry James Cough
Mother	Florence Mabel Cough
Religion	Church of England
Pre-War Occupation	Building Contractor

HISTORY

Singapore	Selarang Camp Changi
Officer Commanding	Johore Bahru, Adam Park
	Sime Road Camps
	Selarang Barracks Changi
POW Number	4/4083
'D' Force Thailand	Commanding Officer of V Battalion
Camps Thailand	Non Pladuk, Kanchanaburi, Bangkok
Return Details 1945	Bangkok-Rangoon by aircraft
	Rangoon-Singapore, HMT *Highland Brigade*
	Singapore (6.10.1945)-Labuan-Morotai-Queensland by aircraft
	Queensland-Perth by ANA aircraft
Additions	On the death of Lieutenant-Colonel M. J. Anketell this Officer was promoted to Battalion Second in Command.

A portrait of a gaunt Major Alf Cough,
drawn by an Indonesian at Kuii Camp, Thailand, October 1943.

HAROLD JOHN COWIE

Rank	Private
Regimental Number	WX8641
Classification	Driver
Company	'B' Company
Enlisted	18.10.1940
Discharged	23.1.1946
Date of Birth	17.10.1914
Place of Birth	Perth, Western Australia
Father	James Cowie
Mother	Florence Amelia Cowie
Religion	Church of England
Pre-War Occupation	Truck Driver

HISTORY

Singapore	Selarang Camp Changi
	Thomson Road (Caldecot Hill Estate Camp)
	River Valley Road
	Selarang Barracks Changi
POW Number	3/7415
Force	'F' Force Thailand
POW Number	13618
Camps Thailand	Shimo Sonkurai
Singapore	Sime Road Camp
	Changi Gaol Camp
Return Details 1945	Singapore-Darwin-Sydney, HMT *Arawa*
	Sydney-Melbourne by troop train
	Melbourne-Perth, HMT *Strathmore*

THOMAS DANIEL CRANE

Rank	Private
Regimental Number	WX16441
Classification	Batman/Runner
Company	Headquarters, 'E' Company, Special Reserve Battalion
Enlisted	10.9.1941
Discharged	17.10.1946
Date of Birth	8.9.1907
Place of Birth	Zeehan, Tasmania
Father	Not Known
Mother	Ada Sarah Crane
Religion	Church of England
Pre-War Occupation	Bogger

HISTORY

Singapore	Selarang Camp and Barracks Changi
'D' Force Thailand	T Battalion, W.O.II, John Dooley Party
Camps Thailand	Chungkai, Non Pladuk
French Indo-China	*Both* Party
Return Details 1945	Saigon-Bangkok-Singapore by aircraft

FREDERICK VICTOR CROSS

Rank	Private
Regimental Number	WX7268
Company	'B' Company
Enlisted	1.8.1940
Discharged	14.7.1945
Date of Birth	7.5.1905
Place of Birth	Mt Magnet, Western Australia
Father	Thomas Henry Cross
Mother	Emma Cross
Religion	Wesleyan
Pre-War Occupation	Miner

HISTORY

Singapore	Selarang Camp Changi
'A' Force Burma	Green Force, No. 3 Battalion
POW Number	1529
Japan	*Rakuyo Maru* Party (rescued by USS *Queenfish*)
Return Details 1944	Saipan-Brisbane-Perth 3.11.1944

STANLEY ALFRED CURRIE

Rank	Corporal
Regimental Number	WX5221
Classification	Technical Storeman
Company	'B' Company Headquarters
Enlisted	26.6.1940
Discharged	20.5.1946
Date of Birth	19.5.1902
Place of Birth	Claremont, Western Australia
Father	Thomas Currie
Mother	Jessie Currie
Religion	Presbyterian
Pre-War Occupation	Driver

HISTORY

Singapore	Selarang Camp Changi
	River Valley Road (October 1943, led a party of 27 men)
	Selarang Barracks Changi
POW Number	1/7422
'D' Force Thailand	S Battalion
POW Number	8726
Camps Thailand	Tarsau (July-October 1943 on a burial party) Nacompaton, Non Pladuk
French Indo-China	*Both* Party
Return Details 1945	Saigon-Bangkok-Singapore by aircraft
	Singapore-Perth by aircraft
	Admitted to 110(P)MH on 24.9.1945 ex-2/14 Australian General Hospital Singapore with Hepatitis.

JOHN GOODE CURTIN

Rank	Private
Regimental Number	WX8735
Classification	Driver
Company	'B' Company
Enlisted	23.10.1940
Discharged	11.4.1946
Date of Birth	8.6.1918
Place of Birth	Norseman, Western Australia
Father	Frances Henry Curtin
Mother	Ethel May Curtin
Religion	Methodist
Pre-War Occupation	Driver

HISTORY

Singapore	Selarang Camp and Barracks Changi
POW Number	4/6043
'D' Force Thailand	Captain Harris Party
French Indo-China	*Both* Party
Return Details 1945	Saigon-Bangkok-Singapore by aircraft
	Singapore-Sydney, HMT *Highland Chieftan*
	Sydney-Melbourne-Perth by troop train

LOUIS JOSEPH DAILY

Rank	Private
Regimental Number	WX8778
Company	'B' Company
Enlisted	23.10.1940
Discharged	13.8.1946
Date of Birth	31.1.1911
Place of Birth	Perth, Western Australia
Father	Aloysius Farquhar Daily
Mother	Agnes Josephine Daily
Religion	Roman Catholic
Pre-War Occupation	Shop Assistant and Fetter's Labourer

HISTORY

Singapore	Selarang Camp and Barracks Changi
'D' Force Thailand	S Battalion
POW Number	8767
Camps Thailand	Chungkai, Tamuang
Japan	*Rashin Maru* Party
Camps Japan	Yamane
	Niihama (No. 4 Party, wharf)
Return Details 1945	Wakayama-Okinawa, USS *Sanctuary*
	Manila-Sydney, HMS *Speaker*
	Sydney-Fremantle, HMT *Dominion Monarch*

JOHN FRANCIS DARE

Rank	Private
Regimental Number	WX9334
Company	'B' Company
Enlisted	30.10.1940
Discharged	28.3.1946
Date of Birth	18.12.1913
Place of Birth	Boulder, Western Australia
Father	Francis Robert Dare
Mother	Not Known
Religion	Methodist
Pre-War Occupation	Bulk Handling Bin Attendant

HISTORY

Singapore	Selarang Camp Changi
'A' Force Burma	Green Force, No. 3 Battalion
POW Number	1526
Camps Burma	Thanbyuzayat Hospital (September 1943)
Camps Thailand	Tamarkan Hospital (16.3.1944), Bangkok (26.4.1944, ulcerated stomach), Nacompaton
Return Details 1945	Thailand-Singapore by aircraft
	No other details are known.

WILLIAM JAMES DAVEY

Rank	Private
Regimental Number	WX8587
Classification	Driver
Company	'B' Company
Enlisted	18.10.1940
Discharged	17.5.1946
Date of Birth	15.2.1908
Place of Birth	Moora, Western Australia
Father	Joseph Davey
Mother	Beatrice Davey
Religion	Roman Catholic
Pre-War Occupation	Barman/Yardman

HISTORY

Singapore	Selarang Camp Changi
	Thomson Road (Caldecot Hill Estate Camp)
	River Valley Road Camp
	Selarang Barracks Changi
POW Number	1/11676
'J' Force Japan	*Wales Maru* Party
Camps Japan	Fukuoka sub-Camp No. 9 Hakensho
Return Details 1945	Nagasaki-Okinawa, U.S. Navy destroyer
	Okinawa-Manila by aircraft
	Manila-Sydney, HMS *Formidable*
	Sydney-Perth by ANA airliner

HARRY BUSSELL De'CASTILLA

Rank	Private
Regimental Number	WX10721
Company	'C' Company
Enlisted	15.1.1941
Discharged	30.4.1946
Date of Birth	25.10.1908
Place of Birth	Perth, Western Australia
Father	Harry De'Castilla
Mother	Violet De'Castilla
Religion	Church of England
Pre-War Occupation	Miner

HISTORY

Singapore	Selarang Camp Changi
'A' Force Burma	Green Force, No. 3 Battalion
POW Number	1506
Camps Burma	Evacuated to Khonkan 55km Camp from Aungganaung 105km Camp on 1.7.1943 and discharged on 17.10.1943
Camps Thailand	Tamarkan, Konkoita, Chungkai, Petchaburi, Kachu Mountain Camp
Return Details 1945	Singapore-Sydney by aircraft
	Sydney-Fremantle, HMT *Otranto* 11.10.1945

PENROD VANCE DEAN

Rank	Lieutenant
Regimental Number	WX6067
Company	'B' Company
Enlisted	30.7.1940
Appointment Terminated	19.12.1946
Date of Birth	9.11.1914
Place of Birth	South Perth, Western Australia
Father	Edward Archibald Dean
Mother	Alice Dean
Religion	Church of England
Pre-War Occupation	Commercial Traveller

HISTORY

Singapore	Selarang Camp Changi
POW Number	3/5847
Camps Singapore	Outram Road Prison
	Levelling Party Changi Aerodrome
	X3 Party
	Changi Gaol Camp (Garden Control Party)
Return Details 1945	Singapore-Darwin-Sydney, HMT *Arawa*
	Sydney-Melbourne by troop train
	Melbourne-Perth by aircraft

ROY ALFRED DEVESON

Rank	Private
Regimental Number	WX6362
Classification	Technical Storeman
Company	'C' Company Headquarters
Enlisted	16.7.1940
Discharged	12.12.1945
Date of Birth	20.3.1920
Place of Birth	Buckingham Mill near Collie, Western Australia
Father	Alfred James Deveson
Mother	Emily Gertrude Victoria Deveson
Religion	Church of England
Pre-War Occupation	Factory Worker

HISTORY

Singapore	Selarang Camp Changi
	Thomson Road (Caldecot Hill Estate Camp)
	River Valley Road Camp
	Selarang Barracks Changi
'J' Force Japan	*Wales Maru* Party
POW Number	530
Camps Japan	Fukuoka sub-Camp No. 9 Hakensho
POW Number	1067
Return Details 1945	Nagasaki-Okinawa, U.S. Navy destroyer
	Okinawa-Manila by aircraft
	Manila-Sydney, HMS *Formidable*
	Sydney-Perth by ANA aircraft

VICTOR JOHN ALEXANDER DEWAR

Rank	Private
Regimental Number	WX8238
Company	'C' Company
Enlisted	4.6.1940
Discharged	20.2.1946
Date of Birth	24.10.1906
Place of Birth	Kookynie, Western Australia
Father	Samuel Sherman Dewar
Mother	Elizabeth Dewar
Religion	Baptist
Pre-War Occupation	Gold Miner

HISTORY

Singapore	Selarang Camp Changi
'A' Force Burma	Green Force, No. 3 Battalion
POW Number	1476
Camps Thailand	Tamarkan, Nacompaton, Tamunag
Return Details 1945	Thailand-Singapore by aircraft
	Singapore-Sydney, HMT *Highland Chieftan*
	Sydney-Perth by troop train

GORDON THOMAS DICKIE

Rank	Corporal (Promoted 14.6.1951)
Regimental Number	WX9328
Company	'A' Company
Enlisted	30.10.1940
Discharged	4.9.1953
Date of Birth	26.4.1910
Place of Birth	Suffolk, England
Father	Thomas Dickie
Mother	Gladys Dickie
Religion	Church of England
Pre-War Occupation	Farmhand

HISTORY

Singapore	Selarang Camp Changi
	Johore Bahru, Adam Park
	Selarang Barracks Changi
POW Number	1/7508
'D' Force Thailand	S Battalion
POW Number	8769
Camps Thailand	Tamuang
Japan	*Rashin Maru* Party
POW Number	4766
Camps Japan	Yamane
	Niihama
Return Details 1945	Wakayama-Okinawa, USS *Sanctuary*
	Okinawa-Manila-USS *Bingham*
	Manila-Morotai, Darwin by PBY Catalina aircraft A24-306
	Darwin-Perth by aircraft

ANDREW ALFRED DICKSON

Rank	Private
Regimental Number	WX9310
Company	'A' Company
Enlisted	30.10.1940
Discharged	9.9.1949
Date of Birth	14.8.1918
Place of Birth	Wyalkatchem, Western Australia
Father	Alexander Dickson
Mother	Not Known
Religion	Methodist
Pre-War Occupation	Farmhand

HISTORY

Java	'Blackforce'
'A' Force Burma	Java Party No. 4, Williams Force
POW Number	4640
Camps Burma	Kun Knit Kway, Reptu, Thanbyuzayat
Camps Thailand	Kanchanaburi, Chumphon, Bangkok, Petchaburi, Kachu Mountain Camp
Return Details 1945	Kachu Mountain Camp-Singapore by aircraft
	Singapore-Fremantle, HMT *Highland Brigade*

PETER JOHN DIMOPOULOS

Rank	Private
Regimental Number	WX13869
Company	Battalion Headquarters
Enlisted	4.6.1941
Discharged	23.1.1946
Date of Birth	29.7.1923
Place of Birth	Greece
Father	John Dimopoulos
Mother	Panorea Dimopoulos
Religion	Church of England
Pre-War Occupation	Driver

HISTORY

Singapore	Selarang Camp Changi
	Sarangoon Road Camp
	Selarang Barracks Changi
'D' Force Thailand	V Battalion (see Lieutenant-Colonel Malcolm, Kanchanaburi Base Camp No. 1)
Camps Thailand	Kanchanaburi Aerodrome Camp
	Kao Rin Specialist Camp
Return Details 1945	Thailand-Singapore by aircraft
	Singapore-Fremantle, HMT *Moreton Bay*
Additions	Rabaul 2.8.1946-15.8.1946 and 29.11.1946-23.5.1947
	(As an interpreter for the Japanese War Crimes Trials)

EDGAR ALBERT DIX

Rank	Private
Regimental Number	WX12924
Classification	Electrician
Attached 2/4th	A.A.O.C.
Enlisted	14.5.1941
Discharged	18.1.1946
Date of Birth	20.4.1907
Place of Birth	Kalgoorlie, Western Australia
Father	Edgar Java Dix
Mother	Clara Dix
Religion	Church of England
Pre-War Occupation	Radio Parts Manufacturer and Wire Winder

HISTORY

Singapore	Selarang Camp and Barracks Changi
	Kranji Hospital Woodlands (29.4.1944)
	Changi Gaol Camp
POW Numbers	1/7514 and 3/7577
Return Details 1945	Singapore-Labuan, 2/1st H.M. Australian Hospital Ship *Manunda* 14.9.1945
	Labuan-Morotai-Darwin-Perth by aircraft
Additions	Soldier was selected for 'F' Force but remained in Singapore as essential personnel due to his trade skills and recurring stomach problems.

MELVILLE ROY DOCKING

Rank	Private
Regimental Number	WX14856
Company	'A' Company
Enlisted	7.7.1941
Discharged	11.2.1946
Date of Birth	16.9.1921
Place of Birth	Subiaco, Western Australia
Father	Victor Roy Docking
Mother	Mary Elizabeth Docking
Religion	Methodist
Pre-War Occupation	Bread Carter

HISTORY

Singapore	A. G. H. Roberts Barracks Changi
	Selarang Barracks Changi
POW Number	1/7519
Force	'F' Force Thailand
POW Number	13927
Camps Thailand	Shimo Sonkurai, Tanbaya (Burma), Kanchanaburi
Singapore	Selarang Barracks Changi
	X3 Party
	Changi Gaol Camp
Return Details 1945	Singapore-Darwin-Sydney, HMT *Arawa*
	Sydney-Melbourne by troop train
	Melbourne-Fremantle, HMT *Strathmore*
Additions	Wounded in action at Buona Vista on 15.2.1942. Admitted to the 2/9th Field Ambulance with a shrapnel wound to the right buttock. Transferred to the 2/13th Australian General Hospital. Soldier was a patient at the Australian General Hospital Roberts Barracks until July 1942. Due to the partial paralysis caused by damage to the sciatic nerve and loss of the use of the right foot, this soldier was given an 'E' Medical Classification. Soldier worked in the cook house for a time on light duties to promote his recovery.

GEORGE JAMES DOODSON

Rank	Private
Regimental Number	WX6917
Classification	Cook
Company	'B' Company Headquarters
Enlisted	30.7.1940
Discharged	25.1.1946
Date of Birth	14.7.1910
Place of Birth	Derby, England
Father	John James Doodson
Mother	Rosanna Doodson
Religion	Church of England
Pre-War Occupation	Fruit, Vegetable and Poultry wholesale business

HISTORY

Singapore	Selarang Camp and Barracks Changi
	X3 Party
	Changi Gaol Camp
Return Details 1945	Singapore-Darwin-Sydney, HMT *Arawa*
	Sydney-Melbourne by troop train
	Melbourne-Fremantle, HMT *Strathmore*

BERNARD PATRICK DOOLAN

Rank	Sergeant
Regimental Number	WX9391
Company	Headquarters Company
Enlisted	21.11.1940
Discharged	18.2.1946
Date of Birth	7.5.1910
Place of Birth	Geraldton, Western Australia
Father	Patrick Doolan
Mother	Nellie Doolan
Religion	Roman Catholic
Pre-War Occupation	Truck Driver

HISTORY

Singapore	Selarang Camp Changi
'A' Force Burma	Green Force, No. 3 Battalion
POW Number	2668
Camps Thailand	Tamarkan, Chungkai, Non Pladuk, Kachu Mountain Camp, Petchaburi, Nacompaton, Nakom Nayok (see Danny Bevis Diary)
Return Details 1945	Thailand-Singapore by aircraft
	Singapore-Fremantle, HMT *Circassia*

JAMES JOHN DORE

Rank	Corporal (Acting Sergeant, Japan)
Regimental Number	WX8617
Awards	Mentioned in Despatches
Company	'A' Company
Enlisted	18.10.1940
Discharged	25.1.1946
Date of Birth	17.3.1919
Place of Birth	Cottesloe, Western Australia
Father	Harold Ignatius Dore
Mother	Ina Dore
Religion	Presbyterian
Pre-War Occupation	Labourer

HISTORY

Singapore	Selarang Camp Changi
	Havelock Road Camp
	Thomson Road (Caldecot Hill Estate Camp)
	Selarang Barracks Changi
POW Numbers	1/7531 and 3/6307
'J' Force Japan	*Wales Maru* Party
Camps Japan	Kobe (Mitsubishi and Toyo Steel)
	Kawasaki Camp, Maruyama Park
	Wakinohama Camp
Return Details 1945	Yokohama-Okinawa, C54 Skymaster aircraft
	Okinawa-Manila, B24 Liberator aircraft
	Manila-Sydney, HMS *Formidable*
	Sydney-Fremantle, HMT *Dominion Monarch*
Additions	Wounded in action at Ulu Pandan on 12.2.1942. Admitted to the 2/13th Australian General Hospital with a shrapnel wound to the left leg. Transferred to the 2/10th Australian General Hospital on 6.3.1942. Discharged to unit ex-Australian General Hospital, Roberts Barracks Changi on 14.4.1942.

By the KING'S Order the name of
Corporal J.J. Dore,
2/4 Aust. M.G. Bn
was published in the Commonwealth Gazette on
6th March, 1947.
as mentioned in a Despatch for distinguished service.
I am charged to record
His Majesty's high appreciation.

Minister of State for the Army.

FREDERICK JOHN DORRINGTON

Rank	Corporal
Regimental Number	WX9557
Company	'B' Company
Enlisted	4.12.1940
Discharged	15.7.1946
Date of Birth	17.12.1905
Place of Birth	London, England
Father	Not Known
Mother	Louise Elizabeth Dorrington
Religion	Church of England
Pre-War Occupation	Wool Classer

HISTORY

Singapore	Selarang Camp Changi
'A' Force Burma	Green Force, No. 3 Battalion
POW Number	2719
Camps Burma	Reptu 30km, Medical orderly (8.4.1943-28.10.1943)
Camps Thailand	Tamarkan, Bangkok, Nacompaton
Return Details 1945	Thailand-Singapore by aircraft
	Singapore-Fremantle, HMT *Moreton Bay*

OWEN ALFRED DOUST

Rank	Private
Regimental Number	WX17881
Company	'A' Company
Enlisted	4.12.1941
Discharged	31.1.1946
Date of Birth	21.5.1922
Place of Birth	Bridgetown, Western Australia
Father	Leonard Harold Doust
Mother	Ellen Doust
Religion	Church of England
Pre-War Occupation	Clerk

HISTORY

Singapore	Selarang Camp Changi
	Johore Bahru, Adam Park
	Selarang Barracks Changi
	Great World, Havelock Road and River Valley Road Camps
	Selarang Barracks Changi
'D' Force Thailand	S Battalion
POW Number	8770
Camps Thailand	Kanu II, Kanu I River Camp (evacuated by barge to Tarsau with typhus), Tardan, Konkoita, Kinsaiyok, Tarsau, Tamarkan, Chungkai, Kachu Mountain Camp, Bangkok
Return Details 1945	Thailand-Singapore by aircraft
	Singapore-Fremantle, HMT *Highland Brigade*

CLAUDE DOW

Rank	Private
Regimental Number	WX17591
Company	'E' Company, Special Reserve Battalion
Enlisted	10.11.1941
Discharged	9.1.1946
Date of Birth	5.4.1917
Place of Birth	East Perth, Western Australia
Father	John Henry Dow
Mother	Sussanna Maud Dow
Religion	Church of England
Pre-War Occupation	Wine Worker

HISTORY

Singapore	A. G. H. Roberts Barracks Changi
	Adam Park
	Sime Road Camp
	Selarang Barracks Changi
'D' Force Thailand	S Battalion
POW Number	8771
Camps Thailand	Kanu II, Hintok Road Camp, Tamarkan, Tamuang
Japan	*Rashin Maru* Party
POW Number	1604
Camps Japan	Yamane (drill sharpener)
	Niihama (repair shop)
Return Details 1945	Wakayama-Okinawa, USS *Sanctuary*
	Okinawa-Manila, USS *Bingham*
	Manila-Darwin, PBY Catalina aircraft A24-382
	Darwin-Perth, B24 Liberator (11.10.1945)
Additions	Soldier was listed as missing from 11.2.1942. He lost his way following the ambush at South-West Bukit Timah and made his way to the coast where he managed to escape by boat to one of the nearby islands to the south of Singapore. He held out there until he contracted beri-beri and in his weakened state, he was handed over to bounty hunters by local Malays who in turn handed him over to the Japanese. Soldier was put in gaol, as he describes it, for two weeks, where he was questioned by the Japanese. It is likely that soldier was actually sent to the Kempeitai Headquarters in the YMCA building on Stamford Road Singapore. Once the Japanese were satisfied that this story was authentic he was sent was to Changi where he was admitted to the Australian General Hospital at Roberts Barracks.

THOMAS FRANCIS DOYLE

Rank	Private
Regimental Number	WX7299
Company	'D' Company
Enlisted	1.8.1940
Discharged	5.3.1946
Date of Birth	1.6.1902
Place of Birth	Fremantle, Western Australia
Father	Joseph Doyle
Mother	Nora Doyle
Religion	Roman Catholic
Pre-War Occupation	Line Foreman

HISTORY

Java	'Blackforce'
Camps Java	Bicycle Camp Batavia
'A' Force Burma	Java Party No. 4, Williams Force
POW Number	4539
Camps Thailand	131km, 133km, Kanchanaburi, Nacompaton (evacuated seriously ill 29.4.1944-9.1.1945), Bangkok
Return Details 1945	Thailand-Singapore by aircraft
	Singapore-Fremantle, HMT *Tamaroa*

ARTHUR MONTAGUE DRAPER

Rank	Corporal (Promoted 24.1.1942)
Regimental Number	WX7777
Awards	Mentioned in Despatches
Company	'B' Company
Enlisted	10.8.1940
Discharged	4.2.1946
Date of Birth	6.7.1903
Place of Birth	Perth, Western Australia
Father	Thomas Percy Draper
Mother	Mabel Draper
Religion	Church of England
Pre-War Occupation	Station Manager

HISTORY

Singapore	Selarang Camp Changi
	Thomson Road (Caldecot Hill Estate Camp)
	Selarang Barracks Changi
POW Number	3/6309
'J' Force Japan	*Wales Maru* Party
POW Numbers	Kobe 600 and Toyama 59
Camps Japan	Kobe (Showa-Denki), Nagoya, Toyama
Return Details 1945	Yokohama-Okinawa-Manila by aircraft
	Manila-Sydney, HMS *Formidable*
	Sydney-Fremantle, HMT *Dominion Monarch*

ROBERT DRYSDALE

Rank	Private
Regimental Number	WX7943
Company	'B' Company
Enlisted	13.8.1940
Discharged	10.4.1946
Date of Birth	18.11.1905
Place of Birth	Edinburgh, Scotland
Father	David Drysdale
Mother	Not Known
Religion	Presbyterian
Pre-War Occupation	Chaff Cutter

HISTORY

Singapore	Selarang Camp Changi
	Havelock Road Camp
	River Valley Road Camp
	Selarang Barracks Changi
POW Number	1/7556
'H' Force Thailand	'H' Force Group No. 3
Camps Thailand	Kanu II Malayan Hamlet, Kanchanaburi (8.9.1943)
Singapore	Sime Road Camp (December 1943)
	Changi Gaol Camp
	Adam Park (June 1944)
	Havelock Road Camp (November 1944)
	X1 Party
	P Party
	Changi Gaol Camp
Return Details 1945	Singapore-Darwin-Sydney, HMT *Arawa*
	Sydney-Melbourne by troop train
	Melbourne-Fremantle, HMT *Strathmore*

JOHN ALLAN DUGGIN

Rank	Private
Regimental Number	WX10199
Classification	Driver
Company	Not Known
Enlisted	18.12.1940
Discharged	5.12.1945
Date of Birth	14.2.1912
Place of Birth	Bowden, South Australia
Father	John Duggin
Mother	Catherine Duggin
Religion	Church of England
Pre-War Occupation	Millhand

HISTORY

Singapore	Selarang Camp Changi
	Johore Bahru, Adam Park
	Selarang Barracks Changi
'D' Force Thailand	V Battalion
Japan	*Aramis* Party
POW Number	622
Camps Japan	Fukuoka sub-Camp No. 17, Omuta
Return Details 1945	Nagasaki-Okinawa, USS *Haven*
	Okinawa-Manila by aircraft
	Manila-Morotai-Darwin, PBY Catalina aircraft A24-201
	Darwin-Melbourne-Perth by aircraft

JOHN SHARP DUNCAN

Rank	Private
Regimental Number	WX8584
Company	'B' Company
Enlisted	18.10.1940
Discharged	8.1.1946
Date of Birth	19.3.1919
Place of Birth	Dunfermline, Scotland
Father	Robert Paterson Duncan
Mother	Margaret Moodie Duncan
Religion	Presbyterian
Pre-War Occupation	Butcher

HISTORY

Singapore	Selarang Camp and Barracks Changi
	River Valley Road Camp
	Alexandra Hospital (clean up party)
	Johore Bahru (cement party for hospital repair)
	Shell Refinery, Pulau Bukom (see the story, *'Who Really Was The First?'*)
	X10 Party
	Changi Gaol Camp
Return Details 1945	Singapore-Darwin-Sydney, HMT *Arawa*
	Sydney-Melbourne by troop train
	Melbourne-Fremantle, HMT *Strathmore*

CECIL HENRY DUNN

Rank	Private
Regimental Number	WX7236
Company	'B' Company Headquarters
Enlisted	1.8.1940
Discharged	21.3.1946
Date of Birth	12.8.1901
Place of Birth	Mount Morgan, Western Australia
Father	Mathew Dunn
Mother	Lillian Dunn
Religion	Roman Catholic
Pre-War Occupation	Fitter, Tractor Driver and Gold Mine Amalgamator

HISTORY

Singapore	Selarang Camp Changi
	Johore Bahru, Adam Park
	Selarang Barracks Changi
POW Number	3/7631
'D' Force Thailand	T Battalion, W.O.II John Dooley Party
French Indo-China	*Both* Party
Return Details 1945	Saigon-Bangkok-Singapore by aircraft
	Singapore-Sydney, HMT *Highland Chieftan*
	Sydney-Perth by troop train

NORMAN LENARD DUNNELL

Rank	Private
Regimental Number	WX17595
Company	'D' Company
Enlisted	10.11.9141
Discharged	29.3.1946
Date of Birth	11.4.1921
Place of Birth	Subiaco, Western Australia
Father	Harry Cyril Dunnell
Mother	Ruby Beatrice Dunnell
Religion	Church of England
Pre-War Occupation	Carpenter and Apprentice Baker

HISTORY

Singapore	Selarang Camp Changi
	River Valley Road Camp
	Selarang Barracks Changi
POW Number	3/7638
'D' Force Thailand	V Battalion
Japan	*Aramis* Party
Camps Japan	Fukuoka sub-Camp No. 17, Omuta
Return Details 1945	Nagasaki-Okinawa, USS *Haven*
	Okinawa-Manila by aircraft
	Manila-Morotai-Darwin, PBY Catalina aircraft A24-359
	Darwin-Perth by aircraft

WILLIAM DUNWOODIE

Rank	Private
Regimental Number	WX9266
Company	'A' Company
Enlisted	30.10.1940
Discharged	17.12.1945
Date of Birth	20.3.1918
Place of Birth	Northumberland, England
Father	Bernard Dunwoodie
Mother	Ann Dunwoodie
Religion	Roman Catholic
Pre-War Occupation	Labourer

HISTORY

Java	'Blackforce', attached to 2/3rd Machine Gun Battalion
Camps Java	Bicycle Camp Batavia
'D' Force Thailand	Java Party No. 6, P Battalion
Camps Thailand	Kachu Mountain Camp
Return Details 1945	Kachu Mountain Camp-Singapore by aircraft
	Singapore-Fremantle, HMT *Highland Brigade*
Additions	Soldier was captured with Lt. Colin Blakeway's group. This group was instructed to lay down arms on 8.3.1942 but they continued to remain at large for a further seven days until a shortage of food forced their surrender to the Japanese on 15.3.1942.

ARCHIBALD HENRY DYSON

Rank	Private
Regimental Number	WX7599
Classification	Driver
Company	'C' Company
Enlisted	6.8.1940
Discharged	23.5.1946
Date of Birth	25.7.1920
Place of Birth	Broome, Western Australia
Father	George Harry Dyson
Mother	Myra Dyson
Stepfather	Edward James Ribe
Religion	Church of England
Pre-War Occupation	Factory Worker and Truck Driver

Singapore	Selarang Camp Changi
	Thomson Road (Caldecot Hill Estate Camp)
	Selarang Barracks Changi
POW Number	3/7653
'D' Force Thailand	S Battalion
POW Number	8772
Camps Thailand	Tarsau (refueling trains, did not accompany S Battalion to Kanu II), Kanchanaburi
Japan	*Rashin Maru* Party
POW Number	1606
Camps Japan	Yamane
	Niihama
Return Details 1945	Wakayama-Okinawa, USS *Sanctuary*
	Okinawa admitted to the 233rd General Hospital on 19.9.1945
	Okinawa-Manila, not known but likely by aircraft
	Manila-Sydney, HMS *Formidable*
	Sydney-Melbourne-Perth by aircraft
Additions	Wounded in action at Hill 200, Ulu Pandan on 11.2.1942. Soldier received a shrapnel wound to the left buttock but remained on duty.
	Sydney admitted to the 113(C)MH
	Melbourne admitted to the 115(H)MH
	Perth admitted to the 110(P)MH 8.11.1945

ROY ELLIOTT ECCLESTONE

Rank	Private
Regimental Number	WX16947
Company	'E' Company, Special Reserve Battalion
Enlisted	8.10.1941
Discharged	11.3.1946
Date of Birth	2.2.1904
Place of Birth	Donnybrook, Western Australia
Father	William Ecclestone
Mother	Ada Jane Grace Ecclestone
Religion	Methodist
Pre-War Occupation	Carpenter

HISTORY

Singapore	Selarang Camp Changi
'A' Force Burma	Green Force, No. 3 Battalion
POW Number	3081
Camps Burma	Reptu 30km Camp
Camps Thailand	Tamarkan, Nacompaton, Bangkok
Return Details 1945	Thailand-Singapore by aircraft
	Singapore-Fremantle, H.M. Hospital Ship *Karoa*

EDWIN FINLAY ELLIOT

Rank	Private
Regimental Number	WX5064
Classification	Driver
Company	'C' Company Headquarters
Enlisted	23.7.1940
Discharged	4.12.1945
Date of Birth	4.3.1917
Place of Birth	Footscray, Victoria
Father	Edwin Finlay Elliot
Mother	Alice Victoria Elliot
Religion	Methodist
Pre-War Occupation	Truck and Tractor Driver

HISTORY

Singapore	Selarang Camp Changi
	Thomson Road (Caldecot Hill Estate Camp)
	Great World and River Valley Road Camps
	Selarang Barracks Changi
POW Numbers	3/7684 and 14122
'H' Force Thailand	'H' Force Group No. 3
Camps Thailand	Kanu II Malayan Hamlet, Kanchanaburi (6 weeks in hospital)
Singapore	Sime Road Camp
	Levelling Party Changi Aerodrome
	X3 Party
	Changi Gaol Camp
Return Details 1945	Singapore-Darwin-Sydney, HMT *Arawa*
	Sydney-Melbourne-Adelaide-Perth by troop train

JAMES STUART ELLIOT

Rank	Private
Regimental Number	WX8619
Company	'A' Company
Enlisted	18.10.1940
Discharged	11.1.1946
Date of Birth	13.12.1919
Place of Birth	Perth, Western Australia
Father	Stuart Elliot
Mother	Constance Elliot
Religion	Church of England
Pre-War Occupation	Wood Turner

Singapore	Selarang Camp Changi
	Johore Bahru, Adam Park
	River Valley Road Camp
	Selarang Barracks Changi
POW Number	1/7614 and 3/7686
'D' Force Thailand	S Battalion
POW Number	8773
Camps Thailand	Kanu II, Hintok Road Camp, Tarsau, Chungkai, Tamuang
Japan	*Rashin Maru* Party
POW Number	1609
Camps Japan	Yamane
	Niihama
Return Details 1945	Wakayama-Okinawa, USS *Sanctuary*
	Okinawa-Manila, USS *Bingham*
	Manila-Morotai-Darwin-Perth, B24 Liberator aircraft A72-379

AUGUSTUS EVELYN ERSKINE

Rank	Private	
Regimental Number	WX20164	
Company	'E' Company, Special Reserve Battalion	
Enlisted	12.11.1941	
Discharged	26.9.1946	
Date of Birth	7.12.1901	
Place of Birth	Bunbury, Western Australia	
Father	Evelyn Pierpoint Erskine	
Mother	Amy Erskine	
Religion	Church of England	
Pre-War Occupation	Miner	

HISTORY

Singapore	Selarang Camp Changi
'A' Force Burma	Green Force, No.3, Battalion
POW Number	3069
Camps Thailand	Tamarkan, Bangkok (go-downs)
Return Details 1945	Thailand-Rangoon by aircraft
	Rangoon-Singapore, HMT *Highland Brigade*
	Singapore-Fremantle, HMT *Moreton Bay*
Additions	Wounded in action on 13.2.1942. Admitted to the 2/10th Australian General Hospital with four machine gun bullets to the left chest. Discharged to unit on 24.2.1942.

BENJAMIN EVANS
a.k.a. Benjamin Tiley-Evans

Rank	Private
Regimental Number	WX9497
Company	'D' Company
Enlisted	4.12.1940
Discharged	4.7.1946
Date of Birth	17.8.1916
Place of Birth	South Wales
Father	Tudor Evans
Mother	Tydfil Irene Evans
Religion	Church of England
Pre-War Occupation	Railway Employee

HISTORY

Singapore	Selarang Camp Changi
	Thomson Road (Caldecot Hill Estate Camp)
	Selarang Barracks Changi
POW Number	1/11725
Force	'F' Force, Thailand
Camps Thailand	Shimo Sonkurai (medical orderly), Kami Sonkurai
Singapore	Changi Gaol Camp Hospital
	Kranji Hospital Camp Woodlands from 28.5.1944
Return Details 1945	Singapore-Labuan, 2/1st H.M. Australian Hospital Ship *Manunda*
	Labuan-Darwin-Broome-Perth, PBY Catalina aircraft
	Admitted to 110(P)MH on 2.10.1945
Additions	Shell shocked at Buona Vista on 13.2.1942 and evacuated on 15.2.1942.

FRANCIS CLYDE EVANS

Rank	Corporal (Promoted on 7.2.1942)
Regimental Number	WX14172
Company	'E' Company, Special Reserve Battalion
Enlisted	11.6.1941
Discharged	13.2.1946
Date of Birth	25.6.1922
Place of Birth	Leonora, Western Australia
Father	Clifford Statin Howard Evans
Mother	Ivy Lillian Evans
Religion	Methodist
Pre-War Occupation	Mine Supervisor

Singapore	Selarang Camp Changi
	Johore Bahru, Adam Park
	River Valley Road Camp
	Selarang Barracks Changi, (Forest Party)
POW Number	4/6105
'D' Force Thailand	V Battalion
Camps Thailand	Kinsaiyok (low bridges, cuttings and hauling timber) soldier fell ill at this camp and doctors convinced the Japanese that some of the sick should be permitted to travel south on a truck which was heading in that direction. The Japanese agreed to allow six sick men to travel south and one of these was Cpl. Frank Evans. He was admitted to hospital at Tamarkan and, when discharged three months later, worked on the Tamarkan bridge. His next camp was Nacompaton where a Hospital Camp was to be constructed to accommodate the men moving south following the construction of the Burma-Thailand rail link. At this stage Frank was selected for one of the Japan or French Indo-China Parties, but instead remained in Thailand and moved from Non Pladuk to Kao Rin to construct the Specialist Hospital Camp. Frank was recovered at wars end from Tamuang from where he moved to the Sports Stadium Camp at Bangkok.
Return Details 1945	Bangkok-Singapore, R.A.F. Lancaster aircraft
	Singapore-Morotai-Wewak-Townsville, by aircraft
	Townsville-Brisbane-Sydney-Melbourne-Adelaide-Kalgoorlie, by troop train
	Detrained at Kalgoorlie and travelled to Leonora to attend to his sick mother, Ivy, before continuing his journey to Perth.
	Admitted to 110 (P)MH before moving out to Point Walter Camp, Bicton.
Additions	Wounded in action at Bukit Timah on 13.2.1942. Admitted to the 2/10th Field Ambulance with a gunshot wound to the left leg. Transferred to the 2/13th Australian General Hospital on 16.2.1942. Discharged to unit on 22.2.1942

KENNETH SAMUEL EVANS

Rank	Private
Regimental Number	WX17269
Company	'E' Company, Special Reserve Battalion
Enlisted	15.10.1941
Discharged	19.12.1945
Date of Birth	12.12.1919
Place of Birth	Bayswater, Western Australia
Father	Joseph Gordon Evans
Mother	Alice Mary Evans
Religion	Church of England
Pre-War Occupation	Not Known

HISTORY

Singapore	Selarang Camp Changi
'A' Force Burma	Green Force, No. 3 Battalion
POW Number	3079
Camps Thailand	Tamarkan, Chungkai, Tamuang, Bangkok
Return Details 1945	Thailand-Singapore by aircraft
	Singapore-Fremantle, HMT *Moreton Bay*

RONALD LUMLEY EVANS

Rank	Private
Regimental Number	WX10057
Classification	Signaller
Company	Headquarters Company
Enlisted	13.12.1940
Discharged	8.2.1946
Date of Birth	12.12.1919
Place of Birth	Brighton, Sussex, England
Father	Joseph Gordon Evans
Mother	Alice Mary Evans
Religion	Church of England
Pre-War Occupation	Stationhand

HISTORY

Singapore	Selarang Camp Changi
'A' Force Burma	Green Force, No. 3 Battalion
POW Number	3082
Camps Thailand	Tamarkan, Chungkai, Linson Wood Camp, Bangkok
POW Number (Linson)	12141
Return Details 1945	Thailand-Singapore by aircraft
	Singapore-Labuan, 2/1st H.M. Australian Hospital Ship, *Manunda*

JACK CLIFFORD EWEN

Rank	Corporal (Promoted on 11.2.1942)
Regimental Number	WX9101
Company	'A' Company
Enlisted	30.10.1940
Discharged	27.3.1946
Date of Birth	1.11.1913
Place of Birth	Mt Hawthorn, Western Australia
Father	David Alexander Ewen
Mother	Amelia Maud Ewen
Religion	Church of England
Pre-War Occupation	Bricklayer

Singapore	Selarang Camp Changi
	Johore Bahru, Adam Park
	Selarang Barracks Changi
POW Number	1/7640
Force	'F' Force Thailand
Camps Thailand	Sonkurai (cook house), Shimo Sonkurai, Kami Sonkurai, Konkoita
Singapore	Selarang Barracks Changi
	Kranji Hospital Camp Woodlands
	X8 Party
	Changi Gaol Camp (cook house)
Return Details 1945	Singapore-Darwin-Melbourne, 1st Netherlands Military Hospital Ship, *Oranje*
	Melbourne 115(H)MH
	Melbourne-Perth by troop train to 110(P)MH
Additions	Wounded in action at Buona Vista on 15.2.1942. Admitted to 2/9th Field Ambulance with gun shot wounds to the lower left leg and left shoulder. Transferred to the 13th Australian General Hospital at St Patrick's School on 17.2.1942. Discharged to unit ex-A. G. H. Roberts Barracks Changi on 8.5.1942.

ARTHUR ERNEST FARMER

Rank	Private
Regimental Number	WX9199
Company	'A' Company
Enlisted	30.10.1940
Discharged	22.1.1946
Date of Birth	30.11.1904
Place of Birth	London, England
Father	Septimus William Farmer
Mother	Martha Farmer
Religion	Presbyterian
Pre-War Occupation	Railway Employee

HISTORY

Java	'Blackforce'
'A' Force Burma	Java Party No. 4, Williams Force
POW Number	4645
Return Details 1945	Thailand-Singapore by aircraft
	Singapore-Fremantle, HMT *Tamaroa*

ANDREW FEE

Rank	Private
Regimental Number	WX5088
Classification	Driver
Company	'C' Company
Enlisted	23.7.1940
Discharged	11.1.1946
Date of Birth	15.10.1901
Place of Birth	Belfast, Ireland
Father	Andrew Fee
Mother	Helen Fee
Religion	Presbyterian
Pre-War Occupation	Ship Riveter

HISTORY

Singapore	Selarang Camp Changi
'A' Force Burma	Green Force, No. 3 Battalion
Camps Burma	Khonkan 55km Camp
Camps Thailand	Tamarkan, Chungkai, Bangkok
Return Details 1945	Thailand-Singapore by aircraft
	Singapore-Sydney, HMT *Highland Chieftan*
	Sydney-Melbourne-Perth by troop train

EDWARD THOMAS FELTHAM

Rank	Warrant Officer Class 2 (Promoted on 24.1.1942)
Regimental Number	WX225
Company	'D' Company Headquarters
Enlisted	11.12.1940
Discharged	21.2.1946
Date of Birth	16.5.1909
Place of Birth	Southern Cross, Western Australia
Father	George Watt Feltham
Mother	Martha Agnes Feltham
Religion	Church of England
Pre-War Occupation	Joiner's Mate

HISTORY

Singapore	Selarang Camp and Barracks Changi
POW Number	1/7663
'D' Force Thailand	S Battalion
POW Number	8715
Camps Thailand	Tonchan, Kanu II, Kanu I River Camp (evacuated with typhus 11.7.1943), Tarsau (evacuated on 8.8.1943) Chungkai, Tamuang, Tamarkan, Nacompaton, Chumphon, Nacompaton
Return Details 1945	Thailand-Singapore by aircraft
	Singapore-Fremantle, HMT *Circassia*
Additions	Wounded in action at Buona Vista on 15.2.1942. Admitted to the 2/9th Field Ambulance with a shrapnel wound to the left foot. Taken to C.C.S. on Holland Road. Transferred to the 2/13th A.G.H. at St Patrick's School. Transferred to the A.G.H. at Roberts Barracks Changi. Transferred to No. 2 Convalescent Depot on 5.6.1942 and discharged to unit on 8.9.1942.

CHARLES GILL FERRIE

Rank	Private
Regimental Number	WX5217
Company	'C' Company
Enlisted	23.7.1940
Discharged	19.12.1945
Date of Birth	15.11.1901
Place of Birth	Ayreshire, Scotland
Father	Not Known
Mother	Not Known
Religion	Presbyterian
Pre-War Occupation	Stationhand

HISTORY

Singapore	Selarang Camp Changi
	Johore Bahru, Adam Park
	Selarang Barracks Changi
POW Numbers	1/7669 and 3/7743
'D' Force Thailand	S Battalion
POW Number	8778
Camps Thailand	Kanu II, Chungkai
Return Details 1945	Thailand-Singapore by aircraft
	Singapore-Fremantle, HMT *Moreton Bay*

HURTLE STANLEY FIDGE

Rank	Sergeant
Regimental Number	WX7663
Company	'C' Company
Enlisted	10.8.1940
Discharged	21.5.1947
Date of Birth	29.12.1915
Place of Birth	Bute, South Australia
Father	Herbert Hall Fidge
Mother	Matilda Sharman Fidge
Religion	Methodist
Pre-War Occupation	Farmhand

HISTORY

Singapore	Selarang Camp Changi
'A' Force Burma	Green Force, No. 3 Battalion
POW Number	1332
Japan	*Rakuyo Maru* Party, Kumi No. 35
Singapore	River Valley Road (Jeep Island, dry dock)
	Changi Gaol Camp Hospital (ulcer in the left eye, removed from the Japan draft)
	Transferred to Changi Administration on 28.1.1945
	X10 Party
Return Details 1945	Singapore-Darwin-Sydney, HMT *Arawa*
	Sydney-Melbourne by troop train
	Melbourne-Fremantle, HMT *Strathmore*

CHARLES FIELDER

Rank	Private
Regimental Number	WX9070
Classification	Rangetaker
Company	'C' Company
Enlisted	25.10.1940
Discharged	12.6.1946
Date of Birth	26.2.1916
Place of Birth	Geraldton, Western Australia
Father	George Fielder
Mother	Lena Fielder
Religion	Presbyterian
Pre-War Occupation	Miller at York Flour Mill

HISTORY

Java	'Blackforce'
Camps Java	Bandoeng (9.3.1942-13.4.1942), Bicycle Camp Batavia (13.4.1942-3.1.1943)
'D' Force Thailand	Java Party No. 6, P Battalion
Camps Thailand	Nakom Nayok, Bangkok
Return Details 1945	Thailand-Singapore by aircraft
	Singapore-Queensland by aircraft
	Brisbane-Sydney-Melbourne-Perth by troop train

THOMAS ALBERT FINLAY

Rank	Private
Regimental Number	WX7886
Company	'B' Company
Enlisted	13.8.1940
Discharged	14.2.1946
Date of Birth	1.11.1917
Place of Birth	Collie, Western Australia
Father	James Alexander Finlay
Mother	Edith Finlay
Religion	Methodist
Pre-War Occupation	Shop Assistant

HISTORY

Singapore	Selarang Camp and Barracks Changi
POW Number	4/6118
'D' Force Thailand	S Battalion
POW Number	8774
Camps Thailand	Kanu II, Non Pladuk
Japan	*Rashin Maru* Party
POW Number	1611
Camps Japan	Yamane
	Niihama
Return Details 1945	Wakayama-Okinawa, USS *Sanctuary*
	Okinawa-Manila, USS *Bingham*
	Manila-Morotai-Darwin-Perth, B24 Liberator aircraft A72-379

THOMAS FIRNS

Rank	Private
Regimental Number	WX7225
Classification	Carpenter
Company	Headquarters Company
Enlisted	1.8.1940
Discharged	8.1.1946
Date of Birth	9.6.1900
Place of Birth	Serpentine, Western Australia
Father	Charles Firns
Mother	Eliza Firns
Religion	Church of England
Pre-War Occupation	Gold Prospector

HISTORY

Singapore	Selarang Camp Changi
	Johore Bahru, Adam Park
	Selarang Barracks Changi
	Changi Gaol Camp
Return Details 1945	Singapore-Darwin-Sydney, HMT *Arawa*
	Sydney-Melbourne by troop train
	Melbourne-Fremantle, HMT *Strathmore*

GEORGE FISHER

Rank	Private
Regimental Number	WX5132
Classification	Rangetaker
Company	'C' Company
Enlisted	23.7.1940
Discharged	26.2.1946
Date of Birth	18.6.1915
Place of Birth	Perth, Western Australia
Father	George Fisher
Mother	Ethel Fisher
Religion	Church of England
Pre-War Occupation	Shop Assistant and Farmhand

HISTORY

Java	'Blackforce'
Camps Java	Bandoeng, Tjimahi, Bicycle Camp Batavia (recovered 18.9.1945)
Return Details 1945	Batavia (22.9.45) Balikpapan-Morotai (30.9.45) Higgins Field Far North Queensland, Townsville-Brisbane by aircraft
	Brisbane-Sydney, Melbourne-Perth by troop train (13-17.10.1945)

BASIL FITZGERALD

Rank	Private
Regimental Number	WX8586
Company	'A' Company
Enlisted	18.10.1940
Discharged	11.3.1946
Date of Birth	30.9.1902
Place of Birth	Collie, Western Australia
Father	Not Known
Mother	Not Known
Religion	Church of England
Pre-War Occupation	Poultry Farmhand and Orchard Worker

HISTORY

Singapore	Selarang Camp Changi
	Johore Bahru, Adam Park
	Selarang Barracks Changi
POW Number	2/12245
'D' Force Thailand	S Battalion
POW Number	8776
Camps Thailand	Chungkai, Kanchanaburi, Nikhe-Nikhe–Sonkurai area
Return Details 1945	Thailand-Singapore by aircraft
	Singapore-Fremantle, H.M. Hospital Ship *Karoa*
Additions	Shell shocked at Ulu Pandan on 12.2.1942 (evacuated)

THOMAS MARTIN FITZGERALD

Rank	Corporal (Promoted on 24.1.1942)
Regimental Number	WX5425
Classification	Cook
Company	'C' Company Headquarters
Enlisted	27.7.1940
Discharged	6.2.1946
Date of Birth	12.4.1903
Place of Birth	Perth, Western Australia
Father	James Fitzgerald
Mother	Annie Fitzgerald
Religion	Church of England
Pre-War Occupation	Greengrocer

HISTORY

Singapore	Selarang Camp Changi
'A' Force Burma	Green Force, No. 3 Battalion
POW Number	1366
Camps Burma	Khonkan 55km Camp
Camps Thailand	Petchaburi, Nakom Chassi
Return Details 1945	Thailand-Singapore by aircraft
	Singapore-Fremantle, HMT *Highland Brigade*

CHARLES FLAKEMORE

Rank	Lance Corporal
Regimental Number	WX8657
Company	'B' Company Headquarters
Enlisted	23.10.1940
Discharged	7.1.1946
Date of Birth	8.6.1910
Place of Birth	Tasmania
Father	Joseph Flakemore
Mother	Agnes Flakemore
Religion	Church of England
Pre-War Occupation	Labourer

HISTORY

Singapore	Selarang Camp and Barracks Changi
'D' Force Thailand	S Battalion
POW Number	8775
Camps Thailand	Chungkai, Nacompaton
Return Details 1945	Thailand-Singapore by aircraft
	Singapore-Fremantle, HMT *Highland Brigade*

JAMES JOSEPH FLANAGAN

Rank	Private
Regimental Number	WX7864
Company	'B' Company
Enlisted	30.8.1940
Discharged	24.5.1946
Date of Birth	16.11.1915
Place of Birth	Collie, Western Australia
Father	Not Known
Mother	Ethel May Flanagan
Religion	Church of England
Pre-War Occupation	Wire Mattress Weaver

HISTORY

Singapore	Selarang Camp Changi (17.2.1942-25.3.1942)
	River Valley Road Camp (25.3.1942-20.12.1942) Soldier was on a Bukit Timah work party in August 1942 when he fractured the upper bone (humerus) in his right arm. Admitted to the A. G. H. at Roberts Barracks Changi on 9.8.1942.
	Selarang Barracks Changi
'D' Force	Captain Fred Harris Party
POW Number	4782
Camps Thailand	Kanchanaburi, Kinsaiyok, Hindato, Konkoita, Tarsau, Non Pladuk
Japan	*Aramis* Party
POW Number	602
Camps Japan	Fukuoka sub-Camp No. 17, Omuta
	Fukuoka sub-Camp No. 21, Nakama
Return Details 1945	Nagasaki-Manila
	Manila-Morotai
	Darwin-Perth, B24 Liberator aircraft A72-379

JOHN HUGH FLANIGAN

Rank	Private
Regimental Number	WX9777
Company	'C' Company Headquarters
Enlisted	6.12.1940
Discharged	15.2.1946
Date of Birth	2.5.1908
Place of Birth	Perth, Western Australia
Father	William Flanigan
Mother	Elizabeth Ann Flanigan
Religion	Presbyterian
Pre-War Occupation	Cabinet Maker

HISTORY

Singapore	Selarang Camp Changi
'A' Force Burma	Green Force, No. 3 Battalion
POW Number	2887
Camps Burma	Khonkan 55km Camp
Camps Thailand	Tamarkan, Kachu Mountain Camp, Petchaburi, Bangkok (see Danny Bevis Diary)
Return Details 1945	Bangkok-Rangoon by aircraft
	Rangoon-Singapore, HMT *Highland Brigade*
	Singapore-Fremantle, HMT *Moreton Bay*

NEAVE FLARTY

Rank	Private
Regimental Number	WX17374
Company	'E' Company, Special Reserve Battalion
Enlisted	22.10.1941
Discharged	8.4.1946
Date of Birth	22.10.1922
Place of Birth	Moora, Western Australia
Father	Not Known
Mother	Margaret Flarty
Religion	Church of England
Pre-War Occupation	Farmhand

HISTORY

Singapore	Selarang Camp and Barracks Changi
'D' Force Thailand	T Battalion
Camps Thailand	Kinsaiyok, Ubon
Return Details 1945	Thailand-Singapore by aircraft
	Singapore-Fremantle, HMT *Highland Brigade*
Additions	Wounded in action at Bald Hill, Bukit Timah on 11.2.1942. Admitted to Alexandra Hospital on 12.2.1942 with a shrapnel wound to the right knee. Discharged to unit on 23.2.1942.

ALFRED ERNEST FOCH

Rank	Lance Corporal
Regimental Number	WX8679
Company	'B' Company
Enlisted	23.10.1940
Discharged	28.3.1946
Date of Birth	23.10.1898
Place of Birth	London, England
Father	Nicholas George Foch
Mother	Amy Sarah Foch
Religion	Church of England
Pre-War Occupation	Miner

HISTORY

Singapore	Selarang Camp Changi
'A' Force Burma	Green Force, No. 3 Battalion
POW Number	2721
Camps Burma	Reptu 30km Camp
Return Details 1945	Thailand-Singapore by aircraft
	Singapore admitted to the 2/14th Australian General Hospital on 10.10.1945
	Singapore-Fremantle, H.M. Hospital Ship *Karoa*

CYRIL ALBAN FOGARTY

Rank	Lance Corporal
Regimental Number	WX7709
Classification	Driver/Mechanic
Company	'A' Company
Enlisted	10.8.1940
Discharged	8.8.1946
Date of Birth	12.6.1902
Place of Birth	Sydney, New South Wales
Father	Daniel Alban Fogarty
Mother	Florence Catherine Fogarty
Religion	Roman Catholic
Pre-War Occupation	Labourer

HISTORY

Singapore	Selarang Camp Changi
'A' Force Burma	Green Force, No. 3 Battalion
POW Number	2763
Camps Thailand	Tamarkan, Nikhe-Nikhe, Nacompaton
Return Details 1945	Thailand-Singapore by aircraft
	Singapore-Fremantle, 2/1st H.M. Australian Hospital Ship *Manunda*

GORDON FOOT

Rank	Private
Regimental Number	WX15719
Company	'C' Company
Enlisted	13.8.1941
Discharged	11.3.1946
Date of Birth	11.8.1920
Place of Birth	Highgate Hill, Western Australia
Father	George Foot
Mother	Lydia Ann Foot
Religion	Church of England
Pre-War Occupation	Orchardist

HISTORY

Singapore	Selarang Camp Changi
	Serangoon Road Camp
	Selarang Barracks Changi
'D' Force Thailand	S Battalion
POW Number	8777
Camps Thailand	Kanu II, Nakom Chassi, Chumphon, Kachu Mountain Camp
Return Details 1945	Thailand-Singapore by aircraft
	Singapore-Fremantle, HMT *Highland Brigade*

ROBERT ARTHUR FOSTER

Rank	Private
Regimental Number	WX12427
Company	'B' Company
Enlisted	6.5.1941
Discharged	22.1.1946
Date of Birth	17.9.1922
Place of Birth	Perth, Western Australia
Father	Harold Foster
Mother	Kate Ella Mary Foster
Religion	Church of England
Pre-War Occupation	PMG Employee

HISTORY

Singapore	Selarang Camp Changi
'A' Force Burma	Green Force, No. 3 Battalion
POW Number	4661
Camps Burma	Khonkan 55km Camp
Camps Thailand	Tamarkan, Nikhe-Nikhe, Nacompaton, Bangkok
Return Details 1945	Thailand-Singapore by aircraft
	Singapore-Fremantle, HMT *Circassia*

JAMES ERIC FRASER

Rank	Private
Regimental Number	WX6506
Classification	Despatch Rider
Company	'D' Company
Enlisted	6.7.1940
Discharged	4.12.1945
Date of Birth	26.3.1915
Place of Birth	Mount Hawthorn, Western Australia
Father	James McIntosh Fraser M.P.
Mother	Ellen Fraser
Religion	Roman Catholic
Pre-War Occupation	Clerk with the Perth City Council

HISTORY

Singapore	Selarang Camp Changi
'A' Force Burma	Green Force, No. 3 Battalion
POW Number	1522
Camps Burma	Khonkan 55km Camp
Camps Thailand	Tamarkan, Nacompaton (on camp construction party), Bangkok, Non Pladuk
French Indo-China	*Both* Party, Kumi No. 41
Return Details 1945	Saigon-Bangkok-Singapore by aircraft
	Singapore-Labuan-Morotai-Darwin-Perth, B24 Liberator aircraft 25.9.1945
Additions	Wounded in action on 8.2.1942 and admitted to the 2/13th A.G.H. suffering from exhaustion and a bayonet wound to the left hand. Discharged to unit on 8.3.1942.

BASIL MELVILLE FROST

Rank	Private
Regimental Number	WX15422
Company	Headquarters Company
Enlisted	28.7.1941
Discharged	8.5.1946
Date of Birth	8.4.1913
Place of Birth	Kalgoorlie, Western Australia
Father	William Frost
Mother	Isabel Frost
Religion	Presbyterian
Pre-War Occupation	Labourer

HISTORY

Java	'Blackforce'
'A' Force Burma	Java Party No. 4, Williams Force
POW Number	4661
Camps Burma	Khonkan 55km Camp (evacuated to Tamarkan Hospital)
Japan	*Rakuyo Maru* Party, Kumi No. 38
Singapore	Changi Gaol Camp Hospital (evacuated with an infected leg August 1944)
	Transferred to Changi Administration on 28.1.1945
	X3 Party
Return Details 1945	Singapore-Darwin-Sydney, HMT *Arawa*
	Sydney-Melbourne by troop train
	Melbourne-Perth by ANA airliner

HARRY CHARLES FUHRMANN

Rank	Sergeant (Promoted 11.2.1942)
Regimental Number	WX7852
Awards	Distinguished Conduct Medal
Company	'C' Company
Enlisted	13.8.1940
Discharged	19.6.1946
Date of Birth	14.8.1909
Place of Birth	Bunbury, Western Australia
Father	Frederick Ernest Fuhrmann
Mother	Margaret Mary Fuhrmann
Religion	Roman Catholic
Pre-War Occupation	Coal Miner

HISTORY

Singapore	Selarang Camp Changi
'A' Force Burma	Green Force, No. 3 Battalion
POW Number	1325
Camps Thailand	Tamarkan, Nacompaton, Bangkok
Return Details 1945	Thailand-Singapore by aircraft
	Singapore-Fremantle, HMT *Moreton Bay*
Additions	Wounded in action at Ulu Pandan on 12.2.1942. Admitted to the 2/13th Australian General Hospital with a gunshot wound to the right shoulder. Discharged to unit on 22.2.1942. NCO suffered from paralysis to the right hand caused by a poisoned bamboo in March 1944 and a tropical ulcer to the left hand in February 1945.

RODNEY CHARLES FULLERTON

Rank	Sergeant (Promoted 29.1.1942)
Regimental Number	WX8119
Company	'C' Company
Enlisted	16.8.1940
Discharged	14.2.1946
Date of Birth	13.8.1913
Place of Birth	Northam, Western Australia
Father	William John Fullerton
Mother	Alice Fullerton
Religion	Church of England
Pre-War Occupation	Bank Officer

HISTORY

Singapore	Selarang Camp and Barracks Changi
	Changi Gaol Camp
	Kranji Hospital Woodlands
	X6 Party
	Changi Gaol Camp
POW Number	1/7752
Return Details 1945	Singapore-Darwin-Sydney, HMT *Arawa*
	Sydney-Melbourne-Adelaide-Perth by troop train
Additions	Wounded in action at 0900 hours on 11.2.1942 at Reformatory Road, Ulu Pandan. NCO was admitted to Field Ambulance with a gunshot wound to the right thigh, a gunshot wound to the lower left femur and three gunshot wounds to the left leg. Transferred to Alexandra Hospital then to the 2/10th Australian General Hospital.

ARTHUR RAYMOND GAMBLE

Rank	Private
Regimental Number	WX9132
Classification	Despatch Rider
Company	'C' Company
Enlisted	30.10.1940
Discharged	13.12.1945
Date of Birth	25.10.1918
Place of Birth	Perth, Western Australia
Father	Robert Gamble
Mother	Winifred Myrtle Gamble
Religion	Methodist
Pre-War Occupation	Farmer

HISTORY

Singapore	Selarang Camp Changi
	Johore Bahru, Adam Park
	Sime Road Camp (quarry at Bukit Timah)
	Selarang Barracks Changi (Garden Control Party)
POW Number	1/7767
'H' Force Thailand	'H' Force Group No. 3
Camps Thailand	Kanu II Malayan Hamlet, Kanu IIIa Kanu I River Camp,
	Kanchanaburi (evacuated sick by barge with cholera 26.6.1943-11.9.1943)
Singapore	Sime Road Camp (transferred to hospital at Changi Gaol Camp)
	Levelling Party Changi Aerodrome
	P Party (Johore Bahru)
Return Details 1945	Singapore-Darwin-Sydney, HMT *Arawa*
	Sydney-Melbourne by troop train
	Melbourne-Fremantle, HMT *Strathmore*

PETER ALAN GARDINER

Rank	Sergeant (Promoted 24.1.1942)
Regimental Number	WX10925
Company	'D' Company
Enlisted	17.2.1941
Discharged	22.3.1946
Date of Birth	14.2.1921
Place of Birth	Perth, Western Australia
Father	Harold Alan Gardiner
Mother	Edith Alice Gardiner
Religion	Church of England
Pre-War Occupation	Storeman

HISTORY

Singapore	Selarang Camp Changi
	Johore Bahru, Adam Park
	Selarang Barracks Changi
POW Number	4/4494
'D' Force Thailand	V Battalion
Camps Thailand	Kinsaiyok, Brankassi, Hindaine, Hindato, Non Pladuk, Nacompaton, Bangkok (go-downs), Motor Transport Camp Bangkok, Bangkok Racecourse seven days, Bangkok University Camp
Return Details 1945	Thailand-Singapore by aircraft
	Singapore-Fremantle, HMT *Moreton Bay*
Additions	Wounded in action on 8.2.1942, spent three days behind enemy lines before being evacuated to hospital. NCO rejoined unit in the line at Holland Village Cemetery, Buona Vista on 15.2.1942. NCO was the half brother of WX15905 E. G. Moir.

CLAUDE WILLIAM GAULT

Rank	Private
Regimental Number	WX10622
Classification	Signaller
Company	Headquarters Company
Enlisted	14.1.1941
Discharged	30.6.1944
Date of Birth	3.1.1914
Place of Birth	York, Western Australia
Father	John Gault
Mother	Elizabeth Gault
Religion	Church of England
Pre-War Occupation	Storeman

HISTORY

Singapore	Last seen at Ulu Pandan and reported missing from 18.2.1942. Soldier was shell shocked on 13.2.1943 and remained unconscious for seven hours. He was evacuated from No. 1 Malaya General Hospital to Columbo from where he was returned to Australia, disembarking at Melbourne on 6.4.1942 ex-HMT *Stirling Castle*. Soldier returned to Western Australia and after a period in hospital and three weeks convalescing, he was posted to the 423rd AA Gun Station. On his first shoot, headaches forced his transfer to the 4th Australian Signal Training Unit. From here he was again transferred to the 51st Water Transport Company.
Australia	

RONALD JACK GIBBONS

Rank	Sergeant (Promoted on 24.1.1942)
Regimental Number	WX7607
Company	'C' Company
Enlisted	10.8.1940
Discharged	25.2.1946
Date of Birth	16.7.1918
Place of Birth	Perth, Western Australia
Father	George Harold Gibbons
Mother	Sheila Aileen Gibbons
Religion	Church of England
Pre-War Occupation	Farmhand

HISTORY

Singapore	Selarang Camp Changi
	Johore Bahru, Adam Park
	River Valley Road Camp
	Selarang Barracks Changi
POW Number	4/4495
'D' Force Thailand	S Battalion
POW Number	8719
Camps Thailand	Tonchan, Hintok Road Camp (cholera), Tarsau (evacuated sick), Kinsaiyok, Nacompaton, Non Pladuk
French Indo-China	*Both* Party
Return Details 1945	Saigon-Bangkok-Singapore by aircraft
	Singapore-Labuan-Morotai-Brisbane-Sydney, by aircraft
	Sydney-Melbourne-Perth by troop train

PERCIVAL JOHN GIBBS

Rank	Private
Regimental Number	WX8607
Classification	Driver/Mechanic
Company	'B' Company Headquarters
Enlisted	18.10.1940
Discharged	27.6.1948
Date of Birth	9.7.1909
Place of Birth	Perth, Western Australia
Father	Frederick John Gibbs
Mother	Susannah Gibbs
Religion	Church of England
Pre-War Occupation	Truck Driver

HISTORY

Singapore	Selarang Camp Changi
'A' Force Burma	Green Force, No. 3 Battalion
Camps Thailand	Tamarkan, Chungkai, Hindato, Pratchinburi, Nakom Nayok, Lopburi, Bangkok
Return Details 1945	Thailand-Singapore by aircraft
	Singapore-Fremantle, HMT *Tamaroa*

THOMAS CROSBY GIBSON

Rank	Private
Regimental Number	WX8900
Classification	Driver
Company	'C' Company
Enlisted	25.10.1940
Discharged	14.1.1946
Date of Birth	30.3.1911
Place of Birth	Cranbrook, Western Australia
Father	George Crosby Gibson
Mother	Mary Gibson
Religion	Church of England
Pre-War Occupation	Bus Driver

HISTORY

Singapore	Selarang Camp Changi
	Johore Bahru, Adam Park
	Selarang Barracks Changi
POW Number	4/6156
'D' Force Thailand	S Battalion
POW Number	8779
Camps Thailand	Kanu II, Tamuang
Japan	*Rashin Maru* Party
POW Numbers	1615 and 445
Camps Japan	Yamane
	Niihama
Return Details 1945	Wakayama-Okinawa, USS *Sanctuary*
	Okinawa-Manila, USS *Bingham*
	Manila-Sydney, HMS *Speaker*
	Sydney-Fremantle, HMT *Dominion Monarch*

WILLIAM MARCUS GIDDENS

Rank	Private
Regimental Number	WX5335
Company	'A' Company (transferred from Bn. Hq's on 22.11.1941)
Enlisted	27.7.1940
Discharged	14.12.1945
Date of Birth	3.5.1920
Place of Birth	Bunbury, Western Australia
Father	Henry Boradlaugh Giddens
Mother	Maude Hilda Giddens
Religion	Church of England
Pre-War Occupation	Dairyhand

HISTORY

Singapore	Selarang Camp Changi
	Johore Bahru, Adam Park
	Selarang Barracks Changi
POW Number	4/6157
'D' Force Thailand	S Battalion
POW Number	8781
Camps Thailand	Kanu II, Rin Tin, Tamarkan, Chungkai, Nacompaton, Nakom Chassi
Return Details 1945	Thailand-Singapore by aircraft
	Singapore-Labuan-Moroatai-Sydney by aircraft
	Sydney-Melbourne-Perth by troop train

FRANCIS LESLIE GILES

Rank	Private
Regimental Number	WX8788
Company	'D' Company Headquarters
Enlisted	23.10.1940
Discharged	15.2.1946
Date of Birth	20.3.1908
Place of Birth	Fremantle, Western Australia
Father	Albert Edward Giles
Mother	Lilly Giles
Religion	Roman Catholic
Pre-War Occupation	Locomotive Fireman

HISTORY

Singapore	Selarang Camp and Barracks Changi
POW Number	4/6159
'D' Force Thailand	V Battalion
Camps Thailand	Nakom Nayok
Return Details 1945	Thailand-Singapore by aircraft
	Singapore-Melbourne by aircraft
	Melbourne-Perth by troop train

JAMES GILMOUR

Rank	Private
Regimental Number	WX8623
Classification	Scout
Company	'A' Company
Enlisted	18.10.1940
Discharged	13.12.1945
Date of Birth	2.8.1921
Place of Birth	Ayr, Scotland
Father	Hugh Gilmour
Mother	Helen Knox Gilmour
Religion	Presbyterian
Pre-War Occupation	Nurseryman

HISTORY

Singapore	Selarang Camp Changi
	Johore Bahru, Adam Park
	Sime Road Camp
	Selarang Barracks Changi
'D' Force Thailand	S Battalion
POW Number	8780
Camps Thailand	Kanu II, Kanu I River Camp, Tarsau (evacuated by barge with cholera), Konkoita, Kinsaiyok, Tarsau, Chungkai, Tardan, Kachu Mountain Camp
Return Details 1945	Thailand-Singapore by aircraft
	Singapore-Fremantle, HMT *Highland Brigade*

JOHN BARRY GILMOUR

Rank	Lance Corporal
Regimental Number	WX8622
Company	'A' Company
Enlisted	18.10.1940
Discharged	14.6.1946
Date of Birth	3.5.1919
Place of Birth	Ayr, Scotland
Father	Hugh Gilmour
Mother	Helen Knox Gilmour
Religion	Presbyterian
Pre-War Occupation	Factory Hand

HISTORY

Singapore	Selarang Camp Changi
	Thomson Road (Caldecot Hill Estate Camp)
	Selarang Barracks Singapore
POW Number	3/7896
'J' Force Japan	*Wales Maru* Party
Camps Japan	Kobe (Showa-Denki)
	Kawasaki Camp-Maruyama Park, Wakinohama
Return Details 1945	Yokohama-Okinawa by aircraft
	Okinawa-Manila, B24 Liberator aircraft
	Manila-Sydney, HMS *Formidable*
	Sydney-Fremantle, HMT *Dominion* Monarch

GEORGE GLASS

Rank	Private
Regimental Number	WX7595
Classification	Driver
Company	Battalion Headquarters
Enlisted	6.8.1940
Discharged	24.4.1946
Date of Birth	21.3.1904
Place of Birth	Belfast, Ireland
Father	Not Known
Mother	Not Known
Religion	Church of England
Pre-War Occupation	Barman/Yardman

HISTORY

Java	'Blackforce'
Camps Java	Bicycle Camp Batavia
'A' Force Burma	Java Party No. 4, Williams Force
POW Number	4540
Camps Burma	Beke Taung 40km, Aungganaung 105km
Camps Thailand	Kanchanaburi-British Army Hospital at Chulalongkorn Bangkok
Return Details 1945	Thailand-Singapore by aircraft
	Singapore-Fremantle, H.M. Hospital Ship *Karoa*

STEPHEN JOHN GLEESON

Rank	Private
Regimental Number	WX16736
Company	Not Known
Enlisted	8.9.1941
Discharged	3.12.1945
Date of Birth	16.4.1919
Place of Birth	Boulder, Western Australia
Father	Stephen Joseph Gleeson
Mother	Beatrice Elizabeth Gleeson
Religion	Church of England
Pre-War Occupation	Brick Worker

HISTORY

Singapore	Selarang Camp and Barracks Changi
'H' Force Thailand	'H' Force Group No. 3
Camps Thailand	Kanu II Malayan Hamlet, Kanchanaburi
Singapore	Changi Gaol Camp
Return Details 1945	Singapore-Melbourne, 1st Netherlands Military Hospital Ship *Oranje*
	Melbourne-Perth by troop train
Additions	Soldier's right leg was amputated. Remained at Kanchanaburi when 'H' Force returned to Singapore due to illness but returned to Singapore after December 1943.

PERCY GOLDEN

Rank	Private
Regimental Number	WX6980
Company	'A' Company
Enlisted	30.7.1940
Discharged	14.6.1946
Date of Birth	29.6.1906
Place of Birth	Croydon, England
Father	Charles Golden
Mother	Lily Golden
Religion	Church of England
Pre-War Occupation	Labourer

HISTORY

Java	'Blackforce'
Camps Java	Bicycle Camp Batavia
'A' Force Burma	Java Party No. 4, Williams Force
POW Number	4644
Camps Thailand	Tamarkan, Nacompaton
Return Details 1945	Thailand-Singapore by aircraft
	Singapore-Fremantle, HMT *Moreton Bay*

JOHN GORRINGE

Rank	Sergeant (Promoted on 11.2.1942)
Regimental Number	WX9336
Awards	British Empire Medal
Company	'B' Company
Enlisted	30.10.1940
Discharged	11.12.1945
Date of Birth	18.1.1913
Place of Birth	Subiaco, Western Australia
Father	Thomas Gorringe
Mother	Eleanor Gorringe
Religion	Methodist
Pre-War Occupation	Butcher and Farmhand

HISTORY

Singapore	Selarang Camp and Barracks Changi
POW Number	1/7833
Force	'F' Force Thailand
Camps Thailand	Shimo Sonkurai
	Kanchanaburi (7.1.44-30.3.1944 beri-beri)
Camps Burma	Tanbaya Hospital Camp (temporary medical staff)
Singapore	Changi Gaol Camp
Return Details 1945	Singapore-Darwin-Sydney, HMT *Arawa*
	Sydney-Melbourne by troop train
	Melbourne-Fremantle, HMT *Strathmore*
Additions	This NCO was admitted to the 2/13th Australian General Hospital with malaria on 16.2.1942 and was not discharged to unit until 9.3.1942. Sergeant Gorringe for nearly two years was the most senior 2/4th NCO at Changi and as well as the excellent work he did there, he was also placed in charge of the cookhouse.

SYDNEY GORRINGE

Rank	Private
Regimental Number	WX9335
Company	'B' Company
Enlisted	30.10.1940
Discharged	7.5.1946
Date of Birth	24.9.1916
Place of Birth	Perth, Western Australia
Father	Thomas Gorringe
Mother	Eleanor Gorringe
Religion	Methodist
Pre-War Occupation	Farmhand

HISTORY

Singapore	Selarang Camp and Barracks Changi
POW Number	4/6168
'D' Force Thailand	S Battalion
POW Number	8783
Camps Thailand	Chungkai, Nacompaton, Bangkok
Return Details 1945	Thailand-Singapore by aircraft
	Singapore-Fremantle, HMT *Circassia*
Additions	Soldier's left leg was amputated below knee due to a tropical ulcer on 30.9.1943.

NORMAN ANGUS GOUGH

Rank	Private
Regimental Number	WX8582
Company	'A' Company
Enlisted	18.10.1940
Discharged	13.11.1945
Date of Birth	20.10.1905
Place of Birth	Mile End, South Australia
Father	Richard Felix Gough
Mother	Rachel Gordon Gough
Religion	Church of England
Pre-War Occupation	Commercial Traveller and Wood Merchant

HISTORY

Singapore	Selarang Camp Changi
	Sime Road Camp
	Selarang Barracks Changi
	Changi Gaol Camp
POW Number	1/2931
Return Details 1945	Singapore-Darwin, HMT *Arawa*
	Darwin-Perth, B24 Liberator aircraft
Additions	Soldier wandered into Regimental Aid Post and collapsed. He was shell shocked and had an injury to his back which caused partial paralysis. Evacuated to St Joseph's School then to the 2/13th Australian General Hospital at St Patrick's School on 16.2.1942. Admitted to the 2/10th Australian General Hospital on 7.3.1942 and discharged to unit on 7.4.1942.

NORMAN FREDERICK THOMAS GOUGH

Rank	Private
Regimental Number	WX17310
Company	'E' Company, Special Reserve Battalion
Enlisted	20.10.1941
Discharged	6.2.1946
Date of Birth	13.11.1922
Place of Birth	Leederville, Western Australia
Father	James Harold Gough
Mother	Jessie Sarah Gough
Religion	Roman Catholic
Pre-War Occupation	Storeman and Miner

HISTORY

Singapore	Selarang Camp Changi
	Johore Bahru, Adam Park
	Sime Road Camp
	Thomson Road (Caldecot Hill Estate Camp)
	Selarang Barracks Changi
POW Number	4/6169
'D' Force Thailand	V Battalion
POW Number	2246
Camps Thailand	Kinsaiyok, Rin Tin, Hindato, Brankassi, Hindaine, Brankassi, Hindato, Non Pladuk, Tarsau, Non Pladuk No. 1 and No. 2 Camps
Japan	*Aramis* Party
POW Number	598
Camps Japan	Fukuoka sub-Camp No. 17 Omuta
Return Details 1945	Nagasaki-Okinawa-USS *Cape Gloucester*
	Okinawa-Manila, USS *Bingham*
	Manila-Morotai-Darwin, PBY Catalina aircraft A24-354
	Darwin-Melbourne-Perth by aircraft

NORMAN HERBERT GRANT

Rank	Lance Sergeant (Promoted 8.10.1941)
Regimental Number	WX8228
Classification	Driver
Company	'C' Company Headquarters
Enlisted	16.8.1940
Discharged	29.3.1946
Date of Birth	3.8.1911
Place of Birth	Fremantle, Western Australia
Father	Thomas George Grant
Mother	Dora May Grant
Religion	Roman Catholic
Pre-War Occupation	Truck Driver and Miner

HISTORY

Singapore	Selarang Camp Changi
'A' Force Burma	Green Force, No. 3 Battalion
POW Number	2682
Japan	*Awa Maru* Party, Kumi No. 41
POW Number	1585
Camps Japan	Fukuoka sub-Camp No. 17 Omuta (underground supervisor)
Return Details 1945	Nagasaki-Manila, USS *Lunga Point*
	Manila-Sydney, HMS *Speaker*
	Sydney-Fremantle, HMT *Dominion Monarch*

CHARLES WILLIAM GRAY

Rank	Corporal (Promoted on 24.1.1942)
Regimental Number	WX10378
Company	'B' Company
Enlisted	18.12.1940
Discharged	7.1.1946
Date of Birth	9.11.1914
Place of Birth	Ravensthorpe, Western Australia
Father	Charles Herbert Gray
Mother	Mary Edith Gray
Religion	Church of England
Pre-War Occupation	Gold Miner

HISTORY

Singapore	Selarang Camp Changi
	Johore Bahru, Adam Park
Force	Japan 'B' Party Korea, *Fukkai Maru*
POW Numbers	331 and 271
Camps Korea	Keijo (warehouse)
	Konan (carbide factory)
Return Details 1945	Korea-Manila, USS *Mercy* and HMS *Collosus*
	Manila-Darwin-Perth, PBY Catalina aircraft A24-377

LEONARD GREAVES

Rank	Corporal
Regimental Number	WX8373
Classification	Driver
Company	'A' Company
Enlisted	3.9.1940
Discharged	11.1.1946
Date of Birth	15.4.1915
Place of Birth	Greenhills, Western Australia
Father	Richard Broddon Greaves
Mother	Mary Alice Greaves
Religion	Church of England
Pre-War Occupation	Timber Worker

HISTORY

Singapore	Selarang Camp Changi
'A' Force Burma	Green Force, No. 3 Battalion
POW Number	2919
Camps Burma	Reptu 30km Camp
Camps Thailand	Tamarkan
Japan	*Awa Maru* Party (soldier remained at Saigon)
Return Details 1945	Saigon-Bangkok-Singapore by aircraft
	Singapore-Sydney, HMT *Highland Chieftan*
	Sydney-Perth by troop train
Additions	Wounded in action at Buona Vista on 15.2.1942. Admitted to the 2/13th Australian General Hospital on 16.2.1942 with a shrapnel wound to the lumbar region of his back. Discharged to unit on 22.2.1942.

ALFRED REDVERS GREEN

Rank	Warrant Officer Class 2
Regimental Number	WX9558
Classification	Electrical Fitter
Attached 2/4th	88 Light Aid Detachment
Enlisted	4.12.1940
Discharged	12.4.1946
Date of Birth	18.4.1901
Place of Birth	Galveston, Tasmania
Father	Robert James Green
Mother	Elizabeth Rachael Green
Religion	Church of England
Pre-War Occupation	Electrical Fitter

HISTORY

Singapore	Selarang Camp Changi
'A' Force Burma	Green Force, No. 3 Battalion
POW Number	2649
Camps Thailand	Tamarkan
Return Details 1945	Thailand-Singapore by aircraft
	Singapore-Fremantle, HMT *Moreton Bay*
Additions	Suffered deafness to the right ear caused by an explosion on 15.2.1942.

CHARLES EDWARD GREEN

Rank	Major
Regimental Number	WX3435
Awards	Member of the British Empire
	Mentioned in Despatches
Company	Battalion Headquarters
Enlisted	11.11.1940
Appointment Terminated	11.1.1946
Date of Birth	30.7.1902
Place of Birth	Perth, Western Australia
Father	Charles Edward Green
Mother	Eliza Bassett Green
Religion	Church of England
Pre-War Occupation	Warehouse Manager at Fauldings Pty Ltd

HISTORY

Singapore	Selarang Camp Changi
'A' Force Burma	Green Force, No. 3 Battalion (Commanding Officer)
POW Number	1284
Camps Thailand	Tamarkan, Chungkai, Kanchanaburi, Petchaburi, Kachu Mountain Camp
Return Details 1945	Thailand-Singapore by aircraft
	Singapore-Fremantle, HMT *Highland Brigade*
Additions	Major Green was promoted to Lieutenant-Colonel on the death of Lieutenant-Colonel Anketell. In his capacity as the Commanding Officer of the 2/4th Machine Gun Battalion and Green Force he was taken by the Japanese and placed into solitary confinement for refusing to sign a no escape declaration. He was sent to Thanbyuzayat and was not released until he had signed this document which he did under duress. On his release on 12.10.1942 he rejoined his Prisoner of War workforce in the rubber plantation at Kendau, the 4.8km Camp. At wars end Lt.Col. Green was called upon to lead a liaison mission to Ubon near the Thai-Loatian border. After this he returned to Bangkok and was assigned the task of commanding all Allied ex-Prisoners of War in the Petchaburi-Kachu Mountain area before returning to Singapore.

Captain Jack Thompson, Captain Avon Smith-Ryan
Major Charles Green, in front

THOMAS HENRY GREEN

Rank	Corporal (Promoted on 11.2.1942)
Regimental Number	WX7869
Company	'B' Company
Enlisted	13.8.1940
Discharged	9.1.1946
Date of Birth	8.3.1918
Place of Birth	West Perth, Western Australia
Father	Edward Green
Mother	Constance Kate Green
Religion	Church of England
Pre-War Occupation	Coal Miner and Timber Worker

HISTORY

Singapore	Selarang Camp and Barracks Changi
POW Number	1/7862
'D' Force Thailand	S Battalion
POW Number	8728
Camps Thailand	Chungkai, Nikhe-Nikhe, Kanchanaburi
Return Details 1945	Thailand-Singapore by aircraft
	Singapore-Fremantle, HMT *Tamaroa*

HENRY JOSIAH GREGORY

Rank	Private
Regimental Number	WX5086
Classification	Batman/Runner
Company	'B' Company
Enlisted	23.7.1940
Discharged	11.2.1946
Date of Birth	18.1.1904
Place of Birth	Adelaide, South Australia
Father	Gilbert Gregory
Mother	Not Known
Religion	Methodist
Pre-War Occupation	Woodcutter

HISTORY

Singapore	Selarang Camp and Barracks Changi
POW Number	4/6176
'D' Force Thailand	S Battalion
POW Number	8784
Camps Thailand	Kanu II, Chungkai, Tamuang
Return Details 1945	Thailand-Singapore by aircraft
	Singapore-Fremantle HMT *Moreton Bay*

RONALD KEITH GREGORY

Rank	Private
Regimental Number	WX9202
Company	'A' Company
Enlisted	30.10.1940
Discharged	27.11.1946
Date of Birth	4.11.1910
Place of Birth	Kalgoorlie, Western Australia
Father	George Henry Gregory
Mother	Janet Margaret Ronald Gregory
Religion	Presbyterian
Pre-War Occupation	Miner

HISTORY

Singapore	Selarang Camp and Barracks Changi
POW Number	1/7869
Force	'F' Force Thailand
Camps Thailand	Shimo Sonkurai, Tanbaya Hospital Camp Burma (3 months), Kanchanaburi
Singapore	Sime Road Camp
	Kranji Hospital Woodlands (10 months)
	Changi Gaol Camp
Return Details 1945	Singapore-Labuan by aircraft
	Labuan-Morotai-Melbourne, 2/2 H.M. Australian Hospital Ship *Wanganella*
	Melbourne-Perth by troop train

WILLIAM RICE GREGORY

Rank	Private
Regimental Number	WX8625
Classification	Rangetaker
Company	'A' Company
Enlisted	18.10.1940
Discharged	7.1.1946
Date of Birth	19.11.1912
Place of Birth	Armadale, Western Australia
Father	Joseph Gregory
Mother	Isabella Gregory
Religion	Church of England
Pre-War Occupation	Miner

HISTORY

Java	'Blackforce'
'A' Force Burma	Java Party No. 4, Black Force
POW Number	454?
Camps Thailand	131km, 133km, Kanchanaburi (13.1.1944)
Return Details 1945	Thailand-Singapore by aircraft
	Singapore-Fremantle, HMT *Moreton Bay*

KEITH GEORGE GRIFFITH

Rank	Corporal
Regimental Number	WX15247
Classification	Cook
Company	'A' Company
Enlisted	23.7.1941
Discharged	15.1.1946
Date of Birth	19.4.1922
Place of Birth	Bunbury, Western Australia
Father	Mark Griffith
Mother	Ada Griffith
Religion	Church of England
Pre-War Occupation	Pastry Cook

HISTORY

Singapore	Selarang Camp Changi
'A' Force Burma	Green Force, No. 3 Battalion
POW Number	1503
Camps Burma	Reptu 30km (26.3.1943)
Camps Thailand	Tamarkan, Bangkok, Nakom Chassi, Nacompaton, Bangkok
Return Details 1945	Bangkok-Singapore by aircraft
	Singapore-Fremantle, HMT *Highland Brigade*
Additions	Wounded in action at Buona Vista and admitted to the 2/13th Australian General Hospital from the 2/10th Field Ambulance with shrapnel wounds to the wrist, left knee and left thigh. Discharged to unit on 22.2.1942.

WILLIAM DUNCAN GRUNDY

Rank	Private
Regimental Number	WX10693
Classification	Signaller
Company	Headquarters Company
Enlisted	15.1.1941
Discharged	27.2.1946
Date of Birth	22.11.1911
Place of Birth	Perth, Western Australia
Father	Not Known
Mother	Amy Constance Grundy
Religion	Methodist
Pre-War Occupation	Miner

HISTORY

Singapore	Selarang Camp Changi
	Johore Bahru, Adam Park
	Selarang Barracks Changi
'D' Force Thailand	T Battalion
Camps Thailand	Chungkai
French Indo-China	*Both* Party
Returrn Details 1945	Saigon-Bangkok-Singapore by aircraft
	Singapore-Sydney, HMT *Highland Chieftan*
	Sydney-Melbourne-Perth by troop train
Additions	This soldier may have been involved with T Battalion and or the Capt. Fred Harris, Sgt. Eddie Derkenne or W.O.II John Dooley Parties.

HORACE VICTOR WENTWORTH GWILLIAM

Rank	Private
Regimental Number	WX16383
Company	Headquarters Company
Enlisted	8.9.1941
Discharged	3.5.1946
Date of Birth	5.10.1922
Place of Birth	Hertfordshire, England
Father	John Gwilliam
Mother	Minnie Gwilliam
Religion	Church of England
Pre-War Occupation	Farmhand

HISTORY

Singapore	Selarang Camp Changi
	Johore Bahru, Adam Park
	Selarang Barracks Changi
POW Number	4/6182
'D' Force Thailand	V Battalion
Camps Thailand	Kinsaiyok, Brankassi, Ubon
Return Details 1945	Bangkok-Singapore by aircraft
	Singapore-Fremantle, HMT *Moreton Bay*

GEORGE WHITTINDALE GWYNNE

Rank	Captain
Regimental Number	WX3450
Awards	Mentioned in Despatches
Company	'D' Company Headquarters
Enlisted	14.12.1940
Appointment Terminated	10.1.1946
Date of Birth	3.8.1904
Place of Birth	West Perth, Western Australia
Father	Lewis Howard Gwynne
Mother	Madeline Isabel Gwynne
Religion	Church of England
Pre-War Occupation	Barrister and Solicitor

HISTORY

Singapore	Selarang Camp Changi
	Thomson Road (Caldecot Hill Estate Camp)
	River Valley Road Camp
	Selarang Barracks Changi
POW Number	3/5779
Force	'F' Force Thailand
Camps Thailand	Shimo Sonkurai, Kami Sonkurai, Nikhe, Tanbaya Camp Burma, Kanchanaburi
Singapore	Leveling Party at Changi Aerodrome Camp
	Changi Gaol Camp
Return Details 1945	Singapore-Darwin-Sydney, HMT *Arawa*
	Sydney-Melbourne by troop train
	Melbourne-Fremantle, HMT *Strathmore*
Additions	This Officer was promoted to Command 'D' Company on the death of Lieutenant-Colonel M. J. Anketell and Major Alf Cough's promotion as battalion second in command.

GILBERT VALENTINE HADDEN

Rank	Private
Regimental Number	WX7213
Company	'D' Company
Enlisted	1.8.1940
Discharged	18.1.1946
Date of Birth	23.6.1908
Place of Birth	Kalgoorlie, Western Australia
Father	Not Known
Mother	Not Known
Religion	Presbyterian
Pre-War Occupation	Miner and Prospector

HISTORY

Singapore	Selarang Camp and Barracks Changi
POW Number	3/7979
'D' Force Thailand	S Battalion
POW Number	8789
Camps Thailand	Kanu II, Chungkai, Ubon
Return Details 1945	Thailand-Singapore by aircraft
	Singapore-Fremantle, HMT *Highland Brigade*

LLOYD FOSTER HADDEN

Rank	Private
Regimental Number	WX9139
Classification	Driver
Company	'B' Company
Enlisted	30.10.1940
Discharged	8.2.1946
Date of Birth	31.12.1916
Place of Birth	Kalgoorlie, Western Australia
Father	Not Known
Mother	Lilly Emma Hadden
Religion	Church of England
Pre-War Occupation	Farmer and Truck Driver

HISTORY

Singapore	Selarang Camp Changi
	Johore Bahru, Adam Park
	Sime Road
	Selarang Barracks Changi
POW Number	4/6184
'D' Force Thailand	Captain Harris Party
Camps Thailand	Kinsaiyok, Non Pladuk, Nikhe Wood Camp
Return Details 1945	Thailand-Singapore by aircraft
	Singapore-Fremantle, HMT *Moreton Bay*

RALPH WILLIAM HADFIELD

Rank	Corporal (Promoted on 24.1.1942)
Regimental Number	WX7246
Classification	Rangetaker
Company	'C' Company
Enlisted	1.8.1940
Discharged	2.5.1946
Date of Birth	12.8.1917
Place of Birth	Leonora, Western Australia
Father	Herbert Thomas Hadfield
Mother	Nancy Teresa Hadfield
Religion	Roman Catholic
Pre-War Occupation	Dairyman and Truck Driver

HISTORY

Singapore	Selarang Camp Changi
	Johore Bahru, Adam Park (4.4.1942-27.12.1942)
	Selarang Barracks Changi (27.12.1942-14.3.1943
POW Number	4/4500
'D' Force Thailand	S Battalion
POW Number	8730
Camps Thailand	Tarsau (27.3.1943-24.4.1943)
	Kanu II (25.4.1943-11.7.1943
	Hintok River Camp (11.7.1943-23.8.1943)
	Tarsau (23.8.1943-26.4.1944)
	Tamuang (26.4.1944-21.6.1944)
Japan	*Rashin Maru* Party
POW Number	1546
Camps Japan	Yamane (10.9.1944-18.5.1945)
	Niihama (18.5.1945-13.9.1945)
Return Details 1945	Wakayama-Okinawa, USS *Sanctuary*
	Okinawa-Manila, USS *Bingham*
	Manila-Sydney, HMS *Speaker*
	Sydney-Melbourne-Perth by troop train

JAMES NOEL HALL

Rank	Private
Regimental Number	WX8690
Classification	Driver/Stretcher Bearer
Company	Battalion Headquarters
Enlisted	23.10.1940
Discharged	14.2.1946
Date of Birth	25.12.1904
Place of Birth	Arkholme, Lancashire, England
Father	Arthur Hall
Mother	Elizabeth Hall
Religion	Church of England
Pre-War Occupation	Farmer and Miner

HISTORY

Singapore	Selarang Camp Changi
	Thomson Road (Caldecot Hill Estate Camp)
	River Valley Road Camp
	Selarang Barracks Changi
POW Number	1/2252
'D' Force Thailand	V Battalion
Camps Thailand	Brankassi, Hindaine, Kuii, Non Pladuk, Ubon
Return Details 1945	Thailand-Singapore by aircraft and admitted to the 2/14th Australian General Hospital
	Singapore-Fremantle, H.M. Hospital Ship *Karoa*

WILLIAM ARTHUR HALLIGAN

Rank	Corporal (Promoted on 24.1.1942)
Regimental Number	WX8807
Company	'B' Company
Enlisted	23.10.1940
Discharged	12.3.1946
Date of Birth	28.9.1918
Place of Birth	Geraldton, Western Australia
Father	James Edge Halligan
Mother	Nellie Francis Halligan
Religion	Roman Catholic
Pre-War Occupation	Miner and Hoist Driver

HISTORY

Singapore	Selarang Camp and Barracks Changi
'D' Force Thailand	S Battalion
POW Number	8786
Camps Thailand	Kanu II, Konkoita, Tarsau, Nacompaton
Return Details 1945	Thailand-Singapore by aircraft
	Singapore-Perth, PBY Catalina aircraft 18.10.1945
Additions	Soldier was missing from 10.2.1942 but had joined up with 'A' Company 2/4th Machine Gun Battalion and fought with them until surrender on 15.2.1942.

REGINALD JOHN HAM

Rank	Private
Regimental Number	WX6975
Classification	Driver
Company	'D' Company
Enlisted	30.7.1940
Discharged	23.1.1947
Date of Birth	18.1.1914
Place of Birth	Mosman Park, Western Australia
Father	John Walter Ham
Mother	Emily Mary Ham
Religion	Methodist
Pre-War Occupation	Painter's Assistant

HISTORY

Java	'Blackforce'
'A' Force Burma	Java Party No. 4, Williams Force
POW Number	4642
Camps Thailand	131km, 133km, Kanchanaburi, Chumphon, Petchaburi, Kachu Mountain Camp
Return Details 1945	Thailand-Singapore by aircraft
	Singapore-Fremantle, HMT *Highland Brigade*

ALBERT JAMES HAMBLEY

Rank	Private
Regimental Number	WX10745
Classification	Signaller
Company	Headquarters Company
Enlisted	15.1.1941
Discharged	24.1.1946
Date of Birth	2.11.1921
Place of Birth	Mount Barker, Western Australia
Father	Sidney Ernest Hambley
Mother	Anne Hambley
Religion	Methodist
Pre-War Occupation	Farmhand

HISTORY

Singapore	Selarang Camp Changi
'A' Force Burma	Green Force, No. 3 Battalion
POW Number	1742
Camps Thailand	Tamarkan
Japan	*Awa Maru* Party, Kumi No. 40
POW Numbers	1455 and 136
Camps Japan	Fukuoka sub-Camp No. 17
Return Details 1945	Nagasaki-Manila, details unknown
	Manila-Morotai-Darwin-Perth, B24 Liberator aircraft A72-379
Additions	Wounded in action on 10.2.1942 and admitted to the 2/13th Australian General Hospital with a shrapnel wound to the back. Discharged to unit on 23.2.1942.

ERNEST EDGAR HAMBLEY

Rank	Lance/Sergeant (Promoted on 11.2.1942)
Regimental Number	WX4991
Company	'B' Company
Enlisted	23.7.1940
Discharged	9.1.1946
Date of Birth	28.4.1917
Place of Birth	Mount Barker, Western Australia
Father	Sidney Ernest Hambley
Mother	Anne Hambley
Religion	Methodist
Pre-War Occupation	Miner

HISTORY

Singapore	Selarang Camp and Barracks Changi
POW Numbers	1/7916 and 14757
Force	'F' Force Thailand
Singapore	Selarang Barracks Changi
	X3 Party
	Changi Gaol Camp
Return Details 1945	Singapore-Darwin-Melbourne, 1st Netherlands Military Hospital Ship *Oranje*
	Melbourne-Perth by troop train

HARRY HAMMER

Rank	Staff Sergeant (Promoted on 9.2.1942)
Regimental Number	WX8718
Classification	Driver
Company	Company Headquarters (replaced W.O. II V. Keay)
Enlisted	23.10.1940
Discharged	29.11.1945
Date of Birth	18.2.1904
Place of Birth	Boulder, Western Australia
Father	Harry Hammer
Mother	Martha Hammer
Religion	Church of England
Pre-War Occupation	Tearooms Proprietor

HISTORY

Singapore	Selarang Camp Changi
'A' Force Burma	Green Force, No. 3 Battalion
Camps Thailand	Tamarkan, Chungkai, Tamuang
Return Details 1945	Thailand-Singapore by aircraft
	Singapore-Fremantle, HMT *Tamaroa*
Additions	This NCO saw action at Jurong Road, Ulu Pandan and Buona Vista.

ROBERT DOUGLAS HAMPSON

Rank	Acting Sergeant (Promoted on 4.3.1942)
Regimental Number	WX7123
Company	'A' Company
Enlisted	1.8.1940
Discharged	20.6.1945
Date of Birth	2.8.1914
Place of Birth	Not Known
Father	John Hampson
Mother	Eileen Hampson
Religion	Roman Catholic
Pre-War Occupation	Bicycle Builder

HISTORY

Java	'Blackforce'
Camps Java	Bicycle Camp Batavia
'A' Force Burma	Java Party No. 4, Williams Force
POW Number	3867
Camps Burma	Apalon 80km Camp
Camps Thailand	Tamarkan
Japan	*Rakuyo Maru* Party, Kumi No. 37 (rescued by USS *Barb)*
Return Details 1944	Saipan-Guadalcanal-Brisbane-Perth
Additions	This NCO was in charge of the guard at an ammunition dump near Meester Cornelis. He was located at the Cornelis Barracks for about seven days before moving to the civil aerodrome at Kemajoran located near Tanjong Priok. Here again he was placed in charge of the guard. Following the surrender, Doug Hampson and Jack Cocking met Lieutenant Colin Blakeway at the tea plantation outside Arinem from where they decided to head for the coast in the hope of flagging down a passing ship or boat.

Doug Hampson following his rescue in 1944.

THOMAS HAMPTON

Rank	Warrant Officer Class 2
Regimental Number	WX9405
Company	'C' Company Headquarters
Enlisted	21.11.1940
Discharged	31.7.1946
Date of Birth	27.1.1917
Place of Birth	Claremont, Western Australia
Father	Thomas Hampton
Mother	Murial May Hampton
Religion	Church of England
Pre-War Occupation	Shop Assistant

HISTORY

Singapore	Selarang Camp Changi
'A' Force Burma	Green Force, No. 3 Battalion
POW Number	1311
Camps Burma	Meiloe 75km (evacuated to Thanbyuzayat for six months with malaria)
	Reptu 30km, Tanbaya
Camps Thailand	Tamarkan, Chungkai, Linson Wood Camp, Chungkai, Tamuang, Bangkok
POW Number (Linson)	12079
Return Details 1945	Thailand-Singapore by aircraft
	Singapore-Fremantle, HMT *Moreton Bay*

GEORGE HANCOCK

Rank	Private
Regimental Number	WX7987
Classification	Clerk
Company	'D' Company Headquarters
Enlisted	13.8.1940
Discharged	24.5.1946
Date of Birth	14.1.1900
Place of Birth	Leicester, England
Father	John Hancock
Mother	Charlott Sophia Hancock
Religion	Methodist
Pre-War Occupation	Cashier

HISTORY

Singapore	Selarang Camp Changi
'A' Force Burma	Green Force, No. 3 Battalion
POW Number	9355
Camps Thailand	Tamarkan, Banderra, Chao Puraya River, Nacompaton
Return Details 1945	Thailand-Singapore by aircraft
	Singapore-Fremantle, HMT *Moreton Bay*

LEONARD HORACE HANCOCK

Rank	Private
Regimental Number	WX9365
Classification	Scout
Company	'B' Company
Enlisted	4.11.1940
Discharged	26.2.1946
Date of Birth	17.5.1901
Place of Birth	Broken Hill, Victoria
Father	Not Known
Mother	Not Known
Religion	Church of Christ
Pre-War Occupation	Not Known

HISTORY

Singapore	Selarang Camp Changi
'A' Force Burma	Green Force, No. 3 Battalion
POW Number	9356
Camps Burma	Khonkan 55km (1.7.1943)
Camps Thailand	Tamarkan, Nacompaton
Return Details 1945	Thailand-Singapore by aircraft
	Singapore-Fremantle, HMT *Tamaroa*

ROBERT HANSEN

Rank	Private
Regimental Number	WX15736
Company	'D' Company
Enlisted	13.8.1941
Discharged	22.1.1946
Date of Birth	20.8.1912
Place of Birth	Bridgetown, Western Australia
Father	Magnus Christian Henrich Hansen
Mother	Topsy Hilda Hansen
Religion	Church of England
Pre-War Occupation	Main Roads Department

HISTORY

Java	'Blackforce'
Camps Java	Bicycle Camp Batavia
'A' Force Burma	Java Party No. 4, Williams Force
POW Number	4664
Camps Thailand	Tamarkan, Kanchanaburi, Bangkok
Return Details 1945	Thailand-Singapore by aircraft
	Singapore-Fremantle, HMT *Highland Brigade*

EDWARD CHARLES HARDEY

Rank	Private
Regimental Number	WX12157
Company	'D' Company
Enlisted	2.5.1941
Discharged	14.12.1945
Date of Birth	27.8.1902
Place of Birth	Bunbury, Western Australia
Father	Edward James Hardey
Mother	Alice Mary Hardey
Religion	Roman Catholic
Pre-War Occupation	Kangaroo Hunter

HISTORY

Singapore	Selarang Camp Changi
'A' Force Burma	Green Force, No. 3 Battalion
POW Number	2923
Camps Thailand	Tamarkan
Japan	*Awa Maru* Party
POW Number	1517
Camps Japan	Fukuoka sub-Camp No.17, Omuta
Return Details 1945	Nagasaki-Manila details unknown
	Manila-Morotai-Darwin-Perth, B24 Liberator aircraft A72-379
Additions	Wounded in action on 10.2.1942 and admitted to the 2/10th Field Ambulance then to the 2/13th Australian General Hospital with a gunshot wound to the right buttock and leg. Transferred to the 2/10th Australian General Hospital on 6.3.1942. Discharged to unit on 27.3.1942.

Edward Charles Hardey and his wife Florrie, on their wedding day

NORMAN JOSEPH HARRIS

Rank	Sergeant (Promoted on 24.1.1942)
Regimental Number	WX4985
Company	'B' Company
Enlisted	23.7.1940
Discharged	22.5.1946
Date of Birth	23.10.1910
Place of Birth	Fremantle, Western Australia
Father	Not Known
Mother	Clara Matilda Harris
Religion	Roman Catholic
Pre-War Occupation	Railway Construction

HISTORY

Singapore	Selarang Camp Changi
	Thomson Road (Caldecot Hill Estate Camp)
'J' Force Japan	*Wales Maru* Party
POW Number	587
Camps Japan	Kobe (Showa-Denki)
	Nagoya (15.2.1945-28.5.1945)
	Toyama (28.5.1945-5.9.1945)
Return Details 1945	Yokohama-Okinawa-Manila by aircraft
	Manila-Sydney, B24 Liberator aircraft
	Sydney-Melbourne by troop train
	Melbourne-Perth by ANA airliner
Additions	This NCO was evacuated to Field Ambulance then to the 2/10th Australian General Hospital with headache on 2.2.1942. He was discharged from hospital to a rest home but he became lost and joined 'B' Company Headquarters, remaining with them until he rejoined No. 9 Platoon at the Botanical Gardens on 13.2.1942.

WILLIAM DENIS HARRIS

Rank	Private
Regimental Number	WX8695
Company	Battalion Headquarters
Enlisted	23.10.1940
Discharged	2.5.1946
Date of Birth	1.6.1903
Place of Birth	Birmingham, England
Father	Not Known
Mother	Not Known
Religion	Church of England
Pre-War Occupation	Labourer

HISTORY

Java	'Blackforce', attached to 2/2nd Pioneer Battalion
'A' Force Burma	Java Party No. 4, Williams Force
POW Number	4653
Camps Thailand	Kanchanaburi
Return Details 1945	Thailand-Singapore by aircraft
	Singapore-Fremantle, HMT *Circassia*

BERNARD GEORGE HARRISON

Rank	Private (Promoted Sgt. on 27.8.1943)
Regimental Number	WX7745
Classification	Driver
Company	'D' Company
Enlisted	10.8.1940
Discharged	31.1.1944
Date of Birth	21.2.1919
Place of Birth	Subiaco, Western Australia
Father	George William Harrison
Mother	Lillian Francis Harrison
Religion	Church of England
Pre-War Occupation	Engine Cleaner

HISTORY

Singapore   When being led out from the west coast on the night of 9.2.1942 by Sergeant Ron Arbery 'D' Coy 16 Platoon, contact was lost with soldier who, it was later heard, had escaped to Australia. Soldier disembarked at Fremantle ex-*Edindale*, on 5.3.1942. Soldier was Taken on Strength, General Details Camp Claremont ex-Batavia, the same day.

Additions   **Australia**
1. 13th Training Battalion 1.4.1942
2. 25th Divisional Cavalry Training Squadron 23.8.1942
3. 3rd Australian Motor Brigade 2.11.1942
4. 4th Motor Regiment, 1st Armoured Division 3.11.1942
5. NCO's Course 5.4.1943

NORMAN PATRICK HAYES

Rank	Private
Regimental Number	WX8374
Company	'A' Company
Enlisted	4.9.1940
Discharged	24.1.1946
Date of Birth	24.11.1915
Place of Birth	Boulder, Western Australia
Father	Not Known
Mother	Philippa Hayes
Religion	Roman Catholic
Pre-War Occupation	Cleaner

HISTORY

Singapore	Selarang Camp and Barracks Changi
'D' Force Thailand	S Battalion
POW Number	8787
Japan	*Rashin Maru* Party
Camps Japan	Yamane
	Niihama
Return Details 1945	Wakayama-Okinawa, USS *Sanctuary*
	Okinawa-Manila, USS *Bingham*
	Manila-Morotai-Darwin, PBY Catalina aircraft A24-254
	Darwin-Melbourne-Perth, C47 Dakota
Additions	Soldier re-enlisted on 1.3.1946 (WX500258) but was discharged on 23.12.1946.

WILLIAM THOMAS HAYWOOD

Rank	Corporal (Promoted on 11.2.1942)
Regimental Number	WX9175
Classification	Driver
Company	'A' Company
Enlisted	30.10.1940
Discharged	5.12.1945
Date of Birth	25.12.1909
Place of Birth	Goomalling, Western Australia
Father	William Haywood
Mother	Mary Haywood
Religion	Church of England
Pre-War Occupation	Farmer and Bus Driver

HISTORY

Singapore	Selarang Camp Changi
'A' Force Burma	Green Force, No. 3 Battalion
POW Number	1474
Japan	*Awa Maru* Party, Kumi No. 41
POW Number	1618
Camps Japan	Fukuoka sub-Camp No. 17
Return Details 1945	Nagasaki-Okinawa, USS *Cape Gloucester*
	Okinawa-Manila details unknown
	Manila-Darwin-Perth, B24 Liberator aircraft A72-379

JOHN CHARLES HEFFERNAN

Rank	Private
Regimental Number	WX6968
Company	'A' Company
Enlisted	30.7.1940
Discharged	16.1.1947
Date of Birth	26.8.1908
Place of Birth	Midland Junction, Western Australia
Father	Thomas Hefferran
Mother	Not Known
Religion	Roman Catholic
Pre-War Occupation	Milk Vendor and Water Borer

HISTORY

Singapore	Selarang Camp and Barracks Changi
'D' Force Thailand	S Battalion
POW Number	8788
Camps Thailand	Kanu II, Kinsaiyok, Chungkai
Return Details 1945	Thailand-Singapore by aircraft
	Singapore-Fremantle, HMT *Highland Brigade*

CLARENCE GORDON HENDERSON

Rank	Private
Regimental Number	WX7642
Company	'C' Company
Enlisted	10.8.1940
Discharged	2.7.1946
Date of Birth	25.7.1917
Place of Birth	Bunbury, Western Australia
Father	Robert Clarence Henderson
Mother	Ada Henderson
Religion	Church of England
Pre-War Occupation	Taxi Driver and Mechanic

HISTORY

Java	'Blackforce'
Camps Java	Bicycle Camp Batavia
'D' Force Thailand	Java Party No. 6, P Battalion
Japan	*Rashin Maru* Party
POW Number	575
Camps Japan	Fukuoka sub-Camp No. 13, Saganoseki (copper smelter)
	Omine Divisional Camp No. 6 (coal mining)
Return Details 1945	Nagasaki-Hong Kong by U.S. aircraft carrier
	Hong Kong-Manila by ship
	Manila-Morotai-Darwin-Perth, PBY Catalina aircraft A24-377
Additions	Wounded in action Singapore receiving a gunshot wound to the right hand that caused a stiff middle finger which was amputated in November 1944. Whilst in Japan an accident necessitated the amputation of two more fingers on the right hand on 27.2.1945.

ROBERT GORDON HENDERSON

Rank	Private
Regimental Number	WX8384
Company	Headquarters Company
Enlisted	19.9.1940
Discharged	1.5.1946
Date of Birth	31.12.1906
Place of Birth	Aberdeen, Scotland
Father	Robert Clarence Henderson
Mother	Ada Henderson
Religion	Presbyterian
Pre-War Occupation	Baker

HISTORY

Singapore	Selarang Camp Changi
	Thomson Road (Caldecot Hill Estate Camp)
	River Valley Road Camp
	Selarang Barracks Changi
	Changi Gaol Camp
Return Details 1945	Singapore-Labuan, 2/1st H.M. Australian Hospital Ship *Manunda*
	Labuan, admitted to the 2/6 Australian General Hospital (21.9.1945)
	Labuan-Darwin by aircraft
	Darwin-Perth, B24 Liberator aircraft
Additions	Arthritis to the left hip is possibly the reason this soldier remained on Singapore Island.

IAN DAVID HEPPINGSTONE

Rank	Private
Regimental Number	WX8525
Classification	Rangetaker
Company	'C' Company
Enlisted	18.10.1940
Discharged	26.4.1946
Date of Birth	22.7.1900
Place of Birth	Bunbury, Western Australia
Father	David Eedle Heppingstone
Mother	Adelaide Louise Heppingstone
Religion	Church of England
Pre-War Occupation	Prospector

HISTORY

Singapore	Selarang Camp Changi
	Johore Bahru, Adam Park
	Selarang Barracks Changi
POW Number	4/6215
'D' Force Thailand	S Battalion
Camps Thailand	Tarsau (spent twelve months at this camp due to illness)
	Tamuang, Chungkai
	Konkoita (road repairs)
	Kanchanaburi, Petchaburi, Kachu Mountain Camp, Bangkok
Return Details 1945	Thailand-Singapore by aircraft (admitted to the 2/14th A.G.H. 30.9.1945)
	Singapore-Fremantle, H.M. Hospital Ship *Karoa*

FREDERICK HERMON

Rank	Private
Regimental Number	WX7976
Classification	Driver
Company	'A' Company
Enlisted	13.8.1940
Discharged	3.5.1946
Date of Birth	10.6.1913
Place of Birth	Northam, Western Australia
Father	Frederick Hermon
Mother	Alberta Eva Hermon
Religion	Church of England
Pre-War Occupation	Farmhand

HISTORY

Singapore	Selarang Camp Changi
'A' Force Burma	Green Force, No. 3 Battalion
POW Number	1504
Camps Thailand	Tamarkan, Bangkok
Return Details 1945	Thailand-Singapore by aircraft
	Singapore-Fremantle, HMT *Moreton Bay*

ARTHUR SIDNEY HEWBY

Rank	Warrant Officer Class 2
Regimental Number	WX8207
Company	'B' Company Headquarters
Enlisted	16.8.1940
Discharged	31.1.1946
Date of Birth	22.7.1900
Place of Birth	Gingin, Western Australia
Father	Arthur George Hewby
Mother	Not Known
Religion	Church of England
Pre-War Occupation	Publican

HISTORY

Singapore	Selarang Camp Changi
	Serangoon Road Camp
	Selarang Barracks Changi
POW Number	4/4506
'D' Force Thailand	V Battalion
Camps Thailand	Chungkai, Ubon
Return Details 1945	Thailand-Singapore-Sydney by aircraft
	Sydney-Melbourne-Perth by troop train

STANLEY RAYMOND HICKEY

Rank	Private
Regimental Number	WX18170
Company	'A' Company
Enlisted	17.12.1940
Discharged	7.2.1946
Date of Birth	29.5.1921
Place of Birth	Narrogin, Western Australia
Father	Leslie Ernest Hickey
Mother	Iveline Muriel Hickey
Religion	Church of England
Pre-War Occupation	Farmhand

HISTORY

Singapore	Selarang Camp and Barracks Changi
POW Numbers	1/8029 and 3/8112
'D' Force Thailand	Captain Harris Party
Camps Thailand	Kanchanaburi, Non Pladuk
French Indo-China	*Both* Party
Return Details 1945	Saigon-Bangkok-Singapore by aircraft
	Singapore-Morotai-Sydney by aircraft
	Sydney-Melbourne-Perth by troop train

GEORGE HALLEY HICKS

Rank	Private
Regimental Number	WX9290
Company	'D' Company
Enlisted	30.10.1940
Discharged	14.12.1945
Date of Birth	21.12.1910
Place of Birth	Northam, Western Australia
Father	James Hicks
Mother	Ellen Hicks
Religion	Church of England
Pre-War Occupation	Chaff Cutter

HISTORY

Singapore	Selarang Camp and Barracks Changi
POW Number	4/6218
'D' Force Thailand	Captain Harris Party
Camps Thailand	Kanchanaburi, Non Pladuk
French Indo-China	*Both* Party
Return Details 1945	Saigon-Bangkok-Singapore by aircraft
	Singapore-Morotai-Sydney by aircraft
	Sydney-Melbourne-Perth by troop train
Additions	Soldier suffered from shell shock and was evacuated to the 2/10th Australian General Hospital on 12.2.1942. Discharged to unit on 20.2.1942.

WILLIAM HICKS

Rank	Private
Regimental Number	WX5206
Classification	Driver/Mechanic
Company	'D' Company
Enlisted	26.7.1940
Discharged	14.6.1946
Date of Birth	29.3.1913
Place of Birth	Boulder, Western Australia
Father	John Hicks
Mother	Linda Hicks
Stepfather	Arthur Henry Pascoe
Religion	Church of England
Pre-War Occupation	Forestry Worker

HISTORY

Singapore	Selarang Camp Changi
	A. G. H. Roberts Barracks Changi
	Tanjong Pagar Camp
	Selarang Barracks Changi
	Kranji Hospital Woodlands (28.5.1944)
	W Party
	Woodlands Camp
POW Number	1/8030
Return Details 1945	Singapore-Labuan, 2/1st H.M. Australian Hospital Ship *Manunda*
	Labuan, admitted to the 2/4th Australian General Hospital (21.9.1945)
	Labuan-Morotai-Brisbane, HMAS *Manoora*
	Brisbane-Sydney by troop train
	Sydney-Fremantle, HMT *Dominion Monarch*
Additions	Wounded in action on 15.2.1942 at Buona Vista. Admitted to the 2/9th Field Ambulance 15.2.1942 with a shrapnel wound to the median nerve of the left arm. Soldier transferred to the 2/13th Australian General Hospital on 16.2.1942. Discharged to unit on 27.4.1942. To Kranji Hospital ex-Changi Gaol Camp on 28.5.1944.

WILLIAM HAMILTON HICKSON

Rank	Corporal
Regimental Number	WX9559
Classification	Electrical Fitter
Attached 2/4th	88 Light Aid Detachment
Enlisted	4.12.1940
Discharged	31.1.1946
Date of Birth	3.1.1920
Place of Birth	Mount Lawley, Western Australia
Father	Charles Hamilton Hickson
Mother	Mildred Ethel Hickson
Religion	Church of England
Pre-War Occupation	Electrical Engineer

HISTORY

Singapore	Selarang Camp Changi
'A' Force Burma	Green Force, No. 3 Battalion
Camps Burma	Aungganaung 105km Camp
Return Details 1945	Thailand-Singapore by aircraft
	Singapore-Fremantle, HMT *Moreton Bay*
Additions	Soldier embarked on HMT *Zealandia* at Fremantle with the 2/6th Field Park Company as 86 Light Aid Detachment on 30.5.1941. Transferred to 88 Light Aid Detachment, 8th Division Salvage Unit and then attached to the 2/4th Machine Gun Battalion, date unknown.

ALAN McKAY HILL

Rank	Private
Regimental Number	WX6602
Classification	Cook
Company	Headquarters Company
Enlisted	17.7.1940
Discharged	15.2.1946
Date of Birth	11.4.1904
Place of Birth	Melbourne, Victoria
Father	Roland Hill
Mother	Catherine Finlayson Hill
Religion	Church of England
Pre-War Occupation	Orchardist, Farmer and Miner

HISTORY

Singapore	Selarang Camp Changi
'A' Force Burma	Green Force, No. 3 Battalion
POW Number	3083
Camps Burma	Reptu 30km Hospital Camp
Camps Thailand	Tamarkan, Nacompaton, Kao Rin
Return Details 1945	Thailand-Singapore by aircraft
	Singapore-Perth, PBY Catalina aircraft (8.10.1945)

RONALD HILL

Rank	Private
Regimental Number	WX7705
Company	'A' Company
Enlisted	10.8.1940
Discharged	13.2.1946
Date of Birth	25.9.1916
Place of Birth	North Fremantle, Western Australia
Father	Richard Hill
Mother	Mary Alice Hill
Religion	Methodist
Pre-War Occupation	Butcher

HISTORY

Singapore	Selarang Camp Changi
	Johore Bahru, Adam Park
	A. G. H. Roberts Barracks Changi (August 1942)
	River Valley Road Camp
	Selarang Barracks Changi
	Kranji Hospital Woodlands (hepatitis)
	Tanjong Pagar
	W Party
	X4B Party
	Changi Gaol Camp
POW Number	3/8113
Return Details 1945	Singapore-Perth, Duke of Gloucester's aircraft *'Endeavour'*.

JOHN BEDFORD HILLS

Rank	Private
Regimental Number	WX6778
Company	'D' Company
Enlisted	19.7.1940
Discharged	4.12.1945
Date of Birth	29.3.1905
Place of Birth	Adelaide, South Australia
Father	Frank Hills
Mother	Edith Hills
Religion	Church of England
Pre-War Occupation	Clerk and Miner

HISTORY

Singapore	Selarang Camp and Barracks Changi
POW Number	4/6223
'D' Force Thailand	S Battalion
POW Number	8790
Camps Thailand	Kanu II, Tarsau, Tamuang, Tarsau, Tamuang, Nacompaton, Tamarkan
	Petchaburi, Kachu Mountain Camp
Return Details 1945	Thailand-Singapore by aircraft
	Singapore-Fremantle, HMT *Highland Brigade*
Additions	This soldier appears to have suffered greatly from Malaria and spent most of his time as a prisoner in Thailand close to hospital camps.

FRANCIS HINDS

Rank	Private
Regimental Number	WX8597
Company	'B' Company
Enlisted	18.10.1940
Discharged	17.12.1945
Date of Birth	17.1.1911
Place of Birth	Maylands, Western Australia
Father	Thomas Hinds
Mother	Emily Hinds
Religion	Roman Catholic
Pre-War Occupation	Plumber and Brick Machinist

HISTORY

Singapore	Selarang Camp Changi
	Thomson Road (Caldecot Hill Estate Camp)
	River Valley Road Camp
	Selarang Barracks Changi
POW Number	3/8121
Force	'F' Force Thailand
Singapore	Changi Gaol Camp
	Levelling Party Changi Aerodrome
	X6 Party, P Party
	Changi Gaol Camp
Return Details 1945	Singapore-Darwin-Sydney, HMT *Arawa*
	Sydney-Melbourne by troop train
	Melbourne-Fremantle, HMT *Strathmore*

FRANK HINNRICHSEN

Rank	Private
Regimental Number	WX8198
Company	Battalion Headquarters
Enlisted	16.8.1940
Discharged	9.1.1946
Date of Birth	3.4.1907
Place of Birth	Perth, Western Australia
Father	Jurgen Gorot Hinnrichsen
Mother	Amy Margaret Hinnrichsen
Religion	Church of England
Pre-War Occupation	Barman

HISTORY

Singapore	Selarang Camp and Barracks Changi
POW Number	1/11866
'J' Force Japan	*Wales Maru* Party
POW Number	763
Camps Japan	Kobe (Showa-Denki)
	Kawasaki Camp, Maruyama Park
	Fukuoka sub-Camp No. 26, Usui
Return Details 1945	Nagasaki-Okinawa, USS *Marathon*, Okinawa-Manila, C54 aircraft
	Manila-Sydney, HMS *Speaker*

HAROLD GERARD HOCKEY

Rank	Private
Regimental Number	WX9240
Company	'B' Company
Enlisted	30.10.1940
Discharged	20.12.1945
Date of Birth	12.3.1903
Place of Birth	Newport, Wales
Father	Sydney Christopher Hockey
Mother	Elizabeth Hockey
Religion	Baptist
Pre-War Occupation	Labourer

HISTORY

Singapore	Selarang Camp Changi
	Johore Bahru, Adam Park
	Sime Road Camp
	Selarang Barracks Changi
POW Numbers	1/8044 and 3/8121
'D' Force Thailand	Details not known but possibly with Captain Harris Party
Camps Thailand	Kinsaiyok, Nacompaton, Non Pladuk
French Indo-China	*Both* Party
Return Details 1945	Saigon-Bangkok-Singapore, by aircraft
	Singapore-Morotai-Sydney-Melbourne-Perth, by aircraft
Additions	Wounded by a U.S.A.A.C. P38 Lightning aircraft whilst in transit to Phan Rang.

PATRICK GEORGE HODGINS

Rank	Private
Regimental Number	WX9350
Classifications	Driver
Company	'B' Company
Enlisted	30.10.1940
Discharged	17.12.1945
Date of Birth	30.4.1914
Place of Birth	Sandstone, Western Australia
Father	George Hodgins
Mother	Mary Ann Hodgins
Religion	Roman Catholic
Pre-War Occupation	Farmer

HISTORY

Singapore	Selarang Camp Changi
	Johore Bahru, Adam Park
	River Valley Road Camp
	Selarang Barracks Changi
'H' Force Thailand	'H' Force Group No. 3
Singapore	Sime Road Camp
	X10 Party
	Changi Gaol Camp
Return Details 1945	Singapore-Melbourne by ship
	Melbourne-Perth. No details are known

SYDNEY MERVYN HOGBEN

Rank	Private
Regimental Number	WX8984
Classification	Motorcycle Orderly
Company	'B' Company Headquarters
Enlisted	25.10.1940
Discharged	31.1.1946
Date of Birth	5.11.1915
Place of Birth	Fremantle, Western Australia
Father	Edwin Hogben
Mother	Elizabeth Hogben
Religion	Methodist
Pre-War Occupation	Storeman

HISTORY

Singapore	Selarang Camp Changi
	Johore Bahru, Adam Park
	River Valley Road Camp
	Selarang Barracks Changi
'D' Force Thailand	S Battalion
POW Number	8785
Camps Thailand	Kanu II, Hintok Road Camp (March-July 1943), Tamuang, Chungkai, Kanchanaburi
Japan	*Rashin Maru* Party
POW Number	1631
Camps Japan	Yamane
	Niihama
Return Details 1945	Wakayama-Okinawa, USS *Sanctuary*
	Okinawa-Manila, USS *Bingham*
	Manila-Sydney, HMS *Speaker*
	Sydney-Fremantle, HMT *Dominion Monarch*

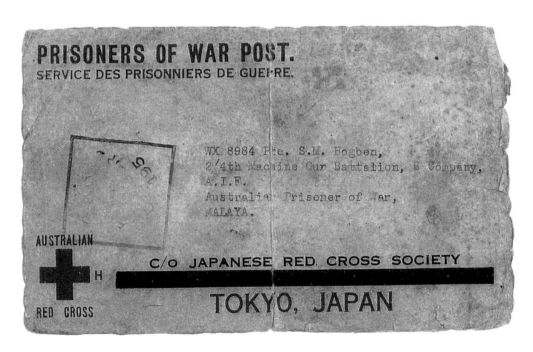

WALTER HOLDING

Rank	Private
Regimental Number	WX17634
Company	'E' Company, Special Reserve Battalion
Enlisted	12.11.1941
Discharged	29.11.1945
Date of Birth	13.8.1919
Place of Birth	Bassendean, Western Australia
Father	Walter Holding
Mother	Hilda Rose Holding
Religion	Church of England
Pre-War Occupation	Engine Cleaner and Driver (Railways)

HISTORY

Singapore	Selarang Camp Changi
	Johore Bahru, Adam Park
	River Valley Road Camp
	Selarang Barracks Changi
POW Number	1/8062
Force	'F' Force Thailand
Camps Thailand	Shimo Sonkurai, Sonkurai, Kami Sonkurai
Singapore	Levelling Party Changi Aerodrome
	P Party
	Changi Gaol Camp
Return Details 1945	Singapore-Darwin-Sydney, HMT *Arawa*
	Sydney-Melbourne by troop train
	Melbourne-Fremantle, HMT *Strathmore*
Additions	Soldier became lost behind enemy lines following the ambush at South-West Bukit Timah. Soldier walked down West Coast Road and eventually met up with No. 9 Platoon 'B' Company 2/4th Machine Gun Battalion.

HUBERT MERVYN HOLLAND

Rank	Private
Regimental Number	WX17997
Classification	Batman/Runner
Company	'B' Company
Enlisted	10.12.1941
Discharged	17.12.1945
Date of Birth	22.2.1921
Place of Birth	Wagin, Western Australia
Father	Charles Newton Holland
Mother	Estelle Holland
Religion	Church of England
Pre-War Occupation	Railway Engine Cleaner and Farmhand

Singapore	Selarang Camp Changi
	Johore Bahru, Adam Park
Force	Japan 'B' Party Korea, *Fukkai Maru*
Camps Korea	Keijo (remained behind due to illness)
Camps Japan	Fukuoka sub-Camp No. 13, Saganoseki
	Omine Divisional Camp No. 6
POW Number	333
Return Details 1945	Nagasaki-Hong Kong-Manila, U.S. Navy aircraft carrier
	Manila-Morotai-Darwin-Perth, PBY Catalina aircraft A24-77

CHARLES HOLMES

Rank	Private
Regimental Number	WX9286
Company	'D' Company
Enlisted	30.10.1940
Discharged	28.5.1946
Date of Birth	15.12.1912
Place of Birth	Doncaster, Yorkshire, England
Father	Simion John Holmes
Mother	Lilian May Holmes
Religion	Church of England
Pre-War Occupation	Farmhand

HISTORY

Singapore	Selarang Camp Changi
'A' Force Burma	Green Force, No. 3 Battalion
POW Number	1521
Camps Burma	Khonkan 55km Camp
Camps Thailand	Tamarkan, Bangkok
Return Details 1945	Singapore-Fremantle, H.M. Hospital Ship *Karoa*

LESLIE NORMAN HOLTZMAN

Rank	Corporal (Promoted on 11.2.1942)
Regimental Number	WX7618
Company	'C' Company
Enlisted	10.8.1940
Discharged	8.8.1946
Date of Birth	18.12.1920
Place of Birth	Bunbury, Western Australia
Father	Norman Guy Holtzman
Mother	Hilda Olive Holtzman
Religion	Methodist
Pre-War Occupation	Plumber and Fibrous Plasterer

HISTORY

Singapore	Selarang Camp Changi
'A' Force Burma	Green Force, No. 3 Battalion
POW Number	1369
Camps Burma	Reptu 30km, Alepauk 18km, Reptu 30km
Camps Thailand	Tamarkan
Japan	*Awa Maru* Party, Kumi No. 40
POW Number	1486
Camps Japan	Fukuoka sub-Camp No. 17, Omuta
Return Details 1945	Nagasaki-Okinawa, USS *Cape Gloucester*
	Manila-Morotai-Darwin-Perth, B24 Liberator aircraft A72-379

WILLIAM HOPTON PATRICK HOOD

Rank	Corporal
Regimental Number	WX7471
Classification	Clerk
Company	Headquarters Company
Enlisted	6.8.1940
Discharged	25.1.1946
Date of Birth	27.3.1901
Place of Birth	Southend-on-Sea, England
Father	Samuel Hood
Mother	Louisa Hood
Religion	Church of England
Pre-War Occupation	Builder

HISTORY

Singapore	Selarang Camp Changi
'A' Force Burma	Green Force, No. 3 Battalion
POW Number	2737
Camps Burma	Khonkan 55km (1.7.1943 tropical ulcer)
Camps Thailand	Tamarkan, Nacompaton
Return Details 1945	Thailand-Singapore by aircraft
	Singapore-Perth, PBY Catalina aircraft

DOUGLAS RADCLIFFE HORN

Rank	Corporal (Promoted on 24.1.1942)
Regimental Number	WX9418
Company	'D' Company
Enlisted	2.12.1940
Discharged	11.2.1946
Date of Birth	21.1.1916
Place of Birth	Perth, Western Australia
Father	Alexander Cecil Radcliffe Horn
Mother	Blanche Eva Victoria Horn
Religion	Church of England
Pre-War Occupation	Bank Clerk

HISTORY

Singapore	Selarang Camp Changi
	Johore Bahru, Adam Park
	Selarang Barracks Changi
POW Number	4/4513
'D' Force Thailand	S Battalion
POW Number	8729
Camps Thailand	Kanu II, Tarsau, Chungkai, Tamuang
Japan	*Rashin Maru* Party
POW Number	1549
Camps Japan	Yamane (copper mine)
	Niihama (furnace attendant and No. 4 Party on the wharves)
Return Details 1945	Wakayama-Okinawa, USS *Sanctuary*
	Okinawa-Manila, USS *Bingham*
	Manila-Sydney, HMS *Speaker*
Additions	Soldier captured on the west coast of Singapore in the vicinity of the Sungei Berih. Additional POW Numbers were issued being: No. 355 at Tarsau and No. 379 at Moji in Japan.

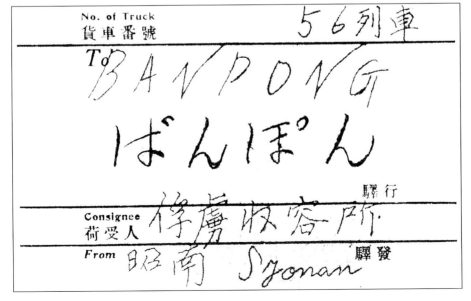

This consignee card was souvenired by Doug 'Trader' Horn,
in transit from Singapore to Thailand in 1943.

347

MELVILLE WILLIAM HORTIN

Rank	Private
Regimental Number	WX9323
Classification	Scout
Company	'B' Company
Enlisted	30.10.1940
Discharged	17.12.1945
Date of Birth	22.11.1913
Place of Birth	Bully Acre, South Australia
Father	Willaim Lawrence Hortin
Mother	Jane Hortin
Religion	Methodist
Pre-War Occupation	Share Farmer

HISTORY

Singapore	Selarang Camp and Barracks Changi
	Kranji Hospital Woodlands
POW Number	1/8093
Return Details 1945	Singapore-Darwin -Labuan, 2/1st H.M. Australian Hospital Ship *Manunda*
	Labuan-Darwin-Broome-Perth, PBY Catalina (2.10.1945)
Additions	Admitted to 2/9th Field Ambulance with shell shock. Transferred to the 2/13th Australian General Hospital on 16.2.1942 and discharged to unit on 21.2.1942. This soldier suffered from asthma when it rained. Because the extensive concrete areas at Changi aggravated his condition, he was transferred to Kranji Camp Woodands, a dirt camp. Asthma was the reason that Pte. Hortin and Pte. Lush were not sent away from Singapore.

Note: There were usually three reasons for retention in Singapore, these being: age, health or that the Soldier provided an essential service in the way of trade skills to the Changi Cantonment.

AUBREY HOSKING

Rank	Lance Corporal
Regimental Number	WX10097
Classification	Signaller
Company	Headquarters Company
Enlisted	13.12.1940
Discharged	7.2.1946
Date of Birth	24.2.1919
Place of Birth	South Perth, Western Australia
Father	Edward Hosking
Mother	Violet Louisa Hosking
Religion	Church of England
Pre-War Occupation	Clerk at the Crown Law Court

HISTORY

Singapore	Selarang Barracks Changi (clerical)
	Garden Control Party
	Levelling Party Changi Aerodrome
	A. G. H. Roberts Barracks Changi
	Convalescent Depot
	Changi Gaol Camp
Return Details 1945	Singapore-Labuan by aircraft (malaria)
	Morotai (3 weeks)-Balikpapan, 2/2 H.M. Australian Hospital Ship *Wanganella*
	Brisbane-Sydney-Melbourne-Perth by troop train
Additions	Wounded in action at Ulu Pandan on 12.2.1942. Admitted to the 2/13th Australian General Hospital. Soldier lost five inches of tibia and it was a full year before he could walk again. Japanese gave him a 'B' Medical Classification, the second highest classification for the medically unfit.

LIONEL ROSEBURY HOUNSLOW

Rank	Private
Regimental Number	WX20025
Company	Headquarters Company
Enlisted	8.9.1941
Discharged	12.4.1946
Date of Birth	11.3.1903
Place of Birth	Perth, Western Australia
Father	Albert Edward Hounslow
Mother	Mary Hounslow
Religion	Church of England
Pre-War Occupation	Commercial Traveller

HISTORY

Singapore	Selarang Camp Changi
'A' Force Burma	Green Force, No. 3 Battalion
POW Number	6285 (Ramsay Force No. 1 Battalion)
Camps Thailand	Petchaburi, Kachu Mountain Camp, Bangkok
Return Details 1945	Bangkok-Rangoon by aircraft
	Rangoon-Singapore, HMT *Highland Brigade*
	Singapore-Australia by ship
Additions	This soldier's POW Number indicates that he was a member of Ramsay Force. It is uncertain if he was at the aerodrome camp at Victoria Point Burma. In this case it is likely he fell sick somewhere along the way and fell in with Ramsay Force. Ramsay and Green Forces were later combined at Meiloe, 75km Camp.

CLIFFORD THOMAS HOWE

Rank	Sergeant (Promoted on 5.2.1942)
Regimental Number	WX15099
Attached 2/4th	A.A.O.C. Armourer
Enlisted	16.7.1941
Discharged	2.9.1947
Date of Birth	17.12.1902
Place of Birth	Lowfell, Gateshead, Newcastle, England
Father	Thomas James Howe
Mother	Jane Margaret Howe
Religion	Presbyterian
Pre-War Occupation	Bin Attendant, Pattern Maker and Mechanic

HISTORY

Singapore	Selarang Camp Changi
	Johore Bahru, Adam Park (i/c of workshops)
	Sime Road Camp (i/c of workshops)
	Selarang Barracks Changi
POW Number	4/4514
Force	'F' Force Thailand
Camps Thailand	Shimo Sonkurai, Tanbaya (Burma)
Singapore	Sime Road Camp
	Kranji Hospital Woodlands
	Changi Gaol Camp (Garden Control Party)
Return Details 1945	Singapore-Darwin-Sydney, HMT *Arawa*
	Sydney-Melbourne by troop train
	Melbourne-Fremantle, HMT *Strathmore*
Additions	NCO was transferred from 88 L.A.D. to A.A.O.C. Armourer Sergeant on 6.2.1942.

JAMES HOWE

Rank	Private
Regimental Number	WX6967
Company	Battalion Headquarters
Enlisted	30.7.1940
Discharged	4.2.1946
Date of Birth	16.6.1909
Place of Birth	Hemel Hempstead, England
Father	Not Known
Mother	Louisa Howe
Religion	Church of England
Pre-War Occupation	Farmer

HISTORY

Singapore	Selarang Camp Changi
'A' Force Burma	Green Force, No. 3 Battalion
POW Number	1513
Camps Burma	Reptu 30km to Thanbyuzayat (27.10.1942 on a work party)
Japan	*Rakuyo Maru* Party, Kumi No. 40
French-Indo China	Soldier remained at Saigon and did not return to Singapore and therefore Japan.
Return Details 1945	Saigon-Bangkok-Singapore by aircraft
	Singapore-Fremantle, HMT *Circassia*

WILLIAM ROBERT HOWSON

Rank	Private
Regimental Number	WX16981
Company	Headquarters Company
Enlisted	13.10.1941
Discharged	28.2.1946
Date of Birth	6.8.1911
Place of Birth	Midland Junction, Western Australia
Father	Robert William Howson
Mother	Jane Howson
Religion	Methodist
Pre-War Occupation	Boilermaker's Assistant

HISTORY

Singapore	Selarang Camp and Barracks Changi
POW Numbers	1/8100 and 3/8192
Force	'F' Force Thailand
Camps Thailand	Tanbaya (Burma), Kanchanaburi
Singapore	Sime Road Camp
	Kranji Hospital Woodlands
	X10 Party
	Changi Gaol Camp
Return Details 1945	Singapore-Darwin-Sydney, HMT *Arawa*
	Sydney-Melbourne by troop train
	Melbourne-Fremantle, HMT *Strathmore*

LAURENCE SLADE HUMMERSTON

Rank	Private
Regimental Number	WX10931
Company	'C' Company
Enlisted	14.2.1941
Discharged	25.2.1946
Date of Birth	12.3.1919
Place of Birth	Kalgoorlie, Western Australia
Father	Harry Goldsmith Hummerston
Mother	Ada Mary Hummerston
Religion	Church of England
Pre-War Occupation	Miner and Farmer

HISTORY

Singapore	Selarang Camp Changi
	Johore Bahru, Adam Park
	Selarang Barracks Changi
'D' Force Thailand	V Battalion
Camps Thailand	Kinsaiyok, (evacuated to Chungkai due to a work accident)
	Tamarkan, Tamuang, Non Pladuk
Japan	*Aramis* Party
POW Number	1455
Camps Japan	Fukuoka sub-Camp No. 17, Omuta
Return Details 1945	Kyushu Island-Okinawa-Manila by U.S. aircraft
	Manila-Sydney, HMS *Formidable*

MALCOLM ASHTON HUNTER

Rank	Corporal (Promoted on 1.3.1942)
Regimental Number	WX9130
Company	'B' Company
Enlisted	30.10.1940
Discharged	25.1.1946
Date of Birth	9.10.1917
Place of Birth	Northam, Western Australia
Father	Ashton Hunter
Mother	Ruby Stella Hunter
Religion	Methodist
Pre-War Occupation	Farmer

HISTORY

Java	'Blackforce', attached to 'C' Company 2/3rd Machine Gun Battalion
'D' Force Thailand	Java Party No. 6, O Battalion
POW Number	6911
Camps Thailand	Hintok Road Camp (evacuated 2.9.1943, cholera)
Return Details 1945	Thailand-Singapore by aircraft
	Singapore-Fremantle, HMT *Moreton Bay*

WALTER WILBOUR HUTCHINSON

Rank	Corporal
Regimental Number	WX7332
Company	Headquarters Company
Enlisted	6.8.1940
Discharged	4.2.1946
Date of Birth	3.1.1906
Place of Birth	Foster, South Australia
Father	David Hutchinson
Mother	Evelyn Hutchinson
Religion	Methodist
Pre-War Occupation	Railway Ganger

HISTORY

Singapore	Selarang Camp Changi
	Thomson Road (Caldecot Hill Estate Camp)
	River Valley Road Camp
	Selarang Barracks Changi
POW Number	3/8226
'J' Force Japan	*Wales Maru* Party
Camps Japan	Kobe (Showa-Denki)
	Kawasaki Camp, Maruyama Park, Wakinohama
Return Details 1945	Yokohama-Okinawa by C54 aircraft
	Okinawa-Manila, B24 Liberator aircraft
	Manila-Sydney, HMS *Formidable*

CHARLES HENRY IRONMONGER

Rank	Corporal
Regimental Number	WX8327
Company	'C' Company Headquarters
Enlisted	21.8.1940
Discharged	13.12.1945
Date of Birth	5.5.1899
Place of Birth	Corby, Northamptonshire, England
Father	William Ironmonger
Mother	Sarah Jane Ironmonger
Religion	Church of England
Pre-War Occupation	Dairy Farmer

HISTORY

Singapore	Selarang Camp and Barracks Changi
	Garden Control Party
	A. G. H Roberts Barracks Changi
	Kranji Hospital Woodlands
	Changi Gaol Camp
POW Number	3/8250
Return Details 1945	Singapore-Darwin-Sydney, HMT *Arawa*
	Sydney-Melbourne by troop train
	Melbourne-Fremantle, HMT *Strathmore*

JOHN ISAAC

Rank	Private
Regimental Number	WX7889
Company	Headquarters Company
Enlisted	13.8.1940
Discharged	11.2.1946
Date of Birth	28.2.1908
Place of Birth	Abergavenny, Wales
Father	Benjamin Howell Isaac
Mother	Lilly Isaac
Religion	Church of England
Pre-War Occupation	Miner

HISTORY

Singapore	Selarang Camp Changi
'A' Force Burma	Green Force, No. 3 Battalion
POW Number	3073
Camps Thailand	Tamarkan, Bangkok
Return Details 1945	Thailand-Singapore by aircraft
	Singapore-Fremantle, HMT *Moreton Bay*

HUIA ALBERT JACKSON

Rank	Private
Regimental Number	WX8750
Classification	Motorcycle Orderly
Company	'B' Company Headquarters
Enlisted	23.10.1940
Discharged	3.4.1946
Date of Birth	18.5.1905
Place of Birth	Foxton, New Zealand
Father	Albert Jackson
Mother	Elizabeth Jackson
Religion	Church of England
Pre-War Occupation	Braceman

HISTORY

Singapore	Selarang Camp and Barracks Changi
	Garden Control Party
	A. G. H. Roberts Barracks Changi
	X10 Party
	Changi Gaol Camp
Return Details 1945	Singapore-Darwin-Melbourne, 1st Netherlands Military Hospital Ship *Oranje*

THOMAS MARSHALL JACKSON

Rank	Lance Corporal
Regimental Number	WX8813
Classification	Driver
Company	'B' Company
Enlisted	23.10.1940
Discharged	22.3.1946
Date of Birth	4.8.1916
Place of Birth	Dwellingup, Western Australia
Father	Thomas Jackson
Mother	Elizabeth Jackson
Religion	Presbyterian
Pre-War Occupation	Millhand and Prospector

HISTORY

Singapore	Selarang Camp Changi
	Serangoon Road Camp
	Selarang Barracks Changi
POW Number	4/6257
'D' Force Thailand	T Battalion
Camps Thailand	Non Pladuk
French Indo-China	*Both* Party
Return Details 1945	Saigon-Bangkok-Singapore by aircraft
	Singapore-Labuan-Morotai-Darwin-Perth by aircraft
Additions	The exact details of this soldier's movements in Thailand are unknown. There is the possibility that he may have been involved with T Battalion and or with the Captain Fred Harris, Sergeant Eddie Derkenne, or W.O.II John Dooley Parties.

HAROLD JACOBS
a.k.a. Harold Cater-Jacobs

Rank	Sergeant (Promoted on 11.2.1942)
Regimental Number	WX10804
Company	'D' Company
Enlisted	15.1.1941
Discharged	29.3.1946
Date of Birth	29.1.1919
Place of Birth	Hemsworth, Yorkshire, England
Father	Isaiah Jacobs
Mother	Florence Jacobs
Religion	Methodist
Pre-War Occupation	Storeman

HISTORY

Singapore	Selarang Camp Changi
	Johore Bahru, Adam Park
	River Valley Road Camp
	Selarang Barracks Changi
POW Number	4/4518
'D' Force Thailand	S Battalion
POW Number	8731
Camps Thailand	Kanu II, Kanu I River Camp (evacuated to Tarsau by barge)
	Chungkai, Tamuang, Kanchanaburi
Japan	*Rashin Maru* Party
POW Number	1532
Camps Japan	Yamane (copper mine)
	Niihama (copper refinery)
Return Details 1945	Wakayama-Okinawa, USS *Sanctuary*
	Okinawa-Manila, USS *Bingham*
	Manila-Sydney, HMS *Speaker*
	Sydney-Melbourne-Perth by troop train
Additions	This NCO acted as No. 13 Platoon Commanding Officer on the wounding of Lieutenant M. E. Wankey on 8.2.1942.

TREVOR ERNEST JOHN JAMES

Rank	Private
Regimental Number	WX8610
Company	'B' Company
Enlisted	18.10.1940
Discharged	17.1.1946
Date of Birth	20.3.1917
Place of Birth	Victoria Park, Western Australia
Father	William Edward James
Mother	Annie Blanche James
Religion	Church of England
Pre-War Occupation	Bootmaker and Driver

HISTORY

Singapore	Selerang Camp Changi
	Johore Bahru, Adam Park
	River Valley Road Camp
	Selarang Barracks Changi
'D' Force Thailand	S Battalion
POW Number	8794
Camps Thailand	Kanu 11, Hintok Road Camp, Kinsaiyok, Tarsau, Chungkai, Tamuang
Japan	*Rashin Maru* Party
POW Numbers	471 and 1641
Camps Japan	Yamane
	Niihama (copper refinery and wharves)
Return Details 1945	Wakayama-Okinawa, USS *Sanctuary*
	Okinawa-Manila, USS *Bingham*
	Manila-Sydney, HMS *Speaker*
	Sydney-Fremantle, HMT *Dominion Monarch*

A group of 'B' Company men. Trevor is in the front row, third from right.

DONALD KEITH JAMIESON

Rank	Corporal (Promoted on 9.2.1942)
Regimental Number	WX7467
Company	'A' Company
Enlisted	6.8.1940
Discharged	18.1.1946
Date of Birth	10.6.1920
Place of Birth	Narrogin, Western Australia
Father	William Charles Jamieson
Mother	Florence Mary Jamieson
Religion	Presbyterian
Pre-War Occupation	Commercial Traveller

HISTORY

Singapore	Selarang Camp and Barracks Changi
POW Number	1/8162
'D' Force Thailand	T Battalion
Camps Thailand	Tarsau, Chungkai, Non Pladuk
French Indo-China	*Both* Party
Return Details 1945	Saigon-Bangkok-Singapore by aircraft
	Singapore-Fremantle, HMT *Tamaroa*
Additions	The exact details of this NCO's movements in Thailand are unknown. There is a possibility that he may have been involved with T Battalion and or with the Captain Fred Harris, Sergeant Eddie Derkenne, or W.O.II John Dooley parties.

GILBERT JAPP

Rank	Private
Regimental Number	WX8702
Classification	Driver
Company	'B' Company Headquarters
Enlisted	23.10.1940
Discharged	15.1.1946
Date of Birth	3.1.1902
Place of Birth	Carnoustie, Angus, Scotland
Father	Charles Japp
Mother	Mary Anne Japp
Religion	Presbyterian
Pre-War Occupation	Brewery Employee and Prospector

HISTORY

Singapore	Selarang Camp and Barracks Changi
'D' Force Thailand	S Battalion
POW Number	8795
Camps Thailand	Chungkai, Nacompaton, Petchaburi, Nakom Chassi
Return Details 1945	Thailand-Singapore by aircraft
	Singapore-Fremantle, HMT *Circassia*

RONALD RALPH JEFFERY

Rank	Lance Corporal
Regimental Number	WX7697
Classification	Scout
Company	'B' Company
Enlisted	10.8.1940
Discharged	17.3.1972
Date of Birth	28.4.1917
Place of Birth	Victoria Park, Western Australia
Father	Albert Jeffery
Mother	Stella Jeffery
Religion	Roman Catholic
Pre-War Occupation	Teamster

HISTORY

Singapore	Selarang Camp and Barracks Changi
POW Number	4/6263
'D' Force Thailand	S Battalion, (Capt. Fred Harris party)
POW Number	8796 (S Battalion)
Camps Thailand	Non Pladuk
French Indo-China	*Both* Party
Return Details 1945	Saigon-Bangkok-Singapore by aircraft
	Singapore-Brisbane by aircraft
	Brisbane-Sydney-Melbourne-Perth by troop train

WILLIAM LAURENCE JEFFERY

Rank	Private
Regimental Number	WX17576
Company	'E' Company, Special Reserve Battalion
Enlisted	5.11.1941
Discharged	25.3.1946
Date of Birth	29.1.1922
Place of Birth	Geraldton, Western Australia
Father	Alfred James Jeffery
Mother	May Jeffery
Religion	Roman Catholic
Pre-War Occupation	Farmhand

HISTORY

Singapore	Selarang Camp Changi
	Johore Bahru, Adam Park
	Selarang Barracks Changi
'D' Force Thailand	V Battalion
Japan	*Aramis* Party
POW Number	632
Camps Japan	Fukuoka sub-Camp No. 17, Omuta
Return Details 1945	Nagasaki-Okinawa, USS *Cape Gloucester*
	Okinawa-Manila, USS *Bingham*
	Manila-Morotai-Darwin, PBY Catalina aircraft A24-354
	Darwin-Melbourne-Perth by aircraft

THOMAS KING JENKINS

Rank	Private
Regimental Number	WX8730
Company	'B' Company
Enlisted	23.10.1940
Discharged	9.1.1946
Date of Birth	18.6.1906
Place of Birth	Esperance, Western Australia
Father	Harry Jenkins
Mother	Sarah Jenkins
Religion	Church of England
Pre-War Occupation	Mines Foreman

HISTORY

Singapore	Selarang Camp and Barracks Changi
POW Number	4/4624
'D' Force Thailand	S Battalion
POW Number	8797
Camps Thailand	Chungkai
Return Details 1945	Thailand-Singapore by aircraft
	Singapore-Fremantle, HMT *Tamaroa*

HENRY JOSEPH JOHNSON

Rank	Private
Regimental Number	WX15640
Company	'E' Company, Special Reserve Battalion
Enlisted	6.8.1941
Discharged	14.12.1945
Date of Birth	22.9.1920
Place of Birth	Adelaide, South Australia
Father	Joseph Norman Johnson
Mother	Olive Gertrude Johnson
Religion	Methodist
Pre-War Occupation	Farmhand

HISTORY

Singapore	Selarang Camp and Barracks Changi
'D' Force Thailand	S Battalion
POW Number	8793
Camps Thailand	Chumphon, Petchaburi, Kachu Mountain Camp, Bangkok (see Danny Bevis Diary)
Return Details 1945	Thailand-Singapore by aircraft
	Singapore-Fremantle, HMT *Highland Brigade*

ALFRED JAMES JONES

Rank	Private
Regimental Number	WX7510
Company	'D' Company
Enlisted	6.8.1940
Discharged	23.1.1946
Date of Birth	21.2.1922
Place of Birth	East Perth, Western Australia
Father	James Johnstone Jones
Mother	Evelyn Lillian Jones
Religion	Church of England
Pre-War Occupation	Vineyard Worker

HISTORY

Singapore	Selarang Camp Changi
	Johore Bahru, Adam Park
	Havelock Road Camp
	Selarang Barracks Changi
POW Number	3/6323
'J' Force Japan	*Wales Maru* Party
POW Number	662
Camps Japan	Kobe (Showa-Denki), Nagoya, Toyama
Return Details 1945	Nagoya-Yokohama
	Yokohama-Okinawa-Manila by aircraft
	Manila-Sydney, HMS *Formidable*
	Sydney-Fremantle, HMT *Dominion Monarch*

EVAN BARTLETT JONES

Rank	Private
Regimental Number	WX10897
Company	'B' Company
Enlisted	31.1.1941
Discharged	28.11.1945
Date of Birth	31.5.1917
Place of Birth	Lismore, New South Wales
Father	Alan Henry Bartlett Jones
Mother	Eileen Jones
Religion	Church of England
Pre-War Occupation	Bank Clerk

HISTORY

Singapore	Selarang Camp Changi
	Serangoon Road Camp
	Selarang Barracks Changi
'J' Force Japan	*Wales Maru* Party
POW Number	796
Camps Japan	Kobe (Showa-Denki)
	Kawasaki Camp, Maruyama Park, Wakinohama
Return Details 1945	Yokohama-Okinawa , C54 Skymaster
	Yokohama-Manila, B24 Liberator aircraft
	Manila-Sydney, HMS *Speaker*
	Sydney-Fremantle, HMT *Dominion Monarch*

LAURENCE DANIEL KEARNEY

Rank	Private
Regimental Number	WX17452
Company	'E' Company, Special Reserve Battalion
Enlisted	27.10.1941
Discharged	2..5.1945
Date of Birth	15.6.1914
Place of Birth	Mintaro, South Australia
Father	Daniel Kearney
Mother	Anna Louise Kearney
Religion	Roman Catholic
Pre-War Occupation	Dairyhand

HISTORY

Singapore	Selarang Camp Changi
'A' Force Burma	Green Force, No. 3 Battalion
POW Number	3085
Japan	*Rakuyo Maru* Party, Kumi No. 37 (rescued by USS *Sealion II*)
Return Details 1944	Saipan-Guadalcanal-Brisbane-Perth
Additions	Wounded in action South-West Bukit Timah on 11.2.1942. The bullet entered through the back at the spine and exited through the left shoulder. There is also evidence to suggest that soldier was bayoneted by the Japanese but feigned death to escape capture. By the time this man was admitted to the Australian General Hospital at Roberts Barracks Changi he was also suffering from exposure to the elements. Discharged to unit on 16.3.1942.

FRANCIS HERBERT KEIRLE

Rank	Private
Regimental Number	WX9915
Classification	Signaller
Company	Headquarters Company
Enlisted	11.12.1940
Discharged	18.1.1946
Date of Birth	7.5.1909
Place of Birth	Fremantle, Western Australia
Father	Alfred Keirle
Mother	Not Known
Religion	Church of England
Pre-War Occupation	Cartage Contractor

HISTORY

Singapore	Selarang Camp and Barracks Changi
POW Numbers	3/8404 and 15476
'H' Force Thailand	'H' Force Group No. 3
Camps Thailand	Kanu II Malayan Hamlet (cholera, 20.6.1943)
	Kanu I River Camp (evacuated by barge, 11.9.1943)
	Kanchanaburi
Singapore	Sime Road Camp, X3 Party
	Changi Gaol Camp
Return Details 1945	Singapore-Darwin-Sydney, HMT *Arawa*
	Sydney-Melbourne by troop train
	Melbourne-Fremantle, HMT *Strathmore*

CLEMENT CHARLES KEITEL

Rank	Private
Regimental Number	WX7541
Classification	Cook
Company	Headquarters Company
Enlisted	6.8.1940
Discharged	18.2.1946
Date of Birth	10.8.1899
Place of Birth	Adelaide, South Australia
Father	Clement Keitel
Mother	Margaret Keitel
Religion	Church of England
Pre-War Occupation	Cartage Contractor

HISTORY

Singapore	Selarang Camp and Barracks Changi
	A. G. H. Roberts Barracks Changi (A. G. H. Staff from 18.1.1944 to 5.5.1944)
	X3 Party
	Changi Gaol Camp
POW Numbers	4/6282 and 15475
Return Details 1945	Singapore-Darwin-Sydney, HMT *Arawa*
	Sydney-Melbourne by troop train
	Melbourne-Fremantle, HMT S*trathmore*
Additions	Soldier had a history of Bronchitis.

EDGAR CHARLES KEMP

Rank	Corporal
Regimental Number	WX7624
Company	'D' Company
Enlisted	10.8.1940
Discharged	14.12.1945
Date of Birth	17.4.1907
Place of Birth	Plaistow, Westham, East Sussex, England
Father	Albert James Kemp
Mother	Rachael Clark Kemp
Religion	Church of England
Pre-War Occupation	Dairyhand

HISTORY

Singapore	Selarang Camp Changi
	Johore Bahru, Adam Park
	Selarang Barracks Changi
'D' Force Thailand	S Battalion
POW Number	8733
Camps Thailand	Kanu II, Hintok Mountain Camp, Tarsau, Tardan, Konkoita, Kinsaiyok, Chungkai, Tamarkan, Kanchanaburi, Nacompaton, Changmai, Nakom Nayok, Bangkok
Return Details 1945	Bangkok-Singapore by aircraft
	Singapore-Fremantle, HMT *Moreton Bay*
Additions	Wounded in action on 10.2.1942 fighting his way out from the west coast. Soldier received a shrapnel wound to the bicep of the left arm.

LESLIE WILLIAM SAMUEL KEMP

Rank	Private
Regimental Number	WX8543
Classification	Rangetaker
Company	'B' Company
Enlisted	18.10.1940
Discharged	3.1.1947
Date of Birth	21.3.1911
Place of Birth	Shepherd's Bush, London, England
Father	William James Kemp
Mother	Amelia Olive Hippel Kemp
Religion	Church of England
Pre-War Occupation	Gold Assayer

HISTORY

Singapore	Selarang Camp and Barracks Changi
POW Number	4/6289
'D' Force Thailand	S Battalion
POW Number	8798
Camps Thailand	Kanu II, Hintok Road Camp, Kinsaiyok, Tarsau, Tardan, Chungkai
Return Details 1945	Singapore-Labuan-Morotai-Townsville by aircraft
	Townville-Sydney by troop train
	Sydney-Fremantle, HMT *Otranto*

ROBERT HENRY KENMIR

Rank	Private
Regimental Number	WX16340
Company	'D' Company Headquarters
Enlisted	3.9.1941
Discharged	13.6.1946
Date of Birth	18.4.1904
Place of Birth	Durham, England
Father	Not Known
Mother	Rose Ann Kenmir
Religion	Church of England
Pre-War Occupation	Labourer

HISTORY

Singapore	Selarang Camp Changi
'A' Force Burma	Green Force, No. 3 Battalion
POW Number	1534
Camps Thailand	Tamarkan
Return Details 1945	Thailand-Singapore by aircraft
	Singapore-Fremantle, HMT *Tamaroa*

MERVYN ST JOHN KENNEDY

Rank	Corporal
Regimental Number	WX10910
Classification	Signaller
Company	Headquarters Company
Enlisted	7.2.1941
Discharged	23.1.1946
Date of Birth	6.1.1919
Place of Birth	Perth, Western Australia
Father	Michael St John Kennedy
Mother	Rose St John Kennedy
Religion	Roman Catholic
Pre-War Occupation	Clerk

HISTORY

Singapore	Selarang Camp Changi
	Mount Pleasant Camp
	Thomson Road (Caldecot Hill Estate Camp)
	River Valley Road Camp
	Selarang Barracks Changi
POW Numbers	3/8392 and 15517
Force	'F' Force Thailand
Singapore	X3 Party
	Changi Gaol Camp
Return Details 1945	Singapore-Darwin-Sydney, HMT *Arawa*
	Sydney-Melbourne by troop train
	Melbourne-Fremantle, HMT *Strathmore*
Additions	Acted as Signals Officer attached to 'B' Company Headquarters. This soldier worked closely with Captain Tom Bunning who spoke highly of his work. A comment from an old friend: - 'He was a lovely gentleman to share a beer with. A twinkle in his eye and had a great sense of humour'.

WALLACE GEORGE BRUCE KENNEY

Rank	Corporal (Promoted on 11.2.1942)
Regimental Number	WX8532
Company	'D' Company
Enlisted	18.10.1940
Discharged	8.3.1946
Date of Birth	29.12.1913
Place of Birth	Trafalgar, Western Australia
Father	Alexander B. Kenney
Mother	Mimmie Matilda Kenney
Religion	Church of England
Pre-War Occupation	Health Quarantine Officer

HISTORY

Singapore	Selarang Camp Changi
	Thomson Road (Caldecot Hill Estate Camp)
	River Valley Road Camp
	Selarang Barracks Changi
	Changi Gaol Camp
Return Details 1945	Singapore-Melbourne, 1st Netherlands Military Hospital Ship *Oranje*
Additions	Admitted to 2/13th Australian General Hospital with a shrapnel wound to the right arm. Transferred to No. 2 Convalescent Depot on 12.2.1942 and discharged to unit on 20.2.1942.

JAMES HUNTER KING

Rank	Private
Regimental Number	WX8178
Classification	Driver
Company	'C' Company Headquarters
Enlisted	16.8.1940
Discharged	28.2.1946
Date of Birth	28.11.1910
Place of Birth	Wanneroo, Western Australia
Father	Lawrence Patrick King
Mother	Blanche Maude King
Religion	Roman Catholic
Pre-War Occupation	Miner

HISTORY

Singapore	Selarang Camp Changi
	Johore Bahru, Adam Park
	Sime Road Camp
	Selarang Barracks Changi
'D' Force Thailand	V Battalion
Camps Thailand	Non Pladuk, Kanchanaburi, Kinsaiyok, Nacompaton (hospital), Kinsaiyok, Linson Wood Camp, Non Pladuk (hospital), Bangkok (go-downs)
Return Details 1945	Bangkok-Singapore by aircraft
	Singapore-Fremantle, H.M. Hospital Ship *Karoa*

WILLIAM JOHN KING

Rank	Private
Regimental Number	WX6429
Company	'A' Company
Enlisted	16.7.1940
Discharged	11.1.1946
Date of Birth	14.3.1911
Place of Birth	London, England
Father	Arthur George King
Mother	Emily King
Religion	Church of England
Pre-War Occupation	Rock Drill Fitter

HISTORY

Singapore	Selarang Camp Changi
	A. G. H. Roberts Barracks Changi
	Selarang Barracks Changi
	X3 Party
	Changi Gaol Camp
POW Numbers	3/8418 and 15573
Return Details 1945	Singapore-Darwin-Sydney, HMT *Arawa*
	Sydney-Melbourne by troop train
	Melbourne-Fremantle, HMT *Strathmore*
Additions	As soldier was admitted to Australian General Hospital with a scalded left forearm on 24.4.1942 until 1.5.1942, it is feasible that he may have worked in the cookhouse for a time.

CLAUDE KNOTT

Rank	Private
Regimental Number	WX7616
Classification	Driver
Company	'A' Company
Enlisted	10.8.1940
Discharged	20.12.1945
Date of Birth	17.7.1917
Place of Birth	Hitchen, Hereford, England
Father	Fred Ernest Lloyd Knott
Mother	Mabel Dithkey Knott
Religion	Church of England
Pre-War Occupation	Well Sinker

Singapore	Selarang Camp Changi
'A' Force Burma	Green Force, No. 3 Battalion
POW Number	2899
Camps Thailand	Non Pladuk
Japan	*Awa Maru* Party, Kumi No. 41
POW Number	1598
Camps Japan	Fukuoka sub-Camp No. 17, Omuta
Return Details 1945	Nagasaki-Manila, USS *Lunga Point*
	Manila-Morotai-Darwin, PBY Catalina aircraft A24-377
	Darwin-Perth, B24 Liberator aircraft A72-379
Additions	Kingsley Fairbridge Farm Schoolboy.

LESLIE KRASNOSTEIN

Rank	Private
Regimental Number	WX7446
Classification	Driver
Company	Headquarters Company
Enlisted	6.8.1940
Discharged	29.4.1946
Date of Birth	17.6.1905
Place of Birth	Palestine
Father	Jacob Krasnostein
Mother	Malka Krasnostein
Religion	Jewish
Pre-War Occupation	Wool Buyer

HISTORY

Singapore	Selarang Camp and Barracks Changi
'D' Force Thailand	V Battalion
Camps Thailand	Hindaine, Non Pladuk
Japan	*Aramis* Party
Camps Japan	Fukuoka sub-Camp No. 17, Omuta
Return Details 1945	Nagasaki-Manila, USS *Lunga Point*
	Manila-Morotai-Darwin, PBY Catalina aircraft A24-359
	Darwin-Perth, B24 Liberator
Additions	Wounded in action Jurong Road on 10.2.1942. Admitted to the 2/13th Australian General Hospital with a shrapnel wound to the right shoulder. Transferred to the 2/9th Field Ambulance on 15.2.1942 and discharged to unit on 21.2.1942.

FRIEDRICH GODFRIED KUHL

Rank	Private
Regimental Number	WX8336
Classification	Driver
Company	Battalion Headquarters
Enlisted	26.8.1940
Discharged	7.3.1946
Date of Birth	26.3.1907
Place of Birth	Essen, Germany
Father	Not Known
Mother	Not Known
Religion	Lutheran
Pre-War Occupation	Farmer

HISTORY

Java	'Blackforce'
Camps Java	Bicycle Camp Batavia
'A' Force Burma	Java Party No. 4, Williams Force
POW Number	4560
Camps Burma	Aungganaung 105km (malaria 21.9.1945 evacuated to Tamarkan)
Camps Thailand	Tamarkan, Nacompaton
Return Details 1945	Thailand-Singapore by aircraft
	Singapore-Fremantle, HMT *Tamaroa*
Additions	Wounded in action by high explosive bomb, receiving a shrapnel wound to the left knee.

JACK GEORGE ALEXANDER KYRIAKOS

Rank	Private
Regimental Number	WX10715
Classification	Signaller
Company	Headquarters Company
Enlisted	15.1.1941
Discharged	7.12.1945
Date of Birth	2.1.1921
Place of Birth	Darwin, Northern Territory
Father	George Kyriakos
Mother	Christina Kyriakos
Religion	Greek Orthodox
Pre-War Occupation	Cook

HISTORY

Singapore	Selarang Camp Changi
	Johore Bahru, Adam Park
	Mount Pleasant Camp
	Selarang Barracks Changi
Force	'F' Force Thailand
POW Number	361
Camps Thailand	Shimo Sonkurai, Sonkurai, Shimo Nikhe
Singapore	Sime Road Camp
	Changi Gaol Camp
Return Details 1945	Singapore-Darwin-Sydney, HMT *Arawa*
	Sydney-Melbourne by troop train
	Melbourne-Fremantle, HMT *Strathmore*

ANDREW LAMBIE

Rank	Private
Regimental Number	WX9528
Company	'C' Company
Enlisted	4.12.1940
Discharged	20.12.1945
Date of Birth	23.7.1920
Place of Birth	Larkhall, Scotland
Father	Andrew Lambie
Mother	Helen Lambie
Religion	Presbyterian
Pre-War Occupation	Labourer

HISTORY

Singapore	Selerang Camp Changi
	Johore Bahru, Adam Park
	Selarang Barracks Changi
POW Number	4/6309
'D' Force Thailand	S Battalion
POW Number	8803
Camps Thailand	Kanu II, Hintok Road Camp, Kinsaiyok, Tamuang
Japan	*Rashin Maru* Party
POW Number	1653
Camps Japan	Yamane
	Niihama
Return Details 1945	Yokohama-Okinawa, USS *Sanctuary*
	Okinawa-Manila, USS *Bingham*
	Manila-Morotai-Darwin, PBY Catalina aircraft A24-70
	Darwin-Adelaide, B24 Liberator aircraft
	Adelaide-Perth, ANA airliner

KENNETH STANLEY LANCE

Rank	Corporal (Promoted on 11.2.1942)
Regimental Number	WX15951
Company	'E' Company, Special Reserve Battalion
Enlisted	21.8.1941
Discharged	22.1.1946
Date of Birth	3.5.1916
Place of Birth	Fremantle, Western Australia
Father	Alfred Josiah Lance
Mother	Ella May Lance
Religion	Methodist
Pre-War Occupation	Clerk

HISTORY

Singapore	Selerang Camp Changi
'A' Force Burma	Green Force, No. 3 Battalion
POW Number	3055
Camps Thailand	Tamarkan, Bangkok, Nacompaton
Return Details 1945	Thailand-Singapore by aircraft
	Singapore-Fremantle, HMT *Moreton Bay*

RAYMOND MALCOLM LANDER

Rank	Sergeant (Promoted on 29.1.1942)
Regimental Number	WX11228
Classification	Technical Storeman
Company	Headquarters Company
Enlisted	1.4.1941
Discharged	5.2.1946
Date of Birth	7.5.1898
Place of Birth	Perth, Western Australia
Father	Titus Lander
Mother	Julie Lander
Religion	Church of England
Pre-War Occupation	Clerk

HISTORY

Singapore	Selarang Camp Changi
'A' Force Burma	Green Force, No. 3 Battalion
POW Number	2657
Camps Burma	Reptu 30km
Camps Thailand	Banderra, Chao Puraya River
Return Details 1945	Bangkok-Rangoon by aircraft
	Rangoon-Singapore, HMT *Highland Brigade*
	Singapore-Sydney by aircraft
	Sydney-Melbourne-Perth by troop train

FREDERICK HENRY LANDWEHR

Rank	Private
Regimental Number	WX4877
Classification	Cook
Company	'A' Company
Enlisted	10.7.1940
Discharged	19.12.1945
Date of Birth	18.2.1921
Place of Birth	West Perth, Western Australia
Father	Henry Frederick Landwehr
Mother	Gertrude Landwehr
Religion	Roman Catholic
Pre-War Occupation	Plaster Fixer

HISTORY

Singapore	Selerang Camp Changi
	Johore Bahru, Adam Park
	Selarang Barracks Changi
POW Number	4/6311
'D' Force Thailand	S Battalion
POW Number	8804
Camps Thailand	Tarsau, Konkoita, Bangkok
Return Details 1945	Bangkok-Singapore by aircraft (admitted to the 2/14th A.G.H.)
	Singapore-Perth by aircraft
Additions	Fred was affectionately known as the 'The Singing Cook'.

IVAN WILLIAM LAWER

Rank	Private
Regimental Number	QX6599
Classification	Driver
Enlisted	31.5.1940
Discharged	20.12.1945
Date of Birth	4.12.1917
Place of Birth	Wilson's Downfall, New South Wales
Father	Frederick Lawer
Mother	Mary Ann Lawer
Religion	Church of England
Pre-War Occupation	Labourer

HISTORY

Singapore	Selarang Barracks Changi
	Thompson Road (Caldecot Hill Estate Camp)
	Serangoon Road Camp
'D' Force Thailand	T Battalion, W.O.II John Dooley Party
Camps Thailand	Kanchanaburi (mechanic), Kinsaiyok, Chungkai, Tamuang, Pratchai, Non Pladuk, Changmai (driving for Japanese), Banderra, Chao Puraya River, Lampang, Bangkok
Return Details 1945	Bangkok-Singapore by aircraft
	Singapore-Fremantle, HMT *Moreton Bay*
	Perth-Sydney, PBY Catalina aircraft
Additions	Wounded in action 11.2.1942. Soldier was with ammunition supply unit. At Murai, soldier received a shrapnel wound to the left forearm and was evacuated to the 2/9th Field Ambulance on 14.2.1942 before being transferred to the 2/10th Australian General Hospital. Ivan transferred to the 2/4th from the 27th Brigade A.A.S.C. on 2.4.1942 to join his brother Reg Lawer. At Tamuang, Reg was selected for Japan whilst Ivan remained in Thailand for the duration of the war.

REGINALD FREDERICK LAWER

Rank	Private
Regimental Number	WX8810
Classification	Driver
Company	'B' Company
Enlisted	23.10.1940
Discharged	19.12.1945
Date of Birth	23.8.1908
Place of Birth	Stanthorpe, Queensland
Father	Frederick Lawer
Mother	Mary Ann Lawer
Religion	Church of England
Pre-War Occupation	Bogger

HISTORY

Singapore	Selarang Camp Changi
	Thompson Road (Caldecot Hill Estate Camp)
	Serangoon Road Camp
	Selarang Barracks Changi
'D' Force Thailand	T Battalion, W.O.II John Dooley Party
Camps Thailand	Tamuang, Kanchanaburi, Non Pladuk
Japan	*Aramis* Party
POW Number	599
Camps Japan	Fukuoka sub-Camp No. 17
Return Details 1945	Nagasaki-Okinawa-Manila
	Manila-Morotai (admitted to 2/9 A.G.H.), evacuated by aircraft to Brisbane
Additions	It is not known for certain if this soldier was a member of T Battalion. Soldier's brother Ivan is definitely listed so it might be reasonably assumed that these two men remained together (as their histories indicate) until their separation in 1944 when Reg was selected for Japan.

MICHAEL JOHN LEAHY

Rank	Private
Regimental Number	WX9312
Company	'B' Company
Enlisted	30.10.1940
Discharged	19.6.1946
Date of Birth	10.11.1916
Place of Birth	Toodyay, Western Australia
Father	Michael Joseph Leahy
Mother	Mary Leahy
Religion	Roman Catholic
Pre-War Occupation	Farmer and Truck Driver

Singapore	Selarang Camp Changi
	Johore Bahru, Adam Park
	River Valley Road Camp
	Selarang Barracks Changi
POW Number	3/8491
'J' Force Japan	*Wales Maru* Party
POW Number	795
Camps Japan	Kobe (Mitsubishi wharves)
	Notogawa sub-Camp No. 9, Osaka (19.5.45-10.9.1945)
Return Details 1945	Yokahama-Okinawa, U.S. Navy hospital ship
	Okinawa Manila, B24 Liberator
	Manila-Morotai-Darwin-Adelaide-Perth by aircraft
Additions	Wounded in action at Tengah on 9.2.1942. The Japanese had located his section and zeroed in on them. Admitted to 2/13th Australian General Hospital at Alexandra Hospital with a shrapnel wound to the left arm. Transferred to No. 2 Convalescent Depot on 12.2.1942. Discharged to unit on 15.2.1942. Soldier was admitted to Kobe Hospital for three months and to Osaka Stadium Prisoner of War Hospital, Itchioka for six months. On his return to Australia he was admitted to 110 (P)MH for two months.

ROBERT WILLIAM LEARMONTH

Rank	Lieutenant
Regimental Number	WX10107
Attached 2/4th	Reinforcement Officer (Taken on Strength 13.8.1941)
Company	'A' Company
Enlisted	13.12.1940
Appointment Terminated	24.11.1945
Date of Birth	10.8.1915
Place of Birth	Subiaco, Western Australia
Father	Archibald Learmonth
Mother	Thirza Charlotte Learmonth
Religion	Methodist
Pre-War Occupation	Bank Officer

HISTORY

Singapore	Selarang Camp and Barracks Changi
POW Number	4/4105
'H' Force Thailand	'H' Force Group No. 6, Officer's Party
Camps Thailand	Wanyai, Tonchan, Hintok Road Camp, Hintok River Camp, Krian Krai,
	'H' Force No. 1 Sub-Section, Konkoita sub camps
Singapore	Sime Road Camp
	Changi Gaol Camp
Return Details 1945	Singapore-Darwin-Sydney, HMT *Arawa*
	Sydney-Melbourne by troop train
	Melbourne-Fremantle, HMT *Strathmore*
Additions	Officer commanded No. 5 Platoon 'A' Company from 13.2.1942.

CHARLES DONALD LEE

Rank	Lieutenant
Regimental Number	WX9387
Company	'B' Company
Enlisted	16.11.1940
Appointment Terminated	7.12.1945
Date of Birth	14.12.1912
Place of Birth	Swanbourne, Western Australia
Father	John Edwin Lee
Mother	Elsie Gertrude Lee
Religion	Church of England
Pre-War Occupation	Government Wool Appraiser

HISTORY

Singapore	Selarang Camp Changi
Camps	Johore Bahru, Adam Park
	Selarang Barracks Changi
POW Number	4/4106
'H' Force Thailand	'H' Force Group No. 3
Camps Thailand	Kanu II Malayan Hamlet
	'H' Force No. 1 Sub-Section, Konkoita sub camps
Singapore	Sime Road Camp (December 1943)
	Changi Gaol Camp
Return Details 1945	Singapore-Darwin-Sydney, HMT *Arawa*
	Sydney-Melbourne by troop train
	Melbourne-Fremantle, HMT *Strathmore*

KENNETH GEORGE LEE

Rank	Lieutenant
Regimental Number	WX10108
Attached 2/4th	Reinforcement Officer (Taken on Strength 13.8.1941)
Company	Headquarters Company
Enlisted	13.12.1940
Appointment Terminated	13.1.2.1945
Date of Birth	25.5.1917
Place of Birth	Subiaco, Western Australia
Father	George Lee
Mother	Ida Eleanor Lee
Religion	Methodist
Pre-War Occupation	Chartered Accountant

HISTORY

Singapore	Selarang Camp Changi
'A' Force Burma	Green Force, No. 3 Battalion
POW Number	1293
Camps Burma	Khonkan 55km Camp
Camps Thailand	131km, 133km (Williams Force), Tamarkan, Kanchanaburi, Nacompaton (hospital staff)
Return Details 1945	Singapore-Perth, PBY Catalina aircraft

LESLIE HERBERT LEE

Rank	Private
Regimental Number	WX7230
Company	'B' Company
Enlisted	1.8.1940
Discharged	8.10.1946
Date of Birth	23.6.1914
Place of Birth	Northam, Western Australia
Father	George William Lee
Mother	Not Known
Religion	Presbyterian
Pre-War Occupation	Labourer

HISTORY

Java	'Blackforce'
'A' Force Burma	Java Party No. 4 to Singapore and joined Java Party 5a, Robertson Force
Camps Thailand	Nacompaton
Return Details 1945	Thailand-Singapore by aircraft
	Singapore-Sydney-Melbourne-Perth
	No further details are known.

LESLIE WALLACE LEE

Rank	Private
Regimental Number	WX15744
Company	'A' Company
Enlisted	13.8.1941
Discharged	20.2.1946
Date of Birth	7.8.1916
Place of Birth	No Man's Lake (Via Narrogin), Western Australia
Father	William Joseph Lee
Mother	Emily Lee
Religion	Church of England
Pre-War Occupation	Farmhand

HISTORY

Java	'Blackforce'
POW Numbers	1602 and 2/17232
Camps Java	Bicycle Camp Batavia
'D' Force Thailand	Java Party No. 6, O Battalion
POW Number	6654
Camps Thailand	Tarsau (evacuated sick on 1.9.1943)
Return Details 1945	Thailand-Singapore by aircraft
	Singapore-Fremantle, HMT *Highland Brigade*
Additions	Soldier was captured at Garoet on 9.3.1942.

JOHN BREMNER LEITH

Rank	Private
Regimental Number	WX4917
Company	'C' Company
Enlisted	23.7.1940
Discharged	12.3.1946
Date of Birth	2.9.1901
Place of Birth	Ross Shire, Scotland
Father	John Leith
Mother	Jane Bremner Leith
Religion	Presbyterian
Pre-War Occupation	Dairyhand

HISTORY

Singapore	Selarang Camp Changi
	Johore Bahru, Adam Park
	Selarang Barracks Changi
POW Number	3/8509
'H' Force Thailand	'H' Force Group No. 3
Camps Thailand	Kanu II Malayan Hamlet, Kanchanaburi (evacuated with beri-beri on 10.9.1943)
Singapore	Sime Road Camp
	Changi Gaol Camp (November 1944-August 1945)
Return Details 1945	Singapore-Darwin-Sydney, HMT *Arawa*
	Sydney-Melbourne by troop train
	Melbourne-Fremantle, HMT *Strathmore*

KENNETH EDGAR LESSELS

Rank	Private
Regimental Number	WX10806
Classification	Stretcher Bearer
Company	Battalion Headquarters
Enlisted	15.1.1941
Discharged	16.4.1946
Date of Birth	25.3.1919
Place of Birth	Swanbourne, Western Australia
Father	William David Lessels
Mother	Mary Lucy Josephine Lessels
Religion	Roman Catholic
Pre-War Occupation	Yardman

HISTORY

Singapore	Selarang Camp Changi
	Johore Bahru, Adam Park
	Selarang Barracks Changi
POW Number	4/6328
'H' Force Thailand	'H' Force Group No. 3
Camps Thailand	Kanu II Malayan Hamlet, Kanchanaburi (evacuated with cholera 21.6.1943)
Singapore	Sime Road Camp
	Levelling Party Changi Aerodrome
	X6 Party
	Changi Gaol Camp
Return Details 1945	Singapore-Darwin-Sydney, HMT *Arawa*
	Sydney-Melbourne-Perth by troop train

LAURENCE HAROLD LEWIS

Rank	Private
Regimental Number	WX11316
Company	'D' Company Headquarters
Enlisted	5.4.1941
Discharged	3.4.1946
Date of Birth	14.11.1913
Place of Birth	Darkan, Western Australia
Father	Harold Silas Lewis
Mother	Emily Lewis
Religion	Church of England
Pre-War Occupation	Benchman

HISTORY

Java	'Blackforce'
'A' Force Burma	Java Party No. 4, Williams Force
POW Number	4647
Camps Thailand	Tamarkan, Ubon
Return Details 1945	Thailand-Singapore by aircraft
	Singapore-Fremantle, HMT *Moreton Bay*

THOMAS HUGH LEWIS

Rank	Private
Regimental Number	WX7441
Classification	Despatch Rider
Company	'D' Company
Enlisted	6.8.1940
Discharged	13.6.1946
Date of Birth	21.5.1921
Place of Birth	Holyhead, Wales
Father	Richard Lewis
Mother	Margaret Anne Lewis
Religion	Church of England
Pre-War Occupation	Farmhand

HISTORY

Singapore	Selarang Camp Changi
	A. G. H. Roberts Barracks Changi
	Selarang Barracks Changi
	Changi Gaol Camp
POW Number	1/8387
Return Details 1945	Singapore-Darwin-Sydney, HMT *Arawa*
	Sydney-Melbourne by troop train
	Melbourne-Fremantle, HMT *Strathmore*
Additions	Shell shocked on 14.2.1942. Also evacuated to the Australian General Hospital at Roberts Barracks Changi on 18.11.1942 with an early case of encephalitis supposedly caused by multiple bee stings. Soldier was in a state of coma for nearly three weeks. He suffered a speech disability and the muscles of one eye were also effected, but it is said that this soldier maintained a bright and happy disposition. The Japanese awarded him an 'A' Medical Classification.

THOMAS ALFRED LIMBOURN

Rank	Lance Corporal
Regimental Number	WX8960
Company	'A' Company
Enlisted	25.10.1940
Discharged	10.4.1946
Date of Birth	20.10.1909
Place of Birth	Wimbledon, England
Father	John Joseph Limbourn
Mother	Eliza Mary Limbourn
Religion	Church of England
Pre-War Occupation	Stereotyper

Singapore	Selarang Camp Changi
'A' Force Burma	Green Force, No. 3 Battalion
POW Number	8960
Camps Thailand	Tamarkan, Chungkai, Kanchanaburi, Tamuang
Return Details 1945	Thailand-Singapore by aircraft
	Singapore-Fremantle, HMT *Moreton Bay*
Additions	Tom Limbourn entered Burma at Victoria Point with Green Force. He became sick at Ye in September 1942 and was later discharged at Tavoy. From Tavoy, he moved north to Moulmein and then onto Thanbyuzayat, possibly with Stringer's draft No. 2 ex-Victoria Point. At this point, Tom re-joined Green Force at the 4.8km Camp and moved to Thetkaw, the 14km Camp.

At Kendaw, Tom became sick again and separated from Green Force. When interviewed by the author, Tom said he had joined up with some of the Dutch Prisoners of War. This is interesting because Tom's POW No. (8960) was within the numbers allocated to a Dutch group, Draft No. 10, under Captain Van der Schaaf. On his discharge from hospital, he moved to the Kun Knit Kway Camp where he was engaged on bridge building. Tom later joined up again with his mates in Green Force as follows: Black Anderson and Williams Forces, eventually massed at Kun Knit Kway. The first two groups to move out to alleviate overcrowding were Black and Anderson Forces, who moved forward to Meiloe 75km Camp in March 1945. It was here that Tom would join up again with Green Force who later moved forward to Aungganaung 105km Camp. From this camp, Tom continued south into Thailand with Williams Force until the completion of the rail link.

JAMES LIND

Rank	Private	
Regimental Number	WX16332	
Company	Headquarters Company	
Enlisted	3.9.1941	
Discharged	23.11.1945	
Date of Birth	22.9.1905	
Place of Birth	Peebles, Scotland	
Father	James Lind	
Mother	Catherine Lind	
Religion	Presbyterian	
Pre-War Occupation	Farmer	

HISTORY

Singapore	Selarang Camp Changi
'A' Force Burma	Green Force
POW Number	2926
Camps Burma	Khonkan 55km Hospital Camp (placed on staff)
Camps Thailand	Tamarkan, Bangkok (medical orderly)
French Indo-China	*Both* Party, Kumi No. 41
Return Details 1945	Saigon-Bangkok-Singapore by aircraft
	Singapore-Brisbane by aircraft
	Brisbane-Sydney-Melbourne-Perth by troop train
Additions	Wounded in action 15.2.1942. Admitted to the 2/13th Australian General Hospital with a gunshot wound to the right temporal region on 16.2.1942. Discharged to unit 21.2.1942. Soldier was originally on the *Awa Maru* Party but missed the draft due to illness and joined the *Both* Party which departed Singapore for French-Indo China on 2.2.1945.

ANDREW JAMES LOLLER

Rank	Private
Regimental Number	WX9321
Company	'D' Company
Enlisted	30.10.1940
Discharged	9.8.1946
Date of Birth	20.6.1914
Place of Birth	Kellerberrin, Western Australia
Father	James Leslie Loller
Mother	Rossietta Melba Loller
Religion	Methodist
Pre-War Occupation	Boring Contractor

HISTORY

Singapore	Selarang Camp and Barracks Changi
	Changi Gaol Camp
POW Number	1/8414
Return Details 1945	Singapore-Darwin-Melbourne, 1st Netherlands Military Hospital Ship *Oranje*
Additions	Wounded in action on west coast by a mortar round at 2330 hours on 8.2.1942. Admitted to 2/9th Field Ambulance on 13.2.1942 with a shrapnel wound to the right knee, both legs and his back. Transferred to the 2/13th Australian General Hospital on 16.2.1942. Transferred to 2/9th Field Ambulance on 22.2.1942. The soldier's right leg was amputated above the knee on 6.4.1942 and he was awarded an 'A' Medical Classification by the Japanese. Soldier later worked in the hospital cookhouse at the Changi Gaol Camp.

ARTHUR HAROLD STEPHEN LONDON

Rank	Private
Regimental Number	WX12717
Classification	Fitter
Attached 2/4th	Australian Army Ordnance Corps
Enlisted	9.5.1941
Discharged	1.2.1946
Date of Birth	8.7.1908
Place of Birth	Broken Hill, South Australia
Father	Dean London
Mother	Rosena London
Religion	Church of England
Pre-War Occupation	Chief Engineer, Western Mining Corporation, Kalgoorlie

HISTORY

Singapore	Selarang Camp and Barracks Changi
	Changi Gaol Camp
Return Details	Singapore-Darwin-Melbourne, 1st Netherlands Military Hospital Ship *Oranje*
Additions	Private London was the drainage engineer for the Garden Control Party with the temporary rank of Sergeant. This was due to the fact that he had men working under his command for the duration of this party.

JOSEPH LEWIS LONSDALE

Rank	Private
Regimental Number	WX16727
Company	'B' Company Headquarters
Enlisted	24.9.1941
Discharged	29.4.1946
Date of Birth	15.5.1923
Place of Birth	West Melbourne, Victoria
Father	Douglas Lonsdale
Mother	Blanche Emily Lonsdale
Religion	Church of England
Pre-War Occupation	Sales Assistant

HISTORY

Singapore	Selarang Camp Changi
	Thomson Road (Caldecot Hill Estate Camp)
	River Valley Road Camp
	Selarang Barracks Changi
'D' Force Thailand	V Battalion
Camps Thailand	Kinsaiyok, Brankassi, Hindaine, Brankassi, Non Pladuk
Japan	*Aramis* Party
POW Number	627
Camps Japan	Fukuoka sub-Camp No. 17, Omuta
Return Details 1945	Nagasaki-Okinawa, USS *Cape Gloucester,* Okinawa-Manila, details unknown
	Manila-Sydney, HMS *Speaker*
	Sydney-Fremantle, HMT *Dominion Monarch*

HARRIE ROBERT LOVE

Rank	Private
Regimental Number	WX7285
Classification	Trade Group I
Company	'A' Company
Enlisted	1.8.1940
Discharged	18.3.1946
Date of Birth	29.6.1905
Place of Birth	Bunbury, Western Australia
Father	Henry Love
Mother	Mary Elizabeth Love
Religion	Church of England
Pre-War Occupation	Truck Driver

HISTORY

Java	'Blackforce'
'A' Force Burma	Java Party No. 4, Black Force
Singapore	A. G. H. Roberts Barracks Changi
	Selarang Barracks Changi
	X3 Party
	Changi Gaol Camp
Return Details 1945	Singapore-Darwin-Sydney, HMT *Arawa*
Additions	Soldier arrived in Singapore on 12.10.1942. This soldier was evacuated to the A.G.H. at Roberts Barracks Changi and did not continue his journey to Burma. Soldier's age or trade skills may have influenced this decision.

HARRY LUCAS

Rank	Acting Corporal
Regimental Number	WX13752
Classification	Driver/Mechanic
Company	'A' Company
Enlisted	28.5.1941
Discharged	17.5.1946
Date of Birth	11.10.1919
Place of Birth	Windsor, England
Father	Frank Lucas
Mother	Alice Lucas
Religion	Church of England
Pre-War Occupation	Farmhand

HISTORY

Singapore	Selarang Camp Changi
'A' Force Burma	Green Force, No. 3 Battalion
POW Number	1496
Camps Burma	Khonkan 55km Camp
Camps Thailand	Tamarkan
Japan	*Awa Maru* Party, Kumi No. 40
POW Number	1509
Camps Japan	Fukuoka sub-Camp No. 17, Omuta
Return Details 1945	Nagasaki-Manila, details unknown
	Manila-Morotai-Darwin, PBY Catalina aircraft A24-357
	Darwin-Perth by aircraft
Additions	Wounded in action at Hill 200, Ulu Pandan on 12.2.1942 and admitted to the 2/13th Australian General Hospital with shrapnel and gunshot wounds to the left thigh. Transferred to the 2/10th Australian General Hospital on 7.3.1942. Discharged to unit on 23.3.1942.

CHRISTOPHER ROBERT LUSH

Rank	Private
Regimental Number	WX9146
Company	'C' Company
Enlisted	30.10.1940
Discharged	14.12.1945
Date of Birth	20.1.1922
Place of Birth	Carlisle, Western Australia
Father	Christopher Lush
Mother	Annie Lush
Religion	Church of England
Pre-War Occupation	Apprentice Carpenter

HISTORY

Singapore	Selarang Camp Changi
Camps	Johore Bahru, Adam Park
	Sime Road Camp
	Selarang Barracks Changi
	Kranji Camp Woodlands
	Changi Gaol Camp
Return Details 1945	Singapore-Darwin-Sydney, HMT *Arawa*
	Sydney-Melbourne by troop train
	Melbourne-Fremantle, HMT *Strathmore*
Additions	This soldier suffered from asthma and was sent to Kranji Camp Woodlands. (see also Pte. M. W. Hortin)

ROBERT RUSSELL LYLE

Rank	Private
Regimental Number	WX8675
Company	Headquarters Company
Enlisted	23.10.1940
Discharged	20.3.1946
Date of Birth	27.11.1916
Place of Birth	Busselton, Western Australia
Father	Lewis Laurence Lyle
Mother	Sarah Lyle
Religion	Church of England
Pre-War Occupation	Miner

HISTORY

Singapore	Selarang Camp Changi
	Serangoon Road Camp
	Selarang Barracks Changi (Garden Control Party)
	X6 Party
	Changi Gaol Camp
Return Details 1945	Not Known
Additions	Wounded in action at Ulu Pandan on 10.2.1942. Admitted to the 2/13th Australian General Hospital with a gunshot wound. The bullet had entered through the arm and exited through his back. He also had a bayonet wound to the stomach. This soldier was a vocalist with the Concert Party.

RONALD RUBEN LYMN

Rank	Private
Regimental Number	WX17515
Company	'E' Company, Special Reserve Battalion
Enlisted	31.10.1941
Discharged	9.11.1945
Date of Birth	11.8.1914
Place of Birth	Adelaide, South Australia
Father	Thomas Dundee Lymn
Mother	Rosetta Robins Lymn
Religion	Church of England
Pre-War Occupation	Miner

HISTORY

Singapore	Selarang Camp Changi
	Johore Bahru, Adam Park
	Selarang Barracks Changi
POW Number	4/6352
'J' Force Japan	*Wales Maru* Party
POW Number	691
Camps Japan	Kobe (Showa-Denki)
	Nagoya, Toyama
Return Details 1945	Yokohama-Okinawa-Manila by aircraft
	Manila-Sydney-B24 Liberator aircraft A72-146
	Sydney-Melbourne by troop train
	Melbourne-Perth by ANA airliner

GORDON LAWRENCE LYNAM

Rank	Private
Regimental Number	WX7847
Company	Headquarters Company
Enlisted	13.8.1940
Discharged	28.2.1946
Date of Birth	12.1.1920
Place of Birth	Bridgetown, Western Australia
Father	George Herbert Lynam
Mother	Esme Beatrice Lynam
Religion	Roman Catholic
Pre-War Occupation	Butcher's Assistant

HISTORY

Singapore	Selarang Camp Changi
'A' Force Burma	Green Force, No. 3 Battalion
POW Number	2905
Camps Thailand	Tamarkan, Non Pladuk, Bangkok (go-downs), Ubon
Return Details 1945	Thailand-Singapore by aircraft
	Singapore-Fremantle, HMT *Moreton Bay*

WALTER ERNEST LYNN

Rank	Lance Corporal
Regimental Number	WX7204
Company	'D' Company
Enlisted	1.8.1940
Discharged	20.12.1945
Date of Birth	8.2.1913
Place of Birth	Claremont, Western Australia
Father	Arthur Ernest Lynn
Mother	Jessie Anne Lynn
Religion	Church of England
Pre-War Occupation	Carpenter, Baker and Miner

HISTORY

Singapore	Selarang Camp Changi
'A' Force Burma	Green Force, No. 3 Battalion
POW Number	2759
Camps Thailand	Tamarkan, Kanchanaburi, Petchaburi, Kachu Mountain Camp
Return Details 1945	Thailand-Singapore by aircraft
	Singapore-Fremantle, HMT *Highland Brigade*

JOHN KENNETH ALEXANDER MacDONALD

Rank	Private
Regimental Number	WX17566
Company	Headquarters Company
Enlisted	5.11.1941
Discharged	15.7.1946
Date of Birth	21.5.1907
Place of Birth	Fremantle, Western Australia
Father	Not Known
Mother	Harriet MacDonald
Religion	Church of Christ
Pre-War Occupation	Locomotive Driver and Miner

HISTORY

Singapore	Selarang Camp Changi
'A' Force Burma	Green Force, No. 3 Battalion
POW Number	1518
Camps Thailand	Tamarkan, Nakom Nayok, Bangkok
Return Details 1945	Thailand-Singapore by aircraft
	Singapore-Fremantle, HMT *Tamaroa*

GRAHAM CHARLES MacKINNON

Rank	Lieutenant
Regimental Number	WX3707
Company	'B' Company
Enlisted	10.6.1940
Appointment Terminated	8.2.1946
Date of Birth	10.12.1916
Place of Birth	Bridgetown, Western Australia
Father	Charles Archibald MacKinnon
Mother	Rhoda Myrtle MacKinnon
Religion	Methodist
Pre-War Occupation	Salesman

HISTORY

Singapore	Selarang Camp Changi
	Johore Bahru, Adam Park
	Selarang Barracks Changi
	Kranji Hospital Woodlands (pellegra 29.5.1944)
	Changi Gaol Camp
POW Number	1/10159
Return Details 1945	Singapore-Labuan by aircraft
	Labuan-Morotai-Sydney, 2/1st H.M. Australian Hospital Ship *Wanganella*
	Sydney-Melbourne-Perth by ambulance train

KENNETH THOMAS MacLENNAN

Rank	Sergeant (Promoted on 29.1.1942)
Regimental Number	WX8377
Classification	Driver
Awards	Mentioned in Despatches
Company	'A' Company
Enlisted	12.9.1940
Discharged	3.10.1946
Date of Birth	14.8.1912
Place of Birth	Laverton, Western Australia
Father	Not Known
Mother	Not Known
Religion	Methodist
Pre-War Occupation	Truck Driver

HISTORY

Singapore	Selarang Camp Changi
'A' Force Burma	Green Force, No. 3 Battalion
POW Number	1309
Camps Thailand	Tamarkan (hospital), Bangkok, Nacompaton
Return Details 1945	Thailand-Singapore by aircraft
	Singapore-Fremantle, HMT *Circassia*
Additions	Wounded in action on 12.2.1942. Shrapnel wound to the right thigh. Wounded for a second time on 15.2.1942 at Buona Vista. Admitted to the 2/13th A.G.H. with multiple shrapnel wounds to the right thigh, back, back of right knee, sole of foot and forearm. Transferred to the 2/10 Australian General Hospital 22.2.1942. This NCO took command of No. 4 Platoon on the night of 12/13.2.1942 when Lt. Manning was killed. It was noted that he did an excellent job even though he was wounded.

WILLIAM MacLEOD

Rank	Private
Regimental Number	WX17302
Company	'E' Company, Special Reserve Battalion
Enlisted	17.10.1941
Discharged	15.3.1946
Date of Birth	28.10.1907
Place of Birth	Greenock, Scotland
Father	Not Known
Mother	Effie MacLeod
Religion	Presbyterian
Pre-War Occupation	Powerhouse Attendant

HISTORY

Singapore	Selarang Camp and Barracks Changi
	Changi Gaol Camp
	X1 Party
	P Party
POW Number	3/8928
Return Details 1945	Singapore-Darwin-Sydney, HMT *Arawa*
	Sydney-Melbourne by troop train
	Melbourne-Fremantle, HMT *Strathmore*

ARTHUR MELVILLE MAGILL

Rank	Corporal
Regimental Number	WX16886
Awards	Military Medal
Company	'E' Company, Special Reserve Battalion
Enlisted	6.10.1941
Discharged	1.3.1946
Date of Birth	30.1.1919
Place of Birth	Collie, Western Australia
Father	Arthur William Magill
Mother	May Eva Magill
Religion	Church of England
Pre-War Occupation	Boiler Attendant

HISTORY

Singapore	Escaped to Sumatra
POW Number	275
Camps Sumatra	Gloe Gloer Camp
	Atjeh Party
	Pakan Baroe-Moearo Railway
Return Details	Singapore-Darwin-Sydney, HMT *Arawa*
	Sydney-Melbourne by troop train
	Melbourne-Fremantle, HMT *Strathmore*
Additions	Wounded in action at Bulim Village 9.2.1942. Soldier received gunshot wounds to the neck and armpit from a light automatic weapon. Soldier was wounded again at South-West Bukit Timah on 11.2.1942 this time receiving a gunshot wound to the third and fourth fingers of the right hand and a gunshot wound to the leg.

REGINALD GORDON MAGOR

Rank	Private
Regimental Number	WX8656
Classification	Driver
Company	Headquarters Company
Enlisted	23.10.1940
Discharged	2.7.1946
Date of Birth	3.6.1920
Place of Birth	Subiaco, Western Australia
Father	Gordon Alfred Magor
Mother	Doris Irene Magor
Religion	Church of England
Pre-War Occupation	Driver

HISTORY

Singapore	Selarang Camp Changi
	Johore Bahru, Adam Park
	Selarang Barracks Changi
POW Number	3/8596
'D' Force Thailand	V Battalion
Camps Thailand	Brankassi, Non Pladuk
Japan	*Aramis* Party
POW Number	582
Camps Japan	Fukuoka sub-Camp No. 17, Omuta
Return Details 1945	Nagasaki-Manila, USS *Lunga Point*
	Manila-Morotai-Darwin, PBY Catalina aircraft A24-354
	Darwin-Melbourne, B24 Liberator aircraft
	Darwin-Perth by aircraft

JOHN WILLIAM MALTHOUSE

Rank	Private
Regimental Number	WX7239
Classification	Batman/Runner
Company	'D' Company
Enlisted	1.8.1940
Discharged	23.1.1946
Date of Birth	2.2.1915
Place of Birth	Aleerton, South Australia
Father	John William Malthouse
Mother	Florence May Malthouse
Religion	Church of England
Pre-War Occupation	Miner

HISTORY

Singapore	Selarang Camp Changi
'A' Force Burma	Green Force No. 3 Battalion
POW Number	1507
Camps Thailand	131km, 133km (Williams Force), Tamarkan, Kanchanaburi, Bangkok
Return Details 1945	Thailand-Singapore by aircraft
	Singapore-Fremantle, HMT *Moreton Bay*
Additions	Shell shock Ulu Pandan on 12.2.1942. Evacuated to the 2/10th Australian General Hospital. Discharged to unit on 20.2.1942.

ERIC HORSLEY MANN

Rank	Private
Regimental Number	WX5175
Classification	Rangetaker
Company	'D' Company
Enlisted	26.7.1940
Discharged	8.2.1946
Date of Birth	25.12.1915
Place of Birth	Pinjarra, Western Australia
Father	Heneage William Mann
Mother	Elsie May Mann
Religion	Church of England
Pre-War Occupation	Salesman

HISTORY

Singapore	Selarang Camp Changi
	Serangoon Road Camp
	Selarang Barracks Changi
POW Number	4/6388
'D' Force Thailand	S Battalion
POW Number	8810
Camps Thailand	Kanu II, Tamuang, Non Pladuk
Japan	*Rashin Maru* Party (remained on Singapore)
French Indo-China	*Both* Party
Return Details 1945	Saigon-Bangkok-Singapore by aircraft
	Singapore-Brisbane by aircraft
	Brisbane-Sydney-Melbourne-Perth by troop train

RONALD FREDRICK MANTHORPE

Rank	Corporal (Promoted on 5.2.1942)
Regimental Number	WX11472
Classification	Fitter
Attached 2/4th	Australian Army Ordnance Corps
Enlisted	9.4.1941
Discharged	24.5.1946
Date of Birth	17.8.1901
Place of Birth	Inglewood, Victoria
Father	Herbert James Manthorpe
Mother	Maggie Manthorpe
Religion	Presbyterian
Pre-War Occupation	Motor Mechanic

HISTORY

Singapore	Selarang Camp Changi
	Johore Bahru, Adam Park
	Selarang Barracks Changi
POW Number	4/4543
'D' ForceThailand	V Battalion
Camps Thailand	Chungkai (hospital), Bangkok (go-downs), Japanese Transport Camp repairing trucks with Jack Swift and Wally Bow.
Return Details 1945	Thailand-Rangoon by C47 aircraft
	Rangoon-Singapore, HMT *Highland Brigade*
	Singapore-Darwin-Perth by PBY Catalina aircraft

JAMES CHARLES MANTON

Rank	Private
Regimental Number	WX8015
Company	Battalion Headquarters
Enlisted	13.8.1940
Discharged	7.12.1945
Date of Birth	28.1.1896
Place of Birth	Melbourne, Victoria
Father	Not Known
Mother	Not Known
Religion	Church of England
Pre-War Occupation	Platelayer (railways)

HISTORY

Singapore	Selarang Camp Changi
'A' Force Burma	Green Force, No. 3 Battalion
POW Number	3167
Camps Burma	Reptu 30km, Khonkan 55km (medical orderly)
Camps Thailand	Tamarkan Hospital (7.1.1944), Nacompaton
Return Details 1945	Thailand-Singapore by aircraft
	Singapore-Fremantle, HMT *Highland Brigade*

BRYAN HARRY MANWARING

Rank	Sergeant
Regimental Number	WX7438
Company	'C' Company
Enlisted	6.8.1940
Discharged	22.5.1946
Date of Birth	23.4.1913
Place of Birth	Worthing, England
Father	Frederick William Manwaring
Mother	Hannah Manwaring
Religion	Church of England
Pre-War Occupation	Clerk

HISTORY

Singapore	Selarang Camp Changi
'A' Force Burma	Green Force, No. 3 Battalion
POW Number	1326
Camps Thailand	Tamarkan
Japan	*Rakuyo Maru* Party (remained behind sick at Saigon)
Return Details 1945	Saigon-Bangkok-Singapore by aircraft
	Singapore-Sydney, HMT *Highland Chieftan*
	Sydney-Melbourne-Perth by troop train

LESLIE JAMES MARRIOT

Rank	Private
Regimental Number	WX7124
Company	'C' Company
Enlisted	1.8.1940
Discharged	1.2.1946
Date of Birth	1.1.1916
Place of Birth	Mt Magnet, Western Australia
Father	Phillip Marriot
Mother	Edith Mary Marriot
Religion	Roman Catholic
Pre-War Occupation	Miner

HISTORY

Singapore	Selarang Camp and Barracks Changi
'D' Force Thailand	V Battalion
Camps Thailand	Non Pladuk, Nacompaton, Bangkok (go-downs)
Return Details 1945	Thailand-Singapore by aircraft
	Singapore-Sydney, HMT *Highland Chieftan*
	Sydney-Melbourne-Perth by troop train

SAMUEL THOMAS MARTIN

Rank	Private
Regimental Number	WX16341
Company	Headquarters Company
Enlisted	3..9.1941
Discharged	4.4.1946
Date of Birth	5.12.1919
Place of Birth	Northam, Western Australia
Father	Henry James Martin
Mother	Ethel May Martin
Religion	Roman Catholic
Pre-War Occupation	Labourer

HISTORY

Java	'Blackforce'
'A' Force Burma	Java Party No. 4, Williams Force
POW Number	4489
Camps Burma	Khonkan 55km Camp
Camps Thailand	Tamarkan, Bangkok
Return Details 1945	Thailand-Singapore by aircraft
	Singapore-Fremantle, HMT *Highland Brigade*
Additions	Soldier was evacuated sick from Khonkan to Tamarkan in 1943 and was still at Tamarkan on 6.9.1944.

FREDERICK NOEL MATTHEWS

Rank	Private
Regimental Number	WX17000
Company	'E' Company, Special Reserve Battalion
Enlisted	13.10.1941
Discharged	28.2.1946
Date of Birth	23.12.1923
Place of Birth	Liverpool, England
Father	Not Known
Mother	Elizabeth Mathews
Religion	Church of England
Pre-War Occupation	Farmhand

Singapore	Selarang Camp Changi
	Adam Park, Johore Bahru
	Selarang Barracks Changi
POW Number	3/8657
'D' Force Thailand	S Battalion
POW Number	8814
Camps Thailand	Hintok River Camp, Kinsaiyok, Tamuang
Japan	*Rashin Maru* Party
POW Number	1667
Camps Japan	Yamane
	Niihama
Return Details 1945	Wakayama-Okinawa, USS *Sanctuary*
	Okinawa-Manila, USS *Bingham*
	Manila-Sydney, HMS *Speaker*
	Sydney-Melbourne-Perth by troop train
Additions	Kingsley Fairbridge Farm Schoolboy.

ROY MATTHEWS

Rank	Lance Corporal
Regimental Number	WX7042
Classification	Clerk
Company	Company Headquarters
Enlisted	30.7.1940
Discharged	8.4.1946
Date of Birth	21.9.1920
Place of Birth	Ogmore Vale, Glenmorgan, South Wales
Father	William John Matthews
Mother	Gwen Matthews
Religion	Baptist
Pre-War Occupation	Driver

HISTORY

Singapore	Selarang Camp Changi
	Mount Pleasant Camp
	River Valley Road Camp
	Selarang Barracks Changi
POW Number	3/8658
'D' Force Thailand	S Battalion
POW Number	8815
Camps Thailand	Kanu II, Hintok Road Camp, Hintok River Camp, Kinsaiyok, Konkoita, Tamarkan, Chungkai, Tamuang, Petchaburi, Kachu Mountain Camp, Ratburi, Nakom Nayok, Lopburi, Bangkok (see Danny Bevis Diary)
Return Details 1945	Thailand-Singapore by aircraft
	Singapore-Fremantle, HMT *Moreton Bay*

WILFORD NEVILLE MATSON

Rank	Private
Regimental Number	WX16347
Classification	Batman/Runner
Company	Battalion Headquarters
Enlisted	3.9.1941
Discharged	11.2.1946
Date of Birth	16.7.1924
Place of Birth	Midland Junction, Western Australia
Father	Not Known
Mother	Gladys Beryl Matson
Stepfather	George Rodwell
Religion	Church of England
Pre-War Occupation	Postal Assistant

HISTORY

Singapore	Selarang Camp Changi
	Thomson Road (Caldecot Hill Estate Camp)
	River Valley Road Camp
	Selarang Barracks Changi
POW Number	3/8660
'D' Force Thailand	V Battalion
Camps Thailand	Kinsaiyok, Brankassi, Hindaine, Kuii, Tamuang, Tamajao (line maintenance party), Tamarkan, Non Pladuk, Tamuang, Non Pladuk, Wampo-Tavoy Escape Road (evacuated sick to Kanchanburi), Nacompaton Hospital (ex-Tavoy 22.5.1945) Bangkok.
Return Details 1945	Thailand-Rangoon by aircraft
	Rangoon-Singapore, HMT *Highland Brigade*
	Singapore-Fremantle, HMT *Circassia*

JACK MAUDE

Rank	Private
Regimental Number	WX13285
Company	'A' Company
Enlisted	21.5.1941
Discharged	20.3.1946
Date of Birth	4.4.1911
Place of Birth	Cambridge, England
Father	Dr Jacques Maude
Mother	Not Known (professional ballet dancer)
Religion	Church of England
Pre-War Occupation	Banana Plantation Worker

Java	'Blackforce'
Camps Java	Bicycle Camp Batavia
'A' Force Burma	Java Party No. 4, Williams Force
POW Number	4752
Camps Burma	Reptu, Tanyin, Taungzun, Anganan No. 2 100km Camp
Camps Thailand	Kanchanaburi
Japan	*Awa Maru* Party, Kumi No. 42
POW Number	13064
Camps Japan	Fukuoka sub-Camp No. 24 Sendyu
Return Details 1945	Nagasaki-Okinawa, U.S. Navy ship
	Okinawa-Manila, PBY Catalina aircraft
	Manila-Morotai-Darwin, PBY Catalina aircraft A24-377
	Darwin-Perth, PBY Catalina
Additions	Jack's father was a doctor who was killed serving with the French Army during WWI. Jack had been sent out to Australia from Swanley Boys Orphanage in Kent to the Kingsley Fairbridge Farm School.

FRANCIS GERALD McCAFFREY

Rank	Lieutenant
Regimental Number	WX3440
Company	'A' Company
Enlisted	1.3.1937
Appointment Terminated	24.5.1949
Date of Birth	23.9.1918
Place of Birth	Albert Park, Victoria
Father	John Francis McCaffrey
Mother	Not Known
Religion	Roman Catholic
Pre-War Occupation	Regular Soldier

HISTORY

Singapore	Selarang Camp Changi
'A' Force Burma	Green Force, No. 3 Battalion
POW Number	3440
Camps Thailand	Tamarkan, Kanchanaburi, Bangkok
Return Details 1945	Thailand-Singapore by aircraft
	Singapore-Fremantle, HMT *Tamaroa*
Additions	Officer was promoted to Captain Australian Staff Corps on 14.4.1947. He attended the Japanese War Crimes Trials at Rabaul from 30.4.1946-21.6.1946. His appointment was terminated on 24.5.1949, 'D' Class medically unfit. He was appointed 2 i/c of 'A' Company 2/4th Machine Gun Battalion on the appointment of Major Saggers to the Special Reserve Battalion.

LESLIE WILLIAM McCANN

Rank	Private
Regimental Number	WX17837
Company	'E' Company, Special Reserve Battalion
Enlisted	1.12.1941
Discharged	4.3.1946
Date of Birth	31.3.1922
Place of Birth	Subiaco, Western Australia
Father	Thomas McCann
Mother	Ivy Muriel McCann
Religion	Church of England
Pre-War Occupation	Butcher and Truck Driver

HISTORY

Singapore	A. G. H. Roberts Barracks Changi (ex-Changi Gaol Civil Internment Camp)
	Selarang Barracks Changi
	Changi Gaol Camp (Hygiene and Garden Control Parties and storeman)
POW Number	1/8466
Return Details 1945	Singapore-Darwin-Sydney, HMT *Arawa*
	Sydney-Melbourne-Perth by troop train
Additions	Wounded in action South-West Bukit Timah on 11.2.1942. Soldier received mortar fragments to his right leg and shooting by a Japanese firing squad.

CLARENCE JOHN McDONALD

Rank	Lance Corporal
Regimental Number	WX8620
Company	'A' Company
Enlisted	18.10.1940
Discharged	9.1.1946
Date of Birth	29.11.1916
Place of Birth	Geraldton, Western Australia
Father	William Donald McDonald
Mother	Beatrice Maude McDonald
Religion	Church of England
Pre-War Occupation	Railway Porter

HISTORY

Singapore	Selarang Camp and Barracks Changi
POW Number	4/4536
'D' Force Thailand	S Battalion
POW Number	8470
Camps Thailand	Kanu II, Hintok Road Camp, Hintok River Camp, Kinsaiyok, Konkoita, Tarsau (hospital), Tamuang, Tamarkan, Chungkai, Petchaburi, Kachu Mountain Camp, Lopburi, Nakom Nayok, Bangkok (see Danny Bevis Diary)
Return Details 1945	Thailand-Singapore by aircraft
	Singapore-Fremantle, HMT *Tamaroa*

COLIN KEITH McDONALD

Rank	Lance Corporal
Regimental Number	WX5163
Classification	Driver
Company	'C' Company
Enlisted	23.7.1940
Discharged	25.1.1946
Date of Birth	24.4.1902
Place of Birth	Kojonup, Western Australia
Father	Not Known
Mother	Not Known
Religion	Methodist
Pre-War Occupation	Truck Driver

HISTORY

Singapore	Selarang Camp Changi
'A' Force Burma	Green Force, No. 3 Battalion
POW Number	2774
Camps Thailand	114km 3.12.1943 (attached to Williams Force), Ratburi, Nacompaton
Return Details 1945	Thailand-Singapore by aircraft
	Singapore-Fremantle, HMT *Circassia*

WILLIAM McEWEN

Rank	Private
Regimental Number	WX8790
Company	Headquarters Company
Enlisted	23.10.1940
Discharged	4.2.1946
Date of Birth	10.3.1902
Place of Birth	Glasgow, Scotland
Father	Robert McEwen
Mother	Not Known
Religion	Presbyterian
Pre-War Occupation	Prospector

HISTORY

Singapore	Selarang Camp Changi
'A' Force Burma	Green Force, No. 3 Battalion
POW Number	3075
Camps Burma	Khonkan 55km (1.7.1943)
Camps Thailand	Tamarkan (hospital 29.4.1944)
Return Details 1945	Thailand-Singapore by aircraft
	Singapore-Fremantle, HMT *Tamaroa*

WILLIAM ALEXANDER McEWEN

Rank	Private
Regimental Number	WX20095
Company	'E' Company, Special Reserve Battalion
Enlisted	1.10.1941
Discharged	4.3.1946
Date of Birth	1.1.1919
Place of Birth	North Fremantle, Western Australia
Father	Charles Henry McEwen
Mother	Mary Catherine McEwen
Religion	Church of England
Pre-War Occupation	Orchard Worker

HISTORY

Singapore	Selarang Camp Changi
'A' Force Burma	Green Force, No. 3 Battalion
POW Number	3070
Camps Burma	Reptu 30km (medical orderly 26.3.1943)
Camps Thailand	Tamarkan, Petchaburi, Linson Wood Camp, Nacompaton
POW Number (Linson)	12173
Return Details 1945	Thailand-Singapore by aircraft
	Singapore-Fremantle, HMT *Tamaroa*

ALFRED JOSEPH McGHEE

Rank	Private
Regimental Number	WX9145
Company	'A' Company
Enlisted	30.10.1940
Discharged	18.4.1946
Date of Birth	1.10.1906
Place of Birth	Boulder, Western Australia
Father	William James McGhee
Mother	Isabella Jane McGhee
Religion	Church of England
Pre-War Occupation	Lift Operator at Boans Pty Ltd

HISTORY

Singapore	Selarang Camp Changi
'A' Force Burma	Green Force, No. 3 Battalion
POW Number	1494
Camps Burma	Khonkan 55km (July-October 1943, evacuated with tropical ulcers on 6.11.1943)
Return Details 1945	Thailand-Singapore by aircraft
	Singapore-Fremantle, HMT *Tamaroa*
Additions	Evacuated to the 2/9th Field Ambulance suffering from exhaustion. Transferred to the 2/13th Australian General Hospital at Roberts Barracks Changi on 10.3.1942. Soldier's right leg was amputated above the knee due to tropical ulcers on 4.1.1944. Evacuated to Tamarkan Hospital and discharged on 27.4.1944. Soldier was then moved to Bangkok in April 1944 and was recovered at Nacompaton at the end of August 1945.

JOSEPH MICHAEL McGINTY

Rank	Corporal (Promoted on 14.2.1942)
Regimental Number	WX7436
Company	Headquarters Company
Enlisted	6.8.1940
Discharged	19.3.1946
Date of Birth	15.9.1917
Place of Birth	Perth, Western Australia
Father	Michael Patrick McGinty
Mother	Not Known
Religion	Roman Catholic
Pre-War Occupation	Furniture Maker and Flenser

HISTORY

Singapore	Selarang Camp and Barracks Changi
Force	'F' Force Thailand
Return Details 1945	Singapore-Darwin-Sydney, 1st Netherlands Military Hospital Ship *Oranje*
	Sydney-Melbourne-Perth by troop train

FRANCIS THOMAS McGLINN

Rank	Private
Regimental Number	WX8478
Company	'C' Company
Enlisted	18.10.1940
Discharged	30.1.1946
Date of Birth	29.8.1909
Place of Birth	Northam, Western Australia
Father	Thomas McGlinn
Mother	Helen Margaret McGlinn
Religion	Methodist
Pre-War Occupation	Farmhand

HISTORY

Singapore	Selarang Camp Changi
	Thompson Road (Caldecot Hill Estate Camp)
	River Valley Road Camp
	Selarang Barracks Changi
POW Number	3/8884
'D' Force Thailand	S Battalion
POW Number	8818
Camps Thailand	Kanu II, Kanu I River Camp, Tarsau, Chungkai, Tamuang
Japan	*Rashin Maru* Party
POW Numbers	78 *(Rashin Maru)* and 499
Camps Japan	Yamane, Niihama
Return Details 1945	Wakayama-Okinawa, USS *Sanctuary*
	Okinawa-Manila, USS *Bingham*
	Manila-Morotai-Darwin, PBY Catalina aircraft A24-354
	Darwin-Perth, B24 Liberator aircraft
Additions	Wounded in action at Hill 200, Ulu Pandan on 11.2.1942 and admitted to the 2/13th Australian General Hospital with a shrapnel wound to the left foot. Discharged to unit on 26.2.1942.

LAURENCE JAMES McGRATH

Rank	Acting Sergeant (Promoted on 28.8.1943)
Regimental Number	WX8611
Awards	Mentioned in Despatches
Company	'B' Company
Enlisted	18.10.1940
Discharged	16.11.1945
Date of Birth	14.9.1916
Place of Birth	Kalgoorlie, Western Australia
Father	Francis James McGrath
Mother	Jean McGrath
Religion	Church of England
Pre-War Occupation	Manager at State Building Supplies

HISTORY

Java
Australia
New Guinea

Remained onboard HMT *Aquitania* at Java and returned to Australia sick. Admitted to 110 (P)MH on 25.1.1942 and discharged to unit on 31.3.1942. Soldier went on to serve at Wewak, Lae and Aitape with the rank of A/Sgt. from 28.8.1943. He was Mentioned in Despatches whilst serving with the 43rd Water Transport Company. There was an explosion on a landing barge which caused a fire to break out. Acting Sergeant McGrath exposed himself to the flames and rescued an unconscious soldier.

JOHN ALEXANDER McGREGOR

Rank	Lance Corporal
Regimental Number	WX12835
Classification	Clerk
Company	'B' Company Headquarters
Enlisted	15.5.1941
Discharged	13.6.1946
Date of Birth	20.9.1903
Place of Birth	Guildford, Western Australia
Father	Charles Hutton McGregor
Mother	Clara Jane McGregor
Religion	Church of England
Pre-War Occupation	Insurance Clerk

HISTORY

Singapore

Selarang Camp Changi
Outram Road Prison
Changi Gaol Camp
Pasir Panjang Work Party (18.3.1945)

POW Number
2/9769

Return Details 1945
Singapore-Darwin-Sydney, HMT *Arawa*
Sydney-Melbourne by troop train,
Melbourne-Fremantle, HMT *Strathmore*

Additions
Escaped from Changi with Lieutenant Penrod Dean. Captured on 6.4.1942 at Pontian Kechil in Johore State by Malay Police and handed over to the Imperial Japanese Army on 7.4.1942. Sentenced to two years solitary confinement at H.M. Prison Outram Road.

ROBERT JAMES McKENZIE-MURRAY

Rank	Private
Regimental Number	WX15838
Company	'A' Company
Enlisted	18.1.1941
Discharged	11.12.1945
Date of Birth	13.7.1916
Place of Birth	Perth, Western Australia
Father	William Alexander McKenzie-Murray
Mother	Olive May McKenzie-Murray
Religion	Roman Catholic
Pre-War Occupation	Commercial Traveller

HISTORY

Singapore	Selarang Camp Changi
	Thompson Road (Caldecot Hill Estate Camp)
	River Valley Road Camp
	Selarang Barracks Changi
POW Number	1/12032
Force	'F' Force Thailand
Camps Thailand	Shimo Sonkurai, Tanbaya (hospital), Kanchanaburi (hospital)
Singapore	Levelling Party Changi Aerodrome
	P Party
	X10
	Changi Gaol Camp
Return Details 1945	Singapore-Darwin-Sydney, HMT *Arawa*
	Sydney-Melbourne by troop train
	Melbourne-Fremantle, HMT *Strathmore*
Additions	The following is a description of this soldier's movements during 1943-1945:
	Departed Singapore for 'F' Force on 19.4.1943.
	Departed on twenty-three day march on 25.4.1943.
	Arrived at Shimo Sonkurai Camp on 17.5.1943.
	Departed for Tanbaya Hospital Camp Burma on 30.8.1943.
	Departed Burma by train on 28.11.1943.
	Arrived Kanchanaburi 'F' and 'H' Force Hospital Camp on 4.12.1943.
	Departed Kanchanaburi on 14.12.1942.
	Arrived Singapore on 18.12.1943 and on 25.12.1943 occupied huts opposite Selarang Barracks.
	Spent Christmas in the Garden and Wood area.
	Moved to Changi Gaol Camp on 10.5.1944.
	All men on the Levelling Party remained behind.
	All civilians moved to Adam Park and Sime Road Camps.
	Soldier moved to Levelling Party at Changi Aerodrome on 14.6.1944.
	Removed from Levelling Party six days later due to repeated malaria attacks. Captain George Gwynne placed soldier on mess duties and made Medical Classification 3B.
	Moved back to Levelling Party on 26.4.1945.
	On 10.7.1945 marched into No. 2 Camp outside Changi Gaol Camp.

CHRIS McLENNAN

Rank	Corporal (Promoted on 24.1.1942)
Regimental Number	WX7608
Company	'C' Company
Enlisted	10.8.1940
Discharged	31.1.1946
Date of Birth	9.10.1920
Place of Birth	Beverley, Western Australia
Father	Gilbert Henry McLennan
Mother	Grace Lavina McLennan
Religion	Church of England
Pre-War Occupation	Motor Mechanic

HISTORY

Singapore	Selarang Camp Changi
	Mt Pleasant Camp
	Thompson Road (Caldecot Hill Estate Camp)
	Selarang Barracks Changi
POW Number	3/6456
'D' Force Thailand	S Battalion
Camps Thailand	Kanu II, Kanu III, Hintok Road Camp, Tarsau, Non Pladuk, Tamuang, Konkoita, Kinsaiyok, Tamarkan, Chungkai, Petchaburi, Nacompation, Bangkok
POW Number	8734
Return Details 1945	Bangkok-Singapore by aircraft
	Singapore-Sydney, HMT *Highland Chieftan*
Additions	Wounded in the face at Hill 200, Ulu Pandan on 11.2.1942 but remained on duty. At Konkoita the work involved the raising the height of a bridge and at Kinsaiyok a railway loop line was built.

CHARLES PETER McLOUGHLIN

Rank	Private
Regimental Number	WX9825
Company	'C' Company
Enlisted	6.12.1940
Discharged	13.3.1946
Date of Birth	24.1.1920
Place of Birth	Northampton, Western Australia
Father	James Archibald McLoughlin
Mother	Violet Minnie Mcloughlin
Religion	Church of England
Pre-War Occupation	Timber Worker

HISTORY

Java	'Blackforce'
Camps Java	Leles, Bandoeng, Bicycle Camp Batavia
'A' Force Burma	Java Party No. 4, Williams Force
POW Number	4738
Camps Thailand	131km, 133km, Kanchanaburi, Tamarkan, Nikhe Wood Camp, Petchaburi, Lopburi, Nakom Nayok, Bangkok
Return Details 1945	Thailand-Singapore by aircraft
	Singapore-Fremantle, HMT *Tamaroa*

WILFRED NOEL KAIN McNULTY

Rank	Private
Regimental Number	WX8834
Classification	Signaller
Company	Headquarters Company
Enlisted	23.10.1940
Discharged	8.2.1946
Date of Birth	12.12.1906
Place of Birth	Wallsend, England
Father	Not Known
Mother	Maude Evelyn McNulty
Religion	Roman Catholic
Pre-War Occupation	Miner

HISTORY

Singapore	Selarang Camp and Barracks Changi
POW Number	4/6377
'D' Force Thailand	V Battalion
Camps Thailand	Tamarkan, Non Pladuk, Chumphon, Petchaburi, Kachu Mountain Camp
Return Details 1945	Thailand-Singapore by aircraft
	Singapore-Fremantle, HMT *Highland Brigade*

CYRIL JOHN McPHERSON

Rank	Private
Regimental Number	WX7675
Company	'B' Company
Enlisted	10.8.1940
Discharged	1.2.1946
Date of Birth	1.8.1914
Place of Birth	Meckering, Western Australia
Father	Hugh McPherson
Mother	Ethel Margaret McPherson
Religion	Church of England
Pre-War Occupation	Farmhand

HISTORY

Singapore	Selarang Camp and Barracks Changi
'D' Force Thailand	S Battalion
POW Number	8813
Camps Thailand	Konkoita
Return Details 1945	Thailand-Singapore by aircraft
	Singapore-Fremantle, HMT *Highland Brigade*

AMBROSE McQUADE

Rank	Sergeant
Regimental Number	WX8243
Company	'C' Company
Enlisted	16.8.1940
Discharged	14.12.1945
Date of Birth	8.8.1897
Place of Birth	York, Western Australia
Father	Ambrose McQuade
Mother	Mary Ann McQuade
Religion	Church of England
Pre-War Occupation	Prospector and Railway Sleeper Cutter

HISTORY

Singapore	Selarang Camp Changi
	Johore Bahru, Adam Park
	Sime Road Camp
	Changi Gaol Camp
POW Number	4/6379
Return Details 1945	Singapore-Darwin-Sydney, HMT *Arawa*
	Sydney-Melbourne by troop train
	Melbourne-Fremantle, HMT *Strathmore*

JAMES McSKENE

Rank	Private
Regimental Number	WX6203
Company	'D' Company Headquarters
Enlisted	13.7.1940
Discharged	27.5.1946
Date of Birth	11.7.1908
Place of Birth	Midland Junction, Western Australia
Father	Not Known
Mother	Not Known
Religion	Roman Catholic
Pre-War Occupation	Labourer

HISTORY

Singapore	Selarang Camp Changi
	Sime Road Camp
	Selarang Barracks Changi
POW Number	3/8958
'H' Force Thailand	'H' Force Group No. 3
Camps Thailand	Kanu II, Kanchanaburi (beri-beri October 1943)
Singapore	Sime Road Camp
	Changi Gaol Camp
Return Details 1945	Singapore-Sydney, HMT *Highland Chieftain*
	Sydney-Melbourne Perth by troop train

ERIC MEAKINS

Rank	Private
Regimental Number	WX7241
Company	'A' Company
Enlisted	1.8.1940
Discharged	14.12.1945
Date of Birth	1.2.1918
Place of Birth	Mt Lawley, Western Australia
Father	Joseph Henry Meakins
Mother	Charlotte Smith Meakins
Religion	Church of England
Pre-War Occupation	Milk Vendor

HISTORY

Singapore	Selarang Camp and Barracks Changi
'D' Force Thailand	S Battalion
POW Number	8806
Japan	*Rashin Maru* Party
POW Number	1677
Camps Japan	Yamane, Niihama
Return Details 1945	Wakayama-Okinawa, USS *Sanctuary*, Okinawa-Manila, USS *Bingham*, Manila-Morotai-Darwin, PBY Catalina aircraft A24-377 Perth by B24 Liberator aircraft A72-379

JOHN BLAIN MELLOR

Rank	Private
Regimental Number	WX8441
Company	'A' Company
Enlisted	18.10.1940
Discharged	12.4.1946
Date of Birth	25.8.1907
Place of Birth	Claremont, Western Australia
Father	Colin Mellor
Mother	Not Known
Religion	Methodist
Pre-War Occupation	Clerk

HISTORY

Singapore	Selarang Camp Changi Thomson Road (Caldecot Hill Estate Camp) River Valley Road Camp Selarang Barracks Changi
POW Number	1/8665
'D' Force Thailand	S Battalion
POW Number	8807
Camps Thailand	Nacompaton
Return Details 1945	Thailand-Singapore by aircraft, Singapore-Sydney (details unknown) Sydney-Fremantle, HMT *Otranto*
Additions	Wounded in action Ulu Pandan on 12.2.1942. Admitted to A.G.H. on 16.2.1942 with shrapnel wounds and discharged to unit on 21.2.1942.

DAVID VICTOR MENTIPLAY

Rank	Lieutenant
Regimental Number	WX228
Company	Battalion Headquarters, Special Reserve Battalion
Enlisted	10.12.1940
Appointment Terminated	20.4.1949
Date of Birth	21.10.1917
Place of Birth	Geraldton, Western Australia
Father	David Mentiplay
Mother	Ethel Mentiplay
Religion	Methodist
Pre-War Occupation	Butcher

HISTORY

Singapore	Selarang Camp Changi
	Johore Bahru, Adam Park
	Selarang Barracks Changi
POW Number	1/809
'H' Force Thailand	'H' Force, Group No. 6, Officer's Party
Singapore	Sime Road Camp
	Changi Gaol Camp
Return Details 1945	Singapore-Perth, Duke of Gloucester's aircraft, *'Endeavour'*
Additions	This Officer was wounded in action at South-West Bukit Timah on 11.2.1942. He witnessed Japanese soldiers bayoneting wounded men, which infuriated him to such a degree that he rushed at the perpetrators, killing several of them. For his efforts he received a bayonet wound through the neck and leg. He was admitted to the 2/13th Australian General Hospital and was later discharged to his unit on 25.2.1942. This officer commanded the Western Australian Victory Parade contingent in London on 8.6.1946. Promoted to the rank of Captain on 25.7.1947.

JOSUAH WILLIAM MEREDITH

Rank	Private
Regimental Number	WX8319
Company	'C' Company
Enlisted	20.8.1940
Discharged	10.1.1946
Date of Birth	11.6.1917
Place of Birth	Fremantle, Western Australia
Father	John Thomas Meredith
Mother	Euphemia Mary Meredith
Religion	Church of England
Pre-War Occupation	Miner

HISTORY

Singapore	Selarang Camp Changi
	Johore Bahru, Adam Park
	Selarang Barracks Changi
	Pulau Blakang Mati
	Changi Gaol Camp
Return Details 1945	Singapore-Darwin-Sydney, HMT *Arawa*
	Sydney-Melbourne by troop train
	R.A.A.F. Laverton (Victoria)-Perth, B24 Liberator aircraft

HUBERT JAMES MILLAR

Rank	Private
Regimental Number	WX9826
Classification	Driver
Company	'C' Company
Enlisted	6.12.1940
Discharged	7.12.1945
Date of Birth	18.8.1921
Place of Birth	Mundaring, Western Australia
Father	William Duncan Millar
Mother	May Millar
Religion	Church of England
Pre-War Occupation	Shop Assistant

HISTORY

Java	'Blackforce', attached to the 2/2nd Pioneer Battalion
Camps Java	Bicycle Camp Batavia
'A' Force Burma	Java Party No. 4, Williams Force
POW Number	4648
Camps Thailand	131km, 133km, Tamarkan, Kanchanaburi, Linson Wood Camp, Petchaburi, Kachu Mountain Camp, Nakom Nayok, Bangkok
Return Details 1945	Thailand-Rangoon by aircraft
	Rangoon-Singapore, HMT *Highland Brigade*
	Singapore-Fremantle, HMT *Tamaroa*

ALBERT MILLER

Rank	Private
Regimental Number	WX7885
Company	'C' Company
Enlisted	13.8.1940
Discharged	4.2.1946
Date of Birth	16.12.1913
Place of Birth	Collie, Western Australia
Father	Thomas Miller
Mother	Eliza Miller
Religion	Church of England
Pre-War Occupation	Miner

HISTORY

Singapore	Selarang Camp and Barracks Changi
'H' Force Thailand	'H' Force Group No. 3
Camps Thailand	Kanu II Malayan Hamlet, Kanu IIIa (Tampie North), Kanchanaburi
Singapore	Sime Road Camp
	Changi Gaol Camp
Return Details 1945	Singapore-Darwin-Sydney, HMT *Arawa*
	Sydney-Melbourne by troop train
	Melbourne-Fremantle, HMT *Strathmore*

EDWIN ERNEST MILLER

Rank	Private
Regimental Number	WX8013
Classification	Driver
Company	'B' Company Headquarters
Enlisted	14.8.1940
Discharged	6.2.1946
Date of Birth	14.10.1911
Place of Birth	Perth, Western Australia
Father	Otto Charles Miller
Mother	Charlotte Miller
Religion	Church of England
Pre-War Occupation	Farmhand

HISTORY

Singapore	Selarang Camp Changi
	Thomson Road (Caldecot Hill Estate Camp)
	River Valley Road Camp
	Selarang Barracks Changi
POW Number	3/8702
Force	'F' Force Thailand
Singapore	X10 Party
	Changi Gaol Camp
Return Details 1945	Singapore-Darwin-Sydney, HMT *Arawa*
	Sydney-Melbourne by troop train
	Melbourne-Fremantle, HMT *Strathmore*

REGINALD JAMES MILLER

Rank	Lance Corporal
Regimental Number	WX13338
Company	'A' Company
Enlisted	21.5.1941
Discharged	9.5.1946
Date of Birth	6.2.1916
Place of Birth	Waroona, Western Australia
Father	Richard Herb Miller
Mother	Thelma Miller
Religion	Methodist
Pre-War Occupation	Butcher

HISTORY

Singapore	Selarang Camp Changi
	Mount Pleasant Camp
	Selarang Barracks Changi
POW Number	3/8703
'D' Force Thailand	Captain Fred Harris Party
Camps Thailand	Kinsaiyok
Japan	*Aramis* Party
POW Number	542
Camps Japan	Fukuoka sub-Camp No. 17, Omuta
Return Details 1945	Nagasaki-Okinawa-Manila
	Manila-Sydney, HMS *Speaker*

THOMAS ALBERT HENRY MINCHIN

Rank	Private
Regimental Number	WX9222
Classification	Driver/Mechanic
Company	'A' Company
Enlisted	30.10.1940
Discharged	10.1.1946
Date of Birth	15.10.1910
Place of Birth	Earlstown Lane, England
Father	Thomas Charles Minchin
Mother	Edith Emily Minchin
Religion	Salvation Army
Pre-War Occupation	Rock Driller

HISTORY

Singapore	Selarang Camp Changi
'A' Force Burma	Green Force, No. 3 Battalion
POW Number	1497
Camps Thailand	Nakom Nayok (see Danny Bevis Diary)
Return Details 1945	Thailand-Singapore by aircraft
	Singapore-Fremantle, HMT *Tamaroa*

KEITH BEDFORD MITCHELL

Rank	Private
Regimental Number	WX11629
Company	'D' Company
Enlisted	9.4.1941
Discharged	16.1.1946
Date of Birth	11.1.1903
Place of Birth	Dongara, Western Australia
Father	William Bedford Mitchell
Mother	Fanny Priscilla Mitchell
Religion	Church of England
Pre-War Occupation	Grazier

HISTORY

Singapore	Selarang Camp Changi
'A' Force Burma	Green Force, No. 3 Battalion
POW Number	1524
Camps Burma	Khonkan 55km (1.7.1943 as medical orderly)
Camps Thailand	Kanchanaburi, Bangkok (medical orderly), Nacompaton, Linson Wood Camp
Return Details 1945	Thailand-Singapore by aircraft
	Singapore-Fremantle, HMT *Moreton Bay*
Additions	Wounded in action at 0400 hours on 9.2.1942. Admitted to the 2/13th Australian General Hospital on 10.2.1942 with a gunshot wound to the left hand. Transferred to No. 2 Convalescent Depot on 12.2.1942 before being discharged to unit on 16.2.1942.

PETER JOSEPH MOATE

Rank	Private
Regimental Number	WX13562
Company	'C' Company Headquarters
Enlisted	24.5.1941
Discharged	23.5.1946
Date of Birth	30.3.1920
Place of Birth	Greenhills, Western Australia
Father	Samuel Joseph Moate
Mother	Theresa Moate
Religion	Roman Catholic
Pre-War Occupation	Railway Porter, W.A.G.R.

HISTORY

Java	'Blackforce', attached to 2/3rd Machine Gun Battalion
Camps Java	Garoet, Bandoeng , Bicycle Camp Batavia, Makasura
'D' Force Thailand	Java Party No. 6, O Battalion
POW Number	6918
Camps Thailand	Hintok Road Camp, Tarsau (evacuated with a tropical ulcer), Nacompaton
Return Details 1945	Thailand-Singapore by aircraft
	Singapore-Australia, no details are known

GEORGE MOIR

Rank	Private
Regimental Number	WX9339
Classification	Driver
Company	'C' Company
Enlisted	30.10.1940
Discharged	18.1.1946
Date of Birth	15.1.1917
Place of Birth	Albany, Western Australia
Father	George Clement Moir
Mother	Evangelene Moir
Religion	Church of England
Pre-War Occupation	Farmhand

HISTORY

Singapore	Selarang Barracks, Changi
	Thomson Road (Caldecott Hill Estate Estate)
	River Valley Road Camp
	Selarang Barracks Changi (Garden Control Party)
'D' Force Thailand	S Battalion
POW Number	8823
Camps Thailand	Tarsau, Kanu II, Hintok Road Camp
Japan	*Rashin Maru* Party
POW Number	1687
Camps Japan	Yamane, Niihama
Return Details 1945	Wakayama-Okinawa, USS *Sanctuary*
	Okinawa-Manila, USS *Bingham*
	Manila-Morotai-Darwin, PBY Catalina aircraft A24-355
	Darwin-Perth, B24 Liberator aircraft A72-379

LLOYD OWEN MOIR

Rank	Private	
Regimental Number	WX9338	
Classification	Driver	
Company	'C' Company	
Enlisted	30.10.1940	
Discharged	25.1.1946	
Date of Birth	21.6.1914	
Place of Birth	Albany, Western Australia	
Father	George Clement Moir	
Mother	Evangelene Moir	
Religion	Church of England	
Pre-War Occupation	Farmhand	

HISTORY

Singapore	Selarang Camp Changi
	Thomson Road (Caldecott Hill Estate Camp)
	River Valley Road Camp
	Selarang Barracks Changi
POW Number	3/8731
'D' Force Thailand	S Battalion
POW Number	8821
Camps Thailand	Kanu II, Hintok Road Camp, Pratchai
Return Details 1945	Thailand-Singapore by aircraft
	Singapore-Darwin-Perth by PBY Catalina aircraft
Additions	Suffered some deafness in the right ear as a result of an explosion.

Andrew Donald Moir   *Collier Moir*   *Lloyd Owen Moir*
WX9337   *WX9338*

ALFRED JOHN MORGAN

Rank	Private
Regimental Number	WX9233
Classification	Rangetaker
Company	'D' Company
Enlisted	30.10.1940
Discharged	9.1.1946
Date of Birth	17.1.1919
Place of Birth	Katanning, Western Australia
Father	James Alfred Morgan
Mother	Mary Ann Edith Morgan
Religion	Church of England
Pre-War Occupation	Grocer's Assistant and Clerk

HISTORY

Singapore	Selarang Camp Changi
	Johore Bahru, Adam Park
	River Valley Road Camp
	Selarang Barracks Changi
POW Number	3/8762
'D' Force Thailand	S Battalion
POW Number	8816
Camps Thailand	Kanu II, Hintok Road Camp, Hintok River Camp, Kinsaiyok, Tamuang, Konkoita, Hindato (landslide on line), Kinsaiyok, Tamarkan, Chungkai, Kachu Mountain Camp, Petchaburi, Nakom Nayok, Lopburi, Nakom Nayok, Bangkok
Return Details 1945	Bangkok-Singapore by aircraft
	Singapore-Fremantle, HMT *Moreton Bay*

OWEN MORRIS

Rank	Private
Regimental Number	WX6173
Classification	Bootmaker
Company	'B' Company
Enlisted	13.7.1940
Discharged	19.12.1945
Date of Birth	31.3.1919
Place of Birth	Glenlin via Bridgetown, Western Australia
Father	Thomas Morris
Mother	Annie Morris
Religion	Church of England
Pre-War Occupation	Butcher

HISTORY

Singapore	Selarang Camp Changi
	Johore Bahru, Adam Park
	Selarang Barracks Changi
POW Number	4/6425
'D' Force Thailand	S Battalion
POW Number	8811
Camps Thailand	Kanu II, Konkoita, Tarsau (12 months), Wampo, Tamajao Wood Camp, Tamarkan, Nikhe, Sonkurai, Nakom Nayok
Return Details 1945	Thailand-Singapore by aircraft
	Singapore-Fremantle, HMT *Tamaroa*

WILLIAM RICHARD MORRIS

Rank	Private
Regimental Number	WX8200
Classification	Storeman
Company	'C' Company
Platoon	10 Platoon
Enlisted	16.8.1940
Discharged	4.5.1944
Date of Birth	20.10.1901
Place of Birth	Kalgoorlie, Western Australia
Father	William Morris
Mother	Catherine Jane Morris
Religion	Church of England
Pre-War Occupation	Prospector

HISTORY

Java	Evacuated sick ex-Java. Embarked on HMT *Stirling Castle* at Ceylon on 13.3.1942
Australia	and disembarked at Melbourne on 28.3.1942. Transferred to 5th Military District disembarking HMT *Egra* on 13.4.1942. Classified medically fit on 27.4.1942 and Taken on Strength with the 2/3rd Machine Gun Battalion on 20.5.1942. Admitted to hospital on 25.11.1942 after an explosives accident and evacuated to the 113th Australian General Hospital. Transferred to the 115th Australian General Hospital on 18.12.1942. Soldier's right hand was amputated above the wrist on 9.2.1944.

ARTHUR EDWARD MORRISON

Rank	Private
Regimental Number	WX15746
Company	'D' Company
Enlisted	13.8.1941
Discharged	28.2.1946
Date of Birth	26.11.1916
Place of Birth	North Perth, Western Australia
Father	Sam Morrison
Mother	Martha Nellie Morrison
Religion	Baptist
Pre-War Occupation	Farmhand and Rabbit Trapper

HISTORY

Java	'Blackforce', attached to 2/2nd Pioneer Battalion. (captured at Garoet 9.3.1942)
POW Number	2/13612
Camps Java	Bicycle Camp Batavia
'A' Force Burma	Java Party No. 4, Williams Force
POW Number	4639
Camps Thailand	116km, 122km, 131km, 133km, Tamarkan, Kanchanaburi (March-April 1944), Chungkai, Non Pladuk, Nacompaton, Sonkurai-Nikhe Defence Line, Tamuang, Bangkok
Return Details 1945	Thailand-Singapore by aircraft
	Singapore-Fremantle, HMT *Moreton Bay*
Additions	This soldier suffered from tropical ulcers to the feet at the 105km Camp Burma and was treated at Kanchanaburi and Chungkai for this complaint.

JOHN CAMPBELL MORRISON

Rank	Lieutenant
Regimental Number	WX9384
Attached 2/4th	Reinforcement Officer (Taken on Strength at Darwin)
Company	'A' Company
Enlisted	19.11.1940
Appointment Terminated	4.2.1946
Date of Birth	27.10.1908
Place of Birth	Guildford, Western Australia
Father	James de Burgh Morrison
Mother	Hilda Morrison
Religion	Church of England
Pre-War Occupation	Clerk at the Perth Tourist Bureau

HISTORY

Singapore	Selarang Camp Changi
	Johore Bahru, Adam Park
Force	'B' Force Borneo
Sarawak	Lintang Officer's Camp, Kuching
Return Details 1945	Kuching-Morotai-Sydney, 2/2 H.M. Australian Hospital Ship *Wanganella*
	Sydney-Melbourne-Perth by troop train
Additions	Evacuated to the 2/13th Australian General Hospital on 11.2.1942 with a high temperature which was diagnosed as dengue fever. Discharged to unit on 21.2.1942. Replaced by Lieutenant G. Branson during his absence.

ALBERT EDWARD MORRISSEY

Rank	Private
Regimental Number	WX15751
Company	'A' Company
Enlisted	13.8.1941
Discharged	14.1.1946
Date of Birth	13.10.1914
Place of Birth	Perth, Western Australia
Father	William Frances Morrissey
Mother	Marjorie Morrissey
Religion	Roman Catholic
Pre-War Occupation	Miner

HISTORY

Singapore	Selarang Camp Changi
	Johore Bahru, Adam Park
	Selarang Barracks Changi
POW Number	3/8773
'D' Force Thailand	S Battalion
POW Number	8809
Japan	*Rashin Maru* Party
POW Number	1690
Camps Japan	Yamane
	Niihama
Return Details 1945	Wakayama-Okinawa, USS *Sanctuary*
	Okinawa-Manila, USS *Bingham*
	Manila-Sydney, HMS *Speaker*
	Sydney-Melbourne-Perth by troop train.

RAYMOND MULLER

Rank	Private
Regimental Number	WX4941
Company	'C' Company
Enlisted	23.7.1940
Discharged	13.12.1945
Date of Birth	5.3.1919
Place of Birth	Perth, Western Australia
Father	Richard Muller
Mother	Annie Muller
Religion	Church of England
Pre-War Occupation	Dairyman

HISTORY

Singapore	Selarang Camp Changi (17.2.1942-4.4.1942)
	Johore Bahru, Adam Park (4.4.1942-25.6.1942)
	Selarang Barracks Changi (25.6.1942-9.10.1942)
	River Valley Road Camp (9.10.1942-24.12.1942)
	Selarang Barracks Changi (24.12.1942-14.4.1943)
POW Number	3/8789
'D' Force Thailand	S Battalion
POW Number	8820
Japan	*Rashin Maru* Party
POW Number	1691
Camps Japan	Yamane (10.9.1944-18.5.1945)
	Niihama (18.5.1945-12.9.1945)
Return Details 1945	Wakayama-Okinawa, USS *Sanctuary*
	Okinawa-Manila, USS *Bingham*
	Manila-Sydney, HMS *Speaker*
	Sydney-Melbourne-Perth by troop train
Additions	Evacuated to Australian General Hospital at Roberts Barracks Changi with beri-beri. Transferred to No. 2 Convalescent Depot on 25.9.1942. Discharged to unit on 6.10.1942.

ARTHUR REGINALD MURDOCH

Rank	Private
Regimental Number	WX12599
Company	'A' Company
Enlisted	9.5.1941
Discharged	20.5.1946
Date of Birth	27.2.1914
Place of Birth	Port Pirie, South Australia
Father	Melbourne Arthur Murdoch
Mother	Bessie Dibing Murdoch
Religion	Methodist
Pre-War Occupation	Miner

Singapore	Selarang Camp Changi
	Johore Bahru, Adam Park
	Evacuated to Australian General Hospital at Roberts Barracks on 10.11.1942
	River Valley Road Camp (1.12.1942-23.12.1942)
	Selarang Barracks Changi (23.12.1942-14.3.1943)
'D' Force Thailand	S Battalion (later V Battalion)
POW Number	8808
Camps Thailand	Kuii, Tamuang
Japan	*Rashin Maru* Party
POW Number	1693
Camps Japan	Yamane
	Niihama
Return Details 1945	Wakayama-Okinawa, USS *Sanctuary*
	Okinawa-Manila, USS *Bingham*
	Manila-Sydney, HMS *Speaker*
	Sydney-Melbourne-Perth by troop train
Additions	It is believed that this soldier arrived at Tarsau with dysentery and a fever and joined up with V Battalion on or about 29.4.1943.

JAMES LEWIS MURDOCH

Rank	Private
Regimental Number	WX5336
Company	'D' Company
Enlisted	27.7.1940
Discharged	14.2.1946
Date of Birth	6.10.1922
Place of Birth	Donnybrook, Western Australia
Father	John Murdoch
Mother	Agnes Murdoch
Religion	Church of England
Pre-War Occupation	Labourer

HISTORY

Java	'Blackforce'
'A' Force Burma	Java Party No. 4, Williams Force
POW Number	4588
Camps Burma	Reptu 30km, Beke Taung 40km Camps
Camps Thailand	Tamarkan, Ubon, Bangkok
Return Details 1945	Bangkok-Singapore by aircraft
	Singapore-Fremantle, HMT *Moreton Bay*

LOUIS McGUFFY MURRAY

Rank	Private
Regimental Number	WX10796
Company	'A' Company
Enlisted	15.1.1941
Discharged	11.1.1946
Date of Birth	3.4.1919
Place of Birth	Scotland
Father	James Murray
Mother	Agnes Murray
Religion	Roman Catholic
Pre-War Occupation	Pastry Cook

HISTORY

Singapore	Selarang Camp and Barracks Changi
POW Number	4/6436
'D' Force Thailand	V Battalion
POW Number	2272
Camps Thailand	Nacompaton, Bangkok (go-downs)
Return Details 1945	Thailand-Singapore by aircraft
	Singapore-Sydney, HMT *Highland Chieftan*
	Sydney-Melbourne-Perth by troop train

EDWIN JOHN MURTAGH

Rank	Private
Regimental Number	WX10792
Company	'B' Company
Enlisted	15.1.1941
Discharged	21.12.1945
Date of Birth	3.3.1919
Place of Birth	Crumpsal, Manchester, England
Father	Percy John Murtagh
Mother	Mary Agnes Murtagh
Religion	Church of England
Pre-War Occupation	Dairy and Farmhand

HISTORY

Singapore	Selarang Camp Changi
'A' Force Burma	Green Force, No. 3 Battalion
POW Number	1532
Japan	*Awa Maru* Party, Kumi No. 42
Camps Japan	Fukuoka sub-Camp No. 24, Sendyu
Return Details 1945	Nagasaki-Manila, U.S. Navy ship
	Manila-Sydney, HMS *Formidable*
	Sydney-Melbourne-Perth by troop train
Additions	Wounded in action at Tengah on 9.2.1942 and admitted to Field Ambulance with a shrapnel wound to the left shoulder and left eyebrow. Transferred to the 2/13th Australian General Hospital on 17.2.1942. Transferred to the 2/9th Field Ambulance on 7.3.1942 and discharged to unit on 1.4.1942.

SAMUEL EDWARD NASH

Rank	Private
Regimental Number	WX15457
Classification	Cook
Company	'C' Company
Enlisted	29.7.1941
Discharged	7.1.1946
Date of Birth	6.8.1907
Place of Birth	London, England
Father	Robert Nash
Mother	Jane Charlotte Nash
Religion	Church of England
Pre-War Occupation	Cook

HISTORY

Singapore	Selarang Camp Changi
	Johore Bahru, Adam Park
	River Valley Road Camp
	Selarang Barracks Changi
	X10 Party
	Changi Gaol Camp
POW Numbers	1/8791 and 3/8963
Return Details	Recovered Changi Gaol Camp on 4.9.1945. Embarked on the 1st Netherlands Military Hospital Ship *Oranje*. Transferred to the 107th Australian General Hospital Melbourne. Admitted to the 115th Heidelberg Military Hospital and then admitted to 105th Adelaide Military Hospital. Deplaned Perth ex-Adelaide on 11.10.1945 and admitted to the 110th Perth Military Hospital.
Additions	Evacuated to the Australian General Hospital at Roberts Barracks Changi, from 6.8.1942-17.8.1942.

HAROLD FREDERICK NEILSON

Rank	Private
Regimental Number	WX5220
Classification	Driver
Company	'B' Company
Enlisted	26.7.1940
Discharged	31.1.1946
Date of Birth	23.1.1912
Place of Birth	Kalgoorlie, Western Australia
Father	Not Known
Mother	Elizabeth Neilson
Religion	Methodist
Pre-War Occupation	Bread Carter

HISTORY

Singapore	Selarang Camp Changi
	Johore Bahru, Adam Park
	Selarang Barracks Changi (worked in the cookhouse)
	Changi Gaol Camp Hospital (16.10.1944)
	Kranji Hospital (2.11.1944)
	Discharged to unit at Changi Gaol Camp on 11.12.1944
POW Number	4/6444
Return Details 1945	Singapore-Darwin-Sydney, HMT *Arawa*
	Sydney-Melbourne by troop train
	Melbourne-Fremantle, HMT *Strathmore*
Additions	Admitted to 2/9th Field Ambulance on 7.2.1942 in possession of a letter from the 2/4th Machine Gun Battalion R.M.O. stating that soldier was suffering from indigestion. Admitted to the 2/10th Australian General Hospital with dyspepsia. Discharged to unit on 21.2.1942. Admitted to Australian General Hospital Roberts Barracks Changi with a duodenal ulcer on 21.3.1943.

CECIL THOMAS NELSON

Rank	Lance Corporal
Regimental Number	WX14031
Company	Headquarters Company
Enlisted	11.6.1941
Discharged	6.2.1946
Date of Birth	19.3.1917
Place of Birth	Fremantle, Western Australia
Father	Edward Nelson
Mother	Olive Nelson
Religion	Church of England
Pre-War Occupation	Baker

Singapore	Selarang Camp Changi
	Serangoon Road Camp, (evacuated to Australian General Hospital at Roberts Barracks Changi with acute appendicitis on 7.8.1942)
	Selarang Barracks Changi
POW Number	1/8808
Force	'F' Force Thailand
Camps Thailand	Shimo Sonkurai
Camps Burma	Tanbaya 30km Hospital Camp
Singapore	Selarang Barracks Changi
	Changi Gaol Camp
Return Details 1945	Singapore-Perth, Duke of Gloucester's aircraft *'Endeavour'*.

GEORGE EDWARD NEVILE

Rank	Private
Regimental Number	WX9256
Company	'D' Company
Enlisted	30.10.1940
Discharged	19.12.1945
Date of Birth	22.3.1918
Place of Birth	Perth, Western Australia
Father	George Howard Nevile
Mother	Doreen Ann Nevile
Religion	Church of England
Pre-War Occupation	Shop Assistant

HISTORY

Singapore	Selarang Camp Changi
	Thompson Road (Caldecott Hill Estate Camp)
	River Valley Road Camp
	Selarang Barracks Changi
'D' Force Thailand	S Battalion
POW Number	8824
Camps Thailand	Kanu II, Tarsau, Konkoita, Nakom Nayok, Bangkok
Return Details 1945	Thailand-Singapore by aircraft
	Singapore-Fremantle, HMT *Moreton Bay*
Additions	Wounded in action on 10.2.1942 receiving a shell burn to the left leg. Soldier remained on duty.

ARCHIE GERALD NEWELL

Rank	Private
Regimental Number	WX8749
Company	'B' Company
Enlisted	23.10.1940
Discharged	18.12.1945
Date of Birth	15.10.1905
Place of Birth	Higham Ferrers, Northants, England
Father	John Newell
Mother	Dorothy Newell
Religion	Methodist
Pre-War Occupation	Miner

HISTORY

Singapore	Selarang Camp Changi
	Johore Bahru, Adam Park
	Selarang Barracks Changi
POW Number	4/6446
'D' Force Thailand	S Battalion
POW Number	8826
Camps Thailand	Kanu II, Chungkai
Japan	*Rashin Maru* Party
POW Number	1695
Camps Japan	Yamane
	Niihama
Return Details 1945	Wakayama-Okinawa, USS *Sanctuary*
	Okinawa-Manila, USS *Bingham,*
	Manila-Sydney, HMS *Speaker*
	Sydney-Fremantle, HMT *Dominion Monarch*

ALFRED NEWTON

Rank	Private
Regimental Number	WX9207
Classification	Cook
Company	'D' Company
Enlisted	30.10.1940
Discharged	2.4.1946
Date of Birth	13.10.1905
Place of Birth	Hyson Green, Nottingham, England
Father	Alfred Newton
Mother	Not Known
Religion	Church of England
Pre-War Occupation	Farmhand

HISTORY

Singapore	Selarang Camp and Barracks Changi
'D' Force Thailand	T Battalion
POW Number	4/12648
Camps Thailand	Non Pladuk, Kanchanaburi, Bangkok (go-downs)
Return Details 1945	Thailand-Singapore by aircraft, No other details are known

WILLIAM JOHN NICHOLAS

Rank	Private
Regimental Number	WX10809
Company	'B' Company
Enlisted	15.1.1941
Discharged	13.2.1946
Date of Birth	3.8.1919
Place of Birth	Goomalling, Western Australia
Father	Evan Hamelin Nicholas
Mother	Maud Cecilia Nicholas
Religion	Roman Catholic
Pre-War Occupation	Engineering Student and Clerk

HISTORY

Singapore	Selarang Camp and Barracks Changi
'D' Force Thailand	W.O.II John Dooley Party
French Indo-China	*Both* Party
Return Details 1945	Saigon-Bangkok-Singapore by aircraft
	Singapore-Labuan-Morotai-Darwin-Perth by aircraft
Additions	Wounded in action Pasir Panjang on 14.2.1942 and admitted to the 2/9th Field Ambulance with a bayonet wound to the left leg and torso. Admitted to the 2/13th Australian General Hospital on 16.2.1942. Discharged to unit on 22..2.1942. Soldier was possibly a member of T Battalion.

SAMUEL NINYETTE

Rank	Private
Regimental Number	WX16417
Company	'D' Company
Enlisted	10.9.1941
Discharged	28.2.1946
Date of Birth	15.3.1917
Place of Birth	Beverley, Western Australia
Father	Jack Ninyette
Mother	Rosie Ninyette
Religion	Salvation Army
Pre-War Occupation	Farmhand

HISTORY

Java	'Blackforce'
Camps Java	Bicycle Camp Batavia
'A' Force Burma	Java Party No. 4, Williams Force
POW Number	4666
Camps Thailand	131km, Kanchanaburi, Konkoita (21.7.1944)
Return Details 1945	Thailand-Singapore by aircraft
	Singapore-Fremantle, HMT *Highland Brigade*

HARRY CLAUDE NORRIS

Rank	Lance Corporal
Regimental Number	WX10790
Company	'C' Company
Enlisted	15.1.1941
Discharged	21.12.1945
Date of Birth	6.1.1920
Place of Birth	Watford, England
Father	Claude Edward Norris
Mother	Elizabeth Norris
Religion	Roman Catholic
Pre-War Occupation	Stationhand

HISTORY

Singapore	Selarang Camp Changi
	Johore Bahru, Adam Park
	Selarang Barracks Changi
'D' Force Thailand	S Battalion
POW Number	8742
Camps Thailand	Kanchanaburi, Non Pladuk, Chumphon, Petchaburi, Kachu Mountain Camp, Bangkok
Return Details 1945	Thailand-Singapore by aircraft
	No other details are known
Additions	Shell shocked at Buona Vista and evacuated on 15.2.1942.

GERARD NORTHEY

Rank	Sergeant (Promoted on 24.1.1942)
Regimental Number	WX9407
Classification	Cook
Company	Headquarters Company
Enlisted	21.11.1940
Discharged	13.6.1946
Date of Birth	2.1.1907
Place of Birth	Edinburgh, Scotland
Father	Not Known
Mother	Not Known
Religion	Presbyterian
Pre-War Occupation	Butcher and Cook

HISTORY

Singapore	Selarang Camp Changi
'A' Force Burma	Green Force, No. 3 Battalion
POW Number	2678
Camps Thailand	Wampo, Tamarkan, Chungkai, Tamuang
Return Details 1945	Thailand-Singapore by aircraft
	Singapore-Fremantle, HMT *Tamaroa*

ALBERT WILLIAM NORTON

Rank	Private
Regimental Number	WX8493
Company	'A' Company Headquarters
Enlisted	18.10.1940
Discharged	9.1.1946
Date of Birth	25.7.1918
Place of Birth	Perth, Western Australia
Father	Albert Norton
Mother	Margaret Norton
Religion	Roman Catholic
Pre-War Occupation	Shop Assistant

HISTORY

Singapore	Selarang Camp Changi
	Johore Bahru, Adam Park
	Selarang Barracks Changi
POW Numbers	1/8839 and 3/9017
'D' Force Thailand	S Battalion
POW Number	8827
Camps Thailand	Kanu II, Kanu III, Tarsau (July 1943-January 1944 working in the tropical ulcers ward), Chungkai, Tamuang, Nacompaton, Non Pladuk.
Japan	*Rashin Maru* Party
POW Number	1697
Camps Japan	Yamane
	Niihama (copper refinery)
Return Details 1945	Wakayama-Okinawa, USS *Sanctuary*
	Okinawa-Manila, USS *Bingham*
	Manila-Morotai-Darwin, PBY Catalina aircraft A24-377
	Darwin-Perth by B24 Liberator aircraft
Additions	Soldier was an experienced Lewis gunner so was transferred from No. 5 Platoon to 'A' Company Headquarters as a Bren gunner.

WILFRED HAROLD NOTTLE

Rank	Private
Regimental Number	WX9181
Company	'C' Company
Enlisted	30.10.1940
Discharged	19.12.1945
Date of Birth	4.10.1918
Place of Birth	York, Western Australia
Father	Richard James Nottle
Mother	Amy Nottle
Religion	Church of England
Pre-War Occupation	Rabbit Trapper and Farmhand

HISTORY

Singapore	Selarang Camp Changi
	Johore Bahru, Adam Park
	Selarang Barracks Changi
'D' Force Thailand	S Battalion
POW Number	8825
Japan	*Rashin Maru* Party
POW Number	1698
Camps Japan	Yamane
	Niihama (wharf)
Return Details 1945	Wakahama-Okinawa (admitted to the 233rd General Hospital), USS *Sanctuary*
	Okinawa-Manila (admitted to the 248th General Hospital)
	Manila-Sydney, HMS *Formidable*
	Sydney admitted to 113(C)MH
	Melbourne admitted to 115(H)MH
	Melbourne-Perth by aircraft admitted to 110(P)MH
Additions	Soldier had been knocked off the wharf at Niihama in August 1945 and had fractured his left ankle. He was admitted to the camp hospital where he remained for three weeks.

JOSEPH PATRICK O'MEARA

Rank	Private
Regimental Number	WX7981
Classification	Driver
Company	'D' Company
Enlisted	13.8.1940
Discharged	14.3.1946
Date of Birth	13.4.1919
Place of Birth	Doodlakine, Western Australia
Father	Jeremiah James O'Meara
Mother	Alice O'Meara
Religion	Roman Catholic
Pre-War Occupation	Teamster and Farmhand

HISTORY

Singapore	Selarang Camp and Barracks Changi
POW Number	4/6467
'D' Force Thailand	S Battalion
POW Number	8829
Camps Thailand	Kanu II, Chungkai
Return Details 1945	Thailand-Singapore by aircraft
	Singapore-Fremantle, HMT *Moreton Bay*
Additions	Wounded in action at Buona Vista on 15.2.1942. Admitted to the 13th Australian General Hospital on 15.2.1942 with a shrapnel wound to the left thigh. Discharged to unit on 28.2.1942.

WILLIAM DARCY O'NEILL

Rank	Private
Regimental Number	WX8828
Classification	Technical Storeman
Company	'B' Company Headquarters
Enlisted	23.10.1940
Discharged	12.10.1943
Date of Birth	25.4.1902
Place of Birth	Fremantle, Western Australia
Father	Not Known
Mother	Not Known
Religion	Church of England
Pre-War Occupation	Mine Manager

HISTORY

Java	Attached to 2/3rd Machine Gun Battalion. Evacuated sick to the hospital ship
Australia	*Wu Sui* which departed Tanjong Priok, Batavia approximately 20.2.1942. Soldier was admitted to the 12th Australian General Hospital Colombo. Discharged from Hospital on 12.10.1943 on his return to Melbourne ex-HMT *Stirling Castle*.

BERNARD MATTHEW O'SULLIVAN

Rank	Lieutenant
Regimental Number	WX9390
Attached 2/4th	Reinforcement Officer (Taken on Strength 10.9.1941)
Company	Headquarters Company (R.Q.M. from 8.2.1942)
Enlisted	16.11.1940
Appointment Terminated	6.12.1945
Date of Birth	9.11.1920
Place of Birth	Leederville, Western Australia
Father	Leonard John O'Sullivan
Mother	Jennie O'Sullivan
Religion	Roman Catholic
Pre-War Occupation	Judge's Associate

HISTORY

Singapore	Selarang Camp Changi
	Serangoon Road Camp
	Sime Road Camp
	Selarang Barracks Changi
POW Number	4/4114
'H' Force Thailand	'H' Force Group No. 3
Singapore	Sime Road Camp
	Selarang Barracks Changi
	Changi Gaol Camp
Return Details 1945	Singapore-Perth, Duke of Gloucester's aircraft *'Endeavour'*.

ALEXANDER SUTHERLAND OAG

Rank	Private
Regimental Number	WX8481
Company	'A' Company
Enlisted	18.10.1940
Discharged	22.4.1947
Date of Birth	19.3.1903
Place of Birth	Edinburgh, Scotland
Father	Alexander Oag
Mother	Agnes Joan Glascow Haywood Oag
Religion	Church of England
Pre-War Occupation	Bread Carter

Singapore	Selarang Camp Changi
	Johore Bahru, Adam Park
	Selarang Barracks Changi
POW Number	4/6470
'D' Force Thailand	S Battalion
POW Number	8828
Camps Thailand	Tarsau, Tonchan South, Tonchan Central, Kanu III, Tonchan Central, Kinsaiyok, Hintok River Camp, Tamuang
Japan	*Rashin Maru* Party
POW Number	395
Camps Japan	Ohama Camp No. 9B
Return Details 1945	Wakayama-Okinawa, USS *Consolation*
	Okinawa-Manila, USS *Haskell*
	Manila-Sydney, HMS *Speaker*
	Sydney-Fremantle, HMT *Dominion Monarch*

ANTHONY HENRY RUPERT ODLUM

Rank	Captain
Regimental Number	WX11001
Classification	Engineering Officer
Attached 2/4th	88 Light Aid Detachment
Enlisted	14.1.1941
Appointment Terminated	18.1.1946
Date of Birth	12.6.1916
Place of Birth	Moora, Western Australia
Father	William Henry Odlum
Mother	Grace Odlum
Religion	Church of England
Pre-War Occupation	Electrical Engineer

HISTORY

Singapore	Selarang Camp Changi
	Adam Park
	Selarang Barracks Changi
	Changi Gaol Camp
POW Number	4/4113
Return Details 1945	Singapore-Sydney, HMT *Duntroon*
	Sydney-Melbourne by troop train
	Melbourne-Fremantle, HMT *Strathmore*

GORDON SPURGEON OHRT

Rank	Sergeant (Promoted on 29.1.1942)
Regimental Number	WX9345
Company	'A' Company
Enlisted	30.10.1940
Discharged	6.2.1946
Date of Birth	17.4.1919
Place of Birth	Johannesburg, South Africa
Father	Frank Millard Ohrt
Mother	Marjorie Ohrt
Religion	Church of England
Pre-War Occupation	Farmhand

HISTORY

Singapore	Selarang Camp Changi
'A' Force Burma	Green Force, No. 3 Battalion
POW Number	2664
Camps Thailand	Tamarkan, Chungkai, Linson Wood Camp, Tamuang, Kanchanaburi, Nacompaton, Bangkok
POW Number (Linson)	12090
Return Details 1945	Thailand-Singapore by aircraft
	Singapore-Fremantle, HMT *Circassia*

PETROS VASSILIOUS OMIRIDIS

Rank	Private
Regimental Number	WX12156
Classification	Batman/Runner
Company	'A' Company
Enlisted	2.5.1941
Discharged	17.10.1946
Date of Birth	26.6.1909
Place of Birth	Grasdain, Macedonia
Father	Petros Omiridis
Mother	Maria Omiridis
Religion	Greek Orthodox
Pre-War Occupation	Stonemason

Singapore	Selarang Camp Changi
POW Numbers	1/8882 and 3/9051
'J' Force Japan	*Wales Maru* Party
POW Number	643
Camps Japan	Kobe (Showa-Denki)
	Kawasaki Camp, Maruyama Park
	Wakinohama
Return Details 1945	Yokohama-Okinawa by aircraft
	Okinawa-Manila by aircraft
	Manila-Sydney, HMAS *Quiberon*
	Sydney 113(C)MH
	Melbourne 115(H)MH
	Detrained Perth and admitted to 110(P)MH
Additions	Wounded in action Jurong Road on 10.2.1942. Admitted to the 2/13th Australian General Hospital on 11.2.1942 with a bayonet wound to the left leg. Discharged to unit on 23.2.1942.

ALBERT WILFRED LANCE PARK

Rank	Private
Regimental Number	WX16448
Company	Headquarters Company
Enlisted	10.9.1941
Discharged	18.2.1946
Date of Birth	27.6.1922
Place of Birth	Fremantle, Western Australia
Father	William Henry Park
Mother	Gwendoline Park
Religion	Church of England
Pre-War Occupation	Truck Driver

HISTORY

Singapore	Selarang Camp Changi
	Johore Bahru, Adam Park
	Selarang Barracks Changi
POW Number	1/8915
'J' Force Japan	*Wales Maru* Party
POW Numbers	805 and 268
Camps Japan	Kobe
	Notogowa-Osaka sub-Camp No. 9
Return Details 1945	Yokohama-Manila, USS *Goodhue*
	Manila-Sydney, HMS *Formidable*
	Sydney-Melbourne-Perth by troop train

ALBERT SYDNEY PARKE

Rank	Private
Regimental Number	WX7724
Company	'A' Company
Enlisted	10.8.1940
Discharged	23.5.1946
Date of Birth	3.7.1914
Place of Birth	Donnybrook, Western Australia
Father	Sydney Spencer Parke
Mother	Kathleen Mary Parke
Religion	Methodist
Pre-War Occupation	Orchard Worker

HISTORY

Singapore	Selarang Camp Changi
'A' Force Burma	Green Force, No. 3 Battalion
POW Number	1530
Camps Thailand	Khonkan 55km (medical orderly from 7.7.1943-19.10.1943)
	Tamarkan, Nacompaton, Bangkok
Return Details 1945	Thailand-Singapore by aircraft
	Singapore-Perth, no details are known

CHARLES SPENCER PARKE

Rank	Private
Regimental Number	WX7738
Company	'A' Company
Enlisted	10.8.1940
Discharged	21.2.1946
Date of Birth	13.8.1916
Place of Birth	Brunswick Junction, Western Australia
Father	Sydney Spencer Parke
Mother	Kathleen Mary Parke
Religion	Methodist
Pre-War Occupation	Coal Miner

HISTORY

Singapore	Selarang Camp Changi
	Johore Bahru, Adam Park
	Selarang Barracks Changi
POW Number	1/12129
'D' Force Thailand	V Battalion
Camps Thailand	Kinsaiyok, Hindaine, Kanchanaburi, Non Pladuk
Japan	*Aramis* Party
POW Number	601
Camps Japan	Fukuoka sub-Camp No. 17, Omuta
Return Details 1945	Nagasaki-Manila, USS *Lunga Point*
	Manila-Morotai-Darwin, PBY Catalina aircraft A24-377
	Darwin-Perth, B24 Liberator aircraft A72-379

DOUGLAS PARKER

Rank	Private
Regimental Number	WX8642
Company	'B' Company
Enlisted	18.10.1940
Discharged	11.1.1946
Date of Birth	6.9.1914
Place of Birth	Bunbury, Western Australia
Father	Richard Edward Winsett Parker
Mother	Jessie Parker
Religion	Church of England
Pre-War Occupation	Salesman, Window Dresser and Storeman

HISTORY

Singapore	Selarang Camp Changi
'A' Force Burma	Green Force, No. 3 Battalion
POW Number	1528
Camps Thailand	Tamarkan, Tamuang
Return Details 1945	Thailand-Singapore by aircraft
	Singapore-Fremantle, HMT *Highland Brigade*

REGINALD PASCALL

Rank	Private
Regimental Number	WX12336
Company	'A' Company
Enlisted	2.5.1941
Discharged	31.1.1946
Date of Birth	5.11.1920
Place of Birth	Kent, England
Father	Not Known
Mother	Elizabeth Pascall
Religion	Church of England
Pre-War Occupation	Farmhand

HISTORY

Singapore	Selarang Camp and Barracks Changi
'D' Force Thailand	S Battalion
POW Number	8832
Camps Thailand	Chungkai
Japan	*Rashin Maru* Party
POW Number	1703
Camps Japan	Yamane
	Niihama
Return Details 1945	Wakayama-Okinawa, USS *Sanctuary*
	Okinawa-Manila, USS *Bingham*
	Manila-Morotai-Darwin, PBY Catalina aircraft A24-354
	Darwin-Perth, B24 Liberator aircraft
Additions	Kingsley Fairbridge Farm Schoolboy.

THOMAS ANTHONY PASCOE

Rank	Private
Regimental Number	WX7409
Classification	Driver
Company	'D' Company
Enlisted	6.8.1940
Discharged	6.6.1945
Date of Birth	11.9.1911
Place of Birth	Cornwall, England
Father	Thomas Pascoe
Mother	Elizabeth Woods Pascoe
Religion	Methodist
Pre-War Occupation	Shop Assistant

HISTORY

Singapore	Selarang Camp Changi
'A' Force Burma	Green Force, No. 3 Battalion
POW Number	1533
Japan	*Rakuyo Maru* Party, Kumi No. 35 (rescued by USS *Pampanito*)
Return Details 1944	Saipan-Guadalcanal-Brisbane-Perth 1.11.1944

JOHN STANLEY PASS

Rank	Private
Regimental Number	WX5123
Classification	Driver
Company	'C' Company
Enlisted	23.7.1940
Discharged	22.3.1946
Date of Birth	16.6.1899
Place of Birth	Norton, England
Father	John Pass
Mother	Sarah Pass
Religion	Church of England
Pre-War Occupation	Prospector

HISTORY

Singapore	Selarang Camp and Barracks Changi
	Changi Gaol Camp
Return Details 1945	Singapore-Darwin-Melbourne, 1st Netherlands Military Hospital Ship *Oranje*
	Melbourne-Perth by troop train
Additions	Wounded in action at Ulu Pandan on 11.2. 1942. Admitted to Field Ambulance with a shrapnel wound to the heel of the right foot. Transferred to the 2/13th Australian General Hospital then to the 2/10th Australian General Hospital on 4.3.1942. This soldier was awarded an 'E' Medical Classification by the Japanese in October 1942. He served with the Royal Marine Artillery from 1916 to 1923 and on his arrival in Australia in the Militia from 1932 to 1940 when he enlisted in the 2nd A.I.F. He passed away in New Zealand on 14.7.1976.

JOSEPH PEARCE

Rank	Lance Sergeant
Regimental Number	WX9268
Company	'D' Company
Enlisted	30.10.1940
Discharged	27.2.1946
Date of Birth	28.2.1917
Place of Birth	Wagin, Western Australia
Father	Thomas Pearce
Mother	Emma Pearce
Religion	Church of England
Pre-War Occupation	Farmer

HISTORY

Singapore	Selarang Camp Changi
	Thomson Road (Caldecot Hill Estate Camp)
	Adam Park Camp
	Selarang Barracks Changi
'D' Force Thailand	S Battalion
POW Number	8735
Camps Thailand	Kanu II, Hintok Road Camp, Hintok River Camp, Kinsaiyok, Konkoita, Tamarkan, Petchaburi, Kachu Mountain Camp, Bangkok, Lopburi, Nakom Nayok, Bangkok
Return Details 1945	Bangkok-Singapore by aircraft
	Singapore-Fremantle, HMT *Moreton Bay*
Additions	Wounded in action north Lim Chu Kang Road at 'D' Company No. 13 Platoon position at 1130 hours on 8.2.1942. Admitted to the 2/9th Field Ambulance with shrapnel wounds to the leg and burns to the body. NCO was transferred to the 2/10th Australian General Hospital on 9.2.1942 and discharged to unit on 23.2.1942.

Joe Pearce in February 2002, at the No. 13 Platoon position, on the night of 8th/9th February 1942

DONALD DAVID PEARSON

Rank	Private
Regimental Number	WX13816
Company	'B' Company
Enlisted	3.6.1941
Discharged	11.12.1945
Date of Birth	5.2.1905
Place of Birth	Claremont, Western Australia
Father	Not Known
Mother	Mary Pearson
Religion	Church of England
Pre-War Occupation	Inspector with Western Australian Trustees Company

HISTORY

Singapore	Selarang Camp Changi
	Johore Bahru, Adam Park
	A. G. H. Roberts Barracks Changi (beri-beri)
	Selarang Barracks Changi
POW Number	1/8951
'H' Force Thailand	'H' Force Group No. 3
Camps Thailand	Kanu II Malayan Hamlet, Kanchanaburi
Singapore	Sime Road Camp (15.2.1942-4.5.1942)
	Changi Gaol Camp
Return Details 1945	Singapore-Darwin-Sydney, HMT *Arawa*
	Sydney-Melbourne by troop train
	Melbourne-Fremantle, HMT *Strathmore*

ROBERT MAYNARD PHELPS

Rank	Captain
Regimental Number	WX3465
Company	Headquarters Company
Enlisted	10.12.1940
Appointment Terminated	18.3.1946
Date of Birth	29.11.1911
Place of Birth	Geraldton, Western Australia
Father	Abraham Phelps
Mother	Edith Winifred Phelps
Religion	Church of England
Pre-War Occupation	Clerk

HISTORY

Singapore	Selarang Camp Changi
'A' Force Burma	Green Force, No. 3 Battalion
Camps Burma	Khonkan 55km (medical orderly)
Camps Thailand	Tamarkan, Kanchanaburi, Bangkok
Return Details 1945	Bangkok-Singapore by aircraft
	Singapore-Fremantle, HMT *Tamaroa*
Additions	Attached to the 7th Indian Division Headquarters and Allied Command, Bangkok 1945.

HARRY PICKETT

Rank	Private
Regimental Number	WX9055
Classification	Signaller
Company	Headquarters Company
Enlisted	25.10.1940
Discharged	20.6.1945
Date of Birth	9.3.1916
Place of Birth	Geraldton, Western Australia
Father	Harry Pickett
Mother	Margaret Emily Pickett
Religion	Church of England
Pre-War Occupation	Butcher

HISTORY

Singapore	Selarang Camp Changi
'A' Force Burma	Green Force, No. 3 Battalion
POW Number	3166
Japan	*Rakuyo Maru* Party, Kumi No. 37 (rescued by USS *Pampanito*)
Return Details 1944	Saipan-Guadalcanal-Brisbane-Perth 1.11.1944

THOMAS WILLIAM PIERSON

Rank	Sergeant (Promoted on 28.1.1942)
Regimental Number	WX9238
Company	Battalion Headquarters
Enlisted	30.10.1940
Discharged	24.6.1946
Date of Birth	19.3.1898
Place of Birth	West Hartlepool, England
Father	Albert Victor Pierson
Mother	Not Known
Religion	Church of England
Pre-War Occupation	Farmhand

HISTORY

Singapore	Selarang Camp Changi
	Thomson Road (Caldecot Hill Estate Camp)
	Adam Park Camp
	River Valley Road Camp
	A.G.H. Roberts Barracks Changi (16.2.1943-May 1943)
	Selarang Barracks Changi
POW Number	6133
Force	'F' Force Thailand
Camps Thailand	Shimo Sonkurai Hospital (May-September 1943)
	Kanchanaburi (November 1943-May 1944)
Singapore	Changi Gaol Hospital (May-June 1944)
	Kranji Hospital Woodlands (June-December 1944)
	Changi Gaol Hospital (December 1944-September 1945)
Return Details 1945	Singapore-Labuan by aircraft
	Labuan-Morotai-Brisbane, 2/2nd H.M. Australian Hospital Ship *Wanganella*
	Brisbane-Sydney-Melbourne-Perth by troop train

CHARLES ROSSITER PIGGOTT

Rank	Lance Corporal
Regimental Number	WX13027
Company	'C' Company
Enlisted	15.5.1941
Discharged	22.3.1946
Date of Birth	10.3.1917
Place of Birth	Bridgetown, Western Australia
Father	Frederick Charles Piggott
Mother	Elizabeth Gertrude Piggott
Religion	Methodist
Pre-War Occupation	Orchardist

HISTORY

Singapore	Selarang Camp Changi
'A' Force Burma	Green Force, No. 3 Battalion
POW Number	1482
Camps Burma	Khonkan 55km (1.7.1943)
Camps Thailand	Tamarkan, Chungkai, Kachu Mountain Camp, Nakom Nayok, Lopburi, Nakom Nayok, Bangkok (see Danny Bevis Diary)
Return Details 1945	Bangkok-Singapore by aircraft
	Singapore-Fremantle, HMT *Moreton Bay*

THOMAS PILMOOR

Rank	Private
Regimental Number	WX17393
Classification	Temporary Batman/Runner
Company	Battalion Headquarters
Enlisted	27.10.1941
Discharged	27.2.1946
Date of Birth	4.7.1917
Place of Birth	Driffield, Gloucestershire, England
Father	Robert Pilmoor
Mother	Sarah Pilmoor
Religion	Methodist
Pre-War Occupation	Yardsman

HISTORY

Singapore	Selarang Camp Changi
'A' Force Burma	Green Force, No. 3 Battalion
POW Number	3057
Camps Thailand	Tamarkan, Chungkai, Kanchanaburi, Ratburi, Lopburi, Nacompaton, Bangkok
Return Details 1945	Bangkok-Singapore by aircraft
	Singapore-Fremantle, HMT *Moreton Bay*
Additions	Kingsley Fairbridge Farm Schoolboy. Soldier was selected for Japan, but missed the draft due to appendicitis.

ROBERT SIDNEY PIMLOTT

Rank	Private
Regimental Number	WX20157
Company	Battalion Headquarters (Regimental Police Corporal)
Enlisted	10.11.1941
Discharged	6.12.1945
Date of Birth	31.1.1912
Place of Birth	Port Pirie, South Australia
Father	Sidney Halford Pimlott
Mother	Annie Pimlott
Religion	Methodist
Pre-War Occupation	Farmer

HISTORY

Singapore	Selarang Camp Changi
'A' Force Burma	Green Force, No. 3 Battalion
POW Number	1519
Camps Thailand	Tamarkan, Nacompaton
Return Details 1945	Thailand-Rangoon by aircraft
	Rangoon-Singapore, HMT *Highland Brigade*
	Singapore-Fremantle, HMT *Tamaroa*

ALBERT LESLIE PITTS

Rank	Private
Regimental Number	WX7626
Classification	Rangetaker
Company	'D' Company
Enlisted	10.8.1940
Discharged	6.3.1946
Date of Birth	29.1.1918
Place of Birth	Partridge Green, Sussex, England
Father	David John Pitts
Mother	Maria Pitts
Religion	Church of England
Pre-War Occupation	Farmer

HISTORY

Singapore	Selarang Camp Changi
'A' Force Burma	Green Force, No. 3 Battalion
POW Number	1537
Camps Burma	Thanbyuzayat (sick 28.9.1942)
	Khonkan 55km (evacuated sick 1.7.1943 and September 1943)
Camps Thailand	Tamarkan, Chungkai, Kachu Mountain Camp (Theatrical Party), Bangkok, Nakom Nayok, Lopburi, Nakom Nayok, Bangkok (see Danny Bevis Diary)
Return Details 1945	Thailand-Singapore by aircraft
	Singapore-Fremantle, HMT *Circassia*
Additions	Soldier was wounded in action at 0200 hours on 9.2.1942. Admitted to Field Ambulance with a shrapnel wound to the left thigh. Transferred to the 2/10th Australian General Hospital on 18.2.1942. Discharged to unit on 24.2.1942.

EDWARD CHARLES STEVEN POPHAM

Rank	Private
Regimental Number	WX9263
Company	'A' Company
Enlisted	30.10.1940
Discharged	9.1.1946
Date of Birth	25.11.1901
Place of Birth	London, England
Father	Edward James Stanford Popham
Mother	Sophia Ellen Popham
Religion	Baptist
Pre-War Occupation	Labourer

HISTORY

Singapore	Selarang Camp Changi
	A. G. H. Roberts Barracks Changi (8.3.1942, typhus)
	Serangoon Road Camp
	Selarang Barracks Changi
POW Number	4/6517
'D' Force Thailand	S Battalion
POW Number	8833
Camps Thailand	Chungkai, Bangkok
Return Details 1945	Thailand-Singapore by aircraft
	Singapore-Darwin-Perth, PBY Catalina aircraft
	Admitted to 110(P)MH on 18.10.1945 with beri-beri.

BERTRAM FREDERICK POULTON

Rank	Private
Regimental Number	WX9764
Company	'D' Company
Enlisted	6.12.1940
Discharged	18.12.1945
Date of Birth	24.11.1907
Place of Birth	Derby, England
Father	Bertram Frederick Poulton
Stepfather	Walter Cove
Mother	Daisy Annie Poulton
Religion	Church of England
Pre-War Occupation	Painter

Singapore	Selarang Camp Changi
	Johore Bahru, Adam Park
	Selarang Barracks Changi
POW Number	3/9219
'D' Force Thailand	S Battalion
POW Number	8830
Camps Thailand	Kanu II, Tarsau, Chungkai, Tamuang
Japan	*Rashin Maru* Party
POW Number	216
Camps Japan	Ohama Camp 9B
Return Details 1945	Wakayama-Okinawa, USS *Consolation*
	Okinawa-Manila, USS *Haskell*
	Manila-Sydney, HMS *Speaker*
	Sydney-Fremantle, HMT *Dominion Monarch*

ARTHUR LINDSAY ROY POWELL

Rank	Corporal (Promoted on 24.1.1942)	
Regimental Number	WX9554	
Classification	Carpenter	
Company	Headquarters Company	
Enlisted	4.12.1940	
Discharged	16.1.1946	
Date of Birth	16.7.1918	
Place of Birth	Northampton, Western Australia	
Father	Arthur Powell	
Mother	Clara Evelyn Powell	
Religion	Church of England	
Pre-War Occupation	Carpenter	

HISTORY

Singapore	Selarang Camp Changi
	Johore Bahru, Adam Park
	Selarang Barracks Changi
POW Number	4/4561
'D' Force Thailand	V Battalion
Camps Thailand	Brankassi, Pratchai, Bangkok
Return Details 1945	Thailand-Singapore by aircraft
	Singapore-Fremantle, HMT *Circassia*

FREDERICK FRANCIS PRITCHARD

Rank	Private
Regimental Number	WX8739
Classification	Driver
Company	Headquarters Company
Enlisted	23.10.1940
Discharged	14.11.1946
Date of Birth	8.6.1904
Place of Birth	Kalgoorlie, Western Australia
Father	Francis James Pritchard
Mother	Isabella Kate Pritchard
Religion	Church of England
Pre-War Occupation	Miner

HISTORY

Singapore	Selarang Camp Changi
'A' Force Burma	Green Force, No. 3 Battalion
POW Number	2903
Camps Thailand	Tamarkan, Nacompaton
Return Details 1945	Bangkok-Singapore by aircraft
	Singapore-Sydney, HMT *Highland Chieftan*

FRANCIS KENNETH PRITCHARD

Rank	Private
Regimental Number	WX8716
Classification	Driver
Company	Headquarters Company
Enlisted	23.10.1940
Discharged	6.12.1945
Date of Birth	14.3.1914
Place of Birth	Northam, Western Australia
Father	Francis James Pritchard
Mother	Isabella Kate Pritchard
Religion	Church of England
Pre-War Occupation	Shop Manager

HISTORY

Java	
Fremantle	
Port Moresby	
Ramu Valley	
Port Moresby	
Townsville	
Brisbane	
Morotai	
Balikpapan	

Soldier remained onboard HMT *Aquitania* at Fremantle. He had fallen ten feet onto his right foot on 15.1.1942 and twisted his knee. He did not trans-ship at Ratai Bay, Java with the battalion but remained onboard the *Aquitania* and returned to Fremantle due to synovitis to the knee. An operation was performed and soldier's right leg was placed in plaster for three months. Soldier then convalesced for four months and after the plaster was removed, he was Taken on Strength as reinforcements for the 2/4th Machine Gun Battalion on 17.7.1942. Taken on Strength with the 35th Infantry Battalion on 25.9.1942 and then the reformed 2/2nd Pioneer Battalion on 12.12.1942. Embarked Fremantle HMT *Duntroon* on 23.7.1943 and disembarked at Port Moresby on 28.7.1943. Soldier saw action at Ramu Valley when the 2/2nd Pioneers were brought in to replace the 2/16th Battalion. This soldier disembarked at Balikpapan from LST 632 (Landing Ship Tank) sometime after 13.5.1945.

HAROLD EDWARD PROCTER

Rank	Private
Regimental Number	WX6172
Classification	Driver
Company	'A' Company
Enlisted	13.7.1940
Discharged	19.6.1946
Date of Birth	12.8.1905
Place of Birth	Lancashire, England
Father	William Procter
Mother	Rosa Procter
Religion	Methodist
Pre-War Occupation	Farmhand

HISTORY

Singapore	Selarang Camp Changi
	Johore Bahru, Adam Park
	A. G. H. Roberts Barracks Changi (beri-beri and avitaminosis July-September 1942)
	Selarang Barracks Changi
'J' Force Japan	*Wales Maru* Party
POW Number	703
Camps Japan	Kobe (factory and dock work)
	Kawasaki Camp, Maruyama Park
	Fukuoka sub-Camp No. 26, Usui
Return Details 1945	Nagasaki-Okinawa, USS *Marathon*
	Okinawa-Manila, C54 aircraft
	Manila-Sydney, HMS *Speaker*
	Sydney-Fremantle, HMT *Duntroon*
Additions	Wounded in action at Hill 200, Ulu Pandan on 12.2.1942. Admitted to Field Ambulance with a shrapnel wound to the back and left arm. Admitted to the 2/13th Australian General Hospital on 16.2.1942 and discharged to unit on 21.2.1942.

JOHN HENRY LLOYD PRYCE

Rank	Private
Regimental Number	WX8725
Classification	Signaller
Company	Headquarters Company
Enlisted	23.10.1940
Discharged	4.12.1945
Date of Birth	20.7.1908
Place of Birth	England
Father	Not Known
Mother	Ellen Pryce
Religion	Church of England
Pre-War Occupation	Miner and Poultry Farmer

HISTORY

Java	'Blackforce'
'D' Force Thailand	Java Party No. 6, P Battalion
Camps Thailand	Petchaburi, Kachu Mountain Camp
Return Details 1945	Thailand-Rangoon by aircraft
	Rangoon-Singapore, HMT *Highland Brigade*
	Singapore-Fremantle, HMT *Highland Brigade*
Additions	Transferred to the 2/2nd Casualty Clearing Station on Java. Captured on 9.3.1942 at Bandoeng. Soldier was on duty with the 1st Allied General Hospital.

EPHRAIM ALBERT PUMMELL

Rank	Lance Corporal
Regimental Number	WX9946
Classification	Bootmaker
Attached 2/4th	Australian Army Ordnance Corps
Enlisted	11.12.1940
Discharged	11.12.1945
Date of Birth	4.8.1914
Place of Birth	Leicester, England
Father	Ephraim Edward Pummell
Mother	Ethel Pummell
Religion	Church of England
Pre-War Occupation	Boot Repairer

HISTORY

Singapore	Selarang Camp Changi
	Serangoon Road Camp
	Selarang Barracks Changi
POW Number	4/6526
Force	'F' Force Thailand
Camps Thailand	Shimo Sonkurai
Singapore	A. G. H. Roberts Barracks Changi (big toe on right foot amputated early 1944)
	Changi Gaol Camp
Return Details 1945	Singapore-Darwin-Sydney, 1st Netherlands Military Hospital Ship *Oranje*
	Sydney-Melbourne-Perth by troop train

CECIL GEORGE QUINN

Rank	Private
Regimental Number	WX9285
Company	'D' Company
Enlisted	30.10.1940
Discharged	9.1.1946
Date of Birth	27.7.1903
Place of Birth	Wagin, Western Australia
Father	Francis Philip Daniel Quinn
Mother	Harriet Quinn
Religion	Church of England
Pre-War Occupation	Barber

HISTORY

Singapore	Escaped to Sumatra
Sumatra	Atjeh Party
	Pakan Baroe-Moearo Railway
Return Details 1945	Sumatra-Singapore by aircraft
	Singapore-Sydney, HMT *Highland Chieftan*
	Sydney-Melbourne-Perth by troop train
Additions	Soldier was wounded in action north Lim Chu Kang Road on 9.2.1942. He was wounded again on 11.2.1942 receiving a shrapnel wound to the left foot.

DANIEL ADAIR CORMACK QUINN

Rank	Private
Regimental Number	WX5054
Classification	Cook
Company	'A' Company
Enlisted	23.7.1940
Discharged	30.8.1946
Date of Birth	24.8.1895
Place of Birth	Grimsby, England
Father	Thomas Quinn
Mother	Ada Quinn
Religion	Church of England
Pre-War Occupation	Farmer and Driver

HISTORY

Singapore	Selarang Camp Changi
	River Valley Road Camp
	A. G. H. Roberts Barracks Changi (August 1942-January 1943)
	Selarang Barracks Changi
	Changi Gaol Camp
	Kranji Hospital Woodlands
POW Number	1/9038
Return Details 1945	Singapore-Perth-Duke of Gloucester's aircraft *'Endeavour'*
	Soldier was evacuated to 110(P)MH ex-2/14th Australian General Hospital Singapore.

JAMES PATRICK QUINN

Rank	Lance Corporal
Regimental Number	WX7831
Company	Headquarters Company
Enlisted	13.8.1940
Discharged	20.6.1946
Date of Birth	25.7.1907
Place of Birth	Dalry, Scotland
Father	Henry Quinn
Mother	Agnes Mary Quinn
Religion	Roman Catholic
Pre-War Occupation	Miner and Teamster

HISTORY

Singapore	Selarang Camp Changi
'A' Force Burma	Green Force No. 3 Battalion
POW Number	1446
Camps Thailand	Tamarkan, Bangkok, Nacompaton
Return Details 1945	Singapore-Perth, PBY Catalina aircraft
Additions	Wounded in action on 13.2.1942 and admitted to No. 1 Malaya General Hospital with a shrapnel wound to the left hand resulting in the loss of the fourth finger. Discharged to unit on 27.2.1942.

JOHN ARGENT RABONE

Rank	Private
Regimental Number	WX7511
Company	Headquarters Company
Enlisted	6.8.1940
Discharged	28.1.1947
Date of Birth	27.3.1905
Place of Birth	Birmingham, England
Father	Clement William Rabone
Mother	Lydia Rabone
Religion	Church of England
Pre-War Occupation	Quarryman

HISTORY

Singapore	Selarang Camp Changi
'A' Force Burma	Green Force, No. 3 Battalion
POW Number	9350
Camps Burma	Reptu 30km (medical orderly), Kyondaw 95km, Aungganaung 105km
Camps Thailand	Tamarkan, Pratchai
Return Details 1945	Thailand-Singapore by aircraft
	Singapore-Fremantle, HMT *Circassia*

ARTHUR RALPH

Rank	Private
Regimental Number	WX20107
Company	'E' Company, Special Reserve Battalion
Enlisted	8.10.1941
Discharged	21.12.1945
Date of Birth	16.5.1906
Place of Birth	Albany, Western Australia
Father	William Ralph
Mother	Susan Ralph
Religion	Church of England
Pre-War Occupation	Stevedore and Shed Worker

HISTORY

Singapore	Selarang Camp Changi
	Selarang Barracks Changi
	Pulau Blakang Mati (November 1943-August 1945)
	Kranji Camp Woodlands
POW Number	2/9269
Return Details 1945	Singapore-Darwin-Sydney, HMT *Arawa*
	Sydney-Melbourne by troop train
	Melbourne-Fremantle, HMT *Strathmore*
Additions	Dislocated ligaments in right knee on 12.2.1942. Evacuated to Alexandra Hospital until the end of hostilities. Discharged to unit on 22.2.1942.

JACK KENNETH RAMSBOTTOM

Rank	Private
Regimental Number	WX14836
Company	'A' Company
Enlisted	4.7.1941
Discharged	5.2.1946
Date of Birth	18.11.1922
Place of Birth	Ramsgate, Kent, England
Father	Not Known
Mother	Mrs Buckthorpe (nee Ramsbottom)
Religion	Church of England
Pre-War Occupation	Farmhand

HISTORY

Singapore	Selarang Camp Changi
	River Valley Road Camp
	Mount Pleasant Camp
	Selarang Barracks Changi
'J' Force Japan	*Wales Maru* Party
POW Number	714
Camps Japan	Kobe
	Kawasaki Camp, Maruyama Park
	Wakinohama
Return Details 1945	Yokohama-Okinawa by aircraft
	Okinawa-Manila by aircraft
	Manila-Sydney, HMS *Formidable*
	Sydney-Melbourne-Perth by troop train
Additions	Kingsley Fairbridge Farm Schoolboy. After his discharge in 1946 this soldier re-enlisted in the Australian Regular Army in 1950 under the legally adopted name of John Kenneth Lane with the Regimental No. 5/1507. He served sixteen years with the Western Command Band before being posted to the Army Apprentices School in Victoria, where he served a further two years as a music teacher before retiring with the rank of Staff Sergeant. This eighteen years additional service qualified him for the Long Service and Good Conduct Medals. After his discharge from the Regular Army, he served another year as Bandmaster of the Western Command Reserve Band with the rank of W.O. I. He was a member of the Combined Army bands which performed at the opening ceremony of the Melbourne Olympics in 1956.

JOHN RANDALL

Rank	Corporal
Regimental Number	WX9563
Classification	Butcher
Attached 2/4th	88 Light Aid Detachment
Enlisted	4.12.1940
Discharged	5.2.1946
Date of Birth	1.6.1905
Place of Birth	King William Town, South Africa
Father	Herbert Randall
Mother	Florence Randall
Religion	Church of England
Pre-War Occupation	Blacksmith and Mechanic

Java	'Blackforce', attached to 2/2nd Pioneer Battalion
Camps Java	Bandoeng, Tjimahi
'A' Force Burma	Java Party No. 4 Party, Williams Force
Japan	*Awa Maru* Party (remained behind at Singapore due to illness)
French Indo-China	*Both* Party
Return Details 1945	Saigon-Bangkok-Singapore by aircraft
	Singapore-Fremantle, 2/1st H.M. Australian Hospital Ship *Manunda*

GEORGE LINTON REAY

Rank	Private
Regimental Number	WX16281
Classification	Stretcher Bearer
Company	Battalion Headquarters
Enlisted	1.9.1941
Discharged	4.1.1946
Date of Birth	9.5.1904
Place of Birth	Newcastle, England
Father	William Reay
Mother	Esther Reay
Religion	Church of England
Pre-War Occupation	Farmhand

HISTORY

Singapore	Selarang Camp and Barracks Changi
	Changi Gaol Camp
POW Number	1/9060
Return Details 1945	Singapore-Darwin-Sydney, HMT *Arawa*
	Sydney-Melbourne by troop train
	Melbourne-Fremantle, HMT *Strathmore*
Additions	The following note was removed from this soldier's paybook and is now held by the Australian War Memorial in Canberra:

"It is with pleasure that I express my appreciation to you on the completion of one year's duty with the Forestry Company of the A.I.F. Prisoner's of War Camp Changi. Your duties have been arduous and at times very irksome but you have continued despite the adverse conditions to perform the essential duties of procuring firewood. Without your continued loyalty and devotion to this special work the health and comfort of the A.I.F. would not have been so good as it was. My thanks to each one of you and I hope the period of duty will soon draw to a close."

Signed:

Brigadier General Callaghan

ARTHUR JOHN REES

Rank	Private
Regimental Number	WX6129
Company	'C' Company
Enlisted	13.7.1940
Discharged	19.2.1946
Date of Birth	6.4.1917
Place of Birth	Midland Junction, Western Australia
Father	Joseph Rees
Mother	Margaret Rees
Religion	Church of England
Pre-War Occupation	Barman and Yardman

HISTORY

Singapore	Selarang Camp and Barracks Changi
POW Number	4/6537
'D' Force Thailand	S Battalion
POW Number	8840
Camps Thailand	Kanu II, Chungkai
Return Details 1945	Thailand-Singapore by aircraft
	Singapore-Fremantle, HMT *Moreton Bay*

WILLIAM WALTER REEVES

Rank	Private
Regimental Number	WX7621
Company	'C' Company
Enlisted	10.8.1940
Discharged	25.1.1946
Date of Birth	23.12.1901
Place of Birth	Prestbury, Gloucestershire, England
Father	George Reeves
Mother	Alice Jane Reeves
Religion	Church of England
Pre-War Occupation	Stevedore and Railway Employee

HISTORY

Singapore	Selarang Camp Changi
	Thomson Road (Caldecot Hill Estate Camp)
	Selarang Barracks Changi
POW Number	3/9303
'D' Force Thailand	S Battalion
POW Number	8839
Camps Thailand	Kanu II, Kao Rin, Nacompaton, Prachuab Kirikhan-Mergui Escape Road, Petchaburi
Return Details 1945	Thailand-Singapore by aircraft
	Singapore-Fremantle, HMT *Highland Brigade*

VERNON SPENCE REID

Rank	Private
Regimental Number	WX17857
Company	'A' Company
Enlisted	3.12.1941
Discharged	14.12.1945
Date of Birth	2.5.1919
Place of Birth	Pingelly, Western Australia
Father	Maude Hemingway Reid
Mother	Rose Reid
Religion	Church of England
Pre-War Occupation	Farmhand

HISTORY

Singapore	Selarang Camp Changi
'A' Force Burma	Green Force, No. 3 Battalion
POW Number	1498
Camps Thailand	Tamarkan, Bangkok (go-downs)
Return Details 1945	Thailand-Singapore by aircraft
	Singapore-Fremantle, HMT *Circassia*
Additions	Wounded in action at Buona Vista on 15.2.1942. Soldier was evacuated to 2/9th Field Ambulance at St Andrews Cathedral a few hours before surrender with shrapnel wounds to the left hip, right leg and right rapiteal space. Transferred to the 2/13th Australian General Hospital until discharged to unit on 22.2.1942.

LESLIE GORDON RICHES

Rank	Lieutenant
Regimental Number	WX11046
Company	'D' Section, 4th Reserve Motor Transport Company
Enlisted	28.2.1941
Appointment Terminated	26.4.1946
Date of Birth	14.11.1896
Place of Birth	Broken Hill, New South Wales
Father	Henry James Riches
Mother	Caroline Riches
Religion	Church of England
Pre-War Occupation	Orchardist

HISTORY

Singapore	Selarang Barracks Changi
	Thomson Road (Caldecot Hill Estate Camp)
	Selarang Barracks Changi
'D' Force Thailand	V Battalion
Camps Thailand	Kinsaiyok, Brankassi, Kuii (evacuated sick), Nacompaton
Return Details 1945	Singapore-Fremantle, HMT *Tamaroa*

ERNEST RICKETTS

Rank	Private
Regimental Number	WX6799
Company	'C' Company
Enlisted	20.7.1940
Discharged	1.5.1946
Date of Birth	3.3.1904
Place of Birth	Derby, England
Father	Not Known
Mother	Not Known
Religion	Church of England
Pre-War Occupation	Labourer

HISTORY

Singapore	Selarang Camp Changi
'A' Force Burma	Green Force, No. 3 Battalion
POW Number	2908
Camps Burma	Khonkan 55km (July 1943)
Camps Thailand	Tamarkan, Non Pladuk, Petchaburi, Kachu Mountain Camp, Bangkok
Return Details 1945	Bangkok-Rangoon by aircraft,
	Rangoon-Singapore, HMT *Highland Brigade*
	Singapore-Fremantle, H.M. Hospital Ship *Karoa*

RICHARD WILLIAM RIDGWELL

Rank	Private
Regimental Number	WX14197
Company	'B' Company Headquarters
Enlisted	11.6.1941
Discharged	13.2.1946
Date of Birth	25.1.1918
Place of Birth	Perth, Western Australia
Father	Alfred George Ridgwell
Mother	Myrtle Ivy Ridgwell
Religion	Church of England
Pre-War Occupation	Mechanical Fitter

HISTORY

Singapore	Selarang Camp Changi
	Johore Bahru, Adam Park
	Sime Road Camp
	Selarang Barracks Changi
POW Number	4/6544
'D' Force Thailand	S Battalion
POW Number	8834
Camps Thailand	Kanu II, Hintok Road Camp, Kinsaiyok, Konkoita, Tarsau, Tamarkan, Chungkai, Nakom Nayok, Bangkok
Return Details 1945	Thailand-Singapore by aircraft
	Singapore-Morotai-Wewak-Townsville by aircraft
	Townsville-Sydney-Melbourne-Perth by train

ROBERT RONALD RIEBE

Rank	Private
Regimental Number	WX8952
Classification	Despatch Rider
Company	'D' Company
Enlisted	25.10.1940
Discharged	24.1.1946
Date of Birth	10.5.1920
Place of Birth	Bayswater, Western Australia
Father	Charles Joseph Riebe
Mother	Wilhelmina Riebe
Religion	Methodist
Pre-War Occupation	Clerk

HISTORY

Singapore	Selarang Camp Changi
	Johore Bahru, Adam Park
	Selarang Barracks Changi
POW Number	4/6546
'D' Force Thailand	S Battalion
POW Number	8837
Camps Thailand	Kanu II, Chungkai, Non Pladuk, Sonkurai-Nikhe Defence Line
Return Details 1945	Thailand-Singapore by aircraft
	Singapore-Fremantle, HMT *Highland Brigade*

WILLIAM ROBERT RITCHIE

Rank	Private
Regimental Number	WX15743
Awards	British Empire Medal
	Mentioned in Despatches
Classification	Stretcher Bearer
Company	Battalion Headquarters
Enlisted	13.8.1941
Discharged	15.1.1946
Date of Birth	7.12.1903
Place of Birth	Lisbon, County Antrim, Ireland
Father	Robert John Ritchie
Mother	Molly Ritchie
Religion	Church of England
Pre-War Occupation	Sheep Farmer

HISTORY

Singapore	Selarang Camp Changi
'A' Force Burma	Green Force, No. 3 Battalion
POW Number	2751
Return Details 1945	Thailand-Singapore by aircraft
	Singapore-Fremantle, H.M. Hospital Ship *Karoa*

STANLEY HENRY GEORGE ROBERTS

Rank	Private
Regimental Number	WX7750
Company	'A' Company
Enlisted	10.8.1940
Discharged	18.7.1943
Date of Birth	1.12.1903
Place of Birth	Boulder, Western Australia
Father	William Roberts
Mother	Isabella Roberts
Religion	Church of England
Pre-War Occupation	Storekeeper

HISTORY

Java	'Blackforce', attached to 2/3rd Machine Gun Battalion
Additions	Soldier was returned to Australia sick and arrived in Melbourne on 28.3.1942. No other details are known.

CLAUDE WILFRED ROBERTSON

Rank	Private
Regimental Number	WX7331
Classification	Driver
Company	'B' Company Headquarters
Enlisted	6.8.1940
Discharged	29.4.1946
Date of Birth	28.8.1903
Place of Birth	Perth, Western Australia
Father	Andrew Robertson
Mother	Agnes Berlette Robertson
Religion	Church of England
Pre-War Occupation	Miner

HISTORY

Singapore	Selarang Camp and Barracks Changi
'D' Force Thailand	S Battalion
POW Number	8835
Camps Thailand	Kanu II, Chungkai, Tamuang, Tardan
Return Details 1945	Singapore-Fremantle, HMT *Highland Brigade*
Additions	It is possible that this soldier returned to Singapore via Rangoon.

DONALD CHARLES ROBERTSON

Rank	Private
Regimental Number	WX16427
Company	'B' Company
Enlisted	10.9.1941
Discharged	6.11.1946
Date of Birth	29.8.1917
Place of Birth	Northam, Western Australia
Father	Charles Aloysius Robertson
Mother	Ada Miriam Robertson
Religion	Church of England
Pre-War Occupation	Administrator, New Guinea Patrol Officer

HISTORY

Java	'Blackforce'
'A' Force Burma	Java Party No. 4, Williams Force
POW Number	4590
Camps Burma	Beke Taung 40km Camp (2.7.1943)
Camps Thailand	131km, 133km, Kanchanaburi, Tamarkan, Kanchanaburi, Rin Tin, Tamarkan
Return Details 1945	Thailand-Singapore by aircraft
	Singapore-Perth, PBY Catalina aircraft

JOHN ROBINSON

Rank	Private
Regimental Number	WX10351
Company	'C' Company
Enlisted	18.12.1940
Discharged	6.6.1946
Date of Birth	5.4.1918
Place of Birth	Cottesloe, Western Australia
Father	Harry Quinn Robinson
Mother	Josephine Robinson
Religion	Church of England
Pre-War Occupation	Orchard Worker

HISTORY

Singapore	Selarang Camp Changi
'A' Force Burma	Green Force, No. 3 Battalion
POW Number	3193
Camps Burma	Reptu 30km Camp
Camps Thailand	Tamarkan, Bangkok, Nacompaton (acting Sergeant Cook), Bangkok
Return Details 1945	Thailand-Singapore by aircraft
	Singapore-Fremantle, HMT *Moreton Bay*

ERIC REGINALD ROGERS

Rank	Private
Regimental Number	WX9005
Company	'C' Company
Enlisted	25.10.1940
Discharged	2.5.1946
Date of Birth	28.9.1905
Place of Birth	Gravesend, Berkshire, England
Father	William James Rogers
Mother	Emma Rogers
Religion	Church of England
Pre-War Occupation	Farmhand

HISTORY

Singapore	Selarang Camp Changi
'A' Force Burma	Green Force, No. 3 Battalion
POW Number	3168
Camps Thailand	Tamarkan, Nacompaton (1944-30.8.1945)
Return Details 1945	Thailand-Singapore by aircraft
	Singapore-Fremantle, HMT *Circassia*

ANDREW MIDDLETON ROGIE

Rank	Private
Regimental Number	WX8652
Classification	Cook
Company	'D' Company
Enlisted	23.10.1940
Discharged	17.12.1946
Date of Birth	14.9.1902
Place of Birth	Aberdeen, Scotland
Father	John Rogie
Mother	Lizzie Middleton Rogie
Religion	Presbyterian
Pre-War Occupation	Farmer and Orchard Owner

HISTORY

Singapore	Selarang Camp Changi
	Sime Road Camp
	Selarang Barracks Changi
	Kranji Hospital Woodlands
	Changi Gaol Camp
POW Number	4/6556
Return Details 1945	Singapore-Darwin-Sydney, HMT *Arawa*
	Sydney-Melbourne-Adelaide by troop train
	Adelaide-Perth by aircraft
Additions	Shell shocked at Buona Vista on 15.2.1942 but remained on duty.

EDWARD JOHN RONAN

Rank	Private
Regimental Number	WX16269
Company	'E' Company, Special Reserve Battalion
Enlisted	27.8.1941
Discharged	1.2.1946
Date of Birth	27.12.1917
Place of Birth	Mingenew, Western Australia
Father	George Ronan
Mother	Alice Ronan
Religion	Church of England
Pre-War Occupation	Miner

HISTORY

Singapore	Selarang Camp and Barracks Changi
POW Number	4/6557
'D' Force Thailand	V Battalion
Camps Thailand	Non Pladuk, Ubon
Return Details 1945	Thailand-Singapore by aircraft
	Singapore-Fremantle, HMT *Highland Brigade*

STEPHEN EDGAR ROOTS

Rank	Private
Regimental Number	WX15893
Company	'A' Company
Enlisted	20.8.1941
Discharged	4.12.1945
Date of Birth	14.12.1921
Place of Birth	Albany, Western Australia
Father	Stephen Roots
Mother	Ethel Blanche Roots
Religion	Church of England
Pre-War Occupation	Truck Driver

HISTORY

Singapore	Selarang Camp Changi
	Johore Bahru, Adam Park
	A.G.H. Roberts Barracks Changi (appendicitis on 24.4.1942)
	Selarang Barracks Changi
Force	Japan 'B' Party Korea
Camps Korea	Keijo (shrine and warehouse, 25.9.1942-13.9.1943)
POW Number	347
	Konan (carbide factory, 14.9.1943-21.9.1945)
POW Number	528
Return Details 1945	USS *Mercy* for two weeks (U.S. hospital ship) at Pusan
	British Destroyer D50 from USS *Mercy* to the HMS *Colossus*
	Pusan-Manila, HMS *Colossus*
	Manila-Morotai-Darwin, PBY Catalina aircraft A24-377
	Darwin-Perth by aircraft

WILLIAM LOWES ROSEL

Rank	Private
Regimental Number	WX7835
Classification	Driver
Company	'C' Company
Enlisted	13.8.1940
Discharged	6.3.1946
Date of Birth	29.10.1908
Place of Birth	Victoria
Father	John Frederick Michael Rosel
Mother	Mary Ann Rosel
Religion	Congregational
Pre-War Occupation	Miner

HISTORY

Singapore	Selarang Camp Changi
	Thomson Road (Caldecot Hill Estate Camp, 8.5.1942-September 1942)
	River Valley Road (go-downs, September 1942-23.12.1942)
	Selarang Barracks Changi (Trailer and Garden Parties, 24.12.1942-7.5.1943)
POW Number	3/9402
'H' Force Thailand	'H' Force Group No. 3
Camps Thailand	Kanu II Malayan Hamlet (11.5.1943-12.8.1943)
	Bampong (13.8.1943-4.12.1943)
	Kanchanaburi (1.10.1943)
Singapore	Sime Road Camp (1.1.1944)
	Havelock Road Camp
	Changi Gaol Camp
Return Details 1945	Singapore-Sydney, 1st Netherlands Military Hospital Ship *Oranje*
	Sydney-Melbourne by troop train
	Melbourne-Perth by aircraft

DOUGLAS GODFREY ROSS

Rank	Private
Regimental Number	WX10066
Classification	Signaller
Company	Headquarters Company
Enlisted	13.12.1940
Discharged	7.2.1946
Date of Birth	16.11.1920
Place of Birth	Narrogin, Western Australia
Father	Robert Ross
Mother	Mildred Annie Ross
Religion	Methodist
Pre-War Occupation	Carpenter

Singapore	Selarang Camp Changi
	Johore Bahru, Adam Park
	Selarang Barracks Changi
	Levelling Party Changi Aerodrome
	Changi Gaol Camp
	X1 Party
	P Party
	Changi Gaol Camp
POW Number	4/6561
Return Details 1945	Singapore-Sydney, 1st Netherlands Military Hospital Ship *Oranje*
	Sydney-Melbourne-Perth by troop train

ARTHUR JOHN CHARLES ROWLAND

Rank	Sergeant (Promoted on 26.3.1943)
Regimental Number	WX17293
Company	'E' Company, Special Reserve Battalion
Enlisted	16.10.1941
Discharged	10.12.1945
Date of Birth	11.9.1920
Place of Birth	West Norwood, England
Father	Jack Rowland
Mother	Louisa Rowland
Religion	Church of England
Pre-War Occupation	Coach Builder and Blacksmith

HISTORY

Additions	Soldier received a gunshot wound to the right thigh on 11.2.1942 and was listed as missing in action. It is believed that he escaped to Sumatra. Soldier was admitted to the 2/12th Australian General Hospital at Columbo, Ceylon, on 9.3.1942. Embarked on HMT *Stirling Castle* for Australia on 13.3.1942 and disembarked at Melbourne on 6.4.1942. Disembarked Fremantle from the British ship *Egra* on 13.4.1942. On 13.3.1944 Taken on Strength with the 2/3rd Machine Gun Battalion and joined the 1st Australian Machine Gun Training Company on 6.8.1944.

CORNELIUS RYAN

Rank	Private
Regimental Number	WX8734
Classification	Rangetaker
Company	'B' Company
Enlisted	23.10.1940
Discharged	14.2.1946
Date of Birth	23.9.1913
Place of Birth	Victoria Park, Western Australia
Father	John Joseph Ryan
Mother	Sarah Ryan
Religion	Roman Catholic
Pre-War Occupation	Miner and Boiler Attendant

HISTORY

Singapore	Selarang Camp Changi
	Johore Bahru, Adam Park
	Selarang Barracks Changi
POW Number	4/6572
'D' Force Thailand	S Battalion
POW Number	8836
Camps Thailand	Tarsau (contracted malaria so remained behind to work at barge landing)
	Kanu II, Kanu I, Tarsau, Tamajao Wood Camp, Non Pladuk, Chao Puraya River
	(bridge repair), Banderra, Bangkok (go-downs)
Return Details 1945	Thailand-Singapore by aircraft
	Singapore-Fremantle, HMT *Circassia*

ERIC WILLIAM RYAN

Rank	Private
Regimental Number	WX16767
Company	Headquarters Company
Enlisted	29.9.1941
Discharged	8.5.1946
Date of Birth	26.2.1921
Place of Birth	Port Augusta, South Australia
Father	William Joseph Ryan
Mother	Violet Jane Ryan
Religion	Church of England
Pre-War Occupation	Truck Driver

HISTORY

Singapore	Selarang Camp Changi
'A' Force Burma	Green Force, No. 3 Battalion
POW Number	2927
Camps Burma	Khonkan 55km (left leg amputated above the knee 21.10.1943, due to a tropical ulcer)
Camps Thailand	Tamarkan Hospital (25.12.1943)
	Bangkok (medical orderly) Nacompaton
Return Details 1945	Thailand-Singapore by aircraft
	Singapore-Fremantle, HMT *Highland Brigade*

ALBERT ERNEST SAGGERS

Rank	Major
Regimental Number	WX3454
Company	'A' Company Headquarters
Enlisted	21.11.1940
Appointment Terminated	1.2.1946
Date of Birth	29.11.1899
Place of Birth	Parramatta, New South Wales
Father	Ernest Saggers
Mother	Annabella Saggers
Religion	Church of Christ
Pre-War Occupation	Footwear Merchant

HISTORY

Singapore	Selarang Camp Changi
	Serangoon Road Camp
	Sime Road Camp
	Selarang Barracks Changi
POW Number	4127
'H' Force Thailand	'H' Force Group No. 3 (2i/c and i/c of pay and records)
Singapore	Sime Road Camp
	Changi Gaol Camp
	Kranji Hospital Camp Woodlands
	2/14th Australian General Hospital
Return Details 1945	Singapore-Perth, Duke of Gloucester's aircraft *'Endeavour'*

ARTHUR GILBERT SAUNDERS

Rank	Private
Regimental Number	WX9272
Classification	Driver
Company	'D' Company
Enlisted	30.10.1940
Discharged	10.1.1946
Date of Birth	10.9.1919
Place of Birth	Narrogin, Western Australia
Father	Frederick John Saunders
Mother	Lily Saunders
Religion	Church of England
Pre-War Occupation	Truck and Tractor Driver

HISTORY

Singapore	Selarang Camp Changi
	Thomson Road (Caldecot Hill Estate Camp)
	Selarang Barracks Changi (Bootmaker at Changi)
	Levelling Party Changi Aerodrome
	Changi Gaol Camp
	X3 Party
POW Numbers	3/9458 and 1/7604
Return Details 1945	Singapore-Darwin-Sydney, HMT *Arawa*
	Sydney-Melbourne by troop train
	Melbourne-Fremantle, HMT *Strathmore*

HAROLD EDWARD SAW

Rank	Lance Sergeant
Regimental Number	WX9045
Company	'A' Company
Enlisted	25.10.1940
Discharged	5.12.1945
Date of Birth	20.9.1918
Place of Birth	Perth, Western Australia
Father	Harold James Saw
Mother	Annie Saw
Religion	Presbyterian
Pre-War Occupation	Farmer and Truck Driver

HISTORY

Singapore	Selarang Camp Changi
	Johore Bahru, Adam Park
	Sime Road Camp
	Selarang Barracks Changi
POW Number	4/4752
'D' Force Thailand	S Battalion
POW Number	8723
Camps Thailand	Kanu I, Hintok Road Camp, Tamuang, Nikhe (bridge repair), Nakom Nayok, Bangkok
Return Details 1945	Thailand-Singapore by aircraft
	Singapore-Labuan-Morotai-Sydney by aircraft
	Sydney-Melbourne-Perth by troop train

THOMAS KEITH SAWYER

Rank	Private
Regimental Number	WX7256
Company	'C' Company
Enlisted	1.8.1940
Discharged	1.2.1946
Date of Birth	13.8.1909
Place of Birth	Menzies, Western Australia
Father	Thomas Sawyer
Mother	Mary Sawyer
Religion	Roman Catholic
Pre-War Occupation	Millhand

HISTORY

Singapore	Selarang Camp Changi
'A' Force Burma	Green Force, No. 3 Battalion
POW Number	3125
Camps Thailand	Tamarkan, Nakom Nayok, Bangkok
Return Details 1945	Thailand-Singapore by aircraft
	Singapore-Fremantle, HMT *Tamaroa*

MERVYN STEWART SCALA

Rank	Lance Corporal
Regimental Number	WX12202
Company	Headquarters Company
Enlisted	2.5.1941
Discharged	30.5.1946
Date of Birth	27.3.1907
Place of Birth	Maylands, Western Australia
Father	Dominic Scala
Mother	Blanche Scala
Religion	Roman Catholic
Pre-War Occupation	Forestry Worker

HISTORY

Singapore	A. G. H. Roberts Barracks Changi
	Selarang Barracks Changi
	Kranji Hospital Woodlands
	Changi Gaol Camp
POW Number	1/9217
Return Details 1945	Singapore-Darwin-Sydney, HMT *Arawa*
	Sydney-Melbourne by troop train
	Melbourne-Fremantle, HMT *Strathmore*
Additions	Soldier was wounded in action at Ulu Pandan on 12.2.1942. Evacuated to the 2/13th Australian General Hospital at St Patrick's School with a gunshot wound to the left forearm. This caused a compound fracture to both bones. Transferred to the 2/10th Australian General Hospital on 7.3.1942 and transferred again to the No. 2 Convalescent Depot ex-A. G. H. Roberts Barracks Changi on 26.9.1942. Soldier was given a 'D' Medical Classification by the Japanese.

JOHN HENRY SCHURMANN

Rank	Sergeant
Regimental Number	WX5007
Company	'A' Company
Enlisted	23.7.1940
Discharged	11.4.1946
Date of Birth	13.10.1918
Place of Birth	Collie, Western Australia
Father	Henry William Schurmann
Mother	Margaret Isabel Schurmann
Religion	Church of England
Pre-War Occupation	Farmhand

HISTORY

Singapore	Selarang Camp Changi
'A' Force Burma	Green Force, No. 3 Battalion
POW Number	1334
Camps Thailand	Tamarkan, Chungkai, Linson Wood Camp, Kachu Mountain Camp, Bangkok, Nakom Nayok, Bangkok
POW Number (Linson)	12091
Return Details 1945	Thailand-Singapore by aircraft
	Singapore-Fremantle, HMT *Circassia*
Additions	This NCO was a member of the War Graves Party.

AUBREY VINCENT SCHUTS

Rank	Private
Regimental Number	WX8562
Company	'B' Company
Enlisted	18.10.1940
Discharged	15.1.1946
Date of Birth	7.8.1913
Place of Birth	Perth, Western Australia
Father	Joseph Schuts
Mother	Mary Ellen Schuts
Religion	Roman Catholic
Pre-War Occupation	Farmer

HISTORY

Singapore	Selarang Camp Changi
	Johore Bahru, Adam Park
	River Valley Road Camp
	Selarang Barracks Changi
'D' Force Thailand	S Battalion
POW Number	8846
Japan	*Rashin Maru* Party
POW Number	409
Camps Japan	Ohama Camp 9B
Return Details 1945	Wakayama-Okinawa, USS *Consolation*
	Okinawa-Manila, USS *Haskell*
	Manila-Sydney, HMS *Speaker*
	Sydney-Fremantle, HMT *Dominion Monarch*

JAMES LAPPIN SCOTT

Rank	Private
Regimental Number	WX12949
Company	'C' Company
Enlisted	14.5.1941
Discharged	17.12.1945
Date of Birth	22.2.1910
Place of Birth	Bridgetown, Western Australia
Father	Arthur Joseph Scott
Mother	Alice Mary Scott
Religion	Roman Catholic
Pre-War Occupation	Locomotive Driver

HISTORY

Singapore	Selarang Camp Changi
'A' Force Burma	Green Force, No. 3 Battalion
POW Number	2888
Camps Thailand	Tamarkan, Bangkok
Return Details 1945	Thailand-Singapore by aircraft
	Singapore-Fremantle, HMT *Highland Brigade*
Additions	Shell shocked at Ulu Pandan on 12.2.1942 (evacuated).

ROBIN ROY SEMPLE

Rank	Private
Regimental Number	WX7532
Company	'D' Company
Enlisted	6.8.1940
Discharged	14.3.1946
Date of Birth	23.5.1912
Place of Birth	Fremantle, Western Australia
Father	Robert Semple
Mother	Cecelia Semple
Religion	Protestant
Pre-War Occupation	Miner

HISTORY

Singapore	Escaped to Sumatra
Camps Sumatra	Padang, Gloe Gloer Camp (Medan)
Singapore	*Hirukiku Maru* Party
Singapore Camps	River Valley Road Camp
	X4B Party
	W Party
	Changi Gaol Camp
	Tanjong Pagar Camp
Return Details 1945	Singapore-Darwin-Sydney, HMT *Arawa*
	Sydney-Melbourne-Perth by troop train
Additions	Wounded in action on 9.2.1942. Gunshot wounds to both legs and left upper arm.

NIGEL JOHN SHEEDY

Rank	Private
Regimental Number	WX8430
Classification	Driver
Company	Headquarters Company
Enlisted	18.10.1940
Discharged	15.2.1946
Date of Birth	12.4.1910
Place of Birth	Woodville, South Australia
Father	Michael Joseph Sheedy
Mother	Letesia Mary Sheedy
Religion	Roman Catholic
Pre-War Occupation	Barman and Mechanic

HISTORY

Singapore	Selarang Camp Changi
'A' Force Burma	Green Force, No. 3 Battalion
POW Number	3087
Camps Burma	Khonkan 55km Camp (2.7.1943)
Japan	*Awa Maru* Party, Kumi, No. 42
Camps Japan	Fukuoka sub-Camp No. 24, Sendyu
POW Number	13097
Return Details 1945	Nagasaki-Manila
	Manila-Morotai-Darwin-Perth, PBY Catalina aircraft A24-377

ARTHUR ROY SHIER

Rank	Private
Regimental Number	WX18151
Company	'A' Company
Enlisted	18.12.1941
Discharged	29.11.1945
Date of Birth	7.6.1905
Place of Birth	Guildford, Western Australia
Father	John Shier
Mother	Not Known
Religion	Church of England
Pre-War Occupation	Labourer

HISTORY

Singapore	Selarang Camp Changi
	Johore Bahru, Adam Park
	Selarang Barracks Changi (Garden Control Party)
Force	'F' Force Thailand
Camps Thailand	Kanchanaburi (appendix and gall bladder operations)
Singapore	Kranji Hospital Woodlands (20.10.1944-February 1945)
	Changi Gaol Camp, X4B Party, W Party, Tanjong Pagar Camp
Return Details 1945	Singapore-Perth, Duke of Gloucester's aircraft *'Endeavour'*

WILLIAM LINDSAY SHORT

Rank	Private
Regimental Number	WX8693
Classification	Cook
Company	'A' Company
Enlisted	23.10.1940
Discharged	15.1.1946
Date of Birth	22.5.1904
Place of Birth	Bath, England
Father	James Lindsay Short
Mother	Emily Gertrude Short
Religion	Church of England
Pre-War Occupation	Miner

HISTORY

Singapore	Selarang Camp and Barracks Changi
	Changi Gaol Camp
POW Number	1/9276
Return Details 1945	Singapore-Darwin-Sydney, HMT *Arawa*
	Sydney-Melbourne by troop train
	Melbourne-Fremantle, HMT *Strathmore*
Additions	Wounded in action at West Bukit Timah on 7.2.1942. Admitted to Field Ambulance with shrapnel wounds to the buttocks, legs and arms. Transferred to the 2/13th Australian General Hospital on 17.2.1942 and to the 2/10th Australian General Hospital on 7.3.1942. Admitted to A. G. H. Roberts Barracks Changi on 27.5.1942 with an abscess to the right leg. Discharged to unit on 28.5.1942. Transferred to the No. 2 Convalescent Depot on 28.9.1942. Soldier suffered a permanent disability to his right leg as a result of his wounds.

RONALD HENRY SIMKIN

Rank	Private
Regimental Number	WX8141
Classification	Driver
Company	'C' Company Headquarters
Enlisted	16.8.1940
Discharged	17.6.1946
Date of Birth	22.9.1917
Place of Birth	Geraldton, Western Australia
Father	Herbert Simkin
Mother	Annie Mary Simkin
Religion	Church of England
Pre-War Occupation	Farmer and Mechanic

HISTORY

Singapore	Selarang Camp Changi
'A' Force Burma	Green Force, No. 3 Battalion
POW Number	2922
Camps Thailand	Tamkarkan, Chungkai, Bangkok, Nacompaton
Return Details 1945	Thailand-Singapore by aircraft
	Singapore-Fremantle, HMT *Circassia*
Additions	Soldier had a toe on his left foot amputated in 1944.

NORMAN EDWARD SIMMONDS

Rank	Private
Regimental Number	WX7576
Company	'C' Company
Enlisted	6.8.1940
Discharged	20.2.1946
Date of Birth	12.7.1915
Place of Birth	Perth, Western Australia
Father	Not Known
Mother	Bertha Florence Simmonds
Religion	Church of England
Pre-War Occupation	Market Gardener

HISTORY

Java	'Blackforce'
'D' Force Thailand	Java Party No. 6, P Battalion
Camps Thailand	Nakom Nayok
Return Details 1945	Thailand-Singapore by aircraft
	Singapore-Fremantle, HMT *Circassia*

ROY ALBERT SIMMONDS

Rank	Private
Regimental Number	WX16952
Company	'B' Company
Enlisted	8.10.1941
Discharged	14.3.1946
Date of Birth	23.7.1919
Place of Birth	Collie, Western Australia
Father	Josiah Edward Simmonds
Mother	Hilda Maud Simmonds
Religion	Church of England
Pre-War Occupation	Miner

HISTORY

Singapore	Selarang Camp Changi
	Thomson Road (Caldecot Hill Estate Camp)
	River Valley Road Camp
	Selarang Barracks Changi
'D' Force Thailand	S Battalion
POW Number	8847
Camps Thailand	Kanu II, Kanu I, Tarsau ,Chungkai, Tamuang
Return Details 1945	Thailand-Singapore by aircraft
	Singapore-Fremantle, HMT *Circassia*

ALFRED SING

Rank	Private
Regimental Number	WX16424
Company	'A' Company
Enlisted	10.9.1941
Discharged	21.5.1945
Date of Birth	8.10.1919
Place of Birth	Northam, Western Australia
Father	Not Known
Mother	Emily Jane Sing
Religion	Church of England
Pre-War Occupation	Rabbit Trapper

HISTORY

Java	'Blackforce', attached to the 2/2nd Pioneer Battalion
	(two weeks guard duties and carting from wharves to Tjililitan Aerodrome)
Camps Java	Bicycle Camp Batavia
'A' Force Burma	Java Party No. 4, Williams Force
POW Number	4660
Camps Burma	Beke Taung 40km, Reptu 30km Camps
Camps Thailand	131km, 133km, Tamarkan, Kanchanaburi
Japan	*Rakuyo Maru* Party, Kumi No. 38 (rescued by USS *Sealion II*)
Return Details 1944	Saipan-Guadalcanal-Brisbane-Perth 1.11.1944

JOHN BARTLEY SKELTON

Rank	Private
Regimental Number	WX6681
Company	'B' Company
Enlisted	19.7.1940
Discharged	9.1.1946
Date of Birth	10.4.1915
Place of Birth	Fremantle, Western Australia
Father	Philip Skelton
Mother	Emma Wilhelmina Skelton
Religion	Church of England
Pre-War Occupation	Clerk

HISTORY

Singapore	Selarang Camp Changi
	Johore Bahru, Adam Park
	Selarang Barracks Changi
POW Number	4/6614
'D' Force Thailand	S Battalion
POW Number	8848
Camps Thailand	Chungkai
Return Details 1945	Thailand-Singapore by aircraft
	Singapore-Fremantle, HMT *Highland Brigade*

ALEXANDER JULIAN SMITH

Rank	Private
Regimental Number	WX6441
Company	'D' Company
Enlisted	16.7.1940
Discharged	9.1.1946
Date of Birth	6.4.1916
Place of Birth	Fremantle, Western Australia
Father	Julian Alfred Smith
Mother	Ellen Smith
Religion	Roman Catholic
Pre-War Occupation	Butcher

HISTORY

Singapore	Selarang Camp Changi
	Johore Bahru, Adam Park
	Selarang Barracks Changi
POW Number	4/6634
'D' Force Thailand	V Battalion
Camps Thailand	Non Pladuk (evacuated to hospital on 23.9.1943)
French Indo-China	*Both* Party
Return Details 1945	Saigon-Bangkok-Singapore by aircraft,
	Singapore-Townsville-Brisbane by aircraft
	Brisbane-Sydney-Melbourne-Perth by troop train

HAROLD MERVYN SMITH

Rank	Private
Regimental Number	WX17448
Company	'E' Company, Special Reserve Battalion
Enlisted	27.10.1941
Discharged	11.1.1946
Date of Birth	16.2.1922
Place of Birth	Bunbury, Western Australia
Father	Alexander Smith
Mother	Christina Miller Smith
Religion	Church of England
Pre-War Occupation	Labourer

HISTORY

Singapore	Escaped to Sumatra
Camps Sumatra	Padang, Gloe Gloer Camp
Singapore	*Hirukiku Maru* Party
Camps Singapore	Changi Gaol Camp (21.7.1944)
Return Details 1945	Singapore-Darwin-Sydney, HMT *Arawa*
	Sydney-Melbourne by troop train
	Melbourne-Fremantle, HMT *Strathmore*
Additions	Soldier was listed as missing following the ambush at South-West Bukit Timah. He later suffered a burst appendix and this may be the reason he was evacuated to Changi and also the reason why he did not return to Sumatra.

JACK EDWARD SMITH

Rank	Private
Regimental Number	WX12252
Company	'D' Company
Enlisted	2.5.1941
Discharged	25.3.1946
Date of Birth	17.8.1919
Place of Birth	England
Father	John Henry Smith
Mother	Alice Smith
Religion	Church of England
Pre-War Occupation	Farmhand

HISTORY

Singapore	Selarang Camp Changi
'A' Force Burma	Green Force, No. 3 Battalion
POW Number	2930
Camps Thailand	Tamarkan
Return Details 1945	Thailand-Singapore by aircraft
	Singapore-Fremantle, HMT *Highland Brigade*

JOHN STEWART SMITH

Rank	Private
Regimental Number	WX6841
Company	'C' Company
Enlisted	20.7.1940
Discharged	24.1.1946
Date of Birth	17.8.1918
Place of Birth	Bunbury, Western Australia
Father	Alexander Smith
Mother	Christina Miller Smith
Religion	Church of England
Pre-War Occupation	Dairyhand

HISTORY

Singapore	Selarang Camp Changi
	Johore Bahru, Adam Park
	Selarang Barracks Changi
POW Number	4/6635
'D' Force Thailand	S Battalion
POW Number	8844
Japan	*Rashin Maru* Party
Camps Japan	Yamane
	Niihama (ore trucks)
Return Details 1945	Wakayama-Okinawa, USS *Sanctuary*
	Okinawa-Manila, USS *Bingham*
	Manila-Morotai-Darwin, PBY Catalina aircraft A24-377
	Darwin-Perth, B24 Liberator aircraft A72-379

JAMES STANLEY SMITH

Rank	Lance Corporal (Promoted on 1.3.1942)
Regimental Number	WX7893
Company	'C' Company
Enlisted	13.8.1940
Discharged	4.3.1946
Date of Birth	17.4.1906
Place of Birth	Manchester, England
Father	Joseph Smith
Mother	Not Known
Religion	Church of England
Pre-War Occupation	Timber Worker

HISTORY

Java	'Blackforce'
'A' Force Burma	Java Party No. 4, Williams Force
POW Number	3932
Camps Burma	Khonkan 55km Camp
Camps Thailand	Tamarkan
Return Details 1945	Thailand-Singapore by aircraft
	Singapore-Fremantle, HMT *Moreton Bay*

JOHN WILFRED SMITH

Rank	Lance Corporal
Regimental Number	WX7784
Classification	Section Orderly
Company	'B' Company
Enlisted	10.8.1940
Discharged	20.2.1946
Date of Birth	4.3.1907
Place of Birth	Bishop Auckland, England
Father	Not Known
Mother	Elizabeth Jane Smith
Religion	Church of England
Pre-War Occupation	Miner

HISTORY

Singapore	Selarang Camp and Barracks Changi
POW Number	4/4582
'D' Force Thailand	S Battalion
POW Number	8744
Camps Thailand	Kanu II, Chungkai, Kachu Mountain Camp, Petchaburi, Chumphon, Nakom Chassi, Bangkok
Return Details 1945	Thailand-Singapore by aircraft Singapore-Fremantle, HMT *Highland Brigade*

ROY SMITH
a.k.a. Lionel Charles Evans

Rank	Private
Regimental Number	WX13552
Company	'D' Company
Enlisted	24.5.1941
Discharged	10.1.1946
Date of Birth	28.3.1915
Place of Birth	Churchstanton, Taunton, Somerset, England
Father	John Evans
Mother	Annie Evans
Stepfather	Charles Edward Smith
Religion	Church of England
Pre-War Occupation	Fisherman

HISTORY

Singapore	Selarang Camp Changi Johore Bahru, Adam Park Selarang Barracks Changi
'D' Force Thailand	S Battalion
POW Number	8842
Camps Thailand	Tarsau, Kanu II, Kanu I, Tarsau, Tamarkan, Chungkai, Nakom Chassi, Chumphon, Petchaburi, Kachu Mountain Camp
Return Details 1945	Thailand-Singapore by aircraft Singapore-Fremantle, HMT *Highland Brigade*
Additions	Legally adopted by Charles Edward Smith. Shell shocked at Ulu Pandan on 12.2.1942. Evacuated to St Joseph's Hospital on 13.2.1942. Discharged to unit on 20.2.1942.

WALTER JOHN SMITH

Rank	Private
Regimental Number	WX8506
Classification	Driver
Company	88 Light Aid Detachment
Enlisted	18.10.1940
Discharged	8.2.1946
Date of Birth	26.1.1917
Place of Birth	Beverley, Western Australia
Father	W.R. Smith
Mother	M.M. Smith
Religion	Church of England
Pre-War Occupation	Electrician

HISTORY

Java	'Blackforce'
'D' Force Thailand	Java Party No. 6, O Battalion
POW Number	6922
Camps Thailand	Tamuang
Return Details 1945	Thailand-Singapore by aircraft
	Singapore-Melbourne, HMT *Otranto*
	Melbourne (R.A.A.F. Laverton)-Perth by B24 Liberator aircraft

AVON REAH SMITH-RYAN

Rank	Captain
Regimental Number	WX3453
Company	'B' Company Headquarters
Enlisted	30.5.1940
Appointment Terminated	18.1.1946
Date of Birth	3.5.1908
Place of Birth	Northam, Western Australia
Father	Thomas Smith-Ryan
Mother	Hilda Mary Smith-Ryan
Religion	Methodist
Pre-War Occupation	Bank Officer

HISTORY

Singapore	Selarang Camp Changi
	Adam Park
	Selarang Barracks Changi
	Levelling Party Changi Aerodrome
	Changi Gaol Camp
POW Number	4/4128
Return Details 1945	Singapore-Darwin-Sydney, HMT *Arawa*
	Sydney-Melbourne by troop train
	Melbourne-Fremantle, HMT *Strathmore*

CLIFFORD JOSEPH SPACKMAN

Rank	Corporal
Regimental Number	WX7715
Company	'D' Company
Enlisted	10.8.1940
Discharged	13.2.1946
Date of Birth	27.2.1917
Place of Birth	Pingelly, Western Australia
Father	Joseph Spackman
Mother	Alice Mary Spackman
Religion	Roman Catholic
Pre-War Occupation	Dairyhand

HISTORY

Singapore	Selarang Camp Changi
	Johore Bahru, Adam Park
	Selarang Barracks Changi
POW Number	3/6557
'D' Force Thailand	V Battalion
Camps Thailand	Nacompaton, Ubon, Bangkok
Return Details 1945	Thailand-Singapore by aircraft
	Singapore-Fremantle, HMT *Highland Brigade*
Additions	Wounded in action at 0300 hours on 9.2.1942. Admitted to the 2/13th Australian General Hospital on 10.2.1942 with shrapnel wounds to the left thigh and right leg. Discharged to unit on 22.2.1942. Admitted to the A. G. H. Roberts Barracks Changi on 24.4.1942 with an infected shell wound to the right leg. Transferred to the No. 2 Convalescent Depot on 25.6.1942 and discharged to unit on 27.9.1942.

CLIFFORD DUDLEY SQUANCE

Rank	Private
Regimental Number	WX16885
Company	'E' Company, Special Reserve Battalion
Enlisted	6.10.1941
Discharged	2.7.1946
Date of Birth	23.7.1920
Place of Birth	Round Hill, Moora, Western Australia
Father	William Francis Squance
Mother	Elsie Olive Squance
Religion	Congregational
Pre-War Occupation	Miner

HISTORY

Singapore	Escaped to Sumatra
Camps Sumatra	Padang, Gloe Gloer Camp (Medan)
Singapore	*Harukiku Maru* Party
Camps Singapore	River Valley Road Camp
Sumatra	Pakan Baroe-Moearo Railway
Return Details 1945	Sumatra-Singapore by aircraft (admitted to the 2/14th Australian General Hospital)
	Singapore-Perth, Duke of Gloucester's aircraft *'Endeavour'*
Additions	Wounded in the left shoulder. Listed as missing from Bald Hill, South-West Bukit Timah from 11.2.1942.

JOSEPH FREDERICK STARCEVICH

Rank	Private
Regimental Number	WX8758
Company	'B' Company
Enlisted	23.10.1940
Discharged	13.2.1946
Date of Birth	20.8.1915
Place of Birth	Laverton, Western Australia
Father	Joseph Starcevich
Mother	Gertrude May Starcevich
Religion	Roman Catholic
Pre-War Occupation	Farmer and Miner

HISTORY

Singapore	Selarang Camp Changi
	Johore Bahru, Adam Park
	Selarang Barracks Changi
POW Number	4/6657
'D' Force Thailand	Captain Fred Harris Party
Camps Thailand	Kanchanaburi, Tarsau, Hintok, Kinsaiyok, Hindato, Konkoita, Tarsau, Non Pladuk
Japan	*Aramis* Party
POW Number	603
Camps Japan	Fukuoka sub-Camp No. 17, Omuta
Return Details 1945	Nagasaki-Okinawa, USS *Cape Gloucester*
	Okinawa-Manila, USS *Bingham*
	Manila-Morotai-Darwin, PBY Catalina aircraft A24-379
	Darwin-Perth, B24 Liberator aircraft A24-379
Additions	This soldier's leg was injured in a rock fall below ground on 5.1.1945. The leg in question was amputated over fifty years later.

HAROLD WILLIAM STEELE

Rank	Private
Regimental Number	WX9419
Company	'C' Company Headquarters
Enlisted	4.12.1940
Discharged	25.1.1946
Date of Birth	1.12.1917
Place of Birth	Glen Forrest, Western Australia
Father	Harold William Steele
Mother	Florence Steele
Religion	Church of England
Pre-War Occupation	Forestry Worker

HISTORY

Java	'Blackforce'
'A' Force Burma	Java Party No. 4, Williams Force
POW Number	43??
Camps Thailand	Kanchanaburi, Tamarkan, Pratchinburi, Linson Wood Camp, Petchaburi, Kachu Mountain Camp
Return Details 1945	Thailand-Singapore by aircraft
	Singapore-Fremantle, HMT *Highland Brigade*

DOUGLAS FRANCIS STERRETT

Rank	Corporal
Regimental Number	WX8596
Classification	Rangetaker
Company	'A' Company
Enlisted	18.10.1940
Discharged	13.2.1946
Date of Birth	23.10.1913
Place of Birth	Maylands, Western Australia
Father	William Edward Sterrett
Mother	Dorothy Sterrett
Religion	Church of England
Pre-War Occupation	Clerk and Salesman

HISTORY

Singapore	Selarang Camp Changi
	Adam Park, River Valley Road Camp
	Selarang Barracks Changi
POW Number	1/9396
Force	'F' Force Thailand
Singapore	Levelling Party Changi Aerodrome
	Changi Gaol Camp
	P Party
	Changi Gaol Camp
Return Details 1945	Singapore-Darwin-Sydney, HMT *Arawa*
	Sydney-Melbourne by troop train
	Melbourne-Perth, HMT *Strathmore*

ALFRED STEVENS

Rank	Sergeant
Regimental Number	WX227
Company	'A' Company
Enlisted	11.12.1940
Discharged	8.12.1946
Date of Birth	29.5.1913
Place of Birth	Perth, Western Australia
Father	Walter George Stevens
Mother	Annie May Stevens
Religion	Methodist
Pre-War Occupation	Engine Driver (Union Flour Mills)

HISTORY

Singapore	Selarang Camp Changi
	Adam Park
Force	'B' Force Borneo
Kuching-Sarawak	Arrested and sentenced by the Kempeitai
Singapore	H.M. Prison Outram Road
	Changi Gaol Camp
Return Details 1945	Singapore-Darwin-Sydney, HMT *Arawa*
	Sydney-Melbourne by troop train
	Melbourne-Fremantle, HMT *Strathmore*

REGINALD HARRY STEWART

Rank	Lance Corporal
Regimental Number	WX7324
Classification	Cook
Company	'D' Company Headquarters
Enlisted	6.8.1940
Discharged	13.3.1946
Date of Birth	30.1.1913
Place of Birth	London, England
Father	Donald Stewart
Mother	Florence Marie Stewart
Religion	Church of England
Pre-War Occupation	Pastry Cook

HISTORY

Singapore	Selarang Camp Changi
'A' Force Burma	Green Force, No. 3 Battalion
POW Number	2900
Camps Burma	Reptu 30km Camp
Camps Thailand	Tamarkan, Nakom Nayok, Bangkok
Return Details 1945	Thailand-Singapore by aircraft
	Singapore-Fremantle, HMT *Moreton Bay*
Additions	Wounded in action at Buona Vista on 15.2.1942. Admitted to the 2/9th Field Ambulance with a shrapnel wound to the right thigh. Discharged to unit on 27.4.1942.

WALTER JOSEPH STONE

Rank	Private
Regimental Number	WX8041
Company	'A' Company
Enlisted	16.8.1940
Discharged	21.2.1946
Date of Birth	5.3.1912
Place of Birth	Geraldton, Western Australia
Father	Patrick James Stone
Mother	Not Known
Religion	Roman Catholic
Pre-War Occupation	Labourer

HISTORY

Singapore	Selarang Camp Changi
	Selarang Barracks Changi
	X10 Party
	Changi Gaol Camp
POW Number	4/6679
Return Details 1945	Singapore-Darwin-Sydney, HMT *Arawa*
	Sydney-Melbourne by troop train
	Melbourne-Fremantle, HMT *Strathmore*

NORMAN LESLIE STRIBLEY

Rank	Private
Regimental Number	WX9058
Company	'D' Company
Enlisted	25.10.1940
Discharged	21.1.1946
Date of Birth	7.2.1913
Place of Birth	Subiaco, Western Australia
Father	Thomas Charles Stribley
Mother	Emily Josephine Stribley
Religion	Church of England
Pre-War Occupation	Labourer

HISTORY

Singapore	Selarang Camp and Barracks Changi
POW Number	3/9683
'D' Force Thailand	S Battalion
POW Number	8843
Camps Thailand	Kanu II, Chungkai, Nacompaton, Bangkok
Return Details 1945	Thailand-Singapore by aircraft
	Singapore-Fremantle, HMT *Circassia*
Additions	Shell shocked at Ulu Pandan on 12.2.1942. Admitted to the 2/13th Australian General Hospital and discharged to unit on 20.2.1942.

REGINALD HAROLD STRIBLING

Rank	Private
Regimental Number	WX9827
Classification	Driver
Company	'C' Company
Enlisted	6.12.1940
Discharged	11.1.1946
Date of Birth	18.1.1919
Place of Birth	Victoria Park, Western Australia
Father	Cecil Sydney Stribling
Mother	Elsie Isabel Stribling
Religion	Church of England
Pre-War Occupation	Storeman

HISTORY

Java	'Blackforce'
'A' Force Burma	Java Party No. 4, Williams Force
POW Number	4651
Camps Thailand	131km, 133km, Kanchanaburi, Tamarkan, Petchaburi, Nakom Chassi, Bangkok
Return Details 1945	Thailand-Singapore by aircraft
	Singapore-Fremantle, HMT *Tamaroa*

WILLIAM STRUTHERS

Rank	Private
Regimental Number	WX8738
Classification	Driver
Company	Headquarters Company
Enlisted	23.10.1940
Discharged	7.2.1946
Date of Birth	20.2.1907
Place of Birth	Leslie, Scotland
Father	William Struthers
Mother	Annie Struthers
Religion	Presbyterian
Pre-War Occupation	Farmhand and Miner

HISTORY

Singapore	Selarang Camp Changi
	Johore Bahru, Adam Park
	Selarang Barracks Changi
'D' Force Thailand	V Battalion
Camps Thailand	Non Pladuk, Ubon
Return Details 1945	Thailand-Singapore by aircraft
	Singapore-Fremantle, HMT *Highland Brigade*

PERCY ALFRED STURTRIDGE

Rank	Sergeant
Regimental Number	WX10794
Company	'C' Company
Enlisted	15.1.1941
Discharged	7.12.1945
Date of Birth	26.5.1918
Place of Birth	Dongara, Western Australia
Father	William Sturtridge
Mother	Eliza Marian Sturtridge
Religion	Church of England
Pre-War Occupation	Carpenter

HISTORY

Singapore	Selarang Camp Changi
	Thomson Road (Caldecot Hill Estate Camp)
	Mt Pleasant Camp
	Selarang Barracks Changi
POW Number	1/9423
'D' Force Thailand	S Battalion
POW Number	8722
Camps Thailand	Tarsau, Kanu II, Kanu I, Hintok Road Camp, Tarsau, Non Pladuk, Nacompaton
	Prachuab Kirikhan-Mergui Escape Road, Petchaburi
Return Details 1945	Thailand-Singapore by aircraft
	Singapore-Fremantle, HMT *Highland Brigade*

JOSEPH SUMNER

Rank	Private
Regimental Number	WX9134
Classification	Cook
Company	'C' Company
Enlisted	30.10.1940
Discharged	23.7.1946
Date of Birth	2.12.1900
Place of Birth	Bolton, England
Father	James Sumner
Mother	Not Known
Religion	Agnostic
Pre-War Occupation	Shearer

HISTORY

Singapore	Selarang Camp Changi
	Johore Bahru, Adam Park
	Selarang Barracks Changi
POW Number	4/6689
'D' Force Thailand	S Battalion
POW Number	8845
Camps Thailand	Kanu II, Hintok Road Camp, Nacompaton
Return Details 1945	Thailand-Singapore by aircraft (admitted to the 2/14th Australian General Hospital)
	Singapore-Fremantle, H.M. Hospital Ship *Karoa*

WILLIAM THOMAS SWANN

Rank	Private
Regimental Number	WX17907
Company	'E' Company, Special Reserve Battalion
Enlisted	7.12.1941
Discharged	13.3.1946
Date of Birth	16.8.1920
Place of Birth	London, England
Father	Robert Walter Swann
Mother	Annie Swann
Religion	Church of England
Pre-War Occupation	Tractor Driver

HISTORY

Singapore	Selarang Camp and Barracks Changi
	X6 Party
	Changi Gaol Camp
POW Number	3/9500
Return Details 1945	Singapore-Darwin-Sydney, HMT *Arawa*
	Sydney-Melbourne by troop train
	Melbourne-Fremantle, HMT *Strathmore*

JOSEPH SWARTZ

Rank	Private
Regimental Number	WX4924
Classification	Driver
Company	'C' Company Headquarters
Enlisted	23.7.1940
Discharged	12.1.1946
Date of Birth	5.3.1912
Place of Birth	North Perth, Western Australia
Father	Maurice Swartz
Mother	Fanny Swartz
Religion	Hebrew
Pre-War Occupation	Truck Driver

HISTORY

Singapore	Selarang Camp Changi
	Johore Bahru, Adam Park
	Selarang Barracks Changi
POW Number	4/6695
'D' Force Thailand	V Battalion
Camps Thailand	Hindaine, Chungkai, Non Pladuk
Japan	*Aramis* Party
Camps Japan	Fukuoka sub-Camp No. 17, Omuta
POW Number	526
	Fukuoka sub-Camp No. 1
POW Number	421
	Moji Camp No. 4
Return Details 1945	Nagasaki-Okinawa-Manila by aircraft
	Manila-Sydney, HMS *Formidable*
	Sydney-Melbourne-Perth by troop train

JOHN CECIL SWIFT

Rank	Sergeant
Regimental Number	WX12378
Classification	Fitter
Attached 2/4th	Australian Army Ordnance Corps
Enlisted	3.5.1941
Discharged	15.4.1946
Date of Birth	23.4.1916
Place of Birth	Perth, Western Australia
Father	Cecil Swift
Mother	Hilda Rachel Urquhart Swift
Religion	Methodist
Pre-War Occupation	Motor Mechanic

HISTORY

Singapore	Selarang Camp Changi
	Johore Bahru, Adam Park
	Thomson Road (Caldecot Hill Estate Camp)
	Selarang Barracks Changi
POW Number	4/4596
'D' Force Thailand	V Battalion
Camps Thailand	Kinsaiyok, Hindaine, Hindato, Nacompaton, Bangkok (go-downs), Japanese Transport Camp with Wally Bow and Ron Manthorpe
Return Details 1945	Bangkok-Rangoon by aircraft
	Rangoon-Singapore, HMT *Highland Brigade*
	Singapore-Fremantle, HMT *Moreton Bay*

GEORGE DOUGLAS TANNER

Rank	Private
Regimental Number	WX16324
Company	Headquarters Company
Enlisted	3.9.1941
Discharged	4.3.1946
Date of Birth	12.1.1922
Place of Birth	London, England
Father	Not Known
Mother	Not Known
Religion	Church of England
Pre-War Occupation	Farmhand

Singapore	Selarang Camp Changi
	Johore Bahru, Adam Park
	Selarang Barracks Changi
POW Number	4/6700
'D' Force Thailand	V Battalion
Camps Thailand	Brankassi (only camp on V Battalion), Non Pladuk
Japan	*Aramis* Party
Camps Japan	Fukuoka sub-Camp No. 17, Omuta
POW Number	653
Return Details 1945	Nagasaki-Manila, U.S Navy Ship
	Manila-Morotai-Darwin, PBY Catalina aircraft A24-354 (admitted to hospital with lung problems).
	Darwin-Perth, B24 Liberator aircraft, transferred to 110(P)MH
Additions	Kingsley Fairbridge Farm Schoolboy.

ALBERT LESLIE TAPPER

Rank	Private
Regimental Number	WX9157
Company	'D' Company
Enlisted	30.10.1940
Discharged	17.4.1946
Date of Birth	11.12.1917
Place of Birth	Perth, Western Australia
Father	Albert Leslie Tapper
Mother	Mary Margaret Bane Tapper
Religion	Church of England
Pre-War Occupation	Grocer and Farm Contractor

HISTORY

Singapore	Selarang Camp Changi
'A' Force Burma	Green Force, No. 3 Battalion
POW Number	1523
Camps Burma	Khonkan 55km Hospital Camp (medical orderly)
Camps Thailand	Tamarkan, Chungkai, Nacompaton, Rin Tin, Nacompaton, Bangkok
Return Details 1945	Thailand-Singapore by aircraft
	Singapore-Perth, Duke of Gloucester's aircraft *'Endeavour'*

EDWARD GEORGE TAYLOR

Rank	Private
Regimental Number	WX8180
Company	'D' Company
Enlisted	16.8.1940
Discharged	3.9.1948
Date of Birth	9.8.1919
Place of Birth	Narrogin, Western Australia
Father	George Cuthbert Taylor
Mother	Elsa Marjorie Taylor
Religion	Baptist
Pre-War Occupation	Stationhand

HISTORY

Singapore	Selarang Camp Changi
	Selarang Barracks Changi (Forest Party and Coconut Party)
	Changi Gaol Camp
POW Number	1/9458
Return Details 1945	Singapore-Darwin-Sydney, HMT *Arawa*
	Sydney-Melbourne by troop train
	Melbourne-Fremantle, HMT *Strathmore*

GEORGE TAYLOR

Rank	Private
Regimental Number	WX8448
Company	'C' Company
Enlisted	18.10.1940
Discharged	26.2.1946
Date of Birth	6.12.1920
Place of Birth	Hamilton, Scotland
Father	Robert Taylor
Mother	Isobel Taylor
Religion	Roman Catholic
Pre-War Occupation	Clerk at the Bunbury Courthouse

HISTORY

Singapore
Sumatra
Ceylon
Australia
Bougainville

Listed as missing in action, believed killed at Sungei Jurong. It was later discovered that soldier had escaped to Sumatra and had been picked up by the HMAS *Hobart* at Padang on the west coast of Sumatra and taken to Ceylon. On arrival at Columbo on 9.3.1942 he was admitted to the 2/12th Australian General Hospital. On 13.3.1942. he boarded the *Stirling Castle* and disembarked at Melbourne on 6.4.1942. From Melbourne to Fremantle he sailed onboard the *Egra*, disembarking on 13.4.1942. On his return to Australia he was Taken on Strength with the reformed 2/3rd Machine Gun Battalion on 1.7.1942. Soldier served on Bougainville with the 58th Australian Corps Field Park Company.

JOHN TAYLOR

Rank	Private
Regimental Number	WX14733
Classification	Blacksmith
Company	'C' Company
Enlisted	2.7.1941
Discharged	18.12.1945
Date of Birth	28.6.1902
Place of Birth	Bellevue, Western Australia
Father	Charles Albert Taylor
Mother	Mary Taylor
Religion	Church of England
Pre-War Occupation	Storeman

HISTORY

Singapore	Selarang Camp Changi
	Johore Bahru, Adam Park
	Sime Road Camp
	Selarang Barracks Changi
	Changi Gaol Camp
POW Number	1/13071
Return Details 1945	Singapore-Darwin-Sydney, HMT *Arawa*
	Sydney-Melbourne by troop train
	Melbourne-Fremantle, HMT *Strathmore*

JOHN ALEXANDER TAYLOR

Rank	Private
Regimental Number	WX4986
Classification	Driver
Company	'B' Company Headquarters
Enlisted	23.7.1940
Discharged	30.11.1945
Date of Birth	3.8.1914
Place of Birth	Greenbushes, Western Australia
Father	George Taylor
Mother	Florence Victoria Pearl Taylor
Religion	Church of England
Pre-War Occupation	Butcher

HISTORY

Singapore	Selarang Camp Changi
Force	Japan 'B' Party Korea
Camps Korea	Keijo (blast furnace 25.9.1942-13.9.1943)
POW Number	336
	Konan (warehouse 14.9.1943-21.9.1945)
POW Number	520
Return Details 1945	Konan-Jinsen by train, USS *Mercy II* (hospital ship)
	Jinsen-Manilla, HMS *Colossus*
	Manila-Morotai-Darwin, PBY Catalina aircraft A24-377
	Darwin-Perth by aircraft

THOMAS ERIC TEASDALE

Rank	Corporal (Promoted on 24.1.1942)
Regimental Number	WX10865
Company	'B' Company
Enlisted	21.4.1941
Discharged	11.3.1946
Date of Birth	4.9.1919
Place of Birth	Northam, Western Australia
Father	Herbert William Teasdale
Mother	Mary Elizabeth Teasdale
Religion	Church of England
Pre-War Occupation	Farmer

HISTORY

Singapore	Selarang Camp and Barracks Changi
POW Number	4/4599
'D' Force Thailand	S Battalion
POW Number	8736
Camps Thailand	Nacomapton, Bangkok
Return Details 1945	Thailand-Singapore by aircraft (admitted to the 2/14th Australian General Hospital) Singapore-Fremantle, 2/1st H.M. Australian Hospital Ship *Manunda*

FRANK DAWSON THAXTER

Rank	Private
Regimental Number	WX7248
Classification	Fitter
Attached 2/4th	Australian Army Ordnance Corps
Enlisted	1.8.1940
Discharged	15.3.1946
Date of Birth	12.9.1918
Place of Birth	Ravensthorpe, Western Australia
Father	Ralph Arthur Thaxter
Mother	Barbara Elsie Thaxter
Religion	Methodist
Pre-War Occupation	Miner

HISTORY

Singapore	Selarang Camp Changi
	Johore Bahru, Adam Park
	A. G. H. Roberts Barracks Changi
	Selarang Barracks Changi
POW Number	4/15469
'D' Force Thailand	V Battalion
POW Number	2298
Camps Thailand	Kinsaiyok, (evacuated to Chungkai), Non Pladuk, Tamajao Wood Camp, Tamarkan, Nacompaton, Prachuab Kirikhan-Mergui Escape Road, Petchaburi
Return Details 1945	Thailand-Singapore by aircraft
	Singapore-Kuching-Labuan-Morotai-Maruka-Biak-Townsville-Brisbane by aircraft
	Brisbane-Perth by troop train.

ARCHIBALD WILLIAM THOMAS

Rank	Captain
Regimental Number	WX3424
Company	'A' Company Headquarters
Enlisted	21.11.1940
Appointment Terminated	11.12.1945
Date of Birth	8.8.1904
Place of Birth	Fremantle, Western Australia
Father	Horace Thomas
Mother	Elizabeth Thomas
Religion	Presbyterian
Pre-War Occupation	Bank Officer

HISTORY

Singapore	Selarang Camp Changi
'A' Force Burma	Green Force, No. 3 Battalion
POW Number	1287
Camps Burma	Reptu 30km Camp
Camps Thailand	Tamarkan, Chungkai, Bangkok, Nacompaton, Bangkok
Return Details 1945	Bangkok-Rangoon by aircraft
	Rangoon-Singapore, HMT *Highland Brigade*
	Singapore-Darwin-Perth by aircraft
Additions	This officer was appointed as Commanding Officer of 'A' Company on Major Saggers taking command of the Special Reserve Battalion.

WILLIAM LLEWELLYN THOMAS

Rank	Private
Regimental Number	WX7480
Company	'D' Company
Enlisted	6.8.1940
Discharged	14.5.1946
Date of Birth	4.11.1917
Place of Birth	Jardee, Western Australia
Father	Arthur Compton Thomas
Mother	Helena May Thomas
Religion	Church of England
Pre-War Occupation	Labourer

HISTORY

Singapore	Selarang Camp and Barracks Changi
'D' Force Thailand	S Battalion
POW Number	8851
Camps Thailand	Nacompaton
Return Details 1945	Thailand-Singapore by aircraft
	Singapore-Fremantle, HMT *Circassia*
Additions	Shell shocked at Hill 200, Ulu Pandan on 12.2.1942. Soldier was evacuated with minor shrapnel wounds to both legs on 13.2.1942.

NORMAN HARDING EDWARD THOMPSON

Rank	Lance Corporal
Regimental Number	WX10927
Company	'A' Company
Enlisted	18.2.1941
Discharged	11.12.1945
Date of Birth	28.5.1909
Place of Birth	Subiaco, Western Australia
Father	Edward Arthur Thompson
Mother	Winifred Thompson
Religion	Roman Catholic
Pre-War Occupation	Hairdresser

HISTORY

Singapore	Selarang Camp Changi
	Johore Bahru, Adam Park
	Selarang Barracks Changi
'D' Force Thailand	S Battalion
POW Number	8745
Japan	*Rashin Maru* Party
POW Number	1557
Camps Japan	Yamane
	Niihama
Return Details 1945	Wakayama-Okinawa, USS *Gloucester*
	Okinawa-Manila, USS *Bingham*
	Manila-Morotai-Darwin, PBY Catalina aircraft A24-355
	Darwin-Perth, B24 Liberator aircraft A72-379

ERIC GERRARD THOMSON

Rank	Private
Regimental Number	WX10117
Classification	Rangetaker
Company	'B' Company
Enlisted	13.12.1940
Discharged	25.1.1946
Date of Birth	27.6.1920
Place of Birth	Arbroath, Scotland
Father	William Thomson
Mother	Elizabeth Thomson
Religion	Presbyterian
Pre-War Occupation	Clerk and Storeman

HISTORY

Singapore	Selarang Camp and Barracks Changi
POW Number	4/6719
'D' Force Thailand	Captain Fred Harris Party
French Indo-China	*Both* Party
Return Details 1945	Saigon-Bangkok-Singapore by aircraft
	Singapore-Brisbane by aircraft
	Brisbane-Perth by troop train

WILLIAM WALTER TISCHLER

Rank	Private
Regimental Number	WX15712
Company	Headquarters Company
Enlisted	13.8.1941
Discharged	11.1.1946
Date of Birth	16.8.1918
Place of Birth	Fremantle, Western Australia
Father	Not Known
Mother	Not Known
Religion	Roman Catholic
Pre-War Occupation	Yardman

HISTORY

Singapore	Selarang Camp Changi
'A' Force Burma	Green Force, No. 3 Battalion
POW Number	1514
Japan	*Awa Maru* Party, Kumi No. 41
Return Details	No details are known
Additions	Soldier was transferred to Changi Gaol Camp Administration on 28.1.1945.

PERCY REEVE TOMKINS

Rank	Private
Regimental Number	WX8139
Company	'C' Company
Enlisted	16.8.1940
Discharged	18.12.1945
Date of Birth	5.7.1916
Place of Birth	Midland Junction, Western Australia
Father	Thomas Claud Tomkins
Mother	Lucy Mary Tomkins
Religion	Church of England
Pre-War Occupation	Yardman, Wood Cutter, Farmhand and Railway Employee

HISTORY

Singapore	Selarang Camp Changi
	Thomson Road (Caldecot Hill Estate Camp)
	River Valley Road
	Selarang Barracks Changi
'D' Force Thailand	S Battalion
POW Number	8850
Camps Thailand	Kanu II, Kanu I, Tarsau (evacuated sick), Non Pladuk
Japan	*Rashin Maru* Party
POW Number	1753
Camps Japan	Yamane
	Niihama
Return Details 1945	Wakayama-Okinawa, USS *Cape Gloucester*
	Okinawa-Manila, USS *Bingham*
	Manila-Morotai-Darwin, PBY Catalina aircraft A24-355
	Darwin-Perth, B24 Liberator aircraft A72-379

THOMAS HORACE TOMKINS

Rank	Lieutenant
Regimental Number	WX7996
Company	'D' Company
Enlisted	13.8.1940
Appointment Terminated	25.11.1946
Date of Birth	28.8.1912
Place of Birth	Midland Junction, Western Australia
Father	Thomas Claud Tomkins
Mother	Lucy Mary Tomkins
Religion	Church of England
Pre-War Occupation	Railway Employee

HISTORY

Singapore	Selarang Camp Changi
'A' Force Burma	Green Force, No. 3 Battalion
POW Number	2640
Camps Thailand	Tamarkan, Kanchanaburi, Bangkok
Return Details 1945	Thailand-Singapore by aircraft
	Singapore-Fremantle, HMT *Tamaroa*

KENNETH DUDLEY TUCKER

Rank	Sergeant (Promoted on 24.1.1942)
Regimental Number	WX8357
Company	'B' Company
Enlisted	18.10.1940
Discharged	12.12.1946
Date of Birth	4.9.1918
Place of Birth	Bunbury, Western Australia
Father	Frederick Roland Tucker
Mother	Ethel Tucker
Religion	Church of England
Pre-War Occupation	Bank Officer

Singapore	Selarang Camp Changi (17.2.1942-4.4.1942)
	Adam Park, Sime Road Camp (4.4.1942-27.12.1942)
	Selarang Barracks Changi (27.12.1942-14.3.1943)
POW Number	4/4605
'D' Force Thailand	S Battalion
POW Number	8724
Camps Thailand	Kanchanaburi (18.3.1943-25.3.1943)
	Tarsau (25.3.1943-25.4.1943)
	Kanu II (25.4.1943-23.6.1943)
	Kanu I, Tarsau (23.6.1943-19.7.1943), escorted sick to Tarsau by barge
	Chungkai (19.7.1943-25.5.1944), Wood Party (1.9.1943-30.4.1944)
	Tamuang (25.5.1944-23.6.1944)
Japan	*Rashin Maru* Party
POW Number	1538
Camps Japan	Yamane (10.9.1944-18.5.1945) copper mine
	Niihama (18.5.1945-12.9.1945) wharves
Return Details 1945	Wakayama, USS *Sanctuary*
	Okinawa-Manila, USS *Bingham*
	Manila-Morotai-Darwin, PBY Catalina aircraft A24-359
	Darwin-Perth, B24 Liberator aircraft

JAMES UNSWORTH

Rank	Warrant Officer Class 2 (acted as W.O.I Changi)
Regimental Number	WX9385
Classification	Signaller
Company	Company Headquarters
Enlisted	16.11.1940
Discharged	12.6.1946
Date of Birth	22.5.1893
Place of Birth	Bolton, Lancashire, England
Father	William Unsworth
Mother	Mary Unsworth
Religion	Roman Catholic
Pre-War Occupation	Miner

HISTORY

Singapore	Selarang Camp Changi
'A' Force Burma	Green Force, No. 3 Battalion
POW Number	2641
Camps Burma	Reptu 30km (medical orderly)
Camps Thailand	Tamarkan, Chungkai, Bangkok, Nacompaton
Return Details 1945	Thailand-Singapore by aircraft
	Singapore-Darwin-Sydney, HMT *Duntroon*
	Sydney-Melbourne by troop train
	Melbourne-Fremantle, HMT *Strathmore*

CYRIL JACK VIDLER

Rank	Private
Regimental Number	WX8585
Company	'A' Company
Enlisted	18.10.1940
Discharged	9.5.1946
Date of Birth	13.12.1919
Place of Birth	Surrey, England
Father	Jack Vidler
Mother	Hilda May Vidler
Religion	Church of England
Pre-War Occupation	Grano Worker

HISTORY

Java	'Blackforce, attached to 'C' Coy 2/3rd Machine Gun Battalion
'A' Force Burma	Java Party 5A, Robertson Force
POW Number	10628
Camps Thailand	Nikhe-Sonkurai Defence Line, Nacompaton, Bangkok
Return Details 1945	Thailand-Singapore by aircraft
	Singapore-Fremantle, HMT *Tamaroa*

COLVILLE DENUYS JARDINE VINCENT

Rank	Lieutenant
Regimental Number	NX46354
Enlisted	4.7.1940
Appointment Terminated	22.11.1945
Date of Birth	5.3.1920
Place of Birth	Kyogle, Newcastle, New South Wales
Father	Ernest Lloyd Vincent
Mother	Helen Irving Vincent
Religion	Church of England
Pre-War Occupation	Bank Officer

HISTORY

Singapore	Selarang Barracks Changi
	Thomson Road (Caldecot Hill Estate Camp)
	River Valley Road Camp
	Selarang Barracks Changi
POW Number	3/5929
'H' Force Thailand	'H' Force Group No. 6, Officer's Party
Singapore	Changi Gaol Camp
Return Details 1945	Singapore-Darwin-Brisbane, HMT *Arawa* 20.10.1945
Additions	Embarked overseas with 2/20th Battalion. Attended Officers' School in Changi and commissioned on 12.12.1941. Transferred to the 2/29th Battalion, Pioneer Platoon. Transferred to 2/4th Machine Gun Battalion from the 2/29th Battalion on 14.1.1943.

SELWYN DESMOND VINEY

Rank	Sergeant
Regimental Number	WX9372
Classification	Clerk
Company	Battalion Headquarters
Enlisted	8.11.1940
Discharged	29.11.1945
Date of Birth	8.5.1915
Place of Birth	Launceston, Tasmania
Father	Roy Ulverston Viney
Mother	Minnie Kathleen Victoria Viney
Religion	Church of England
Pre-War Occupation	Clerk

HISTORY

Singapore	Selarang Camp and Barracks Changi
	A. G. H. Roberts Barracks Changi
	Changi Gaol Camp
POW Number	1/9575
Return Details 1945	Singapore-Darwin-Sydney, HMT *Arawa*
	Sydney-Melbourne by troop train
	Melbourne-Fremantle, HMT *Strathmore*
Additions	Wounded in action on 14.2.1942. Evacuated to the 2/10th Australian General Hospital with a perforated shrapnel wound to the left hip. Transferred to No. 2 Convalescent Depot ex-A. G. H. Roberts Barracks Changi on 9.8.1942.

ERIC JOHN WADDELL

Rank	Private
Regimental Number	WX9236
Company	'C' Company
Enlisted	30.10.1940
Discharged	7.12.1945
Date of Birth	24.8.1920
Place of Birth	Narrogin, Western Australia
Father	Arthur Lynn Waddell
Mother	Beatrice Dorothea Waddell
Religion	Presbyterian
Pre-War Occupation	Farmhand

HISTORY

Singapore	Selarang Camp Changi
	Thomson Road (Caldecot Hill Estate Camp)
	River Valley Road Camp
	Selarang Barracks Changi
'D' Force Thailand	S Battalion (soldier separated from the main group at Tarsau, see 'D' Force, U Battalion)
POW Number	8855
Camps Thailand	Tarsau, Tonchan Central, Tonchan Spring Camp (cookhouse, water carrying duties and wood party), Tarsau (cholera), Tamuang, Non Pladuk, Nikhe-Nikhe Wood Camp, Kanchanaburi, Tamuang, Bangkok (go-downs), Nakom Nayok, Phitsanulok, Takuri, Bangkok
Return Details 1945	Thailand-Singapore by aircraft
	Singapore-Fremantle, HMT *Tamaroa*

GABRIEL JOHN WADE

Rank	Private
Regimental Number	WX17879
Company	'B' Company
Enlisted	4.12.1941
Discharged	28.2.1946
Date of Birth	18.11.1920
Place of Birth	Perth, Western Australia
Father	Seaton John Wade
Mother	Annie Wade
Religion	Roman Catholic
Pre-War Occupation	Shop Assistant

HISTORY

Singapore	Selarang Camp Changi
	Thomson Road (Caldecot Hill Estate Camp)
	River Valley Road Camp
	Selarang Barracks Changi
	Pulau Blakang Mati (reinforcement party 5.11.1943)
	Changi Gaol Camp
	Kranji Camp Woodlands
Return Details 1945	Singapore-Darwin-Sydney, HMT *Arawa*
	Sydney-Melbourne by troop train
	Melbourne-Fremantle, HMT *Strathmore*

HENRY WILLIAM WAGHORN

Rank	Private
Regimental Number	WX5021
Company	'A' Company
Enlisted	23.7.1940
Discharged	7.2.1946
Date of Birth	1.5.1920
Place of Birth	Claremont, Western Australia
Father	Alfred Edward Waghorn
Mother	Agnes Elizabeth Waghorn
Religion	Presbyterian
Pre-War Occupation	Gardener

HISTORY

Singapore	Selarang Camp and Barracks Changi
POW Number	1/9584
'D' Force Thailand	S Battalion
POW Number	8852
Camps Thailand	Kanu II, Tarsau, Tardan, Chungkai, Nacompaton, Bangkok
Return Details 1945	Thailand-Singapore by aircraft
	Singapore-Sydney by aircraft
	Sydney-Fremantle, HMT *Dominion Monarch*

JOHN WILLIAM WAINWRIGHT

Rank	Staff Sergeant
Regimental Number	WX9560
Classification	Fitter
Attached 2/4th	88 Light Aid Detachment
Enlisted	4.12.1940
Discharged	1.5.1946
Date of Birth	20.12.1902
Place of Birth	Newcastle, England
Father	William Wainwright
Mother	Hannah Isabel Wainwright
Religion	Roman Catholic
Pre-War Occupation	Motor Mechanic

HISTORY

Singapore	Selarang Camp and Barracks Changi
POW Number	3/6215
Force	'F' Force Thailand
Camps Thailand	Shimo Nikhe, Shimo Sonkurai, Kanchanaburi (24.11.1943)
Camps Burma	Tanbaya (4.9.1943)
Singapore	Selarang Barracks Changi
	Changi Gaol Camp
Return Details 1945	Singapore-Sydney, HMT *Duntroon*
	Sydney-Melbourne by troop train
	Melbourne-Fremantle, HMT *Strathmore*
Additions	This NCO operated the oil fueled burners which were used for cooking rice at Selarang Barracks. These were later converted to run on wood fuel.

ARTHUR LEWIS WALKER

Rank	Private
Regimental Number	WX16370
Company	'A' Company
Enlisted	8.9.1941
Discharged	11.1.1946
Date of Birth	23.1.1915
Place of Birth	Perth, Western Australia
Father	Not Known
Mother	Not Known
Religion	Baptist
Pre-War Occupation	Labourer

HISTORY

Singapore	Selarang Camp Changi
	Johore Bahru, Adam Park
	Selarang Barracks Changi
'D' Force Thailand	S Battalion
POW Number	8858
Camps Thailand	Kanu II, Tamuang
Japan	*Rashin Maru* Party
POW Number	320
Camps Japan	Ohama Camp 9B
Return Details 1945	Wakayama-Okinawa, USS *Consolation*
	Okinawa-Manila, USS *Haskell*
	Manila-Sydney, HMS *Speaker*
	Sydney-Fremantle, HMT *Dominion Monarch*

HERBERT JOHN WALL

Rank	Private
Regimental Number	WX12989
Company	'C' Company
Enlisted	14.5.1941
Discharged	31.1.1946
Date of Birth	13.10.1922
Place of Birth	Dongolocking, Dumbleyung, Western Australia
Father	Roy Henry Wall
Mother	Edith Annie Wall
Religion	Methodist
Pre-War Occupation	Millhand

Singapore	Selarang Camp Changi
'A' Force Burma	Green Force, No. 3 Battalion
POW Number	1520
Camps Burma	Khonkan 55km
Camps Thailand	Kanchanaburi, Non Pladuk
Japan	*Rakuyo Maru* Party, Kumi No. 35 (rescued by the Imperial Japanese Navy)
POW Number	290
Camps Japan	Sakata
Return Details 1945	Sakata-Sendai by train
	Sendai-Yokohama, HMS *Wakeful*
	Yokohama-Okinawa-Manila by aircraft
	Manila-Sydney, HMS *Formidable*
	Sydney-Melbourne-Adelaide by troop train
	Adelaide-Perth by aircraft

EDWARD WILLIAM WALLIN

Rank	Private
Regimental Number	WX17962
Company	'E' Company, Special Reserve Battalion
Enlisted	10.12.1941
Discharged	10.1.1946
Date of Birth	28.7.1920
Place of Birth	Fremantle, Western Australia
Father	Edward William Wallin
Mother	Maude Orontes Wallin
Religion	Church of England
Pre-War Occupation	Printer

HISTORY

Singapore	Selarang Camp Changi
	Thomson Road (Caldecot Hill Estate Camp)
	Selarang Barracks Changi
Force	'F' Force Thailand
Camps Thailand	Shimo Sonkurai, Shimo Nikhe
Singapore	Selarang Barracks Changi
	Changi Gaol Camp
Return Details 1945	Singapore-Darwin-Melbourne, 1st Netherlands Military Hospital Ship *Oranje*
	Melbourne-Perth by troop train

VINCENT WALLIS

Rank	Private
Regimental Number	WX16442
Company	'A' Company
Enlisted	10.9.1941
Discharged	17.12.1945
Date of Birth	13.7.1918
Place of Birth	Boulder, Western Australia
Father	Robert John Wallis
Mother	Catherine Maude Wallis
Religion	Church of England
Pre-War Occupation	Diamond Driller

HISTORY

Singapore	Selarang Camp Changi
	Thomson Road (Caldecot Hill Estate Camp)
	Selarang Barracks Changi
POW Number	1/12334
Force	'F' Force Thailand
Camps Thailand	Kami Sonkurai (April-November 1943)
	Kanchanaburi Hospital Camp (November 1943-30.4.1944)
Singapore	Changi Gaol Camp (May 1944-September 1945)
Return Details 1945	Singapore-Darwin-Melbourne, 1st Netherlands Military Hospital Ship *Oranje*
Additions	Wounded in action at Buona Vista on 15.2.1942. Admitted to the 2/13th Australian General Hospital with a shrapnel wound to the left shoulder. Discharged to unit on 23.2.1942.

BERNARD JAMES WALSH

Rank	Lance Corporal
Regimental Number	WX7466
Classification	Driver
Company	Headquarters Company
Enlisted	6.8.1940
Discharged	25.1.1946
Date of Birth	27.1.1915
Place of Birth	Sandstone, Western Australia
Father	James Henry Walsh
Mother	Nell Walsh
Religion	Roman Catholic
Pre-War Occupation	Truck Driver

Singapore	'Blackforce', Attached to 2/3rd Machine Gun Battalion
Camps Java	Bandoeng, Bicycle Camp Batavia, Makasura
'D' Force Thailand	Java Party No. 6, O Battalion
POW Number	6519
Camps Thailand	Hintok Road Camp, Hintok River Camp, Tarsau, Tamuang
Japan	*Rashin Maru* Party
POW Number	389
Camps Japan	Fukuoka sub-Camp No. 17, Omuta
Return Details 1945	Manila-Sydney, HMS *Speaker*
	Sydney-Fremantle, HMT *Dominion Monarch*
Additions	It is not known which camp this soldier was sent to after his arrival at Moji. It is known that he was not at Ohama Camp 9B or Niihama, so it is feasible that his camp was Fukuoka No. 17. This soldier's Japanese POW number is within the set of numbers allocated to the prisoners at this camp.

ALEXANDER BRIAN WALTON

Rank	Lieutenant
Regimental Number	WX10363
Company	'A' Company
Enlisted	18.12.1940
Appointment Terminated	27.2.1946
Date of Birth	25.2.1912
Place of Birth	Subiaco, Western Australia
Father	David Storry Walton
Mother	Amy Beatrice Walton
Religion	Methodist
Pre-War Occupation	Solicitor and Barrister

HISTORY

Singapore	Selarang Camp Changi
	Adam Park
	Selarang Barracks Changi
POW Number	4/4131
Force	'E' Force Borneo
Sarawak	Lintang Officer's Camp Kuching
Return Details 1945	Kuching-Labuan-Morotai-Sydney, 2/2nd H.M. Australian Hospital Ship *Wanganella*
	Sydney-Melbourne, 2/9th H.M. Australian Hospital Ship
Additions	Officer was evacuated on 12.2.1942 and was replaced by Lieutenant R. Learmonth on 13.2.1942.

MILTON ERIC WANKEY

Rank	Lieutenant
Regimental Number	WX9392
Awards	Military Cross
Company	'D' Company
Enlisted	16.11.1940
Appointment Terminated	1.3.1946
Date of Birth	4.5.1918
Place of Birth	Narrogin, Western Australia
Father	Edward Adolphus Wankey
Mother	Beryl Viola Wankey
Religion	Church of England
Pre-War Occupation	Letter Press Machinist

HISTORY

Singapore	Selarang Camp and Barracks Changi
	A. G. H. Roberts Barracks Changi
	Changi Gaol Camp
POW Number	1/872
Return Details 1945	Singapore-Darwin-Melbourne, 1st Netherlands Military Hospital Ship *Oranje*
	Melbourne-Perth by aircraft
Additions	Wounded in action at 2330 hours on 8..2.1942 at the 'D' Company No. 13 Platoon position at the northern end of Lim Chu Kang Road. Transferred to the 2/10th Australian General Hospital ex-2/9th Field Ambulance on 10.2.1942. Transferred to the 2/13th Australian General Hospital on 17.2.1942 where this officer's lower right leg was amputated. Transferred to the 2/9th Field Ambulance on 22.2.1942. Transferred to the Australian General Hospital at Roberts Barracks Changi on 11.3.1942. Discharged to unit on 26.3.1942. Officer was awarded an 'A' Medical Classification by the Japanese.

FREDERICK THOMAS WARD

Rank	Private
Regimental Number	WX7913
Classification	Driver
Company	'B' Company
Enlisted	13.8.1940
Discharged	25.1.1946
Date of Birth	20.7.1917
Place of Birth	Maylands, Western Australia
Father	Frederick Ward
Mother	Kathleen Eileen Ward
Religion	Roman Catholic
Pre-War Occupation	Truck Driver and Mechanic

HISTORY

Singapore	Selarang Camp Changi
	Adam Park
	River Valley Road Camp
	Selarang Barracks Changi
'D' Force Thailand	S Battalion
POW Number	8859
Camps Thailand	Kanu II, Kanu I, Hintok Road Camp, Kinsaiyok, Tamarkan
Japan	*Rashin Maru* Party
Camps Japan	Fukuoka sub-Camp No. 13, Saganoseki
	Fukuoka sub-Camp No. 17, Omuta
Return Details 1945	Soldier made his own way to a U.S.A.A.C. base and was flown to Manila
	Manila-Sydney, HMS *Formidable*

JOHN WARRINGTON

Rank	Private
Regimental Number	WX10382
Classification	Cook
Company	'D' Company
Enlisted	18.12.1940
Discharged	17.4.1946
Date of Birth	25.2.1901
Place of Birth	England
Father	John Warrington
Mother	Rose Warrington
Religion	Roman Catholic
Pre-War Occupation	Fetter (railways)

HISTORY

Singapore	Selarang Camp Changi
	Thomson Road (Caldecot Hill Estate Camp)
	River Valley Road Camp
	Selarang Barracks Changi
'D' Force Thailand	T Battalion No. 4 Section, under the command of W.O.II John Dooley
Camps Thailand	Wampo, Kanu II, Non Pladuk, Ubon
Return Details 1945	Thailand-Singapore by aircraft
	Singapore-Fremantle, HMT *Moreton Bay*
Additions	Admitted to the 2/9th Field Ambulance on 1.2.1942 with a knee injury. Discharged to unit on 6.2.1942.

WALTER STAFFORD WATKINS

Rank	Private
Regimental Number	WX8356
Company	Battalion Headquarters
Enlisted	29.8.1940
Discharged	13.6.1946
Date of Birth	5.3.1908
Place of Birth	London, England
Father	Not Known
Mother	Kate Watkins
Religion	Church of England
Pre-War Occupation	Labourer

HISTORY

Java	'Blackforce'
'A' Force Burma	Java Party No. 3, Williams Force (advance party with Lieutenant C. J. Mitchell)
POW Number	4589
Camps Burma	Reptu 30km Camp (25.3.1943)
Camps Thailand	131km, 133km, Kanchanaburi, Tamarkan, Chungkai
Return Details 1945	Thailand-Singapore by aircraft
	Singapore-Fremantle, HMT *Moreton Bay*

ARTHUR HENRY WATSON

Rank	Lieutenant
Regimental Number	WX9381
Company	Headquarters Company (From 'C' Coy 25.10.1941)
Enlisted	4.12.1940
Appointment Terminated	30.5.1951
Date of Birth	20.6.1912
Place of Birth	Perth, Western Australia
Father	Arthur Raynor Watson
Mother	Not Known
Religion	Presbyterian
Pre-War Occupation	Salesman

Singapore	Selarang Camp Changi
'A' Force Burma	Green Force, No. 3 Battalion
POW Number	2634
Camps Burma	Reptu 30km Camp
Camps Thailand	Tamarkan, Kanchanaburi, Bangkok, Nacompaton, Petchaburi, Kachu Mountain Camp, Bangkok
Return Details 1945	Thailand-Singapore by aircraft
	Singapore-Morotai-Darwin-Melbourne by aircraft
	Melbourne-Perth, B24 Liberator aircraft
Additions	Wounded in action Jurong Road on 10.2.1942. Admitted to the 40th Field Ambulance with shrapnel and bayonet wounds to the right hand. Transferred to the 2/13th Australian General Hospital then to the 2/9th Field Ambulance on 22.2.1942. Transferred to the Australian General Hospital at Roberts Barracks Changi on 11.3.1942. Discharged to unit on 17.3.1942. This soldier enlisted in the Permanent Military Force on 8.8.1930 and served until his discharge as an R.S.M. W.O.I on 31.8.1938. He re-enlisted with the P.M.F. on 3.9.1939 with whom he served until 2.12.1940 when he enlisted with the 2nd A.I.F. on 4.12.1940. This officer's commission as a T/Capt. was terminated due his being graded medically unfit..

ELLIOTT ALFRED ALEXANDER WATT

Rank	Private
Regimental Number	WX8502
Classification	Driver
Company	'A' Company
Enlisted	18.10.1940
Discharged	28.11.1945
Date of Birth	21.10.1917
Place of Birth	Cottesloe, Western Australia
Father	Alexander Watt
Mother	Lily Watt
Religion	Presbyterian
Pre-War Occupation	Storeman

HISTORY

Singapore	Selarang Camp Changi
	Mt Pleasant Camp
	Thomson Road (Caldecot Hill Estate Camp)
	Selarang Barracks Changi (Trailer Party)
POW Number	3/9896
'D' Force Thailand	S Battalion
POW Number	8857
Camps Thailand	Kanu II, Tarsau, Chungkai, Konkoita, Chungkai, Petchaburi, Nakom Nayok, Bangkok
Return Details 1945	Bangkok-Singapore by aircraft
	Singapore-Fremantle, HMT *Highland Brigade*
Additions	Shell shocked at Buona Vista on 15.2.1942. Evacuated to the Regimental Aid Post three hours before surrender. Discharged to unit on 20.2.1942.

ERIC GEORGE WATT

Rank	Private
Regimental Number	WX9067
Company	'C' Company
Enlisted	25.10.1940
Discharged	14.2.1946
Date of Birth	17.9.1911
Place of Birth	Southern Cross, Western Australia
Father	William Dunbil Watt
Mother	Bertha Watt
Religion	Church of England
Pre-War Occupation	Farmhand

HISTORY

Singapore	Selarang Camp Changi
	Serangoon Road Camp
	River Valley Road Camp
	Selarang Barracks Changi
POW Number	4/6776
'H' Force Thailand	'H' Force Group No. 3
Camps Thailand	Hintok Road Camp, Kanu II, Kanchanaburi
Singapore	Sime Road Camp
	Pasir Panjang
	A. G. H. Roberts Barracks Changi
	Kranji Hospital Woodlands
	Changi Gaol Camp
Return Details 1945	Singapore-Darwin-Melbourne, 1st Netherlands Military Hospital Ship *Oranje*
	Melbourne-Perth by troop train
Additions	This soldier suffered greatly from beri-beri, dysentery and malaria. He was one of many sick at Kanu II Malayan Hamlet, who was cared for by Alby Miller and Jock Leith.

TOM MURRAY WATTERS

Rank	Private
Regimental Number	WX10761
Company	Headquarters Company
Enlisted	15.1.1941
Discharged	16.1.1946
Date of Birth	1.9.1907
Place of Birth	Aberdeen, Scotland
Father	Not Known
Mother	Sarah Murray Watters
Religion	Presbyterian
Pre-War Occupation	Miner

HISTORY

Java	'Blackforce'
Camps Java	Bandoeng, Bicycle Camp Batavia, Makasura (May 1943)
Return Details 1945	Java-Balikpapan-Morotai-Darwin-Perth by aircraft
Additions	Soldier served with the Territorial Army in the United Kingdom.

THOMAS SYLVESTER WAYMAN

Rank	Private
Regimental Number	WX7502
Classification	Driver
Company	Headquarters Company (Q.M. Store)
Enlisted	5.8.1940
Discharged	7.12.1945
Date of Birth	24.6.1913
Place of Birth	Perth, Western Australia
Father	Frederick Walter Wayman
Mother	Hilda Wayman
Religion	Church of England
Pre-War Occupation	Bus Driver

HISTORY

Java	'Blackforce'
Camps Java	Bicycle Camp Batavia (April 1942-January 1943)
'D' Force Thailand	Java Party No. 6, P Battalion
Camps Thailand	Hintok Road Camp, Hintok River Camp, Kinsaiyok, Konkoita, Tamuang, Nacompaton
Japan	*Rashin Maru* Party
POW Number	1760
Camps Japan	Yamane, Niihama
Return Details 1945	Wakayama-Okinawa, USS *Sanctuary*
	Okinawa-Manila, USS *Bingham*
	Manila-Morotai-Darwin, PBY Catalina aircraft A24-306
	Darwin-Perth, B29 Superfortress *'Waltzing Matilda'*

ALBERT SIDNEY AUSTIN WEBB

Rank	Private
Regimental Number	WX17804
Company	'A' Company
Enlisted	27.11.1941
Discharged	10.5.1946
Date of Birth	17.1.1917
Place of Birth	Fremantle, Western Australia
Father	Herbert Webb
Mother	Fanny Webb
Religion	Church of England
Pre-War Occupation	Gardener

HISTORY

Singapore	Selarang Camp Changi
	Johore Bahru, Adam Park
	Selarang Barracks Changi
POW Number	4/6782
'D' Force Thailand	S Battalion
POW Number	8861
Camps Thailand	Kanu II, Kanu I (evacuated with hepatitis), Tarsau, Kinsaiyok, Konkoita, Tamarkan, Chungkai, Petchaburi, Lopburi, Nakom Nayok, Bangkok
Return Details 1945	Thailand-Singapore by aircraft
	Singapore-Fremantle, HMT *Moreton Bay*

CLIFFORD WEBB

Rank	Private
Regimental Number	WX9219
Classification	Driver
Company	'D' Company
Enlisted	30.10.1940
Discharged	11.3.1946
Date of Birth	7.6.1912
Place of Birth	Kalgoorlie, Western Australia
Father	Phillip Joseph Webb
Mother	Elizabeth Hannah Webb
Religion	Baptist
Pre-War Occupation	Labourer

HISTORY

Singapore	Selarang Camp Changi
	Thomson Road (Caldecot Hill Estate Camp)
	River Valley Road Camp
	Selarang Barracks Changi
	Changi Gaol Camp
POW Numbers	1/9653 and 3/9907
Return Details 1945	Singapore-Darwin-Melbourne, 1st Netherlands Military Hospital *Oranje*
	Melbourne-Perth by troop train (admitted to 110(P)MH suffering from malnutrition)
Additions	Shell shocked at Hill 200, Ulu Pandan on 12.2.1942. Admitted to the 2/13th Australian General Hospital and discharged to unit on 20.2.1942.

CLAUDE WILLIAM WEBBER

Rank	Private
Regimental Number	WX16254
Company	'D' Company Headquarters
Enlisted	27.8.1941
Discharged	4.3.1946
Date of Birth	12.11.1908
Place of Birth	Bunbury, Western Australia
Father	Frederick Webber
Mother	Mary Webber
Religion	Roman Catholic
Pre-War Occupation	Miner

HISTORY

Singapore	A. G. H. Roberts Barracks Changi (March 1942-April 1943, as staff)
	Selarang Barracks Changi
POW Number	1/9656
Force	'F' Force Thailand
Camps Thailand	Shimo Sonkurai
Singapore	Selarang Barracks Changi
	Kranji Hospital Woodlands
	Changi Gaol Camp
Return Details 1945	Singapore-Melbourne, HMT *Largs Bay*
	Melbourne-Fremantle, HMT *Strathmore*
Additions	Admitted to the 2/13th A.G.H. with conjunctivitis on 7.2.1942 and was diagnosed with a corneal ulcer to the left eye. Transferred to the 2/9th Field Ambulance on 8.2.1942 and discharged to unit on 28.2.1942. It is believed that soldier transferred to the 2/9th Field Ambulance joining his brother George.

CHARLES NEWDEGATE WEDGE

Rank	Lieutenant
Regimental Number	WX9553
Awards	British Empire Medal
Company	'C' Company
Enlisted	4.11.1940
Appointment Terminated	21.1.1947
Date of Birth	7.6.1919
Place of Birth	London, England
Father	Charles George Wedge
Mother	Gertrude Ellen Wedge
Religion	Church of England
Pre-War Occupation	Driver

HISTORY

Singapore	Selarang Camp Changi
	Johore Bahru, Adam Park
	Sime Road Camp
	Selarang Barracks Changi
POW Number	4/4132
'D' Force Thailand	S Battalion
POW Number	8713
Camps Thailand	Kanu II, Kanu I (escorted approximately 115 sick to Tarsau by barge)
	Tarsau (2 months), Chungkai (6 months), Kinsaiyok, Rin Tin, Hindato, Tamarkan, Kanu IIIa (Tampie North), Kinsaiyok (4 months), Tamarkan, Chungkai, Tamuang Kanchanaburi, Nakom Nayok, Bangkok
Return Details 1945	Bangkok-Rangoon by aircraft
	Rangoon-Singapore-Fremantle, HMT *Highland Brigade*
Additions	Promoted to Captain and posted to 110 (P)M.H. as Company Officer in December 1945.

HUGO CLARENCE WELLS

Rank	Corporal (Promoted 11.2.1942)
Regimental Number	WX7757
Company	'D' Company
Enlisted	10.8.1940
Discharged	6.2.1946
Date of Birth	11.12.1919
Place of Birth	Guildford, Western Australia
Father	Clarence Wells
Mother	Margo Wells
Religion	Salvation Army
Pre-War Occupation	Farmhand

HISTORY

Singapore	Selarang Camp Changi
'A' Force Burma	Green Force, No. 3 Battalion
POW Number	2720
Japan	*Awa Maru* Party, Kumi No. 41
POW Number	11034
Camps Japan	Fukuoka sub-Camp No. 17, Omuta
Return Details 1945	Nagasaki-Manila, USS *Lunga Point*
	Manila-Sydney, HMS *Speaker*
	Sydney-Fremantle, HMT *Dominion Monarch*

STANLEY KEITH WENN

Rank	Private
Regimental Number	WX7641
Company	'C' Company
Enlisted	10.8.1940
Discharged	8.2.1946
Date of Birth	23.9.1912
Place of Birth	Bunbury, Western Australia
Father	Henry Wenn
Mother	Mable Wenn
Religion	Church of England
Pre-War Occupation	Stevedore

HISTORY

Singapore	Selarang Camp Changi
	Johore Bahru, Adam Park
	A. G. H. Roberts Barracks Changi (Potts fracture to the right tibia 13.11.1942)
	Selarang Barracks Changi
'J' Force Japan	*Wales Maru* Party
POW Number	721
Camps Japan	Kobe, Notogawa
Return Details 1945	Okinawa-Manila, USS *Goodhue*
	Manila-Sydney, HMS *Formidable*
	Sydney-Perth by troop train

PERCIVAL LEONARD WESTLAKE

Rank	Private
Regimental Number	WX9570
Company	'D' Company
Enlisted	4.12.1940
Discharged	25.1.1946
Date of Birth	28.1.1917
Place of Birth	Aldershot, England
Father	George Arthur Henry Westlake
Mother	Marie Adele Westlake
Religion	Church of England
Pre-War Occupation	Farmhand

HISTORY

Singapore	Selarang Camp and Barracks Changi
POW Number	3/9960
'D' Force Thailand	S Battalion
POW Number	8853
Camps Thailand	Kanu II, Chungkai, Nacompaton
Return Details 1945	Thailand-Singapore by aircraft
	Singapore-Fremantle, H.M. Hospital Ship *Karoa*
Additions	Kingsley Fairbridge Farm Schoolboy. Soldier received shrapnel wounds to the right knee and abdomen on 8.2.1942.

JACK LOGAN WHEELOCK

Rank	Private
Regimental Number	WX8753
Company	'B' Company
Enlisted	23.10.1940
Discharged	13.3.1946
Date of Birth	16.1.1919
Place of Birth	Carnarvon, Western Australia
Fathe	Darcy Logan Wheelock
Mother	Edna Elizabeth Wheelock
Religion	Church of England
Pre-War Occupation	Printer

HISTORY

Singapore	Selarang Camp Changi
	Johore Bahru, Adam Park
	Selarang Barracks Changi
'D' Force Thailand	Captain Fred Harris Party
Camps Thailand	Kanchanaburi, Tarsau, Kinsaiyok, Tamarkan, Non Pladuk
French Indo-China	*Both* Party
Return Details 1945	Saigon-Bangkok-Singapore by aircraft
	Singapore-Australia, no other details are known

ARTHUR THOMAS WHITE

Rank	Private
Regimental Number	WX9333
Company	'B' Company
Enlisted	30.10.1940
Discharged	19.12.1945
Date of Birth	20.11.1915
Place of Birth	Brookton, Western Australia
Father	Jeremiah White
Mother	Amy White
Religion	Church of England
Pre-War Occupation	Truck Driver and Miner

HISTORY

Singapore	Selarang Camp Changi
'A' Force Burma	Green Force, No. 3 Battalion
POW Number	1527
Camps Thailand	Tamarkan, Chungkai, Petchaburi, Kachu Mountain Camp
Return Details 1945	Thailand-Singapore by aircraft
	Singapore-Brisbane by aircraft
	Brisbane-Perth by troop train
Additions	Soldier listed as missing from 10.2.1942. He joined up with 'A' Company and fought with them until the surrender on 15.2.1942.

CLIVE WHARTON WHITE

Rank	Private
Regimental Number	WX8814
Company	'C' Company
Enlisted	23.10.1940
Discharged	15.1.1946
Date of Birth	1.5.1917
Place of Birth	Esperance, Western Australia
Father	Arthur Wharton White
Mother	Elsie May Hannah White
Religion	Church of England
Pre-War Occupation	Butcher

HISTORY

Singapore	Selarang Camp and Barracks Changi
POW Number	4/6793
'D' Force Thailand	S Battalion
POW Number	8864
Camps Thailand	Kanu II, Hintok Road Camp, Hintok River Camp, Kinsaiyok, Konkoita, Tamarkan, Tamuang, Petchaburi, Nakom Nayok, Bangkok
Return Details 1945	Thailand-Singapore by aircraft
	Singapore-Fremantle, HMT *Highland Brigade*

HENRY CHARLES FREDERICK WHITE

Rank	Private
Regimental Number	WX9002
Classification	Acted as Cook (not trade grouped as such)
Company	'D' Company
Enlisted	25.10.1940
Discharged	20.5.1946
Date of Birth	9.3.1915
Place of Birth	Katanning, Western Australia
Father	Henry Mathew White
Mother	Rachael Maude White
Religion	Church of England
Pre-War Occupation	Truck Driver

HISTORY

Singapore	Selarang Camp Changi
	Thomson Road (Caldecot Hill Estate Camp)
	River Valley Road Camp
	Selarang Barracks Changi
POW Number	3/9970
'D' Force Thailand	Captain Fred Harris Party
Camps Thailand	Shimo Nikhe (sighted by Captain George Gwynne 'F' Force)
	Non Pladuk, Ubon
Return Details 1945	Thailand-Singapore by aircraft
	Singapore-Fremantle, HMT *Moreton Bay*

ROBERT GREIGSON WHITELAW

Rank	Private
Regimental Number	WX9076
Company	'B' Company
Enlisted	25.10.1940
Discharged	14.3.1946
Date of Birth	10.9.1902
Place of Birth	Saltcoats, Scotland
Father	Not Known
Mother	Elizabeth Whitelaw
Religion	Presbyterian
Pre-War Occupation	Tractor Driver

HISTORY

Singapore	Selarang Camp Changi
	Johore Bahru, Adam Park
	Selarang Barracks Changi
POW Number	4/6799
'D' Force Thailand	S Battalion
POW Number	8862
Camps Thailand	Kanu II, Tamarkan (hospital 16.7.1943-24.11.1943)
	Chungkai (24.11.1943-7.4.1944)
Japan	*Rashin Maru* Party
POW Number	419
Camps Japan	Ohama Camp 9B
Return Details 1945	Wakayama-Okinawa, USS *Consolation*
	Okinawa-Manila, USS *Haskell*
	Manila-Sydney, HMS *Speaker*
	Sydney-Fremantle, HMT *Dominion Monarch*

DAVID LESLIE ARCHIBALD WHITEMAN

Rank	Corporal
Regimental Number	WX7477
Company	'A' Company
Enlisted	6.8.1940
Discharged	1.2.1946
Date of Birth	13.6.1917
Place of Birth	Perth, Western Australia
Father	Oswald Archibald Claude Whiteman
Mother	Catherine Mary Whiteman
Religion	Church of England
Pre-War Occupation	Printer

Singapore	Selarang Camp Changi
	Johore Bahru, Adam Park
	Selarang Barracks Changi
POW Number	4/4610
'D' Force Thailand	S Battalion
POW Number	8737
Camps Thailand	Kanu II, Tarsau (sick for 12 months), Kinsaiyok, Konkoita, Tamarkan, Chungkai, Kanchanaburi, Nakom Nayok, Bangkok
Return Details 1945	Thailand-Singapore by aircraft
	Singapore-Fremantle, HMT *Tamaroa*

ROBERT GEORGE WHITFIELD

Rank	Sergeant
Regimental Number	WX10561
Company	'C' Company
Enlisted	3.1.1941
Discharged	24.1.1946
Date of Birth	4.5.1922
Place of Birth	Guildford, Western Australia
Father	George Ernest Whitfield
Mother	Haidee Cora Whitfield
Religion	Church of England
Pre-War Occupation	Storeman

HISTORY

Singapore	Selarang Camp Changi
	Johore Bahru, Adam Park
	Selarang Barracks Changi
'D' Force Thailand	S Battalion
POW Number	8725
Camps Thailand	Kanu II, Kanu I (brought up supplies from the river camp), Tarsau, Nacompaton
Japan	*Rashin Maru* Party
POW Number	1540
Camps Japan	Yamane
	Niihama (wharf and refinery)
Return Details 1945	Wakayama-Okinawa, USS *Consolation*
	Okinawa-Manila, USS *Bingham*
	Manila Morotai-Darwin, PBY Catalina aircraft A24-70
	Darwin-Adelaide, B24 Liberator aircraft
	Adelaide-Perth, ANA airliner
Additions	Wounded in action at Hill 200, Ulu Pandan on 12.2.1942. Admitted to the 2/13th Australian General Hospital with a shrapnel wound to the right forearm. Discharged to unit on 27.2.1942.

HUGH WILKES

Rank	Private
Regimental Number	WX9179
Classification	Batman/Runner
Company	Battalion Headquarters, Special Reserve Battalion
Enlisted	30.10.1940
Discharged	22.3.1946
Date of Birth	30.7.1921
Place of Birth	Bathgate, Scotland
Father	Ernest James Wilkes
Mother	Eliza Kisia Wilkes
Religion	Presbyterian
Pre-War Occupation	Plumber and Radiator Specialist

HISTORY

Singapore	Selarang Camp Changi
	Johore Bahru, Adam Park
	Selarang Barracks Changi
POW Number	4/6809
'D' Force Thailand	V Battalion
Camps Thailand	Kinsaiyok, Hindaine, Brankassi, Kuii, Non Pladuk
Japan	*Aramis* Party
POW Number	596
Camps Japan	Fukuoka sub-Camp, No. 17, Omuta
Return Details 1945	Nagasaki-Manila, USS *Lunga Point*
	Manila-Morotai-Darwin, PBY Catalina aircraft A24-354
	Darwin-Perth, B24 Liberator aircraft
Additions	Soldier was an original member of the Battalion (No. 6 Platoon) but was Taken off Strength when he injured his knee at Northam Camp and was sent down to the 110(P)MH. He rejoined the unit at Fremantle in January 1942 as a reinforcement.

MICHAEL HENRY WILKINS
a.k.a. Percival Henry Wilkins

Rank	Private
Regimental Number	WX17604
Company	'E' Company, Special Reserve Battalion
Enlisted	10.11.1941
Discharged	4.4.1946
Date of Birth	22.1.1920
Place of Birth	Geraldton, Western Australia
Father	Not Known
Mother	Not Known
Religion	Roman Catholic
Pre-War Occupation	Apprentice Plasterer

Singapore	Selarang Camp Changi
	Havelock Road Camp
	River Valley Road Camp
	Selarang Barracks Changi
'D' Force Thailand	V Battalion
Camps Thailand	Kinsaiyok, Brankassi, Non Pladuk
Japan	*Aramis* Party
POW Number	855
Camps Japan	Fukuoka sub-Camp No. 17, Omuta
	Fukuoka sub-Camp No. 12, Miyata
Return Details 1945	Nagasaki-Manila, details not known
	Manila-Morotai-Darwin, PBY Catalina aircraft A24-377
	Darwin-Perth, PBY Catalina

MERVYN WILFRED WILKINSON

Rank	Private
Regimental Number	WX10049
Classification	Signaller
Company	Headquarters Company
Enlisted	13.12.1940
Discharged	1.2.1946
Date of Birth	7.6.1909
Place of Birth	East Guildford, Western Australia
Father	Charles James Wilkinson
Mother	Isabel Augusta Wilkinson
Religion	Methodist
Pre-War Occupation	Cost Accountant

HISTORY

Java	'Blackforce', attached to the 2/2nd Pioneer Battalion
Camps Java	Garoet, Bicycle Camp Batavia
'A' Force Burma	Java Party No. 5A, Robertson Force and later attached to Williams Force
POW Number	10683
Camps Thailand	131km, 133km, Kanchanaburi (evacuated to Nacompaton 19.8.1944),
	Prachuab Kirikhan-Mergui Escape Road (evacuated to Nacompaton June 1945),
	Bangkok
Return Details 1945	Bangkok-Singapore by aircraft
	Singapore-Sydney, HMT *Highland Chieftan*
	Sydney-Melbourne-Perth by troop train

ALFRED GEORGE WILLIAMS

Rank	Private
Regimental Number	WX1138
Classification	Cook
Company	'C' Company Headquarters
Enlisted	4.12.1939
Discharged	19.12.1945
Date of Birth	9.11.1915
Place of Birth	Chipping Norton, Oxfordshire, England
Father	Walter Alfred James Williams
Mother	Fanny Williams
Religion	Church of England
Pre-War Occupation	Cleaner

HISTORY

Java	'Blackforce'
'A' Force Burma	Java Party No. 4, Williams Force
Camps Java	Bicycle Camp Batavia
POW Number	4488
Camps Burma	Reptu 30km Hospital Camp
Camps Thailand	131km, 133km, Kanchanaburi, Tamarkan, Chungkai, Kinsaiyok, Bangkok
Return Details 1945	Thailand-Singapore by aircraft
	Singapore-Sydney, HMT *Highland Chieftan*

GEORGE DAVID WILLIAMS

Rank	Private
Regimental Number	WX8672
Classification	Driver
Company	Headquarters Company
Enlisted	23.10.1940
Discharged	4.3.1946
Date of Birth	12.9.1915
Place of Birth	Perth, Western Australia
Father	Richard Walter Williams
Mother	May Williams
Religion	Congregational
Pre-War Occupation	Miner

HISTORY

Singapore	Selarang Camp Changi
	Johore Bahru, Adam Park
	Mount Pleasant Camp
	Selarang Barracks Changi
POW Number	4/6812
Force	'F' Force Thailand
Camps Thailand	Shimo Sonkurai, Nikhe
Singapore	Selarang Barracks Changi
	X8 Party
	Changi Gaol Camp
Return Details 1945	Singapore-Darwin-Sydney, HMT *Arawa*
	Sydney-Melbourne by troop train
	Melbourne-Fremantle, HMT *Strathmore*

HERBERT WILLIAM WILLIAMS

Rank	Lance Corporal
Regimental Number	WX7011
Company	'A' Company
Enlisted	30.7.1940
Discharged	6.2.1946
Date of Birth	7.1.1908
Place of Birth	Redruth, Cornwall, England
Father	Herbert Williams
Mother	Annie Williams
Religion	Church of England
Pre-War Occupation	Miner and Orderly at Meekatharra Hospital

HISTORY

Singapore	Selarang Camp and Barracks Changi
	A. G. H. Roberts Barracks Changi
	X10 Party
	Changi Gaol Camp
POW Number	1/12383
Return Details 1945	Singapore-Darwin-Sydney, HMT *Arawa*
	Sydney-Melbourne by troop train
	Melbourne-Fremantle, HMT *Strathmore*
Additions	Soldier was wounded in action at Hill 200, Ulu Pandan on 12.2.1942. Admitted to 2/13th Australian General Hospital ex-2/9th Field Ambulance with a bayonet wound to the middle finger on the left hand. The finger in question was amputated. Discharged to unit on 22.2.1942. Admitted to A.G.H. on 26.11.1942 with a fractured left elbow. Discharged to unit on 26.12.1942. Admitted to A.G.H. on 6.2.1943 again with a fractured left elbow. Discharged to unit on 2.4.1943.

ROBERT EDGAR WILLIAMS

Rank	Private
Regimental Number	WX7263
Company	'C' Company
Enlisted	1.8.1940
Discharged	7.1.1946
Date of Birth	5.1.1904
Place of Birth	Trafalgar, Western Australia
Father	Thomas Andrew Williams
Mother	Ellen Beatrice Williams
Religion	Church of England
Pre-War Occupation	Drover, Miner and Truck Driver

HISTORY

Singapore	Selarang Camp Changi
'A' Force Burma	Green Force, No. 3 Battalion
POW Number	1489
Camps Burma	Thanbyuzayat (evacuated to hospital 10.10.1942)
	Reptu 30km Hospital Camp (26.4.1943, acted as a medical orderly)
Camps Thailand	Tamarkan Hospital (8.1.1944), Nacompaton, Bangkok
Return Details 1945	Thailand-Singapore by aircraft
	Singapore-Fremantle, HMT *Moreton Bay*
Additions	Soldier experienced some deafness to the right ear following a bomb blast.

ROBERT SYDENHAM WILLIAMS

Rank	Private
Regimental Number	WX16956
Company	'E' Company, Special Reserve Battalion
Enlisted	8.10.1941
Discharged	4.4.1946
Date of Birth	5.12.1908
Place of Birth	Fremantle, Western Australia
Father	Not Known
Mother	Blanche Williams
Religion	Church of England
Pre-War Occupation	Butcher

HISTORY

Singapore	Selarang Camp and Barracks Changi
	A. G. H. Roberts Barracks Changi
	Changi Gaol Camp
POW Numbers	1/9729 and 3/10001
Return Details 1945	Singapore-Melbourne, 1st Netherlands Military Hospital Ship *Oranje*
	Melbourne-Perth by troop train
	Evacuated to 110(P)MH with beri-beri and malaria

RALPH THOMAS WILLIAMS

Rank	Acting Corporal
Regimental Number	WX7499
Company	'D' Company
Enlisted	6.8.1940
Discharged	11.3.1946
Date of Birth	12.4.1919
Place of Birth	Fremantle
Father	Albert Andrew Williams
Mother	Blanche Annie Williams
Religion	Church of England
Pre-War Occupation	Storeman

HISTORY

Singapore	Selarang Camp and Barracks Changi
'D' Force Thailand	S Battalion
POW Number	8854
Camps Thailand	Tarsau (July 1943-June 1944)
	Konkoita (June 1944-September 1944)
	Tamarkan (September 1944-December 1944)
	Chungkai (December 1944-March 1945)
	Petchaburi (March 1945-July 1945)
	Nakom Nayok (July 1945-August 1945)
	Bangkok (September 1945)
Return Details 1945	Thailand-Singapore by aircraft
	Singapore-Fremantle, HMT *Tamaroa*
Additions	Shell shocked at Ulu Pandan on 12.2.1942.

JOHN WILSON

Rank	Private
Regimental Number	WX17370
Company	'D' Company
Enlisted	22.10.1941
Discharged	28.1.1947
Date of Birth	23.4.1906
Place of Birth	Creiff, Perthshire, Scotland
Father	Robert Wilson
Mother	Jessie Wilson
Religion	Church of England
Pre-War Occupation	Miner

HISTORY

Singapore	Selarang Camp and Barracks Changi
POW Number	4/6827
Force	'F' Force Thailand
Camps Thailand	Shimo Sonkurai, Kanchanaburi Hospital
Camps Burma	Tanbaya
Singapore	Kranji Hospital Woodlands (critically ill beri-beri, malaria and dysentery)
	Changi Gaol Camp
Return Details 1945	Singapore-Darwin-Sydney, HMT *Arawa*
	Sydney-Melbourne by troop train
	Melbourne-Fremantle, HMT *Strathmore*
Additions	Soldier was missing in action from 9.2.1942. He rejoined unit on 15.2.1942.

JAMES GRAHAM WILSON

Rank	Lieutenant
Regimental Number	WX9394
Company	'C' Company
Enlisted	18.11.1940
Appointment Terminated	15.3.1946
Date of Birth	4.4.1920
Place of Birth	Wickepin, Western Australia
Father	George Edward Wilson
Mother	Cora Wilson
Religion	Church of England
Pre-War Occupation	Law Student

HISTORY

Singapore	Selarang Camp Changi
'A' Force Burma	Green Force, No. 3 Battalion
POW Number	1292
Camps Thailand	131km, 133km, Kanchanaburi, Tamarkan, Bangkok
Return Details 1945	Bangkok-Rangoon by aircraft
	Rangoon-United Kingdom, HMT *Orbita* (disembarked 9.11.1945)
	United Kingdom-Fremantle, HMT *Stirling Castle* (disembarked 16.2.1946)
Additions	Wounded in action at Reformatory Road, Ulu Pandan on 12.2.1942. This officer received a shrapnel wound to the (mastoid area) neck. He was admitted to the 2/13th Australian General Hospital on 12.2.1942 and discharged to unit on 21.2.1942.

RAYMOND COOPER WILSON

Rank	Lance Corporal
Regimental Number	WX8014
Company	'A' Company
Enlisted	13.8.1940
Discharged	8.2.1946
Date of Birth	29.10.1916
Place of Birth	Scotland
Father	James Brown Wilson
Mother	Emily Elizabeth Wilson
Religion	Presbyterian
Pre-War Occupation	Farmer

HISTORY

Singapore	Selarang Camp Changi
'A' Force Burma	Green Force, No. 3 Battalion
POW Number	1450
Camps Burma	Khonkan 55km Hospital Camp (medical orderly 6.7.1943)
Camps Thailand	Tamarkan Hospital (29.2.1944), Tamuang, Kanchanaburi
Return Details 1945	Thailand-Singapore by aircraft
	Singapore-Fremantle, HMT *Moreton Bay*

ALFRED DALY WINTER

Rank	Lance Corporal
Regimental Number	WX8110
Classification	Rangetaker
Company	'D' Company
Enlisted	16.8.1940
Discharged	30.5.1945
Date of Birth	7.12.1914
Place of Birth	Gaulle, Ceylon
Father	William Sextus Daly Winter
Mother	Annie Gertrude Elizabeth Winter
Religion	Church of England
Pre-War Occupation	Miner

HISTORY

Singapore	Selarang Camp Changi
'A' Force Burma	Green Force, No. 3 Battalion
POW Number	2775
Japan	*Rakuyo Maru* Party, Kumi No. 36 (rescued by USS *Pampanito*)
Return Details 1944	Saipan-Guadalcanal-Brisbane-Perth, 1.11.1944
Additions	Wounded in action on 11.2.1942. Soldier received a shrapnel wound to the lower back and leg but remained on duty.

WALTER VICTOR WINTER

Rank	Private
Regimental Number	WX10373
Company	'B' Company Headquarters
Enlisted	18.12.1940
Discharged	2.5.1945
Date of Birth	19.7.1919
Place of Birth	Coventry, England
Father	Walter Victor Winter
Mother	Annie Winter
Religion	Church of England
Pre-War Occupation	Labourer

HISTORY

Singapore	Selarang Camp Changi
'A' Force Burma	Green Force, No. 3 Battalion
POW Number	2901
Camps Burma	Khonkan 55km
Japan	*Rakuyo Maru* Party, Kumi No. 36 (rescued by USS *Pampanito*)
Return Details 1944	Saipan-Guadalcanal-Brisbane-Perth, 1.11.1944

WILLIAM JOHN WOLFE

Rank	Private
Regimental Number	WX16426
Company	Headquarters Company
Enlisted	10.9.1941
Discharged	21.12.1945
Date of Birth	15.8.1913
Place of Birth	Perth, Western Australia
Father	Richard Wolfe
Mother	Katherine May Wolfe
Religion	Roman Catholic
Pre-War Occupation	Shop Assistant

HISTORY

Singapore	Selarang Camp Changi
'A' Force Burma	Green Force, No. 3 Battalion
POW Number	3095
Camps Thailand	Tamarkan
Return Details 1945	Thailand-Singapore by aircraft
	Singapore-Fremantle, HMT *Tamaroa*
Additions	Wounded in action and admitted to the 2/13th Australian General Hospital on 11.2.1942 with a shrapnel wound to the right knee.

THOMAS ASHTON WOOD

Rank	Private
Regimental Number	WX5073
Classification	Driver
Company	'D' Company
Enlisted	23.7.1940
Discharged	4.12.1945
Date of Birth	22.5.1920
Place of Birth	St Pancras, England
Father	Thomas Ashton Wood
Mother	Ellen Elizabeth Wood
Religion	Church of England
Pre-War Occupation	Farmhand

HISTORY

Singapore	Listed as missing from 9.2.1942, soldier had escaped to Java
Return Details 1945	Recovered at Batavia, Java-Singapore by aircraft
	Singapore-Fremantle, HMT T*amaroa*

HAROLD JAMES WORSDELL

Rank	Private
Regimental Number	WX5204
Classification	Driver
Company	'D' Company
Enlisted	26.7.1940
Discharged	11.1.1946
Date of Birth	12.6.1915
Place of Birth	Rushall, Wiltshire, England
Father	Henry Worsdell
Mother	Martha Emily Worsdell
Religion	Methodist
Pre-War Occupation	Farmer

HISTORY

Singapore	Selarang Camp Changi
	Johore Bahru, Adam Park
	Selarang Barracks Changi
POW Number	4/6843
'H' Force Thailand	'H' Force Group No. 3
Camps Thailand	Kanu II Malayan Hamlet (cholera)
Singapore	Sime Road Camp
	X10 Party
	Changi Gaol Camp
Return Details 1945	Singapore-Darwin-Sydney, HMT *Arawa*
	Sydney-Melbourne by troop train
	Melbourne-Fremantle, HMT *Strathmore*

ALFRED WORTH

Rank	Private
Regimental Number	WX7440
Company	'D' Company
Enlisted	6.8.1940
Discharged	11.1.1946
Date of Birth	20.11.1914
Place of Birth	Subiaco, Western Australia
Father	Alfred Worth
Mother	Elsie Worth
Religion	Methodist
Pre-War Occupation	Printer

HISTORY

Singapore	Selarang Camp Changi
	Johore Bahru, Adam Park
	Selarang Barracks Changi
POW Number	4/6844
'D' Force Thailand	S Battalion
POW Number	8856
Camps Thailand	Kanu II, Kinsaiyok, Konkoita, Tamuang
Japan	*Rashin Maru* Party
POW Number	225
Camps Japan	Ohama Camp 9B
Return Details 1945	Wakayama-Okinawa, USS *Consolation*
	Okinawa-Manila, USS *Haskell*
	Manila-Sydney, HMS *Speaker*
	Sydney-Melbourne-Perth by troop train

CYRIL TOM WRIGHT

Rank	Private
Regimental Number	WX18142
Company	Battalion Headquarters
Enlisted	17.12.1941
Discharged	14.1.1946
Date of Birth	11.9.1914
Place of Birth	England
Father	John Albert Wright
Mother	Ada Clay Wright
Religion	Church of England
Pre-War Occupation	Miner

HISTORY

Singapore	Selarang Camp and Barracks Changi
	Coconut and Forestry Parties
	Changi Gaol Camp
Return Details 1945	Singapore-Darwin-Sydney, HMT *Arawa*
	Sydney-Melbourne by troop train
	Melbourne-Fremantle, HMT *Strathmore*

RONALD WILLIAM WYLLIE

Rank	Private
Regimental Number	WX12593
Company	'C' Company
Enlisted	9.5.1941
Discharged	11.2.1946
Date of Birth	6.6.1916
Place of Birth	Claremont, Western Australia
Father	Thomas Wyllie
Mother	Mary Wyllie
Religion	Presbyterian
Pre-War Occupation	Miner and Trucker

HISTORY

Singapore	Selarang Camp Changi
	Johore Bahru, Adam Park
	Selarang Barracks Changi
POW Number	4/6853
'D' Force Thailand	V Battalion
Camps Thailand	Brankassi, Non Pladuk, Ubon
Return Details 1945	Thailand-Singapore by aircraft
	Singapore-Fremantle, HMT *Moreton Bay*

JACK LEONARD YEATES

Rank	Private
Regimental Number	WX9003
Company	'A' Company
Enlisted	25.10.1940
Discharged	25.11.1946
Date of Birth	27.2.1905
Place of Birth	Adelaide, South Australia
Father	Not Known
Mother	Not Known
Religion	Presbyterian
Pre-War Occupation	Stationhand

HISTORY

Singapore	Selarang Camp and Barracks Changi
	Thomson Road (Caldecot Hill Estate Camp)
	Changi Gaol Camp
	Kranji Camp Woodlands
POW Number	1/12405
Return Details 1945	Singapore-Labuan, 2/1st H.M. Australian Hospital Ship *Manunda*
	Labuan-Morotai by aircraft
	Morotai-Melbourne-Perth by aircraft
Additions	Shell shocked at Ulu Pandan 12.2.1942. Two toes on right foot were amputated in 1944 due to tropical ulcers.

THOMAS WILLIAM ZEEB

Rank	Private
Regimental Number	WX9379
Classification	Cook
Company	'B' Company Headquarters
Enlisted	15.11.1940
Discharged	1.2.1946
Date of Birth	4.11.1903
Place of Birth	Kalgoorlie, Western Australia
Father	Charles Zeeb
Mother	Elizabeth Zeeb
Religion	Church of England
Pre-War Occupation	Truck Driver

HISTORY

Singapore	Selarang Camp Changi
	Johore Bahru, Adam Park
	Selarang Barracks Changi
POW Number	4/6859
'H' Force Thailand	'H' Force Group No. 3
Camps Thailand	Kanu II Malayan Hamlet, Kanchanaburi (1.10.1943)
Singapore	Sime Road Camp
	Changi Gaol Camp
Return Details 1945	Singapore-Darwin-Melbourne, 1st Netherlands Military Hospital Ship *Oranje*
	Melbourne-Perth by aircraft

The richest food source of the combined Vitamins B¹, B² and P.P.

(the anti-pellagric factor)

He's doing his bit for his Dad ...

Young Peter loves Vegemite . . . and his mother loves giving it to him . . . but he's not getting so much these days, as his mother says: "It's nearly all going to Daddy, Peter." And she's right! The Vegemite is needed for our fighting men.

As you know, Vegemite is a concentrated extract of yeast, which contains three vital vitamins—B¹, B² and P.P. (the anti-pellagric factor). That is why Vegemite is so necessary to our fighting men at home and overseas.

B¹—is the Nerve Vitamin. To have a strong, well stomach, and a normal, healthy intestinal tract, we need an ample supply of vitamin B¹. Vegemite is one of the richest natural food sources of this vitamin.

B²—is the Growth Vitamin. When you get too little of the vitamin B² it means poor growth and under-nourishment. Vegemite is rich in this vitamin B². It helps proper growth and all-round development of the body.

P.P.—(anti-pellagric factor). Vegemite keeps skin clear and healthy because it supplies the system with the right amount of the skin-clearing vitamin known as P.P. Yes! Vegemite is a concentrated food. Rich food and energy values are packed into Vegemite.

So if you notice less Vegemite in your local shop, just remember that until we have won this war a lot of it will be going to the troops! Vegemite — the concentrated extract of yeast — the richest food source of the combined vitamins B¹, B² and P.P. (anti-pellagric factor). The food that helps keep the troops fighting.

VEGEMITE *is with the Troops!*

He's doing his bit for his Dad …

Colour Plate 1

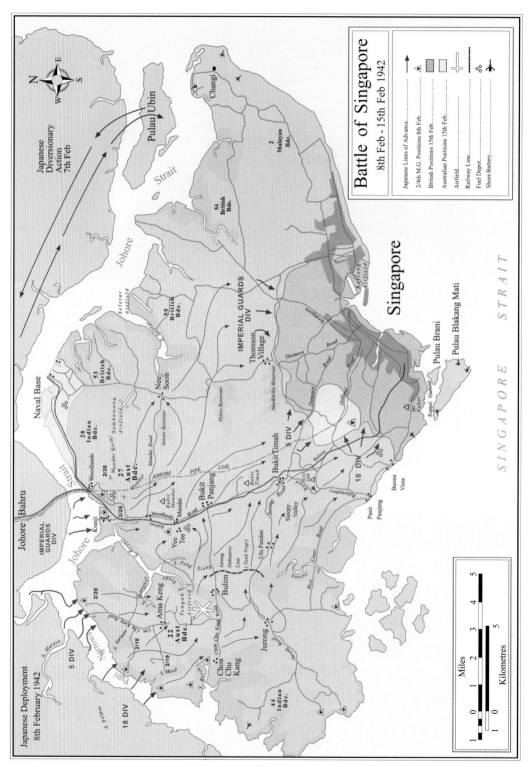

Map No. 9 The Battle of Singapore

Colour Plate 2

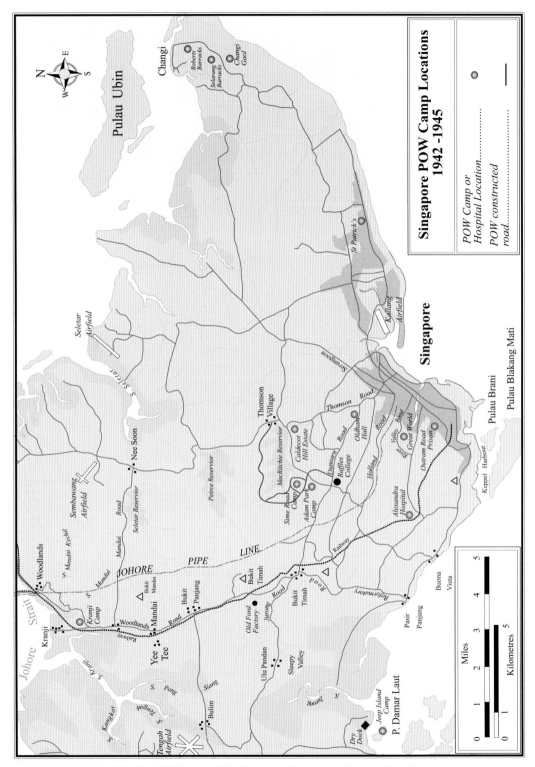

Map No. 10 Prisoner of War Camps on Singapore and general locations

Colour Plate 3

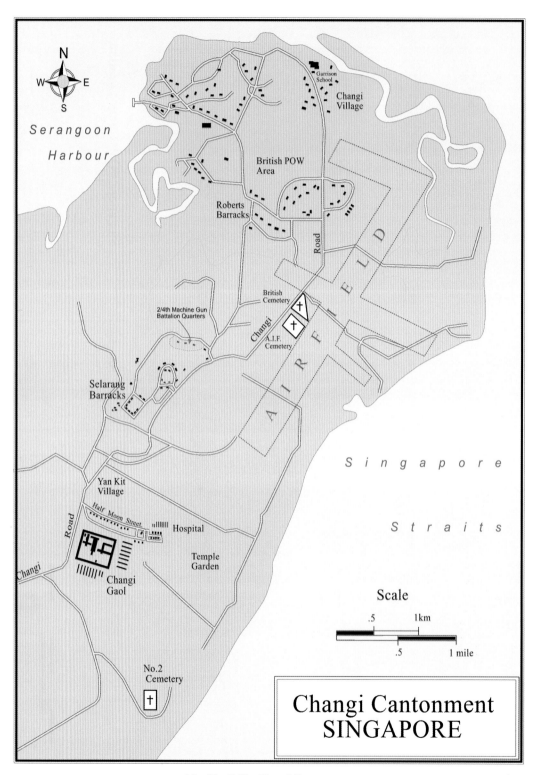

Map No. 11 The Changi Cantonment

Colour Plate 4

Form B5.　　　　10M/23/6/42　　　　Serial No....................................

AUSTRALIAN RED CROSS SOCIETY
MESSAGE SERVICE

(To be written in English, in BLOCK letters)

1. Sender—

    Name..

    Christian Name...

    Street..

    County...

    Country..

2. * Message—

    ....

    ....

    ....

    ....

    ....

    ....

    ....

3. Addressee—

    Name..

    Christian Name...

    Street..

    County...

    Country..

4. † Relationship of Sender to Addressee...

5. Signature of Sender... Date..........................

6. Signature of Authorised Witness §...

7. Message to be sent by (a) Air Mail, 2/-　 } Strike out words inapplicable.
   　　　　　　　　　　(b) Surface Mail, 6d. }

* Of not more than 25 words, conveying family news only.

† Messages may be sent only by the following: Grandparents, parents, spouses, children, grandchildren, brothers, sisters, uncles and aunts (that is to say, full brothers or sisters of either parent only), and persons actually engaged to marry.

§ Authorised witnesses: A nominated Red Cross official, minister of religion, bank manager, justice of the peace, police officer, or postmaster.

Australian Red Cross Message Service Form

Colour Plate 5

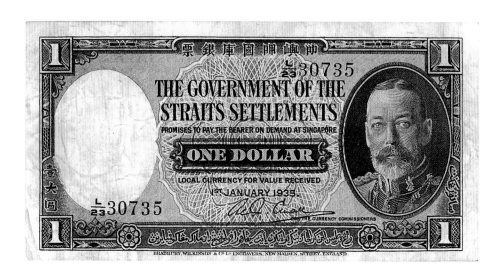

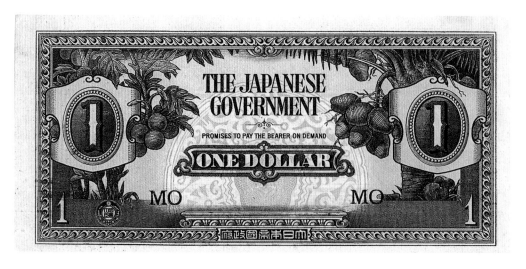

Singapore and Japanese occupation currency

Colour Plate 6

Lyle Curnow at father's grave Kranji War Cemetery

Colour Plate 7

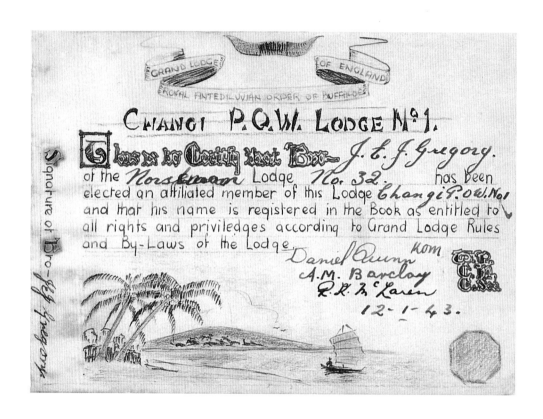

Royal Order of Buffalos, Lodge No. 1, Changi

The Royal Order of Buffaloes
Changi Lodge Singapore

Member	Original Lodge Western Australia	Lodge No.
T. W. Allen K.O.M.	Sir H. Woodward Lodge	5
G. H. Branson	Erlistoun Lodge	68
W. Burgess	Wiluna Lodge	73
G. Burslem	Edna Mae Lodge	69
T. D. Crane	Norseman Lodge	32
J. Cook	Bayswater Lodge	18
J. G. Curtin	Dundas Lodge	32
T. H. Dorizzi	Avon Lodge	43
F. L. Giles	Cue Orient Lodge	36
J. E. J. Gregory	Norseman Lodge	32
R. K. Gregory	Norseman Lodge	32
G. V. Hadden	Emu Lodge	60
A. S. Hewby	Emu Lodge	60
W. Hicks	Palmerston Lodge	83
H. G. Hockey	Albany Lodge	21
T. K. Jenkins	Norseman Lodge	32
I. W. Jones	Mt. Palmer Lodge	47
C. C. Keitel	Mt. Palmer Lodge	47
D. T. Manning	Edna Mae Lodge	69
R. F. Manthorpe	Wiluna Lodge	34
I. W. Lawer	Erlistoun Lodge	68
R. F. Lawer	Erlistoun Lodge	68
R. R. Lyle	Dundas Lodge	59
D. M. O'Leary	Cue Orient Lodge	36
A. E. Powell	Orient Lodge	25
D. A. C. Quinn K.O.M.	Regent Lodge	45
J. E. Pearson	Mt Magnet Lodge	
C. Ryan	Dundas Lodge	59
R. W. Ridgwell	Sons of Gwalia Lodge	48
F. A. Toovey	Orient Lodge	2
H. Tysoe	Orient Lodge	23
J. Warren-Smith	Midland Lodge	4
C. W. Webber	Orient Lodge	22
J. L Wheelock	Norseman Lodge	32
C. W. White	Esperance Lodge	65
G. D. Williams	Coolgardie Lodge	37
R. S. Williams	'Koolinda' Floating Lodge	7
R. Wyllie	Beria Lodge	41

Listing of 2/4th Machine Gunners who were members of the Changi Buffalo Lodge

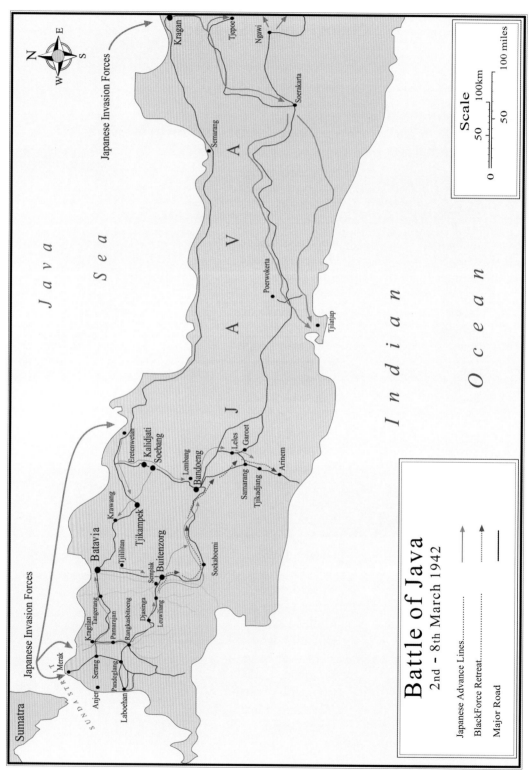

Map No. 12 Battle of Java

Colour Plate 10

Netherlands East Indies and Japanese occupation currency

Colour Plate 11

Kuta Raja

Tenal Gajoe

Blang
Kedjeren

Belawan

Gloe Gloer

Medan

Kota Tjane

Siamtar

S.S.
Van Waerwijck
26 June 1944 ✝

MALAYA

Kuala
Lumpur

S O U T H

Lake
Toba

Sibolga

Bengkalis

Strait of Malacca

Siak River

Singapore

C H I N A

S E A

Pakan Baroe

Kampar River

Fort
De Kock

Indragiri River

I N D I A N

Solok

Moearo

Padang

Batang Hari River

Djambi

Banka
Is.

O C E A N

Palembang

BenKulen

Lahat

Bengkalis

Pakan Baroe - Moeara
POW Railway

N
W   E
S

Siak   River

Teloebetoeng

Oosthaven

Ratai
Bay   Java

Pakan Baroe   Camp No.1

Kampar - Kanan

Kampar River

Lipatkain
Camp No. 7

Kampar - Kiri

Kota Baroe
Camp No. 8

Fort
De Kock

Spur Line

Tapoei

Indragiri River

Pandjang

Logas
Camp No. 9

Moearo
Camp 13

Solok

Padang

50   100km

0   50   100 miles

S U M A T R A

POW Constructed Railway ......

POW Camp................................ •

Scale   0   50   100km

50   100 miles

Map No. 13 Sumatra

Colour Plate 12

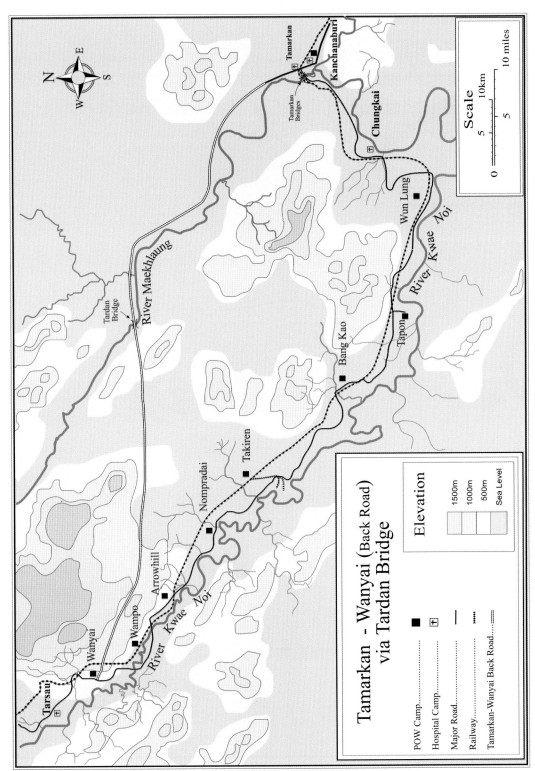

Map No. 15 Burma-Thailand Railway showing the back road via Tardan

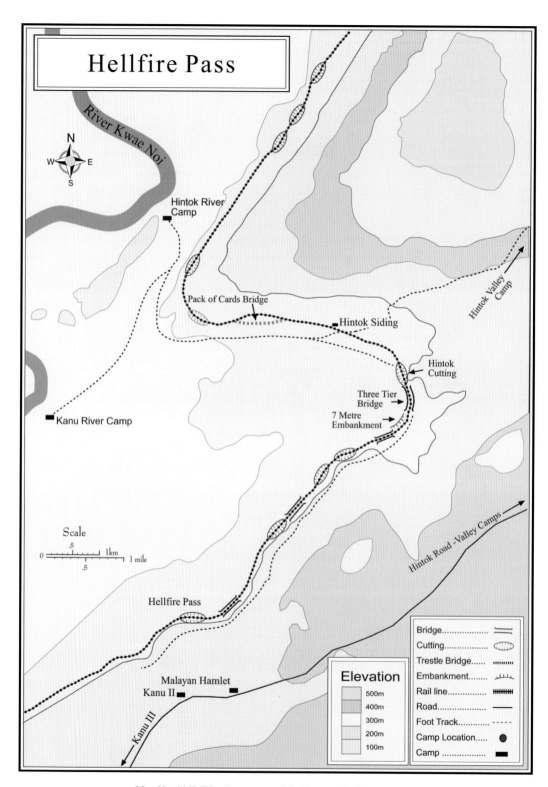

Map No. 16 Hellfire Pass sector of the Burma-Thailand Railway

Colour Plate 14

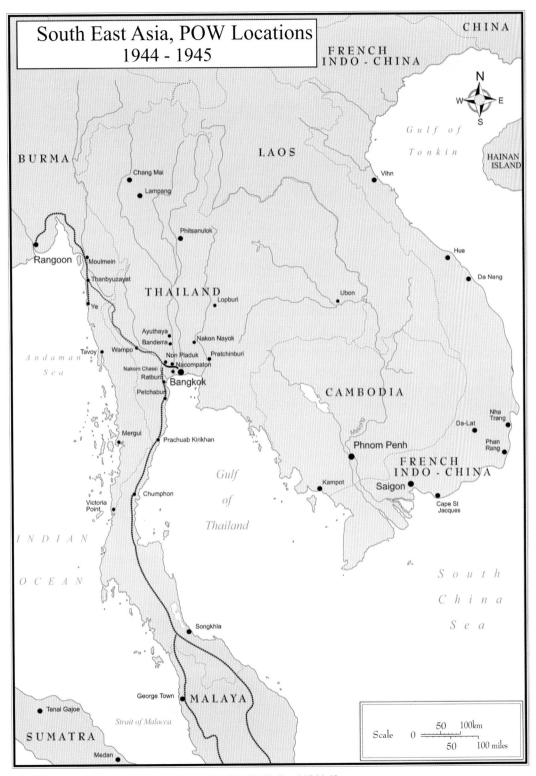

South East Asia, POW Locations 1944 - 1945

CHINA

FRENCH INDO - CHINA

LAOS

Gulf of Tonkin

HAINAN ISLAND

BURMA

Chang Mai

Lampang

Vihn

Phitsanulok

Hue

Rangoon

Moulmein

Da Nang

Thanbyuzayat

THAILAND

Lopburi

Ye

Ubon

Ayuthaya

Andaman Sea

Tavoy

Wampo

Banderra

Nakon Nayok

Non Pladuk

Pratchinburi

Nakom Chassi

Nacompaton

Ratburi

Bangkok

CAMBODIA

Petchabun

Da-Lat

Nha Trang

Mergui

Prachuab Kirikhan

Phnom Penh

Phan Rang

Gulf

FRENCH INDO - CHINA

Kampot

Chumphon

of

Saigon

Victoria Point

Thailand

Cape St Jacques

INDIAN

South

OCEAN

China

Sea

Songkhla

George Town

MALAYA

Tenal Gajoe

Scale   0   50   100km

Strait of Malacca

50   100 miles

SUMATRA

Medan

Map No. 17 Thailand 1944-45

Colour Plate 15

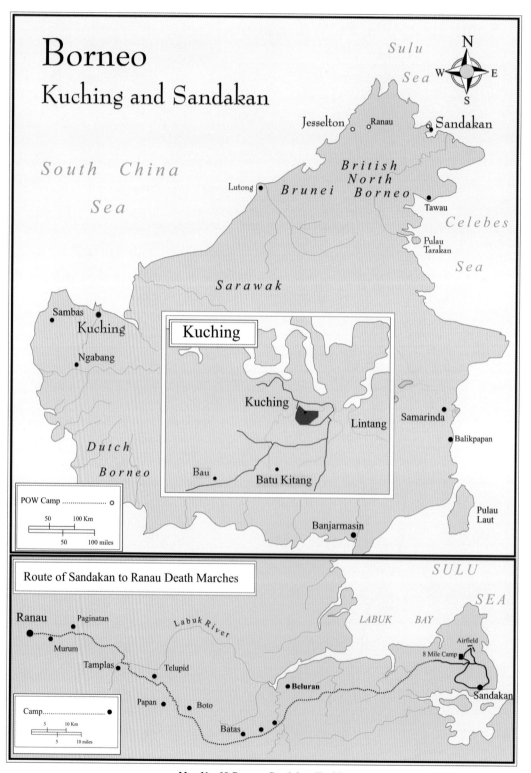

Map No. 18 Borneo, Sandakan Kuching

Colour Plate 16

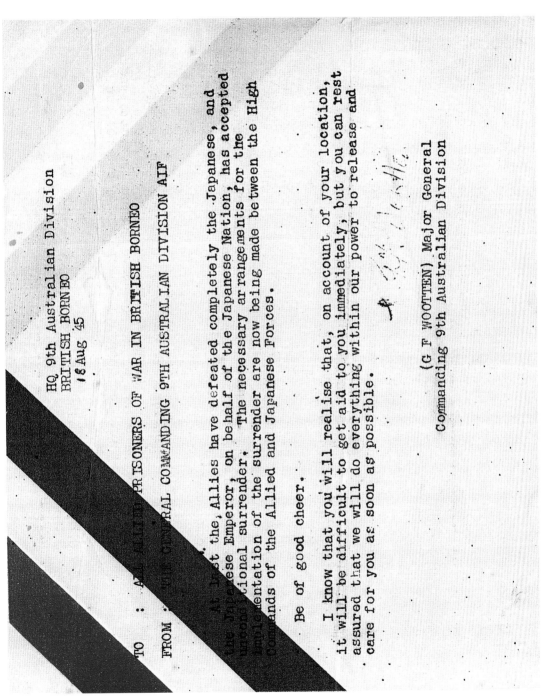

HQ 9th Australian Division
BRITISH BORNEO
18 Aug '45

TO : ALL ALLIED PRISONERS OF WAR IN BRITISH BORNEO

FROM : THE GENERAL COMMANDING 9TH AUSTRALIAN DIVISION AIF

At last, the Allies have defeated completely the Japanese, and the Japanese Emperor, on behalf of the Japanese Nation, has accepted unconditional surrender. The necessary arrangements for the implementation of the surrender are now being made between the High Commands of the Allied and Japanese Forces.

Be of good cheer.

I know that you will realise that, on account of your location, it will be difficult to get aid to you immediately, but you can rest assured that we will do everything within our power to release and care for you as soon as possible.

(G F WOOTTEN) Major General
Commanding 9th Australian Division

A copy of the leaflet dropped from aircraft advising all Allied Prisoners of War of Japan's surrender. This leaflet was dropped over Lintang Barracks Kuching but it is unknown if it was also dropped over Sandakan.
Property of William Pallet R.A.A.F and donated by his daughter Mrs Diane Kerr.

Colour Plate 17

"H.M.S. PINAFORE"

Produced by Capt. R. Spiers

Sunday, 12th March, 1944

CAST

Rafe Rackstraw	Lieut. J. Morrison
Dick Deadeye	Lieut. B. Walton
Buttercup	Lieut. R. Topham
Capt. Corcoran	Lieut. M. Phillips
Sir Joseph Porter	Lieut. A. J. Walker
Josephine	Lieut. M. Lambe
Sister	Lieut. H. Grenfell
Cousin	Lieut. M. Carment
Aunt	Lieut. R. Ewin
Bosun	Capt. J. Throssell
Bosun's Mate	Capt. F. Gaven
First Seaman	Capt. L. Jackson
Second Seaman	Major J. Workman
Crew	Capts. R. May, C. Young,
	Lieuts. K. Moore, J. Doswell,
	Chaplain O'Donovan & Mr. Fleming

LIEUT BRIAN WALTON AS "DICK DEADEYE"

SYNOPSIS

The story of **H.M.S. Pinafore** by Gilbert & Sullivan is known to all. Changes from the original opera were made only where absolutely necessary.

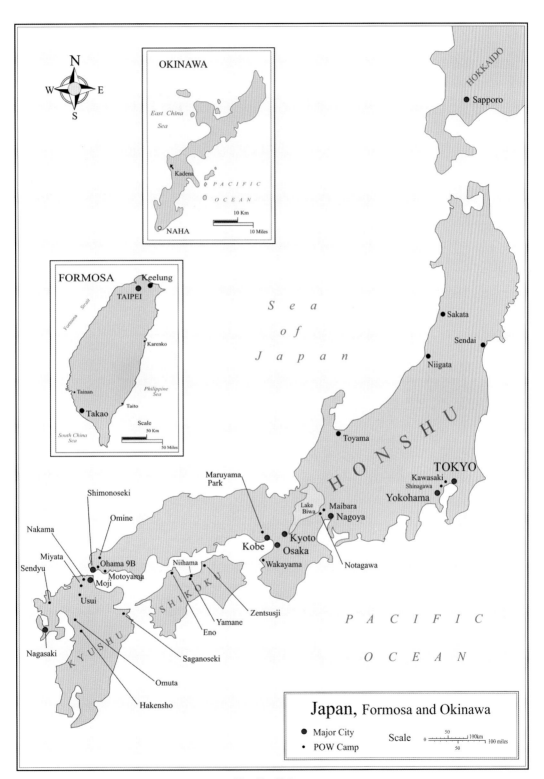

OKINAWA

East China Sea

Kadena

PACIFIC

OCEAN

10 Km

NAHA

10 Miles

FORMOSA

Keelung

TAIPEI

Formosa Strait

Karenko

Tainan

Philippine Sea

Taito

Takao

South China Sea

Scale

50 Km

50 Miles

HOKKAIDO

Sapporo

Sea

of

Japan

Sakata

Sendai

Niigata

Toyama

H O N S H U

Maruyama Park

Shimonoseki

Omine

Nakama

Miyata

Sendyu

Ohama 9B

Motoyama

Moji

Usui

Niihama

S H I K O K U

Yamane

Eno

Zentsusji

Nagasaki

K Y U S H U

Saganoseki

Omuta

Hakensho

Lake Biwa

Maibara

Nagoya

Kyoto

Kobe

Osaka

Wakayama

Notagawa

TOKYO

Kawasaki

Shinagawa

Yokohama

P A C I F I C

O C E A N

Japan, Formosa and Okinawa

● Major City

• POW Camp

Scale

0   50   100km

50   100 miles

Map No. 19 Japan

Colour Plate 19

Trooper 1563A Colin Cameron 4th A.L.H. Regt, WWI

Colour Plate 20

Bill Calyon

Colour Plate 21

Dudley Squire

Colour Plate 22

Tom Shelton died POW Thailand

Colour Plate 23

J.E.J. Gregory

Colour Plate 24

A.J. Bell who was killed attempting to escape Singapore

Colour Plate 25

Lt. Charles 'Mick' Wedge and family

Colour Plate 26

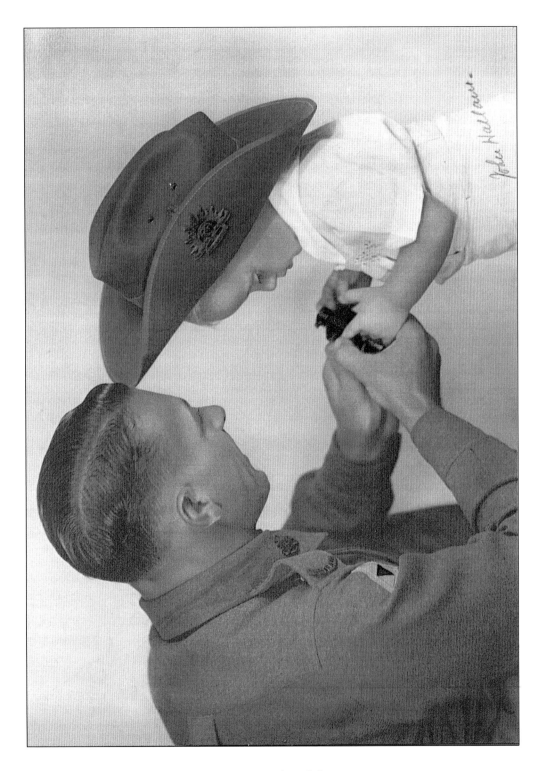

Les Kemp and son Colin

Colour Plate 27

Lt. Eric Wankey MC

Colour Plate 28

Chapter One

Michael Joseph Anketell
10.10.1890 – 13.2.1942

In his book, *Defeat into Victory*, Field Marshall William Slim described a battalion as being one of the four best commands in the Service because: "it is a unit with a life of its own; whether it is good or bad depends on you alone; you have at last a real command". [1]

On 7th November 1940 it was announced by the Minister for the Army, Francis Forde, that Lt-Col M. J. Anketell, was to form and train the 2/4th Australian Machine Gun Battalion. From the outset it was obvious that Lt-Col Anketell would leave his own indelible stamp upon the Battalion. The greatest influence upon Michael had been his father Richard John Anketell, an Engineer and surveyor of note who had opened up large tracts of Australia in the course of his work.

Michael's military career began on 3rd March 1916, when at the age of 25 years and 3 months he volunteered for service with the A.I.F., departing Australia for overseas service on 20th January 1917 with the 7th reinforcements for the 44th Battalion.

By January 1918, twenty-two months after his enlistment, Michael had risen to the rank of Lieutenant.

On his return to Australia in 1919, Michael joined the Australian Military Forces (Militia) where he eventually rose to the rank of Lt-Col and was appointed to command the 28th Battalion in February 1937.

In addition to his military pursuits, Michael had always been a very keen sportsman and competitor. One of his achievements included being a founding member of the YMCA in

Western Australia. It was the YMCA with whom he travelled interstate in 1913 to compete in a team gymnastic competition, in which he took out the highest individual aggregate.

In 1929, Michael, again in gymnastics, won the Senior Grade Paterson Cup. To top it off, he played 'A' grade football in the W.A.F.L.,[2] 'A' Grade cricket and was also a keen yachtsman. His obsession with physical fitness was the cause of many a tired muscle and footsore machine gunner, following some of his marathon battalion training marches.

Lt-Col Anketell's last words on the battlefield on Singapore were reputed to have been 'hold the left flank'. Surely this would epitomise the man Michael Joseph Anketell as a fighter to the last. Wounded in action on 12th February, he was evacuated by ambulance to the Alexandra Hospital but failed to regain consciousness and passed away the following morning.

The name Anketell has certainly left its legacy in the state of Western Australia with a suburb, streets and the Anketell Cup yacht race trophy being competed for annually in memory of a man who was affectionately yet respectfully known simply as 'Mick'.

This sketch was drawn by Lt-Col Michael Anketell

---

[1]   Field Marshall Sir William Slim, *Defeat into Victory.* Cassell & Co Ltd 1956, p.9.
[2]   West Australian Football League.

Why the 2/4th Machine Gun Battalion was sent to Singapore

The 2/4th Machine Gun Battalion's destiny was decided principally because of the British Government's decision to construct a Fleet Naval Base facility on Singapore Island.

Following the Great War of 1914–18, the realisation that wars were no longer isolated to countries, but could escalate into global conflicts, resulted in the United States and Japan initiating ambitious ship building programmes. This would effectively change the greatest concentration of naval strength from the Mediterranean Sea and Atlantic Ocean to the Pacific Ocean rim, with the United States of America, Japan and Britain being the major players. This would mean that if Britain wished to retain control of home waters as well as its interests in the Far East, then a two ocean fleet would be required, meaning that a fleet naval base facility in the Far East would need to be constructed.

To this end, Singapore's geo-strategic location was important to Britain being situated at the gateway of the Indian and Pacific Oceans, the Malacca Strait between Sumatra and Malaya, the Sunda Strait between Sumatra and Java and the South China Sea. These corridors would allow the fleet a line of communication to India, Burma, Borneo, Hong Kong, Australia and New Zealand. Economically, the British controlled Malaya was the chief outlet for rubber, tin, bauxite, silver, lead and tungsten. Also important was Singapore's proximity to the Netherlands East Indies where a rich and readily available source of fuel oil could be obtained for the new generation of oil fueled warships.

Japan had been aware that British interests in the pacific were mainly commercial and posed no strategic threat to her, so initially, was keen not to upset the balance of power in the Pacific. However, the decision to go ahead with the Singapore Naval Base now meant that Singapore would present itself as a potential military target. In fact, any military facility in this region would have presented itself as a barrier which would have to be contained if Japan hoped to seize the rich oil fields of Sumatra in the Netherlands East Indies.

For if Japan was to contemplate waging and maintaining a prolonged war against Britain and the United States of America, simultaneously, then it was clear that she would need to secure these oil reserves for her own needs. Without oil, the 'blood of war', Japan's military machine would grind to a halt. The Japanese had predicted, that based on their oil reserves, this would occur within the first six months of initiating hostilities.

The Singapore Naval Base was officially opened on 15th February 1938 and was heralded by one newspaper reporter as the Gibraltar of the Far East. Successive Australian governments had generally placed a great deal of faith in the British Singapore Naval Base strategy, believing it would keep an increasingly belligerent Japan at arm's length. In Australia, the catch phrase 'yellow peril' would strike fear into the heart of the average citizen, who could easily conjure up images of Japanese soldiers wading up Australian beaches.

Despite a failure to make an official declaration of war, confirmation of Japan's true intentions came in December 1941 with the news of aerial attacks against the U.S. Pacific Fleet at Pearl Harbor and seaborne landings in Thailand at Singora and Patani and at Kota Bahru in Malaya.

There was probably no one else more concerned by these recent developments than the Australian Prime Minister, Mr John Curtin. Curtin's earlier pacifist ideologies had undergone a metamorphosis through the 1920's and 30's to a point where he had become extremely passionate about the subject of Australia's defence. This latest Japanese move was fair warning that it was time for Australia, with its relatively small population, large land mass and predominately British ancestry to break from tradition and face up to the fact that it needed to seek help from the United States of America.

By 17th December 1941 Maj-Gen Gordon Bennett, the General Officer Commanding the Australian 8th Division in Malaya, was more than a little concerned at the speed of the Japanese advance towards Singapore. So much so that he cabled Lt-Gen Vernon Sturdee, the Chief of General Staff, in Melbourne to request reinforcements. He also took the opportunity to write to the Minister for the Army the Rt. Hon Francis Forde.

Moreover, the Deputy Chief of General Staff, Maj-Gen John Northcott, passing through Malaya on his way back to Australia from the Middle East, met with Bennett. Listening to Bennett's predicament, Northcott added his weight to his request for reinforcements by cabling Sturdee on 18th December recommending that the 2/4th Machine Gun Battalion be despatched to Singapore immediately.

The next day, the Minister of External affairs, the Rt. Hon. Mr Herbert Evatt, received Cablegram No. 63 from Australia's representative in Singapore, Mr Vivian Bowden.[3] Mr Bowden had made his own appraisal of the situation and was under no illusion about the possible fate of Singapore:

> 'Understand Gordon Bennett has reported fully to the army regarding the military situation and has expressed his views regarding reinforcements required. I feel strongly that before further Australian troops are committed every possible guarantee should be taken that they will not be abandoned with those already here. In my view real defence strength of Malaya falls far short of previous publicity and I feel assurances should be sought immediately from the United Kingdom Government that Malaya will not continue to be regarded as a secondary theatre of war and that reinforcements and supplies of modern arms and equipment will be rushed here even at cost of slowing down African offensive.'[4]

On 23rd December 1941, meeting No. 1629[5] of the Advisory War Council took place in Canberra and goes a long way to explain how the final decision to despatch the 2/4th to Singapore was reached. The minutes were taken in an abridged shorthand scrawl, however, enough information can be gleaned from these notes to follow the topic of conversation. In attendance at the meeting were the following members of the Advisory War Council:

The Prime Minister and Minister for Defence the Rt. Hon Mr John Curtin

The Leader of the Opposition the Rt. Hon Mr Robert Menzies

The Minister for the Army the Rt. Hon Mr Francis Forde

The Minister for Air and Civil Aviation the Hon Mr Arthur Drakeford

The Minister for the Navy the Hon Mr Norman Makin

The Minister for Supply and Shipping Hon Mr John Beasley

The Attorney-General and Minister for External Affairs the Rt. Hon Mr Herbert Evatt

Member for the Opposition Rt. Hon Mr Percy Spender

Member for the Opposition the Hon Mr John McEwen

Member for the Opposition the Rt. Hon Mr William Hughes

---

3   V. G. Bowden, Australian Government Representative in Singapore 1941–1942
4   AA: A981, War 42, National Archives of Australia
5   Series A5954 File 813/2, Notes on War Cabinet and Advisory War Council Meetings, National Archives of Australia

The following are excerpts from this meeting regarding the future deployment of the 2/4th Machine Gun Battalion:

Forde:
'*Concerning the position of A.I.F. troops in Malaya, I have had a telephone conversation with the Chief of General Staff and apparently the Chiefs of Staff met this morning An urgent letter was sent to them from the Chief of General Staff requesting that a machine gun battalion be sent to Malaya immediately. We could release the 2/4th Machine Gun Battalion at present in Darwin.*'

Evatt:
'*A cablegram from Vivian Bowden has also arrived.*'

Hughes:
'*It would make all the difference in the world if the A.I.F. in Malaya had a machine gun battalion.*'

Curtin:
'*Gentlemen in the absence of strong naval and air forces aren't we adding to the holocaust if we say we won't send them?*'

Spender:
'*If we say we won't send them then aren't we writing Singapore off? I feel we should send these troops otherwise it might appear that we are leaving our forces in Malaya to it. I believe that if the answer is to be yes then we should send them without delay as we can't say at this stage of the war that Singapore will definitely fall.*'

Beasley:
'*The disposition of Japanese forces is not confined to Malaya as they are also in the Philippines, Bonin Islands and elsewhere. How can we say that they won't attempt a landing at Darwin?*'

Spender:
'*That may be true but we can send other forces to Darwin to relieve the 2/4th Machine Gun Battalion.*'

Drakeford:
'*If we do send the battalion of machine gunners and their equipment we will have to replace them with a militia unit.*' [6]

Beasley:
'*Responsibility for Malaya is not entirely ours. However in Australia's case its defence is our responsibility and we need to face up to this fact.*'

Hughes:
'*If we don't send additional troops to Malaya there will be public outcry.*'

---

6   The 19th Light Horse Machine Gun Regiment dismounted from Victoria replaced the 2/4th Machine Gun Battalion

Beasley:

'*I agree to reinforcement.*'

McEwen:

'*It isn't sound thinking that because there's been Japanese landings on the Philippines and Bonin Islands that they will also attempt a landing at Darwin. I personally feel that a landing at Darwin is remote as there are no early indicators.*'

Spender:

'*It's obvious that more fighting men are needed up there. I find it difficult to refuse Bennett's request as we can't write off Singapore just yet. The additional troops may make all the difference in the long run and of course we must stand by our fellows already there.*'

Makin:

'*The longer the delay to the fall of Singapore the more time it will give us to prepare for the defence of Australia.*'

Menzies:

'*Any adequate force might delay the enemy advance in Malaya and even if it's just for a fortnight it might be worthwhile.*'

Beasley:

'*At this stage it's not very hopeful that they'll hold the Philippines or Malaya.*'

Spender:

'*There's also a gloomy view in Melbourne and Bennett has cabled Sturdee about how seriously he views the situation.*'

Forde:

'*But properly equipped Singapore can be defended.*'

Curtin:

'*I believe it should be done. We can replace the 2/4th with militia, however if we send them we must see to it that a naval escort is available. If we don't send them today then tomorrow may be too late.*'

Beasley:

'*If we send them at least we have done our duty in accordance with our obligations.*'

Curtin:

'*Then gentlemen the decision is made. The 2/4th Machine Gun Battalion who are now in Darwin will move before 30th December 1941. There will be an 8 inch Royal Australian Navy cruiser in Port Moresby which will sail south to Sydney with the 2/4th to pick up the 1800 infantry reinforcements whence the convoy will continue on whatever course is decided upon. The Navy is to get in touch with the Commander in Chief Far East to see as to what further escort is available. There's an armed merchant cruiser in Darwin at present which can escort the 2/4th Machine Gun Battalion to Port Moresby where the 8 inch cruiser can then escort.*'

(630) <u>DESPATCH OF ADDITIONAL AUSTRALIAN TROOPS TO MALAYA.</u>

The Minister for the Army stated that he had received advice from the Chief of the General Staff that the Chiefs of Staff, after consideration of representations made by the G.O.C., A.I.F., Malaya, recommended that approval be given for the despatch of an A.I.F. Machine Gun Battalion to Malaya. They considered that this would provide an additional striking force which was likely to prove of vital importance to the A.I.F. in Malaya. They also recommended that 1800 reinforcements be sent to Malaya. Shipping would be available at an early date and it was intended to provide 8-inch cruiser escort. It was also proposed that the 400 personnel from the Armoured Brigade, the despatch of whom to Malaya was authorised by War Cabinet on 22nd December, should proceed at the same time.

The following recommendations were submitted by the Advisory War Council :-

(a) That approval be given for the despatch to Malaya of an A.I.F. Machine Gun Battalion from Darwin.

(b) That Vickers guns and light machine guns required for the equipment of the Battalion should be sent to Malaya with the troops, but that anti-tank rifles should not be despatched.

(c) That steps be taken immediately for the replacement of the Machine Gun Battalion and equipment at Darwin by the despatch from Southern States of A.M.F. troops and equipment. The A.M.F. troops and equipment should arrive at Darwin concurrently with the departure of the A.I.F. Battalion, if possible. If this cannot be arranged, it is to be ensured that the interval in time between the departure of the A.I.F. troops and the arrival at Darwin of A.M.F. troops and equipment is reduced to the absolute minimum. Special steps should be taken to enable this to be done.

(d) That 1800 reinforcements for the A.I.F. in Malaya be also despatched.

(e) That the Machine Gun Battalion, reinforcements and also 400 personnel from the Armoured Brigade should be provided with an 8-inch cruiser escort. The Naval authorities are to approach the Commander-in-Chief, Far Eastern Fleet, with a view to the strengthening of the escort to the greatest degree possible.

(Note: The above recommendations were taken as the decision of War Cabinet (Minute No. 1629)).

The Minister for Supply and Development considered that reinforcements should be sent to Malaya in accordance with our obligations to maintain the A.I.F. there, but that, in view of the requirements of Home Defence, we should not accept any commitment for the despatch of troops to Malaya over and above those required to maintain the A.I.F.

Secretary.

PRIME MINISTER.

533

The Australian Official History *Government and the People* [7] has this to say;

> *'The War Cabinet also decided to send 1,800 reinforcements for the maintenance of the A.I.F., already in Malaya. Next day in response to representations from the G.O.C., A.I.F. Malaya, Maj-Gen Gordon Bennett, it was decided to send to Malaya an A.I.F. machine gun battalion stationed at Darwin, replacing it there by units of the Australian Military Forces. All these measures were taken after consultation with the Advisory War Council and on its recommendation.'*

So it was decided on 23rd December 1941 that the 2/4th Machine Gun Battalion would join the bulk of the 8th Division in Singapore. Prime Minister Curtin's first obligation, without question was of course to Bennett who had been asking for reinforcements. As well as Bennett, Curtin also had an obligation to the families in Australia who had loved ones in the 8th Division. These were the people that would be waiting at home for any news of the men.

Despite assurances by Britain over a period of two decades that the Singapore Naval Base would be the last word in her Far Eastern Imperial defence, there was still a moral obligation for Australia to support Britain in the struggle to retain Singapore.

There is one point to add in regard to the decision by the Prime Minister, Mr John Curtin, concerning the despatch of the 2/4th Machine Gun Battalion to Singapore. Perhaps above all else weighing on Curtin's mind at this time was the fact that it was imperative that Australia demonstrate to the United States of America that as a fledgling nation it was doing all it could to help itself. It would be heartening to think that the 2/4th Machine Gun Battalion's contribution on the battlefield went some way towards slowing down the Japanese advance towards the Australian mainland, thus allowing the time needed for the preparation for Australia's defence and for the return of the 6th, 7th and 9th Australian Divisions from the Middle East.

The Minister for the Navy, the Hon Mr Norman Makin's statement to the Advisory War Council of 23rd December 1941, summarised the situation:

'The longer the delay to the fall of Singapore the more time it will give us to prepare for the defence of Australia.'

The 2/4th Machine Gun Battalion, about to depart Winnellie Camp Darwin, New Year's Eve 1941

---

[7] Paul Hasluck, The Government And The People, Australia in the War of 1939–1945, Civil Volume II, Australian War Memorial 1970 p.17

Fremantle Revisited

When the 2/4th Machine Gun Battalion received embarkation orders for overseas service, many amongst the ranks were elated that finally they would be given the opportunity to show their mettle in battle. Little did these men realise that their excitement would soon turn to despair. Darwin had not been a popular posting with the machine gunners, so when the Minister for Labour and National Service, the Hon Mr Edward Ward, informed the men of their embarkation orders and that they were to be granted leave in Fremantle, understandably spirits rose. The thought of a few days furlough in Sydney and the chance to be reunited with loved ones in Fremantle after a six month absence gave the men of all ranks plenty to talk about.

The brief stopover in Sydney was marred by the tragic loss of Bill Haldane. Bill who was a member of 'B' Company fell overboard between the *Aquitania* and the wharf and drowned sometime during the night of 8th–9th January 1942.

The next port of call was Fremantle, the *Aquitania* dropping anchor in Gage Roads at 0830 hours on 15th January. It was intended that the *Aquitania* would call into Fremantle only long enough to replenish her water, fuel and embark reinforcements and then in a race against time, continue her northward voyage towards Singapore.

The Commanding Officer Troops on convoy "MS 2" was Col. Chas H. Lamb. Colonel Lamb had promulgated orders that during the Fremantle stopover, no leave was to be granted to the troops onboard the *Aquitania*. These instructions were issued to Lt-Col M. J. Anketell and the other group commanders. When advised of the situation Lt-Col Anketell said that he did not expect trouble from the men in his battalion.

The ship's Staff Officer Major L. C. Allen and the Captain of the Day were responsible for posting guards and sentries. An anchorage guard of two Officers, three Sergeants, three Corporals and thirty Privates was mounted immediately the *Aquitania* dropped anchor. A guard from Western Command also embarked for the duration of the stay at Fremantle. As launches and tugboats towing lighters came alongside, men appeared on deck in readiness to go ashore.

A rumour had circulated amongst the troops that the ship's company had been granted shore leave until 1300 hours the following day. This rumour proved to be false as the *Aquitania* was under orders to weigh anchor at 1100 hours on 16th January. With trouble looming, the guard was doubled on exits and gun ports and all Officers and NCO's not on essential duties were placed on picquet duty. This strengthening of the guard was to no avail as by 1030 hours approximately forty troops had managed to squeeze out of portholes and scramble down hawsers.

The first wave of ship breakers were obviously determined to get ashore and by their actions brought home the reality that a riot and possible bloodshed could ensue. The launch with the first ship breakers compelled their helmsman to take them ashore, a request he duly obliged, despite a call requesting the Navy to intercept the launch. Orders were cabled to the Military Police and the Garrison Battalion Guard ashore to form a reception committee and take the first wave of the ship breakers into custody. This military manoeuvre, like the naval plan, did not eventuate and a request to the tug Masters not to tow the lighters ashore also proved useless.

Seeing the first wave go ashore further troops tried their luck at scaling down hawsers and ropes onto lighters. Officers were instructed to go onto the lighters and to plead with the men to return to the ship, but by this time it seems hearts were ruling minds as many men steadfastly refused to budge. Approximately 1,300 troops, including, its believed about half the 2/4th Machine Gun Battalion, broke ship that day and proceeded ashore. Strong shore patrols of Western Command personnel with a large proportion of motor transport patrolled the Fremantle area, Perth City and suburbs during 15th and 16th January with the result that about 150 troops were apprehended and returned to the *Aquitania*. Between 0700 hours and 1030 hours a further

650 troops returned to the ship. When the convoy was due to sail at 1100 hours on 16th January there were still 500 troops absent, but between 1030 hours and 1330 hours another 350 to 400 troops returned onboard. Some of these men had made it back to Fremantle wharf and had been shepherded out of harms way by the troops of the Garrison Battalion Guard and pointed in the direction where they could find transport out to Gage Roads

Others were not as fortunate and were apprehended by the M.P.'s. Many were assured they would be ferried back out to their ship. Unfortunately for the ship breakers the M.P.'s were under orders so their motives were not in the troops best interests as they were taken into custody and given a cell for the night at Fremantle Prison. The prison was being used as a detention barracks for the A.I.F. as all the civilian inmates had been relocated to Barton's Mill Prison. The final tally of 169 imprisoned 2nd A.I.F. personnel consisted of eighty-one Sydney reinforcements and eighty-eight 2/4th machine gunners.[8]

Many years after the event Bert Norton wrote of his experiences as a ship breaker:

'*The battalion expected leave in Fremantle but we were told that no leave was to was to be granted. We heard that the ship's crew had been granted a 24hr leave pass. The ship's Captain had made a request to Western Command to grant us leave, but the answer came back no, because we were not under orders of Western Command. In the heat of the moment everyone who could, went AWL, by climbing down ladders and ropes onto water lighters.*

We got into Fremantle harbour and a Company of old soldiers from the Garrison Battalion were waiting for us with fixed bayonets. They weren't happy about the situation and neither were we. Their C.O. asked us, 'are you all West Australians?' to which everyone shouted 'YES'. He then said, 'come up onto the wharf'. He then marched us all out to the main gate, where he said 'be off, and don't forget to come back in the morning'.

A large Mills and Wares van pulled up and the driver gave about 50 of us a lift into Perth. He dropped me at the corner of St George's Terrace and Milligan Street. I walked down Spring Street to 210 Mounts Bay Road to my parents home where I stayed for an hour with the family. I then made my way to Barrack Street to catch a ferry across the Swan River to South Perth. The Master said the M.P.'s were picking all men with a 2/4th colour patch on their hatband, so forewarned, I turned mine inside out.

I stayed at home with Thelma for the night and in the morning Eddie and Audrey Pummell came and told me the M.P.'s were grabbing all those who were AWL and taking them to Fremantle Prison. As a result I didn't have time to say goodbye to my family. Eddie, Audrey, Thelma and I then caught a Metro bus into Fremantle. The driver warned me to keep down as the M.P.'s were checking every bus from their vehicles. If they saw uniforms onboard, they were stopping the bus and checking military ID's.

When we arrived at Beaconsfield we changed to a tram. The bus driver advised us to ask the tram driver to stop as close as possible to the wharf. We got to the wharf, where we could see the M.P.'s taking men into custody and then taking them to Fremantle Prison. Eddie and I managed to get onboard the Zepher, then the Aquitania. Once back onboard I was sent to man an AA mount on top deck. We left Fremantle that afternoon, all except for about 90 men from the 2/4th left inside Fremantle Prison. These men were later captured on Java. We never did find out the name of the Officer who had issued order for the roundup.'[9]

---

[8]   (Note: there were five 2/4th who for reasons of age or health were taken off battalion strength at Fremantle therefore lowering the total number of machine gunners who failed to re-board the *Aquitania* from ninety-three to eighty-eight men).

[9]   Summary of Albert Norton's experience as a ship breaker donated by his son Robert Norton.

Partly compensating for the loss of these men from 2/4th were 145 reinforcements for the battalion who had travelled overnight by train from Northam Army Camp. This group included, six Officers, four Sergeants and 134 other ranks.

Additionally, there was one stowaway who thought he would like to try his luck with the machine gunners. This man was Henry Christopher, a.k.a. Hugh Christopher 'Horse' Oswald. Originally 'Horse' was a reinforcement for the 2/16th Battalion but whilst on pre-embarkation leave he fell ill and missed his draft. Determined to see some action 'Horse' waited for his moment and stowed away on the *Aquitania*. On 7th November 1943 at Kanchanaburi Base Hospital 'Horse' died as a result of dysentery. When the *Aquitania* weighed anchor and steamed out of Gage Roads on the afternoon of 16th January. It is said that there were many glassy eyed machine gunners in the cells at the Fremantle Prison.The next day these men were transferred to the Claremont Details Camp where they remained until 30th January 1942, at which time they were escorted back to Fremantle. They embarked onboard HMT *Marella*, which set course for Singapore. As destiny so often influences our life, these men from the 2/4th would not complete the voyage to Singapore. As the *Marella* approached Java it was apparent that Singapore was a lost cause as the Imperial Japanese Army closed the ring around Singapore City. As a consequence a decision was made to land these troops at Tanjong Priok, the Port of Batavia where they would also experience action in the forthcoming weeks.

That is the story as it occured and one that has been recounted faithfully utilising official records.[10] The whole ship-breaking episode has not fared well with at least one historian, who has levelled criticism at the 2/4th Machine Gun Battalion for as is claimed, 'a major breakdown of discipline among their better trained comrades in Fremantle'.[11] Unquestionably the actions of some Australian soldiers on Singapore has drawn some degree of disrepute upon the 8th Division and in turn the 2nd A.I.F. Whether the AWL episode at Fremantle and the 2/4th's involvement can be blamed for a lack of training and fighting spirit by some troops during the Battle of Singapore really is a moot point. However, whilst on the subject, history does not record the exact number of machine gunners who were in the first wave of ship breakers.

There were 2,502 men who embarked at Sydney consisting of 120 Officers, 128 Warrant Officers and Sergeants and 2,254 other ranks. The Australian Official History *Japanese Thrust* states that there were 1907 all ranks, largely reinforcements for other units that arrived with the 2/4th Machine Gun Battalion. The end note on this subject goes onto say:

> '*The arrival of such reinforcements in Malaya may be explained partly by the fact that the practice had developed of sending raw recruits to the Middle East where they received their basic training under expert instructors in the excellent training organization that had been developed there. This does not however excuse the blunder of sending untrained men forward (early in January) to a division then going into battle. Even if there was a shortage of untrained reinforcements in Australia early in December, the needs of the 8th Division could have been foreseen.*'[12]

Colonel Lamb's report stated that, in his opinion, Lt-Col Anketell, his Officer's and NCO's sympathies were with the men. Nevertheless, back onboard the *Aquitania*, Lt-Col. Anketell was very busy relieving a number of his NCO's of their chevrons and many more of his other ranks of several pounds, from their paybooks.

Perhaps at this point it might be preferable to let the men from the 2/4th Machine Gun Battalion describe their feelings. This battalion had been interstate for six months and many men now had infant children whom they had never seen. One such man was Lieutenant Frank

10   MP729/7 File 42/422/68 Western Command Convoy "MS2" National Archives of Australia
11   Peter Elphick, Singapore *The Pregnable Fortress,* Hodder & Staughton 1995, p.288
12   Lionel Wigmore, *Japanese Thrust* Australia in th War of 1939–45, Army Volume IV Australian War Memorial Canberra 1957 p.258

Curnow. Frank had remained onboard the *Aquitania* and missed meeting his newborn son Lyle. Frank later wrote to his wife describing his disappointment:

'What I wouldn't have given to have had just one glimpse of that young fella of mine.'

Lieutenant Francis Lyle Curnow was killed in action at Ulu Pandan, Hill 200 on 12th February 1942. Another man who wrote home and mentioned this episode was Eddie Burton Eddie died at Sandakan in Borneo as a member of 'E' Force on 21st February 1945.

> Pte E.G.Burton
> A Coy 2/4" MG Bn.
> AIF Abroad
>   Dear Mum
>   Well here I am
> writing again and it is Sunday evening.
> We are still at Sea and do not yet
> know where we are bound for.
>   Well we went up before the colonel
> this afternoon and I did the two stripes
> and also a £2 fine with it. Still why
> worry it was well worth it, and if
> the boat should call into Fremantle
> again tomorrow I would be one of the
> first off again.
>   The weather is not the best as we
> have not seen the sun since we left
> Fremantle.
>   I am OK.
>   Well Mum this is just a short note.
> to let you know I am getting along alright
> and I will write again as soon as we land.
> some place xxxxxxx Lots of Love, Eddie

Sgt Percy Sturtridge also wrote:

> 'It would be difficult to adequately express in words the emotions felt by the men of the 2/4th on that day which we so eagerly awaited, and which now had become a mockery to us. Six months away from home and loved ones, the certainty that within weeks we would be in action and still no leave.'

The question which still remains unanswered is why eighty-eight trained machine gunners and support personnel who were all trained as infantry were kept behind bars as the *Aquitania* weighed anchor and set sail towards Singapore. Whether the soldier was a driver, a cook or a member of the Vickers machine gun section, the battalion's fighting strength was effectively weakened. Someone had issued the order to restrain these men from re-boarding their ship but who that person was remains a mystery.

Sir Earle Page[13] wrote[14] concerning his struggle to convince the British to send more reinforcements to Singapore. Page's writing aptly fits the situation and is a suitable ending to the story of the 2/4th Machine Gun Battalion's brief interlude at Fremantle.

> *'I then argued vigorously for continued reinforcements for Singapore. I held that Australians had been sent to Singapore with a definite promise of reinforcements and the Australian government would never consent to the desertion of its fighting men. To withhold reinforcements would be entirely fatal to the campaign, and would then threaten lives and fortunes of the men already there.'*

Australian reinforcements disembark at Singapore
Two 2/4th reinforcements, Roy 'Toona' Simmonds leads Richard 'Dick' Ridgwell

---

13   Earle Christmas Grafton Page, The Australian Government's representative to the British War Cabinet 1941–42
14   Sir Earle Page, *Truant Surgeon* Angus & Robertson 1963, p.326

Japanese Battlefield Tactics

The Battle for Malaya had gone so badly for Britain that the Japanese soldier quickly earned a reputation as being invincible. This was a far cry from the picture that had been painted of him and the ridicule he attracted as a short, slant eyed, bespectacled little man who would be no match for a trained soldier of the British Empire. Some of these little soldiers in the Imperial Guards (Konoye Division) were in fact over six feet tall. Much of this myth concerning the Japanese soldiers' fighting ability can be accredited to his battle tactics which he used to full effect. Lt-Gen Percival explains in his report:

619: *'The campaign in Malaya probably provided the first instance of operations between forces armed and equipped on modern lines being conducted in a country almost wholly covered with jungle or plantations of various types. There was therefore little previous experience on which to draw as a guide for the conduct of this particular type of warfare. It is well known that such a country favours the attacker. It makes the defence of a position a difficult and hazardous operation unless the flanks of that position rest securely on natural obstacles.'*

620: *'The Japanese, in accordance with their strategy of a vigorous offensive, invariably attacked with the least possible delay. They seldom made frontal attacks. Their usual tactics were to probe the front and search for the flanks. Having found the flanks they would then push mobile forces round to attack our communications which usually followed a single road. They also employed widely infiltration tactics by individuals and small parties of men as a means of creating alarm, the use of trees as fire positions, and the use of noise, i.e., fireworks and crackers resembling machine-guns in action as a weapon of war. In order to keep up a relentless pressure the Japanese staged attacks both by day and night.'* [15]

These tactics of probing, encirclement and infiltration were used to effect in Malaya and Singapore. By the time the Japanese came into contact with *Blackforce*[16] on Java Brigadier Blackburn had been suitably briefed and had put into place a defence plan to counter his opponents tactics.

Win Annear of 'D' Company No. 16 Platoon later wrote of his experiences coming out from the west coast of Singapore. These few lines explain very well the difficulties encountered by these men in attempting to withdraw to a safer position. If anything this firsthand report highlights the speed and constant pressure which these tactics place upon an adversary.

'When the nips landed on Singapore my guns were cut off. We tried to get through to Singapore township. We broke through the Jap lines several times, but they moved too quickly for us, and we found ourselves behind their lines again and again we were ambushed, in fact, three times. We eventually got into a boat and tried to make it by water, arriving at an island off Singapore on the Monday night after the show was over. By this time I only had two of my original men with me, the others that had not been killed had been separated in ambushes etc.' [17]

---

[15] Second Supplement to the London Gazette Friday 20th February 1948 Operations of Malaya Command, from 8th December 1941 to 15th February 1942 Report by Lt-Gen A. E. Percival, CB, DSO, MC, Formerly GOC Malaya. Section LXII.-Tactics paragraphs 619–620

[16] Lt-Col A. S. Blackburn VC, CMG, CBE, LLB, ED Commanding Officer of the 2/3rd Machine Gun Battalion was appointed to command all A.I.F. troops on Java to be known as *Blackforce*

[17] From a letter written by Richard Winston Annear to his family, donated by Clive Annear

Sungei Kranji-Sungei Jurong Defence Line
(Tank Trap)

This imaginary north-south running line on the western side of Singapore connects the Sungei Kranji on the northwest coast to the Sungei Jurong on the southwest coast. The line effectively shortens a 40,000 yard coastline to a 4,000 yard defensive line. Work was commenced as late as 3rd February 1942 on the digging of an Anti-Tank ditch as part of the defensive line. Except for swamp at its northern and southern extremities the Kranji–Jurong area was sparsely timbered, offering fields of fire of up to 250 yards that would have been ideal for the Vickers machine guns. By the time of the Japanese attack on the west coast of Singapore on the night of 8th February, whilst work on the Anti-Tank ditch had been completed nothing had been done to prepare infantry positions.

> *'Had a more whole-hearted attempt been made regarding this position, some of the disasters which were to befall may have been averted. What is certain is that battalions would have had the opportunity to prove their mettle instead of being disintegrated and defeated in small packets.'* [18]

Machine Gunners or Infantry?

Maj-Gen Gordon Bennett had criticised the British for their retention of 1918 vintage textbook methods. He believed that the method of beach defence whereby a long thin line of posts along a beach without depth as used, was outdated. Bennett preferred the more modern tactic of defending a shorter frontage and bringing forward reserve units once it was known where the enemy intended to execute their main landing. [19]

By the time the last troops had crossed the causeway, the decision had already been made to defend the entire 72 miles of Singapore's coastline. Most historians have generally taken the view that Lt-Gen Arthur Percival had given this order, however, the originator it seems was really Air Vice Marshall Sir Robert Brooke-Popham. Despite this revelation, Lt-Gen Percival had remained mute to this fact. The Wavell Report paragraph ten explains:

> *'Sir Robert discusses the defensive preparations. He had to make a decision between the two schools of thought: to defend the beaches or to hold the line inland. He gave orders for the defence of the beaches.'* [20]

One of the major drawbacks which confronted the 2/4th Machine Gun Battalion within the Singapore defence strategy was their close proximity to the coast which made them a prime target for enemy artillery. This can be directly related to the 'B' Company No. 8 and 9 Platoons and 'D' Company No. 13 Platoon positions. Once the Vickers guns had either been withdrawn, overrun, or all ammunition spent, then the advantage of these weapons over a clear frontage is lost in preference to lighter automatic weapons, the likes of Bren or Thompson machine guns. These weapons are better suited for close jungle fighting.

---

18   AWM54 File 553/5/23 Part 2 Report on Operations of 8th Australian Division A.I.F. in Malaya compiled from the narrative by Col. C. H. Kappe MBE, p.s.c. Australian War Memorial Canberra, p.99
19   Louis Allen, *Singapore 1941-1942*, Davis-Poynter Limited, London 1977, p.192
20   The Wavell Report, Public Records Office, London File PREM 3/168/3, p.3

So in this scenario, and realising that Australian 2nd A.I.F. machine gun battalions were formed as motorised units, the machine gunners were often frustrated by being unable to use the very effective Vickers machine gun over open ground. Save a few occasions during the course of the battle where some platoons had the opportunity to use this weapon, the battalion was generally relegated to an infantry roll. The casualties incurred by the 2/4th Machine Gun Battalion, in particular at Hill 200, Ulu Pandan, is testimony to this fact.

Lim Chu Kang Road Revisited 1942-2002

'D' Company No. 13 Platoon

Of the thousands of Australian tourists who visit Singapore each year most would probably search for a bargain along Orchard Road, sample the culinary delights of Singapore's many hawker stalls or perhaps sip on a pink gin at the Raffles Hotel. Others, in a quest to try and make sense of the Japanese invasion on Singapore in 1942 might make a visit to the Kranji War Cemetery, Changi Chapel, Sentosa Island (formerly Pulau Blakang Mati) or join one of the Battlefield tours under offer from the Singapore Tourist Bureau. It would be a safe bet however, none of these Australian tourists would ever dream of visiting a remote site located near the end of Lim Chu Kang Road on Singapore's northwest coast. It is also likely that the majority of Singaporeans as they go about their daily routines, are unaware that on this remote corner of their island is the place believed by historians to be the place where the Japanese first set foot on their island on the night of 8th February 1942.

Just to the east of the Sungei China at the end of a track within the Buloh Estate stood a two foot high stone retaining wall. Projecting out from this wall was a jetty at the end of which was a rotunda or gazebo. A little further along the wall was a shark proof swimming enclosure.

Lieutenant Eric Wankey, the Commanding Officer of No. 13 Platoon, had decided to mount his three remaining Vickers machine guns in three separate gun pits along this wall. It was impossible to dig gun pits because of the proximity to the water's edge and Singapore's high water table, so in this case the defences were sand bags raised above the height of the stone retaining wall. Originally there had been four Vickers machine guns, however, on Saturday 7th February Sgt. Ron Arbery had been placed in command of a supernumerary platoon, being No. 16 Platoon, and assigned to the defence of an area further to the south within the 2/19th Battalion's area. With Sergeant's Ron Arbery and Des Colevas went several men, being extra gun numbers and one of No. 13 Platoon's Vickers medium machine guns. All that stood between the troops of the Imperial Japanese Army's 5th Division on Singapore at this remote location were approximately thirty-five men of No. 13 Platoon, their three Vickers machine guns and with an allocation of 20,000 rounds of ammunition per gun.

This platoon had been attached to the Australian 2/20th Battalion to strengthen their defence of the northwest coast of Singapore. At 1000 hours on the morning of 8th February 1942 the Japanese commenced their artillery barrage of the west coast of Singapore which would not be lifted until 2200 hours that night.

Late in the morning at approximately 1130 hours the Vickers machine gun in the No. 1 pit received what was close enough to a direct hit. Sergeant Joe Pearce and Corporal Bill Paterson were wounded and Pte. Bob Pratt was killed outright. Corporal Edgar Hunt and Pte.'s Norm Venemore, Tom Beard and Ken Lally checked the gun and found it to be still fully serviceable, testimony to this weapon's robustness. However, so as not to take any unnecessary risks this gun was now sited between the other two Vickers. In pit No. 2 were Pte.'s George Neville and Johny Browning and in pit No. 3 were Pte.'s Lin MacDonald and Jack McCarthy being the numbers one and two on each gun.

John Morgan recalls,

'As it was my watch, on seeing a black mass on the water approaching our position, I called "13 Platoon Action" and commenced firing at the enemy. Gun crews were on the scene and were firing in a matter of seconds.'

The first wave of Japanese had commenced their attack about thirty minutes before the artillery barrage was lifted. It was roughly at this time, 2200 hours that the first wave of enemy leapt from their landing barges and began wading ashore. Some of the barges were sunk and as the enemy spilled into the water they attempted to move around the flanks of No. 13 Platoon's position where they were promptly taken care of by the spare gun numbers and troops from the 2/20th Battalion. One man in particular, Franz 'Brack' Bracklemann had a burning desire to bayonet a Japanese and not only did he fulfil his wish, it is now battalion folklore that with great zeal he may have accounted for as many as eight of the enemy.

About fifteen minutes later a second wave approached No. 13 Platoon's position. This time one barge was moored offshore on a fish trap and a Japanese mortar crew commenced firing. The Japanese knew how to use the mortar to good effect, and many of the battalion's casualties over the next seven days were as result of this weapon. A short time later a mortar round made a direct hit on the Vickers gun that Lt. Wankey and Pte. Jimmy Loller, his No. 2 had been firing. Although the gun did not suffer serious damage Lt. Wankey and Pte. Loller were both wounded. Lt. Wankey was to later have his right leg amputated and likewise Pte. Loller, his left leg. At this time Sgt. Harold 'Jake' Jacobs took over command of No. 13 Platoon. Sergeant Jacob's first order was for Driver Gil Saunders to evacuate the wounded to the Casualty Clearing Station. The story 'Jake' later recorded is one of utter chaos as successive waves of Japanese barges came head long at No.13 Platoon. As the Japanese attempted to come in along the jetty or envelop No. 13 Platoon's position by way of the flanks the machine gunners engaged the enemy with hand grenade, rifle and bayonet.

At close to 0230 hours the ammunition situation was becoming critical and 'Jake' gave the order to destroy the three Vickers machine guns. The remaining men moved out in single file in an easterly direction. Progress along a barely discernable track at night was extremely slow and certainly not helped by the smoke from the oil tank fires in the vicinity of the Woodlands area. Heavy small arms fire could be heard off to the right as the men arrived at dawn at the Sungei Kranji. This water course in their path proved difficult to cross however, with the aid of a purloined fishing boat the crossing was made in three trips. About four of the men had become disorientated along the way and had become lost. For the remainder, much to the relief of Major Alf Cough and Capt. George Gwynne they arrived at 'D' Company Headquarters located about one mile from the Sungei Kranji.

On the sixtieth anniversary of the 'Fall of Singapore' two of the original members of No. 13 Platoon, Joe Pearce and John Morgan travelled to Singapore for the occasion and returned to that isolated location at the end of Lim Chu Kang Road. Joe Pearce recalls this experience:

'My feelings on finding our old gun emplacement site on the Buloh Estate initially was one of excitement. Finally here we were at the same spot after all these years. The jetty, which had been enlarged was still there and is still used by the owners of a large residence which is there now but of course wasn't in 1942. Back then, there was a two storeyed house with an orchard and palm trees. This was where our slit

trenches were but now this whole area is overgrown with jungle. Part of the wall where our guns were set up has been extended on one end. The middle section of this wall has been lowered to about half of its original height but nevertheless you could still roughly work out where our three guns were sited.

I sat down quietly and my mind reflected back to that fateful day when the Japanese artillery barrage started and pounded us continually for seven hours. First Bob Pratt, Bill Paterson and myself were knocked out. Later when the Japs tried to land, Eric Wankey, Jim Loller and Tom Beard were carted out. Lin MacDonald, Fred Tregenza were ambushed on the way out, never to be seen again. Later as POW's Edgar Hunt, Jack McCarthy in 'D' Force, Bill Paterson in 'F' Force, Ron Langdon in 'H' Force, Johny Browning and 'Comet' Shirley in Sandakan Borneo. There was also Harry Carter, Norm Venemore, Jim and Lacy Gibbs drowned going to Japan and Ken Lally killed in a mining accident, all never to see Australia again.

Then the fight to stay alive for three and a half years until war's end and the joy of seeing Australia again and our family and friends. Our loves, lives and ambitions realised, children to raise, beautiful life. Now just John Morgan and myself from No. 13 Platoon back at the landing after 60 years. All these memories good and bad, of life I feel very lucky and humble for my life's experience and say a prayer for our fifteen that never saw Australia again.'

Joe Pearce   25th April 2002

Who Really were the First?

On the night of 8th February 1942 the Japanese 5th and 18th Divisions launched the first attack across the Strait of Johore against the Australian 22nd Brigade positions on the western sector of Singapore. Was this in fact the first attempt at a landing on Singapore or had the Japanese Imperial Guards (Konoe Division) been the first to earn this distinction? The first hint of this may be found in the diary of Capt. Avon Smith-Ryan. He mentions that at Adam Park [21] a Japanese Officer had told him that the Imperial Guards Division had actually been the first to attempt a landing on Singapore at the important Causeway Sector. [22]

The basis of this claim was an incident that occurred on the night of 8th February 1942. Lieutenant Frank Smyth of the 2/30th Battalion had taken out a small boat into the Strait with Pte.'s Calvert and Barnes as a listening and observation post. This was set up about 200 yards from the Johore shoreline and 300 yards to the west of the Causeway. Departing from the 27th Brigade's sector at 2030 hours they gathered information on the location of some Japanese light machine gun positions whereupon they turned the boat around and headed back in towards Singapore.

Sighting another boat about 400 yards to their right Lieutenant Smyth decided to head towards it, believing that it might be another group of Australians on a fact finding mission. When about 50 yards separated the two craft, Lt. Smyth could tell that it was a larger boat than theirs and that there were about seven or eight men onboard. This would be correct because the boats used by the Guards for their feint on Pulau Ubin on the night of 7th–8th February held eight men according to *Singapore 1941–1942 The Japanese Version* by Masanobu Tsuji. [23]

Lieutenant Smyth challenged the Japanese who immediately set a course to ram this officer and his crew. When the two boats were almost on top of each other it is reported that Lt. Smyth leapt into the Japanese boat, released a hand grenade and leapt back into his own boat. The three Australians on a prearranged plan then capsized their boat and swam in different directions back towards the Australian lines. Cries for help were heard from Lt. Smyth but the two Privates were unable to locate him in the darkness and his body was never found. Machine gun fire broke out from the opposite shore and a call for defensive fire went up. Capt. Smith-Ryan's diary now takes up the story:

> '*A grenade exploded over the far side of the Strait and later cries for help were heard down on the wire in the water. Various odd shots were fired, the reason for this is not clear. I went down to the foreshore and found the 2 i/c of the infantry company who declared the voice to be that of the CSM (Lt. Smyth had been promoted that day). The two men got back by way of the Causeway but the CSM was not seen again. I went down to Corporal Sanderson's* [24] *section and returned to Corporal Teasdale's* [25] *area. Just as I was leaving there, machine gunfire broke out on the other side of the Strait. I would say about 12 guns at a minimum. Not very much later, Anderson the infantry company commander 'A' Company 2/30 Battalion from down*

---

[21] Adam Park was a high-class residential area about a mile and a half from the Royal Singapore Golf Club, which was used as a POW working camp whilst scenic roads and the 'Fallen Warriors' shrine atop Bukit Batok were being constructed.

[22] PR00592 Item 10, Captain Avon Smith-Ryan Diary, Australian War Memorial, Canberra. Captin Smith-Ryan was Second in Command of 'B' Company 2/4th Machine Gun Battalion.

[23] Colonel Masanobu Tsuji who was the Chief of Operations and Planning of the Japanese XXV Army orchestrated the Japanese campaign down to the last detail. His book *Singapore 1941-1942* The Japanese Version of the Malyan Campaign of World War II, Oxford University Press Singapore 1991, describes the Malaya and Singapore Campaigns from the Japanese viewpoint.

[24] Sanderson is WX8777 Cpl. John Sanderson, Section Corporal No. 9 Platoon 'B' Company 2/4th Machine Gun Battalion.

[25] Teasdale is WX10865 Cpl. Thomas Eric Teasdale Section Corporal No. 8 Platoon 2/4th Machine Gun Battalion.

at the front decided that something was wrong and sent up four reds (Four red Very lights, signalling a call for CDF). Down came ten guns, gosh it was good to hear and they fired like a dream, 1 minute saturation, 1 minute normal and 3 minutes of intermittent fire. Lt. Don Lee[26] had six Vickers guns under his command and at this time Lt. Graham MacKinnon[27] had four. The guns were equipped with Mk VIIIZ ammunition[28] to cover the longer distances across The Strait. It seems quite feasible from talking with Japanese during our later work that an attempt to land at the Causeway that night was abandoned.'[29]

The Australian official history *The Japanese Thrust* has this to add to the story:

'Vickers machine gunners blazed at the Japanese, and 25 pounders and 4.5 inch howitzers joined in the fire, which lasted for about half an hour. The Australian gunners in this area were aided by a beach-light, which illuminated barges about 700 yards to the left of the causeway. This exchange, to the accompaniment of much yelling from the Japanese, was followed a little later by another burst of fire from their side, but no other engagement occurred during the night. Very lights seen shooting skyward from the 22nd Brigade's sector gave a hint, however, of enemy assault in that direction.'[30]

The 2/30th Battalion unit history *Galleghan's Greyhounds* states:

'It was subsequently believed that the Japanese were attempting diversionary tactics to cover the first crossings and landings in the 22nd Brigade area, to the west and where Japanese success signals were observed going up from the Island shores. Information was later received from a Japanese officer indicating that an attempt to land in the Battalion area was to have been made as a diversion, but the heavy fire had broken up their troop concentrations.'[31]

On the night of 7th-8th February the Japanese Imperial Guards had been tasked with creating a feint. This took the form of a cross-strait landing opposite the Changi Cantonment on Pulau Ubin. In all, 400 men and two mountain guns were landed. This landing and the increased activity of Japanese artillery opposite the eastern sector of Singapore was designed to convince British Malaya Command that the first landings would be in the vicinity of the Causeway on the north coast of the island.

In fact, the west coast of Singapore had already been earmarked for special attention on the day and night of 8th February 1942. Nevertheless the Japanese Imperial Guards Commander (Lt-Gen T. Nishimura) was still not happy. He sought permission to also attack on the night of 8th February.

The Japanese side of the story confirms that the guards were keen to make their presence felt;

'Originally Army orders for the assault on Singapore grouped the Konoe Division

---

26   Lee is WX9387 Lt. Charles Donald Lee Commanding Officer of No. 9 Platoon 'B' Company 2/4th Machine Gun Battalion. [Author's note: Talking to several of the men from 'B' Company, including Don Lee, it is believed, that due to some confusion at the time that not all six of the Vickers guns of No. 9 Platoon came into action.]

27   MacKinnon is WX3707 Lt. Graham MacKinnon, Commanding Officer of No. 8 Platoon 'B' Company 2/4th Machine Gun Battalion.

28   MK VIIIZ ammunition was used for longer ranges. It was estimated that from the Causeway to the Imperial Guard's front line positions was approximately 1200 yards.

29   PR00592 Item 10 Captain Avon Smith-Ryan Diary, Australian War Memorial Canberra

30   Lionel Wigmore, *Japanese Thrust* Australia in the War of 1939–1945 Army Volume IV Australian War Memorial Canberra p.318

31   A. W. Penfold, W. C. Bayliss, K. E. Crispin *Galleghan's Greyhounds* The Story of the 2/30 Battalion A.I.F. 2/30th Bn. Association Sydney 1979 p.191

as the second line, but the commander of the division emphatically demanded a modification of the orders because of his fervent desire to attack shoulder to shoulder with the other two divisions, and the army Commander acceded to his request.' [32]

Mansanobu Tsuju also has this to say:

'General Yamashita revised his orders accordingly, and this matter later gave rise to serious problems.' [33]

Mansanobu Tsuju also states a very interesting point:

> *'Although the whole Army admired the Konoe Imperial Guards for the manner in which they had carried out the duties assigned them, they had a reputation for occasionally taking pride in defying Army orders.'* [34]

The incident with Lt. Smyth and the 2/4th's Vickers machine guns on the night of 8th February had given the Australians fair warning of the Imperial Guards' intentions and this was the pre-cursor to further trouble the following night.

The British Official History has this to say:

> *'The 5th and 18th Divisions practised carrying collapsible boats and boarding on the 4th February 1942 on the Sungei Muar. As both these divisions had had considerable experience in river crossing operations and, as 5th Division had received specialist training in amphibious operations prior to the 8th December 1941, extensive rehearsal was not considered necessary. The Guards Division practised boarding landing craft on 8th February 1942 in an area near its embarkation point. The craft used for the actual crossing of the Strait of Johore were manhandled to the launching points in order to ensure secrecy.'* [35]

On the night of 8th February, the 5th and 18th Divisions moved out from under the cover of the jungle canopy and with their various landing craft prepared to make a landing against the Australians on the west coast of Singapore. On the west coast there were huge gaps between the posts of the 22nd Brigade's positions where as the defensive positions of the 27th Brigade on the Causeway Sector were more concentrated due to the narrower frontage. On the Causeway Sector the Guards Division, conscious of the Singapore Naval Base oil storage tanks, were fearful that this oil might be released into the Johore Strait and ignited, thus creating a wall of fire in their path.

To counter this possibility, the Japanese bombed these tanks, setting them alight. This handicapped their observation of military targets caused by a thick pall of black smoke, [36] which billowed above Singapore. Nevertheless it seems it gave them peace of mind. The Guards now readied themselves for a second time on the night of 9th February.

---

[32] Masanobu Tsuji *Singapore 1941–1942* The Japanese Version, Oxford University Press 1991, p.243–244
[33] ibid p.233
[34] ibid p.234
[35] Maj.-Gen. Stanley Woodburn Kirby CB, CMG, OBE, MC, The History of The Second World War *The War Against Japan* Volume I, HMSO London 1957, Appendix 26.
[36] The oil tanks that were set alight at the Singapore Naval Base at Sembawang, should not be confused with the petrol tanks at the Woodlands tank farm. Considering that these tanks would have been under observed Japanese artillery range it is difficult to understand why they had not destroyed these tanks prior to their cross strait invasion. There are at least two possible answers to this question, the first being that the petrol tanks were underground. Unfortunately history books on this subject do not record whether these tanks were in fact above or underground, so it is difficult to prove this theory. The second answer might be that the Japanese hoped to conserve this petro-chemical resource for their own use once Singapore was under their control. There were also oil storage terminals at Kranji, Pulau Bukom, Pulau Sebarok in the Malacca Straits, and Pulau Sambu in the Straits of Singapore.

The *Japanese Thrust* sums up the situation at this time:

> '*Meanwhile having staged the diversionary landing on Ubin Island, the Japanese Guards Division had been assembling for the attack on the Causeway Sector. The width of suitable landing points between the Causeway and the Kranji was considered too narrow to allow more than one battalion to cross the Strait at a time, and the Japanese Command feared that the operation would involve heavy casualties.*'[37]

At 2100 hours the 4th Imperial Guards Regiment launched their assault against the Australian 27th Brigade positions. Some of the boats were sunk, some Japanese landed and became lost in the darkness, and others came ashore at Sungei Kranji, Sungei Mandai and Sungei Mandai Kechil. At first progress was slow and the rising tide left many cut off in swampy ground. Many of the invaders were cut to pieces by the cross fire from the Vickers machine guns. More landing craft arrived and by midnight of 9th February the three forward companies from the 2/26th Battalion were forced back about 500 yards into the Kranji Peninsula.

In front of the 2/30th positions between the Sungei Mandai and the Sungei Mandai Kechil was the Woodlands tank farm containing 2,000,000 gallons of petrol.[38] The order came down through the chain of command that the 2/26th although in trouble, were not to withdraw until these tanks had been destroyed which were located near the Causeway in the 2/30th Battalion's area. This was in the process of being done when the truck bringing up the Australian Officer, Lt. A. B. Watchorn of the 2/12th Field Company Engineers along with the explosives was destroyed. Undeterred, Lt. Watchorn ordered that the valves on the tanks be opened, allowing petrol in the storage tanks to flow out into the the river system and with the aid of the incoming tide, out into the Strait. In the meantime a second and more successful attempt was made to bring explosives forward to finish the job. This was done and at 0430 hours on 10th February 1942 the Woodlands tank farm was demolished. What awaited the follow up waves of Japanese certainly was a warm reception. The Australians in this sector poured as much fire as possible into the Guards prior to withdrawing from the Causeway.

Masanobu Tsuji describes the carnage:

> '*The Konoe Division just as they commenced to cross the Strait near the Causeway, became caught in petroleum to which the enemy set fire. The front line regiment was enveloped in fire while on the water and was almost annihilated.*'[39]

Permission was sought from Lt-Gen Yamashita to cancel the attack on the Causeway Sector and allow the Guards Division to come in behind the 5th Division on the west coast. Yamashita was not impressed by the whole affair and said that as far as he was concerned the Guards could do what they pleased and he would take Singapore with the 5th and 18th Divisions. It appears that Yamashita and Nishimura were long standing rivals and that 'there existed a high level of animosity between the two Japanese Generals'.[40] The Japanese were surprised that the Johore Strait had not been flooded with oil prior to the attack on the Australian 22nd Brigade sector.

---

37 Lionel Wigmore, *Japanese Thrust* Australia in the War of 1939–45 Army Volume IV Australian War Memorial Canberra 1957 p.331

38 '*Enormous stocks of petrol and oil were destroyed by the naval authorities and by the oil companies themselves. Fires made by this burning oil sometimes continued for two or three weeks. Smoke sometimes hid the sun and soot blackened the town.*' Ivan Simson formerly Chief Engineer, Malaya Command, *Singapore Too Little Too Late*, Leo Cooper London 1970, p.98

39 Masanobu Tsuji *Singapore 1941–1942* The Japanese Version, Oxford University Press 1991 p.243

40 Ian Ward, *Snaring The Other Tiger*, Media Masters Singapore 1996 p.34.

The Australians, having been ordered to withdraw allowed the Imperial Guards to gain a foothold on the Causeway–Kranji Sector. No doubt this withdrawal saved loss of face for the Konoe Division before their commander and the eyes of the Japanese 5th and 18th Divisions. Evidence might now suggest that the Japanese Imperial Guards were granted permission to attack on the night of 8th, but under the stipulation that they not launch their attack until the 5th and 18th Divisions had gained a foothold on Singapore. If this was the case, then it is very likely that the Guards had indeed defied Army orders and launched their attack earlier than they had been authorised. This then is likely what is meant by Masanobu Tsuji's statement that: 'this gave rise to serious problems later.'

> *'The Prince's Forces', as the elite Imperial Guards were known, had not seen action since the Russo-Japanese War in the early years of the century. Very conscious of this fact, Nishimura was anxious to have his troops notch up some quick battlefield successes to dispel widely held concerns over the Guards' lack of combat experience.'* [41]

Ultimately the question must be asked, in an effort to claim its share of glory, had the Imperial Guards in fact attempted the first landing on Singapore. If this is so, had it firstly all gone very wrong when Lt. Smyth and Pte.'s Calvert and Barnes interrupted their plans? Why had Capt. Avon Smith-Ryan been told that the Guards had made the first attempt at a landing on the night of 8th February 1942 if it wasn't true? And why were only men from the 2/4th Machine Gun Battalion sent from Adam Park Camp to Johore Bahru in April 1942 to erect a shrine to honour the fallen from the Imperial Guards Division?

Captain Booth's Report

The following is a copy of a communication received from Capt. E. H. Booth the Commander of 'D' Company 2/30th Battalion addressed to Major Charles Green 2/4th Machine Gun Battalion:

> *'As requested the following are the details of the engagement of my company with the enemy on 12th February 1942 in which Lt. G. MacKinnon who was attached with his platoon and 4 guns displayed outstanding courage and devotion to duty and in my opinion deserves some sort of recognition for this.*
>
> *On the morning of 11th February 1942 the 2/30th Battalion withdrew under orders from the Causeway sector to vicinity of Mandai crossroads and occupied a new defensive position with companies disposed from crossroads to the Singapore–Malaya pipeline astride the road. 'D' Company position was such that it was responsible for the protection of the right flank of the 2/30th Battalion and as the most likely method of enemy approach appeared to be along the pipeline the company was disposed astride this and on the forward slopes of the high ground just north of Mandai Road at this point.*
>
> *Lt. MacKinnon's platoon with 4 medium machine guns at this stage came under command of 'D' Company 2/30th and the co-operation, intelligence and energy of MacKinnon and his men was noticeable from the start. MacKinnon himself made many reconnaissance missions in order to find the best possible gun positions for the tasks I gave him and throughout the whole day of 11th February he spent his time improving the general fire plan of my position. After reconnaissance patrols at*

---

[41]   Ian Ward, *Snaring The Killer They Called God*, Media Masters Singapore 1992 p.90

night and a fighting patrol at dawn had made contact with the enemy north and along the pipeline at 0910 hours on 12th February he launched a heavy attack in the general direction south along Sungei Mandai and on 'D' Company's position.

At this time the 2/30th Battalion were in the process of carrying out an orderly withdrawal (not in close contact) with the object of counter attacking Bukit Panjang further south. 'D' Company automatically became a vanguard for the battalion and much depended on the time we could hold off the enemy attack. MacKinnon had to bring his guns back from their trucks at great speed and under fire. These guns were remounted and were maintained in action despite heavy fire and some casualties for nearly two hours for which period the position was held. MacKinnon himself proved fearless under fire, personally directing the fire of the guns on many occasions.

When an Indian Regiment on our right flank was known to have withdrawn east along Mandai Road I decided to withdraw and it was not until every man of my company were successfully out of the position that MacKinnon brought his guns out. He did everything possible to save these guns but by the time they were loaded on his truck and his Platoon Sergeant (Sgt WX8809 Richard Sandilands) had been killed during the process he was about completely surrounded by the enemy and I consider he did the only thing possible when he had to finally abandon them after attempting to destroy both truck and guns in the face of enemy fire.

The final withdrawal of his men across the Bukit Mandai whilst under exceptionally heavy fire was also a tribute to the courage and the outstanding leadership of Lt. MacKinnon.' [42]

Signed E. H. Booth Capt.

Officer Commanding 'D' Company 2/30th Battalion A.I.F.

Lt. Graham Charles MacKinnon, the Officer Commanding No. 8 Platoon 2/4th Machine Gun Battalion, was recommended for the Military Cross by the Commanding Officer of the 2/4th, Major Charles Edward Green. There is also a report on this action the 2/30th Battalion unit history. [43]

Report by WX7777 Corporal Arthur Draper

'Last Friday I went out on a party under command of Captain E. H. Booth of the 2/30th Battalion. We buried the remains of some of the unknown and on a cross, placed a small disc in memory of the 2/30th and 2/4th killed in that action. Unfortunately time was limited but I was able to have a look around. There was no trace of Dick Sandilands or Donald (Do-Dah) Day. As luck would have it the man who was beside WX8736 Bob (Bloocher) Smith when he was killed was in the party. He took me to the spot and a body had been buried or rather earth covered over it where he fell. He was the only man killed in that area and a mess tin of the old pattern like ours was alongside the mound. I am quite convinced that it was Bob's without a doubt. Back at the hill where Ray Carruthers was last seen the remains of two men were found about 300 to 400 yards up from the road. A helmet

---

42   Report by Captain E H. Booth 2/30th Battalion A.I.F. handed to Major Charles Green 2/4th Machine Gun Battalion. Item donated by Major Green's daughter, Mrs Barbara Brand

43   A. W. Penfold, W. C. Bayliss, K. E. Crispin *Galleghan's Greyhounds* The Story of the 2/30th Battalion A.I.F. 2/30th Bn. Association Sydney 1979 p.206–209

covered with hessian and bearing Gilbert Japp's name and Regimental number was alongside. Also there was a haversack bearing Laurie McGrath's name and Regimental number nearby. (McGrath returned to Australia sick, January 1942, Author) *It may be Carruthers but if so he had a varied collection of gear. It is an almost hopeless task trying to identify any of the remains. Sorry I could not find out anything definite.'* [44]

Signed

WX 7777 O8/O11 Draper

Arthur Draper

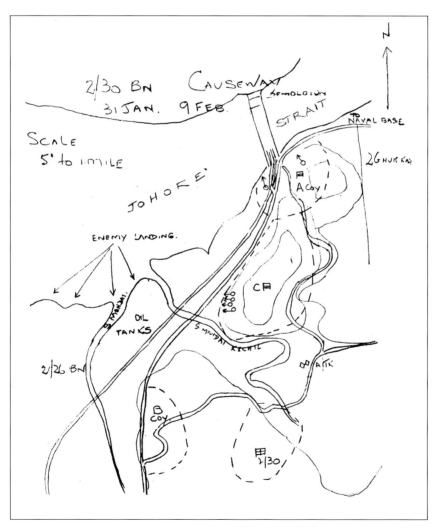

27th Brigade Dispositions Causeway Sector – Hand drawn Map.
This map clearly shows the Sungei Mandai and Sungei Mandai Kechil as well as the location of the Woodlands Tank Farm.

[44]   Report by Arthur Draper handed to Major Charles Green. Item donated by Mrs Barbara Brand

South-West Bukit Timah (Sleepy valley) 11.2.1942

At 1800 hours on 7th February 1942 Major Bert Saggers, the Commanding Officer of 'A' Company 2/4th, Machine Gun Battalion was ordered to form a Divisional Reserve Battalion for the 8th Division. The battalion was to be known as the Special Reserve Battalion and was to comprise two companies, 'A' and 'B', made up of Australian Army Service Corps personnel, and 'E' Company. 'E' Company was to be formed from the reinforcements for the 2/4th who had embarked on 16th January at Fremantle. The question may be asked as to why there were no 'C' and 'D' companies included within this unit? The answer is simple really, there just weren't enough spare men to form these other two companies.

We will take up the story of the Special Reserve Battalion at 0100 hours on 11th February 1942. At this time the battalion was positioned on a bare feature astride Jurong Road. Small arms fire could be heard at Bukit Timah Village, about a mile to the rear. Jurong Road was the only road on which to retire and this ran through Bukit Timah Village.

It was at about this time that firing could be heard on the right flank where a British unit was located. At 0200 hours firing was also heard on the left flank. Major Saggers realised that he would have to get the battalion off this bare feature before first light or stand the chance of coming under attack from observed enemy small arms fire from the other slopes in the area. Lieutenant Vic Mentiplay, Major Saggers' Liaison Officer, had brought back information that the British Commander was ready to withdraw his unit to a better position about 400 yards to the rear.

At daybreak Major Saggers moved his men down one side of the feature whilst the British moved around the other side via Jurong Road. The new position was on a slightly rising slope in a rubber plantation. At this point in time the heads and shoulders of the enemy could be seen against the silhouette of dawn's light. The Japanese pushed up to meet this body of troops using the rubber as cover as they advanced.

The heights of Bukit Timah and Bukit Timah Village were a Japanese strategic objective. Bukit Timah was the highest point on the island at 481 feet. Bukit Timah Village being the juncture of north, south, east and west running thoroughfares, was located at a pivotal point on the island. It was obvious that the Japanese intended to keep this area under their control. From this position the Japanese could swing southeast to Buona Vista and enter Singapore City from the south thereby closing the British escape route via Keppel Harbour.

On coming into view, the enemy immediately engaged and by 0730 hours fighting had become intense along the entire line. Orders came from the senior ranking British Commander that the combined force was to retire. The time was 0850 hours and the force was to be ready to move at 0900 hours. Promptly at 0900 hours 'E' Company launched a vigorous bayonet attack. Fourteen of the enemy were killed and two were captured. The remainder of the enemy in the vicinity fled for their lives.

This action cleared the area to successfully allow the troops to disengage and the formation was now to retire in three columns. The Indians were to withdraw on the left flank, Australians in the centre and the British on the right flank. The men marched about a mile through dense scrub when they came upon a saucer like depression of open country about 600 yards long by 400 yards wide ahead of them. On the left was an embankment about 3 feet high on which a barbed wire fence ran along its length. On the far side of the depression there were several native huts.

The three columns moved forward in column of route until they were about 200 yards from these huts when suddenly all hell broke loose. The enemy had prepared an ambush and from the left and right flanks and in front from the native huts were pouring in mortar, light automatic and small arms fire into the three columns of retreating troops. The three columns then broke and started to intermingle. The main cause of this was the more numerous Indians who panicked, some gesturing with a piece of white cloth, their wish to surrender. As the huts ahead of the men were approached they were raked with light automatic weapons to clear the enemy from their path.

On passing through the huts there was still 150 yards to go until a small rise and comparative safety was reached. Eventually Reformatory Road was reached and on crossing the men again came under further enemy light automatic fire. After crossing the railway line a head count was made of the Special Reserve Battalion and of the original 200 men who had commenced the withdrawal action an hour earlier, eighty now remained. Some of the men who had been wounded in the carnage had been forced to remain behind and seek cover.

One eyewitness account tells us the final seconds of Lieutenant Vic Warhurst:

> '*His thigh was shattered. That evening he asked me to bandage his leg. I was wounded myself and made an attempt to get to Lt. Warhurst when I heard voices. Five Japs appeared on the scene and bayoneted him whilst he lay on the ground. After they left, the bayonet with rifle attached was left sticking out of his lifeless body. It was a .303 rifle presumably his own as he was carrying a rifle in action.*'[45]

The Aftermath

At Sime Road Camp on 8th December 1942 the Japanese had granted Major Saggers permission for a burial party to return to the scene of the ambush at South-West Bukit Timah in an attempt to locate the bodies of the dead. Led to the spot by a local Chinese, the group managed to locate about thirty bodies. Their trip wasn't as successful as they had hoped as they were hampered by the long lalang, or wild grass and time did not allow for proper burials.

As was the case with Hill 200, Ulu Pandan the men were angered by the fact that ten months had elapsed before permission was granted to take out a burial party. At the scene it was discovered that the bodies of the enemy had been collected amidst the bodies of Indian Sepoys, British and Australian troops. There were areas that were pitted with slit trenches where the bodies could easily have been laid out and covered over.

On 21st December 1942, the same day as Major Cough's party was permitted to return to Hill 200, Major Saggers led a burial party to the area for the second time. The bodies of thirty-two men were located at one spot and they were buried in a common grave at map reference: 753147. Identification was difficult however, the remains of Albert Annetts was located and given a proper burial. At another location a cigarette case inscribed with the initials J. T. was found. This was thought to have belonged to Lt. Jimmy Till the original battalion R.S.M. Crosses were placed at the head and foot of the common graves with the following inscription.

Killed in Action
11th February 1942
In this common grave lay the remains of those whose names appear below
Buried 21st December 1942

Rest in Peace

---

45   Permission was sought and granted by Mrs Joan Warhurst, Lt. Vic Warhurst's widow, to publish this information.

Hill 200, Ulu Pandan IV (Mapanyang) 12.2.1942

The following is an abridged report of the 2/4th Machine Gun Battalion's involvement at Hill 200, Ulu Pandan IV. On 11th February Lt-Col M. J. Anketell, was ordered to equip all the machine gunners of his battalion that he could possibly muster. He was to send them forward to fight as infantry on the 22nd Australian and 44th Indian Brigade's fronts. During the day the Australians and Indians had little respite from Japanese machine gun and mortar fire, as well as air attacks by enemy aircraft.

The first solid group to arrive on the scene at the 22nd Brigade's front was a mixed company of about ninety 2/4th machine gunners. These men had made slow progress due to enemy air activity, but managed to occupy Hill 200, Pandan IV at 1700 hours. At about the same time the Signals No. 1 and AA No. 2 Platoons under the command of Capt. McEwin also took up positions approximately 300 yards to the south of feature Hill 200 atop a small hill. By 0930 hours on the morning of 12th February, the strength of the Australians had reached about 800 men with the 2/4th supplying about half of this number.

During the night of 11th–12th February the Australian artillery did a good job in keeping the enemy quiet. The next day, however, was a different story. The Japanese 18th Division continued to push in between the Australian and Indian positions near the Ulu Pandan-Holland Road junction. In an attempt to get behind the 22nd Brigade's position, the Japanese began an infiltration movement around the northern flank of the machine gunners on Ulu Pandan IV.

The enemy, in their attempt to outflank the Australians, had moved into a long gully between the Gordon Highlanders' position and those of the 2/4th on Ulu Pandan IV. Two detachments of machine gunners were sent to an area in the vicinity of a railway bridge on Holland Road. Here they moved into the gully and halted any further penetration by the enemy. All efforts by the Japanese to occupy this high feature had been thwarted, so the enemy had to remain content to pour in machine gun, mortar and spasmodic artillery fire, to little effect.

Just before midday on the 12th the enemy attempted to bring forward reinforcements from the north by truck. This convoy ran into trouble in the shape of an armoured car detachment led by the 2/4th's Cpl. Oliver Stanwell. Corporal Stanwell's crew destroyed the reconnaissance car and thirteen trucks by the time they had finished their work; this action successfully blocking the road to the enemy for some time. Oliver Stanwell was another machine gunner that would not return from 'E' Force in Borneo.

By 1500 hours on the 12th the Japanese had broken through the Indians and captured Hill 150. This necessitated an adjustment to the 2/18th Battalion's positions to counter the enemy's flanking manoeuvre. At about 1700 hours a patrol sighted some stationary Japanese transport vehicles. This was an indication that the enemy had brought up fresh troops with the intention of moving in behind the left flank of the 2/18th Battalion's position. By 1800 hours heavy fire was now being taken to the left rear of the 2/18th Battalion however, the fire was heavier on the 2/4th Machine Gun Battalion positions on Ulu Pandan IV.

The enemy by this time had captured Hill 130 which offered them excellent cover and it was for this reason this feature would have been too costly in lives to regain. At dusk it was decided to reform the line by slightly withdrawing the left flank of the 2/4th Machine Gun Battalion and filling the gap between the 2/4th and the 2/18th with another composite unit. Between 1700 and 2000 hours a great deal of action developed forward of the 2/4th's positions and the situation was becoming serious. The hills opposite the 2/4th on Hill 200, Ulu Pandan IV, were literally infested with Japanese who were too far away to harm with small arms and machine gun fire. A CDF from the artillery was made but because of poor signal communications these guns could not be ranged in accurately on the enemy. This meant that an ideal opportunity to inflict heavy loss upon the enemy was lost.

The Australians were now experiencing their first taste of the 150mm (5.9 inch) mortar nicknamed the 'flying pig'. The pig was in fact the Model 93 (1933) smooth bore muzzle loaded mortar which had a range of 2,100 metres or 2,300 yards. The projectile for this weapon weighed in at 56lbs and contained 14lbs of explosive. The 'flying pig' is really only renowned for the noise it made when its missile was airborne and for the huge hole it made in the earth when it landed. It couldn't be said that this weapon ever inflicted any harm upon the men of the 2/4th but it certainly must have terrified a few of them. It was about 2130 hours that Lt-Col Anketell was badly wounded.[46]

Captain Colin Cameron had accompanied the Colonel around his 'C' Company area. Because 'C' Company had lost hills L, K and H, Lt-Col Anketell, Capt. Cameron and Major Robertson, who was commanding a company from the 2/20th Battalion, were on reconnaissance to define a new perimeter. Captain Cameron reported to Major Cough, 'D' Company, that the Col. had been badly wounded by mortar or artillery shell burst. The R.M.O., Capt. Anderson, dressed the Colonel's wound and sent him back to Alexandra Hospital. Meanwhile the battle to hold Ulu Pandan had only just begun, the following narrative is taken from Col. Thyer's report which gives a good description of events as they affected the 2/4th Machine Gun Battalion:

> '*Neither the noise tactics nor the intensity of the hostile fire perturbed the machine-gunners who waited patiently until the enemy came to within one hundred and fifty yards and then opened up a steady and concentrated fire on the crowded enemy. Those who got through this barrage of rifle and machine-gun bullets were dealt with by hand grenades. One Japanese attack after another was thrown back with heavy losses. Shortly afterwards Brigade orders to withdraw were issued, but it was not until 2220 hours that the Bn. received its instructions.*
>
> *By this time the enemy had gained the lower slopes of Pandan IV and Hill 130 from which he was pouring small arms fire into the rear of 'C' Company and on a smaller knoll 300 yards to the south. The battalion closed into a tighter perimeter stubbornly resisting the enemie's (sic) attacks. In the heavy fighting this unit suffered heavily in killed and wounded, included in the latter was Lt-Col Anketell, the CO, who later died of wounds.*
>
> *By this time the MG Bn. was completely surrounded and because of its inability to organise a detachment to cover the withdrawal it was obvious that the battalion was not yet out of danger. To relieve the pressure a counter-attack with the bayonet was put in and the Japanese put to flight. In every encounter with the A.I.F. they would not face the bayonet.*'[47]

Captain McEwin had reformed his Signals and AA Platoons on the track near the road and led them up this track to a point opposite Hill 200 where he attacked with both platoons. The Japanese were holding the northeast slope of the hill and the attack pushed back to the crest. There were some 2/4th killed and many wounded in this attack and these men were sent back. Captain McEwin pushed on again to take the crest of the hill with what is believed to have been about twenty men. On reaching the crest they attempted to consolidate their old pits, but the enemy came back strongly and only about four or five machine gunners came out.

---

[46] On the subject of Lt.-Col Anketell's wounding Maj-Gen Gordon Bennett wrote: 'Some shells also fell on the 2/4th Machine Gun Battalion's Headquarters, wounding the commanding officer Lieutenant-Colonel Anketell.' Lieut.-Gen H. Gordon Bennett, previously General Officer Commanding Australian Imperial Force, Malaya *Why Singapore Fell* Angus & Robertson 1944 p.173

[47] AWM File 553/5/23 Part 2 Report on Operations of 8th Australian Division A.I.F. in Malaya compiled from the narrative by Col. C. H. Kappe MBE, p.s.c. Australian War Memorial Canberra p.159

'With the aid of the damaged trucks placed across the road, four officers and three other ranks covered the withdrawal of the 50 or more casualties to the Regimental Aid Post. By 0300 hours on the 13th, the battalion now reduced to 250 all ranks, was back on Cemetery Hill near Buona Vista Road triangle where it bivouacked for a well earned respite. The West Australians had acquitted themselves magnificently. During the critical hours between 1700 hours and 2300 hours they had been supported by artillery, who despite the fact that their range was at times so short that the rounds fell among our troops, did invaluable work in relieving the pressure on Pandan IV.' [48]

Adam Park

At Adam Park the prisoners had been in part employed on the clearing and construction of the 'Fallen Warriors' shrine on Bukit Batok. The Japanese went to a great deal of trouble to locate the bodies of their dead, cremate the corpses and lay the ashes at this shrine. This led to repeated unsuccessful requests by Major Cough to gain permission for a search party to be sent back to Hill 200, Ulu Pandan, to locate, identify and bury the bodies of 2/4th who had participated in a bayonet charge to recapture the position on the night of 12th February 1942.

On 29th May 1942 there was trouble at Adam Park as over sixty men were caught outside the wire. They were all given seven days detention and fed one meal per day of plain rice. Most had been out shopping on the black market however three of the men from the 2/4th being Joe Swartz, Joe Meredith and Lawrance Nybo had actually been out searching for bodies of 2/4th at Hill 200. They had been successful in locating the still unburied corpses of Len Helliwell, Allan Brown and Keith 'Bully' Hayes, Frank Curnow, Doug Royce and Ossie McEwin.

This news came with disbelief to many who couldn't fathom how the Japanese could care for their own dead and leave their enemies' unburied corpses to the elements and marauding pigs. Finally after months of negotiations, Major Cough was permitted to take out a burial party with Capt. John Hill and about twenty men from the 2/4th on 21st December 1942, from Sime Road Camp. Twenty-seven bodies were identified and given a decent burial. Major Cough's diary relates:

> *'I could see Doug Royce, pouring vast quantities of beer into that same skull. I could hear Frank Curnow (he roomed next to me at Woodside) say good morning to the picture of his baby son. I saw McEwin, six feet two of dignity and hauteur, who in a toss of that now silent skull, would say in an Oxford drawl, not at all old boy, not at all. We called him Galloping Gertie because of his daring horsemanship in the camps of pre war days. These were some of the things that occurred to me as I committed them to their last resting place, reminding me of the horrors of war. The utter waste of lives. The heartbreaks at home for so many.'* [49]

Captain McEwin, the Officer Commanding Headquarters Company, was found at the crest of the hill with a bullet wound through the skull. Lieutenant Curnow, the Commander of No. 1 Platoon Signals, was killed outright in the advance. Lieutenant Royce, the Commander of No. 2 Platoon AA, was wounded at the crest and crawled back a little way. His men wanted to help him back to the lines but he refused their help.

---

[48] ibid p.159
[49] Major Alf Cough's Diary, privately published and loaned to the author by his son, Alan

Two Came Home – *The Firing Squads*

There were seven members from the 2/4th Machine Gun Battalion who were taken by the Imperial Japanese Army for execution. In all seven cases there does not seem to be any apparent motive except the fact that they were machine gunners. Considering the punishment dealt out by the 2/4th during the Battle of Singapore this was probably reason enough for the Japanese to take vendettas out on the men. Captain Avon Smith-Ryan's diary for 15th February 1942 states:

> '*We were ordered to join the rest of the battalion at the Chinese Cemetery off Holland Road at 1800 hours. I found the rest of 'B' Company there as well as Major Green, Anderson, Thomas, Raphael, Thompson and later Tom Bunning. About midday on the 16th we fell in and walked to the Raffles College padang remaining there for two days. Thompson, Raphael and one other were whisked away on a truck and haven't been seen since. RSM Airey was also taken.*' [50]

The first three men were Capt. Jack Thompson, Lt. Geofrey Raphael and Pte. James Brown.

Major Green's report states:

> '*Captain Thompson, Lieutenant Raphael and Private Brown were with the unit at Buona Vista on 15th February 1942, the date of capitulation of Singapore. On the 16th a portion of the unit was moved to Holland Village and thence to Raffles College Square. During the afternoon of the 16th whilst we were concentrated at Raffles Square a Japanese soldier entered the square and ordered Captain Thompson, Lieutenant Raphael and Private Brown (who were standing at the end of a column) to accompany him. They were marched to the roadside where they were placed on a truck.*' [51]

It is believed that these three were questioned on the Monday, Tuesday, Wednesday and on Thursday 19th February at 1715 hours were executed with their hands tied behind their backs. The reason for this act is still open to conjecture.

The other four battalion members were all in a second firing squad but were not all collected from the same location. The first two men were Privates Les McCann and Rupert Millhouse. During the ambush at South-West Bukit Timah on Wednesday 11th February, Les McCann was wounded in the right leg by mortar fire and took refuge in one of the native huts at the opposite side of the clearing. On 13th February he was joined by Rupert Millhouse who had received four machine gun bullets to the right leg.

The next day the two men decided to move out towards the West Coast Road. That evening they received medical attention at the Mohammedan's Institute, where on 15th February they were informed that all British forces had surrendered to the Japanese. On the morning of 16th February McCann and Millhouse moved out again along West Coast Road where they met three other Australians near Pasir Panjang Village. At the entrance of a house the five men were stopped by the Japanese sentries and ushered inside. They were then locked in a room fitted with barred windows. At about 1800 hours that evening were taken outside and put on a truck. At the gate they met another Japanese who was escorting more Australians, including R.S.M. Fred Airey and Private Harold Ockerby; the remainder were all members of the 2/18th Battalion. R.S.M. Airey had been conscripted to drive trucks for the Japanese for the purpose of collecting Japanese bodies to be taken to the crematorium.

---

50   PR00592 Item 10, Captain Avon Smith-Ryan Diary Australian War Memorial Canberra
51   Report by Major Charles Green on the disappearance of Capt. Thompson, Lt. Raphael and Pte. Brown. Original copy loaned by Major Green's daughter Mrs Barbara Brand

Lieutenant's Curnow, Royce and Raphael

It was here that R.S.M. Airey met up with Harold Ockerby, the former driver to Lt-Col Anketell. During the time on the truck the Japanese tried several times to relieve the R.S.M. of his haversack but he obstinately refused to hand it over to his captors Unbeknown to the Japanese the haversack contained the Battalion Headquarters battle diary. After driving for quite some time, it appeared that the driver was unable to find his destination and returned to the starting point at the house. R.S.M. Airey was later questioned and told the Japanese officer that they were all machine gunners. At this some of the men spoke out stating that they were in fact drivers from the 2/18th Battalion. McCann notes that from dawn on 18th February the Japanese appeared decidedly unfriendly. At 1730 hours the entire group of fifteen men were taken one by one and their hands tied behind their backs.

This group of unfortunates who had probably done nothing more than be in the wrong place at the wrong time were then marched down the road in single file to the jeers of Japanese soldiers lining the road. Turning north onto Reformatory Road, the group were marched a further 400 yards then halted and lined up with their backs parallel to a small stream. The location as later identified by McCann is thought to have been at map reference 753097. Seven Japanese soldiers then appeared on the scene and lined up in file about 10 yards in front of them. The men were ordered to about face and the sound of rifle bolts being worked was heard fom behind. McCann recalls telling himself that the situation was not looking too good. Suddenly there was the all too familiar crack of rifles being discharged. McCann was knocked unconscious, the force of the bullet entering his rib cage had tilted him over the edge of the steep bank on which he was standing.

A temporary lapse in proceedings indicated that all the men had either fallen into the creek or on the bank above. The Japanese firing squad then advanced several paces and fired a second volley into the limp bodies until they were satisfied that all sign of life had expired. McCann remained still for what he believed was five minutes and then hearing no sound freed himself of his bindings, struggled to his feet and moved off along the stream. R.S.M. Airey on the other hand hearing the crack of rifles discharging forcibly, threw himself into the stream, at this stage he was unharmed. When the Japanese fired the second volley he was grazed on the forehead and with blood running over his face, gave the appearance that he had received a fatal head wound.

On hearing the Japanese voices fade into the distance and after what R.S.M. Airey thought was a safe period of time he opened his eyes and looked around. Checking all the bodies he believed that everyone had been executed and made good his escape. If R.S.M. Airey is correct, then it is feasable that McCann may have been unconscious for longer than he thought. After having gone a short distance McCann lost consciousness until just before sunrise the following day.

At this stage McCann did not know the extent of his wounds only that his shirt was soaked in blood and that he was in pain. The bullet in fact had entered his back under the shoulder blade between the fourth and fifth ribs and exited at the fifth rib. There was no damage to the heart, however his left lung had collapsed. McCann redressed his leg wound but was unable to do anything about his chest wound. He then moved back to the location of the massacre and discovered that the Japanese had felled a rubber tree in a half-hearted attempt to conceal the bodies and the war crime. Making his way to a hut he remained there for two days until he felt strong enough to continue.

Times and dates now meld into one over the next week as McCann gradually made his way ever closer to Singapore City. Eventually finding himself at Singapore General Hospital, he was treated by the Japanese and eventually released to Changi Gaol, which at this time was being used as a civilian internment camp. Les McCann rejoined the 2/4th at Selarang Barracks Changi on 14th October 1942. He had survived his ordeal but Rupert Millhouse had not been so lucky. R.S.M. Airey thought Pte. Millhouse gallant to the last as he let his executioners know exactly what he thought of them with his last breath of life. R.S.M. Airey managed to escape from Singapore, firstly to Sumatra then south to Java, where suffering from the effects of starvation he was handed over by local people to the Japanese at Samarang. It was here that he would meet up with other Australians and finished up in Thailand on the Burma–Thailand railway with 'D' Force in the Hintok area. Fred Airey and Les McCann would both survive their execution and the Prisoner of War experience, for they were the two who came home.

Harold Ockerby, the C.O.'s Driver – Note the 2/4th Colour Patch on bumper

Selarang Barracks Changi

On 17th February 1942 the 14,972 men of the 8th Division that were able to walk, were marched the 17 miles to Selarang Barracks Changi. This Barracks was situated on the north-eastern tip of Singapore on the Changi Peninsula, within the Changi Cantonment. This military establishment consisted of the Roberts (Royal Artillery), Kitchener (Royal Engineers), as well as the Birdwood, Selarang, Wavell and Teloh Paku Camps. In addition, to accommodate the Punjabis of the AA Regiment, there were two barracks blocks (India Barracks) and a number of wooden huts.

The Changi Cantonment was in fact a small city with a hospital, gaol, cinemas, sporting facilities, married quarters, school and all the amenities required by the officers and enlisted ranks and their families within Changi and its environs. The seven three-storeyed concrete buildings of Selarang where the A.I.F. would be billeted had been the former home of the 2nd Battalion Gordon Highlanders. The A.I.F. area was situated on 140 acres on rising ground that was grassed and dotted with palms and trees. The buildings were roughly quadrilateral with about 800 yards between two sides and 1,100 yards between the other two. Following the move to Selarang, the 2/10th and 2/13th Australian General Hospitals combined to form the Australian General Hospital (A.G.H.) which was established from early March 1942 in two of the buildings at Roberts Barracks. Like Selarang, this barracks consisted of a number of three-storeyed concrete buildings that like most of the other buildings at Changi had suffered some degree of bomb damage.

At first the Japanese were reasonably lax with their treatment of their new wards and preferred, in the A.I.F.'s case, for the Australians to be autonomous and operate under their own administration. Up until 12th March 1942, when the individual areas of Changi were wired and patrolled, the men had been free to roam the Changi Cantonment to trade on the black market. From about the end of August 1942 the Japanese began to organise Changi as a POW camp proper. This might explain why some of the earlier groups, for instance 'A' and 'B' Forces, that departed Singapore before the end of August were never allocated Singapore Prisoner of War numbers.

In addition to the obvious deterrent or challenge that barbed wire presented to the men of the A.I.F. there was also the presence of the Sikhs. These men had been employed as British Admiralty Police and had been persuaded by the Japanese to work for them as guards. Naturally these Sikhs were not popular with the Australians for swapping their allegiance but more importantly for limiting their movements at night around the Changi Cantonment after dark.

In May 1944 the Selarang boarders were evicted and moved to the Changi Gaol Camp which had its own hospital and medical staff. The reason behind this move from Selarang to Changi Gaol was because as Allied aircraft appeared in the skies over Singapore in increasing numbers during 1944, it was becoming clear to the Japanese Imperial Army Headquarters on Singapore that Japan was losing the war. It was therefore decided to construct an additional fighter aerodrome that was to be built by Prisoner of War labour (called the Levelling Party) on the site of the Birdwood Camp sports ground opposite Selarang Barracks. The earth airstrip comprised a main runway, cross-runway and a dispersal road at its southern end. Completed on 25th May 1945, the aerodrome took twenty months to construct.

The prisoners who moved to the Changi Gaol were those who for reasons of health, age or essential trade skills had remained on Singapore. Also included were those Prisoners of War who had journeyed to Thailand in 1943 as members of either 'F' or 'H' Forces and who had returned to Singapore in December 1943. Whilst at both Selarang and Changi Gaol Camps men moved in and out on various work parties in Johore Bahru and around Singapore Island.

The 2/4th Story

The 2/4th's part within Selarang story began at the Raffles College Square where the Japanese had ordered the Battalion to assemble following the Battle of Singapore. On the evening of Tuesday 17th February at 1830 hours the 2/4th Machine Gun Battalion set off in column for the march towards the Changi Cantonment, arriving at Roberts Artillery Barracks at 0300 hours the following morning. The men slept on the oval and in the morning moved to their new billets in three officer's bungalows to the north of Selarang Barracks.

These three bungalows were numbered S8 which became house No. 36, S7 which became house No. 35 and S6 which became house No. 34. It is assumed that the S means that these bungalows were attached to Selarang. There were approximately 192 men from HQ's Coy 2/4th in house No.38 under the command of Capt. 'Bob' Phelps, 255 men from 'A' and 'B' Coy's in house No.35 under the command of Capt. Tom Bunning and 235 men from 'C' and 'D' Companies in house No.34 under the command of the newly promoted Major Colin Cameron.

The men quickly set to work building mess huts, sleeping huts, bunks and tables. The engineers soon had five wells sunk so that water was running for showers and cooking needs. The officers slept in an Officer's Dormitory, being one room in each of the three houses. There doesn't appear to have been too many complaints at this early stage of captivity and as working parties, the likes of the Adam Park group moved out, more space became available. By the time 'A' Force moved out all the remaining 2/4th had been concentrated in house No. 35. This appears to have been the situation until the Selarang Barracks incident in September 1942.

On August 30th 1942 all Prisoners of War were urged by the Japanese to sign a pledge not to escape. Upon their refusal under the terms of the Geneva Convention, all British and Australian prisoners were congregated into the barracks square at Selarang Barracks until such time as they agreed to sign. The 'Selarang Square Incident' coincides with the arrival of the new Japanese Commandant and the clamp down on security within the Changi Cantonment. Eventually under orders the men signed the pledge, but they did so under duress. Following the Selarang incident it appears that what was left of the 2/4th billeted in bungalow No. 35 were moved into Selarang Barracks occupying half of the second floor of building No. 2. Until the return of what was left of 'F' and 'H' Forces from December 1943 and the move to Changi Gaol Camp in May 1944 life at Selarang could be described as fairly routine.

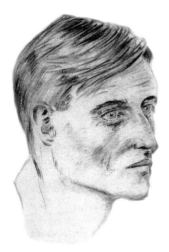

Sketch of Aub Hosking, who, due to his wounds remained in the Changi area from 1942–1945.

Smokes

For those with a penchant for tobacco all manner of concoctions would be inhaled over a three and a half year period. In the early days a man may have been lucky enough to score a job on the go-downs[52] at River Valley Road. Here with a little Aussie ingenuity cigarettes were easy pickings at the warehouses. However, as the supplies and the black market began to dry up, desperate times called for desperate measures as men were now forced to improvise. Stories of prisoners using wafer thin rice paper from bibles (holy smoke) or the splitting of the paper from cement bags are common. Every leaf and obnoxious weed was experimented with until a special blend was discovered. Captain Avon Smith-Ryan, who was obviously a connoisseur, wrote in his diary about this fine art whilst a Prisoner of War on Singapore.

> '*A couple of boongs in adjacent houses acted as our unofficial canteen and we spent our few dollars sparingly on bread rolls at 8 cents each and butter at 50 cents, jam 80 cents and numerous other luxuries. Soap, toothpaste, talcum powder, and boong tobacco. This was my introduction to this detectable weed. I bought a few dollars worth, about 5 ounces. It was a dark brown and when smoked turned out to be aromatic. Yes, very very aromatic– it stank and in addition you could taste the dark brown and wished you couldn't. Well I gave it away after giving fair warning of what I was giving them. My next purchase was more successful, a Sumatran weed and fair enough. A bit on the strong side and no doubt my throat will eventually realise its potency, but it's a fair smoke. Baring papers too and they are really the best for boong tobacco. Of course I had since opened the butts of my Virginian cigarettes and it's surprising how a little blend of this makes the present smoke quite decent. I wonder how I'll be greeted at say Sharps on the corner of Barrack and Hay Streets in Perth with a request for 2 ounces of the best boong and butts. This last package cost 5 dollars for 20 ounces, which is cheaper than smoking in Australia. Papers are*

---

52   It appears that word 'go-down' is the English language translation derived from the Malay word 'gudang' which means warehouse.

2 cents a packet, again cheaper. This compared with the price through the fence at Changi for Virginians from fifty cents to one dollar a packet is real economy.' [53]

Jack Maude recalls:

'Except as a kid I'd never smoked but was forced to take up the habit in Burma just to stave off the pangs of hunger. We thought of little else as POW's except food and smoking seemed to alleviate the problem. You could buy a Burmese cigar (cheroot) for 5 cents and sometimes you would even trade your food in exchange for tobacco.' [54]

Win Annear wrote to his family in Western Australia from the 2/14th Australian General Hospital the day following his evacuation from Sumatra:

'I have received several letters from you, one particularly good one from Mother which gave all the family news in brief. The letter eventually went the way as all the others, used for cigarette papers. It was rather funny all the same. We smoked the twenty-five word ones first, round the edges, then the address, then the signature, then eventually the body of the letters. Chaps would say "Well my people won't mind, they will be glad I have a smoke, or "I can't tell my wife I smoked her letters", but paper was always short. As far as I was concerned I smoked all round the letters then sent them off without worrying. Anyhow I knew them by heart.' [55]

Work Parties at Changi Camps

Amongst the many tasks that were carried out at Selarang and Changi Gaol Camps, the following are of note:

Forest Party
It was the job of this party to collect or fell firewood for the camp kitchens and hospital.

Trailer Party
The method used to transport the necessities of daily life by trailer. Truck and car bodies were stripped of their chassis and replaced with flat platforms. There were as many as twenty men in a party but this depended on the size and weight of the chassis and the load it was required to carry. The men would pull and push these wheeled skeletons whilst the Japanese guards merely went along for the ride at the helm. Several serious accidents occurred under this arrangement, so obviously the chore was not as simple or safe as it sounds.

Coconut Party
The job of this party was to collect coconuts from the trees around the local area. Edward 'Snow' Taylor was on this party for a time.

Saltwater Party
It was the job of this party to collect saltwater from the Changi Beach to be boiled for its salt content for cooking and to produce saline solution for the hospital.

---

53   PR00592 Item 10, Captain Avon Smith-Ryan Diary Australian War Memorial Canberra
54   Jack Maude Diary donated to the author
55   From a letter written by Richard Winston Annear to his family and loaned to the author by Clive Annear

Garden Control Party

At both camps, Selarang Barracks and Changi Gaol, gardens were established from the outset so as the men's rice diets could be supplemented with vegetables. Amongst the crops cultivated were tapioca, sweet potato, spinach, cucumber and sweet corn. Major Colin Cameron and Lt. Kevin Boyle with their green thumbs were the first to represent the battalion in this area of the Prisoner of War existence. Having been allotted ground and tools they soon had five acres planted with tapioca, spinach and sweet potato on the outside of the wire at Selarang. They also had a further three acres planted in the house area inside the wire. When Colin and Kevin ventured north with 'A' Force in May 1942, Captain Tom Bunning took over as Garden Control Officer.

The additional food and nutritional value the vegetables provided was vital to men's survival. Large numbers of men toiled in these gardens for the common good. Private Arthur London, A.A.O.C., an engineer by trade, was appointed as drainage engineer. Because he had men working under his command he was promoted to the rank of T/Sgt. for the term of his employment on the Garden Control Party.

With the move to the Changi Gaol Camp there was an urgency to get the gardens under cultivation a soon as possible. Capt. Tom Bunning started on Thursday 1st June 1944. He was allocated a spot of about 8 acres which was planted with tapioca and other vegetables. The new garden area was known as Tanah Merah. Captain Bunning's biggest problem at the new camp garden was manpower. As 1944 moved into 1945 it was obvious that despite reaping harvests of tons of vegetables it was easy to see that physically the men were losing on average four to five pounds in body weight at the new camp. The problem was exacerbated during the course of 1945 as the Japanese grew more desperate as the war drew to a close. Their demands for labour on work parties, particularly Tunnelling Parties around Singapore and Johore deprived the gardens of workers and as a result the gardens tended to take a back seat to Japanese military priorities.

The Concert Party

The Concert Party's work on Singapore has been reasonably well documented. This multi-national band of merry makers did more than just entertain the troops. Their performances lifted the prisoners' morale and if only for a short time, took their minds off their miserable existence, death and empty stomachs. The Concert Party was represented by at least one member of the 2/4th, being Robert Lyle, who was an accomplished vocalist. The Concert Party made all their own props as well as producing and choreographing all their productions, for which they must be congratulated. The A.I.F. concert party was disbanded in March 1945 by order of the Japanese for no other reason than a certain item on the repertoire had displeased them.

Bukit Timah

On 4th April 1942 2,800 A.I.F. moved out of Selarang Barracks Changi to the Bukit Timah area in the vicinity of the MacRitchie Reservoir. The 2/4th had been ordered to supply 300 men for the occasion, under the command of Major Alf Cough. Lieutenant Graham MacKinnon had left Selarang Barracks at 0900 hours on 4th April with an advance party of twenty-three other ranks with the rations and cooking utensils. The main body of A.I.F. did not complete the march to Adam Park Camp until late that evening, at which time Major Cough was ordered to report to the Japanese Headquarters where he was told he must relocate his men with some of their officers to Johore Bahru the following morning.

Johore Bahru

Johore Bahru, or J.B. as it is more commonly known, is the most southern province of Malaya and is connected to Singapore by the Causeway. This had been partially demolished by the British before the Battle of Singapore, but had since been repaired by the Japanese. This time the men moved in trucks saving many a footsore prisoner, following the previous day's march to Adam Park. The men were billeted in two large two-storeyed homes.

The task set aside for the machine gunners was to construct a shrine to the dead from the Japanese Imperial Guards, (Konoe) Division. The work at J.B. consisted of reclaiming some muddy ground, the setting up of a memorial garden and the construction of the shrine. The 4 metre spire of the shrine has not survived the test of time, however, the base still exists today. The lower base dimensions were approximately 2 and a half metres by 4 metres with a second base of proportionately smaller dimensions which rested on the lower base.

The work at J.B. had been relatively easy and the Japanese guards that accompanied the men from Adam Park had been a congenial lot. They even located a piano and supplied the transport to move it to one of the houses for the men's entertainment in the evenings before lights out. However, by the 30th April 1942, twenty-five days after their arrival, all work had been completed and the 2/4th returned to Adam Park Camp to begin another phase of their Prisoner of War experience.

Adam Park Revisited

At this stage it is worth mentioning a few points about the following work force at Bukit Timah. All orders from Japanese overseers to the Prisoners of War on work parties had to go through the officers. All officers carried the rank of Captain and as such wore a badge of rank of one star. W.O.2 William 'Blue' Burgess, 'A' Company's C.S.M. unofficially wore his one star, permitted for the occasion, as he was acting as the Adjutant at Adam Park. There were five sub-camps in this area being Adam Park, Sime Road, Thomson Road (Caldecot Hill Estate) Mount Pleasant Estate and Lornie Road. Three of the camps were former housing estates and the other two were atap[56] style native hutted camps. It seems that men from all these billets or camps worked in the same area, on the one job. All the camps were located on the southern perimeter of the MacRitchie Reservoir and are generally referred to as the Bukit Timah, Adam Park or Thomson Road work force. The camps themselves should be seen not as Prisoner of War camps with barbed wire, guard posts and searchlights but as housing from the well to do, to its simplest form in the case of the hutted camps.

The Royal Singapore Golf Club's course was considered to be one of the best in the world with its water hazards and course layout. The course and clubhouse were located on the south-west corner of MacRitchie Reservoir which itself was located roughly in the middle of Singapore. The Japanese had decided to use this locale as a site for the 'Fallen Warriors Shrine.' The water hazards were converted into miniature lakes with rustic bridges and ornamental gardens. On one side of the course was a thickly wooded hill, (Bukit Batok) which was about 350 feet high. The Japanese had decided that this would be the perfect site for their shrine, so the top of the hill was levelled to form a plateau in the centre about 50 yards square. Leading up to the plateau a stairway was built using granite slabs; these had been honed by the local Chinese artisans and placed into position by the prisoners.

---

[56]   The huts derive their name from the roofs, which were constructed using the broad atap palm leaf

The shrine itself was a long length of highly polished teak wood which the Japanese had proudly polished themselves. Other work in this area included the cutting of a road through virgin jungle, scenic drives and the Divine Bridge 'Syonan Binzya'. This crossed a finger of the reservoir and led to the approach road that continued up to the steps of the Shrine.

There were seven steam, and three diesel driven road rollers as well as several tar boilers to macadamize the roads at Adam Park. One of the better known stories to come out of this camp was how the Australian road roller drivers had convinced their Japanese guard that they needed (puff puff makan), or in other words, food for their plant machinery. Once the drivers had managed to get their message across to their guard each driver would be issued with two gallons of petrol on a daily basis, which was then sold on the black market. This ruse continued until the day that a Japanese guard with perhaps a little better understanding of engines put a stop to this little pantomime. Bill 'Bullets' Struthers was one prisoner involved in this episode which must have provided many laughs for the Australians, at the expense of the Japanese.

Adam Park Camp

Adam Park was a well to do residential area about one and a half miles from the Royal Singapore Golf Club. This estate was about half a mile square situated amid a series of small hills and valleys that were always green. Winding sealed roads followed the contours through leafy tree lined avenues up and down the slopes of the hills. Across from the camp was an expanse of hollow ground about a quarter of a mile wide. On the far side, was a major thoroughfare that had been cordoned off with barbed wire and was patrolled by Indian Sepoys who had gone across to the Japanese. Towards the end of November 1942 Major Cough and some of the men from the 2/4th moved to the Sime Road Camp.

Sime Road Camp

Sime Road Camp was located closer to the golf links about a mile from Adam Park. Here the accommodation was not as palatial as Adam Park, being native huts that were scattered and spread over a wide area. The huts were typical atap style built on concrete bases. This group was moved back to Selarang Barracks Changi on 27th December 1942.

Thomson Road (Caldecot Hill Estate) Camp

Thomson Road was located on the southeast side of the MacRitchie Reservoir. The houses were the former homes of British troops. The task allotted to the men accommodated at this camp was to cut a scenic drive through virgin jungle. This ran from a point approximately three miles north of the camp on Thomson Road, to the Royal Singapore Golf Club to where the 'Fallen Warriors Shrine' was being constructed. Records indicate that a number of 2/4th went from Thomson Road to the River Valley Road Camp prior to their return to Selarang Barracks Changi.

Mount Pleasant Camp

This camp was located about 200 yards to the south of the Thomson Road Camp. The accommodation consisted of comfortable two-storeyed homes that formerly housed government officials. The men at this camp moved to Mount Pleasant on 5th May 1942 but a month later were moved again to the Thomson Road Camp. In addition to the draft from Selarang Barracks, some of the men had come from the Great World and River Valley Road Camps, having left Selarang Barracks the previous March.

Lornie Road Camp

A workforce of 750 men arrived at Lornie Road on 5th May 1942. Records available indicate that there were no 2/4th machine gunners at this camp, as they were mostly men from the 2/19th and 2/20th Battalions. This camp was located on Lornie Road on the south side of the MacRitchie Reservoir adjacent to Adam Park Camp. The men lived in seven two-storeyed houses, the former residences of R.A.F. personnel.

Great World, River Valley Road and Havelock Road Camps

Great World was an amusement park that had been erected before the war with the intent to disperse and accomodate the Chinese population of Chinatown in the event of Japanese aerial bombing of the city precinct. Great World was later closed and the prisoners were moved to the adjacent River Valley Road Camp. Accommodation at Great World was atap huts.

River Valley Camp was surrounded by barbed wire and guards were posted. Corporal Stan Currie led a party of twenty-seven men from the 2/4th to River Valley Road Camp on 30th October 1942. River Valley Road would later become one of several transit camps where men who had returned to Singapore would mark time whilst they waited for available shipping before being forwarded to Japan or Saigon.

Housing at Havelock Road was ground level and single-storey atap huts. A canal ran between River Valley Road and Havelock Road Camps, however there was a footbridge that connected the two whereby the men were permitted to cross and mix with each other. The bonus for the men at these three camps, as opposed to the other work camps around Singapore was the opportunity to pilfer from under the Japanese guards' noses. Work parties were employed loading rice trains, loading and unloading ships in the harbour and at the go-downs or warehouses on the docks. These go-downs contained a plentiful supply of food stocks, alcohol and cigarettes. There were as many as fifty-nine members from 2/4th at Havelock Road who would, like the rest of the work parties around Singapore, return to Selarang Barracks in December 1942.

Serangoon Road Camp

Major Bert Saggers took a party of 278 A.I.F. to Serangoon Road Camp on 25th May 1942. This camp had been an internment camp for the Chinese and consisted of atap huts even less palatial than the Sime Road Camp. This group shared their accommodation with a number of British Prisoners of War and were employed at the Ford Motor Works. The factory was located close to Bukit Batok where the shrine to the 'Fallen Warriors' was being built. The Ford factory is also where Lt-Gen Arthur Percival surrendered all British forces to Lt-Gen Tomoyuki Yamashita at 1810 hours on 15th February 1942. On 31st October 1942 Major Saggers' group left this camp and moved to Sime Road Camp until 27th December whereupon they moved back to Selarang Barracks Changi.

Alexandra Hospital

The Alexandra Hospital was a British Military Hospital built for the use by the British garrison on Singapore. The hospital is nestled in the corner of Ayer Raja and Alexandra Roads. On Friday 13th February 1942 Japanese troops entered the rear of the hospital via Ayer Raja Road and massacred many of the staff and patients. It is conclusive that the Commanding Officer of the 2/4th Machine Gun Battalion Lt-Col M. J. Anketell was not involved in this horrific episode as he had already passed away at 0745 hours on that morning.

Oldham Hall

Oldham Hall was a boarding school where the 2/10th Australian General Hospital had set up operations. The hospital later moved to the Cathay Theatre in the centre of the city. Tom Edwards was brought into Oldham Hall on the morning of 12th February 1942, but by the time he arrived for treatment he had already died as a result of his wounds. Tom was buried on the padang or open area adjacent to the boarding school. So ended the life of a man who was recognised for his actions on Singapore and who had also been awarded a Military Medal with the British Army in the First World War.

H.M. Central Prison -- Outram Road

Outram Road Prison was a military as well as a civilian prison for Indian and Chinese offenders. It was a three-storeyed building, each cell being approximately 10 feet long, 6 feet wide and 14 feet high. There was a small iron barred window about 12 feet from the ground that permitted the minimum amount of light to filter through into the cell.

After the Fall of Singapore the Kempeitai or Japanese Military Police became the new landlords of the prison from August 1942. Kempeitai Headquarters on Singapore was based at the YMCA building on Stanford Road. This was not a place for the fainthearted as screams were constantly heard coming from the basement.

At Outram Road Prison beatings, strict discipline, filth and starvation were the norm and a sojourn at this establishment tested a man's mind and body to its breaking point. In each cell, the accoutrements included a metal bucket, obviously for bodily functions, a block of wood with a curvature to rest the head, three planks of wood about seven feet long on which to lie and one threadbare blanket. A twenty-second birdbath from a bucket of fresh water was permitted once a week and the latrine bucket was also emptied weekly.

There were three members of the 2/4th Machine Gun Battalion who were sentenced for crimes against Japan and sent to Outram Road. These men were Lt. Penrod Dean, Cpl. John McGregor and Sgt. Alf Stevens. Dean and McGregor had collaborated in an escape bid leaving the island at 2300 hours on 17th March 1942. Unfortunately their daring plan failed and after being captured by Malay Police on 6th May 1942 at Pontian Kechil in Johore State they were handed over to the Japanese authorities. Dean and McGregor were each sentenced to two years solitary confinement.

Alf Stevens on the other hand was a member of 'B' Force in Borneo and was arrested on 26th July 1943 at Sandakan for his part in the operation of a radio. He was sent to Kuching, the Kempeitai Headquarters in Borneo, where he was sentenced on 19th October 1943 to six years penal servitude. Alf Stevens was in reality one of the lucky few to be sent to Sandakan because had he remained he most certainly would have perished like the other Prisoner's of War on 'B' Force. Stevens was evacuated to the Changi Gaol Hospital on 5th January 1945 suffering from beri-beri and tropical ulcers whereupon he was also returned to Outram Road until war's end.

Alf passed away in 1979 on the 9th putting green at the Mandurah golf course in Western Australia. Penrod Dean served his term in solitary confinement and hard labour. During the course of his stay he learnt how to speak Japanese and as a result was invited as one of Australia's ten witnesses at the Tokyo War Crimes trials in 1946. John McGregor was evacuated to the Australian General Hospital at Roberts Barracks Changi on 19th July 1943 suffering skin problems and failing eyesight whence he was returned to Outram Road. Penrod Dean and John McGregor were both released from Outram on 18th May 1944 having served their time in purgatory.

Pulau Blakang Mati 1942–45

Pulau Blakang Mati was an island situated in the Strait of Singapore, due south of Singapore City. The island is more commonly known today as Sentosa Island, a popular tourist location. The advance party arrived on 22nd April 1942 and was followed by the main body of 170 men from the 2/18th Battalion. Although there was a mixture of men from British and Australian units, predominately the island was a 2/18th Battalion domain. Accommodation was in two barracks buildings, 'Australia House' and 'British House'. The barracks were equipped with showers, latrines and kitchens so in terms of Prisoner of War accommodation, Blakang Mati was quite luxurious.

The work by the prisoners was for a Japanese Army Supply Unit that was supplying the Imperial Japanese Army Air Service and involved the handling of aviation fuel, oil and bombs. The sick were evacuated to either of the Changi Hospitals and men were sent out to take up their position in the work force. There were seven members from the 2/4th on Pulau Blakang Mati, one of which was detached to the Keppel Harbour Camp on W Party in 1945.

Orchard Road Camp

This camp was situated close to the heart of Singapore on Orchard Road and was considered by the men to be a reasonably good camp. It consisted of three, two-storeyed huts and was surrounded by a high fence over which private residences and a park could be seen. Work at this camp was generally working at Keppel Harbour on the go-downs. Its close proximity to Keppel Harbour made it a perfect choice to use as a transit camp for those prisoners that were later destined to be shipped out of Singapore to Japan. Towards the end of the war men from this camp dug what were supposedly sewerage trenches at the Alexandra Hospital, however, this work was no doubt the advance party for the work which X.4c Party would continue in August 1945.

Pasir Panjang (Yokota Tai Camp) 31.7.45 – 19.8.45

This camp was located to the west of Keppel Harbour on the southern side of the Ayer Raja Road on the south side of a hill west of Alexandra oil tank farm. It was under the command of Lt. D. McGregor of the 2/18th Battalion. A mixed party of 140 men had marched into this camp from Keppel Harbour at 1030 hours on 31st July 1945 and a second party of 160 men followed at 1430 hours from Tanjong Pagar Camp the same day. The accommodation was in a large block of brick go-downs still under construction, so there was no lighting and the men were forced to sleep on the earthen floor, on mats that were provided on request to the Japanese. The men were employed on digging storage pits into the hills around Gillman Barracks. Two tunnels were dug into the hills about 15 to 18 metres apart for about 40 metres then turned in at right angles to meet each other. There was one member of 2/4th previously on Pulau Blakang Mati on this party.

Tanjong Pagar Camp

This camp was adjacent to the wharf at Keppel Harbour. There were three members from the 2/4th at this camp at the end of the war and all had been on X.4b, the advance party for W Party at Keppel Harbour.

Pulau Damar Laut (Jeep Island) Dry Dock

This island was west of the mouth of the Sungei Jurong on the southwest side of Keppel Harbour. A new graving dock reputed to be large enough to refit ships of up to 10,000 tons was commenced in 1944. The dock was located on the sheltered north side of the Pulau Damar Strait on Singapore Island. Some of the Australian Prisoners of War were quartered in the camp on the southern end of Pulau Damar Laut and others were quartered at the River Valley Road Transit Camp. Either way, prisoners would commute daily by motorised barges from the small island or from River Valley Road Camp to the dry dock work site.

The island camp consisted of six large huts with galvanized iron roofs, wooden walls and floors. There was very little in the way of facilities on the island and this situation included the rations and water supply. The island derived its name from its commandant who was a short stocky man with the usual Japanese bad temper. As well as Australians, the workforce comprised Dutch and British prisoners who were quartered at the Havelock Road Transit Camp. There were two shifts on the dry dock, the night shift being worked by the prisoners and the day shift by forced coolie labour. Excavation work on the 525 by 100 foot dry dock which had a depth of 45 feet was done entirely by pick and shovel. When the first transit Prisoner of War force left Singapore destined for Japan aboard the *Rakuyo Maru* in September 1944, the dock was only half complete to a depth of about 20 to 25 feet. More than half of the men who embarked on the *Rakuyo Maru* worked on the dry dock, and the remainder worked in the vicinity of the dock near the River Valley Road Camp.

Kranji Camp

Kranji Camp was located on the east side of the main Woodlands Road near the 15 milestone just opposite the petrol storage tanks. Also located in this area was an Indian Hospital and this may have been used later as the Kranji Camp Hospital. Kranji Camp like Great World, River Valley Road, Havelock Road and Alexandra Hospital was a transit camp. Between 5,000 and 11,000 Prisoners of War are believed to have passed through these camps during the period of May to September 1944. The work at Kranji involved the maintenance of the pump station, general engineering, road making and the digging of pits in the sides of hills for the storage of petrol. Generally all the work entailed the handling of petrol.

Changi Gaol Camp

The Changi Gaol was a modern concrete structure originally built to hold 550 Asian and fifty European civil prisoners. On 26th March 1944 the Japanese announced that all Allied Prisoners of War were to be transferred to the Changi Gaol Camp. This was to include the remnants from 'F' and 'H' Forces who had returned to Singapore following their time on the railway. Some of these men had been sent to Sime Road Camp so they could be kept in isolation as a precaution against cholera and small pox. The majority, however, were sent to either the Australian General Hospital at Roberts Barracks or to Selarang Barracks, Changi.

On 12th April 1944 the Japanese announced that the men at Sime Road Camp were to be included in the move. The gaol had been the home to civilian prisoners who were transferred to the Sime Road Camp. The Changi Gaol was about one mile from Selarang Barracks situated on the main road to Singapore. The order to move really took the Prisoners of War by surprise and pushed administration and organisational skills to the limit. On 1st May 1944 the movement of stores began. Suddenly huts were being demolished at a rate of three per day. Literally everything at Selarang Barracks had to be moved by trailer parties. There were twenty of these, each one with a complement of twenty men making two trips per day. On 9th May the main body of A.I.F. started to move to the gaol and the men from Sime Road Camp also arrived.

By 1st June the move had been completed. One might say that everything that wasn't bolted to the floor had gone with the men. Outside and adjacent to the southern wall of the gaol were fifteen 100 metre long atap huts for which the Japanese had supplied the building materials. These huts were intended to accommodate 200 prisoners however, the actual number would have been nearer 250. The permanent coolie lines were brick structures and were located on the east side of the gaol. On the north side were permanent two-storeyed buildings along Half Moon Street.

The temporary hospital was set up on the eastern side, and could handle 1,200 patients. In addition a convalescent depot, was set up in the old warders quarters also located on Half Moon Street. On 7th June the order came to set up a new hospital at Kranji some 22 miles away. Kranji was a hutted camp on the main Johore Bahru–Causeway road. The camp had been set up when the Prisoners of War were employed at Bukit Timah erecting the 'Fallen Warriors Shrine' at Bukit Batok. The Kranji Camp at Woodlands could accommodate 350 prisoners and the Kranji Hospital could handle the same number of patients. The Kranji Hospital was to care for the epidemic cases or heavy sick and the Changi Gaol Hospital the light sick. Kranji Hospital was to be run by the British and Changi Gaol Hospital by the Australian medical personnel.[57]

The officers of all nationalities were, as had occurred in Thailand, separated from the other ranks and were billeted in atap huts in the staff coolie lines outside the walls of the gaol. The reasoning behind this decision was that with the tide of war going against Japan there was a fear that an uprising by the prisoners, led by their officers could eventuate. For this reason the officers where separated from the other ranks from early September 1944 and were not permitted to enter the gaol to visit the men without prior permission. Inside the gaol Sgt. John Gorringe was the senior 2/4th Machine Gun Battalion NCO. From the outset it was obvious that space was going to be at a premium in the gaol camp. Figures seem to vary from one source to the next, however it seems that there were in the region of 6,300 men inside the gaol and 4,000 outside the walls. As local work parties began to move out in 1945, the problem with space was eased.

---

[57] Heavy sick might for example be someone who was bed ridden with beri-beri or cholera whilst in Japanese eyes, light sick might be someone suffering from an attack of malaria or dysentry

P1 and P2 Parties 7.5.45 – 1.8.45

No details are known of P1 party but it is assumed that it was at the same camp as the P2 Party. There were fifty-one A.I.F. on P2 party which was located one mile to the northwest of Johore Bahru and three quarters of a mile from Q party. This was a newly built camp to accommodate 200 men. From 3rd August 1945 to 10th August 45 this party worked on the excavation of tunnels with Q party. Work stopped until 14th August 45 and then recommenced on clearing and digging until 18th August 45 when like Q party the work finished. There were four members from the 2/4th in P2 party.

Q Party 10.1.45 – 8.8.45

This camp was situated two miles north of Johore Bahru on the main road. Accommodation consisted of three 40 metre long atap huts equipped with electric light and showers. The first task given to the prisoners, 140 of which were A.I.F., was to build a wall, the construction of which continued until 25th February 1945 when this workforce was put to work on a large Japanese ordnance dump. On 30th March another job was commenced. This time it was the digging of tunnels, a task that continued until 8th August 1945. The work then stopped for a few days and then recommenced at the Japanese Military Barracks in Johore until all work ceased on 18th August 1945.

W Party 6.4.45 – 20.8.45

This camp was under the command of Capt. R. Swartz of the 2/26th Battalion and was situated on Keppel Road near Mount Faber on reclaimed land. Accommodation for the prisoners consisted of two atap huts that were described as being on raised platforms and in good condition. Party X.4b from Changi Gaol Camp on 6th April 1945 acted as the advance party. Work commenced on 10th April 1945. All work until the latter part of the stay involved the digging of tunnels. There were three members from the 2/4th at this camp who had come originally with X.4b Party and were later recovered at Tanjong Pagar Camp at the end of the war. One hundred men from Pulau Blakang Mati later marched into the Keppel Harbour Camp on 17th April 1945. In this group was one member from the 2/4th Machine Gun Battalion. A mixed group of 140 prisoners made up of Australians, British, two Americans and one Canadian again moved from Keppel Harbour Camp to the new Pasir Panjang (Yokota Tai Camp) on 31st July 1945. In this group was again one man from the 2/4th who had been detached ex-Pulau Blakang Mati to Pasir Panjang Camp.

X Parties – Singapore 1945

The common denominator in all these X Parties and indeed most of the work groups which left Changi Gaol Camp during 1945 it appears was tunnelling. At this stage in the proceedings it was obvious that Japan's war was over. Nevertheless, the Japanese garrison on Singapore initiated a programme of excavating tunnels to store ammunition and for the use as air raid shelters in what they saw as their last ditch effort to prolong the inevitable, total collapse of their war effort. Some of the prisoners believed that they were to be herded into the tunnels like cattle and the entrances blown. Two very bright flashes of light over Japan in August 1945 put an end to this theory, which proved to be well founded.

X.1 Party 28.3.45 – 30.4.45

Under the command of Capt. D. Duffy 2/30th Battalion, this party consisted of men from the 2/29th and 2/30th Battalions. Work consisted of excavating tunnels at Johore Bahru. The men worked on a daily rota of one hour on, one hour off due to the inadequate ventilation, and by 1945 the men's poor physical condition. The work was dangerous with frequent falls of earth. The prisoners were accommodated in an old barracks and a large house which were located about two miles apart. On 24th April 1945 the work force was merged at the barracks. Most of the men on this party had been up country so malaria was prevalent amongst their ranks. Following his work with X.1 Party, Capt. Duffy led another group, being the A.1 Party, on tunnelling duties from 7th May 1945. There were eight companies on this party totalling 282 men. No other details are known on this group.

X.2 Party

Departed 29th April 1945 to Kranji. This party consisted of 665 British Prisoners of War.

X.3 Party 1.4.45 – 20.8.45

This party was under the command of Capt. Fred Stahle of the 8th Division Signals. It consisted of seven officers and 377 other ranks. This included one officer from the 2/4th, being Lt. Penrod Dean, who was accompanied by thirteen other ranks from the battalion. The work site was at Choa Chu Kang Road to the north of Bukit Panjang, approximately 400 yards west of Bukit Timah Road. The work consisted of the excavation and construction of tunnels, trenches and weapons pits.

X.4a Party 17.6.45

Located at Bukit Timah and contained fifty A.I.F. No other details are known. *(See also Orchard Road camp)*

X.4b Party 6.4.45

The Pasir Panjang-Keppel Harbour Camp consisted of fifty A.I.F. This group acted as the advance party for W Party. There were three members of the 2/4th on this party. *(See Tanjong Pagar Camp)*

X.4c Party 10.4.45 – 17.8.45

This party worked in the vicinity of River Valley Road under the command of Capt. Bowring of the 2/29th Battalion. The work consisted of tunnelling for defensive purposes. The last few weeks before the end of the war the men constructed machine gun pits, in particular around the Alexandra Hospital.

X.5 Party 12.4.45

The following three groups (X.5, X.6 and X.7) had consisted of fifty-one A.I.F. and fifty-one British.

X.6 Party 26.5 45

Work consisted of tunnelling around Singapore and Johore Bahru.

X.7 Party 29.5.45

There were twenty-seven men from the 2/4th spread between these three groups.

X.8 Party 4.7.45 – 17. 8. 45

Under the Command of Warrant Officer A. Crawford. The work consisted of tunnelling in the vicinity of Jurong Road. The A.I.F. contingent was housed in huts. There were three members from the 2/4th on this party.

X.9 Party 29.5.45

Possibly in the Singapore area consisting of 200 A.I.F. but no other details are known.

X.10 Party

Comprised 1,000 prisoners to dig tunnels in the hills about 2-3 miles from Changi Gaol Camp. There were members of the 2/4th on this party including Jim Duncan but no other details are known.

X.11 Party 28.7.45

This group worked in the area of Johore Bahru, but no other details are known.

Chapter Two

Java and the 'Malay Barrier'

Holland's surrender to Germany on 15th May 1940 brought fears that an opportunist Japan could take advantage of the situation. Concerns that Japan might make a move on the islands of the Netherlands East Indies instigated a pledge of support from the Australian Government for the following reasons. Firstly, because these islands to the north of Australia were considered as being vitally important to Australia's outer defence perimeter. This island chain comprised from west to east, Sumatra, Java, Bali, Lombok, Sumbawa, Flores, Sumba and Timor, hence the term 'Malay Barrier'.

Secondly because British and American pledges of military aid were not forthcoming. As far as Australia's interests were concerned it was felt that an attack against the islands included within the 'Malay Barrier' or the Portuguese half of Timor would make it a relatively easy task for Japan to conduct air raids against Darwin.

Generally the Australian Chiefs of Staff were keen to establish air forces within the 'Malay Barrier', however, the Chief of Air Staff was against sending his aircraft and personnel to the islands unless there were army garrisons there to protect the airfields. The Australian Chief of General Staff, Lt-Gen V.A.H. Sturdee, reluctantly agreed to send the 2/22nd Battalion to Rabaul on New Britain for this purpose and to send the other two battalions from the 23rd Brigade, the 2/21st and the 2/40th Battalions, to Darwin in readiness to move to Ambon and Timor.

> *'On 5th December, three days before the Japanese onslaught from Pearl Harbour(sic) to Malaya, the Netherlands East Indies Government asked Australia to send aircraft to Ambon and Timor in accordance with the long-standing agreement. The Australian War Cabinet approved, and, at dawn on 7th December, two flights of Hudsons (of No. 13 Squadron) flew to Laha Field on Ambon and one flight (of No. 2 Squadron) to Koepang. That day Brigadier Lind, at Darwin, received orders to move the 2/21st Battalion to Ambon and the 2/40th Battalion to Timor.'* [1]

---

[1]   Lionel Wigmore, *Japanese Thrust* Australia in the War of 1939–45 Army Volume IV Australian War Memorial Canberra, p.419

The 2/4th Machine Gunners on Java

By now it should be no secret that ninety-three members of the 2/4th Machine Gun Battalion failed to re-board HMT *Aquitania* on the morning 16th January 1942. The defaulters concerned were detained at the Fremantle Prison before being transferred to the Claremont Details Camp where they were charged and fined. There were five of these men who would not continue their journey overseas for reasons of age or health.

On 30th January 1942 these remaining eighty-eight men were transported to Fremantle with their Escort Officer Lt. Colin Blakeway. On 30th January 1942 convoy "MS 3" departed Fremantle. This small convoy, escorted by HMAS *Canberra* consisted of seven tankers destined for Palembang on Sumatra and four cargo ships for Tanjong Priok, the Port of Batavia on Java. One of these four cargo ships was the 7,475 ton SS *Marella,* which was carrying the machine gunners and their escort officer.

It had been intended that when these machine gunners were put ashore on Java they would tranship for the onward passage to Singapore. However at this stage not even eighty-eight reinforcements could influence the final outcome on Singapore. Instead these men disembarked at Tanjong Priok on 13th February 1942 and moved to their barracks at Meester Cornelis, an older European area on the southern side of Batavia. Batavia was divided into three sections, the northern section was the old town, to the south was the new town of Weltevreden, and further south of this new town was Meester Cornelis. The natural growth of these three towns now formed the municipality of Batavia and together covered about 66 square miles. Under the command of Lt. Colin Blakeway the 2/4th machine gunners now found themselves as reinforcements for Java and were assigned guard duties at ammunition dumps within the Batavia area, tasked with the movement of stores from the wharves to the aerodromes. Following the landing of the Australian troops from HMT *Orcades* on 19th February, the 2/4th reinforcements joined either the 2/3rd Machine Gun Battalion or the 2/2nd Pioneer Battalion for airfield defence at either the Kemajoran or Tjililitan Aerodromes.

There is one other member from the 2/4th who managed to make his own way to Java. This man was the battalion R.S.M., Fred Airey. R.S.M. Airey had managed to evade his executioners on Singapore by making his way up the Indragiri River to Padang on the west coast of Sumatra. R.S.M. Airey knew that if he was recaptured and it was discovered that he had narrowly escaped a massacre on Singapore he might not be so lucky the second time. Continuing his bid for freedom he set off from Padang to the south via the Mentawai Islands until he reached a point somewhere on the south coast of Java. As exhaustion and hunger sapped his strength he was passed over to the Japanese by the local Javanese. This occured at a place called Samarang located to the southeast of Bandoeng to the west of Garoet. R.S.M. Airey fearing that his secret might be discovered passed himself off as an officer with the rank of Lieutenant, a rank he kept until the end of the war. R.S.M. Fred Airey was to travel up into Thailand with Lt-Col E. E. Dunlop's Java Party No. 6 where he took over duties as quartermaster on 'D' Force O Battalion at the Hintok Road camp.

Australia's Dilemma

Of all the years of the Second World War, 1942 was Australia's most perilous. Japan had conducted an unprecedented series of successful land, sea and air campaigns that had gained her far more territory than anyone would ever imagine possible in so short a period of time. With Malaya firmly in Japanese hands by the end of January 1942 and Singapore destined for a similar fate, a feeling of panic gripped the civilian population of Australia, particularly after the first Japanese air raid on Darwin. Under mutual agreement between the British and Australian

Governments it was decided that the battle seasoned troops from the Australian 6th and 7th Divisions (and later the 9th Division) were needed to fight the Japanese a little closer to home. The Australian Government had been thinking along these lines but was surprised when the British first put forward the suggestion of these Divisions' return. Nevertheless the transfer of these troops from the Middle East to Java and home to Australia turned into a battle itself and many strongly worded cables were exchanged between the Australian and British Prime Ministers before the matter was finally resolved.

The Australian Prime Minister, John Curtin, caused a sensation at home and overseas when on 27th December 1941 he had the courage of his conviction to publish an article in the Melbourne *Herald* newspaper, part of which read:

> 'Without inhibitions of any kind, I make it quite clear that Australia looks to America, free of any pangs as to our traditional links or kinship with the United Kingdom.'[2]

In hindsight this may have been a cleverly worded statement by the use of the word *kinship,* because in December 1940 Winston Churchill had written:

> 'If Australia is seriously threatened by invasion we should not hesitate to compromise or sacrifice the Mediterranean position for the sake of our kith and kin.'[3]

When Britain had decided to build the Singapore Naval Base it was under the understanding that it would despatch a powerful fleet to the Far East when necessary. Singapore's defences and Australia's defence policy were naively based around this assumption. A generation of Australians were raised on this promise, yet the fleet never did arrive. Winston Churchill was decidedly upset by Curtin's newspaper article, as was President Franklin Delano Roosevelt. Yet despite what Roosevelt may have thought of Curtin at the time, the United States required a continental landmass from which to launch operations against Japan. Beyond politics, Australia with it common roots, language, ports, facilities and excellent geographic location was exactly what America needed.

The intention had originally been to transport the Australian 6th and 7th Divisions to the Netherlands East Indies where the 7th Division would defend southern Sumatra and the 6th Division would defend central western Java. It was predicted that the whole of the 7th Division, (which was the first Australian division to depart the Middle East) would not arrive equipped and ready for action prior to 15th March 1942, at the earliest.

From a total of 3,400 troops that had boarded the fast transport ship HMT *Orcades*, a composite force to be known as *Boost Force* consisting predominately of 2/3rd machine gunners and 2/2nd pioneers was put ashore at Oosthaven on the southern end of Sumatra on 15th February 1942. This formation of 2,570 troops which was organised into four battalions were ferried into shore at 2100 hours. On reaching the harbour at Oosthaven a message was received for *Boost Force* to return to the *Orcades*. Intelligence reports had been received that the Japanese had already secured a foothold on Sumatra by landing paratroops at the Palembang Airfield (P1) on the 14th and had followed this up with an amphibious landing on 15th February. The oil refineries at Palembang were one of the Far East's richest. The two enormous oil refineries that were capable of producing large quantities of 100 octane aviation fuels were all but demolished except for two smaller plants, thus denying these facilities to the Japanese. As a result of the earlier Japanese landings on Sumatra *Boost Force* was ferried back

---

2   Kristin Williamson, *The Last Bastion* Lansdowne Press 1984, p.419
3   Winston Churchill, The Second World War Volume II *Their Finest Hour* App. A Prime Minister's Personal Minutes and Telegrams May–December 1940, Cassell & Co. Ltd London 1949, p.628.

out to the waiting *Orcades* to be transported to Tanjong Priok in Java, where they arrived on 17th February and eventually disembarked on 19th February.

M.I. SERIAL No. ....SD.5704....

SECRET
(Cipher Office Classification)

DECIPHERED MESSAGE

TO ...ARMY MELBOURNE...............

FROM .ABDACOM BATAVIA............

ORIGINATORS No/s	ORIGINATORS DATE
0251/ 15/2 OP/1785	

TIME MESSAGE REC. ....0330.....

DATE ....16/2................

CIPHER OFFICE DISTRIBUTION –
3 COPIES D.S.D.
1 COPY CIPHER LOG

CHECKED BY

REF MY SIGNAL OF 13TH FEB (.)

PERSONAL FOR STURDEE FOR INFORMATION OF PRIME MINISTER (.)

OP/1785

DECISION NOW TAKEN DIVERT FIRST AUSTRALIAN SHIP CONTAINING 2/3

M.G. BN. 2/2 PIONEER BN 2/6 FIELD COY AND OTHER SMALLER UNITS

TOTALLING 3400 FROM OOSTHAVEN IN SOUTH SUMATRA TO BATAVIA

M.L.W.
0530

16/2

Copy of Cipher sent to Lt-Gen V. A. H. Sturdee advising him of the decision to land Boost Force on Java.

A barrage of high level cables had preceded their landing at Batavia. But as the 2/4th Machine Gun Battalion had been sacrificed towards an already lost cause on Singapore, similarly were these Corps troops from the 1st Australian Corps attached to the 7th Division and with them eighty-eight reinforcement 2/4th machine gunners and their escort officer. The advance units who had sailed onboard the *Orcades* were the:

2/3rd Machine Gun Battalion *(less some officers, NCO's and some other ranks)*
2/2nd Pioneer Battalion
2/6th Field Company of Engineers
2/2nd Casualty Clearing Station
105th General Transport Company
'C' Company No. 10 Platoon, 1st Australian Corps Headquarters Guard Regiment.

Unquestionably this was a fine body of troops but certainly not a balanced formation to be thrown into action against a numerically superior Japanese force. By 17th February, the Japanese were rapidly closing the trap door on Java from the east and west. The Japanese invasion of Bali, one of the islands within the 'Malay Barrier' island chain occurred on 18th February. Darwin was subjected to an aerial attack on 19th February and on the 20th the Japanese, employing paratroops for the second time in less than a week, occupied the airfield at Koepang on Timor. This not only meant that Timor could serve the Japanese as a forward air base from which to launch further air strikes against the Australian mainland, but also that the fighter air reinforcement route between Darwin and Java was severed. The Japanese now commanded the seas and islands to the north, west and east of Java. The fate of the troops on Java was now sealed because there was no chance that any further Australian units would be committed when the security of Australian mainland was under threat of invasion. The Supreme Allied Commander South-West Pacific, General Archibald Wavell sent a most secret cipher telegram to the British joint staff mission in Washington on 18th February 1942.[4]

Paragraphs 2 and 3 from this document state that:

(2) *'My general conclusion is that successful defence of Java with resources available and in sight extremely doubtful if Japanese act rapidly and in strength as there is every likelihood they will. Report this morning indicates that advance on Bali or Lombok is now taking place.'*

(3) *'Effective Dutch fighting force only four mobile brigades of three battalions each with little artillery. 80% are native troops. Remainder Dutch forces are static scattered over island. One squadron 3 Hussars with light tanks and about 1200 Australian troops are being landed for aerodrome defence remainder of Australian troops in Orcades are unarmed. General ter Poorten agrees that troops now available can do little to stop invasion.'*

A few days after this cipher was sent General Wavell's command as Supreme Allied Commander of the American British Dutch Australian Command (ABDACOM) was dissolved and the responsibility for the defence of Java was passed to Lt-Gen Hein ter Poorten of the Netherlands East Indies Army. There was now nothing left for General Wavell to command. Hong Kong, Malaya and Singapore had been lost as had most of the islands of the Netherlands East Indies.

---

4   AWM54 File A2663 Copies of most secret Cipher Messages "A" Commander in Chief South-West Pacific To War Office Australian War Memorial Canberra.

Lieutenant-Colonel A. S. Blackburn VC – *Blackforce*

On 21st February 1942 Lt-Col Arthur Seaforth Blackburn, the Commanding Officer of the 2/3rd Machine Gun Battalion, was promoted to the rank of Brigadier and appointed to command all A.I.F. troops on Java, to be now known as *Blackforce*. All the same, Brigadier Blackburn was to come under the direct control of the Dutch Commander in Chief Lt-Gen Hein ter Poorten. *Blackforce* was organised on a brigade basis of three battalions consisting of approximately 2,900 Australian,[5] British and American troops as follows:

No. 1 Battalion
The 2/3rd Machine Gun Battalion under the command of Lt-Col Lyneham
One section from the 2/6th Field Company
One officer and a number of other ranks ex-Singapore and a proportion of the reinforcement draft from Australia. (Total strength: 700)

No. 2 Battalion
The 2/2nd Pioneer Battalion under the command of Lt-Col J.M. Williams with the reinforcements from the Middle East
One section from the 2/6th Field Company. (Total strength: 900)

Allied Troops attached to No. 2 Battalion
The American 131st Field Artillery Regiment (less 'E' Battery)
The British 'B' Squadron Kings Own Hussars (equipped with 16 light tanks)
A British signals section from one of the five Anti-Aircraft units (Total strength: 900)

No. 3 (Reserve) Battalion (organised into 8 Platoons)
A Composite Battalion under the command of Capt. (T/Maj.) J.C. de Crespigny
The remainder of the 2/6th Field Company (less two sections)
'C' Company No. 10 Platoon, 1st Australian Corps Headquarters Guard Regiment as well as those troops ex-Singapore and the reinforcement draft ex-Australia not allocated to the other two battalions. This third battalion was formed on 28th February when all surplus reinforcements were allotted to this unit. This included Lt. Colin Blakeway and forty of the eighty-seven 2/4th machine gunners who were transferred across from the 2/3rd Machine Gun Battalion on this day. (Total strength: 400)

The 2/2nd Casualty Clearing Station and No. 1 Allied General Hospital

The 2/2nd Casualty Clearing Station under the command of Lt-Col E. E. Dunlop, was transported directly from Tanjong Priok to Ursuline Sisters' Christylijk Lyceum Girls' High School in the centre of Bandoeng, where the staff set up to operate as a general hospital to be known as No. 1 Allied General Hospital. The whole of the medical equipment that was unloaded from the *Orcades* went with the 2/2nd Casualty Clearing Station to Bandoeng where this unit remained throughout the action on Java. The hospital operated until 18th April 1942 at which time it was closed down with only a few hours notice, the staff and patients being marched 6 miles to a native prison at Tjimahi. Firstly they were moved to two separate camps at Tjimahi before being moved for a third time to Camp No. 12, the former Dutch 15th Depot Battalion

---

5   Not all of the 3,400 troops of the 1st Australian Corps who sailed on the *Orcades* had disembarked at Tanjong Priok. Also some troops who had escaped capture on Singapore proved to be unsuitable and were returned to Australia on the last ship to depart Java.

Barracks at Bandoeng. During the eighteen days that the hospital was in operation it had handled a creditable 1,351 cases. After the surrender, and up to the hospital's closure, there had still been a steady stream of sick and convalescent patients moving in and out of this hospital.

The 2/3rd Reserve Motor Transport Company

Brigadier Blackburn envisaged problems with his supply column and so he placed Major (T/Lt-Col) C. M. Black the Commanding Officer of the 2/3rd Reserve Motor Transport Company to command four sections from the 2/3rd R.M.T. to handle the movement of petrol, ammunition, supply and workshop. This unit was credited with having done excellent work down the length of the Malay Peninsula. Many of the men were veterans of the First War and were over 45 years of age and so it was for this reason they were evacuated to what was believed to be the safety of Java.

Later Lt-Col Black would command Black Force during the construction period of the Burma-Thailand rail link. This force should not be confused with the combatant *Blackforce* which fought on Java. Likewise Lt-Col. J. M. Williams, the commanding officer of the 2/2nd Pioneer Battalion, was to command Williams Force, also on the Burma–Thailand rail link.

Preparations Begin

When the 7th Division had departed the Suez Canal each unit's equipment had not necessarily been loaded onboard the ship on which it was sailing. For instance, when the 2/3rd Machine Gun Battalion disembarked at Tanjong Priok they did so without their Vickers machine guns. As a result *Blackforce* was insufficiently armed except for rifles and a few Thompson machine guns and Brens. Most of these arms (for want of a better word) had been scrounged. In addition all units were under strength but in particular the 2/3rd Machine Gun Battalion, was seven Officers and a number of NCO's under establishment. Overall the men from the 2/4th were dispersed amongst the three battalions with the greater number going to Major de Crespigny's No. 3 Reserve Battalion.

On 24th February, Brigadier Blackburn was briefed by General Wavell on the eve of his departure, that as his was practically the only trained British Force on Java capable of going into action against the Japanese, and ordered him to assist the Dutch by placing his troops in offensive operations wherever possible. Brigadier Blackburn following his reconnaissance of all the defence positions west of Batavia, decided to concentrate his forces in the Buitenzorg area at a tea plantation 8 miles to the west of Buitenzorg at a place called Tjampea. Although access into and out of the plantation was limited due to the very narrow access roads, Tjampea did offer good air cover from Japanese fighter and reconnaissance aircraft and there were adequate buildings to offer shelter for his troops.

On 28th February pioneers and machine gunners went into position covering the stone bridge across the Tjianten River at Leuwiliang. Up until this time No. 8 Platoon from the 2/2nd Pioneers had been sent out from Semplak Airfield to cover the area astride the Leuwiliang–Buitenzorg Road.

The Topography of Western Java

The sector of Java west of the capital Batavia can be divided into a grid much like that of a noughts and crosses game. The two east-west running lines would be represented by the two main roads that were known as Road No. 1 and Road No. 2. Firstly Road No. 1 ran mostly through flat open country from the west coast of Java at Merak and Anjer and followed the north coast east via Serang, Kragilan, Balaradja and Tangerang to Batavia. The main Dutch defensive position covering Batavia was at Tangerang where Road No. 1 crossed the deep Tjisadane River. Secondly Road No. 2 ran from the west coast at Laboehan and ran roughly through the centre of Java mostly through rubber plantations via Pandeglang, Rangkasbitoeng, Djasinga and Leuwiliang to Buitenzorg.

The two north-south running grid lines would be represented firstly by the Tjioedjoeng River about 50 miles to the west of Batavia and Buitenzorg. This river was impassable unless bridged especially at this time of the year when water levels were high. The two main bridges across this river were at Kragilan and further to the south at Rangkasbitoeng. This river began in the high mountainous country near the south coast of Java and flowed to the Java Sea on the north coast. A good road ran along the east bank of the Tjioedjoeng River and connected Roads No. 1 and No. 2 between Kragilan and Rangkasbitoeng.

Approximately half way along this road was a concrete dam at Pamarajan at which point vehicular traffic could cross the Tjioedjoeng River and exit to the south via a good road that led to the dam from the west. Brigadier Blackburn had pressed the Dutch to demolish this dam to deny the enemy a crossing point but despite his protests this was not done for the reason that there were not enough explosives. As a result the Japanese used this crossing to great advantage when their advance along the No. 1 Road was delayed. Nevertheless the bridges that crossed the Tjioedjoeng River on Road No. 1 at Kragilan and Road No. 2 at Rangkasbiteong were demolished once the Japanese had landed.

The last line of the grid is formed by the Tjisadane River of which one branch of this river flows to the west of Buitenzorg (Tjaipaes River) and the other branch, (Tjianten River) that flows through the town of Leuwiliang. These two branches of the Tjisadane River then join a little further north near a place called Tjltempoean before continuing north through Tangerang to the west of Batavia. Another road of importance was the north-south running No. 3 Road between Batavia and Buitenzorg.[6]

The Netherlands East Indies Army

The Netherlands East Indies regular army (the KNIL-Koninklijk Netherlands Indisch Leger) on Java consisted of about 25,000 men made up of a force of four infantry regiments, each of three battalions. In addition to their regular forces, there was a Home Guard with further 40,000 men but like their regular counterparts their ability to hold back a Japanese onslaught was in question. Only about one man in forty was actually a Dutchman, the greater portion of this Dutch army being indigenous peoples. For this reason and after further discussions with Lt-Gen ter Poorten, the Dutch Commander in Chief, it was decided to use *Blackforce* as a mobile striking force ready to attack the invading Japanese wherever and whenever the opportunity arose. However, in accordance with orders issued prior to disembarkation these troops from the 1st Australian Corps were allocated for airfield defence.

The Dutch Plan For The Defence Of Java

The Dutch troops were to be divided into four area commands for the defence of Java being Batavia, north central Java, south Java and east Java. The bulk of the Dutch forces were under

---

6   AWM54 File 559/2/2 Report by Brigadier A. S. Blackburn on operations of the A.I.F. in Java Feb/Mar 42. Australian War Memorial Canberra

the command of Maj-Gen Schilling and would be deployed to hold Batavia, and its Port of Tanjong Priok, the largest port in all the Netherlands East Indies. Bandoeng, 80 miles to the southeast of Batavia was the Headquarters of the Netherlands East Indies Army and was also the Indies Government administrative centre of Java. Buitenzorg some 35 miles to the south of Batavia was an important government town and several administrative offices were there as well as the palace of the Governor-General. Sourabaya on the eastern end of Java was also considered as being worth defending, as this was where the Dutch Naval Base was located. By the time of the Japanese landings on Java the Imperial Japanese Navy had virtually swept the seas clean of Allied warships around Java. As well as the Allied troops that have been mentioned there were five British Anti-Aircraft regiments used specifically for airfield defence however, two of these regiments were without their guns.

The Airfields

The original plan had been to use the Australians for static airfield defence against enemy paratroops at Kemajoran, Tjililitan, Tjisaoesk and Tjileungsir all in the vicinity of Batavia and at Semplak near Buitenzorg. The 2/3rd Machine Gun Battalion and the 105th Australian General Transport Company were allotted the task of airfield defence at Kemajoran Aerodrome as were some 2/4th machine gunners and the 2/2nd Pioneer Battalion, the Guards platoon and a section from the 2/6th Field Company were allocated the task of defending Tjililitan Aerodrome with the help of some 2/4th machine gunners. British troops who were better suited to this type of defence would replace the Australians who, from 26th February began to concentrate at Tjampea.

Kemajoran Aerodrome
Kemajoran Aerodrome was located to the northeast of Batavia's residential area, Weltevreden and about 2 and a half miles in from the coast. It was a first class commercial airport having only been completed in July 1940. It was in operational use by the Japanese who called it Jyakaruta after the old native town of Djakatra. Shortly after the arrival of the 2/3rd Machine Gun Battalion 'B' Company was detached to the defence of the airfield at Semplak. The remainder of the battalion prepared their defences until 26th February when they began to move to the tea plantation at Tjampea.[7]

Tjililitan Aerodrome
Tjililitan Aerodrome was also a first class aerodrome located 8 miles to the southeast of Kemajoran Aerodrome and close to the old residential area of Meester Cornelis. The 2/2nd Pioneer Battalion, the Guards platoon and a section from the 2/6th Field Company were moved to Tjililitan Aerodrome on landing at Tanjong Priok. A warning order was issued to 'B' and 'C' Companies of the 2/2nd Pioneer Battalion and the Guards platoon to prepare to move to Semplak near Buitenzorg. The next day this group moved out and reinforcements (including Hubert 'Dusty' Millar) from the Fremantle reinforcement pool were brought in to replace those who had been transferred further south. On 22nd February Japanese aircraft made a raid on Tjililitan and as a result the Allied aircraft based there were flown out. The remaining pioneers were also transferred as the Australians began to concentrate in the Tjampea–Leuwiliang area.[8]

---

[7]   Allied Geographical Section SWPA, Special report No. 112 Java Australian War Memorial Canberra
[8]   ibid

Semplak Airfield

At 0930 hours on 22nd February Japanese aircraft also raided Semplak Airfield, which was located to the northeast of Leuwiliang. Six R.A.A.F. Hudson aircraft from No. 1 Squadron were destroyed on the ground and some damage was also caused to a hanger and ground installations. At the time 'B' and 'C' Companies from the 2/2nd Pioneer Battalion, the Guards platoon and 'B' Company 2/3rd Machine Gun Battalion were based here.

The Japanese Landing

The Japanese 16th Army formations utilised for the invasion of Java were:

> 2nd Division (West Java)
> 230th Infantry Regiment (West Java)
> 48th Division (East Java)
> 56th Regimental Group–Sakaguchi Detachment (East Java)[9]

28th February – 1st March 1942

At 1800 hours on 28th February 'B' Company 2/3rd Machine Gun Battalion took up a defensive position on high ground 1 mile to the west of Buitenzorg. Likewise at 1830 hours 12 Platoon 'D' Company 2/2nd Pioneer Battalion also took up positions that had been prepared by the Dutch to the left of the road so as to cover the Tjianten Bridgehead at Leuwiliang. At this time the final arrangements were being made for the allotment of surplus reinforcements to Major de Crespigny's No. 3 Reserve Battalion at Tjampea. On this day Lt. Blakeway and forty reinforcements from the 2/4th Machine Gun Battalion were transferred from the 2/3rd Machine Gun Battalion to the No. 3 Reserve Battalion. Later that evening 'B' Company and the other two platoons of 'D' Company 2/2nd Pioneer Battalion moved from Tjampea and took up positions near the Tjianten Bridge and waited.

The Japanese invasion of western Java took place before dawn on the morning of 1st March 1942. Brigadier Blackburn was notified by telephone at 2300 hours on 28th February with the news that the Japanese were landing on the western end of Java and elsewhere on the north coast. The Japanese indeed had landed, the 2nd Division coming ashore at Merak and Banten Bay located on either side of the landform St Nicolas Point. This was the most northwest extremity of Java at the northern exit of the Sunda Strait.

By dawn on 1st March the scene at the Tjianten Bridge was a hive of activity. Armoured car patrols were sent out, listening posts were sent forward as well as to the flanks to detect the earliest contact with the enemy; and defensive positions were improved. By 0900 hours on 1st March the latest report received was that Dutch troops on Western Java had fallen back to the line of the Tjoedjoeng River but as yet had not made contact with the Japanese column. By 1400 hours a report was received that advance elements from the Japanese column had reached the Tjioedjoeng River and that the Dutch troops had demolished the bridge near Kragilan before falling back to the east towards Balaradja. Although the Dutch troops had put

---

[9]   The Japanese 48th Division and the 56th Regimental Group landed on Java at Kragan which is located on the northeast coast of Java to the west of Sourabaya. Because these troops were not involved in the fighting with *Blackforce,* they then will not be covered in this story.

up some resistance, by the afternoon of 1st March they had been overwhelmed and the road junction at Serang was in enemy hands. The Japanese 2nd Division then advanced eastward in two columns, the main body moving on Road No. 1 towards Batavia, whilst one regiment swung south towards Pandeglang to pick up Road No. 2 from Rangkasbitoeng via Djasinga. Because the Dutch troops had demolished bridges ahead of the main Japanese column it was experiencing delays, so on 3rd March a second regiment was swung south to pick up Road No. 2. As predicted by Brigadier Blackburn this was achieved by moving south along the Kragilan–Rangkasbitoeng Road that followed the east bank of the Tjioedjoeng River, and by then crossing the concrete dam at Pamarajan. The column on Road No. 2 was now the stronger of the two Japanese columns as it advanced towards the Dutch at Djasinga and *Blackforce* at Leuwiliang.

At Maj-Gen Schilling's request Brigadier Blackburn proceeded to Maj-Gen Schilling's Headquarters for a conference, arriving at 1445 hours on 1st March. Brigadier Blackburn was advised that it had been decided to counterattack the Japanese 230th Infantry Regiment at Soebang to the north of Bandoeng at dawn on 2nd March. Maj-Gen Schilling suggested that a detachment be left at Leuwiliang whilst the remainder of *Blackforce* be used to support the Dutch in this action. Brigadier Blackburn then explained to Maj-Gen Schilling that this would involve a move of over 125 miles into unfamiliar territory and showed little prospect of success. The proposed move Brigadier Blackburn believed would have placed the defence of the area around Leuwiliang and Buitenzorg at risk. As a result of Brigadier Blackburn's objections this plan was dropped and *Blackforce* would be left to its own resources for the remainder of this short campaign.

Brigadier Blackburn could not have been back in the Leuwiliang area long because at 1700 hours the Dutch Officer in Command at Rangkasbitoeng appeared at Leuwiliang and reported that his troops had been heavily engaged and pursued by the Japanese all day and that he had been unable to hold the position at Djasinga. When the Dutch commander was questioned by Brigadier Blackburn as to how many casualties his force had suffered he replied that he had one man wounded.

Brigadier Blackburn now spoke with Maj-Gen Schilling over the phone about the present situation and put forward his view that the Japanese should be attacked on Road No. 2. Maj-Gen Schilling agreed and offered Brigadier Blackburn the use of a Dutch infantry regiment currently positioned at Buitenzorg. Brigadier Blackburn immediately took up the offer. It was suggested that these local troops, being familiar with the area could follow a track around the back of Tjampea, where they could cross the river 2 miles down stream (to the north) of Leuwiliang then swing back south to attack the enemies' left flank and rear. Whilst this was happening, *Blackforce* it was intended, would advance across the bridge at Leuwiliang and make a frontal assault against the Japanese column advancing along Road No. 2. This plan was approved and by 2030 hours Brigadier Blackburn and the Dutch Commander of the infantry regiment that was to be involved in the action had worked out the finer details of the attack.

After the plans for this proposed attack against the Japanese column had been made the phone rang and Maj-Gen Schilling informed Brigadier Blackburn that he had been ordered by Lt-Gen ter Poorten to send not only the offered infantry regiment but all Dutch troops defending Road No. 2 including those in the vicinity of Buitenzorg for a planned attack on the right flank of the Japanese 230th Regiment. The 230th had landed 80 miles to the east of Batavia at Eretanwetan and were advancing on Bandoeng from the north. The objectives of this formation were to capture the airfield at Kalidjati and to then cut the Batavia–Bandoeng railway before advancing on Bandoeng.

At this stage Brigadier Blackburn was concerned about his right flank being exposed now that the Dutch were withdrawing their troops. Brigadier Blackburn then posed the question as to what his orders were considering the Japanese were advancing in column of route along Road No. 2 now that virtually all Dutch Forces on Western Java were being withdrawn to the east to stem the tide of the Japanese advance on Bandoeng. Maj-Gen Schilling replied that he had no orders for him, so under the circumstances Brigadier Blackburn felt that he had no choice except to pull back *Blackforce* to the southeast of Buitenzorg where he could protect each of his flanks on a river. Brigadier Blackburn then called his commanders and ordered them to have their units ready to move at 0400 hours on the morning of 2nd March.

2nd March 1942

At 0420 hours, just after his force had begun to move out of the Leuwiliang–Tjampea area Brigadier Blackburn received a telephone call from Maj-Gen Schilling saying that he had decided to leave him two companies of Dutch troops to cover his right flank and that he was to take over responsibility for the defence of Road No. 2. Brigadier Blackburn immediately ordered his column to cease their withdrawal and to take over the defence from the Dutch.

Brigadier Blackburn now ordered Lt-Col Williams to take a company of his No. 2 Battalion and place them in a defensive position covering the Leuwiliang Bridge. Likewise Lt-Col. Lyneham with a company from his No. 1 Battalion was to take up position half to three quarters of a mile to the rear of the No. 2 Battalion. Major de Crespigny, was ordered to hold his No. 3 Battalion as a mobile reserve ready to move out and protect the flanks of the other two battalions.

Brigadier Blackburn expected the enemy to probe and attempt to move around his flanks so he also ordered patrols to be sent out for a distance of 2 miles from both flanks to check any Japanese patrols intending to outflank *Blackforce*. Brigadier Blackburn was now satisfied that with the forces at his disposal that *Blackforce* was now disposed in depth for the defence of the river crossing. He had already been suitably briefed by Lt-Col. Ian Stewart, OBE, MC, the Commanding Officer of the Argyll and Sutherland Highlanders on the nature of Japanese battle tactics so he was well aware of their tactic of encircling their enemies' flanks.

The commander of 'B' Squadron of the King's Own Hussars was ordered to bring his light tanks forward at dawn on 2nd March to cover the approaches of the Leuwiliang Bridge across the Tjianten River. As infantry support Brigadier Blackburn also ordered two companies from No. 1 Battalion forward. They were briefed to be ready to cross the bridge and advance towards Djasinga and recapture the position from the enemy. At this stage the Dutch had not been advised that *Blackforce* was to take over the defence of the stone bridge so Lt-Col Williams rushed forward by car. Just as he arrived at the bridge at dawn, charges were detonated and the bridge collapsed in a pile of rubble before his eyes. The destruction of this bridge now prevented any effective offensive action against the advancing Japanese.

Lt-Col Tharpe commanding the American 131st Field Artillery Regiment was now ordered to also take up positions with his artillery. This was to be in the general region of the bridge to cover the approaches from the west along Road No. 2. By 0900 hours this position was fully occupied by all troops involved. At 0930 hours Lt-Col Williams ordered his No. 6 Platoon move forward and to the right of No. 4 Platoon and that No.'s 11 and 12 Platoons should switch positions The 2/3rd machine gunners (less their Vickers machine guns) were incorporated into the defence plan and were positioned to the left and rear of the companies defending the bridge.

That morning Lt-Col Williams had sent out a patrol towards Djasinga with orders to remain there and send back a report. When this patrol arrived at Djasinga it discovered no evidence of enemy occupation which would indicate that the Dutch troops had abandoned their positions.This then begs the question, how had the single Dutch casualty occurred. Not only had Djasinga been abandoned without justification but it also meant that the bridge over the Tjianten River at Leuwiliang had been demolished prematurely. The Australian patrol at

Djasinga encountered three Japanese armoured fighting vehicles at about 1000 hours but because the Australians were not in sufficient numbers to engage, they withdrew back to the Leuwiliang position.

At 1115 hours the three armoured vehicles arrived on the scene on the western side of the Leuwiliang Bridge. Deciding not to engage the Japanese at this time but instead to retain the element of surprise the defenders remained concealed. One of the enemy armoured vehicles now turned about and headed back west to report the situation to the Commander of the main Japanese column. Observation of the approach to the crossing at Leuwiliang was restricted due to heavy jungle in this area and also because the road swung sharply to the west. Shortly after, Japanese infantry were seen closing on bicycles along the road as well as on foot. By 1400 hours it was ascertained that a considerable Japanese force was bearing down on *Blackforce*.

Lt-Col Williams now despatched a platoon to the south and a patrol to the north to watch for any outflanking movements. He then ordered his troops to open fire, which by all accounts took the Japanese completely by surprise and inflicted many casualties. This included several high-ranking Japanese Officers who at the time were surveying the damage to the bridge. The platoon that had been sent to the south by Lt-Col Williams encountered some Japanese endeavouring to cross the Tjianten River upstream (to the south) so as they could work around the left flank of *Blackforce*, whilst the patrol sent northwards reported enemy moving north along the western bank with the same intention.

Just to the north of *Blackforce's* positions was a small knoll on the eastern bank of the river. Lt-Col Williams had sent a company to occupy this feature which remained in this position during the entire operation and stopped many of the enemy from infiltrating north and crossing the river to come in behind *Blackforce's* right flank. This company denied the enemy freedom of movement to the north despite being under almost continuous heavy small arms and mortar fire. Evidence would indicate that the grenade discharger and the mortar were the Japanese soldier's preferred weapons because reviewing the records of the men of the 2/4th Machine Gun Battalion following the Battle of Singapore, a great number of the fatalities and casualties had been as a result of shrapnel from these weapons. The Japanese had a selection of these weapons that propelled projectiles from 50mm to 150mm.

Meanwhile, back at Leuwiliang enemy attacks increased during the day. *Blackforce's* positions opposite the bridge were under constant mortar fire as well as accurate small arms fire, particularly from snipers firing from tree tops. During the night of 2nd–3rd March enemy fire eased considerably but active patrolling of the eastern side of the river was maintained all through the night. It was discovered that the enemy under the cover of darkness were moving a considerable distance to the south and infiltrating across the river. To counter this flanking movement Brigadier Blackburn ordered a company from No. 2 Battalion to move out and set up a defensive position and a second company from No. 1 Battalion to move around the enemies' left flank in readiness to attack at dawn. This operation was extremely successful, except for the fact that three officers were taken prisoner whilst out reconnoitring the area. Lieutenant C. G. Brettingham-Moore from the 2/3rd Machine Gun Battalion was now the only officer remaining. He had taken over command and had directed the attack against the enemy, an act for which he was awarded the Military Cross.

3rd March 1942

From dawn on 3rd March Japanese pressure increased and by the afternoon Brigadier Blackburn decided to place the American 131st Field Artillery Regiment into action for the first time. The 131st's report saw the enemy reply with infantry weapons and mortar fire. Still the

The demolished bridge at the Tjianten River, Leuwiliang
Photograph donated by Bill Haskell

Japanese persevered and still their attempts to cross the Tjianten River during the day and night of the 3rd–4th March were thwarted. The Japanese had been steadily working further and further south causing grave concern to Brigadier Blackburn who was forced to counter the enemies' movement by extending his front. The Japanese with their numerical strength could well afford to play this game, however, Brigadier Blackburn was hamstrung by having the use of only three battalions. If his front continued extending then he was going to lose the advantage of defence in depth. This would mean that once the Japanese had managed to circle around his flank he would have no reserve left with which to counter their movements and be forced to withdraw his troops to the east

Brig. Blackburn explains in his own words:

> '*Generally speaking the plan which I had ordered all my forces to adopt was to appear to give way in the centre whenever or wherever an enemy attack was delivered and at the same time, to send out fighting patrols or units on each flank. The centre then stopped their withdrawal after about 300–400 yards and the flanking troops then swing in swiftly towards the original centre of the position, thus encircling not only the enemy's center(sic) but also the outflanking parties which in every case he sent out on one or both flanks to endeavour to encircle my force. These tactics were very highly successful and appeared to cause much concern.*' [10]

---

[10]   AWM54 File 559/2/2 Report by Brigadier A. S. Blackburn on operations of the A.I.F. in Java Feb/Mar 1942 Australian War Memorial Canberra p.8

During the day of 3rd March hammering could be heard on the opposite bank of the Tjianten River indicating that the enemy might be building rafts to attempt a river crossing. Brigadier Blackburn decided to set a trap for the Japanese on the opposite bank and ordered Lt-Col Tharp to place a certain number of his artillery in such a position that if the Japanese attempted anything untoward the 131st could bring their artillery to bear along the road leading west from the demolished bridge. He then ordered Lt-Col Williams to withdraw his troops 350–400 yards to the rear, but to do this in such a way that it could be observed by the enemy who he hoped would believe were being withdrawn to the east. Patrols were left in place at the bridge to observe and report on the enemies' movements. Two companies of infantry, one 800 yards to the north and the other 1,000 yards to the south were also left in position ready to attack at dawn on 4th March and to mop up any of the enemy who were trapped in the void created by the pocket. The night passed without incident but patrols reported that although no enemy tanks had crossed there was considerable movement of infantry troops across the river.

4th March 1942

At dawn on 4th March *Blackforce's* attack was delivered and was a complete success, except that the enemies' strength was not as great as has been hoped. At 0930 hours Maj-Gen Schilling requested a meeting with Brigadier Blackburn, which took place at 1020 hours. Maj-Gen Schilling explained that his troops on Road No. 1 at Tangerang were being attacked but were holding their positions. He also said that the counterattack against the Japanese column at Soebang had met with initial success but because of lack of infantry support, the counterattack had failed to halt the enemy. This now meant that the situation in central Java had deteriorated with the road and railway leading into Bandoeng now under enemy control. Maj-Gen Schilling also explained that he had received a warning order to evacuate Batavia by withdrawing his forces back to Bandoeng, but that he was still awaiting final orders.

The danger at this stage of the battle was that with the Japanese advancing on Bandoeng, and with Batavia about to be evacuated the Allied troops on Western Java were being bottled up in the area between Leuwiliang and Bandoeng. As a consequence Maj-Gen Schilling's plan was modified for *Blackforce* to hold back the enemy, believing that 24 hours would be long enough from the time of receipt of his orders. He hoped this would be enough time for the garrison at Batavia to escape using both the road and railway south to Bandoeng. These two senior officers then worked out a plan in which *Blackforce* would hold the road and railway until 1430 hours on 5th March which should allow the Batavia Garrison enough time to evacuate. Maj-Gen Schilling said that he would send as much traffic as possible unobtrusively south on the road on the afternoon of 4th March.

The two men then discussed the planned withdrawal of *Blackforce* from the Leuwiliang–Tjampea area. Maj-Gen Schilling said that he desired that *Blackforce* should act as a rear guard throughout the entire withdrawal moving part of his force to Soekaboemi on the night of 4th–5th March, but only if the enemy were not pressing too hard and if it was possible to break off contact. He then said he would like *Blackforce* to be prepared to move on the night of the 5th–6th March. Brigadier Blackburn agreed to these proposals and then returned to his headquarters.

On arrival he found that the enemy had moved a considerable force about 3 and a half miles to the south of the Tjianten Bridge along a road that ran parallel with the river and had succeeded in making a crossing. Brigadier Blackburn at once ordered a company from No. 1 Battalion to move out and pin down this force before they had the opportunity to outflank his positions. He gave his company commanders the discretion to either drive back the enemy across the river or hold them, depending on the situation, but also made them aware of the plan to withdraw over the 4th–5th March.

The company from No. 1 Battalion got to within about a quarter of a mile from the enemy, who were disposed in a long line to the south but at that time had made no effort to advance north towards *Blackforce's* positions at Leuwiliang. The company commander had given each of his platoons a different sector of responsibility each some distance apart and ordered them to attack and drive the enemy back. These attacks by the three platoons were all delivered between 1700 and 1830 hours with the result that no further enemy movement was made up until the time of the final evacuation at 1530 hours on 5th March. Regretfully contact was lost with these troops in this company from No. 1 Battalion. It was later discovered that the withdrawal order did arrive but that those troops who were not overwhelmed by the enemy did attempt to circle around and join up with the main force. However they were unable to do so and had no option but to head for the mountains where they later joined up with some other Dutch and British troops. These troops managed to remain at large until their capture in early August 1942. This company from No. 1 Battalion had fought with great courage and it is possible that had the enemy not been attacked and held back they may have infiltrated around the left flank of *Blackforce*, which would have not only placed the evacuation of the Dutch garrison at Batavia in danger but this would have also necessitated a withdrawal from the Leuwiliang defence position.

Brigadier Blackburn now fine-tuned his plans for the final withdrawal of his force to the east. He decided that he would leave behind five light tanks from the King's Own Hussars and one company from No. 1 Battalion. While the rest of his troops withdrew this rearguard was to be located in a strongly held defensive position with their left and right flanks resting on a small river astride the road leading east away from Leuwiliang. One company was to reconnoitre and be prepared to take up position 1,000 yards to the rear of the former if necessary, while another company was also tasked with holding a defensive position astride the road and flanked on either side by a river about 1 mile to the southeast of Buitenzorg. This second defensive position was to be used to extricate and extract the forward troops if they became too heavily engaged during the actual withdrawal.

Brigadier Blackburn was not so much concerned with Japanese armour because with the bridge destroyed a crossing would be difficult and this in turn would affect time delays upon the enemy. Furthermore, the rear guard company had their position well covered by Bren guns and he was confident that it would take a large-scale attack to drive these troops out of their positions. What concerned him most was that the only way of withdrawing his troops through Buitenzorg was across a well constructed steel bridge over the deep Tjiliwoeng River. This was obviously going to create a bottle neck along his retreating column.

At about 1700 hours on 4th March it was reported that the Japanese were concentrating their mortar and bringing forward a considerable number of trucks and or armoured cars. By this time the second Japanese column which had been turned south on 3rd March must have arrived or at least been close to arriving at Leuwiliang area. As mentioned, observation of Japanese movements on the opposite bank of the Tjianten River was obstructed by heavy jungle and the sharp bend in the road. All the same the last 200-300 yards of approach road to the bridge on the western side of the Tjianten River was open to observation. For this reason Lt-Col Tharp was instructed not to engage minor targets for the following reasons. Firstly, so that the enemy could not position his artillery, and secondly so as the enemy might remain unaware of the number of artillery pieces *Blackforce* possessed and take greater risks by exposing their position. Brigadier Blackburn now ordered Lt-Col Tharp's 131st Regiment to lay down a barrage with his artillery which managed to silence at least five Japanese mortar crews and destroyed an unknown number of vehicles. From now until the final withdrawal at 1530 hours the following day nothing more was heard from the enemy, particularly their mortars which had been a constant nuisance to *Blackforce*.

Soon after dark on the night of 4th March the first of the Dutch troops moving down from Batavia passed through Buitenzorg. From then on a steady stream of vehicles passed through during the night. By holding the east bank of the Tjianten River at Leuwiliang *Blackforce* had allowed enough time for demolitions to be completed and for the Dutch garrison at Batavia to evacuate to the south before the Japanese occupation on 5th March. The destruction of the bridge over the Tjianten River had allowed sufficient time for the Batavia garrison to escape but this now only exacerbated Brigadier Blackburn's problems by restricting the offensive movements of his troops to the east of Leuwiliang.

As planned, the forward companies' withdrawal was completed by 2100 hours thanks to a heavy rainsquall that aided concealment. At 2200 hours on 4th March Brigadier Blackburn received a report that it appeared as if the Japanese were massing for an attack on the western side of the river. As a result of this information he ordered all fire to cease from 2245 to 2315 hours, at which time intense small arms fire was to be opened up on the opposite bank of the river in an effort to deceive the enemy into believing there was no withdrawal but rather an attack was about to be launched. This small arms fire was at first answered with heavy fire from the Japanese but after a while it rapidly dwindled, causing Brigadier Blackburn to believe the enemy had fallen back. At this he issued the order at 0030 hours on 5th March for his force to commence withdrawal at 0215 hours. The remaining troops were loaded onto vehicles and transported to Soekaboemi, which was reached on the morning of 5th March.

5th March 1942

The withdrawal proceeded without incident except for a report at 0130 hours that the enemy had penetrated the area of the No. 3 Reserve Battalion at Tjampea, but this later proved to be false. The road heading southeast towards Soekaboemi was very congested but nevertheless *Blackforce* reached the town where they concentrated for the night on the outskirts of the town with one company acting as a rear guard. Soon after dawn Brigadier Blackburn sent out a patrol to Buitenzorg which reported back at about 1100 hours with the information that the position there was quiet. The Dutch had given the all clear once the last of their troops had evacuated Batavia and had reached Buitenzorg; and at this the rear guard withdrew from Leuwiliang without incident. *Blackforce* was to see no more action after Leuwiliang. Meanwhile, following a conference by senior Allied officers at Bandoeng on the evening of 5th March Brigadier Blackburn was ordered to withdraw his troops to the east of Bandoeng.

6th March 1942

Blackforce commenced the move from Soekaboemi to Bandoeng soon after dark on the night of 6th March but progress was very slow due to the fact that the bridge at Tjirandang had been heavily mined. This meant that only one vehicle could cross at a time and even then only at a speed of 5 m.p.h.

7th March 1942

The next morning at dawn on 7th March Brigadier Blackburn received a message that Dutch resistance could cease, that Bandoeng might be declared an open city, and that he was cleared to take independent action. Should this happen he was advised to withdraw to the mountains in southwest Java. At this time *Blackforce* was to the east of Bandoeng and a study of the map showed no roads that he could move his force to the southwest of Java without moving back through Bandoeng. Such a move appeared impossible in view of the Dutch warning that Bandoeng might be declared an open city. Brigadier Blackburn decided that it was feasible to move his force to the mountains south of Garoet with the intention of reaching the south coast of Java. Over the next two days Brigadier Blackburn reconnoitred the mountain country to the south of Bandoeng in the vicinity of Garoet and arranged for food dumps to be made.

8th March 1942

At 2100 hours on 8th March Lt-Gen ter Poorten broadcast to all Allied forces fighting on Java that all resistance had ceased and that troops were to lay down their arms.

> *'The Malay barrier was thus shattered and the gateway to the Indian Ocean open. The Allied fleet in the Far East had been destroyed. In three months the Japanese had completed the conquest of Malaya and the Netherlands East Indies and had gained possession of all the resources of the rich southern area for which they had gone to war.'* [11]

Brigadier Blackburn learnt of this latest development about one hour later, and immediately issued orders that his forces were to withdraw to an area near Tjikadjang where they could cover the road to the south coast. Brigadier Blackburn then attempted to get a wireless message through to the Australian Government but to no avail as wireless communications had ceased before it was sent. *Blackforce* remained in position in the area of Tjikadjang and in the vicinity of a tea plantation at Arinem just to the southwest of Tjikadjang. It had been hoped that by communicating with Australia and making their way to the coast at Tjilatjap there was a possibility they might be rescued by the navy. However, the Japanese had already taken Tjilatjap on 7th March so it was highly unlikely that a naval evacuation would take place considering Japanese air and naval dominance.

It was now in the best interest of the troops to surrender because there was neither food nor medicine to sustain such a force as this in the mountains without unnecessary loss of life. Now was time to accept the fact that Java was securely in Japanese hands. After the news of the official surrender all *Blackforce's* vehicles were lined up in convoy fashion and run with their chokes on, the oil sumps and radiators having been pierced with iron bars. After about 10 minutes of running the engines seized thus denying their use to the Japanese.

Blackforce was a mixed force of Australians, British and Americans who were thrown into a battle as a composite group. The fact that the Japanese advance was impeded for nearly 72 hours is a credit to Brigadier Blackburn and the determination and fighting ability of these men. On 12th March Brigdier Blackburn was one of three commanders who had been driven to the Imperial Japanese Army Headquarters at Bandoeng where an unconditional surrender was signed:

> *'When Brigadier Blackburn entered the room, General Maruyama, the Japanese commander and his staff stood up. Through an interpreter Blackie asked the reason and was informed that they wished to pay a tribute to his troops. They could not understand how so small a force could have held them up for so long.'* [12]

---

[11] Maj-Gen Stanley Woodburn Kirby CB, CMG, OBE, MC, The History of the Second World War *The War Against Japan* Volume I HMSO London 1957, p.449
[12] John Bellair *Snow to Jungle* A History of the 2/3rd Machine Gun Battalion Allen & Unwin 1987, p.105–106

The Japanese admitted later that *Blackforce* had accounted for at least 500 Japanese casualties during the action at the Tjianten River and still found it hard to believe that they had only opposed a brigade and not a division. There is one point that does come to light concerning the Imperial Japanese Army following this action on Java. It would appear that whilst Japanese infantry was mobile and on the offensive using their strategem of encirclement infiltration and speed to gain them ground, then everything was as it should be. However, once they met a determined defence as they had on this occasion at the Tjianten River it appears they were reluctant to follow through with the momentum of their attack.

The Australian Chief of General Staff, Lt-Gen V. A. H. Sturdee had written a paper prior to the date that units from the 1st Australian Corps landed at Tanjong Priok. This report is important because it concerns the breaking up of balanced Australian formations and tossing them piecemeal at the enemy to either be killed or captured and is obviously a subject that deeply concerned Lt-Gen Sturdee. The Australian 8th Division had been broken up in this way to the detriment of the division. Firstly its armour was removed and sent to the Middle East. Then the three battalions of the 23rd Brigade were sent to defend Rabaul, Ambon and Timor, which left Maj-Gen. Gordon Bennett with only two of his three brigades. Amongst other corps troops his Pioneer Battalion was taken from him and up until the eleventh hour his Machine Gun Battalion. A similar situation confronted the Australian 7th Division except this time in reverse when some of its corps troops were landed on Java, only to meet the same fate as the men in the 8th Division.

The following paragraph is taken from Lt-Gen Sturdee's report dated 15.2.1942, in which he expresses his view about the breaking up of balanced formations:

> '*In view of the present situation in the S.W. Pacific Area and of information which has just come to my knowledge, I consider that the future employment of the A.I.F. requires immediate reconsideration by the war cabinet.*
>
> *So far in this war against Japan we have violated the principle of concentration of forces in our efforts to hold numerous small localities with totally inadequate forces, which are progressively overwhelmed by vastly superior numbers. These small garrisons alone without adequate reinforcement or support never appeared to have any prospect of withstanding even a moderate scale of attack. In my opinion, the present policy of trying to hold isolated islands with inadequate resources needs review.*' [13]

Brigadier Blackburn also wrote:

> '*To the many men who took part in the campaign in Java and to the many people in Australia, it seemed at the time that the landing of Australian troops in that island was a needless waste of men. I can say, however, without hesitation, that the resistance put up by that small force of Australians against a crack Japanese Division was not wasted. At that critical time, March 1942, every day, perhaps every hour, during which the Japanese advance on Australia was delayed, meant a big gain to this country. Without attempting to make comparisons, I say that the fight put up by the Australian troops on Java caused considerable delay to the Japanese plans for invasion.*' [14]

---

[13]   Lionel Wigmore, *Japanese Thrust* Australia in the War of 1939–45 Army Volume IV Appendix No. 5 Future Deployment of A.I.F. General Sturdee's Paper of 15th February 1942 paragraph 3 Australian War Memorial Canberra 1957, p.675

[14]   From the foreword written by Brigadier A. S. Blackburn for Walter Summons, *Twice Their Prisoner* Oxford Press 1946

Based on Brigadier Blackburn's view, which appears echoes the Hon Mr Norman Makin's statement of 23rd December 1941 that the Japanese must be delayed as long as possible. It might be reasonably put that the actions of the Australians in Malaya, Singapore and Java caused the Japanese Government to seriously reconsider their plans for a possible invasion of Australia. During the course of these three campaigns on numerous occasions the Japanese soldier had come up against his Australian counterpart and had been mauled. The Japanese by this time must have reasoned that if Australians were to fight as they had done on a foreign soil, then how determined were they likely to defend their own homeland? Was the 8th Division's and to a lesser degree, the 1st Australian Corps' sacrifice in human life and suffering in vain? If the answer is no, then as a nation Australia owes these men a great debt of gratitude and they should be remembered more so for their achievements on the battlefield than for their experiences as Prisoner's of War.

Prisoners of the Japanese

The troops had been told that they were free to try escape if they wished. Some of the men, the likes of Alf Sing, Doug Hampson, Jack Cocking, 'Bluey' Walsh and Tom Wayman went towards the south coast with a group under the leadership of Lt. Blakeway, in the hope of avoiding capture. As strange as it sounds Alf, Doug and Jack were three of only eleven men onboard the *Rakuyo Maru* who were torpedoed and later rescued by the Americans in 1944.This group remained on the south coast of Java for a few days and as Tom Wayman remembers all they had to eat was bully beef and chocolate. Parties were sent out, travelling up to 60 miles in either direction in an attempt to find a means of escape. Eventually dysentery and malaria began to take a toll on the men so when an officer arrived on the beach with a message that they would be machine gunned if they didn't make there way back to Leles it was decided that this was their only option. On the most part *Blackforce* had remained in the vicinity of the tea plantation at Arinem, whilst the medical staffs had remained the whole time at Bandoeng.

As 1943 dawned many of the Australians would relocate to either Burma or Thailand as members of the Java Parties to work as forced labour on the Burma–Thailand rail link. Later one member from the 2/4th would finish up in Borneo on 'E' Force and several others would transit through Singapore and work on the Sumatran Pakan Baroe–Moearo Railway. The camps covered below are the main areas where Prisoners of War were imprisoned on Java.

Leles

The camp at Leles was occupied from 14th March 1942 being a square where the Javanese held their markets. The market place consisted of several buildings about 12 feet wide with just enough covering overhead to shade the vendor's stalls. Most of the prisoners at Leles were moved to the Bicycle Camp at Batavia between 30th March and 14th April 1942. The first group of about fifty prisoners left in late March 1942 as the advance party with the intention that they would build a camp prior to the main group of prisoners arriving. This, however, never eventuated as they were billeted at the Koan School at Glodok, a suburb in Batavia when they were moved to the Bicycle Camp at Batavia in May 1942.

Garoet

On 14th April 1942 a group of mostly 2/3rd machine gunners left Leles for Garoet where they remained until 22nd June. The camp was located in the High School buildings which were serviced with light, water and sewerage. In June they were then moved to Bandoeng to Camp No. 12, the 15th Depot Battalion Barracks Camp where they met up with other Australians from the 2/2nd Casualty Clearing Station.

Bandoeng-Tjimahi

The main Prisoner of War camp at Bandoeng was Camp No. 12 in the former 15th Depot Battalion Barracks at Kampement Streat Bandoeng. Members from the 2/3rd Machine Gun Battalion moved to this camp on 22nd June 1942. Many of those who had remained at large were, when captured, imprisoned in a concentration camp at Soekaboemi, (Doug Carter was one such man) and in June they were transferred to Tjimahi. This was presumably to concentrate all Prisoners of War on Western Java into one area. Some prisoners were also placed into the Soekamiskin Prison to the east of Bandoeng. The Soekamiskin Prison, (Maurice Caldwell was at this prison from the 15th February 1942 to 5th February 1944) was for Dutch, British, American, Ambonese and Mendaonese Prisoners of War and Indonesian convicts. Once the 1st Allied General Hospital was closed down the patients and staff were marched 6 miles from Bandoeng to a native prison, being the Landsop Camp at Tjimah.from here they were then moved to No. 4 Camp, which was possibly the 4th Battalion Barracks at Tjimahi, before again being moved back to Camp No. 12, the former Dutch 15th Depot Battalion Barracks at Bandoeng.

Bicycle Camp Batavia

The Bicycle Camp at Batavia was located at a place called Senen in the older part of the city at Weltevreden. It was the former barracks to the 10th Battalion Bicycle Unit, Netherlands East Indies Army. In May 1942 the camp was almost completely filled with British and Australian Prisoners of War. Work parties would leave the camp to do labouring jobs around the environs of Batavia or on the wharves at Tanjong Priok. Tasks included roadwork, rolling steel drums, or sorting out motor vehicle parts, as there was a General Motors assembly plant at Tanjong Priok. On 14th May British and Dutch troops were moved to another camp and the Australians from Glodok Prison and the advance party from Leles, were transferred to the Bicycle Camp. There were two 2/4th at this camp being Edgar Jones who died in July 1942 and William Nicholls who died the following October.

Glodok Prison Batavia

Glodok Prison with its high walls and cramped cells was a gaol built by the Dutch and was located close to the port area of Batavia. Reports state that conditions at this camp were very bad with living spaces so crowded that men were forced to sleep in passageways. Australians were still there in May 1943.

Makasura

This camp was just to the south of Meester Cornelis on the Meester Cornelis-Tjilititan Road. In May 1943 there were still about 500 British, Dutch and Australian Prisoners of War here working in the vegetable market garden. It was from this camp that men who were included in Java Party No. 6 (Dunlop Force) departed for Singapore and Thailand on 4th January 1943. They had been transferred to Makasura from Bandoeng on 6th November 1942. This might then tell us that those members from the 2/4th that were on the Java No. 6 Party were likely at Bandoeng for most of their stay on Java. Desmond Jackson tells us that this camp at Makasura was located in a kapok plantation and describes the camp as

> '*A pleasant, heavily populated locality, abundant with tropical growth. High barbed-wire fences divided the camp into three small sections comprising a barracks area, a parade ground and an exercise yard. We spent most of our time in the barracks area where our living quarters were particularly crude bamboo huts.*' [15]

---

15   Desmond Jackson, *What Price Surrender* Allen & Unwin Sydney 1989, p.26

Chapter Three

Burma and Japan's Strategic Objectives

Although Burma's value to Japan lay in its resources of rice, oil and wolfram, used in the manufacture of tungsten for armaments, there was also strategic motives. Japan had been at war with China since 1937 but had been unable to achieve a decisive victory. Burma also protected Japan's newly won landward approaches to Thailand, Malaya and Singapore. China was being supplied U.S. lend lease military hardware by way of the Burma Road which ran for 350 miles from Lashio in Burma to Kunming, the provincial capital of Yunnan in China. Lashio was connected to Rangoon via a rail link through Mandalay. Burma's capital, Rangoon was also important because it was Burma's only seaport and was also a crucial link in the British air reinforcement route from India to Malaya and Singapore.

In Burma these British airfields were from north to south, Moulmein, Tavoy, Mergui and Victoria Point. They were all located on Burma's Tenasserim Peninsula a 500 mile long tail that hangs below Burma and shares the Kra Isthmus with Thailand and Malaya. Once Japan expanded her empire in the Pacific and had occupied China, French Indo-China, Thailand, Malaya, Singapore and the islands of the Netherlands East Indies it was just a matter of taking Burma. This would then create a buffer zone to keep the Allies out of this immensely resources rich area. Once Singapore with its fleet naval base was captured followed later by Rangoon the Royal Navy would have nowhere else to operate except Trincomalee in Ceylon and Australia.

On 16th December 1941 a battalion from the Japanese 143rd Infantry Regiment moving across the Kra Isthmus captured the British airfield at Victoria Point. The 15th January 1942 saw the Japanese move against the second airfield at Tavoy. The British had hoped to keep Tavoy in their possession but the Japanese moved too quickly for its defenders and by 19th January the airfield was securely in Japanese hands. Now that Victoria Point and Tavoy were captured Mergui and this was isolated and was evacuated between 20th and 23rd January. All that remained to gain control of the whole Tenasserim Peninsula was to capture Moulmein, and Japan would be standing at the gates of Rangoon. Japan also knew that time was of the essence because the longer they delayed the more time Britain would have to reinforce Burma. This very nearly occurred with Australian troops who would later fight the Japanese in New Guinea.

On 30th and 31st January the Japanese 55th Division took Moulmein against stubborn resistance by its British defenders. The knock out blow to Rangoon had finally arrived with Moulmein's loss, because Japanese bombers would now be within range of Rangoon. It should come as no surprise that the first ports of call for the three battalions of 'A' Force were Victoria Point, Mergui and Tavoy where the prisoners were put to work on airfield repairs.

The 'A' Force Story

In May 1942 the Japanese announced they would require a force of 3,000 men to be drawn from the 8th Division. This force being the first group to depart Singapore was named 'A' Force and its composition was as follows:

Headquarters	Commander	Brigadier A. L. Varley	2/18th Battalion
Engineering	"	Major J. A. Shaw	2/12th Field Company
Medical Det	"	Lt-Col T. Hamilton	2/4th Casualty Clearing Station
No. 1 Battalion	"	Lt-Col G. R. Ramsay	2/30th Battalion
No. 2 Battalion	"	Major D. R. Kerr [1]	2/10th Field Regiment
No. 3 Battalion	"	Major C. E. Green	2/4th Machine Gun Battalion

On 14th May 'A' Force embarked at Singapore on two ships. Headquarters, No. 2 and No. 3 Battalions sailed on the *Toyohashi Maru* and No. 1 Battalion and the medical detachment on the *Celebes Maru*. Sailing past Medan on the northeast coast of Sumatra two small ships and a sloop transporting British Prisoners of War joined the convoy. These were the men who would be known as the British Sumatra Battalion. They had been captured by the Japanese at Padang in Sumatra and were moved north to Belawan, the port of Medan on 9th May 1942. Included amongst these ranks was Lt-Col Albert Coates A.A.M.C. who was destined to become the Senior Medical Officer on the Burma side of the rail link. Arriving off Victoria Point on 21st May, Green Force (named after its commander, Major Charles Green) and 1,016 Prisoners of War disembarked. On 23rd May, Lt-Col Ramsay's No. 1 Battalion disembarked at Mergui along with the British Sumatra Battalion and on 25th May the remainder of the prisoners in this convoy disembarked at Tavoy. The men would now be set to work on runway repairs at all three locations, before moving north to begin work on the Burma–Thailand rail link.

Victoria Point

Green Force was now broken down into two groups, the first group comprising 600 all ranks to work at the airfield camp, located about seven miles from the Victoria Point townsite. The remaining 416 men in the second group were based at Victoria Point and were accommodated in houses along the waterfront. Work here consisted of unloading aviation fuel drums and rice from ships, rolling, stacking and loading fuel drums onto trucks for the airfield, and roadwork.

The airfield group was accommodated in huts on the western slopes of a range of hills. This was on the eastern side of the airfield about 1,000 yards north of the Japanese garrison. Major Green pointed out the inadequacies of the housing and the problem of overcrowding. Soon the

---

[1] On arrival at Tavoy, Lt-Col C. G. W. Anderson became the Commander of No. 2 Battalion and Major Kerr became his Second in Command. From this point the battalion was to be known as Anderson Force until its amalgamation with Williams Force on 3rd January 1943.

men had pulled down some huts around the airfield and rebuilt them at their camp, thereby temporarily alleviating the housing problem. Camp improvements from hereon continued as the men settled into their new surroundings.

Towards the end of May, work commenced on the airfield. The Japanese had grand ideas about improvements, but without the equipment to carry out these tasks it would be impossible. Also some unexploded mines had been discovered and searches for these soon became a daily occurrence. In all, four unexploded mines were discovered. The former owners had damaged the runway before their departure, leaving it pitted with craters which had to be filled before the airfield could be made serviceable again. There were a total of forty craters in the runway and these consisted of eleven small craters about two feet six inches in diameter by 6–8 feet deep. Also there were twenty-nine larger craters about 25 feet in diameter and varying between 10 and 20 feet deep. These had been made with crater charges in galvanized piping with about 50lbs of gelignite. Other work consisted of levelling and rolling the runway, loading sand onto trucks, unloading and ramming sand, carrying sand in bags, filling bags, wiring the camp and roadwork.

At 1000 hours on 8th July 1942 it was reported that NX10420 Pte. Robert Goulden was missing. This man was a cook and had transferred across to the 2/4th so that Claude Webber could join his brother George, who was also a member of the 2/9th Field Ambulance. Goulden made good his escape but had become lost and decided to surrender to the Burmese Police whence he was handed back to the Japanese. He was returned to the airfield camp and at 1030 hours on 12th July was interviewed by Major Green. He had told the Major he had been worried about his wife who had been sick. At the time Goulden did not know that his wife had given birth to his son Howard on 6th March 1942. Major Green pleaded Goulden's case explaining his anguish, but the Japanese insisted that Goulden knew the rules governing escape. He was executed by firing squad at 1200 hours on 12th July 1942. Robert Goulden's death had been used as an example of what would happen to Prisoners of War who were caught trying to escape. The irony is that the Japanese firing squad then honoured this man by presenting arms to his lifeless body before marching off. Goulden's body was buried at 1400 hours in Lot No. 30 of the English Section of the cemetery at Victoria Point, the funeral service being conducted by Padre F. X. Corry, 2/4th Machine Gun Battalion.

From the end of July 1942 men from the Victoria Point Camp started to arrive on the scene to help with the work on the airfield. This was an early indicator that another move was afoot. By 10th August the airfield was being cleared of refuse, the rollers moved and tools stacked away.

Tavoy-Ye-Lamaign-Moulmein

Green Force was now split into two detachments, the first under Major Green and the second under Major J. Stringer from the 2/26th Battalion. From this point the two detachments leap frogged each other until they joined forces again at Kendau, the 4.8km Camp, and the first construction camp on the Burma side of the rail link. The first detachment left Victoria Point on 6th August and arrived at Tavoy three days later. They had embarked on two ships, one with only the identification No. 593, being a small coal ship and the other ship named *Tatu Maru*.

The 15th August saw the initial draft of the first detachment leave Tavoy by truck and arrive at Ye the same day. This was followed on 17th August by the remainder of the force in the second draft who also arrived at Ye the same day. Work on the last and most northern of the three airfields was completed by mid September. All ranks, less the sick, marched out of Ye to Thanbyuzayat via Lamaign, over 25th and 26th September 1942, arriving at Thanbyuzayat on 28th September. On 1st October all ranks of Major Green's first detachment who had left Victoria Point on 6th August marched out to the Kendau 4.8km Camp. As the end of October drew nearer so did the end of the southwest monsoon and soon the men in Green Force would be hard at work constructing the rail link from the Burma end. Work had already begun on the Thailand side by a British work force.

This now left Stringer's second detachment which had left Victoria Point on 13th August aboard the ship No. 593. This ship, after disembarking the first detachment from Green Force, returned to Victoria Point to transport the second and smaller draft. This group arrived at Tavoy on 15th August and on 20th August boarded the *Unkai Maru* for passage to Moulmein, on the Salween River. Over 23rd and 24th October they travelled by train from Moulmein for Thanbyuzayat. On 26th October Major Springer's second detachment marched into Kendau 4.8km Camp and Green Force was once again united. Green Force now became No. 3 Battalion of the Burma Administration Group No. 3, under the command of the Japanese 5th Railway Regiment. Each prisoner was issued with a wooden plaque with his Prisoner of War number inscribed into the wood.

The Tragedy and the Triumph

Many personal accounts have been published concerning the Prisoner of War experience and the Burma–Thailand Railway. Usually these reminiscences do not take the form of fun filled scenic tours but are a record of brutality, enslavement, privation, humiliation, starvation, disease, filth, death and despair. Understandably, these are not subjects that an ex-Prisoner of War would discuss with his wife or children over the dinner table. It is likely that an ex-prisoner might tell of incidents which involved mateship, ockerism, larrikinism, bravery, heroism, leadership, pride, loyalty, dignity and humour.

His mind might flash back to the time he watched on helplessly as his mate was beaten to a pulp by a Japanese, Formosan or Korean guard. He might remember the time he knelt beside that same beaten body, now devoid of all strength as it drifted peacefully into an unbroken sleep. He might also remember the time when he himself was shivering with fever. This was the same mate who sold his wristwatch so he could purchase a duck egg to aid him recover. He might remember seeing a fellow prisoner wipe the sweaty brow of his feverish mate in some squalid hospital camp on the line and have observed almost a mother's love in the eyes of the carer as this man tried unsuccessfully to raise a smile from those withered parched lips. He might remember seeing the camp cemeteries fill with crosses and recall the smell in his nostrils as the corpses of the cholera victims were burnt on the funeral pyre.

Then again, scenes and memories such as these may have been totally erased from his memory. But one thing is for sure, he most certainly would remember seeing the Union Jack flap in the breeze for the first time in three and a half years and have spared a thought for his mates who were not there to see it with him. This is the story of the Burma–Thailand Railway, a story that is related not so much to shock or solicit pity for the men who endured its privations, but to raise the reader to new and higher level of knowledge and understanding. Perhaps then it can be explained, when as a child you wondered why your father whispered when he was in the company of his mates from the battalion.

The Burma – Thailand Railway

The Burma Section

There were several reasons behind the Japanese wanting to build a rail link between Non Pladuk, the 000.00 kilometre point in Thailand, and Thanbyuzayat in Burma, the 414.92 kilometre point. At the top of the list was the Japanese military's involvement in the China–Burma Theatre. The Imperial Japanese Army had to be supplied, so it was imperative that a line of communication be established between Bangkok, the capital of Thailand and Burma. There were three ways this could be achieved. By sea from Bangkok to Rangoon, by road, or by rail.

Firstly we will look at the sea route and Japan's merchant shipping. Following six months of war, Japan's newly won territories were spread far and wide. A wartime propaganda picture had been painted of a Japanese octopus with its tentacles wrapped around the islands of the Pacific and landmass of the Far East. Even though, by June 1942 the Japanese were realising that these tentacles were stretched to the limit and here in lay Japan's dilemma. Japan's Achilles heel was her merchant marine. Merchant shipping had to be shared between the Army, Navy and the Japanese home islands' needs. The Japanese population had to be fed and Japanese industry had to be supplied with the raw materials required to maintain her war effort.

One of the biggest mistakes Japan made is that she did not allow for the fact that war is a battle of attrition. Japan knew that her ability to wage a prolonged war was limited but hoped that a series of crippling blows to the Allies might bring them to their knees and force a parley at the peace table. Nevertheless by May 1942 Japan had already lost over 300,000 tons of shipping but unlike the United States of America, did not possess the power base of industry to keep up with supply and demand. Whereas Britain protected her convoys against German U Boats in the North Atlantic, Japan had not taken Allied submarine action against her merchant marine fleet into consideration. This would later cause havoc amongst Japanese shipping, virtually reducing Japan's merchant marine to a fleet of rowboats.

In the second instance a road was not practical because in the mountainous terrain of Thailand and Burma, rainfall during monsoon months is measured in feet not inches. A road in these conditions would not have stood up to this sort of punishment. Finally there was the possibility that the railway option could be achieved either by utilising one of two existing rail links between Bangkok and Non Pladuk or through the centre of Thailand from Bangkok to Phitsanulok. From Thanbyuzayat in Burma the existing rail system ran south to Ye and north to Moulmein. From Moulmein it was possible to travel by train directly to Rangoon. The existing rail system within Japanese controlled territory connected Korea, Manchuria, China and French Indo-China to Bangkok, then continued west to finish at Non Pladuk. From Non Pladuk an artery of Thailand's railway system ran south down the Kra Isthmus to connect Thailand with Malaya and Singapore and obviously from Singapore it was only a short voyage to either Sumatra or Java.

There was at least one problem concerning the construction of such a railway that could be solved easily enough and that problem was labour. Japan, following her rapid and decisive victories over the Allied powers had suddenly found herself with a massive labour pool from which to draw a workforce, despite the fact that this would defy every rule of the Geneva Convention, governing the treatment of Prisoners of War.

So it should now be seen that Japan's only solution would be to establish a line of communication between Thailand and Burma and to build a railway with Prisoners of War and coolie labour recruited from within what Japan called the Greater South East Asia Co-Prosperity Sphere. This was Japan's notion that the nations of Asia should unite and cast the white man from their soil under Japanese supervision of course.

The decision to go ahead with the project to build a one-metre gauge railway line from Non Pladuk in Thailand to Thanbyuzayat in Burma was finally approved by Tokyo on 20th June 1942,. This route would allow the use of the rivers to assist with the problems of transport. It also meant that the railway would run along the spine of the mountain ranges as opposed to across them as would be the case if the Phitsanulok to Moulmein route had been chosen.

An earlier survey to assess the feasibility of building such a rail link had been made but the consensus of opinion was that to build a railway over this untamed malaria ridden terrain in such a harsh climate would be economic suicide. Regardless, the Japanese decided to go ahead with their plan.

The railway was to ultimately be the responsibility of the Southern Army Railway Corps. Burma was the responsibility of the 5th Railway Regiment. This section of line was again split into two Burma Prisoner of War Administration Groups being Group No. 3 and No. 5. There were 2/4th in both of these groups that were to eventually be disbanded on 17th July 1944. The Thailand side of the railway was under the control of the 9th Railway Regiment being Group Nos. 1, 2, 4 and 6, with Groups No. 4 and 6 also having members of the 2/4th amongst their ranks. There were two other groups that did not come under either Burma or Thailand railway administrative control. These were 'F' and 'H' Forces, which remained attached to the Singapore administration and returned to Singapore from December 1943.

In addition to the two Japanese Railway Regiments which consisted of 5,000 men, there was also a Materials Workshop of 1,000 men based mainly at Non Pladuk with the remainder at Thanbyuzayat. A Railway Regiment consisted of a Headquarters, four Battalions and a Supply Depot, altogether about 2,500 men. There were also Bridging Units, a Signals Unit and with all the other Japanese support personnel it has been estimated that there were about 13,500 Japanese assigned to the railway. As there were Korean and Formosan guards on the railway, they would come under the general term of Japanese. These guards, particularly the Koreans, quickly established a reputation for their uncontrollable brutality which they would unleash upon the prisoners.

Even before the official sanction had arrived from Tokyo, preparations were already under way to collect materials for the railway. The Malayan rail system lost 333 miles of track alone not to mention 5,600 wagons, thirty locomotives and the rest can be left to the imagination. A 170 mile stretch of line was lifted between Rangoon and Toungoo in Burma and this was supplemented with still more rails from Java in the Netherlands East Indies. Rails were of different weights and were of British, German (Krupps) and Australian (BHP) manufacture. No circular rails were provided, but instead straight rails were cut into shorter lengths to enable bends in the line to be negotiated. There was one commodity however that was in abundance in Burma and Thailand and that was wood. It was utilised to build bridges, corduroy roads, the construction of the atap huts for the camps, to fire the locomotives and to make railway sleepers.

The terrain on the Burma side of the railway is generally kinder than the Thailand side, being flatter, and the jungle and bamboo less dense. However, the Burma section, in comparison to the Thailand section, was somewhat handicapped in that it did not have rivers running parallel to the railway. The river was the lifeline in Thailand, being the means by which supplies, materials and the sick could be transported south and local traders could tout their foodstuffs. In Burma the rivers tend to cross the rail link, but at no point are they of any value as a means by which men or supplies could be transported. This meant that supplies and the evacuation of the sick had to be by truck if roads were passable, or else by motor rail or on foot. The condition of roads was also dependent upon the seasonal monsoon rains.

From the coastal plain, where Thanbyuzayat sits on the western extremity, the railway travels south over the many tributary rivers across the Sedaung Taung Hills, through the valleys of the Mezali and Zami Rivers. Ascending to a plateau at the three Pagodas Pass at the 113km point, the terrain begins to gently descend again towards Nihke. The first 20-30 kilometres heading out from Thanbyuzayat is level or gently undulating country covered with a thick low scrub. From this point the terrain becomes less friendly with hills covered in sparse jungle and dense undergrowth.

Work on the railway trace at first consisted of clearing the dense undergrowth, felling trees and building embankments and excavating cuttings. In the hillier country the track would serpentine around hills following the natural gradients and for this reason high embankments and deep rock cuttings that would become the trademark of the Thailand side were rare. Two wide rivers, Mezali and Zami, had to be bridged as did many smaller rivers and ravines. In all there were six rivers in Burma that would need to be bridged. Besides the Zami and Mezali, there were the Apalon, Winyaw, Khonkan, and Myettan rivers. All these rivers and ravines equated to a grand total of 688 bridges, which had to be built, the majority of these in wood.

The climate over the length of the rail link was similar except that the rainfall in the northern end is much heavier than in the south. The rains begin in May and finish in October with the heaviest falls from July to August. From November to January the weather is colder, especially when the bitter north wind is blowing. From February to April the climate becomes progressively warmer with a fine powdery dust around camps, which instantly turns into a morass as soon as the first rains arrive in May. A point of note at this early stage is that the railway construction camps were not always located close to the line. It was not uncommon for the men on the work parties to walk from 5 to 7 miles to the worksite and return back to camp at the end of their shift, often in pitch darkness.

Burma Camps

Thanbyuzayat	414.92–000.00km	Ronshii	355.77–059.15km
Kendau	410.12–004.80km	Kami Mezali	348.66–066.26km
Wagale	406.37–008.55km	Mezali	342.83–072.09km
Thetkaw	401.34–013.58km	Meiloe	339.92–075.00km
Alepauk	396.39–018.53km	Apalon	337.25–077.67km
Kun Knit Kway	391.02–023.90km	83k Camp	332.09–082.83km
Reptu	384.59–030.33km	85k Camp	329.92–085.00km
Tanyin	379.92–035.00km	Kyondaw	319.88–095.04km
Beke Taung	374.40–040.52km	Anganan No. 2	314.92–100.00km
Anankwin	369.06–045.86km	Aungganaung *(Anganan No. 1)*	310.63–104.29km
Tanbaya	361.60–053.52km	Payathonzu	306.92–108.00km
Khonkan	359.92–055.00km	110k Camp	304.92–110.00km
Taungzun	357.60–057.32km	Three Pagodas Pass	301.92–113.00km

Note: In the table above, the distances in the left hand column are north from Non Pladuk and in the right hand column are south from Thanbyuzayat. Whilst accuracy is desired, these distances should be looked upon as approximate. All distances in this instance are stated in kilometres. Those camps highlighted, are Hospital Camps.

Organization of POW's by Groups

'The Battalion was the basic unit, original strengths varying from 600 to 1,000 P.O.W. Each Bn. had at first a fairly generous proportion of officers and o.r. staffs, but later on these were very much reduced. Each group contained a number of Bn.'s, which were normally kept as homogenous units. The number of P.O.W. in any working camp was presumably based on work to be done, so that a camp might have from half a Bn. to five or six. In a few camps Bn.'s from more than one group might be present, for example, at Kinsaiyok which in May 1943 was the point of contact of No's 4 and 6 Gp's. At each group HQ a reasonably accurate card index system of Bn.'s was kept by a P.O.W. Officer and o.r. clerks under Japanese direction. In the later stages of the period under review, Bn.'s on the line were so reduced by sickness and death (one was below 10 in Dec 43) that many of them were formed up into "composite" Bn.'s for local administration. One such Bn. had men of no less than twelve original Bn.'s. P.O.W. were however, on paper, retained in their original Bn.'s and generally speaking it was not until March 1944 that these units were officially scrapped, and the basic unit became the Group.' [2]

The structure of the work parties within the battalions was such. Kumis consisted of thirty to fifty men that were commanded by one of their own officers, called a Kumichi, equivalent in rank to a Lieutenant. When two kumis were joined they were known as a han and were commanded by a Hancho, equivalent to a Captain.

The 'speedo' May–November 1943

'In mid-January 1943 a Japanese staff officer (Maj-Gen Shimoda) from the control centre of the Burma–Thailand railway was summoned to Imperial General Headquarters in Tokyo to give a progress report on the construction achieved to date. To his surprise and shock he was ordered to ensure that the railway was completed by May 1943. The staff officer, we are told, was amazed by this reckless command and explained what at the time was the volume of work still to be done and stressed the difficulties involved. Eventually a three month postponement was agreed; the railway to be operational by the end of August 1943.' [3]

The 'speedo' period effectively began along the entire length of the railway in April–May 1943 and ended in November that year with the two ends meeting in October. All the same, there were parts of the railway that would still require some serious attention before the Burma–Thailand Railway would be anywhere near operational. The Japanese were to pay a high price for treating their human labour force as a limitless resource, because as early as June 1943 many of the Prisoners of War and coolies alike were either dead or too sick to work. Japan's earlier run rate of victories against the Allies between December 1941 and June 1942 was now on the decline. It was for this reason that work on the rail link into the Burma Theatre was given a higher priority. When Maj-Gen Shimoda returned from Tokyo with news of the new time schedule for the completion of the railway, it was not well received by his two subordinates. As these orders from Tokyo were passed down the chain of command, the burden would be passed to the labour-force, that is the coolies and the ubiquitous Prisoners of War.

---

2   AWM54 554/2/1 Report on Conditions of Life and Work of Prisoners of War in Burma and Siam by Brigadier C. A. McEachern, *Australian War Memorial Canberra*
3   Clifford Kinvig, *River Kwai Railway* The story of the Burma–Siam Railroad, Braseys 1992, p.100

As sickness began to take a toll of this labour pool and coolies headed for the jungle in droves the workload on the Allied Prisoners of War became steadily heavier. For this reason 'F' and 'H' Forces were brought up from Singapore to shore up the deficiencies in the centre and upper sections of the rail link. Those who were left after the completion of the railway, were sent back to Singapore in tatters. However preceding 'F' and 'H' Forces, Dunlop Force or 'D' Force O, P, Q and R Battalions were brought up from Java in January 1943. This group was followed by 'D' Force's S, T, U and V Battalions, in a succession of trains out of Singapore in March 1943.

There are a few points to note before the story of the individual groups who worked to build the Burma–Thailand Railway begins. As the rail link snaked its way south from Thabyuzayat and north from Non Pladuk the two ends would meet near Konkoita. Although Thanbyuzayat was the starting point in Burma, the 000.00km point was at Non Pladuk in Thailand. When a workforce is covered, it is done so as a group. It is to be realised that splinter groups or small parties of men may have been required to rush through the construction of a bridge or help lay a section of railway line away from the main group.

Although distances along the railway trace have been quoted in kilometres, (km) in some cases lengths and heights are given in miles, yards and feet because this is how the prisoners themselves have quoted them. Obviously anyone from a British background would use the Imperial weights and measures system and the Japanese and countries in the Far East that had been colonised by the French or Dutch would be accustomed to the metric system. One example is the distance from the 'D' Force Kanu II Camp in Thailand that according to maps was about 400 metres from the Hellfire Pass Cutting. The actual distance if walked was probably closer to 1 mile. These differences should not be viewed as a failing or a departure from accuracy but only as a general guide.

Cholera

If there was one word which struck fear into the Japanese and the Prisoners of War alike then it would be cholera. This disease was so rapid and lethal in its effect that what was left of a man's body was cremated in an attempt to control its spread. Cholera went hand in hand with the monsoon rains in Burma and Thailand. The rains fall from May to October with the heaviest falls in July and August. The first known cases of cholera it is believed appeared in Burma and Thailand around June 1943. This was during the 'speedo' period when the men were pushed to the limit with regards to the steadily increasing working hours and demands on them on little more than starvation rations. These elements created a situation where the men's bodies were at their lowest ebb and just ripe for the cholera bacillus.

'*Vibrio cholerae, is a rather weakly, if mobile, organism; it dies at a temperature above 60 degrees centigrade, is easily killed by drying and cannot live in the presence of acid. But when conditions are right it thrives alarmingly and can be a deadly infection; in epidemic conditions up to 50 per cent of those inflicted by it can die. In May 1943 the conditions in the Kwai camps were ideal for its spread. The camps lay, first of all quite near to the global seat of cholera at the junction of the great rivers of what are now north-east India and Bangladesh from which it is easily spreads southwards in the monsoon conditions which at the time affected the whole region. Furthermore the River Kwai proved the perfect medium for its spread, being heavily alkaline and containing much calcium leached by the rains from the limestone catchment area.*

Finally, the crowded and insanitary conditions of the camps, the poor latrine arrangements, the primitive cooking facilities and the debilitation and disorganisation of the coolie labour forces in particular, provided the optimum conditions for the dissemination of the bacillus, it being found in the faeces of those suffering from it and spread in contaminated water and by flies which now swarmed in clouds about the camps.[4]

The *War Diaries of Weary Dunlop*, explains perfectly the effects of cholera on the human body:

'The orderlies have made little bed pans out of cut-down tins placed in little wooden boxes but of course nothing can deal entirely with the gushing faecal contamination. With these intolerable cramps and abdominal pains and delirium there can be no silence and the air is full of groans, cries for relief and curses in weak husky voices. They look so dreadfully emaciated and unrecognisable almost from the beginning and their discomfort is terrible. The saline drips, although they bring relief from cramps, cause their own special misery in that they necessitate lying quietly without much movement of one arm which remains extended. The symptoms and signs of this disease are unforgettable. The piteous shrinkage and dehydration, the earthy cyanosis, faint husky voice, agonising cramps and abdominal pains, rapid breathing and icy cold breath, the clammy almost pulseless cold limbs and terminal restlessness and delirium. One rather disconcerting aspect of the patient is cholera sleep, the habit of or lying with the eyelids open and the eyes turned up so that the pearly whites stare from between the lids. Almost all complain of roaring in the ears in the early stages.'[5]

The Migration of Disease

With the huge Japanese demands for Prisoner of War and coolie labour the likes of Chinese, Malays, Tamils, Thais etc a situation was created whereby the peoples of Asia where subjected to certain diseases that were not prevalent in their particular indigenous locations. For instance, a native of Malaya may never have come in contact with a disease in his area but conversely his people may have built up immunity over decades to a more prevalent disease. The same could be said for a Tamil, a Burmese or Thai. The consequence was that when these indigenous peoples came into contact with each other the result was that a disastrous situation developed as diseases were spread and multiplied out of control. The Japanese in fact helped to spread disease throughout Asia by their practice of moving their multinational labour force far and wide. The consequence of all these men and diseases being concentrated into this region of Burma and Thailand would have adverse effects on the Allied Prisoners of War. In most cases the Japanese carried out frequent testing and inoculation for cholera and several other diseases however, many of these drugs were out of date and proved to be ineffective in the control of disease. Australian doctors were absolutely fastidious about enforcing hygiene upon their wards in the primitive conditions of base hospital and working camps. However as coolie labour and other nationalities with lower standards of hygiene migrated freely up and down the length of the railway it proved to be an impossible task to stem the spread of disease. A good example in this case would be Lt. Banno's refusal to isolate an outbreak of cholera at Konkoita and its spread throughout the 'F' Force camps until this disease eventually claimed 750 Allied Prisoners of War.

---

4   ibid p.131
5   E. E. Dunlop *The War Diaries of Weary Dunlop* Penguin Books 1997, p.263

Atap Hut Accommodation

'The initial task on arrival was to clear the jungle and carry bamboo and atap from the river to construct huts. The construction of these huts was new to the Prisoner of War but eventually they evolved scientific plans. The huts were typical coolie accommodation in the east. They were generally from 80 to 100 metres long with king-post trusses at approximately 3 metre intervals so that the hut was divided into sections known as bays. Into such a section approximately 3 metres by 3 metres as many as 20 men were packed. The roofs were of atap palm leaves. These leaves were bent over thin sticks 1 metre long, the whole producing a sort of water-proof flap of crisp brown leaves 1 metre by 30 centimetres. Sleeping accommodation consisted of 1 inch diameter bamboos laid side by side and lashed with strips of tree bark to a framework of stout 2 inch bamboos. This formed platforms about 2 metres wide running the whole length of the hut. Two types of hut were in vogue in the early days. One with a central gangway 2 metres wide with platforms down either side and the other with a double width platform filling in the centre, entrance being affected by crawling under the eaves which were about three feet off the ground. Both these types of hut were quite inadequate to cope with the monsoon conditions. The inside resembled a gloomy, dark, smelly cavern in which men ate, slept, were ill and died. An individual space consisted of a strip of platform about 27 inches (or roughly 70 centimetres) wide. This crowding was a sure means of spreading disease and was a great mental strain.' [6]

Interior of an Atap Hut
Courtesy Australian War Memorial

---

[6]   AWM54 File 554/2/1 Report on Conditions, Life and Work of Prisoners of War in Burma and Siam by Brigadier C. A. McEachern, Australian War Memorial Canberra

Hospital Camps – Burma

Thanbyuzayat–Reptu–Khonkan

The Prisoners of War realised at an early stage that working for the Japanese on the Burma–Thailand rail link was going to entail a great deal of human suffering and misery. The cost of the railway in physical terms was going to be counted in headstones, unless the men were given all the help possible by way of medical facilities. About January 1943 Thanbyuzayat was recognized as a base hospital, possibly because of the fact that that there were 1,600 patients admitted. The hospital was situated opposite the railway station and workshops. From February–March 1943 the work on the rail link became steadily harder and as the Japanese Engineers demands for work increased, so did the sick rolls. The Japanese refused to acknowledge that the human body is not a machine.

Early March saw the 30km Reptu Camp established as a hospital camp, but on the orders of the Japanese it was closed as quickly as it was opened and the hospital's patients were transferred back to the Thanbyuzayat Hospital Camp. On 12th June 1943, a visit by Allied bombers to the railway workshops and marshalling yards killed five Australians when two bombs went astray and fell inside the camp compound. On 15th June the aircraft returned in force with the result that another thirteen Australians were killed and double this number were wounded. The next day the Japanese ordered that all patients be moved to the disused Kendau 4.8km, Wegale 8km and Alepauk 18km Camps. The Japanese headquarters was set up at the 4.8km Kendau Camp, located within the Moulmein rubber plantation.

Eventually all these hospital patients were concentrated back at the Reptu 30km Hospital Camp which was reopened. By June most of the major camps were forward of the Meiloe 75km Camp. At this time the Japanese admitted that they had a problem getting supplies to the men at the forward camps at Meiloe 75km, Aungganaung 105km and the Payathonzu 108km, and in any case they couldn't see the sense of transporting food for men who couldn't work. This Japanese attitude was met with the suggestion that a hospital should be set up at the Khonkan 55km Camp and the sick from 105km and 108km Camps be evacuated back to this camp. This plan of action was agreed upon, and the 55km opened on 30th July 1943. Brigadier Varley, the Commander of 'A' Force, also suggested that the men from the Meiloe 75km Camp be moved back. This was done and the patients moved by road and rail to the Khonkan 55km Camp under the command of Lt-Col Albert Coates.

Coates was to Burma what Dunlop was to Thailand, each being a fine surgeon in his own right. Khonkan 55km Camp was destined to become one hospital camp that many men would never forget, if they survived to tell the tale, that is. Many a tropical ulcerated gangrene infected leg parted company with its host. In many cases there was little choice but to amputate the infected limb, or lose the patient. The R.M.O. from the 2/4th Machine Gun Battalion, Capt. Claude Anderson, was to be one of several mainstay medicos at the 105km Camp. Claude spent from 1st September to 19th October 1943 at the Khonkan 55km Camp, whereupon he returned to the Aungganaung 105km Camp. In November 1943 the Reptu 30km Hospital Camp was closed and patients transferred forward to the Khonkan 55km Camp. Once work had begun on the railway, Brigadier Varley pushed for the Chaplains to be distributed along the length of the rail link.

It was common practice that if a man needed time to convalesce following his admission into a hospital camp then he might work for a time as an orderly or be given tasks around the hospital or camp. In this way his return to a construction camp and the likelihood of being 'blitzed' by the Japanese Engineers to go out on daily work parties was delayed. There is of course one more hospital camp in Burma that has not been covered in this section and that was Tanbaya, located very close to Khonkan at the 53.52km point. Tanbaya Camp was specifically set up to cope with the sick on 'F' Force, so therefore will be covered in the 'F' Force story.

Green Force

The camps on the Burma side of the rail link have not been covered in as much detail as the camps on the Thailand side, and the reasons for this are three-fold. Firstly, because books, like *Ghosts in Khaki*, *Slaves of the Son of Heaven*, *Blue Haze* and *Behind Bamboo*[7] all do justice to this section of the rail link, so there seems little point in going over old ground. Secondly, because the distance over which the railway was constructed in Burma was only in the region of 25% of the total distance of the rail link; and thirdly, because the terrain over which the railway was built in Burma was generally kinder than that in Thailand and employed far fewer Prisoners of War.

Kendau 4.8km Camp 1.10.1942 – 1.12.1942

This camp was located within the Moulmein rubber plantation, about 100 yards from the railway line. Accommodation was in atap huts that were open on one side. The camp had been taken over after Burmese natives had occupied it and as a result was in an appallingly filthy state. The kitchen and latrines were built and a general effort was made to improve the huts. Railway work commenced with the excavation of embankments and cuttings. On 1st December 1942 Green Force marched out to Thetkaw, the 14km Camp.

Thetkaw 14km Camp 1.12.1942 – 28.3.1943

Green Force was employed mainly on bridge building at this camp. There were several collapses here where men, including the Japanese, were badly injured. This camp was an improvement on the previous camp at Kendau and some attempt had been made at preparation prior to the men arriving.

Meiloe 75km Camp 28.3.43 – 11.5.43

It was here that Ramsay and Black Force's from Java, and Green Force from Singapore joined forces. The main party marched out of the Kun Knit Kway 26km Camp on 18th March 1943. Green Force joined them from the 14km Camp on 28th March. Lt-Col Ramsay was now appointed the commander of this camp which was located in a valley near the Mezali River. On 1st April the last of the sick from the 26km Camp arrived.

Aungganaung 105km Camp 11.5.1943 – December 1943

The entire force was marched to this new camp at 2100 hours after putting in a full day's work at Meiloe. The wet season had set in and the roads were in a poor condition, as were the men who were forced to march through a known cholera ridden area. Captain Claude Anderson recalls marching at the tail end of this column picking up items of kit that the men had discarded along the way. The camp was situated on a slope, the huts being the usual vermin infested filthy

---

7   Les Cody, *Ghosts in Khaki*, The History of 2/4th Machine Gun Battalion A.I.F., Hesperian Press Perth 1997. Roy Whitecross, *Slaves of the Sun of Heaven* Dymocks 1952. Leslie Hall G., *Blue Haze* Published by Leslie Gordon Hall 1985. Rohan Rivett, *Behind Bamboo* Penguin Books Australia 1991.

native atap type. In December 1943 Major Green was informed that the rail link was completed and that a small force was to be left behind under the command of Lt-Col Williams. Some of these men remained as part of a railway maintenance party. There were however several 2/4th men who continued with William's No. 1 Mobile Force into Thailand. Amongst this group were Padre F. X. Corry, Lieutenants Kevin Boyle, Graham Wilson, Ken Lee and Private John Malthouse. From Java Party No. 5a Robertson Force, Ted Cosson and Merv Wilkinson were included.

Lt-Col Anderson was advised to take command of all Australian personnel from Brigadier Varley and Ramsay and Black Forces were to combine under the command of Lt-Col Ramsay. Green and Anderson Forces were to also combine under the command of Major Green. The two newly combined Ramsay and Green Forces now moved by rail in six parties to Tamarkan Camp in Thailand. Although an improvement on the railway construction camps, the appearance of bombs being dropped on the bridge adjacent to the camp caused many to feel uneasy. The continuing story of the 2/4th in Group No. 3 will be covered in the Thailand post railway section 1944-1945.

Black and Williams Forces

Java Parties No's. 3 and 4

In addition to the Singapore Prisoner of War labour pool, the Japanese could also call upon their labour reserves from Java. In total twenty-six parties left Java between September 1942 and January 1945. Although the majority of these men were Netherlands East Indies troops (Indonesians), there were 3,980 A.I.F. troops from the 1st Australian Corps and the 8th Division who were included amongst this aggregate of 39,377 men. Out of this number the 3,449 who left Java almost all to a man were sentenced to a term of bondage on either the Burma or Thailand ends of the rail link.

The pathfinders were Java No. 3 Party under the command of Lt. C. J. Mitchell from the 2/2nd Pioneer Battalion. This party included one member of the 2/4th Machine Gun Battalion, being Walter Watkins. The next group to depart Batavia was Java Party No. 4 under the Command of Lt-Col J. M. Williams. This party departed Tanjong Priok aboard the 2,676 ton cargo ship, *Kinmon Maru,* on 8th October 1942 and disembarked on 12th October at Singapore, where Lt. Mitchell's advance party was reunited with Java Party No. 4 at Changi. Two days later on the 14th October, Java Parties No. 3 and 4 departed Singapore aboard the *Maebashi Maru*. Rangoon was their next port of call. Arriving on 23rd October they transhipped to the smaller *Yamagata Maru* which departed Rangoon and sailed up the Salween River in Burma to Moulmein arriving late on the following day. Accommodation for the prisoners whilst at Moulmein was to be at the local native gaol.

Java Party No. 4 was now organised into two groups. These, like previous groups, were named after their commanding officers, and in this case Black Force after the Commanding Officer of the 2/3rd Reserve Motor Transport Company, Lt-Col C. M. Black and Williams Force after the Commanding Officer of the 2/2nd Pioneer Battalion, Lt-Col J. M. Williams. Williams Force also included 272 of the ship's complement from the HMAS *Perth*. There were approximately forty-three members of the 2/4th Machine Gun Battalion in Williams Force and six in Black Force. On the morning of 26th October Williams and Black Forces marched the 2 miles to South Moulmein railway station where their 40 mile train journey to Thanbyuzayat would begin. Williams and Black Force were then incorporated into Burma Administration Group No. 3 which we know also included Green, Ramsay and Anderson Forces.

Tanyin 35km and Beke Taung 40km Camps

Williams Force was transferred to the Tanyin 35km Camp the next day. This camp's accommodation consisted of two atap huts that were open on one side. There was a native well about 500 yards from the camp and also a stream about the same distance away. Like Williams Force, Black Force also commenced work at the 40km Beke Taung Camp the following day.

Kun Knit Kway 26km Camp

Black Force was not in residence at the Beke Taung 40km Camp long when the water supply failed, so on 29th November 1942 they were compelled to move back to the Kun Knit Kway 26km Camp. Between 14th and 25th December Ramsay Force also moved into the 26km Camp to join Black Force. This camp was very open, being situated at the end of a valley leading up into the mountains and dense jungle. There was a section of line at the 26km that was 2 and a half miles in length on which there were six cuttings and three embankments. Each of the six cuttings was 55 yards deep and from 80 to 250 yards long. In the same section there were six small and two large bridges, one of which contained about 60 yards of two tier scaffolding about 60 feet above the ravine.

Anderson Force

Alepauk 18km Camp

Anderson Force now enters the story, having commenced work on the railway on 5th October 1942. They were based out of Thanbyuzayat and began work with the building of an embankment. This task was completed by 10th October whence Anderson Force moved by a day march along a rough road to the Alepauk 18km Camp.

Tanyin 35km Camp

On 3rd January 1943 Anderson Force moved by motor transport to join Williams Force at the 35km Tanyin Camp. Williams and Anderson Forces now combined and moved back along the trace to the Kun Knit Kway 26km Camp on the night of 27th March 1943. The 26km Camp appeared to have been in for an overcrowding problem, except that on 13th March the advance party for the now combined Black and Anderson Forces moved out of the 26km Camp for the Meiloe 75km Camp. The main party moved out on 18th March on a 30 kilometre march by way of the railway trace. Green Force at this stage was still at the 14km Thetkaw Camp but moved out to the 75km Camp arriving on 28th March 1943. The history of Black, Green and Ramsay Forces will now continue from the Meiloe 75km Camp.

Anankwin 45km Camp 24.4.43 – 13.5.43

The combined Anderson and Williams Forces left the Tanyin 35km Camp by train on the evening of 24th April 1943 to the Anankwin 45km Camp. From this camp onwards, the Japanese did not permit the movement from one camp to the next during working hours, so as not to interfere with railway construction work. The men would carry their tools and personal belongings to the job in the morning and at the end of day would move on to the next camp, often in the dark.

Williams No. 1 Mobile Force

Taungzun 57km Camp 13.5.43 – 13.7.43

The next move for Williams Force was on 13th May when the force moved by rail motor to the Taungzun 57km Camp. It was at this camp that Williams and Anderson Forces were designated as No. 1 Mobile Force. The work now consisted of serious railway construction with sleeper laying, ballasting, and rail laying gangs; with this mobile construction force keeping apace of the ever forward thrust of the rail link towards the Thai border.

Linda Goetz Holmes wrote:

> '*No doubt the Japanese couldn't believe their luck at capturing a whole battalion of rugged Australians – and an engineering unit at that! So it is not surprising that Williams Force became the core of No. 1 Mobile Force – and mobile it was: on the move constantly, under worsening weather, supply and jungle conditions.*' [8]

Mezali 72km Camp 13.7.43 – 1.9.43

On 13th July 1943 Williams No. 1 Mobile Force moved by rail motor and marched to their next camp, the Mezali 72km Camp.

Apalon 77km Camp 1.9.43 – 11.9.43

Movement was during the day by rail, motor and march. This camp was located within a bamboo hollow. A small stream flowed near the camp kitchen. The condition of this camp when occupied by Robertson Force during April and May is described as having been in a bad state.

Kyondaw 95km Camp 11.9.43 – 17.9.43

There was a day movement by march to this camp, except for those too sick to walk who were transported by rail.

---

[8] Linda Goetz Holmes, *4,000 Bowls of Rice*, Allen & Unwin 1993, p.26

Payathonzu 108km Camp 17.9.43 – 21.9.43

This was a night march except for the sick, medical and kitchen staffs. This camp was located 108km from Thanbyuzayat or 306 kilometres from Non Pladuk. George Ramage from the 2/4th died from dysentery at this camp on 23rd September 1943.

Kami Sonkurai 116km Camp 21.9.43 – 25.9.43

This camp was just over the Burmese border into Thailand in the vicinity of the Changaraya No. 5 Camp. Movement was both by rail motor and a 4 kilometre march, for the sick, medical and kitchen staff. The remainder marched from the work site. At this camp, the native coolie cholera hut was situated adjacent to the prisoners' huts that were positioned on the slope of a hill; with the occupied Burmese huts on the top of the hill, a situation was created whereby food and excreta was being washed down the side of the hill through the prisoners' lines. The camp was located a distance from the line that ran around the base of the hill on which the camp was situated. After this camp all moves were made during the monsoon period. This was the worst camp occupied by any force from Burma Administration Group No. 3 and this is not surprising considering the fact that the British at the nearby 'F' Force camp at Changaraya lost 200 of their men from cholera. This was a consequence of having to share their accommodation with 500 Burmese coolies.

122km Camp 25.9.43 – 26.12.43

This camp would have been in the vicinity of the Sonkurai No. 2 Camp at the 294km point on the rail link. This was the place where the 600 Bridge had been constructed by the British on 'F' Force at a great cost in human life. The majority of the men marched to this camp, however eighty sick and the baggage were transported by rail motor. This was a better camp than the 116km, but was still overcrowded. The grounds of this camp were not awash with mud, but just the same there were no atap palm leaves on the huts so they offered little protection from the weather.

Nikhe-Nikhe 131km Wood Camp 26.12.43 – 11.1.44

This camp by calculation would have been located near the 283.92km point between the Shimo Sonkurai Camp at the 290.00km point and the new Headquarters Camp at the 281.80km point. It was located high in the ranges, so was quite cold at night. Movement to this camp was by a day's march for all the men. Those too sick to walk were carried on stretchers. On 26th December, 1943 the sick were moved to the 281.80km Camp, and on 11th–12th January 1944 this group moved by train over a period of 24 hours to Kanchanaburi in Thailand. From here the sick marched 5 kilometres back to Tamarkan Base Hospital Camp No. 2. At the Nikhe-Nikhe Wood Camp there was a series of small hills. Rail laying was suspended whilst cuttings were excavated through these obstacles. Once the cuttings were completed the rail laying gangs recommenced, which was on 13th October 1943.

Nikhe 133km Camp 11.1.44 – 25.1.44

This camp would have been located near the 281.80km point just north of the Nikhe Old Headquarters Camp at the 276.00km point and was the last camp on the rail link for Williams

Force. The two ends of the rail link had been joined on 17th October 1943 at Upper Konkoita–Lower Teimonta at the 262.87 km point. On 25th January Williams No. 1 Mobile Force moved north back to the border at the Changaraya 113.97km–300.95km Camp and about ten days later moved back to the 104.29km Camp at Aungganaung where they met up with the remnants of Australian work groups still in Burma. These included Robertson's Java Party No. 5a, Burma Administration Group 5 Burma, who had been employed on woodcutting for the steam locomotives.

Aungganaung 105Km Camp Burma 5.2.44 – 25.3.44

This camp was at the 310.63km point from Non Pladuk. Williams group was still in Burma in March 1944 but it was about this time that the fittest were being selected for Japan, and some prisoners were sent to the collection centre at Tamarkan. Williams No. 1 Mobile Force, like so many of the other forces, was about to commence the move south where a new chapter of their Prisoner of War experience would begin. On 22nd March the Aungganaung 105km Camp was machine gunned by two B24 Liberator bombers and as a result, two days later, the remainder of the men at this camp began the move south to Kanchanaburi in Thailand. The accommodation in all the above construction camps had been the same, being long atap huts with central or side aisles. The aisle floors were earth, always damp and often flooded. The roofs were usually in poor condition and it was not uncommon for the men to be wet for days on end. In almost all cases, not only for Williams No.1 Mobile Force but also for many of the forces in Burma and Thailand, camps had been previously occupied by native coolies and were in a deplorable condition. Often these camps were awash with filth, excreta and dead, bloating corpses. Usually advance parties would attempt to clean up the camps before the main group arrived, but this was not always possible when men left at night, or departed from their last construction job, and moved to the next campsite on the rail link. Therefore it really was anyone's guess what would await the men as they arrived at their next camp tired, hungry and more often than not sick.

Aunggaunang 105km Camp, Burma

Robertson Force

Java Party No. 5A

Java Party No. 5a was the third group to depart Java that contained men from the A.I.F. There were four members of the 2/4th on this party. They were Ted Cosson, Merv Wilkinson, Cyril Vidler and Les Lee. Les was an original in Java Party No. 4, however, illness whilst in transit through Singapore forced him to miss the draft, and he joined up with No. 5a Party when they departed for Burma. The commander of the Australian contingent was Major L. J. Robertson from the 2/6th Field Company Engineers. This group departed the Bicycle Camp Batavia for Tanjong Priok on 11th October 1942 bound for Singapore aboard the *Nichi Maru*. Arriving on 16th October they settled in for a two and a half month respite at Changi and on 7th January this party departed Singapore by train for Prai on the Malayan mainland opposite Penang. It was here that they boarded two transport ships, the *Nitimei Maru* and the *Moji Maru,* and departed Penang under Japanese Naval escort. On the afternoon of 15th January two B24 Liberator bombers attacked these ships and their escorts. One of the transports, the *Nitimei Maru,* took two, possibly three direct hits and sank in about 10 minutes. After loitering in the area for about 6 hours, 968 survivors, mostly Dutch, were rescued and the *Moji Maru* continued her voyage. Reaching Moulmein on 17th October. Between 24th–28th January Robertson Force Burma Administration Group 5, as it would now be known, marched out to its first camp on the railway the Alepauk 18km Camp.

Alepauk 18km Camp 26.1.43 – 23.3.43

Anderson Force had vacated this camp on 3rd January 1943 and joined Williams Force at the Tanyin 35km Camp. Work for Robertson's men began on 26th January mainly with excavation and bridgework.

85km Camp 23.3.43 – 6.4.43

The advance party left for the next 85km Camp on 22nd January and was followed the next day by the main group. The new camp was located in mountainous heavily timbered hills in an area of partly cleared Jungle. Water was supplied by a small stream which ran past this camp.

80km Camp 6.4.43 – 29.5.43

Orders were suddenly received for a move to the 80km Camp. The entire camp aided by two trucks and many ox carts were used to carry baggage and those men too sick to walk. This camp was located about a bamboo hollow but proved to be very hot after 1000 hours. Work here consisted of bridge work and digging.

Anganan No. 2 100km Camp 29.5.43 – 26.1.44

About twenty prisoners from this camp were detached to the 83km Camp but still remained part of the parent group. From 27th–29th December 1943 the first of the sick from Robertson Force Java 5a Party were evacuated south by train to Kanchanaburi in Thailand. On 26th

January 1944 the remainder of Robertson Force marched into the Aungganaung 105km Camp and were absorbed into Anderson Force, or more accurately Green Force. The remnants of Robertson Force were moved to Kanchanaburi by rail on 24th March 1944.

An R.A.F. Liberator bombing a section of the railway.

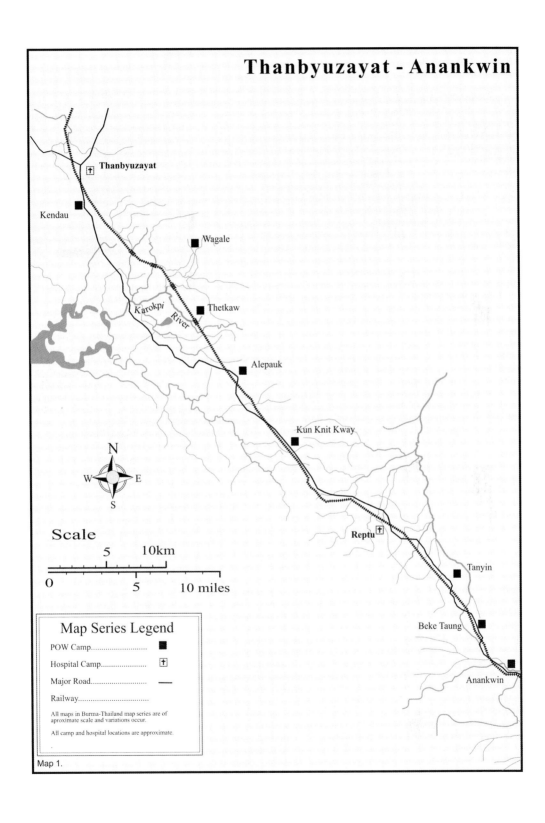

Thanbyuzayat - Anankwin

Thanbyuzayat

Kendau

Wagale

Karokpi River

Thetkaw

Alepauk

Kun Knit Kway

N
W   E
S

Reptu

Tanyin

Scale

5   10km

0

5   10 miles

Beke Taung

Anankwin

Map Series Legend

POW Camp............................ ■

Hospital Camp...................... ✝

Major Road........................... —

Railway.................................

All maps in Burma-Thailand map series are of
aproximate scale and variations occur.

All camp and hospital locations are approximate.

Map 1.

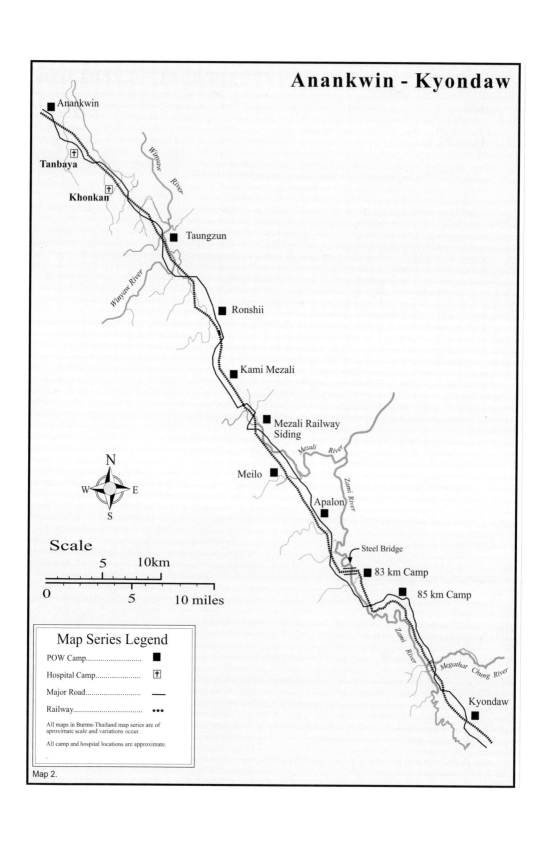

Anankwin - Kyondaw

Anankwin

Tanbaya

Khonkan

Winyaw River

Taungzun

Winyaw River

Ronshii

Kami Mezali

Mezali Railway
Siding

Mezali River

Meilo

Zami River

Apalon

N
W   E
S

Steel Bridge

83 km Camp

85 km Camp

Scale

5   10km

0

5   10 miles

Zami River

Megathat Chung River

Kyondaw

Map Series Legend

POW Camp............................ ■

Hospital Camp...................... ✝

Major Road........................... ——

Railway................................. ●●●

All maps in Burma-Thailand map series are of
aproximate scale and variations occur.

All camp and hospital locations are approximate.

Map 2.

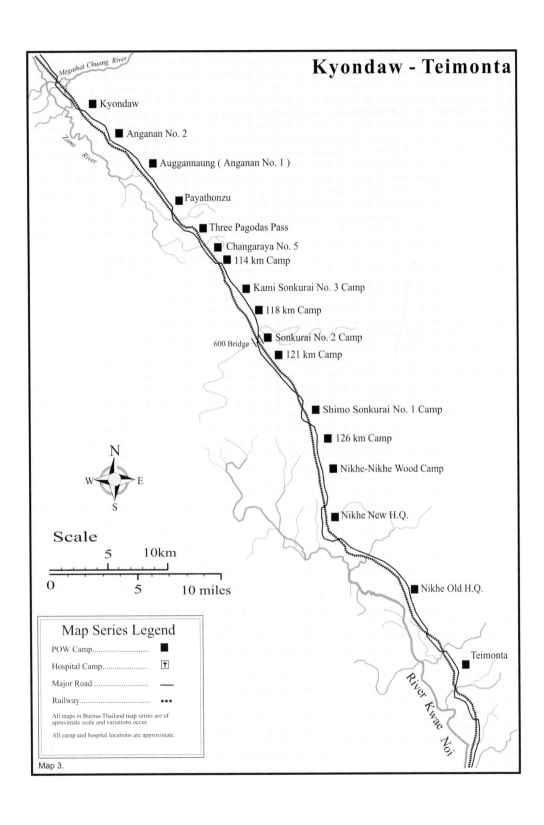

Kyondaw - Teimonta

Megathat Chuang River

Kyondaw

Zami River

Anganan No. 2

Auggannaung (Anganan No. 1)

Payathonzu

Three Pagodas Pass

Changaraya No. 5

114 km Camp

Kami Sonkurai No. 3 Camp

118 km Camp

600 Bridge

Sonkurai No. 2 Camp

121 km Camp

Shimo Sonkurai No. 1 Camp

126 km Camp

Nikhe-Nikhe Wood Camp

Nikhe New H.Q.

N
W   E
S

Nikhe Old H.Q.

Teimonta

River Kwae Noi

Scale

5   10km

0

5   10 miles

Map Series Legend

POW Camp.......................... ■

Hospital Camp.................... ✝

Major Road.......................... —

Railway.................................. •••

All maps in Burma-Thailand map series are of
aproximate scale and variations occur.

All camp and hospital locations are approximate.

Map 3.

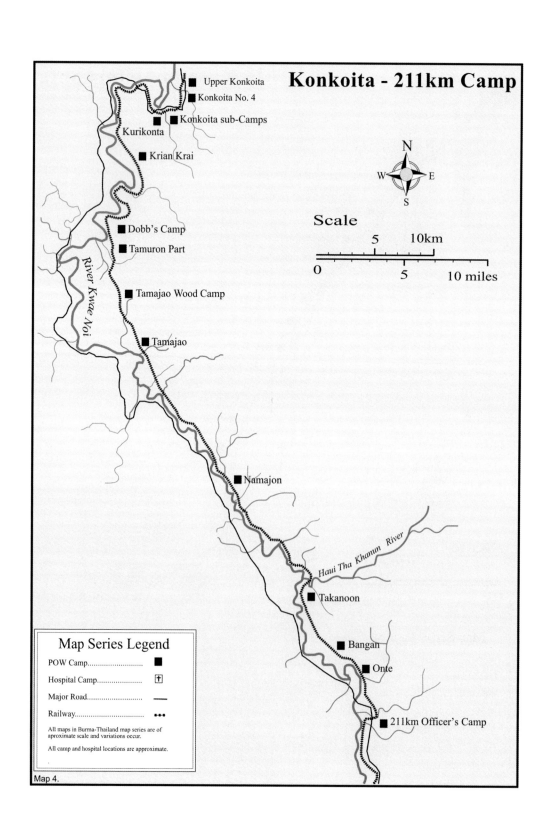

Konkoita - 211km Camp

■ Upper Konkoita

■ Konkoita No. 4

■ Konkoita sub-Camps
■ Kurikonta

■ Krian Krai

■ Dobb's Camp

■ Tamuron Part

■ Tamajao Wood Camp

■ Tamajao

River Kwae Noi

N
W E
S

Scale

5   10km

0   5   10 miles

■ Namajon

Haui Tha Khamun River

■ Takanoon

■ Bangan

■ Onte

■ 211km Officer's Camp

Map Series Legend

POW Camp........................ ■

Hospital Camp.................... ✝

Major Road.........................

Railway................................ ●●●

All maps in Burma-Thailand map series are of
aproximate scale and variations occur.

All camp and hospital locations are approximate.

Map 4.

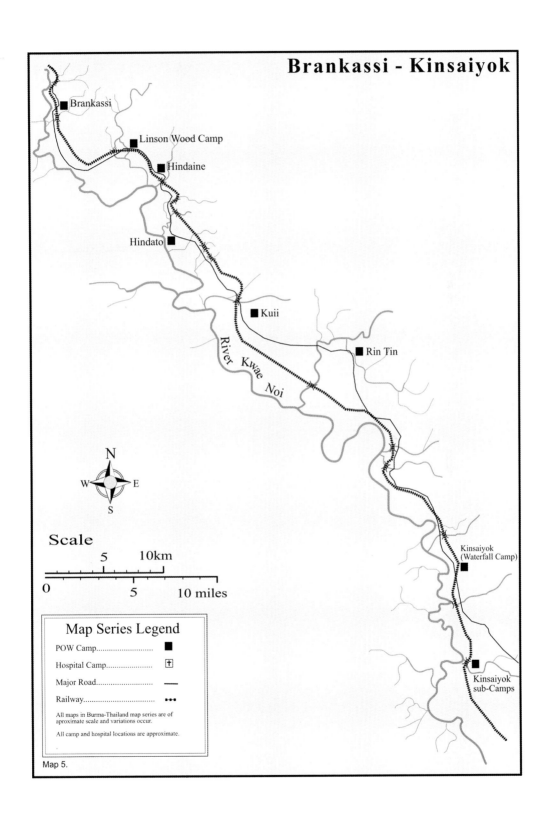

Brankassi - Kinsaiyok

Brankassi

Linson Wood Camp

Hindaine

Hindato

River Kwae Noi

Kuii

Rin Tin

N
W E
S

Scale

5   10km

0   5   10 miles

Kinsaiyok
(Waterfall Camp)

Kinsaiyok
sub-Camps

Map Series Legend

POW Camp............................ ■

Hospital Camp...................... ☩

Major Road........................... ——

Railway................................ ▪▪▪

All maps in Burma-Thailand map series are of
aproximate scale and variations occur.

All camp and hospital locations are approximate.

Map 5.

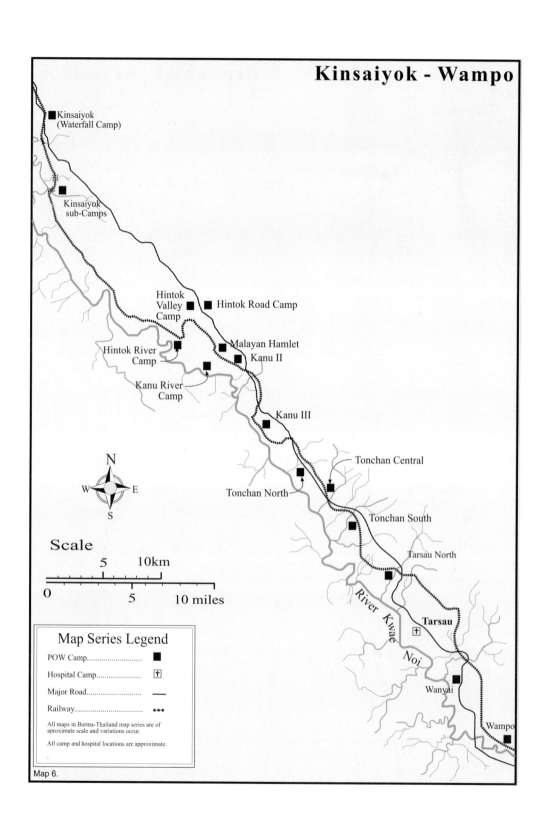

Kinsaiyok - Wampo

Kinsaiyok
(Waterfall Camp)

Kinsaiyok
sub-Camps

Hintok
Valley
Camp

Hintok Road Camp

Malayan Hamlet

Hintok River
Camp

Kanu II

Kanu River
Camp

Kanu III

Tonchan Central

Tonchan North

Tonchan South

Tarsau North

N
W   E
S

Scale

5   10km

0

5

10 miles

River Kwae

Noi

Tarsau

Map Series Legend

POW Camp............................ ■

Hospital Camp..................... ✝

Major Road........................... —

Railway................................ •••

All maps in Burma-Thailand map series are of
aproximate scale and variations occur.

All camp and hospital locations are approximate.

Wanyai

Wampo

Map 6.

Arrowhill - Chungkai

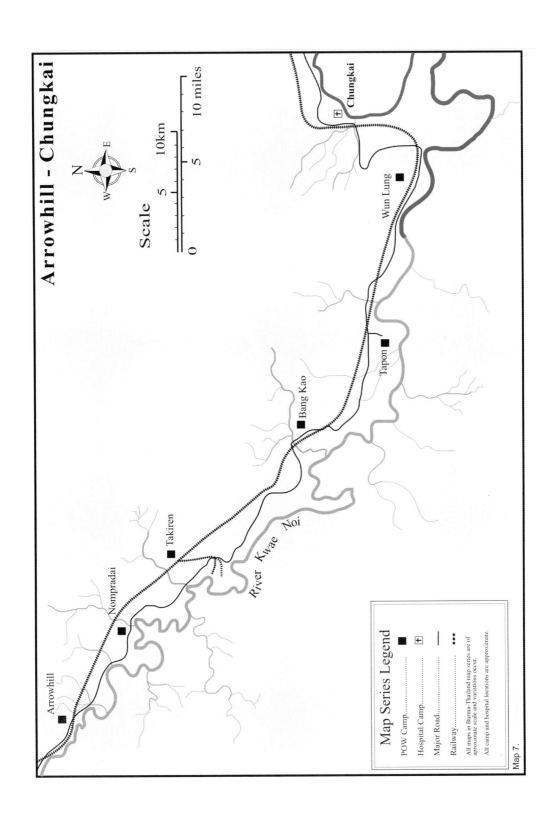

N
W — E
S

Scale

5   5   10km

0   5   10 miles

Arrowhill

Nompradai

Takiren

River Kwae Noi

Bang Kao

Tapon

Wun Lung

Chungkai

Map Series Legend

POW Camp..................... ■

Hospital Camp................ ⊞

Major Road..................... ——

Railway........................... ┆┆┆

All maps in Burma-Thailand map series are of aproximate scale and variations occur.

All camp and hospital locations are approximate.

Map 7.

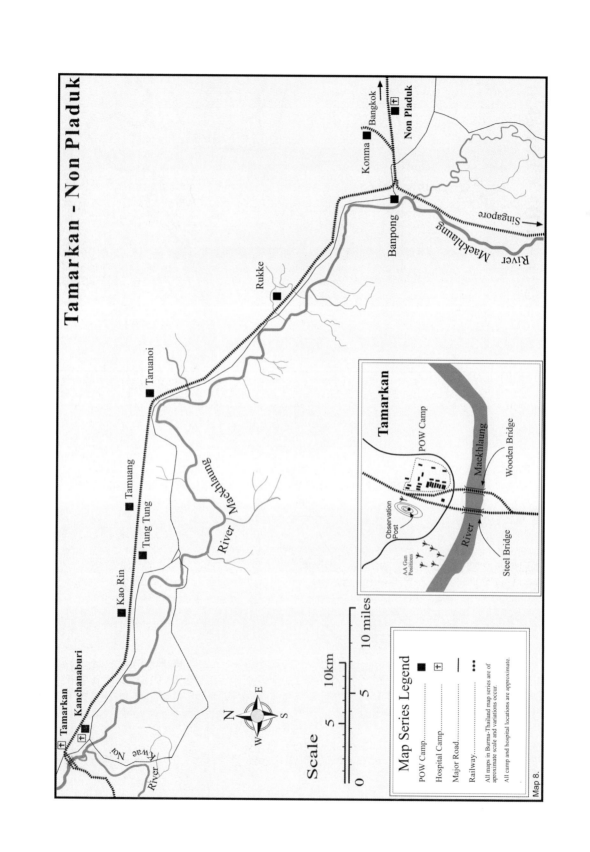

Tamarkan - Non Pladuk

Non Pladuk

Bangkok

Konma

Banpong

Singapore

River Maekhlaung

Rukke

Taruanoi

Tamuang

Tung Tung

River Maekhlaung

Kao Rin

Tamarkan
Kanchanaburi

River Kwae Noi'

Tamarkan

POW Camp

Maekhlaung

Wooden Bridge

Observation Post

River

Steel Bridge

AA Gun Positions

Scale

N
W E
S

5   10km
0   5   10 miles

Map Series Legend

POW Camp............................... ■

Hospital Camp......................... ✚

Major Road..............................

Railway.....................................

All maps in Burma-Thailand map series are of aproximate scale and variations occur.

All camp and hospital locations are approximate.

Map 8.

The Burma -- Thailand Railway

The Thailand Section

Many of the reasons behind the Japanese decision to build the Burma–Thailand Railway have already been discussed, so now all that remains is to fill in the blanks as far as the Thailand section is concerned. The first point is that Siam officially became Thailand in 1939. Despite this fact the railway is still sometimes referred to as the Burma–Siam Railway. We understand that the 000.00km point for the start of the new rail link from the Thailand end was Non Pladuk. It was from here that the railway linked with the Malayan railway system and it was also at Non Pladuk that the Japanese Materials Workshop was based.

From Non Pladuk the railway sets out over reasonably level country for the first 50.32 kilometres to Kanchanaburi. Between these two towns was a good metalled road along which railway construction materials and supplies could be conveyed. Tamarkan is another 4.68 kilometres further on and is the point where the railway veers left and makes a river crossing to the next location named Chungkai. From Chungkai to Wun Lung at the 68.59km point the railway travels over level open country that is covered in a low sparse scrub. From Wun Lung the country starts to transform as the jungle becomes thicker with clumps of prickly bamboo. Beyond Arrowhill at the 108.14km point the hills begin to dominate the landscape as the railway hugs the terrain at the 114.04km point at Wampo. Beyond Tarsau at the 130.30km point the gradient rises steeply and suddenly, with landscape transformed into rugged, wild hilly jungle. This high ground continues past Kinsaiyok to Kuii at the 190.48km point where a higher level of plateau is reached. Here the vegetation begins to change again from mostly dense bamboo jungle to more open scrub; and stunted trees begin to dominate. As the railway edges still further northwards, the country begins to gently fall away again towards Takanoon at the 218.15 km point. The vegetation remains unchanged right through to the Burmese border at the Three Pagodas Pass at the 301.92 km point. The two ends of the railway would meet at Upper Konkoita–Lower Teimonta at the 262.87km point on 17th October 1943. The official ceremony took place eight days later on 25th October.

The work on the Thailand side consisted of a number of varied tasks that included clearing of the jungle, tree felling, rock cutting, ballasting of the line, bridge and viaduct building, embankments and cuttings. In the dry season the Kwae Noi was navigable by barges towed by motorboats up to Takanoon; and in the wet, to Kurikonta at the 257.70km point. Williams No. 1 Mobile Force would work their way down to New Headquarters Camp at Nikhe at the 281.80 kilometre point, or if calculated from Thanbyuzayat the 133.12km point. If our addition is correct this should total to 414.92 kilometres and that is in fact the length of the Burma–Thailand Railway.

Without doubt the most influential parts of Thailand's topography which would dictate the course the railway were the rivers Kwae Noi, or little Kwae and the Maekhlaung, or big Kwae. In terms of importance the Kwae Noi would win hands down because the Thailand section of the railway followed the east bank of this river right up to its origins at the Burma–Thailand border. Therefore the River Maekhlaung was not as important as the River Kwae Noi by virtue of the fact that the Kwae Noi was the main line of communication for the Railway.

The confluence of these two rivers and the site mistakenly chosen by the Japanese Engineers to bridge the Maekhlaung River would be paid for in the long run by human sacrifice and suffering. The Japanese Engineers needed to get the Maekhlaung bridged and the site chosen was at Tamarkan. Once crossed, the railway follows the Kwae Noi in a southwest direction for about 25 kilometres, whereupon the river and railway swing roughly northwest towards the Burmese border. Although identified on post-war maps of the Burma–Thailand Railway as Chungkai, and also being known by the prisoners as Chungkai, there is no village or landmark here that would have identified this location as being Chungkai. This is where the problem began because the actual village at the site of Chungkai, is called Khao Pun. It is understood that an error was made when the Japanese Engineers misread their own survey map of the railway.

Another mystery is why the Japanese sited a bridge at a location where two major rivers converged, thereby creating a flood plain during the monsoon season when both these river's levels rise? It is believed that the correct location for the crossing should have been further north near the village of Lat-Ya, where the hill is known as Chongkai. Had the railway crossed the Maekhlaung at the village of Lat-Ya and headed in a northwest direction towards Tarsau, the railway would have been shorter and the double viaduct at Wampo and the cutting at Chungkai would have been unnecessary.

From Kanchanaburi, heading north, there was a twisting jungle track to where the river was crossed by barge at Tardan. Later a camp was established here and a wooden bridge was built across the Maekhlaung further north near the village of Takatai. This bridge was later washed away when the monsoon waters rose and a Prisoner of War party was despatched to make repairs. Strangely the bridge was still called the Tardan Bridge, perhaps not because of its location but by virtue of the fact that it replaced the barge crossing so therefore inherited its name. Once this thoroughfare from Tamarkan crosses the Tardan Bridge over the Maekhlaung it heads northwest towards the village of Wanyai at the124.85km point.

The only time this jungle road or track from Tamarkan is mentioned as actually having been used as a means to travel north is in the 'F' Force report. Also in Major Bert Saggers' Diary there is a mention of using this route to Tarsau. Apart from H6 Officer's Party who travelled by train to Wanyai in late May 1943 it is assumed that the majority of Australians in 'D', 'F' and 'H' Forces moved via this road and this would explain why 'D' force T Battalion arrived at Tarsau and then back tracked to the Wampo area.

Returning now to Tamarkan, the first bridge to be erected at this location was a low wooden bridge, about one and a half feet above the water, designed only to get men and supplies across the Maekhlaung so the railway could be commenced as soon as possible. There were two other bridges at Tamarkan capable of carrying rail traffic. Firstly there was a wooden bridge completed in February 1943 and 100 metres upstream the more majestic looking concrete and steel spanned bridge, completed the folowing April. The steel bridge spanned 300 metres across the Maekhlaung and was constructed with eleven 20 metre steel spans. These two bridges were the lifeline of the railway and as such attracted a great deal of attention from Allied bomber aircraft. Although the movie 'Bridge on the River Kwai' was filmed in Ceylon, it is generally accepted by tourists that the steel bridge over the Maekhlaung is the bridge the movie depicts. Although this steel bridge was sited at Tamarkan, Kanchanaburi has expanded over the years since the war, and it has eventually taken over Tamarkan.

The first group to leave Singapore for work on the Thailand side of the railway was entirely British. It consisted of five groups, A, B, C, D and E Battalions each of 600 men and left by train on every alternate day from 18th June 1942. Arriving at Non Pladuk the prisoners were marched the 2 kilometres to Konma, where a staging camp was to be set up for the thousands of prisoners who would transit through Non Pladuk, before heading up country to the railway construction camps. By 24th June 1942 the first of these British Battalions was hard at work building the transit camp and the base workshop for the Japanese materials depot at Non Pladuk. The first group of prisoners to pass through Non Pladuk that contained 2/4th machine gunners was Dunlop Force ex-Java. They would soon be reunited with old friends as 'D' Force massed in the Hintok-Kanu sector of the railway.

As 1943 drew to a close, Prisoners of War who had worked as slave labour in Burma and Thailand began to migrate south again. Those who had survived their mental and physical ordeal either by sheer will power, the help of a mate, or an overworked doctor, witnessed things they never thought possible. As Lt. Don Lee travelled south from Konkoita, he committed to memory in utter amazement some of the feats that had been achieved by a multi-national Prisoner of War and coolie workforce. Don later wrote: [9]

> *'The railway was incredible in many ways. Bridges three tiers high (60' or more), one three-quarters of a mile long, enormous causeways and cuttings and the waterfall. We went behind the fall of water, between the curtain of water and the rock face.*
>
> *Then there was the place where huge platforms had been lowered down the cliff-face, holes drilled into the rock and enormous logs inserted. The railway was built onto the jutting logs and from our open truck we looked down to see boiling white rapids 200' below. It was like looking out of an aeroplane window.'*

Thailand Camps

Changaraya No. 5 Camp	300.95–113.97km
114km Camp	300.92–114.00km
Kami Sonkurai No. 3 Camp	298.00–116.92km
118km Camp	296.00–118.00km
Sonkurai No. 2 Camp (600 Bridge)	294.02–120.90km
121km Camp	293.92–121.00km
Shimo Sonkurai No. 1 Camp	290.00–124.92km
126km Camp	288.92–126.00km
Nikhe-Nikhe Wood Camp	283.92–131.00km
Nikhe-New Headquarters Camp	281.80–133.12km
Nikhe-Old Headquarters Camp	276.00–138.92km
Teimonta	273.06–141.86km
Upper Konkoita–Lower Teimonta	262.87–152.05km
Konkoita No. 4 Camp	262.53–152.39km
Konkoita sub-Camps	257.70–157.22km
Kurikonta	256.92–158.00km
Krian Krai	250.13–164.79km
Dobb's Camp	246.00–168.92km
Tamuron Part	244.19–170.73km
Tamajao Wood Camp	238.92–176.00km
Tamajao	236.80–178.12km
Namajon	229.14–185.78km
Takanoon	218.15–196.77km
Bangan	214.00–200.92km
Onte	213.00–201.92km
211km Officer's Camp	211.00–203.92km
Brankassi	208.11–206.81km
Linson Wood Camp	202.50–212.42km
Hindaine	200.00–214.92km

---

[9]   Don Lee, *A Yarn or Two*, Access Press 1944, p.87

Hindato	197.75–217.17km
Kuii	190.48–224.44km
Rin Tin	180.53–234.39km
Kinsaiyok (Waterfall Camp)	171.72–243.20km
Kinsaiyok sub-Camps	167.66–247.26km
Hintok River Camps	158.00–256.92km
Hintok Road-Hintok Valley Camps	156.00–259.00km
Malayan Hamlet (later Kanu IIIa-Tampie North)	153.72–261.20km
Kanu I River Camp	158.00–256.92km
Kanu II Camp 'D' Force Camps	152.30–262.62km
Kanu III Camp (later Kanu IIIr-Tampie South)	147.52–267.40km
Tonchan North	142.92–272.00km
Tonchan Central-Spring Camp	139.05–275.87km
Tonchan South-Waterfall Camp	134.00–281.00km
Tarsau North	133.30–281.62km
Tarsau	130.30–284.62km
Wanyai	124.85–290.07km
Wampo (3 camps)	114.04–300.88km
Arrowhill	108.14–306.78km
Nompradai	102.00–312.92km
Takiren	097.89–317.03km
Bang Kao	087.93–326.99km
Tapon	077.66–337.26km
Wun Lung	068.59–346.33km
Chungkai (Kao Pon)	057.30–357.62km
Tamarkan	055.00–359.92km
Kanchanaburi	050.32–364.60km
Pak Prage	048.00–366.92km
Kao Rin (Specialist camp)	046.92–368.00km
Tung Tung	041.00–373.92km
Tamuang	038.90–376.02km
Taruanoi (Tarawa)	025.89–389.03km
Rukke	013.38–401.54km
Banpong	005.13–409.79km
Konma Transit Camp	002.00–412.92km
Non Pladuk	000.00–414.92km

Note: In the table above, the distances in the left hand column are north from Non Pladuk and in the right hand column, south from Thanbyuzayat. Whilst accuracy is desired these distances should be looked upon as approximate. All distances in this instance are stated in kilometres. Those camps highlighted are Hospital Camps.

Thailand Base Hospitals

The first hospitals in Thailand were established at the southern end of the railway at Kanchanaburi, Chungkai and Tarsau. These camps were ususaly in better condition than the jungle camps, although accommodation was the same, with overcrowding being commonplace. The worst period for the base hospitals was from September 1943 towards the end of the railway construction period, when thousands of sick Prisoners of War were evacuated by barge, rail and road to these already overcrowded hospitals. The Japanese policy was that if sick Prisoners of War were unable to work, then they were deemed useless and therefore better off dead. Their reasoning being that at least then they wouldn't have to be fed. It was common practice amongst the Australian camps to set up canteen funds whereby the meagre wages paid to the prisoners could be pooled and used to purchase additional food from local traders. These traders plied their goods up and down the River Kwae Noi to the Japanese and Prisoners of War alike. Whenever possible, foodstuffs were purchased to aid the rapid recovery of the sick. One food item that was eagerly sort after for its nutritional value was the egg.

Tarsau Hospital

This hospital was established in November 1942 and remained in operation until April 1944, during which time 15,029 patients had been admitted. The camp was situated on the River Kwae Noi 130.30 kilometres from Non Pladuk, unquestionably inside the jungle belt. This hospital was poorly sited close to the river. Accommodation in this camp consisted of eighty-four atap huts, all in the usual state of collapse, and in fact some did, on top of their inhabitants. From July 1943 this hospital grew from a camp hospital to a base hospital for the whole of 'D' Force Thailand Administration Group 4. At the beginning of 1944 the sick at Tarsau were graded and the heavy sick were sent to Nacompaton; and the light sick to Chungkai.

Kanchanaburi Base No. 1 Camp

This hospital was established in January 1943 by Lt-Col Malcolm R.A.M.C. and was in operation until December 1943. When 'D' Force V Battalion staged through Kanchanaburi on their way up to Kinsaiyok, Peter Dimopoulos who had managed to learn Japanese during his time at Changi was commandeered by Lt-Col Malcolm to act as an interpreter. Peter remained at this camp until 23rd December 1943 whence he moved to the Aerodrome Camp located in the centre of Kanchanaburi. Peter stayed here until 29th January 1944 until he was moved again, about 5 miles away to the Kao Rin Specialist camp, where he saw out the end of the war. This hospital was to serve the sick Prisoners of War generally on 'D' Force on the Thailand side of the railway. It is also worth noting that late in July 1943 evacuations of sick from 'H' Force to this hospital camp had commenced before the completion of the 'H' and 'F' Force Hospital. The camp was under the command of Lt-Col P. Toosey ('D' Force) who was the most senior British officer connected with the Burma–Thailand Railway. Like Tarsau and Chungkai it was one of the larger base hospitals. All three bore the brunt as remnants of human beings were evacuated south from the construction camps in the jungle. This was particularly so during the 'speedo' months from May to August 1943. By January 1944 the majority of the prisoners were concentrated in the Kanchanaburi area where there were three camps. These were Tamarkan, Kanburi Camp No. 1 and Kanburi Camp No. 2. Kanchanaburi and Kanburi should not be mistaken as being different locations as they are actually the same place. Kanchanaburi is where the Commonwealth War Graves Cemetery is now located and no doubt is a familiar name to many ex-Prisoners of War and their families who have made the pilgrimage to Thailand. For this reason Kanchanaburi has been chosen over Kanburi as the more generally accepted name.

The 'F' and 'H' Force Hospital – Kanchanaburi

As mentioned, the 'F' and 'H' Force Hospital at Kanchanaburi; with its new atap huts was completed on 27th August 1943. This was 12 hours before the first sick began to arrive from up river. Overcrowding in all eight huts and twenty-eight wards soon became commonplace.

Initially, sixty patients were accommodated in each hut, but soon after 100 became the norm. The sick from 'H' Force and later 'F' Force placed a heavy demand on medical personnel. This necessitated the forming of a medical group known as 'L' Force on which Peter Dimopoulos from the 2/4th was a member. Patients from 'H' Force alone numbered 2,296 sick. As soon as the sick recovered they were sent to the 'Fit Camp', about 2 miles away located in a jungle clearing. Conditions at the 'Fit Camp' were greatly improved with better food and treatment by the Japanese. This helped to relieve the pressure on the 'F' and 'H' Force Hospital Camp. As well as the 'D' Force and 'F' and 'H' Force Hospitals, there was also a Tamil Hospital next door to the 'F' and 'H' Force Hospital.

Tamarkan No. 2 Hospital Camp

This base hospital was opened in May 1943 and was one of the better hospitals. It was closed in December 1943 and its patients were transferred to Chungkai.

Chungkai No. 3 Hospital Camp

The hospital was opened in November 1942 and remained in operation until it was closed in June 1945. During this time 19,975 cases had been treated with an average of 2,000 patients at any one time.

Non Pladuk

This camp throughout served as a base for the railway workshops. This hospital was established in October 1942. The only problem with this camp was its close proximity to the railway workshops being a military target to Allied bombers. There were two camps at Non Pladuk, the No. 1 Camp and the No. 2 Hospital Camp. This was just one of the several camps where Prisoners of War were selected as fit to travel to Japan.

The 'D' Force Story

Although 'D' Force contained 2,220 A.I.F., the entire force spanned from A to Z Battalions, the 21st to 24th Battalions and a party ex-Saigon. These battalions which included 2,780 British and Dutch troops, totalled 5,000 Prisoners of War. Following the departure of 'A' Force in May 1942, the next group to leave the confines of Singapore with a significant head count of 2/4th was 'D' Force. This group departed Singapore by train, beginning with S Battalion on 14th March 1943, under the command of Major G. Schneider from the 2/10th Field Regiment. This group was followed by T Battalion on 16th March under the command of Major E. J. Quick of the 4th Anti-Tank Regiment and V Battalion on the 17th March under the command of Major Alf Cough of the 2/4th Machine Gun Battalion. Finally, U Battalion on 18th March under the command of Captain Reg Newton of the 2/19th Battalion. Lt-Col McEachern was to command the four Battalions and his headquarters was incorporated into S Battalion by order of the

Japanese. Now with Lt-Col E. Dunlop's group of O, P, Q and R Battalions already in position since late January 1943, the A.I.F component of 'D' Force consisted of O, P, Q, R, S, T, U and V Battalions.

Like their predecessors, the A.I.F component ex-Singapore was also given Company No.'s and these were S Battalion No. 17 Company, T Battalion No. 18 Company and U Battalion No. 2 Company. All these battalions were assigned to the Thailand Administration Group 4, however, it would transpire that V Battalion was segregated from the other Australian formations and assigned to the Thailand Administration Group 6. The battalions that contained 2/4th in Group 4 were S, and to a much lesser degree, T Battalion who were amalgamated about May 1943. Also there was at least one member from the 2/4th in U Battalion. The four battalions by this time had all passed through Non Pladuk. There weren't too many of these men that were sad to see the end of the four-day train journey. As one man put it 'Fancy being sea sick on a bloody train'.

From Kanchanaburi the battalions were marched to a staging camp and left to their own resources, for some up to ten days. Major Alf Cough's V Battalion were destined to work further north and how this came about can be explained by his report:

> 'For 6 days the party sold clothes etc and purchased food from the Thais, it was like a picnic, the guards were unconcerned. Suddenly guards and trucks arrived without warning. A Jap officer screamed, guards ditto, men moved and eventually all men were on nondescript vehicles with much overcrowding and heading for the jungle.' [10]

Group 4 Battalions would now work in the area from Wampo, north to Kinsaiyok, which was the demarcation camp between the 'D' Force Group 4 Battalions and V Battalion Group 6. Major Cough's V Battalion camps would run further north from Kinsaiyok to Takanoon. We will leave V Battalion at this stage and concentrate on the Group 4 camps.

The 'D' Force Group 4 area was easily the busiest and most congested along the entire length of the rail link. The terrain was mountainous and rugged, which only made the excavation of cuttings through rock faces and bridge building all the more difficult. Taking into account the jungle, mountain, escarpments, hills and valleys in the area between Kanu III and Hintok River Camp there were six cuttings including the four major cuttings, two at Hellfire Pass, the one at Hintok and finally the Compressor Cutting. There were nine bridges including the Three Tier and Pack of Cards Bridges; two major embankments being the Seven Metre and the embankment that would replace the Pack of Cards Bridge once the railway line was rerouted. In addition there were eight ledges from Hellfire Pass to the Three Tier Bridge that had to be built up to compensate for the sloping terrain.

With regard to the Hellfire Pass cuttings, one cutting was 500 yards in length and rose 25 feet high, followed by the more difficult to excavate 80 yard by 80 foot high cutting, a little further along the line. Still further along, as the line headed roughly southwest towards the Kwae Noi was the Hintok Cutting followed by the Compressor Cutting, so called because air compressors and jackhammers were brought in to speed up the excavation process. Beyond Hellfire Pass was the cantankerous 400 yard long by 80 foot high Three Tier Bridge. This bridge is more often than not confused with the ten foot high Pack of Cards Bridge. Ray Parkin mentions the Pack of Cards Bridge:

> 'The long trestle bridge the Tamils were building has collapsed like a house of cards. It now lies flat, with the trestles intact.' [11]

---

10   Major Alf Cough's Diary donated by his son Alan Cough
11   Ray Parkin, *Into the Smother* Hogarth Press 1963, p.167

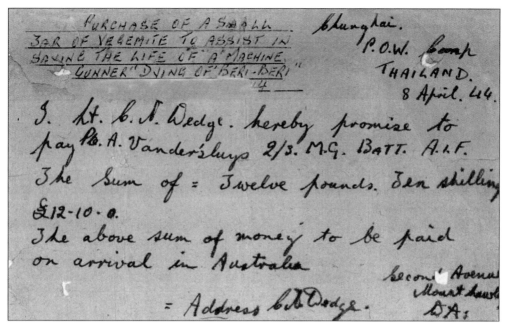

An I.O.U. from Lt. 'Mick' Wedge for the purchase of a small jar of Vegemite to aid the recovery of Bill Rodda who was suffering with beri-beri.

The purpose of the Pack of Cards Bridge was only intended as a stopgap. It was constructed so that the railway line could be pushed through, due to the delay in building up the intended embankment which had fallen behind schedule. On some maps of this area, a disused section of railway line approximately 400 yards long is shown. This in fact is the Pack of Cards Bridge. Once the embankment had been completed the railway line was rerouted and the Pack of Cards rail course closed down. There may also be some confusion caused by the naming of Kanu Camps. Like the Hintok Road Camp that has several aliases, the Kanu Camps also appear to have been labelled with various names. In this story Kanu I or Lower Kanu is the River Camp. Kanu II will be either the 'D' Force Camp or the 'H' Force Kanu II Malayan Hamlet Camp. However, the Kanu area is more complicated than just a few variations of a theme. Kanu IIIa (advance camp) later went through a name change to Tampie North and Kanu IIIr (rear camp) became Tampie South. The Kanu Camps which ran from north to south (omitting Kanu I River Camp) were as follows:

> Kanu II Malayan Hamlet (later Kanu IIIa–Tampie North)
> Kanu II–'D' Force Camp
> Kanu III (later Kanu IIIr–Tampie South)

A marshalling yard and siding was located about 400 yards south of the KIII Camp, which would position it at about the 147.15km point. Bert Norton had been sent back from Kanu II in June 1943 to a clearing where he and about twenty other prisoners were to set up a hutted camp. It was here that a later work force was to arrive and construct a marshalling yard and siding. It is worth noting that there were many sidings and marshalling yards along the length of the Burma–Thailand rail link. The picture the mind might paint of a 414.92 kilometre railway line from Non Pladuk to Thanbyuzayat could not be further from the truth. The fact is there were sidings, loop lines and marshalling yards in place, so that if the situation arose where a north-bound and south-bound train should meet then one could switch into a siding and allow the other to pass.

On a final note, in the course of research and interviewing ex-Prisoners of War who had worked on the Hellfire Pass Cutting, it was enquired as to whether a compressor was used at Hellfire Pass or only at the Compressor Cutting near the Hintok River Camp. This question is answered in Don Lee's book which reveals that:

> '*At first there were several jackhammers pounding away at the rock. Over the next week or two these gradually broke down and they couldn't seem to repair or replace them. Practically all the drilling was done by hand with one man holding a cold-chisel and another belting it with a 10lb hammer.*' [12]

In a war crimes affidavit, Sgt. N. Boese from the 2/15th Field Regiment explains his work at Hellfire Pass:

> '*The work was on a rock cutting about 300 yards long, 100 feet deep at its deepest point and about 20 feet wide. I was in charge of 24 men who worked 12 on jackhammer and 12 on compressor.*'

Visitors to the Hellfire Pass Memorial may have noticed jackhammer scores in the rock face. These two eyewitness reports should now explain fully how they got there.

Dunlop Force

Java Party No. 6

The fourth group to leave Java was Party No. 6 or Dunlop Force, as it has been popularised after its Commanding Officer Lt-Col E.E. 'Weary' Dunlop of the 2/2nd Casualty Clearing Station. This party left the Makasura Camp for the port of Tanjong Priok on 4th January 1943, embarking on the *Usu Maru* and disembarked three days later at Singapore. They were then moved as a group to the Changi Cantonment where they were accommodated in the British area to the north of Selarang Barracks. This was only to be a brief stay, as Dunlop's Java Party began to move out by train on 19th January. Arriving at Non Pladuk on 24th January they were then transported by truck to Tarsau via Tardan and then north to Kanu III, which they reached on 25th January. Dunlop Force was to be the first Australian force to work on the southern end of the railway in Thailand and was now incorporated into 'D' Force Thailand Administration Group 4.

This force from Java has somehow managed to retain its identity over the years as Dunlop Force and is rarely referred to as part of 'D' Force, yet the four battalions, three Australian

---

12   Don Lee, *A Yarn or Two* Access Press1994, p.72
13   AWM54 File 1010/4/16 War Crimes Affidavit by NX32581 Sgt. N. W. C. Boese, Australian War Memorial Canberra

and one Dutch were all incorporated into this workforce. The first two battalions were O Battalion under Major H. Greiner of the 2/3rd Machine Gun Battalion, and P Battalion under the command of Major F. Woods who was the Australian Liaison Officer during the Battle of Java. The third was Q Battalion under the command of Capt. J. Hands also from the 2/3rd Machine Gun Battalion and last but not least was the Dutch R Battalion under the command of Capt. Smits. Whilst O and P Battalions retained close ties with the 2/4th machine gunners of S and T Battalions, Q and R Battalions tended to always remain one step ahead of the other two battalions of 'D' Force.

The numbers allocated by the Japanese to these Australian Battalions from Java were O Battalion No. 25 Company, P Battalion No. 26 Company and Q Battalion No. 20 Company. Whilst these numbers may appear insignificant they are the designated Company No.'s as allocated by the Japanese and are sometimes the key that unlocks the secret as to which particular group each Prisoner of War belonged. There were twenty men from the 2/4th Machine Battalion split equally between O Battalion No. 25 Company and P Battalion No. 26 Company.

Kanu I River Camp (Lower Kanu) 25.1.43 – 12.3.43

Following a not uneventful trip from Tarsau, when at times the prisoners were forced to dismount and push their transport up the steep inclines into the Kanu III area, O and P Battalions arrived safely at their stepping off point on 25th January 1943. They then continued on foot, slowly worming their way down the steep mountainside following the track past a British camp to the yet to be established camp site area for the Kanu I River Camp. The trees in this jungle patch had been cleared but that was all that had been done prior to their arrival. The prisoners' first task would be to build the Japanese their accommodation, headquarters and stores huts before concentrating on their own lodgings. By 1st February a kitchen had been erected, one hut about 55 yards long by 7 yards wide was completed, a second hut had been commenced with most of the roof thatched with atap, and a third hut was on the way from the ground up. By 14th February the framework for another five huts, the hospital and officers quarters were completed but were held up by the lack of material to thatch the roofs. March 7th saw all the huts with sleeping platforms, or chungs constructed, so at least the men were off the ground even if they were still under the stars.

It appears the location for this camp did not suit the Japanese. The easiest explanation for this would be that this camp was too far away from the projected route of the railway. As a consequence of a Japanese decision, the men's labour setting up this camp was for nought as the camp was abandoned, and O and P Battalions moved back up the mountain on 17th March 1943. In fact the time and labour spent setting up this camp was not lost because the cholera patients from Malayan Hamlet, Kanu II and III Camps would be brought down the mountain to this camp and kept in isolation before being barged down river to one of the established Hospital Base Camps. That is if they survived the treacherous trek on foot or by stretcher down the mountainside, and then their period of isolation.

Hintok Road Camp 12.3.43 – 1.7.43

Hintok Road Camp over the years seems to have attracted several different names. It is common to see this camp referred to as Hintok Road, Hintok Jungle or Hintok Mountain Camp, depending on whoever is relating the story. It is known that there were other camps in this area accommodating other national groups or coolie labour gangs, however, in this story it will be known only as Hintok Road Camp. This camp was approximately 156 kilometres from Non Pladuk. The Hintok Road Camp was like the Kanu II and III Camps, being located in the higher mountainous country of Thailand.

On 12th March the first batch of 100 men from O Battalion moved out on foot from the Kanu I River Camp to their next camp at Hintok Road. The route taken was back along the track that they had used to come into this camp the month before. This track went up the side of the mountain to the plateau and then north along the road past the yet to be established Kanu II Camp. Within seven days the remainder of O and P Battalions had moved up from the Kanu I River Camp to join the advance party at the Hintok Road Camp. At this camp there were a few huts that had been erected by Dutch prisoners, but the camp was in such a filthy state that the existing huts and lean-to's were sent up in smoke. Lt-Col Dunlop described the camp at Hintok Road as like a Chinatown with many crazy looking huts. The new inhabitants then set to work by pitching tents and constructing bamboo sleeping platforms and floors within.

'*In one camp (Hintok) a spring was dammed and water conducted several hundred yards by bamboo piping to a system of showers, dixie washing points, etc; all devised from bamboo. This water system was also used for continuous flow cooling of condensers in our distilled water plant.*' [14]

As soon as the men of O and P Battalions began to arrive at Hintok Road Camp they were sent on to railway work as the establishment of the new camp assumed a lower priority. One of the difficulties with this camp, as with the Kanu II and III Camps, was the distance from the barge landings on the River Kwae Noi. Hintok Road Camp was about 7 kilometres from the nearest barge landing and its location necessitated that food supplies had to be manhandled over some very steep and slippery terrain before it could be brought into the camp. The most common route if heading down the mountain towards the river was through the Hintok Valley Camp, up the ladder and down the escarpment to the Hintok River Camp. Work at the Hintok Road Camp began with the felling of trees to clear the way ahead of the railway and the building of an embankment. Between April 3rd and 18th the work steadily increased as the embankment drew closer to its maximum height which would give this monument of labour its name, the Seven Metre Embankment. This man made feature was immediately prior to the Three Tier Bridge.

By 25th April 1943, the day that 'D' Force S Battalion arrived at the Kanu II embankment, work gave way to the excavation of cuttings. Following the arrival of S Battalion, about 200 men were sent forward on 28th April to Hintok Road Camp to bring O and P Battalions up to strength, as sickness had began to take its toll on their numbers. At this time 230 men from Hintok Road Camp were in hospital, too sick to labour on the railway. Now that the 'D' Force contingent from Singapore had arrived, with Lt-Col McEachern at the helm, Lt-Col Dunlop persuaded the Japanese commander to relieve him as an administrator so as he could concentrate on carrying out his true profession as a surgeon. This proposal was sanctioned and from April 1943 Lt-Col McEachern also took over the command of Hintok Camp.

Because the work on the last cutting out of Hintok, the Compressor Cutting, was falling behind schedule an air compressor and twelve jack-hammer operators had been brought up to speed up its forward progress. By 20th July all of the hospital cases at the Hintok Road Camp had been moved down to the Hintok River Camp. The group remaining at the Road Camp won out when the hospital was relocated from the tents in the low lying area of the Road Camp into the huts the Japanese had vacated. This made life a little more tolerable for not only the sick,

---

14 AWM54 File 554/5/5 Report on working camps and hospitals in Thailand by Lt-Col E. E. Dunlop, Australian War Memorial Canberra

but for the medical staff. As the sick at the Hintok Road Camp recovered, they were also moved down to the Hintok River Camp.

The first case of cholera appeared at Hintok Road Camp on 19th June 1943, three days after the first reported case at the Kanu II Malayan Hamlet Camp. The Japanese were absolutely terrified of cholera and so it was their policy to segregate any cholera cases to a lower lying area downstream of the camp's water supply. In this way there was less chance of contaminating the camp's water supply. During the height of the cholera epidemic at Hintok Road, three water stills were put into operation. These were manufactured from stolen petrol piping coiled inside bamboo jackets.

With the stills working day and night, 120 pints of saline solution was produced daily. This saline solution was administered to cholera patients by using improvised infusion sets manufactured from stethoscope tubing, tin cans and discarded Japanese saki bottles.

One man who stands out as an unsung hero is the 2/4th's very own Jim Allpike. During the cholera epidemic Jim made round trips up and down the ladder at the cliff face at the Hintok Valley Camp with two demijohns of this saline solution, and carried these down the slippery track to Hintok River Camp in an attempt to save the lives of the cholera patients. Mention Jim Allpike's name to anyone who knew him and immediately there is a nod of approval, that is an unspoken yet respectful acknowledgement of the work that this man did as a Prisoner of War at this camp. When the Hintok Road Camp was evacuated, the three stills were dismantled and transferred down to the River Camp where they were put back into operation again.

Hintok River Camp 1.7.43 – 17.9.43

The information on the general movements of O and P Battalions was taken from a statement made by Major F. Woods.[15] The date given as 1st July 1943 seems was the date that he took over command of this camp following his move down from the Hintok Road Camp. It seems likely though that this camp was established prior to this date. When referring to Hintok River Camp, it is to be noted that there was more than just one camp at this river site. There was of course the River Camp for O and P Battalions who were joined later by S and T Battalions. According to a hand drawn sketch made in 1986 by an ex-Prisoner of War, there was also an Officer's Camp, an Australian Camp, a British Camp and a Tamil Camp. However, this could not be guaranteed as being the last word on the subject of camps in this vicinity.

On arrival at an uncleared site in the jungle near the River Kwae Noi, the eighty men from Hintok Road Camp were informed that this was to be the site for their next camp. It was to be a tented camp and so the task was to clear the ground and pitch the tents before nightfall. The new site fell in the shadow of tall trees and bamboo, but was judged as being a reasonably good site in comparison to other camps in Thailand. Here was a barge landing, and the distance from the river to high ground where the camp was situated, depended upon the rains and the height of the river.

The Hintok River Camp was closer to the work site which was for the purpose of the excavation of the Compressor Cutting and Pack of Cards Embankment. On 29th June men from the 'H' Force Groups, H1, H5 and H6 began to move down the mountain from Hintok Valley Camp to an overflow camp at Hintok River. By August 1943 what was left of the fittest of men from 'D Force O, P, S and T Battalions also began to gather at this camp, and in September what was again left of these four battalions was combined into one formation known as 'Kawa' or river.

---

15   MP742/1 File 336/1/636 Statement by formerly QX6100 Major F. A. Woods on war crimes committed by Japanese during POW existence Java and Thailand during the period 3rd April 1942–15th August 1945, National Archives of Australia

An equivalent British formation comprising 'D' Force E, J and W Battalions was combined and called 'Yama' or mountain. The names given to these two formations should be self explanatory when taking into consideration the terrain. By the middle of September the Hintok sector was completed and those that had not been isolated due to cholera or evacuated down the River Kwae Noi to Tarsau and later Tamuang were relocated to the Kinsaiyok Camp.

Kinsaiyok Camp 17.9.43 – 6.12.43

Kinsaiyok was to grow to be a major rail terminus with a number of loop lines, a materials shed and water standpipe. There were a number of Kinsaiyok Camps between the main Waterfalls Camp at the 171.72km point and several sub-camps between here and the 167.66km point. There were also several bridges in this area that would require the return of work parties in 1944 to cut timber for the locomotives and keep up the maintenance to these bridges. On 17th September 1943 the remaining but diminished workforce of the fittest men travelled the four hours by barge to the next camp at Kinsaiyok. At this time there were only twenty-five men from the original 427 men remaining from O Battalion who had marched into Kanu I River Camp.

Kinsaiyok was by all accounts a reasonably big camp situated on flat swampy ground close to the River Kwae Noi. The camp had been established in February 1943 and could handle from 1,000 to 2,000 sick at one time. Accommodation was the typical long atap huts, however, some of these huts were in such a state of disrepair, they were replaced. The camp, being close to the river, made trading with the Thai merchants for additional foodstuffs possible. The work at Kinsaiyok consisted mostly of felling trees and then clearing the way back towards Hintok River Camp for the rail laying gangs. With the 'speedo' period almost over, the prisoners were employed on maintenance duties. The railway had been pushed through at such a frenzied pace that it was necessary to go back and upgrade sections that weren't up to the task of carrying rail traffic.

According to the report by Major Woods concerning O and P Battalions, it is assumed that what was left of S and T Battalions were at Hintok Road Camp from 6th December 1943 to 13th January 1944. From 13th January to 13th February 1944 they were at Hintok River Camp whence the remnants of O, P, S and T Battalions were moved south to Tarsau until 28th April 1944, so ending for some 2/4th machine gunners a year out of their lives building a railway for the Japanese war effort.

'D' Force S and T Battalions

Apart from the group that left Singapore with Major Charles Green on 'A' Force, 'D' Force S Battalion contained the largest number of men from the 2/4th Machine Gun Battalion who were to work on the Thailand end of the rail link. On 14th March 1943 the men in S Battalion having travelled up from Singapore by train arrived at Non Pladuk on 18th March. The next day they travelled by truck the 49 kilometres from the transit camp at Konma to Kanchanaburi. Following the brief stopover at Kanchanaburi, S and T Battalions then moved out to Tarsau, presumably having moved via Tardan. Whilst at Tarsau, S Battalion over the next several weeks was engaged on clearing the path ahead for the rail laying gangs. The two battalions then parted company, as S Battalion would head north and T Battalion south.

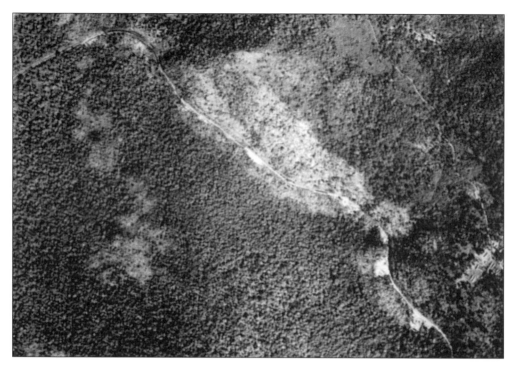

Hellfire Pass – Kanu II – Hintok Area

Kanu II Camp 25.4.43 – 16.7.43

'D' Force S Battalion, after their stay at Tarsau, moved to the 'D' Force Camp at Kanu II, arriving on Anzac Day, 25th April 1943. This camp was located 152.30 kilometres north of Non Pladuk on top of a plateau above the Kanu I River Camp. The camp was under canvas apart from the atap structures which included the hospital, Japanese Headquarters and the guard's and stores huts. On 28th April 200 men from S Battalion were sent up to assist 'D' Force O and P Battalions now at the Hintok Road Camp. The Hellfire Pass cutting would dictate the prisoners' lives at Kanu II Camp over the next several months. Hellfire Pass was simply a rock face that stood in the way of the railway line and the only way around the dilemma was to cut a passage through this monolith. This was achieved by a method the prisoners termed hammer and tap. This entailed the labour intensive process of drilling out holes in the rock, inserting explosives and blasting. Whilst another section of rock was being prepared for blasting, other prisoners would follow up and clear away the rock and debris in baskets.

With the wet season approaching, cholera was expected as a matter of course and several tents were pitched away from the main camp about 350 yards into the jungle. These tents were now the cholera isolation area for Kanu II and III camps. When it was suspected that a man had contracted cholera, he was segregated from the others for a period of up to six weeks until the doctor gave the all clear.

One such case was Jim Gilmour. Jim contracted cholera on 28th June 1943 and was banished by Capt. Phil Millard A.A.M.C. to the cholera isolation tented area at Kanu II. When Jim arrived he searched for somewhere to sleep for the night but all the cholera tents were full. Jim eventually found a narrow corridor in a tent where he slept the night. In the morning he awoke having survived a disease that can dehydrate and wither a man's body, suffocating all life from it in less than eight hours. To his surprise, Jim discovered that he had slept the night in the morgue tent and the narrow gap he had found to lie was alongside the rows of corpses. Jim's experience highlights the fact that not every Prisoner of War who contracted cholera succumbed to this dreaded disease.

The sick from Kanu II Camp were evacuated down to Kanu I River Camp for the first time on 4th July 1943 and from there they were either barged down the River Kwae Noi to Tarsau or one of the other base hospital camps. During his stay at Kanu II Camp Lt. 'Mick' Wedge, the senior officer from the 2/4th on S Battalion made three return trips escorting the sick down river to Kanchanaburi.

Wampo and Kanu II Camps

Meanwhile, 'D' Force T Battalion had also moved out of Tarsau about 12 kilometres to the south. A camp was set up on a creek bed near the junction of a river where an embankment was being built up. After two weeks this group moved further south downstream of an established British camp at Wampo. The Wampo camps were situated approximately 114 kilometres from Non Pladuk and 16 kilometres south of Tarsau. There were three camps at Wampo being North, Central and South so it is difficult to say where T Battalion was actually camped.

The Australians had been brought in to assist the British with the work that consisted of earth moving for an embankment. The path for the railway alongside the River Kwae Noi had been progressing slowly in preparation for the construction of viaducts at the 103km and 109km points. The pressure was on to finish the job and shifts were worked around the clock. The final shift produced a thirty-hour spurt of energy with no doubt a measure of Japanese Engineer's standover tactics that would see the embankment job through to its finale. One of the viaducts was the Double Viaduct, a wooden bridge perhaps not unlike the Pack of Cards Bridge at Hintok that was at least 400 yards long and built around the side of the cliff face, supported 25 feet above the River Kwae Noi. There was then a gap of about 600 yards, followed by another viaduct in the region of 150 yards long, hence the name double viaduct.

T Battalion now marched north for two and a half days to join S Battalion in the area of Kanu II Camp. The date has been quoted as also being 25th April 1943, however, this is believed to be incorrect with sometime in early May 1943 being closer, as this was when S and T Battalions were amalgamated. To substantiate this claim, Capt. Reg Newton of U Battalion noted that T Battalion came through Tarsau on 8th May 1943 and dropped off fifty sick before continuing 20 kilometres further north. Within half a day of their arrival, they were again at work on the Hellfire Pass Cuttings. Before the new camp was even established half of the T Battalion was sent to work on this cutting. Around the middle of July 1943 what was left of S and T Battalions at Kanu II were broken down indiscriminately as 2/4th machine gunners were sent to Hintok Road Camp and Hintok River Camp. The story of 'D' Force S and T Battalions should now continue within the story of 'D' Force O and P Battalions at Hintok River Camp.

Kanu I River (Lower Kanu) Camp

Following the cholera outbreak at Kanu II, this camp was evacuated beginning in mid July and all cholera patients were moved down from Kanu II and III to the Kanu I River Camp. Like the jungle camps at Malayan Hamlet and Kanu II, the cholera patients at Kanu I were also isolated under canvas away from the main group. The remainder of the non-cholera sick were in no better shape and were only at the Kanu I Camp about two weeks before being evacuated by barge to

The cliff-hugging Viaduct at Wampo

Tarsau or one of the other hospital base camps further south along the River Kwae Noi. Work at Kanu I Camp during the excavation of the Hellfire Pass Cuttings comprised mainly the unloading of supply barges and evacuation of the sick to hospital camps down river. There were atap huts at Kanu I River Camp that had been built earlier by 'D' Force O and P Battalions on their arrival in January 1943. Although this camp was abandoned by this group in March 1943, deemed valueless as a working camp, it was still of value as a barge landing and supply route up the side of the mountain into Kanu II and III Camps.

'D' Force U Battalion

This battalion left Singapore on 18th March 1943 under the command of Capt. Reg Newton of the 2/19th Battalion. Arriving at Non Pladuk four days later they were marched the 2 kilometres to the transit camp at Konma. The following day on 23rd March this group rode onboard open flat railway trucks to Kanchanaburi. The three other battalions of 'D' Force, namely S, T and V Battalions had already arrived at Kanchanaburi, having departed Singapore before U Battalion. It was here that Capt. Fred Harris reluctantly agreed to command a 225 strong Prisoner of War work party that the Japanese had ordered be separated and remain behind to load ballast onto trains. Amongst this party were several members of the 2/4th Machine Gun Battalion, including Joe Starcevich and James Flanagan. These two men had eaten some pork and this rich meat was blamed for causing them some stomach problems. When their group moved out for Kanchanaburi, ill health forced them to remain behind. There is a valid argument that because

U Battalion were the tail-enders from the Australian contribution to 'D' Force they tended to gather in some of the stragglers into their group at the lower camps in Thailand as they moved north from Kanchanaburi. This appears to be true in the case of Tom Cato, who it appears by his diary entries, joined U Battalion ex-S Battalion at Tarsau in June 1943. On 4th April the Japanese arrived to pick up U Battalion in a convoy of trucks to take them to their next destination, Tarsau. This came as a pleasant surprise as they were under the impression that they were going to march to their next camp.

Tarsau Camp 4.4.43 – 24.5.43

Captain Newton's U Battalion on arrival at Tarsau erected their tents and immediately began work on the line. This work entailed the clearing of the path ahead of the rail laying gangs and the building up of embankments. The rail link at this stage did not extend past Kanchanaburi because of the route chosen by the Japanese would have to pass through the Chungkai Cutting and over the viaducts at Wampo where 'D' Force T Battalion was currently working.

Tarsau North Camp 24.5.43 – 2.6.43

On 24th May U Battalion moved up the line to Tarsau North and set up a new camp. Although Tom Cato had travelled up from Singapore with S Battalion, his is a good case in point for not becoming locked into set ideas about the movements of Prisoners of War along the rail link. Tom was a locomotive fireman with the Western Australian Government Railways at the East Perth depot. He had enlisted in the A.I.F. in his lunch break with his mate Danny Bevis. There may be several reasons why Tom remained at Tarsau whilst the rest of S Battalion proceeded to the Kanu II Camp. An obvious choice might be sickness. It is possible he may have been removed from S Battalion by the Japanese to be used as a vehicle driver or for some other job. Or perhaps it was because Tom was born in Broken Hill, N.S.W. and both the 2/19th and 2/20th Battalions were raised in New South Wales. Whatever the reason it appears that Tom was now part of U Battalion, for a while at least.

Tonchan Camp 2.6.43 – 28.6.43

They had only just settled in to their new surroundings, when on 2nd June U Battalion moved up to Tonchan South. On 29th June U Battalion marched to Tonchan Central where the barge landing for the Tonchan camps was located. After several false starts the men loaded themselves and their gear onto the barges and began the trip up river to Kanu I River Camp. Once ashore they started out on the trek up the mountain track to the Kanu II area. This was the same march that O and P Battalions had made the previous March on their way through Kanu II to establish the Hintok Road Camp.

Kanu II Camp 30.6.43 – 10.7.43

This group, along with the other workforces in this area, were to work on the Hellfire Pass Cuttings. Whilst at Kanu II, a similar situation arises as to that of T Battalion's, in that it is difficult to say where exactly the U Battalion camp was located. However, it was most likely in the vicinity of the 'D' Force S Battalion camp at Kanu II. Leaving Kanu II around 10th July U Battalion moved back down the mountain to the Kanu I River Camp and proceeded to Hintok

River Camp. Maps of this area indicate that there was a foot track between the Kanu I and Hintok River Camps.

Hintok River Camp 11.7.43 – 16.7.43

From the Hintok River Camp to the work site, the incline was so steep that it took an hour to reach in the mud. The job was at the Hintok Cutting and when this task was completed, U Battalion then moved further up to the Three Tier Bridge which Captain Newton also refers to as the Pack of Cards Bridge. Around mid July orders were received to move U Battalion back down river by barge to the British camp at Tonchan Central.

Tonchan Central Camp 17.7.43 – 21.9.43

This crowded camp was located on flat ground between the River Kwae Noi and the railway line which by this time had already been laid past this point. Newton's U Battalion now set to work on the main road north and ballasting of the railway line and bridgework. Two work parties left this camp, one going to Tonchan Spring Camp and the other to a camp in the Kanu II area that the Prisoners of War referred to as the fly camp. Both these splinter parties from U Battalion were engaged on repair and maintenance work. On 21st September all the non-sick back at Tonchan Central Camp were barged to the Rin Tin Camp. It was at this point that Tom Cato separated from the main group of U Battalion.

Rin Tin Camp

Rin Tin had been a Dutch camp, or to be specific, a Netherlands East Indian camp. The Dutch had colonised the Netherlands East Indies (Indonesia) and as a consequence many local Netherlands East Indians had Dutch names because of interracial marriages. Australians would cringe when they learnt that they were following up these Dutch-Indonesian Prisoners of War because of their less than acceptable standards of hygiene. Work at Rin Tin consisted of maintenance with repairs to embankments and bridges. Whilst at Rin Tin Capt. Newton ventured north about 9 kilometres back up the line to Kuii where he came across Major Alf Cough's V Battalion. Newton wrote:

> '*In the middle of about 1,500 Indonesians we found the 2/4 m/gunners. Alf Cough and Les Riches and their chaps crowded round and poured out their story of being placed under the command of the Indonesians from the moment they had arrived and, had been working on all the usual things, embankments, bridges, cuttings etc and had lost a number of men. Things had gone hard with them with the Japanese "treatment" and being under the Dutch command as they had no control of their work figures and always received the thin end from the Dutchies; they had had little medical attention as it was centred mainly on the Indonesians and above all they had no representation on the rations and in the kitchens and consequently had to take what they were given.*' [16]

---

[16] R. W. Newton, *The Grim Glory of the 2/19th Battalion A.I.F.* Sydney 1975, p. 617

Major Alf Cough's V Battalion made the greatest sacrifice of all the Australian battalions in 'D' Force Groups 4 and 6 originating from Singapore. The figures are as follows:

> S Battalion Group 4 lost 14.2%
>
> T Battalion Group 4 lost 21.2%
>
> U Battalion Group 4 lost 5.2%
>
> V Battalion Group 6 lost 50.0%

Tonchan Central Camp

On 17th November 1943 Capt. Newton was ordered to return to Tonchan Central. On arrival he was informed that a new camp was to be set up. This new campsite was to be beside the old camp on flat level ground, the establishment of which was tackled with gusto and in the mould of O and P Battalions' example at the Hintok Road Camp. A bamboo tube reticulation system was constructed to enable fresh water to be piped in from the nearby spring into the camp. On 11th December U Battalion was given orders to prepare to move to Kanu IIIr–Tampie South the next day.

Kanu IIIr – Tampie South Camp

The battalion started out on 13th December 1943 and began the steep trek up to the Tampie Camp where there was a marshalling yard and siding 400 yards to the south. It will be remembered that in June 1943 Bert Norton and about twenty other Prisoners of War moved south from Kanu II to clear the jungle for this siding camp and marshalling yard. Captain Newton tells us:

'On arrival at Kanu IIIr-Tampie South, U Battalion started cutting timber for the steam locomotives'.

There were also permanent gangs here available 24 hours a day for the replenishment of water for the steam locomotives. At this time there were already about 500 British established at this camp which comprised B and C Battalions from 'D' Force. As well as these duties other men from U Battalion were engaged on track ballasting and repairs. A programme of construction continued at this camp which was destined to become semi-permanent in terms of the railway construction camps as the native village of Tampie began to spring up in the vicinity of this camp. Captain Newton makes a point of mentioning the local Thai villagers:

> *'Now that the railway was through the Thais were now making their way up country and setting up villages at the main railway sidings. Tampie being a marshalling yard was larger in size than most and we had about 50 Thais in the area within 2 months'.*
>
> *'On 28th March 1944 orders were received to stand by for the long awaited move south'.* [17]

There were delays encountered except this time instead of blaming Japanese organisation it was due to Allied bombing attacks on the now complete Burma-Thailand Railway. On 5th April 1944 what remained of U Battalion was loaded onto a train and embarked on a rickety journey south to Tamuang, 12 kilometres south of Kanchanaburi.

---

[17]   Ibid p.623

'D' Force V Battalion Group 6

This group left Selarang Barracks, Changi on 17th March 1943, moving by trucks to the Singapore Railway Station where they entrained for the four day guided tour north through Malaya into Thailand. As we take up the story of 'D' Force V Battalion we join Major Cough's group on 29th March 1943 heading further north from their staging camp at Kanchanaburi, once again aboard trucks. They staged overnight at Tarsau where one man died. At this time Tarsau was under the command of Capt. J. Hands from the 2/3rd Machine Gun Battalion who had also been placed in command of 'D' Force Q Battalion ex-Java. The following is a general description of where these men of V Battalion were located.

Kinsaiyok Camp 31.3.43 – 1.5.43

On 31st March V Battalion arrived at Kinsaiyok camp which was already occupied by 300 British and 600 Dutch Prisoners of War. Major Cough's V Battalion at this stage consisted of five officers and 482 other ranks. Of all the 'D' Force battalions, fate would deal out a heavy blow to this group. From the men who marched into Kinsaiyok on 31st March 1943 many less would march out the following December. Tom Gough, who at this stage had not attained his 21st birthday, had made up his mind that he would survive this ordeal. This particular Kinsaiyok Camp was situated on the bank of the River Kwae Noi. Described as being not too bad, the accommodation was atap hut, each one sheltering about 200 men. Along the side of each hut was a long bench called a chung. This was about 7 feet wide and made from flattened out bamboo on which the men would sleep. The first task at Kinsaiyok was to cut a track through the jungle ahead of the rail laying gangs and the excavation of a long cutting. Seven men died at this camp during the thirty-two day stay. On 2nd May V Battalion was on the move again to the north staging overnight at Rin Tin Camp. The next day they set out, arriving at Hindato Camp at the 197.75km point where they once again staged overnight. Hindato was the Headquarters for 'D' Force Group 6 under the command of Major Shida. The following day they moved on another 10 kilometres to Brankassi Camp, where they arrived on 5th May 1943.

Brankassi–Onte–Bangan Camps 5.5.43 – 10.7.43

`Brankassi Camp was located at the 208.11km point on the rail link. Working conditions, accommodation and food here were exactly the same as those as they would encounter from July at the Hindaine Camp. Brankassi Camp was judged as being worse than Kinsaiyok, the mud contributing to the discomfort. Accommodation here was twenty-two men per 10 feet by 12 feet tent that were described as being very old and threadbare. There were no flies on the tents, and water would enter when it rained heavily. The beds were made from bamboo slats and were raised about two feet from the ground.

Twenty-seven men died in this camp including five machine gunners, one of these men being William 'Bill' Andrew Dwyer who had been in a weak and delirious state thought to be brought on by a bout of cerebral malaria. Tom Gough stated that 'Bill' was in the cholera tent at the time because lime had been spread on the ground around the tent. A Japanese Engineer Corporal by the name of 'Black Cat' had taken great delight in beating 'Bill' unconscious and then pushing bamboo sticks into his ears and eyes. 'Bill' had stood up magnificently to this savagery but died on the night of 22nd August 1943. Lieutenant 'Scotty' Howell from the 2/3rd Reserve Motor Transport Company was a witness therefore 'Bill' was probably on W Party (*see Hindaine Camp*) when he was savagely attacked. Tom Gough was also on this party.

On 6th May V Battalion was split up when 172 other ranks under the command of W.O. Glen Blyden of the 2/3rd Ordnance Stores Company were detailed to continue 6 kilometres north of Brankassi to a clearing in the jungle, to a place called Onte. Major Cough in his diary mentions Onte where there was a wooden bridge constructed across the River Kwae Noi. W.O. Arthur Hewby was with this party, but arrived sick and returned to Brankassi where it is presumed he remained. Following the work at Onte the men moved north approximately another 4 kilometres to Bangan.

Hindaine Camp 10.7.43 – 31.8.43

This camp was located about 8 kilometres south of Brankassi, close to Hindato on a small tributary of the River Kwae Noi. This would place it around the 200km point. This camp was also under canvas and as usual the tents would not do what they were designed to do.

Major Alf Cough wrote:

> '*This camp is just hell, the whole area a sea of black stinking mud, very little food; and men dying every day. For the last three weeks we have eaten nothing but rice and dried fish; for three weeks prior to that we had rice and dried cabbage, at the rate of one cupful of rice plus a dessert spoon of fish or cabbage. The men cannot last out much longer unless we get some decent food and medical supplies. I am tired of reading burial services, and watching my men die without being able to lift a hand to help them; they are full of courage and keep their chins up until the last moment.*' [18]

On 27th July Lt. 'Scotty' Howell was detached to Brankassi with about eighty other ranks as W Party. 'D' Force V Battalion now consisted of three separate groups, one at Onte, one at Hindaine and W Party at Brankassi. On 10th August forty of the heavy sick including Capt. John Hill were evacuated. A total of twenty-eight men died at this camp including several machine gunners. These figures are perhaps an indicator of this camp's remote location and how important it was for the prisoners to be able to do business with the local traders. On 30th August Major Cough was ordered to take one hundred of his fittest men to the next camp, Kuii. The remainder of this group returned to Brankassi Camp.

Kuii Camp 31.8.43 – 18.12.43

Kuii was located at the 190.48km point about ten kilometres south of Hindaine Camp. Located about 4 kilometres from the River Kwae Noi this atap hutted camp was already established and occupied by 1,700 Dutch which is mentioned by Capt. Newton in the 'D' Force U Battalion story. After coming down river by barge from Hindaine, work commenced on 1st August with every available man in camp and continued until 17th December 1943. Lieutenant Les 'Pard' Riches and twenty-nine other ranks (heavy sick) were evacuated on 11th August. A total of fifty-two men including sixteen machine gunners died at this camp. On 18th December 1943 the remaining officer Major Alf Cough and eighteen other ranks from the original party were evacuated to Non Pladuk. Three of these other ranks died within three days of their arrival. Out of the original 500 men, 200 had died by December 1943 and another twenty had died by March

---

18   Major Alf Cough Diary loaned to the author by Alan Cough

1944. Had V Battalion remained with the Australians instead of the Dutch it is certain that many more of these men would have stood a better chance of walking out of the jungle at the end of 1943.

Tom Gough was one of those who did walk out of the jungle, as he said he would. By this time he had attained the mature age of twenty-one years whilst in residence at the Tarsau Camp. It is likely that Tom had seen things that other men would not see or experience in a lifetime of living.

'D' Force-Miscellaneous Work Groups

Captain Fred Harris, Sergeant Eddie Derkenne, W.O.II John Dooley

Every effort has been made to document the sector where it is thought each member of the 2/4th Machine Gun Battalion worked on the rail link. However, there are still a few enigmas concerning Thailand so perhaps the best way to begin is allow Capt. Reg Newton explain quoting from the 2/19th Battalion unit history *Grim Glory* concerning the 'D' Force U Battalion move from Kanchanaburi:

> '*About two hours after receiving the news that we would move up tomorrow, the I.J.A. came back and told us to leave 225 behind as a work party for them and that no sick would be left behind at Kanburi P.O.W. hospital (British). As it was our policy not to leave any group behind anywhere without an officer backstop, Captain Fred Harris was selected to stay. He did not like the idea (nor did anybody else) of being dropped off from the main group and very forcibly said so, and then asked that he have his own choice of N.C.O.'s. So W.O. II Geoff Riach and Sgt. Laurie Sheather from 2/19 Bn., W.O. II Ken Cullen, Sgt. Eddie Derkenne and Sgt. Ben Raven from 2/20 Bn. with several Corporals including Abbie Hutchins, Eric Saunderson from 2/19 and Ern Parkinson of 2/20 Bn. remained behind. Some of the party were sick and it was thought that with a British P.O.W. hospital nearby they had a better chance than go on. The splintering of the P.O.W. battalion group continued.' Some of Fred Harris's party of 225 finished up in three locations in Japan, some finished up in Saigon, a few back at Changi, and the others spread over camps in Thailand.*' [19]

The following is Capt. Harris' and Sgt. Derkenne's stories as explained in their war crimes affidavits.

Captain Fred Harris:

> '*I was in captivity at Kanburi camp, Thailand from the 1st April 1943 until the 27th May 1943. I was in charge of a working party of approximately 200 men, half English, half Australian. We were working on a night shift, loading ballast trains on the Kanburi River.*' [20]

---

[19]   R. W. Newton, *The Grim Glory of the 2/19th Battalion A.I.F.* Sydney 1975, p.579
[20]   AWM54 File 1010/14/66 War Crimes Affidavit by NX34662 Capt. F. L. Harris, Australian War Memorial Canberra

Sergeant Eddie Derkenne:

> '*From Kanburi I went to the British General Hospital, where I remained during April for a little over a fortnight. I then went to Kinsiok jungle camp No. 2 where I remained from May until August 1943. There were 32 Australians in this camp. We were engaged in bridge building work. Capt. Atkins was in charge of the party of English and I was in charge of the 32 Australians. He left me to look after my own men as best I could. Another NCO and myself went out and eventually got the tents erected and made another jungle camp outside the other one. From Kinsiok I went to Konkwita where I remained from August until December 1943. There were 45 Australians in this camp and we were engaged in building embankments for the railway. When we first arrived at Konkwita, we slept in tents which were very old and holey; some of the men had only groundsheets and bits of bamboo to keep them off the ground. We were evacuated from Konkwita to Hindata, which was the headquarters of the Japanese in charge of the Thailand Prisoners of War.*'[21]

In the 2/20th Battalion unit history Sgt. Eddie Derkenne again relates his experiences:

> '*The only time I thought I was going to die was at Kinsoika. I joined Capt. Harris' party there and we worked on the bridge building at Jungle Camp No. 2 even though I had the hospital armband on the Japs gave you. From there I went to Hindata where I got hepatitis and Harris said you can't go out with the working parties you stay here.*'[22]

It is likely that nineteen or more members of the 2/4th were connected with Capt. Harris. This party is recorded as being at Non Pladuk on 4th March 1944. Some of these men were then selected for the Saigon Party and concluded their war in French Indo-China. On the other hand Sgt. Derkenne from the 2/20th Battalion found himself included on the *Aramis* Party which was despatched to Japan. Tom Gough, who was a member of Major Cough's V Battalion, was also selected for Japan and sailed onboard the *Aramis*. The common denominator is that both men worked in Thailand in the Kinsaiyok, Hindaine, Hindato area. The selection of prisoners who were to be included on this party as well as the Saigon party was made at Non Pladuk. It will be remembered that when the remnants of Major Cough's V Battalion emerged from their jungle camps that they were moved to Non Pladuk.

The following members of the battalion are believed to have been on the Capt. Harris Party: Ron Badock (Kinsaiyok only), Thomas 'Lance' Barnett, Ron Brown, John 'Taddy' Curtin, James Flanagan, Lloyd Hadden, George Hicks, Ray Hickey, Ron Jeffery, Reg Miller, Noel Outrim, Joe Starcevich, Henry White and Jack Wheelock.

Last but not least is W.O. II John Dooley from the 2/3rd M.A.C. (Motor Ambulance Convoy) who kept a roll of 'D' Force T Battalion Company No.18 Section No. 4. Warrant Officer Dooley mentions that he was at Kanchanaburi on the railway ballast party but was not with Capt. Harris's group, but instead remained at Kanchanaburi until early June 1943. Ivan Lawer recalls working on a big cutting to the north of Kanchanaburi which is thought to have been the Chungkai Cutting. Originally a tunnel was to be cut through this rock face but because the Japanese did not have any experienced tunnelling engineers, this Chungkai Tunnel became the Chungkai Cutting. Although the H6 Officer's Party passed through this cutting by train on 28th May 1943, it is quite possible the cutting required widening in sections if the excavation work had been pushed through in a hurry. As has been mentioned tracing the movements of the

---

[21] AWM54 File 1010/14/42 War Crimes Affidavit by NX45924 Sgt. E. J. Derkenne, Australian War Memorial Canberra

[22] Don Wall, *Singapore and Beyond* The Story of 2/20th Battalion Don Wall 2/20th Battalion Association, East Hills N.S.W. 1985, p.162

men from the 2/4th can be a hit and miss affair and we must keep an open mind to suggestion, as anything is possible where the Japanese were involved.

The following members of the battalion are believed to have been with W.O. II John Dooley:

Thomas Crane, Cecil Dunn, Reg and Ivan Lawer, Alf Newton and John Warrington.

The 'H' Force Story

'H' Force consisted of six groups or parties within 'H' Force from H1 to the H6 Officer's Party. Two of these six groups contained members of the 2/4th Machine Gun Battalion, being H3 and the H6 Officer's Party. The officers, like the other ranks in 'H' Force, were expected to participate on the labouring tasks on the rail link. This is a fair indication that by April–May 1943 the Japanese were running out of Prisoners of War to call upon from what they must have initially thought was a limitless labour pool. The reason 'H' Force was despatched to the Thailand side of the railway was to beef up the labour force in the middle section where problems were being experienced and progress had fallen behind schedule.

Like 'D' Force V Battalion, which had been separated from the Japanese Thailand Administration Group 4, 'H' Force Groups were similarly separated and neglected because they would remain under Singapore's administrative umbrella and not Thailand's. This might also explain why the sick from 'H' Force were not evacuated down river by barge to Tarsau, but instead were moved by train to the Kanchanaburi Hospital Camp. 'H' Force was represented by 705 Australians between the H3 and H6 Groups, part of a total Prisoner of War labour force of 3,270 men. 'F' Force began the move out of Singapore in thirteen trains from 18th April 1943. The first 'H' Force train to depart Singapore was on 5th May 1943 virtually on top of the last 'F' Force train to leave Singapore. This fact in itself must indicate how desperate the Japanese were to complete the Burma–Thailand rail link before the time limit set by Tokyo Headquarters had expired.

'H' Force Group 3

'H' Force Group 3 consisted of an all Australian force under the command of Lt-Col R. F. Oakes. Major Bert Saggers was to be Lt-Col Oakes' second in command and in charge of the group's pay and records. This group departed Singapore on the morning of 8th May 1942 and arrived at Non Pladuk four days later on 12th May where they moved into the transit camp at Konma. There is little doubt and much evidence to suggest that H3 Group participated in the same route march from the transit camp at Konma to their railway construction camp at Kanu II Malayan Hamlet. It is then suggested that anyone with a particular interest in H3 Group should also read the section in 'F' Force concerning the march north from Konma to Kanu II Malayan Hamlet Camp.

The next day 13th May at 2300 hours they marched out of camp and arrived at their first rest camp at 1000 hours the following day. That night they were back on the road again, arriving at Kanchanaburi at 0900 hours where they camped in an open paddock. During the night the local Thais crept amongst the sleeping men and stole whatever they could escape with. Following a day's rest the men moved, that night arriving at the Temple Camp which the 'F' Force columns had passed through. The rest of the march is the same as 'F' Force even down to hiring twenty oxen and carts to carry their gear forward from this camp to the Tardan Bridge Camp. This routine of marching by night and stopping at rest camps continued in stages of 15 miles for a total distance of 90 miles. The Kanu III Camp was reached at 0400 hours on 21st May and from here to the Malayan Hamlet Camp it was about 4 miles. Nevertheless this march took three hours to complete. [23]

Kanu II Malayan Hamlet Camp – May to September 1943

Although this group started out as an Australian workforce, by the time it had arrived at Malayan Hamlet it had collected 114 British and some prisonerss ex-Java along the way. On 30th May an additional ninety-eight stragglers marched in. Ultimately there would be approximately 500 Australian, 200 British and some Americans at this camp. Of these, 106 British and 111 Australians would die at this camp. The workforce was split into four shifts, from A to D, each shift consisting of one hundred men. Two shifts worked during the daylight hours and the other two shifts, the hours of darkness.

There is an entry in Capt. Tom Bunning's diary that relates to H3 Group at Malayan Hamlet which is worthy of note and is perhaps a good example of how some people rise above adversity to help others less fortunate than themselves:

'One of our men was sent to hospital two days ago, Watt of 'C' Company, with a very bad abscess. He apparently had a lot of sickness up north, beri-beri, malaria and dysentery and speaks highly of Leith and Miller, both of 'C' Company. They apparently did an amazing job for other M.G.'s in looking after and washing them and also in scrounging food for them. Stories of such as this help to restore one's faith in human nature,' [24]

These men were Eric Watt, John 'Jock' Leith and Alby Miller.

The Malayan Hamlet campsite was on uncleared slightly sloping ground. A small area about the size of a lawn bowls green was cleared on the afternoon of their arrival on 21st May and twenty tents were pitched. The camp was located roughly 450 yards to the east of the Hellfire Pass Cutting and to the north of the 'D' Force S Battalion camp, it is believed about 1.42 kilometres. The road from Tarsau passed to the right of both the Kanu II and Malayan Hamlet Camps. From this road a track led to the Hellfire Pass Cutting that was just over a kilometre on foot as there was no other way of getting there. A stream ran just to the south of the Malayan Hamlet Camp that was crossed by a bridge on the Kanu to Hintok access road. Another stream also ran to the south of the Kanu II 'D' Force Camp that similarly was crossed by bridge on the same road.

Over the next two days the camp was enlarged and bamboo floors were laid inside the tents. Water was drawn from the small stream, but the precaution was taken to boil this water before drinking. The first working party was called for by the Japanese Engineers on 24th May, however, after the long journey from Singapore and the work involved in setting up the camp, officers experienced some difficulties in getting the men to work.

On 16th June at 1000 hours the first case of cholera appeared in this camp and by 1630 hours this man had died. The cholera epidemic had been expected to arrive as the weather

---

23   Major Bert Saggers' Diary loaned to the author by his son, Ian Saggers
24   Captain Tom Bunning's Diary privately published by the Bunning family and loaned to the author

closed in for the monsoon and two tents were pitched in the jungle about 165 yards from the main camp. This caused some concern because cholera had also appeared at the Kanu II and Hintok Road Camps by this time. One saving grace was that at least the water supply was taken from separate streams.

After cholera appeared at the Kanu II Malayan Hamlet Camp fifty-nine British were brought up on 18th June from Kanu III and set up a new camp called Kanu IIIa or KIII Advance Camp as it was to be known. On 25th August eighty-three Australians from Groups H3 and H6 joined the 'H' Force No. 1 Sub-Section and travelled by train to the Konkoita area in a last minute dash to complete the railway in that sector. On 8th September the first Australian party from 'H' Force consisting of stretcher cases was evacuated to Kanchanaburi. Over the next few days another four parties were also evacuated, totalling about 500 men; leaving about twenty-five men to clean up the campsite. On 16th September the rear party who had been at Tonchan Spring Camp came forward to Kanu IIIa (Tampie North Camp) and joined the other Australians before this last group also moved down to Kanchanaburi.

Kanu IIIa (Tampie North)

This new camp, Kanu IIIa, became the new Imperial Japanese Army Administrative Headquarters for the 'H' Force Singapore Administration under the command of Lt-Col Oakes. Both camps were combined for administrative purposes. This camp was set up on the opposite side of the road to the Malayan Hamlet Camp at the 153.72km point. There were some protests about the sanity of moving men up from Kanu III to the Kanu II–Malayan Hamlet area where cholera was prevalent. In addition to the atap buildings of the Japanese Administrative Headquarters office, mess and sleeping quarters there was also four tents in use by the Prisoners of War.

Kanu IIIr (Tampie South)

This camp was situated amongst jungle approximately 4 kilometres to the south of the Kanu IIIa Camp at the 147.52km point. This camp consisted of about thirteen tents that were described as being in poor condition. 'H' Force H4 Group moved into this camp. Cholera patients from this camp and also Kanu II Malayan Hamlet were evacuated down the precipitous mountain track on improvised bamboo stretchers to the Kanu I River Camp. This hazardous journey took four to five hours and several cholera patients died as a result of falling off stretchers.

The 'F' and 'H' Force Hospital Kanchanaburi

The evacuation of the sick to Kanchanaburi had commenced prematurely on 20th July 1943 before the 'F' and 'H' Force Hospital had been completed. For the next month these sick were possibly accommodated at the 'D' Force Base Hospital Camp No. 1 until their own hospital was finished on 27th August and ready to accept them. As soon as the men were classified fit they were transferred to this 'Fit Camp,' located two miles away in a jungle clearing. On 19th November 1943 the first party of 500 left under the command of Lt-Col T. H. Newey as an advance party back to Singapore. Newey had come into Kanchanaburi from Konkoita with 'H' Force No. 1 Sub-Section, which had arrived at Kanchanaburi between 8th–12th November 1943. Between 20th November and 10th December 1943, 'H' Force returned to Singapore en-masse by train, with the exception of some seriously ill men who would not return until May

'H' Force Group 3 Officers – Lt. Bernie O'Sullivan , Maj. Bert Saggers and Lt. Vic Mentiplay

anyone back at Singapore would learn of the conditions being experienced at the construction camps on the Burma–Thailand the rail link.

Sime Road Camp December 1943 – May 1944

On arrival at Singapore some of the men, including 185 Australians, were taken by truck to the atap hutted camp at Sime Road. The sick had been taken to the Australian General Hospital at Roberts Barracks Changi and the balance returned to Selarang Barracks from where they had departed the previous May. It was at the Sime Road Camp where 'H' Force was officially disbanded. In May 1944 they were moved into their new quarters at the Changi Gaol Camp. The exception to the rule is that some of the first Prisoners of War to return from 'F' and 'H' Force moved into the cells at Changi Gaol during March 1944; and alternatively some prisoners moved into the Gaol Camp from Sime Road as late as June. Obviously the civilian internees in residence at the gaol had to be evicted before the Prisoners of War from Selarang Barracks Changi could move in, and vice versa. Before all the above could occur, room had to made at Sime Road Camp. Don Wall of the 2/20th Battalion, who was also a member of 'F' Force, remembers still being able to smell perfume in the cells that had just been vacated by the women. The writings of Capt. David Nelson would indicate that some of the men from 'F' and 'H' Forces who had returned to Singapore from Thailand from December 1943 were sent to Sime Road Camp to be kept in quarantine, in case they were carriers of disease, like smallpox and cholera that might possibly be introduced onto Singapore Island.

'At this time all ranks were being vaccinated in the event that small-pox might have been brought in by the forces from Thailand..' [25]

David Nelson also wrote:

'I was at I.J.A. Headquarters all day and met Lt.'s Jusuke Terai, Takeuchi and Saji now with 'H' Force, and members of 'F' Force who are housed temporarily in Syme Road hutted camp, possibly for a period of quarantine against a spread of cholera or small-pox from Thailand.' [26]

An epidemic would be the last thing the Japanese would wish for with the levelling of a new airfield at Changi about to commence, not to mention the tunnelling and defence works that would be initiated during 1945 as Japan's war drew to its inevitable end.

H6 Officer's Party

On 17th May 1943, 320 officer Prisoners of War, including sixty-eight Australian officers and one other rank, being the medical orderly, departed Singapore like the five 'H' Force groups had before them. Arriving at Non Pladuk on 21st May they went into the transit camp at Konma. It had been raining and on arrival the camp was found to be a sea of mud, a foot deep. The five huts, each about 120 feet in length, were constructed of bamboo and atap with no sides and an earthen, or to be more correct, a mud floor. They stayed at this transit camp for two days during which time it rained intermittently but heavily the whole time. Leaving Konma they marched 49 kilometres over the next two nights until they reached Kanchanaburi where they moved into a crowded tented camp. It also rained heavily at Kanchanaburi during their stay over the next two days. It was here that two 14 feet by 12 feet tents were issued for the sixty-eight men of the A.I.F. component for the duration of their stay in Thailand.

On 28th May after a six-hour wait at the railway station, they travelled by train to the 125km point on the rail link at Wanyai. This would indicate that the railway had been pushed through to Tarsau through the Chungkai Cutting and around the viaducts at Wampo by this time. We know that 'D' Force T Battalion had finished their work at Wampo and had passed through Tarsau, dropping off their sick on 8th May. This information is important because it gives an indication as to how the construction of the rail link north from Non Pladuk was progressing. The men made another night march that ended at the bivouac site at Tarsau North. The following day there was another march, up steep hills which brought this group into Tonchan South where 'H' Force Group H5 had arrived two days earlier.

Tonchan South Camp May – July 1943

On arrival the officer's in H6 Party commenced the setting up of what was to be a permanent camp. This entailed clearing the jungle of heavy infestations of bamboo and timber, pitching of tents, and laying sleeping platforms inside the tents. The commander of the H5 Group felt compelled to assist the H6 Officer's Party by helping out with tentage.

---

[25] David Nelson, *The Story of Changi Singapore* Changi Publication Company Perth 1976, p.126
[26] Ibid p.131

The railway line crossed the road from east to west about 1 mile to the south of this camp where it then turned north and ran parallel with the road, about 1 and a half miles away, between the camp and the River Kwae Noi. The ground sloped to the railway line but then fell away sharply in the last mile to the Kwae Noi where there was a perpendicular fall of about 100 feet to the river. The current ran so swiftly that even close to the bank where its strength is weakest, it would have been impossible to swim against it. There was another group at Tonchan South at this time, being Capt. Reg Newton's 'D' Force U Battalion, who were camped on the opposite side of the road. The U Battalion Camp is described as being placed on an escarpment overlooking a wide valley with a stream running through the camp.

It was at Tonchan South that the officers in Group H6 learnt that they were to be recruited into the labour force. This news was not met with a resounding hurrah, but rather a strongly worded protest by the H6 Officer's Group commander, Lt-Col W. Whittenbury. The Col. was in possession of a letter from the Japanese commanding officer back in Singapore stating that this officer's group were not required to engage in manual labour. Needless to say the Japanese can be very persuasive when their orders are questioned. For the next four to five days the H6 Officer's Party worked on clearing bamboo. These grew in clumps to a height of 80–90 feet and were on average about 9 inches in diameter. Following this task they were moved to a part of the line where a cutting was being excavated and an embankment built. This job was about 2 and a half to 3 miles from the camp. The rail link passing, along a mountain range, as it did, necessitated the excavation and construction of a succession of cuttings, embankments and wooden bridges.

About the middle of June 1943 cholera broke out amongst the Tamils in the camps beside and behind the 'H' Force Camp at Tonchan South. The real concern was that disease might spread by way of the creek that ran, as mentioned, through the U Battalion Camp between the Japanese Camp and the Tamil and 'H' Force Camps. At this point when cholera had only just surfaced at Hintok and Kanu Camps these Tamils were already dying in droves. As the work demands on the railway were being met, the first of H6 Group ordered to leave Tonchan South was to include 110 officers. When the order came on 28th June for this party to move north to the Hintok River Camp only twenty-eight A.I.F. officers fell in with cooking gear and tents for the march. On 1st July two additional parties which included five A.I.F. officers, under the command of Lt. Ross Ambrose, moved north to the Hintok Valley Camp. On 7th July a further six A.I.F officers under Major G. McKay also moved to the Hintok Valley Camp despite the fact that none of these men were completely fit. After only three weeks at Hintok Valley Camp they joined the other officers at the Hintok River Camp.

Hintok Valley Camp June – July 1943

This camp was situated in the worst possible position, between the Hintok Road Camp and the base of a limestone cliff. The camp was to be the new home of H1 Group which was the first party from the 'H' Force component to arrive. These prisoners were also the first from 'H' Force to work on what appears as if it may have been the Three Tier Bridge and the Hintok Cutting. From the end of June to early July H5 Group arrived at Hintok River Camp and subsequently moved up the escarpment along the slippery track to the Hintok Valley Camp where they joined the officers from H6 Group.

The close proximity of Tamils, who were also accommodated at the Hintok Valley Camp, greatly concerned the men from 'D' Force O and P Battalions, who were located across the road at the nearby Hintok Road Camp. For these men to get to some of the lower work sites along the Hintok section of the rail link it was required that they walk along a muddy track through the middle of the Hintok Valley Camp. These men from Groups H1, H5 and H6, the majority being British, were suffering badly as disease, sickness and death did its best to diminish their ranks. Altogether 141 British and three Australian Prisoners of War died at the Hintok Valley Camp.

The ground on which the Hintok Valley Camp was sited was a swamp. A stream ran past Hintok Road Camp and then doubled back on itself in a U shape, flowing back in the opposite direction past the Hintok Valley Camp. To get to the lower reaches of the railway trace where construction and excavation was still being carried out it was necessary to climb a ladder and then follow a steep track down the escarpment. This camp was about two miles from the path of the line that would later make a westerly bend after the Three Tier Bridge, then a northerly bend towards Kinsaiyok after the Pack of Cards Bridge and Compressor Cutting. This meant that the intended path for the railway was between the Hintok Road and Valley Camps and the River Kwae Noi.

Accommodation at this camp consisted of fifteen tents, eleven of which were only outer fly sheets and the remaining four tents were inner fly sheets. An attempt at erecting a hospital was made, however this was little more than four uprights and an atap palm leaf roof, which did little to keep the rain at bay. Commencing from 29th June 1943 men from this camp began to move out to the overflow camp at Hintok River which at least had the advantage of being closer to the lower worksites. Towards the end of July 1943 the Hintok Valley Camp was closed down and all who could walk were evacuated to the Hintok River Camp. Those too sick to walk, which included some cholera patients were left to their fate.

Tonchan South Camp Revisited July – August 1943

Conditions at Tonchan South had improved during July for the remaining officers of H6 Group. Earlier in the month the Japanese had ordered that the worst of the sick be evacuated to Kanchanaburi Base Hospital Camp. As the 'F' and 'H' Force Hospital Camp was not completed until 27th August these men must have been admitted to the 'D' Force Hospital at Kanchanaburi. This was done in the middle of the month, the sick being transported south by rail. As some of those on the sick list recovered they were sent north again. What was left of the Australians at Tonchan South after 24th August were moved north to Tonchan Spring Camp and on 16th September were sent forward to Kanu IIIa Camp to join the remnants of the Australians from 'H' Force, before being sent south again to the 'Fit Camp' at Kanchanaburi.

Hintok River Camp July – August 1943

Conditions for H6 Officer's Group at this camp were improved with regard to food, however, the accommodation for the next two months was again tents that were overcrowded. On arrival at about 1700 hours the men had to clear the jungle site, establish a kitchen and cart water approximately 100 yards up a steep hill from the river to the camp. From the original thirty-nine A.I.F. officers that had left Tonchan South between the end of June to early July it was only these twenty-eight who remained. The crowded accommodation situation was only relieved when one of the officers was admitted to hospital seriously ill. Rations improved at this camp, being close to the River Kwae Noi with local purchase possible from barges, which pulled in regularly. Lieutenant 'Bob' Learmonth was one of the officers from the 2/4th (and a member of H6 Officer's Group), being one of several reinforcement officers who had joined the battalion at Fremantle on 16th January 1942. Lieutenant Learmonth had managed to document his personal experiences in a diary:

'We had plenty of eggs 6 to 8 a day, imitation milk, brown sugar, bananas, peanuts and jam. Prices were eggs 10–15 cents, milk $1.50, sugar 40 cents, peanuts 50 cents, jam $2.50 an 8oz tin, cigarettes 50 cents for twenty.' [27]

The work was mainly on the Compressor Cutting that was about a mile away from the camp, and later ballasting on the line when the rail laying gangs came through. For the next two months at the Hintok River Camp work demands were reasonable however the work was in three shifts and was described as being hard.

'The Jap Engineers on the cutting were more organised than any we had previously seen. There was no time wasted. Instead of men with hammers and augers boring holes, pneumatic drills were being operated. The cutting resounded with the din of this drilling and with the shouting of the Japs. Instead of rocks being carried seventy yards to be dumped, trucks moved this material. The stones were first of all picked and shovelled into baskets so that a supply was maintained to be emptied into the trucks immediately they arrived on each trip. The line had to pass through the cutting by a certain date. We were cutting a path through a hill, a distance of one hundred and fifty yards to the centre and seventy to eighty feet deep.' [28]

It has already been stated that this Kanu–Hintok area was the most difficult section of the entire 414.92 kilometres of railway. The Pack of Cards Bridge was hurriedly constructed as a temporary substitute for the Pack of Cards Embankment which had fallen behind schedule. A compressor had been brought in to also speed work at this the last cutting on the exit side of this Hintok area as the rail link serpentined towards Kinsaiyok. Lieutenant 'Bob' Learmonth describes the scene at night at the Compressor cutting: [29]

'The scene at that cutting resembled Dante's Inferno. It was lit by scores of flares. These caused the shadows of the workers to assume grotesque shapes. Nearly naked bodies glistened with sweat. The din was terrific. The pneumatic drills, the trucks running backwards and forwards filling and emptying their loads of rock. The clang of picks and shovels failed to drown out the shouting and screaming of the overseers as they ensured that the work was proceeding faster than humanly possible.'

It is not known exactly when the work on the Compressor Cutting was commenced. It could have been as early as April, however sometime in May seems feasible. Lieutenant Learmonth then goes on to describe the journey from Hintok Valley Camp to the Hintok River Camp except this time it is from the opposite direction:

'At intervals perhaps a dozen of us managed to get a day off as a rest or we considered it as such. Hintok Road Camp lay several miles away from us on the other side of the mountains. This camp was in a bad way with a cholera epidemic. Rations arrived by motor launch and had to be transported which means carried to them. I always volunteered for the job. The path a mere track through the jungle was slippery with a thin layer of mud and rose steeply on our side of the summit of the mountain. At that point it rose steeply for thirty or forty feet where a ladder had been built and fell away on the other side, over rocks and through deep bogey mud a foot deep. A most difficult ascent and descent unhampered and this was done with a 140 pound bag of rice.' [30]

27 Lt. Bob Learmonth's Dairy loaned to the author by Dr. G. Paul
28 Ibid
29 Ibid
30 Ibid

It appears from Lt. 'Bob' Learmonth's diary that following the completion of the Compressor Cutting, the work continued. The railway line had been laid, however, there was only the barest of room for the trains to pass through the cutting without touching the rock face.

> '*The main job for the next few weeks was to widen and roughly level off the sides which at that time overhung in places and falls of rock were both numerous and dangerous. The pneumatic drills were at work on the face above us. Charges were blown several times during the morning. A limited amount of rock and debris was thus thrown onto the line and this would rapidly be cleared if a train arrived. The job had its compensations. While a train was passing through the party had a short rest and a smoke.*' [31]

The remainder of the men from H5 and H6 Groups who were not required at Konkoita were ordered to move back to the Tonchan Spring Camp on 28th August 1943 where they remained until 20th September. As the construction of the rail link drew to a close these men, as with the all the survivors of 'H' Force, began to move south to either the 'F' and 'H' Force Hospital or 'Fit Camp' at Kanchanaburi.

'H' Force No. 1 Sub-Section

Konkoita Camp August – November 1943

On 26th August 1943, fourteen officers and seven other ranks from H6 Group departed Hintok River Camp for Konkoita. This group was part of 400 prisoners including eighty-three Australians from 'H' Force designated No. 1 Sub-Section 'H' Force under the command of a British Officer, Lt-Col T. H. Newey, who had been in command of H5 Group. Hintok Siding, which is located between the Three Tier Bridge and the Compressor Cutting, was where this sub-section boarded a train that would take them north into 'F' Force country. Arriving at Takanoon the men detrained and started out on a march that would take them three days to complete.

On arrival the 400 men were split into two groups with the officers going to Lower Konkoita and the other ranks to the Upper Konkoita–Lower Teimonta area. The overland trek for the officers would take them along jungle tracks via Tamuron Part, Krian Krai and finally onto one of the Konkoita sub-Camps located at Lower Konkoita near Kurikonta. The Officer's Camp was sited on undulating ground about 100 yards from the River Kwae Noi on a promontory in between two bends in the river. According to Lt. 'Bob' Learmonth's diary this was a Japanese staging camp for their invasion of Burma. Immediately on arrival, a start was made to clear the jungle and pitch the tents. Work on the railway, which had fallen behind in this section, commenced about three days after arrival at Konkoita and continued up until November. Four British died at this camp, the cause of which has been put down to the following: The difficult march to get to this camp, the heavy rain, leaking tents, long working hours, seven days a week, and the fact that they worked in mixed gangs with Tamils and Chinese. It is to be remembered the 'speedo' was still active and that the two ends of the rail link would not be joined until 17th October 1943. Lt. Don Lee explains:

---

[31]   Ibid

'My particular party worked on a bridge about a quarter of a mile from the camp gate.
The bridges, as usual on the railway, had no plates or bolts; everything was
joggled or morticed.' [32]

As the work came to an end this 'H' Force Sub-Section moved south by train to Kanchanaburi. The sick were evacuated to the Kanchanaburi 'F' and 'H' Force Hospital Camp and the remainder to the 'Fit Camp'. So ended the ordeal for the officers of 'H' Force some of whom had never been subjected to manual labour.

The 'F' Force Story

Together 'F' and 'H' Forces made up a combined British, Australian and Dutch labour force of 10,270 Prisoners of War. The difference between these two forces and previous forces which had departed Singapore to work on the Burma–Thailand rail link, was thus. Where as previous forces had been amalgamated into the Burma or Thailand Railway Administrations, 'F' and 'H' Forces remained under the control of the Singapore Administration, and at the end of the their usefulness, were returned to Singapore.

From the outset the Japanese had totally misrepresented to the prisoners their reasons for wanting to form 'F' Force. They stated that the reason for wanting to move such a large force away from the Changi Cantonment was because the food situation on Singapore Island was deteriorating. When the Japanese were informed that 7,000 fit men could not be mustered, they lowered their selection criteria and granted permission for up to 30% light sick to be included. The reason they gave being that 'F' Force was not to be a working party and that there would be no manual labour or marching except from the train to the nearby camp. Transport, they stated would be provided for the sick, and canteens would also be set up for the purchase of extra food. Gramophones, blankets, clothing and mosquito nets, it was promised, would be issued on arrival at the new camp, however, it was stipulated that all tools and cooking gear were to be taken. The abyss this force fell into was caused by British and Australian naivety in believing the Japanese rhetoric. This episode is commented on by Capt. Reg Newton:

> *'This was one of the biggest "come in sucker" incidents of the A.I.F. P.O.W. period*
> *during the 1939-1945 war and although many minor incidents had been experienced*
> *of a similar nature by work parties who had been out in the cold, cold world, from the*
> *very early days of incarceration, there was not anybody senior enough left in Changi*
> *with a knowledge of Japanese habits and promises to issue a strong warning.'* [33]

The prisoners were led to believe they were leaving Singapore for a land of 'milk and honey', a place where the sick would have a better chance of recovery with good food, in a pleasant hilly place with good recreational facilities. They were lured even further into this fairytale by being permitted to take bandsmen's instruments and various other personal items that would otherwise have been left at Singapore had the truth been known. At this stage it is presumed that no one expected, or suspected that they would return to Singapore.

In overall command of 'F' Force was Lt-Col S. Harris, the commander of the British 18th Division area at Changi. Lt-Col G. Kappe from Headquarters 8th Division Signals would command the Australians. The Australian 27th Brigade had been kept relatively intact since the

---

32   Don Lee, *A Yarn or Two* Access Press Sydney 1994, p.82
33   R. W. Newton, *The Grim Glory of the 2/19th Battalion A.I.F.* Sydney 1975, p.646

Fall of Singapore and so this brigade group formed the basis for the organisation for 'F' Force. The Australian component was split into five proportionate sized battalions. As well as the 27th Brigade Headquarters and medical component for the force were the three 27th Infantry Brigade commanding officers being Major C. Tracey 2/26th Battalion, Col. S. Pond 2/29th Battalion and Major N. Johnson 2/30th Battalion.

The A.I.F. contribution to 'F' Force was 3,666 men, with the British making up the difference, bringing this force to its total of 7,000 men. From British ranks there were to be 2,037 deaths and Australia's 1,060, making a total of 3,097 men. Expressed in percentages, this equates to a death rate of 44.75%. Although there were many more British deaths than Australian (61% as opposed to 28%), these percentages really are irrelevant because what is important is the fact that the Japanese in their quest for 'speedo' managed to decimate almost half of a 7,000 strong Prisoner of War workforce in seven months. If a comparison were to be drawn between 'F' Force in Thailand and 'B' and 'E' Forces in Borneo, it would be seen that these three forces have a similar history. Where as 'B' and 'E' Forces were at first treated reasonably well, this situation deteriorated to the point where they were deliberately starved and needlessly marched to Ranau from Sandakan. Those that were too sick to march or fell behind on the march were systematically massacred until the few that survived did so by escaping. 'F' Force on the other hand were ruthlessly marched north into Thailand, starved, denied the medicines they so desperately required; and those that could be coaxed or driven from their hospital beds were mercilessly worked to death.

'F' Force was organised to move north from Singapore in thirteen trains, the numbers of prisoners in each train dependant on the space allocated by the Japanese for stores and baggage. The first train loaded with Australians departed Singapore on the morning of Sunday 18th April 1943. This first train was closely followed by five more trainloads of Australians with the British on the remaining seven trains. Following the usual four to five day 'cattle class' train journey from Singapore, each of the thirteen trains deposited their human cargo at Non Pladuk, leaving thirteen columns of weakened, hungry and no doubt confused Prisoners of War wondering when they could expect to move to their new camp. The march was made to the nearby transit camp at Konma where a check parade took place and every prisoner was issued with a 'hat number' or in other words a Prisoner of War number. Initially it was thought that 'F' Force had not been issued with these numbers because they remained under the Singapore Administration. Evidence now suggests that 'F' Force was actually issued with two sets of numbers, one for Singapore and one for Thailand.

No transport had been provided for the cartage of the heavier stores and equipment from the station to the transit camp, so all this excess baggage had to be manhandled by men who were already physically drained or sick following their train journey from Singapore. It was at Konma that the men were advised that a 300 kilometre route march lay ahead of them. This must have been heartbreaking news for some men who were forced to leave behind the extra clothing and possessions that they were convinced they should bring with them. A great deal of this personal kit that could not be carried or traded with the local Thais was immediately transformed into ballast and discarded. For the officers it was a different story. Also under advice from the Japanese, the officers had brought everything they owned with them including all their personal effects. As a consequence of this misinformation, the majority of this kit was left behind unguarded in the open, under a tarpaulin where it was to be pilfered by the guards and the local Thais.

This was not the first time pilfering had affected the lives of the men in 'F' Force and indeed many Australian soldiers on Singapore. After the cessation of hostilities it was later discovered that many of the men's kit bags had been ransacked. Whether the culprits were Australian, British, Indian, Japanese or Chinese has never been stated, however, this must be one of the lesser known incidents that occurred on Singapore.

Captain Avon Smith-Ryan made comment in his diary on this distasteful episode: [34]

> *'The kit bag situation was bad. What the Imperial Japanese Army did not take, apparently our army did. I had my good brown cloth jacket brought out to me at Adam Park and that is the only item I received from two kit bags, a leather grip and a big trunk.'*

Earlier promises by the Japanese that the men were moving to a 'Health Camp' did not look promising. After the initial shock that a long march lay ahead of them some men were actually looking forward to this new adventure. With bellies full following a trading frenzy with the local Thai vendors most believed they were ready to start out on their trek north. But once the first stage of the march had begun it did not take very long for the effects of tiredness, aches, pains and sore feet to set in after the train journey from Singapore. Fourteen months earlier this forced march would not have bothered any of these men, but having been forced to survive on a staple diet of rice to which the men were unaccustomed their health had deteriorated.

The following narrative is an example of one column of Australians who marched from the Konma transit camp the 290 kilometres to the 'F' Force No.1 railway construction camp at Shimo Sonkurai. Actual dates are not important as generally the march took between seventeen and twenty days, depending upon the rest periods spent at staging camps and generally was the same throughout. The only difference as far as the Australians are concerned was the final destination. One of the first problems encountered even before the first Australian columns set out, was to split the medical stores into six or more separate panniers. The majority of the marching was carried out during the hours of darkness making movement hazardous, and the chance to gain complete rest during daylight hours virtually impossible.

The first two stages of the march were over the sealed road between Konma and Kanchanaburi. From hereon the marching was conducted initially over a gravel road, then over an unsealed jungle track. Although rarely stated this continuous stream of men did not arrive at Kanchanaburi, cross the bridge at Tamarkan and continue their march north to Tarsau along the projected route of the rail link. In fact the route taken was along the track which the rail link from Kanchanaburi should have taken. This was past Chonkai to the river crossing at Tardan then northwest to the village of Wanyai and then Tarsau. This was certainly not the first time this back road had been used as 'H' Force Group H3 had taken this same route, as did the Australian Battalions within 'D' Force.

The March North

The first day's march out of Konma is stated as being a distance of 24 kilometres to a village on the railway line called Taruanoi, also known as Tarawa. This camp consisted of an open area about 450 yards from the Maekhlaung River.

> *'One of the first sights we got used to in Thailand were vultures sitting in all the trees right through the town. Whether this was an omen or not I don't know.'* [35]

When the time came to move off on the second night's march, being the next 24 kilometres to Kanchanaburi, the men's bellies had again been reinforced with food, thanks to the local Thai vendors. Kanchanaburi was reached the next morning and by this time the numbers of sick were beginning to increase. The camp at Chiriku known as the Desert Camp, so named because of the water supply situation and its location which was about a mile from the Kanchanaburi Hospital, and about the same distance from the river. The only shelter available at this staging

---

34 PR00592 Item 10 Capt. Avon Smith-Ryan's Diary, Australian War Memorial Canberra
35 Narrative loaned to the author concerning 'F' Force written by Wally Holding a member of 2/4th Machine Gun Battalion

area was one open sided hut and the only water available in the vicinity of the camp was a dirty brown variety which could be purchased from a local Thai's well at a cost of 5 cents per bucket. This brown liquid then had to be boiled to ensure it was safe to drink. A planned day of rest did not eventuate as it was announced that the men had to assemble at Kanchanaburi Hospital for a 'glass rodding'. This can only be described as an unceremonious jab up the back passage with a glass rod to test for amoebic dysentery and pestis (plague). (It was common practice amongst the Japanese that when a glass rod was not readily available a length of bamboo was substituted.) As well as being subjected to this indignity a blood test for malaria and smallpox vaccinations were also administered. On returning to the campsite a meal was hastily prepared and eaten, gear packed and then it was back on the road again.

For this next section of the night march, two water filling points had been arranged by the Japanese so as water bottles could be refilled with boiling water. As the sealed road passed under them, the way ahead was now over an unsealed road that could be best described as a track. The weaker men and sick in the column now began to lose ground and had to be assisted or carried on stretchers which in turn placed extra burdens upon the stronger and fitter men. The next staging camp at Wampoh or Tarkujong (Temple Camp) was reached the next morning. It was situated on a flat area of ground amidst clumps of bamboo near the Maekhlaung River close to an old Siamese temple. There were no other buildings nearby that might have offered any form of shelter. Itinerant Thai vendors that had been shadowing the men set up stalls, however, as the distance from Non Pladuk increased so did the vendor's prices, whilst the quality of the food decreased.

The men set off again that night on a 26 kilometre march along the track that was beginning to ascend with each kilometre covered. Already some of the personal gear that the men had brought with them from Singapore was being discarded into the jungle on either side of the road. As well as the Thai food vendors, there were two stages where oxen and carts were hired from Thais and these were used to transport the heavier loads and some of the sick, relieving some of the strain on the stronger men over the earlier stages of the route march. By daylight the column had arrived at the Bridge Camp (Bamboo Crossing Camp) at Tardan. Once again this camp was just a cleared area of ground with little shade except for that provided by some bamboo. Expecting another night march, the men were informed that a day of rest would be granted.

The next stage was another 24 kilometre march which would bring the column from the back blocks of the Maekhlaung River cross country to Wanyai, closer to the River Kwae Noi and Tarsau, where men from 'D' Force were presently working. The outskirts of Tarsau were reached at dawn and as the men approached this camp, work parties from Tarsau were seen heading out to work. After some delays an area was allocated to set up camp and a few tents were issued. Permission was sought from the Japanese to leave the sick at Tarsau, but despite some initial banter and some rough treatment only some of the more seriously ill were granted permission to remain. The harsh reality was that these men were still under the Singapore Administration's jurisdiction and were not the Thailand Administration's problem. This situation would not improve during the course of 'F' Force's stay in Thailand and was fair warning of the problems that were still to be encountered, thus highlighting the petty jealousies that would be encountered between the Japanese Burma–Thailand–Singapore Administrations, not to mention at an even lower level of collaboration between the camp guards and the railway construction engineers. In the end, as was always the case, it would be the Prisoners of War on 'F' Force who would suffer.

A night march out of Tarsau now followed the main service road for the rail link north. Long stretches of this road were corduroyed, which made marching at night all the more difficult and as a result the incidence of sprains and even broken limbs caused by falls increased over these sections. Each one of the rest camps from here now bore the same name as a railway construction camp, however, there was little to be seen that would suggest this because at this stage the rail link was still a long way from completion. As the column set out north again an already rough road was only made worse with the onset of the rains. Daily thunderstorms started on 30th April and the monsoon broke on 17th May, just after the Australian columns reached their final destinations at Upper Konkoita–Lower Teimonta and Shimo Sonkurai.

From Tarsau north on all the stages the Japanese had set up rest points roughly mid-way where water was available and a one hour rest break was permitted. This break would give the stragglers time to catch up with the main column, however, not necessarily the additional time required to allow them sufficient time to rest when they did catch up.

The plan was then modified with the stragglers now being positioned at the head of the column in the hope that they would set the pace rather than keep up with it.

This was tiger country in more ways than one and at each stop the Japanese lit big bamboo fires. There was also a very real danger of stragglers being attacked by Thai bandits if they fell too far behind the main column. There were several instances reported where Prisoners of War and their guards fought off gangs of bandits. One Thai received a hearty belt across the face with a full water bottle from an Australian Prisoner of War who was obviously in no mood for fun and games. It is believed that as many as twenty prisoners who went missing from the thirteen columns could have met their Maker at the hands of these bandits who were armed with edged weapons.

The next stopover was at Kanu III where a rest period was made a little easier by the shade afforded by the thick clumps of bamboo. The march this time was shorter and with all the columns of 'F' Force was made during daylight hours. This distance was a relatively short one which saw the men arrive at Kinsaiyok. It was here where that a full night's rest was allowed. The next camps were Rin Tin, Hindato and Brankassi. Hindato was christened the Stockyard Camp because the prisoners were herded into what might be looked upon as a rough stockyard. Brankassi was named the Hitler Camp because the resident guards at this camp took charge of the columns and were obsessed with discipline; handing out punishment for the slightest misdemeanour.

A rest day at Brankassi now brought the column to the end of a fourteen day march since first setting out from Non Pladuk. The rains were now becoming more frequent which made movement in darkness over the roads and bridges all the more treacherous. The next staging camp was Takanoon (Whale Meat Camp) that was described as being the best jungle camp to date. The bivouac area was a cleared site on a hill which to everyone's surprise had not been fouled by coolies. Plenty of shade and a fast flowing stream nearby gave all a good opportunity to catch up on much needed rest and a chance to wash and rejuvenate the mind and body.

Having set out late in the afternoon the next camp Tamuron Part (Fresh Pork Camp) was not reached until first light the following day. The men were then told that the next stage was only a short one, but by now they had become expert at judging distance and became very disgruntled when they discovered that the distance was actually about 18 kilometres to the next camp at Konkoita. There were to be several railway construction camps at Konkoita (Brigade or Cholera Camp) and this was the first camp the column had arrived at that could be called a proper camp as opposed to a staging area. With the exception of the first two columns that halted at Konkoita, the expected day's rest was cancelled for the third column which was forced to continue through to the next camp at Shimo Nikhe, called the Assembly Camp. After the first 3 kilometres, steep ascents and descents came one after the other. This final stage to Shimo Sonkurai No. 1 camp for most of the Australians would end a route march of approximately 290.00 kilometres.

From the first train the first column to embark on the march from Non Pladuk, only about half of the men made the full distance from start to finish. Some of the weaker men and sick had been left behind at the staging camps to act as cooks, or otherwise were left to recover and continue the march with a later column marching north. A note here is that as the prospect of the numbers of sick men increasing, the guards believed the only solution was to limit the numbers to be left behind from each column and force the remainder at bayonet point, if necessary. All the same there must have been an almost continuous cycle of men falling out of the march, recovering, moving on and being replaced by other less fit men who themselves would continue the march with a later column. This situation helps to highlight the difficulty in keeping track of prisoners under these circumstances.

It was at Konkoita that the commander of A.I.F. troops, Lt-Col Kappe, contacted Lt-Col Harris, the 'F' Force commander. Lt-Col Harris and his staff had travelled up from Singapore in train No. 7, the first train to transport the first of the British columns. Lt-Col Harris then travelled north by motor transport from Tarsau to Shimo Nikhe ahead of the thirteen columns with the Japanese force commander, Col. Banno. It was at Konkoita where there had been an outbreak of cholera amongst the coolie labour force. As each of the thirteen columns of Australians and British staged through Konkoita, cholera was contracted by the prisoners and very effectively spread throughout the construction camps. Colonel Banno was approached directly and asked that Konkoita be avoided at all costs, but although sympathetic he said that there was nothing he could do. Ultimately there was also nothing that could be done for the 750 men on 'F' Force who later died as a result of this horrid disease.

The arrival on site of the first and subsequent columns had caught the Japanese unprepared. This after all was the 'speedo' and in an effort to move 'F' Force up north and into the construction camps as fast as possible before the monsoon rains began, Japanese organisation had crumbled under the pressure. By the end of May 1943 the men who had lasted the distance were distributed amongst several different camps. In most cases these camps consisted of the native style atap huts without the atap being provided for the roofs. These atapless huts would remain in this state for some weeks and this only resulted in more needless deaths from pneumonia. At all the camps the roofing was generally completed within the first two weeks of arrival but the atap palm leaf was used so sparingly that all the huts leaked.

By the end of June only 700 men from what was by now a workforce of only 5,000 prisoners were at work on a daily basis and out these 700 men about half were fit enough for heavy labouring jobs. From the original 7,000 men who had left Singapore, it is estimated that about 1,350 had failed to complete the march to their appointed camps either having fallen sick, died or been ambushed by Thai bandits. Additionally Col. Pond's Battalion, comprising 700 men, was commandeered at Konkoita by Lt. Maruyama to work for the Japanese Railway Engineers. By this time the main land artery, the road from Non Pladuk had been cut by the monsoon rains. These rains began in earnest on 17th May and would last until 2nd October 1943, making the road impassable and effectively closing the back door on 'F' Force. After 20th May no wheeled vehicles could get into the southern area camps where the bulk of the Australians in 'F' Force were concentrated.

Although the Kwae Noi River was being used by barges to bring in merchandise as far north as Nikhe Village for the Thai shopkeepers and by the Japanese to bring in supplies and war materiel destined for Burma, the medical supplies for 'F' Force were still at Non Pladuk despite repeated requests to Col. Banno to have these barged north. It appears that supply could not keep up with demand as the ration scale at one of the 'F' Force camps was drastically reduced in June. This situation was not helped by the fact that from the end of July even the roads between the camps were impassable and the problem was exacerbated by several of the bridges being in urgent need of repair. There also appears to be a disparity between the quality and the supply of food between the 'F' Force camps. Where as one camp may have received regular supplies of canteen goods from the local Thai merchants, another may have received no external supplies and even poorer camp supplies. It appears that with 'F' Force, each camp's situation was localised and dependent upon the whims of the most senior Japanese.

As the numbers of sick increased, it became necessary at each camp to reinforce the medical personnel with combatant personnel to care for the sick. This was achieved by using convalescent patients as medical orderlies. Shimo Nikhe, an Australian camp, pioneered the use of combatant officers as Wardmasters and for hospital register work, called Wardmustering, thereby relieving the medical personnel of these duties so as they could get on with the job of caring for the sick. This practice soon spread to other camps due to the scheme's success. The negative side of this arrangement was that the Japanese were monitoring the numbers of combatant officers working in the hospital as opposed to the numbers of other ranks working on camp duties such as the cookhouse, sanitation, burial party and wood collecting, plus any other chores as required by the camp guards. In effect the officers were actually working to save their own men, however, the Japanese didn't see it that way. There was to be an agreed number of prisoners working in camp and so by having officers working in the hospital, this exceeded this agreed number. The Japanese therefore saw this as a way of demanding more other ranks for railway construction work. Because there was a certain amount of aptitude and proficiency involved with camp duties, it was found to be impossible to have a rota system whereby men were alternated between camp duties and construction work. As sick men came into hospital they were replaced on the line with convalescents who were then sent out to perform construction work.

'F' Force Camps

'To visualise conditions it is necessary to remember that everything described took place in incessant rain, day and night.' [36]

Later when the evacuation of the sick to Tanbaya in Burma took place, several camps were closed down and the Prisoners of War were concentrated at the two main camps at Kami Sonkurai and Sonkurai with the New Headquarters Camp being established at Nikhe. Once Changaraya, Nikhe and Shimo Nikhe were about to close the order came through on 2nd August 1943 to regroup at Sonkurai and Kami Sonkurai so as each camp could supply the same number of prisoners for the Japanese Engineers on the line. Patients who were too sick to be evacuated to the newly established Tanbaya Hospital Camp in Burma and were expected to die, were ordered to remain with their carers until told otherwise. The following is a list of the construction camps where 'F' Force and a sub-section from 'H' Force worked over a distance of 82.80 kilometres.

Changaraya No. 5 Camp	300.95km
Kami Sonkurai No. 3 Camp	298.00km
Sonkurai No. 2 Camp	294.02km
Shimo Sonkurai No. 1 Camp	290.00km
Nikhe-Nikhe Camp (future site of the Wood Camp)	283.92km
Nikhe-New Headquarters Camp	281.80km
Shimo Nikhe-Old Headquarters Camp	276.00km
Teimonta Camp	273.06km
Upper Konkoita-Lower Teimonta	262.87km
Konkoita No. 4 Camp	262.53km
Konkoita sub-Camps	257.70km
Kurikonta	256.92km

---

36   AWM54 File 554/7/2 Part 1 History of 'F' Force. Report by Lt-Col S. W. Harris, OBE, R.A., Australian War Memorial Canberra

Krian Krai	250.13km
Tamuron Part	244.19km
Tamajao (future site of a wood camp)	238.92km
Namajon	229.14km
Takanoon	218.15km

Tanbaya 53km Hospital Camp Burma

This camp was 53.52 kilometres from Thanbyuzayat, or if travelling from Non Pladuk at the 361.60km point on the rail link. Lt-Col Harris had pointed out the fact to Col. Banno that there was no organisation for an 'F' Force Base Hospital in existence and suggested that Tarsau or Banpong might be suitable for this purpose. This suggestion was met with an immediate point blank refusal. Colonel Banno would not allow sick prisoners to be evacuated south whilst 'F' Force was in the grip of a cholera epidemic, stating that the road was impassable and would remain so even after the monsoon. If Col. Banno had taken the time to listen to common sense, then he may have pondered for a moment on the sense of staging columns through Konkoita, a known hot area for cholera and would have isolated and controlled the spread of this disease in the first place. Orders were eventually issued for the evacuation of 1,700 patients and medical personnel to move further north to Tanbaya by road and rail. The actual number of sick that were moved to Tanbaya was over 1,900, mainly as a result of the efforts of the Japanese Engineers at Sonkurai No. 2 Camp. Major Bruce Hunt A.A.M.C. was to be the Officer Commanding Tanbaya Hospital. Major Hunt was the second most senior Medical Officer of the Australian contingent of 'F' Force. When the cholera epidemic broke out, the Senior Medical Officer was detained further south and so Major Hunt was appointed to take up the post for the five main 'F' Force camps being camp No.1 Camp Shimo Sonkurai, No. 2 Camp Sonkurai, No. 3 Camp Kami Sonkurai, No. 4 Camp Konkoita and No. 5 Camp Changaraya.[37]

> *'He is an officer with a most resolute personality and possesses outstanding organising ability. Physically powerful and capable of remarkable endurance, he heavily overtaxed these two qualities in the interests of the sick of the Force during the seven months in Thailand and Burma.'*

The move to Tanbaya Hospital Camp was to be through three staging camps Changaraya, Kyondaw and Ronshii. The Japanese gave assurances that all preparations would be in place to receive the advance party which departed on 30th July 1943. As soon as the advance party left for Tanbaya, an order was passed down the line to close Changaraya No. 5 Camp, Nikhe, the Old Headquarters Camp and Shimo Sonkurai No. 1 Camp. The selection as to which of the sick prisoners should be sent to Tanbaya posed a problem. If men in too delicate a condition were sent, they might not survive the journey and in fact a total of forty-three patients out of the 1,900 died in transit. On the other hand if they remained at any one of the 'F' Force construction camps, there was a danger that their health might deteriorate beyond the point of no return. The evacuation of the sick to Tanbaya nevertheless commenced and continued through August and into September 1943. The selection criteria for transfer to Tanbaya as dictated by the Japanese was to be for chronic patients only, who in the considered opinion of the medical officers would be unfit for work for a period of at least two months. Men suffering from infectious diseases and those in a dangerously ill condition who might not complete the journey to Tanbaya were not to be included.

---

[37]   AWM54 File 554/7/2 Part 2 Summary of Medical Report Britsh and Australian POW, April 1943–April 1944 by Lt-Col Huston, R.A.M.C. Australian War Memorial Canberra

The Tanbaya Hospital Camp was a hutted camp. Patients were segregated into the various wards according to the complaint or disease. The Wardmustering system which was initiated at Shimo Sonkurai was also incorporated. From approximately 900 patients that departed Tanbaya for Kanchanaburi on 24th November 1943 only two men failed to complete the five to six day journey. A medical staff of 102 personnel had been left behind to care for 218 patients. Major Hunt had predicted that ninety to one hundred of these men would die and he was not far out, as the actual number was ninety-six.

About mid-December it was realised that the water supply at Tanbaya was not going to last much longer. On 31st January 1944, five officers and 109 other ranks moved out for Kanchanaburi. On the following day, 1st February, the remaining five officers and ninety-five other ranks also moved out. There were 763 mounds left in the ground at the Tanbaya Hospital Camp cemetery.

Wardmustering at Tanbaya

Major Hunt wrote on Wardmustering as follows:

Details of medical administration were as follows: Patients were segregated as far as was possible according to their complaints; this facilitated treatment and prevented much cross-infection. Thus one ward was devoted solely to dysentery, one ward to pure dysentery and ulcers combined with dysentery, two wards to ulcers and three wards to general medical diseases, chiefly malaria and beri-beri. Each ward contained in the earlier stages approximately 190 patients and was under the control of a Wardmaster. The Wardmaster was a combatant officer, usually of company commander status or above; he had as his assistants an Assistant Wardmaster, usually a subaltern, two NCO's who acted as CSM and CQMS respectively and a clerk. The Wardmaster was responsible for nominal rolls, for discipline, for hut cleanliness, for messing, for canteen supplies and in general for everything which took place in the ward except such matters as involved technical medical knowledge or skill. He had in addition, through the medical officers or Senior Nursing NCO supervisory control over the activities of the nursing orderlies in regard to their non-technical functions. This system of Wardmuster control, first developed at Shimo Sonkurai Camp and further extended in Burma, proved of the greatest possible assistance in running the hospital. Discipline and general ward efficiency were very much better than they usually were under NCO control; in particular messing functioned much more efficiently and with much less complaint than is usually the case. I was particularly fortunate in having a very able body of Wardmasters; they worked, ate and slept in their wards and were completely devoted to their duties and to the interests of their patients. I should like here to express formally my appreciation of their valuable services, Wardmasters were (in numerical order of their wards) Lieut I. Perry [2/1 Heavy Bty A.I.F.], Capt R. Walker [2/26 Bn A.I.F.]; Major R. Hodgkinson [R.A.S.C.], Major W. Auld [R.O.A.C.)]; Capt B.Berry [2/10 Fd Regt A.I.F.] Major D Price [R.C.O.S.]; Capt G. W.Gwynne [2/4 MG Bn A.I.F.] and LT-Col Ferguson [18 Div HQ]. [38]

---

38 AWM54 File 554/7/2 Part 1Report by Major Bruce Hunt A.A.M.C. Formerly commander Tanbaya Hospital Camp Burma, Australian War Memorial Canberra

Changaraya Camp No. 5

This camp was located one kilometre south of the Burma–Thailand border at the 300.95km point. The 27th May signalled the arrival of the first party of 383 British at this camp, followed later that day by a further 318, all under the command of Major Gairdner. It was discovered that part of the accommodation was occupied by 500 Burmese coolies with whom the cookhouse would have to be shared as would the cooking utensils, as none were provided for the British to use. After a protest was lodged they were issued with their own cooking utensils and permitted to build another cookhouse for their own use. On the second night in camp, two cases of cholera were reported and so a cholera isolation hut was set up, however, within a week cholera had taken a firm grip of the camp.

> '*The general situation of the camp when we arrived was nothing short of unbelievable filth. The Burmese had thrown all their unwanted rice and other food all over the camp and particularly near their own huts. Incidentally, there were parties of Burmese in every hut in our area, including those occupied by my men, and had 'shat' indiscriminately everywhere. The flies were a menace, remains of slaughtered animals and skins were in the undergrowth all around the cookhouse in every degree of decomposition.*' [39]

When Changaraya Camp was shut down, 310 men from this camp moved south to join the Australians who were also moving into Kami Sonkurai Camp. The British at this camp had lost one third of their men as a result of the cholera epidemic.

Kami (Upper) Sonkurai No. 3 Camp

This camp was first occupied by a party of 393 Australians on 25th May 1943 under the command of Capt. G. Allan A.A.S.C. Located at the 298.00km point on the rail link the accommodation at this camp was similar to that at Shimo Sonkurai Camp. There were two rows of atap huts, although these were not quite in the same layout. The camp was located at the base of three steep hills. These formed a swampy low lying valley into which water ran into the camp from all sides and turned it into a quagmire when it rained. The rail link, road and a river ran parallel to the camp, the river being about 200 yards from the road. Only a portion of the huts had been roofed with atap palm leaves.

By order of the Japanese Engineers the water supply had to be drawn from a creek on the north side of the camp near a compound where the cholera infected coolies had been segregated. Within a day of arriving at this camp, with the exception of some essential personnel and thirty-five sick, the men were put to work on the rail link. By the end of the first week the sick had risen to 160 of which some were cases of cholera. A request was made to set up a cholera isolation hut, but it was not until after a visit on 5th June by Major Bruce Hunt from Shimo Sonkurai that approval was given to set up a small hut on the opposite side of the road away from the main camp.

On 8th June Capt. R. Swartz of the 2/26th Battalion was sent from Shimo Sonkurai Camp by Major Johnson to take over command of Kami Sonkurai Camp from Capt. Allan who had fallen ill. This change of command was the result of a visit by Major Bruce Hunt, who reported the prevalence of cholera up and down the line as well as the poor state of health of Capt. Allan. By now the number of sick had soared to 216 and seven men had died from the eleven who had been diagnosed with having cholera. Taking into account the sick,

---

[39] AWM54 File 554/7/2 Part 1 paragraph 14, Report by Major Gairdner British Army, Australian War Memorial Canberra

essential camp personnel and medical personnel, the average daily figure for men for construction work on the rail link during June and July never rose above ninety.

Captain Swartz engaged in some camp reorganisation which included the setting up of a hospital at the end of one of the huts for the non-cholera patients. The only medical stores on site were those that had been brought up with the column from Non Pladuk. By the middle of June the cholera epidemic at Kami Sonkurai had been beaten but not before fifteen deaths from thirty-five diagnosed cases. After repeated requests some medical supplies were obtained through the Japanese at the end of July. In addition, also by request, mosquito nets and extra blankets were supplied. Kami Sonkurai was to eventually become the best camp in the 'F' Force group. Food was better and more varied, no reduction in rations was made for the sick, the Japanese Engineers were less demanding, and working hours were fewer, the only exception being that there were no rest days. Also on the negative side there were no outside canteen supplies available to promote the rapid recovery of the sick, but this was supplemented by collecting edible jungle roots and shoots as well as an edible type of spinach.

> *'We had a lot of trouble with the trucks not getting through, it was the top camp at Kami Sonkurai. When the trucks could not get through because of the condition of the road and bridges that had been washed away the stores could not get through. We then had to walk up via Three Pagodas Pass into Burma to collect rice at the 105k camp, for our camp. They picked the fittest of the blokes to go, usually about 20 of us and they were accompanied by a guard.'* [40]

From this point we will return to Shimo Sonkurai Camp where the first party is about to move to Kami Sonkurai Camp. This was due to the closure of the camp following the evacuation of the sick to Tanbaya. The march which took place on 28th July from Shimo Sonkurai to Kami Sonkurai took the seven officers and 295 other ranks five hours to complete. Out of these 302 men, 173 had to be admitted to hospital immediately on arrival, some of whom never left the hospital alive. In addition to the four parties of about 650 men from Shimo Sonkurai, there were also approximately 310 British from Changaraya and 360 from Nikhe. By 8th August 1943 this camp totalled 1,690 men of whom 670 were British and 1,020 were Australians. Generally the British from Changaraya were in a poorer state of health than the Australians. During the cholera epidemic they had lost 200 of their number from their original 701 men.

As British and Australians poured into this camp they were again greeted by the sight of roofless atap huts, and less than adequate latrines. Only a few Burmese had been employed on roofing the huts with the result that demand had exceeded supply, meaning that some men were forced to sleep out in the open. Some of the sick were forced to sleep in huts in which the floors were collapsing. The latrine had broken its banks and effluent was running through the camp and under the floor of the huts used as the hospital.

The order came down the chain of command that no Englishmen were to work in the cookhouse or on camp duties. As there were only about seventy fit men amongst the British, this order placed a heavy burden upon the Australians who, as there was no other option, were substituted for British until they were fit enough to resume construction work. This situation resulted in the increased death rate of Australian Prisoners of War during September and October 1943. Nevertheless, the Japanese seemed determined to undermine the British by bringing them to their knees. This predicament was not made any easier by the enforced segregation of British and Australians in hospital, meaning duplication of wards and twice as much work for the medical staff.

---

[40] Narative loaned to the author concerning 'F' Force written by Wally Holding, a member of the 2/4th Machine Gun Battalion

It would be heartening to think that the treatment of both British and Australian Prisoners of War improved but alas some pitiful stories emerged from this camp of men almost crawling back into camp in pouring rain at the end of a days' work.

On 10th August 1943 cholera struck at Kami Sonkurai when a man who had collapsed on the job and had been returned to camp was diagnosed with this disease. By September nearly fifty men including ten Australians had died from cholera.

Work at this stage of construction began with a 3 mile march to the job site before being set to work on a deep cutting, bridge building and felling trees. By the beginning of September 1943 it had been hoped that the railway construction work in this section would have been completed, but despite the fact that 3,000 Burmese coolies were also working in this area the work continued. The closeness to the completion of the rail link meant that the men at Kami Sonkurai for the first two and a half weeks of September experienced their worst period at this camp, which was not made any easier by the rain which continued through the whole of the month. It was stated by the Japanese that the rail link must pass through Kami Sonkurai by 15th September 1943. Yet it wasn't until 16th September that this section of rail link was even ready for the rail laying gangs.

This particular section of the rail was being laid by Williams No. 1 Mobile Force who continued down from Burma into Thailand as far south as Nikhe. Williams Force was setting a cracking pace and laying 2 and a half kilometres of track per day. To achieve this meant work on earthworks and bridges had to be accelerated which meant that working hours also had to be extended.

Leslie Hall wrote:

'Of all the Forces on the Burma side of the death railway, not one suffered more than the No. 1 Mobile Force. This Force, which combined Anderson and Williams Forces, had to ballast, sleeper and lay the rails of the line. It was the fastest, hardest task on the whole project.

Trains loaded with sleepers, leading bogie and rails, would be shunted up to the end of the last rail laid. From then on it was work at a furious pace, ensured so by waddy wielding engineers and guards.

The men worked in pairs running ahead and laying sleepers, the empty bogie would be pulled off the rails to the side, then the rails had to be unloaded and laid, a pair at a time. Eighteen or twenty men, depending on availability, would, from both sides grasp a rail and carry it to the drop point on the loose-laid sleepers. Each rail would be pulled into position, fish-plated and bolted; holes would be drilled into the sleeper, either side of the joint, a dog-spike driven in, one in the middle and the other end of the rail laid. The bogie pulled off, then the next one shunted forward. That pattern continued until the whole train was unloaded.

Following the laying gang came the dog-spikers; they had to spike the rails to the sleepers, one to each side of the rail on the straight and two on each curve. The team of four workers; one armed with a steel bar that weighed about 25lb (to start, got heavier as the work proceeded at a pace) had to lever the sleeper hard against the rail as the augerman drilled the two holes, then came the hammermen, each with a 12lb (hammer) tool. They had to drive the dog-spikes home straight.

Occasionally, one, due to weariness, would miss-hit a spike, bend it and the hawk-eyed engineers or guards, always on the lookout for such a happening, would whip into an immediate fury and thrash the hammer-wielder unmercifully.' [41]

Throughout September the Japanese were blasting rock in a nearby quarry that was only 50 yards from one of the British hospital wards. Rocks were continually crashing in through the

---

[41]   Leslie Hall, *The Blue Haze* published by the author 1985, p.197

roofs of these wards and absolutely terrified the patients inside. One British prisoner received a broken arm and many others narrowly missed being killed by the falling debris. October was a better month as the pressure eased a little for now the rail link was finally completed. The repercussions of the previous two months, however, was reflected in the higher death rates, in particular amongst the Australians whose deaths had risen from 50% in September to 75% in October. Men who had fallen ill in August and September and who had bravely clung to life finally succumbed as a direct result of the unchanging food and medical situation in this camp. We saw this same situation occur with Major Alf Cough's 'D' Force V Battalion where men died not because they were at Hindaine and Kuii but as a result of the fact they had been at Hindaine and Kuii.

Sonkurai No. 2 Camp

This camp was located at the 294.02km point on the rail link. The British columns No.'s 7, 8 and 9 arrived here on 20th May 1943. The camp consisted of three huts being 150, 200 and 250 feet long. The guards, Prisoner of War officers and NCO's were quartered in the smallest hut and the other ranks were quartered in the other two roofless huts. This was a problem that took the Burmese coolies two weeks to resolve. The latrines and cookhouse were adequate, however, a day was spent cleaning the camp surrounds of foliage. On 22nd May the British columns No.'s 10 and 11 arrived bringing the camp's strength up to 1,600 men. Cholera broke out at this camp on 23rd May, probably because like all the previous columns to date they had staged through Konkoita. By the end of May sixty-three men had died of the disease. By the beginning of August as a result of sickness, starvation and the brutal treatment dealt out by the Japanese Engineers these British numbered less than 1,000 men. The task had been to construct a large bridge, known as the 600 Bridge, across the river adjacent to the camp. The river at this point was 60 yards wide and was crossed by the 600 Bridge, which not only carried the railway line but also the road. The bridge was finally completed on 20th August 1943.

> '*The country around the "600" bridge was wild and untamed. Half a mile above the "600" bridge was the confluence of five rivers. In a mighty line 500 yards long these rivers each roared over a ten feet high natural step gashed through the jungle-clad earth. From the seething, booming cauldron beneath the rivers, the water flowed away down two great rivers. With the wet season at its height enormous trees swirled and bobbed through the mad current like matchsticks.*' [42]

Five days after the 600 Bridge's completion, the first party left from Sonkurai for the Tanbaya Hospital Camp. The British who worked on this bridge included some very sick men who were unmercifully punched, kicked and beaten with bamboo sticks and wire whips. This was done not so much as a matter of discipline but as psychological tool to drive others to greater achievement beyond their physical strength.

On 4th August the camp began to fill with Australians. The first party of about 300 arrived from Shimo Sonkurai and they were joined by a second party on 7th August under Major Tracey with seven officers, 143 fit and 147 hospital patients. Also a mixed group of British and Australians joined this camp from Nikhe. On 24th September another 230 Australians marched in from Shimo Sonkurai. This party was from a group of 500 sick that were left at Shimo Sonkurai destined for Tanbaya in Burma. Only 277 of these men actually made it to Tanbaya and the remainder were sent to Sonkurai. Also on 7th November another 107 from Pond's Battalion who had moved to Nikhe when Teimonta Camp was closed joined Tracey's group at

---

42   Roy Whitecross, *Slaves of The Son of Heaven* Dymock's 1953, p.103

Sonkurai. On arrival Major Tracey was greeted by the situation in which the entire structure of camp administration had collapsed, perhaps accelerated by the higher than normal number of officers sick in hospital. A concerted effort was made to 'put things right' following the arrival of the Australians. Immediately new cookhouses were constructed, old latrines were filled in and new ones dug, food sterilisation points were established and a wood supply readied. The raising of morale throughout the camp, particularly with the British, was instantaneous.

Working conditions were no better at Sonkurai than at any of the other 'F' Force construction camps, the urgency at Sonkurai camp being the completion of the 600 Bridge. On 11th November 1943 road and railway construction work at Sonkurai ceased. The evacuation on 2nd November of 620 British and Australian prisoners to Tanbaya at least relieved some of the burden upon the administrative and medical personnel. With the evacuation of these sick, the co-operation established between the British and Australian administrative officers, could be described as the best it had been for several months. During August alone 268 Prisoners of War had died at Sonkurai. On 17th November ten days after Col. Pond's Party from Nikhe had arrived at Sonkurai, an advance party departed Sonkurai for Kanchanaburi. From hereon men would begin to leave, signalling the closure of this camp and yet another page of the Prisoners of War story and the Burma–Thailand rail link.

Shimo (Lower) Sonkurai No. 1 Camp

Located at the 290.00km point on the rail link, accommodation at this camp, the biggest of the three Sonkurai Camps, consisted of two rows of atap huts running parallel to the north-south road. Except for eight tents to cover the bamboo frame of the officer's quarters, no other overhead protection existed. The exposure of the roofless huts to the elements had weathered them to the extent that it would have been preferable if they had been demolished and rebuilt. The huts were about 200 feet long and were expected to house 2,500 men, but under protest and possibly the outbreak of cholera at Shimo Sonkurai this was later amended to 2,000 men. Latrines had been dug on the hillside above the level of the huts so that when it rained they flooded, and the effluent flowed down the hill into the camp. The only water supply, described as being meagre, was from a small stream between the main camp and the huts occupied by the Japanese Engineers. This stream crossed the road in two places sandwiching the huts of the main camp between its flow. The first group of 1,000 Australians in columns No. 3 and 4 (Party No. 1) under the command of Major Tracey, 2/26th Battalion, arrived on the morning of 15th May after twenty-one days on the road. The next day all fit men were sent out to work.

The 16th May saw the first case of cholera reported at Shimo Nikhe Headquarters Camp. The victim was an Australian Private who had come through Konkoita with Major Johnson, in No. 5 column. A cholera isolation hut was immediately set up at Shimo Nikhe and by the evening another three cases had surfaced. Despite representations to defer the movement forward of further columns to Shimo Sonkurai, this did not sway the decision of Col. Banno, the Japanese commander. Thus on the 17th May the second group of 820 men in columns No. 5 and 6 (Party No. 2), under the command of Major Johnson, marched into Shimo Sonkurai joining Major Tracey's columns No. 3 and 4 in (Party No. 1). Major Johnson, being the senior officer, now took over command of the camp from Major Tracey. It was then advised that one of the men who had just arrived with column No. 5 that morning had been diagnosed with a suspected case of cholera. A cholera isolation hut was set up and the matter was reported to the Japanese camp commander, Lt. Fukuda. Later that day two more possible cases of cholera were admitted to the isolation hut by Capt. Lloyd Cahill, the only Medical Officer in camp. Lt. Fukuda associated the introduction of cholera with the arrival of the No. 2 Party, not that this had anything to do with No.'s 1 and 2 Parties also staging through Konkoita from where the cholera epidemic had emanated.

The next morning Major Bruce Hunt, leading a medical team, arrived with Capt. Taylor, from the A.A.M.C. with seven Australian and eight British volunteer medical orderlies who had previously been inoculated against cholera. On the northern end of the camp was a bamboo covered hill and this was selected as the best location to set a cholera isolation hospital. This topographic feature was then to be known as 'Cholera Hill' and would be the place where the cholera patients were banished to serve out their purgatory. At the peak of the cholera epidemic this hospital on the hill housed 128 patients.

The hospital was commenced on 19th May and was constructed by slinging tent canvas over a bamboo framework. It rained whilst it was being built and leaked after it was finished. A delivery of another ten tents saw the majority of these go to 'Cholera Hill.' Colonel Banno learning of the cholera outbreak at Shimo Sonkurai, arrived on the scene and held a conference with Lt. Fukuda and Majors Hunt and Johnson. Colonel Banno more or less intimated from the outset that the responsibility and control of the spread of this disease at Shimo Sonkurai was the responsibility of the Senior Camp Officer and the Senior Medical Officer, in other words, Majors Johnson and Hunt. Major Johnson pointed out to Col. Banno the most unsatisfactory state of the camp and a very strong argument was presented for the supply of atap to properly roof the huts. He also requested that he be permitted to keep back enough men from the Japanese Engineers for new camp construction such as a cookhouse, latrines, water sterilisation points and the reinforcement of sections of huts where the floors had collapsed under the men's weight. It was also pointed out to Col. Banno that these men had not been properly vaccinated against cholera before they had left Singapore.

Major Hunt had brought with him enough serum to vaccinate 1,400 men. However on 20th May another 163 men marched into camp bringing the camps strength up to approximately 1,997 men. Surprisingly, within days seventy tents and atap roofing material was delivered into camp. After spending several miserable nights under the stars enough atap arrived to complete the huts. This delivery was most welcome and by 30th May all the huts had been roofed. This was possibly the first and last time anyone actually succeeded in getting the message through to Col. Banno and managed to raise a positive response from him. Most heartening was also the supply of cholera serum that also arrived with this unexpected delivery.

By this time the first man to be admitted to the isolation hospital had died of the disease. The method used to combat cholera at Shimo Sonkurai was an intravenous injection by syringe of a saline solution creek water and kitchen salt. This method was crude to say the least and admittedly not as technically advanced as the improvised still that was in operation at the Hintok Road Camp, but nevertheless it did contribute to the saving of some lives. The cholera epidemic at Shimo Sonkurai arrived in two waves. In the first wave of cholera that had originated from Konkoita, of the twenty cases five died up to 23rd May. The second wave which had originated from within the Shimo Sonkurai Camp from 24th–31st May was a little more serious. This time from 164 cases, fifty-one men died. From the 209 cases of cholera at Shimo Sonkurai, 101 died including some of the volunteer cholera medical orderlies. However, by 1st June camp hygiene had improved to the point where the real threat of a cholera epidemic had subsided.

Although it is true that cholera killed a total of 750 men from 'F' Force, by far the most deadly of the diseases was dysentery which was promoted by malnutrition and aided and abetted by beri-beri, malaria or both with a touch of tropical ulcer for good measure. Although cholera could suck the life out of a man's body there were other diseases that were just as prevalent. The following is a list of just some of the more common varieties; typhus, spinal meningitis, smallpox, diphtheria, jaundice, pneumonia, pleurisy, all types of malaria, amoebic and bacillary dysentery, cardiac beri-beri and tropical ulcers. As well as 'Cholera Hill' at Shimo Sonkurai there was if we can call it such, the 'normal hospital' which comprised six of the twelve huts. The first block of three huts housed the mild dysentery patients, one hut the severe dysentery patients, one for malaria and one for the hospital personnel.

Work at Shimo Sonkurai up to 24th May was on the rail link, but with the constant rain making the road virtually impassable, work was switched from railway construction work to road work, much to the displeasure of the Japanese Engineers. The work at Shimo Sonkurai for the next five to six weeks now consisted of repair and corduroying of the main north-south road. Also, new roads had to be built to allow access into the camp before the embankment work on the rail link could commence. Work on railway construction recommenced on 4th June 1943. Towards the end of July the closing of Shimo Sonkurai and move to Kami Sonkurai was to come with the evacuation of the sick to Tanbaya in Burma. On 26th July orders were issued to commence the move of 302 prisoners to the Kami Sonkurai Camp.

The move began on 28th July and comprised seven officers and 295 other ranks. With the exception of a very small minority, most of this party were made up of sick and patients from the convalescent depot. The road was in such a muddy state that the move had been delayed because so many sick needed to be carried on stretchers. As well as the stretcher cases, the men's personal gear, camp cooking equipment the likes of heavy cast iron rice boilers and cooking utensils, mosquito nets and blankets had to also be carried. On 1st August the remaining 500 prisoners were ordered to move to Kami Sonkurai. This excluded about thirty men who were to move to Tanbaya Hospital, assigned to camp maintenance. This order was then cancelled and changed so that 300 would now move to Sonkurai (this number was to eventually be 597 with Major Tracey's party) and the remaining 200 would transfer to Kami Sonkurai as previously planned. The Japanese wanted to mix Australian and British troops, believing it would improve morale, hygiene and decrease the death rates that were much higher at the British Sonkurai and Changaraya Camps. It was decided that the stretcher cases would also go to Kami Sonkurai as the hospital there was better than the one at Sonkurai. Major Tracey also took a party of 297 to Sonkurai and on 5th August, from Shimo Sonkurai another thirty-two Australians marched to Kami Sonkurai followed by another eighty-two men, two days later. All that remained at Shimo Sonkurai now were 500 patients and thirty maintenance personnel awaiting the move to Tanbaya. Of these only 277 men actually transferred to Burma, the remainder moving to Sonkurai in September.

Shimo Sonkurai camp was now considered a hospital camp from 5th August, as the huts were filled with coolies amongst whom another cholera epidemic broke out. There were 151 mounds left behind in the Prisoners of War burial ground at Shimo Sonkurai and 101 of these were as a direct result of cholera. Padres Polain and Walsh had cleared the ground and had prepared the site for the cemetery for the internment of the ashes. Later, rough crosses were erected over each grave with the name of the dead man burnt into the wood. The sad reality is that all these crosses could so easily have been avoided if the Japanese Force Commander, Colonel Banno had worked with his Prisoners of War officers and medical personnel instead of against them, in an attempt to control the spread of this disease.

Nikhe – New Headquarters Camp

This camp was located at the 281.80km point on the rail link. Colonels Banno and Harris with about fifty men moved up to set up their new headquarters at this camp about 12th June 1943. The site chosen was the concentration point for the railway with a loop line, engine shed, water standpipe and camouflaged shunting tracks. Rations were better here, which has been put down to the fact that it was a railway centre and because it was possible to purchase canteen supplies locally. The camp itself was set in a depression that turned into a quagmire when it rained, like most of the camps along the entire length of the rail link. At Nikhe the Japanese supplied a small hut as an isolation ward for cholera about half a mile from the main camp. The location was beneficial in quelling the spread of this disease at Nikhe, but under the circumstances, made the supply of food and water to the patients all the more difficult. The main work at this camp was the corduroying of the road and clearing the jungle ahead of the rail laying gangs. On 6th November 281 men from Pond's Battalion marched, staggered or were carried into this camp. From these, 107 men moved to Sonkurai Camp further north.

In December 1943 Nikhe, being a railway centre, was used as an assembly point for the movement of Prisoners of War back to Kanchanaburi. It would be the duty of the party at Nikhe to supply cooked food and boiled water for the trainloads of men as they passed through on the journey south to Kanchanaburi between 18th–27th November 1943. Their other duty was to relieve the trains of the dying and dead.

Shimo (Lower) Nikhe Base Camp and Old Headquarters Camp

This camp was located on the 276.00km point on the rail link. It was here that the Australian and British parties were organised before being sent to the main camps. This was to be the Headquarters Camp for 'F' Force under the commands of Colonels Banno and Harris and at no time was used as a construction camp, the prisoners here either being too sick to work or otherwise struck down with cholera. As the men's health improved they were moved to the New Headquarters Camp and hospital camp at Nikhe, to the north.

The camp was situated in a partly cleared jungle hollow with partially finished atap huts and seven large roofless huts and there was a stream that flowed near this camp. Colonel Banno naturally had his own roofed hut and the guards occupied the partially roofed huts, whilst the prisoners were left with the roofless huts. This was to include buildings for the hospital and cookhouse, so there was nowhere for the men to shelter.

The first group of prisoners arrived on 13th May and included Column No. 3 (Tracey) and the stragglers from Columns No.'s 1 and 2 (Pond). The most that were in this camp at any one time was 1,075 of which 450 were Australians. From these there were eleven deaths, six being from cholera. A number of the Australians, 360 in fact, left this camp in early August and moved on to the Kami Sonkurai Camp, whilst others moved to the new hospital at Tanbaya in Burma. Colonels Banno and Harris had by this time moved to their headquarters at Nikhe on 11th June, but it was to be some weeks before Shimo Nikhe Camp was closed down.

As the numbers of sick rose and accumulated at Shimo Nikhe, a hospital was set up under canvas from old British tents slung over bamboo hut frames instead of using atap palm leaf as roofing. This canvas, because of its age and condition and the fact that the framework over which it was slung did not have sufficient angle for the rain to run off caused it to leak like a sieve. The insistence by the Japanese that canvas be used as a substitute for atap was repeated at Nikhe Camp.

Colonel Pond's Battalion

Upper Konkoita – Lower Teimonta 16.5.43 – 21.6.43

At Konkoita 700 Australians from columns No.'s 1 and 2 under the command of Lt -Col S. Pond from the 2/29th Battalion were stopped from moving any further north and were placed under the command of Lt. Maruyama of the Imperial Japanese Army Engineers. This group was made up of men mainly from the 2/29th Battalion. There was at least one member from the 2/4th with Pond's Battalion being Wally Worth. This party was detached from the Singapore Administration of 'F' Force until they rejoined what was left of the main force at Nikhe in December 1943.

It was at this camp that cholera first broke out on 15th May 1943. Because of this cholera outbreak Col. Pond's Battalion was hurriedly moved the next day (16th May) to Upper Konkoita–Lower Teimonta, below Shimo Nikhe. Pond's Battalion occupied at least twelve separate camps between May and November 1943. Already this group differentiated itself from the other Australians in 'F' Force, firstly by being separated and attached to the Japanese Engineers; secondly because of the number of camps they transferred to during their stay in Thailand; and thirdly because the man whose command they were to be under was quite an unpleasant fellow. Lieutenant Maruyama was known to be cruel, ruthless and dishonest with his rationing of food to the prisoners. This man was formerly the director of the anti-communist squad and chief training instructor to the Tokyo Police Force. He was 38 years of age, stood 5 foot 10 inches tall and was in fine physical condition. He demanded that a certain standard of work be produced from his Prisoners of War workforce which was simply impossible to produce. By 17th May the monsoon had broken which turned the camp into a quagmire. At this time only two thirds of the prisoners were sleeping under canvas, the remainder being forced to sleep on the muddy ground under the floors of incomplete huts or make shift lean-tos made from ground sheets, bamboo and leaves. Under these conditions the sick rate rose alarmingly with beri-beri, dysentery and diarrhoea, but in particular malaria. The worst news of all was that cholera had by now caused several deaths.

This is not surprising as Col. Pond's Battalion was located at the nucleus of the cholera outbreak amongst the coolies. With cholera now dictating the terms of everyday life Lt. Maruyama quarantined the camp, ceased road works and placed the sick on reduced rations.

An attack of dysentery may appear insignificant when compared to cholera, however it should be understood that dysentery can kill a man just as effectively as cholera and there are no sub-classifications of dead. During a typical night a man might be forced to make seven or eight trips to the latrines, which at Upper Konkoita were situated about seventy yards away. There were two types of latrines, the nine foot deep covered type and the shallow trench type. A visit to the latrines would entail a slippery, slimy trek cross country in the darkness, feeling every inch of the way with ones bare feet until the edge of the latrine was located. Often nature would not wait and this resulted in the ground in the vicinity of the latrines becoming fouled and as a consequence excreta and maggots were carried back to the sleeping areas. Here the sick prisoner would once again lie down, soaked to the skin under a wet blanket beneath a leaking tent or lean-to.

Work at this camp consisted of bridge building, the felling and carrying of trees, road works, and the corduroying of roads, a necessity during the monsoon. This so called road has been likened to a bush stock route, which gives an indication as to what was already in place and that which had to be improved upon into some form of usable thoroughfare. Due to the fact that the ration situation at Upper Konkoita was becoming serious, it was decided to move 316 of Col. Pond's Battalion to the Old Headquarters Camp, at this stage still situated at Shimo Nikhe.

On 8th June 1943 the first party from Col. Pond's Battalion began the move out, taking two days and eighteen hours to reach Shimo Nikhe, a distance of only 12 kilometres. Lt-Col Kappe, who had accompanied this forward party of Col. Pond's, met up with Lt-Col Harris, the 'F' Force commander, who felt that Pond's Battalion would be established at the New Headquarters Camp at Nikhe. Moving on from Shimo Nikhe Col. Pond's forward party set up a tented camp by the river about one kilometre south of where the New Headquarters Camp was to be established. On 12th June another seventy of Col. Pond's men arrived at Nikhe followed by a further ninety-two on 16th June, practically all these men being either three day malaria cases or else suffering from diarrhoea. This third party had to endure the burden of their own gear, wet tents, heavy coils of wire, engineer's tools and in some cases the guard's packs and their rifles. This left only the sick and enough medical personnel and carers at Upper Konkoita–Lower Teimonta. When it was time to move again, fifty-four sick were left behind at Shimo Nikhe Hospital for later transfer to the new Nikhe Hospital.

The situation for Pond's Battalion at the end of June was 636 men with 458 classified as sick and very few from the remainder who were not suffering from exhaustion. From 18th June until 2nd July the withdrawal of Pond's Battalion commenced from the Nikhe River Camp back to Upper Konkoita–Lower Teimonta where the balance of the battalion was picked up en route. Then it was on to Konkoita, Krian Krai, Tamuron Part and finally Takanoon.

Why Col. Pond's Battalion was moved north to the new Headquarters Camp at Nikhe in the first place and then turned around and marched south again to Takanoon is beyond comprehension. The only suggestions might be for reasons of rations or the Japanese Engineer's demands for construction work on the rail link. A shuttle system was employed whereby the fittest of the unfit went forward to the next staging point, erected tents, dug latrines and prepared the cookhouse before returning to the previous camp to carry forward the stretcher cases. As well as these responsibilities, these men had to go back and dig out ox carts from the mud that were laden with Japanese gear. At Konkoita during a two-day halt the battalion was accommodated in huts that had only just been evacuated the previous day due to deaths from cholera. Burmese coolies were still in residence at this camp and were permitted to move amongst Col. Pond's Battalion and continue to spread their vomit, spit and excreta throughout the campsite.

Takanoon Camp 3.7.43 – 3.9.43

There were four camps at Takanoon between the 218.15km camp and the Japanese Headquarters Camp at the 206.00km point. By now with the monsoon in full swing, the road was impassable except to some Japanese six wheeled vehicles that were managing to bring rations into Nikhe from Burma. To the north of Takanoon, bridges were repeatedly being washed away making supply convoys into the New Headquarters Camp at Nikhe irregular, and this reflected on the amount and frequency that rations were coming into the railway construction camps. Not only was food in short supply, but most Prisoners of War by this time were dressed only in tattered shorts or g-strings and were without boots. This situation promoted the incidence of trench feet and cuts which led to tropical ulcers forming.

From Tamuron Part the battalion continued the move south in two parties to Takanoon, where the first party arrived on 3rd July 1943. The area allotted for the pitching of tents only had a perimeter of 70 by 30 yards and this included a section of ground that was too steep to erect tents. Protests were made because this chosen site was wedged between the bend in a creek, the road and path of the projected railway line, so there was little room to expand the camp. These protests fell upon deaf ears, namely Lt. Maruyama's. The confined space allocated for this camp with tents packed in close together and guy ropes branching off in all directions did not allow for a standard camp layout with paths and shortcuts to latrines. All improvements inside camp had to be carried out by officers and the sick who were unable to be employed on railway construction work because of their fragile condition.

Despite a week of hard work on the establishment of this camp there was little to show for the effort and many men were still sleeping on ground sheets in the open. The start of a typical working day at Takanoon and for that matter the majority construction camps throughout Burma and Thailand, with few exceptions, would begin with reveille at 0700 hours in pitch darkness and usually in rain. The men would line up in a queue taking their turn to sterilise their mess tin by dipping it into boiling water. They would then move to the mess line to receive their rice and then squat or stand in the rain whilst they ate their breakfast. Once the breakfast ceremony was over, they would then line up for their lunch issue to be carried out to the job. The working party would fall in whilst efforts were made to blitz more workers from the sick parade and at 0815 the work party would move out of camp to work. Generally it can be said that all times observed were in Tokyo time, which was ahead of Thailand time being further east.

On arrival at the work site the men would be split into teams of four men, one man on the pick to cut the rock face, one man on the shovel and two men to carry away the rubble in bamboo stretcher like baskets. It only needed one man in the four man team to fall sick for the allotted quota of work to fall behind schedule with the result that a guard was usually close by and willing to use a bamboo stick on the offender. Another problem encountered was the quality of the tools that were issued. Baskets were prone to break on a regular basis that involved delays repairing them. Shovels were made from the unused tin from petrol drums bent double, picks were blunt and made little impression in rock and tool handles were made from jungle timber and invariably promoted blisters to hands. An hour and a half was taken off for lunch which was later reduced to one hour as the rail link drew closer to its completion. Usually meal breaks coincided with torrential downpours of rain, or for at least the first six weeks at Takanoon they did. Last light at this time of the year was around 2115 hours and this usually signalled the end of the working day.

The work party would now collect up and count all the tools and baskets and number of prisoners before the march back to camp in darkness. Arriving back at about 2215 hours the same sterilisation and messing procedure would start all over again. It was perhaps a quick dip in the river to wash off the mud or join the sick parade outside the medical officer's tent or it was off to catch as much sleep as possible between visits to the latrines before the same routine began all over again the next day. The first case of cholera at Takanoon appeared on 9th July 1943, with another forty cases appearing before the end of the week. All told there were to be sixty-two cases of cholera at this camp, which led to the establishment of a cholera isolation hospital on the other side of the road consisting of two tents and a marquee.

Very soon the camp was sub divided into three separate areas, the main camp and attached hospital, the fit camp 200 yards away and the cholera isolation hospital. The main camp and its hospital consisted of one marquee and a tent that were cordoned off by a menacing bamboo fence that the flies and the 'vibrio cholerae' organism were expected to respect.

Digressing for a moment, here is an example of how a nation so technologically advanced that they had built one of the best fighters of the Pacific War in the Mitsubishi Zero. A nation whose warships were a match for any Royal Navy or United States Navy warship. A nation who had invented a night vision binocular and persevered until they had developed the oxygen powered 'Long Lance' torpedo which wreaked havoc in the Solomon Islands against the U.S. Navy. This was after the British had given up on the project, believing that the development of such a torpedo was impossible. These were the same people that intended to establish the 'Greater South East Asia co-Prosperity Sphere' and who were preparing to lead the collective peoples of the Far East into a new era free of the white colonialist master. Yet they still believed that a bamboo fence was the answer to containing cholera in the closed environment of a Prisoner of War camp. This bamboo quick fix was not the first time this method of keeping cholera under control had been utilised because it had been used previously at the Australian camp at Shimo Sonkurai.

Once it was established that a prisoner was not a cholera carrier the all clear was signalled and the potential offender was transferred from the main camp to the fit camp. On 26th July 1943, seventy sick were evacuated by barge to Wanyai 5 kilometres to the south of Tarsau. Wanyai will be remembered as being the location where 'F' Force passed through on their march up from Non Pladuk. A medical team known as 'K' Force had left Singapore at the end of June to establish coolie hospitals at base and jungle camps in Thailand. 'K' Force had set up a hospital camp at Wanyai near a coolie camp and another coolie hospital was set up at Nikhe. The only reason seen for sick being sent to Wanyai is because the 'F' and 'H' Force Hospital at Kanchanaburi was not completed until 27th August 1943. Nevertheless it has been recorded that the first sick began to depart the construction camps for Kanchanaburi from 20th July 1943. It is also recorded that some sick from 'H' Force were permitted to move into the 'D' Force Hospital at Kanchanaburi under sufferance by the Japanese Thailand Administration until the 'F' and 'H' Force Hospital was ready to accept patients.

It is interesting that the same situation occurred on 'H' Force whereby the evacuation of the sick to Kanchanaburi had commenced prematurely on 20th July 1943. The fact that the sick men from both 'F' and 'H' Force began the move south to the 'F' and 'H' Force Hospital at Kanchanaburi before its completion would indicate either the wrong message had been sent by the Japanese or else the message had been misinterpreted.

On 10th August five officers and ninety-five of the fittest other ranks were moved about 3 kilometres north for a separate task which may have been in the vicinity of Namajon. At this time the pace of the work began to increase and this is reflected in the fact another eighty men were evacuated by barge to Wanyai on 16th August. This group was followed by the third and final party of eighty sick on 31st August 1943 to Kanchanaburi, now that the hospital was completed and ready to accept patients. This group included about thirty-four stretcher cases which were left behind at Tamuron Part under the care of Lt. Vietch. During their two month stay fourteen of these sick died. On their arrival by barge from Tamuron Part the remaining stretcher cases from this original group were barged down to Kanchanaburi with another sixty-one convalescing patients from Takanoon who up to this time had been under quarantine orders. It was now time for Col. Pond's Battalion to move again except for sixty sick, one officer and several carers. This small group was evacuated to Kanchanaburi by barge on 30th October 1943.

Teimonta Camp 7.9.43 – 6.11.43

All that remained now of Pond's original Battalion of 700 was 287 men. On 3rd September the first party of one hundred men departed for Teimonta to the north. This first party, instead of being the advance party as was the usual practice, were in fact the less fit from the battalion. The reasoning behind this move being that the Japanese had allowed four days for these men to complete the march. The march did take four days and included a rest stop for one day at Tamuron Part at a coolie camp. One night was also spent at Krian Krai at the 250.13km point where a party from Java, part of 'D' Force extended a hand of hospitality to these men supplying them with shelter and food. The rest of Col. Pond's Battalion having joined the lead party brought the strength of the battalion up to 294 men.

The first two weeks accommodation at Teimonta was spent in a two-storeyed coolie hut noted for its darkness, squalor and a stench which combined forces with the latrines that were located very close by. Whilst work continued on the rail link a new hut was built on higher ground about 300 yards away from the coolie quarters. This new hut which was occupied on 21st September was by far the best and cleanest the men in Pond's Battalion had experienced to date. The negative side was, thanks to the brief stay with the coolies, eight men had contracted pneumonia and cases of scabies and lice had increased. But on a positive note the monsoon rains ceased on 2nd October.

As the guards began to spread the rumour of a move to Changi, it was obvious that the rail link was nearing completion. The rail laying gangs reached Teimonta on 15th October 1943 as did the first train. Men were taken off work parties in the cuttings and put to work breaking rock in the quarry to supply stone for ballast for the line. Two days later the two ends met at the 262.87km point at Upper Konkoita–Lower Teimonta where Col. Pond's Battalion had moved to on 16th May 1943, following the cholera outbreak at Konkoita.

For the last ten days of October, on a daily basis a party of one hundred men was called for to carry the Japanese Engineer's railway construction equipment from Nikhe to Teimonta or otherwise from Teimonta to Sonkurai.

The path taken for this return journey was along the newly completed railway line. On several occasions empty trains passed by whilst sick men struggled with bundles of tools and in one instance a 300lb anvil without the slightest sign of concern for their predicament from their Japanese overseers or for that matter the engine drivers.

Nikhe Camp – November 1943

On 6th November 1943 Col. Pond's Battalion amalgamated with the other remnants of 'F' Force and began the move to the new 'F' Force Headquarters Camp at Nikhe for the second time. Out of a total of 281 men all that remained of Col. Pond's Battalion at Teimonta were seventy who were in hospital, and twenty-six who were stretcher cases. Of the 211 men left, eighty were sick and could only just manage to get themselves and their own gear to Nikhe. This means that 131 men had to carry all the camp gear, assist the frail and carry those on stretchers. Most stretcher bearers' limit of endurance and strength was 100 yards before their charge had to be lowered and a short respite taken before moving off again. It has been said that war is a battle of attrition. The construction of the Burma–Thailand rail link, in respect to the Prisoner of War was one battle of attrition that the Japanese were well on the way to losing. Had the railway not been completed when it was, it would be a fair comment that 'F' Force would have been totally obliterated. The night the battalion arrived at Nikhe, a party of 107, which was probably all that were capable of any sort of movement, were ordered to carry on a further 12 kilometres north to Sonkurai. The following day these 107 men were incorporated into Major Tracey's party until their return to Kanchanaburi.

'H' Force No. 1 Sub-Section

From the 'H' Force story we know that 400 Prisoners of War including some eighty-three Australians with the officers from H6 Officer's Group departed Hintok Siding on 29th August 1943.

On arrival they were split up and trekked for three days, with the officers going to the area of Lower Konkoita, possibly at one of two Konkoita sub-Camps in the area of Kurikonta. The officers worked on a bridge at this camp that may possibly have been in the vicinity of the Fukushima wooden bridge over the River Kwae Noi near Konkoita, or several of the other minor railway bridges that crossed tributaries that ran into the Kwae Noi. The other ranks it is believed moved to the Upper Konkoita–Lower Teimonta area. This is where the two ends of the rail link met and were joined on 17th October 1943.

Back to Kanchanaburi and Singapore

In November 1943 'F' Force began the train journey south via Kanchanaburi back to Singapore.

As the prisoners massed at Nikhe (a railway concentration point), no time was allowed for organisation as men were hurriedly loaded aboard the first train available that was heading south. Any feelings of relief that a man may have had after being packed into open trucks under a hot tropical sun, after long delays, train derailments and hurried transfers from one train to another soon turned to frustration. These factors and long periods between meals with the lack of drinking water only promoted sickness as it had done during the train journey north from Singapore to Non Pladuk. At least forty-six men died during the course of this journey south.

The first party to arrive at Kanchanaburi consisted of fifty men from the Kami Sonkurai Camp. These men should have been used as an advance party to prepare for the arrival of follow up parties. This, however, did not occur and as train loads of 'F' Force arrived at all hours of the night and day there really had been no preparations made for their arrival apart from the 'F' and 'H' Force Hospital and 'Fit Camp' at Kanchanaburi. Whilst the Japanese supplied rations these did not improve from those of the construction camps at Kanchanaburi, but at least local purchase from the Thai vendors was available. Despite this fact 186 men of 'F' Force died in the first three weeks at Kanchanaburi. To reiterate, the Australians in 'F' Force had suffered a 28% death rate whilst the British faired much worse at 61%.

The Australians, however, had had the advantage of arriving at their camps before the monsoon rains broke when the roads and tracks north were in a much better condition.

Soon after arrival at Kanchanaburi it was announced that two parties of 500 fit men would be leaving Thailand and would be expected to work on arrival at a new destination with Sumatra, Japan and Singapore all mentioned as possibilities. It had been impossible to find 1,000 fit men whilst they were employed on railway construction work and the situation had not improved. The first party of 500, which included some sick, had departed on 2nd December 1943 and arrived the next day at the Bangkok docks to the news that the next stage of their journey was to be by sea. This party remained camped in a go-down on the docks for the next week.

On 10th December this party embarked as deck cargo aboard a 4,000 ton steamer that docked at Singapore four days later. With the exception of the first party, all the remaining parties from 'F' Force arrived back at Singapore by train up to 23rd December. By April 1944 all 'F' Force had been returned to Singapore after the sickest of the men, mostly dysentery and beri-beri cases, had been held over at the Kanchanaburi 'F' and 'H' Force hospital.

The Tanbaya Hospital in Burma was evacuated on 20th December 1943 and all patients were brought south to Kanchanaburi and then forwarded on to Singapore.

Of the men from 'F' Force who returned to Singapore about 95% were heavily infected with malaria. About 80% were classified as general debility and half required hospitalisation for extended periods because of dysentery, beri-beri, chronic malaria, skin diseases and malnutrition.

A group of 165 Australians and 175 British, probably those for isolation were sent to Sime Road Camp as possible carriers of small pox or cholera. Those who required urgent medical treatment were sent to the Australian General hospital at Roberts Barracks and the remainder were returned to Selarang Barracks Changi.

The medical classification of personnel returned from Thailand was as follows:

Class 1	(Heavy Duty)
Class 2	(Light Duty)
Class 3	(Very Light Duty)
Class 4	(Temporarily Unfit)
Class 5	(Admitted to the Australian General Hospital)

There were also Japanese letter classifications for repatriation purposes that ran from 'A' to 'E'. Following the Battle of Singapore 'Andy' Toovey, who was bed ridden, and Eric Wankey, who had had his leg amputated were rated as 'A' Classification, so 'A' must have been the highest and 'E' the lowest. With this information we know that on 22nd April 1944, 700 men classified as 3 'B' no duty were moved from Selarang Barracks to Sime Road Camp.

Also on this date 700 men, by now medically cleared by the Japanese, transferred from the Sime Road Camp back to Selarang Barracks to work on the Levelling Party for the proposed new runway at Changi. The following was taken from an 'F' Force report yet could so easily be applied to any report about men from the 7th or 8th Australian Divisions who died as a result of being a Prisoner of War of the Imperial Japanese Army:

> 'Every unit had lost original men and soldiers of proved quality; many mothers and wives and children in Australia had lost loved ones. All could have been saved by the simple precaution of prior inoculation, by a more humane appreciation of the medical requirements for white men, already weakened by over 12 months on a vitamin-deficient diet entering a known cholera and dysentery area. Whatever revelations the future may bring, the men who have survived this experience will retain an indelible memory and recollection of our enemy's lack of humanity during the period, and the Australian public after the war will do well to remember these events when considering a relationship with this northern neighbour.' [43]

On 23rd December 1943 'F' Force ceased to exist. No doubt this would have been a fitting Christmas present for those that had survived this journey to the land of 'milk and honey.'

The Concentration of Prisoners of War in Thailand 1944

Between December 1943 and April 1944 the majority of the Prisoners of War who had worked on the Burma–Thailand rail link had been brought south to camps in Thailand at Chungkai, Tamarkan, Kanchanaburi, Tamuang, Non Pladuk and Nacompaton. Following the insanity of the 'speedo' period during 1943 conditions and rations began to improve.

A well-built base hospital was in operation at Nacompaton which was now accepting patients from Chungkai, Kanchanaburi and Non Pladuk however, by this time it was too late to save some of the men who had already gone past the point of no return.

During February 1944 the Japanese began to make arrangements to send parties of prisoners to the Japanese home islands. Originally it was the intention to send workers with technical skills or knowledge who could be utilised in heavy industry. This might have been possible except for the fact that no Australian was prepared to admit to having a trade or skill that would aid the Japanese war effort. As a result the skilled labour base that the Japanese, Koreans or Formosans had not beaten, starved or worked to death were simply not available, or otherwise were not volunteering for conscription into the Japanese home islands work force.

---

[43] AWM54 File 554/7/2 Part 2 Summary of Medical Report, British and Australian POW April 1943–April 1944 by Lt-Col Huston R.A.M.C. Australian War Memorial Canberra

When the Japanese realised that their original plan would not come to fruition it was then stated that it was the intention of the Japanese Government to send 10,000 Prisoners of War, mostly from the enlisted ranks, with just enough officers to control them to Japan for general labouring work.

Instead of being used in heavy industry these ex-railway workers would now be put to work in the mines and factories to help make up for the shortage of labour in Japan. These men were selected for their physical fitness, however it soon became obvious that when the Japanese were not selecting men with a dark skin colour or freckles, or anyone with a skin disease, that the Japanese intended to show off their human prizes to the local populations back home in Japan.

This occured with the men from the 2/4th who were sent to Korea, with 'B' Force at Sandakan and 'J' Force at Kobe.

Because the Japanese selection criteria only went skin deep, men who appeared to be healthy were sent to Japan despite that fact that they were suffering from attacks of malaria. Some men actually wanted to go to Japan, and unbeknown to the Japanese, slight variations to the original Japanese selections were made by the Australian medical staffs. After selection, those chosen were tested for the usual favourites, amoebic dysentery and pestis and were then given the various inoculations. This workforce of 10,000 men was drawn from the various Prisoner of War groups between April and June 1944.

The first group of prisoners who had migrated down from Burma would eventually board the *Rakuyo Maru*, a passenger-cargo ship of 9,419 tons. Many of these men would never complete this voyage whilst others, the lucky ones, would return home to Australia carrying with them the first news of the so called infamous Burma–Thailand Railway.

Richard 'Dick' Ridgwell, a member of 'D' Force S Battalion,
who would remain in Thailand during 1944–1945
and eventually be recovered from Bangkok.

Chapter Four

The Borneo Story

The Prisoners of War on 'B' and 'E' Forces who were transported to the picturesque town of Sandakan in British North Borneo were involved in the greatest tragedy to befall Australian servicemen during WWII. In this instance it is not the intention to reopen the file on Sandakan but to only relate the facts of 'B' and 'E' Forces as they affected the men from the 2/4th Machine Gun Battalion. By doing so we may better understand the sequence of events which led to their deaths. The battalion's contribution to these two Forces was thirty-three and thirty-six men respectively. Of these sixty-nine men the only survivors were Lt. John Morrison and Sgt. Alf Stevens from 'B' Force and Lt. Brian Walton from 'E' Force.

Just one of the many tragedies pertaining to the 2/4th and indeed for the small town of Toodyay in Western Australia was the loss of the three Dorizzi brothers, Tom, Gordon and Bert. There was also Reg Ferguson, another born and bred Toodyay lad, who adopted 'Gunner' the battalion's canine mascot, or was it the other way around? Rolf Newling was a member of 'B' Force and his two brothers Rexford and Oswald also died while with Major Alf Cough's 'D' Force V Battalion in Thailand. There was Bob 'Lofty' Chipperfield, a six foot eight inch tall gentle giant of a man from London who began his life in Australia as a Kingsley Fairbridge Farm Schoolboy, as did Syd Osborne. Remember Eddy Burton who was fined for being AWL in Fremantle and wrote home to his mother stating that he would have done it again if the situation arose? Eddy was a member of 'E' Force and died at Sandakan, in February 1945. Last but by no means least was Arthur 'Codge' Thorns, who is believed to be the last man from the 2/4th Machine Gun Battalion to have died at Ranau on 1st August 1945. Codge supposedly died of malaria but it is almost certain that the mosquito involved was either the 7.7mm bullet strain or the tempered steel proboscis strain.

It was evident that after the Japanese surrender in Borneo that nearly all the death certificates had been falsified. Irrespective of the cause of death, natural or otherwise, the majority of these death certificates stated the cause of death as being either malaria, beri-beri or dysentery. Personal belongings which were later discovered at Sankakan or at some remote location along the track between Sandakan and Ranau do not necessarily mean that the soldier was actually there.

We can read of this happening in the Arthur Draper Report where Laurie McGrath's haversack was discovered in the vicinity of the Mandai Crossroads, yet Laurie McGrath had returned to Australia sick in January 1942 having never set foot on Singapore, or for that matter on Java. This facet of the Prisoner of War experience at Sandakan should not be seen as irregular because as men died it would be natural for their belongings to be distributed amongst their mates within their own unit or amongst the other prisoners. It is for this reason that the author is reluctant to make statements about the place or cause of death unless convinced they are based on fact.

Over half a century has passed since news of his tragedy came to be known. Every year at memorial services around Australia, the families and friends of these men unite, lay wreaths and join in prayer to remember their passing. There would be very few people at these annual reunions around Australia who wouldn't be asking themselves the same question, what actually happened between Sandakan and Ranau in 1945?

'B' Force

Japanese control of Borneo took a very high priority because of the major oil reserves associated with this island. By the end of January 1942 the whole of the former British and Dutch controlled Borneo was under their control. It was then decided to construct an airfield at Sandakan for the following reasons. Firstly, so they could better protect their convoys, control the skies, and seaward approaches around Sandakan and Northern Borneo in the event of an Allied invasion. Secondly, because this airfield would also serve as a refueling point for Japanese aircraft en-route to other bases held by the Imperial Japanese Navy and Army.

The camp at Sandakan was established as a branch of the larger Kuching Prisoner of War camp which was also the Borneo headquarters to the Kempeitai, the feared Japanese Military Police.

On 8th July 1942, the men of 'B' Force departed Changi under the command of Lt-Col A.W. Walsh of the 2/10th Field Regiment A.I.F. and boarded the *Ubi Maru*, the ship that would transport them to British North Borneo. This force comprised 1,494 Australians of which 145 were officers.

During the course of an interview Yuki Tanaka, the author of *Hidden Horrors,* had with the Japanese staff officer from the Kuching Headquarters the staff officer stated that the ship was not the *Ubi Maru*, as we are to understand but rather the *Ume Maru*. The reference, *Merchant Shipping Losses During WWII* makes no mention of the *Ubi Maru* however it does list the *Ume Maru* as a cargo-passenger ship of 5,859 tons. Therefore it can only be assumed that this information is correct and the ship was in fact the *Ume Maru*. [1]

Sandakan

Sandakan was the capital of the State of British North Borneo, now called Sabah. The town was built close to the foreshore on Sandakan Harbour at the entrance of which sat Berhala Island where in excess of ninety civilians, including most of the British officials were interned at the leper quarantine station. The industrial quarter of Sandakan was to the west of the town where the power station and timber mills were located. There were three good partially

---

[1]   Yuki Tanaka, *Hidden Horrors* Japanese War Crimes in WWII, Westview Press 1996. End notes for Chapter One
      p.220 Item 10. Interview with Yamada Masaharu.

macadamized main roads that led into the town, namely Labuk (Beluran) Road, Sibuga Road and Leila Road.

Looking back across the town from the waterfront the buildings that stood out were a clock tower, Fort Pryer with its constabulary buildings and gaol, and the customs buildings near the wharf. The town consisted of mostly single storey buildings and to the left of the waterfront there was the native water village. Most of the European residents at Sandakan had built their homes on the low range of hills that ran across the back of the town.

Following the capitulation of British North Borneo on 19th January 1942 the Japanese changed the name of the town from Sandakan to Elopura and made it the capital of the Japanese State of East Borneo. Arriving at Sandakan on 18th July 1942 the Australian Prisoners of War aboard the *Ume Maru* were disembarked and paraded on the oval situated between the native village and the town. It was here the men were displayed like zoo animals before a curious local population. The Japanese took great pleasure in trying to humiliate their white prisoners in front of the indigenous peoples of Asia. The locals were told that these Australians had been captured in their own country and that Australia was now part of the Japanese Empire. As every wireless in the town had been confiscated the locals were none the wiser, but by the same token not completely convinced. Herein lies the key to the secret of Sandakan and the reason why so many people would suffer as a result. The Kempeitai were absolutely obsessed with controlling the local populace by denying them access to information by way of overseas wireless broadcasts

Once the Prisoners had been searched, counted and fed they marched off in groups under close guard to the nearby Catholic Mission School. Early the next morning they were marched back to the oval and once again counted by their Formosan guards.[2]

The prisoners were then marched to the camp which was located approximately 8 miles from the township and about one mile from the turn off on the Baluran–Labuk Road. The Sandakan main camp, originally built by the British as an internment camp for about 300 Japanese residents now living at Sandakan, was now to be known as Sandakan No. 1 Prisoner of War Camp. The camp was built on the site of the old British Government Experimental Agriculture Farm and comprised about twenty single-storey wooden buildings. The Japanese then added about another twenty native style atap huts that were used by the other ranks and could accommodate about fifty men per hut. The more substantial wooden buildings were used for the A.I.F. administration office, quartermaster's store, hospital and officer's accommodation.

Francis Armstrong 21.8.1912 – 30.7.1942

The first casualty at Sandakan was a man from the 2/4th Machine Gun Battalion, Frank Armstrong. Despite having a history of stomach problems Frank decided to go ahead and enlist in the 2nd A.I.F in August 1940. He had been admitted to the Australian General Hospital at Roberts Barracks Changi on 3rd May 1942 with what was diagnosed as a peptic ulcer and was discharged back to the unit two weeks later. Despite his medical history he was included on the 'B' Force draft. Frank died on 30th July 1942, twelve days after his arrival at Sandakan. This episode is mentioned in Peter Firkin's book *From Hell to Eternity* in which Firkins states:

> *'On one occasion not long after arrival at Sandakan, Captain D.G.Picone, who had been the medical officer in an artillery unit was preparing to operate on a prisoner who had suffered a burst duodenal ulcer. Being night time, and the operation being urgent, Dr Picone borrowed a stronger globe from the guardhouse. He had just given*

---

2   Ibid p.12

the first injection of the anaesthetic when a Japanese burst into the theatre. 'Who had given you permission to perform this operation?' he was asked.

'No one. It is an urgent operation', replied Picone.

'Who gave you permission to take this globe from the guardroom?' the guard continued.

'With that the Japanese beat Picone with his wooden baton and made him stand to attention for two hours outside the guardhouse while the patient waited.' [3]

All the guards at Sandakan camp were Formosans (Taiwanese) under the command of their Japanese Imperial Army and Kempeitai Officers. Needless to say Frank Armstrong was the victim and died due to the guard's intervention. Frank was buried at the European section of the Sandakan cemetery located close to town, his grave being marked with a wooden cross with a metal plate bearing his name, rank and number. Padre A. H. Thompson conducted the burial service. Frank's body was exhumed at the end of the war and now rests in peace at the Labuan War Cemetery.

If there is one consolation to come out of this episode it was that at least Frank's family know that he died of natural causes and not at the hands of some Formosan guard or Japanese soldier. One fact that comes to light from this incident is that Frank's Prisoner of War number was 1,467 of the 1,494 issued to the prisoners in 'B' Force. Therefore these numbers must have been issued between his arrival on 18th July and his death on 30th July. No Prisoner of War numbers were issued on Singapore as 'B' Force left prior to August 1942. The fact that Frank's was the highest Prisoner of War number amongst the 2/4th machine gunners in 'B' Force might indicate that Frank was one of the last to disembark from the *Ume Maru* which may also be an indication as to his state of health at the time.

Another point is that no Koreans or Formosans were pressed into Japanese military service prior to May 1942. Both the Koreans and Formosans were considered by the Japanese as being of a lower class than themselves and were treated as such. It is for this reason that they were not used as combatant troops. However, by making this changing of the guard, so to speak, they effectively relieved Japanese front line troops for other duties. The status of the Koreans and Formosans within the Japanese military hierarchy was even lower than the lowest private in the Imperial Japanese Army.

It then stood to reason that if a lowly Japanese private could punish a Korean or Formosan guard, then there wasn't much hope of immunity for the prisoners, regardless of rank. This situation was accepted as a fact of life as the guards vented their pent up resentment upon the prisoners. In the guard's eyes the prisoners were disgraced for allowing themselves to be taken prisoner in the first place and were to be treated with contempt. However, this attitude where east meets west was not isolated to Borneo because it was endemic along the entire length of the Burma–Thailand rail link and the many other Prisoner of War camps throughout the Far East. In the Japanese military system brutality was accepted as a way of life, therefore it is not difficult to see how easy it would have been to dehumanise the prisoners, whereby they are looked upon not as human beings but as commodities, merely slaves of the Emperor of Japan.

Operation Market Garden – The Underground

The following narrative is intended to introduce the main players and sequence of events that led to the arrest by the Kempeitai of Sgt. Alf Stevens and to try and make some sense out of the insanity for the massacre of so many Prisoners of War. A Prisoner of War civilian

---

3   Peter Firkins, *From Hell to Eternity* Westward Ho Publishing Company 1979, p.12

underground intelligence network, secret radio and transmitter, several escape attempts, the eventual isolation of Borneo by Allied operations and air raids on the Sandakan airfield and camp meant one thing, that the Australian and British Prisoners of War at Sandakan would all be marked men. Japanese fears that the prisoners led by their officers would rise up against them in the event of an Allied invasion, and the order that no Prisoners of War were to be handed back to the Allies ensured that they would be the victims of a plan to starve, brutalise and murder them. The Japanese were adamant that not even one Prisoner of War would survive to tell his story. They very nearly achieved this goal.

The Players

The period at Sandakan No. 1 Camp from the time of 'B' Force's arrival in mid-July to the end of the month was probably the most serene period that the prisoners would encounter prior to their demise. Security at Sandakan in the early days was reasonably lax.

It was around the end of July 1942 that Lt-Col Walsh sought, and was granted permission from the Japanese for his officers to establish a vegetable garden outside the confines of the camp. This request was genuine as Lt-Col Walsh was only looking at a means by which to keep his officers occupied during daylight hours and of course to supplement the camp's rations with vegetables. On arrival at Sandakan Capt. L. Matthews, 8th Division Signals, established an intelligence network that consisted of about twenty officers and NCO's. Now that permission had been granted to establish a camp vegetable garden Capt. Matthews managed to make contact with a Malayan by the name of Dick Maginal who was employed by the Japanese as a gardener in the camp. There is one thing that seems to stand out in the Sandakan story and that is the loyalty and respect the local population had for the former British Colonial Administration.

This loyalty would cost many their lives and yet there was never any doubt as to their allegiance. Maginal was sympathetic towards the prisoners and not only made it known to Matthews but also informed him that there were civilians from Sandakan interned on Berhala Island that were being guarded by local constabulary and Japanese soldiers. He then managed to set up a meeting between Sandakan No. 1 Camp and Berhala Island via Cpl. Ahbin.

Ahbin was the local policeman at the eight-mile post on the Beluran-Labuk Road at the turn off into No. 1 Camp. He was not only permitted to visit the Sandakan No. 1 Camp but also the Civilian Internees Camp on Berhala Island, thus it was possible for Matthews to establish a link between these two camps. The British Commandant of Police and Ahbin's boss to whom he was loyal was Major Rice-Oxley.

Although interned on Berhala Island Major Rice-Oxley was able to establish a phantom command and issue orders to his men from time to time through collaboration with Matthews. In this way preparations were put into place in the event of an Allied invasion. Another of Major Rice-Oxley's faithful men on Berhala Island was Cpl. Koram who will enter the story a little later.

It was also during this period that contact was made with the Senior Medical Officer at Sandakan Hospital Doctor J. P. Taylor thanks to Cpl. Ahbin. The first contact with Dr Taylor, who incidentally was an Australian, was made by Lt-Col E. Shepphard, from the 2/10th Field Ambulance and Lt. N. Sligo, R.A.N. Lieutenant Sligo held the job of Canteen Officer but was in fact 'B' Force's Intelligence Officer. These two men had been granted permission to walk into Sandakan Township and make contact with Dr Taylor for the purpose of obtaining medical supplies for the camp.

What actually transpired was that the ground work for an intelligence network was established, with Dr Taylor to act as the middle man in an organisation that would assist the prisoners by raising money and assisting with preparations for escape attempts. Some others in this clandestine group were Mr. G. Mavor, the manager and Chief Engineer of the Sandakan Electric Supply, and his wife who were both confined to the powerhouse bungalow. There was also Mr. A. Phillips, the manager of the British North Borneo Trading Company and his Malayan wife who were permitted to carry on business as usual. Shortly after the meeting with Dr Taylor, Lt. Sligo died of dysentery and his position as Intelligence Officer was taken over by Capt. Matthews. Dr Taylor and friends were considered by the Japanese as essential personnel and were not transferred to Berhala Island but rather permitted to work and remain at Sandakan under a form of house arrest. Captain Matthews arranged to have Taylor smuggle a parcel of medical supplies into the camp by leaving it at prearranged place where it could be collected by the Wood Party later.

This detail was under the command of Lt. R. Wells also from the 8th Division Signals. Lieutenant Wells, a wireless expert was placed in charge of the Wood Party whose responsibility was to supply wood for cooking and for the camp's wood-fired, electricity generating boiler. As Capt.Matthews' movements within the Garden Party became more and more restricted Lt. Wells who had the run of the surrounding area with his Wood Party was taken into Capt. Matthews' confidence and made second in command of the intelligence network. Through Dick Maginal, Capt. Matthews was also introduced to Ah Ping who was in the employ of Mr. Mavor as the foreman at the Sandakan No. 1 Camp powerhouse. Another trusted employee of Mavor's was the powerhouse Chief Engineer, Ah Kong.

Welcome to Radio Sandakan

When 'B' Force had left Singapore they had managed to smuggle out some wireless parts. These parts were added to with the aid of local Chinese merchants who were displeased about being put out of business by the Kempeitai. During September 1942 Dick Maginal obtained a crystal detector and headphones. Corporal Ahbin managed to procure two wireless valves through Lamberto Apostle, the houseboy to Mr. G. Brown, the Assistant to the Conservator of Forests and Director of Agriculture. Mr. Brown at this time was interned on Berhala Island but would later be transferred to Lintang Barracks Kuching.

From Ah Ping the route plans for electrical and telephone lines were also obtained. Three prisoners with the expertise, Lt. A. Weyton and Cpl.'s Small and Mills had a wireless receiver operational by 4th November 1942. The network even went so far as to being able to convert the camp AC electrical supply to DC by the very resourceful fabrication of a chemical rectifier. As the power generator was located some distance from the prisoner's barracks the fluctuating power output was so low that it would need to be increased if it was hoped to receive world news broadcasts.

Lieutenant Wells arranged with Ah Ping that extra wood would be supplied to the powerhouse so that an increase in the camp's power generation could be made at 2200 hours each night. That in itself was simple enough with Wells in charge of the wood collection party and able to supply additional fuel, but Wells now had Ah Ping seek permission from the Japanese for extra manpower to be made available to help run the powerhouse. The Japanese consented to Ah Ping's request and this is where Sgt. Alf Stevens from the 2/4th Machine Gun Battalion enters the story. Sergeant Stevens prior to his enlistment had been an engine driver, or boiler attendant, at the Union Flour Mills in the Western Australian country town of Kellerberrin. Sergeant Stevens who had been indoctrinated into the underground network would now act as the middleman between Capt. Matthews, Ah Ping and Ah Kong.

Through Sgt. Stevens, news could be passed back to Ah Ping at the powerhouse and Cpl. Ahbin who could then supply Dr Taylor with the latest update on the war and the underground from the Sandakan No. 1 Camp end. The system worked well thanks to the ingenuity of the prisoners and the help of the British civilians and local community. Unfortunately when this underground network came crashing down, Prisoners of War, civilian internees and local people alike would become victims to Kempeitai's notorious heavy handedness.

The Sandakan Escapes

Captain Matthews was one who believed that obtaining arms in the event of an Allied invasion should take a high priority. Ahbin had brought Alex Funk who was an overseer at the Public Works Department into the underground and put him in touch with Capt. Matthews. Funk had local Chinese contacts that were in touch with Filipino guerrillas on Batu Batu Island in the southern Philippines. Funk supplied Matthews with a pistol and some ammunition as well as a map of British North Borneo.

Through Funk, contact was then established with Filipino guerrillas who were happy to supply two machine guns, twenty-seven rifles and about 2,500 rounds of ammunition. This little cache of weapons and ammunition was hidden at the 15 mile peg on the Beluran–Labuk Road for the day that an armed uprising might hopefully occur. Up to this time the wireless receiver and the intricate underground network of prisoners, civilian internees and local population had been kept a secret from the Japanese. There was however one thing that could not be kept a secret and that was the number of prisoners trying their luck at bids for freedom.

Shortly after arrival at Sandakan there were several escape attempts. As mentioned in the early days the security at Sandakan No. 1 Camp had been quite lax. On Friday 31st July 1942, eleven Australian Prisoners of War attempted to escape. There were three separate groups, one group of two men, one group of four men and the last group of five men. The first two groups were all members of the A.A.S.C., although they had departed camp at different times they joined up outside the wire and headed north. After three days the group of four men acted on false information that Mr. Phillips could help them.

Changing plan and probably by now realising the futility of their bid for freedom they headed back to Sandakan and sought shelter and assistance from Phillips. The only problem was that Phillips lived across the road from the Sandakan Headquarters of the Kempeitai. On 8th August 1942 when a Japanese learned he was harbouring escapees, Phillips was left with no option but to hand in these men to the Kempeitai. Phillips had only managed to remain in town because the Japanese frequented his trading company and as his wife was Malayan there was a certain amount of influence from the local population. Under these circumstances it is easy to see Phillips' precarious situation. If he had been arrested and tortured this would surely have placed the underground network and many innocent lives in jeopardy. The Kempeitai would most certainly have then been indiscriminate as to whom they selected for questioning and subjected to torture. The two other A.A.S.C. men who escaped were recaptured 40 miles down the coast on 25th August after being betrayed by some locals. These local people were villagers, and rewards offered by the Japanese were too much of a temptation not to accept. This was the same situation as in Burma and Thailand where locals would hand in escaped prisoners for rewards from the Japanese. Also, as in Burma and Thailand the jungles, rivers and swamps were as great an enemy to the prisoners as the Japanese were.

It is for these reasons that escapes were not more common than they actually were. It is also to be remembered that the Japanese were extremely intolerant of escape bids and in most cases the perpetrators were shot. Meanwhile, there were still the five prisoners from Sandakan, all members of the 2/29th Battalion, still at large. These men managed to hold out for seven months but were picked up on 27th January 1943, attempting to sail south towards Australia. The only reason that this group had been able to hold out as long as they had was due in part to the intervention of Dr Taylor and his Chinese contacts. So far the Australian run rate for successful escapes was not too good.

The next attempt was made by two men who absconded from the airfield on 20th February 1943 but their attempt could be described as little more than a stroll in the park as they were recaptured as quickly as they had escaped. Another escape bid by three men was made on 30th April which now brought the total to sixteen men who had tried to escape from Sandakan. Two of these men were sighted by the Japanese and shot on 11th May but the third man, Sgt. Wallace managed to make it to Berhala Island with help from Heng Joo Ming, a local Chinese lad who will be introduced shortly. Wallace would make another escape bid with members of 'E' Force in June 1943.

'E' Force

The next force to depart Changi was 'E' Force consisting of 500 A.I.F. and 500 British Prisoners of War. There were thirty-six men from the 2/4th Machine Gun Battalion in 'E' Force which later included Thomas Green. Because 'E' Force departed Singapore after August 1942 they had remained on the island long enough to be issued with their Singapore Prisoner of War numbers.

The Australians came under the command of Major J. Farley of the 2/20th Battalion, however the force commander was the British Lt-Colonel Whimster. This force embarked on the small tramp steamer *de Klerk* which departed Singapore on the morning of 28th March 1943. Amongst this group were several Australians who were already planning their escape.

The first port of call was Kuching, the capital of Sarawak, where the prisoners would remain for eight days before moving on again. Once ashore the Australians were moved out along the Lintang Road to the Batu Lintang Military Camp located about one and a half miles to the south of Kuching. There were about seventy buildings of sawn timber and atap roofing each 100 feet long by 15 feet wide, raised about 3 feet from the ground. About forty-five of these buildings were used as barracks, the Australians being crammed into three of these.

The camp was the former home to the 2nd Battalion of the 15th Punjabi Regiment but was now used to accommodate British and Australian officers and other ranks, civilian men, women and children, Netherlands East Indians, priests, and of course the guards. When British prisoners began to arrive at the camp during 1942 they were put to work on the airfield. There were a few Australians captured on Java amongst those at Lintang Barracks and one of these men from the 2/4th was Thomas William Green. Tom had departed Java on 12th October with Java Party No. 4 to Singapore. This was the group that departed with Williams and Black Forces from Tanjong Priok onboard the *Kinmon Maru*. It would appear that Tom was left behind at Changi when Black and Williams Forces moved north to Burma. The simplest explanation for this would be sickness, as only the sick would have been taken off the draft and sent to the Australian General Hospital at Roberts Barracks Changi.

On 3rd February 1943 men from Java Parties No. 1 and 2 (British) and Parties No. 3, 4 and 5a (Australian) a total of 104 men left Singapore for Kuching. Major Farley was informed by Major Suga Tatsuji, the head of POW camps in Borneo, that no combatant officers were to accompany the men to Sandakan.

As a result Major Farley, one other officer and fifteen other ranks were removed from the draft and these men were replaced with seventeen other ranks that had arrived in February. Tom

Green was one of these seventeen men. Tom's future had already been decided for him before his arrival at Sandakan. Major Farley now appointed Capt. R. Richardson from the 2/20th Battalion with Capt. R. Steele his second in command. The civilian internees from Berhala Island were now in residence at Lintang Barracks. Included in this group was Major Rice-Oxley who on departure had handed over control of the police to Capt. Matthews. On 9th April 1943 the Australian contingent of 'E' Force marched out of Lintang Barracks to board the *Taka Maru*, a small cargo ship of only 887 tons. The previous day 200 British from Jesselton (Kota Kinabalu) arrived at Sandakan. It took five days for the *Taka Maru* to edge its way around the top of the Borneo coastline via Labuan Island to replenish its coalbunkers before continuing onto Sandakan. These Prisoners of War in 'E' Force were not to join the other Australians at Sandakan No. 1 Camp at this stage as they disembarked at Berhala Island. This camp had been opened on 15th August 1942. Living conditions at the camp were reasonably good, the prisoners being quartered in wooden houses that had been erected before the war. The camp was located near the beach and the prisoners were permitted to swim in the harbour under the guard's supervision.

Four days later on 18th April the remainder of the British, 576 men from Jesselton, also moved to Sandakan. These three groups were kept segregated and not permitted by the Japanese to join into one force. There was now to be three camps at Sandakan, No. 1 Camp for the Australians of 'B' Force, No. 2 Camp for the British and No. 3 Camp for the Australians of 'E' Force.

The Berhala Island Escapes

The Intelligence Officer for 'E' Force was Lt C. Wagner of the 2/18th Battalion. Lieutenant Wagner made contact with Cpl. Koram and informed him of his intention to escape. Lieutenant Wagner then gave Koram a message to pass to Capt. Matthews at Sandakan No. 1 Camp but before this could be carried out Koram had a most unexpected meeting with a U.S. Navy submarine. Koram had been out in his perahu fishing when the submarine surfaced before his eyes.

A Filipino guerrilla fighter who had been working with the Americans passed Koram a note that offered to help anyone who wanted to escape. Koram was instructed to pass the note to a white man, which Koram dutifully did, passing it onto Dr Taylor who in turn passed it to Capt. Matthews.

On 4th June a barge appeared at the jetty on Berhala Island to transport 'E' Force to the mainland so now it was imperative that if there were to be an escape attempt that it would have to be soon. Preparations were well in place as arranged by Dr Taylor, Capt. Matthews and Lt. Wells and on the night of 5th June eight prisoners absconded, including Sgt. Wallace from 'B' Force who had been hiding out on Berhala Island. The group divided themselves into two, with the three other ranks, Pte's. Butler, McLaren and Kennedy in one group and the four officers, Capt. Steele and Lt.'s Wagner, Blow and Gillon as well as Sgt. Wallace.

When the Australians of 'E' Force on Berhala Island assembled on 6th June in readiness to make the move to Sandakan No. 3 Camp, it was obvious to the Japanese that something was amiss. Indeed something was amiss as the seven escapees were nowhere to be seen. Their absence had been covered up well until the moment of truth when it was discovered by the guards. Three of the men, had stolen a canoe and were on their way to a prearranged rendezvous point where they would transfer to a perahu which would transport them to Tawi Tawi Island, where they arrived on 14th June 1943. The others had created the illusion that they had escaped Berhala Island when in fact they were still hiding out on the island. The five men remained out of sight for three weeks until when on 26th June they were picked up by a boat and also taken to Tawi Tawi Island in what would prove to be a nerve wracking voyage. It was on Tawi Tawi that the eight men were reunited on 30th June 1943.

History records that out of the twenty-three Prisoners of War who attempted to escape it was only these eight men from Sandakan and Berhala Island that were successful. Their success would not have been possible without the assistance of the civilian and local population.

In the meantime the remainder of 'E' Force had been moved to Sandakan No. 3 Camp located under a mile from No. 1 Camp. Instead of being ferried to the wharf at Sandakan 'E' Force was taken up the Sibuga River to the north of the airfield where they then disembarked and marched to Sandakan No.3 Camp. Like 'B' Force before them, 'E' Force was to also be employed on the airfield.

Sandakan Airfield

At about the time of Frank Armstrong's death, 30th July 1942, the Japanese Guard Commander Capt. Hoshijima Susumi addressed the prisoners and informed them that they were to build an airfield at Sandakan. Capt. Hoshijima had been appointed as the Engineering Officer in charge of construction of the airfield but was also ordered to take over the duties as camp commandant from Lt. Okahara. This was a post for which he was not entirely suited, nor it seems, particularly interested in taking responsibility for. As a result he left a great deal of the daily running of the camp to his subordinates.

Before the Japanese invasion of British North Borneo the only operational airfield in the vicinity was at Tarakan Island in Dutch Borneo. In British North Borneo sites had been surveyed at Jesselton (Kota Kinabalu), Sandakan and Kudat but no airfields had been constructed. The site for the Sandakan airfield was the one which had been selected by the R.A.F. before the war. This was five miles to the northwest of Sandakan Town between the 7 and 8 mile pegs on the Labuk–Beluran Road. On the seaward side of the proposed airfield site was a mangrove swamp, to the south were low hills that rose to the back of Sandakan.

The materials to be used for the construction of the airfield could be quarried locally being coral from the coast and sandstone from the hills. So there was really nothing stopping the Japanese in their endeavour, now that they had the available materials and the manpower to complete the task. Work on the construction of the airfield began at the end of August 1942. At the end of September 1942 the officers that had accompanied 'B' Force were informed that they would also be required to work on the airfield. Private Tom Burns of the 2/20th Battalion kept a diary until sometime prior to his death in July 1945 when the diary was buried for safe keeping, and retrieved at the end of the war. Private Burns' diary entry for August 1942 reads:

> '*We all start working on building a road about 300 yards from the camp. This road finished will lead to the aerodrome, which we are going to build. It will take 12 months to complete the aerodrome, which is 3 miles from our camp. The Japs demand a certain number of men and we have to supply them. I see a lot of trouble starting here before long as the food is getting very short and the guards are belting our boys.*'[4]

The guards that were especially guilty of beating the prisoners were eight particularly nasty characters who were formed into a 'bash gang' when it was decreed that work on the airfield was progressing too slowly. The 'bash gang' was suitably equipped with pick handles, bad tempers and short fuses. They had no compunction whatsoever in bashing whoever they thought was not doing their job. However, instead of culling out individuals these overseers would bash entire kumis consisting of anything up to fifty Prisoners of War. Admittedly the Australians had been stalling for time at the construction site, as well as carrying out some odd acts of sabotage

---

[4] B3856 File 144/14/40 National Archives of Australia

whenever possible, but by the time they realised their mistake the 'bash gangs' had already arrived onsite to punish the offenders. The majority of the ground clearing work had already been done by the local Chinese and 3,000 Javanese who had been brought in to work on the airfield. Incidentally these Javanese were the labour force who had cut the track, or rentis, from the end of the sealed section of the Labuk Road through to Ranau. All the same, some clearing work was still required to be done by the prisoners which included the removal of stumps and the clearing and burning of the piles of debris. Once the ground at the airfield site was cleared of vegetation and rubble it required levelling.

Originally the Japanese had planned for only one runway. The east-west running No. 1 runway was the first to be constructed and would on completion be 5,350 feet long by 260 feet wide with dispersal loops on its northern side. As the tide of war began to turn against the Japanese, a decision was made to construct a second runway, the north-south running No. 2 runway which would on completion be 4,800 feet long and 260 wide with dispersal loops on the western side. When completed the airfield with its two runways would accommodate a considerable number of aircraft and its strategic position and facilities would determine it to be considered a major air base capable of operating bomber aircraft.

The runways were originally planned to be 2,788 feet in length, however for these runways to accept larger bomber aircraft they would need to be extended to at least 4,600 feet in length. Here was the problem because at both ends of the two runways the terrain fell away meaning that it would require extensive landfill before the proposed extensions could continue. In the same way that Prisoners of War on the Burma–Thailand rail link were being driven by their overseers on starvation rations with little or no medical supplies, the long term effect of poor food and the non-existence of medical supplies at Sandakan was also beginning to take its toll on 'B' Force.

As work on the airfield began to fall behind schedule more British prisoners from Jesselton as well as the Australians from 'E' Force were brought in to boost the workforce. When 'E' Force arrived so did additional Formosan guards to augment those already at Sandakan, boosting their numbers to around one hundred. The No. 1 runway was completed in September 1943 and now every effort was being made to also complete the second runway, but this goal was still over a full year away.

On 10th October 1944 the U.S. Navy began attacks on the Japanese southern island of Okinawa. The following day, attacks were also initiated against Japanese forces on the Philippine island of Luzon. In a series of air raids from October 1944 using the twin tailed P38 Lightnings, B25 Mitchell light bombers and B24 Liberator heavy bombers, the Americans and Australians together bombed and strafed Sandakan airfield. Altogether they destroyed in the region of sixty Japanese aircraft on the ground. On Christmas Day 1944, B24 Liberators finally put the airfield out of commission.

After 10th January 1945 work on the Sandakan airfield ceased. From now on the prisoners' labour would be used for another purpose along the track between Sandakan and Ranau.

Before the Prisoners of War at Sandakan were marched off into the interior we must first return to 1943 and complete the story concerning the illicit radio that had been operation since November 1942 and the eventual betrayal of the underground.

Radio Sandakan Revisited

It was around April–May 1943 when Capt. Matthew's Sandakan No. 1 Camp underground group decided to build a radio transmitter. Some parts had already been smuggled in by members of 'E' Force but the remaining parts that were required would need to be obtained through the local merchants and trusted local operatives in the underground. One such friend was a fresh faced young local Chinese man named Heng Joo Ming. Sergeant Wallace made acquaintance with Joo Ming who because of his youthful looks was permitted by Lt. Okahara to sell food to the prisoners at the airfield. It was also Joo Ming who harboured Sgt. Wallace after his escape from the No. 1 Camp and who again managed to smuggle Wallace across to Berhala Island. Joo Ming had been persuaded in the early stages of radio manufacture to help the Australians to obtain the parts they needed for the receiver and now he agreed to help to obtain parts to build a transmitter. It is from this time that the days of the entire underground network at Sandakan were numbered.

The perpetrator was Joo Ming's business associate, an Indian by the name of Dominic Koh, who was convinced that Joo Ming had tried to swindle him out of some money. He knew or otherwise suspected Joo Ming's involvement with the underground and attempted to blackmail him. Joo Ming vehemently denied Koh's allegations, refusing to be blackmailed. On 16th July 1943 Koh informed a local Chinese, Jackie Lo, who had been acting as an informant for the Japanese at the camp.

Not only would many innocent people be tortured and killed by the Kempeitai by this act of greed and betrayal, but also his action was the stimulus that would lead to the ultimate extermination of all but six Prisoners of War. Now that the whistle had been blown on the underground, Joo Ming and his father were seized by the Kempeitai, and under the pain of torture gave the names of other Chinese members involved with the underground. Other members of the underground including Capt. Matthews, Dr Taylor and Ahbin were also arrested. On 22nd July the camp was raided and two pistols, a map and an incriminating note was found in one of Lt. Wells' boots, but still no radio or parts were discovered.

A second search of the camp was conducted on 24th July and this time a list of parts that had been smuggled into camp was discovered. Following Lt. Wells' arrest and after being subjected to torture he produced some parts for an incomplete radio transmitter in the hope that this would convince them that these were the only parts in his possession. The Kempeitai however were not convinced and ultimately the transmitter was handed in as interrogations and torture continued on the Australians, civilians and local population over the next three months until the Kempeitai were satisfied and closed the file on what they were to call the 'Sandakan Incident'.

To help understand the paranoia experienced by the Kempeitai it is necessary to mention several other so called incidents. The previous month, June 1943 the 'Haga Incident' had occurred at Banjarmasim on the southeast coast of Borneo. Dr B. J. Haga, after whom the incident was named, was the Dutch Governor of East and West Kalimantan. The Kempeitai had raided the house of a Netherlands East Indian radio mechanic and not surprisingly discovered a radio transmitter claiming that it had been used by the local resistance group to communicate with the Allies. Over the next few months, 257 people were tortured and or murdered by the Kempeitai including Dr Haga and his wife.

Next, a baseless rumour was circulated that an armed uprising was about to take place at Pontianak on the west coast of Borneo. This time the Imperial Japanese Navy equivalent of the Kempeitai took control of the situation. Out of a total of 1,500 Indians, Chinese and Netherlands East Indians who were arrested, the majority were tortured and killed on the basis of this rumour. However one event that was not fabricated by the Kempeitai and one that convinced them that they were in fact facing a real uprising occurred at Jesselton, in October 1943. A Chinese man who had been trained by American operatives in the Philippines was put ashore by submarine to organise and recruit a resistance movement from young local men. On 10th October 1943, about one hundred local men rose up against the Japanese at Jesselton killing about sixty Japanese and Formosan residents. It would take the Japanese three months to quell this uprising.

Because of the 'Sandakan and Haga Incidents', the Pontianak tortures and the uprising at Jesselton the Kempeitai began to lose faith in their own ability to control British North Borneo and consequently invented their own conspiracy theories. Added to this fuel was the reality that Japan was losing the war to the Allies who were moving ever closer towards Borneo. Captain Matthew's underground organisation was never intended to mobilise until such time of an Allied invasion of Sandakan.

Looking back now over events from the time of 'B' Force's arrival in July 1942 to January 1945 when the airfield was made totally unserviceable, the following events had occurred. An underground intelligence network had been uncovered involving Australian Officers and enlisted men, trusted European civilians, local constabulary and members of the local population. A radio and parts to build a transmitter were discovered in the possession of the Australians. Sixteen prisoners had escaped and fifteen were either shot or captured. A further seven prisoners escaped, including Sgt. Wallace who had escaped earlier and was hidden by the underground, this making eight the total number who had successfully escaped Sandakan and Berhala Island.

The uprising in Jesselton, the 'Haga Incident' at Banjarmasim and the imagined uprising at Pontianak, were all episodes that helped to seal the fate of the British and Australian Prisoners of War at Sandakan.

Returning now to the time of the closure of the 'Sandakan Incident' in 1943. On 15th October 1943 following the removal of most of the British Officers, all but eight of the Australian Officers were moved to Lintang Barracks Kuching on twenty minutes notice. On 25th October 1943 those who had been arrested at Sandakan where sent to Kuching by ship for trial. This included twenty-eight Australians, forty-eight of the local population plus five European civilians from Sandakan. Of the Australians, Lt. John Morrison and Sgt. Alf Stevens from the 2/4th were included. Lieutenant Morrison was acquitted of any crime against the Imperial Japanese Army, however, Sgt. Stevens was sentenced to six years penal servitude to be served at Outram Road Prison, Singapore, for his part in the underground and the operation of the radio receiver. Sergeant Stevens had been arrested on 26th July 1943, sentenced on 2nd March 1944 and arrived at Outram Road Prison on 11th March 1944 where he remained until his release at the end of the war. Sergeant Stevens also had a hand to play in the immobilising by sabotage of a heavy piece of earthmoving equipment at Sandakan.

Sandakan–Ranau – 1945

Following the 'Sandakan Incident' the prisoner's rice and food rations were reduced. From the time of 'B' Force's arrival to their ultimate deaths the rice ration would steadily be reduced to the point where the men were surviving on little more than a handful of rice per day.

On 17th October 1943 'B' and 'E' Forces were amalgamated, most likely in the belief that they could better control the subversive activities of the Australians if they were all together. In August 1944 the Morotai Islands fell and the Japanese garrison stationed there was withdrawn to Borneo. The Japanese garrison at Sandakan was increased in September and this placed increased demands upon the food stocks. As it was becoming increasingly difficult to ship in food from Sarawak due to Allied action against Japanese shipping, the Sandakan garrison began to stock pile their food.

This situation is reflected in the health of the prisoners who by the end of 1944 were all suffering from malnutrition, or some form of tropical disease. An Allied air raid that occurred on 14th October had also destroyed a fair portion of the crops in the Sandakan environs which only exacerbated the food supply problem. The decision to trim the prisoners' rations to a level that would only just sustain life was not made by Hoshijima but by Lt-Gen Yamawaki Masataka of the Borneo Defence Force Headquarters at Kuching, later renamed the 37th Army.

The ulterior motive was that in the event of an Allied invasion the Prisoners of War would be so weak that they would be of little use to the invading forces.

> '*By March 1945 the Japanese had stockpiled huge quantities of food and medical supplies in preparation for the expected Allied invasion. Presumably these stockpiles were intended only for the Japanese personnel. The storage room beneath commandant Hoshijima's house contained more than 90 metric tons of rice and 160,000 quinine tablets. After the war, Allied forces found other stockpiles in the Sandakan area containing more than 786,000 quinine tablets, '19,600 Vitamin A and D tablets, large numbers of Vitamin B and C tablets, and a great deal of medical and surgical equipment. Nothing from this stockpile was supplied to the POW's.*' [5]

This latest development at Sandakan can now be seen as a direct result of the events that led to the arrest of Capt. Matthews and the discovery of the Sandakan underground network. The Japanese were plainly scared of the ramifications of what may have happened if the prisoners had risen up in retaliation against three years starvation and brutality. A search of the camp at the end of 1944 resulted in the confiscation of knives and scissors.

The First Sandakan–Ranau Death March

In North Borneo Allied Tactical Air Forces had subjected Sandakan to a heavy series of air attacks.

> '*This town was practically wiped out, and the Japanese in the town and nearby areas were harried daily by bombing and machine-gun fire. The general tactical plan in Borneo was to prevent the enemy consolidating positions or concentrating in any one area. First T.A.F. aircraft were used to attack any sign of concentration. Attacks were made on stores areas, keeping the enemy on the move, preventing him from growing food supplies and driving him into the jungle. This policy was continued in August until the war ended.*' [6]

The taking of Palawan Island just to the north of Borneo and the fear that an attack might be launched against Brunei instigated a reorganisation of the 37th Army's positions. This situation brought about the decision to move two of the three Japanese battalions now based at Sandakan to Jesselton and to utilise the Prisoners of War as carriers whence they would be relocated to a new camp at Tuaran, 35 kilometres to the north of Jesselton. Because there was no road between Sandakan and Jesselton, the Japanese had sought the help of a Dusun tribesman by the name of Kulang to advise them as to the best route to take between the two locations. Kulang's sympathies were in no way inclined towards the Japanese and so he mapped a route that encompassed every obstacle that was possible to place in the path of the trekkers. Had he known that it would be Australian and British Prisoners of War who would suffer as a direct consequence of his deviousness he may have been a little less harsh in his selection of the terrain that the parties would need to traverse.

The lead party on the first march from Sandakan to Ranau, a distance of 164 miles, set out on 28th January 1945. The plan was that of the 470 prisoners, 370 Australians and one hundred

---

5   Yuki Tanaka, *Hidden Horrors* Japanese War Crimes in WWII, Westview Press 1996, p.43
6   George Odgers, *Air War Against Japan 1942–1945* Australia in the War of 1939–45, Air Volume II, Australian War Memorial Canberra 1968, p.490

British were to set out in small groups in nine parties over consecutive days. The last party on the first march departed on 6th February. Each party was under the control of the guards, who were regular Japanese soldiers, however, there were also Formosan guards who were intermingled amongst these soldiers of Nippon.

Prior to the first party setting out, all the Japanese platoon commanders were summoned for a briefing. Orders were issued that no prisoners were to be left behind, no matter what the reason. The Japanese platoon commander of the last party on the first march was taken aside and instructed in no uncertain terms that any Prisoner of War left behind, or for that matter any stragglers who were encountered along the track, were to be disposed of.

The intention had been to make supply drops at intervals along the intended route. An issue of rice was made before the commencement of each march at the 15 mile peg at end of the sealed section on the Labuk–Baluran Road. This issue of rice was meant to last the first four days of the march until the first supply drop at Maunad was reached. These drops which were set up by Japanese Quartermaster Corps soldiers were to be at Maunad at the 49 mile point, Sapi at the 60 mile, Boto at the 103 mile, Papan at the 120 mile and Paginatan at the 138 mile and the last drop before Ranau at the 164 mile point on the march.

The distance from Ranau to Jesselton was another 76 miles further east. Not that this mattered because none of the prisoners would have the opportunity to tread this path. Each of the emaciated Prisoners of War on the first march was to carry a mixed load of food, ammunition or anything required of them by the Japanese. The system worked out by the Japanese for the planned supply drops of food failed almost immediately. There had been sufficient food for the first party but not for the other parties following up behind. In the end, men were going days without food and what food there was in the possession of the prisoners was being pilfered by the guards to supplement their own meals. The first party that had set out on Sunday 28th January arrived at Ranau on Monday 12th February 1945.

The wet season did not finish in this area of Borneo until the end of February, so prisoner and guards alike had been forced to slog through heavy mud along the track. This not only took its toll on the weak, sick and starved Prisoners of War but some of the guards as well. Under these conditions, with the state of the track and the lack of food whereby the supposedly fit guards were finding the going tough, it would be naive to think that the guards would help prisoners even if they had been permitted to do so by their officers.

On arrival at Ranau the guards from the first party now moved onto Jesselton whilst those of the prisoners who had avoided a bullet or bayonet were to remain at Ranau. The food situation had not been relieved on arrival at Ranau and prisoners continued to die from disease, malnutrition and the workloads which had been placed upon them. On several occasions from 22nd February, parties of the fittest prisoners that had reached Ranau were chosen to carry twenty kilogram bags of rice the 26 miles back down the track to Paginatan. Many of these unfortunates would never complete the round trip. It was later stated by one of the six survivors from the march that it was believed that this rice was for the consumption of the guards and not the prisoners.

The Second Sandakan–Ranau Death March

The situation back at Sandakan had become worse since the departure of the nine parties on the first march to Ranau. Indiscriminate bombing by the Allies over Sandakan had killed at least thirty prisoners; a wood collecting party had been attacked, the pilots believing that they were Japanese soldiers. The food situation, despite the huge stockpiles of food under Capt. Hoshijima's house had become critical. The camp had been over run by rats due to the fact that Allied bombing and strafing attacks had disrupted their food supply. The rats were particularly prevalent in the camp hospital where 400 seriously ill prisoners were admitted. On 17th March Capt. Hoshijima received orders to the effect that all Prisoners of War were to be exterminated.

With the constant Allied bombing and the Australian invasion of Tarakan on 1st May 1945, Sandakan was looking as if it was about to be transformed into a war zone. Captain Hoshijima was replaced by Capt. Takakuwa Takuo around 17th May 1945. Captain Takakuwa was a combatant officer and it seems better suited to the task of removing the remaining Prisoners of War from Sandakan.

On 27th May Sandakan was bombarded by Allied warships and also bombed by aircraft. Captain Takakuwa decided that his only option was to move every prisoner that was capable of walking to Ranau. Of the 824 Prisoners of War left alive at Sandakan it was believed by the Japanese that 536, being 439 Australians and 97 British, were in some sort of condition to depart Sandakan on foot. This then meant that 288 prisoners were left behind at Sandakan. By this time all the prisoners had been congregated in the wired section of the Australian No. 1 Camp.

On 29th May the original British No. 2 Camp and the Australian 'E' Force Camp were razed to the ground. Later that day Capt. Takakuwa ordered that all patients be moved out into the open and the buildings set alight. The 536 prisoners that were to embark on the second march were gathered on the parade ground and sorted into eleven groups of approximately fifty prisoners. There would be 147 guards spread over the eleven kumis but they were not all Formosans, as there were Japanese guards included in this second march. The eleven groups were then split into three parties.

The second Sandakan–Ranau march began on the night of 29th May 1945. As soon as the prisoners left the camp all the remaining buildings, except for some still being used by the Japanese, were burnt down. The march continued throughout the night until the column came to a halt the following afternoon and rested that night. Already it was apparent that some of the prisoners would be lucky if they would be able to march much further. Whereas on the first march, orders were issued to dispose of any prisoner who fell behind or attempted escape, on the second march the Japanese guards were indiscriminately selecting prisoners, herding them off into the jungle and ridding themselves of their burden.

This action may very well be an indication that the Japanese guards were worried about the possibility that Allied soldiers might be following close behind and were attempting to put as much distance as possible between themselves and Sandakan. Obviously the prisoners in their present state of health would only slow them down.

Three days after departing Sandakan it was always Lt. Watababe Genzo's or S/Sgt. Tsuji's special group of Formosan guards that followed up the rear to eliminate any prisoners who were too sick or weak to go any further. The Formosans in these two groups were constantly rotated so as no guard missed out on an opportunity to eliminate a prisoner either by rifle butt, bullet or bayonet. According to evidence given at war crimes trials, these murders were not carried out by any of the Japanese soldiers, as it was the Formosan guards who were forced to conduct these executions.

The prisoners by this time were all well aware of what their fate would be if they failed to keep up with the column. They would hear the sounds of gunshots in the distance and they passed enough decomposing bodies along the track to convince them of the seriousness of the situation. Prisoners would shake hands when one of them fell out. It was almost as if the chosen were accepting the fact they were soon to die and were going to their death with a feeling of anticipation of finally being at peace. They knew that soon their tired bodies would be at rest, far away from this insane world of death, hunger and misery.

When the last of the three groups had arrived at Ranau on 25th June 1945 out of the 536 prisoners who had departed Sandakan twenty days earlier there were 183 prisoners left alive.

The Final Days at Sandakan

The 288 prisoners that had been left behind at Sandakan were forced to improvise with any materials they could scrounge and assemble into some form of shelter. In addition the prisoners had also been forced to forage for food, as they had not received rations from the Japanese for some time. A Japanese S/Sgt. and sixteen Formosan guards had been left behind with the remaining prisoners.

When a Lt. Moritake returned to Sandakan with orders to remove, quote 'all Prisoners of War from Sandakan' Lieutenant Moritake selected seventy-five prisoners and placed them in the charge of 2nd Lt. Iwashita along with thirty-seven Japanese soldiers and instructed him to march them to Ranau. Of the seventy-five Prisoners of War that departed on 9th June 1945 none survived. This now left in the region of 185 prisoners remaining at Sandakan. This number had shrunk to fifty by 12th July.

A few days earlier Lt. Moritake had been ordered by Capt. Takakuwa to leave the Sandakan area as soon as possible and to dispose of the surviving prisoners along the track on the way to Ranau. Lieutenant Moritake selected twenty-three prisoners who he thought might be able to make the march, but rather than take them along he had them executed immediately; the remaining twenty-seven prisoners were too sick to be marched. On 13th July, these remaining twenty-seven prisoners were taken to the airfield by twelve Formosan guards and shot. Their bodies were then thrown into a trench and covered with earth.

On 16th July 1943 an Indian by the name of Domonic Koh betrayed the Sandakan underground because he believed that he had been swindled out of a few dollars. On 13th July 1945 as a consequence of this act a deathly silence fell upon the once picturesque little town of Sandakan.

The Final Days at Ranau

At the end of June 1945 there were 189 Prisoners of War remaining at Ranau. When the 183 survivors from the second march arrived they were put to work immediately without rest, building atap huts for themselves and the Japanese officers. As Ranau had also been subjected to Allied air attacks, Capt. Takakuwa decided to establish another Prisoner of War camp ten kilometres away in the jungle which would offer better cover from marauding aircraft. This camp was the 110 mile camp, where Arthur 'Codge' Thorns was still alive on 28th July.

Naturally the prisoners were employed on all the manual labouring as well as water carrying from the valley below. The new camp was completed on 18th July and at this time there were about seventy-two prisoners left alive. The prisoners that were suffering from dysentery were forced to sleep on the ground under the floor of the single storyed prisoners hut. Those who were not suffering were permitted to sleep inside the hut.

On 28th July, on information received from a guard, that all the prisoners were soon to be murdered, two men, W.O. Bill Stipcewich and Pte. Herman Reither escaped. Only one of these men, W.O. Stipcewich would live to tell the story; Reither dying within a few days of his escape. Altogether only six prisoners would escape and survive the Sandakan to Ranau Death Marches. At this time, there were thirty-eight prisoners left alive at Ranau including Capt. P .G. Picone who had operated on Frank Armstrong on 30th July 1942. By 1st August there were thirty-three prisoners left alive when the death order was given. The prisoners were broken up into groups on this day and between 1000 hours and 1300 hours were taken into the jungle, and were either shot or bashed to death. If this information is correct then Arthur Stanley 'Codge' Thorn's date of death would be 1st August 1945 not 8th August as has been quoted and recorded by the Commonwealth War Graves.

Lintang Officer's Camp – Kuching

As mentioned, the Australian officers had been transferred to Lintang Barracks Kuching on 15th October 1943. It will be remembered that 'E' Force passed through this camp on their way to Sandakan. The officers had only been given twenty minutes notice, just enough time to collect their belongings before being bundled onboard a river steamer bound for Kuching.

There were two officers from the 2/4th who were sent to this camp. One of these was Lt. John Morrison who had been arrested by the Kempeitai because he had been found with a note in his possession from Lt. Brian Walton. At the time Brian was still on Berhala Island and had managed to get the note to John to inform him that his wife Elsie had given birth to a baby girl. He was arrested by the Kempeitai on 8th September 1943 and spent fifty-four days in a native gaol at Sandakan, before being sent to Kuching for trial. Lieutenant Morrison was tried by a military court but found to be not guilty of any crime against the Imperial Japanese Army and was subsequently released to Lintang Barracks.

The other officers arrived at their new home on 22nd October 1943 and settled into the Lintang compound. The internees at Lintang were a multi-racial group of both gender and sections of the compound were wired off into nine distinct areas. The officers found their quarters were to be three huts and a kitchen, enclosed in an area on about one acre. Each hut could accommodate about 150 officers and twenty other ranks. The other ranks were employed on kitchen and general duties.

Unlike Sandakan, the officers were not required to work, so they found themselves with a great deal of spare time on their hands. Whilst at Sandakan a group of thespians had already distinguished themselves with the quality of their productions. Their first effort at Sandakan had been staged on 8th December 1942. It was a little production called 'Radio Rubbish'. It seems ironic now that the first production had the word radio in the title. It is perhaps no less ironic that the second and last major production at Sandakan was called 'Let's Boong it On'. Lieutenant John Morrison was already accredited with having a splendid singing voice and was well known for his leading rousing singing sessions on the way back to camp at Sandakan after a hard day's work at the airfield.

Once the officers had organised their individual creature comforts, they set to work on establishing a vegetable garden inside their wired off area. Once established, the garden only required a few hours tending each day. It wasn't long before the thespians were at it again, this time with a musical comedy. For the Gilbert and Sullivan fans amongst the audience, an old favourite, "**H.M.S. Pinafore**" was staged on 12th March 1944. The 2/4th Machine Gun Battalion was well represented with both Lt.'s John Morrison and Brian Walton taking on two of the main singing parts. Following "**H.M.S. Pinafore**", there was a break in production as scabies broke out in one of the huts, the one that was used to stage the productions.

Now the hut was used exclusively for those suffering from this contagious skin disease, and with the effects of malnutrition, the scabies epidemic was proving difficult for the medical staff to eradicate. Each man in the Officer's Camp was soon categorised into one of two groups, the scabies sufferers and the clean skins. Perhaps the most important factors at the Officer's Camp at Lintang Barracks was that they kept their morale high by keeping themselves busy with their staged productions.

On 18th August 1945 leaflets were dropped over Borneo including Sandakan and Kuching informing all Japanese forces that the war was over. The Japanese, however, thought these to be Allied propaganda and ignored these leaflets. A second leaflet drop was made over Kuching a few days later and it was only then that the Japanese believed the war was in fact over.

On 13th September 1945 Lt.'s John Morrison and Brian Walton boarded the 2/2nd Australian Hospital Ship *Wanganella*. The ship arrived at Morotai on 19th September and these two 2/4th officers were admitted to the 2/9th Australian General Hospital. One week later on 26th September they again boarded the *Wanganella* that sailed for Sydney where they disembarked and travelled by train via Melbourne and home to Perth. Like the majority ex-Prisoners of War who returned home to Western Australia, they were admitted to the 110 (PMH) Perth Military Hospital on 21st October 1945.

For Lt. John Morrison Christmas 1945 would be spent with a wife Elsie who he had not seen for over three and a half years, and a baby daughter he had only known for two months.

The Sumatra Story

There were a number of members from the 2/4th Machine Gun Battalion who managed to escape Singapore Island only to be captured on the island of Sumatra in the Netherlands East Indies. This escape route went across the Durian Straits between Singapore and Sumatra, then traced the Indragiri River, one of several east-west flowing rivers past the towns of Tembilihan, Rengat as far Ayer Molek. From Ayer Molek it was necessary to move on foot to Padang on the southwest coast of Sumatra.

It was at Padang that these fugitives hoped they would be rescued by a ship and evacuated to safety. The author believes that following the evacuation of the British and French Forces at Dunkirk an event which was repeated on a smaller scale following the failed Greece and Crete Campaigns, that a 'Dunkirk mentality' existed amongst Commonwealth troops. Simply put, this meant that if the army got into trouble it was expected the navy would come to their rescue and pluck them from the beaches. We saw this happen in 1915 at Gallipoli and we would see it happen again with troops from *Blackforce* when headed towards the beaches on the south coast of Java.

The men from the 2/4th who made good their escape did not all travel together as the following will explain. Firstly, there were the three 2/4th relocated from Java to Sumatra by the Japanese; being Harold Booth, Noel Banks and Robert McAskil. McAskil departed Java in Party No. 20 arriving at Singapore on 21st May 1944. This party was taken to River Valley Road Transit Camp where testing was carried out to assess the health of the men before they were forwarded to Japan. McAskil was removed from the draft which was reduced from 777 to 772 men. The ship he would have eventually boarded, was sunk off Nagasaki by a U.S Submarine on 24th June 1944. However, there was to be no reprieve for Robert Ramsay McAskil because he died from cardiac beri-beri whilst at Kampoeng near Kota Baroe in Sumatra on 28th March 1945. Noel Banks and Harold Booth were transported to Singapore on 27th June 1944 from the Bicycle Camp Batavia on Java Party No. 22, arriving at Singapore on 1st July 1944. All three men were sent to Pakan Baroe but this episode will be covered later in the story.

Included in another group that left Singapore were Clifford 'Squasher' Squance, Arthur Magill, Ron MacLellan from Queensland, an English soldier, an Indian Sepoy and the two Rush brothers from the 2/18th Battalion. Five of these men had been caught in the Japanese ambush at South-West Bukit Timah on 11th February 1942. Arthur Magill had been wounded in the neck and armpit at Bulim Village two days earlier. The second time around, Arthur had his rifle shot out of his right hand receiving two gunshot wounds to his third and fourth fingers, and his leg. Cliff Squance, who had also been wounded in the left shoulder still managed to escape the scene of the ambush and assisted Arthur Magill over an embankment. The two machine gunners then made for the coast where they met up with another three fugitives. This small group borrowed a dinghy from a seaside resort near Pasir Panjang that was equipped with an outboard motor.

By this time there were the five men in the dinghy but before too long the Rush brothers were also taken onboard. The seven men motored for some time against the outgoing tide but eventually the outboard ran out of petrol and they were forced to put into an island somewhere in Keppel Harbour, close to Singapore City. A vote was taken, and it was decided to continue with their escape to Sumatra where it was hoped they would be rescued. They then traded the dinghy with some locals for what they believed would be in exchange for transport to Sumatra. Instead in the darkness the men were taken in the general direction of Sumatra and dropped off at a large island. They remained on this island for four days until the local natives acted out of concern as to what the Japanese might do to them if they were caught harbouring soldiers from Singapore.

In the end the locals plucked up the courage and transported the seven to another island where they were again left to their own resources. It was here that a Chinese junk arrived and picked them up. There were already about 120 men aboard the junk and about the same number were waiting on the island to board. The junk made Sumatra but required a tow from a Dutch launch for a way up the swift flowing Indragiri River. Records list a Chinese ship named the *Hung Jao* which was sunk by its own crew on 9th March 1942 in the Indragiri River due to engine failure. This ship had been contracted to collect survivors from Singapore and the fact that it was towed up the Indragiri River may well be an indication that it was the ship that 'Squasher' and Arthur had managed to secure a berth on during their escape. However, this was far from the only incident where a fleeing ship or boat was assisted.

The Indragiri River was not an easy river to navigate and eventually they were forced to disembark at Ayer Molek and began the trek across Sumatra on foot towards Padang. Both 'Squasher' and Arthur because of their wounds, stopped at a hospital at Sawahunto for treatment, whereupon they continued their trek overland. Like so many others on the same quest, time ran out and they were captured by the Japanese at Padang. The experiences of 'Squasher' and Arthur are probably typical of most who tried their luck at escaping Singapore via Sumatra.

Richard Winston Annear escaped from Singapore some time after Monday 16th February 1942. By this time Singapore was firmly under Japanese control. As 'Win', whilst in the company of two other men from the 2/4th, had made it as far as an island off Singapore, he could see no reason why they should surrender and suggested they make a break for Sumatra. The other two men however were not as keen on the idea and as 'Win' says, 'my two blokes were tired and hungry and so decided to go back to Singapore and give themselves up'. 'Win' decided to go it alone and so now we will let him tell the remainder of his story.

> *'I had forty dollars on me so I paid a native one dollar to row me to the next island were I picked up with some other chaps.*
>
> *From here we set off towards Sumatra and after many trials and foodless days we arrived at Sumatra at a town called Rengat. There we met up (unfortunately) with an organised evacuation party which only slowed our travel. We eventually made the other coast of Sumatra tired and hungry at a place called Padang, but by the time of our arrival we were two days too late and the last boat had already gone and the next one was sunk coming in. We were lucky that we missed these boats as very few of them got through the Japanese net.*
>
> *Just before the Japs took Padang six of us decided to head south. All the Padang chaps were taken prisoner on the 17th March. We, after much walking made a tea plantation and from there we took to the jungle where we stayed for two months eating weeds or rice, brown beans and trapping our own deer, the longest we went*

without meat was three days. Eventually the natives gave us away and we found ourselves back at Padang POW Camp on 9th May. All the chaps there were starving and we were as fat as butter, then we starved along with them. Six weeks later we were moved by truck to Medan in northern Sumatra.' [7]

Another party of would be escapees from the 2/4th would not all be so lucky. 'Win' Annear's brother Dudley, Roy Semple and Albert Bell attempted to escape later in the week from the west coast of Singapore. These three men were members of D' Company No. 15 Platoon.

It is believed that thy were overtaken by Japanese troops and went to ground. Sometime on 14th February 1942 they attempted to flee the island by boat but were spotted and attacked by Japanese troops. Roy Semple was lucky to make it, even though he received a wound to the upper left chest. Dudley Annear and Albert Bell were not so lucky during the execution of their escape bid.

Dudley and Albert are both believed to have been in or near the boat when they were hit by mortar fire, and as a result Albert Bell was killed outright and Dudley died later. Roy Semple still managed to escape to Sumatra, despite his wounds and made his way to Padang where he was also taken prisoner. In the letter to his family 'Win' makes no mention of ever meeting up with his brother on Singapore following the Japanese landing so it can only be assumed that they made their bids to escape independent of each other.

The remaining members of the 2/4th who also managed successful escapes were Ted Hopson from 'B' Company No. 7 Platoon who escaped on the Sunday night 15th February 1942. There was also Cecil Quinn from 'D' Company No. 13 Platoon who was wounded in action at Lim Chu Kang Road, Alfred Burgess and Harold Smith from 'E' Company Special Reserve Battalion.

In the Bag

On St Patrick's Day, 17th March 1942, the Japanese arrived in Padang and took over control from the Dutch. There was to be no fighting as the Dutch had declared Padang an open city.

The prisoners who had been quartered in the Chinese School at Padang were permitted to remain for a few more days until their transfer to a Dutch Army barracks. Conditions were quite good at this camp with plenty of room, organised sport and lectures, and even though the food was rationed it improved when the Dutch took over the cooking duties.

After about two weeks in this camp the Japanese made it known that in two days, 500 prisoners would be departing Padang. Included in this group was Lt-Col Albert Coates from the 10th Australian General Hospital. On 9th May Lt-Col Coates was ordered to fall in with this group of British from the three services who called themselves the British Sumatra Battalion.

Moving north to Belawan the Port of Medan on the northeast coast of Sumatra they would board the *England Maru* on 15th May and sail to Burma to work on the rail link to Thailand. Thankfully Lt-Col Coates was included in this draft as he will always be remembered for his work and devotion to duty at the Khonkan 55km Camp in Burma during 1943.

Gloe Gloer Camp – Medan

On 13th June 1942 the remainder of the prisoners, except the Indians, were loaded onto trucks and driven north on a journey that would take five days. Leaving Padang they headed off parallel to the west coast via Fort de Kock to Loebock Sekapi for the first night's stop. The

---

[7]   Taken from a letter written by Richard Winston Annear to his family. Item loaned to the author by Clive Annear

second night they stayed at the Dutch Army barracks at Sibolga. The third night was spent at Larung as the journey now took the men across the interior of Sumatra towards the east coast past Lake Toba. The fourth night was spent at Siamtar and on the fifth day (17th June) they arrived at Belawan, located a few kilometres from Medan, the largest town in northern Sumatra.

At first the men were accommodated in coolie labourer's huts adjacent to the wharf. They would work here for the next few days loading scrap iron and rubber onto ships destined for Japan. The prisoners would return to the wharves later but on 20th June they were ushered onto railway trucks and transported to their next camp. This was a Dutch Army barracks called Gloe Gloer No. 1 Camp, located about 2 kilometres from Medan. There, the prisoners were accommodated in six long barracks buildings that ran side by side. There was a parade ground, sports ground, Japanese officers' and guard's buildings, all located inside an eight feet high wall.

The prisoners were soon put to work on daily work parties. At first the men would finish their allotted daily quota of work so as they could return to barracks. However, like every other Prisoner of War camp it was soon realised that the sooner they finished the sooner they would be given other tasks to complete.

The place they were put to work was at the Socony Oil Depot where they filled petrol into drums. This job lasted about seven to eight weeks until the Japanese discovered that the fuel being put into the drums was for some reason contaminated. The next job allocated to the prisoners was the excavation of a moat around a temple and shrine to honour the fallen.

As we learnt at Adam Park on Singapore with the construction of the 'Fallen Warriors Shrine' at Bukit Batok, the Japanese prefer to have some form of a water channel and bridge crossing on the approach to their shrines.

On the completion of the shrine, the next job was of all things the construction of a racecourse. At about this time, the Japanese guards were relieved by Koreans. At first they were timid and somewhat nervous, however, it did not take them long to learn their trade and soon bashings and brutal treatment were commonplace.

Atjeh Party

On 7th March 1944 after days of rumours the word was out that a working party was to be sent to Northern Sumatra where a road was to be constructed. This party would include fifty Australians under the command of Lt. Tranter from the 2/29th Battalion. The next day, those selected to leave on this party were loaded onto trucks and were driven into the interior where they would remain for the next seven months. Included in this group were George Quinn, Ted Hopson and Arthur Magill. On the first day of their journey they travelled 308 kilometres to a place called Kota Tjane. This was located about 10 kilometres to the north of Laubaleng in the heartland of Sumatra. They stayed here for two days billeted in a schoolhouse, then it was back onboard the trucks. Thinking that they were to continue the journey they were surprised when the trucks turned around and headed back from whence they had just come.

The next day, 13th March 1944 it was on the road again as the work party set off on a 145 kilometre march to a still undisclosed destination. The first night's stopover was at Gunung, and the second at Maloek. After four day's marching, on 17th March the men arrived at their final destination, Blang Kedjeren. They were accommodated in a former Dutch Army barracks that was to be known by the prisoners as the Hospital Camp.

The sick and those unable to march any further were left here, some never to be seen again. The next day it was on the road again until they finally reached their camp at Tenal Gajoe. This was the territory of the Atjeh or Achinese natives. These people were renowned for being fierce headhunters and had never been completely subdued during the Dutch colonisation of Sumatra.

There were two camps at this location in the mountains, one for the British and Australians, and one for the Dutch. The work at this camp kept the prisoners busy for about three weeks. Then, on 3rd May 1944, as the road they were building progressed, they moved further north to another location at Kedjeren.

It had been necessary to leave Ted Hopson behind at Tenal Gajoe because he was suffering from appendicitis. It had not been possible to operate because at the time he was also suffering from dysentery. By not being able to operate for fear of infection Ted died on 26th April 1944.

Ted was a popular and a well liked man amongst the group and has been described as being a good bloke, an Australian's way of saying that you were a decent person. Ted's body was brought forward to the camp at Blang Kedjeren where a coffin was constructed and this popular 2/4th machine gunner was laid to rest about 100 yards from the camp. There was a stonemason amongst the prisoners who cut a headstone that was placed at the head of his grave. The work on the road continued at a location to the east between the old campsite and the new. On 6th October 1944 it was time to move back to Medan. The prisoners set out in three columns as they had done on the journey north. As the columns passed Ted Hopson's grave all paid respect to their friend with a snappy and respectful 'eyes left'.

The men arrived back at a rest camp just outside of Medan on 11th October, five days after they had set out from Blang Kedjeren. After a week's rest on reduced rations the prisoners were shaken back to reality with the news that they on the move again. Leaving the haven of the rest camp the men were marched the 3 miles to the railway station where after a short journey they detrained and were loaded onto trucks.

Using the same route as they had travelled on the way to Medan they headed back towards Fort de Kock on the west coast of Sumatra. They were billeted for three days in the old Police Barracks at Bukit Tinggi, and then it was back on a train for a lengthy journey this time to a place called Moearo. The date was 21st October 1944.

The prisoners were now to learn that like their brothers on the Burma–Thailand rail link they were to build a three foot six inch gauge railway line between Pakan Baroe and Moearo, a distance of 220 kilometres.

In addition to this main line there was also a shorter two foot five and one half inch narrow gauge 20 kilometre spur line which branched off the main line at the 119km point. However, before the story of the railway is told it is necessary to return to Medan.

Harukiku Maru – SS *Van Waerwjick* Party

When the fifty men departed the Gloe Gloer camp on 8th March 1944, there were forty-nine Australians left behind, including Roy Semple, 'Win' Annear, 'Squasher' Squance, Alf Burgess and Harold Smith. On 24th June 1944 they were alerted to be ready to leave for Singapore. The following day trucks turned up at the Gloe Gloer Camp to transport the prisoners to the port of Belawan to board the ship that would transport them to Singapore.

The ship was the SS *Van Waerwjick*, a 3,040 ton passenger-cargo ship that had been captured by the Japanese on 3rd March 1942. As was the Japanese custom, the ship was given a Japanese name, in this case *Harukiku Maru*.

The men arrived at the docks at around noon and were crammed into the fore and aft holds of the ship. A Japanese corvette was to act as escort to this small convoy that included two tankers and two transport ships. The *Harukiku Maru* sailed from Belawan at about 1500 hours on 25th June and headed out into the Malacca Straits, where it was joined by the other ships in the convoy.

On 26th June at 1350 hours at position Latitude 3 degrees-15 minutes North, Longitude 99 degrees 46-minutes east, two mighty explosions amidships rocked the ship, and sent it to the depths. Two torpedoes had been fired from the HMS/M *Truculent* which was depth charged, causing her to hit the bottom at 68 feet. There was no loss of life from the 2/4th but 167 others went down with the ship.

The survivors after having spent four hours treading water were rescued by one of the Japanese tankers. They then continued their voyage onboard this tanker to Singapore where they disembarked and were taken to River Valley Road Transit Camp. Of the four men from the 2/4th, 'Win' Annear and 'Squasher' Squance would return to Sumatra to work on the Pakan Baroe–Moearo railway. Harold Smith was sent to the hospital with appendicitis on 21st July. Alf Burgess had suffered a head injury from the sinking of the *Harukiku Maru*.

As mentioned earlier, three men had arrived at Singapore on Java Parties No. 20 and No. 22 between 21st May and 1st July 1944. It is believed that it would have been sometime between the 7th July and 8th August 1944 that these three men from Java, McAskil, Booth and Banks, as well as 'Win' Annear and 'Squasher' Squance, were transported to Pakan Baroe to work on the railway. They would work mainly between Loeboeksakat at the 23km point and Logas at the 140km point on the railway. The entire draft of 1,257 prisoners who were destined for Pakan Baroe had been split into smaller drafts. They were transported from Singapore directly up the Siak River on an old ferryboat named the *Elizabeth*, otherwise known as the 'white boat'.

The size of this ferry and the fact that it could not carry many passengers might suggest why these men were transported in several parties between 7th July and 8th August 1944.

The township of Pakan Baroe was a small port about 90 miles along the Siak River from its mouth. This river was deep enough to accommodate ships of up to 800 tons all year round. Because the Japanese were losing so much shipping to the Allies it was decided that in the event of an Allied attack on Western Sumatra, Japanese reinforcements from Singapore would be brought in by sea, utilising the shelter of the islands between Singapore and Sumatra. The Japanese troops would then be brought straight up the Siak River to Pakan Baroe.

At this time there was no railway, however, there were roads that connected Pakan Baroe to Padang on the west coast and Oosthaven on the south coast. As usual, labour was not a concern to the Japanese as there were still enough Prisoners of War who could be set to the task. There were 513 Prisoners of War who would lose their lives building on this railway, not to mention the many prisoners and Romeshas (Netherlands East Indian conscripts) who would lose their lives when their ship, the *Junyo Maru* was torpedoed by a British submarine on 18th September 1944 whilst in transit from Java to Sumatra. These figures fade into obscurity when compared to the loss of life and the massive effort that the Japanese put into the building of the Burma–Thailand Railway. It is possibly for this reason that the Pakan Baroe–Moearo Railway has been cast under the shadow of the Burma–Thailand Railway.

On 24th May, work began on the railway from the Pakan Baroe, the 000.00 kilometre point. The rails and locomotives for this railway were removed from an existing railway on the east coast of Sumatra between Medan and Belawan. As well as Sumatra, railway materials were procured from Java and Malaya. The construction of the Pakan Baroe–Moearo Railway was made more difficult by virtue of the fact that the first 60 kilometres had to be built through swamps.

The following is a list of the railway construction camps and their approximate distances from the 000.00 point at Pakan Baroe.

Pakan Baroe	Camp No. 1	000.00km
Tengkirang Hospital	Camp No. 2	005.00km
Koebang	Camp No. 2a	015.00km
Teratakboeloeh	Camp No. 3	018.00km
	Camp No. 4a/b	019.00km
Loeboeksakat	Camp No. 5	023.00km
Soengei Pagar	Camp No. 6	036.00km
	Camp No. 7a	069.00km
Lipatkain	Camp No. 7	075.00km
Kota Baroe	Camp No. 8	111.00km
Logas	Camp No. 9	142.00km
Loeboek Ambatjan	Camp No. 10	160.00km
Pinto Batoe	Camp No. 11	176.00km
Siluewah	Camp No. 12	200.00km
Moearo	Camp No. 13	220.00km
Tapoei–Petai spur line	Camp No. 14	118.00/119.00km

Construction began on 26th October 1944 and finished one week after the end of the Pacific War, on 22nd August 1945.

There were a great many similarities between this railway and the Burma–Thailand Railway with respect to the type of work, rations and treatment meted out to the prisoners by the Korean guards. However, as there is only limited information available on this subject this narrative must be looked upon as a precis and not as a detailed report. What is more important is that the prisoners receive the recognition they deserve for their work on this railway.

It appears that although the Australians worked at as many as eleven of the fourteen camps, the main camps they were concentrated in were the No.'s 2, 5, 8, 9, 10, 11, 12 camps and the No. 14 Spur Line Camp. The railway ran roughly north-south and slightly west as it crossed the equator near Camp No. 7 at Lipatkain.

There were large bridges across the rivers Kampar Right and Kampar Left. Also there was another large bridge further south that crossed the Indragiri River near Moearo. From Moearo the line headed east along the Indragiri or Koeattan River Valley for 70 kilometres until it joined up with the north-south line from Pakan Baroe. The prisoners who had been brought down from Medan on 25th October 1944 found themselves at Camp No. 14, Tapoei–Petai spur line camp. The first job was the construction of a trellis bridge over a deep gorge. When the bridge was completed the men were then put to work excavating a 200 metre long cutting that lay between the recently completed bridge and the head of the spur line at Petai. When the work had been completed on this 20 kilometre spur line the prisoners were then put to work laying the rails on the main line between Pakan Baroe and Moearo.

In about March 1945 they were moved to Camp No. 8 at Kota Baroe where there were a great number of prisoners of many nationalities. Work only started from the Moearo end of the line in March 1945 when it appeared the progress was going too slowly. In addition to the Australians from Medan now working at Camp No. 8 there were still the Prisoners of War who were brought to Singapore from Java and were then transported to Pakan Baroe.

Their first camp was the No. 2 Hospital Camp at Tengkirang at the 5km point. These prisoners were put to work on the rail laying gangs, as most of the clearing of the jungle ahead of the line had already been done. This group proceeded south through most of the camps until they reached Camp No. 8 at Kota Baroe.

It was here that one day, some of the men proceeded up the spur line where they met up with some old mates from the original group from Medan. The second group from Java and Singapore continued to work their way south staying for a time at the No.'s 10, 11 and 12 Camps.

Korean guards who had been overseers on the Burma–Thailand railway had been brought in to speed things up. Soon the same cries of 'speedo-speedo' that had echoed through the jungles of Burma and Thailand and the same bashings for the slightest misdemeanor were to be repeated in Sumatra.

By June 1945 the group from Medan was also moving south and it was around this time whilst at Camp No. 9 at Logas they were moved to Camp No. 10 at Loeboek Ambatjan. It was at Camp No. 10 that they would learn the war was over.

The news of Japan's surrender filtered through to the prisoners, yet still the Japanese persisted with pushing ahead with the railway until the last link in the railway was laid on 22nd August 1945, one week after the official Japanese surrender. The Prisoners of War now made their own arrangements to move themselves north by train to Camp No. 2 at Tengkirang. This is where the hospital and a nearby airfield were located and where they could be evacuated.

There were two men from the 2/4th Machine Gun Battalion who died during the construction of the Sumatran railway. The first man was Robert McAskil who died as a result of cardiac beri-beri at 0300 hours on 28th March 1945 at the 106km point on the railway. This was at a place called Kampoeng near Kota Baroe, the area where Camp No. 8 was located. The second man was Harold Vernon Booth who also died from beri-beri at the No. 2 Hospital Camp on 15th April at Tengkirang, five kilometres south of Pakan Baroe.

The Evacuation of Sumatra

The repatriation of the ex-prisoners from South-East Asia began on 18th August 1945. It was organised by R.A.P.W.I., which stood for Recovery of Allied Prisoners of War, and Internees. By 10th October they had already evacuated 18,500 Allied Prisoners of War from Thailand.

However, in the case of Sumatra there is a little known story. It became known on 13th October 1945 that the ex-Prisoners of War on Sumatra, included a number of Australian nurses, who were in need of urgent attention. It was also understood that the Sumatran ex-Prisoners of War were in a poor state of health and if something wasn't done as soon as possible then there would be even more needless loss of life.

On 16th September a Douglas C47 transport plane was flown to Pakan Baroe where a review of the local situation was made by Major Windsor A.A.M.C. from the 2/14th Australian General Hospital. The report that came back to Singapore from Major Windsor was that there were 169 Australian servicemen in the area; and although morale was good, the conditions under which these men were living, were in this officer's opinion, unbearable. Also, the officer reported that the hospital was in a poor condition and immediate evacuation by air was recommended. It was thus decided to make Sumatra the No. 1 priority ahead of Thailand for the evacuation of ex-Prisoners of War.

Before this officer left Singapore on the morning of 16th September it had been the intention that three C47 aircraft would do at least two return trips each that day. Back at Pakan Baroe all motor transport, most of which was in a state of disrepair, was mustered to transport the worst cases from the hospital to the airfield 5 kilometres away. By 1500 hours on 16th September the equivalent of three planeloads of ex-prisoners were at the airfield awaiting evacuation to Singapore. When the rescue teams arrived at Pakan Baroe and saw the state of some of the ex-prisoners who had worked on the Sumatra railway, they were reduced to tears.

Prior to Japan's surrender, men were forced to eat fungus and bark from trees just to keep themselves alive. Apart from the aircraft that had returned to Singapore that day, no aircraft returned to Pakan Baroe for the planned second evacuation. When queried why this was so the officer in charge of the operation was informed that the R.A.A.F. had been directed that no further aircraft were to be sent to Pakan Baroe. On hearing this, Major Windsor returned to Singapore and on his orders a C47 aircraft was returned to Pakan Baroe to evacuate at least one more plane load of sick. Had this not occurred, these unfortunates would have been forced to remain out in the open that night; being too frail to return the 5 kilometres to the Hospital Camp.

A conference was arranged immediately on the return of the officer in charge, in which it came out that the British D.D.M.S. had cancelled the flights because he believed that there was not sufficient accommodation on Singapore. It was then pointed out at the conference that because of the fragile condition of these men, how imperative it was that they be evacuated to Singapore as soon as possible. It was agreed and decided that all aircraft must be made available for this human airlift. As a result of the officer in charge questioning the sanity of the orders issued to the R.A.A.F. by a higher ranking officer, these mercy flights continued on 17th September with the evacuation of all British and Australian ex-Prisoners of War from Sumatra to Singapore.

The Australians on arrival at Singapore were admitted to the 2/14th Australian General Hospital for immediate care. Three of these men of the 2/4th Machine Gun Battalion were flown directly from Singapore to Guildford Airport in Perth Western Australia a week later on 24th September 1945.

Following a warm homecoming with their families they were admitted to the 110 Perth Military Hospital. These three men from Sumatra were Richard 'Win' Annear, Noel Banks and 'Squasher' Squance, who flew home on Duke of Gloucester's Avro York aircraft, *'Endeavour'*.

The Duke of Gloucester had graciously loaned his personal aircraft so that some of the sick ex-prisoners could be evacuated back home as soon as possible rather than wait for an available ship.

Alf Burgess returned onboard the 1st Netherlands Military Hospital Ship *Oranje*, Arthur Magill returned onboard the *Arawa* and Cecil Quinn returned onboard the *Highland Chieftain*. That is the Story of Sumatra as it affected some of the men from the 2/4th Machine Gun Battalion. It is a story that has not been overly publicised, but nevertheless it is one of the most interesting stories that involved men from this battalion.

The Story of (Chosen) Korea

There were five members of the 2/4th Machine Gun Battalion who managed to see the sights of Korea. These five were Ted Roots, Jack Taylor, Jim Clancy, Bill Gray and Hubert 'Dutchy' Holland. They boarded the *Fukkai Maru*, a 3,829 ton passenger-cargo ship on 16th August 1942. The Australian contingent of 115 was part of a 1,000 strong work party. The remainder of this party was made up of 885 British prisoners which was designated Japan 'B' Party.

There is no evidence to suggest that Singapore Prisoner of War numbers were ever issued to these five men prior to their departure. This would fall in line with the theory that these numbers were not issued to Prisoners of War on Singapore until sometime after August 1942. These 1,000 prisoners, were only the icing on the cake as the real prize was the forty-seven man Senior Officer's Party.

There was not an officer in this group under the rank of full Colonel, and included Lt-Gen A. E. Percival, the former G.O.C. Malaya, Singapore's former Governor Sir Shenton Thomas and Brigadier Arthur Blackburn ex-Java. This Officer Party, designated simply as the 'Special Party' was made up to a compliment of 400 men by the inclusion of engineers and technicians. At first it was the Japanese intention that all 1,400 men would be loaded aboard the *Fukkai Maru* but because Lt-Gen Percival had protested against the cramped accommodation the working party remained and the officers, engineers and technicians embarked aboard another transport the 17,526 ton *Kamakura Maru*.

The *Fukkai Maru* was fitted with wooden platforms constructed around the bulkheads of its four holds. Nevertheless this was the best accommodation available under the circumstances. The two ships sailed in convoy under an armed escort via Cape St. Jacques (Vung Tau) then anchored in the estuary of the Riviere de Saigon in French Indo-China. This wide estuary was a regular assembly point for Japanese ships to form up before continuing their onward voyages. That was until U.S. Navy submarines transformed this estuary into a virtual elephant's graveyard of Japanese shipping. The *Fukkai Maru* and *Kamakura Maru* fortunately for the prisoners, managed to depart unscathed and arrived at Takao in Formosa (Taiwan) on 29th August 1942.

Formosa

Takao is located on the southwest coast of Formosa (Taiwan) island. The senior officers, engineers and technicians disembarked from their transport whilst the 1,000 prisoners onboard the *Fukkai Maru* were put to work over the next two weeks unloading bauxite from the holds of the *Fukkai Maru* for the nearby aluminium plant.

Bill Gray, who was suffering from oedema of the ankles, was ferried ashore for medical treatment and was later returned to the *Fukkai Maru*. Leaving Formosa behind them the *Fukkai Maru* sailed in convoy towards Korea arriving at the port of Fusan (Pusan) on the south coast on 22nd September 1942.

On the morning of 24th September the 1,000 strong work party disembarked and were marched through Fusan. This was the Imperial Japanese Army's way of showing off their white slaves before the people of this fair city before they entrained for their first camp, Keijo. The prisoners were then split into two groups, with four of the five machine gunners remaining at Keijo whilst Jim Clancy travelled another 20 miles to (Inch'on) or Jinsen with the second group. Jim would later move to the Hoten Camp in Manchuria.

The new Divisional Camp at the port town of Jinsen in the Keikido Prefecture was located in the southwest part of the city on the road leading to Keijo. Since the (Sino) Chinese-Japanese War Keijo and Jinsen and the eight towns along the 24 mile railroad connection had mushroomed industrially, with most of this development serving Japan's military needs.

The Prisoner of War camp at Jinsen had originally been an Imperial Japanese Army barracks. It consisted of three black barracks buildings and five huts making up an area of about 16,000 square metres, surrounded by a wooden fence. Returning now to Keijo, and the four other machine gunners, this camp was surrounded by local mud brick homes with thatched or iron roofs. The main building in which the prisoners were quartered was a four-storeyed brick structure with wooden floors and staircases. This building, prior to being converted into a Prisoner of War camp, was a spinning mill. The only barrier between the camp and the local residents was a high barbed wire topped wooden fence that encircled the camp.

Work at Keijo was a mix of chores from stoking furnaces, working on a shrine, loading and unloading railroad trucks stacked with rice, iron, flour and timber.

Konan

On 13th September 1943 Jack Taylor, Ted Roots and Bill Gray were transferred to their next camp at Konan, which was located on the northeast coast of Korea approximately 200 miles from Keijo. Prisoners of War were also brought into Konan from Jinsen in September 1943. Altogether there were about 330 men from Jinsen and Keijo at Konan of which fifty-one were Australians, including the three machine gunners. These three men, were to now remain at Konan until the end of the war pending their release by the Russian Army on 21st September 1945.

This camp was built on reclaimed land adjacent to a swamp. The men were accommodated forty to a room in which they slept, lived and ate. These huts were about 50 feet long by 25 feet wide and were arranged in such a way that they formed the letter H. Work at Konan consisted of either working in warehouses, shifting limestone or stoking furnaces at the carbide factory. It was here that a three-man team would stoke one of the four electric furnaces for twenty minutes before taking a forty minute respite from the intense heat. These furnaces operated at a temperature of 3,000 degrees Fahrenheit. In each eight hour shift each Prisoner of War would stoke the furnace eight times bringing his total time at the heat face to two hours and twenty minutes. The shifts on the limestone kilns were also on three eight-hour shifts.

Whereas a man on the Burma–Thailand Rrailway had to endure tropical heat and monsoonal rains, these men in Korea and for that matter Japan had to endure extremes of cold. In an effort to keep warm, men huddled around stoves in their huts or barracks where temperatures were frequently just a few degrees above freezing point. As many as six blankets were issued to help the men stay warm during winter. On 1st June 1945 Ted Roots developed pneumonia and did not return to Konan camp until the end of July 1945.

Fukuoka sub-Camp No. 13 Saganoseki

When the other three men had departed for Konan, 'Dutchy' Holland had remained at Keijo as he was suffering from dysentery, and unable to travel. On 10th October 1944 'Dutchy' departed Korea for Japan where he met up with Clarrie Henderson at Fukuoka sub-Camp No. 13 Saganoseki. Clarrie had been included in the *Rashin* (Byoki) *Maru* Party which had been split up at Moji.

A number of 2/4th were sent to the Fukuoka No. 13 Camp, but when this camp was closed down, Clarrie and 'Dutchy' remained together and moved to the Omine No. 6 Camp. The two remaining 2/4th members, being Joe Beattie and Fred Ward, were moved to the Fukuoka sub-Camp No. 17 Omuta. Fukuoka sub-Camp No. 13 Saganoseki was located on the northeast coast of Kyushu Island. Living conditions at this camp were quite reasonable but the food although regular was inadequate. The prisoners worked at a copper refinery in three shifts, either tending the furnaces or loading trucks with copper ore. Between September 1944 and May 1945 these four men worked at a copper smelter before moving on to Omine Divisional Camp No. 6 or Fukuoka sub-Camp No. 17 Omuta.

Omine Divisional Camp No. 6

Omine was a coal mining town located on the west side of Honshu Island. The coal mine at Omine had been closed down before the war because it had proven unproductive and thus uneconomic to continue working. The mine was brought back into production to help meet wartime demands for coal, using Prisoner of War labour that was both cheap and expendable. Its full designation was Detachment 6, Yamaguchi, Konoda-Shi. Motoyama Coal Mine (Motoyama Tanako).

The camp itself was situated near a railroad in the vicinity of Higashi in the Prefecture of Mamaguchi. The prisoners accommodation was a two-storeyed barracks that had been constructed using a bamboo framework covered with mud to form the external walls.

From May 1945 until his release on 19th September 1945 'Dutchy' worked as a powder monkey in this mine. When it was time to return home he moved by train to Nagasaki on 22nd September 1945. At Nagasaki he boarded a U.S.N. aircraft carrier to Hong Kong then proceeded on this ship to Manila. On 12th October he was reunited with Bill, Ted and Jack joining them for the remainder of the journey home to Australia.

Konan Camp – Korea

On 12th July 1945, code breakers intercepted a message from the Japanese Foreign Minister to the Japanese Ambassador in Moscow, ordering him to pass on to the Russians an urgent request from the Japanese Emperor Hirohito to plead for peace. This was just days before Marshal Joseph Stalin was to meet President Harry Truman and Prime Minister Winston Churchill at the Potsdam Conference.

On 6th August 1945 the first atomic bomb exploded over the Japanese city of Hiroshima. Three days later a second bomb was exploded over the Port City of Nagasaki. This was also the day that Russia began its advance against the Japanese in Manchuria.

On 10th August 1945, following the exploding of the second atomic bomb over Japan, President Truman gave orders to cease military action to allow Emperor Hirohito some time to either accept or refuse his terms for an 'unconditional surrender'. At 1200 hours on 15th August 1945 the Japanese listened to a pre-recorded radio announcement by Emperor Hirohito that Japan had accepted the terms of the 'unconditional surrender' and so ended war in the Pacific. However, it would transpire that Japan would not be a signatory to the instrument of surrender until 2nd September 1945. The United States and Russia, the only powers who were in a position to supply troops, agreed to divide Korea between them for the purpose of disarming Japan. The dividing line as agreed by these two great military powers was to be taken as being the 38th parallel. However the Russians had entered North Korea before the Japanese surrender on 15th August. They defeated the Japanese in the north, removed the Japanese Military Administration and replaced it with an organised Korean Communist Administration.

In hindsight, what we can now see developing is a Communist Russia who really was in no hurry to see Japan surrender. This would give her the time needed to retaliate against Japan for some previous wrong doings dating back to the Russo-Japanese war of 1904–1905 and also to promote the cause of Communism in China and Korea.

The Americans on the other hand did not arrive in Korea in force until 8th September. Having no means of replacing the Japanese Administration in South Korea, the Americans kept the Japanese Administration in place for several more months.

The three machine gunners following their recovery, now left Konan by train for Jinsen where they were taken aboard the American hospital ship USS *Mercy(II)* for a long overdue medical check up and sample some western food before being sent on their way to Manila aboard the aircraft carrier HMS *Colossus*. Once they had reached Manila they were reunited with Jim Clancy whom they had left behind at Keijo. All four men then boarded an R.A.A.F. Catalina flying boat Serial No. A24-377 on 12th October 1945. Flying via Morotai and Darwin they finally landed at Crawley Bay on the Swan River, Perth Western Australia on 17th October 1945.

Hoten Camp – Manchuria

It will be remembered that Jim Clancy had parted company with the other three machine gunners when he transferred to Jinsen on 9th November 1942. Jim was once again moved, however this time it was to Hoten (Mukden or Wenkuatuan) Camp in Manchuria where he remained from 21st November 1942 until his release at the end of the war.

Hoten camp was located 12 miles from Mukden on the Tungling Road, having been established on 28th October 1942. The camp consisted of three newly built two-storeyed Imperial Japanese Army barracks with double glazed windows and wooden floors. The camp was surrounded by a brick wall and high voltage electric cable. Jim was engaged in work at the Honga Kiasha carbide factory which supplied tools for the Japanese.

Rumours began to circulate at Hoten and the other Prisoner of War camps in the area about 10th August that the war would soon be over. On 14th August the number required for factory work was reduced, and on 16th August all work ceased. It was on 16th August that U.S. Army paratroopers arrived to break the good news concerning Japan's surrender the previous day. On 20th August, the Russians arrived to disarm the Japanese, and on 24th August evacuation of the officers and the sick began. On 30th August an American recovery team arrived on site whereupon the men moved by train to Port Arthur and then by the U.S.N. ships *Refuge* and *Noble* to Okinawa before continuing to Manila. They then embarked on the British aircraft carrier HMS *Formidable* on 4th October 1945 and docked at Sydney on 13th October whence Jim travelled by train to Western Australia. So ends the story of five machine gunners who were perhaps luckier than most by being selected to go to Korea and Japan as opposed to the Burma–Thailand Railway, or even worse, to Sandakan in Borneo.

The hangar deck on HMS *Colossus*
The ship's aircraft had been off loaded at Singapore so that camp stretchers could be set up to accomodate ex-Prisoners of War.

The Story of 'J' Force – Japan

This group of 900 prisoners, 600 British and 300 Australians departed Singapore on 15th May 1943.

It has become the practice for authors to group 'J' Force and the subsequent 'J' or Japan Parties together, however, surviving 'J' Force members become most indignant when anyone except themselves are referred to as 'J' Force. For this reason any 2/4th Machine Gun Battalion members who departed Singapore with later Japan Parties shall be identified by the name of the ship in which they sailed.

This method of identification should also simplify the tracking of the men by way of their final destination in Japan once they had arrived and disembarked from their ships. The men of 'J' Force like those in 'F' Force were told they were going to a rest camp. This was a contradiction of terms because under the Japanese doctrine of no work no food there was no chance that the Japanese would tolerate a situation where Prisoners of War would be fed without earning their keep. By comparison, the hand that 'F' Force was dealt as opposed to that of 'J' Force was like comparing chalk to cheese.

There was, however, one major difference between these two forces, being that 'F' Force was not in a situation where U.S.A.A.C. B29 Superfortress bombers would rain incendiary bombs upon them.

The Voyage To Japan

Embarking on the *Wales Maru*, 'J' Force was formed in Singapore under the command of Lt-Col L. J. A. Bryne from the 8th Division A.A.S.C. There appears to be some question as to the correct spelling of this ship on which these men sailed. The Joint Army Naval Assessment Committee document *Japanese Naval and Merchant Shipping Losses During World War Two By All Causes*, states that name of the ship was the *Wales Maru* and that it was a passenger-cargo ship of 6,586 tons.

Those that travelled on her seem to remember her as an old and slow ship, with a top speed of around 6 knots, that perhaps should have been scrapped years before. The Japanese had seized literally thousands of tons of foreign shipping during their lightning five-month campaign in 1942. Also in some cases, ships that the Japanese had purchased for scrap metal before the war were still in service and this may have been the case with the *Wales Maru*.

The *Wales Maru* set off from Singapore on 15th May 1943 with the 900 men divided and crammed into three of its four holds. The first port of call in French Indo-China was the estuary of the Riviere de Saigon at Cape St Jacques. The *Wales Maru* lay anchored off the coast for three days as the convoy's numbers swelled. As stated in the story of Korea, the estuary was a collecting point where convoys would arrive, break up and form up with other ships depending on final destinations. This was until U.S. Navy submarines discovered this fact and quickly put the cat amongst the pigeons.

The *Wales Maru* weighed anchor and set sail on 23rd May, reaching Takao on the southwest coast of Formosa on 29th May 1942. Departing Takao on 2nd June, the tropical heat of Singapore that these men had become accustomed to was now giving way to light showers and cooler air temperatures.

On 5th June at 10.00 hours all hell broke loose aboard the *Wales Maru*. A U.S. Navy submarine had fired two torpedoes into the convoy but had failed to score a hit. The Japanese armed escort, thought to be a sloop, dropped depth charges on the submarine whilst the other ships in the convoy fired their deck guns. According to shipping loss records it does not show that any of the Japanese ships were lost, however, it appears that the propeller shaft of the *Wales Maru* may have received some damage during the foray when the depth charges exploded.

Forced to reduce speed to about three knots the geriatric *Wales Maru* was soon left behind to fend for herself. On 7th June a collective sigh of relief by the *Wales Maru's* human cargo signalled the arrival of these 900 prisoners to Moji in Japan.

Moji

The two cities of Shimonoseki on Honshu Island and Moji on Kyushu Island form two of the most important transportation and communication centres in Japan. These ports have practically unlimited anchorage and good port facilities capable of handling the largest of vessels. The heavy traffic in the strait that separates the two cities arose from Kyushu's large coal exports and concentrations of heavy industry and trade with Korea, Manchuria, China, and the Netherlands East Indies.

Now in full view of the public on the wharf, a medical examination and glass rod test was conducted aboard the *Wales Maru*. Covered previously in the story of the Burma–Thailand Railway, this glass rectal examination again highlights Japanese paranoia concerning amoebic dysentery and pestis. The prisoners in 'J' Force were now divided into three parties. No. 1 Party was made up of approximately 150 sick and invalid, who it was claimed, were being sent to a rest camp near Moji. Included in this group of one hundred British and fifty Australians were machine gunners Roy Deveson and William 'Pop' Davey.

The promise of a rest camp could hardly be described as such as they both found themselves working down coalmines at Fukuoka sub-Camp No. 9 Hakensho on Kyushu Island. This camp will be covered a little later within the Kobe story.

No. 2 Party, was composed of 250 Australians including the other eighteen members of the 2/4th Machine Gun Battalion in 'J' Force. No. 3 Party was made up of 500 British who travelled with No. 2 Party, but remained on the train and continued to another camp.

At dusk the men in parties two and three boarded a ferry that took them across the strait to Shimonoseki where they berthed at the ferry landing. This landing was situated at the northern limit of the southern wharves. From the ferry landing it was only a matter of yards to the railway station where the men entrained for Kobe.

Osaka – Kobe – Kyoto

Kobe is built along a narrow section of the north coast of Osaka Bay at the western extremity of the Osaka plain. Kobe began life as a tiny fishing village but was opened up to foreign trade in 1867. In 1892 the city was granted a charter and soon developed into a prosperous port with the help of the Sino-Japanese War of 1894–95 and the Russo-Japanese War of 1904–05 that soon saw this port outstrip Yokohama, by volume of imports and exports.

The Osaka–Kobe–Kyoto area was the most highly industrialised in the Japanese Empire and it produced vast quantities of war materials, the commercial district being near the waterfront on the coastal plain. This area produced 25% of all Japan's rolled iron and steel products approximately 30% of her naval and merchant ships and 30% of her marine engines. Wartime production in this area also included the manufacture of aircraft, engines, parts and ordnance. There can be little doubt now as to the value of this area and its attractiveness to American B29 bombers.

Kobe House

After travelling all night the men arrived at the city of Kobe and detrained at Sannomiya Railway Station. Forming up, they then marched a short way down a street called Naka Machi Dore where they assembled on the YMCA sports ground known as Yoenchi Park. This uneven sided park was virtually opposite Kobe House. It was here where the men were issued with their Prisoner of War numbers and divided into sections before crossing the road to their new home.

This was a red brick three storeyed warehouse turned army barracks and was now to be known as Kobe House. This camp consisted of two warehouses bounded on three sides by streets. Two of the streets ran north-south past Kobe House and were connected by a long narrow partially covered alleyway that ran through this warehouse camp. At each end of this alleyway there were high heavy wooden spiked gates. Between the two main buildings was an array of old wooden houses and offices used by the Japanese camp staff and guards. In one of these houses was the camp hospital.

Kobe House was located about half a mile back from the harbour's edge with its wharves and warehouses. Like those who went to Korea, the prisoners at Kobe lived, slept and ate in their new quarters. The Australians occupied the first two floors of the warehouse overlooking the park. As well as Australians there were also in residence at Kobe, British from Hong Kong, a few Americans from Manila and a mix of foreign seamen.

The staple diet at Kobe was rice, beans, vegetables, meat and fish. Because the Australians had arrived at Kobe reasonably well equipped, issues of clothing were denied, however, blankets were issued; and winter and summer military style clothing and the distinctive Japanese two toed boots would be issued later. The Australian Official History states that: 'The Australian group contained a large proportion of over-age men and all were considered to be convalescents on departure from Changi.' [8]

Amongst the 2/4th Machine Gun Battalion draft included for Kobe there were several men in their twenties and forties, however, most were in their thirties, being the average age of the Australians at Kobe House. One fact that does stand out however, is that four of the men included in 'J' Force had worked at Thomson Road Camp (Caldecot Hill Estate) and had been admitted to the Australian General Hospital at Roberts Barracks Changi in 1943 with amblyopia. This is impaired vision, caused by a B group vitamin deficiency. It is interesting to note that amongst the Australians in 'J' Force there had been 146 cases of amblyopia recorded at Changi before their departure. Several others had also received medical treatment for various complaints during the latter part of 1942 and early part of 1943. This evidence does not indicate any set pattern as far as selection of 2/4th members in 'J' Force but it may substantiate the statement that some of these men were in fact convalescing at the time of their selection.

There were perhaps only a few minor annoyances of note at Kobe House. The first was the assimilation of the Australians with the British and Americans. The latter had been at Kobe House longer than the Australians and as you might expect, they had become somewhat territorial. This difficulty was nevertheless overcome as the Australians found their way, and once they had commenced working outside the Kobe House gates and flexed their muscles as expert scroungers, they soon gained ground within the pecking order at Kobe House. The other annoyance perhaps a little more serious, was the state of the latrines that emptied into shallow cement pits.

These pits, which were about 30 feet long and 4 feet wide, were then emptied at irregular intervals by a coolie bucket brigade. This meant that they were frequently overflowing, with the area crawling with maggots and swarming with flies. This was especially so during the summer months. With the Australians on the first and second floors, and given the location of the stairs

8   Lionel Wigmore, *Japanese Thrust*, Australia in the War of 1939–45 Army Volume IV, Australian War Memorial Canberra 1957, p.624

it was unavoidable that some foreign matter was finding its way upstairs into the living, sleeping and eating areas.

On 15th June, after a brief respite following their travels, and a crash course in Japanese, the Australians now found themselves ready to enter the Kobe workforce like first graders ready for their first day at school.

John Lane's (Jack Ramsbottom) book tells us of some of the local Kobe companies and factories where the men were contracted out to work:

> '*The Japanese companies of Mitsui, Mitsubishi, Sumitomo, Kamagumi, Ohamagumi, Utsumigumi, Takahama, Kobe-go, and Sempaku soon became as familiar to us as Coles and Woolworth's. All these firms had large warehouses scattered along the huge artificially constructed waterfront, and most of the Aussies were allocated to these places. However there were three factories situated some ten miles east of Kobe, to which about seventy of us were detailed to work. This group comprised the Showa Denki carbon works, Yoshihara vegetable oil processors and Toyo steel foundry.*' [9]

David Bergamini tells us:

> '*When Japan started out on the road to modernisation the nation's economy fell into the hands of the three great cartel families of Mitsuis of the Mitsui Company, the Iwasakis of the Mitsubishi Company and the Sumitomos of the Sumitomo Company. Between these three families they controlled Japan's heavy industry, foreign trade and banking.*' [10]

Some of the Prisoners of War at Kobe house now found themselves enlisted into the union of stevedores, so it is probably best to describe the Kobe docks area first. The warehouses were constructed by firms the likes of Sumitomo and Mitsubishi, and had railroad sidings adjacent to the main piers. These warehouses were of a modern concrete construction, multiple floored and earthquake proof.

Transit sheds of wood or steel and corrugated iron construction also lined most of the piers. Freight lines connected all the main wharves with the Tokaido–Sanyo railroads and there were also four freight yards that served the waterfront section of Kobe. Takahama Quay was the collection point for general domestic cargo, and when the opportunity arose gave plenty of scope for scrounging and looting.

Alex Dandie explains:

> '*There were two gangs which worked in the Railway Goods Yards, one of which was at the Southern end of the city, and was called the 'coal job' because the gang had to empty railway trucks of coal. The gang at the Northern Goods Yards or Mintagowa Job, worked on platforms of train terminals or in nearby goods yards. The types of goods, which passed through their hands was very varied. They lent themselves to reasonable pickings.*' [11]

As time went on, the prisoners became more proficient at the art of looting. If caught there was the risk of reprisal but in most cases the prize outweighed the punishment. Apart from some injuries in their new jobs as wharf lumpers and factory hands there wasn't too much to complain about. Food was adequate with the midday meal supplied by the company or factory for which

---

9   John Lane, *Summer Will Come Again* Fremantle Arts Centre Press 1987, p.65.
10   David Bergamini, *Japan's Imperial Conspiracy* William Morrison & Company 1971, p.333–334.
11   Alex Dandie, *The Story of 'J' Force* Published by the author 1985, p.78.

the prisoners were contracted out to work. The weather was pleasant with light showers and temperatures between eighteen and thirty degrees Celsius.

As the months passed the humidity rose and apart from some cases of dengue and diarrhoea there was nothing much else of note to report. As October and November arrived so did heavy colds and influenza. November 1943 also saw the only death of a 2/4th machine gunner from Kobe House, that being Harry Tysoe. Harry had been admitted into hospital on 7th November 1943 suffering from influenza and acute beri-beri. Sadly he passed away on 26th November 1943 as a result of progressive cardiac failure and beri-beri. Harry's body was cremated at Kobe and his ashes were enshrined at Zuganji, Osaka. Lance Park and Wally Hutchinson were two others that also succumbed to pneumonia between November 1943 and January 1944.

The Australians were now discovering what it was like to live through a Japanese winter but strangely enough as the weather became colder the Australian's health appeared to improve. Blanket issues now increased from three to five per man as men struggled to keep warm. A dry winter now changed into a wet spring, however, by May 1944 Kobe was experiencing warm days and cool nights.

On 15th February 1945 a party of twenty Australians left Kobe house under the command of Lt. K. W. Goddard A.A.S.C., to live-in at the Showa-Denki factory. Initially there was one 2/4th in this party, Arthur Draper, who was later followed by Alf Jones, Norm Harris and Ron Lymn.

On 17th March 1945, Kobe was initiated into its baptism of fire by American B29 Superfortress bombers with their lethal loads of incendiary bombs. At 0530 hours between waves of bombers the prisoners were hustled to the sports ground across the road where slit trenches had been prepared. This raid was the pre-cursor to more regular raids by increasing numbers of American bombers.

Early in May 1945, a party of Australians which included Harold Procter and Frank Hinnrichsen moved out to Fukuoka sub-Camp No. 26 Usui. On 20th May another party of Australians departed Kobe House for Maibara, included in this group was Gerry Arthur and Edwin Clarke. The third party of Australians departed Kobe House for Notogawa Camp also on 20th May and there were three machine gunners included in this group, being Jack Leahy, Lance Park and Stan Wenn.

By this time the prisoners at Kobe or those who had just recently left, had lost on average four to six kilograms in weight. With the three parties leaving, the Australian contingent at Kobe House now consisted of seventy-six men.

June 1945 was the month that would sound the death knell for Kobe House. On the morning of 5th June, B29's appeared in the skies over Kobe. Just as breakfast had begun, sirens sounded the alarm, warning of an impending air raid. The first of the incendiaries whistled their way in from the B29's far above and exploded into walls of flames. These incendiaries were followed by 500lb oil filled bombs that were designed to keep the incendiary fires burning.

The remaining Australian residents at Kobe House were in luck this day. As Kobe House burned there was no chance of escape, as the Japanese guards, in their panic to seek out shelter from the firestorm, had failed to unlock the heavy side gates which led out onto the street. As a consequence, the Australians were trapped inside a burning building whilst the B29's wrecked havoc over Kobe. Fortunately, one of the heavy gates at the end of the alleyway was hit by a bomb and blown off its hinges. Invitations were not necessary as the Australians streamed across the road to the sports ground and dived into slit trenches. The losers in this raid were the Japanese guards. When the air raid warning was sounded they headed straight for their air raid shelter that received a direct incendiary splash. The Japanese guards were then watched as they ran screaming from their shelter, covered from head to foot in flames.

As with the previous raid on 17th March 1945 a strong wind had sprung up, making it dangerous to move about freely amongst burning embers and sparks. The eventual departure of the B29's left an eerie silence over Kobe except of course for the sound of burning buildings, roofs crashing in and explosions from combustible materials in local warehouses. Later in the day when the fires had died down some rice was cooked on the sports ground. After sunset the prisoners from Kobe House were mustered, and the march began to Kawasaki Camp about 8 miles away in the foothills above Kobe.

On 21st June this Kobe party departed Kawasaki Camp and moved to Wakinohama Camp, which was located about one and a half miles from the ruins of Kobe House. The greatest concern to the men at this stage was the food situation. A great deal of the local food stocks had been burnt in the incendiary raids and it now became necessary to feed on salvaged rice. This necessitated thorough washing before consumption to separate the shrapnel fragments, dirt and incendiary material.

At 1200 hours on Wednesday 15th August 1945 sirens blew a long blast. This was the signal for all in Japan to stand by the nearest wireless set to listen to a broadcast by Emperor Hirohito. This as mentioned in the Korea story was a pre-recorded message. The amazing thing is that except for those close to Hirohito, no one in Japan had ever heard his voice. All the Prisoners of War at Wakinohama Camp were herded into the furthest part of the camp away from the wireless in the Japanese guard's office.

After about a half an hour the guards reappeared from the camp office looking most despondent. The camp was abuzz with guesses as to the reason for the wireless broadcast but by now most had an inkling of what had happened. That night the camp commander at Wakinohama made a special announcement to the Prisoners of War to the effect there would be no more bombs and no more sirens and that they could sleep in peace this night, the war was over.

Within a few days the prisoners had taken over the camp and were beginning to enjoy their freedom for the first time in a long time. Clandestine raids were made on the warehouses on the docks, with sugar and cigarettes being prime targets. On 28th August the first food and clothing supply drops were made over Wakinohama. Forty-four gallon drums, with or without parachutes, were literally raining from the sky and were also random in their selection of a final resting place. Houses, roads, tram and power lines all came in for special attention.

On 29th August old mates were again united as men wandered in from Notogawa and Maibara Camps. The first American recovery teams showed up at Wakinohama Camp on 6th September. Once the formalities of recording each man's name, age, date of birth, nationality, address of next of kin were taken, they were examined to ascertain their state of health, categorised accordingly and issued with a coloured ticket. This ticket dictated the urgency with which each ex-Prisoner of War was to be evacuated. This could be via hospital ship, navy transport or by aircraft.

At this time there were 545 ex-Prisoners of War at Wakinohama Camp. After all the formalities had been attended to, a general questionnaire (interrogation form) filled in and a cable message form had been completed, it was time to commence the long journey back home to loved ones and familiar scenes. This return journey for the Australians at Wakinohama Camp began with a short march, or a ride, to the Kobe Railway Station. A special train was waiting that would take these men to Yokohama.

For the next stage of their journey home, they climbed aboard a C54 Skymaster aircraft. The first stop was Kadena Airfield on Okinawa where they arrived on 8th September. On 10th September it was off again, this time onboard a B24 Liberator bomber. Finally, after five and a half hours flying, the B24's set down at Clarke Field, 60 miles out of Manila. From Clarke Field the men transferred to Dakota C47 transports to Nielson Airfield whence they were taken to recovery Camp No. 3. On 5th October, twelve of the original twenty members of 'J' Force embarked on the aircraft carrier HMS *Formidable* for Sydney where they disembarked on 13th October 1945.

The Wharves at Kobe

Alex Dandie wrote:

> *'Dock work or stevedoring was carried for various firms. The jobs involved the loading of railway trucks from warehouses and loading and unloading of ships and barges, which were drawn up to the dockside, taking the goods into the warehouses or direct to the railway trucks.'* [12]

The following is a description of the work engaged in by the Prisoners of War at some but not all warehouses on the Kobe docks.

Mitsui

The Mitsui warehouse handled an array of goods from tin ingots and rubber bales to stores belonging to the Imperial Japanese Army. On the second floor of this concrete warehouse was the treasure trove that the prisoners christened the 'canteen', for it was here that items like tins of pink and red salmon, milk, and cigarettes could be procured at a very reasonable cost.

It transpired that it had been possible to duplicate a key to the 'canteen' with the help of some of the men who were at the time working at Toyo steel foundry. Fortunately there were two locksmiths amongst the Australians that had been selected for 'J' Force. This simple twist of fate was to reap great rewards because if these two Australians had been sent to work on the Burma–Thailand rail link it is certain that their skills would have been completely wasted.

Mitsubishi

Jim Dore worked here for about twelve months, as did Gerry Arthur and Edwin Clarke for a time. The men would leave Kobe House at 0715 hours and commence work at 0730 hours, an indication as to the close proximity of the wharves to the camp. Mitsubishi was a complex of massive multi-storeyed warehouses that contained mostly Imperial Japanese Army supplies including tempting items like emergency ration packs and army issue cigarettes.

Ohamagumi

Australians worked at this warehouse for the first time from December 1943. The site was located on the southern section of the Kobe docks near the Kawasaki shipyards where members of 'C' Force were working. For the men from Kobe House to get to the Ohamagumi warehouse, it meant a tram ride and a march that took one hour each way. Work consisted of stevedoring on the wharf or working in the warehouse on which a railway goods yard was located on one side. Sometimes the work was quite heavy, but this depended on the height of the tide. If the tide was low then a system of planks was arranged so that the freight could be man handled up from the barges to the dock. Sometimes the cargo was loaded straight onto the waiting railway trucks and other times it was stacked into the warehouses. The cargo that was handled the most was soya beans and sugar.

Takahama

This company was a subsidiary of the Mitsubishi group of companies and was considered one of the best jobs along the Kobe waterfront. This quay handled general and domestic cargo.

---

[12] Ibid p.60

A great deal of the spoils from Japan's newly won Empire entered Kobe through this warehouse, so naturally there was a vast selection of goods for the taking. Takahama was British territory and the Australians only got a look in on the rare occasion when a position in a work gang needed to be filled.

Sempaku

This company appears to have had the monopoly of unloading ships that were stood out in the Kobe Harbour. The Prisoners of War in this gang would be taken out into the harbour to the ship in question and then proceed to unload its cargo into barges that would be then towed to the docks. The main goods that were handled were soya beans, rice, sugar, copra and barley. It could be said anything that came in a sack and was heavy was handled this way. These sacks could weigh anything from 180–220lbs.

Other cargo that might also be handled were 2 foot by 3 foot bales of rubber, crated goods, or as now realised, anything of value that Imperial Japanese Army had leeched from its new, and by this time, decreasing Empire.

The Factories at Kobe

Showa-Denki

Showa-Denki was a graphite factory some distance from Kobe house. John Gilmour worked at this factory for nine months and explains:

> 'We used to leave Kobe House at 7am and marched about half a mile to the railway station. Here we caught an electric train which took us about fifteen miles towards the factory. Once we had all detrained it was about another three mile march to the Showa-Denki factory.' [13]

As well as John Gilmour, Evan Jones, Frank Hinnrichsen, Peter Omiridis and Wally Hutchinson, all worked at Showa-Denki for a time. Having journeyed with the Yoshihara and Toyo workers to Koshen Station the Showa-Denki workforce would travel a few more stations before alighting from the train at Showa-Denki.

This was where carbon electrodes were manufactured in a process in which graphite was used. The graphite dust settled onto every surface, into every corner of the factory and in every nook and cranny on the men's bodies. With the added negative that there was nothing of marketable value worth looting from Showa-Denki, this job was perhaps the least popular.

Most of the prisoners were employed on keeping up the supply of coke used to fire the kilns. One bonus for workers at Showa-Denki was the daily hot bath to wash off the collection of dirt and grime after the day's work.

On 15th February 1945, twenty Australians from Kobe House, including Arthur Draper, accompanied Lt. K. W. Goddard to Showa-Denki. This group was to eventually number about one hundred men; a mixture of Australians, British and Americans. As mentioned, also included in this later group would be Alf Jones, Norm Harris and Ron Lymn.

There was an aircraft factory next door to Showa-Denki that had come in for some special attention by the Americans, so when this happened the group was moved on to the north coast to a place called Toyama. At least two exceptions were known to be Arthur Draper and Norm Harris who both moved to Nagoya camp for three months before moving on again to Toyama in May 1945.

---

[13] Ibid p.51

Yoshihara

This was a vegetable oil processing factory. Jack Ramsbottom (John Lane) and Stan Wenn worked for a period here. Setting off for work at about 0700 hours the prisoners on this job would march to the railway station where they boarded an electric train and headed north. After a journey of about 12 miles to a station called Koshen, the Yoshihara factory and Toyo steel plant workers were ushered off the train, whilst the Showa-Denki workers continued on their way for about another three miles.

It was back to shank's pony now as these two groups marched to their respective jobs. The Toyo steel gang parted company first as the Yoshihara workers continued on for another 500 yards along a canal until the gates of the factory appeared before them. The prisoners left their packs that contained their midday meal and then donned a tatty green uniform and prepared for work.

John Lane wrote:

> 'Yoshihara processed a variety of products including copra, peanuts, cotton, and rape seed, and castor beans, with the oil being syphoned off into four gallon tins and the residue being bagged.' [14]

The produce to be processed was brought up the canal to the factory site in barges. This was then unloaded and brought into the factory. These 150lb bags were manhandled in the same manner as described at the docks at the Ohamagumi Quay. Sometimes, depending on the tide, a 20 foot drop between the landing along the canal down to the barge might be commonplace. Any contraband that was possible to be slipped through the net passed the Japanese guards was carried back to Kobe House. As there was nothing worth stealing from Toyo the two work parties would meet back at Koshen Station and, in a flash the ill gained goods were transferred to the Toyo workers who were less likely to be searched as thoroughly as the Yoshihara workers.

Toyo

Jim Dore worked at this factory following his twelve-month stint on the wharves. The men travelled the 12 miles to the Toyo steel foundry in a special electric train. At least three other members of the 2/4th worked here, being Edwin Clark, Gerry Arthur and Arthur Draper.

The work here was similar to that at Showa-Denki in that small rail carts were brought to the furnaces from the scrap heaps and from the furnaces to the slag heaps. This was also a dirty job and on a scale was about as popular as Showa-Denki.

The Fukuoka sub-Camps – Kyushu Island

Altogether there were something like twenty-seven Fukuoka sub-Camps, and each one might be owned and operated by a different Japanese company. Coal resources on Kyushi Island were extensive and the estimated deposits on this island alone represented about 49% of Japan's reserves. In 1936 total production of coal from Kyushu was 29,600,000 metric tons most of which went to the Kobe–Osaka industrial district.

Whilst Fukuoka itself is the largest city on Kyushu Island with its own seaport, the actual Fukuoka coal mining camps are spread out through the northern part of Kyushu with the locations of the individual company mines identified by the nearby village. It has proven almost impossible to pin point the exact locations of some of these camps, however, every effort has been made to at least give an approximation of where the camp or mine was located.

---

[14]   John Lane, *Summer Will Come Again* by Fremantle Arts Centre Press 1987, p.67

Fukuoka sub-Camp No. 9 – Hakensho

The Japanese designation for this camp was Fukuoka, Mizumaki-Cho. The mine was owned by the Nippon Mining Company (Nippon Kogyo). There were two members of the 2/4th at Fukuoka sub-Camp No. 9 Hakensho and they were Roy Deveson and William 'Pop' Davey who it will be remembered were segregated on arrival at Moji and sent to a so called rest camp. This rest camp proved to be a coal mine located on the island of Kyushu southwest of Moji, east of Nagasaki between Omuta and Kumamoto. The mine was located about a quarter of a mile to the west of the camp.

The train journey to the camp on 7th June 1943 took about two hours. As well as the mixed British and Australian party comprising 150 prisoners there was already an established work force of Dutch and Netherlands East Indians (Indonesians) and Americans in residence. The British and Australians kept themselves separate from the Dutch by way of both administration and accommodation, moving into three barracks on the northeast corner of the camp. Discipline at this camp was strict, food limited and there was no opportunity like there had been at Kobe to scrounge for extras. No writing materials were permitted and the good news was that there were only two and a half years to go until the end of the war. As coal mines go this one was not considered to be a safe place to work. The shafts in this mine had not been properly timbered which caused several falls of rock. Cave-ins were commonplace and injuries and deaths a regular occurrence thanks to the unsafe state of the mine and Japanese incompetence.

Alex Dandie wrote:

> '*The ever present fear of becoming a future fine specimen of fossil was bad enough, but made infinitely worse by the Japanese, whose minds had hardly progressed from the fossil state.*' [15]

As 1944 gave way to 1945 it was obvious that the Japanese were preparing themselves for an invasion on Kyushu. The camp was under the flight path of American B29's from Okinawa as they flew over on their twice-daily raids. It was now a part of every day life to see searchlights pointing skywards, followed by the puffs of smoke from Japanese AA bursts that were usually too low to hit the B29's. From this camp it was possible to see the bursts of light in the distance for instance over Moji as the American planes pulverised their target selected for that day. Ultimately, as at every other Prisoner of War camp in Japan, men were informed that they were now free men. The Japanese commandant at Fukuoka sub-Camp No. 9 assembled the prisoners and obviously feeling uncomfortable about the whole affair made the following announcement.

> '*Japanese Government have discussed the war with America and Great Britain and all countries have agreed to say war is finished. We know all men have enjoyed working in beautiful Japan. When you go home to your own country, you will tell all your families, how beautiful Japan is.*' [16]

The skies above Kyushi were now free of American bombers until the morning of 28th August when a lone B29 flew over the camp and dropped leaflets that stated that a food supply drop would be made in two hours.

The period from the cessation of hostilities had not been made any easier by the Japanese guard's belligerence either as a consequence of Japan's defeat, or by the critical shortage of

---

[15]   Alex Dandie, *The Story of 'J' Force* Published by the author 1985, p.244
[16]   Ibid p.269

food or both. All was made well as the planned food drop eventuated, thereby relieving a desperate situation. The prisoners remained in camp for about one month before recovery teams appeared on site. The men were then transported to Nagasaki by train where they too saw the devastation caused by the atomic bomb. Here they boarded a U.S. Navy destroyer to Okinawa and were then flown to Manila.

Once at Manila, Roy and 'Pop' embarked on the HMS *Formidable* with other members of the 2/4th Machine Gun Battalion and began their homeward bound journey to Sydney. Both men then returned home to Western Australia by aircraft.

In closing the story of Fukuoka No. 9 it is to be noted that there is a possibility that both Roy Deveson and William Davey may have been included in work parties to Fukuoka sub-Camp No. 6 Hajenjo and Fukuoka sub-Camp No. 15. In both these men's interrogation reports they stated that they had been at these camps. Unfortunately there is not enough information to substantiate their claims or pin point the exact locations of these two camps.

Fukuoka sub-Camp No. 26 – Usui

The Japanese designation for this camp was Fukuoka, Kaho-Gun. The mine was owned by the Aso Mining Company (Aso Kogyo). There were two members from the 2/4th that left Kawasaki Camp on 12th June 1945 for Fukuoka sub-Camp No.26 Usui. These two men were Frank Hinnrichsen and Harold Procter. The party of 200 men that included some of 'C' Force had departed Sannomiya Railway Station at 1800 hours in two carriages. They arrived at Moji the next morning having travelled from Shimonoseki to Moji through the Kammon undersea tunnel.

Detraining at Moji, they would change trains twice more before reaching their final destination at Fukuoka sub-Camp No. 26, Usui, on the island of Kyushu. The location of the mine camp at Fukuoka No. 26 was located on an east-west line between the city of Fukuoka and the town of Yamada. The camp itself was located about a mile from the railway station and about a quarter of a mile from the township, nestled in a valley behind a mountain range. On arrival the prisoners moved into a new camp, which it is thought, was meant to house Japanese civilian mine workers after the war. Accommodation was in ten huts that were all connected by a roofed passageway. A 10 foot high electrified wooden fence surrounded the camp.

There were two jobs allocated to the prisoners at this camp. Firstly, there was work underground in the coalmine which, the like Omine No. 6, had been put back into production to feed Japan's steel industry. Secondly, there was work in the camp market garden.

This party at Fukuoka No. 26 was considered to be a convalescent party, yet still men were expected to work below ground on fourteen-hour shifts. Every camp in Japan was the same; men were expected to do physically demanding manual labour whilst their health deteriorated and the ration situation in Japan deteriorated.

On 16th August 1945 the by now ex-Prisoners of War were informed by their Japanese overseers that the war was over. All the same it took some time, 19th September, in fact before they were recovered by the U.S. military and sent on their way home on the first leg of their journey by train via Nagasaki. Once aboard USS *Marathon* the ship set sail for Okinawa where C54 transports were boarded on 25th September for the flight to Manila. Harold and Frank, after the usual formalities, boarded HMS *Speaker* a Royal Navy aircraft carrier which would take then as far as Sydney on their homeward journey.

Camps on Honshu Island

Nagoya

Nagoya is located in central Honshu Island to the east of Kobe. When Arthur Draper and Norm Harris left Showa-Denki they first came to a place called Nagoya. They were in residence here from 2nd February to 28th May 1945 whence they again moved to Toyama camp. It is believed that there were twenty men in this group under Lt. K. W. Goddard. All that is known is these twenty men were harshly treated. There was a base camp and five Nagoya sub-Camps but it cannot be said with any authority which camp these men moved to.

Toyama Camp

This camp was a sub-Camp of the Nagoya group of camps. As mentioned it is believed that four members from the 2/4th were first sent from Showa-Denki to Nagoya on 29th May 1945. They moved by train from the Showa-Denki via Nagoya for three months then to Toyama Camp, that was located to the northeast of Kobe on the north coast of Honshu Island.

The camp was located on open ground in the midst of a rice padi about a mile from Toyama which lies close to the seaport of Aomori. The men were employed mostly on the docks unloading iron ore for the local steel mill, and salt and beans. Food at this camp was no different to other camps at this time, being limited and of poor quality.

It was not until about three weeks after the end of the war, 6th September in fact, that the prisoners were recovered by U.S. Marines. They were transported by train to Nagoya where they then boarded a barge and were ferried out to a U.S. Navy hospital ship. Once given a clean bill of health they then boarded a U.S. Navy destroyer that took them to Yokohama, from where they were then flown to Okinawa and then to Manila.

At Manila, like all the Australian ex-Prisoners of War, they were processed, and arrangements made for their onward journey home by the 3rd Australian Prisoner of War Reception Group. Alf Jones and Arthur Draper returned to Sydney on the HMS *Formidable* and then the *Dominion Monarch* to Fremantle. Norm Harris and Ron Lymn returned from Manila on an R.A.A.F. B24 Liberator bomber Serial No. A24-146 to Sydney. From there they caught a train to Melbourne and were flown home to Perth aboard an ANA airliner, arriving home on 27th September 1945.

Kawasaki Camp-Maruyama Park

This camp was located at Maruyama Park and was located about eight miles away from Kobe House in a northwest direction in the foothills of Kobe. The reason it is also known as Kawasaki Camp is because it housed members of 'C' Force from Singapore who were engaged in work at the Kawasaki shipyards. Accommodation at this camp was in a 100 foot long wooden hut. Food consisted of a basic diet of rice and vegetable stew.

The days of the 'free for all' at the dockside warehouses was well and truly over. Almost all the Prisoners of War who had not by this time been sent to camps further away from Kobe and out of harms way, were now at Maruyama Park.

Following the incendiary raid on 5th June the remaining prisoners at Kobe House were evacuated to Kawasaki Camp. Peter Omiridis was one machine gunner who was included in this group.

On 12th June a group of fifty prisoners which included some 'C' Force, departed for Fukuoka sub-Camp No. 26, and on 21st June, fifty men from this group, the remnants of Kobe, now moved to Wakinohama camp.

Wakinohama

On 21st June 1945 the remaining group of fifty prisoners at Maruyama Park moved down from the foothills to Wakinohama Camp. This was a partially burnt out brick building that was once used as a school located about 1 and a half miles from Kobe House. Amongst the 2/4th machine gunners now at this camp were John Gilmour, Jack Ramsbottom, Wally Hutchinson, Peter Omiridis and Jim Dore. The close proximity of Wakinohama to the Kobe docks was soon taken advantage of as soon as the siren was sounded on the end of the war.

Maibara-Osaka sub-Camp No.10

The Japanese designation for this camp was Shiga, Maibara-Machi, Yaeuchiko Kankatsu. Two members of the 2/4th Machine Gun Battalion were sent to this camp on 19th May 1945 and on the next day the camp was officially opened. The camp was located on the outskirts of the village of Maibara in the Shiga Prefecture. The two 2/4th machine gunners were Gerry Arthur and Edwin Clarke.

Information received from ex-Prisoners of War from Maibara Camp who had made a social call to Wakinohama on 1st September, stated that the camp was approximately six hours away by train and about ten minutes away from Lake Biwa. Accommodation consisted of grass-roofed huts no doubt similar to the atap variety that was so common in Burma and Thailand. Water for the camp was drawn from a well that very quickly ran dry unless it rained frequently. Work at Maibara was the construction of a dyke to enable the lake to be emptied so that rice, barley and sorghum (tropical grass) could be planted for food.

The prisoners at this camp were not aware that the war had finished until 20th August. Following their visit to Wakinohama they were sent back to Maibara with the good news, and were much healthier thanks to the air drops by the B29's over Wakinohama.

Notogawa-Osaka sub-Camp No. 9

The Japanese designation for this camp was Shiga, Notogawa-Cho, Nakamiko Kankatsu. Three members of the 2/4th, Stan Wenn, Lance Park and Jack Leahy were amongst a party sent to Notogawa from Kobe on 20th May 1945 under S/Sgt. Keith Pescod. Notogawa Camp was approximately 60 miles to the north of Osaka and 4 and a half miles to the southwest of Maibara Camp. Rations at this camp were limited and most of the prisoners who had been sent here after Kobe House, lost between four and eight kilograms in weight. Food was mainly rice and tainted meat supplemented by what fresh water mussels could be collected from the lake. Work at this camp, like Maibara, was the reclaiming of land from Lake Biwa so that crops could be planted.

The Rakuyo Maru Story

Between December 1943 and March 1944 the *Rakuyo Maru* Party departed their camps at Tamarkan, Banpong or Non Pladuk. By this time the prisoners had been inoculated twice against cholera, twice against pestis (plague) and once against tuberculosis.

The senior officer who would be in command of this group was Brigadier A. L. Varley from the 2/18th Battalion. Brigadier Varley had also been the senior Australian officer on 'A' Force in Burma and was well known and respected for standing his ground against the Japanese.

The 717 Australians on this *Rakuyo Party* were organised into six kumis, No.'s 35–40 of approximately 150 men each. On 27th March 1944, the first three kumis departed Tamarkan for Kanchanaburi where they would board a train for the short journey to Non Pladuk. The prisoners were accommodated at the transit camp at Konma. which has been mentioned on several occasions within the 'D', 'F' and 'H' Force stories. The first party remained here for several days whilst the other kumis caught up. Now as before the kumis departed in stages through Bangkok on their way to Phnom Penh in Cambodia. Here they would board a river boat named the *Long Ho* that would take them the rest of the way to Saigon in French Indo-China.

French Indo-China

After a brief stay at Saigon the prisoners were taken even further down river to the estuary of the Riviere de Saigon at Cape St Jacques where they boarded a ship for onward passage to Japan. The Japanese realised the danger of moving the Prisoners of War by ship from this staging point because of the American submarine blockade. Instead, it was decided that it would be safer to move the *Rakuyo Maru* Party back to Singapore from where they could be shipped to Japan. First though, it was back to Saigon where the prisoners were put to work on docks, go-downs and various jobs at the Tan Son Nhut civil aerodrome just north of Saigon.

The first man to pass away from the 2/4th and possibly the *Rakuyo Maru* Party was Albert Struthoff. Albert fell ill on 23rd June 1944 and died in a rest room as a result of pneumonia and dysentery at 2100 hours on 19th September. His death certificate was signed on 21st September by Captain Sugiyama Tomokichi, an officer with the Imperial Japanese Army Medical Department. Albert was buried at the Chi Hoa Cemetery Saigon and his remains were exhumed and reburied at Kranji War Cemetery after the war.

On the move again, the first two kumis set out on the journey back to Singapore on 24th June and were followed by the others up until 28th June 1944. It is noted that a few sick prisoners remained behind, so then it must be assumed that Albert had not been in a fit state to travel at this time. Albert's Japan POW number was 1657 so it must also be assumed that these numbers were issued to the prisoners before they commenced their journey.

Another man from the 2/4th who remained behind and was transferred to the Saigon rolls with the British Prisoners of War already in residence, was James Howe. However, one member of the 2/4th who does not appear on the kumi lists yet is believed to have been on this *Rakuyo Maru* Party and remained behind in Saigon due to illness was Bryan Manwaring.

When the trains carrying the *Rakuyo Maru* Party arrived at the Non Pladuk rail terminus it was observed by the prisoners that they were now heading south towards Singapore. On 4th July the train carrying the *Rakuyo Maru* Party finally crossed the causeway onto Singapore Island where they then moved into the River Valley Road Transit Camp.

Singapore 4.7.1944 – 4.9.1944

As well as the River Valley Road Transit Camp a number of the *Rakuyo Maru* Party were to work on the excavation of the dry dock opposite Pulau Damar Laut, otherwise known as Jeep Island. They would work here from 27th July to 3rd September 1944 when it was finally announced that the *Rakuyo Maru* Party was again on its way. There were some members of the 2/4th who at the last moment would be excused. Murray Cheyne was one, who on 14th July, was sent to Changi Gaol Camp hospital from River Valley Road suffering from malaria and pneumonia. On regaining his health, and being a Pay Sergeant, he was later transferred to

Changi Administration on 28th January 1945. Basil Frost was another from the battalion who was sent to Changi Gaol Camp hospital with an infected leg.

When in August 1944 the time came to embark on the *Rakuyo Maru* Party it was discovered that there was not enough room to take the Australian kumis No.'s 35–40, so the last kumi was deleted from the passenger list. The members amongst the 2/4th that were included in this kumi No. 40 were Vic Barnett, Bill Cake, Harry Lucas, Albert Hambley and Les Holtzman. All these men would be included in the draft that would sail onboard the *Awa Maru* to Japan at the end of December 1944.

The *Rakuyo Maru* was a passenger-cargo ship displacing 9,419 tons having been built by the Mitsubishi Company at Nagasaki and launched in 1921. On the morning of 4th September 1944 the Australians who were included in the final draft of the *Rakuyo Maru* Party, (718 in all) were marched up the gangway and were crammed into the number two hold of three holds on this ship. The fortunate prisoners who could not be accommodated below were to travel as open cargo on the top deck of the ship.

The other ship in the convoy that would meet the same fate as the *Rakuyo Maru* was the *Kachidoki Maru* which was also transporting 1,500 British Prisoners of War to Japan. The British who had come down to Singapore, were accommodated at the Havelock Road Transit Camp on the opposite side of the canal at the River Valley Road Transit Camp. These British prisoners had travelled down the Malayan Peninsula directly from Tamuang camp, thus avoiding the scenic route via Saigon. Together the British, Australians and sole American on these two ships would form a draft of 2,218 men destined for Japan. By this time there was an element of apprehension felt by the Prisoners of War as to whether or not they would actually arrive at their final destination, considering the strong presence of Allied submarines in the seas between Singapore and Japan.

The two ships now moved out to the roadstead where they remained at anchor for the next thirty-six hours. On the morning of 6th September two more passenger-cargo ships and two tankers joined the *Rakuyo* and *Kachidoki Maru's*. These six ships were then joined by their four escorts and now this small convoy headed northeast.

Whilst discomfort was caused by the cramped conditions, and although the food rations were the usual meagre portions, the greatest concern to the prisoners aboard the *Rakuyo Maru* was the drastic water shortage. Men like rats in the dark of night left the safety of their hold to seek out sources of water. On 10th September, the fifth afternoon at sea, the heavens opened up as if in answer to a prayer and deluged the convoy with torrential rain. Prisoners, topside grabbed anything that would collect rainwater including gaping open mouths. The next day, the convoy was joined by another three freighters and three warships. At about 0530 hours on Tuesday 12th September 1944 the convoy was attacked by three U.S. Navy submarines.

The Torpedo Attack

As quickly as the attack had begun one of the tankers, a cargo ship and an escort were on their way to the depths. Before there was time to take in what was happening, the prisoners aboard the *Rakuyo Maru* were alerted to the fact that it was their turn, when two torpedoes from the *Sealion II* slammed into the starboard side of the ship. Fortunately, one torpedo hit forward near the No.1 hold in the region of the chain locker, and the other midships just aft of the bridge in the engine room. When the two torpedoes struck home there were no great explosions or walls of seawater, in fact, the wake up call that something had happened was described as a dull thud.

The *Rakuyo Maru* would take twelve hours to sink as her hull settled about twelve feet deeper in the water. The *Rakuyo Maru* was carrying a shipment of rubber blocks weighing about 30lbs each and these have been attributed to the ships buoyancy. Nevertheless, precautions had been put into practice by briefing the prisoners on how to abandon ship. These briefings helped to lessen the panic when the reality hit home that the ship was actually sinking.

Six Japanese warships now homed in on the *USS Sealion II* dropping their depth charges where they thought the submarine to be located. No major damage was suffered by the *Sealion II* but she was as good as pinned down whilst the Japanese escorts skimmed the surface looking for her. It was now the turn of the other American submarines, *Growler* and *Pampanito* to wreak havoc upon the convoy.

The scene around the *Rakuyo Maru* was by this time chaotic. Japanese soldiers and sailors scrambled into lifeboats concerned with one thing only, saving themselves. The water was awash with oil from the tanker, and patches of the sky were ablaze as oil burnt away on the surface of the water. Those without life preservers and who could not swim panicked and drowned, whilst others were pushed into the burning oil by the strong current. Others, already in the water were either being killed or knocked unconscious by objects that were being tossed overboard. Instead of these objects saving lives they were doing the opposite and this was despite the fact that all the prisoners on the *Rakuyo Maru* had been warned of this danger by sailors from the R.A.N.

When it was realised that the *Rakuyo Maru* was not in immediate danger of sinking, the rush subsided and some men including Phil Beilby even ventured back onboard in search of food and water. By 0600 hours most of the British and Australians from the *Rakuyo Maru* were in the water. Approximately fifty-two minutes later the commander of the submarine, *Growler* fired six torpedoes at a Japanese frigate achieving two positive hits on the Japanese warship. Another Japanese frigate followed up the chase for the *Growler* dropping depth charges at random. In the book *Return From The River Kwai* the story of these Japanese frigates in pursuit and the subsequent depth charging of the *Growler* is explained:

Barney Barnett described the sensation as 'horrible, like it was squeezing your stomach into your throat'.

John Langley also explains:

'It was about the worst experience I have ever had. First there was a slight tingling in the spine like an electric shock. Then the concussion. You vomited and moved your bowels at the same time.' [17]

In an interview the author had with Harry Pickett from the 2/4th Machine Gun Battalion he explained:

'We took a blast in the water when a Jap frigate depth charged a submarine. It felt like as if vertebrae down my spine were separating from the concussion in the water.'

Harry went on to say:

'When the yanks rescued me my body was covered in small punctures where the globules of oil that were spitting to the surface made indentations in my skin.'

The oil and diesel fuel that covered the surface of the water also covered the bodies of the prisoners in the water. It was was not the slimy film that coated these half naked bodies in the water, or the slippery film that coated everything that was buoyant enough to keep them afloat that was the problem; it was the irritation and burns caused to the skin by the oil and diesel fuel and the exposure to sunlight and salt water.

---

17   Joan and Clay Blair, *Return from the River Kwai* McDonald & James 1979, p.145

Instructions for shipwrecked Australian sailors, provided in lifeboats and rafts issued suggestions for the treatment:

'of various conditions of the skin such as burns, sunburn, frostbite, abrasions, cracked skin caused by sun and salt water burns (boils). When leaving a floundering ship, men were likely to receive cuts and bruises, perhaps from the incrustations of barnacles on the lower sides and bottom. These injuries could be so irritated by fuel oil, salt water and burning sun so as to become septic.' [18]

The Survival Factor

By mid morning of the 12th, the prisoners from the *Rakuyo Maru* had split into two groups. The first and biggest of these groups consisted of about 900 men. By this time they had drifted some distance from their original position. The second and smaller group, which had stayed in closer to the sinking *Rakuyo Maru* consisted of about 350 men.

After surviving the trials of the Burma rail link these men would now need to call on every ounce of strength left in their minds and weakened bodies. Over the next several days their lives would be suspended from a very tenuous thread. In this situation, bobbing about in the middle of an ocean, under a blazing sun, covered in oil with nothing to eat or drink there was nothing that could be done to ease their pain. There was nothing that even mates could do to help except reassure each other that they would soon be rescued. Yet both submarine commanders were oblivious to the fact that there were Allied Prisoners of War in the water, some of whom were already feeling the effects of the sinking and depth charging.

At approximately 1730 hours on 12th September the *Rakuyo Maru* finally slid under the surface with hardly a sound, except for the hiss of air escaping from the hulk. The *Rakuyo Maru's* position in the South China Sea was Latitude 18 degrees-42 minutes North, Longitude 114 degrees-30 minutes East, and it was here that most of the prisoners remained on the first night.

Whilst the *Rakuyo Maru* was bidding its final farewell, two Japanese frigates and a cargo-passenger ship were looming ever larger on the horizon. Hopes of rescue soared but they needn't have, as the Japanese only picked up their own within the vicinity of the *Rakuyo Maru* and refused to pick up any of the prisoners in the water, only waving in contempt. This act might appear cruel but considering Japan's situation at this stage of the war and what was happening at Sandakan in Borneo and what was potentially about to happen in Thailand and on Singapore it is surprising that these survivors were not machine gunned in the water. It is perhaps no consolation but the passenger-cargo ship that picked up the Japanese survivors was the *Kachidoki Maru*. It was torpedoed by the *Pampanito* the following day with 900 British Prisoners of War, but it is anyone's guess as to how many of the rescued Japanese were aboard.

At least now, with the departure of the Japanese, this had made available eleven lifeboats and odd items of flotsam and jetsam which was quickly put to good use by the prisoners. During the first day in the water there were repeated attempts to organise rafts into groups for mutual assistance. Large groups remained together but as days turned into nights these groups began to drift apart and it was obvious that the numbers of men on the rafts were diminishing. This was particularly so during the hours of darkness when men fell asleep and slipped off the oil covered rafts never to resurface.

One of the very real dangers of men ship wrecked at sea is that they might drink seawater. Many gave in to this craving and gulped seawater, this only made them delirious which in turn, placed others at risk.

---

[18]   Alan S.Walker, *Medical Services of the R.A.N. and R.A.A.F.* Australia in the War of 1939–45, Medical Volume IV p.94

Meanwhile, the two U.S. Navy submarines *Sealion II* and the *Pampanito* remained on patrol off the Hainan coast over 13th–14th September in the hope of scoring a few more Japanese ships. At 1630 hours, as the *Pampanito* cruised on the surface towards two wisps of smoke the bridge watch reported the sighting of life rafts and lifeboats in the water. Believing that these were Japanese survivors the commander of the *Pampanito* decided to keep tracking the smoke on the horizon. By 1700 hours the *Pampanito* was close enough to distinguish that the smoke was coming from two Japanese freighters. At 1915 hours the *Pampanito* dived to wait for darkness before pressing its attack.

Just under thirty minutes later at 2013 hours *Pampanito* surfaced but had lost contact with its prey. Remaining on task, the submarine searched for the ships until two small pips appeared on the radar screen. The *Pampanito* pursued these but as it turned out the two pips were small trawlers which the submarine's commander felt were not worth wasting torpedoes on whilst there was still bigger prey in the vicinity.

The *Pampanito* now broke off the search for remnants of the Japanese convoy and decided to rendezvous with the *Sealion II* at 0700 hours the following morning, 15th September 1944. The two submarines met as planned and it was then decided that together they would head east on the surface which would take them back through the area of the initial *Sealion II-Growler* attack on the Japanese convoy. At sunrise the two submarines formed a line 20 miles apart as they sailed due east.

Rescue – The Luck Factor

At about 1800 hours on 15th September the officer of the day and the bridge lookout aboard the *Pampanito* spotted a lifeboat and a large quantity of debris in the water. The position was Latitude 18 degrees-42 minutes East and Longitude 114 degrees-00 minutes North, which was slightly north of where the *Sealion II* and *Growler* had attacked the convoy and where the *Rakuyo Maru* had been torpedoed. As it turned out the lifeboat was empty but ten minutes later two more life rafts were sighted with men, who were waving madly. The first raft was a conglomeration of hatch covers and timber which was keeping about fifteen men buoyant. The Americans truly believed that these survivors were Japanese and made preparations to dispose of them accordingly.

Then in an instant the realisation that these were Allied servicemen was made clear when someone on the raft called up to the American submariners that they were all British and Australian Prisoners of War. The crew of the *Pampanito* went into action immediately. Bales of rags were sent up from below to wipe off the crude oil. On the second raft there were about nine men. Then a raft was passed with a single occupant. Part of the head was missing and so it was supposed that a shark had been involved. Then there was a third raft, then a fourth. Altogether about fifty elated men were rescued in the immediate vicinity.

The submarine then headed south where another two rafts had been sighted and this netted the Americans another thirteen survivors. Meanwhile the *Pampanito* was alerted to another ship in the area but as it turned out it was the *Sealion II* that had been requested to help with the rescue. The *Pampanito* had broken radio silence to alert U.S. Fleet Headquarters at Pearl Harbor to the fact that there were possibly many Allied Prisoners of War that needed to be rescued urgently.

Meanwhile, the crew of the *Pampanito* observed that the *Sealion II* was dead in the water so reasoned that its crew were also picking up survivors. On this day, the *Pampanito* rescued seventy-three British and Australian Prisoners of War. These survivors were suffering from shock, exposure, exhaustion, dehydration, starvation and skin sores. Small quantities of liquids were administered to the survivors who were receiving the best of care that the crew of the

United States submarine *Pampanito* could administer. The crew of the submarine also unselfishly volunteered to surrender their bunks to the survivors without being asked by their commander.

On board the *Pampanito* at this time were five 2/4th machine gunners being, Alf and Wally Winter, Jack Cocking, Tom Pascoe and Harry Picket. The *Pampanito* now headed towards the American held island of Saipan, which was reached on the morning of 20th September. All the survivors, excepting two British who had died, were then transferred to small boats and ferried ashore to cheers and waves goodbye from their former hosts. At 1715 hours the commander of the *Sealion II* had received a request for help to search for survivors. At this time the submarine was about 28 miles to the northeast of the last reported position of the *Pampanito*. The commander of the *Sealion II* immediately changed course and increased speed towards the scene of the rescue. Debris was first sighted at 1750 hours and a few minutes later the submarine passed through a heavy oil slick. At 1830 hours the first of many dead bodies floated past, but moments later the first calls for help were heard. It was an hour before sunset so time was now of the essence.

The submarine's crew sprang into action, some diving into the water to assist the survivors in the water as others stood by on the hauling out party. The first raft took a line and the first survivor came aboard at 1837 hours. From now until dark it was an all out race to rescue as many men as possible. By dark fifty survivors had been rescued. It could not be estimated how many survivors were still alive amongst the debris but it is thought that there were still many. Regardless, the *Sealion II* could only have picked up a limited number of survivors in any case. Of these, two were from the 2/4th, being Alf Sing and Laurie Kearney. This rescue had taken place sixty hours after the *Rakuyo Maru* was torpedoed, the survivors having gone without water and food for two days and three nights.

Like the *Pampanito*, the *Sealion II* started out on its five-day cruise to Saipan where it arrived at 1115 hours on 20th September. There were two other U.S. Navy submarines that would also rescue survivors from the *Rakuyo Maru*, the *Queenfish* and the *Barb*. But it wouldn't be until 0400 hours on 16th September that the two submarine commanders would learn of the urgent need for their services. The two submarines headed in the direction of the survivors and as they did the indications were that a storm was brewing.

Both submarines arrived at the search area at 0530 hours on 17th September. This was about one and a half hours before sunrise. It was realised that with the wind speed increasing and the seas whipping up that it could be a limited search. Over four hours passed, when at 0950 hours the bridge lookout on the *Barb* spotted some debris stretching as far as the eye could see. The two submarines changed course and proceeded to engulf their vessels in wreckage.

It was about 1230 hours when some bodies went floating past. At this time it was questioned whether men could survive this long, and the feasibility of continuing the search was doubtful. But at 1255 hours it was reported that two rafts with five men had been sighted through the high periscope. It was just after 1300 hours when the first three survivors were brought onboard. *Barb* then found another survivor and this was followed by another group until there were fourteen onboard. There was only one 2/4th machine gunner in this group being Doug Hampson.

Now it was the turn of the *Queenfish* whose crew rescued another eighteen survivors, bringing the total to thirty-two between the two submarines. Taken aboard the *Queenfish* from the 2/4th were Vic Cross and Phil Beilby and Harry Bunker. Altogether from the 2/4th Machine Gun Battalion there were eleven men who were rescued by the four American submarines.

The *Queenfish* and *Barb* now also headed towards Saipan with their fragile human cargo. The increase in wind and rising seas had by now turned into a typhoon but by all accounts this in no way affected the appetites of the *Rakuyo Maru* survivors, who exulted in the knowledge that they were now safe and above all, free men. On 25th September, the two submarines arrived at Saipan where again the survivors were put ashore for some tender loving care at the U.S. Army Hospital on Saipan. The survivors would now move on, except for six men including Vic Cross who was still too sick to travel.

On 28th September, the remaining eighty-six survivors boarded the troopship *Alcoa Polaris* destined for Guadalcanal in the Solomon Islands. They would remain here for several days before boarding the U.S. Navy minesweeper, USS *Mondanock* that would take them as far as Brisbane, where they disembarked on 18th October 1944. From Brisbane the men from Western Australia would board an aircraft that would transport them the remainder of the way home. They landed back in Western Australia on 1st November 1944. Their war was now over, but not forgotten as the information they would provide would help to compile intelligence reports for the continued Allied assault against Japan. The detailed information they brought home would be the first since the February 1942 concerning the treatment of Prisoners of War, the construction of the Burma–Thailand rail link, as well as intelligence concerning Singapore and Java. Sadly some families would be informed by eye witness accounts about how their loved ones were killed in action or else had died as Prisoners of War, building the Japanese their railway.

These were supposed to be happy times for the survivors, however they were bombarded with questions and it was occasionally their solemn duty to inform relatives that their loved one had since passed away. This duty must have been heart wrenching considering what they had seen and endured. Instead of being able to put these real life experiences behind them they were kept busy fending off questions and letters from family and friends that just wouldn't let them forget.

All of these eleven men were nominated by Major Charles Green to receive the British Empire Medal. Not one of these men received this award. Perhaps Major Green understood what they had endured above and beyond their experience on the Burma–Thailand Railway.

The Rakuyo Maru Survivors
Back row: Alf Winter, Doug Hampson, Harry Bunker, Alf Sing, Laurie Kearney, Phil Beilby, Jack Cocking
Front row: Wally Winter, Harry Picket, Tom Pascoe (Absent, Vic Cross)

The Other Survivors

There were three other survivors from the sinking of the *Rakuyo Maru*. These three men were Bert Wall, 'Aussie' Climie and Syd Clayden. Bert Wall was picked up with 135 others by a Japanese corvette on the morning of 14th September. The following day they were delivered safely to Hainan Island and transferred to a tanker along with the survivors of the *Kachidoki Maru*. The prisoners couldn't believe their ears when they were told that they were to travel to Japan aboard a tanker. This seemed like waving a red rag to a bull with American submarines continually prowling the seas in search of prey.

On 16th September, they were transferred to another ship, the whale processing ship *Kibibi Maru*. Unbeknown to them at the time they had just been transferred to a whale factory ship that had been converted to carry fuel oil. All the prisoners who had been rescued following the sinking of the *Rakuyo Maru* and the *Kachidoki Maru* were billeted in the cavernous space between decks where the whales were flenched.

On the same day as the prisoners boarded the *Kibibi Maru* it set sail for Japan as part of a small convoy of ships. On 20th September, the *Kibibi Maru* arrived at Keelung on the northern tip of Formosa, but it was only here a day or two before getting under weigh again for Moji in Japan. Twice the *Kibibi Maru* was forced back into Keelung by alarms that American submarines were operating in the area. Finally, on the third attempt on the 24th September the ship made a break for the open seas. The voyage from Keelung to Moji would take four days, and every minute of the voyage the prisoners were fearful that they would again be torpedo fodder for American submarines. On the 28th, the *Kibibi Maru* docked at Moji, but rather than feeling concern about being deeper in enemy held territory, the men were actually relieved to at last be out of harm's way.

The prisoners, of whom about eighty were Australians, were issued with their new POW numbers and split up into their various work parties. There were thirty Australians who went to Sakata on the northwest coast of Honshu Island, one of these men being Bert Wall. The other camp where the remaining fifty Australians were sent was Kawasaki, mid-way between Yokohama and Tokyo.

Sakata Camp

This party left Moji by train on 29th September bound for Yokohama where issues of a drab green jacket, shirt and trousers were made to the prisoners. They arrived at Sakata on 3rd October 1944. This camp was a rice warehouse, formerly surrounded by a barbed wire fence forming a compound approximately 75 yards long by 50 yards wide. This building was now converted into a Prisoner of War dormitory by adding a wooden floor. The floor was approximately 8 feet from the ground and was reached by scaling almost vertical wooden ladders into the building. It was covered with straw tatami mats on which the men slept in winter with their meagre issue of three blankets. Dysentery was common at this camp, however some assistance was received from the British and American staff at the Shinagawa Hospital in this area.

Work was a mixture of stacking and loading timber, carting coal and smelter work which was one of Bert Wall's assignments. The men at this camp were released on 13th September 1945. They were taken by a R.N. destroyer, HMS *Wakeful* to Yokohama whereupon they were flown to Okinawa and then Manila compliments of the U.S.A.A.C. It was here that Bert Wall embarked on the R.N. aircraft carrier HMS *Formidable* to Sydney. On 13th November 1945 he arrived back in Western Australia one year and twelve days after the other survivors from the *Rakuyo Maru*.

Kawasaki Camp No. 14D

Prisoners of War were usually contracted out to civilian companies so it is sometimes difficult, as it is in this case, to accurately determine the exact location of particular camps. In the 2/20th Battalion unit history *Singapore and Beyond*[19] there is mention of the Shibaura Electric Company which states that the factory was about 2 and a half miles from the camp. This factory is listed as Tokyo Shibaura Electric Co., Section 13-Niigata-Shi and appears to be a likely candidate as to where 'Aussie' Climie and Syd Clayden were employed. It would be fair to say that the camp and the factory were reasonably close to the docks area of Tokyo Bay to the southeast of the city. American intelligence from March 1945 reported a camp as the Shibaura Camp that was close to the docks and was protected by a high concrete wall on one side. The remainder of the story concerning 'Aussie' Climie and Syd Clayden will have to be surmised.

In March 1945 American B29 pathfinders had marked out the area that was to receive special attention. This raid was followed by the main force of B29's their loads of M47A2 jellied petroleum (incendiary) bombs. The fires would burn continually for a week before they were extinguished or otherwise ran out of fuel. However, well before the total damage was done the prisoners were moved away from the camp to an open paddock area. The incendiary raid lasted for four hours, it being estimated that literally hundreds of B29's had been involved in this air raid over the Tokyo–Kawasaki environs.

Over four square miles of real estate had been obliterated and nothing remained of the prisoners' former home, so they were moved into the factory building. The air raids continued and on the night of 13th–14th July 'Aussie' Climie, who had been amidst the action on Hill 200, Ulu Pandan was killed. 'Aussie' was not the only prisoner to die this night, as he was just one of eight Australians.

Shinagawa Main Camp Hospital

This camp is thought to have been located to the south of the Kawasaki Camp and factory from where they had just spent their last days as Prisoners of War. This hospital where British and American medical staff were in residence had also been used by some prisoners from the Sakata camp. This is listed as being Syd Clayden's last camp, having been recovered on 5th September 1945. He was ferried out to a U.S.N. hospital ship, USS *Benevolence*, which would transport him to Manila. From here he boarded the R.N. aircraft carrier HMS *Speaker* that took him back to Sydney. So ends the story of the *Rakuyo Maru* Party. There were eleven men rescued who survived, one was recovered from Sakata and one from Shinagawa. The remainder of these men from the 2/4th Machine Gun Battalion went to their watery graves. Like their fellow machine gunners who were included in 'B' and 'E' Forces Borneo they are remembered on the Labuan War Memorial.

---

[19]   Don Wall, *Singapore and Beyond* The Story of the Men of the 2/20th Battalion, 2/20th Battalion Association, East Hills NSW 1985, p.225

The Aramis Story

The *Aramis* is one ship that made the voyage from Singapore to Moji that seems to have escaped the attention of many historians. Although obscure it still transported nineteen members from the 2/4th Machine Gun Battalion to Japan. Most of these nineteen men were the survivors from Major Alf Cough's 'D' force V Battalion or else had been on 'D' Force T Battalion. The common denominator it seems is that all these men were selected for Japan whilst at Non Pladuk. There were two camps at Non Pladuk, Camp No. 1 and Camp No. 2 being the Hospital Camp.

The *Aramis* had been a troopship for the French Foreign Legion. This ship was built at Bordeaux and registered at Marseilles in 1922. Being a military transport ship there is no record of it in Lloyds Shipping Register, that is until 1931 when it is recorded that the Aramis had a change of name to the *Chenonceaux*. This would indicate that the ship was sold and therefore recorded in Lloyds.

Whilst researching the story of the Saigon party it was discovered that there were three Messageries Maritimes liners, the *Athos II, D'Artagnan* and the *Chenonceaux* that could navigate the Riviere de Saigon, all ships having a length of 500 feet and a draught of 30 feet.

The *Aramis* or *Chenonceaux* was a 14,825 ton oil fuelled ship with four decks. Working on this theory it is possible that the name the prisoners saw painted across the bow was the old name *Aramis* which was showing under the weathered paint, or else a brass plaque with the name *Aramis* was sited by one of the prisoners somewhere onboard the ship.

Below decks, to their surprise, the prisoners discovered that there were bunks for their use that had been previously occupied by Japanese soldiers. The party was brought down to Singapore from Non Pladuk by train where they entered the River Valley Road Transit Camp. As Tom Gough recorded they boarded the *Aramis* on 2nd June. It seems likely that the *Chenonceaux* did not sail for several days as it waited out at the roadstead for its armed naval escort. Once at Moji this group was sent to their camp at Fukuoka sub-Camp No. 17 Omuta.

On 5th November 1944 Joe Swartz and Bill Dwyer were sent to Fukuoka sub-Camp No.1. This camp was the Western Army District Intendance Department. Joe would stay at this camp until 5th May until he was again moved to the Moji No. 4 Camp where he worked on the wharves until the end of the war. Bill Dwyer however succumbed to acute colitis on 5th May 1945. His body was cremated by the Japanese but instead of being enshrined in Japan his ashes finished up at Labuan War Cemetery, possibly carried by an Australian or other Allied serviceman.

The 2/4th and 2/6th Australian General Hospitals had been set up at Labuan and some ships carrying ex-Prisoners of War called into Labuan on the way to Australian eastern ports. There will be more on this subject of ashes and the stance taken by the Australian Government. Another casualty from the 2/4th was Ken Lally who died at Fukuoka sub-Camp No. 17 Omuta. Ken was crushed between two coal trucks below ground in the coalmine. As a result, Ken died of suffocation on 23rd March 1945 with his body being cremated by the Japanese and enshrined at the Yokohama War Cemetery.

Fukuoka sub-Camp No. 12 – Miyata

The Japanese designation for this camp was Fukuoka, Miyata-Machi and is noted as being located outside of Kaijima coal mine (Kaijima-Machi). The camp was situated in the hills about 10 miles to the northeast of Fukuoka City and consisted of twenty single-storey wooden huts with tiled roofs. The huts were the former barracks to the civilian mine workers. Surrounding the camp was a 12 foot high electric fence. At some stage 'Mick' Wilkins was moved from Fukuoka sub-Camp No. 17 to Fukuoka sub-Camp No. 12 Miyata where he remained until Japan's surrender.

Fukuoka sub-Camp No. 21 Nakama

The Japanese designation for this camp was Fukuoka, Nakama-Cho, Taisho Mining Company (Taisho Kogyo). James Flanagan was sent to this camp from Fukuoka sub-Camp No. 17, Omuta and remained here until the end of the war. This camp was located about 15 kilometres to the southwest of Moji almost on the north coast of Kyushu Island. It was yet another coalmine that had been reopened. The prisoners put in a two-shift rota working either the day or night shift with a rotation every ten days. As American air raids in the area increased the prisoners were forced to spend increasingly more time below ground. Shortly after Japan's surrender food drops were made over the camp by American B29's and again it was not long before the now ex-Prisoners of War at Fukuoka sub-Camp No. 21 were being moved down to Nagasaki for the journey home. James returned from Manila via Darwin by PBY Catalina and B24 Liberator aircraft.

The Rashin (Byoki) Maru Story

The *Rashin Maru* was a passenger-cargo ship of 5,454 tons. The prisoners who sailed in her had christened the ship *Byoki Maru*, Byoki being the Japanese word for sick. Put in simple terms, the *Rashin Maru* was a rust bucket. The origin of this ship was that it had been built in Canada and launched as the *Canadian Prince* in 1917. It was then sold to the Japanese for scrap in 1923 but instead the Japanese had elected to keep it in service. It had been bombed and burnt out in the Java Sea and was towed back to Singapore where because of a shortage of ships it was patched up sufficiently to make the voyage back to Japan. There was no bridge deck, but in its place was a wooden jury bridge erected aft on the poop deck.

The Prisoners of War who would be selected for the *Rashin Maru* Party came from the Tamuang area and all had worked on the Thailand side of the rail link on 'D' Force. Instead of travelling via the Saigon route the prisoners were transported by train directly to Singapore and moved into the River Valley Road Transit Camp. They had left Thailand on 22nd June 1944, arrived in Singapore on 27th June and by 4th July were aboard the *Rashin Maru*. There was one man from the 2/4th who did not travel at this time, possibly due to illness, being Eric Mann who would join the Saigon Party in February 1945.

By now the reader should be well aware of the risk involved in sailing to Japan aboard a Japanese ship. The *Rashin Maru* was lucky not to have been sunk. Ex-Prisoners of War who had sailed on her jokingly suggested that the Americans didn't believe she was worth wasting a torpedo on. This would certainly not be true and in any case the ship was sunk one week before the Japanese surrendered on 15th August 1945.

The Voyage

As well as the *Rashin Maru's* commercial cargo of rubber and tin there were approximately 1,660 prisoners, which included 900 Australians. The *Rashin Maru* made for the North Borneo coast and anchored off Miri in Sarawak on 8th July 1944. This old hulk was a coal burner so regular stops would be needed to replenish its coalbunkers. The ship weighed anchor on 10th July but remained in close to the coast of North Borneo as it would during most of the voyage to Japan. The ship anchored off Palawan Island and continued again the next morning, tracking along the west coast of Mindoro Island in the Philippines Islands group. Just on sunset on 16th July the *Rashin Maru* sailed through the Bataan Peninsula between Bataan and the fortified island of Corregidor and anchored in Manila Bay in the island of Luzon. There was a lengthy stopover at Luzon, in fact after fifteen days the ship had still not been replenished with coal and rations because it was impossible to get barges alongside. For this reason the *Rashin Maru* moved to a protected area of the harbour into calmer waters where the coaling and rationing of the ship was now made possible.

On 9th August the *Rashin Maru* again set sail in convoy with seventeen other ships. The Prisoners of War onboard had already spent twenty-two days at anchor in Manila Bay, but worse was yet to come. Suddenly the prisoner's senses were awakened to the fact that they were under attack. The convoy now broke up in the chaos and the *Rashin Maru* put into Lingayen Gulf at the opposite side of the landmass that juts out on the west coast of Luzon Island. On 13th August the little *Rashin Maru* nosed out of the Lingayen Gulf under a threatening overcast sky, and into seas fraught with danger. Soon the *Rashin Maru's* plates were groaning under the strain as the ship was tossed about the ocean.

The Captain thankfully was a cautious man, indicated by the manner in which he had steered the ship abeam of any landform in sight. Again realising that the ship would be in danger from a typhoon, he put into the leeward side of Mabudi Island. This haven offered a sheltered anchorage formed by the triangle of the three Bataan Islands. At 0800 hours on 14th August the *Rashin Maru* set sail once again, arriving at Takao on the southern end of Formosa on 15th August. The next port of call was Keelung on the northern end of Formosa. Both Takao and Keelung will be remembered from the Korea and *Rakuyo Maru* stories.

Following several attempts to depart Keelung, only to be forced back again by U.S. Navy submarines, the *Rashin Maru* made Naha on the island of Okinawa on 30th August. Finally, after sailing from Kagoshima on the southern end of Kyushu Island and along the west coast of Kyushu the *Rashin Maru*, after seventy long days and nights finally put into the port of Moji on 7th September 1944.

So ended a journey for the prisoners who for nearly two and a half months, were crammed into the holds of a decrepit old hulk that had been taunted by American submarines and tossed about like a cork in a bathtub thanks to the force of a typhoon. There were no welcoming crowds or brass bands but the prisoners certainly knew they had reached Moji because the Captain of the *Rashin Maru* slammed the ship alongside the wharf in his keenness to tie up alongside. He had done a good job to come as far as he had unscathed, but probably only due to the fact he had captained the ship the entire way on his own nervous energy.

The Prisoners of War were now herded down the gangway, lined up along the wharf and pondered in utter amazement how in the world they had come as far as they had. The prisoners were now split into kumis of 150 men and sent on their way to their designated camps which will now be covered in detail. The first camp and one which would receive a number of the men from the 2/4th Machine Gun Battalion was Niihama on the northern coast of the Inland Sea island of Shikoku.

Yamane and Niihama

The Yamane–Niihama area was vital to Japan's war effort. This region was important for its ore processing, chemical and manufacturing plants. Included in this was metal casting, marine engines, stone crushing machines, ship building and mining machinery, copper smelting, aluminium, alumina, nickel, ammonia, sulphuric acid, coke ovens, explosives, methyl alcohol, phosphates, chlorine, caustic soda and a silk spinning mill.

The prisoners bound for Niihama were put onto a train which headed off in an easterly direction from Moji along the Japanese main island of Honshu. This group of over 250 Australians was now under the command of Lt. Ralph Sanderson from the 2/19th Battalion. When they detrained at Tokoyama they were then put onto a barge and towed across the Inland Sea to the port of Matsuyama on Shikoku Island. They were then bundled onto trucks and driven to the Niihama Railway Station from where they were marched 1 and a half miles to their new camp at Yamane.

This camp had only recently been completed judging by the weathering of the timber used in its construction. The camp was divided into the two distinct areas that were enclosed by a high wooden fence. One section was for prisoners and the other for the guards, camp offices and parade ground. The Australian prisoner's accommodation was in hut No. 1, a two-storeyed building about 200 feet long, by 30 feet wide. The construction of the buildings in this camp was virtually the same as the Niihama Camp, which will be covered shortly.

The prisoners were brought to this location to work below and above ground at the Sumitomo Besshi copper mine. The mine was located in the Besshi Mountain at an elevation 2,000 feet above sea level, approximately 7 and a half miles to the south of and overlooking the Port of Niihama. Two mine shafts extended eastward from their entrances for 5 miles into the hills. The mine was not only rich in copper but also gold and bauxite, used in the manufacture of aircraft.

The mine kept 100,000 people gainfully employed and there is no doubting that Niihama's industry that encompassed an area of 12 and a half miles only existed because of the mine. The copper, aluminium and chemical refineries and foundry of the Yamane–Niihama area were an important contributor towards Japan's war effort. The copper, bauxite and gold ore was taken from the mine in railway ore cars to the wharf between machinery and chemical plants where it was shipped to Shikan Island for refining. The ores once refined were shipped back to the foundry, machinery, chemical and aluminium plants at Niihama.

The Besshi Copper Mine

It was around 11th September 1944 that the Prisoners of War began work at the mine. Their first, and presumably a typical day at the Besshi copper mine, was as follows: After breakfast they were marched to the Niihama Railway Station where they were unceremoniously piled into open railway ore trucks for the trip up the mountain. On arrival at the mine the men were paraded outside the mine offices and introduced to Capt. Takuji Marukami. In a display of swordsmanship before a captive Prisoner of War audience he convinced all who were paraded before him that they must work hard to mine the copper ore for Japan or he would have their heads. Captain Marukami, from this time forth earned himself the nick name 'lolly lopper,' attributed to his impressive demonstration of swordsmanship.

Most, but not all the men, were to work below ground. Some of the machine gunners were to work above ground on mine maintenance and repair duties. Jim Elliot and Edwin Adams worked in the carpentry shop and Claude Dow worked as a drill sharpener. There were many 2/4th Machine Gun Battalion members that were to work below ground in Japan, however, this mine would take its toll upon this battalion. The first casualty from the 2/4th at Yamane was Roy 'Dickie' Hindle. Roy died on 30th September 1944 as a result of an underground rock fall. Roy's body was cremated and his ashes were carried by an Australian officer to Manila. From there they were forwarded onto Labuan War Cemetery for burial.

Another casualty although not fatal was that of Arch 'Strawb' Dyson who in January 1945 was pinned between a copper ore truck and a wall injuring both his legs. Tom Wayman was another who suffered injury. Working below ground repairing iron water pipes that had corroded through, Tom's hand was crushed causing severe nerve damage. On 18th May 1945 the prisoners were moved from work at the Besshi copper mine to the wharves, smelters and refineries of Niihama. The reason for this move was simply because the men's health had flagged so much that they were of no further use to the Japanese at the mine site.

Niihama

The camp at Niihama, although different to Yamane, was of much the same construction. The barracks walls were constructed from pine wood and interlaced with a bamboo and an earth mixture plastered about 3 inches thick. The roof was also made of pine with a natural fibre mating or bark laid over it. The latrines and pigsty were located at the end of the barracks. Unlike the barracks at Yamane, which was one long building, this barracks was divided into two sections with the entrance in the centre instead of at each end as it was at Yamane. One half of the barracks was the sleeping quarters and the other for messing. The floor of the sleeping quarters was covered around the walls and down the centre with grass tatami mats.

Following their arrival at Niihama the prisoners were allocated to the jobs that would keep them employed for the final months until Japan's surrender. Fred 'Cowboy' Matthews who was placed on light duties due to a tropical ulcer on his leg, worked in the cookhouse at Yamane and Niihama. Work was allocated to the prisoners at the copper refinery, No. 4 Party on the wharf, warehouses, iron foundry or stoking blast furnaces. At the engineering machinery foundry included amongst the Australian prisoners was Andrew 'Mick' Lambie who would clean up the castings as they were released from their moulds.

Several 2/4th who were employed on the wharves like the Kobe group, had the opportunity to scrounge extra food in the form of sweet potato and maize flour. Some of this crew were Bob Whitfield, Ken Tucker, Wilfred 'Bill' Nottle, Ray Muller, Lou Daily, Tom Conway and George Moir. At war's end Bob Whitfield took his Japanese overseer and showed him the places where they used to hide the contraband. No doubt the Japanese overseer was impressed with the Australians' ingenuity. In August, 'Bill' Nottle was knocked off the wharf by a crane and fractured his left ankle. This accident put him in the camp hospital for four weeks. Frank McGlinn whose diary was called upon to remind us of some facts about Niihama was one member from the 2/4th on the refining of the copper. In this process Frank wrote:

'There were 36 large vats of sulphuric acid and bluestone which had water running through them. In each vat was placed 22 plates of impure copper. Then another set of 22 plates that were painted with kerosene and which had had a tar like coating applied around the edges of them. The vats had a weak electric current running through them, which would cause the copper to leave the larger plates and form a thin layer of copper to form over both surfaces of the smaller prepared plates. It was our job to strip the sheet of surplus copper and repeat the process of coating the plates with the kerosene and tar. If you had any scabs on your skin they would fester because of the acid we were using. This was not the best job as the acid dropping on your clothes cut them away and we are all nearly as naked as the day we were born. This Sumitomi firm does not believe in reissuing clothing, although they did give us a pair of white cotton shorts a few days before the end of the war.' [20]

---

[20] Frank McGlinn's Diary loaned to the author by his sister Mrs Pearl Cockburn

Another 2/4th member who worked at this refinery was Harold 'Jake' Jacobs. Trevor James, Reg Pascall and John 'Stewy' Smith were at the beginning of the production line. They were part of a five-man team whose job it was to unload the copper ore trucks and reload them with coal, whilst other members of the 2/4th were gainfully employed stoking the blast furnace. On 1st August 1945 most of the A.I.F. units at Niihama ran sweeps amongst themselves as to what day they thought the war would finish. There were thirty-one 2/4th in a unit sweep at one pound each and each man drew a day from a hat. It was agreed that if it did not finish in August that the sweep was to be carried over into September. The day announced by the *West Australian* Newspaper was 15th August, the winner being 'Mick' Lambie.

On 15th August the word around Niihama was that the war was at last over. The prisoners had been stood down from their various jobs whereupon they returned to camp. It would be another five days before Capt. Marukami would inform them that the war might be over as fighting had been suspended.

Lieutenant Ralph Sanderson had assembled the men and made them aware of the impending danger of placing oneself between a supply aircraft and terra firma. He issued orders that if anything was air dropped by the Americans, everyone was to stay clear and he would arrange for ten of the strongest men to retrieve the supplies. There indeed was the danger of serious injury or even death as errant airborne medical, clothing and food containers dropped over Prisoner of War camps throughout Japan.

In the meantime Lt. Sanderson had asked for additional rations which were not forthcoming. Naturally the men couldn't see the reason for being starved now that the war was as good as over so they killed one of 'lolly lopper's' pigs and cooked up a stew, tossing a couple of chickens into the pot for good measure. On 25th August the Japanese delivered 900 bottles of Asahi brand beer to the camp.

On 28th August an American B29 made the first Red Cross, clothing and food drop over the Niihama Camp. The plane which had a large letter T painted on its tail fin and PW-SUPPLIES on the underside of its wings came in and circled over Niihama. It then came in at about 500 feet and dropped its load of supplies which were stacked in forty-four gallon drums. These were meant to float to the ground under the canopy of a parachute, however, some of these failed to open and the men just had enough time to get out of the way before some of the canisters came crashing to the ground. The first load dropped on the Japanese guardroom, office and cookhouse and on the other side of the fence into the sea that was only 20 yards from the camp.

Another two planes came over the camp and repeated the experiment dropping their loads on the nearby town and Besshi Mountain. A big sign was then displayed on the roof of the barracks, which said 'THANKS YANKS.' This was along with the Australian, British and Dutch flags. Red Cross representatives visited the camp on 4th September but there was no definite news at this stage as to when the men would be sent home. Nevertheless they hadn't been forgotten as B29's were dropping supplies into the camp on an almost daily basis.

Finally the big day that every ex-prisoner at Niihama had been waiting for arrived; they were on their way home. The machine gunners packed for 'Strawb' Dyson who had, only had his first walk without the aid of crutches two days previous. He had been bed ridden since his accident in the mine at Yamane back in January 1945. The sick left the camp at 0800 hours and the remainder had to be ready to move out at by 0900 hours. At about 1015 hours they started the march to Niihama station to catch the train which they boarded at midday. The train followed the coast in a westward direction to Tadotsu on the coast where there were some 109 American ex-Prisoners of War from Zentsuji Camp. The train then headed east again to Takamatsu where a ferry was boarded at Eno that would take the men back across the Inland Sea to the main island of Honshu. The journey continued through Osaka and as they looked out they could see the devastation caused by the American bombing of Kobe. The train stopped at Wakayama at 1000 hours on 14th September 1945. It was now time for medical examinations, fumigations and interrogations before they were finally taken out into Osaka Bay on the landing ship USS *Cabildo*. Then at 1830 hours that evening they boarded the hospital ship, USS *Sanctuary*. There were certainly no complaints coming from the members of the 2/4th Machine Gun Battalion. This hospital ship was probably the cleanest thing they had seen since leaving Australia. The *Sanctuary* set sail on 15th September and headed towards Okinawa, however, the ship was forced off course by a typhoon, which put it one day behind schedule. The *Sanctuary* arrived at Okinawa three days later whereupon the men were taken by landing barge to the (Amphibious Personnel Assault) ship APA225 USS *Bingham*. All from the 2/4th embarked except for 'Bill' Nottle and 'Strawb' Dyson who instead were taken ashore for some further attention in hospital.

The USS *Bingham* arrived at Manila on 26th September where the men, once ashore, were taken by truck to the reception camp seventeen miles away. The majority of the ex-Prisoners of War from Japan would transit through this camp and catch up with old friends and the latest news. Bert Wall was one that arrived on 27th September, and having left Changi in May 1942 had not seen these men for nearly three and a half years, so there was lots of old news to catch up with. Most of these men would now return to Australia aboard the British aircraft carrier HMS *Speaker* which would deliver them safely home to No. 9 Wharf Pyrmont, Sydney Harbour on 15th October 1945. The full complement of aircraft on both HMS *Speaker* and HMS *Formidable* had been off loaded at Singapore to make room for the ex-prisoners. Each man was allotted a camp stretcher with clean linen and blankets. These stretchers were lined up in long rows in the hanger decks of both aircraft carriers.

Some of the members of the 2/4th at Niihama however returned home by other means than the HMS *Speaker*. Tom Wayman for instance left Cavite Bay Manila aboard an R.A.A.F. PBY Catalina seaplane Serial No. A24-306 and flew via Morotai to Darwin. Tom was at an outdoor cinema in Darwin when his name was called out over the public address system. When he reported to the guardroom he was told to collect his gear and that he was going home. Tom's taxi for this leg of his journey was an American B29 Superfortress with the name *Waltzing Matilda* painted on the side of its fuselage. This particular aircraft was being used by the Australian Government to promote the sale of War Bonds and after its arrival in Perth would make a promotional trip to the Western Australian goldfields.

Niihama Camp
Back row: Thomas Gibson, Albert Norton, Fred 'Cowboy' Matthews, Ralph Hadfield
Front row: George Chatfield, Norm Thompson, Claude Dow, Andrew 'Mick' Lambie

Ohama Camp No. 9B

As mentioned, the prisoners onboard the *Rashin Maru* were split up at Moji and sent to their various camps. One group of 250 Australians under the command of Capt. Reg Newton from the 2/19th Battalion were sent to work in the coal mine at Ohama 9B Camp, arriving on 8th September 1944. Included in this group were seven members of the 2/4th Machine Gun Battalion. Alf Worth who was one of these men, told the author that the 2/4th men were mixed up with men from the 2/3rd Machine Gun Battalion and that is how it came to be that they became separated.

This camp was built on the southwest side of a peninsula that jutted out from the western tip of Honshu Island into the Inland Sea about 15 miles from Shimonoseki and 10 miles west of Ube. The Hamlet of Ohama and the camp were perched on the side of a hill that sloped down towards the water's edge. The camp was surrounded by a high barbed wire topped wooden fence and consisted of two long two-storeyed wooden buildings where the prisoners were to sleep, and a third single-storey multipurpose building. A corridor ran down the whole length of the northern side of each barracks building giving access to twelve rooms that could accommodate ten men each. On the floor of each room there were ten grass tatami mats on which the prisoners would sleep. The building's second-storey was reached by means of central and end stairways.

As well as the prisoners barracks buildings there was also a third building that ran between these two buildings and was used as the cookhouse, mess, mine administration office, Japanese Sgt.'s office, bulk store, boiler room and bathing room. One of the barracks buildings, the older of the two, was already occupied by some British Prisoners of War. The Australians were to move into the second and newer of the two buildings. Once the men had found their preferred place to sleep they were led away in groups of sixty-five to the bathing room, after which the heads of the prisoners were shaved. They were then photographed and these bald-headed mug shots were displayed near the Japanese Administrator's office.

As a result of the two and half month voyage from Singapore a number of the prisoners were not well and required medical attention. One month prior to the arrival of the Australians a hospital had been established in one of the buildings. These men had come from the jungles of Thailand and most were still suffering from bouts of malaria, dysentery and deficiency diseases.

The Mine Work

About one week after their arrival that the Australian prisoners were subjected to a physical examination by the mine's Japanese doctor. The men were classified into three categories; those suitable for camp duties only, those able to work below ground, and those who could only work on the surface. All the Australians were initially given work on the surface for a period of one month however after this time those selected to do mine work were given regular mine duties on an eight hour shift rota.

Surface work varied greatly from light to heavy camp maintenance chores depending on the health of the prisoner in question. Heavy work on the surface was carried out by those who were exempted from underground work by reason of perhaps a heart condition or hernia. These men were utilised loading timber for the mine, repairing the mine's coal trucks, the sawmill, workshops, working in the camp market garden or cutting wood for the cookhouse.

Light work above ground was little different to the heavier work they had been doing underground except that their food ration was reduced accordingly. Japanese thinking during the entire Prisoner of War period was, no work – no food. Sick men were put on reduced rations because they could not work, yet the reason they were sick was because of the poor rations in the first place. Had the Japanese instead reasoned that if they increased the rations and for that matter the medicines, the sick and weak would have regained their strength and therefore been able to return to the workforce.

The coal mine at Ohama was a drift mine which meant that the seams of coal ran close to the surface whereby the coal was excavated by means of long sloping tunnels or 'drifts' that ran out beneath the sea bed. The eight hour shifts were timed at the coal face and so by the time a shift was relieved and returned to the surface the prisoners might be absent from camp as long as nine or ten hours.

The prisoners would begin their shift by lining up to be issued with a miner's lamp. Invariably these leaked battery acid or refused to hold a charge, only increasing the strain upon the men's eyes as their illumination dimmed. The shift of Prisoners of War miners would then make their way down a long steeply inclined limestone drift to the coal seams. This now placed the prisoners in the region of 70 to 80 feet below the seabed which meant that the ceiling was always wet and likely to crumble. Shoring timbers were needed to prop up the ceiling otherwise cave-ins would occur either trapping, injuring or killing the men below ground.

Like the majority of the Japanese mines that were brought back into service during the war they were all in a state of disrepair due to poor maintenance, and Ohama 9B was no exception to the rule. The coal was mined either by a conveyor which worked along a face for 200–300 feet. This was dangerous work because the ceiling kept collapsing as the coal supporting it was removed. Another method of excavation was stall work, which was a little safer in that it consisted of narrow galleries like veins that ran into main arteries. The galleries were about 6 to 8 feet wide and about the same in height. Small ore trucks running on rails would carry the coal out the main arteries where it would then be taken to the surface with the aid of electrical winches. All the same, ceiling collapses were common with this method of excavation and this often forced the tunnels to reduce down to as low as three feet in height, just enough clearance to bring up the ore trucks to the coal face.

Another problem was that shoring timbers supplied to the prisoners were always of an inferior quality to that which was supplied to the Japanese miners. Breathing air was brought into the mine only by the exhaust air from pneumatic jackhammers and this made the atmosphere underground oppressive and stale. Each gang of prisoners had a Japanese overseer who did not necessarily have any knowledge of mining, and this only worsened the conditions below ground. It was only by virtue of the fact that there were British and Australian Prisoners of War with mining experience that would on many occasions help to avoid fatal accidents and injury. There were times, usually towards the end of the month, when the Japanese pushed the prisoners at a frenzied pace to increase the quota of coal removed from the mine.

The jungles of Burma and Thailand were a world away but this did not mean a departure from the brutality that the prisoners had been subjected to during the construction of the rail link. Japanese civilian mine workers were prone to and quite capable of administering their own fair share of punishment, as they deemed necessary. Like so many other Prisoner of War camps scattered around Japan, on 15th August 1945 there was a strange calm felt, that would instil a renewed hope they might soon all be free men. The first food and medical supplies were not air dropped over Ohama Camp from B29's until 31st August. The Ohama prisoners had watched across the water as supplies had been dropped over the Motoyama camp but were forced to wait several more days until they too would receive their share. In the meantime, Capt. Jack Hands from the 2/3rd Machine Gun Battalion had managed to arrange transport around the bay to the Motoyama Camp and returned with some medicines and enough food for two days. When it was time to leave Ohama 9B the men boarded a train which took them across Honshu to the port of Wakayama. Here they boarded a U.S. Navy hospital ship USS *Consolation* that would take them to Okinawa. At Okinawa they transferred to an American liberty ship, the USS *Haskell* (a name that Bill Haskell from the 2/3rd Machine Gun Battalion remembers very well) which took them to Manila. The last leg of the voyage home to Australia was aboard the R.N.

aircraft carrier HMS *Speaker* that would deliver the men safely to Sydney. From Sydney to Perth some of the men would return home aboard HMT *Dominion Monarch* whilst others travelled by train.

Ohama 9B Camp
Back row: Aub Schuts, Bob Whitelaw, Bert Poulton.
Front row: Alec Oag, Alf Worth, Arthur Walker – Inset: Sgt. Douglas Carter

Fukuoka sub-Camp No. 13 – Saganoseki

So far the *Rashin Maru* Party had been split up between Niihama on Shikoku Island and Ohama 9B on Honshu Island, however, there was another location where men from the 2/4th were sent once they had landed at Moji. This was Fukuoka sub-Camp No. 13 Saganoseki on Kyushu Island. As mentioned in the Korea story, this camp was located on the northeast coast of Kyushu Island where the men worked in three 8 hour shifts tending the four blast furnaces at an old copper refinery. The refinery had been brought back into service to meet wartime demands. There were four blast furnaces at the refinery that were in operation twenty-four hours a day. The camp at Saganoseki, had been built atop a slagheap; the prisoners judging by its condition that it was reasonably new. Each room in the barracks building accommodated six men, and to the prisoners who had roughed it in the jungles this was the Ritz Hotel. Although the food was just adequate it was still an improvement on what they were used to. In May 1945 this camp was closed down due to a shortage of raw material to refine. As a result, two roughly equal groups of 100 Australian prisoners were transferred to Fukuoka sub-Camp No. 17 Omuta and No. 6 Camp Omine. Fred Ward and Joe Beattie were transferred to Omuta arriving on 30th June 1945 and the other two machine gunners 'Dutchy' Holland and Clarrie Henderson were sent to the Omine No. 6 Camp.

Fukuoka sub-Camp No. – 17 Omuta

The Japanese designation for this camp was Fukuoka, Omuta-Shi. Mitsui Miike Mining Company (Mitsui Miike Kogyo Sho). Fukuoka sub-Camp No.17 Omuta was located on the western side of Kyushu Island mid way between Fukuoka and Nagasaki. The camp itself was situated between the town of Omuta and the sea. In fact the camp was built on land that had been reclaimed by spilling the workings from the mine into the bay thereby extending the coastline. This camp, which was the largest Prisoner of War camp on Kyushu Island was nestled amongst other buildings and consisted of thirty-three (later increasing to thirty-eight) single-storey wooden buildings that had been the former labourer's quarters. Each barrack building had ten rooms leading off a corridor that in total could sleep fifty men per hut. The buildings were roofed with corrugated iron and the camp was surrounded by a twelve foot high electrified fence. In each room was the standard Japanese tatami mat and a sleeping platform raised about 6 inches above the ground.

The camp had been opened on 10th August with the arrival of 500 American prisoners from the Philippines. When the *Rashin Maru* group arrived at Fukuoka sub-Camp No. 17 the prisoners who had made the voyage aboard the *Aramis* in June 1944 were already in residence. There were 144 Australians in this group which included eighteen men from the 2/4th Machine Gun Battalion. They had arrived in camp on 19th June having three weeks earlier been in Thailand, the majority being the survivors from Major Cough's V Battalion. Surprisingly this group was described as being in good physical condition possibly due to the relatively brief voyage from Singapore. By the end of the war there would be thirty-one 2/4th machine gunners at this camp. The work here would comprise of coal mining, working in the local zinc refinery, working in the market garden and constructing huts and air raid shelters in the confines of the camp. The separate tasks were allocated to the prisoners by nationality. The British worked at the zinc foundry and the Dutch on the coalbunkers near the camp and also the coaling of ships. The Americans and the Australians worked below ground in the coalmines.

Fukuoka sub-Camp No. 17 – Omuta

Down The Mines

Work in the coalmine where 75% of the prisoners in camp were employed was labour intensive and the mining equipment they were supplied with to use underground was antiquated and prone to regular failure. On arrival in Japan these men most of whom had worked out in the open on the Burma–Thailand rail link where given a brief period of training by Japanese civilian mine employees on how to be miners.

Roy Whitecross explains:

> '*On the last day of our training we were taken down the mine, not to work, just to see what the mine was like and to learn the underground routine. Everyone was eager to see first hand what a coal mine was like. Fifteen hundred feet below we left the train and walked along a rough, stone - littered tunnel. Our inspection party moved on. On we went, passing steel coal skips, with a capacity of two and a half tons of coal, drawn by electric locomotives, which drew their power from a single overhead wire. In some parts of the mine, strings of coal-laden skips were hauled up from the lower levels by means of a steel cable and winch. That cable was another hazard. Sometimes it lay in the centre of the track, hidden by the shadows and rubble. When the signal was given to the winchman to haul the trucks attached to it, the cable tightened and, at the bends of the tunnel, whipped across and whined against the timbers at the inner side. In the early days in the mine many men were caught by that steel cable before we learned always to walk on the outside of the curves. Finally we made our way back to the main tunnel and were carried by the train to the surface.*' [21]

---

21   Roy Whitecross, *Slaves of the Son of Heaven* Dymocks 1952, p.190–191

For some men the thought of being crushed by collapsing ceilings, suffocation, blast injuries or for some the simple fear of having to work in a confined space was just too much to handle. Of course any apprehension shown by the prisoner workers was met with the usual Japanese method of persuasion and brutality. The war crimes affidavit by Lou Lonsdale who arrived with the *Aramis* Party on the 19th June 1944 describes the work underground:

> '*We were worked 8 or 9 hours a day on shift work in the mine and were actually away from camp about 12 hours because we had to march about 2 miles to the mine and back again. In the mine the work was divided into three sections. Work in the extraction section consisted of blasting the coal wall and shovelling the coal into trucks and elevators for carriage to the surface. In the preparation section the work consisted of building rock walls along the tunnels as the coal was taken out to make it as safe as possible. In the exploration section the work consisted of tunnelling through from given points making new laterals and the coal. There were Japanese and Koreans working in the mine at the same time as the PW and Chinese labour battalions worked in an adjoining mine, which connected with the mine we were working in. Reports came to us that the Americans had originally owned the mine and had abandoned it as they considered it was unsafe to extract any more coal from it. When we arrived at Omuta we found that the mine had been re-opened and we were taking out pillars of coal which should have been left there for safety measures. In some parts of the mine the laterals had sunk so low we were bent almost double while carrying tools such as jack hammers, shovels, picks, etc and heavy logs for timbering. There were quite a lot of falls of coal and rock in the mine but ironically mostly the Japanese suffered in these falls.*' [22]

Roy Whitecross now gives us an excellent description of exactly how the coal forms below ground and the method by which it is extracted:

> '*The formation of coal in the mine fell into two main categories. In one, coal was found in a seam which usually measured about six to ten feet from the top to bottom and five to six feet wide. In these cases the coal was extracted from the end of the seam so that a tunnel was formed which had for its dead end a face of coal the size of the seam. As the tunnel was extended it was timbered to prevent the roof falling in. Provided the timbering kept pace with the extraction of coal, these tunnels were reasonably safe. The other principle formation consisted of " islands " of coal about six feet thick and extending over an area measuring perhaps fifty yards long by sixty to seventy yards wide. These deposits were worked by the " long wall " system. Here a tunnel was driven beside the coal deposit and then the tunnel extended sideways into the mass of coal. Along the fifty-yard face a long wall team of about thirty men worked. As the coal was extracted the roof was timbered, but owing to the huge space formed, these workings were always more dangerous. Sometimes the railway line was run in beside the face, which meant that after being blasted the coal was shovelled directly into the trucks. In other cases it was impracticable to run trucks into the face, and a conveyor trough was used to take the coal won from the face out to the nearest tunnel along which trucks ran.*' [23]

It was not until 15th September 1945; about four weeks after Japan's surrender, that the men would depart Omuta. In fact at one stage they thought they would never be rescued and this

---

22   AWM54 File 1010/4/92 War Crimes Affidavit by WX16727 Pte. J. L. Lonsdale, Australian War Memorial Canberra
23   Roy Whitecross, *Slaves of the Son of Heaven* Dymocks 1952, p.219–220

prompted them to lay out white painted rocks on the ground displaying the letters PW. As was common in most Prisoner of War camps in Japan some men became impatient and decided to find their rescuers before they found them. Fred Ward made his way to a U.S.A.A.C. base near Nagasaki and hitched a ride direct to Manila. For the others the journey was a little longer. Following a train journey to Nagasaki some of the men sailed directly to Manila aboard the USS *Lunga Point*, a light fleet aircraft carrier. The *Lunga Point* was a sister ship to the *Cape Gloucester* which also transported ex-Prisoners of War to Okinawa before being transferred to Manila. At least two 2/4th from Fukuoka sub-Camp No. 17 travelled to Okinawa aboard the hospital ship USS *Haven*. This ship was also a sister ship to the *Benevolence*, *Sanctuary* and *Consolation*. Some of the men were flown by B24 Liberator from Okinawa to Manila whilst others were taken by landing barge out to the amphibious personnel assault ship USS *Bingham* which was also carrying 2/4th from Niihama. Once at Manila where they had arrived on 26th September some men returned by aircraft and others by either the HMS *Formidable* or *Speaker*.

The Awa Maru Story

The *Awa Maru* was a passenger-cargo ship of 11,249 tons that transported seventeen members from the 2/4th Machine Gun Battalion to Moji in Japan. It was here where they would be assigned to camps at Fukuoka sub-Camp No.17 Omuta, Fukuoka sub-Camp No. 22 and Fukuoka sub-Camp No. 24 Sendyu. The ill fated *Rakuyo Maru* Party had travelled to Saigon in French Indo-China in late March 1944 only to be diverted to Singapore before embarking on their voyage to Japan.

Similarly the *Awa Maru* Party would follow suit, travelling to Saigon before also being diverted to Singapore where they would board the *Awa Maru*. It is worth noting that these two parties had been part of 'A' Force working on the Burma end of the rail link. The *Rakuyo Maru* Party originally consisted of kumis 35 to 40, with each kumi being made up of approximately 150 Prisoners of War. All of kumi No. 40, as well as some sick from the other kumis were transferred to the Changi Gaol Camp or hospital, were destined not to travel to Japan at this time. Instead the fit prisoners in kumi No. 40 would be included on the *Awa Maru* Party with kumis No. 41 and 42.

One member of the 2/4th and Kumi No. 41 who did not sail aboard the *Awa Maru* to Japan was James Lind, who may have fallen ill and missed his draft by being in hospital. Another 2/4th member with a similar history to James Lind's was John Randall from the 88th Light Aid Detachment. Both men nevertheless were included in the Saigon Party that left Singapore on 2nd February 1945.

A pattern can be seen with the shipping of prisoners to Japan. The prisoners who did not transit via Saigon but were transferred directly to Singapore where they would board the transports *Rashin Maru* and the *Aramis*, were all members of 'D' Force. Why 'A' Force was sent to Saigon and then back to Singapore whilst 'D' Force went directly to Singapore is not known. However, the answer may be that it was just a coincidence, or on the other hand it could be connected with the Japanese Burma and Thailand Railway Administrations.

Regardless, the ever present threat of American submarines made it blatantly clear that as few ships as possible would be permitted to slip through the blockade.

The *Awa Maru* Party was moved to Saigon from the Tamarkan, Kanchanaburi Non Pladuk, area, where they had passed selection for Japan. Taking the same route as the *Rakuyo Maru*

Party via Bangkok and Phnom Penh the party arrived at Saigon on 15th April and remained until 15th August 1944. The prisoners were billeted in the ex-French Foreign Legion barracks on the Rue Jean Eudel which ran behind and parallel with the docks on the Saigon River. There was also an immigration building on the Rue Jean Eudel that was used as a Prisoner of War camp. During their time in French Indo-China several attempts were made to transport the party to Japan but with the American submarine blockade in place this was proving impossible.

During their four-month sojourn in French Indo-China, the prisoners were put to good use either working at the go-downs, wharves or on general labouring chores. On 15th August the party was ferried back to Phnom Penh where they would board a train that would eventually deliver the party to Singapore on 22nd August. One member of the 2/4th who may have remained behind even though he does not appear on the kumi lists is Harold Clayden. It is noted that Harold was in Saigon on 20th August 1944 and was recovered on 6th September 1945. Looking closely at the dates it is assumed that he was left behind in Saigon when the *Awa Maru* Party moved back to Singapore. Another in the same position is thought to have been Leonard Greaves.

Predictably the *Awa Maru* Party was moved to the River Valley Road Transit Camp to await available shipping to Japan. From this time until 15th December 1944 when they would finally board the *Awa Maru* the men were kept busy loading and unloading ships at Keppel Harbour. Some of this group, including Jack Maude, worked for a time on the dry dock opposite Jeep Island.

On 16th December 1944 the *Awa Maru* with its human cargo of 525 Australian, American and Dutch Prisoners of War aboard moved out to the roadstead where it would wait for the remainder of the convoy to assemble. All 525 prisoners were crammed into one hold that had been modified by adding two platforms that effectively provided three tiers of cramped sleeping space. In addition, the passageways were also crammed with sleeping prisoners. The convoy set sail on 26th December, the *Awa Maru* reaching its destination of Moji unscathed on 15th January 1945. On arrival the party was divided into several smaller groups. The majority of the 2/4th men were sent to Fukuoka sub-Camp No. 17, Omuta except for three men who were sent to Fukuoka sub-Camp No. 24, Sendyu.

Fukuoka sub-Camp No. 17 – Omuta

A description of this camp and the work in the coalmines has been given in the *Rashin Maru* story. There were thirteen 2/4th on the *Awa Maru* Party who would join the Australian, British and American Prisoners of War workforce at this camp. One man, Norm Grant, an ex-miner was made an underground supervisor in the coalmine because of his past experience.

Fukuoka sub-Camp No. 22

The Japanese designation for this camp was Fukuoka, Kaho-Gun. The mine was owned by the Sumitomo Mining Company (Sumitomo Kogyo). A group of ninety Australians went to this camp from Moji. They were accommodated in a reasonably good building that slept ten to a room. The first three weeks were spent as a rest period following their voyage from Singapore where they had been digging air raid shelters. After this respite they were employed in the coalmine which was located about one mile from the camp. Initially the food ration was meagre but improved a little after the work commenced down the mine. There was a particularly nasty Japanese Sgt. at this camp who was rather lavish with his bashings, which he would administer en masse. By the time of Japan's surrender in August 1945 there was not a fit Prisoner of War prisoner in camp. For months prior there had not been an issue of meat or fish in camp. On 15th February 1945 Henry Cooper was transferred to this camp from the Fukuoka sub-Camp No. 17 Omuta camp.

Fukuoka sub-Camp No. 24 – Sendyu

The Japanese designation for this camp was Nagasaki, Kita Matsuura-Gum. The mine was owned by the Sumitomo Mining Company (Sumitomo Kogyo). In Japanese, kita means north, and ura means coast or beach. This camp was located approximately seventy kilometres to the north of Nagasaki towards the northwest coast of Kyushu near a town called Emukae which itself is located close to Matsuura. When the atom bomb was dropped on Nagasaki it was reported that the prisoners at Fukuoka sub-Camp No. 24 could see the nuclear fallout to the southwest. There were about 250 prisoners from the *Awa Maru* Party including Jack Maude, Ted Murtagh and 'Mick' Sheedy from the 2/4th who were selected for this camp. For the first six weeks at this camp the food ration was satisfactory although deficient in meat. After this time the ration began to reduce. Camp accommodation was a row of wooden huts on either side of the compound that was surrounded by a nine-foot high wooden fence. Sleeping arrangements were tatami mats spread out on the floor of the huts. Work at Sendyu consisted of three eight-hour shifts down the nearby coal mine which had been reopened to assist Japan's war effort. Before the prisoners actually ventured down the mine they were given basic instruction on the surface by their Japanese civilian supervisors. This mine was nowhere near the scale of either the Ohama or Omuta mines as the prisoners were forced to excavate coal from spaces as small as three feet from floor to ceiling. Shovels of coal were tossed over the shoulder into a trough conveyor belt that would carry the coal away from the face to skips that took it to the surface. As the coalface was worked deeper into the seam the conveyor would be moved in closer to the Prisoner of War miners. At the same time Japanese miners would shore up the roof of the tunnel with timber. These tunnels could be for example 40 feet long, 8 feet wide by 4 feet high. At 1102 hours on 9th August 1945, *Fat Boy*, a plutonium bomb exploded over Nagasaki. At the time, Jack Maude was working underground in the coalmine. In his own words:

'*As usual the shift went down the mine about 700-800 feet underground. After having been down a few hours there was a terrible deafening roar and we were thrown about by some unexplainable force. At the time we were sure the Yanks had blown in the mine head and all our camp above had been obliterated, such was the force of the explosion. Our few civilian guards were in a frenzy by now with the dust visibility below ground was down to zero. Our battery-powered miner's lamps that were fitted to our helmets were of little use. The Nips by now had managed to stop all the mine machinery which wasn't much anyway, chiefly just the moving belt buckets that we had to keep filled as the coal was hacked out of the face. We were fairly resigned to the fact that by now we were buried alive, which was not my idea of a Christian burial. By this time the guards were scurrying all over the place screaming at the top of their lungs. They seemed far more terrified than any of us, which was one good aspect of the whole thing, if we were to be buried alive then so would they beside us.*

After a few hours the dust below ground in the mine settled down a little and we able to make our way to the main shaft. The skips that pulled us to the top by windlass was out of order. We could do little but wait until the winches up top began working again to bring us up to the surface. After another hour we decided that we would have to climb up a steep gradient if we to have any hope of survival. There were about 40 of us clawing our way up to the surface for what seemed like hours. We just kept on going up and ever up the line and the sleepers were our guide. It was just as well our battery headlamps held out which enabled us to proceed slowly upward, resting frequently as we were weak and had little strength for this exhausting mammoth climb. Our main concern was that when we reached the surface that the mine head would be blown in. We reasoned that this was possible but as the air seemed to be getting fresher we were sure that there would be some sort of an opening enabling us to escape when we reached the surface.

We eventually reached the surface after moving at seemed like a snail's pace for hours. We could see light at the end of the tunnel and everything appeared to be normal except the guards had disappeared and all the machinery, the winches and pulleys were out of order. With great relief we hauled ourselves out into late afternoon light. I remember the sun, it was so warm and inexplicably bright and the joy and relief to have made it! Word filtered into the camp that a super bomb had been dropped and completely destroyed Nagasaki. Our camp was in the hills a distance from the centre of the explosion. We would witness and see the enormity and full horror and total destruction it had caused when we moved to Nagasaki.' [24]

The Phoenix Rises

It is customary in Japan to cremate the bodies of the dead, so naturally when Prisoners of War passed on, their bodies were also cremated. There were five members of the battalion who died in Japan. From these five, three of these men's ashes would remain in Japan however, two urns made it as far as Labuan Island off the north coast of Sabah, Borneo.

The three machine gunners whose ashes remained in Japan were:

WX4927 Austin Newman Climie
WX9318 Kenneth Lally
WX9226 Harry Tysoe

The two members of the battalion whose ashes made their way to Labuan Island off the northeast coast of Borneo were:

WX8869 Herbert Roy 'Dickie' Hindle
WX20076 William Dwyer

In the case of Herbert Roy Hindle, it appears that the urns containing the ashes of several men from the Island of Shikoku were carried back to Manila by an Australian officer. The urns containing their ashes were then passed on to Lt. J. Williams from the War Graves Unit at Manila. It appears then that in accordance with Australian Government policy these ashes were then transported to the nearest Commonwealth War Graves Cemetery. In the case the cemetery on Labuan Island. In relation to William Dwyer who died at Fukuoka sub-Camp No. 1 it can only be assumed that a similar situation occurred whereby an Allied servicemen carried the ashes of this man as far as Manila. The following newspaper clipping came from The *Herald* dated 9th January 1946 and sums up the Australian Government's stance on this subject.

---

[24] Jack Maude Diary donated to the author

POW ASHES WILL STAY ABROAD

CANBERRA.—It is unlikely that urns containing the ashes of AIF prisoners-of-war who died in Japanese captivity will be returned to Australia.

Allied troops recently discovered a number of urns in Japan.

It was explained officially today that in principle there could be no difference between bringing back the ashes of dead soldiers and bringing back their bodies.

The Government had ruled earlier in the war that because of shipping difficulties, the bodies of dead servicemen could not be returned to Australia from foreign countries or from the islands north of Australia.

The War Graves Commission was appointed to ensure proper and reverent burials and to beautify and maintain the cemeteries.

Newspaper clipping from "The Herald" – 9th January 1946

The Both *Story*
Saigon Party – French Indo-China

This Saigon Party was the last group to leave Thailand for overseas. Identified as a Japan Party they would travel no further than Saigon in French Indo-China where they would serve out the remainder of their time as Prisoners of War. There was a total of 2,030 prisoners in this party, most being British with a small proportion of Netherlands East Indian Dutch and 200 Australians. Of these, there were twenty-two members from the 2/4th Machine Gun Battalion. Two of these men, James Lind and John Randall had already been to Saigon with the *Awa Maru* Party so were already in Singapore. Taking a close look at the origins of this group of machine gunners it will be seen that they were quite a mixed bunch. Coming from 'D' Force, 'A' Force and also Williams No. 1 Mobile Force from Java they had come together at Singapore to form the Saigon Party. Whilst at Singapore the prisoners were billeted at the River Valley Road Transit Camp and were put to work on the mandatory chores on the docks loading and unloading ships. This group departed Singapore on 2nd February 1945 aboard the small 1,489 ton ship *Both*. This ship was the grandfather of them all having been built in 1890 and registered at Batavia. It was in the service of owners Koninkl Paketv Matts (KPM) when seized by the Japanese. The *Both* was also one of the seven Dutch ships that carried Australian troops from convoy "MS 2" into Singapore when they transshipped from the *Aquitania* at Ratai Bay, Java on 20th January 1942. The convoy was made up of four ships plus two armed Japanese ships,

745

a destroyer and a corvette. Loaded into the holds of the *Both* were the familiar 30lb rubber blocks and on deck was an array of earth-moving equipment that was destined for Japan. On 6th February the 6,968 ton cargo ship *Engen Maru* was sunk by the U.S. Navy submarine *Pampanito*. In the early hours of 7th February the 6,892 ton cargo ship *Taigo Maru* was also sunk by an American submarine. The following day the 3,520 ton passenger-cargo ship *Eifuku* was sunk by the *Pampanito*. By this time the Japanese escorts had departed the scene. It was likely, the Captains of the Japanese warships reasoned that it wasn't worth risking two warships to protect an old, slow coal burning 3,000 merchant ship that would probably fall prey to an American submarine anyway. At this point the *Both* was approximately 300 kilometres to the south of Cape St Jacques so the ship's Captain did the only thing he thought would save his ship; he set a course straight for Cape St Jacques. As the *Both* sailed up the Riviere de Saigon evidence that American submarines had the upper hand in this war, was everywhere. In excess of twenty ships including an aircraft carrier could be seen sitting on the bottom of the river.

The Port of Saigon lies about thirty miles up the Riviere de Saigon. The port has a river frontage of 5 kilometres extending from the mouth of the Canal de la Derivation to just beyond the Arroyo de l'Avalanche. The wharves that handled the commercial traffic are located in the southern region of the port that is divided by the Arroyo Chinois. The naval dockyards and arsenal lie to the north of the town. The wharves were constructed of steel and concrete and there are numerous go-downs adjacent to the wharves that run at right angles to the river. The average go-down would be in the region of 150 feet long by 50 feet wide and behind these warehouses a railway line runs to the main rail terminus in Saigon.

The *Both* docked at about 1500 hours on 8th February 1945. Once ashore the Australians in this Saigon Party were grouped together and directed by the Japanese to a go-down where they remained for the first few days. The Australians in this Saigon party were now split up, with thirty being incorporated into Group No. 8 and the remainder incorporated into Group No. 10. The prisoners in Group No. 8 continued to work in the docks area until their recovery in September 1945. The Australians in Group No. 10 remained at this location for the next few weeks; the only difference now between Saigon and Singapore was the latitude and longitude as the men were put to work on various jobs around the docks area.

The next move for those in Group No.10 was to an aerodrome where they would be employed on drainage work. The airfield that the Australians were put to work is thought to have been at Long-Thanh which was located approximately 20 miles to the east of Saigon. After about four weeks, approximately 8th April, the party set off again towards Phan Rang on the coast before heading north. Two groups left by train and one group by truck but it was the second train that was bombed and strafed by an American Lockheed P38 Lightning aircraft. Although several men were killed in the attack Harold Hockey was lucky to only receive wounds to the left breast, left leg and buttocks. When the machine gunners had marched through Perth on 7th March 1941 following their marathon march down from Northam Army Camp a child had thrust a small ivory lamb in Harold Hockey's hand. Harold regarded the gift from the child as a good luck charm and carried on his person when he departed Australia for Singapore.

The whole party eventually arrived at Dran on the Da-Lat Plateau. Situated at 1,500 metres above sea level, Dran was a hill station about 100 miles east-north-east of Saigon. The airfield at Da-Lat where Group No.10 were to be put to work was about 2 miles to the west-north-west of the town. The first chore was to erect buildings for the Japanese, followed by the carting of stone to use as landfill for the runway. Group No. 10 remained on the airfield construction job at Da-Lat until 20th July 1945 when they were marched back to Dran. It was here where they would board a train which would transport them back to Saigon.

On arrival they were billeted with some British prisoners who had been in Saigon for some time and were in a camp on the Rue Catinant adjacent to the docks. The huts in this camp were rated as being very good and were even supplied with electric light, a commodity almost forgotten by these men from Australia. After about a week the Australians were transferred to the French Foreign Legion barracks on the Rue Jean Eudel where they remained for the last month of the war. About twenty Australians from Group No. 10 had been transferred to Phnom Penh whilst the remainder of Group No. 10 were to be sent to a location 500 kilometres to the north of Phnom Penh. However, the surrender by Japan instigated the return of the twenty to Saigon and cancellation of the order to despatch the others.

There were six deaths in this Saigon Party with 265 Australians being recovered at the end of the war. These now ex-Prisoners of War at Saigon were recovered by the Americans on 6th September 1945. They were flown via Bangkok where they continued their journey by Douglas C47 aircraft back to Singapore arriving on 20th September. It is not to be forgotten that there were other members of the 2/4th who had finished up in French Indo-China and were returned to Australia via Singapore. These men were James Howe, Bryan Manwaring, Harold Clayden and Leonard Greaves.

Most of the 2/4th Machine Gun Battalion who were members of this Saigon Party were eventually flown back to Australia. John Randall returned aboard the 2/1st Australian Hospital Ship *Manunda*. Several others boarded the *Tamaroa* that sailed directly to Fremantle whilst a few others boarded the *Highland Chieftain* to Sydney returning to Western Australia by train or aircraft from Melbourne.

Thailand 1944–1945

Following the construction of the Burma–Thailand Railway, the majority of prisoners were concentrated in Thailand where after a brief respite following the 'speedo' were put to work on other tasks. Probably the most immediate task was the maintenance of the railway line and bridges that had collapsed due to either the monsoon rains, Allied bombing or sabotage by the prisoners. There was also the upkeep of wood to fuel the locomotives.

As 1944 drew to a close and 1945 dawned the Japanese were beginning to accept the fact that they were losing the war. It was now that the prisoners were put to work building airfields and defensive positions in the event the Allies invaded Thailand. Additionally there was the excavation of tunnels to conceal ammunition and the construction of escape routes from within Thailand to the Burmese coast at Tavoy and Mergui.

By March 1944 the majority of prisoners were brought out of the jungles and concentrated in the main camps at Nacompaton, Non Pladuk, Tamuang, Kanchanaburi, Tamarkan and Chungkai. Some prisoners were retained at Tarsau until the end of April 1944 and at Apalon in Burma until February 1945. At Tarsau about 1st April 1944 the sick were graded, the heavy sick being sent to Nacompaton and the light sick to Chungkai.

Of all these prisoners we can now remove from the story those men from 'A' and 'D' Forces who were considered fit enough to travel to Japan, as well as the last of those men from 'F' and 'H' Forces who had all returned to Singapore by April 1944. From May 1944 parties of prisoners were sent back up-country to work at anyone of over sixty camps between Kinsaiyok and Sonkurai. Many of these camps were built on sites that had been previously occupied by coolie labourers. In reality, the prisoners were returning to conditions reminiscent of the 'speedo' period during 1943.

The early work on both ends of the railway, where the country was relatively flat had been carried out reasonably well with firm roadbeds and wide cuttings. However as the two ends progressed into the jungles and rocky mountainous country in Thailand the standard of work deteriorated. The railway would require constant maintenance if the Japanese ever expected it to deliver anywhere near the proposed tonnages of war materiel that was required by their front line troops fighting in Burma.

Another problem that the Japanese would encounter was that now the rail link was completed, the track, bridges and rolling stock immediately became targets for Allied aircraft. Also, it was not uncommon for rolling stock to do just that, roll off the track due to the poor ballasting of the rail bed, or for trains to derail because they had taken curves at too high a speed. Extreme caution was also exercised by engine drivers on some bridges that were so rickety that they swayed from side to side under the weight of the locomotive and its rolling stock.

There were very few railway stations as such, just loop lines, sidings and concealed sections of track where trains could pass each other or halt so that wood fuel and water could be replenished. In cases where bridges had been washed away by the rains or damaged by Allied bombing, it was the practice to employ Prisoner of War labour to ferry one train's cargo across a river to another train waiting on the opposite bank so that the line of communication for the carriage of Japanese troops and war materiel could continue northwards into Burma. As soon as a bridge was put out of commission, a workforce of prisoners or coolies with pre-cut timbers at the ready, went to work immediately to repair the damage, working day and night until the repair work was completed.

From the end of 1944 to mid 1945 the concrete and steel span bridge at Tamarkan was targeted no less than seven times. The first three raids achieved little more than superficial damage, the fourth raid managed to inflict some minor damage to the wooden disused railway bridge downstream. However, on 13th February 1945 a raid by American B24 Liberators managed to knock out three of the eleven spans of the bridge. The Tamarkan Camp was set back from the river but the railway line ran past the northern side of this camp. Over to the north of the camp sited on a hill was a Japanese observation post, and located between the river and the camp were six Japanese AA guns. The Japanese had used these guns in anger which only drew unnecessary attention to the camp. There were casualties from these Allied air raids as prisoners were forced to dive for cover every time the ominous drone of bomber aircraft was heard overhead. The Japanese realising that they would lose their labour force if they didn't act quickly, began to move groups of prisoners across the river to the camp at Chungkai.

The author's uncle, Cpl. Danny Bevis, was a member of the 2/4th Machine Gun Battalion. Dan kept a diary[25] and documented his travels from Northam Army Camp until his return to Fremantle in October 1945. As he worked at many of the locations that are pertinent to the Thailand story during the years from 1944–1945 his diary will be used as a guide. Other camps throughout Thailand where members from the 2/4th were sent are also covered. However, in common with the period of construction of the rail link it is impossible to state exactly where each man was located for the final twenty months as Prisoners of War without detailed interrogation forms.

The Danny Bevis Diary

Tamarkan

'*Arrived at Tamarkan on 2nd January 1944. Food good for six weeks to build up the Japan Party, later torpedoed. Camp is 60 yards from bridge of eleven steel spans and a large AA position. Surrounded by observation post, nip engineers, cavalry camp and railway line. Twenty one planes over 29th November 1944. Four*

---

[25] Danny Bevis Diary loaned to the author by his son Mervyn Bevis

bombs dropped on camp, 18 killed and 38 wounded. Non Pladuk show 30th November, 62 buildings, workshops etc, wiped out. Bombs and bullets in camp 93 killed and 310 wounded. Kanchanaburi bombed 13th December 1944. Several more raids at Tamarkan in December and quiet until 28th January 1945. Wooden bridge destroyed and repaired by us. One plane, one bomb, lost one whisky. 5th February, AA half a mile from camp, nip engineers and bridge bombed, 1,000lb. First Red Cross parcels received 23rd May 1944, 6 men to one parcel. First mail 28th May 1944.'

Chungkai

'Left Tamarkan 12th February 1945. March to Chungkai over bridge, broke all records going over. Arrived Chungkai, 6 kilometres, same day. Next day, 13th February bridge blown to pieces. Left Chungkai 19th February 1945.'

Non Pladuk

'Arrived Non Pladuk 20th February 1945. Spent a night of expectancy as previous raid very noticeable. Nothing standing except portion of the POW camp. In train 4 hours before leaving for Kachu Mountain 21st February. Detrained at blown bridge at Ratburi, Thai's hostile to nips, pontoons over river.'

Kachu Mountain

'March to Kachu Mountain 86 kilometres (53) miles. Self picked up in truck 15 miles out (malaria) and arrive Kachu Mountain 22nd February. The rest arrive in a bad way on the 24th February. Building 2 aerodromes No. one, 8 kilometres from camp. No. two, 3 kilometres from camp. Conditions and nips, no good. Self malaria all the time, nearly passed out. Twenty-six planes go over 28th April 1945, strafing drome. Machine gun mounted by nips outside hospital hut. Plenty blackwater fever. Storms every night, 7 huts blown down in typhoon. I eat python and armadillo, not too bad.'

This camp was established in February 1945, and had attained a strength of 2,526 by March which consisted of an approximately equal number of British and Australian Prisoners of War. The main work here was the construction of a landing strip and aerodrome. The campsite itself was originally a padi field and after tackling many difficulties the camp was quite reasonable as Prisoner of War camp standards go. The work at this camp whilst hard was reasonable and the men's health generally improved as did relations with the Japanese. For about ten days prior to 18th August 1945 everyone in camp suspected that something was afoot. Work on the aerodrome ceased on 15th August and on 18th August at 1945 hours the Japanese Commandant announced that hostilities had ceased. Red Cross parcels and clothing that had been confiscated by the Japanese were made available immediately. This airstrip would at the end of the war become a collecting and forwarding point for ex-Prisoners of War. As men came into this camp from surrounding areas they would be processed and forwarded onwards by aircraft, initially to Rangoon and then directly to Singapore. In July 1945 1,000 prisoners were transferred from Kachu Mountain Camp to Petchaburi.

Petchaburi

'Left Kachu Mountain 1st July 1945. March to Petchaburi (18 miles). Self in truck after 10 miles, malaria again.'

This camp was located 100 miles to the southwest of Bangkok and according to Dan Bevis, about 12 miles from the Kachu Mountain Camp. The camp at Petchaburi consisted of eleven atap buildings. Prisoners were engaged in the digging of a canal from the railway line to allow the unloading of river barges directly onto the railway stock. They were also put to work digging air raid shelters and constructing weapons pits for Anti-Aircraft emplacements. Major Charles Green, 2/4th Machine Gun Battalion, took over command of this camp on 6th September 1945 following his mission to accept the Japanese surrender at Ubon a week earlier.

Ratburi

'Train to Ratburi , damage of previous planes evident. Stopped for night sitting up. Chinese say war one more month, he was right.'

There were two camps at Ratburi, one on an island in the middle of a river and the other on the Bangkok side of the river about 2 miles distant. At both camps the prisoners were operating a ferry service due to the fact that the bridges over the river had been destroyed by Allied aircraft. The prisoners ran a relay service transferring goods from one train to another. A small group of prisoners from Tamuang had also arrived at Ratburi in February 1945 and were put to work on road and rail maintenance.

Nacompaton

'Through Nacompaton, largest pagoda ever seen. There are hundreds of legless and armless men here, bridge blown to pieces.'

Nacompaton had been set up from December 1943 as a large hospital and convalescing camp. There were several members from the 2/4th who were involved with the construction of this camp, including Eric Fraser and Frank 'Blue' Evans. This is where men like Tom Barbour, Syd Gorringe, Eric Ryan and Allan Bamford, to name just a few who had limbs amputated, and would remain at this camp until the end of the war. The camp itself was located about 30 miles to the west of Bangkok. As well as the amputees (amps) there were many Prisoners of War who were sent to this camp to build up their strength following the construction of the rail link. As their health improved slightly they were again called upon to depart Nacompaton on work parties. On Japan's surrender in August 1945 Nacompaton also became an Allied Forces collection centre for ex-Prisoners of War who were then either moved out via Bangkok to Singapore direct or via Rangoon to Singapore.

Bangkok

'Arrive Bangkok 3rd July 1945. Bombs have wreaked havoc at station and railway workshops. Took barge to go-downs. Big raids two weeks previous. Lofty Holdman killed, roofs wrecked. Do not like it here very much. Left go-downs 6th July 1945. Arrive Pratchanburi 6th July. Left 0100 hours 7th July for Nakom Nayok.'

Nakom Nayok

'March was murderous and at end of 45 kilometres men were all in. Nips would not pick up sick. Had been going with no food or boots for 33 hours continuous. Tried to refuse to march when three quarters of the distance was covered on account no water, but rifle and bayonet won the argument so we staggered on. Arrived Nakom Nayok on 7th July 1945. Long hours and hard work digging dugouts, ammo dumps etc., in hills 8 kilometres away. Plenty of lightning and storms, under water constantly. Cannot dig latrines on account of water. Cement bags were split for cigarette papers. Left Nakom Nayok on 4th August 1945.'

Work for the prisoners at Nakom Nayok consisted mainly of digging. The digging of trenches or tunnels into the side of a hill to store supplies and petrol drums, thought to have been aviation fuel for the Imperial Japanese Army Air Service.

Lopburi

'Arrive Lopburi 4th August 1945. One hundred yards to two tarmacs, three transmitting stations and trucks, petrol dumps, hangers and nips galore. Surrounded by military objectives and confined to an area 75 yards square, under tents. Two hundred in party and instructed that if any air activity not to move out of area or would be shot. One B29 over and all keyed up for eventualities as one nip plane came from hanger to have a go at him. Nothing happened, nip plane crashed. Self route planned for escape if needed.'

Nakom Nayok

The Australians at Nakom Nayok had organised themselves into three groups which would all escape in different directions if it became necessary. [Apparently the same arrangements had been made at Lopburi–author]. Lopburi was located about 100 miles to the north of Bangkok.

'Told on evening of 16th August that we were to move back to Nakom Nayok next morning 17th August 1945. Thai's shower truck with food etc and we had an idea something had happened.'

'On arrival at Nakom Nayok we were elated to see Yank, British and Dutch flags flying and were notified that war had finished. Plane dropped men and supplies on 1st September; what a sight. One man through roof of hut, also some parcels when chutes failed to open. Again on 3rd and 4th September more supplies, clothes and medicine. One plane dare devil flyer, very exciting. Lady Edwina Mountbatten visits camp.'

A bund at Chungkai Camp, Thailand

Nakom Nayok
Standing: Les Cody, Seated: Para Sgt., Roy Matthews, Syd Webb, Clive 'Potty' White, Ralph Williams, John Morgan

Bangkok

Situated at the Klong Toi Ports, there were twelve go-downs in four groups to the southeast of the city. Not all the warehouses accommodated prisoners that by June 1945 were estimated, by Allied intelligence sources, to be in the region of 1,000 men. At the end of the war the ex-Prisoners of War were billeted at either the Sports Stadium Camp or the Tamasaart University Camp.

> *'Left Nakom Nayok 13th September 1945. Arrive Bangkok at Tamasaart University 13th September. Wonderful buildings, King's Palace, pagoda etc in Bangkok. On 24th September left Bangkok 0850 hours Don Muang Aerodrome and flew 900–1,000 miles to Singapore, arriving after 5 hours 25 minutes flying time at 1415 hours. Bad weather on leaving, crossed Gulf of Siam and South China Sea, thence east coast of Malaya. Views of padi fields, rivers and jungles, magnificent. Had a couple of nasty bumps over South China Sea. All Aussie crew onboard a Dakota plane. Height mostly 10,000 feet. Present quarters at Singapore just like civilization again and had my first drink of beer in three and three quarter years. This was a record. Left Singapore Tamaroa 29th September 1945.*
> *Home, West Aussie at last, 10th October 1945.'*

Other Camps and Work Parties Thailand 1944–1945

Banderra-Chao Puraya River

Banderra lies to the southwest of Lopburi, to the south of the old Thai capital of Ayuthaya. A work party was sent to repair a bridge that crosses the Chao Puraya River on the Bangkok–Changmai railway line. These men were recovered at Bangkok, ex-Banderra.

Changmai

Work at this camp consisted of digging tunnels into the mountain and the construction of concrete pillboxes and defensive positions for a possible last stand action against the Allies. Apparently there was an officer from the 2/4th Machine Gun Battalion in charge of the 150 Australians in this group, however as most of the officers had been separated from the enlisted men at the beginning of 1945 this officer may have in fact been a Warrant Officer. Ivan Lawer was one member from the 2/4th who worked at this location.

Chumphon

Chumphon is located on the east coast of peninsula Thailand, 3 and a half miles inland from Chumphon Bay. North of Chumphon is the narrowest part of peninsula Thailand. Work at this camp comprised the repair of a bombed out bridge that as soon as it was repaired, was bombed by Allied aircraft again. The north–south railway between Singapore and Non Pladuk ran through Chumphon, so it can be seen that it was important, like the other towns on this line as part of the Japanese link between Singapore, Bangkok and Burma.

Hindato – Kinsaiyok – Konkoita

These were just a few of the many maintenance camps along the length of the Thailand side of the railway that appear in some of the men's records, so it can only be assumed that at some stage these three camps were frequented by 2/4th machine gunners. John Morgan spent some time at Hindato clearing a landslide off the line. By early 1944 Kinsaiyok had been transformed into a major rail terminus. One of the tasks at Konkoita was to build the bridge higher than the river's monsoon water level and at Kinsaiyok work included the construction of a loop line for the steam locomotives.

Kao Rin

This medical specialist camp which was located 5 miles from Kanchanaburi has been mentioned before as Peter Dimopoulos worked here as a translator for most of his time in Thailand. There were at least two other 2/4th at this camp at the end of the war. Again, one was Frank 'Blue' Evans and the other was Alan Hill who was assigned to the specialist party on 20th March 1944 as a cook.

Lampang

This village of Lampang or Lampon is located approximately 25 miles to the south of Changmai in northern Thailand on the Bangkok–Changmai State Railway line. It would seem like those recovered here at the end of the war were engaged in digging tunnels in the hills for the Japanese at Changmai.

Linson Wood Camp

This camp was located on the 202.50km point, sandwiched between Brankassi to the north at the 208.11km point and Hindato to the south at the 197.75km point. If the reader can imagine the Burma–Thailand rail link, take a right turn at the 202.50km point and then travel about 800 metres along a track upon which vehicles could travel, then the Linson Wood Camp would be discovered. Parallel to this track ran a tramway which was used to bring the cut timber from the jungle up adjacent to the main railway line for the steam locomotives. Linson is an important camp as far as the 2/4th Machine Gun Battalion is concerned. At least ten of its members were included in the work party and four men from Major Cough's V Battalion buried in the small cemetery at Linson, situated about 100 metres in from the main road and railway. These four deceased were, Fred Whitacker, 'Mick' Geary, Jack McCarthy and John Clare.

The 2/4th machine gunners that were sent to this camp were done so to cut and stack fire wood for the steam locomotives. There appears to have been three drafts of prisoners to this camp which included British, Australian and Dutch Prisoners of War. Three of the senior 2/4th members at this camp were W.O.II Tom Hampton, Sgt. Gordon Ohrt and Sgt. Jack Schurmann, who was placed in charge of the canteen. This was a job that he was apprehensive about taking responsibility for but nevertheless one that he accepted and performed admirably.

On Friday 22nd December 1944 Tom Hampton was stretchered into camp from the work site complaining of pains in his stomach. By 2300 hours that night the medical orderlies all agreed that he should be operated on for a duodenum inflammation. The Japanese Sgt. in charge was woken from his sleep and realising the urgency of the situation allowed a prisoner, accompanied by one of his Corporals, to go back down to the 201.00km Camp and have Capt. P. T. Millard, the A.I.F. surgeon, return to examine the patient. Captain Millard on arrival at Linson decided to operate at once. Tom was carried by stretcher to the 201.00km camp where he arrived at about 0230 hours on 23rd December. The operation was performed at 0400 hours and was a complete success.

One of the men who helped to stretcher Tom down to the 201.00km Camp was Bill Carlyon. Bill was one of five indigenous Australians in the 2/4th Machine Battalion. This fact is mentioned not because of the fact that Bill was an Australian aboriginal serving in the 2nd A.I.F. but because Tom never forgot the debt he owed Bill, and these two machine gunners formed a special friendship that lasted for decades after they were released from captivity.

Tom and his party had left Chungkai for Linson on 27th August 1944. It was four months later on Tuesday 2nd January 1945 that Tom was evacuated south, back to Chungkai. Likewise the other prisoners at this camp were sent south to Chungkai sometime in early 1945 probably before mid February as the steel spanned bridge at Tamarkan was still being visited by Allied bombers and as we know from Danny Bevis's Diary, the three spans were not knocked out until 13th February 1945.

Nakom Chassi

Ken Griffith was one of about one hundred Australians including several 2/4th who arrived at this camp on 20th May 1945 to reinforce the 300 Dutch already in residence. They would remain at this camp until the end of the war. The camp was located to the west of Bangkok approximately half way between Bangkok and Nacompaton, the work here being similar to that at Ratburi and Petchaburi. A suspension bridge that crossed the north–south flowing Nakom Chassi River had been destroyed and to enable freight to cross the river it was ferried by boat and loaded onto another train. The Australians were split into two working parties of about fifty men each. Working alongside their fellow Dutch Prisoners of War, the Australians dug and maintained canals. Early in July some of the prisoners were also put to work digging air raid shelters alongside the line near the canal. These shelters had to be built above ground due to the amount of water lying about. Anti-Aircraft weapon pits were excavated for the Japanese.

Nikhe-Nikhe Wood Camp 1944 and the Sonkurai–Nikhe Defence Line 1945

Nikhe-Nikhe was mentioned within the Williams Force Story when this group crossed over the border into Thailand and continued rail laying until the completion of the rail link in October 1943. This camp is believed to have been located in the vicinity of the 283.92km point from Non Pladuk just to the north of the New Headquarters Camp at the 281.80km point on the rail link.

A work party was put into Nikhe-Nikhe for three months from August 1944, for the purpose of cutting billets of wood for the wood fired steam locomotives. As stated in the 'F' Force Story, the New Headquarters Camp at the 281.80km point was a rail centre from December 1943. John Waddell was one member from the 2/4th included in this group.

The Sonkurai to Nikhe region is the location chosen by the Japanese for the building of a defensive line that consisted of an Anti-Tank ditch and tunnels in the hillsides. The purpose of this line was to be somewhere the Japanese could make a stand, if forced out of Burma by Allied forces.[26] Work was carried out in the region of Sonkurai and Nikhe between April and August 1945. The exact location of this defence line is not known, however referring to the 'F' Force Story the area around Sonkurai No. 2 Camp at the 294.02km point appears to be perfect for this defence line.

> 'The country around the "600" Bridge was wild and untamed. Half a mile above the
> "600" Bridge was the confluence of five rivers.'[27]

Like most camps in Thailand evidence of Japan's impending defeat was mounting as the food situation worsened, and working hours reverted back to the long hours of the 'speedo' period experienced during the construction of the rail link. When we look at the history of each man who worked in this Sonkurai–Nikhe area, we must ascertain whether he went up in 1944 to cut firewood or in 1945 to build defence works or in some cases both tasks.

Nakom Nayok–Phitsanulok Party

There was only one member from the 2/4th on this party, being John Waddell. This group departed from Nakom Nayok in mid July 1945 and consisted of 800 British and 100 Australians, under the command of a British Warrant Officer and two Medical Officers, Capt. Brereton A.A.M.C. and Capt. Peh S.S.V.F. who was attached to this party. These prisoners were forced to march 375 miles over a period of six weeks for no apparent reason. The fact that only three men on this party died should be seen as a miracle because amongst this group were 105 chronic amoebic dysentery and 250 relapsing malaria cases which only placed a heavier burden upon the fitter prisoners.

It is believed that the route taken was via the old capital of Ayuthaya where the north–south railway line from Phitsanulok joined with the Bangkok line. From here they would have then travelled north via Lopburi and followed the railway north past Nakom Sawan. Everything needed for the journey was pulled and pushed along in carts, with ten prisoners allocated to each cart. The distance travelled each day could vary from as little as 2 or 3 miles to as many as 15 miles. The journey initially had been along a good gravelled road but eventually they were led down a narrow track that was even too narrow for the carts to traverse, so they were dismantled and everything including the carts were carried. At one stage a river was crossed which was possibly the Chao Puraya. The Japanese guards organised two large barges for the river crossing which was successfully navigated.

At this point the guards who may have been destined for the front line fighting in Burma were replaced by a group of geriatric specimens of Japanese manhood. It was about this time that the local Thais informed the prisoners that the war had finished. The prisoners later learned that they were to be killed on 18th August but whether this would have occurred is open to conjecture because unbeknown to the Japanese guards a Major in the British Commandos had

---

26 The reader should also note the mention of the two escape roads. Firstly the Wampo to Tavoy Escape Road and secondly the Prachaub Kirikhan to Mergui Escape Road. Both these escape routes would permit Japanese soldiers to make their way to the coast in the hope of making good their escape. Perhaps what we are seeing here is the Japanese version of the 'Dunkirk mentality'.

27 Roy Whitcross, *Slaves of the Son of Heaven* Dymocks 1952, p.103

been shadowing the prisoners for almost two weeks ready to intervene with his men if necessary. Meanwhile, despite news that the Japanese had surrendered, the prisoner's journey continued until they reached the village of Changmai where they were locked up at night. This routine continued until 31st August when they were finally set free. After a few days they were transferred to a camp at Takuri where an airfield had just been completed. The men were then flown out to Bangkok and then onto Singapore where the Australians in the group would be forwarded to their home ports.

Prachuab Kirikhan-Mergui Escape Road

It is known that there were at least seven members of the 2/4th on this party who were selected from Nacompaton Hospital Camp. The seven men were Percy Sturtridge, Mervyn Wilkinson, Ted Cosson, Greg Burdon, John Warren-Smith, Bill Reeves and Frank Thaxter. Prachuab Kirikhan is located approximately 144 miles to the south-south-west of Bangkok this is roughly half way between Petchaburi to the north and Chumphon to the south on the peninsula part of Thailand that is shared with Burma. The camp at Prachuab Kirikhan was the base camp and from there the prisoners would move out to one of four jungle camps. The object of this exercise was to cut an escape road approximately 94 miles or 150 kilometres in length through virgin jungle from the port of Prachuab-Kirikhan on the east coast of Thailand to the port of Mergui on the west coast of Burma. A buffalo cart track ran to within kilometres of the Maw Daung Pass (via Knong Hin and Glohngwal) at an elevation of 720 feet, which was crossed by a well defined track which then led down into the Tenasserim Valley. This valley was nick named 'Death Valley' by Ted Cosson and the other prisoners who worked on this road.

Like the Burma–Thailand rail link and for that matter the Sumatran Railway the camps on this escape road were marked off in kilometres. Greg Burdon remembers working at the 10 and 15 kilometre points. The Prisoner of War workforce selected for this task experienced conditions reminiscent of the construction period on the Burma–Thailand rail link. Out of those selected only 300 out of the 1,011 could be considered fit enough to be included in the party, and out of these 1,011 prisoners selected by the Japanese Medical Officer Dr Higuchi, 240 would not survive the experience. They were told that they were being transferred to a better hospital camp, information which of course was totally false.

This group left Nacompaton by train on 12th April 1945. When they reached Ratburi they were forced by necessity to change trains due to the bridge having being destroyed by Allied aircraft. It is worth mentioning that the railway line between Singapore up through Malaya travels through Chumphon, Prachuab Kirikhan, Petchaburi and Raturi to Non Pladuk, the starting point for the Burma–Thailand Railway. They then continued their journey south to Prachuab Kirikhan the starting point for the escape road.

Although there was ample rice, food consisted of mostly Chinese radish, sweet potatoes and the occasional dried cabbage and bamboo shoots. The only time meat was supplied was when oxen died and the prisoners were permitted to use the carcass for food. The work was mostly pick and shovel, carrying of stone for the road bed, felling of trees and grubbing bamboo roots, but it is also recorded that there were at least three well constructed timber bridges on this road. The hours of work went from 0830 hours to 1900 hours. The prisoners were broken into parties of approximately thirty and assigned various tasks.

The diet again like that on the Burma–Thailand rail link was insufficient for manual labouring. Accommodation was bamboo huts that proved less waterproof than the atap roofed variety. During the building of this road, Mervyn Wilkinson was evacuated back to Nacompaton in June 1945. Greg Burdon and Frank Thaxter, on completion of the road, marched out towards the Burmese coast pulling ox carts loaded with the sick. They then cut an airstrip in the jungle for three C47 Dakota aircraft to land and firstly evacuate the British ex-Prisoners of War to

Rangoon. Greg and Frank themselves with the other remaining 2/4th and many others were then flown north to the Kachu Mountain Camp where they again met up with Ted Cosson. It was from here that all three men were flown back to Singapore in September 1945.

Wampo–Tavoy Escape Road

There was at least one member from the 2/4th on this party, being Neville Matson. This party consisted of 200 British and 200 Dutch. The task, like that at Prachuab Kirikhan was to cut a 3 metre wide escape road from Wampo through to Tavoy, which was located across the border near the Burmese coast. The distance from Wampo to Tavoy is believed to have been approximately 110 kilometres as the crow flies, however the actual distance taking into account the rugged terrain was considerably further.

This party departed Tamuang Camp for Wampo on 19th December 1944 perched on top of the railway wagons. On arrival at Wampo the prisoners were marched about 7–10 kilometres to their first construction camp where four tents were issued to accommodate the 200 British, and 200 Dutch Prisoners of War. After the first two day's work the prisoners were again marched a further 13 kilometres to their next camp. This march is remembered because it was undertaken at night and after the first 3 kilometres the road petered out forcing the prisoners to grapple their way in darkness through virgin jungle. Rations were carried in by the prisoners, being brought in daily from Wampo which meant a round trip of 26 kilometres, carrying loads from 25 to 40 kilograms in weight.

The escape road was completed on 5th June 1945, however, in Neville Matson's case he was evacuated sick from Tavoy to Nacompaton Hospital on 22nd May 1945. Like most other camps the Japanese were uncooperative when it came to improvement of conditions, rations and medicines. Surprisingly, only thirteen deaths occurred amongst this group, and the majority of these were as a result of malaria.

Pratchai

There is only scant information available on this camp. All that is known is that there were some members from the 2/4th at this camp, which is thought to have been located somewhere between Tamuang and Bangkok. This would then place it somewhere to the west of Bangkok.

Pratchinburi

This camp was located to the south-south-east of Nakom Nayok and it is possible that the Prisoner of War workforce came from the camps in the Nakom Nayok area. Owen Morris and Arthur Morrison were at this camp, the work entailed the digging of tunnels.

Tardan Bridge

This bridge which crossed the Maekhlaung River has been covered in the story of the Burma–Thailand rail link. Repairs were made to this bridge when it was damaged by debris that had been carried down river by the monsoon rains. It is not known how many expeditions were made to repair this bridge but it is certain that Tom Cato was included in a work party that carried out repairs in March–April 1945. A place that is spelt Takabutai, Takatai or Buntai appears in a few of the men's histories including Tom's. This place is thought to be near Tardan and might possibly be Tha Kathi or Kau Hin Tai, which are both villages marked on the map close to Tardan. With a little imagination it would not be difficult to translate these names phonetically into Takati, Takabutai or any number of other variations. Perhaps the most solid piece of evidence that might substantiate this theory is the fact that Tom Cato's next camp was

Tarsau and as we know the bridge at Tardan is where the road crosses the Maekhlaung River and continues north to Wanyai and on to Tarsau.

Tamajao Wood Camp

It was early 1945 when about 500 Prisoners of War were sent to Tamajao to cut wood for the steam locomotives. This camp had originally been an Indian camp of which most of the original inhabitants had died. Within a little over a month after arrival the camp was abandoned as malaria had killed in the region of twenty men and in addition more than 300 men were too sick to work.

Ubon

Allied intelligence reported that there was one large camp about 6 miles north-north-west of Ubon and several smaller camps in the same area with an estimated total of 3,000 Prisoners of War that had been transferred from the Kanchanaburi area. Ubon is located in the northeast corner of Thailand near the Loatian border. The Prisoners of War in this area were put to work constructing airfields. Major Charles Green was flown from Bangkok to Karot near Ubon to accept the local Japanese commander's surrender. This was carried out on 27th August 1945 whereupon Major Green returned to Bangkok. Bill 'Bullets' Struthers mentions in his diary that his group travelled by train from Bangkok via the old capital of Ayuthaya to Ubon.

The Separation of the Officers 1945

It was late in 1944 when it became known of the Japanese intention to separate the officers from the other ranks. This caused some concern because the officer's rank had always been the buffer between the Japanese and the enlisted men. Some officers were better than others, some were stalwarts standing steadfastly against their Japanese overseer's demands for sick men to work on the rail link. This of course covers the doctors including Capt. Claude Anderson who on several occasions received a jolly good bashing for his trouble. The reason for this desire to separate the commissioned from the enlisted ranks is thought to have been so that an organised force of prisoners could not be raised should an Allied invasion eventuate.

In January 1945 all the officers in Thailand excepting certain Medical Officers and Padres were concentrated at Kanchanaburi. It has been mentioned that for work on the Burma–Thailand rail link the Burma and Thailand Administration Groups No. 1 through 6 had been formed. With the officers now concentrated at Kanchanaburi, they now became Group No. 7. The total strength at this Officer's Camp was to be 3,000 British, Australian, Dutch and American officers, plus an equal number of other ranks. Warrant Officers and NCO's now stepped in to take over where their officers had left. The Officer's Camp at Kanchanaburi is described as being congested and dirty with dilapidated huts. A lot of work was required and was carried out to bring the camp to a reasonable standard, this work was completed by May 1945. By the time the dust had settled, some of the officers at Kanchanaburi were moved again to another camp to the north-north-east of their present location.

According to Lt. 'Mick' Wedge, there were about 200 officers in this party including Capt. Archie Thomas and Lt. Kevin Boyle. At the time, Archie Thomas was not well and required constant assistance from 'Mick' and Kevin during the march to the new camp, thought to have been in the Nakom Nayok area. By the time of Japan's surrender, five of these Officer Parties had already been moved away from Kanchanaburi. Contrary to expectations, incidents between the guards and the Warrant Officers and NCO's now that they had taken over the responsibility of the enlisted men actually decreased. It is recorded that certain NCO's did magnificent work in some of the jungle camps.

The Kill all Prisoners Order No. 27

During the course of interviewing the ex-members of the 2/4th Machine Gun Battalion, some of the men had mentioned that it was the Japanese intention to kill them should an Allied invasion occur. This was at first thought to be whimsical except for the fact that the author's uncle, Danny Bevis, made an entry in his diary that substantiated this statement.

'All men go paradise. Did not know until end of war what was meant.' [28]

By chance a document arrived amongst some other files that had been ordered from the National Archives of Australia. The following is a record of the statements made by 1st Lt. Kishio Usuki, I.J.A., in response to questions by Lt-Col. John E. Murray through 2nd Lt. Eichi Nakazono, who was acting as interpreter, at Banh Kwang Gaol, Bangkok, on 17th November 1945.

Lt-Col. Murray:
'I am an American officer, a Lt-Col. In the American Army, and I am investigating war crimes for the United States. I want to ask you some questions concerning statements which have been made by former American POW and I want you to give me truthful replies. What was the proposed plan at Saraburi [located 100 miles N.N.E. of Bangkok-author] to dispose of POW's in the event of an Allied landing?'

Lt. Usuki:
'The following is all I know about the matter. All the main conferences were attended by Branch Commandants, and since as I was only commander of a group beneath No. 4 Branch I did not attend conferences. All I heard was from the Branch Commander Capt. Suzuki. One of the instructions was that no POW's were to be allowed to escape whatsoever. About 11th August 1945 the Staff Officer of Saraburi Branch Camp was called in by Capt. Suzuki, Commander of No 4 Branch. At that time Capt. Suzuki explained Order No. 27 issued by main POW Headquarters in Bangkok.'

Lt-Col. Murray:
'I presume Order No. 27 came direct from Col. Sugasawa?'

Lt. Usuki:
'The order No. 27 to the best of my knowledge was as follows: that all Koreans were to be shipped to Nakom Nayok to the Kobayashi Heidan, and that all POW guards henceforth were to be Japanese. These Koreans were to then be used as labourers for the Japanese Army and that utmost security was to be maintained to keep prisoners from escaping. I received instructions from Capt. Suzuki that huts were to be built to house POW's and that a moat was to be built around these huts large enough to keep POW's from jumping across it; that in case of invasion by allied forces that all POW's would be herded into these huts and Japanese guards would

---

28   Danny Bevis Diary loaned to the author by his son Mervyn Bevis

be put around it. As to the method of disposition of the POW's it was left up to the Branch Commander. The disposition was not given to me and I do not know what steps were to be taken to dispose of the POW's in the event of an Allied invasion.'

Lt-Col. Murray:

'Isn't it a fact that in the discussion in Capt. Suzuki's office you proposed the scheme of soaking the bamboo huts in oil and setting fire to them?'

Lt. Usuki:

'No, I did not say to put oil and gasoline on the huts and burn them, but I did mention the fact that any POW's attempting to escape should be shot without warning.'

Lt-Col. Murray:

'Is it not true that during your conference Capt. Suzuki explained to you that as soon as an Allied landing was made that all POW's in camp would be killed. In other words isn't it true that you had received instructions to kill all POW's as soon as an Allied landing was made?'

Lt. Usuki:

'Yes that is true. I had received instructions that all POW's were to be killed.'

Lt-Col. Murray:

'From whom did you receive instructions to this effect.'

Lt. Usuki:

'From Capt. Suzuki.'

Lt-Col. Murray:

'How was the killing to be accomplished.'

Lt. Usuki:

'The decision as to the method in which the prisoners were to be killed was to be decided on by the Branch Commander, Capt Suzuki, when the time came.'

It is to be noted that this is not the only record of Japanese intent to annihilate Allied Prisoners of War as a copy of one such order was discovered by Jack Edwards, Royal Corps of Signals whilst he was engaged on war crimes after the war on the island of Formosa or Taiwan as it is now known. This document is now held by the United States National Archives at Washington D.C. and in short states:

'Whether they are destroyed individually or in groups, or however it is done, with mass bombing, poisonous smoke, poisons, drowning, decapitation, or what, dispose of them as the case dictates. In any case it is not the aim to allow the escape of a single one, to annihilate them all, and not to leave any trace.'

In Thailand deep trenches or bunds were dug round many of the camps during 1944–45. The soil from these bunds was then piled high on the outer extremity of the bund to limit the view and to add to the inner security of the camp. From this point on it was obvious that the Japanese preferred the prisoners to remain within the confines of the camp when not at work under an armed guard. In some instances machine gun posts had been set up to this end. This facet of the Prisoner of War experience is dealt with in the Japanese Thrust:

'Meanwhile in Thailand base camps the discipline had noticeably tightened. In October 1944 ditches were dug round the perimeter of the camps, sentry posts were built and so placed as to cover the entire camp boundaries. As an additional precaution a series of fences were constructed of both barbed wire and bamboo, and embankments were built round most camps to block the prisoners' view of the surrounding country. In addition regulations prohibiting contact with the Thais were rigidly enforced, the Japanese evidently fearing that the civilians might attempt to enlist prisoners in their resistance movement. Frequent searches were carried out by the Japanese military police, and officers and other ranks were subjected to third degree by the Kempei [Kempeitai–author] *headquarters at Kanburi.'* [29]

If the reader can now reflect back to the Sandakan Story and the tunnels which were dug on Singapore during 1945 then Japanese intentions should now become clear. It would appear the extermination of prisoners was to be left entirely up to the Japanese Branch Commander in each locality as and when the threat of an Allied invasion or occupation appeared imminent, and this final and fatal decision was left up to him. In Sandakan's case the uncovering of the underground movement, the discovery of a radio receiver and parts for a transmitter, combined with Allied air attacks and Japanese paranoia flamed by the Kempeitai must certainly have contributed to the extermination of these men. Many since 1945 have questioned the morality of dropping two atom bombs on Japan. Japan's dilemma was that it had desperately been seeking a way of ceasing hostilities with the Allied powers, without it appearing to the peoples of the Japanese nation, as well as the enemies' of Japan as a 'loss of face.' The dropping of these two new powerful weapons ultimately solved this problem. Had these weapons not been utilised as they were then it is almost certain that there would have been very few men from the 2/4th Machine Gun Battalion left to tell of their experiences.

In reply to a civic welcome held in the Shire of Woorooloo at the end of 1945 for returned servicemen from the district, John Robinson made a speech of which the following is considered a fitting ending to this book concerning *The Men of the 2/4th Machine Gun Battalion.*

'Countless millions saw the Union Jack torn from its position and replaced by symbols of hate and tyranny, and only the blood and determination of the peoples restored it to its old glory. If you had been (and thank God you were not) subject to a foreign flag, I am certain you would agree with me when I say that Our Own Flag is the most precious emblem in our possession.

Lest We Forget is the anthem that will continue to echo from the cenotaph on ANZAC Days but homage will not discharge our obligations unless we take care to preserve the ideals and freedom for which they fell.

I commend you to unfurl the flag over your homes, over your schools and over your public buildings, for it is the embodiment of cenotaphs and the beacon of freedom.

Together we must care for the bereaved, together we must maintain the spirit of co-operation learnt during the war years, and if ever a doubt should creep into your minds that all is not well, walk over to the mast and give the chord a little tug just to make sure our flag is right at the top, LEST WE FORGET.'

THE END

---

[29] Lionel Wigmore, *Japanese Thrust* Australia in the War of 1939–45, Army Volume IV Australian War Memorial Canberra 1957, p.590–591

Lieutenant Les 'Pard' Riches

Major Alf Cough wrote of Les: 'So off went my right hand man. I will miss him, his high morale and rough wit which could nearly always raise a smile from the boys, he also used effectively on me the same bulldust'.

Reg and Ivy Ferguson with their daughters Daphne, Pauline and the 2/4th Machine Gun Battalion's canine mascot, Gunner. Reg died as a Prisoner of War on 'B' Force Borneo in 1945.

Percy and Dorothy Gibbs and their daughters, left to right Marlene, Faye and Beryl

Johny and Thelma (Bennie) Browning and their son Robert. Johny died a Prisoner of War on 'B' Force Borneo in 1945.

Dan and Thelma Bevis and their children left to right, Mervyn, Desmond, Trevor, Beryl and Glenis.
Dan died four years after his return to Australia on 16th September 1949.

Ted Bunce with his wife Doreen and son Terry

Laurence and Enid Harvey. Laurence was Lost at Sea on 12th September 1944 following the sinking of the Rakuyo Maru

B&W Plate 6

George Hancock, Bryan Manwaring and Dorothy Letts, later Mrs Manwaring

Tom Pascoe. Note the pock marks on Tom's arm caused by oil rising to the surface from the sunken Rakuyo Maru

Top: Harry and Junor Elkins. Junor who was born in April 1942 never met her father.
Harry died a Prisoner of War at Brankassi Camp Thailand on 12th August 1943.
Bottom Left: Edward Popham with his son Edward aged 4. Bottom Right: Bert Rubery and his sister Nell.

Top: Vern Hoppe as a boy at Day Dawn Western Australia who died as a Prisoner of War at Kuii Camp Thailand on 19th November 1943. Left: Claude Anderson whilst studying at Prince Alfred College, South Australia. Right: John Mellor

Top: William John King is the younger of these two boys. His older brother WX6038 Arthur George King died as a result of his wounds on 3rd August 1941 whilst serving with the 2/28th Battalion in Libya.
Bottom: Sydney Albert Osborne, London 1924 aged 5. Syd died whilst a Prisoner of War at Sandakan in Borneo.

No. 1 Platoon Signals

Back Row: H. Eastwood, *V.T.W. Hoppe*, M.W. Wilkinson, G.R. Ramage, N. Warne, T. Davidson, C.W. Gault, *A.R. Leishmire*, R.F. Cannon, A.J.L. McIntosh, G.J. Gossage, M. St. J. Kennedy. **Centre Row**: H. Pickett, R.D. McCracken, W.J. Nicholls, E.J. Cosson, J.G.A. Kyriakos, A.J. Hambley, G.L. Taylor, W.E. Clothier, H.A. Walker, *J. Wren*, D.G. Ross, R. D. Maconachie. **Front Row**: W.G. Worth, W.D. Grundy, F.H. Keirle, J.M. Rutherford, B.E. Hansen, F.L. Curnow, J. Unsworth, A.D. Hosking, J.H.L. Pryce, W.N.K. McNulty, R.L. Evans

No. 2 Platoon Ack-Ack

Back Row: J.P. Murphy. R.L. Todd. E.C. Jones, J.M. McGinty, J. Issac, H.R. Harrison, W.J. Tucker, C.B. Thackrah, *D. Stevenson*
Front Row: J. Wilkie, H.W. Scaddan, F.J. Annesley, W.L. Innes, J.D. Royce, C.A. Phillips, J.S. Smith, A.G. Hayes, R.R. Lyle, D.J. Davies

No. 2 Platoon Ack-Ack
Top: This photo includes Gordon Lynam and AA Platoon Drivers Frank Pritchard and Norm Holdman
No. 2 Ack-Ack Platoon Drivers
Bottom: Left to Right: F.K. Pritchard, N.P. Holdman, W.H. Philp, E.H. Sullivan

B&W Plate 14

No. 3 Platoon

This photograph was taken at Mundaring during the march from Northam to Perth. The photograph was donated by the Pummell family and is believed to be No. 3 Platoon.

No. 3 Platoon Drivers

Back Row: *D. Nelligan, Minty?, J. Treasure, T.W. Green, E.H. Sullivan, H.B. Ockerby*. **Centre Row**: *J.N. Hall, N.J. Sheedy, T.M. Davison, H.P. Bennett, H. Hammer, J.R. Williams*. **Front Row**: *L. Krassnostein, J. Sevier, T.J. Butler, N.P. Holdman, W. Struthers*

Pioneers and A.A.O.C.
Back Row: T. Firns, R.J. Kelt, J.C. Swift, J.A. Rabone
Centre Back Row: R.F. Manthorpe, C.H. Dunn (A.A.P.C.), E.A. Pummell, E.L. Preedy, E.A. Dix
Centre Front Row: A.W. Findlay, J. Bagrie, H.J. Cooper
Front Row: R.F. Newling, P.J. Beilby, *W. Jones*, B.P. Doolan

B&W Plate 17

A.A.O.C.
Back Row: J.C. Swift, A.H.S. London, F.D. Thaxter, E.A. Dix
Front Row: P.J. Beilby, R.F. Manthorpe

B&W Plate 18

'A' Company

'A' Company No. 4 Platoon

Back Row: *J. Roberts*, H.W. Waghorn, L. Greaves, H.M. Rubery, *J.A. Connolly*, A.B. Facey, J.O. Street, A.M. Hack, *A.D. Symons*, *A. V. Badger*, C.S. Parke, E. Meakins, *H.H. Taylor*, J.C. Heffernan, E.G. Burton. **Centre Rear Row**: *J.E. Sands*, H.E. Procter, C. Harris, R.C. Wilson, E.J. Clarke, *L. Hunt*, R.J. Baggs, A.A.M. Brazier, E.H. King, F. Nazzari, F. Hermon, F.C. Moore, *C.D. Astill*, L.J. McGrath, R.E. Godfrey. **Centre Front Row**: W.J. King, H.B. Lear, *D.J. McMahon*, E.N. Bates, *W.A. Wilson*, R.D. Hampson, A.W. Thomas, F.G. McCaffrey, W. Burgess, K.T. MacLennan, D.M. O'Leary, M. Armstrong, *E.A. Gill*, A.R. Beattie, M.R. Docking, J. Young. **Front Row**: C.E. Burns, A.S. Oag, R.J. Miller, R. Hill, W.J. Stone, A.J. Barnes.

'A' Company No. 5 Platoon

Back Row: C.R. Bird, D.F. Sterrett, *F.G. Kerwin*, J.B. Gilmour, E.A.A. Watt, J. Scales, W.T. Haywood, R.P. Elvish, A.S. Parke, L. McG. Murray, W.R. Gregory, R.E. Hughes, T.M. McMahon, R.C. Reed. **Centre Row**: L.R. Rayner, L Armstrong, E.J. Ovens, J.S. Elliot, N.H.E. Thompson, L.C. Hellmrich, B. Fitzgerald, R.W. Chipperfield, J.B. Mellor, E.J. Holst, J.K. Ramsbottom, J. Alderton, D.J. Davies, J. Borrow. **Front Row**: C.J. Vidler, S.J. Blewett, N.P. Hayes, A.J. McGhee, J. Gilmour, J.J. Dore, J.H. Schurmann, A.B. Walton, R.H. Cornish, H.E. Saw, R.G. Tuffin, C.J. McDonald, L.G.Willacott, A.W. Norton, T.A.H Minchin.

'A' Company No. 6 Platoon

Back Row: E.J. Waddell, J. Lee, *H.G. Atkins*, E.C.S. Popham, J.A. Brooker, *D.J. Atkins*, J.R. Baker, H. Tysoe, P. Golden, J.C. Ewen, S.H. Gibbs, *W.L. Deeley*, J. Rochester, G. Dorizzi. **Centre Row**: K. Clifton, R.K. Gregory, H.W. Heal, C. Knott, D. Ross, H.T. Bunker, N.A. Gough, A.E. Farmer, L.S. Hodgson, G.T. Dickie, D.A.C. Quinn, A.A. Dickson, *H.S.N. Knudsen*, *P.S. Dore*. **Front Row**: K.K. McDonald, W. Dunwoodie, W.C. Evans, J.H. Shackleton, G.W. Taylor, F.McP. Townsend, A. Stevens, J.G. Wilson, E.J. Howard, D.L.A. Whiteman, T.A. Limbourn, C.A. Fogarty, T.J. Fury, H.W. Williams, *E.G. Masters*.

B&W Plate 22

'B' Company

'B' Company Headquarters

Back Row: J.A. McGregor, G.P. Biggs, G. Japp, H.A. Jackson, A. Brooksbank, W.J. Robinson. **Centre Row**: A. McD.D. Drummond, S.M. Hogben, J.C. Colbey, E.E. Miller, G.J. Doodson, F. Vaughan, C.H. Dunn, J. Hill. **Front Row**: T.W. Zeeb, C. Flakemore, A.S. Hewby, G.McR. Bunning, A.R. Smith-Ryan, R.S. Campbell, V.G. Barnett.

'B' Company No. 7 Platoon

Back Row: A.E. Powell, F.R. Noble, *J. Ritchie*, A.E. Foch, A.T. White, P.G. Hodgins, G.K. Cameron, E.G. Thomson, S.M. Hogben, H. Atkinson, A.S. Thorns. **Centre Back Row**: *J. Thorburn*, S. Gorringe, J.B. Stubbs, J.C. Colbey, R.W. Newling, T. Zeeb, G. Japp, J.N. Cainmanos, G.C. Arthur, M.J. Leahy, J.F. Dare, J.J. Flanagan. **Centre Front Row**: M.W. Hortin, J.A. McGregor, A. Brooksbank, C. Flakemore, R.F. Lawer, H.G. Hockey, J.F. Starcevich, W.R.S. Baker, J.E.J. Gregory, E. M. Hopson, C.L. Collins, T.H. Green, T.A. Finlay. **Front Row**: W.V. Winter, G.P. Biggs, W.A. Halligan, W.E. Breed, N.J. Outtrim, P.V. Dean, J.E. Pearson, D. Holm, V.G. Barnett, H.A. Jackson, *T.W. Greathead*, J.J. Barry.

B&W Plate 25

'B' Company No. 8 Platoon

Back Row: R.F. Carruthers, D.N. Russell, C. Ryan, T.M. Jackson, J.L. Wheelock, L.J. Daily, R.L. Smith, C.W. Gray, J.B. Skelton, *O.K. Harrington*, D.C.J. Hall. **Centre Back Row:** G.H. Edwards, J.A. Taylor, L.H. Lee, C.W. Armstrong, W.H. Hall, L.F. Hadden, *K. Renshaw*, H.C.S. MacMaster, O. Morris, C.W. Robertson, C.J. Burns, W.T. Castles. **Centre Front Row:** *B.C. Evans*, F.V. Cross, F. Vaughan, *R.G. Herron*, H.F. Neilson, A.J. Burns, J. Hill, T.R. Fotheringham, C.H. Dunn, L.P. Walsh, T.K. Jenkins, J.G. Curtin. **Front Row:** D.A. Day, R.C. Badock, D.T. Manning, J. Gorringe, R.H. Sandilands, G.C. MacKinnon, J.F. Helsin, A.M. Draper, E.E. Hambley, C. Mutton.

'B' Company No. 8 Platoon

Entraining at Oakbank, South Australia en route to Darwin, Donald (Do-Dah) Day and Hec MacMaster can easily be identified by the names on their kit bags

'B' Company No. 9 Platoon

Back Row: L.J. McGrath, R. Goodwin, T.E.J. James, R.W. Haldane, F. Hinds, E.E. Miller, D.N.H. Carter, D. Parker, H.J. Cowie, J. Halligan. **Centre Back Row:** W.J. Davey, G.J. Doodson, W.G. Nicholson, R.G. Whitelaw, T.H. Buscombe, A.V. Schuts, H.G. Blakiston, R. Drysdale, W.H. Earnshaw, A. McD.D. Drummond, W.F. Anderton. **Centre Front Row:** F.T. Ward, L.W.S. Kemp, M.A. Hunter, G. Kidd, A. Hackshaw, C.J. McPherson, J.W. Smith, A.G. Newell, H.J. Gregory, J. Warren-Smith, L. O'Neil. **Front Row:** R.A. Briggs, J.J. Lynch, T.E. Teasdale, K.D. Tucker, N.J. Harris, C.D. Lee, J.W. Sanderson, F.J. Dorrington, W.J. Robinson, E.B. Jones, R.R. Jeffery.

'C' Company

'C' Company Headquarters

Back Row: J. Swartz, J.W. Basell, R.H. Simkin, M.A. Bartlett, A. Spooner, C.P. McLoughlin. **Centre Row**: E.F. Elliot, N. Bradshaw, J.W.H. Needham, J.H. King, *W.F.D. Nelson*, N.E. Banks, *Mecklenberg*, H.W. Steele, S.R. Clayden. **Front Row**: A.G. Williams, R.A. Deveson, D.B. Chapman, L. Helliwell, *G. Hassell*, T. Hampton, N.H. Grant, T.M. Fitzgerald

B&W Plate 30

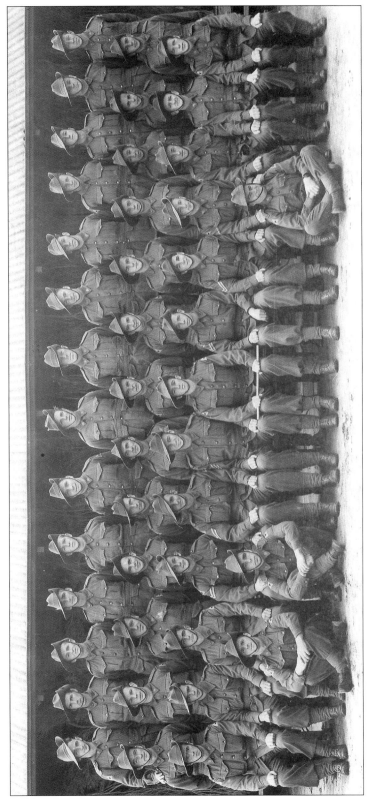

'C' Company No. 10 Platoon

Back Row: D.T. Manning, *R. Reynolds*, W.R. Morris, E.T. Adams, L.S. Hummerston, K.T. Hayes, *R.J. Armstrong*, R.R. McAskil, C.G. Henderson, A.H. Dyson, R.W. Hadfield, L.J. Marriot, N. Jones, F.V. Carroll **Centre Rear Row**: W.W. Reeves, K.G. Moir, L.P. Byrne, F.T. McGlinn, K.J. Howell, E. Ricketts, D.A. Matheson, R.J. Carlile, L.N. Holtzman, *P. Knowles*, G.N. Burslem, _____, S.K. Wenn **Centre Front Row**: J.B. Leith, G.L. Burdon, R.E. Godfrey, H.C. Fuhrmann, H.J.S. Fidge, R.C. Fullerton, V.I. Warhurst, F.W. Webb, _____ J.R. Aberle, C. McLennan, C.K. McDonald, F.J. Baxter, W. McKay **Front Row**: J. Clare, C.W.M. Anderson, C.W. White

B&W Plate 31

'C' Company No. 11 Platoon

Rear Row: A.R. Minchin, V.J.A. Dewar, A. McQuade, E.J. Waddell, J.S. Pass, J. Robinson, D.J. Squire, W.C. Roberts, H.J. Millar, J.S. Clarke, W.L. Rosel **Centre Row**: H.E. McDonough, H.T. Clayden, F. Barker, A. Miller, L.O. Moir, T.C. Gibson, A.V. Cousins, *V. Brambles*, N.W. Fraser, F.W. Toms, C.G. Ferrie, N.A. Gibson **Front Row**: H.S. Werrett, G. Moir, D.E. Bevis, S.E. Foxall, B.H. Manwaring, K.C. Boyle, P.A. Sturtridge, E.J. Rowell, A.A. Adams, A.J. Rees, T.J. Conway

'C' Company No. 11 Platoon

Left to Right: A.N. Climie, A.V. Cousins, D.J. Squire, A. Miller, A.R. Minchin, V.J.A. Dewar, *V. Brambles*

'C' Company No. 12 Platoon

Back Row: R.A. Page, W.H. Nottle, C. Joynes, R.H. Stribling, *J. Woods*, E.G. Watt, L.A.C. Kuhlman, P.R. Beaton, G. Fisher, *B. Brown*, J.McL. Goldie, A.J. Colquhoun, H.C. Norris, R. Muller **Centre Row**: J.S. Smith, A. Lambie, R.J. Gibbons, W.H. Beard, *J. Beaglehole*, J.E. Peers, C.R. Lush, B.C. Jones, S.O'G. Haley, C. Fielder, A.R. Gamble, M.J. Smith, W.P. McCudden, S. Clarke **Front Row:** E.R. Rogers, J.M. Jenkins. *J. Ewings*, I.D. Heppingstone, B.W.J. Clarke, R.J. Kingswell, L.J. Harvey, C.N. Wedge, R.G. Whitfield, P.R. Tomkins, A. Fee, E.L. Nolan, C.L. Heppell, A.P. Spouse

'D' Company

B&W Plate 35

'D' Company No. 13 Platoon

Back Row: R.W. Pratt, *G.L. Parsons*, T.J. Beard, A.H. Carter, R.G. Anderson, _____, R.G. Langdon, E.H. Hunt, G.H. Hicks, A.J. Loller, A. Newton, J.H. Browning, J. McCarthy
Centre Row: T.A. Pascoe, A.T.J. Cato, K. Lally, C.G.Mc Kelly, G.E. Nevile, J.A. Morgan, L.M. MacDonald, W.H. Gibbs, L.G. Gibbs, S.T. Brown, W.F. Baillie, N.J. Venemore,
R.R. Riebe **Front Row**: R.W. Annear, C.G. Quinn, J.Pearce, *R.E. Ardagh*, R.E. Arbery, L. Cody, M.E. Wankey, H. Jacobs, F. Bracklemann, A.F. Shirley, A.G. Saunders, F.T.Tregenza

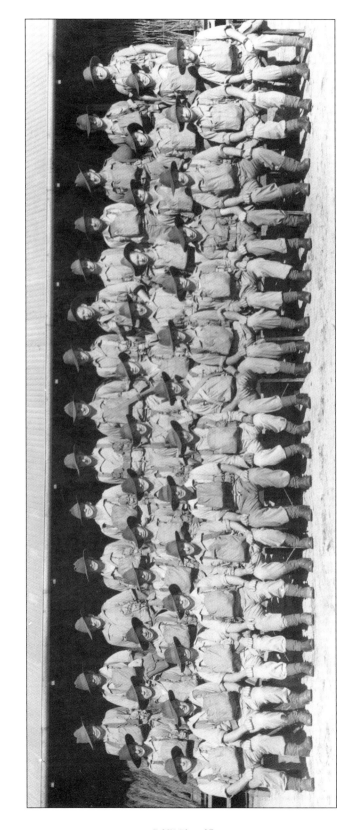

'D' Company No. 14 Platoon

Back Row: *A. Tregillis,* G.V. Hadden, T.H. Edwards, S.A. Osborne, R.S. Barr, W. Hicks, J.P. Clancy, W.L. Thomas, T.A. Wood, D.W. Thomas, B.F. Poulton, J.H. Blackborrow, J.P. O'Meara, T.F. Doyle **Centre Row:** H.J. Worsdell, R.J. Ham, P.L. Westlake, H.A.T. Chilvers, E.J. Hope, A.R. Attenborough, J.E. Smith, A.D. Winter, W.E. Lynn, E.H. Mann, A. Worth, A.J. Jones, T.H. Lewis **Front Row:** *P.G. Moltoni,* B, Evans, A. Cryer, J. MacDonald, W.G.R. Stuart, D.R. Horn, J.V. Colevas, T.H. Tomkins, *A.W.T. Rickard,* H.C. Wells, *H. Turnbull,* L.A. Poyser, I.W. Jones, G. Hancock

'D' Company No. 15 Platoon

Back Row: _____, R.T. Williams, E.J. Leadbitter, E.C. Kemp, F.M. Barrymore, E.T. Hill, D.A. Annear, F.L. Taylor, K.B. Mitchell, R.R. Semple, F. Armstrong, *R.J. Craig,*
J.E. Fraser, A.L. Pitts **Centre Row:** E.G. Moir, G.R. Rouse, _____, P.A. Giese, B.G. Harrison, R.P. Ferguson, _____, L.A. Blair, F.D.J. Clarke, _____, R. Whitford,
G.R. Bousfield, W.J. Beer **Front Row:** C. Holmes, C.J. Spackman, G.T. Shelton, _____, *B.A. Fuller,* J. McSkene, J.T. Meiklejohn, J.F. Solly, J. Thorpe, A.J. Bell, A.L. Tapper,
E.G. Taylor, E. Shackleton, P.A. Gardiner, J.E. Tregenza

B&W Plate 38

Reinforcement Pool Northam 1941
The officer in the front of the column second from right is Lt. Ken Lee. The tall soldier third row back, second from left is believed to be Peter Omiridis. It was from this pool of soldiers that the reinforcements were selected to join the 2/4th Machine Gun Battalion at Fremantle on 16th January 1942

ANZAC Day 1946

Chapter Five

Honours and Awards

WX7852 Acting Corporal Henry Charles Fuhrmann DCM

On 10 February 1942, 'C' Coy came under command 22 Bde. 'A' Pl, which at that time was commanded by A/Cpl. H. C. FUHRMANN, was ordered to defend Adv Bde. HQ. At first light the enemy launched a very heavy attack on the forward Bn. Firing became so intense that A/Cpl. FUHRMANN'S posts were pushed forward. The attack increased in intensity and the forward Bn. was ordered to withdraw and take up a fresh position, with the result that the positions held by A/Cpl. FUHRMANN were now in the front line. The Japanese attacked several times during the day but each time were repulsed. During this action, A/Cpl. FUHRMANN behaved in an outstanding and energetic manner. He fearlessly moved around his posts, directing their fire, encouraging the men and supervising the evacuation of the wounded. Seeing some Indian troops on his flank about to give way, A/Cpl. FUHRMANN rushed across and by his courage and example restored the position. On the 12th February 1942 at ULU PANDAN A/Cpl. FUHRMANN again showed outsanding leadership. A key point in the line had been evacuated and A/Cpl. FUHRMANN was ordered to move forward with two sections and hold it. He held this position for the whole of that day until relieved by his Coy Comd and his behaviour was an inspiration to the men under his command. A/Cpl FUHRMANN'S bearing and behaviour during the whole of the time he was in action was outstanding and worthy of recognition.

Recommended by: A/Maj. C. Cameron O.C. 'C' Coy 2/4 M.G. Bn.
Honour or Award recommended: Distinguished Conduct Medal
Honour or Award granted: Distinguished Conduct Medal
Date of London Gazette: 1st August 1946
Date of Commonwealth of Australia Gazette: 12th September 1946

WX3435 Major Charles Edward Green MBE MID

Major GREEN was a Prisoner of War in Japanese hands from Feb 1942 to August 1945 in Malaya, Burma and Siam. He was a camp commander for nearly the whole of this period. Such a task imposed on him a heavy and continuous mental and physical strain under difficult conditions brought about by brutal and uncivilized Japanese administration and included humiliation and continuous threat of personal violence. Under these conditions Maj. GREEN exhibited marked qualities of leadership, ability, initiative, energy, courage and devotion to duty. Throughout he maintained a determined opposition in endeavouring to modify and resist Japanese demands for sick and dying personnel to do heavy labour. Such work saved many lives.

Recommended by: Maj-Gen C. A. Callaghan. CMG. DSO.VD. 8 Aust Div HQ Melbourne
Honour or Award recommended: Member of the Order of the British Empire
Honour or Award granted: Member of the Order of the British Empire
Date of London Gazette: 6th March 1947
Date of Commonwealth of Australia Gazette: 6th March 1947

His Majesty the King has been graciously pleased to approve of the award 'Mentioned in Despatches' in recognition of gallant and distinguished services in Malaya in 1942.

Honour or Award granted: Mentioned in Despatches
Date of London Gazette: 1st August 1946
Date of Commonwealth of Australia Gazette: 12th September 1946

WX9392 Lieutenant Milton Eric Wankey MC

Lt. WANKEY was O.C. 13 Pl. 2/4 M.G. Bn. and during early action was under command 2/20 Bn. Pl. was sited at the NORTHERN end LIM CHU KANG ROAD. The area was vital to the defence as it was the only solid landing beach in the Bn. sector. During the whole of 8 Feb 1942 the position was subjected to very heavy artillery fire. One gun was put out of action and casualties were heavy. The enemy commenced landing operations at 2130 hrs., barges attempted to land in waves at 10 to 15 minute intervals but were held off by close range M.G. fire and tremendous casualties were inflicted. At 2200 hrs heavy mortar fire caused casualties in the Pl. and Lt. WANKEY himself fired a gun with Pte. LOLLER as his No. 2. They kept this gun in action until 2230 hrs when they were both wounded. Lt. WANKEY was severely wounded in the right knee but remained at his post and controlled the fire of his Pl. until ordered to withdraw by 2/20 Bn. at 0130 hrs. Lt. WANKEY was then evacuated to hospital and later had his leg amputated above the knee. Lt. WANKEY'S devotion to duty, although severely wounded, was an outstanding example of courage, which imbued his men with the determination to hold this key position and so deny the enemy an important bridgehead for a period of four hours.

Recommended by: Major A. J. Cough. Commanding Officer. 'D' Coy 2/4 M.G. Bn.
Honour or Award recommended: Military Cross
Honour or Award granted: Military Cross
Date of London Gazette: 1st August 1946
Date of Commonwealth of Australia Gazette: 12th September 1946

WX16886 Private Arthur Melville Magill MM

Pte. MAGILL A.M. was a member of the 2/4 M.G. Bn. but fought in 'E' Coy. (2/4 M.G. Bn. reinforcements) of the reserve Bn. At BULIM VILLAGE Line on 9th Feb 1942 he was leading his section on a patrol when he encountered an enemy patrol armed with H.M.G. He immediately engaged the enemy and killed five of them. He led his section most gallantly and was wounded in the neck and under the armpit. Three of his section were killed, but he successfully withdrew the remainder to safety. Although wounded, he remained on with his section. At 1430 hrs on 10 Feb 1942 the Bn. withdrew to a position two and a half miles back on the JURONG ROAD. At 0100 hrs on the 11th February 1942, it was realised that the Bn. was surrounded. The Japanese attacked strongly at 0600 hrs when an order for withdrawal was given. During this action, Pte. MAGILL again exhibited splendid powers of leadership. The Bn. was ambushed and had to fight its way out. Pte. MAGILL again led his section with vigour and dash. He was wounded in the hand and had his rifle smashed but continued to fight on by assisting with a Bren gun. Of his section, six were killed and he was wounded three times. This man's comrades spoke very highly of his leadership, and his behaviour throughout the action, despite his wounds, was an outstanding example of courage and devotion to duty.

Recommended by: Major A. E. Saggers. C.O. Reserve Bn.
Honour or Awarded recommended: Distinguished Conduct Medal
Honour or award granted: Military Medal
Date of London Gazette: 1st August 1946
Date of Commonwealth of Australia Gazette: 12th September 1946

WX15743 Private Robert William Ritchie BEM MID

Pte. RITCHIE was the Medical Orderly attached to Capt. C.L. Anderson, M.O. with 3 Bn. 'A' Force. Pte. RITCHIE acted as Medical Orderly during the whole of his POW days. During the whole of this period he displayed outstanding devotion to duty. He worked unceasingly and never spared himself, his personal care and interest was the means of saving many men's lives. He was medical orderly at the notorious 75 and 105 Kilo Camps on the Burma Railway and despite crowded and difficult conditions showed unfailing courage and a quiet determination, which was an inspiration to the sick men in his charge. When cholera broke out at 105 Kilo Camp he immediately volunteered to work in the isolation ward. This work he carried out and worked day and night under extremely grim conditions. He suffered from frequent bouts of malaria but always doggedly carried on with his work. During the whole three and a half years he carried on with his outstandingly good work. He, at all times, set an example of high courage and his quiet determination and absolute reliability was an inspiration to all ranks. He exhibited the same coolness and courage during bombing raids during Nov–Dec 1944 and Jan 1945 at Tamarkan Camp Thailand. This soldier's work during the whole period of captivity is worthy of commendation.

Recommended by: Major C. E. Green C.O. 2/4 M.G. Bn.
Honour or award recommended: British Empire Medal
Honour or Award granted: British Empire Medal
Date of London Gazette: 6th March 1947
Date of Commonwealth of Australia Gazette: 6th March 1947

This soldier acted as Orderly to Capt. C. L. Anderson and showed remarkable devotion to duty. During and after a very heavy artillery bombardment at BUONA VISTA on 15th February 1942, he showed outstanding courage and absolute fearlessness by his care and attention to the wounded. It is recommended that he be granted the award of Mentioned in Dispatches.

Recommended by: Maj-Gen. C. A. Callaghan. CMG. DSO. VD. 8 Aust Div HQ Melbourne
Honour or award recommended: Mentioned in Despatches
Honour or Award granted: Mentioned in Despatches
Date of London Gazette: 1st August 1946
Date of Commonwealth of Australia Gazette: 12th September 1946

WX9336 Sergeant John Gorringe BEM

Sgt. J. GORRINGE was a member of 'F' Force, which moved from Singapore to Thailand in April 1943. I commanded a Coy in this force, which was marched by the Japanese a distance of approximately 190 miles to Shimo Sonkurai Camp. This was a nightmare march through jungle country, with sick men on scanty rations, and morale was stretched to the utmost limits. Sgt. GORRINGE acted as CSM and his conduct and behaviour was an inspiration to all ranks. He never spared himself and his handling and care of tired, dispirited and sick men was worthy of the highest commendation. At Shimo Sonkurai, Sgt. GORRINGE worked in the hospital and upon the outbreak of cholera volunteered to work in the isolation camp. In August 1943 a hospital camp was opened at Tanbaya for 1900 men. Major R. B. Hunt (110 AGH) was S.M.O. In view of Sgt. GORRINGE'S outstanding work he was selected by Major Hunt for work in this camp. He was placed in control (under medical supervision) of 200 cases of tropical ulcers. His devotion to duty and the personal interest and care he took of these sick men was outstanding. He was cheerful under most difficult and trying conditions and his example and firmness was the means of maintaining discipline and morale. I wish to stress that the outstanding qualities of this NCO were maintained throughout the whole of his POW days and he consistently set an example of devotion to duty during difficult and trying times and despite the fact that he himself for quite a long period, suffered from dysentery. I was administering the Ulcer Wards at Tanbaya and Sgt. GORRINGE was Wardmaster of one of them.

Recommended by: Captain G. W. Gwynne C.O. 'D' Coy 2/4 M.G. Bn.
Honour or Award recommended: British Empire Medal
Honour or Award granted: British Empire Medal
Date of London Gazette: 6th March 1947
Date of commonwealth of Australia Gazette: 6th March 1947

WX9553 Lieutenant Charles Newdegate Wedge BEM

Lieutenant Charles Newdegate WEDGE was posted to 110 Perth Military Hospital (Hollywood) as Company Officer with the rank of Captain in December 1945. In the 1969 New Years Honours List he was bestowed with the award of the British Empire Medal for his work with Prisoners of War of the Japanese prior to the cessation of hostilities and on their behalf over two decades at Hollywood Hospital.

Date of London Gazette: 1st January1969
Date of Commonwealth of Australia Gazette: 1st January 1969

WX3464 Captain Claude Anderson A.A.M.C. MID

Capt. ANDERSON was the M.O. attached to 2/4th M.G. Bn. During action on Singapore Island he was outstanding in his tireless devotion to duty. He worked unceasingly and with absolute disregard for his personal safety. At ULU PANDAN on the night of 12/13 February 1942 the Bn. was heavily engaged and practically surrounded by the Japanese. Casualties had been heavy and when a withdrawal order was received from HQ 22 Bde. there was about 40 wounded from various units in the R.A.P. The possibility of being cut off was extremely likely, but Capt. ANDERSON remained at his post and with great calmness and courage successfully organised and carried out the evacuation of the R.A.P. in the face of considerable danger.

At BUONA VISTA on 15 February 1942 the Bn. was subjected to an exceptionally heavy artillery barrage. Many men were severely wounded and owing to the situation quick evacuation was impossible. A Japanese attack appeared imminent, but Capt. ANDERSON realising the position doubled forward from his R.A.P. to the forward posts to attend to the seriously wounded. In this action he showed great courage, and it was a typical example of his bearing under fire and his complete disregard for personal danger.

Recommended by: Major C. E. Green C.O. 2/4th M.G. Bn. 17th December 1945
Honour or Award recommended: Member of the Order of the British Empire
Honour or Award granted: Mentioned in Despatches
Date of London Gazette: 6th March 1947
Date of Commonwealth of Australia Gazette: 6th March 1947

WX3376 Lieutenant-Colonel Michael Joseph Anketell MID

His majesty the King has been graciously pleased to approve of the award Mentioned in Despatches in recognition of gallant and distinguished service in Malaya 1942.

Honour or Award recommended: Mentioned in Despatches
Date of London gazette: 1st August 1946
Date of commonwealth of Australia Gazette; 12th September 1946

WX3451 Major Colin Cameron MID

His Majesty the King has been graciously pleased to approve of the award 'Mentioned in Despatches' in recognition of services rendered whilst a POW in Japanese hands.

Honour or Award granted: Mentioned in Despatches
Date of London Gazette: 6th March 1947
Date of Commonwealth of Australia Gazette: 6th March 1947

WX8617 Corporal James John Dore MID

His Majesty the King has been graciously pleased to approve of the award Mentioned in Despatches in recognition of services rendered whilst a POW in Japanese hands.

Honour or Award granted: Mentioned in Despatches
Date of London Gazette: 6th March 1947
Date of Commonwealth Gazette: 6th March 1947

WX7777 Corporal Arthur Montague Draper MID

His Majesty the King has been graciously pleased to approve of the award Mentioned in Despatches in recognition of services rendered whilst a POW in Japanese hands.

Honour or award granted: Mentioned in Despatches
Date of London Gazette: 6th March 1947
Date of Commonwealth of Australia Gazette: 6th March 1947

WX3450 Captain George Whittindale Gwynne MID

His Majesty the King has been graciously pleased to approve of the award Mentioned in Despatches in recognition of services rendered whilst a POW in Japanese hands.

Honour or Award granted: Mentioned in Despatches
Date of London Gazette: 6th March 1947
Date of Commonwealth of Australia Gazette: 6th March 1947

WX8377 Sergeant Kenneth Thomas MacLennan MID

Sgt. MacLENNAN was Pl. Sgt. of 4 Pl. 'A' Coy. On the night of 12/13 February 1942 his Pl. Comd., Lt. Manning was killed. Sgt. MacLENNAN commanded the Pl. from then on and showed outstanding ability and energy. He was wounded but remained on duty. He set an exceptionally high example of courage and was absolutely fearless. His command of the Pl. was excellent and his leadership was marked. Had circumstances been otherwise it is felt that he certainly would have reached a commissioned rank. It is recommended that he be granted the award of Mentioned in Despatches.

Recommended by: Maj-Gen C. A. Callaghan. CMG. DSO. VD. 8 Aust Div HQ Melbourne
Honour or Award recommended: Mentioned in Despatches
Honour or Award granted: Mentioned in Despatches
Date of London Gazette: 1st August 1946
Date of Commonwealth of Australia Gazette: 12th September 1946

WX8611 Sergeant Laurence James McGrath MID

This man serving as a member of the 43rd Landing Craft Coy went into the flames of a burning barge following an explosion to rescue an unconscious soldier.

Honour or Award granted: Mentioned in Despatches
Date of London Gazette: 14th February 1946
Date of Commonwealth of Australia Gazette: 21st February 1946

Members of the 2/4th Machine Gun Battalion who received nominations for the British Empire Medal, not Awarded

WX12765 Private Philip James Beilby
WX9223   Private Harold Thomas Bunker
WX16369 Private Alfred John Cocking
WX7268   Private Frederick Victor Cross
WX7123   Lance/Sergeant Robert Douglas Hampson
WX17452 Private Laurence Daniel Kearney

WX7409   Private Thomas Anthony Pascoe
WX9055   Private Harry Pickett
WX16424 Private Alfred Sing
WX8110   Private Alfred Daly Winter
WX10373 Private Walter Victor Winter

THE ABOVE SOLDIER, was a member of the party of Ps.O.W. which embarked in a Japanese ship at Singapore on 4 Sept 1944 for transfer to Japan. The ship that they were in was torpedoed at about 0530 hrs on 12 Sept 1944. The Japanese panicked and without showing the slightest interest in the Ps.O.W. deserted the ship in the lifeboats. The Ps.O.W. showing amazing control and discipline threw all rafts and wooden articles, which would float overboard and then progressively made an orderly evacuation of the ship. Depth charges were dropped by the escorting Japanese destroyer affecting many men struggling in the sea. The Japanese then proceeded to rescue their own nationals and when this had been done waved derisively to the Ps.O.W. who showed their magnificent spirit by singing "Rule Britannia". THE ABOVE SOLDIER spent four to five nightmare days on the raft with his comrades. After years of exhausting work on the Burma Railway, in an emaciated state from the conditions under which they had existed on the Japanese transport, covered with filthy oil, without clothing and exposed to the elements for four days and nights without a scrap of food or a drop of water, these men displayed dauntless courage and amazing endurance. It was the outstanding and intrepid spirit of THE ABOVE SOLDIER and his comrades that enabled them to survive this terrifying ordeal, until rescued by a U.S. submarine. As a result of their tenacity and courage they were the means of conveying to Australia the condition of the Ps.O.W. in Japanese hands thereby rendering a very great service.

Recommended by: Major C. E. Green C.O. 2/4 M.G. Bn.

Officers recommended for the Military Cross, not awarded

WX3707 Lieutenant Graham Charles MacKinnon

Lt. MacKINNON was O.C. 8 Pl. 2/4 M.G. Bn. and on 11th February 1942 came under the command 'D' Coy 2/30 Bn. 'D' Coy's position at this time was at the MANDAI CROSSROADS and was responsible for protection right flank 2/30 BN. Lt MacKINNON'S energy and actions at this stage were outstanding and he set a fine example to the men under his command. On the morning 12 Feb 1942, 'D' Coy was acting as rearguard for the withdrawal of 2/30 Bn. which was to carry out a counter attack at BUKIT PANJANG, when the enemy launched a heavy attack on 'D' Coy's position. Lt. MacKINNON'S Pl. had been ordered to withdraw, but when the attack developed he brought his guns back from the truck at great speed and under heavy fire. The guns were re-mounted and he kept them in action and controlled them, and despite casualties and heavy fire, kept them in action for nearly two hours. Lt. MacKINNON during this action was absolutely fearless in his actions. When it was found that an Indian Regt. on 'D' Coy's right flank had withdrawn orders were issued to withdraw the Coy. Lt. MacKINNON'S Pl. covered the withdrawal and remained in action until every man of the Coy had withdrawn. Lt. MacKINNON by this time was practically surrounded. He made every effort to destroy his guns but finally had to withdraw in the face of extremely heavy fire. His Pl. Sgt. was killed and the final withdrawal of his men across the BUKIT MANDAI was an outstanding example of leadership and courage.

Recommended by: Captain E. Booth C.O. 'D' Coy 2/30 Bn.

WX228 Lieutenant David Victor Mentiplay

Lt. D. V. MENTIPLAY was a reinforcement officer of the 2/4 M.G. Bn., seconded to Reserve Bn. where he acted as I.O. During the action, he acted with the utmost coolness and courage. On the morning of the 10th February, Reserve Bn. and British Bn. were holding the Japanese attack astride the JURONG ROAD. Orders were received to withdraw and Lt. MENTIPLAY was ordered to make certain that 'E' Coy, junctioned and made contact with 'A' Coy. He displayed great courage and carried out this task with complete disregard of personal danger. Shortly afterwards the Bn. was practically surrounded and were forced to fight their way clear. During this action Lt. MENTIPLAY saw a Japanese soldier bayoneting one of our wounded, he rushed at the Japanese and received a bayonet thrust through the neck. He threw himself backwards off the bayonet and while on the ground shot the Japanese with his pistol. He was then surrounded, he shot four more Japanese and flung the empty pistol at an L.M.G. crew who, apparently thinking it was a grenade, scattered. Lt. MENTIPLAY then jumped into a native duck pond where he concealed himself until the attack passed on. This action took place on 11th February 1942 about one mile SOUTH of BUKIT TIMAH VILLAGE. Lt. MENTIPLAY made his way back through the Japanese lines to our own lines where he collapsed from his wound. Throughout this action his conduct displayed outstanding courage and bravery.

Recommended by: Major A. E. Saggers. C.O. Reserve Bn.

Officers, NCO's and Other Ranks recommended or nominated for Mentioned in Despatches, not awarded

WX3452 Captain Gavin McRae Bunning

Capt. BUNNING was O.C. 'B' Coy 2/4 M.G. Bn. and came under command 27 Aust. Inf. Bde. Comd Brigadier D. S. MAXWELL. A letter was sent from Brigadier MAXWELL to Maj-Gen. C. A. Callaghan recommending Capt. BUNNING for the award of Mentioned in Despatches.

WX5425 Corporal Thomas Martin Fitzgerald

The above-mentioned NCO was the Coy Cpl. Cook. When the fight for Singapore started he armed himself with a Bren gun, which he used most effectively, and accounted for many of the enemy. He led several patrols into Japanese territory causing loss to them. I consider that his conduct deserves recognition and recommend that he be Mentioned in Despatches.

Recommended by: Major C. E. Green C.O. 2/4 M.G. Bn.

WX9418 Corporal Douglas Radcliffe Horn

Cpl. HORN was a Sec. Comd. In 14 Pl. At all times during action he showed outstanding leadership. During heavy shelling at BUONA VISTA it became necessary for him to assume temporary command of his Pl. He accepted responsibility with calmness and showed complete fearlessness. He carried out all tasks with grim determination and at all times was a fine example to the men of his section.
It is recommended that he be granted the award of Mentioned in Despatches.

Recommended by: Major C. E. Green C.O. 2/4 M.G. Bn.

WX10931 Private Laurence Slade Hummerston

This soldier served in a very soldierly and courageous manner right through the fighting on Singapore Island. He was a Bren gunner and his personal bag of Japanese was extremely high. I personally saw him decimate what looked like a Pl. of Japanese sheltering near a house. The distance was too great to count the bodies but he got most of them. When targets became hard to get he did not hesitate to go looking for them. He was very courageous with plenty of initiative and continued so until ordered to lay down his arms at capitulation. I consider his conduct to be worthy of recognition and recommend that he be Mentioned in Despatches.

Recommended by: Major C. E. Green C.O. 2/4 M.G. Bn.

WX8790 Private William McEwen

This soldier was the water duty man with HQ Coy. The water supply was poor and difficult to obtain, but Pte. McEWEN with dogged determination overcame all difficulties and never failed with the supply of water to the troops. Owing to continued low flying attacks by enemy aircraft, movement of any description was extremely hazardous, but Pte. McEWEN displayed utter fearlessness and with complete disregard of his own personal safety continued with the supply of water to positions however widely dispersed. His devotion to duty was outstanding and was an inspiration to the troops. It is recommended that he be granted the award of Mentioned in Despatches.

Recommended by: Major C. E. Green C.O. 2/4 M.G. Bn.

WX10561 Sergeant Robert George Whitfield

On 12 February 1942 at ULU PANDAN Sgt. WHITFIELD was commanding a Pl. in a forward position. This position was heavily shelled and then attacked by the Japanese. Three successive attacks were thrown back with heavy loss. This was largely due to the leadership of Sgt. WHITFIELD, who by his courage and coolness under heavy fire and pressure from superior numbers set an example of steadiness to his men. His whole behaviour during action was characterised by utter fearlessness and devotion to duty. It is recommended that he be granted the award Mentioned in Despatches.

Recommended by: Major C. E. Green C.O. 2/4 M.G. Bn.

WX9394 Lieutenant J. G. Wilson

During the fighting on the JURONG Road on 12 Feb 1942 and the following day at REFORMATORY Road, Lt. WILSON handled his platoon with outstanding ability. By his fearlessness he set a fine example to his men and the good work done by this Pl. was largely due to his leadership. Although holding an exposed position at REFORMATORY Road under continual mortar and machine gun fire, Lt. WILSON maintained his position most determinedly and repulsed all attacks until he was badly wounded and evacuated to hospital. His conduct was such that it is recommended that he be granted the award of Mentioned in Despatches.

Recommended by: Major C. E. Green C.O. 2/4 M.G. Bn.

Members of the 2/4th Machine Gun Battalion who received Honours or Awards during the First World War

WX11046 Lieutenant Leslie Gordon Riches MC

This officer served as a Lieutenant and original member of the 11th Battalion Regt. No. 925. Lt. Riches participated in the first Landing at Gallipoli and is therefore an original Anzac.

His citation reads:

On 11th August 1918, near Lihons, when the left flank was held up by a strong enemy post and machine-gun nest, he was then sent forward with a party of men from Headquarter's details to dislodge the enemy. He repeatedly led the men against the enemy position, bombing them down the trench, putting an enemy machine-gun post out of action, and capturing the machine-gun. Later, with the assistance of trench-mortar fire, he rushed and captured the enemy position, thus enabling the flank to advance, and allowing the battalion on our left flank to come forward and line up. Throughout the operation he showed conspicuous gallantry and ability to command.

Date of London Gazette: 1st February 1919
Date of Commonwealth of Australia Gazette: 3rd June 1919

WX14495 Private William George Raymond Stuart MM

This soldier served as a Corporal with both the 16th and 48th Battalions Regt. No. 1349. William served with the 16th Battalion at Gallipoli before being transferred to France in 1916. He was taken on battalion strength with the 48th Battalion on 3rd May1917. This soldier received a recommendation on 12th August 1918 for his work on the 8th and 9th August 1918 at Proyart, France. He was also wounded at Hill 63 after Messiness Ridge receiving gunshot wounds to the left thigh and foot. He also served as a S/Sgt. with the 16th Battalion militia as a Vickers machine gun instructor before enlisting for the 2nd A.I.F.

Recommended by: Lt. R. Potts
Date of London Gazette: 24th January 1919
Date of Commonwealth of Australian Gazette: 23rd May 1919

WX13977 RSM George Frederick Airey MM

This NCO served during WWI with the 1/5th East Lancashire Regt. No.203106 in France and at Chanak Turkey with the British army of occupation. During World War One he was recommended for an award for his actions on the night of 18th–19th June 1917 and was awarded the Military Medal.

WX7620 Private Thomas Henry Edwards MM

This soldier served in the British Army in WWI with the Lancashire Fusiliers with the Regt. No. 52912. He was awarded the Military Medal for:

Conspicuous bravery and devotion to duty during the British offensive in the Foret de Mormon on 4th November 1918. In spite of very heavy shell and machine gun fire and numerous casualties this man carried on his duties of runner and guide with great courage for four hours continuously. By his action he maintained communication and was of the greatest assistance in assuring the success of this attack in his sector.

WX15720 Warrant Officer Class 2 Stanley Scott McNeil MM

This NCO served in WWI in the British Army with the Cheshire Regiment, Regt. No. 201075 in the Egyptian Campaign against the Turks. On 4th November 1917 he volunteered with Private Greenwood who fired the gun whilst McNeil held up the enemy with bombs. When the operation was completed McNeil retrieved a Lewis gun that had been impossible to recover during the day owing to heavy enemy fire.

Private Harold Ockerby

Members

who

served

during

World

War

One

Lt. Leslie G. Riches MC

Able Seaman Tom Firns

Sapper Daniel A. C. Quinn

Stan McNeil MM

Thomas Edwards MM

Members of the 2/4th Machine Gun Battalion known to have served with either Australian or British Services during the First World War

WX3376 Lieutenant-Colonel M. J. Anketell

Served as a Lieutenant with 'B' Coy, 44th Battalion France, Regimental No. 3009.

WX8098 Warrant Officer Class 2 William Burgess

Served with the British Army. No other details are known.

WX9316 Private Albert Brooksbank

Served with the West Yorkshire Yeomanry 'Prince of Wales Own 14th of Foot' and transferred to the 7th Armoured Car Company Royal Tank Corps. Soldier served in India for seven years.

WX3451 Major Colin Cameron

Served as Trooper George Clowes Voege Regt. No. 1563A with the 3rd Camel Regiment, the 8th and 4th Australian Light Horse Regiments. Colin was on regimental strength when the mounted charge took place at Beersheba on 31st October 1917 against fortified Turkish positions. He was wounded in action (date unknown) receiving a bullet in the base of the spine. After the First War Colin served as a Captain with the 10th Australian Light Horse Regiment before resigning his commission to enlist in the 2nd A.I.F. with the 2/16th Battalion. He attended the NCO school at Randwick, N.S.W. but was unable to continue with his service due to the wound he had received during his First War service. He then rejoined the 10th Australian Light Horse Regiment before enlisting for a second time in the 2nd A.I.F. whence he became a member of the 2/4th Machine Gun Battalion.

WX5088 Private Andrew Fee

This soldier is known to have served with the Royal Inniskilling Fusiliers and because of his age it is possible that this service was during World War One. No other details are known.

WX8874 Private Alexander William Findlay

This soldier served with the 51st Highland Division in France during World War One. He was also a POW having been captured by the Germans.

WX7225 Private Thomas Firns

This soldier had enlisted in the Royal Australian Navy on 30th September 1918. He served as a stoker, Service No. 6880 at HMAS Cerebus, Westernport Bay Victoria. He also served onboard the HMAS *Melbourne* and HMAS *Sydney* until he received a medical discharge on 9th September 1920.

WX7801 Private Albert Hackshaw

This soldier served with the 28th Battalion, Regt. No. 52068.

WX12157 Private Edward Charles Hardey

This soldier enlisted at Blackboy Hill on 27th August 1917. He departed Australia onboard the HMT *Ormonde* with the 22nd reinforcements for the 28th Battalion, Regt. No. 7310. Edward joined the 51st Battalion on 4th June 1918 with whom he remained with until his discharge on 19th September 1919. He was wounded in the left buttock during his WWI service. Whilst in action on Singapore he was again wounded, this time in the right buttock.

WX8207 Warrant Officer Class 2 Arthur Sidney Hewby

This NCO had worked his way through the ranks to eventually be promoted to 2nd Lieutenant with the 44th Battalion in France. He enlisted for the First War on 24th March 1916 and left Australia with the 7th reinforcements for the 44th Battalion and carried the Regt. No. 1840. He was wounded in action on 20th October 1917 receiving a gunshot wound to the left side.

WX8327 Private Charles Henry Ironmonger

This soldier is believed to have served with the British Army in France with the 11th Essex Regiment as well as the Scottish Rifles (Cameronians). No other details are known.

WX8702 Private Gilbert Japp

This soldier served in the Royal flying Corps as an AC II Class from 1919–1920.

WX8243 Sergeant Ambrose McQuade

This NCO served as a private with the 11th Battalion with the Regt. No. 1590. He was wounded at Gallipoli receiving a gunshot wound to the chest and lung. He was then transferred to the 51st Battalion fighting in France then to the 13th Machine Gun Company that later became the 4th Machine Gun Battalion. Like many First War veterans he stated that he had no previous military service when he enlisted for the second time on 16th August 1940.

WX7336 Private Harold Bertram Ockerby

This soldier enlisted on 11th December 1917 embarking on HMT *Ormonde* on 13th March 1918 with the 22nd reinforcements for the 28th Battalion, Regt. No. 7338. He was transferred to the 51st Battalion with whom he fought in France until the end of the war. Harold was Lt-Col Anketell's driver both men being World War One veterans having fought in France.

WX5123 Private John Stanley Pass

This soldier served with the Royal Marine Artillery from 1916-1923 and onboard the HMS *Hood*. He also served in the Militia, presumably in Australia from 1932-1940 before enlisting in the 2nd A.I.F.

WX5054 Private Daniel Adair Cormack Quinn

This soldier enlisted from the West Australian gold mining town of Kalgoorlie with the A.I.F. on 21st January 1916 and served as a sapper with the 2nd Tunnelling Coy with the Regt. No. 856. He was blown up at Sallon Farm in September 1916 whence he was invalided back to England. He was involved in the mining at Charleroi in Belgium in 1918 and was invalided out of the A.I.F with a tumour on 18th August 1919.

WX9385 Warrant Officer Class 2 James Unsworth

This NCO served with the British Army with the (Duke of Cambridge's Own) Middlesex Regiment (The Diehards) with the Regt. No. 4720. He was wounded three times at Mons where this unit suffered many casualties. He also had previous service in Australia with the 28th Battalion militia.

WX7166 Private Herbert Stanley Werrett

This soldier served in France with the 28th Battalion with the Regt. No. 7386. He also sailed on the HMT *Ormonde* with the 22nd reinforcement that also included Harold Ockerby and Edward Hardey. He was discharged on 17th October 1919.

WX6958 Private John Young

This soldier enlisted on 7th December 1917 and served with the Royal Flying Corps in WWI as a fitter-armourer with No.'s 176 and 274 Squadrons. At the end of the war he served with Palestine Brigade H.Q. and then No.'s 111 and 14 Squadrons achieving the rank of AC 1st Class. He was eventually discharged in July 1926, having experienced first hand the formation of the Royal Air Force. His Service No. was 157766, being a high number because like most fledgling air forces it was still part of the army. This soldier died at Nacompaton in Thailand on the last day of the Second World War on 15th August 1945. He also holds the distinction of being the last man listed on the 2/4th Machine Gun Battalion's Honour Roll.

Members of the 2/4th Machine Gun Battalion who served with the British Commonwealth Occupation Forces Japan or in Korea

WX10609 Sergeant John 'Des' Verdun Colevas

This NCO spent 12 months after the war as guard sergeant at Marrinup Prisoner of War Camp before embarking for Japan with the BCOF with the 66th Battalion. He served in Korea as a Warrant Officer Class 2 and C.S.M. 'D' Coy 3rd Battalion RAR from 1950–1951. He left 3 RAR to return to Australia and became a National Service instructor,. Regt. No. 5/250

WX12427 Private Robert Arthur Foster

This soldier enlisted on 15th August 1950 and was discharged on 10th November 1953. He was wounded in North Korea at 0630 hours on 24th April 1951 receiving a gunshot wound to the left thigh and shrapnel wounds to the right knee and left elbow as well as a slight concussion. He was evacuated to Seoul and then to Kure in Japan where he spent 5 weeks convalescing. His Regt. No.'s were 5/4000058 and 5/2305.

WX7697 Corporal Ronald Ralph Jeffery

This soldier re-enlisted and served with the BCOF at Kure in Japan. His Regt. No. on enlistment was WX500151. Ron went on to the rank of Warrant Officer serving with an Australian Army medical unit.

WX16236 Private Alfred Victor King
a.k.a. Albert John King

This soldier enlisted on 9th August 1950 and landed in Korea on 28th September 1950. He served with the Special Forces Unit 3 RAR and was killed in action on 8th November 1950 after only 42 days in action. His Regt. No. was 5/400008. His remains are buried at the:

United Nations Memorial Pusan Korea.
Sukchon Cemetery
Portion 2, Plot and Row 11, Grave 126

WX228 Lieutenant David Victor Mentiplay

This Officer served with the BCOF from 1947–1949 with the 67th Infantry Battalion and the 3rd Battalion, Royal Australian Regiment.

WX8952 Private Robert Ronald Riebe

This soldier served with the BCOF in Japan. His Regt. No. was WX501060. He was discharged on 9th March 1949.

Chapter Six

The Vickers Machine Gun

The Vickers Mark 1 (Class C) machine was the primary weapon of Australian medium machine gun battalions during the First and Second World Wars. Prior to the First World War, Vickers, Son & Maxim Ltd had manufactured the standard medium machine gun in British service until Hiram Maxim, an American and inventor of the Maxim gun retired in 1911. It was then that the commercial alliance became Vickers Ltd who modified the design and came up with the new Vickers Maxim machine gun that was adopted in November 1912. This weapon saw extensive service with Australian Machine Gun Companies on the Western Front during the First World War. These companies were later formed into Machine Gun Battalions as the worth of this weapon was quickly appreciated. One Vickers machine gun was equivalent to 50 good riflemen and could deliver devastating firepower against an advancing enemy.

The Vickers medium machine gun consists of:

1. The gun, .303 in calibre weighing 42lbs with 7 pints of water in the barrel.
2. The tripod with it its two vernier dials that allow traverse and elevation. Weight 42lbs.
3. The ammunition belt. The ammunition box filled weighed about 21lbs.
4. Instruments.

The gun is water cooled, the barrel being encased in a water jacket that is fitted with filler and drain plugs. The gun carries its own supply of fresh water in a condenser can. As the gun fires it boils the water to create steam which is carried away by means of a steam tube through and an escape hole along a condenser tube to the condenser can. This is an advantage when fresh water is not available.

The tripod consists of a crosshead and elevating gear and wheel. The crosshead pivots in a socket that has three folding legs that were secured by clutch plates. The tripod at 42lbs is a weapon within itself. It was an ungainly creature that the Vickers machine gunners affectionately called the iron octopus. The gun is mounted by opening out the legs of the tripod whilst at the same time supporting the crosshead at the required height. Once the feet of the tripod are securely on the ground the apparatus is secured by tightening the jamming handles.

The gun is secured to the tripod at the crosshead by both the crosshead and elevating joint pins. A direction dial calibrated in degrees is fitted on the socket and this is used in conjunction with an index on the crosshead. The crosshead is held in position by the traversing clamp on the front of the socket. Elevation of the gun is varied by rotating the elevating gear on the tripod by turning the elevating hand wheel thereby the worm screws are extended or contracted thus lowering or raising the muzzle of the gun.

The Vickers machine gun has two rates of fire:
Rapid fire at one belt or 250 rounds per minute, or Normal fire at one belt every two minutes, or 125 rounds per minute. The gun is usually fired at a rate of 250 rounds or one belt per minute, however the gun was generally fired in short service bursts. A service burst is 25 rounds under all conditions, except when on firing on fixed lines, or at a moving target, when it is 50 rounds. With a cyclic rate of 600 rounds per minute the expenditure of ammunition is something that needs to be carefully monitored. Normally 14 belts of ammunition are carried with the gun, amounting to 3,500 rounds with a reserve of 4,500 rounds. The belts are manufactured from canvass and may be reloaded by spare gun numbers for reuse. Ammunition used is the standard Mark VII .303 bullet that is the same round that is fired from the Lee Enfield rifle. Maximum range with this ammunition is 2,700 yards or 2,430 metres.

During the Second World War Mark VIIIZ ammunition was used which allowed the gun to shoot over a greater distance, to at least 4,050 metres. With the Mark VIIIZ ammunition, a different calibration was necessary on the back sight and different range tables were also required to be used.

The Gun Team

There are five men in a Vickers machine gun team and each one must be capable of replacing a gun number who becomes a casualty. When ordered to **Take Post,** No. 1 goes to the tripod, No. 2 to the gun and No. 3 to the condenser can and ammunition. They examine their respective gear and then if correct report **All Correct**. On the order **Mount Gun,** No. 1 mounts the tripod, No. 2 comes forward and mounts the gun on the tripod and No. 3 brings the ammunition and the condenser can. The gun is now ready to begin firing with No. 1 behind the gun, No. 2 on the right hand side to feed the ammunition and No. 3 takes up a position to right and rear of the gun. The spare gun No.'s 4 and 5 stand by and form a chain of supply from the transport. If the supply of ammunition belts becomes critical it is possible that spare numbers will reload the fabric belts with reserve supplies of .303 ammunition.

The ammunition belt is fed into the guide on the right hand side. The crank handle located on the right hand side of the weapon is pulled back to accept the first cartridge which is pulled through by means of a tab on the ammunition belt. Once the first .303 cartridge is engaged by the pawls, the crank handle is pulled back for a second time. The gun is now cocked and ready to fire and is done so by depressing the firing lever which in turn releases the firing pin in the lock and fires the gun. When the gun is mounted, loaded and laid, fire can be opened immediately which is intense and accurate, that can surprise and temporarily demoralise the enemy. Machine gunners need to be well acquainted with the technical workings of the gun and be able to maintain continued firing of the gun except where unavoidable stoppages like blockages or breakages occur and render the weapon unserviceable.

The Organisation of a 2nd A.I.F. Medium Machine Gun Battalion 1939–1945

Machine Gun Battalions are corps troops that are provided on a scale of one per division. They are fully mechanised with both men and weapons being carried in motor transport. Each battalion consists of Battalion Headquarters, Headquarters Company and four Machine Gun Companies.

Battalion Headquarters includes the headquarters staff, medical section and regimental police. Although an Intelligence Officer is provided there is no intelligence section.

Headquarters Companies consist of:

No. 1 Platoon – *Signals*
No. 2 Platoon – *Protection*

This platoon is equipped with four Bren .303 L.M.G.s for anti-aircraft and ground defence, four Boyes anti-tank rifles [1] and each of the four trucks allocated to this platoon carried a motley mounting.

No. 3 Platoon – *Administrative*

There are four Vickers machine gun companies. Each company has its own headquarters and consists of three platoons organised as such:

'A' Company Headquarters and No.'s 4, 5, 6 Platoons
'B' Company Headquarters and No.'s 7, 8, 9 Platoons
'C' Company Headquarters and No.'s 10, 11, 12 Platoons
'D' Company Headquarters and No.'s 13, 14, 15 Platoons [2]

Each Machine Gun Platoon consists of two sections each with two Vickers machine guns giving the battalion a total of forty-eight Vickers machine guns. The No.'s 1 and 2 on the gun are issued with revolvers but in the case of the 2/4th Machine Gun Battalion these were never issued. Each platoon is equipped with a Boyes Anti-Tank rifle. For each platoon six 15cwt trucks are provided. This gives each Company a total of twenty-one vehicles.

The battalion is organised by attaching certain personnel from Battalion Headquarters and the Headquarters Companies to the Machine Gun Companies to enable each Machine Gun Company to be self-contained administratively.

The battalion transport includes 122 vehicles as well as motorcycles, which explains the high number of driver trade groupings in the battalion. The handling of all these vehicles is important to the efficiency of the battalion and so the Transport Sergeant and Corporals and the Light Aid Detachment (L.A.D.) who service these vehicles have a big responsibility resting upon their shoulders to ensure the serviceability of the battalion's transport.

---

[1] No Boyes Anti-Tank rifles were issued to the 2/4th Machine Gun Battalion.
[2] For the defence of the west coast of Singapore, a No. 16 Platoon was formed from the Fremantle reinforcements and spare numbers from 'D' Company.

Battalion Headquarters

Officers

Commanding Officer–Lieutenant Colonel (1)   Second-in-Command–Major (1)

Adjutant–Captain x 1   Intelligence Officer–Lieutenant (1)

Warrant Officers

Regimental Sergeant Major–W.O. I (1)

Sergeants

Orderly Room Sergeants (2)   Provost Sergeant (1)

Sergeant i/c stretcher-bearers (1)

Corporals (1)

Privates (27)

Attached Personnel

A.A.M.C. Regimental Medical Officer–Captain (1)

Total Personnel (38)

Headquarters Company x 3 Platoons

Company Headquarters

Officers

Commanding Officer–Captain (1)

Warrant Officers

Company Sergeant Major (1)   Company Quartermaster Sergeant (1)

Privates (3)

Total Personnel (6)

No. 1 Platoon Signals

Officers

Commanding Officer–Lieutenant (1)

Sergeants (1)

Corporals (1)

Privates (26)

Total Personnel (29)

No. 2 Platoon Anti-Aircraft

Officers
Commanding Officer–Lieutenant (1)

Sergeants (1)
Corporals (1)
Privates (14)

Total Personnel (17)

No. 3 Platoon-Administrative

Officers
Quartermaster–Captain (1)   Lieutenant (1)

Warrant Officers
Regimental Quartermaster Sergeant (1)

Sergeants
Pioneer Sergeant (1)   Sergeant Cook (1)
Transport Sergeant (1)   Technical Stores Sergeant (1)

Corporals (4)
Privates (51)

Total Personnel (62)

Attached Personnel

Sergeants A.A.O.C. Armourer (2)   **Electrician** (1)
Fitters Motor Transport (4)   **Fitter Motor Transport** (Sergeant) (1)
Shoemaker (1)   **A.A.P.C.** (Postal) Sergeant (1)

Total Personnel including No. 3 Platoon (72)

Machine Gun Company Headquarters (4)

Officers
Commanding Officer Captains or Majors (1)   **Second-in-Command**–Captain (1)

Warrant Officers
Company Sergeant Major (1)

Sergeants
Company Quartermaster Sergeant (1)

Corporals (1)
Privates (21)

Total Personnel (26)

Machine Gun Platoons (12) – Machine Gun Sections (24)

Platoon Headquarters (4 x 1)

Officers

Commanding Officer–Lieutenant (1)

Sergeant Technical Stores (1)
Privates (6)

Total Personnel (8)

Machine Gun Platoons (12 x 1)

Sergeants (1)
Corporals (3)
Privates (28)

Total Platoon Personnel (40)

Total Personnel on Battalion Strength all Ranks (746)

The Distribution of Personnel by Trade Grouping

Trade Group I

Bricklayers (2)   No. 3 Platoon Administrative (2)

Trade Group II

Carpenters (3)	No. 3 Platoon Administrative (3)
Cooks (20)	No. 3 Platoon Administrative (4)
	Machine Gun Company Headquarters (4 x 4)
Mechanics (4)	Machine Gun Company Headquarters (4)
Signallers (20)	No. 1 Platoon Signals (20)

Trade Group III

Butcher (1)	No. 3 Platoon Administrative (1)
Clerks (9)	Battalion Headquarters (2)
	Headquarters Company (1)
	No. 3 Platoon Administrative (2)
	Machine Gun Company Headquarters (1 x 4)
Driver Mechanics (15)	No. 3 Platoon Administrative (3)
	Machine Gun Company (3 x 4)
Equipment Repairers (1)	No. 3 Platoon Administrative (1)
Rangetakers (24)	Machine Gun Sections (2 x 12)
Technical Storemen (6)	No. 3 Platoon Administrative (2)
	Machine Gun Company Headquarters (1 x 4)

The Distribution of Non-Trades Personnel

A.A.L.M.G. Detachments (13)	No. 2 Platoon
Ammunition Numbers (16)	Machine Gun Company Headquarters (4 x 4)
Batmen (31)	Battalion Headquarters (6)
	Headquarters Company (1)
	No. 1 Platoon Signals (1)
	No. 2 Platoon Anti-Aircraft (1)
	No. 3 Platoon Administrative (2)
	Machine Gun Company Headquarters (2 x 4)
	Machine Gun Platoons (1 x 12)
Drivers MT (105)	No. 3 Platoon Administrative (25)
	Company Headquarters (5 x 4)
	Platoon Headquarters (1 x 4)
	Machine Gun Platoons (4 x 14)
General Duties Officer's Mess (1)	No. 3 Platoon Administrative
General Duties Sergeant's Mess (1)	No. 3 Platoon Administrative
Medical Officer's Orderly (1)	Battalion Headquarters
Machine Gun Detachments (276)	Machine Gun Company (4 x 69)
Motor Cyclist Orderlies (27)	No. 1 Platoon Signals (6)
	No. 2 Platoon Anti-Aircraft (1)
	Machine Gun Company Headquarters (2 x 4)
	Machine Gun Platoon Headquarters (1 x 4)
	Machine Gun Platoons (2 x 4)
Orderlies (24)	Machine Gun Platoons (2 x 12)
Postmen (1)	No. 3 Administrative Platoon
Regimental Police (3)	Battalion Headquarters
Sanitary Duties (4)	No. 3 Platoon Administrative
Scouts (24)	Machine Gun Platoon Headquarters (2 x 12)
Storemen Non-Technical (6)	Headquarters Company (1)
	No. 3 Platoon Administrative (1)
	Machine Gun Company Headquarters (1 x 4)
Stretcher Bearers (16)	Battalion Headquarters
Transport Corporals (4)	Machine Gun Company Headquarters (1 x 4)
Water Duties (2)	No. 3 Platoon Administrative

Total of all on Strength Ranks Technical and Non-Technical (660)

Australian Army Ordnance Corps Attached

Sergeants (3)
Corporals (1)
Lance Corporals (1)
Privates (4)

Total Personnel all ranks (9)

88th Light Aid Detachment (L.A.D.)

Attached A.A.O.C. Personnel Technical

Commanding Officer–Captain x 1   **Warrant Officer Class 2** x 1

Staff Sergeants x 1

Corporals x 1

Privates x 10

Total Personnel all Ranks (14)

War Establishment of an A.I.F. Machine Gun Battalion

Pistols .455 inch	176	**Machine Guns** (Vickers) .303 inch	48
Rifles .303 inch	570	**Pistols Signal**	24
Anti Tank Rifles (Boyes) .55 inch	18	**Hand Grenades**	180
Light Machine Guns (Brens) .303 inch	13		

A platoon of the 2/4th Machine Gun Battalion in Vickers machine gun training at Lancelin in 1941

The Men of the 2/4th Australian Machine Gun Battalion 1940–1945

The following is a list which comprises all those personnel who departed Fremantle for overseas service, either on Singapore or Java, however, certain facts must be taken into consideration.

In October 1941 whilst in training at Woodside Camp, South Australia there was an exchange of personnel as some men returned to Western Australia, others joined the unit and were Taken on Strength.

It was quite common in Australia during the war of 1939–45 for men to transfer out of their original unit. Some reasons for this occurring may have been attributed to the following: man-powering where a man may have been required to work on the land or an essential war industry, illness, unsuitability, family reunion (where men were claimed by relatives in other units) or to re-enlist in either the R.A.A.F. or R.A.N. as vacancies became available. As some of the 2/4th Machine Gun Battalion's NCO's proved themselves worthy they were Taken off Strength to attend Officer Training School only to rejoin the unit later at either Darwin or Fremantle.

There was the Absent Without Leave episode[1] at Fremantle and the addition of the reinforcement draft from Northam Camp who also joined the battalion at Fremantle.

In January 1942 once landed on Singapore the battalion was reorganised with many of the reinforcements forming the Special Reserve Battalion under the command of Major Bert Saggers. There was also an additional platoon, being No. 16 Platoon made up predominately of men from 'D' Company under the command of Sgt. Ron Arbery.

As casualties were incurred during the Battle of Singapore, officers changed commands or took over other duties and NCO's and other ranks were promoted or demoted as necessity demanded. In many cases NCO's who had lost stripes after Fremantle, as a general rule were reinstated to their original rank. However at least one exception was Sgt. Vic Barnett who acted as an NCO during the Battle of Singapore and although promised the return of his stripes, he was never reinstated to his pre-Fremantle rank. Corporal Jim Dore shared a similar experience by acting as a Sgt. at Kobe House in Japan, yet despite this fact, his promotion was never processed on his return to Australia.

There were some further additions to the battalion nominal roll following hostilities on Singapore Island and those personnel concerned have been included with their own dossier and are also included in the nominal index.

Battalion Headquarters

Commanding Officer
WX3376 Lt-Col. M. J. Anketell

Second in Command Major	**Adjutant**
WX3435 Maj. C. E. Green	WX3434 Capt. J. H. Hill
Intelligence Officer	**Regimental Sergeant Major**
WX3447 Lt. G. A. Raphael	WX13977 W.O.I, G. F. Airey

---

[1]   All ranks are those held during the period between Fremantle and the Fall of Singapore.

Orderly Room Sergeants

WX9372 Sgt. S. D.Viney WX11455 Sgt. A. N. Mantle

Provost Sergeant
WX14644 Sgt. C. V. Smith

Sergeant i/c Stretcher Bearers
WX9238 Sgt. T. W. Pierson

Corporals

WX9031 Cpl. M. J. Brennan WX20157 Pte. R. S. Pimlott

Privates

WX7064 B. W. J. Allpike	WX8198 F. Hinnrichsen
WX8981 E. R. Baker	WX6967 J. Howe
WX8485 A. W. Bamford	WX8336 F. G. Kuhl
WX9340 H. P. Bennett	WX10806 K. E. Lessells
WX8709 R. B. Blaschek	WX8015 J. C. Manton
WX13442 L. N. W. Bullock	WX7336 H. B. Ockerby
WX10365 M. W. Caldwell	WX8826 L. Purchon (To SRBn.)
WX7595 G. Glass	WX7939 C. J. Sawyer
WX8690 J. N. Hall	WX7506 R. L. Sloane
WX8695 W. D. Harris	WX8356 W. S. Watkins

Reinforcements

WX15756 A. J. Burgess	WX16347 W. N. Matson
WX17754 J. Brown	WX17393 T. Pilmoor
WX10841 A. C. Bruce	WX16281 G. L. Reay
WX15707 H. M. Cooper	WX15743 W. R. Ritchie
WX13869 P. J. Dimopoulos	WX15941 J. W. Robinson
WX17745 C. H. Fletcher	WX18142 C. T. Wright
WX16375 J. W. Hunt	

Regimental Medical Officer A.A.M.C. Attached
WX3464 Capt. C. L. Anderson

Chaplain Attached A.A. Ch.D.
NX76253 F. X. Corry

Company Headquarters

Commanding Officer
WX3442 Capt. O. S. McEwin

Company Sergeant Major
WX9385 W.O.II J. Unsworth

Company Quartermaster Sergeant
WX8718 S/Sgt. H. Hammer

Privates

WX7042 L/Cpl. R. Matthews	WX8544 J. Sevier
WX7458 L. O. Peat	

Headquarters Company No. 1 Platoon Signals

Commanding Officer
WX3446 Lt. F. L. Curnow

Sergeants
WX10678 Sgt. B. E. Hansen WX10785 Sgt. J. M. Rutherford

Corporals
WX10910 Cpl. M. St. J. Kennedy

Privates

WX8485 A. W. Bamford	WX9801 R. D. Maconachie
WX7479 R. F. Cannon	WX5584 R. D. McCracken
WX10739 W. E. Clothier	WX9849 A. J. L. McIntosh
WX10048 E. J. Cosson	WX8834 W. N. K. McNulty
WX7909 T. Davidson	WX7645 W. J. Nicholls
WX10114 H. Eastwood	WX9129 E. J. Ovens
WX10057 R. L. Evans	WX9055 H. Pickett
WX10622 C. W. Gault	WX8725 J. H. L. Pryce
WX9062 G. J. Gossage	WX9059 G. R. Ramage
WX10693 W. D. Grundy	WX10066 D. G. Ross
WX10745 A. J. Hambley	WX14775 G. L. Taylor
WX10635 V. T. W. Hoppe	WX9224 H. A. Walker
WX10097 L/Cpl. A. D. Hosking	WX8626 N. Warne
WX9915 F. H. Keirle	WX10049 M. W. Wilkinson
WX10715 J. G. A. Kyriakos	WX10012 W. G. Worth

Reinforcements
WX12202 L/Cpl. M. S. Scala

Headquarters Company No. 2 Platoon Anti-Aircraft

Commanding Officer
WX9383 Lt. J. D. Royce
Sergeants
WX10389 L/Sgt. C. A. Phillips WX9552 Sgt. W. L. Innes

Corporals
WX7905 A/Cpl. F. J. Annesley WX7332 Cpl. W. W. Hutchinson
WX7436 Cpl. J. M. McGinty WX8699 Cpl. C. B. Thackrah

Privates

WX8855 D. J. Davies	WX7426 J. P. Murphy
WX8733 H. R. Harrison	WX7617 H. W. Scaddan
WX8408 A. G. Hayes	WX7893 L/Cpl. J. S. Smith
WX7889 J. Issac	WX7470 R. L. Todd
WX7453 E. C. Jones	WX7484 W. J. Tucker
WX8675 R. R. Lyle	WX8706 J. Wilkie
WX7847 G. L. Lynam	

Reinforcements

WX20018 J. L. Correy
WX15872 L. C. Gray
WX16383 H. V. W. Gwilliam
WX20025 L. R. Hounslow

WX15402 L. Jaensch
WX16332 J. Lind
WX14327 L. R. Nybo

Headquarters Company No. 3 Platoon Administrative

Quartermaster

WX3465 Capt. R. M. Phelps

WX9390 Lt. B. M. O'Sullivan

Regimental Quartermaster Sergeant

WX691 W.O.II E. Bell

Lieutenant

WX9381 Lt. A. H. Watson

Pioneer Sergeant

WX9391 Sgt. B. P. Doolan

Sergeant Cook

WX9407 Sgt. G. Northey

Transport Sergeant

WX9039 Sgt. R. N. Fitzpatrick

WX10910 Cpl. M. St. J. Kennedy

Technical Stores Sergeant

WX11228 Sgt. R. M. Lander

Corporals

WX5050 L/Sgt. J. A. Briggs
WX7471 Cpl. W. H. P. Hood

WX10388 Cpl. K. L. Meads
WX9554 Cpl. A. L. R. Powell

Privates

WX8829 J. Bagrie
WX8720 A. J. Baker
WX7495 L. P. Ball
WX8650 H. J. Bishop
WX7947 A. R. Brown
WX7469 T. J. Butler
WX8445 R. C. Carter
WX8822 H. J. Cooper
WX7804 T. M. Davison
WX7562 H. L. Elkins
WX8874 A. W. Findlay
WX7225 T. Firns
WX6258 J. H. Grace
WX8540 T. W. Green
WX8690 J. N. Hall
WX6602 A. Mc. Hill
WX8384 R. G. Henderson
WX7465 N. P. Holdman
WX7550 W. J. Holt
WX7541 C. C. Keitel
WX9151 R. J. Kelt

WX7446 L. Krassnostein
WX7285 H. R. Love
WX8656 R. G. Magor
WX8790 W. McEwen
WX5196 F. H. New
WX8432 R. F. Newling
WX7902 W. H. Philp
WX7416 E. L. Preedy
WX8739 F. F. Pritchard
WX8716 F. K. Pritchard
WX7831 L/Cpl. J. P. Quinn
WX7511 J. A. Rabone
WX7493 R. G. S. Rennie
WX7904 R. M. Smith
WX7563 E. H. Sullivan
WX8738 W. Struthers
WX9351 J. Treasure
WX7466 L/Cpl. B. J. Walsh
WX7502 T. S. Wayman
WX8672 G. D. Williams
WX7429 F. B. Yensch

Reinforcements

WX15989 J. S. Buckley
WX15785 W. Carlyon
WX20076 W. Dwyer
WX15422 B. M. Frost
WX16446 C. Hobson
WX16981 W. R. Howson
WX17566 J. K. A. MacDonald
WX16341 S. T. Martin
WX14031 C. T. Nelson

WX17458 O. K. Newling
WX16448 A.W. L. Park
WX16324 G. D. Tanner
WX15712 W. W. Tischler
WX15614 R. J. Walker
WX10761 T. M. Watters
WX16274 F. Whitacker
WX16426 W. J. Wolfe

Attached Personnel

Sergeants A.A.O.C. Armourer
WX15099 Sgt. C. T. Howe

WX4921 Sgt. J. T. Taylor

Electrician
WX12924 Pte. E. A. Dix

Fitter Sergeant Motor Transport
WX12378 Sgt. J. C. Swift

Fitters Motor Transport
WX12765 P. J. Beilby
WX12717 A. H. S. London

WX11472 Cpl. R. F. Manthorpe
WX7248 F. D. Thaxter

Shoemaker
WX9946 L/Cpl. E. A. Pummel

A.A.P.C.
WX9388 Sgt. J. M. C. Cheyne

WX8092 Cpl. C. H. Dunn

88th Light Aid Detachment (L.A.D.)

Attached A.A.O.C. Personnel Technical

Commanding Officer
WX11001 Capt. A. H. R. Odlum

Warrant Officer II
WX9558 W.O.II A. R. Green

Staff Sergeants
WX9560 S/Sgt. J. W. Wainwright

WX9562 Sgt. I. E. Thorley

Corporals
WX9561Cpl. A. E. Dahlberg
WX9559 Cpl. W. H. Hickson

WX9563 Cpl. J. Randall

Privates

WX10920 N. E. Bailey

SX11457 E. H. Cole

NX73270 B. J. Howard

WX8435 R. McCann

WX9260 S. E. Neale

NX73279 C. W. Newman

WX8340 N. J. Sheedy

WX8506 W. J. Smith

WX8467 L/Cpl. R. H. C. Spence

WX11744 G. E. Willimott

WX11745 J. F. Willimott

Machine Gun Companies

'A' Company Headquarters

Commanding Officer

WX3454 Maj. A. E. Saggers (SRBn.)

Second in Command

WX3423 Capt. A.W. Thomas

WX3440 Lt. F. G. McCaffrey

C.S.M.

WX8098 W.O.II W. Burgess

C.Q.M.S.

WX8438 S/Sgt. R. M. Wilson

Transport Corporal

WX8867 Cpl. G. W. Taylor

Corporal Cook

WX4945 Cpl. H. R. N. Fawcus

WX15247 Cpl. K. G. Griffith

Corporals

WX8872 L/Cpl. D. F. Anderson

WX6976 L/Cpl. J. M. Clare

WX7709 L/Cpl. C. A. Fogarty

WX8973 L/Cpl. G. G. Mongan

Privates

WX6970 A. J. Barnes

WX4877 F. H. Landwehr

WX8493 A. W. Norton

WX5018 C. B. Shelvock

Reinforcements

WX16389 R. J. Bell

WX17864 B. A. Bendall

WX17860 H. D. Cain

WX16436 G. D. Clifton

WX15783 D. C. Cripps

WX16420 H. A. Davis

WX12575 L/Cpl. G. A. Gorman

WX16439 D. R. Lane

WX16279 E. F. Osborne

WX15829 H. Radburn

WX16356 E. E. Randall

WX18151 A. R. Shier

WX17424 A. Sing

WX15967 D. E. Sutherland

'A' Company No. 4 Platoon

Commanding Officer

WX3440 Lt. F. G. McCaffery

WX8484 Lt. H. J. Manning

Platoon Sergeant
WX8377 Sgt. K.T. MacLennan

Sergeants
WX7123 A/Sgt. R. D. Hampson
WX9345 Sgt. G. S. Ohrt

Corporals
WX7046 Cpl. M. Armstrong
WX8373 Cpl. L. Greaves
WX8707 Cpl. F. Nazzari
WX8174 L/Sgt. D. M. O'Leary

Privates
WX9864 R. J. Baggs
WX9018 E. N. Bates
WX10791 A. R. Beattie
WX14226 L/Cpl. A. A. M. Brazier
WX7702 C. E. Burns
WX7007 E. G. Burton
WX9360 E. J. Clarke
WX8011 H. T. Delaporte
WX14856 M. R. Docking
WX4915 A. B. Facey
WX5335 W. M. Giddens
WX8003 A. M. Hack (SRBn.)
WX7851 C. Harris
WX6968 J. C. Heffernan
WX7976 F. Hermon
WX7705 R. Hill
WX8007 E. H. King
WX6429 W. J. King
WX7043 H. B. Lear
WX7285 H. R. Love
WX7241 E. Meakins
WX13338 L/Cpl. R. J. Miller
WX8076 F. C. Moore
WX8493 A. W. Norton
WX8481 A. S. Oag
WX7738 C .S. Parke
WX6172 H. E. Procter
WX7474 H. M. Rubery
WX8041 W. J. Stone
WX5021 H. W. Waghorn
WX12008 L/Cpl. T. C. Wearn
WX8014 L/Cpl. R.C. Wilson
WX6958 J. Young

Reinforcements
WX15386 R. K. Moran

'A' Company No. 5 Platoon

Commanding Officer
WX10363 Lt. A. B. Walton
WX10107 Lt. R. W. Learmonth

Platoon Sergeant
WX5007 Sgt. J. H. Schurmann

Sergeants
WX9035 Sgt. R. H. Cornish
WX9045 L/Sgt. H. E. Saw

Corporals
WX8617 Cpl. J. J. Dore
WX9175 Cpl. W. T. Haywood
WX8596 Cpl. D. F. Sterrett
WX10927 L/Cpl. N. H. E. Thompson
WX8491 Cpl. R. G. Tuffin

WX8599 J. Alderton
WX8963 L. Armstrong
WX9017 C. R. Bird
WX8631 S. J. Blewett
WX8712 J. Borrow
WX8397 R. W. Chipperfield
WX8681 R. W. Davey
WX8619 J. S. Elliot
WX8381 R. P. Elvish
WX8586 B. Fitzgerald
WX8623 J. Gilmour
WX8625 W. R. Gregory
WX8374 N. P. Hayes
WX8638 L. C. Hellmrich
WX8678 E. J. Holst
WX10795 R. E. Hughes

WX8620 L/Cpl. C. J. McDonald
WX9145 A. J. McGhee
WX8760 T. M. McMahon
WX8441 J. B. Mellor
WX9222 T. A. H. Minchin
WX10796 L. McG. Murray
WX7724 A. S. Parke
WX14836 J. K. Ramsbottom
WX9357 L. R. Rayner
WX8503 R. C. Reed
WX8843 J. Scales
WX8693 W. L. Short
WX8585 C. J. Vidler
WX8502 E. A. A. Watt
WX6071 L. G. Willacott

Reinforcements
WX17857 V. S. Reid

'A' Company No. 6 Platoon

Commanding Officer
WX9384 Lt. J. C. Morrison

WX10372 Lt. G. H. Branson

Platoon Sergeant
WX227 Sgt. A. Stevens

Sergeant
WX7628 Sgt. E. J. Howard

Corporals
WX9101 Cpl. J. C. Ewen
WX15247 Cpl. K. G. Griffith
WX7467 Cpl. D. K. Jamieson

WX10797 Cpl. F. McP. Townsend
WX7477 Cpl. D. L. A. Whiteman

Privates
WX9367 J. R. Baker
WX9288 J. A. Brooker
WX9223 H. T. Bunker
WX9243 K. Clifton
WX9328 G. T. Dickie
WX9310 A. A. Dickson
WX9274 G. Dorizzi
WX12884 T. H. Dorizzi
WX9266 W. Dunwoodie
WX9230 W. C. Evans
WX9199 A. E. Farmer
WX7709 L/Cpl. C. A. Fogarty
WX9270 T. J. Fury
WX9255 S. H. Gibbs
WX8622 L/Cpl. J. B. Gilmour

WX9320 H. W. Heal
WX9231 L. S. Hodgson
WX7616 C. Knott
WX9214 J. Lee
WX8960 L/Cpl. T. A. Limbourn
WX13285 J. Maude
WX8621 K. K. McDonald
WX15838 R. J. McKenzie-Murray
WX9263 E. C. S. Popham
WX5054 D. A. C. Quinn
WX7750 S. H. G. Roberts
WX10808 J. Rochester
WX9253 D. Ross
WX9252 J. H. Shackleton

WX8870 T. E. Gittos
WX6980 P. Golden
WX8582 N. A. Gough
WX9202 R. K. Gregory

WX9226 H. Tysoe
WX16370 A. L. Walker
WX7011 L/Cpl. H. W. Williams
WX9003 J. L. Yeates

Reinforcements

WX12661 W. E. Cake
WX17881 O. A. Doust
WX18170 S. R. Hickey
WX15744 L. W. Lee
WX13752 A/Cpl. H. Lucas
WX15751 A. E. Morrissey
WX12599 A. R. Murdoch

WX12156 P. V. Omiridis
WX12336 R. Pascall
WX15893 S. E. Roots
WX13553 S. F. Spouse
WX16442 V. Wallis
WX17804 A. S. A. Webb

'B' Company Headquarters

Commanding Officer
WX3452 Capt. G. McR. Bunning

Second in Command
WX3453 Capt. A. R. Smith-Ryan

C.S.M.
WX8207 W.O.II A. S. Hewby

C.Q.M.S.
WX9556 S/Sgt. R. S. Campbell

Transport Corporal
WX222 Cpl. T. J. Barnett

Corporal Cook
WX4891 A/Cpl. G. Smith

Corporals

WX5200 A/Sgt. W. J. Robinson

WX5221 Cpl. S. A. Currie

Privates

WX8798 G. P. Biggs
WX9316 A. Brooksbank
WX8808 J. C. Colbey
WX6917 G. J. Doodson
WX8830 A. Mc.D. Drummond
WX7236 C. H. Dunn
WX8657 L/Cpl. C. Flakemore
WX8607 P. J. Gibbs
WX8756 L/Cpl. J. Hill
WX8984 S. M. Hogben

WX8750 H. A. Jackson
WX8702 G. Japp
WX12835 L/Cpl. J. A. McGregor
WX8013 E. E. Miller
WX8828 W. D. O'Neill
WX7331 C. W. Robertson
WX4986 J. A. Taylor
WX5932 F. Vaughan
WX10373 W. V. Winter
WX9379 T. W. Zeeb

Reinforcements
WX16727 J. L. Lonsdale

'B' Company No. 7 Platoon

Commanding Officer
WX6067 Lt. P. V. Dean

Platoon Sergeant
WX8118 Sgt. J. E. Pearson

Sergeants
WX8986 Sgt. D. Holm

Corporals

WX9011 Cpl. G. C. Arthur
WX9229 Cpl. W. E. Breed

WX8807 Cpl. W. A. Halligan

Privates

WX9342 H. Atkinson
WX8429 V. G. Barnett
WX8682 W. R. S. Baker
WX8185 J. J. Barry
WX8798 G. P. Biggs
WX12335 R. E. Brown
WX9261 J. N. Caimanos
WX11226 G. K. Cameron
WX10282 C. L. Collins
WX9334 J. F. Dare
WX7886 T. A. Findlay
WX7864 J. J. Flanagan
WX8679 L/Cpl. A. E. Foch
WX9335 S. Gorringe
WX7869 T. H. Green
WX8674 J. E. J. Gregory
WX8807 W. A. Halligan
WX9365 L. H. Hancock
WX9240 H. G. Hockey

WX9350 P. G. Hodgins
WX9241 E. M. Hopson
WX9323 M. W. Hortin
WX8702 G. Japp
WX8810 R. F. Lawer
WX9312 M. J. Leahy
WX12835 L/Cpl. J. A. McGregor
WX10792 E. J. Murtagh
WX8865 R. W. Newling
WX10809 W. J. Nicholas
WX9413 F. R. Noble
WX13816 D. D. Pearson
WX8840 A. E. Powell
WX8758 J. F. Starcevich
WX9332 J. B. Stubbs
WX10117 E. G. Thomson
WX10289 A. S. Thorns
WX9333 A. T. White
WX10373 W. V. Winter

Reinforcements
WX16952 R. A. Simmonds

'B' Company No. 8 Platoon

Commanding Officer
WX3707 Lt. G. C. MacKinnon

Platoon Sergeant
WX8809 Sgt. R. H. Sandilands

Sergeants

WX9336 Cpl. J. Gorringe

WX4991 L/Sgt. E. E. Hambley

Corporals

WX7777 Cpl. A. M. Draper
WX10095 Cpl. J. F. Helsin

WX10802 Cpl. N. J. Outtrim

Privates

WX7370 C. W. Armstrong
WX8729 R. C. Badock
WX8766 L/Cpl. H. V. Booth
WX7333 A. J. Burns
WX7316 C. J. Burns

WX9139 L. F. Hadden
WX10370 D. C. J. Hall
WX8747 W. H. Hall
WX8756 L/Cpl. J. Hill
WX8813 L/Cpl. T. M. Jackson

WX15690 J. M. Carr
WX7325 R. F. Carruthers
WX8792 W. T. Castles
WX16369 A. J. Cocking
WX7268 F. V. Cross
WX8735 J. G. Curtin
WX8778 L. J. Daily
WX7240 D. A. Day
WX7236 C. H. Dunn
WX7266 G. H. Edwards
WX10803 T. R. Fotheringham
WX10378 C. W. Gray
WX8730 T. K. Jenkins

WX7230 L. H. Lee
WX8689 L/Cpl. H. C. S. MacMaster
WX6173 O. Morris
WX7181 C. Mutton
WX5220 H. F. Neilson
WX7331 C. W. Robertson
WX10164 D. N. Russell
WX8734 C. Ryan
WX6681 J. B. Skelton
WX8736 R. L. Smith
WX8731 T. E. Smith
WX8776 L. P. Walsh
WX8753 J. L. Wheelock

Reinforcements

WX14634 W. G. H. Anderson
WX17997 H. M. Holland
WX17636 H. W. Holland
WX14197 R. W. Ridgwell

WX16427 D. C. Robertson
WX17879 G. J. Wade
WX13161 L/Cpl. H. E. Wright

'B' Company No. 9 Platoon

Commanding Officer
WX9387 Lt. C. D. Lee

Platoon Sergeant
WX4985 Sgt. N. J. Harris

Sergeants

WX8537 Sgt. K. D. Tucker

WX5200 A/Sgt. W. J. Robinson

Corporals

WX9557 Cpl. F. J. Dorrington
WX8777 Cpl. J. W. Sanderson

WX10865 Cpl. T. E. Teasdale

Privates

WX8518 W. F. Anderton
WX7937 H. G. Blakiston
WX7329 R. A. Briggs
WX7790 T. H. Buscombe
WX8240 D. N. H. Carter
WX8641 H. J. Cowie
WX8587 W. J. Davey
WX7943 R. Drysdale
WX8584 J. S. Duncan
WX6262 W. H. Earnshaw
WX9131 R. Goodwin
WX5086 H. J. Gregory

WX8610 T. E. J. James
WX7697 L/Cpl. R. R. Jeffery
WX10897 E. B. Jones
WX8543 L. W. S. Kemp
WX7250 G. Kidd
WX8639 J. J. Lynch
WX8611 L. J. McGrath
WX7675 C. J. McPherson
WX8013 E. E. Miller
WX8749 A. G. Newell
WX7940 W. G. Nicholson
WX5222 L. O'Neil

WX7801 A. Hackshaw

WX8433 R.W. Haldaine

WX8819 J. Halligan

WX8869 L/Cpl. H. R. Hindle

WX8597 F. Hinds

WX9130 M. A. Hunter

WX8642 D. Parker

WX8562 A.V. Schuts

WX7784 J. W. Smith

WX7913 F. T. Ward

WX8765 J. Warren-Smith

WX9076 R. G. Whitelaw

Reinforcements

WX15433 Cpl. J. L. Anderson

WX12427 R. A. Foster

'C' Company Headquarters

Commanding Officer

WX3451 Capt. C. Cameron

Second in Command

WX3448 Capt. G. A. J. Thompson

C.S.M.

WX9405 W.O.II T. Hampton

C.Q.M.S.

WX7504 S/Sgt. D. B. Chapman

Transport Corporal

WX8228 L/Sgt. N. H. Grant

Corporal Cook

WX5425 Cpl. T. M. Fitzgerald

Corporals

WX8327 Cpl. C. H. Ironmonger

Privates

WX10343 N. E. Banks

WX9361 M. A. Bartlett

WX9195 J. W. Basell

WX9090 L/Cpl. N. Bradshaw

WX10358 S. R. Clayden

WX6362 R. A. Deveson

WX5064 E. F. Elliot

WX9777 J. H. Flanigan

WX9755 L/Cpl. L. Helliwell

WX8178 J. H. King

WX8137 L/Cpl. J. W. H. Needham

WX8141 R. H. Simkin

WX7337 L/Cpl. A. Spooner

WX9419 H. W. Steele

WX9134 J. Sumner

WX4924 J. Swartz

WX1138 A. G. Williams

Reinforcements

WX11584 W. C. Case

WX12488 J. W. Clay

WX12663 A. E. Floyd

WX13562 P. J. Moate

WX15457 S. E. Nash

WX12985 L/Cpl. P. J. Negri

WX12628 S. J. Oliver

WX13027 L/Cpl. C. R. Piggott

WX12949 J. L. Scott

WX15869 A. J. Struthoff

WX14733 J. Taylor

WX17882 A. G. Trigwell

WX17863 V. C. Trigwell

'C' Company No. 10 Platoon

Commanding Officer

WX9394 Lt. J. G. Wilson

WX10874 Lt. T. R. Ambrose

Platoon Sergeant
WX8119 Sgt. R. C. Fullerton

Sergeants
WX7852 Sgt. H. C. Fuhrmann

WX7663 Sgt. H. S. Fidge

Corporals
WX239 Cpl. J. R. Aberle

WX7608 Cpl. C. McLennan

WX7618 Cpl. L. N. Holtzman

Privates
WX7622 N. L. Ablett

WX8245 E. T. Adams

WX9123 C. W. M. Anderson

WX8140 F. J. Baxter

WX11573 G. G. Breeze

WX7629 F. Bugg

WX7542 G. L. Burdon

WX7661 G. N. Burslem

WX6155 L. P. Byrne

WX8192 R. J. Carlile

WX9551 F. V. Carroll

WX7163 J. Clare

WX7599 A. H. Dyson

WX7606 R. E. Godfrey (To 'E' Coy)

WX7246 R. W. Hadfield

WX8250 F. Halbert

WX11202 K. T. Hayes

WX7642 C. G. Henderson

WX5181 K. J. Howell

WX10931 L. S. Hummerston

WX9433 N. Jones

WX4917 J. B. Leith

WX7660 D. T. Manning

WX7124 L. J. Marriot

WX9296 D. A. Matheson

WX8261 R. R. McAskil

WX5163 C. K. McDonald

WX8478 F. T. McGlinn

WX7138 W. McKay

WX8012 K. G. Moir

WX8200 W. R. Morris

WX7621 W. W. Reeves

WX6799 E. Ricketts

WX7256 T. K. Sawyer

WX7576 N. E. Simmonds

WX9829 F. W. Webb

WX7641 S. K. Wenn

WX8814 C. W. White

'C' Company No. 11 Platoon

Commanding Officer
WX3483 Lt. K. C. Boyle

Platoon Sergeant
WX10794 Sgt. P. A. Sturtridge

Sergeants
WX7438 Sgt. B. H. Manwaring

WX8243 Sgt. A. McQuade

Corporals
WX8962 Cpl. J. A. Baker

WX9061 Cpl. D. E. Bevis

WX4927 Cpl. A. N. Climie

WX7569 Cpl. S. E. Foxall

WX7662 A/Cpl. A. R. Minchin

WX10793 Cpl. E. J. Rowell

Privates

WX9828 A. A. Adams
WX7587 T. Barbour
WX7164 F. Barker
WX7625 J. S. Clarke
WX10354 H. T. Clayden
WX4912 T. J. Conway
WX9092 A.V. Cousins
WX8238 V. J. A. Dewar
WX5127 C. G. Ferrie
WX10366 N.W. Fraser
WX10944 N. A. Gibson
WX8900 T. C. Gibson
WX9052 H. E. McDonough
WX9826 H. J. Millar
WX7885 A. Miller

WX9339 G. Moir
WX9338 L. O. Moir
WX9887 A. C. Mussman
WX5123 J. S. Pass
WX8856 H. W. Pearce
WX6129 A. J. Rees
WX9358 W. C. Roberts
WX10351 J. Robinson
WX7835 W. L. Rosel
WX9330 D. J. Squire
WX7664 F. W. Toms
WX9236 E. J. Waddell
WX7166 H. S. Werrett
WX7263 R. E. Williams

Reinforcements

WX11279 G. K. Chatfield
WX17706 A. T. Cunningham

WX15719 G. Foot
WX11580 D. S. McGlinn

'C' Company No. 12 Platoon

Commanding Officer
WX9553 Lt. C. N. Wedge

Platoon Sergeant
WX10561 Sgt. R. G. Whitfield

Sergeants

WX7607 Sgt. R. J. Gibbons

WX4949 Sgt. R. J. Kingswell

Corporals

WX9112 A/Cpl. B. C. Jones

WX10822 Cpl. L. J. Harvey

Privates

WX7883 W. H. Beard
WX14855 L/Cpl. P. R. Beaton
WX9136 L/Cpl. B. W. J. Clarke
WX6632 S. Clarke
WX9109 A. J. Colquhoun
WX10721 H. B. De'Castilla
WX5088 A. Fee
WX9070 C. Fielder
WX5132 G. Fisher
WX9132 A. R. Gamble
WX7627 J. McL. Goldie
WX14830 S. O'G. Haly
WX9348 C. L. Heppell

WX8820 W. P. McCudden
WX9825 C. P. McLoughlin
WX8319 J. W. Meredith
WX4941 R. Muller
WX7659 E. L. Nolan
WX10790 L/Cpl. H. C. Norris
WX9181 W. H. Nottle
WX4934 R. A. Page
WX9197 J. E. Peers
WX5054 D. A. C. Quinn
WX9005 E. R. Rogers
WX6841 J. S. Smith
WX9143 M. J. Smith

WX8525 I. D. Heppingstone
WX5118 J. M. Jenkins
WX9297 C. Joynes
WX8077 L. A. C. Kuhlman
WX9528 A. Lambie
WX9146 C. R. Lush

WX8646 L/Cpl. A. P. Spouse
WX9827 R. H. Stribling
WX8448 G. Taylor
WX8139 Pte. P. R. Tomkins
WX12989 H. J. Wall
WX9067 E. G. Watt

Reinforcements
WX12593 R. W. Wyllie

'D' Company Headquarters

Commanding Officer
WX3444 Maj. A. J. Cough

Second in Command
WX3450 Capt. G. W. Gwynne

C.S.M.
WX225 Sgt. E. T. Feltham

C.Q.M.S.
WX9555 S/Sgt. L. Cody

Transport Corporal
WX7789 Cpl. O. M. Stanwell

Corporal Cook
WX7324 L/Cpl. R. H. Stewart

Privates

WX7444 A. R. Attenborough (No.15 and 16 Plns.)
WX9294 W. F. Baillie (No.13 Pln.)
WX7253 W. V. Bow (No.15 Pln.)
WX9278 E. W. H. Bunce (No.13 Pln.)
WX9060 A.T. J. Cato (No.13 and 16 Plns.)
WX7714 F. D. J. Clark (No.15 Pln.)
WX9004 A. Cryer (No.15 Pln.)
WX7997 H. Dorizzi (No.16 Pln.)
WX7999 R. P. Ferguson (No. 15 Pln.)
WX8000 M. H. Geary
WX8788 F. L. Giles

WX7987 G. Hancock (No.14 Pln.)
WX7646 R. B. Hutchison (No.14 Pln.)
WX16340 R. H. Kenmir
WX7640 L/Cpl. F. Lee-Steere
WX224 J. MacDonald (No.15 Pln.)
WX6203 J. McSkene (No.15 Pln.)
WX8652 A. M. Rogie (No.13 Pln.)
WX9272 L/Cpl. A. G. Saunders (No.13 Pln.)
WX7211 C. S. Saunders
WX9080 A. W. Stribley (No.16 Pln.)

Reinforcements
WX11316 L. H. Lewis

WX16254 C. W. Webber

'D' Company No. 13 Platoon

Commanding Officer
WX9392 Lt. M. E. Wankey

Platoon Sergeant
WX10787 Sgt. R. E. Arbery (No. 16 Pln.)

Sergeants
WX10804 Cpl. H. Jacobs

Corporals

WX9327 Cpl. E. H. Hunt

WX8532 Cpl. W. G. B. Kenney

WX9073 Cpl. W. J. Paterson

WX9268 L/Sgt. J. Pearce

Privates

WX9289 R. G. Anderson

WX13468 R. W. Annear

WX9277 T. J. Beard

WX8796 L/Cpl. F. Bracklemann

WX10805 R. J. Brown

WX8789 S. T. Brown

WX9283 J. H. Browning

WX9278 E. W. H. Bunce

WX9326 A. H. Carter

WX9060 A. T. J. Cato (No.16 Pln.)

WX16407 L. G. Gibbs (No.16 Pln.)

WX8958 W. H. Gibbs

WX9290 G. H. Hicks

WX7612 C. G. Mc. Kelly

WX9318 K. Lally

WX9293 R. G. Langdon

WX9321 A. J. Loller

WX9324 J. McCarthy

WX9279 L. M. MacDonald

WX9233 A. J. Morgan

WX9256 G. E. Nevile

WX9207 A. Newton

WX7409 T. A. Pascoe

WX8705 R. W. Pratt

WX9285 C. G. Quinn

WX8952 R. R. Riebe

WX9272 A. G. Saunders

WX8652 A. M. Rogie

WX8535 A. F. Shirley

WX13552 R. Smith

WX9058 N. L. Stribley

WX9280 F. T. Tregenza

WX9292 N. J. Venemore

WX9219 C. Webb

WX9002 H. C. F. White (No.16 Pln.)

Reinforcements

WX17595 N. L. Dunnell

WX17452 L. D. Kearney (No.2 Pln. SRBn.)

WX17000 F. N. Matthews

WX15746 A. E. Morrison

WX17363 C. O. Nash

'D' Company No. 14 Platoon

Commanding Officer
WX7996 Lt. T. H. Tomkins

Platoon Sergeant
WX9282 Sgt. F. K. H. Skinner

Sergeants
WX10609 Sgt. J. V. Colevas (No.16 Pln.)

Corporals

WX9148 Cpl. D. R. Horn

WX7757 Cpl. H. C. Wells

Privates

WX7611 R. S. Barr

WX12469 J. H. Blackborrow

WX7148 M. L. Browne (No.16 Pln.)

WX8123 H. A. T. Chilvers

WX7122 J. P. Clancy

WX9004 A. Cryer

WX7299 T. F. Doyle

WX7620 T. H. Edwards (No.16 Pln.)

WX9497 B. Evans

WX7441 T. H. Lewis (No.16 Pln.)

WX7204 L/Cpl. W. E. Lynn

WX7239 J. W. Malthouse

WX5175 E. H. Mann

WX7981 J. P. O'Meara

WX7634 S. A. Osborne

WX9764 B. F. Poulton

WX7213 G. V. Hadden
WX6975 R. J. Ham
WX7987 G. Hancock
WX5206 W. Hicks
WX6778 J. B. Hills
WX7022 E. J. Hope
WX7646 R. B. Hutchison
WX7510 A. J. Jones
WX7234 I. W. Jones
WX16391 G. B. Kluth
WX8767 P. H. C. Lakeman
WX7320 L. A. Poyser

WX7509 A. W. Rodda
WX6441 A. J. Smith
WX12252 J. E. Smith
WX14495 W. G. R. Stuart (No.16 Pln.)
WX6623 D. W. Thomas
WX7480 W. L. Thomas
WX15897 F. A. Toovey
WX9570 P. L. Westlake
WX8110 L/Cpl. A. D. Winter
WX5073 T. A. Wood (No.16 Pln.)
WX5204 H. J. Worsdell
WX7440 A. Worth

'D' Company No. 15 Platoon

Commanding Officer
WX9393 Lt. J. T. Meiklejohn

Platoon Sergeant
WX7127 Sgt. J. F. Solly

Sergeants
WX10925 Sgt. P. A. Gardiner

WX9325 Sgt. J. E. Tregenza

Corporals
WX7998 Cpl. P. A. Giese
WX7624 Cpl. E. C. Kemp

WX7715 C. J. Spackman
WX7499 A/Cpl. R. T. Williams

Privates
WX13457 D. A. Annear
WX7717 L/Cpl. F. Armstrong
WX7444 A. R. Attenborough (No.16 Pln.)
WX7796 J. J. S. Barrass
WX9589 F. M. Barrymore
WX7636 W. J. Beer
WX9063 A. J. Bell
WX7308 L. A. Blair
WX7600 G. R. Bousfield
WX7253 W. V. Bow
WX10390 W. A. Dwyer
WX7999 R. P. Ferguson
WX6506 J. E. Fraser
WX7745 B. G. Harrison (No.16 Pln.)
WX7029 E. T. Hill (No.16 Pln.)
WX9286 C. Holmes (No.16 Pln.)
WX8425 E. J. Leadbitter
WX224 J. MacDonald

WX6203 J. McSkene
WX11629 K. B. Mitchell
WX9337 A. D. Moir
WX5336 J. L. Murdoch
WX9287 J. R. Osborne
WX7626 A. L. Pitts
WX9295 S. Reid
WX7656 G. R. Rouse
WX7532 R. R. Semple
WX7330 E. Skackleton
WX7623 G. T. Shelton
WX9157 A. L. Tapper
WX8180 E. G. Taylor
WX8450 F. L. Taylor
WX8460 J. Thorpe
WX10382 J. Warrington
WX7499 R. T. Williams
WX7232 R. Whitford

WX15736 R. Hansen   WX16417 S. Ninyette
WX15905 E. G. Moir

No. 16 Platoon

Commanding Officer
WX10787 Sgt. R. E. Arbery (No.13 Pln.)

Platoon Sergeant
WX10609 Sgt. J. V. Colevas (No.14 Pln.)

Corporals
WX9080 L/Cpl. A. W. Stribley (Coy Hq's and No.15 Pln.)

Privates

WX13468 R. W. Annear (No.13 Pln.)   WX7745 B. G. Harrison (No.15 Pln.)
WX7444 A. R. Attenborough (No.15 Pln.)   WX7029 E. T. Hill (No.15 Pln.)
WX7796 J. J. S. Barras (No.15 Pln.)   WX9286 C. Holmes (No.15 Pln.)
WX10805 R. J. Brown (No.13 Pln.)   WX7441 T. H. Lewis (No.14 Pln.)
WX7148 M. L. Browne (No.14 Pln.)   WX7330 E. Shackleton (No.15 Pln.)
WX9060 A. T. J. Cato (Coy Hq's)   WX14495 W. G. R. Stuart (No.14 Pln.)
WX7997 H. Dorizzi (Coy Hq's)   WX8180 E. G. Taylor (No.15 Pln.)
WX7620 T. H. Edwards (No.14 Pln.)   WX9002 H. C. F. White (No.13 Pln.)
WX9497 B. Evans   WX7499 R. T. Williams (No.15 Pln.)
WX16407 L. G. Gibbs (No.13 Pln.)   WX5073 T. A. Wood (No.14 Pln.)
WX8958 W. H. Gibbs (No.13 Pln.)

Reinforcements

WX13079 R. E. Ellis   WX17370 J. Wilson
WX12157 E. C. Hardey

Special Reserve Battalion (SRBn.)

Battalion Headquarters

Commanding Officer
WX3454 Maj. A. E. Saggers

Adjutant   **Intelligence Officer**
WX9406 Lt. C. Odgers   WX228 Lt. D. V. Mentiplay

Batmen

WX8003 A. M. Hack   WX9179 H. Wilkes
WX16323 R. G. Tooze

'E' Company Headquarters

Commanding Officer
NX70433 Lt. V. I. Warhurst

Second in Command
WX8389 Lt. H. DeMoulin

C.S.M.
WX15720 Cpl. S. S. McNeil

R.Q.M.S.
WX8431 Cpl. V. A. Keay

Cooks

WX17915 T. W. Allen

WX6258 J. H. Grace

Orderly Room Clerk
WX6976 L/Cpl. J. M. Clare

Batmen / Runners

WX16441 T. D. Crane

WX7606 R. E. Godfrey (From 'C' Coy)

No. 1 Platoon

Commanding Officer
WX10788 Lt. H. F. Green

Platoon Sergeant
WX17293 Cpl. A. J. C. Rowland

Corporals

WX17251 Cpl. L. G. Ashbolt
WX14022 Cpl. R. Burchell

WX10822 Cpl. L. J. Harvey
WX13515 L/Cpl. A. B. W. Annetts

Privates

WX17793 W. J. Andrews
WX16795 F. C. Chambers
WX20026 W. Cameron
WX16306 J. Cook
WX20086 G. Davies
WX17269 K. S. Evans
WX17974 L. S. Gibson
WX16793 A. M. Hargreaves
WX17582 G. Lake
WX17759 J. S. Livingstone
WX17000 F. N. Matthews

WX17837 L. W. McCann
WX16675 R. J. Millhouse
WX17737 K. Moher
WX20107 A. Ralph
WX20068 H. W. Ralph
WX10808 J. Rochester
WX16885 C. D. Squance
WX17907 W. T. Swann
WX16956 R. S. Williams
WX17973 J. Wilson

No. 2 Platoon

Commanding Officer
WX9382 Lt. J. Till

Platoon Sergeant
WX16883 L/Cpl. N. W. Platts

Corporals

WX14172 Cpl. F. C. Evans
WX15041 Cpl. D. J. Gardner

WX16886 Cpl. A. M. Magill

Privates

WX17545 J. R. Buchan
WX14068 G. A. Dalrymple
WX15873 S. J. Darby
WX17391 M. W. Day
WX20164 A. E. Erskine
WX18022 F. J. Heinz-Smith
WX17634 W. Holding
WX17351 P. G. Hurst
WX17452 L. D. Kearney (No.13 Pln)
WX16355 G. R. Leipold
WX17778 F. J. Ludge

WX17515 R. R. Lymn
WX17639 R. W. Marsh
WX17390 E. M. Munday
WX16674 J. J. Murphy
WX16293 H. H. T. Norton
WX16931 H. C. Oswald
WX8826 L. Purchon
WX16269 E. J. Ronan
WX17899 S. G. Scott
WX17448 H. M. Smith
WX17615 E. J. Thomsett

No. 3 Platoon

Commanding Officer
WX7216 Lt. A. E. Mazza

Platoon Sergeant
WX15951 Cpl. K. S. Lance

Corporals

WX16260 L/Cpl. E. A. Cornell
WX15700 Cpl. J. Kingdon

WX15684 Cpl. J. E. Muldoon

Privates

WX16405 E. J. Burgess
WX17755 M. W. F. Butcher
WX16425 C. N. Chamberlain
WX17591 C. J. Dow
WX16947 R. E. Ecclestone
WX17374 N. Flarty
WX17310 N. F. T. Gough
WX17576 W. L. Jeffery
WX15640 H. J. Johnson
WX20095 W. A. McEwen

WX17302 W. MacLeod
WX17414 J. S. Peters
WX13429 W. N. Poole
WX20074 J. T. Ridley
WX16618 R. W. Roberts
WX17344 A. Slater
WX17594 G. C. Stone
WX17593 H. R. Turner
WX17962 E. W. Wallin
WX17604 M. H. Wilkins

Personnel Taken on Strength
Woodside Camp
South Australia 5.10.1941

WX16389 R. J. Bell ('A' Coy)
WX10841 A. C. Bruce (Bn. Hq's)
WX15989 J. S. Buckley (No.3 Pln.)
WX16405 E. J. Burgess (SRBn.)
WX15785 W. Carlyon (No.3 Pln.)
WX15690 J. M. Carr (No.8 Pln.)
WX16425 C. N. Chamberlain (SRBn.)
WX11279 G. K. Chatfield (No.11 Pln.)
WX16436 G. D. Clifton ('A' Coy)
WX16369 A. J. Cocking (No.8 Pln.)
WX16306 J. Cook (SRBn.)
WX15707 H. M. Cooper (Bn. Hq's)
WX16441 T. D. Crane ('E' Coy-SRBn. Hq's)
WX15783 D. C. Cripps ('A' Coy)
WX16420 H. A. Davis ('A' Coy)
WX13869 P. J. Dimopoulos (Bn. Hq's)
WX10199 J. A. Duggin (Coy not known)
WX15719 G. Foot (No.11 Pln.)
WX15422 B. M. Frost (No.3 Pln.)
WX16407 L. G. Gibbs (No.13 and No.16 Plns)
WX15872 L. C. Gray (No.2 Pln.)
WX15247 K. G. Griffith (No.6 Pln.)
WX16383 H. V. W. Gwilliam (No.2 Pln.)
WX15736 R. Hansen (No.15 Pln.)
WX16446 C. Hobson (No.3 Pln.)
WX16416 C. Holme (Coy not known)
WX16375 J. W. Hunt (Bn. Hq's)
WX16340 R. H. Kenmir ('D' Coy Hq's)
WX16236 A. J. King (Coy not known)
WX16391 G. B. Kluth (No.14 Pln.)
WX16439 D. R. Lane ('A' Coy)
WX15744 L. W. Lee (No.6 Pln.)
WX11316 L. H. Lewis ('D' Coy Hq's)
WX16332 J. Lind (No.3 Pln.)

WX16727 J. L. Lonsdale ('B' Coy Hq's)
WX16341 S. T. Martin (No.3 Pln.)
WX15838 R. J. McKenzie-Murray (No.6 Pln.)
WX8319   J. W. Meredith (No. 12 Pln.)
WX13562 P. J. Moate ('C' Coy Hq's)
WX15905 E. G. Moir (No.14 Pln.)
WX15386 R. K. Moran (No.4 Pln.)
WX15746 A. E. Morrison (No.13 Pln.)
WX15751 A. E. Morrissey (No.6 Pln.)
WX15457 S. E. Nash ('C' Coy)
WX16417 S. Ninyette (No.15 Pln.)
WX16279 E. F. Osborne ('A' Coy)
WX16448 A. W. L. Park (No.3 Pln.)
WX13429 W. N. Poole (SRBn.)
WX15829 H. Radburn ('A' Coy)
WX16356 E. E. Randall ('A' Coy)
WX16281 G. L. Reay (Bn. Hq's)
WX15743 W. R. Ritchie (Bn. Hq's)
WX16427 D. C. Robertson (No.8 Pln.)
WX15893 S. E. Roots (No.6 Pln.)
WX16424 A. Sing ('A' Coy)
WX15869 A. J. Struthoff ('C' Coy)
WX15967 D. E. Sutherland ('A' Coy)
WX16324 G. D. Tanner (No.3 Pln.)
WX15712 W. Tischler (No.3 Pln.)
WX15897 F. A. Toovey (No.14 Pln.)
WX16370 A. L. Walker (No.6 Pln.)
WX15614 R. J. Walker (No.3 Pln.)
WX16442 V. Wallis (No.6 Pln.)
WX10761 T. M. Watters (No.3 Pln.)
WX16254 C. W. Webber ('D' Coy)
WX16274 F. Whitacker (No.3 Pln.)
WX16426 W. J. Wolfe (No.3 Pln.)

Personnel AWL at Fremantle
Western Australia

WX8245	E. T. Adams (No.10 Pln.)
WX7064	B. W. J. Allpike (Bn. Hq's)
WX7905	F. J. Annesley (No.2 Pln.)
WX9367	J. R. Baker (No.6 Pln.)
WX8682	W. R. S. Baker (No.7 Pln.)
WX10343	N. E. Banks ('C' Coy Hq's)
WX7587	T. Barbour (No.11 Pln.)
WX7164	F. Barker (No.11 Pln.)
WX6970	A. J. Barnes (No.4 Pln.)
WX10791	A. R. Beattie (No.4 Pln.)
WX8766	H. V. Booth (No.8 Pln.)
WX7600	G. R. Bousfield (No.13 Pln.)
WX7333	A. J. Burns (No.8 Pln.)
WX6155	L. P. Byrne (No.10 Pln.)
WX10365	M. W. Caldwell ('B' Coy Hq's)
WX9551	F. V. Carroll (No.10 Pln.)
WX8240	D. N. H. Carter (No.9 Pln.)
WX10354	H. T. Clayden (No.11 Pln.)
WX16369	A. J. Cocking (No.8 Pln.)
WX10048	E. J. Cosson (No.1 Pln.)
WX8855	D. J. Davies (No.2 Pln.)
WX9310	A. A. Dickson (No.6 Pln.)
WX7299	T. F. Doyle (No.14 Pln.)
WX8830	A. Mc.D. Drummond ('B' Coy Hq's)
WX9266	W. Dunwoodie (No.6 Pln.)
WX9199	A. E. Farmer (No.6 Pln.)
WX9070	C. Fielder (No.12 Pln.)
WX5132	G. Fisher (No.12 Pln.)
WX7569	S. E. Foxall (No.11 Pln.)
WX15422	B. M. Frost (No.3 Pln.)
WX9270	T. J. Fury (No.6 Pln.)
WX7595	G. Glass (Bn. Hq's)
WX6980	P. Golden (No.6 Pln.)
WX8540	T. W. Green (No.3 Pln.)
WX8625	W. R. Gregory (No.5 Pln.)
WX6975	R. J. Ham (No.14 Pln.)
WX7123	R. D. Hampson (No.4 Pln.)
WX15736	R. Hansen (No.15 Pln.)
WX8695	W. D. Harris (Bn. Hq's)
WX8408	A. G. Hayes (No.2 Pln.)
WX7642	C. G. Henderson (No.10 Pln.)
WX7465	N. Holdman (No.2 Pln.)
WX10795	R. E. Hughes (No.5 Pln.)
WX9130	M. A. Hunter (No.9 Pln.)
WX5118	Cpl. J. M. Jenkins (No.12 Pln.)
WX7453	E. C. Jones (No.2 Pln.)
WX7612	C. G. Mc. Kelly (No.13 Pln.)
WX4949	R. J. Kingswell (No.12 Pln.)
WX8336	F. G. Kuhl (Bn. Hq's)
WX7230	L. H. Lee (No.8 Pln.)
WX15744	L. W. Lee (No.6 Pln.)
WX11316	L. H. Lewis ('D' Coy Hq's)
WX7285	H. R. Love (No.4 Pln.)
WX16341	S. T. Martin (No.3 Pln.)
WX13285	J. Maude (No.6 Pln.)
WX8261	R. R. McAskil (No.10 Pln.)
WX9825	C. P. McLoughlin (No.12 Pln. Hq's)
WX9826	H. J. Millar (No.11 Pln.)
WX13562	P. J. Moate ('C' Coy Hq's)
WX8200	W. R. Morris (No.10 Pln.)
WX15746	A. E. Morrison (No.13 Pln.)
WX5336	J. L. Murdoch (No.15 Pln.)
WX7645	W. J. Nicholls (No.1 Pln.)
WX16417	S. Ninyette (No.15 Pln.)
WX8828	W. D. O'Neill (No.7 Pln.)
WX8856	H. W. Pearce (No.11 Pln.)
WX8725	J. H. L. Pryce (No.1 Pln.)
WX9059	G. R. Ramage (No.1 Pln.)
WX7493	R. G. S. Rennie (No.3 Pln.)
WX7750	S. H. G. Roberts (No.6 Pln.)
WX16427	D. C. Robertson (No.8 Pln.)
WX5200	W. J. Robinson ('B' Coy Hq's & No.9 Pln.)
WX7939	C. J. Sawyer (Bn. Hq's)
WX8843	J. Scales (No.5 Pln.)
WX7576	N. E. Simmonds (No.10 Pln.)
WX16424	A. Sing ('A' Coy)
WX7893	J. S. Smith (No.2 Pln.)
WX8506	W. J. Smith (88 L.A.D.)
WX9419	H. W. Steele ('C' Coy Hq's)
WX9827	R. H. Stribling (No.12 Pln.)
WX8585	C. J. Vidler (No.5 Pln.)
WX15614	R. J. Walker (No.3 Pln.)
WX7466	B. J. Walsh (No.3 Pln.)
WX8356	W. S. Watkins (Bn. Hq's)
WX10761	T. M. Watters (No.3 Pln.)
WX7502	T. S. Wayman (No.3 Pln.)
WX10049	M. W. Wilkinson (No.1 Pln.)
WX1138	A. G. Williams ('C' Coy Hq's)

Voyage Only Officer – Taken on Strength Java

WX10322 Lt. C. Blakeway

Reinforcements Taken on Strength Fremantle, Western Australia 16.1.1942

Officers

WX10874 Lt. T. R. Ambrose (No.10 Pln.)
WX10372 Lt. G. H. Branson (No.6 Pln.)
WX10107 Lt. R. W. Learmonth (No.5 Pln.)

WX10108 Lt. K. G. Lee (Hq's Coy)
WX228　Lt. D. V. Mentiplay (SRBn.)
WX9390　Lt. B. M. O'Sullivan (Hq's Coy)

Sergeants

WX12949 Sgt. J. L. Scott ('C' Coy)

Corporals

WX15433 Cpl. J. L. Anderson (No.9 Pln.)
WX17251 Cpl. L. G. Ashbolt (SRBn.)
WX14172 Cpl. F. C. Evans (SRBn.)
WX15041 Cpl. D. J. Gardner (SRBn.)
WX15720 Cpl. S. S. McNeil (SRBn.)
WX15684 Cpl. J. E. Muldoon (SRBn.)

WX17293 Cpl. A. J. C. Rowland (SRBn.)
WX13515 L/Cpl. A. B. W. Annetts (SRBn.)
WX12575 L/Cpl. G. A. Gorman ('A' Coy)
WX16883 L/Cpl. N. W. Platts (SRBn.)
WX12202 L/Cpl. M. S. Scala (No.1 Pln.)

Privates

WX17915 T. W. Allen ('E' Coy Hq's SRBn.)
WX14634 W. G. H. Anderson (No.8 Pln.)
WX17793 W. J. Andrews (SRBn.)
WX17864 B. A. Bendall ('A' Coy)
WX11573 G. G. Breeze (No.10 Pln.)
WX17754 J. Brown (Bn. Hq's)
WX12335 R. E. Brown (No.7 Pln.)
WX17545 J. R. Buchan (SRBn.)
WX14022 R. Burchell (SRBn.)
WX15756 A. J. Burgess (SRBn. then Bn. Hq's)
WX17755 M. W. F. Butcher (SRBn.)
WX17860 H. D. Cain ('A' Coy)
WX12661 W. E. Cake (No.6 Pln.)
WX20026 W. Cameron (SRBn.)
WX11584 W. C. Case ('C' Coy)
WX16795 F. C. Chambers (SRBn.)
WX12488 J. W. Clay ('C' Coy)
WX16260 E. A. Cornell (SRBn.)

WX20018 J. L. Correy (No.2 Pln.)
WX17706 A. T. Cunningham (No.11 Pln.)
WX14068 G. A. Dalrymple (SRBn.)
WX15873 S. J. Darby (SRBn.)
WX20086 G. Davies (SRBn.)
WX17391 M. W. Day (SRBn.)
WX17881 O. A. Doust (No.6 Pln.)
WX17591 C. J. Dow (SRBn.)
WX17595 N. L. Dunnell (No.13 Pln.)
WX20076 W. Dwyer (No.3 Pln.)
WX16947 R. E. Ecclestone (SRBn.)
WX13079 R. E. Ellis (No.16 Pln.)
WX20164 A. E. Erskine (SRBn.)
WX17269 K. S. Evans (SRBn.)
WX17374 N. Flarty (SRBn.)
WX17745 C. H. Fletcher (Bn. Hq's)
WX12663 A. E. Floyd ('C' Coy)
WX12427 R. A. Foster (No.9 Pln.)

WX17974 L. S. Gibson (SRBn.)
WX16376 S. J. Gleeson (Coy not known)
WX17310 N. F. T. Gough (SRBn.)
WX12157 E. C. Hardey (No.16 Pln.)
WX16793 A. M. Hargreaves (SRBn.)
WX18022 F. J. Heinz-Smith (SRBn.)
WX18170 S. R. Hickey (No.6 Pln.)
WX17634 W. Holding (SRBn.)
WX17997 H. M. Holland (No.8 Pln.)
WX17636 H. W. Holland (No.8 Pln.)
WX20025 L. R. Hounslow (No.2 Pln.)
WX16981 W. R. Howson (No.3 Pln.)
WX17351 P. G. Hurst (SRBn.)
WX15402 L. Jaensch (No.2 Pln.)
WX17576 W. L. Jeffery (SRBn.)
WX15640 H. J. Johnson (SRBn.)
WX17452 L. D. Kearney (No.13 Pln. then SRBn.)
WX15700 J. Kingdon (SRBn.)
WX17582 G. Lake (SRBn.)
WX15951 K. S. Lance (SRBn.)
WX16355 G. R. Leipold (SRBn.)
WX17759 J. S. Livingstone (SRBn.)
WX13752 A/Cpl. H. Lucas (No.6 Pln.)
WX17778 F. J. Ludge (SRBn.)
WX17515 R. R. Lymn (SRBn.)
WX16886 A. M. Magill (SRBn.)
WX17639 R. W. Marsh (SRBn.)
WX16347 W. N. Matson (Bn. Hq's)
WX17837 L.W. McCann (SRBn.)
WX17566 J. K. A. MacDonald (No.3 Pln.)
WX20095 W. A. McEwen (SRBn.)
WX11580 D. S. McGlinn (No.11 Pln.)
WX17302 W. McLeod (SRBn.)
WX17000 F. N. Matthews (SRBn. and No.13 Pln.)
WX16675 R.J. Millhouse (SRBn.)
WX17737 K. Moher (SRBn.)
WX17390 E. M. Munday (SRBn.)
WX12599 A. R. Murdoch (No.6 Pln.)
WX16674 J. J. Murphy (SRBn.)
WX17363 C. O. Nash (No.13 Pln.)
WX12985 P. J. Negri ('C' Coy)
WX14031 C. T. Nelson (No.3 Pln.)
WX17458 O. K. Newling (No.3 Pln.)
WX16293 H. H. T. Norton (SRBn.)
WX14327 L. R. Nybo (No.2 Pln.)
WX12156 P. V. Omiridis (No.6 Pln.)

WX12628 S. J. Oliver ('C' Coy)
WX16931 H. C. Oswald (SRBn.)
WX12336 R. Pascall (No.6 Pln.)
WX17414 J. S. Peters (SRBn.)
WX13027 L/Cpl. C. R. Piggott ('C' Coy)
WX17393 T. Pilmoor (Bn. Hq's then 'D' Coy)
WX20157 R. S. Pimlott (Bn. Hq's)
WX20107 A. Ralph (SRBn.)
WX20068 H. W. Ralph (SRBn.)
WX17857 V. S. Reid (No.5 Pln.)
WX14197 R. W. Ridgwell ('B' Coy Hq's & No.8 Pln.)
WX20074 J. T. Ridley (SRBn.)
WX16618 R. W. Roberts (SRBn.)
WX15941 J. W. Robinson (Bn. Hq's)
WX10808 J. Rochester (SRBn.)
WX16269 E. J. Ronan (SRBn.)
WX16767 E. W. Ryan (No.3 Pln.)
WX17899 S. G. Scott (SRBn.)
WX18151 A. R. Shier ('A' Coy)
WX16952 R. A. Simmonds (No.7 Pln.)
WX17344 A. Slater (SRBn.)
WX14644 C. V. Smith (Bn. Hq's)
WX17448 H. M. Smith (SRBn.)
WX12252 J. E. Smith (No.14 Pln.)
WX13553 S. F. Spouse (No.6 Pln.)
WX16885 C. D. Squance (SRBn.)
WX17594 G. C. Stone (SRBn.)
WX17907 W. T. Swann (SRBn.)
WX14733 J. Taylor ('C' Coy)
WX17615 E. J. Thomsett (SRBn.)
WX16323 R. G. Tooze (SRBn.)
WX17882 A. G. Trigwell ('C' Coy)
WX17863 V. C. Trigwell ('C' Coy)
WX17593 H. R. Turner (SRBn.)
WX17879 G. J. Wade (No.8 Pln.)
WX12989 H. J. Wall (No.12 Pln.)
WX17962 E. W. Wallin (SRBn.)
WX17804 A. S. A. Webb (No.6 Pln.)
WX9179   H. Wilkes (SRBn.)
WX17604 M. H. Wilkins (SRBn.)
WX16956 R. S. Williams (SRBn.)
WX17370 J. Wilson (No.16 Pln.)
WX17973 J. Wilson (SRBn.)
WX18142 C. T. Wright (Bn. Hq's)
WX13161 H. E. Wright (No.8 Pln.)
WX12593 R. W. Wyllie (No.12 Pln.)

Bibliography

Official Histories – Australian War Memorial – Canberra

Australia in the War of 1939–1945 (Army)
Wigmore, Lionel, Volume IV *The Japanese Thrust,* 1957

Australia in the War of 1939–1945 (Navy)
Gill, G. Hermon, *Royal Australian Navy, 1939–42* 1957
Gill, G. Hermon, *Royal Australian Navy, 1942–45* 1968

Australia in the War of 1939–1945 (Air)
Gillison, Douglas, *Air War Against Japan, 1939–42* 1957
Odgers, George, *Air War Against Japan, 1942–45* 1968

Australia in the War 1939–1945 (Civil)
Hasluck, Paul, *The Government and The People, 1939–41* 1952
Hasluck, Paul, *The Government and The People, 1942–45* 1970

Australia in the War of 1939–1945 (Medical)
Walker, Allan S., *Clinical Problems of War,* 1952
Walker, Allan S., *Middle East and Far East,* 1953
Walker, Allan S., *Medical Services of the R.A.N. and R.A.A.F.,* 1961

Official Histories – British – HMSO London

Woodburn-Kirby, Maj-Gen Stanley, *The War Against Japan,* 1957.

General References and Histories of the Second World War

Allen, Louis, *Singapore 1941–1942*, Davis Pointer London 1977.
Bellair, John, *From Snow to Jungle,* A History of the 2/3rd Australian Machine Gun Battalion, Allen & Unwin, Sydney 1987.
Bennett, Lt-Gen H. Gordon, *Why Singapore Fell,* Angus & Robertson Ltd, Sydney 1944.
Bergamini, David, *Japan's Imperial Conspiracy,* How Emperor Hirohito led Japan into war against the West, William Morrow & Company, Inc., New York 1971.
Blair, Joan and Clay, *Return From The River Kwai,* McDonald & Janes, London 1979.
Bowden, Tim, *Changi Photographer,* George Aspinall's record of Captivity, ABC Books 1984.
Buckley, John, OBE, ED., *Australia's Most Perilous Year January 1942–January 1943,* Defence Force Journal No. 72, Special Issue Sept/Oct 1988, Ruskin Press, North Melbourne.
Burfitt, James, *Against The Odds,* The History of the 2/18th Battalion A.I.F., 2/18th Battalion (A.I.F.) Association, Frenchs Forest NSW 1991.

Christie, Robert W. and Robert Christie (editors), *The History of the 2/29th Battalion, 8th Australian Division, A.I.F.* 2/29th Battalion Association, Sale, Victoria 1983.

Clarke, Hugh V., *Last Stop Nagasaki,* Allen & Unwin 1984.

Clarke, Hugh, Burgess-Colin, Braddon-Russell, *Prisoners of War*, Time Life Books, Australia 1988.

Clarke, Hugh V., *Twilight Liberation,* Allen & Unwin 1985.

Coast, John, *Railroad of Death,* Hyperion Press Ltd, London 1946.

Coates, Albert, and Rosenthal Newman, *The Albert Coates Story,* Hyland House, Melbourne 1977.

Cody, Les, *Ghosts in Khaki,* The History of 2/4th Machine Gun Battalion, 8th Division A.I.F., Hesperian Press, Perth 1997.

Connolly, Ray, and Wilson-Bob (editors), *Medical Soldiers,* 2/10th Field Ambulance, 8th Division 1940–1945, 2/10th Field Ambulance Association, Kingsgrove, NSW 1985.

Dandie, A., *The Story of J Force,* Published by author 1985.

Day, David, *The Great Betrayal,* Britain, Australia, and the Onset of the Pacific War 1939–1945, Angus & Robertson (UK) 1988.

Dunlop, E. E., *The War Diaries of Weary Dunlop,* Combined edition of two books, Penguin Books 1997.

Elphick, David, *Singapore – The Pregnable Fortress,* A study in Deception, Discord and Desertion, Hodder & Stoughton London 1995.

Fawcett, Aitken Edward, *The Story of the 2/2nd Australian Pioneer Battalion,* 2/2nd Pioneer Battalion Association, Melbourne 1953.

Firkins, Peter. *From Hell to Eternity,* Westward Ho Publishing Company 1979.

Ford, Roger, *The Grim Reaper* 1996, Sedgwick & Jackson, London 1996.

Goetz Holmes, Linda, *4000 Bowls of Rice,* Allen & Unwin 1993.

Hall, Leslie G., *The Blue Haze,* Published by Leslie Gordon Hall 1985.

Hart, Liddell B.H., *Liddell Hart's History of the Second World War,* Book Club Associates, London 1970.

Henning, Peter, *Doomed Battalion,* The Australian 2/40th Battalion 1940–1945, Mateship and Leadership in War and Captivity, Allen & Unwin, St Leonards, NSW 1995.

Horner, D. M., *High Command,* Australia and Allied Strategy 1939–1945, Allen & Unwin, Sydney 1982.

Horner, David, *Inside The War Cabinet,* Directing Australia's War Effort 1939–1945, Allen & Unwin, NSW 1996.

Hudson, W. J., and Stokes H. J., (editors), Department of Foreign Affairs, *Documents on Australian Foreign Policy 1937–49,* Volume V, July 1941–June 1942, Australian Government Printing Service Canberra 1982.

Janes, *Fighting Ships of World War II,* Tiger Books International, U.K.1998.

Kinvig, Clifford, *River Kwai Railway,* The story of the Burma–Siam Railroad, Brassey's, U.K. 1992.

Kinvig, Clifford, *Scapegoat – General Percival of Singapore,* Brassey's, London 1996.

Lamb, Richard, *Churchill As War Leader – Right or Wrong?* Bloomsbury 1993.

Lane, John, *Summer Will Come Again*, Fremantle Arts Centre Press 1987.

Lee, Don, *A Yarn or Two,* Access Press 1994.

Lodge, A. B., *The Fall of General Gordon Bennett,* Allen & Unwin, Sydney 1986.

Lowe, Peter, *Great Britain and the origins of the Pacific War,* A study of British Policy in East Asia 1937–1941, Clarendon Press, Oxford 1977.

Magarry, Ron, *The Battalion Story,* 2/26th Infantry Battalion, 8th Australian Division A.I.F., Published by the author, Jindalee, Queensland 1994.

Marder, Arthur J., *Old Friends – New Enemies,* The Royal Navy and the Imperial Japanese Navy, Strategic Illusions 1936–1941, Clarendon Press, Oxford 1981.

Marder, Arthur J., Jacobsen-Mark and Horsfield-John, *Old Friends – New Enemies,* The Royal Navy and the Imperial Japanese Navy, The Pacific War 1942–1945, Clarendon Press, Oxford 1990.

McCarthy, John, *Australia and Imperial Defence 1918–39,* A Study in Air and Sea Power, University of Queensland Press 1976.

McGregor, John, *Blood on the Rising Sun,* Bencoolen 1979.

McIntyre, W. David, *The Rise & Fall of the Singapore Naval Base,* Cambridge Commonwealth Press 1979.

Neidpath, James, *The Singapore Naval Base and the Defence of Britain's Eastern Empire 1919–1941.* Clarendon Press, Oxford 1981

Nelson, David, *The Story of Changi,* Changi Publication Company, Australia.

Nelson, Hank, *Prisoners of War – Australians Under Nippon,* ABC Enterprises 1985.

Newton, R.W., *The Grim Glory of the 2/19th Battalion, A.I.F.,* Sydney 1975.

Page, Sir Earle, *Truant Surgeon,* Angus & Robertson 1963.

Parkin, Ray, *Into the Smother,* Hogarth Press 1963.

Penfold, A. W., Bayliss W. C., and. Crispin K. E., *Galleghan's Greyhounds,* The Story of the 2/30th Australian Infantry Battalion, 22nd November 1940 to 10th October 1945, 2/30th Battalion Association, Sydney 1979.

Percival, Lt-Gen A. E., *The War in Malaya,* Eyre & Spottiswoode, London 1949.

Ponting, Clive, *1940 Myth and Reality,* Ivan R. Dee, Publisher, Chicago 1990.

Power, F. W. G., *Kurrah!* An Australian POW in Changi, Thailand and Japan, 1942–1945, McCrae, Australia 1991.

Ramsay, Silver Lynette, *Sandakan – A Conspiracy of Silence,* Sally Milner Publishing 1998.

Rivett, Rohan D., *Behind Bamboo,* Penguin Books, Australia 1991.

Robertson, John, *Australia at War 1939–1945,* William Heinemann, Melbourne 1981.

Robertson, John, and McCarthy, John, *Australian War Strategy 1939–1945,* A Documentary History, University of Queensland Press 1985.

Robinson, Frank, and Hall, E. R. (Bon), *Through Hell and Bomb Blast,* Published by the author 1982.

Roscoe, Theodore, *United States Submarine Operations in World War II,* Naval Institute Press 1988.

Simson, Ivan, S*ingapore – Too Little Too Late,* Leo Cooper, London 1970.

Skennerton, Ian*, 303 Vickers Medium Machine Gun S.A.I.S. No. 8.,* Thai Watana Panich Press Co. Ltd., Bangkok, Thailand 1997.

Skennerton, Ian, *100 years of Australian Service Machine Guns,* Published by I. D. Skennerton 1989.

Slim, Field-Marshall, Sir William, *Defeat into Victory,* Landsborough Publications Ltd, London 1958.

Tanaka, Yuki, *Hidden Horrors*, Japanese War Crimes in World War II, Westview Press 1996.

Thorne, Christopher, *Allies of a Kind,* The United States, Britain, and The War Against Japan, 1941–1945, Hamish Hamilton Ltd, London 1978.

Tsuji, Masanobu, *Singapore 1941–1942,* The Japanese Version of the Malayan Campaign of World War II, Oxford University Press, Singapore 1991.

U.S. War Department, *Handbook on Japanese Military Forces,* Greenhill Books 1991.

Wall, Don, *Heroes at Sea,* Don Wall Publications 1991.

Wall, Don, *Heroes of F Force,* Don Wall Publications 1993.

Wall, Don, *Sandakan – The Last March,* Don Wall Publications 1997.

Wall, Don, *Singapore and Beyond,* The Story of the men of the 2/20th Battalion, Told by the survivors, Don Wall 2/20th Battalion Association, East Hills, NSW 1985.

Ward, Ian, *The Killer they called God,* Media Masters, Singapore 1992.

Ward, Ian, *Snaring The Other Tiger,* Media Masters, Singapore 1996.

Whitecross, Roy, *Slaves of the son of Heaven,* Dymocks 1952.

Williamson, Kristin, *The Last Bastion,* Lansdowne Press, Sydney 1984.

Willmott, H.,P., *Empires in the Balance,* Japanese and Allied Pacific Strategies to April 1942, Orbis Publishing, London 1982.

Woodburn, Kirby, Maj-Gen, Stanley, *Singapore – The Chain of Disaster,* The MacMillan Company, N.Y. 1971.

Sources used for 'Colour Patch'

SINGAPORE

A9716/1   File 1241 R.A.A.F. Intelligence reports – Singapore, National Archives of Australia, Canberra

AWM54   File 135/4/2 Schedule of known cemetries and burial places of A.I.F. personnel who died whilst Prisoners of War of the Japanese in Burma, Siam and Singapore, Australian War Memorial, Canberra

AWM54   554/11/4 Part 12, Report on Singapore Camps and Working Parties, Australian War Memorial, Canberra

AWM54   554/11/29 Chronology of important events of working parties from Changi Prisoner of War Camp Malaya, Australian War Memorial, Canberra

AWM54   554/11/39 A.I.F. War Diary, Changi, February 1942 to August 1945, Australian War Memorial Canberra

B3856   File 144/1/358 Australian Imperial Forces and British Prisoners of War admitted to Outram Road Military Prison, Singapore under the Japanese administration, National Archives of Australia, Melbourne

MP742/1   File 251/5/1187 2/4th Machine Gun Battalion – Promotions, National Archives of Australia, Melbourne

PR00592   Items 1–10 AWM Capt. Avon Smith-Ryan Diary, Australian War Memorial, Canberra

Captain Tom Bunning's Diary 2/4th Machine Gun Battalion, loaned to the author by Mrs Margo Bunning

Major Alf Cough's Report and Diary 2/4th Machine Gun Battalion, loaned to the author by his son Alan Cough

JAVA

Allied Geographical Section S.W.P.A. Special Report No. 112 Java, National Archives of Australia, Perth

AWM54   File 423/4/157 ATIS S.W.P.A. Enemy Publications Feb–March 1942 Accounts of the Netherlands East Indies Campaign, Australian War Memorial, Canberra

AWM54   File 556/2/1 "Java Interlude" The Japanese on the Netherlands East Indies 1942, Australian War Memorial, Canberra

AWM54   File 559/2/2 Report by Brigadier A. S. Blackburn GOC, A.I.F. Java, on Operations of the A.I.F. on Java February–March 1942, Australian War Memorial, Canberra

AWM54   File 627/11/2 Services Reconnaissance Department – Information on Operations Java, Australian War Memorial, Canberra

AWM54   File 627/11/4 Services Reconnaissance Department – Information on Japanese Prisoner of War Camps in Java, Australian War Memorial, Canberra

AWM54   File 779/1/10 An account of one of several drafts of Prisoners of War from Java to Japan, Australian War Memorial, Canberra

B3856   File 140/1/26 Deceased personnel – Java, National Archives of Australia, Melbourne

B3856   File 140/1/41 Nominal Rolls of Prisoners of War and Internees in the Far East, obtained from Japanese records, National Archives of Australia, Melbourne

B3856   File 140/1/60 (85) Nominal Rolls of Deceased POW Java, National Archives of Australia, Melbourne

B3856   File 144/1/361 Australian Prisoners of War movements in South East Asia. Allied Prisoner of War Parties to leave Java, National Archives of Australia, Melbourne

MP742/1   File 336/1/191 Movements Australian Prisoners of War, South East Asia, National Archives of Australia, Melbourne

SUMATRA

AWM52   30/3/15 War Diary for HQ 2 Australian Prisoner of War Reception Group (A.I.F.) August–December 1945, Australian War Memorial, Canberra

AWM54   File 553/6/1 Report on Evacuation from Singapore across Sumatra, February–March 1942, Australian War Memorial, Canberra

AWM54   File 627/9/3 Part 3, Services Reconnaissance Department – Padang, Australian War Memorial, Canberra

AWM54   File 627/9/3 Part 5, Services Reconnaissance Department – Medan, Australian War Memorial, Canberra

AWM54   File 815/2/9 Account of Railway construction in Sumatra by Allied Prisoners of War 1944–1945, Australian War Memorial, Canberra

B3856   File 140/1/61 Australian casualties on Java, Sumatra and surrounding areas, National Archives of Australia, Melbourne

KOREA

Allied Geographical Section S.W.P.A. Special Report No. 109 Seoul Korea, National Archives of Australia, Perth

Allied Geographical Section S.W.P.A. Special Report No. 111 Pusan Korea, National Archives of Australia, Perth

AWM54   File 627/17/1 Part 1, Services Reconnaissance Department Korea X-10 Keijo, X-15 Jinsen, Australian War Memorial, Canberra

Prisoner of War Encampments Cinpac – Cinpoa Bulletin 113–45, Australian War Memorial, Canberra

'A' Force – BURMA

AWM54 1010/4/62 War Crimes Affidavit by Major C. E. Green, Australian War Memorial, Canberra

AWM54 File 554/2/1A Reports on Conditions, Life and Work of Prisoners of War in Burma and Siam by Brigadier C. A. McEachern 1942–1945, Australian War Memorial, Canberra

AWM54 File 554/2/2 Report by Major C. E. Green 2/4th M.G. Bn. Commanding 3rd Battalion, "A" Force and known subsequently, whilst working on the Thai–Burma Railway as "Green Force", Australian War Memorial, Canberra

AWM54 File 554/2/3 Report on "A" Force by Brigadier Varley 1942, Australian War Memorial, Canberra

AWM54 File 554/2/4 Reports on "A" Force. On Conditions of Prisoners of War by Lt-Col C. J. W. Anderson, VC, MC, Australian War Memorial, Canberra

AWM54 554/2/14 Diary of Major L. J. Robertson R.A.E. Commanding Australian Personnel of Thai Prisoner of War Branch 5, Burma 1943–1944, Australian War Memorial, Canberra

Green Force Roll donated by one of the compilers, Les Cody 2/4th Machine Gun Battalion

Summary File on Green Force by Major C. E. Green, Commanding "Green Force" donated by Major Green's daughter, Mrs Barbara Brand

'D' Force – THAILAND

AWM 3DRL 6550 File 1 Nominal roll of deceased Australians Group IV, Australian War Memorial, Canberra

AWM54 File 1010/4/62 War Crimes affidavit by Major Hector George Greiner 2/3rd Machine Gun Battalion, Australian War Memorial, Canberra

AWM54 554/2/1A Report on Conditions, Life and Work of Prisoners of War in Burma and Siam, by Brigadier C. A. McEachern, Australian War Memorial, Canberra

AWM54 File 554/5/1 Report on Kinsaiyok Camp and Hospital and Tarsau Base Hospital 1943–1944, by Lt-Col E. E. Dunlop, Australian War Memorial, Canberra

AWM54 File 554/5/5 Interview and report upon experiences of Prisoners of War, working camps and hospitals in Thailand by Lt-Col E. E. Dunlop, Australian War Memorial, Canberra

Major Alf Cough's Report and Diary 2/4th Machine Gun Battalion, loaned to the author by his son Alan Cough

Map compiled by Ray Parkin from R.A.F. Aerial Photo No. 487, 22/12/1944 and Survey by Ken Bradley A.T.T.C. Donated by Bill Haskell, formerly of the 2/3rd Machine Gun Battalion

'F' Force – THAILAND

AWM54 File 554/7/2 Part 1A History of "F" Force, Report by Lt-Col S.W. Harris O.B.E., R.A., Australian War Memorial, Canberra

AWM54 File 554/7/2 Part 2, Summary of Medical Report, British and Australian POW April 1943–April 1944, by Lt-Col Huston, R.A.M.C., Australian War Memorial, Canberra

AWM54 File 554/11/4 Part 7, 8th Division Army personnel recommended for Honours and Awards, MID whilst POW in "F" Force in Thailand, Australian War Memorial, Canberra

AWM54 File 64, Report on the march from Non Pladuk–Shimo Sonkurai, Australian War Memorial, Canberra

B3856 File 140/1/60 Item 130 "F" Force Roll, National Archives of Australia, Melbourne

MP742/1 File 255/9/618, Report of Activities of A.I.F. "F" Force, National Archives of Australia, Melbourne

'H' Force – THAILAND

AWM54 File 554/8/1 Interim report on A.I.F. Section of "H" Force ex-Changi Camp, Thailand, Period 5th May 1943 to 23rd December 1943, Australian War Memorial, Canberra

B3856 File 140/1/60, National Archives of Australia, Melbourne

MP741/1 File 255/15/1617 Attachment 1 "H" Force report by Lt-Col H. R. Humphries, National Archives of Australia, Melbourne

'L' Force – THAILAND

AWM54 1010/4/43 War Crimes affidavit by Peter John Dimopoulos, 2/4th Machine Gun Battalion, Australian War Memorial, Canberra

AWM54 554/10/1 "L" Force Hospital Party Diary by Lt-Col Malcolm R.A.M.C. 1942–1943, Australian War Memorial, Canberra

THAILAND 1944 – 1945

AWM54 554/2/1 Report on Conditions Life and Work of Prisoners of War in Burma and Siam by Brigadier C. A. McEachern 1942–1945, Australian War Memorial, Canberra

B3856/0 Item 144/14/33 Nominal Roll, Knong Hin–Mergui Escape Road, National Archives of Australia, Melbourne

B3856/0 Item 144/14/134 Report on British A.I.F. working party to Linson Camp, National Archives of Australia, Melbourne

B3856/0 Item 148/1/18 List of Deaths in Linson Prisoner of War Camp Siam, National Archives of Australia, Melbourne

'B' & 'E' Forces – BORNEO

A3269 Item V17, Services reconnaissance Department, Sandakan, National Archives of Australia, Canberra

A4311/8 File 747/5 War Crimes investigations, Final report on North Borneo, National Archives of Australia, Canberra

AWM54 554/3/2 Information regarding Allied Prisoners of War Sandakan, Jesselton and Ranau, Australian War Memorial, Canberra

AWM54 File 627/4/16 Part 18, Services Reconnaissance Department Intelligence Reports Sandakan, Australian War Memorial, Canberra

AWM54 File 627/4/16 Part 21, Services Reconnaissance Department Intelligence Reports 1944, Kuching area, Australian War Memorial, Canberra

AWM54 File 779/3/8 Interrogation of recovered Australian and Allied POW from Borneo 1945, Australian War Memorial, Canberra

AWM226 File 71, Reports, Affidavits etc., concerning war crimes, submitted to the Australian War Crimes Commission, Australian War Memorial, Canberra

Allied Geographical Section Terrain Handbook Sandakan 14th March 1945, Study Number 90, North Borneo Series 1, Department of Defence Allied Geographical Section S.W.P.A., National Archives of Australia, Perth

B3856 File 144/14/140 Diary of Burns? 2/20 Bn., Documents found in a mass grave of 23 Australian Prisoners of War, National Archives of Australia, Melbourne

B3856 File 145/4/147 Report on investigations and Allied Prisoners of War, 8th Australian Division area, 15th August–27th November 1945, National Archives of Australia, Melbourne

Borneo Burlesque Story by Lt. George Forbes, Published privately 1947

The Bulletin October 9th,1946 *The Serviceman*

FRENCH INDO-CHINA

AWM54 File 627/8/1 Services Reconnaissance Department, Saigon 1945, Australian War Memorial, Canberra

AWM54 File 627/8/2 Services Reconnaissance Department French Indo-China March–August 1944, Australian War Memorial, Canberra

B3856 File 144/14/61 Movements POW French Indo-China, National Archives of Australia, Melbourne

Geographical Handbook Series B.R.510 British Naval Intelligence Division December 1943 for the use of persons in H.M. Service only N.p. (London)

Rakuyo Maru PARTY

AWM54 Item 1010/9/109 Report on information from 1942–1944, obtained from recovered Aust PW ex-*Rakuyo Maru*, Australian War Memorial, Canberra

B3856 File 144/1/128 Attachment 1, Phom Penh Roll, National Archives of Australia, Melbourne

B3856 File 144/14/33 National Archives of Australia, Melbourne

JAPAN

A816/1   File 37/301/315 Reports of POW Camps in the Far East including Ohama 9B Camp, National Archives of Australia, Canberra

AWM54   File 554/15/1 Diary by Captain C. R. Boyce, Medical Records "J" Force 8th Div A.I.F. Changi Prisoners of War Camp 1943–1945, Australian War Memorial, Canberra

AWM54   File 627/12/1 Services Reconnaissance Department Report X-B-23 Niihama, Australian War Memorial, Canberra

AWM226 File 80 POW Encampments CINPAC–CINPOA Bulletin No. 113–45, Australian War Memorial, Canberra

Allied Geographical Section S.W.P.A. Special Report No. 107 Inland Sea, National Archives of Australia, Perth

Allied Geographical Section S.W.P.A. Special Report No. 112 Shikoku, National Archives of Australia, Perth

Allied Geographical Section S.W.P.A. Special Report No. 113 Yawata–Shimonosecki, National Archives of Australia, Perth

Allied Geographical Section S.W.P.A. Special Report No. 134 Nagoya, National Archives of Australia, Perth

Allied Geographical Section S.W.P.A. Special Report No. 136 Osaka, National Archives of Australia, Perth

B3856   File 140/1/40 Newspaper cutting relating to the ashes of A.I.F. Prisoners of War who died in Japanese captivity, National Archives of Australia, Melbourne

MP742/1 File 255/9/606 Australian POW's Far East, Japanese Camps Reports, Ohama POW Camp, National Archives of Australia, Melbourne

Frank McGlinn Diary concerning the voyage to Japan aboard the *Rashin Maru* and life at Yamane and Niihama Camps on Shikoku Island Japan 1944–1945. Item donated by Frank's sister Mrs Pearl Cockburn

Nominal Roll of Notogawa Camp as supplied to the author by ex-S/Sgt Keith Pescod

Reinforcements for MALAYA and AWL Fremantle

A1608/1 File AI 45/1/1 Reinforcements for Malaya, National Archives of Australia, Canberra

AWM54   963/15/2 A.I.F. Convoy–H.M.T. "MS2" Voyage No.342, Australian War Memorial, Canberra

AWM54   963/15/11 H.M.T. "MS2" Voyage Report, Australian War Memorial, Canberra

MP729/7 File 42/421/750 Reinforcements for Malaya–Report, National Archives of Australia, Melbourne

MP729/7 F 42/422/68 Western Command Convoy "MS2", National Archives of Australia, Melbourne

The Vickers Machine Gun

AWM54   Item 385/12/1 Vickers Machine Gun, Characteristics, Personnel and co-operation with infantry, Australian War Memorial, Canberra

The Vickers Medium Machine Gun – *The Australasian* July 19th, 1942

Notes on The Organization and the tactical handling of Medium Machine Guns–Military Training Pamphlet No. 31, 1940. Prepared by the Chief of Imperial General Staff, The War Office, February, 1940

Organisation of a WWII Machine Gun Battalion

An Infantry (Machine Gun) Battalion – War Establishment A.I.F. III/1940/32E/2

Other Sources Consulted

A5954/1 File 527/12 Operations of the 8th Division in Malaya 1941/42, National Archives of Australia, Canberra

AWM51   File 125 Report by Major-General H. Gordon Bennett CB, CMG, DSO, VD, GOC Malaya, on Malayan Campaign 7th December 1941 to 15th February 1942, Australian War Memorial, Canberra

AWM52   File 8/5/4 2/4th Machine Gun Battalion Diary Routine Orders Part I, Australian War Memorial, Canberra and Routine Orders Part II, Soldier Career Management Agency, Melbourme

AWM54   File 553/3/4 Operation Report of 8th Division in Malaya, Australian War Memorial, Canberra

AWM54   553/5/23 Part 2 Report on Operations of 8th Division Australian Imperial Force in Malaya, compiled by Colonel J. H.Thyer, CBE, DSO, from the narrative by Colonel C. H. Kappe MBE, p.s.c., Australian War Memorial, Canberra

B3856   File 144/14/8 Original statements made by repatriated Prisoners of War concerning their internment, National Archives of Australia, Melbourne

B3856   File 144/1/275 Nominal Rolls alive Changi Gaol Camp, Kranji, Tanjong Pagar, National Archives of Australia, Melbourne

Nominal Roll Index

WX239   J.R. Aberle, 2
WX7622   N.L. Ablett, 208
WX9828   A.A. Adams, 2
WX8245   E.T. Adams, 208,731
WX13977 G.F. Airey, 209,557,558,
  559,576,773
WX8599   J. Alderton, 210
WX17915 T.W. Allen, 210
WX7064   B.W.J. Allpike, 211,628
WX10874 T.R. Ambrose, 211,645
WX3464   C.L. Anderson, 52,212,
  555,557,608,609,758,767
WX9123   C.W.M. Anderson, 3
WX8872   D.F. Anderson, 213
WX15433 J.L. Anderson, 213
WX9289   R.G. Anderson, 214
WX14634 W.G.H. Anderson, 214
WX8518   W.F. Anderton, 215
WX17793 W.J. Andrews, 3
WX3376   M.J. Anketell, xvii,xviii,4,
  138,251,268,317,321,527,528,535,
  537,554,555,558,568,767,775
WX13457 D.A. Annear, 5,695
WX13468 R.W. Annear, 215,540,
  563,694,695,697,698,701
WX7905   F.J. Annesley, 5
WX13515 A.B.W. Annetts, 6,553
WX10787 R.E. Arbery, 216,542,787
WX7370   C.W. Armstrong, 216
WX7717   F. Armstrong, 6, 677,678,
  684,691
WX8963   L. Armstrong, 217
WX7046   M. Armstrong, 218
WX9011   G.C. Arthur, 218,712,714,
  718
WX17251 L.G. Ashbolt, 219
WX9342   H. Atkinson, 220
WX7444   A.R. Attenborough, 7
WX8729   R.C. Badock, 221,639

WX9864   R.J. Baggs, 7
WX8829   J. Bagrie, 221
WX10920 N.E. Bailey, 8
WX9294   W.F. Baillie, 222
WX8720   A.J. Baker, 8
WX8981   E.R. Baker, 222
WX8962   J.A. Baker, 223
WX9367   J.R. Baker, 223
WX8682   W.R.S. Baker, 9
WX7495   L.P. Ball, 224
WX8485   A.W. Bamford, 224,750
WX10343 N.E. Banks, 225,693,698,
  701
WX7587   T. Barbour, 225,750
WX7164   F. Barker, 226
WX6970   A.J. Barnes, 226
WX222   T.J. Barnett, 227,639
WX8429   V.G. Barnett, 227,720,787
WX7611   R.S. Barr, 9
WX7796   J.J.S. Barrass, 10
WX8185   J.J. Barry, 228
WX9589   F.M. Barrymore, 10
WX9361   M.A. Bartlett, 11
WX9195   J.W. Basell, 228
WX9018   E.N. Bates, 229
WX8140   F.J. Baxter, 229
WX9277   T.J. Beard, 230,542,544
WX7883   W.H. Beard, 11
WX10791 A.R. Beattie, 230,703
WX14855 P.R. Beaton, 231
WX13421 R.C. Beckham, 231
WX7636   W.J. Beer, 12
WX12765 P.J. Beilby, 232,721,724,
  725,769
WX9063   A.J. Bell, 12,695
WX691   E. Bell, 232
WX16389 R.J. Bell, 13
WX17864 B.A. Bendall, 13
WX9340   H.P. Bennett, 14

WX9061   D.E. Bevis, 233,633,
  748–752,754,759
WX8798   G.P. Biggs, 14
WX9017   C.R. Bird, 15
WX8650   H.J. Bishop, 15
WX12469 J.H. Blackborrow, 16
WX7937   H.G. Blakiston, 233
WX7308   L.A. Blair, 234
WX10322 C. Blakeway, 43,286,327
  576,584
WX8709   R.B. Blaschek, 235
WX8631   S.J. Blewett, 235
WX8766   H.V. Booth, 16,693,698,700
WX8712   J. Borrow, 17
WX7600   G.R. Bousfield, 236
WX7253   W.V. Bow, 236,390,482
WX3483   K.C. Boyle, 237,564,610,
  758
WX8796   F. Bracklemann, 238,543
WX9090   N. Bradshaw, 239
WX10372 G.H. Branson, 239,414
WX14226 A.A.M. Brazier, 17
WX9229   W.E. Breed, 240
WX11573 G.G. Breeze, 240
WX9031   M.J. Brennan, 18
WX5050   J.A. Briggs, 18
WX7329   R.A. Briggs, 241
WX9288   J.A. Brooker, 19
WX9316   A. Brooksbank, 241,775
WX7947   A.R. Brown, 19,556
WX17754 J. Brown, 20,557
WX12335 R.E. Brown, 242,639
WX10805 R.J. Brown, 20
WX8789   S.T. Brown, 21
WX7148   M.L. Browne, 21
WX9283   J.H. Browning, 22,543,544
WX10841 A.C. Bruce, 242
WX17545 J.R. Buchan, 243
WX15989 J.S. Buckley, 22

WX7629 F. Bugg, 23
WX13442 L.N.W. Bullock, 23
WX9278 E.W.H. Bunce, 243
WX9223 H.T. Bunker, 244,724,725, 769
WX3452 G.McR. Bunning, 72,244, 364,557,561,564,641,770
WX14022 R. Burchell, 24
WX7542 G.L. Burdon, 245,756,757
WX15756 A.J. Burgess, 245,695,697 698,701
WX16405 E.J. Burgess, 246
WX8098 W. Burgess, 246,565,775
WX7333 A.J. Burns, 247
WX7702 C.E. Burns, 24
WX7316 C.J. Burns, 247
WX7661 G.N. Burslem, 248
WX7007 E.G. Burton, 25,538,675
WX7790 T.H. Buscombe, 248
WX17755 M.W.F. Butcher, 25
WX7469 T.J. Butler, 26
WX6155 L.P. Byrne, 249
WX9261 J.N. Caimanos, 249
WX17860 H.D. Cain, 26
WX12661 W.E. Cake, 250
WX10365 M.W. Caldwell, 250,595
WX3451 C. Cameron, 251,555, 561,564,763,767,775
WX11226 G.K. Cameron, 251
WX20026 W. Cameron, 27
WX9556 R.S. Campbell, 252
WX7479 R.F. Cannon, 27
WX8192 R.J. Carlile, 28
WX15785 W. Carlyon, 252, 754
WX15690 J.M. Carr, 28
WX9551 F.V. Carroll, 253
WX7325 R.F. Carruthers, 29,550
WX9326 A.H. Carter, 29,544
WX8240 D.N.H. Carter, 253,595,737
WX8445 R.C. Carter, 30
WX11584 W.C. Case, 30
WX8792 W.T. Castles, 254
WX9060 A.T.J. Cato, 254,633,757
WX16425 C.N. Chamberlain, 255
WX16795 F.C. Chambers, 31
WX7504 D.B. Chapman, 31
WX11279 G.K. Chatfield, 255,734
WX9388 J.M.C. Cheyne, 256,719
WX8123 H.A.T. Chilvers, 32
WX8397 R.W. Chipperfield, 32,675
WX7122 J.P. Clancy, 256,701,702, 705
WX7163 J. Clare, 33
WX6976 J.M. Clare, 33,754
WX7714 F.D.J. Clark, 34
WX9136 B.W.J. Clarke, 257
WX9360 E.J. Clarke, 257,710,712, 714,718

WX7625 J.S. Clarke, 34
WX6632 S. Clarke, 35
WX12488 J.W. Clay, 258
WX10354 H.T. Clayden, 258,742,747
WX10358 S.R. Clayden, 259,726,727
WX16436 G.D. Clifton, 35
WX9243 K. Clifton, 259
WX4927 A.N. Climie, 36,726,727, 744
WX10739 W.E. Clothier, 260
WX16369 A.J. Cocking, 260,327, 594,724,725,769
WX9555 L. Cody, xi,261,609
WX8808 J.C. Colbey, 261
SX11457 E.H. Cole, 36
WX10609 J.V. Colevas, 262,542,778
WX10282 C.L. Collins, 262
WX9109 A.J. Colquhoun, 37
WX4912 T.J. Conway, 263,732
WX16306 J. Cook, 264
WX8822 H.J. Cooper, 264
WX15707 H.M. Cooper, 37
WX16260 E.A. Cornell, 265
WX9035 R.H. Cornish, 266
NX76253 F.X. Corry, 43,59,85,145, 172,266,599,610
WX20018 J.L. Correy, 267
WX10048 E.J. Cosson, 267,615,756
WX3444 A.J. Cough, 268,321,543, 553,555,556,564,566,622,623,634, 635,636,637,639,661,675,728,738, 754,762,764
WX9092 A.V. Cousins, 38
WX8641 H.J. Cowie, 269
WX16441 T.D. Crane, 269,640
WX15783 D.C. Cripps, 38
WX7268 F.V. Cross, 270,724,769
WX9004 A. Cryer, 39
WX17706 A.T. Cunningham, 39
WX3446 F.L. Curnow, 40,538,556
WX5221 S.A. Currie, 270,567
WX8735 J.G. Curtin, 271,639
WX9561 A.E. Dahlberg, 40
WX8778 L.J. Daily, 271,732
WX14068 G.A. Dalrymple, 41
WX15873 S.J. Darby, 41
WX9334 J.F. Dare, 272
WX8681 R.W. Davey, 42
WX8587 W.J. Davey, 272,707,716
WX7909 T. Davidson, 42
WX8855 D.J. Davies, 43
WX20086 G. Davies, 43
WX16420 H.A. Davis, 44
WX7804 T.M. Davison, 44
WX7240 D.A. Day, 45,550
WX17391 M.W. Day, 45
WX10721 H.B. De'Castilla, 273
WX8389 H.F. DeMoulin, 46

WX6067 P.V. Dean, 144,273,400, 568,569,573
WX8011 H.T. Delaporte, 46
WX6362 R.A. Deveson, 274,707, 716
WX8238 V.J.A. Dewar, 274
WX9328 G.T. Dickie, 275
WX9310 A.A. Dickson, 275
WX13869 P.J. Dimopoulos, 276,621, 753
WX12924 E.A. Dix, 276
WX14856 M.R. Docking, 277
WX6917 G.J. Doodson, 278
WX9391 B.P. Doolan, 278
WX8617 J.J. Dore, 279,712,718, 767,787
WX9274 G. Dorizzi, 47,675
WX7997 H. Dorizzi, 47,675
WX12884 T.H. Dorizzi, 48,675
WX9557 F.J. Dorrington, 280
WX17881 O.A. Doust, 280
WX17591 C.J. Dow, 281,731,734
WX7299 T.F. Doyle, 282
WX7777 A.M. Draper, 282,675,710, 713,714,717,768
WX8830 A. McD.D. Drummond, 48
WX7943 R. Drysdale, 283
WX10199 J.A. Duggin, 284
WX8584 J.S. Duncan, 284,574
WX7236 C.H. Dunn, 285
WX8092 C.H. Dunn, 49
WX17595 N.L. Dunnell, 285
WX9266 W. Dunwoodie, 286
WX20076 W. Dwyer, 50,728,744
WX10390 W.A. Dwyer, 49,636
WX7599 A.H. Dyson, 286,732,733, 734
WX6262 W.H. Earnshaw, 50
WX10114 H. Eastwood, 51
WX16947 R.E. Ecclestone, 287
WX7266 G.H. Edwards, 51
WX7620 T.H. Edwards, 52,568, 773,774
WX7562 H.L. Elkins, 52
WX5064 E.F. Elliot, 288
WX8619 J.S. Elliot, 288,731
WX13079 R.E. Ellis, 53
WX8381 R.P. Elvish, 53
WX20164 A.E. Erskine, 289
WX9497 B. Evans, 290
WX14172 F.C. Evans, 290,750,753
WX17269 K.S. Evans, 291
WX10057 R.L. Evans, 292
WX9230 W.C. Evans, 54
WX9101 J.C. Ewen, 292
WX4915 A.B. Facey, 54
WX9199 A.E. Farmer, 293
WX4945 H.R.N. Fawcus, 55

WX5088　A. Fee, 294,775
WX225　E.T. Feltham, 294
WX7999　R.P. Ferguson, 55,675
WX5127　C.G. Ferrie, 295
WX7663　H.J.S. Fidge, 295
WX9070　C. Fielder, 296
WX8874　A.W. Findlay, 56,775
WX7886　T.A. Finlay, 296
WX7225　T. Firns, 297,774,776
WX5132　G. Fisher, 297
WX8586　B. Fitzgerald, 298
WX5425　T.M. Fitzgerald, 298,771
WX9039　R.N. Fitzpatrick, 56
WX8657　C. Flakemore, 299
WX7864　J.J. Flanagan, 299,632,639
WX9777　J.H. Flanigan, 300
WX17374　N. Flarty, 300
WX17745　C.H. Fletcher, 57
WX12663　A.E. Floyed, 57
WX8679　A.E. Foch, 301
WX7709　C.A. Fogarty, 301
WX15719　G. Foot, 302
WX12427　R.A. Foster, 302,778
WX10803　T.R. Fotheringham, 58
WX7569　S.E. Foxall, 58
WX6506　J.E. Fraser, 303,750
WX10366　N.W. Fraser, 59
WX15422　B.M. Frost, 303,720
WX7852　H.C. Fuhrmann, 304,763
WX8119　R.C. Fullerton, 304
WX9270　T.J. Fury, 59
WX9132　A.R. Gamble, 305
WX15041　D.J. Gardner, 60
WX10925　P.A. Gardiner, 306
WX10622　C.W. Gault, 306
WX8000　M.H. Geary, 60,754
WX7607　R.J. Gibbons, 307
WX16407　L.G. Gibbs, 61,544
WX8607　P.J. Gibbs, 307
WX9255　S.H. Gibbs, 61
WX8958　W.H. Gibbs, 10,62,544
WX17974　L.S. Gibson, 62
WX10944　N.A. Gibson, 63
WX8900　T.C. Gibson, 308,734
WX5335　W.M. Giddens, 308
WX7998　P.A. Giese, 63
WX8788　F.L. Giles, 309
WX8623　J. Gilmour, 310,630
WX8622　J.B. Gilmour, 310,713,718
WX8870　T.E. Gittos, 64
WX7595　G. Glass, 311
WX16376　S.J. Gleeson, 311
WX7606　R.E. Godfrey, 64
WX6980　P. Golden, 312
WX7627　J. McL. Goldie, 65
WX9131　R. Goodwin, 65
WX12575　G.A. Gorman, 66
WX9336　J. Gorringe, 312,571,766

WX9335　S. Gorringe, 313,750
WX9062　G.J. Gossage, 66,71
WX8582　N.A. Gough, 313
WX17310　N.F.T. Gough, 314,636,
　638,639,728
NX10420　R.S. Goulden, 67,599
WX6258　J.H. Grace, 67
WX8228　N.H. Grant, 315,742
WX10378　C.W. Gray, 315,701,702,
　703,704
WX15872　L.C. Gray, 68
WX8373　L. Greaves, 316,747
WX9558　A.R. Green, 316
WX3435　C.E. Green, xviii,43,317,
　549,550,557,598,599,610,725,750,
　758,764,765,767,769,771,772
WX10788　H.F. Green, 68,186
WX7869　T.H. Green, 318
WX8540　T.W. Green, 69,682,683
WX5086　H.J. Gregory, 318
WX8674　J.E.J. Gregory, 69
WX9202　R.K. Gregory, 319
WX8625　W.R. Gregory, 319
WX15247　K.G. Griffith, 320,754
WX10693　W.D. Grundy, 71,320
WX16383　H.V.W. Gwilliam, 321
WX3450　G.W. Gwynne, 140, 321,
　401,543,657,766,768
WX8003　A.M. Hack, 70
WX7801　A. Hackshaw, 70,776
WX7213　G.V. Hadden, 322
WX9139　L.F. Hadden, 322,639
WX7246　R.W. Hadfield, 323,734
WX8250　F. Halbert, 71
WX8433　R.W. Haldane, 71,535
WX10370　D.C.J. Hall, 72
WX8690　J.N. Hall, 324
WX8747　W.H. Hall, 72
WX8819　J. Halligan, 73
WX8807　W.A. Halligan, 324
WX14830　S.O'G. Haly, 73
WX6975　R.J. Ham, 325
WX10745　A.J. Hambley, 325,720
WX4991　E.E. Hambley, 326
WX8718　H. Hammer, 326
WX7123　R.D. Hampson, 327,594,
　724,725,769
WX9405　T. Hampton, 328,754
WX7987　G. Hancock, 328
WX9365　L.H. Hancock, 329
WX10678　B.E. Hansen, 74,162
WX15736　R. Hansen, 329
WX12157　E.C. Hardey, 330,776
WX16793　A.M. Hargreaves, 74
WX7851　C. Harris, 75
WX4985　N.J. Harris, 162,331,710,
　713,717
WX8695　W.D. Harris, 331

WX7745　B.G. Harrison, 332
WX8733　H.R. Harrison, 75
WX10822　L.J. Harvey, 76
WX8408　A.G. Hayes, 76
WX11202　K.T. Hayes, 77,556
WX8374　N.P. Hayes, 332
WX9175　W.T. Haywood, 333
WX9320　H.W. Heal, 77
WX6968　J.C. Heffernan, 333
WX18022　F.J. Heinz-Smith, 78
WX9755　L. Helliwell, 78,556
WX8638　L.C. Hellmrich, 79
WX10095　J.F. Helsin, 79
WX7642　C.G. Henderson, 334,
　703,738
WX8384　R.G. Henderson, 334
WX9348　C.L. Heppell, 80
WX8525　I.D. Heppingstone, 335
WX7976　F. Hermon, 335
WX8207　A.S. Hewby, 336,637,776
WX18170　S.R. Hickey, 336,639
WX9290　G.H. Hicks, 337,639
WX5206　W. Hicks, 338
WX9559　W.H. Hickson, 338
WX6602　A. Mc. Hill, 339,753
WX7029　E.T. Hill, 80
WX8756　J. Hill, 81
WX3434　J.H. Hill, 82,637
WX7705　R. Hill, 340
WX6778　J.B. Hills, 340
WX8869　H.R. Hindle, 83,731,744
WX8597　F. Hinds, 341
WX8198　F. Hinnrichsen, 341,710,
　713,716
WX16446　C. Hobson, 83
WX9240　H.G. Hockey, 342,746
WX9350　P.G. Hodgins, 342
WX9231　L.S. Hodgson, 84
WX8984　S.M. Hogben, 343
WX17634　W. Holding, 344,651,659
WX7465　N.P. Holdman, 84,750
WX17997　H.M. Holland, 344,701,
　703,704,738
WX17636　H.W. Holland, 85
WX8986　D. Holm, 85
WX16416　C. Holme, 86
WX9286　C. Holmes, 345
WX8678　E.J. Holst, 86
WX7550　W.J. Holt, 87
WX7618　L.N. Holtzman, 346,720
WX7471　W.H.P. Hood, 346
WX7022　E.J. Hope, 87
WX10635　V.T.W. Hoppe, 88
WX9241　E.M. Hopson, 88,695,
　696,697
WX9418　D.R. Horn, 347,771
WX9323　M.W. Hortin, 348
WX10097　A.D. Hosking, 348,561

WX20025 L.R. Hounslow, 349
NX73270 B.J. Howard, 89
WX7628 E.J. Howard, 89
WX15099 C.T. Howe, 350
WX6967 J. Howe, 350,719,747
WX5181 K.J. Howell, 90
WX16981 W.R. Howson, 351
WX10795 R.E. Hughes, 90
WX10931 L.S. Hummerston, 351,771
WX9327 E.H. Hunt, 91,542,544
WX16375 J.W. Hunt, 91
WX9130 M.A. Hunter, 352
WX17351 P.G. Hurst, 92
WX7332 W.W. Hutchinson, 352, 710,713,718
WX7646 R.B. Hutchison, 92
WX9552 W.L. Innes, 93
WX8327 C.H. Ironmonger, 353,776
WX7889 J. Issac, 353
WX8750 H.A. Jackson, 354
WX8813 T.M. Jackson, 354
WX10804 H. Jacobs, 355,543,733
WX15402 L. Jaensch, 93
WX8610 T.E.J. James, 356,733
WX7467 D.K. Jamieson, 357
WX8702 G. Japp, 357,776
WX7697 R.R. Jeffery, 358,639,778
WX17576 W.L. Jeffery, 358
WX5118 J.M. Jenkins, 94
WX8730 T.K. Jenkins, 359
WX15640 H.J. Johnson, 359
WX7510 A.J. Jones, 360,710,713, 717
WX9112 B.C. Jones, 94
WX10897 E.B. Jones, 360,713
WX7453 E.C. Jones, 95,595
WX7234 I.W. Jones, 95
WX9433 N. Jones, 96
WX9297 C. Joynes, 96
WX8431 V.A. Keay, 97
WX17452 L.D. Kearney, 361,724, 725,769
WX9915 F.H. Keirle, ii,361
WX7541 C.C. Keitel, 362
WX7612 C.G. Mc. Kelly, 97
WX9151 R.J. Kelt, 98
WX7624 E.C. Kemp, 362
WX8543 L.W.S. Kemp, 363
WX16340 R.H. Kenmir, 363
WX10910 M.St. J. Kennedy, 364
WX8532 W.G.B. Kenney, 365
WX7250 G Kidd, 99
WX16236 A.V. King, 99,778
WX8007 E.H. King, 100
WX8178 J.H. King, 365
WX6429 W.J. King, 366
WX15700 J. Kingdon, 100
WX4949 R.J. Kingswell, 101

WX16391 G.B. Kluth, 101
WX7616 C. Knott, 366
WX7446 L. Krassnostein, 367
WX8336 F.G. Kuhl, 368
WX8077 L.A.C. Kuhlman, 102
WX10715 J.G.A. Kyriakos, 368
WX17582 G. Lake, 102
WX8767 P.H.C. Lakeman, 103
WX9318 K. Lally, 103,542,544, 728,744
WX9528 A. Lambie, 369,732,733, 734
WX15951 K.S. Lance, 369
WX11228 R.M. Lander, 370
WX4877 F.H. Landwehr, 370
WX16439 D.R. Lane, 104
WX9293 R.G. Langdon, 104,544
QX6599 I.W. Lawer, 371,372,640, 753
WX8810 R.F. Lawer, 371,372,640
WX8425 E.J. Leadbitter, 105
WX9312 M.J. Leahy, 372,710,718
WX7043 H.B. Lear, 106
WX10107 R.W. Learmonth, 373, 499,646,647,648
WX9387 C.D. Lee, 374,546,619, 625
WX9214 J. Lee, 106
WX10108 K.G. Lee, 374,610
WX7230 L.H. Lee, 375
WX15744 L.W. Lee, 375
WX7640 F. Lee-Steere, 107
WX16355 G.R. Leipold, 107
WX4917 J.B. Leith, 376,641
WX10806 K.E. Lessells, 377
WX11316 L.H. Lewis, 377
WX7441 T.H. Lewis, 378
WX8960 T.A. Limbourn, 379
WX16332 J. Lind, 379,741,745
WX17759 J.S. Livingstone, 108
WX9321 A.J. Loller, 380,543,544
WX12717 A.H.S. London, 380
WX16727 J.L. Lonsdale, 381,740
WX7285 H.R. Love, 381
WX13752 H. Lucas, 382,720
WX17778 F.J. Ludge, 108
WX9146 C.R. Lush, 348
WX8675 R.R. Lyle, 383,564
WX17515 R.R. Lymn, 384,710,713, 717
WX7847 G.L. Lynam, 384
WX8639 J.J. Lynch, 69
WX7204 W.E. Lynn, 385
WX9801 R.D. Maconachie, 109
WX224 J. MacDonald, 110
WX17566 J.K.A. MacDonald, 385
WX9279 L.M. MacDonald, 110, 543,544

WX3707 G.C. MacKinnon, 386, 546,549,550,564,769,770
WX8377 K.T. MacLennan, 386, 768
WX17302 W. Macleod, 387
WX8689 H.C.S. MacMaster, 111
WX16886 A.M. Magill, 387,693, 694,696,701,765
WX8656 R.G. Magor, 388
WX7239 J.W. Malthouse, 388,610
WX5175 E.H. Mann, 389,729
WX7660 D.T. Manning, 111
WX8484 H.J. Manning, 112,386
WX11472 R.F. Manthorpe, 390,482
WX11455 A.N. Mantle, 112
WX8015 J.C. Manton, 390
WX7438 B.H. Manwaring, 391,719, 747
WX7124 L.J. Marriot, 391
WX17639 R.W. Marsh, 113
WX16341 S.T. Martin, 392
WX9296 D.A. Matheson, 113
WX17000 F.N. Matthews, 392,732, 734
WX7042 R. Matthews, 393
WX16347 W.N. Matson, 394,757
WX13285 J. Maude, 394,563,742, 743
WX7216 A.E. Mazza, 114
WX8261 R.R. McAskil, 114,693, 698,700
WX3440 F.G. McCaffrey, 395
WX17837 L.W. McCann, 396,557, 559,
WX8435 R. McCann, 115
WX9324 J. McCarthy, 115,543, 544,754
WX5584 R.D. McCracken, 116
WX8820 W.P. McCudden, 116
WX8620 C.J. McDonald, 396
WX5163 C.K. McDonald, 397
WX8621 K.K. McDonald, 117
WX9052 H.E. McDonough, 117
WX8790 W. McEwen, 397,771,772
WX20095 W.A. McEwen, 398
WX3442 O.S. McEwin, 118,554, 555,556
WX9145 A.J. McGhee, 398
WX7436 J.M. McGinty, 399
WX11580 D.S. McGlinn, 118
WX8478 F.T. McGlinn, 399,732
WX8611 L.J. McGrath, 400,675, 768
WX12835 J.A. McGregor, 400,568, 569
WX9849 A.J.L. McIntosh, 119
WX7138 W. McKay, 119
WX15838 R.J. McKenzie-Murray, 401

WX7608 C. McLennan, 402
WX9825 C.P. McLoughlin, 402
WX8760 T.M. McMahon, 120
WX15720 S.S. McNeil, 120,773,774
WX8834 W.N.K. McNulty, 403
WX7675 C.J. McPherson, 403
WX8243 A. McQuade, 404,776
WX6203 J. McSkene, 404
WX10388 K.L. Meads, 121
WX7241 E. Meakins, 121,405
WX9393 J.T. Meiklejohn, 16
WX8441 J.B. Mellor, 405
WX228 D.V. Mentiplay, 405,552,
643,770,778
WX8319 J.W. Meredith, 406,556
WX9826 H.J. Millar, 407,583
WX7885 A. Miller, 407,641
WX8013 E.E. Miller, 408
WX13338 R.J. Miller, 408,639
WX16675 R.J. Millhouse, 122,557,
559
WX7662 A.R. Minchin, 122
WX9222 T.A.H. Minchin, 409
WX11629 K.B. Mitchell, 409
WX13562 P.J. Moate, 410
WX17737 K. Moher, 123
WX9337 A.D. Moir, 123
WX15905 E.G. Moir, 124,306
WX9339 G. Moir, 410,732
WX8012 K.G. Moir, 124
WX9338 L.O. Moir, 411
WX8973 G.G. Mongan, 125
WX8076 F.C. Moore, 125
WX15386 R.K. Moran, 126
WX9233 A.J. Morgan, 412,543,753
WX6173 O. Morris, 413,757
WX8200 W.R. Morris, 413
WX15746 A.E. Morrison, 414,757
WX9384 J.C. Morrison, 239,414,
675,687,692,693
WX15751 A.E. Morrissey, 415
WX15684 J.E. Muldoon, 126
WX4941 R. Muller, 416,732
WX17390 E.M. Munday, 127
WX12599 A.R. Murdoch, 416
WX5336 J.L. Murdoch, 417
WX16674 J.J. Murphy, 127
WX7426 J.P. Murphy, 128
WX10796 L. McG. Murray, 418
WX10792 E.J. Murtagh, 418,743
WX9887 A.C. Mussman, 128
WX7181 C. Mutton, 129
WX17363 C.O. Nash, 129
WX15457 S.E. Nash, 419
WX8707 F. Nazzari, 130
WX9260 S.E. Neale, 130
WX8137 J.W.H. Needham, 131
WX12985 P.J. Negri, 131

WX5220 H.F. Neilson, 420
WX14031 C.T. Nelson, 420
WX9256 G.E. Nevile, 421,543
WX5196 F.H. New, 132
WX8749 A.G. Newell, 422
WX17458 O.K. Newling, 132,675
WX8432 R.F. Newling, 133,675
WX8865 R.W. Newling, 133,675
NX73279 C.W. Newman, 134
WX9207 A. Newton, 422,640
WX10809 W.J. Nicholas, 423
WX7645 W.J. Nicholls, 595
WX7940 W.G. Nicholson, 135
WX16417 S. Ninyette, 423
WX9413 F.R. Noble, 135
WX7659 E.L. Nolan, 136
WX10790 H.C. Norris, 424
WX9407 G. Northey, 424
WX8493 A.W. Norton, 425,536,
635,734
WX16293 H.H.T. Norton, 136
WX9181 W.H. Nottle, 426,732,734
WX14327 L.R. Nybo, 137,556
WX8174 D.M. O'Leary, 137
WX7981 J.P. O'Meara, 427
WX5222 L. O'Neil, 138
WX8828 W.D. O'Neill, 427
WX9390 B.M. O'Sullivan, 428,643
WX8481 A.S. Oag, 428,737
WX7336 H.B. Ockerby, 138,557,
774,777
WX9406 C.P. Odgers, 139
WX11001 A.H.R. Odlum, 429
WX9345 G.S. Ohrt, 430,754
WX12628 S.J. Oliver, 139
WX12156 P.V. Omiridis, 430,713,
717,718
WX16279 E.F. Osborne, 140
WX9287 J.R. Osborne, 140
WX7634 S.A. Osborne, 142,675
WX16931 H.C. Oswald, 141,537
WX10802 N.J. Outtrim, 142,639
WX9129 E.J. Ovens, 142
WX4934 R.A. Page, 143
WX16448 A.W.L. Park, 431,710,718
WX7724 A.S. Parke, 432
WX7738 C.S. Parke, 432
WX8642 D. Parker, 433
WX12336 R. Pascall, 433,733
WX7409 T.A. Pascoe, 434,724,
725,769
WX5123 J.S. Pass, 434,777
WX9073 W.J. Paterson, 143,149,
542,544
WX8856 H.W. Pearce, 144
WX9268 J. Pearce, 435,542,543
WX13816 D.D. Pearson, 436
WX8118 J.E. Pearson, 144

WX7458 L.O. Peat, 145
WX9197 J.E. Peers, 145
WX17414 J.S. Peters, 146
WX3465 R.M. Phelps, 436,561
WX10389 C.A. Phillips, 146
WX7902 W.H. Philp, 147
WX9055 H. Pickett, 147,437,721,
724,725,769
WX9238 T.W. Pierson, 437
WX13027 C.R. Piggott, 438
WX17393 T. Pilmoor, 438
WX20157 R.S. Pimlott, 439
WX7626 A.L. Pitts, 439
WX16883 N.W. Platts, 186
WX13429 W.N. Poole, 148
WX9263 E.C.S. Popham, 440
WX9764 B.F. Poulton, 440,737
WX8840 A.E. Powell, 148
WX9554 A.L.R. Powell, 441
WX7320 L.A. Poyser, 149
WX8705 R.W. Pratt, 149,542,544
WX7416 E.L. Preedy, 150
WX8739 F.F. Pritchard, 442
WX8716 F.K. Pritchard, 442
WX6172 H.E. Procter, 443,710,716
WX8725 J.H.L. Pryce, 444
WX9946 E.A. Pummell, 444,536
WX8826 L. Purchon, 150
WX9285 C.G. Quinn, 190,445,
695, 696
WX5054 D.A.C. Quinn, 445,774,777
WX7831 J.P. Quinn, 446
WX7511 J.A. Rabone, 446
WX15829 H. Radburn, 151
WX20107 A. Ralph, 447
WX20068 H.W. Ralph, 151
WX9059 G.R. Ramage, 152,613
WX14836 J.K. Ramsbottom, 448,
709,714,718
WX16356 E.E. Randall, 152
WX9563 J. Randall, 448,741,745
WX3447 G.A. Raphael, 20,153,557
WX9357 L.R. Rayner, 153
WX16281 G.L. Reay, 449
WX8503 R.C. Reed, 154
WX6129 A.J. Rees, 450
WX7621 W.W. Reeves, 450,756
WX9295 S. Reid, 154
WX17857 V.S. Reid, 451
WX7493 R.G.S. Rennie, 155
WX11046 L.G. Riches, 451,634,
637,762,772,773,774
WX6799 E. Ricketts, 452
WX14197 R.W. Ridgwell, 452,539,
673
WX20074 J.T. Ridley, 155
WX8952 R.R. Riebe, 453,778
WX15743 W.R. Ritchie, 453,765,766

WX16618 R.W. Roberts, 156
WX7750 S.H.G. Roberts, 454
WX9358 W.C. Roberts, 156
WX7331 C.W. Robertson, 454
WX16427 D.C. Robertson, 455
WX10351 J. Robinson, 455,761
WX15941 J.W. Robinson, 157
WX5200 W.J. Robinson, 157
WX10808 J. Rochester, 158
WX7509 A.W. Rodda, 158,624
WX9005 E.R. Rogers, 456
WX8652 A.M. Rogie, 456
WX16269 E.J. Ronan, 457
WX15893 S.E. Roots, 457,701,703, 704
WX7835 W.L. Rosel, 458
WX9253 D. Ross, 159
WX10066 D.G. Ross, 458
WX7656 G.R. Rouse, 159
WX10793 E.J. Rowell, 160
WX17293 A.J.C. Rowland, 459
WX9383 J.D. Royce, 160,162,556
WX7474 H.M. Rubery, 161
WX10164 D.N. Russell, 161
WX10785 J.M. Rutherford, 162
WX8734 C. Ryan, 460
WX16767 E.W. Ryan, 460,750
WX3454 A.E. Saggers, 186,395, 461,487,552,553,567,618,641,643, 765,770,787
WX8777 J.W. Sanderson, 162,545
WX8809 R.H. Sandilands, 163,550
WX9272 A.G. Saunders, 461
WX7211 C.S. Saunders, 163
WX9045 H.E. Saw, 462
WX7939 C.J. Sawyer, 164
WX7256 T.K. Sawyer, 462
WX7617 H.W. Scaddan, 164
WX12202 M.S. Scala, 463
WX8843 J. Scales, 165
WX5007 J.H. Schurmann, 463,754
WX8562 A.V. Schuts, 464,737
WX12949 J.L. Scott, 464
WX17899 S.G. Scott, 165
WX7532 R.R. Semple, 465,695, 697
WX8544 J. Sevier, 166
WX7330 E. Shackleton, 166
WX9252 J.H. Shackleton, 167
WX8430 N.J. Sheedy, 465,743
WX7623 G.T. Shelton, 167
WX5018 C.B. Shelvock, 168
WX18151 A.R. Shier, 466
WX8535 A.F. Shirley, 168,544
WX8693 W.L. Short, 466
WX8141 R.H. Simkin, 467
WX7576 N.E. Simmonds, 467
WX16952 R.A. Simmonds, 468,539

WX16424 A. Sing, 468,594,724, 725,769
WX6681 J.B. Skelton, 469
WX9282 F.K.H. Skinner, 169
WX17344 A. Slater, 169
WX7506 R.L. Sloane, 170
WX6441 A.J. Smith, 469
WX14644 C.V. Smith, 170
WX4891 G. Smith, 171
WX17448 H.M. Smith, 470,695, 697,698
WX12252 J.E. Smith, 470
WX6841 J.S. Smith, 470,733
WX7893 J.S. Smith, 471
WX7784 J.W. Smith, 472
WX9143 M.J. Smith, 171
WX13552 R. Smith, 472
WX8736 R.L. Smith, 172,550
WX7904 R.M. Smith, 172
WX8731 T.E. Smith, 173
WX8506 W.J. Smith, 473
WX3453 A.R. Smith-Ryan, 317, 473,545,549,557,562,651
WX7127 J.F. Solly, 121,173
WX7715 C.J. Spackman, 474
WX8467 R.H.C. Spence, 174
WX7337 A. Spooner, 174
WX8646 A.P. Spouse, 175
WX13553 S.F. Spouse, 175
WX16885 C.D. Squance, 474,693, 694,697,698,701
WX9330 D.J. Squire, 176
WX7789 O.M. Stanwell, 176,554
WX8758 J.F. Starcevich, 475,632, 639
WX9419 H.W. Steele, 475
WX8596 D.F. Sterrett, 476
WX227 A. Stevens, 476,568,569, 675,678,680,687
WX7324 R.H. Stewart, 477
WX17594 G.C. Stone, 177
WX8041 W.J. Stone, 477
WX9178 J.O. Street, 177
WX9080 A.W. Stribley, 178
WX9058 N.L. Stribley, 478
WX9827 R.H. Stribling, 478
WX8738 W. Struthers, 479,566,758
WX15869 A. J. Struthoff, 178,719
WX14495 W.G.R. Stuart, 179,773
WX9332 J.B. Stubbs, 179
WX10794 P.A. Sturtridge, 479,538, 756
WX7563 E.H. Sullivan, 180
WX9134 J. Sumner, 480
WX15967 D.E. Sutherland, 180
WX17907 W.T. Swann, 480
WX4924 J. Swartz, 481,556,728
WX12378 J.C. Swift, 390,482

WX16324 G.D. Tanner, 482
WX9157 A.L. Tapper, 483
WX8180 E.G. Taylor, 484,563
WX8450 F.L. Taylor, 181
WX8448 G. Taylor, 484
WX14775 G.L. Taylor, 181
WX8867 G.W. Taylor, 182
WX14733 J. Taylor, 485
WX4986 J.A. Taylor, 485,701,703, 704
WX4921 J.T. Taylor, 182
WX10865 T.E. Teasdale, 486,545
WX8699 C.B. Thackrah, 183
WX7248 F.D. Thaxter, 486,756,757
WX3424 A.W. Thomas, 153,557, 758
WX6623 D.W. Thomas, 183
WX7480 W.L. Thomas, 487
WX3448 G.A. J. Thompson, 20,184, 317
WX10927 N.H.E. Thompson, 317, 488,557,734
WX17615 E.J. Thomsett, 184
WX10117 E.G. Thomson, 488
WX9562 I.E. Thorley, 185
WX10289 A.S. Thorns, 185,675,691
WX8460 J. Thorpe, 186
WX9382 J.J. Till, 68,147,186,553
WX15712 W.W. Tischler, 489
WX7470 R.L. Todd, 187
WX8139 P.R. Tomkins, 489
WX7996 T.H. Tomkins, 490
WX7664 F.W. Toms, 187
WX15897 F.A. Toovey, 188,672
WX16323 R.G. Tooze, 189
WX10797 F. McP. Townsend, 189
WX9351 J. Treasure, 190
WX9280 F.T. Tregenza, 190,544
WX9325 J.E. Tregenza, 191
WX17882 A.G. Trigwell, 191
WX17863 V.C. Trigwell, 192
WX8537 K.D. Tucker, 192,490,732
WX7484 W.J. Tucker, 192
WX8491 R.G. Tuffin, 193
WX17593 H.R. Turner, 193
WX9226 H. Tysoe, 194,710,744
WX9385 J. Unsworth, 491,777
WX5932 F. Vaughan, 194
WX9292 N.J. Venemore, 195,542, 544
WX8585 C.J. Vidler, 492,615
NX46354 C.D.J. Vincent, 492
WX9372 S.D. Viney, 493
WX9236 E.J. Waddell, 493,755
WX17879 G.J. Wade, 494
WX5021 H.W. Waghorn, 494
WX9560 J.W. Wainwright, 495
WX16370 A.L. Walker, 496,737

WX9224 H.A. Walker, 195
WX15614 R.J. Walker, 196
WX12989 H.J. Wall, 496,726,734
WX17962 E.W. Wallin, 497
WX16442 V. Wallis, 498
WX7466 B.J. Walsh, 498,594
WX8776 L.P. Walsh, 196
WX10363 A.B. Walton, 499,675,692
WX9392 M.E. Wankey, 21,355,
500,542,543,544,672,764
WX7913 F.T. Ward, 500,703,741
NX70433 V.I. Warhurst, 64,197,553
WX8626 N. Warne, 197
WX8765 J. Warren-Smith, 198,756
WX10382 J. Warrington, 501,640
WX8356 W.S. Watkins, 502,610
WX9381 A.H. Watson, 502
WX8502 E.A.A. Watt, 503
WX9067 E.G. Watt, 504,641
WX10761 T.M. Watters, 504
WX7502 T.S. Wayman, 505,594,
732,734
WX12008 T.C. Wearn, 198
WX17804 A.S.A. Webb, 505
WX9219 C. Webb, 506
WX8929 F.W. Webb, 199
WX16254 C.W. Webber, 67,506,599

WX9553 C.N. Wedge, 158,507,624,
631,758,766
WX7757 H.C. Wells, 508
WX7641 S.K. Wenn, 508,710,713,
718
WX7166 H.S. Werrett, 199,777
WX9570 P.L. Westlake, 509
WX8753 J.L. Wheelock, 509,639
WX16274 F. Whitacker, 200,754
WX9333 A.T. White, 510
WX8814 C.W. White, 510
WX9002 H.C.F. White, 511,639
WX9076 R.G. Whitelaw, 512,737,
WX7477 D.L.A. Whiteman, 513
WX10561 R.G. Whitfield, 513,732,
772
WX7232 R. Whitford, 200
WX9179 H. Wilkes, 514
WX8706 J. Wilkie, 201
WX17604 M.H. Wilkins, 514,729
WX10049 M.W. Wilkinson, 515,610,
615,756
WX6071 L.G. Willacott, 201
WX1138 A.G. Williams, 516
WX8672 G.D. Williams, 516
WX7011 H.W. Williams, 517

WX7263 R.E. Williams, 517
WX16956 R.S. Williams, 518
WX7499 R.T. Williams, 518
WX11744 G.E. Willimott, 202
WX11745 J.F. Willimott, 202
WX17370 J. Wilson, 519
WX17973 J. Wilson, 203
WX9394 J.G. Wilson, 519,610,772
WX8014 R.C. Wilson, 520
WX8438 R.M. Wilson, 203
WX8110 A.D. Winter, 520,724,725,
769
WX10373 W.V. Winter, 521,724,725,
769
WX16426 W.J. Wolfe, 521
WX5073 T.A. Wood, 522
WX5204 H.J. Worsdell, 522
WX7440 A. Worth, 523,735,737
WX10012 W.G. Worth, 204,666
WX18142 C.T. Wright, 523
WX13161 H.E. Wright, 204
WX12593 R.W. Wyllie, 524
WX9003 J.L. Yeates, 524
WX7429 F.B. Yensch, 205
WX6958 J. Young, 205,777
WX9379 T.W. Zeeb, 525

Name Index

General Index